THE OXFORD HANDBOOK OF

ENVIRONMENTAL AND NATURAL RESOURCES LAW IN INDIA

THE OXFORD HANDBOOK OF

ENVIRONMENTAL AND NATURAL RESOURCES LAW IN INDIA

Edited by

PHILIPPE CULLET, LOVLEEN BHULLAR,

and

SUJITH KOONAN

OXFORD
UNIVERSITY PRESS

OXFORD
UNIVERSITY PRESS

Great Clarendon Street, Oxford, OX2 6DP,
United Kingdom

Oxford University Press is a department of the University of Oxford.
It furthers the University's objective of excellence in research, scholarship,
and education by publishing worldwide. Oxford is a registered trade mark of
Oxford University Press in the UK and in certain other countries

Published in the United States of America by Oxford University Press
198 Madison Avenue, New York, NY 10016, United States of America

British Library Cataloguing in Publication Data
Data available

Library of Congress Control Number is on file at the Library of Congress

ISBN 978–0–19–888468–2

DOI: 10.1093/oxfordhb/9780198884682.001.0001

Printed and bound in India by
Replika Press Pvt. Ltd.

In memory of Manoj Misra (1954–2023)

Foreword

We live, we are told, in the Anthropocene era. An era in which the Earth has witnessed rapid degradation of the environment and destabilising climate change brought about by 'uncaring' models of energy production and 'hyper-consumption' of resources. Greenhouse gases emitted through the production and use of energy from coal, oil, and natural gas have led to the inevitable 'global warming' and unpredictable weather patterns affecting the lives and livelihoods of millions of people across the planet. Humans have, by using up natural resources at a rate that outstrips the Earth's capacity to regenerate them, left a negative footprint on Earth.

In the latest version of the UNDP's Human Development Report, 'Uncertain Times, Unsettled Lives: Shaping our Future in a Transforming World', the authors reflect on a host of issues that are making our lives increasingly uncertain. They talk about the 'confluence of destabilizing planetary pressures with growing inequalities, sweeping societal transformations'.[1] The report tells us that '[r]ecent years have seen more record temperatures, fires and storms around the world, alarming reminders that the climate crisis marches on, alongside other planetary-level changes wrought by the Anthropocene. Biodiversity collapse is one of them.'[2] The Social Progress Index Report for 2021, while evaluating the 'Foundations of Wellbeing' in several countries across the world, has focused on, among other things, 'environmental quality'. Its authors examined four specific parameters: (i) outdoor air pollution attributable deaths, (ii) particulate matter pollution, (iii) species protection, and (iv) deaths from lead exposure.[3] There is thus an increasing awareness of the extent to which human activities, unmindful of consequences, have led us to where we are at present.

The above backdrop underscores the importance of this tome on environmental and natural resource laws in India, which, its editors say, 'comprehensively and extensively covers different dimensions and issues', not only in their traditional sense but the interlinkages with 'non-environmental issues' as well. Developments in the area in India in the past two decades have been rapid, and not always progressive or consistent with the object of meeting the growing challenge of saving our planet for the future generations. It is therefore, necessary for scholars, and policy- and law-makers and enforcers, to continue to reflect on the paths traversed and the choices made, which can serve a guide to

[1] UNDP, *Human Development Report 2021/2022 'Uncertain Times, Unsettled Lives: Shaping our Future in a Transforming World'* (United Nations Development Programme 2022) iii.

[2] ibid 7.

[3] Social Progress Imperative, 2021 Social Progress Index (2021).

future generations. And, hopefully, help them avoid the pitfalls and disasters, mostly human-made.

This book would perhaps remind us of the wise words of Svetlana Alexievich, who won the Nobel Prize for literature in 2015 for documenting the voices of the survivors of the Chernobyl disaster of 1986 when she observed: 'Humanitarian man is lagging behind technological man' and that 'fear is a large part of our lives—more even, than love'.[4] Or for that matter, William Carl Heinrich Hueper, a renowned scientist and the author of *Poison Spring* in which he describes the world's industrial chemicals as a 'global disaster'. According to him, it is in the best interest of mankind that industry makes the proper adaptations by eliminating and reducing environmental and occupational cancer hazards. He asserts that:

> Human beings lack the ability to make appropriate biological adaptations for effectively combating the growing wave of toxic and carcinogenic risks propagated by modern industry, which represent the biological death bombs with a delayed time fuse which may prove to be, in the long run, as dangerous to the existence of mankind as the arsenal of atom bombs.[5]

It is never enough to discuss the possibilities of changes in human behaviour that can be brought about by policy and law and their effective enforcement. A book like this holds out that hope. Let us not give up.

Dr Justice S Muralidhar, Chief Justice, High Court of Orissa

[4] Svetlana Alexievich, *Voices from Chernobyl: The Oral History of a Nuclear Disaster* (trans Keith Gessen, Picador 2006). Text quoted from 'A Conversation with Svetlana Alexievich By Ana Lucic', *Dalkey Archive Press* (2013) <https://www.dalkeyarchive.com/2013/08/02/a-conversation-with-svetlana-alexievich-by-ana-lucic>.

[5] EG Vallianatos with McKay Jenkins, *Poison Spring: The Secret History of Poison and the EPA* (Bloomsbury Press 2014) xii.

Acknowledgements

The editors would like to acknowledge the significant contribution made to the preparation of this volume by Jessy Thomas. We would also like to acknowledge the contribution of Kakoly Pande in copy-editing some of the chapters.

Contents

PART VIII WATER

PART IX HEALTH AND SANITATION

PART X RESOURCE EXTRACTION, INDUSTRIAL DEVELOPMENT, AND ENERGY

PART XI ENFORCEMENT AND LITIGATION

Contributors

Dr **Shawkat Alam**, Professor of International and Environmental Law, Macquarie Law School, Macquarie University, Sydney.

Dr **Arindam Basu**, Assistant Professor, Indian Institute of Technology, Kharagpur.

Dr **Neha Bhadbhade**, Fellow, Society for Promoting Participative Ecosystem Management (SOPPECOM), Pune.

Ms **Sarita Bhagat**, Fellow, Society for Promoting Participative Ecosystem Management (SOPPECOM), Pune.

Dr **Tanvi Bhatkal**, Postdoctoral Researcher, Institute of Development Studies, Sussex, Brighton.

Dr **Lovleen Bhullar**, Assistant Professor, Birmingham Law School, University of Birmingham.

Mr **Vishavjeet Chaudhary**, Advocate, Supreme Court of India, New Delhi and Door Tenant, Lamb Building, London.

Dr **Srinivas Chokkakula**, Senior Fellow and Ministry of Jal Shakti Research Chair, Centre for Policy Research, New Delhi and Senior Research Fellow, School of Public Policy, University of Massachusetts Amherst.

Ms. **Nairita Roy Chaudhuri**, Doctoral Researcher, Tilburg Law School, Tilburg University, Netherlands.

Dr **Nupur Chowdhury**, Assistant Professor, Centre for the Study of Law and Governance, Jawaharlal Nehru University, New Delhi.

Dr **Wendell S.C.L. Cornwall**, Counsellor, Embassy of Grenada to the United States, Washington, DC.

Dr **Philippe Cullet**, Professor of International and Environmental Law, SOAS University of London and Visiting Professor, National Law University Delhi, New Delhi.

Prof **Vinita Damodaran**, Professor, South Asian History, University of Sussex, Brighton.

Dr **Bharat H. Desai**, Professor of International Law, Jawaharlal Nehru Chair and Chairperson, Centre for International Legal Studies, School of International Studies, Jawaharlal Nehru University, New Delhi.

Ms **Preeta Dhar**, Doctoral candidate, SOAS University of London.

Mr **Shyam Divan**, Senior Advocate, Supreme Court of India, New Delhi.

Prof **Navroz Kersi Dubash**, Senior Fellow, Sustainable Futures Collaborative, New Delhi and Adjunct Senior Research Fellow, LKY School of Public Policy, National University of Singapore.

Ms **Shibani Ghosh**, Advocate-on-Record, Supreme Court of India and Visiting Fellow, Sustainable Futures Collaborative, New Delhi.

Prof **Gitanjali Nain Gill**, Professor of Environmental Law, Northumbria University, Newcastle upon Tyne.

Prof **Kaveri Gill**, Non-Resident Senior Fellow, Centre for Excellence in Himalayan Studies, School of Humanities and Social Sciences, Shiv Nadar University (Institution of Eminence) Delhi-NCR.

Ms **Parul Gupta**, Advocate and Advisor to Vindhyan Ecology and Natural History Foundation, Mirzapur.

Ms **Shalini Iyengar**, Doctoral Candidate, Department of Anthropology, Yale University, New Haven, CT.

Ms **Alphonsa Jojan**, Doctoral candidate, Newcastle Law School, University of Newcastle, Australia.

Dr **Stellina Jolly**, Associate Professor, Faculty of Legal Studies, South Asian University, New Delhi and Visiting Senior Research Associate, Research Centre for Private International Law in Emerging Countries, University of Johannesburg.

Dr **Sophy K.J.**, Associate Professor, National Law University Delhi, New Delhi.

Mr **K.J. Joy**, Senior Fellow, Society for Promoting Participative Ecosystem Management (SOPPECOM), Pune.

Dr **Divya Karnad**, Assistant Professor, Department of Environmental Studies, Ashoka University, Sonipat.

Ms **Shomona Khanna**, Advocate, Supreme Court of India, and Founding Member, Legal Resource Centre, New Delhi.

Dr **Arpitha Kodiveri**, Assistant Professor in International Law and Political Science, Department of Political Science, Vassar College, New York.

Dr **Sujith Koonan**, Associate Professor, Centre for International Legal Studies, School of International Studies, Jawaharlal Nehru University, New Delhi.

Dr **Himanshu Kulkarni**, Scientist (Emeritus), Advanced Center for Water Resources Development and Management (ACWADAM), Pune.

Dr **Aruna L.**, Associate Professor and Chairperson—Internship and Placement Cell, CMR University School of Legal Studies, Bengaluru.

Dr **Sharachchandra Lele**, Distinguished Fellow in Environmental Policy and Governance, Ashoka Trust for Research in Ecology and the Environment, Bengaluru and Honorary Professor, Shiv Nadar University (Institution of Eminence) Delhi-NCR, and Adjunct Faculty, Department of Humanities and Social Sciences, Indian Institute of Science Education & Research (IISER) Pune.

Dr **Zainab Lokhandwala**, Lecturer in Sustainability and Environmental Law, University of Essex.

Prof **Roopa Madhav**, Professor of Law (Research), National Law University Delhi, New Delhi.

Dr **Sourav Kumar Mahanta**, Guest Faculty, Post Graduate Department of History, Government Autonomous College, Rourkela.

Prof **Shiju Mazhuvanchery**, Professor of Law, Sai University, Chennai.

Ms **Dhvani Mehta**, Co-Founder, Vidhi Centre for Legal Policy, New Delhi.

Prof **Lyla Mehta**, Professorial Fellow, Institute of Development Studies, Brighton and Visiting Professor, Norwegian University of Life Sciences, Ås, Norwey.

Mr **Haaris Moosa**, Advocate, High Court of Kerala, Kochi.

Prof **M.N. Murty**, Professor (Retired), Institute of Economic Growth, Delhi University, New Delhi.

Dr **Sushama Murty**, Professor, Centre for International Trade and Development, School of International Studies, Jawaharlal Nehru University, New Delhi.

Dr **Birsha Ohdedar**, Lecturer in Climate Change and Environmental Law, SOAS) University of London.

Mr **Aditya Valiathan Pillai**, Fellow and Coordinator for Adaptation and Resilience at the Sustainable Futures Collaborative, New Delhi

Dr **Jagjit Kaur Plahe**, Associate Professor, Department of Management Impact Labs, Monash University, Melbourne.

Prof **Tony George Puthucherril**, Professor of Law, OP Jindal Global University, Sonipat.

Prof **Prabhash Ranjan**, Professor and Vice Dean (Continuing Education), Jindal Global Law School, OP Jindal Global University, Sonipat.

Mr **Abraham Samuel**, Senior Consultant, Society for Promoting Participative Ecosystem Management (SOPPECOM), Pune.

Mr **Kumar Satyam**, Formerly Research Consultant, Advanced Center for Water Resources Development and Management (ACWADAM), Pune.

Uday Shankar, Associate Professor, Rajiv Gandhi School of Intellectual Property Law, IIT Kharagpur.

Prof **Awadhendra Sharan**, Director, Centre for the Study of Developing Societies, New Delhi.

Dr **Aviram Sharma**, Senior Researcher, Post-Growth Innovation Lab, University of Vigo, Pontevedra.

Prof **Charu Sharma**, Vice Dean (OSAI), Director, Centre for Environmental Law and Climate Change, OP Jindal Global University, Sonipat.

Mr **Debadityo Sinha**, Senior Resident Fellow and Lead-Climate & Ecosystems, Vidhi Centre for Legal Policy, New Delhi.

Mr **Sarvajeet Kumar** Sinha, Doctoral candidate, National Institute of Advanced Studies, Bengaluru.

Dr **Anirudh Sridhar**, Assistant Professor, Alliance University, Bengaluru and Visiting Fellow, London School of Economics and Political Science.

Prof **T.R. Subramanya**, Dean, School of Legal Studies, CMR University, Bengaluru.

Mr **Salil Tripathi**, Senior Adviser—Global Issues, Institute for Human Rights and Business, New York.

Mr **Sanjay Upadhyay**, Senior Advocate, Supreme Court of India.

Ms **M.S. Vani**, Trustee, Development Centre for Alternative Policies, New Delhi.

Prof **Virginius Xaxa**, Visiting Professor, Institute for Human Development, New Delhi; formerly Professor of Sociology, Delhi School of Economics and Tata Institute of Social Sciences, Guwahati Campus.

INTRODUCTION

PHILIPPE CULLET, LOVLEEN BHULLAR, AND SUJITH KOONAN*

THIS Handbook is a response to the rapid growth of environmental and natural resources law in India over the past few decades. The discipline is now a distinct field of research and teaching. A Handbook focused on India is required because the country has been at the forefront of jurisprudential developments among countries with similar environmental, geographical, socio-economic, and cultural conditions. Concurrently, India has been receptive to ideas and principles originating in other parts of the world or international law. The growth of environmental and natural resources law in India is sustained in part by growing environmental awareness and in part by the increasingly dire nature of the problems relating to the environment and natural resources, from local issues to the global climate crisis. At the same time, the continuous push for development has not abated, leading to recurrent pressure to weaken existing standards for environmental protection and the use and management of natural resources.

This Handbook combines the multiple strands of the diverse and complex area of environmental and natural resources law. The complexity is reflected at all levels, starting with the choice of the title for this volume. For a long time, natural resources law was understood as something separate from environmental law. The former mainly dealt with using and managing natural resources for economic development. The latter was concerned, to an extent, with preventing and controlling pollution and protecting and conserving the environment from the adverse effects of human actions, including developmental activities. In principle, 'sustainable development' has been framed around the need to integrate protection (environment) and use (development) for decades, but the pre-existing distinction between sectors is yet to be completely erased. This is, for instance, the case with water, where its protection is understood as an environmental matter, whereas the regulation of its use is part of what is known as 'water law', a separate area of regulation. Bringing together the 'environment' and 'natural resources' is a necessity in the 2020s.

* The editors would like to thank Ms Shibani Ghosh for her insightful comments on an earlier draft.

The rest of this introduction first offers the reader some insights into the rationale for this Handbook. This is followed by sections examining the selected frame of reference and the scope and relevance of the Handbook. The introduction then highlights some main themes and how the chapters are organized.

I.1 Rationale for this Handbook

Environmental and natural resources law is a broad discipline covering a variety of issues, including nature conservation, prevention and abatement of pollution, and waste management. It also encompasses concerns related to natural resources, such as forests, water, minerals, and fisheries, and the balance between their use and protection. In addition, certain integral parts of environmental and natural resources law, such as the laws relating to climate change and biodiversity, have become complex and separate areas in themselves. Environmental and natural resources law also connects with distinct but related fields, such as agriculture, food, health, human rights, and trade.

The broad nature of environmental and natural resources law has generated multiple debates, for example, concerning the scope of the 'environment' that forms the subject matter of regulation,[1] as well as the relationship between human beings and the environment.[2] The other issues that the discipline is grappling with include the need to strike the right balance between development and environment,[3] and increasingly, to address the inherent inequity in the relative importance given to the needs and interests of different individuals and communities.[4]

The growth of environmental and natural resources law in India over the past five decades has been phenomenal. Law and policy interventions, as well as case law, recognize the environment and natural resources as important areas of regulation. Environmental regulation pertaining to water and air pollution touches on the lives and activities of most people, directly or indirectly. Issues such as air pollution and climate change have managed to move beyond esoterism and have become part of everybody's routine talk, as in the case

[1] E.g., Andreas Philippopoulos-Mihalopoulos, 'Towards a Critical Environmental Law' in Andreas Philippopoulos-Mihalopoulos (ed), *Law and Ecology: New Environmental Foundations* (Routledge 2011) 18.

[2] E.g., Susan Emmenegger and Axel Tschentscher, 'Taking Nature's Rights Seriously: The Long Way to Biocentrism in Environmental Law' (1993–1994) 6(3) *Georgetown International Environmental Law Review* 545–592.

[3] E.g., Saptarishi Bandopadhyay, 'Sustainable Development and Indian Environmental Jurisprudence' in Shibani Ghosh (ed), *Indian Environmental Law: Key Concepts and Principles* (Orient BlackSwan 2019) 107.

[4] E.g., Geetanjoy Sahu, 'Mining in the Niyamgiri Hills and Tribal Rights' (2008) 43(15) *Economic and Political Weekly* 19–21; D Asher Ghertner, 'The Nuisance of Slums: Environmental Law and the Production of Slum Illegality in India' in Jonathan Shapiro Anjaria and Colin McFarlane (eds), *Urban Navigations: Politics, Space and the City in South Asia* (Routledge 2011) 23.

of air pollution in the National Capital Territory of Delhi and discussions on climate change in the context of frequent floods in the state of Kerala.[5] Efforts to strengthen environmental and natural resources law co-exist with attempts to dilute the existing standards and procedures relating to the protection, use, and conservation of the environment and natural resources, as confirmed by legislative proposals to weaken existing protection standards and procedures,[6] certain judicial decisions,[7] and the dilution of environmental regulation through executive orders.[8]

Environmental and natural resources law has also developed as a distinct field of research and teaching in India. This is evident from the increase in publications[9] and award of grants for research on issues relating to the environment and natural resources.[10] Further, environmental law is a compulsory subject for the undergraduate law degree (LLB) according to the Bar Council of India Rules of Legal Education,[11] and all the law schools in the country teach environmental law. A few universities offer a master's degree (LLM) in environmental and natural resources law.[12]

There has also been an increase in the visibility of environmental and natural resources law in India beyond national borders. In some areas of domestic jurisprudence, Indian law tends to be more developed than in neighbouring South Asian

[5] Shaju Philip, 'Climate Cafés Spark Debate in Rural Kerala on Environmental Issues', *The Indian Express* (2 November 2021) <https://indianexpress.com/article/india/kerala/climate-cafes-spark-debate-in-rural-kerala-on-environmental-issues-7603310/>.

[6] Leo F Saldanha, 'Need for Meaningful and Deeply Democratic Review and Debate on Fundamental Changes Proposed to India's Environment Protection Act, 1986 and Related Laws'—A Discussion Note (2022).

[7] E.g., *Pahwa Plastics Pvt Ltd v Dastak NGO* Civil Appeal No 4795 of 2021. Decided on 25 March 2022 (Supreme Court of India).

[8] E.g., Ayaskant Das, 'Incremental Dilution of India's Environment Regulatory Regime for Benefit of Corporates?', *NewsClick* (26 April 2022) <https://www.newsclick.in/incremental-dilution-india-environment-regulatory-regime-benefit-corporates>.

[9] E.g., Kailash Thakur, *Environmental Protection Law and Policy in India* (Deep and Deep Publications 1997); Aruna Venkat, *Environmental Law and Policy* (PHI Learning 2011); Mohammad Naseem and Saman Naseem, *Environmental Law in India* (Kluwer 2014); P Leelakrishnan, *Environmental Law in India* (LexisNexis 2016). See also Gitanjali N Gill, *Environmental Justice in India: The National Green Tribunal* (Routledge 2016); Shibani Ghosh (ed), *Indian Environmental Law: Key Concepts and Principles* (Orient BlackSwan 2019); Kanchi Kohli and Manju Menon, *Development of Environmental Laws in India* (CUP 2021); Shyam Divan and Armin Rosencranz, *Environmental Law and Policy in India: Cases, Materials, and Statutes* (3rd edn, OUP 2022).

[10] This includes the activities of the Centre for Environmental Law, WWF India, the Centre for Environmental Law Education, Research and Advocacy (CEERA), the South Asia Network on Environmental Law and Policy (SANEL), and Centre for Policy Research—Environmental Law and Governance.

[11] Bar Council of India, Rules of Legal Education 2008 <http://www.barcouncilofindia.org/wp-content/uploads/2010/05/BCIRulesPartIV.pdf>.

[12] E.g., Cochin University of Science and Technology (CUSAT), Tamil Nadu National Law University, Jindal Global Law School, and WWF-India.

countries.[13] India is known for its contributions to developing environmental law. This does not necessarily imply that laws or judgments are effectively implemented or enforced.[14] Further, the understanding of environmental and natural resources issues in India takes into consideration social and human issues to a certain extent.[15] This can be compared with member states of the Organization for Economic Co-operation and Development (OECD) where the understanding of the environment remains much more exclusively focused on science. This tends to sideline other dimensions, including social dimensions.[16]

Environmental and natural resources law in India also reflects a willingness to learn from developments elsewhere. This includes, for instance, the incorporation of the precautionary principle and the polluter pays principle, which has occurred in part by drawing upon binding and non-binding instruments of international environmental law.[17] However, this does not mean that environmental and natural resources law in India follows the principles and norms as articulated in international environmental law. For instance, while incorporating the precautionary principle, the Supreme Court of India preferred to articulate a strong version of the principle as opposed to the weaker version in international environmental law.[18] In certain cases, environmental and natural resources law in India has incorporated novel ideas and principles, which do not have a precedent in international environmental law or other domestic jurisdictions, for instance, the articulation of the principle of absolute liability in the context of hazardous or inherently dangerous industries.[19] This development took place in the aftermath of the Bhopal gas leak disaster.[20] Some progressive features of environmental and natural resources law in India, such as the application of the public trust doctrine in a manner that prevents any undue appropriation,[21] could enable domestic legal systems to leapfrog beyond their international commitments vis-à-vis protection of the environment and natural resources.

The rapid development of environmental and natural resources law in India highlights the need for and presents a unique opportunity to adopt a descriptive and

[13] E.g., Jona Razzaque, *Public Interest Environmental Litigation in India, Pakistan and Bangladesh* (Kluwer Law International 2003); Parvez Hassan, 'Good Environmental Governance: Some Trends in the South Asian Region' (2015) 18 *Asia Pacific Journal of Environmental Law* 169–192. See also Gill (n 9).

[14] Lovleen Bhullar, 'Water Pollution in India: Environmental Rights Litigation as a Solution' (PhD Thesis, SOAS University of London 2018).

[15] E.g., The Scheduled Tribes and Other Traditional Forest Dwellers (Recognition of Forest Rights) Act, 2006. At the same time, this does not imply that the implementation of such laws is effective.

[16] E.g., Nicolas de Sadeleer, *Environmental Principles: From Political Slogans to Legal Rules* (2nd edn, OUP 2021); Katherine Selena Taylor, Sheri Longboat, and Rupert Quentin Grafton, 'Whose Rules? A Water Justice Critique of the OECD's 12 Principles on Water Governance' (2019) 11 *Water* 809.

[17] Ghosh (n 9) chs 3–6.

[18] E.g., Lavanya Rajamani, 'The Precautionary Principle', in Shibani Ghosh (ed), *Indian Environmental Law: Key Concepts and Principles* (Orient BlackSwan 2019) 192.

[19] *MC Mehta v Union of India AIR* 1987 SC 1086 [*Oleum Gas leak* case].

[20] Usha Ramanathan, 'Bhopal: As the Law Develops' (2010) 45(34) *Economic and Political Weekly* 82. See also ch 38 in this volume.

[21] *MC Mehta v Kamal Nath* (1997) 1 SCC 388.

critical account of the same. This Handbook assesses the state-of-the-art environmental and natural resources law in India—both in its traditional sense and considering the interlinkages with 'non-environmental' issues. In addition, it situates existing and emerging concerns relating to the environment and natural resources in the contemporary context and analyses the responses of the makers, interpreters, and implementers of environmental and natural resources law.

Environmental and natural resources law in India has been a focus of extensive academic writing.[22] However, the pace and the magnitude with which the law and related policies in India have been evolving necessitate constant updating and expansion of their coverage. A Handbook that comprehensively and extensively covers different dimensions and issues in the context of environmental and natural resources law meets this requirement. At this juncture, the complexity and diversity of the topics to be covered necessitates the involvement of a large group of experts.

I.2 Integration as the Frame

This Handbook provides a comprehensive account and extensive analytical coverage of several important issues arising in the context of environmental and natural resources law in India. It contributes to the ongoing process of integrating our understanding and analysis of the 'environment' and 'natural resources', which are still too often considered separately in pedagogy, academic research, and law- and policy-making. Such an integration will lead to a better understanding of the connections between conservation, management, and the use of the environment and natural resources. The distinction between natural resources and the environment was always artificial. In fact, the debate should already have been settled in the 1970s. The Stockholm Declaration of 1972 asserted that 'natural resources of the earth, [include] the air, water, land, flora and fauna and especially representative samples of natural ecosystems'.[23] A later study prepared for the United Nations Environment Programme on the definition of natural resources repeated the above assertion and further blurred the distinction between the environment and natural resources.[24] Despite these early attempts at integration, it has taken decades to bring together the 'environment' and 'natural resources'. Some recent publications continue to define natural resources as substances that can be used to sustain life or for economic exploitation.[25]

[22] See fn 9.

[23] Declaration of the United Nations Conference on the Human Environment, Stockholm, 16 June 1972, UN Doc A/CONF.48/14/Rev 1, Principle 2.

[24] UNEP, Definition of Internationally Shared Natural Resources (1978) para 22.

[25] E.g., Julia Dehm, 'Natural Resources' in Koen De Feyter, Gamze Erdem Türkelli, and Stéphanie de Moerloose (eds), *Encyclopedia of Law and Development* (Edward Elgar 2022) 211.

There is an intimate link between the conservation of natural resources, maintenance of ecosystem balance, and sustenance of livelihoods. Yet, the distinction has endured in part because natural resources have often been reduced to a few resources, such as minerals, that could be more easily identified or understood as contributing to economic growth. At the same time, some of the most crucial natural resources, such as forests, have long been understood as falling within the scope of environmental law in India.

This artificial distinction between the environment and natural resources leads to a blinkered view of the field. This is well exemplified in the case of water. Environmental law and water law remain conceived as distinct fields. On the one hand, water is, in principle, part of the scope of environmental law in India, but, in practice, this is limited to a focus on the pollution and control of water pollution, as reflected in the Water (Prevention and Control of Pollution) Act, 1974. Environmental lawyers usually understand water through the lens of this legislation. On the other hand, water law deals extensively with issues related to the use and management of water. It focuses primarily on use, as exemplified by laws relating to irrigation.[26] This is not to say that points of contact have not developed, but they remain insufficient. An example is the emphasis in water law on scarcity, which is an environmental concern. Typically, groundwater laws focus on the use of groundwater in relation to water scarcity.[27] However, this concern usually translates only to measures to restrict the use of groundwater by individual users rather than broader measures to protect aquifers.[28]

This Handbook addresses a range of issues such as conservation, livelihoods, and pollution that are, among other things, part of the umbrella concept of sustainable development. These issues are interconnected and, therefore, need to be considered in tandem. In fact, the interconnectedness of these issues has been the anchor of sustainable development and the Sustainable Development Goals (SDGs), a set of development goals, including those relating to the environment and natural resources.[29] This integrated approach has also been incorporated in the domestic policy framework in India, and NITI Aayog has been tasked with coordinating the development of a synergistic approach to achieve them by 2030.[30]

The concept of sustainable development and the SDGs inform many of the chapters in this Handbook, even if they do not directly address the concept or the goals because

[26] Roopa Madhav, 'Law and Policy Reforms for Irrigation' in Philippe Cullet and others (eds), *Water Law for the Twenty First Century: National and International Aspects of Water Law Reform in India* (Routledge 2010) 205.

[27] E.g., Kerala Ground Water (Control and Regulation) Act, 2002; West Bengal Ground Water Resources (Management, Control and Regulation) Act, 2005.

[28] E.g., Philippe Cullet, 'Groundwater Law in India—Towards a Framework Ensuring Equitable Access and Aquifer Protection' (2014) 26(1) *Journal of Environmental Law* 55.

[29] Sustainable Development Goals and Targets, in UN General Assembly Resolution 70/1, Transforming our World: The 2030 Agenda for Sustainable Development, UN Doc A/RES/70/1 (2015).

[30] The NITI Aayog is described as the apex public policy think tank of the government of India. See NITI Aayog, SDG India Index—Baseline Report (2018) 3.

they focus mostly on the law rather than on policy goals. At the same time, some of the chapters address the constitutive elements of sustainable development, in particular principles and concepts, which form an integral feature of domestic environmental law and, to an increasing extent, natural resources law. In this context, this Handbook includes discussions of the principles of prevention and precaution, the polluter pays principle, and the principle of inter-generational equity in the context of mining and industrial disasters (chapters 36 and 38). These principles are part of environmental and natural resources law in India, first through case law and subsequently through an explicit mandate in the National Green Tribunal Act, 2010.[31]

I.3 Scope and Relevance

This Handbook focuses on India partly due to the vastness of the discipline and the country, including its environment and natural resources and partly because of the lack of literature that offers a single point of reference for learning, teaching, and research purposes. However, the relevance of the Handbook is not limited to readers in India or researchers focusing on environmental and natural resources law in India.

This is due to several reasons. First, issues relating to the environment and natural resources covered in this Handbook also arise in other countries in the global 'South' and the global 'North'. Second, developments in India have influenced the growth of environmental and natural resources law in other countries in South Asia, which have progressively become more independent of these early moorings. Third, globally, India has been a beacon in terms of judicial activism around social and environmental justice.[32] This pro-poor and pro-environment image of the judiciary in India has come under increasing scrutiny in the past couple of decades,[33] but this does not diminish India's contribution to environmental and natural resources jurisprudence globally.

However, this connection between environmental and natural resources law in India on the one hand and international and foreign jurisdictions on the other is not unidirectional. Legal developments in other jurisdictions have exerted some influence on the development of environmental and natural resources law in India. This is, for instance, the case with the public trust doctrine. The Supreme Court of India heavily relied on developments in the US[34] while declaring that the public trust doctrine is part of the law on environmental and natural resources law in India[35].

[31] National Green Tribunal Act, 2010 s 20.

[32] E.g., Hajime Sato, 'The Universality, Peculiarity, and Sustainability of Indian Public Interest Litigation Reconsidered' (2017) 100 *World Development* 59–68.

[33] E.g., Prashant Bhushan, 'Sacrificing Human Rights and Environmental Rights at the Altar of "Development"' (2010) 41(2) *George Washington International Law Review* 389.

[34] *National Audubon Society v Department of Water and Power of the City of Los Angeles*, Supreme Court of California, 17 February 1983, 658 P.2d 709.

[35] *MC Mehta* (n 21).

This Handbook contextualizes and emphasizes the links between several elements of environmental and natural resources law in India and international law. An important manifestation of this link is the fact that several of the environmental statutes in India are part of India's efforts to comply with its obligations under international environmental law. For instance, domestic biodiversity laws were enacted to implement India's international commitments under the Convention on Biological Diversity, 1992, and the Nagoya Protocol on Access and Benefit Sharing, 2010.[36] The Wetland Conservation and Management Rules, 2017, apply to wetlands designated as Ramsar Sites under the Ramsar Convention on Wetlands of International Importance especially as Waterfowl Habitat, 1971.[37] India is a signatory to all the major international legal instruments that prescribe legal obligations on states to protect the coastal and the marine environment. The National Disaster Management Plan (which also refers to the Paris Agreement, 2015 and the SDGs) aligns with the Sendai Framework on Disaster Risk Reduction, 2015. Less explicitly, domestic climate policy and the recent efforts towards the development of a legal regime respond to the international climate regime comprising the United Nations Framework Convention on Climate Change, 1992, the Kyoto Protocol, 1997, and the Paris Agreement, 2015.[38] Beyond multilateral environmental agreements, environmental concerns are also addressed through other regimes, for instance, international investment law (chapter 7). At the same time, international law (based on consensus among all signatory nations) may restrict the scope of domestic law, particularly in the global 'South', as is the case with World Trade Organization (WTO) agreements and the domestic regulatory regime governing agriculture.[39]

The scope of this Handbook extends beyond the existing scholarship on environmental and natural resources law that tends to address a limited number of issues.[40] Existing scholarship has increasingly offered deeper insights into specific aspects of environmental law, such as environmental principles.[41] Bringing together the different strands of environmental and natural resources law will lead to wider recognition of the linkages between different issues. This is well illustrated in the case of climate change, often understood as an all-encompassing environmental issue. At the same time, climate change policy often focuses on energy directly linked with greenhouse gas emissions

36 Convention on Biological Diversity, Rio de Janeiro, 5 June 1992, 1760 UNTS 79; Protocol on Access to Genetic Resources and the Fair and Equitable Sharing of Benefits Arising from their Utilization, Nagoya, 29 October 2010, UN Doc UNEP/CBD/COP/DEC/X/1.

37 Convention on Wetlands of International Importance, Ramsar, 2 February 1971, 996 UNTS 245.

38 UN Framework Convention on Climate Change, New York, 9 May 1992, 1771 UNTS 107; Kyoto Protocol to the United Nations Framework Convention on Climate Change, Kyoto, 11 December 1997, 2303 UNTS 162; Paris Agreement, Paris, 12 December 2015, in the Report of the Conference of the Parties on its Twenty-First Session, UN Doc FCCC/CP/2015/10/Add.1.

39 E.g., Jennifer Clapp, 'WTO Agriculture Negotiations: Implications for the Global South' (2006) 27(4) *Third World Quarterly* 563.

40 E.g., Kanchi Kohli and Manju Menon, *Development of Environmental Laws in India* (CUP 2021); Sairam Bhat, *Natural Resources Conservation Law* (Sage 2010).

41 See generally Ghosh (n 9).

without making links with other sectors, such as labour. It is therefore crucial to understand the different strands of environmental and natural resources law as a whole to ensure progressively improved integration of the environment and natural resources in drafting and implementing laws.

This Handbook provides a comprehensive study of environmental and natural resources law in India. It offers a reference guide for students, researchers, and law- and policy-makers interested in environmental and natural resources law in India. This focus on India notwithstanding, this Handbook deals with issues of more general relevance, such as the relationship between domestic and international law and between law and other disciplines such as economics, history, and political science. Thus, this Handbook is also relevant for students and researchers from other disciplines working on issues relating to the environment and natural resources.

This Handbook introduces different areas of environmental and natural resources law, as well as in-depth engagement with specific topics. At the same time, owing to the constraints of a single volume, each topic is not addressed in as much detail as may be the case in a more focused monograph. Further, although this Handbook attempts to cover as many topics as possible, the list is not exhaustive. In addition, given the space constraints, each chapter highlights major trends without being necessarily comprehensive. As a result, this Handbook maintains a delicate balance between breadth and depth of coverage of environmental and natural resources law in India. Further, there are some unavoidable but limited overlaps in certain parts/chapters in the Handbook, such as concerning land (chapter 17) and forests (chapter 24). At the same time, the Handbook remains true to its intellectual agenda of integrating the 'environment' and 'natural resource' and offering a comprehensive panorama of environmental and natural resources law in India.

While this Handbook covers most of the important issues and aspects of environmental and natural resource law in India in individual chapters, some subjects are dealt with as part of other chapters in this Handbook. For instance, the substantive and procedural dimensions of public interest environmental litigation in India have long been recognized for their pioneering role.[42] The inter-linkages between environmental and natural resources law in India, on the one hand, and administrative law, common law, constitutional law on the other are also acknowledged.[43] Some of the chapters in this Handbook elaborate the specific manifestations of these aspects and contribute to the growing domestic environmental and natural resources jurisprudence (chapter 40).

With contributions from academics, practitioners, and researchers representing different generations, this Handbook offers a representative sample of Indian environmental and natural resources law scholarship that has emerged and evolved over the

[42] E.g., Lavanya Rajamani, 'Public Interest Environmental Litigation in India: Exploring Issues of Access, Participation, Equity, Effectiveness and Sustainability' (2007) 19(3) *Journal of Environmental Law* 293.

[43] E.g., Rosencranz and Divan (n 9).

years. Most contributors are scholars working on the topic they have covered for years. Other chapters are authored by early career researchers, including doctoral scholars. These contributions allow the Handbook to present evolving substantive and methodological perspectives and to engage with novel issues. Most authors are academics, but the Handbook also includes authors with experience at the grassroots level in bureaucracy and activism. Another unique aspect of this Handbook is that some of the authors do not have a legal background, but they have wide-ranging experience in researching legal issues and participating in law- and policy-making at the state and central levels, as well as in litigation relating to the environment and natural resources. This amalgam of authors brings much-needed diversity of perspectives otherwise missing in the existing literature on environmental and natural resources law in India.

I.4 Approach and Themes

The chapters in this Handbook follow a similar structure. First, they provide a clear, panoramic view of the existing law and policy framework about a particular topic, including its historical evolution as and when necessary. In the process, the chapters engage with law and policy instruments and case law (to varying extent) and the relevant literature. This ensures the Handbook can be used as a reference material and a teaching resource. Second, the chapters provide critical reflections on the law and policy framework besides engaging with current and emerging challenges in the field of environmental and natural resources law.

One contribution addresses international law dimensions (chapter 2), two consider South Asian perspectives concerning environmental and natural resources law generally (chapter 3), and water disputes and the environment (chapter 33). Most contributors describe and analyse domestic law in India directly, including constitutional provisions, legislation and case law, policies, and institutions. Chapter 4 focuses on the Constitution of India, 1950. A few rely on case studies for this purpose, for example, in the case of disasters (Sunderbans—chapter 29) and fisheries (customary law of indigenous fisherfolk—chapter 22). While critical reflections may indirectly point towards certain solutions, this Handbook does not prescribe specific solutions to the problems discussed or gaps identified. It is intended to be deliberative and reflective rather than prescriptive.

As explained in Section I.4, the chapters have been written by various authors with different entry points into the topic covered, helping to bring a fresh outlook on environmental and natural resources law to this Handbook. This is why some chapters go beyond a strict legal analysis to offer a broader reading of the policy, social, scientific, or economic context within which the topic falls. The latter translates to the adoption of an interdisciplinary approach in several chapters. For instance, examining the history of laws is essential for understanding their origin, nature, and scope. In addition to a specific chapter on environmental history (chapter 1), this historical perspective is evident in the chapters dealing with fisheries, forest rights, health, and sanitation, among others (chapters 22, 25, 34, and

35). Environmental and natural resources law in India is characterized by an ongoing balancing act between environmental protection and social and economic development (often described as sustainable development) (chapter 10). Other contributions address the principles of prevention, precaution, and polluter pays (chapter 11) and the public trust doctrine (chapter 12). In addition, the traditional command-and-control approach to regulating the environment and natural resources is no longer the only game in town. Economic instruments have entered the fray (chapter 8). The chapter on environmental movements highlights social and political factors as the key elements of any discussion of environmental and natural resources law in India (chapter 5), and specific chapters address these factors regarding food sovereignty and forest rights (chapters 5, 18, and 25). The chapters on agriculture (chapter 19) and biosafety in synthetic biology (chapter 21) examine the links between technology, the environment, and natural resources.

This Handbook uses the term law as a countable and uncountable noun, encompassing the multitude of laws relating to the environment and natural resources in India. There are specific laws in respect of certain issues, for example, biodiversity, forests, and wildlife. In most instances, these particular laws are not comprehensive. In other cases, there are no specific laws to deal with issues, as in the case of climate change. Laws dealing with other issues are often relevant in both situations. Some of the contributions engage with legal pluralism in the form of the notion of common property resources (chapter 17) and customary law of indigenous coastal fisherfolk (chapter 22). Several chapters consider binding laws and non-binding policies,[44] as in the case of climate change (National Action Plan on Climate Change) (chapter 28), the coastal and marine environment (Integrated Coastal Zone Management) (chapter 23), disasters (National Disaster Management Plan) (chapter 29), sanitation (chapter 35), and water (chapter 31).

The Handbook addresses specific topics that form the subject matter of environmental and natural resources law in India. It also addresses several broader themes, some of which run through the Handbook, while others are more specifically linked to certain parts and chapters. At the same time, there are links between the topics covered in different parts of the Handbook. For example, Part VI on 'Forests, ecosystems, and people' must be read with chapters on biodiversity (Part IV), the coastal and marine environment (Part V), climate change (Part VII), and water (Part VIII) among others. Similarly, Part VIII on water is linked to Part V on fisheries and the coastal and marine environment, as well as the chapters on social movements (Part I), land (Part IV), and climate change and disasters (Part VII). In other words, the domestic law framework relating to specific components of the environment and natural resources is not confined to laws with those terms in the title.

Some of the key substantive themes emerging from the different chapters in this Handbook are as follows:

[44] The term 'policy' includes action plans, programmes, etc.

First, it is imperative to examine environmental and natural resources law in India by referring to diverse state and non-state actors, the relationship between the three branches of state in respect of the enactment, implementation, and interpretation of environmental and natural resources law, as well as the economic, social, and environmental justice dimensions of the issues and related laws.

Second, it is almost impossible to study environmental and natural resources law in India without considering the constitutional and/or statutory rights of individuals and the duties of the state. The constitutional rights include the rights to life, health, sanitation, the environment, and water. One chapter engages with the duties of non-state actors including citizens as well as corporations (chapter 13). Environmental law, and to a great extent, natural resources law, is overwhelmingly anthropocentric. Judicial recognition of the rights of nature and constitutional, statutory, and judicial developments in respect of the rights of nature and animals and the corresponding duties of human beings mark a gradual shift towards acknowledging the intrinsic value of non-human beings (chapter 14). Procedural rights of access to information, public participation in decision-making and access to justice complement the substantive components of environmental and natural resources law in India (chapter 15). The chapter on substantive and procedural due process sheds light on issues relating to both law-making and implementation (chapter 16).

Third, the concept of public interest underpins environmental and natural resources law in India. Laws seek to address the complementarity, as well as tensions between forests, wildlife, and forest dwellers to varying extents. In some cases, wildlife protection, forest management or economic development is pitted against the rights of forest communities; in others, conflict exists between wildlife, forests, and forest communities on one hand and economic development on the other. A narrow understanding of public interest excludes forest communities from the decision-making process; a narrow species focus of wildlife laws may undermine the protection of other species (chapters 24, 25, and 26).

Fourth, the implementation and enforcement of environmental and natural resources law can be considered through the lens of statutory provisions relating to penalties and compensation and availability of, and access to, courts and tribunals. Chapters addressing issues such as air pollution (chapter 27), water pollution (chapter 31), and hazardous wastes and substances (chapter 37) consider the scope and limits of relevant statutory provisions and statutory institutions such as pollution control boards. The chapter on penalties and compensation discusses different types of penalties (chapter 40), and there is a separate chapter on liability (chapter 9). The development of public interest litigation before the Supreme Court of India and High Courts at the state level has significantly impacted the field of environmental and natural resources law, at least since the early 1980s. In fact, the rise in environmental litigation even led to the establishing of a distinct body, the National Green Tribunal (NGT), to resolve environmental disputes. In addition to a specific chapter on the NGT (chapter 41) and another chapter that considers compensation before the NGT (chapter 40), several chapters engage with the role of the judiciary in respect of the environment and natural resources in India.

Fifth, administrative boundaries underpin the discussion of certain environmental and natural resources laws. Users of forests include forest communities, private corporations, and members of the public living in other parts of the country. Agriculture-related laws focus on agriculturists in rural areas but exclude consumers in urban and rural areas. Other instances of boundary drawing include the urban versus rural dimension of water use laws (chapter 30), the provision of water and sanitation in urban slums (chapter 35), and interstate dimensions of water sharing and protection (chapter 32). The boundaries are also evident in Schedule V and Schedule VI areas under the Constitution of India (chapter 6), in respect of industrial disasters (chapter 38), municipal solid waste management (chapter 42) in urban areas, and environmental and climate-related disasters in other parts of the country (chapter 29).

Sixth, an individual's class, caste, gender, and/or ethnicity combine to create different modes of discrimination and privilege in respect of the environment and natural resources and related laws in India. The contributions on environmental movements (chapter 5), biodiversity (indigenous communities) (chapter 20), fisheries (indigenous fisherfolk) (chapter 22), forest rights (forest-dwelling communities) (chapter 25), and sanitation (poor women) (chapter 35) engage with the analytical framework of intersectionality to varying extent.

Seventh, some chapters discuss regulatory responses to environmental and natural resources issues that have either emerged or gained more salience over the years but have received insufficient attention in the existing literature. These include regulatory measures in Schedule Areas (chapter 6), the environmental aspects of agricultural law (chapter 18), health law (chapter 34), sustainability issues related to energy (chapter 39), and biosafety in synthetic biology (chapter 21).

Finally, this Handbook must be read in the context of the progressive evolution of environmental and natural resources law in India. The era that witnessed the steady strengthening of environmental safeguards cannot be taken as a given. This means that some of the elements addressed in the chapters of this Handbook may evolve. Some recent developments, such as the notification of the Forest (Conservation) Rules, 2022, the passing of the Wild Life (Protection) Amendment Bill, 2021, and other proposals, are likely to exert significant influence on the contours of environmental and natural resources law in India.[45] Yet, this Handbook addresses topics that will remain relevant regardless of specific regulatory changes. This will ensure the relevance of this volume for years to come.

[45] See also, the *Jan Vishwas* (Amendment of Provisions) Act, 2023, revising penalty amounts under the Public Liability Insurance Act, 1991; the Environment (Protection) Act, 1986 and the Air (Prevention and Control of Pollution) Act, 1981.

I.5 Organization

This Handbook has been organized thematically with eleven parts broadly addressing distinct but interrelated themes or aspects of the law relating to the environment and natural resources in India. Part I provides the background and the context of the Handbook. While it does not examine any specific issue or aspect *per se*, it provides the contextual scenario that is relevant for understanding and analysing the other parts/chapters. It, therefore, looks at the law relating to the environment and natural resources in India from a historical perspective and in the context of the legal framework at international and regional levels. It also provides an overview of the constitutional and statutory framework for the environment and natural resources in India and the contribution of social movements to the discourse. Part II focuses on institutional and regulatory regimes by highlighting the institutional mechanisms in Schedule 5 and 6 areas as identified in the Constitution of India, and analyses economic instruments, liability, and exceptions in investment and trade law to achieve environmental goals. Part III introduces and analyses key existing and emerging substantive and procedural principles of environmental and natural resources law in India. Part IV discusses land, agriculture, and biodiversity. The chapters in this part focus on different kinds of property rights over land, the links between agriculture, environment, and technology from the point of view of sustainability and rights, and biodiversity, including issues of access and benefit sharing and biosafety in the context of evolving technologies. Part V examines fisheries and the marine environment, focusing on the intersection of the environment, natural resources, and the people. In continuation of the focus on specific ecosystems, Part VI examines the law relating to the protection of forests and wildlife in India and how it interacts with the life of forest-dependent and forest-dwelling people.

Part VII concerns air pollution, climate change and environmental disasters, which are interconnected issues. Air pollution is a serious environmental issue in India. Certain air pollutants contribute to climate change, a local, national, regional, and global challenge. The adverse impacts of climate change affect the occurrence and severity of disasters in India. Similarly, Part VIII offers a description and analysis of laws relating to groundwater and the regulation of water quality and pollution in India. An environmental perspective is adopted to examine (a) water sharing between states in India with reference to the distinct legal framework for interstate rivers, and (b) the use and protection of important rivers in India (e.g., Ganges and Brahmaputra) that are transboundary in nature using the existing legal and institutional mechanisms as the starting point. Part IX looks at the intersection of health, sanitation, and the environment from a legal perspective, most importantly to examine the extent to which existing laws on health and sanitation address environmental aspects and consequently contribute to realizing the fundamental rights to health, sanitation, and the environment. Part X addresses the extraction of mineral resources, production of energy, and production and disposal of waste (hazardous, solid, and e-waste) from an environmental angle. Finally, Part XI focuses on two important aspects of enforcement of the law relating to the environment and natural resources in India, that is, the system of penalties and compensation, the role of a specific tribunal—the National Green Tribunal—established for the settlement of environmental disputes, and the role of courts in solid waste management.

PART I

BACKGROUND AND CONTEXT

CHAPTER 1

ENVIRONMENT, NATURAL RESOURCES, AND ENVIRONMENTAL HISTORY

VINITA DAMODARAN AND
SOURAV KUMAR MAHANTA

ABSTRACT

The chapter looks at laws relating to the environment and how these came to be formulated, resource challenges and conflicts facing states and communities, and the development of new regulatory frameworks in colonial India. It attempts to fill the gaps in the literature by focusing primarily on laws related to forests, water, mining, and fisheries in the nineteenth and twentieth centuries covering a long time frame in the context of a broader environmental history of India.

INTRODUCTION

IN this chapter, we take the perspective of political environmental history to examine law and state policy in India from the late eighteenth century until the twentieth century and to understand how it relates to the natural world in the colonial and post-colonial periods. The systematic study of how governments at the regional and national levels approached nature, how interest groups struggled over it, and law and legislation is part of this field of enquiry. The chapter attempts to fill the gaps in the literature on India by focusing primarily on laws related to forests, water, mining, and fisheries in the nineteenth and twentieth centuries, covering a long time frame in the context of a broader environmental history of India. While there has been a lot of discussion in the existing literature on forest laws, there has been less on ownership of minerals and mining-related legislation in India. The post-colonial Indian state's assertion of property rights over its land, minerals, and water sources can be seen as an essential aspect of modern nationalism, but its fostering of a specific type of corporate capitalism is proving highly destructive to the environment and people's livelihoods. Understanding India's environmental history and natural resource legislation in the nineteenth and twentieth centuries against this background of what today is a massive land grab by corporate companies and the state is central to the theme of environmental justice. The rights of communities to land and resources through recourse to customary law can be seen as part of claim making by social movements.

Current interest in natural resources/common property resources law has arisen from a larger interest in colonialism, globalization, land alienation, environmental protection, and rights in the context of a growing resource crisis. The largest country in the world in terms of population and occupying 3.2 million sq km of territory, India's environmental history, including the history of forest destruction, conservation, water pollution, and rights, is critical to current debates on the environment.[1] Many resistance movements in India today have concerns around land, and there are recurrent debates around the question of development for whom? There is a long history of people's struggle against developmental policy and enclosures resulting from colonial law, which resulted in what Guha has called 'a neo-feudal organization of landed property' under the Permanent Settlement of Bengal.[2] Rights accruing to the *zamindari* class were challenged from the nineteenth century through popular struggles for customary law by tribal communities in Eastern India. In the case of the iconic tribal rebellion of Birsa Munda in the 1890s, forest regulation of the colonial state, which restricted the rights of communities to their forests, came under attack.[3] It is important to note that for India, a historical inquiry into a body of law dealing with natural resources is still undeveloped and has remained subsumed within the broader field of environmental history which, in turn, has been dominated by studies on forests. Scholars like Richard Grove, Ramchandra Guha, Mahesh Rangarajan, Ravi Rajan, and Akhileshwar Pathak have made significant contributions to the study of forest legislation, while water rights have been explored in the work of Rohan D'Souza and more recently by Aditya Ramesh.[4] Other areas of natural law have been less systematically studied.

[1] Kilaparti Ramakrishna, 'The Emergence of Environmental Law in the Developing Countries: A Case Study of India' (1984–85) 12(4) *Ecological Law Quarterly* 907.

[2] Ranajit Guha, *A Rule of Property for Bengal: An Essay on the Idea of Permanent Settlement* (Duke University Press 1996).

[3] Suresh K Singh, *The Dust-storm and Hanging Mist: A Study of Birsa Munda and His Movement in Chotanagpur, 1874–1901* (Firma KL Mukhopadhyay 1966).

[4] Richard Grove, *Green Imperialism: Colonial Expansion, Tropical Island Edens and the Origins of Environmentalism, 1600–1860* (CUP 1995); Ramachandra Guha, *The Unquiet Woods: Ecological Change and Peasant Resistance in the Himalaya* (OUP 1989); Mahesh Rangarajan, *Fencing the Forest—Conservation and Ecological Change in India's Central Provinces 1860–1914* (OUP 1996); Rohan D'Souza, *Drowned and Dammed: Colonial Capitalism and Flood Control in Eastern India* (OUP 2006); Aditya Ramesh, 'Custom as Natural: Land, Water and Law in Colonial Madras' (2017) 34(1) *Studies in History* 29.

In this chapter, we show how environmental law in India was located within a particular colonial framework and how different understandings of legal entitlements or rights about common property resulted in law emerging as a critical area of struggle between different actors in specific contexts in colonial India.[5] This is particularly important given the contemporary crisis of the legal system in India where the law is overlooked in the context of sustained land grabs by mining companies enshrining the need to protect private interests at all costs though 'lawfare' or the use of law as a medium of control.[6] By examining legal norms as they emerged in specific historical contexts, we hope to examine 'the ways in which rights to use, own and access resources have been framed by local communities in dialogue with the state'.[7] It is important to highlight in this context how subaltern resistance has taken the form of legal and popular struggle even in the past.

The large rural and tribal or *Adivasi* communities in India are most affected by how laws that affect their ability to access, use, and own resources have been historically framed. The land struggles in Eastern India, for example, have resulted in the passage of some unique tenure laws like the Chotanagpur Tenancy Act, 1908, which was a product of a tribal movement in the late nineteenth century. However, their success was undermined by the forest laws in the region, which were imposed from above by the state and were difficult to challenge. The usurpation of common natural resources over land, whether through state monopoly or a private capitalist body and its legal validity have had a major impact on people's lives in the colonial period as they do now.[8] Many scholars have commented on post-colonial continuities in terms of ecological control and resistance in India.[9] The state ownership of forests and the application of the legal principle of eminent domain have 'continued to erode the customary collective rights of local communities to commons; classification of forests based on the principles of conservation and commercial use which have deprived the rural poor of timber, fodder, firewood, forest lands and produce'.[10] Local norms and practices are flouted and the extensive powers of the Forest Department over the lives and livelihoods of local populations have resulted in the forced displacement of forest-based communities from national parks and wildlife sanctuaries.

[5] Nandini Sundar (ed), *Legal Grounds—Natural Resources, Identity, and the Law in Jharkhand* (OUP 2009). See also Elinor Ostrom, 'Beyond Markets and States: Polycentric Governance of Complex Economic Systems' (2010) 100(3) *American Economic Review* 641.

[6] See Sundar (n 5) 4.

[7] ibid.

[8] Vinita Damodaran, 'Indigenous Agency: Customary Rights and Tribal Protection in Eastern India, 1830–1930' (2013) 76 *History Workshop Journal* 85.

[9] Ashok Swain, 'Democratic Consolidation? Environmental Movements in India' (1997) 37(9) *Asian Survey* 818.

[10] Shalini Randeria, 'Global Designs and Local Lifeworlds: Colonial Legacies of Conservation, Disenfranchisement and Environmental Governance in Postcolonial India' (2007) 9(1) *Interventions—International Journal of Postcolonial Studies* 12.

Such usurpation has been achieved through a complex network of Forest Acts, laws concerning minor forest produce, those governing other common lands, and industrial and agrarian laws and policies. State monopoly over resources has enabled it to make these available to specific private industries and has become the medium through which privatization is facilitated. However, these were not the only reasons the state took over custodianship of forests and game. As Grove has argued, another reason that led to environmental regulations was the fear of the colonial government that unrestricted exploitation of resources such as forests by private enterprise would result in the drying up or desiccation of soils followed by famines and food crisis on a sub-continental scale.[11] The forest reserves that were created excluded local communities and coupled with privatization of common property resources was a historical injustice, which the British and subsequently the independent Indian government have perpetuated on rural and tribal India. As Sundar notes, 'the Indian Forest Act of 1927, like the Indian Penal Code, is a classic example of colonial law that has carried to the post-colonial period unchanged'.[12] Many hundreds of poor tribal communities find themselves languishing in prison for petty forest crimes with no recourse to justice or the law. Also important to note here is that increasing privatization, apart from divesting local communities from access to their natural resources, is also the reason for massive deforestation and other ecological problems.[13] Until the passage of the Scheduled Tribes and Other Traditional Forest Dwellers (Recognition of Forest Rights) Act in 2006, the entire management of forests rested with the Forest Department. This chapter attempts to outline the legislation related to forests in the context of other natural resources and common property law related to water, fishing, and minerals.

1.1 Forest Rights and Conservation Agendas

In India, forest laws were met with resistance like that encountered by the enclosure movement in Britain in the sixteenth century.[14] The East India Company had, from the eighteenth century, been involved in forest exploration, timber trade, and promoting timber plantations. In the nineteenth century, the destructive impact of uncontrolled natural resource exploitation across the colonial world began to give rise to a sophisticated environmentalist response and demands for intervention. The nature of the response to environmental change varied in different territories, but there were also

[11] Grove (n 4) 11. See also Richard Grove, Vinita Damodaran, and Satpal Sangwan (eds), *Nature and the Orient: The Environmental History of South and Southeast Asia* (OUP 1998).

[12] Sundar (n 5) 7.

[13] Damodaran (n 8).

[14] Chester Kirby, 'The English Game Law System' (1933) 38(2) *The American Historical Review* 240.

some common features.[15] It is important to note that while India provided the model for early state forestry legislation elsewhere, many of the ideas on which it drew originated in other parts of the Empire in fragile island environments. Ideas of finitude, extinction, and desiccation, for example, first emerged in the eighteenth century in the context of oceanic islands, which suffered devastation because of what Richards has described as the 'unending frontier' of colonial resource extraction.[16] This growing environmental consciousness was motivated by several factors, most importantly the climatic fear that if unregulated deforestation were to continue, droughts and famines would ensue. By the nineteenth century, early legislative interventions for conservation on islands such as St Vincent, Mauritius, and St Helena were to lead the way to the first comprehensive set of forestry regulations in India in the guise of the Indian Forest Acts of 1865 and 1878.[17] As a model for the custodianship of natural heritage, the Indian case provided much of the basis for debates on environmental intervention and conservation that went on in other parts of the British Empire.[18] It is important to point out here that although it was not until 1865 that the formal structure of an Indian Forest Act was established, the environmental context in which state forestry in India originated had already been going on both in India and elsewhere in the British Empire for many decades.[19] These debates were dominated not only by a production agenda but also, and as importantly, by conservationists and surgeons concerned about the relationships between deforestation, climatic deterioration, disease, agricultural production, and aesthetics.[20] While it has been argued that the Forest Act should be understood primarily as a feature of modern state formation,[21] this obscures a wider variety of imperial agents and motivations. In the context of a modern state agenda within institutions such as forestry, many discordant voices came to be heard in the nineteenth century. This included not only the assertion of different agendas for forestry in terms of the custodianship of natural environments and their flora and fauna but also, for example, debates concerning the rights of indigenous communities, many of whom had begun to voice vociferous resistance to these Acts. This latter concern was increasingly being aired by district officers on the ground as they witnessed the impact of unregulated forest exploitation on local populations.[22]

[15] Richard Grove and Vinita Damodaran, 'Imperialism, Intellectual Networks, and Environmental Change: Unearthing the Origins and Evolution of Global Environmental History' in Sverker Sörlin and Paul Warde (eds), *Nature's End: History and the Environment* (Palgrave Macmillan 2009) 23.

[16] John F Richards, *The Unending Frontier: An Environmental History of the Early Modern World* (University of California Press 2006).

[17] Grove (n 4) 9–12.

[18] Paul Basu and Vinita Damodaran, 'Colonial Histories of Heritage: Legislative Migrations and the Politics of Preservation' (2015) 226 *Past and Present* 240.

[19] Grove (n 4); Guha (n 4); Rangarajan (n 4).

[20] Grove (n 4) 11.

[21] K Sivaramakrishnan, *Modern Forests: State Making and Environmental Change in Colonial Eastern India* (Stanford University Press 1999).

[22] Basu and Damodaran (n 18) 266.

In 1864, an India-wide Imperial Forest Department was established, and a year later, the Indian Forest Act was passed. While the 1865 Act was the first large-scale environmental law implemented in the nineteenth century, it was hurriedly drafted and regarded as incomplete in many respects. Indeed, it was soon superseded by the 1878 Forest Act. This was much more draconian in nature, giving the state absolute control over forested areas, overriding the existing customary practices and rights of indigenous people.[23] By 1880, nearly a fifth of India's land mass came under the control of the Forest Department highlighting a vision of conservation that enshrined the imperial sensibilities of custodianship of men such as Lord Dalhousie and Lord Curzon, who were responsible for the creation of the Kaziranga Reserve Forest (India's first game park) in 1905. As deputy to the Secretary of State for the Colonies in 1906, campaigning for the strengthening of Game Laws across the Empire, Curzon argued that, while 'we are continually using language which implies that we are the trustees for posterity of the Empire ... we are also trustees for posterity of the natural contents of that Empire'.[24]

In Eastern India, the colonial officials argued for the insulation of forests from the pressure of local communities. The state did this by claiming property rights on forests through the Forest Act, 1865, which was re-enacted in 1878. It was claimed that in English law, all unoccupied land was vested in the king, and, therefore, the British state in India had sovereign rights over all forests and wastelands. The customary usage of the local people since time immemorial was interpreted to be at the mercy of the monarch and not a customary right.[25] In the schema of the Forest Act, customary usage was to be treated as a 'concession' granted by the state. Only rights explicitly granted by the earlier rulers were to be treated as rights. 'Customary rights' in effect were extinguished by the Forest Act, 1878, which created three categories of forests—reserved forests, protected forests, and village forests. The forests free from claims were to be constituted as reserved forests, while others were to be created as protected forests awaiting the settlement of claims. However, local ecologies and customs were to leave their influence on law and rights. There was also the issue of private rights.

The period between 1865 and 1878 saw extensive debates on forest law and the recognition of the category of private forests, which included the forest lands of *Inamdar* and other landholders who were proprietors of wastes and forests included in their estates. 'Forests in permanently settled estates of Bengal, *talukdari* estates of Oudh and *zamindari* estates of the Central Provinces were declared private forests, even though they were held by these land controllers under obligation to permit villagers forest produce to meet their needs.'[26] Private forests also included lands under other tenures where the

[23] Ramachandra Guha, 'An Early Environmental Debate: The Making of the 1878 Forest Act' (1990) 27(1) *Indian Economic and Social History Review* 65.

[24] Minutes of Proceedings at a Deputation from the Society for the Preservation of the Wild Fauna of the Empire to the Right Hon. The Earl of Elgin, His Majesty's Secretary of State for the Colonies, 15 June 1906, (1907) 3 *Journal of the Society for the Preservation of the Wild Fauna of the Empire* 24.

[25] As in England, this was subject to much conflict.

[26] K Sivaramakrishnan, 'Conservation and Production in Private Forests: Bengal, 1864–1914' (1998) 14(2) *Studies in History* 244.

government had alienated its right to trees growing on those lands. Sivaramakrishnan has examined in some detail the colonial government's efforts to take over private forests in Bengal, and he argues that even in 1945 when Bengal first enacted a Private Forests Act, this law stopped short of reserving *zamindari* forests.[27] Only with the abolition of *zamindari* estates in 1955 could the forests contained in them become state property. He argues therefore that the property principle enshrined in the Permanent Settlement of Bengal was 'enacted through coalitions cutting across elements in a heterogenous state and differentiated society'.[28]

1.2 Colonial Forestry Policy and Customary Law: the Case of Eastern India

When the Forest Department was constituted in the 1860s, the state of the forests in much of India was poor and chaotic, and the ideas for their administration were extremely vague and the progress of the department was also slow. However, it is important to note that the establishment of the Forest Department gradually stifled the steady erosion of forest areas in India, a process that was reversed once again only during the Depression of the 1930s and, on a much larger scale, after national independence in 1947.[29] It was hoped that the forest rules 'may in time after they have been explained to the landholders, be of some effect in checking the relentless destruction of forest'.[30]

The drafting of proper forest laws for the different provinces in the period 1869–1878 led to debates about the extent to which the long-continued right of the user—to the free collection of small produce, fuel, grass, bamboo grazing, and shifting cultivation in the wastelands—should be regarded as a prescriptive right. On the other hand, the government (as the guardian of all public interests) insisted on the regulation of these rights to render possible good management of the reserved forests in the interests of the country.[31] With forests increasingly being recognized as a revenue resource by the district administration, the clash between foresters and administrators became more apparent. While forest conservancy was adopting a tone that promoted direct control, systematization, and regulation of the extraction of timber from what was perceived to be a dwindling resource of tropical timber, local administrators often urged caution in overriding local rights to forests. The issue of rights, therefore, continued to be an important one for the district administration.[32]

[27] ibid 243.
[28] ibid 244.
[29] *Indian Forester*, vol 10 (Mussoorie 1884).
[30] ibid.
[31] ibid.
[32] ibid.

This was very apparent in the case of Eastern India, where, by the 1880s, forests in Chotanagpur were organized under a variety of arrangements—reserved, protected, privatized, and leased from the political states. It was generally argued that the interests of the agriculturists were amply safeguarded during the creation of the reserved forest.[33] However, the history of forest reservation and the evidence of unrest indicate that the interests of small farmers living adjacent to forests and their commons were far from secure. A closer look at the differing outcomes of forest policy as a result of these diverse pressures, the protection of forests for a variety of reasons, the revenue-generating possibilities of timber production, and the issue of local rights show how these played out in a range of contexts in Chotanagpur, notably the Saranda region and the Porahat forest. In Saranda, the regional administration emphasized the productionist agenda of the Forest Department through the enforcement of 'reserved forests' while in Porahat, the colonial officials protected local rights, given the conflict between the Raj and local indigenous communities in the context of 'protected forests',[34] highlighting the fact that customary and local rights to resources could not be brushed under the carpet.

In 1878, the Indian Forest Act was passed, extending policies regarding 'reserved forests' and 'protected forests' to all the provinces of British India. Every possible safeguard against infringements (by private rights) surrounded the first-class constitution of 'reserved forests', secured by a permanent settlement. The second-class demarcation of 'protected forests', however, offered fewer sufficient guarantees for stability and protection. There were also private forests leased from political states. By 1898, 33,738 square miles of forest were closed to all animals, and 28,146 square miles were closed to browsers throughout India.[35] Systematic forestry commenced after the stabilization of British rule in the latter half of the nineteenth century.

The first decades of forest conservancy in Chotanagpur show a variety of competing interests. While some areas like Saranda were dominated by factors such as timber supply and profits from forests with draconian forest legislation, other areas provided less scope for removing timber as they were involved with supplying local needs. In Saranda, the most stringent forest legislation followed. The principles of scientific forestry were rigorously applied to these forests, which were regarded as an important revenue resource, and the rights of local communities were ignored.

It is clear from colonial accounts that the question of local rights did exercise the colonial government elsewhere and serious attempts were made to protect them as in the case of the Porahat settlement in Eastern India in 1900.[36] It is within these debates that

[33] This section draws on Vinita Damodaran, 'Customary Rights and Resistance in the Forests of Singhbhum' in Daniel J Rycroft and Sangeeta Dasgupta (eds), *The Politics of Belonging in India: Becoming Adivasi* (Routledge 2011) 113–119.

[34] ibid 107.

[35] PJ Phillips, *Revised Working Plan for the Reserved Forests of Saranda and Kolhan Divisions in Singhbhum* (Superintendent of Government Printing 1924).

[36] Deputy Commissioner's Report, 15 September 1905, Chaibasa District Record Room, Singhbhum, District.

one can locate changing and contested ideas of property.[37] That the government had absolutely no right in the Mundari *khuntkhatti* villages was apparent as Macpherson noted 'the government cannot conceivably have any rights in the waste or forest land in these villages'.[38] The question of jungle rights was important to local people and a significant factor in the Birsa Munda rebellion of the 1890s was also recognized in Macpherson's comment that 'with aboriginals jungle rights are ever of supreme importance and in Porahat they are not disposed to accept curtailment of rights or fresh impositions'.[39] In his report, Macpherson set out systematically to protect customary rights of local communities against the onslaught of the proprietor. This attempt to settle customary rights, especially concerning forests, resulting from the impact of the Birsa movement on government opinion. The role of the district administration in recording and emphasizing the importance of local rights against the productionist agenda of the foresters is important here.[40] As Thompson notes:

> the most ambitious project to transpose both the law of property and the sociological model of the landowner into an alien context were the succession of land settlements imposed by the British in India ... communal forms expressed an alternate notion of possession, in the petty and particular rights and usages which were transmitted in custom as the properties of the poor.[41]

However, it is also important to point out that in Chotanagpur, one could say that 'colonialism learnt how to co-exist with tribal land usages and with customary law'.[42]

The debate on customary rights continued after independence. In the post-Independence period, customary access declined even further. Under the Indian Forest Act, 1927, forest land or wasteland could be notified as a reserve forest by a state government, extinguishing the rights of local communities.[43]

1.3 Water and Riparian Rights

Common law was also debated in regarding water issues in the nineteenth century. As legally framed, common law took precedence over riparian rights, which could have been limited by the colonial government. Gilmartin noted that control over water came to

[37] TS Macpherson, 'Final Report on the Operation for the Preparation of the Record of Rights in Paragona Porahat, district, Singhbhum, 1905–1907' (Government Printing 1908).

[38] ibid.

[39] ibid.

[40] ibid.

[41] EP Thompson, *Customs in Common* (Merlin Press 1991) 175.

[42] ibid.

[43] Shyam Divan and Armin Rosencranz, *Environmental Law and Policy in India: Cases, Materials and Statutes* (OUP 2002) 289.

define a central element in the new public character of the colonial state's claim to legitimate authority in India from the 1860s.[44] Throughout the second half of the nineteenth century, as Ramesh has shown through the Irrigation Cess Act of 1865, the Madras government attempted to separate water and land as distinct revenue and value-yielding entities, allowing it to extract revenue from water as separate from land.[45] The government faced severe opposition from *zamindars* to any further legislation that would centralize control over water resources as well as powers to levy fees over water use to the government. This was brought before the Privy Council over the interpretation of the Irrigation Cess Act and in 1917, in a landmark judgment, 'the dispute between the Madras government and the Urlam *zamindari* was resolved in favour of custom which rendered it a physical, historically reified, and 'natural' quality, simultaneously within and outside the encounter between labour and nature'.[46] Riparian rights had begun to come under the purview of the state by the mid-nineteenth century and by the 1870s, the state had allocated to itself the property rights to all water resources under the Northern India Canal and Drainage Act, 1873. The Madras Irrigation and Cess Act, 1865, however, could declare all water the property of the government. Powerful landed interests prevented the government from doing so and raised a wealth of objections in colonial courts. The Urlam case was resolved in favour of the long-standing rights of *zamindars*.

While riparian rights were disputed and taxed between the state and differing interests and landed property were treated as the legal terrain of ownership, D'Souza has argued that river flow regimes became the subject of technical intervention as the British sought to separate land from water for taxation purposes and grant land ownership rights to moving landscapes. As he notes:

> 'The Eastern deltas through the course of the nineteenth century were re-plumbed by the colonial dispensation through a combination of irrigation, drainage and flood control practices... In the colonial land centered imagination the delta appeared as a collection of isolated fluvial elements rather than as a dynamic organic process'.[47]

The state's rights to rivers, to tax water regimes, and to separate land from water even in the most mobile environments were applied in the post-colonial period, showing the land-dominated vision of these governments.

The Constitution of India, 1950, recognized water in Entry 17 of List II (State List), but subject to the provisions of Entry 56 of List I (Union List). Under the Indian Easements Act, 1882, the rights of a riparian, a person who owns the land adjoining a river or a water stream, were recognized. Section 7 of the Act gave every riparian owner the right

[44] David Gilmartin, *Blood and Water: The Indus River Basin in Modern History* (University of California Press 2015).

[45] Ramesh (n 4).

[46] ibid.

[47] Rohan D'Souza, 'Drainage, River Erosion, and Chaurs: An Environmental History of Land in Colonial Eastern India' NMML Occasional Paper (Nehru Memorial Museum and Library 2015).

to continued flow of waters of a natural stream without any destruction or unreasonable pollution and recognized their customary rights under two basic rules: (i) long usage or prescription, and (ii) local custom.[48] However, these rights were not absolute or enjoyable without any external interference but were subject to the government's right to 'regulate the collection, the retention and the distribution of the waters of rivers and streams flowing in natural channels'.[49] In the 1990s, following rapid development and increasing pollution of water sources, the public trust doctrine based on English common law was invoked in several cases relating to water pollution where the state as a trustee of all natural resources was shown to be under a legal duty to protect them.[50] It is important to note here that the colonial history of water pollution, in particular the pollution of the river Ganges occurred in the nineteenth century when ignoring the European experience, colonial officials dumped sewage into the Ganges.[51] In many ways, the riparian rights of communities both in the colonial and post-colonial period similar to other common rights in forests were often ignored by the state and public trust doctrine marginalized for the interests of the state and private interests.

1.4 Minerals and Mines

Coal mining was the earliest modern industry to develop in India. By the nineteenth century, coal was acquiring importance for commerce and conquest. From 1885, the extension of railway lines to the coalfields led to an increase in coal output. The Jharia fields adjacent to Raniganj had been surveyed in 1866 and 1887 but developed after the East India Railways' technical survey in 1890. Jharia's output rose from 1,500 tons to two million tons in six years. By 1900, Indian coal had completely replaced imported coal on the railways.

In the early period, there were no mining laws or government controls on mining operations in India. The exploitation of the coal fields of Bengal started in 1814 with the Raniganj coalfield.[52] This was also linked to railway construction supported by businessmen interested in the textile trade and shipping companies which needed coal at Indian ports. The Bengal Coal Company, established in 1834, dominated the development of the Raniganj coalfield well into the 1860s. The *zamindars* from whom the mining companies obtained mining concessions lacked knowledge of coal mining,

[48] Annie Mampilly, 'Riparian Rights in India' (2017) 29 *Lex Terra* 18p. <https://www.nluassam.ac.in/docs/lex%20terra/Lex_terra_issue_29.pdf>.

[49] ibid.

[50] *MC Mehta v Kamal Nath* (1997) 1 SCC 388; Divan and Rosencranz (n 43) 168–169.

[51] Janine Wilhelm, *Environment and Pollution in Colonial India: Sewerage Technologies along the Sacred Ganges* (Routledge 2020).

[52] Thomas Henry Holland, *Sketch of the Mineral Resources of India* (Nabu Press 1908). See also Dilip Simeon, 'Coal and Colonialism: An Exploratory Essay on the History of Indian Coal' NMML Occasional Paper (Nehru Memorial Museum and Library 1998).

possible damages from mining operations and so on. The companies acquired extensive leases and built-up large reserves of mining land for future exploitation. In their organization of labour, they took over many of the features of the feudal system prevailing in Bengal, leasing land to miners under a system where miners owned labour as well as rent to the company. The excesses of the system in terms of its impact on labour resulted only in minor regulatory mining laws by the end of the nineteenth century.[53]

A new set of mining rules was promulgated in 1899 to regulate the issue of licences for prospecting. These new rules changed the scenario of mineral exploitation in India, and the increase in mining activities in the first half of the twentieth century was mainly due to revised mining rules, facilitating the entry of private entrepreneurs into the mining sphere. It was noted that:

> Prospecting licenses were issuable by the local authority for a period of one year on certain conditions and the license had a right ... to the grant of a mining lease in the case of precious stones. Mining leases were granted by the local government not exceeding 30 years and provided for the payment of dead rent, as well as of royalty at specified rates. The area which a mining lease may extend to varied with respect to different minerals. But there was a provision that the local government may not without the consent of the Government of India, grant to one lessee ... lease over areas exceeding an aggregate of 10 sq. miles.[54]

In addition to the dead rent, which was, except in the case of coal and iron, generally one rupee per acre, the royalty payable was fixed at one *anna* per ton of coal, eight *annas* per forty gallons of oil, 7½ per cent on the net profit in the case of gold or silver, ½ *anna* per ton of ironstone, 2½ per cent on sale value in the case of other metals and 30 per cent on the net profits of each year in respect of precious stones.[55] According to the rules, an exploring licence for one year could be obtained, but gave no exclusive rights and there was no prohibition against free exploration in unoccupied and unreserved lands. Prospecting licences were granted over restricted areas for one year, renewable with the consent of the local government for a second and third term. Such licences carried an indefeasible claim for a subsequent mining lease for any mineral other than precious stones over the same or a restricted area. These rules, however, were applicable only in British India.[56]

Under the revised rules issued in 1913, the 'Exploring license' was abolished. Prospecting licences for a limited period might be granted to persons holding certificates of approval from the local government. Such licences carried a right to a mining lease or, in the case of precious stones, to the first offer of a mining lease that the government of

53 Vinita Damodaran, 'Globalisation and Tribal Histories in Eastern India' in John McNeill, Mahesh Rangarajan, and José Augusto Pádua (eds), *Environmental History: As if Nature Existed* (OUP 2010) 151.

54 House of Commons, 'Statement Exhibiting the Moral and Material Progress and Condition of India, 1901–02' (His Majesty's Stationery Office 1903) 238–239.

55 ibid.

56 ibid.

India might think fit to make. The area let to a single lessee was limited. Rights in respect of petroleum and certain metals of importance in the manufacture of armament might be granted only to British subjects.[57]

In nearly all the coal bearing land in Bengal, mineral rights were conceded permanently with surface ownership. In the coalfields, the collieries acted as the 'industrial variant of the *zamindary* estate', with the *zamindary* managers invariably being Europeans.[58] Many of the larger colliery enterprises took advantage of the Permanent Settlement to acquire extensive *zamindary* estates, and a significant proportion of their employees became their tenants. 'The usual practice was to bind the miners in service tenancy arrangement, under which a small plot of land was given to them in exchange for their labour in the mines.'[59] This arrangement, especially in Raniganj and Giridih, enabled the firms to exert considerable power over their workers.[60] In 1908, the Chotanagpur Tenancy Act prohibited such service arrangements, but they continued unabated until the Depression made it obsolete in the 1930s, and the local colonial officials saw nothing wrong with that deliberate infringement of law.[61] In practically all native or princely states, however, the mineral rights belonged to the respective rulers and concessions were granted for mining and prospecting under rules that involved a certain amount of supervision by the government of India.[62]

Legislation for mining labour was introduced very late in India due to the fierce opposition of mine owners on the one hand and the absence of any effective trade union organization on the other. The Indian Mines Act, 1901, was the first major legislation regarding the safety of mine labour. There were three serious discussions about the introduction of governmental control over mining employment and safety in 1868–70, 1878–80, and 1883–85 before passing the Indian Mines Act, 1901. However, the first concrete proposal for the inspection and regulation of mining operations in India came only in 1890, when the Secretary of State, Lord Cross, while forwarding a copy of the proceedings of the Berlin Conference in 1890, asked the government of India to 'consider the advisability of undertaking legislation for the inspection of mines and regulations of employment therein of women and children'.[63]

To a large extent, the Indian Mines Act, 1901, was a 'protective' labour legislation. The primary emphasis here was on the need to inspect 'mine premises'. The Act empowered the government to frame rules for regulating work in mines. It strengthened the office of

[57] India Office, *Statement Exhibiting the Moral and Material Progress and Condition of India, 1912–13* (His Majesty's Stationery Office 1914) 60.

[58] Sekhar Bandyopadhyay, *From Plassey to Partition: A History of Modern India* (Orient Longman 2004).

[59] CP Simmons, 'Recruiting and Organizing an Industrial Labour Force in Colonial India: The Case of the Coal Mining Industry c. 1880–1939' (1976) 13(4) *The Indian Economic and Social History Review* 463.

[60] ibid 482.

[61] ibid 471.

[62] India Office (n 57) 60.

[63] ibid 60.

the Inspectorate of Mines. Inspectors were empowered to enter and inspect mines and to enquire into mine accidents. The employment of competent managers in mines was also made mandatory. However, the need to regulate the wage and labour time of miners was deferred.[64] The entire framework of this Act was geared towards regulating the working conditions of collieries. As a result, it largely remained unconcerned about conditions of mining of other minerals, which were equally hazardous. This was due to a narrow definition of the word 'mine' consisting of minerals excavations over twenty feet deep. It was only when the Mines Act was re-enacted in 1923 that provisions relating to hours and limitation of employment on the surface and underground were introduced.[65]

For a long time, the debate on the introduction of mining legislation centred on the difference in the nature of mining operations between England and India and to what extent 'mines' are different from 'factories'. The colonial government ignored the safety concerns of Indian mines for a long time and remained blind to the 'dangerous' nature of mine work, especially in underground mines. Two major mine accidents by the end of the nineteenth century alerted the colonial government to the necessity of legislation. In 1897, a disaster in the Kolar Goldfields (in Mysore State) killed fifty-two persons in a shaft accident. This was followed in 1898 by a fire in the Khost Coal Mine in Baluchistan in which forty-seven persons were killed.[66] This finally paved the way for the Mines Act, 1901. International pressure played an important role in making mines legislations.[67] In passing these 'protective' labour legislations, the colonial state displayed a paternalistic attitude. The chief provisions of the Act of 1901 included the definition of a mine 'which was deemed to be any excavation twenty feet below the surface where minerals were searched', and the definition of a child as a person under the age of twelve years. A Chief Inspector of Mines was appointed by the government of India, and inspectors or subordinate officers by local governments. They were granted powers to prohibit the employment of children and women in mines where the conditions, in their opinion, were dangerous for their health and safety. Furthermore, local mining boards and committees were to be appointed to enquire into cases of accidents or dangers considered by the inspector to be the result of mismanagement, and breaches of the law were to be punishable by fines not exceeding Rs. 500 or imprisonment not exceeding three months, or both.[68]

The Act proved defective in several respects, including (1) lack of provisions for regulating the conditions of employment, (2) inadequate provisions for regulating the labour of women and children, and (3) lack of definite division of authority between the central and provincial governments regarding administration. Moreover, ratification of

[64] Sanhati, 'Overview of Coal Mining in India: Investigative Report from Dhanbad Coal Fields (2011) <http://sanhati.com/excerpted/3798/>.

[65] Rajani Kanta Das, 'Labour Legislation in India' (1930) 22(5) *International Law Review* 609.

[66] CP Vinod Kumar, PG Revathi, and KT Rammohan, 'Kolar Gold Mines: An Unfinished Biography of Colonialism' (1998) 33(24) *Economic and Political Weekly* 1467.

[67] ibid.

[68] International Labour Organization, Industrial Labour in India—Studies and Reports Series A (Industrial Relations) No 41 (ILO 1938).

the Hours Convention by the government of India in 1921 made it necessary to amend the Act to conform to the principle of the sixty-hour week. A new Act was therefore passed in 1923 and came into force on 1 July 1924.[69]

This Act made a number of important amendments to the provisions of the Act of 1901: (1) the definition of a mine was extended to include any excavation, irrespective of depth, for searching for or obtaining minerals, (2) the weekly hours of work were limited to fifty-four underground and sixty above ground, (3) working days were limited to six in the week, (4) the definition of 'child' was amended to mean any person under the age of thirteen years, and no child was allowed to be employed in a mine or to be present in any part of a mine which was below ground. Other amendments made more precise the division of the rule-making power between the Governor-General in Council and local governments, reserving to the former, in particular, the power to prohibit, restrict or regulate the employment of women.[70]

In the post-Independence period, three laws were used to acquire land, which included the Land Acquisition Act, 1894, the Coal Bearing Areas (Acquisition and Development) Act, 1957, and the Atomic Energy Act, 1962, for mining atomic materials. In Eastern India, the government subverted protective land laws for indigenous communities and laws related to local governance, such as the Panchayats (Extension to Scheduled Areas) Act, 1996. This continues to result in large-scale land alienation for these communities and widespread unrest and resistance among communities.[71]

1.5 Petroleum and Natural Gas

The legislation related to minerals also included oil and natural gas. Over 40 per cent of India's energy comes from oil and natural gas. Despite the fact that at the time of independence only a percentage of India's energy came from petroleum, India was one of the first of the decolonizing states 'to pursue a public sector oil project, inaugurated under KD Malaviya in 1956 as the Oil and Natural Gas Commission or ONGC, with the stated aim of transforming India into a "self-sufficient" petroleum economy'.[72] The purpose of formation of ONGC was to take control over India's oil resources and to undermine the monetary power of the hard currencies of dollar and sterling.[73] The oil strike in Naharkatiya by the Assam Oil Company was a breakthrough for newly independent India and in the 1950s, KD Malaviya was able to deny Assam oil its legal claim over 'Neharkatiya founding in its place a public sector oil company to produce Indian oil in Indian rupees'.[74]

69 ibid.
70 ibid.
71 Ajitha Susan George, 'Mining and Development: The Paradox' in Sundar (n 5) 157–188.
72 Matthew Shutzer, 'Oil, Money and Decolonization in South Asia' (2022) 258(1) *Past and Present* 212.
73 ibid.
74 ibid.

The government denied that the Assam Oil Company had any right to the Neharkatiya oil under a colonial era licensing agreement of 1938. The legislation relating to petroleum includes the Petroleum Act, 1934, to address operational issues covering the entire value chain of oil production. The main aim of the Act was to consolidate laws relating to the import, transport, storage, production, refining, and blending of petroleum and the regulation of these aspects was vested primarily with the central government. This was followed by the Oilfields (Regulation and Development) Act, 1948,[75] where the central government was granted the power to make rules for regulating mining leases (for offshore blocks). The Act also empowered the central government to determine rates of royalty payable by the holder of the mining lease for onshore as well as offshore blocks. It was in the post-Independence period, however, that the authority of the central government over the development of the sector was further reaffirmed by the powers awarded to it under the Petroleum and Natural Gas Rules, 1959. Under the said rules, even though the respective states own the blocks found within their territory and are responsible for awarding the licences for onshore blocks, they could do so only with prior approval from the central government. Therefore, taking into consideration the Oilfields Act, 1948, and the Petroleum and Natural Gas Rules, 1959, it is clear that the powers enjoyed by the state governments were restricted by the central government with respect to granting of onshore mining licences and deciding upon the royalty and surface rent rates.

With regard to the acquisition of user rights on land where petroleum and/or mineral pipelines have to be laid, the Petroleum and Minerals Pipeline Act was passed in 1962.[76] This Act had provisions relating to the acquisition and utilization of land for laying pipelines and the central government was authorized to acquire the land with the option of either keeping the acquired land or transferring it to either the state government or the corporation for which the land has been acquired. The Act also provided for compensation in case of 'any damage, loss or injury is sustained by any person interested in the land under which the pipeline is proposed to be, or is being, or has been laid'. Further, the liability of paying the compensation lies with the concerned authority, that is, the central or state government or corporation.[77]

As Shutzer argues:

> Malaviya's project to assert greater national sovereignty over oil resources was part of a global effort to reshape resource industries through new forms of international co-operation. This shift was evident in the wave of nationalisations in resource-exporting countries in the 1940s and the early 1950s, the experiences from which

75 Anmol Soni and Anomitro Chatterjee, 'Governance of the Petroleum and Natural Gas Sectors in India: A Status Note' TERI Working Paper Series No 15 (TERI 2014) <https://www.teriin.org/projects/nfa/2008-2013/pdf/working-paper-15-Governance-of-the-petroleum-and-natural-gas-sector-in-india-a-status-note.pdf>.

76 ibid.

77 ibid.

> guided the 'underdeveloped' bloc of nations in the UN to push forward resolutions to recognise the rights of states over natural resources.[78]

This can be seen in the legislative interventions of post-colonial India over oil and natural gas.

1.6 Fisheries

Overfishing of the seas has been one of the biggest environmental problems of the twentieth century. What has changed in the last few decades since what was seen as the peak of marine production is the role of historical knowledge that has led marine scientists to ignore historic changes in marine populations. The rise of two interlinked disciplines, marine environmental history and historical marine ecology, is important in this regard.[79]

The history of state control and management over the coastal fisheries during the pre-colonial and colonial period in India is a very poorly charted terrain.[80] It is argued that for South Asia, as for many other parts of Eastern and Western Asia, rivers have been far more important than the adjacent seas in terms of the value of fish catches and inland fisheries were far more important than marine fisheries.[81] Thus, coastal areas while being much more open to influences from other societies across the sea, were relatively less influenced by their land-based neighbouring communities. The discussion of state control over water resources in contrast to community management took place during the colonial period.[82] An enquiry made by Francis Day in 1868–70 into the freshwater fisheries in India and Burma showed that indiscriminate and wholesale slaughter of fish life took place annually. Day pointed out that unless remedial measures were adopted, this would result in a great diminution in the fresh supply of India. It was, however, in 1897 that the protection of fisheries in India was afforded by legislation with the enactment of the Indian Fisheries Act.

In controlling fisheries, the British came up against landholder interests in Bengal. The Permanent Settlement had given the *zamindars* rights to the fisheries adjoining their lands as part of their income, and particular fisheries (*jalkar*) were parts of *zamindari* estates (*mahah*). The *zamindars* had begun the practice of leasing *jalkar* lands to their sub-tenants or *ijaradars*. Over the nineteenth century, *jalkars* thus came into the possession of *ijaradars*, and access to the fisheries was determined by these groups,

[78] Shutzer (n 72) 236.

[79] Joseph Christensen and Malcolm Tull (eds), *Historical Perspectives of Fisheries Exploitation in the Indo-Pacific* (Springer 2014).

[80] Peter Reeves, 'Regional Diversity in South Asian Inland Fisheries: Colonial Bengal and Uttar Pradesh Compared' (2002) 25(2) *South Asia: Journal of South Asian Studies* 121.

[81] ibid.

[82] ibid 122.

who could charge fishers for access. In 1859, the Bengal government attempted to revoke rights in *jalkar* in navigable rivers but met with strong *ijaradari* opposition. In 1889, they strengthened the law against poaching from *zamindari* fisheries by enacting the Bengal Private Fisheries Act, 1889.

The question of legislation for controlling indiscriminate fishing and slaughter of fish by passing an Act under which fishing may be licensed arose again in 1941, and opinions were sought from the provincial governments. Some provinces like Bengal and Central Provinces drew attention towards practical difficulties in enforcing the existing law or any rules that might be framed for the purpose.[83] The government of Central Provinces argued that if police and forest subordinates were empowered to lodge complaints, another handle would be given to unscrupulous subordinates for the oppression of the aboriginals and other backward peoples, who constituted a large proportion of the residents of the province, and for depriving them of one of the few forms of nutritious food available to them. Second, the effect of trying to compel *mukaddams* and *kotwars* to report such cases would be worse still. These officials would likely either overlook the breaches of rules or use their powers tyrannically against their fellow villagers. In the third place, legislation was argued to be unnecessary in the province because there was no large-scale destruction there except such fish that mostly died in pools that dry up in the summer.[84]

The Bengal government pointed out that the Private Fisheries' Protection Act, 1899, was the only provincial act in force on this issue. In reserved and protected forests, rules made under the appropriate sections of the Forest Act prohibited poisoning of any river or other water, killing fish by explosives, damming or baling water (presumably to take or kill fish, though this is not explicitly stated in the rules) and use of any fixed engine, that is net, cage, trap, or other contrivance to catch fish. As regards areas outside the reserved and protected forests, the Indian Fisheries Act, 1897, forbade and penalized the use of explosives or poison to kill fish in any waters, including the sea, within one marine league of the coast. It further gave the power to make rules regulating the construction and use, in waters which were not private waters, of fixed engines and weirs, and the dimensions of nets together with the mode of using them. Fishing in any specified water was prohibited for a period not exceeding two years. According to the above provisions, rules were framed for the districts of Darjeeling and Jalpaiguri. In respect of private waters, the Fisheries Act gave power to frame similar rules with the consent in writing of the owner or such persons as have, for the time being, any exclusive right of fishery therein.[85] No rules were framed under this section, but the Bengal Legislature passed the Private Fisheries Protection Act, 1899, which penalized poaching in private waters and

[83] ibid.

[84] Government of the Central Provinces and Berar, Revenue Department, No 656/290-XII dated 3 March 1943, From Khan Sahib S I Husain, Under Secretary to Government, Central Provinces, and Berar, to the Secretary, Imperial Council of Agricultural Research, New Delhi (National Archives of India).

[85] ibid.

in general terms the catching or destruction of fish, without permission of the person to whom the right of fishery belonged by any matter including explosives or dynamite. The question of framing rules under sections 6 and 7 of the Indian Fisheries Act, 1897, for the protection of young Hilsa was also discussed in Bengal.[86]

Conclusion

This chapter has shown how environmental law needs to be studied in the context of the environmental history of India and the competing interests for natural resources between the state, private interests, and village communities and the competing motivations for conservation, including climate and desiccation ideas for forest protection. The overwhelming claim of the colonial state to the forests of India did not go unchallenged, as we have seen and continues to be the subject of much conflict. Colonial law, as framed and legislated upon, has had to contend with elite and subaltern challenges that have continued in the post-colonial period. Natural resource law was used to legitimate governmental control and property rights, but popular struggles challenging these laws highlight the importance of the customary law of village communities. While the post-colonial Indian state's assertion of property rights over land, minerals, and water sources can be seen as an essential aspect of modern nationalism, it has failed in protecting many of its national parks and forest reserves against exploitation by private companies, particularly in the way it has allowed mining companies to crisscross forest reserves with mining leases, deforest, pollute, and convert large areas into special economic zones in favour of private interests.

In this context, for the law to effectively protect the environment, a thorough reform of legal and regulatory frameworks is needed, bolstered by institutions and procedures that support both the public good and the rights of communities against corporate takeover and massive land grabs. In a recent landmark ruling, the constitutional court of Ecuador has decided against mining permits issued in Los Cedros, a protected area in the north-west of the country, and has upheld the rights of nature.[87] These laws draw on specific indigenous ideas challenging the priorities of a legal system that 'treats nature as property but corporations as legal persons'.[88] The idea that nature has intrinsic rights should not only be seen as a legal means to prosecute those polluting the land and the water but also in terms of the challenges it poses to the ecosystem services approach

[86] Govt of Bengal, Commerce, Labour and Industries Dept, Fisheries Branch, No 546 dated 12 March 1943, From Asst Sec to the Govt of Bengal to the Secretary, ICAR (National Archives of India).

[87] Patrick Greenfield, 'Plans to Mine Ecuador Forest Violate Rights of Nature, Court Rules' *The Guardian* (2 December 2021) <https://www.theguardian.com/environment/2021/dec/02/plan-to-mine-in-ecuador-forest-violate-rights-of-nature-court-rules-aoe>.

[88] Ruby Russell, 'Rights of Nature, Indigenous Traditions Become Law' *Deutsche Welle* (2 May 2020) <https://www.dw.com/en/environment-nature-rights-indigenous-activism-legal-personhood/a-52186866>.

which commodifies nature and its economic value in terms of clean air, water, and even the concept of a conservation zone. This could bring a whole new and welcome dimension to the debate on environmental law in the Indian context.

Suggestions for Further Reading

Vinita Damodaran, 'Globalisation and Tribal Histories in Eastern India' in John McNeill, Mahesh Rangarajan, and José Augusto Pádua (eds), *Environmental History: As if Nature Existed* (OUP 2010).

Rohan D'Souza, *Drowned and Dammed: Colonial Capitalism and Flood Control in Eastern India* (OUP 2006).

Richard Grove, *Green Imperialism: Colonial Expansion, Tropical Island Edens and the Origins of Environmentalism, 1600–1860* (CUP 1995).

Ramachandra Guha, *The Unquiet Woods: Ecological Change and Peasant Resistance in the Himalaya* (OUP 1989).

Nandini Sundar (ed), *Legal Grounds—Natural Resources, Identity, and the Law in Jharkhand* (OUP 2009).

CHAPTER 2

INTERNATIONAL ENVIRONMENTAL LAW AND ITS INTERFACE WITH INDIA'S DOMESTIC LAW

BHARAT H. DESAI

ABSTRACT

This chapter provides a glimpse into the advent and growth of the body of international environmental law and its role in national law-making in India. It seeks to make sense of the interface between international treaty-making process and the Indian adherence to international environmental obligations, the interaction of international institutions with the domestic institutions, how international environmental law has contributed to the shaping of environmental law in India and how India has contributed to the shaping international environmental law. It examines which lessons can be drawn from the transposition of international environmental law in the Indian domestic law in a context where it has become even more relevant in the context of formal recognition of the Anthropocene epoch on 21 May 2019 based on an 'unmistakable imprint of human activities' on planet Earth.

INTRODUCTION

THE evolution of international environmental law took shape, especially after the first United Nations Conference on the Human Environment in Stockholm in 1972.[1] International environmental law is part of public international law. Hence, the fundamental principles of international law are equally applicable to international environmental law as it has developed as a separate governance and law-making process.[2] The concerted international environmental law-making process has an organic linkage with domestic environmental law-making processes. India is no exception to this global trend.

The traditional law-making process in the field of international law has been premised upon the consent of the states, which remain the primary subjects of international law. The process of deciphering the law as it stands is important. We find different sources such as international conventions, international custom, general principles of law, and other subsidiary means, as prescribed in Article 38(1) of the Statute of the International Court of Justice.[3] International law has had a diversified history in terms of its normative character to govern the relations between sovereign states. Before the advent of codification through treaty-making to give concrete shape to law, various facets of interstate conduct were based upon customary practices and rules among states. For instance, the 1961 Vienna Convention on Diplomatic Relations codified the institution of diplomatic relations that had grown through long-standing customary practices among the states.[4]

In fact, the ground rules concerning 'treaty making' were elevated from customary law into codified form through the 1969 Vienna Convention on Law of Treaties.[5] Thus, both of these major 'institutions' of international law were codified following the painstaking efforts of the International Law Commission—a subsidiary organ of the United Nations (UN) General Assembly (GA)—as it took twenty years (from 1949 to 1969) and eleven years (from 1949 to 1961) for the law on treaties and diplomatic immunities, respectively, to fructify. Those aspects of law that are not covered under these conventions continue to be governed by customary rules. Since the establishment of the UN, the task of progressive development and codification of international law has grown by leaps and bounds.

The domestic legal system, especially in India, practices dualism regarding the application or implementation of international law in its national legal system. The provisions of the Constitution of India, 1950, make it clear that India follows dualism.

[1] United Nations, *Report of the United Nations Conference on the Human Environment*, Stockholm, 5–16 June 1972, UN Doc A/CONF.48/14/Rev 1.

[2] Bharat H. Desai, *International Environmental Governance: Towards UNEPO* (Martinus Nijhoff 2014) chapter 2.

[3] UN, Statute of the International Court of Justice, 1945, 1 UNTS 99.

[4] Vienna Convention on Diplomatic Relations, Vienna, 18 April 1961, 500 UNTS 95.

[5] Vienna Convention on the Law of Treaties, Vienna, 23 May 1969, 1155 UNTS 331.

So, international treaties to which India is a party do not automatically become part of India's domestic law; they require parliamentary legislation. India is expected to respect international law and treaty obligations while enacting laws.[6] The interface between international environmental law and domestic law of India began at the 1972 Stockholm Conference. Thus, India has contributed to both international environmental law and domestic environmental law-making processes simultaneously.[7]

It is in this context that this chapter seeks to make a modest effort to understand the international environmental law-making process. It comprises the subtle normative process at work, including 'global conferencing' resorted to by the UN General Assembly, how it draws upon the basic legal underpinnings of international law, the unique treaty-making enterprise at work, and what this enormous process portends for the protection of the global environment in the Anthropocene epoch.[8] It seeks to provide an understanding of the linkage between international law and its transposition into the domestic law of India.

2.1 International Environmental Law-Making Process

The international environmental law-making process shows that the practice of states has been in favour of prescribing a threshold for specific environmental activity rather than outright prohibition *per se*, such as the United Nations Framework Convention on Climate Change (UNFCCC) that aims at 'stabilization of greenhouse gas concentrations in the atmosphere at a level that would prevent dangerous anthropogenic interference with the climate system'.[9]

Over the years, this technique has taken the form of 'quotas', 'ceilings', 'timetables', 'voluntary commitments', 'nationally determined contributions', and other tools. Interestingly, the process of law-making on most of the sectoral environmental issues has been generally linked to scientific evidence on the issue in question. International environmental institutional mechanisms or programmes often act as catalysts in this

[6] CH Alexander, 'International Law in India' (1952) 1(3) *International & Comparative Law Quarterly* 289, 291.

[7] UN, Women and the Environment (2007) <https://www.un.org/womenwatch/daw/beijing/beijingat10/K.%20Women%20and%20the%20environment.pdf>. See also, UNEP, 'India is Key to the Success of Stockholm+50, as it was in 1972' (2022) <https://www.unep.org/news-and-stories/opinion/india-key-success-stockholm50-it-was-1972>.

[8] On 21 May 2019, the Anthropocene Working Group decided to accept the unmistakable imprint of human activities on Earth and recognized 'Anthropocene' as the new geological epoch. See Bharat H. Desai, 'How India Fares in Fighting Pollution' *The Tribune* (6 June 2019) <https://www.tribuneindia.com/news/archive/comment/how-india-fares-in-fighting-pollution-783964>.

[9] UN Framework Convention on Climate Change, New York, 9 May 1992, 1771 UNTS 107, art 2.

process as they are an integral part of the international environmental law-making process, for instance, the United Nations Environment Program (UNEP).[10]

In the international environmental law-making process, multilateral environmental agreements[11] are the 'predominant legal method for addressing environmental problems that cross national boundaries'.[12] Moreover, they are part of a broader trend of 'increasingly more complex web of international treaties, conventions, and agreements' (based on topic, sector, or territory).[13] In view of the commonalities of interests for the common concerns and the workability of the lowest common denominator approach, 'state sovereignty' *per se* does not pose an insurmountable problem. Depending upon the level of consensus that emerges from negotiations, states are willing to 'share' their prerogative of sovereign consent for regulating a specific problem area in a global *problématique*. The process has been characterized largely by *ad hoc*, need-based, and sectoral responses. Multilateral environmental agreements that emerge from marathon negotiations, spread over a relatively short period, generally enshrine a framework or a skeleton. Many multilateral environmental agreements provide a bare framework, which must be supplemented by 'fleshing out' the subsequent legal instruments (generally known as protocols). In this sense, some hard legal instruments comprise soft obligations at their core (a hard shell with a soft belly). Thus, in the words of Arnold McNair, treaties may be judged from their contents, which will 'affect their legal character as well'.[14]

The emerging framework of multilateral environmental agreements reflects the balance between 'national sovereignty and international interdependence'.[15] The complex regimes created by the varied multilateral environmental agreements have generated debate about the need for, and efficacy of, such forms of international environmental governance.[16] The complex web of these regimes comprises built-in law-making mechanisms, inherent flexibility, large participation of states, the role of non-state actors, and issues of implementation and compliance that need to be taken into account to assess their efficacy.

10 UNEP, About UN Environment Programme (undated) <https://www.unep.org/about-un-environment>.

11 For a detailed study, see Bharat H. Desai, *Multilateral Environmental Agreements: Legal Status of the Secretariats* (CUP 2010).

12 Anonymous, 'Developments in the Law: International Environmental Law' (1991) 104(7) *Harvard Law Review* 1484, 1521.

13 United Nations University, *Inter-Linkages: Synergies and Coordination between Multilateral Environmental Agreements* (UNU 1999) 5, 8.

14 Arnold D McNair, 'The Functions and Differing Legal Character of Treaties' (1930) 11 *British Yearbook of International Law* 100.

15 Richard Elliot Benedick, 'Perspectives of a Negotiation Practitioner' in Gunnar Sjöstedt (ed), *International Environmental Negotiation* (Sage 1993) 229.

16 For a detailed exposition of this idea, see generally, Bharat H. Desai, *International Environmental Governance: Towards UNEPO* (Brill Nijhoff 2014); Bharat H. Desai, *Institutionalizing International Environmental Law* (Transnational Publishers 2004).

There has been enormous growth in international instruments concerning environmental issues.[17] The latest treaty is the much-celebrated 2015 Paris Agreement.[18] The multilateral environmental agreements on many of these issues have, in fact, 'changed over time, just as political, economic, social, and technological conditions have changed over time'.[19]

2.1.1 'Soft' Law as a Convenient Tool

The widely used method of hortatory, inspirational, promotional, or programmatic statements has remained the hallmark of the international environmental law-making process. These statements could be described generally as declarations, conference statements, or statements of principles. The traditional modes of international law-making have evolved, are time-consuming, and have built-in rigidity that must adapt to the sense of urgency necessary to address an environmental issue. In view of this and where states are not yet ready to make concrete commitments, they often prefer to use politically convenient 'soft instruments'. These instruments are less formal than the so-called 'hard law'.

Apart from the language of the instrument, the difference lies in the intended outcome by the states negotiating such a 'soft' instrument. If the parties do not intend an international instrument to establish legal rights and obligations among them, it is generally regarded as devoid of legal character. In fact, the intention of the parties is a material element without which an agreement is regarded as '*sans portée juridique*'.[20] At the normative level, these so-called soft rules or principles generally lack the requisite characteristics of international legal norms proper. Hence, they are legally regarded as non-binding. It would be more appropriate to state that negotiating states design them in such a fashion that they remain uncertain in the application, with 'calculated ambiguity', and generate conflicting signals.[21]

In effect, such built-in drafting ambiguities may create a misleading impression about the legal force of an instrument (calling it non-legal soft law). Still, it can be argued that it 'promotes feelings of international comity and cooperation that are very valuable'.[22] In such cases, states prefer to retain the discretion that is revealed in the language,

[17] Desai (n 11).

[18] Paris Agreement, Paris, 12 December 2015, in Report of the Conference of the Parties on its Twenty-First Session, UN Doc FCCC/CP/2015/10/Add.1.

[19] Edith Brown Weiss, 'The Five International Treaties: A Living History' in Edith Brown Weiss and Harold K Jacobson (eds), *Engaging Countries: Strengthening Compliance with International Environmental Accords* (MIT Press 1998) 89.

[20] *International Status of South-West Africa* Advisory Opinion (1950) ICJ Rep 128, 140.

[21] Oscar Schachter, 'The Twilight Existence of Nonbinding International Agreements' (1977) 71(2) *American Journal of International Law* 297.

[22] Geoffrey Palmer, 'New Ways to Make International Environmental Law' (1992) 86(2) *American Journal of International Law* 259, 269.

such as 'as far as possible and as appropriate' and 'with its particular conditions and capabilities'.[23] Still, soft law instruments could be devoid of legal consequence. As aptly pointed out, there are 'norms of various degrees of cogency, persuasiveness, and consensus which are incorporated in agreements between States but do not create enforceable rights and duties'.[24]

Thus, it is not surprising that soft law has played a significant role in the evolution of normative structure in various areas of international law, such as human rights, economic law, and now environmental issues. It is generally regarded that the hardness or softness of a rule 'does not, of course, affect its normative character'.[25] In fact, it can be considered to reflect the transitory stage of the normative threshold with an inherent expectation that the states party to it 'will gradually conform their conduct to its requirement'.[26]

2.1.2 Tools and Techniques

Soft law norms have their own significance at the normative level. Differences exist regarding their precise effect and their evolution into hard law. The UN General Assembly, as the plenary organ of the UN, has played a significant role in terms of preparing declaratory principles on a variety of subjects. Soft law instruments encompass varied aspects of contemporary global concerns, such as principles of self-determination, decolonization, friendly relations, new international economic order, human rights, and some of the 'common concerns of humankind' (e.g., climate change).

The process undertaken regarding the French initiative and the resultant UN General Assembly resolution concerning a Global Pact for the Environment underscores the soft law technique.[27] As compared to the expectation for a legally binding Global Pact, the UN General Assembly endorsed the report of the *ad hoc* open-ended working group (after three rounds of the Nairobi process during January to June 2019) and 'all its recommendations'.[28] In turn, the UN General Assembly asked the UN Environment

23 Bharat H. Desai and others, *Implementation of the Convention on Biological Diversity: A Retrospective Analysis in the Hindu Kush-Himalayan Countries* (ICIMOD 2011) 3. See also Convention on Biological Diversity, 1992, 1760 UNTS 79, arts 5, 12, 14.

24 RR Baxter, 'International Law in Her Infinite Variety' (1980) 29(4) *International and Comparative Law Quarterly* 549.

25 Prosper Weil, 'Towards Relative Normativity in International Law?' (1983) 77 *American Journal of International Law* 414.

26 Patricia Birnie, 'International Environmental Law: Its Adequacy for Present and Future Needs' in Andrew Hurrell and Benedict Kingsbury (eds), *The International Politics of the Environment: Actors, Interests and Institutions* (Clarendon Press 1992) 53.

27 UN General Assembly Resolution 72/277, Towards a Global Pact for the Environment, UN Doc A/RES/72/277 (10 May 2018).

28 UN, Follow-up to the report of the *ad hoc* open-ended working group established pursuant to General Assembly resolution 72/277; UN General Assembly resolution 73/233, UN Doc A/RES/73/333 (30 August 2019).

Assembly (UNEA) to prepare, at its fifth session, a political declaration.[29] Accordingly, the UNEA-5 adopted the Political Declaration on 4 March 2022.[30] In doing so, the UN General Assembly virtually acts as a 'conductor of a grand orchestra' in the concerted environmental regulatory process.[31] In the emerging scenario, it will become necessary to address environmental issues that have global ramifications, such as 'plastics pollution' as a new common concern of humankind.[32]

Prior to the change in its nomenclature as UNEA, the Governing Council of UNEP (a subsidiary organ of the UN General Assembly) adopted various decisions and guidelines. Several became trendsetters in initiating soft law instruments and, in some cases, even graduated into hard law instruments, such as the 1988 resolution designating climate change as a 'common concern of mankind' led to 1990–1992 negotiations and finally to the adoption of the UNFCCC. In fact, UNEP's Montevideo Programme, now in its fifth phase (2020–2029),[33] was explicitly designed to have such a catalytic role in the development of environmental law, notwithstanding the absence of any explicit mandate in the constituent instrument for this purpose.[34] This appears to be a fine example of the use of implied powers by a subsidiary organ of the UN General Assembly.

In the specific case of international environmental law, a series of such declaratory norms enshrined in the Stockholm Declaration,[35] the World Charter for Nature,[36] the protection of global climate,[37] and the Rio Declaration[38] have made a similar impact on

[29] The UNEP Governing Council was designated the UN Environment Assembly and held its first meeting in Nairobi in June 2014. For a detailed analysis, see Bharat H. Desai, 'The Advent of the United Nations Environment Assembly' (2015) 19(2) *The American Society of International Law Insights* <http://www.asil.org/insights/volume/19/issue/2/advent-united-nations-environment-assembly>.

[30] UNEP, Political declaration of the special session of the United Nations Environment Assembly to commemorate the fiftieth anniversary of the establishment of the United Nations Environment Programme, UN Doc UNEP/EA.SS.1/4 (8 March 2022).

[31] Bharat H. Desai, 'UN General Assembly as the "Conductor of a Grand Orchestra"' in the Discourse on *Global Perspectives on a Global Pact for the Environment* (Columbia Centre on Sustainable Investment, Columbia University, New York, 19 September 2018).

[32] Bharat H. Desai and Balraj K Sidhu, 'Climate Change as a Common Concern of Humankind: Some Reflections on International Law-making Process' in Jordi Jaria Manzano and Susana Borràs (eds), *Research Handbook on Global Climate Constitutionalism* (Edward Elgar 2019) 153. See also Balraj K Sidhu and Bharat H. Desai, 'Plastics Pollution: A New Common Concern of Humankind?' (2018) 48(5) *Environmental Policy and Law* 252.

[33] UN, Fifth Programme for the Development and Periodic Review of Environmental Law (Montevideo Programme V): Delivering for People and the Planet, UN Doc UNEP/EA.4/Res 20 (2019); UNEA res 4/20 of 15 March 2019.

[34] UN General Assembly Resolution 2997(XXVII), Institutional and Financial Arrangements for International Environmental Co-operation, UN Doc A/8901 (15 December 1972) at 43, Part I, para 2(a).

[35] Declaration of the United Nations Conference on the Human Environment, Stockholm, 16 June 1972, UN Doc A/CONF.48/14/Rev 1.

[36] World Charter for Nature, UN General Assembly Res 37/7, 28 October 1982, UN Doc A/RES/37/7; UNGA Resolution 43/53, Protection of Global Climate for Present and Future Generations of Mankind, UN Doc A/RES/43/53 (6 December 1988).

[37] Patricia W Birnie and Alan Boyle, *Basic Documents on International Law and the Environment* (Clarendon Press 1995) 248–251.

[38] Rio Declaration on Environment and Development, 14 June 1992, UN Doc A/CONF.151/26/Rev 1 (vol I), Annex II (1992).

the legal developments in the field. As mentioned earlier, the UN General Assembly-mandated process for a Global Pact for the Environment would also fall in this category of instruments.[39]

2.1.3 Hard Law with a Soft Belly

A formal structure or form of a multilateral treaty (legal) instrument neither provides evidence nor is sufficient to ensure the hardness or binding character of the law. In this context, 'legal hardness' accounts for the legally binding character of a provision. Interestingly, the 1969 Vienna Convention on Law of Treaties does not make it a prerequisite for international treaties to enunciate any specific legal rights and obligations. It merely requires an international agreement to be in 'written form and governed by international law'.[40] It is basically a result of the built-in law-making process and ensures the gradual evolution of a legal regime as political consensus materializes. This, in turn, requires the application of deft legal engineering skills, as the original *ad hoc* instrument remains a work in progress. It entails the innovative legal craft of building the treaty regime brick by brick over a period of time.

There are examples of recent multilateral environmental agreements as 'frameworks' that incorporate soft obligations within a formal multilateral treaty. Some of these agreements portray the miasma (illusion) of a non-legal norm as law due to considerable scientific uncertainty and sharp divisions among the states. Thus, soft law provisions play an important role in forming a normative process in international law, in general, and in international environmental law, in particular. The relative hardness or softness of norms must be judged from the specific context and the content rather than the form in which they are encased. The underlying assumption for soft law instruments is the expectation that states voting in favour of a resolution or adopting it at a multilateral conference will 'gradually conform their conduct to its requirements'.[41] It remains a moot point as to what extent the sheer 'multiplying' of soft law norms propels states to comply with them.[42] However, both hard law and soft law play their roles at their own pace in the development of international environmental law.

In view of the frequent recourse to soft law norms for environmental issues, they may be considered as the delicate 'thin end of the normative wedge' of international

[39] UN General Assembly Resolution 72/277, Towards a Global Pact for the Environment, UN Doc A/RES/72/277 (10 May 2018); UN General Assembly Resolution 73/233, UN Doc A/RES/73/333 (30 August 2019).

[40] United Nations Conference on the Law of the Treaties, First and second sessions, Vienna, 26 March–24 May 1968 and 9 April–22 May 1969, UN Doc A/CONF.39/11/Add.2 (1971).

[41] Birnie and Boyle (n 37) 53.

[42] Manfred Lachs, 'The Challenge of the Environment' (1990) 39(3) *International and Comparative Law Quarterly* 668.

environmental law.[43] Since the evolution of international law is a continuing process, it requires a 'wide range of modalities',[44] and soft law tools are just one of them. The best way to measure the softness of soft law is the attitude and actual behaviour of the states. Two global conventions adopted at the 1992 Rio Earth Summit, namely the UNFCCC and the Convention on Biological Diversity (CBD), provide examples of the in-built soft belly of the hard instrument. Both these instruments followed the framework convention-protocol approach and required follow-up instruments to translate them into action: (i) UNFCCC has two instruments, 1997 Kyoto Protocol and 2015 Paris Agreement, and (ii) CBD has two instruments: 2000 Cartagena Protocol on Biosafety and 2010 Nagoya Protocol on Access to Genetic Resources and the Fair and Equitabl Sharing of Benefits Arising From Their Utilization. Together with the main convention, these instruments constitute a regime on each sectoral environmental issue.

2.1.4 Fulcrum for Law-Making

The process of centralized legalization has taken various forms. Unlike the development of traditional international law, the pace of law-making in this sphere has been relatively faster. Furthermore, it is more in the direction of 'conventional' (treaty) law than customary law. Most of the international legal developments in the field of the environment have taken place outside the precincts of the International Law Commission, which was assigned the task of progressive development and codification of international law. Without a central law-making institution in the environmental field, this task has generally fallen upon the UN General Assembly. The UN General Assembly has played a crucial role in convening global conferences (1972 Stockholm; 1992 Rio de Janeiro; 2002 Johannesburg; 2012 Rio de Janeiro; and 2022 Stockholm). The Rio + 20 Summit produced a landmark document, The Future We Want,[45] that became a precursor to the Sustainable Development Goals.[46] Apart from global conferencing on environmental issues, the UN General Assembly has, from time to time, played a catalytic role in launching a process for international regulatory frameworks such as climate change, biological diversity, and desertification.

As a subsidiary organ of the UN General Assembly, UNEP has played an important role in galvanizing the international law-making process. The constituent instrument of UNEP mandated it to 'promote international co-operation in the field of the environment and to recommend, as appropriate, policies to this end'.[47] In 2014, the Governing

[43] Günther Handl, 'Environmental Security and Global Change: The Challenge to International Law' (1990) 1(1) *Yearbook of International Environmental Law* 8.

[44] Christine M Chinkin, 'The Challenge of Soft Law: Development and Change in International Law' (1989) 38(4) *International and Comparative Law Quarterly* 866.

[45] UN General Assembly Resolution 66/288, The Future We Want, UN Doc A/RES/66/288 (2012).

[46] UN General Assembly Resolution 70/1, Transforming Our World: The 2030 Agenda for Sustainable Development, UN Doc A/RES/70/1 (2015).

[47] UN General Assembly Resolution 2997(XXVII), Institutional and Financial Arrangements for International Environmental Co-operation, UN Doc A/8901 (15 December 1972).

Council of UNEP was designated as the UNEA with universal membership.[48] Some other notable agencies within the UN system, that have roles in this context include the FAO, the WHO, UNESCO, the IMO, and the WMO. The intergovernmental and non-governmental institutions outside the UN system that have contributed to the process include the International Union for the Conservation of Nature (IUCN), the World-Wide Fund for Nature (WWF), the International Law Association (ILA), and the Institute of International Law (IIL).

Interestingly, the subtle change in emphasis from common 'heritage'[49] to common 'concern'[50] at various stages appears to have been made to accommodate conflicting interests of the negotiating states. The common concerns are to be addressed within a multilateral framework based on common but differentiated responsibilities of the contracting states to a global convention (such as the UNFCCC). The usage of this phrase in legal parlance has wide ramifications in terms of both the centralization of environmental law-making and multilateral environmental negotiations. It remains to be seen if this is replicated in addressing the simmering challenge of plastic pollution as a new common concern of humankind.

2.1.5 New Treaty-Making

A sense of urgency is generally inherent in most multilateral environmental negotiations. Unlike traditional international law-making, states cannot now afford the luxury of waiting for the emergence of a hardened customary norm through the practice of states. Instead, soft law norms are often adopted as an instant guideline for regulating the behaviour of sovereign states. Interestingly, even this soft law is often just a prelude to the formulation of hard law as a treaty. One can smell the flavour of soft norms couched in the hard shell. Still, this does not usually pose much of a problem as it suits most states. In recent years, states have preferred to go for the legal soft law contained in many of the multilateral environmental agreements. The framework convention-protocol approach works in tandem as a step-by-step process to build the regime.

In the past, the efforts of negotiating states to go for an all-comprehensive approach, comprising threadbare discussions, finalizing all the issues on the agenda of negotiations, and providing concrete obligations for the parties and a dispute settlement mechanism, have proven to be time-consuming. They did not envisage the use of calculated ambiguity and built-in law-making exercises. In view of the very nature of environmental issues, states prefer to go for exhortatory and/or discretionary language in such agreements. At the same time, they prefer some scientific certainty before accepting concrete obligations. This is especially so as the legally binding obligations

[48] Desai (n 29).

[49] United Nations Convention on the Law of the Sea, Montego Bay, 10 December 1982, 1833 UNTS 3.

[50] UN Framework Convention on Climate Change (n 9); Convention on Biological Diversity (n 23).

would entail some painful measures by states at the domestic level, which can potentially unleash bitter political and economic implications. The Convention on International Trade in Endangered Species of Wild Fauna and Flora, 1973, (CITES) was one of the earliest examples of this approach.[51] The UN Economic Commission for Europe's (ECE) 1979 Convention on Long-Range Transboundary Air Pollution (LRTAP Convention)[52] is another example of this approach. The 1979 Convention on Migratory Species of Wild Animals also follows this genre of treaties containing flexibility and adjustment of the regime through a 'list of species' and providing an umbrella for the development of 'agreements' on specific species.[53]

Such framework conventions play an important role in setting in motion a normative process through an exhortatory agreement to evolve in due course. The process of enshrining precise legal obligations and a timeframe for carrying them out is conditioned by political will (coupled with economic considerations) of the states. Multilateral environmental agreements have generally followed the devices of protocols or agreements to strengthen the main framework conventions. Often, the appendices to the convention also serve the purpose of a protocol (as in the case of CITES and CMS). The climate change regime has followed this familiar trajectory of the 1992 UNFCCC and two subsequent instruments: the 1997 Kyoto Protocol and the 2015 Paris Agreement.[54]

Despite the flexibility and adaptability of this approach, several powerful states whose economic interests are likely to be affected have tried to reduce the lowest common denominator to the barest minimum. Even the negotiation and acceptance of the protocols are often marred by foot-dragging and long delays. It can cripple the legal instrument and raise the abatement costs. For example, the states, including India, would face huge financial losses due to climate change heightened sexual and gender-based violence (SGBV). By 2050, climate change could see 4 per cent of global annual economic output loss to US$23 trillion, and it may hit many poorer parts of the world disproportionately.[55] However, no such special international environmental law instrument addresses this issue.

[51] Convention on International Trade in Endangered Species of Wild Fauna and Flora, Washington, 3 March 1973, 993 UNTS 243.

[52] Convention on Long-Range Transboundary Air Pollution, Geneva, 13 November 1979, 1302 UNTS 217.

[53] Convention on Migratory Species of Wild Animals, Bonn, 23 June 1979, 1651 UNTS 333, App I (Endangered Migratory Species) and App II (Migratory Species to be Subject to Agreements), arts III, IV, V.

[54] For the entire climate change 'process' and all instruments, see <https://unfccc.int/process-and-meetings>.

[55] Bharat H. Desai and Moumita Mandal, 'The Cost of Climate Change Heightened Sexual and Gender-based Violence: A Challenge for International Law' (2022) 52(5–6) *Environmental Policy and Law* 413.

2.2 Interface with the Indian Domestic Law

Environmental protection was earlier seen by many developing nations, including India, as a goal conflicting with developmental priorities. Some even regarded industrialized nations' recommendations that developing nations adopt environmental protection policies as a trap. Giving expression to this feeling, in her address at the 1972 Stockholm Conference, the late Indian Prime Minister, Mrs Indira Gandhi asked:

> How can we speak to those who live in the villages and in slums about keeping the oceans, rivers and the air clean when their own lives are contaminated at the source? The rich countries may look upon development as the cause of environment destruction, but to us it is one of the primary means of improving the environment of living, of providing food, water, sanitation and shelter, of making deserts green and mountains habitable.[56]

In the aftermath of India's participation in the 1972 Stockholm Conference, the government of India enacted the first legislation for water pollution control (1974) followed by another for air pollution control (1981). They explicitly drew a mandate from the 1972 Stockholm Declaration. The Indian national legal mechanisms that act as connecting tools between international environmental law and domestic environmental laws are: (i) the Constitution of India, 1950, (ii) the Environment (Protection) Act, 1986, and the subordinate legislations and rules notified thereunder as well as other subject-specific legislations, and (iii) the judicial pronouncements in a flurry of public interest environmental litigations.

2.2.1 The Constitution of India: Environmental Protection

The Constitution of India is the highest law of the country, and all other national laws made by the Parliament of India, including national environmental legislation, are in accordance with the provisions of the Constitution of India. Even India is a party to any international environmental law that will not automatically apply to India until and unless Parliament makes or adopts any legislation in accordance with the Constitution of India.

[56] Speech of the late Prime Minister of India, Indira Gandhi, on 'Man and Environment' at Plenary Session of the United Nations Conference on Human Environment, Stockholm, 14 June 1972 <http://lasulawsenvironmental.blogspot.in/2012/07/indira-gandhis-speech-at-stockholm.html>.

According to famous jurist Hans Kelsen's 'Pure Theory of Law', the Indian Constitution is the *grundnorm* or basic norm for India.[57] It is the source of law in India. Thus, all the statutes, case law, customary law, etc., are recognized by the Constitution of India.[58] Statutes are enacted by Parliament, State Legislatures, and Union Territory Legislatures in India. There is subordinate legislation in the form of rules, regulations, policies, by-laws, etc., made by the central government, state governments, and other institutions, for example, the Central Pollution Control Board, and local bodies like municipal corporations, *gram panchayats*, and other bodies. Regarding case law, the Supreme Court of India is the highest, and the decisions are binding on all the subordinate courts and tribunals (including the National Green Tribunal (NGT)) as precedents, which is another source of law. Prevailing trends indicate that the churning process at work impinges upon domestic developmental priorities, trends in spreading awareness of environmental law, capacity building, and preparedness to contend with the larger challenges in global environmental negotiations as well as implementation, compliance and enforcement.[59] In essence, they give effect to India's international environmental law obligations under different global instruments.

The above process emanates from in-built provisions of the Constitution of India wherein dualism has been practised in the domestic legal system. International treaties to which India is a party do not automatically become part of the domestic law of India; parliamentary legislation is required. Article 51(c) of the Constitution sets out an obligation to foster respect for international law and treaty obligations through appropriate policy and legislative actions. This obligation is not enforceable in the courts of law because it is placed under the Directive Principles of State Policy, which are non-justiciable but remain 'fundamental in the governance of the country'. Thus, India is expected to respect international law and treaty obligations through the enactment of laws at the domestic level.[60]

Negotiating a treaty is an executive act in India, but implementation within the domestic legal system by adopting legislation is within the exclusive domain of the Parliament of India. Article 253 of the Constitution provides for 'legislation for giving effect to international agreements, treaty, convention, and so on by the Parliament'.[61] Similarly, it is the Parliament that has sole authority to enact a law under Article 246 of the Constitution[62] on the subjects listed under the Union List or List 1 specified in the Seventh Schedule. Entry 14 of the Union List specifies: 'Entering into treaties and

[57] Stanford Encyclopaedia of Philosophy, 'The Pure Theory of Law' (2002) <https://plato.stanford.edu/entries/lawphil-theory/>.

[58] The Constitution of India, 1950, Art 246, Seventh Schedule, and Art 253.

[59] *High-Level Meeting on Compliance with and Enforcement of Multilateral Environmental Agreements*, Colombo (21–22 January 2006) and Geneva (31 May–2 June 2006). The author was a part of these deliberations.

[60] The Constitution of India, Art 37. See also Alexander (n 6) 291.

[61] The Constitution of India, Art 253.

[62] ibid Art 246.

agreements with foreign countries and implementing of treaties, agreements, and conventions with foreign countries.'[63]

Apart from the above provisions, Article 73 of the Constitution defines the scope of executive power of the central government or the Union and provides: 'the executive power of the Union shall extend (a) to the matters with respect to which Parliament has the power to make laws; and (b) to the exercise of such rights, authority and jurisdiction as are exercisable by the government of India by virtue of any treaty or agreement'.[64] Thus, all the above-discussed constitutional provisions have close interlinkages as regards India's international obligations including under an international treaty.

The Indian judiciary has evolved a magnificent jurisprudence to fulfil its onerous responsibility of protecting rights and rendering justice. It has pronounced many path-breaking judgments. In one such case, *Vishakha v State of Rajasthan*, the Supreme Court, while adjudicating upon the applicability of CEDAW 1979 (a treaty ratified by India but no domestic legislation at that time to give effect to its provisions), observed that:

> In the absence of domestic law occupying the field ... the contents of international conventions and norms are significant for the purpose of interpretation ... of the Constitution .... Any international convention not inconsistent with the fundamental rights and in harmony with its spirit must be read into these provisions to enlarge the meaning and contents thereof, to promote the object of the constitutional guarantee.[65]

Thus, a duly ratified treaty could be invoked to construe the nature and ambit of constitutional guarantees. In the absence of any domestic legislation occupying the field, international conventions and norms should be read into the constitutional provisions guaranteeing fundamental rights, provided such a reading is not inconsistent with any domestic legislation.

The Supreme Court in *Vellore Citizens' Welfare Forum v Union of India*, while commenting upon international customary law, observed that:

> [o]nce these principles are accepted as part of Customary International Law there would be no difficulty in accepting them as part of domestic law. It is almost an accepted proposition of law that the rules of Customary International Law which are not contrary to the municipal law shall be deemed to have been incorporated in the domestic law and shall be followed by the courts of law.[66]

In view of the above, India's international obligations, whether incurred under customary international law or treaty law, are relied upon by domestic courts while

63 ibid Seventh Schedule: (Art 246) List I—Union List.

64 ibid Art 73.

65 *Vishakha v State of Rajasthan* AIR 1997 SC 3011; also quoted in SK Verma, *An Introduction to Public International Law* (3rd edn, Satyam Law International 2019) 81.

66 *Vellore Citizens' Welfare Forum v Union of India* AIR 1996 SC 2715.

adjudicating any matter if there is no domestic law on the point, and such reliance on international law is not incongruous with the domestic legal system. India's international obligations are to be read into the domestic legal system to provide meaningful protection to constitutional guarantees. The provisions of the Constitution or any other law could be interpreted using the insights from India's international obligations. In this respect, the official Indian position is understood to reflect the following observation of the National Commission to Review the Working of the Constitution:

> (I)t is left totally to the Executive to not only enter into treaties and agreements but also to decide the manner in which they should be implemented, except where such implementation requires making of a law by Parliament. And the fact of the matter is that once the Executive Government enters into a treaty, it would be, ordinarily speaking, quite embarrassing for the Parliament to reject the treaty.... Theoretically speaking, however, it is always open to the Parliament to disapprove a treaty entered into by the Executive whereupon the treaty will have to (take) effect whatever. Moreover, if any treaty or agreement violates any of the provisions of the Constitution, it would be totally incompetent and ineffective and even the Vienna Convention would not stand in the way.[67]

Article 48A of the Constitution directs the state to take appropriate steps to protect, improve and safeguard the environment, forests, and wildlife. Article 47 directs the state to take all appropriate steps to raise the level of nutrition and the standard of living of its citizens. It also requires the state to improve the conditions of public health. These provisions belong to Part IV of the Constitution and are not judicially enforceable, but the courts have read them in conformity with the international environmental law and expanded the contours of the right to life to include in it the right to a clean environment.[68] The protection and improvement of the natural environment, including forests, lakes, rivers, and wildlife, is also a fundamental duty of every Indian citizen.[69] On the basis of these constitutional provisions, as mentioned earlier, India has enacted a series of national environmental legislations to give respect and implement international environmental law within the national legal system.

[67] National Commission to Review the Working of the Constitution, 'A Consultation Paper on Treaty-Making Power under our Constitution', 8 January 2001 <https://legalaffairs.gov.in/sites/default/files/Treaty-making%20power%20under%20our%20Constitution.pdf>. See also Law and Practice Concerning the Conclusion of Treaties, UN Legal Series ST./Leg./Ser./B/3 (1953) 63; Upendra Baxi, 'Law of Treaties in the Contemporary Practice of India' (1965) XIV *Indian Yearbook of International Affairs* 137.

[68] *Rural Litigation and Entitlement Kendra v State of UP* AIR 1985 SC 652.

[69] Constitution of India, Art 51(A)(g).

2.2.2 Domestic Legislation

The Parliament enacted laws relating to the protection of the environment in India. These laws reflect the interface between international environmental law and domestic environmental law. Several Indian legislations explicitly invoke treaty obligations as enabling authority to give effect to international obligations.

The Air (Prevention and Control of Pollution) Act, 1981, is based on India's respect for international environmental law according to the UN Conference on the Human Environment held in Stockholm in June 1972.[70] Similarly, the Environment (Protection) Act, 1986, is based on India's international obligation to protect the environment in the Stockholm Declaration, 1972, to take the appropriate steps for the protection of the environment.[71] The Biological Diversity Act, 2002, is an example of the implementation of international environmental law that the CBD signed in Rio de Janeiro on 5 June 1992 for the national legal system.[72] The NGT Act, 2010, is another example of a law enacted to implement the Stockholm Declaration, 1972, and:

> decisions were taken at the United Nations Conference on Environment and Development held at Rio de Janeiro in June, 1992, in which India participated, calling upon the States to provide effective access to judicial and administrative proceedings, including redress and remedy and to develop national laws regarding liability and compensation for the victims of pollution and other environmental damage.[73]

The abovementioned invocation of phraseology and style is a self-explanatory methodology for transposing international environmental obligations into the domestic legal system. As a result, this would also explain some delays in India's ratification of multilateral environmental agreements until domestic preparedness makes it possible to undertake and give effect to respective international obligations.

2.2.3 Rules

The Ministry of Environment, Forest and Climate Change (MoEFCC) is the authority that can make the rules. In many cases, the concerned subjects of states (mentioned in the State List under the Seventh Schedule of the Constitution)[74] need to be duly kept in mind. The following rules reflect the interface between international and domestic environmental laws in India. For example, the Hazardous and Other Wastes (Management & Transboundary Movement) Rules, 2016, reflect the fact that India ratified the Basel

70 Air (Prevention and Control of Pollution) Act, 1981, preamble.
71 Environment (Protection) Act, 1986, preamble.
72 Biological Diversity Act, 2002, preamble.
73 NGT Act, 2010, preamble.
74 Constitution of India, Seventh Schedule.

Convention on Transboundary Movement of Hazardous Wastes in 1992 and integrated the protection regime of the Convention domestically to reduce transboundary movement of waste such as tyres, paper, metal scrap, and used electronic items.[75]

The MoEFCC modified the Plastic Waste Management (Amendment) Rules, 2021, to phase out single-use plastic by 2022 because of the adverse impacts of littered plastic on both terrestrial and aquatic ecosystems.[76] It came after India participated in the UNEA 4 (2019) that adopted resolution 6 (marine plastic litter and microplastics).[77]

2.3 Some Important Recent Cases

This section discusses how the Indian higher judiciary (Supreme Court of India and the state High Courts) and the NGT have played a crucial role in implementing the national environmental legislation. As mentioned, almost all the relevant environmental legislation draws its mandates from India's participation in an international conference or an international treaty (as mandated by Article 253). The decided cases do not directly mention or use the provisions of the global environmental instruments (both soft and hard). Since India follows dualism, the judiciary interoperates and implements the provisions of respective national policies (such as the National Environment Policy 2006) and legislations in conjunction with global instruments and India's respective obligations. In many of the decided cases, there are frequent references to the soft instruments (such as the Stockholm Declaration, Rio Declaration, Agenda 21, etc.) as well as the global conventions (such as the 1971 Ramsar Convention, 1972 CITES, 1972 World Heritage Convention, 1979 Basel Convention, and the 1985 Montreal Protocol).

In *Bonani Kakkar v Oil India Ltd*, the case concerned the assessment of damage and destruction to the biodiversity due to a blowout in the Baghjan-5 oil well in Assam, which released a huge amount of toxic gases and, other consequential events, including a fire incident in 2020. The claimant sought restoration of the environment and compensation to the victims for the damage. The NGT held that '[t]he principle of absolute liability is attracted to such incidents in accordance with law laid down in *MC Mehta v Union of India* (1987) 1 SCC 395 and thus the victims are entitled to compensation at least on principle of restitution without proving negligence'.[78] It also directed for remedial

[75] Hazardous and Other Wastes (Management and Transboundary Movement) Rules, 2016. See also National Productivity Council, Capacity Building Programme on Implementation of Waste Management Rules, 2016 (2019) <https://www.npcindia.gov.in/NPC/Files/delhiOFC/EM/Hazardous-waste-management-rules-2016.pdf>.

[76] Plastic Waste Management (Amendment) Rules, 2021, Ministry of Environment, Forest and Climate Change Notification GSR 571(E), 12 August 2021.

[77] United Nations Environment Assembly Resolution 4/6, Marine plastic litter and microplastics, 15 March 2019, UN Doc UNEP/EA.4/Res 6.

[78] *Bonani Kakkar v Oil India Ltd* NGT Principal Bench, New Delhi, Original Application No 43/2020 (EZ), Order of 19 February 2021, paras 24 and 28 (pp 57 and 59).

measures planned by a ten-member committee headed by the Chief Secretary, Assam for 'assessing the damage to the environment and remedial restoration plan, including Dibru-Saikhowa National Park, the Maguri-Motapung Wetland'. Subsequently, the Supreme Court of India decided to reconstitute the committee for remedial action after assessing the environmental damage. It held that it was warranted since 'Oil India cannot be judge in its own cause'.[79]

In *Saloni Singh v Union of India*, the issue was compliance with Plastic and Solid Waste Management Rules at railway premises, prevention of unlawful discharge of effluents, and water management, including recycling and re-use by the Railways. The NGT directed the Railway Administration to evolve a suitable environment management plan covering all aspects of waste management and to 'take further steps in compliance of orders of this Tribunal'.[80]

The case in *Bhanwar Lal Bhargava v State of Rajasthan* concerned the discharge of untreated sewage and industrial effluents on the agricultural land at village Nokha, Bikaner, Rajasthan. The NGT directed the state of Rajasthan to take immediate remedial measures to stop pollution, especially water pollution.[81]

In an application filed by Air Marshal Anil Chopra on environmental and waste management issues in the armed forces' cantonments and military stations, the NGT ordered that 'the authorities will take all necessary measures required for protection of environment at all levels, including proper management of biomedical, domestic, solid, electrical, electronic wastes as per statutory rules. Scientific management of other waste generated in the course of operations of the armed forces like artillery and other ammunition has also to be ensured in the interest of public health, sanitation and environment'.[82]

Conclusion

The experience of the past fifty years shows that the international environmental law-making process is essentially a product of a complex set of factors. Both state and non-state actors have contributed significantly to the process. It brings to the fore a whole set

[79] The Economic Times, 'Oil India Cannot be Judge in Its Own Cause, Will Reconstitute Panel: SC on Baghjan Oil Well Tragedy' *The Economic Times* (23 August 2021) <https://economictimes.indiatimes.com/industry/energy/oil-gas/oil-india-cant-be-judge-in-its-own-cause-will-reconstitute-panel-sc-on-baghjan-oil-well-tragedy/articleshow/85570032.cms?from=mdr>.

[80] *Saloni Singh v Union of India*, NGT Principal Bench, New Delhi, Original Application No 141 of 2014, Order of 18 November 2021.

[81] *Bhanwar Lal Bhargava v State of Rajasthan*, NGT Principal Bench, New Delhi, Original Application No 972/2019, Order of 21 September 2021.

[82] Air Marshal Anil Chopra (Report on Environmental Issues, Waste Management-Armed Forces, General issues of Cantonments and lists major military stations and Cantonments of all the state) NGT Principal Bench, New Delhi, Original Application No 451/2019, Order of 24 May 2021.

of tools and techniques put forward by various states in the wake of intense negotiations in inter-governmental meetings. If one can take an aerial view of the fascinating law-making process in recent decades, it reveals an interesting pattern at work, especially within each cluster of environmental issues. A closer look would also show that it has taken the shape of a piece of fine art and craft that weaves a fabric according to the political compulsions and convenience of the sovereign states even as it considers scientific evidence and requirements of commitments in a legal or non-legally binding instrument.

In fact, the states that finally adopt instruments try to grapple with various legal responses to an environmental problem. The role of civil society appears to be gaining ground both at the stage of multilateral environmental negotiations and influencing the state's attitude at the subsequent stages of signature and ratification. This is underscored by an unprecedented participation of almost 200 countries in the 2021 Glasgow Conference of the Parties of the climate change convention.[83]

In the absence of a central law-making institution, the initiative for an international environmental instrument generally comes from a specialized environmental institution such as UNEP that will act as a catalyst, either on its own accord or in conjunction with another international institution, to initiate intergovernmental negotiations. In other cases, functional international organizations of the UN system have taken the initiative (e.g., the FAO or UNESCO) in matters closely related to their functional jurisdiction. However, it is the UN General Assembly that occupies an important place—as the conductor of a grand orchestra—in providing decisive impetus to the norm-setting and treaty-making process and overall political guidance for the entire process. A closer analysis of the range, scope, and depth of resolutions of the UN General Assembly provides a spectacular view of the entire law-making process to a perceptive connoisseur in the field. These resolutions, couched in familiar UN language, carry their moral force in influencing the conduct of states in areas such as mainstreaming the Sustainable Development Goals for attaining targets in seventeen areas by 2030. Many states do follow up on these resolutions with appropriate domestic action. They also help build consensus regarding the seriousness of the challenge (e.g., common concerns) and the need for requisite global action. The UN General Assembly sometimes sets up intergovernmental negotiating committees to draft an MEA or assign the groundwork to some intergovernmental forum. Initiatives taken by the UN General Assembly on the work assigned to the UN Forum on Forests[84] on the forest issue are examples of this approach.

In the international environmental law-making process, India has played a constructive role, especially during the past fifty two years (1972–2024). On many occasions, the Indian delegations have played a role in moulding the global law-making process and working of the regime-based institutions. As a result, the

[83] Decision 1/CMA.3 Glasgow Climate Pact, Conference of the Parties serving as the meeting of the Parties to the Paris Agreement, 13 November 2021, UN Doc FCCC/PA/CMA/2021/10/Add.1.

[84] For a detailed study of this process, see Bharat H. Desai, 'Forests: International Protection' in R Wolfrum (ed), *Max Planck Encyclopaedia of Public International Law*, vol. IV (OUP 2011) 190–198.

development of Indian environmental legislation has witnessed phenomenal growth over the years. In almost all the cases, by the power enshrined in Article 253 of the Constitution, Parliament enacted legislations to give effect to international obligations. In some cases, special legislation took shape (e.g., the Biological Diversity Act, 2000), whereas in other cases, the delegated legislation was used by invoking the powers vested in the Environment (Protection) Act, 1986. Delegated legislation takes the form of notifications, such as in the case of ozone-depleting substances and hazardous wastes and other cases where existing legislation has been used (forests, wetlands, desertification, etc.). Notwithstanding scholarly suggestions, the Indian Parliament is yet to enact a special 'comprehensive legislation' and 'institutional framework ... for administering and supervising GHG-related regulations' to address the challenge of climate change.[85]

In the post-Stockholm + 50 (2022) period, one hopes that India will be able to provide ideational leadership to effectively address and provide workable legal solutions for global environmental challenges in the coming decades of the twenty-first century. One such potential area could be the suggestion for revival and repurpose of the UN Trusteeship Council (with a new mandate)[86] mooted by this author in a lecture at the World Bank in Washington DC, USA.[87] It could provide a global supervisory forum in the UN system both to oversee select multilateral environmental agreements (such as climate change, biological diversity, and desertification) with universal membership as well as the global commons (the atmosphere, Antarctica, the high seas (the Area), and outer space).[88] A reference to this was made in the 2021 report of the UN Secretary-General for a 'repurposed UN Trusteeship Council'[89] as well as the Indian Prime Minister in his virtual address for 'trusteeship of the planet' at the G-20 Riyadh Summit on 21 November 2020.[90] Hence, it remains to be seen as to what final trajectory it assumes in the future.

[85] Bharat H. Desai, 'India: Greenhouse Gas Mitigation' (2013) 43(4–5) *Environmental Policy and Law* 238, 245–246.

[86] Bharat H. Desai, 'The Repurposed UN Trusteeship Council for the Future' (2022) 52(3) *Environmental Policy and Law* 223; Bharat H. Desai (ed), *Envisioning Our Environmental Future: Stockholm + 50 and Beyond* (IOS Press 2022) 53–65.

[87] For a detailed proposal, see Bharat H. Desai, 'Revitalizing International Environmental Institutions: The UN Task Force Report and Beyond' (2000) 40(3) *Indian Journal of International Law* 455–504.

[88] Desai (n 11).

[89] UN, 'Our Common Agenda: Report of the Secretary-General' (New York 2021) 77 <https://www.un.org/en/content/common-agenda-report/assets/pdf/Common_Agenda_Report_English.pdf>.

[90] Bharat H. Desai, 'Reforms Needed to Meet Environment Goals' *The Tribune* (5 June 2021) <https://www.tribuneindia.com/news/comment/reforms-needed-to-meet-environment-goals-263493>.

Suggestions for Further Reading

Bharat H. Desai, 'Enforcement of the Right to Environment Protection through Public Interest Litigation in India' (1993) 33 *Indian Journal of International Law* 27.

Bharat H. Desai, 'Effectuation of International Environmental Law at the National Level: Some Comparative Trends in South Asia' (2007) 5 *Banyan* 55.

Bharat H. Desai, *Multilateral Environmental Agreements: Legal Status of the Secretariats* (CUP 2010).

Bharat H. Desai, 'The Repurposed UN Trusteeship Council for the Future' (2022) 52(3–4) *Environmental Policy and Law* 223.

Bharat H. Desai (ed), *Envisioning Our Environmental Future: Stockholm+50 and Beyond* (IOS Press 2022).

CHAPTER 3

CROSS-FERTILIZATION OF ENVIRONMENTAL LAW IN THE SAARC

Exploring Substantive and Constitutional Environmental Rights

SHAWKAT ALAM

Abstract

This chapter explores environmental law within the South Asian Association for Regional Cooperation (SAARC), comprising Afghanistan, Bangladesh, Bhutan, India, the Maldives, Nepal, Pakistan, and Sri Lanka. SAARC countries share the constitutional recognition to a right to a clean environment. Whilst this is explicit in newly created constitutions (Afghanistan, Bangladesh, Bhutan, the Maldives, and Nepal), this right has been read into other existing rights (such as the right to life) in older constitutions (India, Pakistan, and Sri Lanka). The former have borrowed principles and ideas from the latter through shared constitutional mechanisms, that is, Directive Principles thus illustrating the cross-fertilization of environmental law within the SAARC. Furthermore, SAARC members share implementation and enforcement challenges, including a lack of technical, human and financial capacity, as well as low environmental literacy. The SAARC can overcome these challenges by improving access to justice to allow maturation of environmental law and to further regional cooperation.

Introduction

The South Asian Association for Regional Cooperation (SAARC) constitutes Bangladesh, Bhutan, India, the Maldives, Nepal, Pakistan, and Sri Lanka, with Afghanistan joining later in 2007. Historically, these countries have been sites of some of the most significant environmental disasters and instances of pollution, and exploitation, which have continued in the post-colonial era. Incidents such as the Bhopal disaster in India, seasonal floods, and cyclones demonstrate an area highly vulnerable to environmental disruption, which is further compounded by systemic underdevelopment and poverty. Notwithstanding all this, these nations have come a long way from rudimentary environmental protection and have demonstrated maturity in environmental legislation, regulation, and institutions, with the judiciary playing a key role in expanding environmental rights within the SAARC. This has been bolstered not only by the fact that SAARC countries share common ecosystems but also by their common legal heritage and traditions, constitutional structures, and legislative frameworks, which have developed in the post-colonial era.

Against this backdrop, this chapter will explore how environmental legal principles permeate the SAARC. SAARC countries have developed their Constitutions and pathways towards independence in the post-colonial era, and the judiciary has been guided by doctrines developed in comparative SAARC jurisdictions that share constitutional mechanisms. More modern SAARC constitutions such as Afghanistan, Bangladesh, Bhutan, the Maldives, and Nepal have been more explicit in recognizing the right to a clean environment. This approach can be compared to places such as India and Sri Lanka that have chosen not to enshrine a constitutional right to a clean environment, and instead rely on expanding environmental rights through other existing rights protected under their respective Constitutions. Many theories posit why environmental constitutionalism cross-fertilizes, including internationalizing constitutional rights to more local political dynamics. This chapter will advocate that when approached from a regional lens, the distinction between global and local factors is diffuse and that legal mechanisms (such as the use of directive principles within Constitutions) can enable cross-fertilization of environmental law, as evidenced in India and Nepal.

In addition, this chapter will discuss the environmental legislative frameworks and supporting institutions in each country, to examine the implementation challenges they share. This chapter will identify a lack of financial, technical, and human resource capacity to fully implement and enforce these laws, and low environmental literacy as key impediments to effective implementation. In light of these findings, this chapter will examine how SAARC can overcome these challenges by further improving access to justice and bolstering regional cooperation to alleviate capacity constraints and promote further cross-fertilization of environmental legal principles.

3.1 SAARC: A Region of Geo-Political Diversity and Shared Legal Traditions

The SAARC was established in 1983 and includes the countries of Bangladesh, Bhutan, India, the Maldives, Nepal, Pakistan, Sri Lanka, and Afghanistan. South Asia covers a diverse area in terms of geographic and ecological diversity, as well as cultural, social, and political diversity. The SAARC region faces hugely demanding climate change challenges, including melting glaciers in the Himalayas, rapid urbanization, declining crop yields, periodic flooding, and rising sea levels.[1] Larger countries such as India possess different capabilities to small island developing states like the Maldives, but also have other developmental challenges, including the pressing need for poverty alleviation, building the capacity for climate change adaptation and mitigation, and the economic capability to perform environmental management and improvement works. For this reason, the SAARC has been atypical in that 'it has emerged from a region of political disharmony and strategic schism, unlike other regionalism projects where political-strategic harmony forms a vital factor in stimulating and facilitating close and extensive cooperation linkages'.[2] Coupled with this divergence, the SAARC is also exposed to significant geo-political change. India's march towards greater global and regional significance, as well as South Asia's history of strained political relationships between countries, such as India-Pakistan, Afghanistan-Pakistan, and India-Nepal, are political realities that impact the effectiveness of the SAARC as a regional organization, as well as the social perception of this group as its own distinct region within the global community. More recently, there has been a push to develop sub-regional organizations given the inherent diversity and divergence present within the SAARC, such as the creation of the Bay of Bengal Initiative for Multi-Sectoral Technical and Economic Cooperation (BIMSTEC), that aligns more strongly with each country's own national interests.

Despite this variation, the SAARC also share a common heritage, allowing these countries to identify as their own distinct region within the global community. The SAARC countries are bounded by their geographical proximity, more so than a cultural or economic proximity and significant power imbalances between SAARC countries exist.[3] The area also has a long history of colonialism to which there is a strong political and ideological commonality driven by 'anti-colonial sentiment'.[4] This history

[1] Baniateilang Majaw, 'Climate Change and South Asian Association for Regional Cooperation: A Regional Response' (2012) 4(2) *International Journal of Social Sciences and Humanity Studies* 71, 73.

[2] K Yhome and Tridivesh Singh Maini, 'Regionalism: SAARC and Beyond' (2017) *ORF* Occasional Paper No 135 <www.orfonline.org/research/regionalism-saarc-beyond/>.

[3] See V. V Desai, 'The Political Economy of Regional Cooperation in South Asia' (Asian Development Bank, July 2010). Available at https://www.adb.org/sites/default/files/publication/28528/wp54-political-economy-south-asia.pdf. Accessed 5 March 2024.>.

[4] Yhome and Maini (n 2).

of colonialism, together with religious and ideological divisions, has contributed to many of modern-day disputes found between SAARC members.[5] Yet, despite this history of long and socially traumatic experience with colonial powers, these states have developed as independent democratic nations and have modelled their legal structures, including their Constitutions, on other post-colonial states and each other. In this respect, the SAARC constitutions have adopted tools such as directive principles, which provide direction to the state to improve the welfare of its citizenry and guide the policy-making apparatus of the state. Together with the adoption of fundamental rights, this also has an important effect of guiding judicial interpretation, and as this chapter will further demonstrate, has an significant impact on expanding environmental rights.

The SAARC is a regional organization primarily focused on economic development, but also considers environmental conservation within the region. To this extent, the SAARC has implemented the Committee on the Environment, which has undertaken technical studies on pressing regional environmental issues, such as the Regional Study on Greenhouse Effects and implemented the recommendations from other technical reports produced by the SAARC Secretariat, such as the Causes and Consequences on Natural Disasters and the Preservation and Protection of the Environment in South Asia. The SAARC Committee on Environment plays a key coordinating role in establishing further regional and bilateral relations to perform climate change adaptation and conservation programmes, including improving cooperation in water-sharing arrangements, strengthening environmental management infrastructure, climate change adaptation and mitigation, and improving forestry management. The Committee also monitors the implementation of the SAARC Environment Action Plan and the SAARC Action Plan on Climate Change. To increase the effectiveness of its environmental mandate, the SAARC has also established several regional centres to improve collaboration and coordination. This includes the SAARC Energy Centre that aims to develop sustainable forest management, the SAARC Disaster Management Centre that provides policy advice and capacity building for disaster risk reduction and management, as well as the SAARC Natural Disaster Rapid Response Mechanism that will assist in carrying out disaster relief. Section 3.2 considers how each country has taken a different approach to environmental protection. Most SAARC countries have implemented framework legislation and sectoral policies to address different aspects of sustainable development and environmental conservation.

[5] Desai (n 3).

3.2 Cross-Fertilization in the SAARC: the Constitutional Recognition of a Right to a Clean Environment

Constitutional recognition of the right to a clean environment reflects the core principles and priorities of society and guides judicial interpretation. Across the SAARC, there are divergent approaches to enshrining the right to a clean environment. While some states take an explicit approach, Constitutions drafted prior to the maturity of the right to a clean environment under international human rights law have been interpreted by relevant appellate courts as granting an implied right in other substantive rights, such as the right to life. This section will establish the different approaches to environmental constitutionalism within the SAARC, with the following section analysing how environmental principles are permeated between members within the region.

The Supreme Court of India has read the right to a clean environment as a liberty that is implied within the right to life enshrined in Article 21 of the Constitution.[6] In *MC Mehta v Union of India*, the Supreme Court of India expanded on the right to life to require the state to undertake positive steps to ensure a clean environment and issued a mandamus order requiring the state to demonstrate its commitment to restoring the quality of the environment.[7] In addition, the Indian Constitution also sets out obligations, or fundamental duties, that individuals hold against the state.[8] This duty is both negative and positive. In *M/s Abhilash Textile v The Rajkot Municipal Corporation*, the High Court determined that an individual could not discharge effluent into public drainage, as it contravened the duty to the environment.[9] In *Virender Gaur v State of Haryana*, the High Court determined that this duty is a positive duty and held that an individual has an active obligation to maintain a hygienic environment.[10] The Indian judiciary have also expanded the right to a clean environment to consist of vital procedural protections for citizens. In *MC Mehta v Union of India*, the petitioner successfully argued that the constitutional duty to protect and improve the environment requires freedom of speech and access to information so that citizens are adequately informed on matters relating to the environment.[11] The Indian judiciary have been receptive to expanding environmental rights, both substantive and procedural, by adopting this broad interpretation of other rights enshrined under the Constitution.

Like India, Pakistan does not have an explicit provision which provides the right to a clean environment. Instead, the judiciary has interpreted existing rights broadly to

[6] See *Subhash Kumar v State of Bihar* (1991) 1 SCC 598.
[7] *MC Mehta v Union of India* (1987) SCR (1) 819.
[8] The Constitution of India, 1950 Arts 48A and 51A.
[9] *M/s Abhilash Textile v The Rajkot Municipal Corporation AIR* 1988 57 [7].
[10] *Virender Gaur v State of Haryana* (1995) 2 SCC 577 [7].
[11] *MC Mehta v Union of India* (1992) 1 SCC 358.

enable such a right, through the right to life. In *Shehla Zia v WAPDA*,[12] Akhtar J noted that if both Article 14 (right to dignity of man) and Article 9 (right to life) are read together, a 'question will arise whether a person can be said to have dignity of man if his right to life is below the bare necessity line without proper food, clothing, shelter, education, healthcare, clean atmosphere and an unpolluted environment'.[13] Later, in *General Secretary, West Pakistan Salt Miners Labour Union (CBA) Khewara, Jhelum v The Director, Industries and Mineral Development, Punjab, Lahore*, Pakistan's judiciary reaffirmed that the right to life 'cannot be restricted to a vegetative life or mere animal existence ... the right to have water free from pollution and contamination is a right to life itself'.[14] Given the parallels with a lack of an explicit right to a clean environment, the Pakistani judiciary have relied on Indian jurisprudence on several occasions to expand the right to life to include a right to a clean environment.[15]

The Constitution of Sri Lanka also does not contain an explicit provision outlining the right to a clean environment. Under Article 27(14), the state has an obligation to protect, preserve and improve the environment for the benefit of the community.[16] Citizens also have a fundamental duty to protect and preserve the environment,[17] which is not a justiciable matter under Article 29 of the Constitution. Nevertheless, the Sri Lankan judiciary has interpreted other existing doctrines broadly to encapsulate the right to a clean environment, much like its Indian and Pakistani counterparts. In particular, the Sri Lankan judiciary have expanded on the doctrine of public trust, whereby the state holds natural resources in the interests of the community. In *Bulankulama v Secretary, Ministry of Industrial Development*, the Supreme Court of Sri Lanka held that the government is a trustee of natural resources and, as such, must protect these resources from exploitation for private commercial gain.[18] This is a seminal case in Sri Lankan environment law as it introduces sustainable development principles, including intergenerational equity and other obligations that Sri Lanka holds in international environmental treaties as relevant considerations during the decision-making process when determining the use of natural resources. More importantly, it further demonstrates the expansion of other existing rights to introduce a right to a clean environment despite the lack of an explicit constitutional provision.

Conversely, other SAARC constitutions have been more explicit in recognizing the right to a clean environment as interpreted by the Indian and Pakistani courts. The more recently drafted Afghan Constitution contains provisions which protect the right to a

[12] *Shehla Zia v WAPDA* PLD 1994 SC 693.

[13] ibid para 712.

[14] *General Secretary, West Pakistan Salt Miners Labour Union (CBA) Khewara, Jhelum v The Director, Industries and Mineral Development, Punjab, Lahore* 1994 SCMR 2061.

[15] ibid. In Shehla Zia (n 12), the Supreme Court applied Indian cases such as *Rural Litigation and Entitlement Kendra v State of UP AIR* 1985 SC 652 and *MC Mehta v Union of India* (n 7) and *MC Mehta v Union of India* (n 11).

[16] The Constitution of the Democratic Socialist Republic of Sri Lanka, 1977, Art 27(14).

[17] ibid Art 28(f).

[18] *Bulankulama v Secretary, Ministry of Industrial Development* (2000) LKSC 18.

healthy environment, with Article 15 of the Constitution requiring the state to adopt the necessary measures to improve forests as well as the living environment.[19] In addition, the Constitution of the Maldives explicitly recognizes the right to a clean environment. Under Article 22, the state 'has a fundamental duty to protect and preserve the natural environment, biodiversity, resources and beauty of the country for the benefit of present and future generations'.[20] The provision is further supported by the obligation for the state to achieve the progressive realization for 'a healthy and ecologically balanced environment' under Article 23 of the Constitution. In addition, citizens hold the same obligation as the state to preserve and protect the environment under Article 67.

An explicit constitutional protection also exists in Bhutan. Under Article 5, the Constitution affirms that 'every Bhutanese is a trustee of the Kingdom's natural resources',[21] and places an obligation on the government to ensure that it protects, conserves, and improves the pristine environment, and among others, secures ecologically balanced sustainable development.[22] The most striking provision of the Constitution of Bhutan is also a quantitative obligation to preserve forest cover, requiring the government to ensure that 60 per cent of the total land mass remains forested for all time.[23] When looking at this requirement in further detail, the 60 per cent threshold provides a rare example of a social, political, and economic right being drafted in quantitative, rather than qualitative terms.[24] Bhutan's existing forest policy prior to the drafting of the Constitution in 2008 provides clues as to why the drafters adopted this requirement; this constitutional provision reflected existing obligations under the Forest Policy, 1974.[25] In terms of standing, the Constitution of Bhutan is also unique in that not only can citizens bring an action if they are an aggrieved party, but the Opposition party plays a special role to file cases where it is in the national interest and 'fulfil the aspirations of the people'.[26]

In Bangladesh, the 2011 amendment to the Constitution, which inserted Article 18A, places an obligation on the state to protect and improve the environment and preserve natural resources, biodiversity, wetlands, forests, and wildlife for present and future

[19] The Constitution of the Islamic Republic of Afghanistan, 2004 Art 15. Note that since the 2021 transfer of power to the Taliban, authorities have indicated a restoration of the 1964 Afghan Constitution, which does not contain this provision.

[20] The Constitution of the Republic of the Maldives, 2008 Art 22.

[21] The Constitution of the Kingdom of Bhutan, 2008 Art 5(1).

[22] ibid Art 5(2).

[23] ibid Art 5(3).

[24] Stephen Turner, 'The Constitution of Bhutan: A Quantitative Environmental Standard' in Stephen Turner and others (eds), *Environmental Rights: The Development of Standards* (CUP 2019) 323, 329.

[25] Thinley Wangdi, Phurba Lhendup, and Norbu Wangdi, 'An Analysis of Forestry Policy, Acts and Rules of Bhutan to Mainstream Climate Change Adaptation' Regional Climate Change Adaptation Knowledge Platform for Asia, Partner Report Series 13 (Stockholm Environment Institution 2013) 3 <www.weadapt.org/sites/weadapt.org/files/legacy-new/knowledge-base/files/521c8788e61b3bhutan-serie-13-cs5-v7-for-web.pdf>.

[26] Constitution of Bhutan Art 18(1); *Government of Bhutan v Opposition Party* Judgment No SC (Hung 11–1) 24 February 2011.

generations.[27] While this provision is not an individual right but rather an obligation held by the state,[28] its language demonstrates strong alignment to equity principles under sustainable development, namely the requirement to consider intergenerational equity. This constitutional provision must also be considered in light of key decisions from the Supreme Court of Bangladesh. In *Dr M Farooque v Government of Bangladesh*, the right to a healthy environment was read into the right to life that is enshrined under Articles 31 and 32 of the Constitution of Bangladesh.[29] In this case, the Supreme Court of Bangladesh determined that the right to life 'encompasses within its ambit, the protection and preservation of environment, ecological balance free from pollution of air and water, sanitation without which life can hardly be enjoyed'.[30] However, much like the Pakistani courts, the Supreme Court of Bangladesh applies an 'aggrieved persons' test to determine whether a complainant has standing. This has led to criticisms that it creates uncertainty for public interest litigation to protect this right,[31] as complainants may not possess the requisite direct and personal interest when litigation is performed by non-government organizations (NGOs) and civil society groups. Yet, as the *Farooque* case demonstrates, the persons' aggrieved test can *bona fide* be espoused to civil society groups where the cause of action can apply to an indeterminate amount of people with respect to a subject matter of great public concern.[32]

Under the Constitution of Nepal, Article 30 provides citizens with the explicit right to a clean environment and provides a constitutional guarantee that victims of environmental pollution and degradation 'shall have the right to be compensated by the polluter as provided by law', reflecting the polluter pays principle.[33] Critically, Article 30 contains an important caveat not replicated in other SAARC constitutions, providing that 'this Article shall not be deemed to obstruct the making of required legal provisions to strike a balance between environment and development for the use of national development works'.[34] This caveat to the right to a clean environment has not been litigated in Nepalese courts, and it remains to be seen how the 'balance between environment and development' is achieved before designated national development work is considered unlawful. In addition, the Constitution also contains many other rights which have been 'greened' and interpreted to enable the right to a clean environment within its purview.[35]

[27] The Constitution of the People's Republic of Bangladesh, 1972 Art 18A.

[28] Under the Bangladesh Constitution, a fundamental right is a right held against the state and not against another private body or person.

[29] *Farooque v Government of Bangladesh* WP No 998 of 1994, CA No 24 of 1995 (25 July 1996), para 101.

[30] ibid.

[31] Jona Razzaque, 'Human Rights and the Environment: The National Experience in South Asia and Africa' (UNEP-OHCHR Expert Seminar on Human Rights and the Environment, Geneva, 2002) <www.researchgate.net/publication/255967177_Human_Rights_and_the_Environment_The_National_Experience_InSouth_Asia_and_Africa>.

[32] South Asia Cooperation for Environment Programme, *Handbook on National Environmental Legislation and Institutions in the Maldives* (SACEP 2001) 21.

[33] The Constitution of Nepal, 2015 Art 30(2).

[34] ibid Art 30(3).

[35] *Surya Prasad Sharma Dhungel v Godavari Marble Industries* WP No 35 of 1992, 10 October 1995.

Finally, Article 51 of the Constitution of Nepal requires the state to undertake certain policies for the betterment of its citizenry guided by Directive Principles.[36] This includes policies regarding agriculture and land reform, development policy, conservation and management of natural resources, and transportation policy. Article 51 requires the state to ensure, *inter alia*, that the state achieves a sustainable use of natural resources and inclusive development.[37] Critically, the Constitution, much like its Sri Lankan counterpart, contains a privative clause which prevents 'questions ... raised in any court as to whether any of the provisions in this Part is implemented or not'.[38] Yet this does not prevent questions as to whether the state has infringed other fundamental freedoms, and there is a body of jurisprudence from environmental litigation demonstrating the constitutionality of large-scale project proposals.[39]

As this section has discussed, SAARC countries explicitly protect the right to a clean environment through constitutional provisions or the judiciary have read into other existing constitutionally protected rights. As demonstrated by the Indian judiciary, this includes both substantive and procedural rights, which, in turn, have been jurisdictions which directly cite this growing area of jurisprudence, as occurred in Pakistan. Despite the divergence in explicitly recognizing constitutional protection towards the environment, as Section 3.3 will illustrate, courts continually borrow ideas and principles from neighbouring SAARC judiciaries, which is only possible given the constitutional mechanisms and legal traditions they share.

3.3 Explaining Cross-Fertilization and Convergence: the Importance of Shared Constitutional Mechanisms in SAARC

There have been many theories which posit why some countries choose to undertake constitutional recognition of the environment. The proliferation of constitutional democracies in the developing world and the internationalization of constitutional rights,[40] the ratification of international environmental law,[41] and the expansion of

[36] Constitution of Nepal Art 50.

[37] ibid Art 51.

[38] ibid Art 55.

[39] E.g., Padam Bahadur Shrestha on his own and as President representing *Environmental Development and Conservation Legal Forum v Kathmandu Metropolitan and Others* (2013) 074-WO-0283 (Supreme Court).

[40] James R May, 'Constituting Fundamental Environmental Rights Worldwide' (2006) 23 *Pace Environmental Law Review* 113.

[41] James R May, 'Constitutional Directions in Procedural Environmental Rights' (2013) 28 *Journal of Environmental Law and Litigation* 27.

environmental legal jurisprudence[42] have all been indicated as reasons why there has been an expansion of constitutional recognition of a right to a clean environment in recent decades. In addition, climate change and the maturity of sustainable development as a principle have also been attributed to increased environmental constitutionalism, especially in developing countries.[43] Yet, as Gellers points out,[44] these explanations do not provide a 'granular social-scientific analysis' of why certain countries have adopted constitutional recognition over others and what factors have led to constitutional recognition.

According to Gellers, Nepal's adoption of environmental constitutionalism is the product of country-specific 'contextual factors' and 'political dynamics' that were present before and during the constitutional drafting process.[45] Contextual factors include a grassroots push for a more responsive government following internal conflict and ongoing (localized) environmental degradation as motivating factors for environmental constitutionalism.[46] In addition, political dynamics such as advocacy, collaboration, and support from civil society actors, and sustained economic and social inequality drove social attention towards environmental issues while the Constitution of Nepal was being drafted.[47] Conversely for Sri Lanka, an emphasis on government stability, coupled with an existing judicial receptiveness to effectively adjudicate environmental disputes, resulted in environmental groups believing that environmental justice can be achieved in Sri Lanka without constitutional reform.[48] As a result, the right to environment is not enshrined under the Constitution of Sri Lanka unlike its Nepalese counterpart.

A central tenant of Geller's findings is this distinction between international and domestic forces which drive the adoption of environmental constitutionalism in a specific country. As Geller notes, a more granular examination of country-specific contexts can provide a causal explanation for adopting environmental constitutionalism, diverging from existing literature that advocates that global trends (e.g., internationalization of constitutional rights) are the determinative factor for environmental constitutionalism. In doing so, Gellers posits that domestic political conditions, history, and structures drive environmental constitutionalism more directly than the international normative context. Yet, when considering the potential for cross-fertilization of environmental law through a regional lens, this distinction between domestic and international sources

[42] Erin Daly, 'Environmental Human Rights: Paradigm of Indivisibility' (2011) *Widener Law School Legal Studies Research* Paper No 11–05.

[43] David R Boyd, *The Environmental Rights Revolution: A Global Study of Constitutions, Human Rights and the Environment* (UBC Press 2012) 9.

[44] Joshua Gellers, 'Environmental Constitutionalism in South Asia: Analyzing the Experiences of Nepal and Sri Lanka' (2015) 4(2) *Transnational Environmental Law* 395, 398.

[45] ibid 402.

[46] ibid 403–405.

[47] ibid 405–407.

[48] ibid 422.

for constitutionalism is challenged when we reflect that many of the domestic causative factors are intimately shared across the SAARC.

SAARC countries share many of the same ecosystems which have suffered environmental decline. But more importantly, many of the same legal mechanisms and traditions are shared across the SAARC, promoting the cross-fertilization of environmental legal principles. As discussed above, the Pakistan judiciary, on several occasions, has relied on Indian jurisprudence to expand the right to life to include a clean environment in lieu of a lack of an explicit provision giving the right to a clean environment.

In addition, there are other constitutional mechanisms where cross-fertilization is illustrated, such as the use of Directive Principles in the Constitutions of India and Nepal to guide policy-making and judicial interpretation. Directive Principles are a constitutional tool which was inspired by the Irish Directive Principles when they declared their independence from the British. Taking *Surya Prasad Sharma Dhungel v Godavari Marble Industries* as a case in point, the Supreme Court of Nepal determined that, in relation to whether environmental NGOs have standing, the petitioner held *locus standi* and relied upon *dicta* from Indian courts which also use Directive Principles to guide constitutional interpretation. It asserted that:

> there has been a constitutional provision which states that the State shall give priority to the protection of the environment and prevent its further damage ... Since the Indian Supreme Court in *Shree Sachidananda Pandey v State of West Bengal* (AIR 1987 section 1109) has propagated a principle on the very Directive Principles of the State, and as the Directive Principles of our Constitution also comprises of the matter of environmental cleanliness, the existence of *locus standi* of the petitioner in the present case cannot be ruled out.[49]

Surya Prasad Sharma Dhungel is a cornerstone ruling for environmental law in Nepal, holding that the right to life enshrined under Article 12(1) of the Constitution of Nepal included the right to a healthy environment. The case highlights that the sharp distinction between international and domestic sources for environmental constitutionalism is diffuse, given that countries within the SAARC region share similar legal mechanisms and traditions *viz* Directive Principles. These mechanisms are especially pronounced as most member countries have transitioned towards a post-colonial legal order following their respective independencies. At various times, South Asian countries adopted a republican Constitution which, unlike Western Constitutions, aimed to empower the state so that it can bring social transformation and economic redistribution.[50] *Surya Prasad Sharma Dhungel* provides an excellent illustration of cross-fertilization at work, with judiciaries adopting doctrines from fellow SAARC jurisdictions in light of their shared use of Directives Principles in constitutional interpretation.

[49] *Surya Prasad Sharma Dhungel v Godavari Marble Industries* WP No 35 of 1992, 10 October 1995.

[50] Rohit De, 'South Asian Legal Traditions' in James Wright (ed), *International Encyclopaedia of the Social and Behavioural Sciences* (2nd edn, Elsevier, Pergamon 2015) 58.

3.4 Environmental Legislative Frameworks, Institutions, and Implementation Challenges Within SAARC Countries

Each country within the SAARC has its own legislative framework to ensure environmental protection. These jurisdictions have responded to rising environmental problems associated with pollution and climate change by enacting various legislative safeguards. However, legislation remains largely ineffective with an inadequate supporting administrative apparatus to enforce these laws. This section will explore the legislative frameworks that provide environmental protection across the SAARC, as well as discuss the existing implementation barriers experienced by their supporting institutions. The legislation used in this analysis is non-exhaustive but presents a comparative approach to how different jurisdictions have established their governance to implement environmental legislation. As this section will explore, some jurisprudence has emerged that strengthens relevant provisions protecting the natural environment, while others are still developing a body of law in this area.

3.4.1 Afghanistan

Afghanistan has undergone significant institutional and legal changes following the conflict during the 2000s. Afghanistan joined SAARC in 2007. However, prior to its inauguration into the SAARC, the Afghan government introduced the Environment Act, 2007, which provided rules on managing natural resources, biodiversity, drinking water, and pollution control, which became a prevalent issue given the impact of war and conflict. The Act established the National Environment Protection Agency under the guidance of expert advice from the United Nations Environment Programme (UNEP). In particular, the UNEP focused on the devastation that warfare has created on wetlands, poor waste management, and a lack of access to clean drinking water.[51] One of the most striking features of the Environment Act is the introduction of measures to improve environmental education. Article 65 and 66 of the Environment Act contains provisions to improve environmental literacy within the Afghan government, as well as training to increase awareness of obligations established under the Act.[52] Capacity constraints remain a real issue in enforcing and implementing the Environment Act, and measures to improve environmental literacy and mainstreaming awareness of climate change and

[51] See David A Taylor, 'Environmental Triage in Afghanistan' (2003) 111(9) *Environmental Health Perspectives* 470.

[52] Environment Act, 2007 (Afghanistan), ss 65 and 66.

other environmental conservation matters[53] enables a whole of government approach that fosters different perspectives to tackle this issue.

3.4.2 Bangladesh

Bangladesh has an extensive history of legislation and policy aimed at preserving the environment and achieving sustainable development. Since the 1970s, Bangladesh sought to control water pollution through the Water Pollution Control Ordinance, 1970, which was later expanded by implementing the Environmental Pollution Control Ordinance, 1977. This arose from the growing water pollution issues at the time, especially in major urban areas such as Dhaka. These Ordinances were narrow and aimed to control private and commercial pollution of air, water, and soil. Later, this was superseded by the National Environmental Policy, 1992, and the National Environmental Management Plan, 1995, which embraced sustainable development and the use of civil society to help monitor compliance, including fisheries and agricultural activities.[54] Since then, the Environmental Conservation Act, 1995, has provided framework legislation to help control and mitigate environmental pollution and integrates the polluter pays principle by creating remedies from polluters.[55] The Act also empowers the government to declare 'ecologically critical areas' that enables the Department of the Environment to undertake enforcement action against entities responsible for damaging the designated regions.[56] To date, areas designated under the Act as ecologically critical areas include the Sundarbans, Cox's Bazar, and St Martin's Island. These designations are important, as they enable civil society to undertake litigation against the government where they have failed to perform protective measures to conserve the designated areas, as demonstrated by the *rule nisi* issued in *BELA v Ministry of Land* and *BELA v Bangladesh*.[57] In support of the Act, the government has also implemented the Environment Conservation Rules, 1997, which stipulate air, water, and noise quality standards, as well as standards for vehicle emissions, effluent, and access to information procedures.

Bangladesh, a least developed country, has also experienced capacity constraints in implementing effective environmental law. However, the country has performed significant reforms to its judiciary, with the Environment Court Act, 2000, establishing

[53] Abdul Azim Doosti and Mohammed Haris Sherzad, *Climate Change and Governance in Afghanistan* (National Environmental Protection Agency 2015) <https://wedocs.unep.org/bitstream/handle/20.500.11822/22447/Report_CC_Governance_Afghanistan_EN_v2.pdf?sequence=1&isAllowed=y>.

[54] Alexandra Clemett, *A Review of Environmental Policy and Legislation in Bangladesh* (Department for International Development 2006) <https://assets.publishing.service.gov.uk/media/57a08c2fe5274a31e0001058/R8161-Section2.pdf>.

[55] Environment Conservation Act, 1995 (Bangladesh) s 9.

[56] ibid s 5(1).

[57] *Bangladesh Environmental Lawyers Association (BELA) v Ministry of Land* Writ Petition No 4286 of 2003; *Bangladesh Environmental Lawyers Association (BELA) v Bangladesh* Writ Petition No 2224 of 2004.

specialized environmental courts that specify its jurisdiction, procedures, and penalties that the Court can issue. This presents an important step in enabling sustainable development within Bangladesh, as the specialized court possesses the technical capacity to adjudicate matters with complex scientific and other specific knowledge aspects and issue orders which ameliorate damage, including damage to the environment or substantive environmental rights. Together with other policies,[58] Bangladesh has also aimed to reduce administrative silos that have the impact of pigeonholing environmental issues with just an environmental government department.[59] Policies such as the Five Year Plans (FYPs) and Perspective Plan—strategic documents which outline the government's immediate development priorities—aim to mainstream sustainable development and environmental issues across the whole of the government to ensure that different institutions tackle environmental degradation cohesively.

3.4.3 Bhutan

Bhutan has a highly centralized environment and forest management system, which has helped the nation preserve its natural resources.[60] Since 1969, Bhutan passed the Forest Act, 1969, which brought all forests under government control. Following this, the government implemented the National Forest Policy in 1974, which maintained that 60 per cent of Bhutan's total land mass must be forested at any one time.[61] Forest areas which are subject to harvesting are regulated by a Forest Management Units (FMU) programme which places an export ban on raw timber since 1999[62] and requires forestry actors to ensure that forested areas are subject to a forestry management programme. However, this highly centralized model of forest management resulted in a loss of community participation. In response, the Bhutan government has reformed the Forest Act, 1969, replacing it with the Forest and Nature Conservation Act 1995, which established community forests that now cover 1.7 per cent of the total country land mass and involve 28.3 per cent of rural households.[63] In addition, the Bhutanese government have also implemented the National Environment Protection Act, 2007, which established

[58] E.g., National Water Policy, 1999; National Sustainable Development Strategy 2010–21.

[59] E.g., Ian Scott and Ting Gong, 'Coordinating Government Silos: Challenges and Opportunities' (2021) 1 *Global Public Policy and Governance* 20.

[60] World Bank, 'Bhutan Forest Note: Pathways for Sustainable Forest Management and Socio-equitable Economic Development' (World Bank 2019) 16–17 <https://documents1.worldbank.org/curated/en/118821562700584327/pdf/Bhutan-Forest-Note-Pathways-for-Sustainable-Forest-Management-and-Socio-equitable-Economic-Development.pdf>.

[61] Wangdi, Lhendup, and Wangdi (n 25).

[62] Purna Chhetri and Kinley Tenzin, 'State of the Forest Genetic Resources in Bhutan—Country Report' (RNR Research and Development Centre—Royal Government of Bhutan 2012) 17 <www.fao.org/3/i3825e/i3825e5.pdf>.

[63] Turner (n 24) 336.

the National Environment Commission which administers and monitors compliance of the 60 per cent forest cover requirement.

In terms of effectiveness, Bhutan suffers from a lack of public awareness and confidence in environmental law. Although understanding of Bhutan's forestry regulations is moderate, awareness of other key pieces of legislation, including the Water Act, 2011, remains low.[64] Interestingly, the study by Dolkar et al reveals that the public and key stakeholders have strong preferences in how environmental law and policy information is disseminated within the media. The study indicates that many actors prefer to receive news on environmental law and policy through radio rather than print media or the internet.[65] To improve public awareness and confidence in environmental law and its supporting institutions, policymakers must be sensitive in how information is disseminated and ensuring that they promote environmental literacy through the platforms most used by their target audience.

3.4.4 India

India has several sectoral policies and laws that respond to sustainable development and climate change through different approaches. Its umbrella law, the Environment (Protection) Act, 1986, enables the government to protect and improve the environment and to prevent, control, and abate environmental pollution. This umbrella legislation has also established several rules and regulations which dictate more specific obligations to manage natural resources. These include the Hazardous and Other Waste (Management and Transboundary Movement) Rules, 2019, the Environmental Impact Assessment Notification, 2006, and the Solid Waste Management Rules, 2016. In addition, there is expected to be significant reform of the draft Chemicals (Management and Safety) Rules[66] and the Manufacture, Storage and Import of Hazardous Chemicals Rules, 1989. Other legislation aims to protect sectoral interests relating to the environment and sustainable development, including the Wild Life (Protection) Act, 1972, and the Forest (Conservation) Act, 1980. The National Green Tribunal Act, 2010, establishes a separate judicial bench which closely monitors the implementation and enforcement of environmental laws in India.

In terms of supporting institutions, environmental legislation is administered by the Ministry of Environment, Forests and Climate Change (MoEFCC). MoEFCC is responsible for planning and coordinating environmental activities, regulations, and standards, with the Central Pollution Control Board (CPCB) and State Pollution Control Boards (SPCB) tasked with implementing and enforcing these standards. However, much like

[64] Jamyang Dolkar and others, 'Public Awareness of Environmental Policies in Bhutan' (2013) *Bhutan Journal of Research & Development* 1.

[65] ibid.

[66] See Indian Chemical Regulation Helpdesk, 'Indian CMSR Draft Rules' (2022) <https://indianchemicalregulation.com/indian-cmsr/>.

other SAARC countries, the CPCB and SPCBs suffer from crippling human and financial resource constraints. The vacancy rate at the SPCBs can range from 43 to 65 per cent, and there is no formal or technical training provided to CPCB or SPCB staff.[67] In addition, the OECD has identified that institutions often lack a wide range of enforcement tools which can be used to address minor to moderate regulatory breaches, such as continued non-compliance with reporting requirements.[68]

India's judiciary and public interest litigation have been crucial in promoting greater enforcement of its existing environmental legislation. The judiciary provides environmental litigants access to a range of court orders that can compel compliance or provide remediation, as well as reduced standing. In recent decades, Indian courts have adjudicated on several large-scale projects that shape environmental legal jurisprudence and how government agencies can achieve sustainable development that balances social, economic, and ecological progress.[69] In *Vellore Citizens' Welfare Forum v Union of India*, the Indian Supreme Court reaffirmed the use of the Brundtland Commission's definition of sustainable development, while also affirming the use of the precautionary principle to require the state government and statutory authorities to 'anticipate, prevent and attack' the causes of environmental degradation.[70] This *dicta* reinforces the positive obligation that the government holds in preserving the environment, and unlike Bangladesh and Pakistan, Indian courts have applied the polluter pays principle when determining liability for industrial pollution accidents.[71]

3.4.5 The Maldives

Environmental protection in the Maldives is primarily governed under the Law on the Protection and Preservation of the Environment (Law No 4/93), which outlines that the environment forms part of the national heritage of the Maldives and is to be preserved for the benefit of present and future generations. Under this framework legislation, project proposals that impact the environment require an Environmental Impact Assessment (EIA), with the legislation empowering the Minister for Environment to terminate projects based on their environmental impact.[72] The National Commission for the Protection of the Environment, established by the President, provide advice to

[67] OECD, 'Environmental Compliance and Enforcement in India: Rapid Assessment' (OECD 2006) 14–15 <https://www.oecd.org/environment/outreach/37838061.pdf>.

[68] ibid 19–20.

[69] *People United for Better Living in Calcutta and Another v State of West Bengal AIR* 1993 Cal 215; *Goa Foundation v Konkan Railway Corporation* AIR 1992 Bom 471; *Bombay Environmental Action Group v State of Maharashtra* AIR 1991 Bom 301. See also Razzaque (n 31).

[70] *Vellore Citizens' Welfare Forum v Union of India* (1996) 5 SCC 647.

[71] *MC Mehta (Tanneries) v Union of India* (1997) 2 SCC 411.

[72] Law on the Protection and Preservation of the Environment (Law No 4/93) (Maldives) ss 5–6.

the Minister to discharge their functions, including planning assessment decisions and advice on significant environmental matters.[73]

Under government arrangements, the Ministry of Planning and Environment, the National Environmental Council, the Ministry for Atolls Administration, the Maldives Water and Sanitation Authority, the Ministry for Fisheries and Agriculture, the Marine Research Section, and the Selected Islands Development Unit each play key roles in environmental administration and monitoring compliance against relevant sectoral policies and laws. Local government administration is provided by Atoll Chiefs who report to the Minister of Atolls Administration and play a crucial role in enabling community participation in conservation decisions. The centrepiece environmental policy for the Maldives government is the National Environment Action Plan (NEAP). In its third iteration, NEAP III established several objectives and goals relating to building climate change resilience, improving ecosystems, healthy communities, and, among others, improving environmental stewardship.[74] This policy is now supported by the National Adaption Programme of Action, which also outlines how the Maldives will improve its resilience against climate change through adaptation and capacity building.[75] This presents an important step in addressing an existential issue to the Maldives, being a collection of low lying tropical atolls that faces a higher risk to sea level rise.

3.4.6 Nepal

The environment in Nepal is primarily governed by the Environment Protection Act, 2019, and its Regulations. The Act provides for the protection of the environment, measures to seek compensation for victims of pollution, management of natural resources, and mitigation of adverse impacts associated with development work and proposals. In 2019, the Act was amended following the decision in *Shrestha v Office of the Prime Minister* which held that the government, under the Constitution, held an obligation to legislate against the negative impacts associated with climate change; an issue which was previously not addressed by the government and required the applicant to obtain a writ of mandamus to compel action on this issue.[76] Under the revised Act, Article 23 requires the state to adopt climate change adaptation plans and provides increased powers with regard to risk management,[77] technological standards,[78] and

[73] South Asia Cooperation for Environment Programme (n 32) 44–45.

[74] See Ministry of Housing, Transport and Environment, 'National Environment Action Plan III' (UNEP) <https://policy.asiapacificenergy.org/sites/default/files/Third-National-Environment-Action-Plan.pdf>.

[75] See Ministry of Environment, Energy and Water, 'National Adaptation Programme of Action (NAPA)' (Government of Maldives 2007) <https://unfccc.int/resource/docs/napa/mdv01.pdf>.

[76] *Shrestha v Office of the Prime Minister* 074-WO-0283 (Supreme Court) (25 December 2018).

[77] Environment Protection Act, 2019 (Nepal) s 26.

[78] ibid s 27.

the ability to perform carbon trading.[79] In addition, the revised Act now creates an Environment Protection Fund that is responsible for the prevention and control of pollution and mitigating the adverse impacts of climate change.

In addition, the institutional arrangements have empowered the Ministry of Population and Environment as the portfolio responsible for the administration and execution of the Act. The Ministry is also responsible for the execution and development of key environmental and sustainable development policies, including the Nature Conservation National Strategic Framework for Sustainable Development (2015–30), which provides an umbrella instrument to implement sustainable resource use, interagency cooperation, valuing ecosystem services and promoting accountability.[80] Supporting this policy are also other key sectoral policies,[81] including the Forest Plan, the development Three Year Plans, the Energy Policy, and housing policy intending to make Nepal more resilient against earthquakes and natural disasters, a prevalent issue given Nepal's geography.

3.4.7 Pakistan

Pakistan contains laws which regulate environmental pollution, development, and sustainable development. The Environmental Protection Act, 1997, espouses the polluter pays principle, requiring polluters to compensate for infringing pollution controls and standards.[82] The Act also establishes the Pakistan Environmental Protection Council, the Environmental Protection Agency, and the Provincial Environmental Protection Agency. The Environmental Protection Council is represented by ministries, NGOs, trade, and industry, as well as journalists and education institutions. The Act has also established environmental magistrates[83] and tribunals,[84] which possess the technical capacity and know-how to adjudicate disputes involving scientific information and other highly specialized knowledge. To date, there are four environmental tribunals established, each housed within their respective provinces within Pakistan; however, this remains a live issue in Pakistan given the limited staff, resources, and expertise provided to these institutions to deliver rulings.[85]

[79] ibid s 28.

[80] Amber Pant, 'Country Report: Nepal—Development of Environmental Law 2015' (2015) 7 *IUCNAEL eJournal* 221, 227–228.

[81] ibid 229.

[82] Environmental Protection Act 1997 (Pakistan) s 11.

[83] ibid s 24.

[84] ibid s 20.

[85] Martin Lau, 'The Role of Environmental Tribunals in Pakistan: Challenges and Prospects' (2018) 20(1) *Yearbook of Islamic and Middle Eastern Law* 1.

3.4.8 Sri Lanka

Sri Lanka is unique in using a combination of both common laws relating to public nuisance and statutory law to protect the environment. Public nuisance is used as the basis to lodge complaints with the Central Environmental Authority as required under the National Environmental Act, 1980.[86] The Act also provides an important framework for regulations which provide Sri Lankans with other substantive and procedural rights, including the right to access information and participate in EIAs, and details a process for development applications and pollution controls.[87] The Act is administered by the Central Environmental Authority, together with the Environmental Council and District Agencies which possess delegated authority. Like the Maldives, the Environmental Council advises the Environment Minister regarding the sustainable management of natural resources. Sri Lankan environmental regulation is further bolstered by supporting sectoral policies and regulations. This includes legislation such as the Coast Conservation and Coastal Resource Management Act 2014, the National Heritage and Wilderness Areas Act 1988, and several public ordinances, including the Forests Ordinance 1907 and the Fauna and Flora Protection Ordinance 1938, which remain central environmental legislation given Sri Lanka's vulnerability to climate change and its impact to its coastal biomes and unique wilderness.

As this section has discussed, each country within the SAARC has implemented a range of environmental laws which address different aspects of environmental protection and sustainable development. However, a key issue that is being experienced across SAARC nations remain implementation challenges. This ranges from a lack of environmental literacy from the public in Afghanistan and Bhutan to a lack of staff and resources within specialized environmental courts in Pakistan. In light of these challenges, some countries such as Bangladesh and Nepal, have performed institutional and capacity building to provide more effective environmental law and policies which aim to remove administrative silos that can mainstream environmental issues across the whole of the government.

86 National Environmental Act No 47 of 1980 (Sri Lanka) s 31.

87 For more information on Sri Lankan EIAs, see Miriya Samarakoon and John S Rowan, 'A Critical Review of Environmental Impact Statements in Sri Lanka with Particular Reference to Ecological Impact Assessment' (2008) 41(3) *Environmental Management* 441, 442.

3.5 Future Challenges for Environmental Law in the SAARC: Access to Justice and Regional Cooperation

In addition to a shared pathway towards post-colonial constitutionalism, most SAARC countries have also witnessed a growth in public interest litigation providing the impetus to mature and develop domestic environmental law. With onerous procedural requirements that were left over from colonial rule, public interest litigation has played a key role in lowering standing requirements, introducing innovative legal remedies, and pushing courts to interpret the constitutional right to life more broadly to include the right to a clean environment, as well as other human rights, including the right to education, right to information, and healthcare. Public interest litigation has been readily adopted in countries such as Bangladesh, India, Nepal, Pakistan, and Sri Lanka to further strengthen court legitimacy. However, there is still significant room for greater access to justice as lower courts often do not possess the resources to consider environmental claims. India has the largest backlog of cases in the world, with thirty million cases awaiting hearing, with procedural delays often providing an incentive structure for legal practitioners to charge additional professional fees and increase litigation costs. In Bangladesh, the Directorate of the Environment has identified over 903 instances of pollution infringements under the Environment Conservation Rules, 1997; however, no action was taken against these entities due to administrative capacity constraints.[88] The SAARC can provide a platform for greater south-south cooperation and knowledge transfer opportunities, such as sharing knowledge in how to improve judicial efficiency and institutionalizing alternative dispute resolution (ADR) mechanisms before matters are litigated before the courts.

Capacity constraints continue to hamper the ability of SAARC countries to enforce existing environmental laws effectively. For this reason, environmental law in several SAARC countries has developed 'a lively jurisprudence through their innovative use of constitutional provisions'[89] to fill the gap between these inadequacies and utilize constitutional remedies to protect the local environment on a case-by-case basis. As a demonstration of this innovation, more recently, the Supreme Court of Bangladesh has recognized the legal personhood of rivers, opining that the state holds certain natural resources, such as rivers, in public trust and the Turag River itself has standing before the court to ensure that laws which address illegal encroachment and pollution are

[88] Mahfuz Ullah, *Environmental Politics in Bangladesh* (CFSD 1999) 153–161.

[89] Ben Boer, 'The Rise of Environmental Law in the Asian Region' (1999) 32(5) *University of Richmond Law Review* 1503, 1515.

enforced.[90] More importantly, the Court determined in this case to refer the National River Conservation Commission Act 2013 for law reform and mandate the state to provide an affidavit of compliance to confirm stronger investigation and compliance powers. Yet SAARC's efforts have predominately focused on relief and rehabilitation rather than prevention and protection against regional impacts associated with climate change, sustainable development, and pollution.[91]

The SAARC is uniquely placed to enable greater regional monitoring and reporting of environmental damage. Yet, SAARC has played a limited role in this regard. While the SAARC Convention on Cooperation on Environment, Delhi, and Thimphu Statements recognize the need for regional cooperation towards climate change,[92] these statements have not created any enforceable obligations on SAARC members, including reporting obligations towards implementation. Despite the absence of enforceable obligations, other regional organizations have successfully implemented capacity-building initiatives. For comparison, the Association of Southeast Asian Nations (ASEAN) improved their capacity to monitor transboundary haze pollution by sharing satellite data with law enforcement and prosecutors to charge companies and landholders who perform illegal burning and land clearing in response to several transboundary haze pollution incidents.[93] There is significant scope for greater regional cooperation to improve the availability of information,[94] especially given that the SAARC country members share ecosystems and possess different capabilities for monitoring and enforcement.

Regional organizations also play a key role in developing strategy and action against climate change and can organize access to technical knowledge to assist smaller developing countries in developing their positions under the climate change regime and improve their decision-making more generally. The SAARC can play a key role given that many of its members share the same environmental priorities and barriers to technical knowledge, which prevent them from developing informed positions when entering multilateral environmental negotiations. Creating a SAARC Regional Centre, in the same tradition as SAARC centres created on other thematic issues (e.g., Disaster

[90] *Human Rights and Peace for Bangladesh and others v Secretary of the Ministry of Shipping and others*, Writ Petition No 13989 of 2016 (Supreme Court of Bangladesh, High Court Division) (judgment dated 30 January 2019 and 3 February 2019). For more information, see Mohammad Sohidul Islam and Erin O'Donnell, 'Legal Rights for the Turag: Rivers as Living Entities in Bangladesh' (2020) 23(2) *Asia Pacific Journal of Environmental Law* 160.

[91] Habib Zafarullah and Ahmed Shafiqul Huque, 'Climate Change, Regulatory Policies and Regional Cooperation in South Asia' (2018) 21(1) *Public Administration and Policy* 22.

[92] SAARC, 'Environment, Natural Disasters and Biotechnology' (2020) <www.saarc-sec.org/index.php/areas-of-cooperation/environment-natural-disasters-biotechnology>.

[93] E.g., Shawkat Alam and Laely Nurhidayah, 'The International Law on Transboundary Haze Pollution: What Can We Learn from the Southeast Asia Region?' (2017) 26(3) *Review of European Comparative and International Environmental Law* 243.

[94] Zafarullah and Huque (n 91).

Management, Energy, or HIV), can establish a platform to allow South Asian countries to obtain access to specialized and technical knowledge, as well as promoting further integration on policy and strategy on climate change.

Conclusion

The SAARC encapsulates a diverse area bounded by geographical proximity rather than cultural or economic proximity. Despite the diversity inherent within SAARC, these countries share the constitutional recognition of a right to a clean environment, albeit either explicitly or implied, by reading the right into other existing, constitutionally protected rights, such as the right to life. Many theories posit why environmental constitutionalism occurs, including the internationalization of constitutionalism, to more localized explanations (including political dynamics), as suggested by Gellers. As this chapter has explored, adopting a regional lens shows that a local-global dichotomy is not clear cut. The cross-fertilization within the SAARC, given the constitutional mechanisms (i.e., Directive Principles) that they share, offers an alternative explanation of how environmental constitutionalism propagates.

Each SAARC country has also developed different sectoral approaches to climate change and environmental conservation. Most SAARC countries have implemented legislation, regulations, and policies to address various aspects of sustainable development and environmental conservation. Yet despite the evolution of environmental law and maturity of supporting institutions, many challenges remain. On a practical level, there is significant scope for capacity building, with SAARC members not possessing the capabilities to undertake proper implementation and enforcement, which is not pursued with the urgency required, given the low rates of environmental literacy within the community. Furthermore, despite public interest litigation's evident and important role in enforcing and maturing environmental law within the SAARC, it remains hindered. Efforts to promote access to justice and regional cooperation that can bolster greater cross-fertilization of ideas will only benefit the effectiveness of environmental law within the SAARC.

Suggestions for Further Reading

Ben Boer, 'The Rise of Environmental Law in the Asian Region' (1999) 32(5) *University of Richmond Law Review* 1503.

Joshua Gellers, 'Environmental Constitutionalism in South Asia: Analyzing the Experiences of Nepal and Sri Lanka' (2015) 4(2) *Transnational Environmental Law* 395.

Parvez Hassan, 'Good Environmental Governance: Some Trends in the South Asian Region' (2015) 18 *Asia Pacific Journal of Environmental Law* 169.

Stephen Turner, 'The Constitution of Bhutan: A Quantitative Environmental Standard' in Stephen Turner and others (eds), *Environmental Rights: The Development of Standards* (CUP 2019) 323.

Habib Zafarullah and Ahmed Shafiqul Huque, 'Climate Change, Regulatory Policies and Regional Cooperation in South Asia' (2018) 21(1) *Public Administration and Policy* 22.

CHAPTER 4

THE ENVIRONMENT, THE CONSTITUTION, AND THE LEGAL FRAMEWORK AT THE NATIONAL LEVEL

SHYAM DIVAN

Abstract

The Constitution of India profoundly influences environmental law making and policy. Express provisions in the Constitution elevate environmental protection to a high national goal. The federal structure created by the Constitution demarcates and distributes law-making power amongst the Union government and the states. The fundamental right to life guaranteed in Part III of the Constitution has been interpreted to embrace the right to a clean environment. The Constitution provides for a dispute resolution machinery through constitutional courts which lay down guiding principles of environmental law. The challenges posed by climate change will require creating new institutions within the constitutional framework that can effectively respond to the drastic impacts that will shortly befall the subcontinent.

Introduction

On 7 October 2021, the Supreme Court pronounced judgment in a batch of cases questioning the *suo motu* jurisdiction of the National Green Tribunal. Asked to examine the law establishing the Tribunal[1] and to decide whether that Act allowed the Tribunal to self-activate cases, the court chose to look beyond the statute. It reached for the Constitution of India.

The court reasoned that the object of establishing the National Green Tribunal was to secure a facet of the right to life guaranteed under Article 21 of the Constitution. The National Green Tribunal was intended to unburden the Supreme Court and the High Courts from exercising their constitutional writ jurisdictions in environmental cases. Indeed, the Tribunal was institutionally designed to take forward the creative work of the constitutional courts in developing environmental law. Holding that the National Green Tribunal could exercise *suo motu* powers, the court emphasized the tribunal's unique character. In addition to its traditional adjudicatory work, the tribunal played an inquisitorial role to prevent and remedy environmental problems. Consequently, similar to the constitutional courts it was designed to relieve, the National Green Tribunal too could self-activate cases in response to pressing environmental issues.[2]

The spirit of the Constitution permeates environmental and natural resources law, as exemplified by the Supreme Court's search for the true character of the National Green Tribunal. The Constitution elevates environmental protection to a high national policy; it demarcates and distributes power among the Union government and the states with respect to law-making in different environmental fields; it circumscribes state power in relation to citizens engaged in activities that utilize natural resources; it provides for dispute resolution platforms in environmental matters; and it enables constitutional courts to lay down guiding principles of environmental law.

Drawing on constitutional history, this chapter lays out the textual provisions in the Constitution pertaining to environmental protection. This is followed by a description of how the Supreme Court derived the fundamental right to a clean environment even where there was no explicit articulation in the constitutional text. The chapter then explains the dichotomy in legislative authority under India's federal structure and the manner in which Parliamentary authority to legislate on environment was shored up. The following section examines the shift in the role and responsibility of the constitutional courts from being the primary dispute resolution forums prior to the National Green Tribunal's establishment to the principal source of environmental law principles. Finally, the chapter examines the main national environmental statutes and suggests framework changes that might assist in responding to global environmental challenges such as climate change.

1 National Green Tribunal Act, 2010.

2 *The Municipal Corporation of Greater Mumbai v Ankita Sinha* (2022) 13 SCC 401.

4.1 Constitutional Provisions

The Constitution of India is the foundational document by which Indians govern themselves. It provides the framework of government and defines the relationship between citizens and the state. All laws including those dealing with the environment and natural resources are subordinate to the Constitution and must comport to constitutional limitations. These limitations relate to who can make the law, how the law is made, and the boundaries which the state must not transgress. The spaces preserved for individual activity and the rules limiting governmental oversight are defined through the enumeration of universal human rights in the fundamental rights section of the Constitution. The text of the Constitution that bears on environmental law is found in the parts dealing with fundamental rights, directive principles of state policy, fundamental duties, and the provisions conferring law-making authority on the Union and state legislatures within the federation.

The Constituent Assembly which drafted the Constitution commenced work in 1946,[3] the year before the nation gained independence from colonial rule.[4] A product of intense deliberations and debate, the Constitution commenced in 1950.[5] It is the longest Constitution in the world, with very detailed provisions. The intricate provisions, the relative ease with which the Constitution is amended, and the evolving national ethos to respect what is in the constitutional document have led to repeated constitutional amendments. Working the Constitution for over seven decades, the people of India have imbibed its values. Emphasising the importance of constitutionalism,[6] the Supreme Court has underscored the importance of this social and political compact as essential for national development, renewal, reform, and progress.[7]

Despite its length, the original constitutional document did not contain any provision that specially recognized environmental values. That came two and a half decades later with the Constitution (Forty-Second) Amendment Act, 1976. The Forty-Second Amendment introduced provisions pertaining to environmental protection and conferred legislative authority on Parliament to make national laws relating to forests and wildlife.[8]

Inspired by a similar concept in the Irish Constitution, Part IV of the Constitution of India sets out the directive principles of state policy. Although, the provisions in this part are not justiciable and cannot be enforced through courts, they are considered complementary to the fundamental rights enumerated in Part III of the Constitution. Directive principles are in the nature of policy goals that the government must endeavour to

[3] The inaugural session of the Constituent Assembly was held on 9 December 1946.

[4] Independence was achieved on 15 August 1947.

[5] The Constitution came into effect from 26 January 1950.

[6] *Navtej Singh Johar v Union of India* (2018) 10 SCC 1.

[7] ibid.

[8] The Constitution (Forty-Second Amendment) Act, 1976 ss 10 and 11.

achieve. Many of the directive principles are in the nature of economic rights that India could not assure its citizens at the time of independence, but which are expected to be realized progressively.

The Forty-Second Amendment inserted Article 48A as a new directive principle. It provides that 'The State shall endeavour to protect and improve the environment and to safeguard the forests and wild life of the country'. It also introduced a new chapter titled Fundamental Duties. Article 51A(g) requires every citizen 'to protect and improve the natural environment including forests, lakes, rivers and wild life, and to have compassion for living creatures'. When read together, Articles 48A and 51A(g) underscore the importance of environmental protection as a high constitutional objective. Consequently, all organs of the state and citizens must have regard to preserving the natural environment.

In the judicial sphere, this constitutional mandate requires that when a question pertaining to ecology and environment comes before the court it 'is not to shrug its shoulders and say that priorities are a matter of policies and so it is a matter for the policy-making authority. The least that the court may do is to examine whether appropriate considerations are borne in mind and irrelevancies excluded'.[9]

4.2 Right to a Clean Environment

The Constitution of India does not have an express fundamental right guaranteeing the right to a wholesome or healthful environment. However, this right has been derived by the Supreme Court through a process of interpretation.

In the mid-1980s, the Supreme Court examined several cases involving environmental despoliation in its jurisdiction under Article 32 of the Constitution. Petitions brought under Article 32 must involve the violation of a fundamental right. Implicit in the reasoning of the Supreme Court in those cases was the unstated premise that environmental degradation violated fundamental right(s).

In the 1990s, the Supreme Court explained that the right to life guaranteed in Article 21 of the Constitution includes the right to enjoy unpolluted air and water.[10] A more detailed articulation followed in *Virender Gaur v State of Haryana*:

> Article 21 protects the right to life as a fundamental right. Enjoyment of life ... including [the right to live] with human dignity encompasses within its ambit, the protection and preservation of environment, ecological balance free from pollution of air and water, sanitation, without which life cannot be enjoyed. Any contra acts or actions would cause environmental pollution. Environmental, ecological, air, water pollution, etc. should be regarded as amounting to violation of Article 21.

[9] *Sachidanand Pandey v State of West Bengal* AIR 1987 SC 1109, 1114–1115.

[10] *Subhash Kumar v State of Bihar* AIR 1991 SC 420, 424.

> Therefore, hygienic environment is an integral facet of right to healthy life and it would be impossible to live with human dignity without a humane and healthy environment.... [T]here is a constitutional imperative on the State Government and the municipalities, not only to ensure and safeguard proper environment but also an imperative duty to take adequate measures to promote, protect and improve both the man-made and the natural environment.[11]

The right to a wholesome environment is not absolute and must be balanced against competing freedoms. The Constitution of India guarantees to citizens the freedom to carry on trade or business subject to reasonable restrictions imposed in the interest of the general public.[12] The fundamental right to equality prevents arbitrary or unreasonable actions by the state.[13] These twin protections allow businesses including industries to operate freely when compliant with environmental laws. Generally, environmental regulations are considered to be reasonable restrictions imposed in the public interest to protect the environment and the health of citizens. Occasionally, limits and restrictions are imposed through Supreme Court orders in the absence of any law.[14] Since the Supreme Court is the highest court and its orders are final, such directions cannot be appealed but may be revisited by the court itself. This type of judge-imposed restriction, ostensibly to protect public health under Article 21, introduces legal risk for enterprises and may leave them without recourse.

4.3 Legislative Competence

India is a federation of states, and the Constitution distributes the fields of legislative authority between the federal and the state governments. This division undergirds the legislative origin of early national environmental laws. The decisions taken at the Stockholm Conference of 1972[15] opened a new avenue for Parliament. The Union Legislature could now use the authority under the Constitution to make laws to implement decisions made at international conferences. As we shall see, recourse by the central government to Article 253 of the Constitution has diminished the federal-state divide relating to legislative competence on environmental subjects. Today, the constitutional scheme permits Parliament to make laws on all aspects of environmental protection by tracing back the law to an international conference. Nevertheless, the history of early environmental legislation continues to cast a shadow on the form and structure of

11 *Virender Gaur v State of Haryana* (1995) 2 SCC 577, 580–581.

12 Constitution of India Art 19(1)(g).

13 ibid, Art 14.

14 *MC Mehta v Union of India* (2016) 4 SCC 269, 277.

15 United Nations Conference on the Human Environment, June 1972, Stockholm.

the pollution control agencies, their capacities, and their effectiveness in implementing environmental laws.

The deliberations in the Constituent Assembly which framed the Constitution suggest that the distribution of legislative authority was influenced primarily by the scheme under the Government of India Act, 1935 and a contest between those who preferred a strong central government and those who wanted a greater devolution of power to the states. The authority to legislate over natural resources implied control over the resource and thus power. Forests and fisheries were important economic resources and were the subject of deliberations at a meeting convened by the Drafting Committee in July 1949. The meeting was attended by premiers of Indian states and the provinces and delegates from central ministries. Provincial representatives opposed the suggestion from the Ministry of Agriculture for legislative authority to be shared over 'forests' and 'fisheries'. The Ministry's effort to link forests and agricultural development failed to persuade the assembly, and the topic 'forests' and 'fisheries' were classified as state subjects.

Part XI of the Constitution governs the political relations between the Union and the states. Parliament may legislate for the entire country, while the state legislatures are empowered to make laws for their respective states. Article 246 of the Constitution divides the legislative subjects between the Union and the states. List I of the Seventh Schedule to the Constitution contains nearly a hundred subjects over which Parliament has exclusive powers to legislate. These include defence, foreign affairs, atomic energy, participation in international conferences, and implementing decisions made at these conferences, shipping, major ports, regulation of air traffic, regulation and development of oilfields, mines and mineral development, and interstate rivers. The state legislatures have exclusive power to legislate with respect to nearly sixty subjects enumerated in List II of the Seventh Schedule, such as public health and sanitation, agriculture, water supplies, land, irrigation and drainage, and fisheries. Under List III, both Parliament and the state legislatures may enact laws with respect to fifty-two subject areas, including forests, the protection of wildlife, mines, and mineral development not covered in the Union List, population control and family planning, minor ports and factories.

The Constitution leans towards a strong Union government by vesting in Parliament residual power to legislate on subjects not enumerated in the three Lists.[16] Moreover, should a central law conflict with a state law on a concurrent subject, the central law prevails. However, a state law passed subsequent to a central law will prevail where it has received Presidential Assent under Article 254.[17]

Parliament is also empowered to legislate in the 'national interest' on matters enumerated in the State List.[18] In addition, Parliament may enact laws on state subjects, for states whose legislatures have consented to a central legislation. The Wild Life

[16] Constitution of India, Seventh Schedule Art 248 and Entry 97, List I. Illustratively, the Gift Tax Act, 1958 and the Commissions of Inquiry Act, 1952 were passed under the residuary power of Parliament.

[17] For instance, the Arbitration (Orissa Second Amendment) Act, 1991 and the UP Industrial Disputes Act, 1947 were held to prevail over the central law since they had received the President's assent.

[18] Constitution of India Art 249.

(Protection) Act, 1972 was passed by Parliament pursuant to enabling resolutions of eleven states under Article 252(1) of the Constitution. This was followed by another important national legislative effort in the Water (Prevention and Control of Pollution) Act, 1974 which was enacted by Parliament pursuant to consent resolutions passed by twelve state legislatures.

4.4 Article 253 and Parliamentary Authority to Enact Environmental Legislation

In the 1970s, amendments to the Constitutional text and global developments in the form of the United Nations Conference on the Human Environment[19] cemented Parliament's authority to enact environmental laws. The Constitution (Forty-Second) Amendment Act, 1976 expanded the concurrent list by moving 'Forests' and 'Protection of Wild Animals and Birds' from List II to List III.

The lively debate in Parliament when the constitutional amendments were considered did not focus on the shift of the legislative entries.[20] While none of the suggestions made during the deliberations yielded any change to the text proposed in the Bill, members welcomed the new directive principle highlighting the importance of environmental protection; and there was a robust discussion on the need for a mechanism such as a Parliamentary Standing Committee, to enforce the directive principles. Among the concerns expressed were the adverse impact of conservation laws on forest dwelling tribal communities, and the need for measures to address industrial pollution, and vehicular pollution in Delhi.[21]

Article 253 of the Constitution empowers Parliament to make laws to implement India's international obligations and any decision made at an international conference, association or other such body. It reads:

> Notwithstanding anything in the foregoing provisions of this Chapter, Parliament has power to make any law for the whole or any part of the territory of India for

[19] Stockholm Conference (n 15).

[20] The Constitution (Forty-Fourth Amendment) Bill, 1976 after passage became the Constitution (Forty-Second Amendment) Act, 1976.

[21] The Bill was debated in the Lok Sabha (Lower House of Parliament) between 25 October 1976 and 3 November 1976 and in the Rajya Sabha (Upper House of Parliament) between 4 and 11 November 1976. See *Lok Sabha Debates*, Eighteenth Session, Fifth Series, Vol LXV, No 5, 29 October 1976, columns 94–117; *Lok Sabha Debates*, Eighteenth Session, Fifth Series, Vol LXV, No 5, 1 November 1976, columns 170–191, and *Parliamentary Debate: Rajya Sabha: Official Report*, Vol XCVIII, No 5, 9 November 1976, columns 158–75; and *Parliamentary Debate: Rajya Sabha: Official Report*, Vol XCVIII, No 5, 10 November 1976, columns 158–172.

> implementing any treaty, agreement or convention with any other country or countries or any decision made at any international conference, association or other body.

Entry 13 of the Union List covers: 'Participation in international conferences, associations and other bodies and implementing of decisions made thereat'.

Parliament has used its power under Article 253 read with Entry 13 of the Union List to enact the Air (Prevention and Control of Pollution) Act, 1981 and the Environment (Protection) Act, 1986.[22] The preambles to both laws refer to the need to implement decisions made at the United Nations Conference on the Human Environment held at Stockholm in 1972. At the conference, nations agreed to preserve natural resources and each country was required to work towards this object.

The preamble to the Biological Diversity Act, 2002 refers to the United Nations Convention on Biological Diversity, signed at Rio de Janeiro on 5 June 1992. The preamble to the National Green Tribunal Act, 2010 refers to both the Stockholm Conference as well as the Rio de Janeiro Conference. The preamble cites the decisions at the Rio conference 'calling upon the States to provide effective access to judicial and administrative proceedings, including redress and remedy, and to develop national laws regarding liability and compensation for the victims of pollution and other environmental damage'.

The broad language of Article 253 and the succession of international conferences to tackle global environmental issues suggests that environmental legislation is the province of Parliamentary enactment. Recourse to Article 253 to enact four major national environmental legislations is a pointer that future legislation will also draw on this source of constitutional authority.

4.5 Federal Issues

The division of power and responsibility under a federal Constitution may result in legislative overreach. While land zoning and development is a state subject under the Constitution relatable to land and local government, Central coastal regulations and Central regulations with respect to ecologically sensitive areas have denuded the states' power in these aspects. Likewise, the Scheduled Tribes and Other Traditional Forest Dwellers (Recognition of Forest Rights) Act, 2006 by requiring the grant of land title documents to forest dwellers, appears to extend over a state subject.

With a view to protect the habitat around wildlife reserves, the central government has notified buffer zones under the Environment (Protection) Act, 1986. The consequential restrictions on industrial activity have strained relations between the centre and some states since the curbs prevent economic activity such as mining mineral

[22] *S Jagannath v Union of India (Shrimp Culture case)* AIR 1997 SC 811, 844, 846.

deposits. Another example of Union–state tensions is the central restrictions imposed in 1991 on new industry in Dahanu Taluka. Although the ecologically sensitive district is rich in horticulture, the state of Maharashtra has lobbied to lift the curbs.

At an administrative level, the establishment of pollution control boards under state control and the working of the forest and wildlife bureaucracies within state administrations results in a dichotomy. Union legislation is enforced and implemented by state agencies resulting in variable implementation across the country.

4.6 Constitutional Machinery for Dispute Resolution

While the Forty-Second Constitutional Amendment introduced provisions to elevate environmental protection to a high constitutional objective, it was the Supreme Court that raised public awareness about environmental harm and sensitized government agencies to the need for strict enforcement. This task was advanced in a series of public interest litigations entertained by the Supreme Court. The court directed hundreds of polluting industrial units to shut operations when they lacked statutory permissions from the pollution control boards;[23] required polluters to establish treatment facilities before resuming production;[24] required municipalities to treat sewage before its discharge into rivers;[25] and involved the local administration in the coercive measures to shut polluters.[26] Separately, the court required educational curricula to cover environmental protection[27] and enlisted government media to increase public consciousness through public information campaigns concerning the environment.[28]

Before the establishment of the National Green Tribunal in 2010, environmental disputes were primarily resolved in the High Courts and the Supreme Court. These constitutional courts entertained petitions under their writ jurisdictions. Generally, writ petitioners complain about a violation of their individual rights by the state. However, since adverse environmental impacts are often diffused across a community, these cases were entertained as public interest litigations. Indeed, the story of environmental litigation since its inception in India in the 1970s is intertwined with the growth of public interest law.

One of limitations with the writ jurisdiction in environmental cases is that the environmental harm must be manifest and egregious. This is because writ courts do not enter into disputed questions of fact, these cases being decided on affidavit. Another related

[23] *MC Mehta v Union of India* AIR 1988 SC 1037.
[24] *MC Mehta v Union of India* AIR 1988 SC 1037.
[25] *MC Mehta v Union of India* AIR 1988 SC 1115.
[26] *MC Mehta v Union of India* AIR 1997 SC 734.
[27] *MC Mehta v Union of India* AIR 1992 SC 382.
[28] ibid.

limitation is that writ courts generally do not award damages and prefer to grant injunctive relief or remedial directions to restore the environment.

The National Green Tribunal is an advance, being equipped to receive evidence, award compensation and parse contested facts. Nevertheless, the constitutional jurisdiction of the High Courts and the Supreme Court remain available to citizens in environmental cases that fall beyond the jurisdiction of the Tribunal. Such cases include cases involving wildlife protection or cases where town and country planning laws are in play. Moreover, at times, the litigant may challenge the constitutional validity of a law or administrative direction. In such cases too, it is the constitutional courts alone which are endowed with the power to invalidate a law or a subordinate legislation.

Decisions of the National Green Tribunal may be appealed to the Supreme Court on a substantial question of law.[29] Under the constitutional scheme, High Courts exercise general supervisory jurisdiction over tribunals.[30] This power is intended to keep in check all tribunals including the National Green Tribunal from committing jurisdictional errors.

4.7 Constitutional Courts and Environmental Law Principles

The system of checks and balances on state power under the Constitution relies on judicial review. This mechanism enables the High Courts in the states and the Supreme Court at the peak of the judicial pyramid to strike executive action and legislation that fail to comport with constitutional requirements. The power of judicial review is an essential feature of the Indian Constitution and is so deeply ingrained that it cannot be extinguished even by constitutional amendment.[31]

The duty of constitutional courts to judicially review state action combined with the general business of appellate judging calls for the articulation of new principles. Typically, a new principle is laid out to resolve the case at hand. However, the robust principles continue to be applied by judges through the doctrine of *stare decisis*.[32] Judicial precedents are valued because they ensure consistency in the outcome of similar matters.

Drawing on its constitutional jurisdiction and to lend heft to environmental jurisprudence the Supreme Court has framed several principles:

29 National Green Tribunal Act, 2010 s 22.

30 Constitution of India Art 227.

31 *L Chandra Kumar v Union of India* (1997) 3 SCC 261.

32 The legal principle requiring cases to be decided according to precedent.

(1) The Supreme Court must accord the highest attention to issues concerning the environment.[33]
(2) The right to a wholesome environment is a facet of the right to life guaranteed under Article 21 of the Constitution.[34]
(3) The polluter pays principle requires the polluter to bear remedial costs and to compensate the victims of pollution.[35]
(4) The precautionary principle requires government authorities to anticipate, prevent and address the causes of environmental pollution. The onus of proof lies on the project proponent to show that the proposal is not environmentally harmful.[36]
(5) Sustainable development is imperative. This doctrine helps cater to present needs without compromising the ability of future generations to satisfy their needs.[37]
(6) Inter-generational equity obliges us to preserve natural resources and pass on to future generations an environment as intact as the one we inherited.[38]
(7) The public trust doctrine requires the state as the trustee of natural resources to preserve them for public use and enjoyment. These resources cannot be converted into private ownership.[39]
(8) Enforcement agencies must strictly enforce environmental laws.[40]
(9) To protect endangered species, decision-makers ought to adopt an ecocentric approach over an anthropocentric approach. Where a species is endangered,

[33] *Tarun Bharat Sangh, Alwar v Union of India* Writ Petition (Civil) No 509 of 1991, Supreme Court, 14 May 1992 (M N Venkatachaliah and B P Jeevan Reddy, JJ).

[34] *Subhash Kumar v State of Bihar* AIR 1991 SC 420, 424; *MC Mehta v Union of India (Delhi Stone Crushing case)* (1992) 3 SCC 256, 257; and *Mantri Techzone Pvt Ltd v Forward Foundation* (2019) 18 SCC 494, 517.

[35] *Indian Council for Enviro-Legal Action v Union of India* AIR 1996 SC 1446, 1466; *Vellore Citizens' Welfare Forum v Union of India* AIR 1996 SC 2715, 2721; *S Jagannath v Union of India* AIR 1997 SC 811, 846, 850; *Bittu Sehgal v Union of India* (2001) 9 SCC 181, 193; *Research Foundation for Science (18) v Union of India* (2005) 13 SCC 186, 200; *Lal Bahadur v State of UP* (2018) 15 SCC 407, 424–425; and *MC Mehta v Union of India* (2018) 18 SCC 397, 446.

[36] *Vellore Citizens' Welfare Forum v Union of India* AIR 1996 SC 2715, 2721; *S Jagannath v Union of India* AIR 1997 SC 811, 846; *A P Pollution Control Board v Prof M V Nayadu* AIR 1999 SC 812, 819; *Arjun Gopal v Union of India* (2017) 16 SCC 267, 269 and *Hospitality Association of Mudumalai v In Defence of Environment and Animals* (2020) 10 SCC 589, 607.

[37] *MC Mehta v Union of India* (2001) 4 SCC 577, 580; *N D Jayal v Union of India* (2004) 9 SCC 362, 381–383; *Amarnath Shrine, In Re* (2013) 3 SCC 247; *Alembic Pharmaceuticals Ltd v Rohit Prajapati* (2020) 17 SCC 157; and *State of Meghalaya v All Dimasa Students Union* (2019) 8 SCC 177, 196.

[38] *State of Himachal Pradesh v Ganesh Wood Products* AIR 1996 SC 149, 159; *Glanrock Estate Pvt Ltd v State of Tamil Nadu* (2010) 10 SCC 96, 109; *Alembic Pharmaceuticals Ltd v Rohit Prajapati* (2020) 17 SCC 157; and *State of Meghalaya v All Dimasa Students Union* (2019) 8 SCC 177, 196.

[39] *MC Mehta v Kamal Nath* (1997) 1 SCC 388; *MI Builders v Radhey Shyam Sahu* AIR 1999 SC 2468, 2498; *Fomento Resorts and Hotels Ltd v Minguel Martins* (2009) 3 SCC 571, 614; *Centre for Public Interest Litigation v Union of India* (2012) 3 SCC 1; *Association for Environment Protection v State of Kerala* (2013) 7 SCC 226, 229 and *Tata Housing Development Company Ltd v Aalok Jagga* (2020) 15 SCC 784.

[40] *Indian Council for Enviro-Legal Action v Union of India* (1996) 5 SCC 281, 294, 301; and *MC Mehta v Union of India* (2004) 6 SCC 588, 618.

the court may apply the 'species best interest standard' to test the validity of state action.[41]

(10) The principle of environmental rule of law requires that the process of environmental decision-making is transparent, responsive and inclusive.[42]

(11) Where actions have long term impacts regard should be had to the 'Seventh Generation sustainability principle', or the 'Great Law of the Iroquois' (as it originates from the Iroquois tribe) which requires all decision making to be tested for benefits that last for seven generations.[43]

These principles lend vitality to the fundamental right to life and enable citizens to enforce the right to a wholesome environment through actions brought against polluters and state agencies.

At times, the principles enunciated by the Supreme Court are engrafted into statutory provisions and must then be followed across cases as a matter of statute law. The National Green Tribunal Act, 2010 requires the Tribunal to decide cases applying the principles of sustainable development, the precautionary principle and the polluter pays principle.[44] Moreover, where environmental harm or personal injury are caused by an accident, the Act engrafts the principle of no-fault liability, a standard previously propounded by the Supreme Court.[45]

4.8 National Environmental Laws

Drawing on diverse sources of legislative authority conferred by the Constitution, India's principal environmental laws are enacted by Parliament and operate nationally. The main workhorse is the Environment (Protection) Act, 1986. This law is an enabling legislation passed in the wake of the world's worst industrial disaster that occurred at Bhopal on 3 December 1984. The Environment (Protection) Act confers the responsibility to frame subordinate legislation to protect the environment on the central government. The scope of the statute is very broad with Parliament defining environment to include: 'water, air and land and the inter-relationship which exists among and between water, air and land, and human beings, other living creatures, plants, micro-organism

[41] *TN Godavarman Thirumulpad v Union of India* (2012) 4 SCC 362, 374; *TN Godavarman Thirumulpad v Union of India* (2012) 3 SCC 277, 283; *Centre for Environment Law, WWF-I v Union of India* (2013) 8 SCC 234, 256; and *MK Ranjitsinh v Union of India* (2021) 15 SCC 1.

[42] *Hanuman Laxman Aroskar v Union of India* (2019) 15 SCC 401; *Bengaluru Development Authority v Sudhakar Hegde* (2020) 15 SCC 63; and *Himachal Pradesh Bus Stand Management and Development Authority v Central Empowered Committee* (2021) 4 SCC 309.

[43] *The Municipal Corporation of Greater Mumbai v Ankita Sinha* (2022) 13 SCC 401.

[44] National Green Tribunal Act, 2010 s 20.

[45] *MC Mehta v Union of India* AIR 1987 SC 1086.

and property'.[46] The primary mandate requires the central government 'to take all such measures as it deems necessary or expedient for protecting and improving the quality of the environment and preventing, controlling and abating environmental pollution'.[47]

The central government has used its power to frame elaborate delegated legislation covering pollution control,[48] hazardous substance regulation,[49] environment impact assessment,[50] waste regulation,[51] the protection of the coast,[52] wetlands,[53] ecologically sensitive areas, and certain other issues.[54]

The national pollution control framework has two other laws: the Water (Prevention and Control of Pollution) Act, 1974 and the Air (Prevention and Control of Pollution) Act, 1981. These laws establish the agencies charged with controlling pollution: the state pollution control boards for each state and the Central Pollution Control Board at the centre. The establishment of these boards under laws that were already in place when the Environment (Protection) Act was enforced has meant that there is no all-purpose federal environment protection agency in India, though this possibility is envisaged by that statute.[55]

The protection of wildlife and the specified plants is regulated under the Wild Life (Protection) Act, 1972. The law enables the creation of protected areas for wildlife and prohibits the hunting of specified species, regardless of their location in or outside these areas. Administered by wildlife wardens and their staff, the Wild Life (Protection) Act also regulates trade in wild animals, animal products and trophies.

Three national laws regulate forest resource conservation and use. The pre-independence Indian Forest Act, 1927 categorizes forests into four groups[56] with reserved forests assigned the highest degree of protection from human interference. Since forests were being decimated, Parliament passed the Forest (Conservation) Act in 1980 to prevent the diversion of forests for non-forest purposes unless the Centre approved. In 2023, the name of the 1980 Act was changed to Van (Sanraskshan Evam Samvardhan) Adhiniyam, 1980. The third national law is the Forests Rights Act of

46 Environment (Protection) Act, 1986 s 2(a).

47 ibid s 3(1).

48 Environment (Protection) Rules, 1986 and Noise Pollution (Regulation and Control) Rules, 2000.

49 Manufacture, Storage and Import of Hazardous Chemicals Rules, 1989 and Hazardous and other Wastes (Management and Transboundary Movement) Rules, 2016.

50 Environment Impact Assessment Notification, 2006.

51 Solid Waste Management Rules, 2016; Construction and Demolition Waste Management Rules, 2016, Bio-medical Waste Management Rules, 2016, Plastic Waste Management Rules, 2016, E-Waste (Management) Rules, 2016.

52 Coastal Regulation Zone Notification, 2019 and Island Coastal Zone Notification, 2019.

53 Wetlands (Conservation and Management) Rules, 2017.

54 Ozone Depleting Substances (Regulation and Control) Rules, 2000; Regulation of Lead Contents in Household and Decorative Paints Rules, 2016.

55 Environment (Protection) Act, 1986 s 3(3).

56 The categories are reserved forests, village forests, protected forests, and non-government (private) forests.

2006,[57] a transformative law seeking to correct a historical wrong by recognizing the rights of forest communities to remain on their land. Before its enactment, forest officers failed to acknowledge the traditional rights of forest communities to dwell in forests and use the forest resources for their livelihood.

The Biological Diversity Act, 2002 creates a system for conservation, sustainable use and the fair and equitable sharing of India's rich biological resources. The Act implements the United Nations Convention on Biological Diversity signed at Rio de Janeiro in 1992. The National Biodiversity Authority established under this law administers the Act and regulates intellectual property rights arising from inventions based on biological resources.

The National Green Tribunal Act, 2010 establishes the National Green Tribunal:

> for the effective and expeditious disposal of cases relating to environmental protection and conservation of forests and other natural resources including enforcement of any legal right relating to environment and giving relief and compensation for damages to persons and property.[58]

The tribunal comprises judicial members as well as experts qualified in environmental sciences and is chaired by a person who was a judge of the Supreme Court or a Chief Justice of a High Court.[59] The tribunal has all India jurisdiction over civil cases involving a substantial question relating to the environment and arising out of the implementation of specified laws.[60] In addition, the tribunal exercises appellate jurisdiction with respect to orders and directions issued by authorities under the specified laws.[61] Decisions of the tribunal may be appealed to the Supreme Court on a substantial question of law.[62]

Conclusion: Emerging Challenges

As our review shows, national environmental legislation emerged in the 1970s and by the end of the next decade, the main pieces of the statutory jigsaw were in place. The lack of initiative on the part of enforcement agencies and their inability to implement pollution control laws and take forward statutory mandates to protect forest resources, fostered judicial interventions by the constitutional courts. Today, environmental law

[57] Scheduled Tribes and Other Traditional Forests Dwellers (Recognition of Forests Rights) Act, 2006.

[58] National Green Tribunal Act, 2010 Long Title and Preamble.

[59] ibid s 5.

[60] ibid s 14. Schedule 1 lists seven central statutes including the Water (Prevention and Control of Pollution) Act, 1974; the Forest (Conservation) Act, 1980; the Air (Prevention and Control of Pollution) Act, 1981; the Environment (Protection) Act, 1986; and the Biological Diversity Act, 2002.

[61] ibid s 16.

[62] ibid s 22.

enforcement is achieved partly through executive action and partly through judicial directions issued by the constitutional courts and the National Green Tribunal.

This fractured enforcement has failed to lift the capacity and resolve of executive agencies despite decades of judicial prompting. The pollution control boards and other environmental bureaucracies have neither the technical and financial capacity nor the political heft to achieve the constitutional goals of protecting the natural environment, the forests and wildlife and the health of the citizenry. In the present milieu, the emerging challenges posed by climate change are a bridge too far for the executive agencies. Radical changes to the design and structure of environmental law enforcement agencies are imperative to respond to complex climate change-related challenges.

The Constitution of India as well as the Environment (Protection) Act, 1986 suggest a way forward. Emerging from the text of the Constitution, strong independent institutions have grown to protect democratic values and to achieve other constitutional goals. Among these institutions are the judiciary, the Election Commission of India, and the Comptroller and Auditor General of India. Each of these institutions, over time, have built capacities and fashioned solutions in response to the unique and daunting problems posed by the size and diversity of the nation. To tackle the enormous challenges triggered by climate change and that lie ahead, there appears a need for a new constitutional office that can respond to the drastic impacts that will shortly befall the sub-continent. While devolution of power and decision-making to the states, local governments and communities will make for a more resilient society, the crafting of a long-term policy with appropriate strategies and time-bound goals requires national conception and co-ordination. It is here that a new constitutional body supported by a national environment protection agency can help create a responsive administrative framework that delivers our constitutional goals.

Suggestions for Further Reading

Anuj Bhuwania, *Courting the People: Public Interest Litigation in Post-Emergency India* (CUP 2017).

Shyam Divan and Armin Rosencranz, *Environmental Law and Policy in India: Cases and Materials* (3rd edn, OUP 2022).

Shibani Ghosh, *Indian Environmental Law: Key Concepts and Principles* (Orient BlackSwan 2019).

Kanchi Kohli and Manu Menon, *Development of Environmental Laws in India* (CUP 2022).

Nawneet Vibhaw, *Environmental Law: An Introduction* (LexisNexis 2016).

CHAPTER 5

ENVIRONMENTAL MOVEMENTS AND LAW

NAIRITA ROY CHAUDHURI

ABSTRACT

Environmental movements in India are grassroots-based calls for just political conditions for sustaining subsistence living. Such movements have a long history dating back to British rule, including peasant revolts in 1859–63 against indigo plantations and 1893 agitations against the commercialization of forests and *Adivasis'* lands; to post-Independence movements against dam-building, seed capitalism, and mining, and the farmers' movements against agricultural neoliberalization. This chapter takes a socio-legal approach by borrowing heterogeneous concepts and sources from social sciences to critically examine the substantive field of law, development, and environmental movements in the context of India's post-coloniality. Through a description of some key post-Independence movements, the chapter shows how they engage in confrontational and non-confrontational strategies to resist the colonial legacy and neoliberal ideology of development, the ontological duality that separates nature and culture and the Westphalian state's legal and political domination over local sovereignty, and their negative ecological and social consequences.

INTRODUCTION

ENVIRONMENTAL movements (EMs) have a long history in India that dates back to British rule, including peasant revolts in 1859–63 against indigo plantations and 1893 agitations against the commercialization of forests and *Adivasis'* lands.[1] However, since India's Independence, grassroot calls for environmental justice magnified in response to rapid industrialization towards nation-building and development.[2] Shah defines EMs as 'struggles of the people on the issues of their livelihood and access to forest and other natural resources'.[3] Guha and Gadgil define the EM as 'organized social activity consciously directed towards promoting sustainable use of natural resources'.[4] In India, they are also framed as 'environmentalism of the poor'—'to distinguish them from the environmentalism born out of affluence' in advanced capitalist countries or among the urban bourgeoisie in the South.[5] Such movements raise concerns of justice in that India's hegemonic developmental strategy largely materializes not only at the cost of subaltern[6] people's means of subsistence but such people are also excluded from framing the parameters of 'development' (intersectional and intergenerational equity, sustainability, plural ontologies, effective participation, and direct democracy).[7] For the sake of this chapter, the term EMs shall connote movements that call for environmental justice[8] and just political 'conditions needed to sustain life'.[9] They are not exclusively about environmental protection but connect with broader material and socio-cultural concerns of grassroots communities' subsistence livelihoods; and include peasant, *Adivasi*, and other EMs led by NGOs/activists.

The role of law in EMs is anything but straightforward. Depending on the discipline, legal scholars and sociologists examine general social movements as a *subject* of analysis to reform the law or describe/critique its normativity; recommend studying *with* social movements as partners to 'cogenerate ideas'[10] and transform the law and its foundations; or investigate the functions of law as means to achieve the movement's goals.[11] This

[1] Arun Kumar Nayak, 'Environmental Movements in India' (2015) 31(2) *Journal of Developing Societies* 249; Brototi Roy and Joan Martinez-Alier, 'Environmental Justice Movements in India: An Analysis of the Multiple Manifestations of Violence' (2019) 2(1) *Ecology, Economy and Society–the INSEE Journal* 77.

[2] Roy and Martinez-Alier (n 1) 3.

[3] Ghanshyam Shah, *Social Movements in India: A Review of Literature* (2nd edn, Sage 2004) 250.

[4] ibid 252.

[5] Madhav Gadgil and Ramachandra Guha, 'Towards a Perspective on Environmental Movements in India' (1998) 59 *Indian Journal of Social Work* 450, 455.

[6] Those who live in a marginalized position in relation to the state apparatus, dominant social structure, and institutions such as the judiciary.

[7] Ashish Kothari and others (eds), *Pluriverse: A Post-Development Dictionary* (Tulika Books 2019); Bina Agarwal, 'Participatory Exclusions, Community Forestry, and Gender: An Analysis for South Asia and a Conceptual Framework' (2001) 29(10) *World Development* 1623.

[8] For the constituents of environmental justice see Usha Natarajan, 'Environmental Justice in the Global South', Sumudu A Atapattu, Carmen G Gonzalez, and Sara L Seck (eds), *The Cambridge Handbook of Environmental Justice and Sustainable Development* (CUP 2021) 39.

[9] Radha D'Souza, *What's Wrong with Rights?: Social Movements, Law and Liberal Imaginations* (Pluto Press 2018) xiv.

[10] Amna A Akbar, Sameer M Ashar, and Jocelyn Simonson, 'Movement Law' (2021) 73 *Stanford Law Review* 821, 5.

[11] Scott L Cummings, 'Law and Social Movements: An Interdisciplinary Analysis' in Conny Roggeband and Bert Klandermans (eds), *Handbook of Social Movements Across Disciplines* (Springer International 2017) 233.

chapter takes a socio-legal approach by borrowing heterogeneous concepts and sources from social sciences to critically examine the substantive field of 'law', development, and EMs.[12] It understands 'law' as a field that transgresses formality and nation-state boundaries to cover 'a set of norms, procedures and authorities' that shape and are shaped by social life.[13] Due to word limitations, the chapter will not describe the EMs in colonial India that resisted formal laws (Indian Forest Act, 1927, Land Acquisition Act, 1894), which violently confiscated subaltern communities' traditional rights to access ecological commons (land and forests) for their subsistence livelihoods. Despite the plurality of EMs in India, a few (with far-reaching effects in terms of global reach and success) EMs after India's Independence would be examined in the context of its 'post-coloniality'[14] because the challenges such as climate change impacts, neo-colonial laws and under-development, which are 'haunting'[15] the subaltern people today relate to India's ongoing coloniality.[16] Section 5.1 provides a critical overview of EMs and their claims, followed by Section 5.2 that expands on the barriers facing EMs and their links with supra-local and global issues. Finally, the chapter ends with a conclusion.

5.1 Environmental Movements Through State-Led Development and Neoliberalism

This section describes the colonial legacy of law and development discourse in post-colonial India through a gradual shift from state-led (economic growth and progress) to neoliberal modes of development. Such contexts subvert the sustainable livelihoods of subaltern people despite the formal recognition of some of their rights. Consequently,

[12] Amanda Perry-Kessaris, *Doing Sociolegal Research in Design Mode* (Routledge 2021) 14.

[13] Sergio Coronado, 'Agrarian Law' in Haroon Akram-Lodhi and others (eds), *Handbook of Critical Agrarian Studies* (Edward Elgar 2021) 187.

[14] The 'post-colonial' framing of India aims to highlight the 'past' and 'present' of colonial power relations (emerging from European colonization) as a continuum rather than looking at them as temporally unrelated categories. It is different from a historical approach in that it engages with a sustained and critical analysis of new forms of power relations/structures in the present that cannot be understood without contextualizing them in European colonization. See Ania Loomba, *Colonialism/Postcolonialism* (3rd edn, Routledge 2015); Bill Ashcroft, Gareth Griffiths, and Helen Tiffin, *Post-Colonial Studies: The Key Concepts* (2nd edn, Routledge 2000); Dipesh Chakrabarty, *Provincializing Europe: Postcolonial Thought and Historical Difference* (Princeton University Press 2000).

[15] Farhana Sultana, 'The Unbearable Heaviness of Climate Coloniality' (2022) *Political Geography* 102638, 2.

[16] Concerning neo-colonial environmental laws, see Kishan Khoday and Usha Natarajan, 'Fairness and International Environmental Law from Below: Social Movements and Legal Transformation in India' (2012) 25(2) *Leiden Journal of International Law* 415; Usha Natarajan and Kishan Khoday, 'Locating Nature: Making and Unmaking International Law' (2014) 27 *Leiden Journal of International Law* 573; Nayak (n 1) 250.

the EMs have been resisting both the state and its nexus with corporations against extractivism and capital accumulation. It further discusses the counter-hegemonic struggles led by EMs to seek transformational justice. They demand for just conditions that sustain life by seeking non-extractive and non-dominating notions of the state, development, sovereignty, and sustainability.

5.1.1 Colonial Law and Development Meet Resistance

Despite formal decolonization from the direct British rule in 1947, independent India continued to follow the path of western ideas of modernization and framed its national development strategies accordingly.[17] India inherited the very colonial superstructure including a sovereign nation-state, 'eminent domain'[18], the ideology of state-led economic growth and progress, 'Enlightenment' and racist assumptions of backwardness/primitiveness in anything traditional, and the ontological duality of nature-culture/humans.[19] In reality, however, rural communities (and especially the *Adivasis*) depend on commons, including forests, rivers, streams, ponds, and other communal spaces for accessing fuelwood, nutrition, drinking water, bathing, and other purposes for meeting their everyday livelihood needs via customary/traditional property regimes and mutual relations between human and non-human natures.[20]

Upon independence, India's trajectory of development vested in materializing large-scale projects such as the construction of dams, mining, and infrastructure-building that required state control over resources and the populations dependent on them. The state obtained elite-consent for such projects by mobilizing the ideological rhetoric of economic growth, human sacrifice, and nation-building for the 'greater common good' wherein the gains from the development would outweigh the costs of sufferings of the rural subalterns.[21] The objective behind say, dam construction was attributed to generating electricity, irrigation (for intensive farming), navigation, and flood control—all of which were indispensable for national development. As dam-building accelerated after the 1950s, so did the anti-dam protests in India's rural areas. The Hirakud dam in

[17] Dipesh Chakrabarty, *The Climate of History in a Planetary Age* (University of Chicago Press 2020).

[18] The notion of eminent domain originated from the Land Acquisition Act, 1894 that was amended in 1984 and allowed the state to acquire rural and tribal lands for public (land reforms and developmental projects) purposes. India's Constitution and land acquisition laws retained the principle of eminent domain because property rights vested with the state were conducive for economic development. See Priya S Gupta, 'The Peculiar Circumstances of Eminent Domain in India' (2012) 49(3) *Osgoode Hall Law Journal* 445; Nayak (n 1) 260; Khoday and Natarajan (n 16) 428.

[19] Khoday and Natarajan (n 16) 415, 425.

[20] Nairita Roy Chaudhuri, 'Exploring Sustainable Degrowth-Based Adaptation to Climate Change-Aggravated Water Scarcity in Parts of Rural India: A Gender Relations Approach' (2022) 9 *The Journal of Gender and Water* 34, 36.

[21] Krishna Mallick, *Environmental Movements of India: Chipko, Narmada Bachao Andolan, Navdanya* (Amsterdam University Press 2021); Arun Kumar Nayak, 'Big Dams and Protests in India: A Study of Hirakud Dam' (2010) 45(2) *Economic and Political Weekly* 69.

Sambalpur in the eastern state of Odisha was the 'first multipurpose river valley project' constructed post-Independence that caused immense protests by the local people who initially claimed a complete halt of the project owing to the submergence of cultivable farmlands (291 villages in Odisha and thirty-four villages in Madhya Pradesh), displacement of several people (around 100,000), and dispossession from communal living and means of livelihood.[22] The movement's claims shifted from defence of traditional livelihoods, displacement, and dispossession, to unequal distribution of the benefits of so-called development in the year 2007 when about 30,000 farmers protested the diversion of dam water meant for irrigation in favour of industries. Unequal allocation of water was legally legitimized via a state government order in 1990.[23]

The 1970s witnessed the Chipko movement in the Himalayan region of erstwhile Uttar Pradesh (now Uttarakhand) which was directed against commercial exploitation of Mandal forests led by the government (i.e., the Forest Department, who in turn subcontracted to a private company).[24] The movement employed the tactic of *Satyagraha*—non-violent civil disobedience or mass refusal to cooperate with state authorities to defend local livelihoods.[25] Local communities from Mandal and nearby villages, under the leadership of Chandi Prasad Bhatt (leader of Dasholi Gram Swarajya Sangh or DGSS, a small industrial corporation, and including mostly hill women (because their gendered responsibilities of fetching fuelwood and fodder were directly impacted) were motivated to hug the trees to protest the state-private corporation nexus of felling the trees.[26] In addition, it mobilized the Gandhian ideology of development that does not exploit humans and living/non-living beings other than humans. The movement was yet another protest to counter the oppressive monopoly of the state over forest laws and policies, to defend the communal right to access the benefits (for small-scale 'industrial' use in the Gandhian sense, in the Mandal village, and subsistence use in the nearby Reni village) of the forests and interconnected ecosystems (water bodies)—all of which may be broadly framed as local livelihood rights.[27] The villagers' main demands aligned with local calls for sovereignty including termination of commercial felling of trees, restoration of traditional rights of local forest-dependent communities to meet their subsistence needs, restoration of local biodiversity through community-centred participation, and development of a localized form of village-economy.[28]

[22] Kishor Kumar Podh, 'Maladies of Development in India—Protest against Large Scale Dams: A Case of Hirakud Dam' (2015) 2(4) *International Journal of Multicultural and Multireligious Understanding* 11, 20.

[23] ibid 21.

[24] Emma Mawdsley, 'After Chipko: From Environment to Region in Uttaranchal' (1998) 25(4) *The Journal of Peasant Studies* 36.

[25] Nayak (n 1) 249, 268.

[26] Bina Agarwal, 'The Gender and Environment Debate: Lessons from India' (1992) 18(1) *Feminist Studies* 119; Mawdsley (n 24) 147.

[27] Mawdsley (n 24) 3.

[28] Mallick (n 21) 54; Mawdsley (n 24) 12.

Coming back to anti-dam protests, one of the most globally popular EMs was the Narmada Bachao Andolan (NBA) mobilized from the mid-1980s.[29] Until this movement, displacement of peoples was normalized as a cost of development; and the tribals did not have formally recognized legal titles to lands. For this reason, they were unable to claim compensation and resettlement due to loss of rights over their means of livelihood, that were caused by developmental projects.[30] The NBA's charisma can be explained by both legal (employing India's public interest litigation culture and the available legal provisions that empower grassroot communities to mobilize environmental justice) and extra-legal (protest mobilization, and local-to-global solidarity across non-state actors) factors. The dam, funded by the World Bank, was planned to be constructed across the states of Gujarat, Madhya Pradesh, Maharashtra, and Rajasthan (a non-riparian state) to deliver drinking water, irrigation, and energy.[31] The movement was led by a woman, a social worker named Medha Patkar, and allied NGOs along with the indigenous peoples (who were displaced by the Sardar Sarovar dam or SSD in the Narmada River) under the banner of the NBA. After the official construction of the SSD started in 1961, the state of Gujarat filed a complaint under the Inter-State Water Disputes Act, 1956 for fair allocation of water among the riparian states.[32] To this effect, the centre constituted the Narmada Water Disputes Tribunal (NWDT) whose final award in 1978 acknowledged that all submerged lands should be acquired by the states and that all people living on these lands should be rehabilitated.[33] In other words, the land was to be returned in exchange for land confiscated.[34] But this came with intersectional negative impacts—some got well-irrigated lands, some received poor-quality farmlands, and the tribals and women who did not have formal land rights lost out.[35] For example, women were denied the right to land compensation because the government perceived men as patriarchal heads who have exclusive ownership rights.[36] They were exposed to further deprivations in resettled places due to their additional care burden in the domestic realm, and patriarchal biases in public spheres and state institutions.

Overall, resentment led to widespread protests to initially claim for resettlement and rehabilitation because, the submergence of large areas of forests not only led to the displacement of *Adivasis* but also deprived them of their means to secure sustainable livelihoods, that is, accessing food, fuel, and medicines.[37] Then their claim shifted to

[29] Balakrishnan Rajagopal, 'The Role of Law in Counter-Hegemonic Globalization and Global Legal Pluralism: Lessons from the Narmada Valley Struggle in India' (2005) 18(3) *Leiden Journal of International Law* 345, 364.

[30] Philippe Cullet, *The Sardar Sarovar Dam Project: Selected Documents* (Routledge 2007) 2; Mallick (n 21) 68–71.

[31] Cullet (n 30) ch 1.

[32] Philippe Cullet, 'Human Rights and Displacement: The Indian Supreme Court Decision on Sardar Sarovar in International Perspective' (2001) 50(4) *International and Comparative Law Quarterly* 973, 974.

[33] Balakrishnan Rajagopal, *International Law from below: Development, Social Movements, and Third World Resistance* (CUP 2003) 356–357.

[34] Cullet (n 32) 974.

[35] Rajagopal (n 29) 361.

[36] Mallick (n 21) 70–72.

[37] Mallick (n 21) 60.

resistance to the entire project and applying pressure on the World Bank to commission an independent review of the project. The result was the Government of India cancelling the World Bank loan and the bank withdrawing itself, but the project continued domestically. Despite the NBA's reluctance to file a case because of fears of courts protecting the 'powerful',[38] it nevertheless challenged the construction of the SSD before the Supreme Court of India in 1994 via a public interest litigation to argue that the affected populations were not heard and represented before the NWDT and that the project came with immense socio-economic and environmental costs which violate human rights and environmental sustainability.[39]

The petition was met with some key moments. In February 1994, the Court declined to stop the construction of the dam because of constitutional barriers concerning jurisdictional issues over water disputes already considered by the NWDT. On 16 December 1994, the Court decided that it was not bound by the tribunal award and issued a stay order on the construction of the SSD until the affected people were rehabilitated. The stay order was confirmed in May 1995 for another four years, however, construction continued on the ground in violation of Court orders.[40] Meanwhile, the NBA branched off to reconstructive approaches by collaborating with local and global alliances and engaging in small-scale social works such as the construction of housing, water conservation, and irrigation schemes, and planting trees.[41] Legal and protest strategies gained them 'public attention'[42] that spread across other regions in India and pressurized the governments to withdraw projects in Rathong Chu in 1997, Bedthi in 1998, and revise the rehabilitation and displacement package in Tehri and Koel Karo.[43] From 1998 to 2000, however, the Court continued to harden its position, and finally in 2000, directed the government to complete the project 'as expeditiously as possible' while effectively resettling the displaced.[44] In all, it failed to look into the non-monetary and human costs of development by adjudicating them in a 'technical manner' without valuing the fundamental contradictions between human rights (subaltern's livelihood rights), environmental sustainability, and development process.[45]

This was followed by another petition in 2002, specifically concerning the irregularities around resettlement and rehabilitation of the affected populations. To this end, the Court passed an order in 2005, 'lamenting' the cash compensation for land given instead of land-for-land compensation as was mandated in the NWDT award.[46] An interview with Medha Patkar in 2016 revealed that several companies continued to

[38] Interview with Prashant Bhushan, counsel to NBA cited in Rajagopal (n 29) 368.

[39] Cullet (n 32) 975.

[40] Rajagopal (n 29) 370.

[41] ibid 371.

[42] Defne Gönenç, 'Litigation Process of Social Movements as a Driver of Norm Transformation?' (2019) 32(1) *Cambridge Review of International Affairs* 43, 49.

[43] Nayak (n 1) 268.

[44] Cullet (n 30) 11–12; Gönenç (n 42) 50.

[45] Cullet (n 32) 986.

[46] Gönenç (n 42) 50.

reap the benefits of the dam at the cost of access to drinking water by local communities thus, lamenting the entire point of the project.[47] Additionally, the Court took a contradictory stance in February 2017 by legitimizing cash compensation, thus abstracting the value of resettlement and rehabilitation processes, agency, and subsistence livelihoods to a narrow monetary frame.[48] Monetization of legal claims into market prices is also observed in other EMs that claimed closure of industrial units because of environmental pollution (e.g., the case of the Sterlite copper smelting unit in Tuticorin, Tamil Nadu) and state-facilitated and industry-led land grabs (e.g., the Tata Motors factory in Singur in West Bengal). The problem with the valorization of legal claims to monetary compensation is that it serves the interests of certain groups who are willing to exchange land for money while devaluing the subjectivities of minority groups whose relationship to lands involves different material realities. Monetization is based on a colonial and dualistic view of land (nature) as 'fungible' or a replaceable commodity and thus, separating it from its social life (identity, culture, subsistence economy).[49] This view of ownership eliminates plural legal realities that operate in rural contexts. For example, agricultural labourers have a customary right to cultivate despite not being legal owners of agricultural lands. Compensation in market terms fails to account for the loss of non-monetary assets like customary rights.[50]

5.1.2 Protection Versus Precarity

After India's economic liberalization in 1991, much emphasis was laid on 'developing' the backward states through increased reliance on the free market. These backward states were also resource-rich and inhabited by tribals. On the one hand, the development-induced displacement of around forty million people and the ongoing EMs pressurised the government to formulate a draft rehabilitation policy.[51] This was an outcome of pressure from intergovernmental organizations (the United Nations through the Rio Conference in 1992), multilateral, and human rights organizations.[52] The Right to Fair Compensation and Transparency in Land Acquisition, Rehabilitation, and Resettlement Act, 2013 was thus passed to redress concerns of displacement. There were further legal attempts in protecting the forest rights of tribals through the passage of the Scheduled Tribes and Other Traditional Forest Dwellers (Recognition of Forest Rights) Act, 2006 (FRA) to undo the historical injustices committed against the tribals who have been living in the forests for centuries.

[47] ibid 50–51.

[48] ibid 50.

[49] Gupta (n 18) 475; Prabhat Pattnaik, 'Neoliberalism and the Crisis in India's Countryside' in Haroon Akram-Lodhi and others (eds), *Handbook of Critical Agrarian Studies* (Edward Elgar 2021).

[50] Pattnaik (n 49) 331.

[51] The National rehabilitation policy for protecting displaced persons in 1993.

[52] Nayak (n 1) 249, 270.

The FRA was passed in the dual contexts of alienation of tribals from their lands and the associated peak in activism.[53] It sought to restore the forest rights of *Adivasis* and prevent their arbitrary eviction and displacement by developmental projects and allow their implementation only with the consent of village assemblies. On the other hand, the National Mineral Policy was introduced to privatize the mining sector in the same year.[54] Despite the passage of protectional legislations, the context of liberalization systematically exposed India's forestlands and tribals to the state-corporate nexus whereby the state enables foreign direct investment in most public sectors.[55] Nevertheless, the FRA was useful to challenge the extractive projects led by POSCO, and Vedanta Aluminium in the state of Odisha before the Supreme Court for lack of prior informed consent. But its implementation remains a challenge because of fragmented forest laws with contradictory provisions; 'epistemic distance'[56] between formal laws and vernacular knowledge; and technicalization of legal language and subjectivity to matters requiring proof of indigeneity, ownership, and performance of identity.[57]

While the PIL culture (liberalization of legal standing for claiming remedies) and employment of constitutional rights (such as the right to life and other fundamental rights) remain useful tools to challenge the extractive sector, the collusion of the state and corporations (domestic/multinational) remains a key barrier to implementing pro-subaltern laws. In several instances, the state resorted to the application of force on protests (the case of Kalinganagar against the Industrial Infrastructure Development Corporation of Orissa, a government body; and the case of Utkal Aluminium Industrial Limited in Odisha).[58] Even though the Constitution of India recognizes equality, and positive discrimination to protect disadvantaged groups, including the Scheduled Tribes and Scheduled Castes, it fundamentally marginalizes other notions of development by promoting a 'secular, rational–scientific nation-state'.[59] The Constitution also centralizes the role of the state in the context of environmental governance by explicitly recognizing the fundamental duty of the state and citizens in environmental protection through the Forty-second Constitutional Amendment. We see the conflicting goals of the state in using its legal sovereignty to formally protect the rights of the *Adivasis* while simultaneously pushing them into precarity, by continuing the civilizing mission

[53] Prakruti Ramesh, 'Rural Industry, the Forest Rights Act, and the Performance(s) of Proof' in Kenneth Bo Nielsen and Patrik Oskarsson (eds), *Industrialising Rural India: Land, Policy and Resistance* (Routledge 2016) 162.

[54] Roy and Joan Martinez-Alier (n 1) 82.

[55] Stein Sundstøl Eriksen, 'From State-Led Development to Embedded Neoliberalism: India's Industrial and Social Policies in Comparative Perspective' in Nielsen and Oskarsson (eds) (n 53) 46.

[56] Robyn Bartel, 'Vernacular Knowledge and Environmental Law: Cause and Cure for Regulatory Failure' (2014) 19(8) *Local Environment* 891.

[57] Colonial-era legislation including the 'Indian Forest Act, 1927, the Wildlife Protection Act, 1972, and the Forest Conservation Act, 1980—differ in their priorities and approaches' that continue to marginalize tribal communities. See Ramesh (n 52) 161; Roy and Joan Martinez-Alier (n 1) 83.

[58] Roy and Joan Martinez-Alier (n 1) 82.

[59] Glyn Williams and Emma Mawdsley, 'Postcolonial Environmental Justice: Government and Governance in India' (2006) 37(5) *Geoforum* 660, 664.

of taming the 'backward' and 'traditional citizens' to become 'modern' on its 'own terms'.[60] Simultaneously, the *Adivasis* use those very protectional laws to resist the state-corporate nexus in acquiring tribal lands.

5.1.3 Reclaiming Communal Sovereignty and Autonomy

Some of the EMs which are ongoing today include Navdanya and the farmers' movements towards farmers' sovereignty and sustainable agriculture.[61] Unlike the previously discussed EMs that resisted development through the direct expropriation of peasants' assets (land, water, forests), these EMs are resisting the neoliberal state's instrumental role in indirect appropriation-cum-exploitation and 'slow violence'[62] on agrarian frontiers and bodies.[63] Sustainable agriculture is gaining importance as an ecological alternative to modern agriculture's excess dependence on chemical fertilizers-cum-pesticides, high-yielding variety seeds, and water that cause degradation of soil-fertility and water quality, biodiversity loss, and greenhouse emissions.[64] Agriculture is an existential sector that is crucial for meeting India's food security, hunger, and malnutrition challenges that are very vulnerable to global warming due to reduced crop yield, increased evapotranspiration, reduced soil moisture, and seasonal disruptions. To top this, farmers fear agri-business firms taking over food systems – all of which immediately threatens their autonomy, especially peasant farmers and agricultural labourers.[65] In this context, both the movements aim to transform the global food production order by radically shifting its control from the hands of multinational-corporations (MNCs) and the state to farmers. They also aim to transform the quality of the food produced and the way it is produced, distributed, and consumed.[66]

The Navdanya movement, mobilized by scholar-activist, Vandana Shiva does so by challenging genetic engineering and patenting of seeds/plant varieties that expropriate

[60] ibid 664.

[61] Mallick (n 21) ch 4; Also see my paper Nairita Roy Chaudhuri, 'Social Movements and Grassroots Discourse of Climate Justice in the Context of Droughts in Semi-Arid Regions: A Case Study in India' (2021) 11(1) *Onati Socio-Legal Series* 69; Lys Kulamadayil, 'Informed Dissent or Misinformed Rebellion? Making Sense of India's Farmer Protests' (*Völkerrechtsblog*, 4 February 2021) <https://voelkerrechtsblog.org/informed-dissent-or-misinformed-rebellion-making-sense-of-indias-farmer-protests/>; Aniket Aga, 'Farm Protests in India Are Writing the Green Revolution's Obituary—Scientific American' *Scientific American* (24 January 2021); Arjun Kumar and Simi Mehta, 'Deconstructing the Enigma of Recent Farmers' Protests in India' (2017) 3(7) *IndraStra Global* 1.

[62] Nixon (2011) cited in Roy and Joan Martinez-Alier (n 1) 84.

[63] Pattnaik (n 49) 331.

[64] Roy Chaudhuri (n 61) 80–81; Andrew Flachs, 'Degrowing Alternative Agriculture: Institutions and Aspirations as Sustainability Metrics for Small Farmers in Bosnia and India' (2022) *Sustainability Science* 1; Trent Brown, *Farmers, Subalterns, and Activists: Social Politics of Sustainable Agriculture in India* (CUP 2018); Vandana Shiva and Kartikey Shiva, *Oneness vs. the 1%* (Chelsea Green 2020).

[65] Brown (n 64) ch 1; Vandana Shiva, *Stolen Harvest: The Hijacking of the Global Food Supply* (University Press of Kentucky 2016).

[66] Vandana Shiva, *Staying Alive: Women Ecology and Development* (North Atlantic Books 2016).

traditional and indigenous knowledge or impair small farmers from freely conserving, exchanging, and reusing them for use in subsequent crop cycles, by resorting to litigation wherever applicable. For example, a public interest litigation filed by Vandana Shiva through the Research Foundation for Science and Technology and Navdanya before the Supreme Court of India in 1999 challenged the procedural lapses (illegal clearance of untested technology) in the way the Ministry of Science and Technology granted permission to Monsanto-Mahyco company to conduct open field trials of genetically modified (GM) Bt cotton in India and commercially selling them to Indian farmers because it amounted to a violation of biosafety rules under the Environment (Protection) Act, 1986.[67] The concerns raised include harmful and irreparable consequences of Bt cotton and GM seeds for commercial plantation on human health, ecology (Bt toxins harming bees, insects, and livestock; GM plants becoming superweeds and herbicide resistant), and farmers' income security (through their continued economic dependence on corporations for buying seeds that were traditionally free and reusable).[68] The case yielded a four-year ban on Bt cotton on the introduction of GM crops, after which the government allowed the commercialization of Bt cotton raising questions on the sides taken by the state.[69] While the case opened doors for future challenges against harmful GM crops, to date several farmers continue to depend on Bt cotton, and are trapped in debt.[70] Other strategies employed by the Navdanya movement include emphasizing the human right to food, and mobilizing environmental justice claims around ecofeminism,[71] and 'Earth democracy', that is, small farmers' collective and legal sovereignty[72] over their seeds, food, and water in the global South—thereby decentralizing sovereignty beyond the confines of the nation-state. The movement promotes seed sovereignty (saving and sharing) because it considers seeds as traditional means of life (e.g., the right to control genomic information of seeds is a vital aspect of food sovereignty)[73] over which farmers ought to have moral communal rights and control towards

[67] Vandana Shiva and Afsar H Jafri, 'Bursting the GM Bubble: The Failure of GMOs in India' (2003) 11(3) *The Ecologist Asia* 6; Vandana Shiva, 'Earth Democracy: Beyond Dead Democracy and Killing Economies' (2010) 21 *Capitalism Nature Socialism* 83; Gigesh Thomas and Johan De Tavernier, 'Farmer-Suicide in India: Debating the Role of Biotechnology' (2017) 13 *Life Sciences, Society and Policy* 3–4.

[68] Shiva (n 67) 83–95.

[69] Shiva and Jafri (n 67); Shiva (n 67) 87.

[70] Marcus Taylor, *The Political Ecology of Climate Change Adaptation: Livelihoods, Agrarian Change and the Conflicts of Development* (Routledge 2017); Shiva (n 67) 87–88; Thomas and De Tavernier (n 67) 11.

[71] Shiva argues that colonialism created ontological hierarchies between nature-humans and feminine-masculine that justifies man's domination over nature and women. Ecofeminism challenges this thought by linking feminism with sustaining the web of life through care, non-violence, and non-domination. See Manisha Rao, 'Ecofeminism at the Crossroads in India: A Review' (2012) 20 *Deportate, esuli, profughe (DEP)* 124; Chhāyā Dātār, *Ecofeminism Revisited: Introduction to the Discourse* (Rawat 2011).

[72] Jack Kloppenburg, 'Re-Purposing the Master's Tools: The Open Source Seed Initiative and the Struggle for Seed Sovereignty' (2014) 41(6) *Journal of Peasant Studies* 1225.

[73] This is because GM seeds are not 'self-pollinating, meaning that, if saved, they will not express the same characteristics, including their increased yields, in the next generation'. See Amy Trauger,

a larger struggle for sustainable agriculture, commoning, and against private property.[74] However, the transformative potential of the Navdanya movement can be interrogated on moral and temporal grounds because Navdanya accepts donations from large corporations, a strategy that does not align with its anti-corporate goals.[75] Even though the movement continues to mobilize peasant farmers based on a moral economy of subsistence living, its dependence on corporate funding may impede its long-term goals of autonomy.

Moving-forward, the 2015 farmers' protests, against the backdrop of severe crop failure due to climate change-aggravated droughts, show that climate justice framed from below offers socially and ecologically sustainable agricultural solutions that can only be addressed by transforming the 'growth-obsessed' notion of development.[76] The movement is chasing shifting targets—from All India Kisan Sangharsh Coordination Committee, a pan Indian network of farmers' attempts to institutionalize farmers' claims in formal legal terms by introducing agricultural bills (or formalizing law from below) through elected representatives, north-western farmers successfully opposing the three neoliberal farm bills introduced by the government to commercialize the agricultural sector, and to finally aiming at transformational justice that transgresses the field of law to questions of development, political economy, and ecology.[77] Their attempt to formalize law from below highlights the importance of formal law for legitimizing grassroot interests, and the disempowering Westphalian[78] state's monopoly over the production of legal knowledge without which grounded claims have no legitimacy. The farmers continue to protest multiple vulnerabilities inherent in India's political economy, which is also embedded in global capitalism, because they are causing agrarian crisis. They are resisting a combination of factors, including declining incomes from selling crops, increasing agricultural input costs, planned underfunding of the agricultural sector, and simultaneous investment in corporate capital by the neoliberal state, debt, urban-biased agricultural policy, capitalist norms of yields and efficiency,

'Seed Sovereignty as Civil Disobedience in Northern India?' in Amy Trauger (ed), *Food Sovereignty in International Context: Discourse, Politics and Practice of Place* (Routledge 2015) 107.

[74] Kloppenburg (n 72) 1234–1235.

[75] Trauger (n 73) 114.

[76] Roy Chaudhuri (n 61) 69.

[77] Kulamadayil (n 61); Aga (n 61); Roy Chaudhuri (n 61) 96; Surinder S Jodhka, 'Why Are the Farmers of Punjab Protesting?' (2021) 48(7) *The Journal of Peasant Studies* 1356; Natasha Behl, 'India's Farmers' Protest: An Inclusive Vision of Indian Democracy' (2022) 116(3) *American Political Science Review* 1141.

[78] With its origins in the Treaty of Westphalia in 1648 in Europe, Westphalian sovereignty refers to a modern nation-state that has exclusive sovereignty (legal and political) over its territory. The principle is criticized because it excludes neo-colonial global forces that transgress territorial boundaries and other conceptual histories of the state in the post-colonies. See Antony Anghie, 'The Evolution of International Law: Colonial and Postcolonial Realities' (2006) 27 *Third World Quarterly* 739; Gurminder K Bhambra, 'The State: Postcolonial Histories of the Concept' in Olivia U Rutazibwa and Robbie Shilliam (eds), *Routledge Handbook of Postcolonial Politics* (1st edn, Routledge 2018) 200–209; Nancy Fraser, 'Social Exclusion, Global Poverty, and Scales of (in)Justice: Rethinking Law and Poverty in a Globalizing World' (2011) 22(3) *Stellenbosch Law Review* 452.

and market-capture of self-reliant small farming through seed patents and unfair global trade terms by the World Trade Organization—all of which are negatively impacting local biodiversity, water availability and farmers' sovereignty.[79]

Farmers' movements are not reactive because India has a longstanding history of farmers' unions engaging in pro-peasant resistance movements and bargaining strategies with the state for claiming equitable land reforms, social security, and economic security.[80] However, certain tipping points such as the passage of the farm laws, and unprecedented droughts caused a peak in protests by farmers resorting to Gandhian forms of direct action (fasting, rallying, strikes). The Navdanya and farmers' movements claim farmers' sovereignty and rights beyond the Westphalian and individualistic frames.[81] They are also challenging extractive webs of capitalism and imperialism by calling for just conditions that 'sustain life'.[82]

5.2 Local-to-Global Struggles, Solidarities, and Barriers to Environmental Justice

Given how economic globalization connects nation-states today, this section critically reflects on the local-to-global issues that affect EMs including the barriers faced, and solidarities forged. The objective is to examine the long terms goals for transformational justice.

5.2.1 Connected Struggles and Networked Solidarity

Resisting large-scale developmental projects requires movement actors to constantly resist the dominating powers of the state, global finance capital, and institutions. This can materialize by strategically connecting local (state, impacts, ideologies, laws) and global (capital, ideologies, NGOs, laws) levels of struggle. While the *chipko* movement successfully caused a fifteen-year legal ban on the felling of trees by calling upon the state, it was unable to achieve its long-term goals of decentralized sovereignty that are delinked from the realms of neoliberal-capitalist globalization and the nation-state. Demands for a 'sound local economy'[83] were translated into a subsequent struggle for a separate state

[79] Flachs (n 64); Pattnaik (n 49); Taylor (n 70) ch 7.

[80] Jodhka (n 77) 1360–1362; Navsharan Singh, 'Agrarian Crisis and the Longest Farmers' Protest in Indian History' (2021) 30(3) *New Labor Forum* 66.

[81] Matthew C Canfield, *Translating Food Sovereignty Cultivating Justice in an Age of Transnational Governance* (Stanford University Press 2022).

[82] D'Souza (n 9) xiv.

[83] Mawdsley (n 24) 12.

of Uttaranchal that could enable 'hill people's political voice'[84] to be heard. However, the movement failed to achieve long-term autonomy because of 'supra-local political, economic and cultural influences'[85] of the state (that corresponds to the executive, legislature, and judiciary), global capitalism, and the ideology of unlimited economic growth that remains hegemonic within the state's governance structures, and the public sphere.[86] Furthermore, the power of the NBA movement is arguably more performative than its real victory in terms of environmental justice.[87]

Ultimately, India's desire for economic development superseded the affected community's claims for alternate modes of development and harvesting water that centre meaningful participation.[88] However, the movement was globally instrumental in calling for an independent review of the costs of large dams funded by the World Bank across the global South, which led to the formation of the World Commission on Dams, and the first internal accountability mechanism within the bank, that is, the Inspection Panel.[89] The review report suggested that projects that do not prioritize human rights norms over those subscribed by the World Bank and other borrower countries should not be implemented.[90] It opened new legal grammar and international standards for affected populations to challenge multilateral organizations that engaged in neo-colonial practices of providing high-interest loans to so-called third-world countries to promote free-market capitalism in the name of development.[91] For the first time in the 1980s, the local population's livelihood claims were articulated through the language of human rights in the dual contexts of international development aid and the North-South divide. In all, if the struggle at the domestic level involves accountability of the colonial superstructure inherited by the post-colonial state, and domestic corporations; at the global level, it involves accountability of the MNCs and multilateral organizations. Connecting the g(local) levels of struggles is strategically materialized through a network of international NGOs, journalists, activists, and academics who mobilize counter-hegemonic norms that transgress nation-state borders—a solidarity-based tactic that makes the NBA, Navdanya and farmers' movements internationally popular.[92] However, popular EMs may come with the risk of highlighting majoritarian concerns that may resonate with globally hot topics while excluding local and intersectional (class, caste, landholding size, gender, ethnicity) needs.[93]

[84] ibid 52.

[85] ibid 11.

[86] Rajagopal (n 33) ch 8.

[87] Gönenç (n 42) 57; María Arquero de Alarcón and others, 'DAM[N]ED: Mechanizing a Sacred River Landscape Redrawing Territorial Systems in the Narmada River Valley' (2018) *New Instrumentalities* 341.

[88] Mallick (n 21); Gönenç (n 42); Arquero de Alarcón and others (n 87) 349.

[89] Cullet (n 30) 2.

[90] Mallick (n 21) 67.

[91] David Harvey, *A Brief History of Neoliberalism* (OUP 2005); Mallick (n 21) 67–68.

[92] Aljazeera, 'From Hinterland to Hollywood, Indian Farmers Galvanise Their Stir' Agriculture News (*Aljazeera*, 26 February 2021) <https://www.aljazeera.com/news/2021/2/26/hinterland-to-hollywood-how-indian-farmers-galvanised-their-stir>; Mallick (n 21); Nayak (n 1) 270–271.

[93] Brown (n 64); Agarwal (n 26) 150–153.

5.2.2 Environmental Justice and Structural Barriers

Through a review of some key EMs discussed above, we see that grassroot communities counter the hegemonic logic of development wherein multiple parties (state and non-state actors) compete or collaborate. Non-state actors include affected subalterns across intersectional identities, courts, NGOs, activists, corporations, and supra-national organizations. Often NGOs/activists due to their class and social privileges play a key role in voicing subaltern concerns by mobilizing legal and political strategies.

We see that the core objectives of the EMs are directed against the colonial legacies of capital accumulation, extractivism, and neoliberalism in the pretext of development, which is often led by the nexus between the state and corporations. They also resist the state's legal and political domination over rural/tribal communal resources by reclaiming ecological democracy (sovereignty and autonomy) over local commons. Lastly, EMs resist the ontological duality that separates the material means of subsistence from environmental and socio-cultural sustainability (sound economy, everyday customary laws and practices embedded in interdependent and proximal relations between human and non-human natures). Movements offer useful sites to understand the conflicting power of formal law. Meaning, law can be a powerful tool (e.g., public interest litigation culture, constitutional rights, FRA, Environment (Protection) Act) used by—grassroots communities to counter the dominating forces of the state, capitalist markets, and elite capture; and such dominating forces to legitimize their interests (e.g., neoliberal farm bills, eminent domain, mineral policies) by oppressing and conflicting with local customary norms and laws (e.g., diverse and informal property regimes, gender roles).

Rights/entitlements and public interest litigation offer legal opportunities for movement actors to defend their sovereignty over local resources and challenge the neoliberal state/corporations/multilateral organizations through confrontational and non-confrontational strategies. Yet, long-term goals of environmental justice face structural and ideological impediments such as state sovereignty, economic growth, and global capitalism; thereby limiting subaltern peoples' agency to legitimize their subjective notions of development. When faced with peasant resistance, legal reform is only able to bring temporary changes to pacify dissent without rectifying the structural drivers of marginalization.[94] To elaborate, if state-cum-industry-led accumulation drives the logic of development, then environmental, and welfare laws (e.g., tribal identity-based FRA) to protect the subalterns will remain surface-level attempts (although useful at this juncture) to reverse the developmental violence because such attempts of reversal reinforce the state-market hegemony and top-down governance.

It also locks-in the subalterns within a dialectical relationship with the state and markets wherein the former both resist and depend on the latter actors by providing

[94] Dean Spade, 'Intersectional Resistance and Law Reform' (2013) 38 *Signs: Journal of Women in Culture and Society* 1031.

coerced consent (e.g., consenting to monetary compensation for displacement); thus, continuing to live precarious lives.[95] As long as the Westphalian nation-state model persists, equity[96] and placed-based (such as geographical scales tied to local and plural socio-cultural contexts) legal realities of local communities need to be at the centre of globally networked anti-capitalist, anti-anthropocentric, anti-colonial, and anti-patriarchal EMs to enable the subalterns to live with dignity and basic needs; while simultaneously degrowing and setting a cap on unending wants of the elite populations.[97]

Conclusion

This chapter highlighted the plurality of EMs in India that cannot be understood without historicizing them in colonial violence. EMs offer useful sites to understand the conflicting power of formal law. EMs also shape legal-norms (agricultural bills, accountability standards for multilateral organizations, decentralized seed sovereignty) and creatively mobilize formal laws (constitutional and human rights, statutes such as the FRA and the Environment (Protection) Act) to aim at transformational[98] changes that counter the hegemonic notion of development which usurp the ecological, economic, social, and cultural spheres of subaltern lives. They raise questions of environmental injustice because natural resources in rural India are used to meet the requirements of the urban-industrial-export sector for which forests, water, and other resources are diverted or destroyed, especially impacting women and marginalized groups even more.[99]

Formal laws are powerful tools for movement actors to demand environmental justice and yet they continue to remain vulnerable because of structural impediments. India's susceptibility to climatic threats (heatwaves, droughts, desertification, floods, sea-level rise) is a further call to overcome these structural barriers by redefining and repurposing an anti-extractive politics of sustainability that welcomes plural onto-epistemological subjectivities; and counters human-centric, patriarchal, and colonial categories of knowledge, development, nature (dualism), gender (hierarchical binarism), work, labour, property, nationalism, state, and capitalist markets.[100]

[95] Partha Chatterjee, 'Democracy and Economic Transformation in India' (2008) 43(16) *Economic and Political Weekly* 53.

[96] That transgresses single axis politics of exclusion towards an intersectional praxis, by considering power relations of gender, caste, class, ethnicity, and other contextual factors. See Spade (n 94) 1046–1051; Sumi Cho, Kimberlé Williams Crenshaw, and Leslie McCall, 'Toward a Field of Intersectionality Studies: Theory Applications and Praxis' (2013) 38 *Signs: Journal of Women in Culture and Society* 785.

[97] For more on what degrowth is, see Jason Hickel, 'The Anti-Colonial Politics of Degrowth' (2021) 88 *Political Geography* 1; Jason Hickel, 'What Does Degrowth Mean? A Few Points of Clarification' (2020) 18 *Globalizations* 1; Chaudhuri (n 20) 43–46.

[98] Zoha Shawoo and CL McDermott, 'Justice through Polycentricity? A Critical Examination of Climate Justice Framings in Pakistani Climate Policymaking' (2020) 20(4) *Climate Policy* 199, 202.

[99] Mallick (n 21) ch 1.

[100] Chaudhuri (n 20); Mallick (n 21) 91.

Suggestions for Further Reading

Kishan Khoday and Usha Natarajan, 'Fairness and International Environmental Law from Below: Social Movements and Legal Transformation in India' (2012) 25(2) *Leiden Journal of International Law* 415.

Krishna Mallick, *Environmental Movements of India: Chipko, Narmada Bachao Andolan, Navdanya* (Amsterdam University Press 2021).

Arun Kumar Nayak, 'Big Dams and Protests in India: A Study of Hirakud Dam' (2010) 45(2) *Economic and Political Weekly* 69.

Balakrishnan Rajagopal, *International Law from Below: Development, Social Movements, and Third World Resistance* (CUP 2003).

Ghanshyam Shah, *Social Movements in India: A Review of the Literature* (2nd edn, Sage 2004).

PART II

INSTITUTIONAL AND REGULATORY DIMENSIONS

CHAPTER 6

GOVERNING THE ENVIRONMENT IN THE FIFTH AND SIXTH SCHEDULE AREAS

VIRGINIUS XAXA

Abstract

This chapter engages with environmental governance in the Fifth and Sixth Schedule areas of the Constitution of India. At the outset, it spells out the broad features of the two schedules besides tracing their lineage in the Constitution. It then focuses on environmental governance under different historical regimes and delineates the key concerns of the people and the environment. Following this, the potential of environmental governance under regimes of contemporary times is discussed. The chapter then analyses the state of the environment in the two scheduled areas and puts forward a perspective for environmental governance based on experiences of the two areas.

Introduction

Governing the environment means engaging with regulatory processes, mechanisms, and organizations through which societal actors influence environmental actions and outcomes. It entails actions of the state alongside diverse non-state actors ranging from the local, and state to national level.[1] Environmental governance in the Fifth and Sixth

[1] International Bureau of Education, Concept of Governance <www.ibe.unesco.org/en/geqaf/technical-notes/concept-governance>.

Schedule areas emanates from the system of administration provided for tribes in the Constitution of India, 1950. The provisions of the Fifth Schedule of the Constitution apply to the administration and control of the scheduled areas and scheduled tribes in any state other than the states of Assam, Meghalaya, Mizoram, and Tripura where tribal areas come under the Sixth Schedule of the Constitution. A Presidential Order must notify both scheduled areas and tribal areas, which could be district or a part thereof.[2] Geographically, these areas are predominantly marked by hills and plateaus and are extensively covered with forests of different types. They are also hotspot zones of biodiversity besides being endowed with rich mineral resources. They have been the destination of extractive economic activities since the colonial period raising the need for attention to environmental governance at the peripheries. After all, the environment has no boundaries.

Initially, the British ruled the areas so described in the same way as they administered other regions. The laws, regulations, rules, and administrative practices regulating the civil and criminal spheres were the same. All these had adverse consequences on tribes, resulting in a series of revolts against the British all through the nineteenth century. These revolts led the British to think of a different system of administration for tribal areas. The Fifth and Sixth Schedules of the Constitution can be traced to this system of administration under the British.

This chapter is organized into six sections. Section 6.1 discusses the evolution of the Fifth and Sixth Schedules of the Constitution. Section 6.2 looks at environmental governance in a historical context, while Section 6.3 assesses the situation of environmental governance in the post-Independence period. Section 6.4 discusses the key concerns of people and the environment in the scheduled areas; and section 6.5 considers the potential of the existing regime concerning environmental governance. Section 6.6 outlines an alternative perspective for environmental governance in the scheduled areas.

6.1 Making of the Fifth and Sixth Schedule Areas

The people who inhabit the Fifth and Sixth Schedule areas are linguistically, socially, and culturally different from the people in the plains of India and are generally referred to as tribes. Each tribe occupies a distinct territory. Their economic, social, and cultural life is intertwined with the land, forest, and water, which are regulated as per customary laws and traditional practices for sustainable livelihood. Lands and forests are generally held either as individual tenure or by a clan or the village community. The key issues of the village, including natural resources management, are discussed and deliberated in the village assembly and the decisions are executed by the village council comprising

[2] The Constitution of India 1950, Art 244(1) and 244(2).

the elders of different clans in the village. Though villages are autonomous and self-governing, they are not without a relationship with other villages, and institutional mechanisms exists to deal with larger issues.

The areas that later came under the Fifth and Sixth Schedules of the Constitution were brought under colonial rule during different phases. As a step to enforce its rule, the colonial rulers extended their civil and criminal regulations, rules, and practices to new areas. The result was a series of revolts all through the late eighteenth century and early nineteenth century resulting in the extension of Regulation X of 1822. This Regulation introduced the concept of a non-regulated system for carrying out the administration of these areas under paternalistic executive.[3] Under this system, regulations and laws framed for general administration were not applicable in these areas. The system allowed tribes to be governed by their customary laws and traditions in respect of both civil and criminal administration. Of course, the powers of tribes especially over criminal matters were severally truncated. Notwithstanding such a provision, the executive that includes governors who often delegated powers to Commissioners, among others, had the discretionary power to extend the general regulations and laws either in toto or in a modified form, which they extended strategically from time to time. It was a kind of paternalistic administration. Such non-regulated tracts came to be known by different names during different phases of British rule. Agency, scheduled district, backward areas, and later excluded and partially excluded areas are notable among them.

The Government of India Act, 1935 classified the non-regulated tracts referred to above into Excluded Areas and Partially Excluded Areas. The Fifth Schedule areas, relatively more accessible, were opened to the outside world through the extension of roads, railways, and other means of communication. This offered opportunities for the movement of people from the plains into these areas for land, trade, commerce, and jobs leading to the presence of non-tribes. The Sixth Schedule areas remained excluded from such development. Consequently, the Partially Excluded Areas which led to the emergence of the Fifth Schedule to the Constitution were brought under the legislative authority of the state. Notwithstanding, the governor was entrusted with special responsibility for administration of the Partially Excluded Areas and had discretionary powers to override the laws enacted by Parliament and state legislatures. In contrast, the Excluded Areas were not brought under the legislative authority of the state. They were to be administered by the governor at his unfettered discretion as per the earlier practice. The Fifth Schedule of the Constitution is thus a lineal descendant of the administration in practice in the Partially Excluded Areas. The Sixth Schedule is an innovation of the Constituent Assembly, which accepted the recommendations of the Bordoloi Sub-Committee on North-East Frontier (Assam) Tribal and Excluded Areas.[4] The Partially Excluded Areas, as per the Constitution, are not exclusively inhabited by

[3] Bani Prasanna Misra, 'Keynote Address' National Seminar on *Governance, Socio-Economic Disparity, and Unrest in the 'Scheduled Areas' of India* (Tata Institute of Social Sciences, Unpublished, Guwahati 2012) 7.

[4] ibid 8.

the tribal population, whereas the Excluded Areas are. Based on the distinction that the Government of India Act, 1935 introduced, the trajectory of governance of tribes and backward tracts moved in two different directions and culminated in the introduction of the Fifth and Sixth Schedules in the Constitution.

The Fifth Schedule of the Constitution provides for distinct administration of tribal majority areas of ten states in mainland India.[5] The key provisions of the Fifth Schedule revolve around the administration and control of scheduled areas and scheduled tribes. The governor, as per the provision, has the discretionary power not to extend any act of Parliament or state legislatures to the scheduled areas or to extend it with such exceptions and modifications as he may deem fit. The governor has also the power to make regulations for peace and good governance in the scheduled areas in concurrence with the Tribes Advisory Council provided for under the Fifth Schedule of the Constitution and submit them to the President for assent. Further, he may repeal any existing law which is applicable in the scheduled areas. In addition to the above, the governor has the power to direct any area or part thereof as a scheduled or non-scheduled area.

The Sixth Schedule of the Constitution provides for the creation of an Autonomous District Council and an Autonomous Regional Council in tribal areas of Northeast India to enable them to maintain and govern as per their customary laws and traditions. The councils enjoy legislative, executive, and judicial power over subjects specified in the Sixth Schedule. Further, laws and regulations passed by Parliament and state legislatures are not applicable in the Sixth Schedule areas unless the governor extends them to these areas.[6] The district council is formed through duly notified elections based on the adult tribal franchise. Ordinarily, the council consists of thirty members out of which four are generally nominated by the governor. The Sixth Schedule of the Constitution provides for an Executive Committee of the District Council to carry on its executive functions. The Chief Executive Member (CEM) is elected by the elected members of the District Council who then selects other Executive Committee members. The CEM has the power to protect the traditional system through legislative, executive, and judicial power as well as to introduce changes in keeping with the demands of society. The legislative power is concerned mainly with land, forest, and social and religious customs. The power to make laws related to land concerns allotment, occupation, or use or setting a part of the land for the purpose of cultivation, grazing, residence, and other non-agricultural purposes. In the case of forests, the regulation of shifting cultivation (*jhum*), earmarking reserved forests, and maintaining the environment, channelising canals or watercourses for agriculture, etc. are the key concerns. The other subject of law-making is social custom especially inheritance, succession, marriage, and divorce. However, the laws will have effect only after receiving assent from the governor.

[5] These ten states are Andhra Pradesh, Telangana, Gujarat, Jharkhand, Chhattisgarh, Himachal Pradesh, Madhya Pradesh, Maharashtra, Odisha, and Rajasthan.

[6] P Chakraborty, *Fifth and Sixth Schedules to the Constitution of India (Updated and Annotated)* (Capital Law House 2011).

In short, whereas the Constitution formally recognizes customary tradition and system of governance in the Sixth Schedule areas, the same is absent in the Fifth Schedule areas. Rather, it is implicit, and the governors can use similar powers in the Fifth Schedule areas.

6.2 Environmental Governance

Until the advent of colonial rule, tribal people had been living and governing their ancestral territories and their environment for centuries through village councils. The village councils regulated the land, forest, and water under their jurisdiction as per customary laws and practices. The conflicts between villages over any issue were resolved through the joint meeting of council members of the concerned villages. If the conflict persisted, it went before the council of a cluster of villages (confederation) that had evolved among many tribes. Tribes used land, forest, and other resources for sustenance and not for accumulation. Further, they had a religious and spiritual relationship with nature. This enabled people to nurture nature as long as the governance of nature was in their hands.

Although placed under a similar historical and administrative arrangement as referred to in section 1 above, the areas under the Fifth and Sixth Schedules of the Constitution moved to a different system of governance in actual practice, especially concerning natural resource management. Thus, most of the regions under the Fifth Schedule were drawn into the land and revenue settlements of the provinces they were part of. They were also drawn into the structure of state forest management such as reserved, protected, and village forests under the Forest Act, 1865. The territory also saw the dispossession of tribals from their land and forest under the Land Acquisition Act, 1894. Further, in independent India, all laws, regulations, and policies framed by Parliament and state legislatures have been extended to the Fifth Schedule areas despite special discretionary powers conferred on the executive under the Constitution to protect and safeguard the tribal people's interests. Tribes are thus tightly integrated with every regulatory mechanism and institutional structure of state governance. In short, laws and policies enacted by Parliament and the concerned state legislature have been imposed in the Fifth Schedule areas. Such laws and policies were not extended to areas under the Sixth Schedule of the Constitution.

Such practice in Fifth Schedule areas has had disastrous consequences on tribes leading to the movement for self-governance. The Panchayat Act (Extension to Scheduled Areas) Act, 1996 (PESA) is an expression of this movement. The Act is an extension of local self-governance in place in rural India but with an exception in the sense that it makes space for the traditional system of governance with the *Gram Sabha* (village assembly) as the cornerstone. This has been the only Act specific to the Fifth Schedule areas. In contrast, the Sixth Schedule areas have been governed by specific laws and rules framed by the concerned Autonomous District Council on subjects specified in the schedule. Among the subjects, social and religious system, customary practices, and traditional governance are notable. Laws enacted by Parliament and state legislatures on such subjects are in general not applicable in these areas.

The Fifth and Sixth Schedule areas are rich in natural resources on the surface and below the surface of the earth. Tribes inhabiting the areas had secured the natural environment for hundreds of years. The state and the market have taken the exploitation of such resources as critical to development with unprecedented consequences for the tribes and the environment. Depletion of forest areas, overexploitation of water and mineral resources, and other related activities such as the development of industries and dams have resulted in ecological instability, drying of rivers and streams, pollution of air, land, and water bodies with enormous harm and problems for humans and non-humans. All these have been important factors of global warming and climate change. In this context, the Schedule areas still represent the best environmental management, and their governance needs careful attention.

6.3 Environmental Governance in Post-Independent India

The political regime in India has often been referred to as the party or coalition of parties in power. However, the regime has also been conceptualized with reference to the imprint that the government may have left on the state and its institutions. Now, if one were to situate the governments keeping in mind ecological governance and the Fifth and Sixth Schedule areas, it would be more pertinent to think of the political regime in the latter sense though the place of the former could not be denied.

In the sense of leaving a distinct imprint on the state, one can broadly discern three distinct regimes in India. Since the vestiges of the earlier regimes have survived, the discussion of the existing regime would be incomplete without reference to the preceding ones. Even though the Fifth and Sixth Schedule areas were somewhat differently administered as mentioned above, control over natural resources gradually shifted from traditional institutions such as individuals, clans, and villages to the colonial state. State management of forests under the garb of scientific management as well as the Land Acquisition Act, 1894, an expression of the doctrine of eminent domain, has been historically more pronounced in the Fifth Schedule areas than the Sixth Schedule areas.

The colonial regime came to an end with India's Independence in 1947. The post-Independence Indian state embarked on a national reconstruction process with the agenda of revamping the economy and society to build a democratic, just, and egalitarian society. In the shaping of this futuristic imagination, the role of the government in power was critical. It left a distinct imprint on the regime. As a socialist regime, the state assumed the role of the key player in social transformation and development. However, unlike under the British when the state was oriented to the interest of Great Britain and capital, in post-Independence India, the role of the state was to promote the needs of the people. Accordingly, planning became an important pillar of development. Yet the space for the private sector was not denied; it was restricted.[7]

The shaping of such a state under the regime did have some positive bearing on the tribal population, including those living in the Fifth and Sixth Schedule areas. The scheduled areas that had remained outside the scope of development (in terms of agriculture, education, and health) were brought under the state development plan and schemes. This did have a positive bearing, especially in respect of education and state employment. Notwithstanding this, the nature and type of natural resource management under the British has continued in post-Independence India in an accelerated form in the name of nation-building and development.

The ushering in of a New Economic Policy in 1991, imbued with the agenda of liberalization, privatization, and globalization marks a major regime shift in the character of the state in India. The New Economic Policy aimed at major structural economic reforms encompassing almost all sectors of the economy. The thrust of the reform has been the integration of the economy with the global economy, dismantling controls, welcoming foreign investment and technology, promoting productivity, and restructuring the public sector through disinvestment by giving greater participation to the private sector. The New Economic Policy also provided for greater autonomy and power to provincial states to mobilize and restructure their economy. The policy had a far-reaching bearing on the Fifth and Sixth Schedule areas, especially the former.

Most of the Fifth Schedule states endowed with rich minerals and other resources have taken advantage of the new policy and have opened up their states for private investment including multinational corporations.[8] Following this, there has been a sharp rise in the growth of industries, coal power projects, and mineral extraction to feed such industries.[9] Such economic activities in the Fifth Schedule areas, as observed earlier, have been going on since the colonial period and were accelerated as a part of the national reconstruction process in post-Independence India. This has led to environmental degradation, depletion of forest cover, and loss of biodiversity including pollution of air, water, and rivers.

Although such developments by the state and corporations have been markedly absent in states with Sixth Schedule provisions, mineral extraction, especially of coal, limestone, and other forms of quarrying traditionally pursued, have acquired momentum in states like Meghalaya without any form of regulatory mechanism. This has led to much damage to the local ecological landscape and the environment resulting in

[7] AR Desai, *Recent Trends in Indian Nationalism* (Popular Prakashan 1973).

[8] Virginius Xaxa, 'Identity, Power and Development: The Kondhs in Orissa, India' in Suzana Sawyer and Edmund Terence Gomez (eds), *The Politics of Resource Extraction: Indigenous Peoples, Multinational Corporations and the State* (Palgrave Macmillan 2012) 180–203.

[9] Kuntala Lahiri-Dutt, Radhika Krishnan, and Nesar Ahmad, 'Land Acquisition and Dispossession: Private Coal Companies in Jharkhand' (2012) 47(6) *Economic & Political Weekly* 39.

the intervention of the Supreme Court on coal mining.[10] Earlier in 1996, felling trees for timber from the forest led to a similar ban by the Supreme Court.[11] The ban was later lifted and harvesting of trees was allowed with the prior approval of the Centre.[12] Accordingly, the Khasi Hills District Council evolved a working scheme for the approval of the Centre.[13] Yet the environmental damage in the Sixth Schedule areas is miniscule in comparison to the Fifth Schedule areas.

6.4 Emerging Concerns and Challenges in the Contemporary Context

A very large majority of tribes make their living off the land, forest, and water even today. A combination of modes of making a living such as agriculture, foraging, fishing, and hunting characterizes their lives. Thus, land and forest have been the life support system of tribes. Even settled agriculturists depend on the forest for a large basket of their food. Yet the situation of people living off these resources today is not the same as it was before. Their land holdings have steadily dwindled with the alienation of land from tribes to non-tribes. This has its genesis in the land and revenue settlement and records of rights introduced by the British.

Tribes' control over forests, another very important source of their life support system, has gone through a similar process. As a part of scientific management, the colonial state drew a 'Charter of Indian Forest' in 1855 and enacted the Indian Forest Act, 1865. The laws related to forest governance were later consolidated in the Indian Forest Act, 1927. These laws brought the forest under the authority and control of the state besides the declaration or notification of any land with trees/bushes as a forest. The Act made provisions for making rules for the preservation of the forest and empowered the forest department to punish anyone for breaches of the Act. The Forest Settlement Officers were instructed to record such rights over the forest to ensure the rights of tribes.[14] Yet claim-making, individual or community, was not free of hassles and people did lose the access and rights they had traditionally enjoyed. The Act of 1927 still refers to the rights

[10] Syeda Ambia Zahan, 'Why Meghalaya Struggles to Prevent Illegal Coal Mining Despite Repeated Tragedies' *Firstpost* (15 June 2021) <www.firstpost.com/india/why-meghalaya-struggles-to-prevent-illegal-coal-mining-despite-repeated-tragedies-9714351.html>.

[11] Tiplut Nongbri, 'Timber Ban in North-East India' (2001) 36(21) *Economic & Political Weekly* 1893.

[12] ibid.

[13] Newsfile, Shillong, 'Meghalaya Allowed to Harvest Trees' *Hindustan Times* (30 October 2005) <www.hindustantimes.com/india/meghalaya-allowed-to-harvest-trees/story-62ATb7STicBF6k20E3srML.html>.

[14] Ritambhara Hebbar, *Ecology, Equality and Freedom: The Engagement with Self-Rule in Jharkhand* (Earthworm Book 2011).

and claims of the forest dwellers and the Forest Settlement Officers with a responsibility to record the rights of earlier owners and claimants.[15]

Post-Independence India took note of the protective provisions prevailing under British rule. It, therefore, made special provisions in the Constitution. Accordingly, almost all states in the Fifth Schedule areas enacted laws restricting the alienation of land from tribes to non-tribes. However, these laws have not been able to fully prevent tribal land alienation. As per the information available with the Ministry of Rural Development in January 1999, 465 thousand cases of alienation of tribal land covering an area of 917 thousand acres had been registered in the Fifth Schedule area states.[16] The 2014 Report of the High-Level Committee on Socio-economic and Health Status of Tribal Communities in India states that as per cases filed under state laws for the restoration of alienated land, the annual report of 2007–08 records 506,307 cases of land alienation involving 9,02,417 acres of land.[17]

In addition, there has also been dispossession and displacement of tribes from their land arising from land acquisition by the state for developmental projects such as dams, irrigation, industries, mines, and thermal and hydro power. The benefits of these projects, however, did not go to tribes either in the form of employment or electrification of their homes and villages, or irrigation of their lands. Between 1951 and 1990, a little over 21 million people were estimated to have been displaced by development projects.[18] Of this, over 16 million have been displaced by dams, and about 2.6 and 1.3 million by mines and industries, respectively.[19] A little over one million have been displaced by other projects, wildlife sanctuaries being the most important among them. Of the total displaced, as many as 8.54 million have been enumerated as tribals.[20] Tribals have thus come to constitute as much as 40 per cent of the displaced population though they comprise less than eight per cent of the total population.[21] The issues of dispossession and displacement have become aggravated following the introduction of the New Economic Policy.[22]

[15] Sharad Kulkarni, 'The Forest Policy and Forest Bill: A Critique and Suggestions for Change' in Walter Fernandes and Sharad Kulkarni (eds), *Towards a New Forest Policy: People's Rights and Environmental Needs* (Indian Social Institute 1983) 84–101.

[16] Government of India, Tenth Five Year Plan, 2002–07, ch 4.2 (Scheduled Tribes) (Planning Commission 2001).

[17] Government of India, Report of the High-Level Committee on Socio-economic and Health Status of Tribal Communities in India (Chairman: Prof Virginius Xaxa) (Ministry of Tribal Affairs 2014) 281–282 <https://archive.nyu.edu/bitstream/2451/36746/2/Tribal%20Committee%20Report%2c%20May-June%202014.pdf>.

[18] Government of India, Report of the Steering Committee on Empowering the Scheduled Tribes for the Tenth Five Year Plan (Planning Commission 2001) Annexure XII <https://niti.gov.in/planningcommission.gov.in/docs/aboutus/committee/strgrp/stg_sts.pdf>.

[19] ibid.

[20] ibid.

[21] ibid.

[22] Binay Kumar Pattnaik, 'Tribal Resistance Movements and the Politics of Development-induced Displacement in Contemporary Orissa' (2013) 43(1) *Social Change* 53.

There is no freedom from the colonial framework of forest administration for forest-dwelling communities. Rather, this framework has got further deeply entrenched. Under the colonial state, there was still some leeway for tribes, as implementation of the framework was not as stringent as in post-Independence India. Tribes still enjoyed some access to the forest for food, shelter, and grazing of cattle. That the situation of the tribes worsened after Independence can be inferred from the restrictions added in the New Forest Policy, 1952 which withdrew the concessions concerning the release of the forest for cultivation, free grazing, and weaning away tribals from shifting cultivation, etc.[23] Further, there was an emphasis on increasing the area under forest as well as on stringent regulation, policing, and revenue earning. Yet this policy was directed more towards bringing land under reserved and protected forests than their actual protection and conservation. There was no halt to the diversion of forest land for non-forest purposes.[24] The concern for the environment gained further momentum resulting in legislation such as the Wild Life (Protection) Act, 1972, the Forest (Conservation) Act, 1980, the Environment (Protection) Act, 1986, etc. All these laws had an adverse effect on tribes, as conservation was thought of as absence of tribal people.[25] At the same time, environmental concerns in the form of social forestry in the 1980s and joint forest management in the 1990s had a bearing on the enhancement of forest cover.

The increasing concern for conservation and the environment among citizens and civil society organizations pushed the forest dwellers into a situation they had never been in before. A PIL paved the way for an order of the Supreme Court that led to the eviction of forest dwellers from 1.52 lakh hectares of forest land between May 2002 to March 2004 out of a total of 13.43 hectares of encroached land.[26] This led to the forceful eviction of about three lakh forest-dwelling households and deprivation of their livelihood during this period. Their houses, crops, and food were destroyed; some women were raped, and men shot at and killed.[27]

Paradoxically, such a situation occurred despite constitutional provisions, legal enactments, and policies protecting tribes. Mass eviction could have been avoided if the governors vested with constitutional power to protect tribal interests had acted as per their constitutional responsibility and, the forest department had complied with provisions in the forest-related laws referred to above. Even the Ministry of Environment and Forests (MoEF) had issued several circulars aimed at regularization of the so-called encroachers or resolution of disputed claims.[28] The tribes had to pay a heavy price for

[23] Subhash C Kashyap, *National Policy Studies* (Lok Sabha Secretariat and Tata McGraw-Hill Company 1990).

[24] ibid 328.

[25] ibid 335–336.

[26] CR Bijoy, 'Forest Rights Struggle: The Adivasis Now Await a Settlement' (2008) 51(12) *American Behavioural Scientist*1764.

[27] ibid 1765.

[28] Madhu Sarin, 'Retrieving Ancestral Rights. The Making of the Forest Rights Act' in Meena Radhakrishna (ed), *First Citizens—Studies on Adivasis, Tribals, and Indigenous Peoples in India* (OUP 2016) 278–306.

the indifference and negligence of the forest department. The Scheduled Tribes and Other Traditional Forest Dwellers (Recognition of Forest Rights) Act, 2006 (FRA) is to be located in this context. The Act, a product of the struggle of hundreds of grassroots organizations under a larger coalition of the Committee for Survival and Dignity (CSD), represents a radical departure from a state-controlled and managed system of governance to people/community-centric governance.

The laws listed above were not extendable in the Sixth Schedule areas as per the provisions in the Constitution. Hence, the tribal communities in the Sixth Schedule areas did not have to go through the eviction drive that tribal people in the Fifth Schedule areas had to. This did mean the absence of laws, regulations, and rules concerning environmental governance. The Sixth Schedule areas were governed by specific laws enacted by the autonomous district councils. Thus, the United Khasi and Jaintia Hills Autonomous District Council enacted the Management and Control of Forests Act, 1958. Similarly, the Garo Hills Autonomous District Council enacted laws such as the Garo Hills (*Jhum*) Regulation, 1954, and the Garo Hills District (Forest) Act, 1958.[29] The forest laws in these two autonomous district councils make provision for declaring certain forests as reserved and protected forests after duly settling the rights of the claimants, and classifying forests as per customary practices of ownership, control, and usage. The executive committee manages the reserved, protected, and unclassed forests. Other forests, such as private, clan, joint-clan, or village communities are managed as per the rules framed by the council from time to time. The different owners of forest must comply with rules framed by the council for the general interest of the forestry. To provide for the regulation and control of the practice of *jhum* (shifting cultivation), laws were framed prohibiting *jhum* in a radius of 400 meters of any water sources, 50 meters on either side of the public works department or council's roads, the area covered by Sal and other valuable tree fixings of the *jhum* cycle, precaution against fire, recuperation of soil in *jhum* area by mandating cultivators to grow quick-growing trees in fallow land, promotion of terrace cultivation, etc. At the same time, extensive reliance on resource royalties puts great pressure on Meghalaya's environment. The demand for increased government-sanctioned timber felling bolsters the Autonomous District Council's royalties, but unscrupulous producers and government officials also cooperate to facilitate illegal felling practices.[30]

The implementation of the Forest Rights Act in the Fifth Schedule areas is far from smooth because of hostility to the Act due to the radical rearrangement of governing forest resources in favour of tribal communities from the top to the bottom of the forest governance authority, as well as the colonial governance mindset of some civil society organizations, which envisions conservation without the presence of people in the

[29] Department of Forests and Environment, Government of Meghalaya, Compendium of Acts and Rules of Autonomous District Councils (2019) <www.megforest.gov.in/docs/Compendium_of_Acts_and_Rules_of_Autonomous_District_Councils.pdf>.

[30] David Stuligross, 'Autonomous Councils in Northeast India: Theory and Practice' (1999) 24(4) *Alternatives* 497.

forest. The forest department has been creating obstacles to the implementation of the Act and thereby regularization of claims on various grounds. It is also reluctant to pass on governance to the *Gram Sabha* by creating all kinds of bottlenecks, often violative of the provisions under the Act such as pushing joint forest management, diversion of forests, or creating protective areas zone without settling the rights of the people. The *Gram Sabha* on the other hand has also been not as proactive as it should have been. This is largely due to their inadequate understanding of the provisions of the Act as well as their capacity to translate them into reality. After all, *Gram Sabha* is the key player in the implementation of the Act, and its capacity building both in respect of PESA and FRA will go a long way in democratizing environmental governance.

At the same time even after twenty-five years since the enactment of PESA, its performance has been dismal due to the sheer indifference and even hostility to it at the state level. All Fifth Schedule states have brought requisite amendments to implement PESA. However, the amendments in most states have diluted the provisions in PESA eroding its ethos and spirit. Even otherwise, there are many states which have not even framed rules for implementation of the Act to date. To ensure people-centric governance, all acts and policies, central and state, related to part IX of the Constitution were to be synchronized with the provisions of PESA. Most central acts related to the environment such as the Indian Forest Act, 1927, the Wild Life Protection Act, 1972, the Forest (Conservation) Act, 1980, etc., and rules and regulations related to these were supposed to be harmonized with PESA. In the absence of such harmonization, the self-rule envisaged under PESA has failed to usher in the expected far-reaching turnaround in what was seen as governance deficit and misgovernance in the scheduled areas. The reasons why PESA failed to deliver include lack of clarity, legal infirmity, bureaucratic apathy, lack of political will, and resistance to change in the power hierarchy.[31]

Notwithstanding such limitations, the *Gram Sabha* has exercised the power provided in PESA for securing land, forest, and religious and cultural systems with varying levels of success. One of the most successful stories has been Vedanta's mining project in the Niyamgiri hill in Kalahandi, State of Odisha. The project having got legally entangled reached the Supreme Court.[32] The judgment of the Supreme Court placed the project before the *Gram Sabha* which rejected it outright.[33] However, Niyamgiri's success is more of an exception than the rule. Many more such projects have come up in the Fifth Schedule states after the *Vedanta* case. Yet success has been rare despite resistance. Lands are being acquired even without consultation with the *Gram Sabha*. Even where there has been consultation and the *Gram Sabha* did not give consent, the state has continued with the project. The only alternative left is to go for litigation which the *Gram Sabh*a is ill-equipped for considering various factors, including resources to fight cases in the court. Given the fact that many states (Jharkhand, Odisha, Chhattisgarh,

[31] CR Bijoy, 'Taking Stock of Forest Rights Act' (2010) *Planet Earth* 15 <www.academia.edu/6171865/Taking_Stock_of_Forest_Rights_Act>.

[32] Xaxa (n 8)192.

[33] ibid 191.

and Madhya Pradesh) have not even framed rules under PESA, the legality of any decision taken by the *Gram Sabha* is shrouded in doubt. In case of projects that need environmental clearance through a public hearing, the concerned company in collaboration with the state authority manipulates the public hearing, and decisions are manufactured in favour of the project.

Environmental problems caused by infrastructure and development projects such as dams and irrigation, roads, mineral exploitation, and industries that have grown manifold in the scheduled areas have not been adequately addressed. These activities have not only led to ecological instability, environmental degradation, and loss of biodiversity but also pollution of air, water, and soil through smoke and dust. Rivers and streams, besides getting dried up because of mineral and industrial activities, are also getting affected by effluents flowing from the industries. Smoke, particles, and wastes (solid and liquid) flowing from these projects have also polluted lands and fields with crops. These have also affected the health of people living in these areas who have been now exposed to many health problems. At the same time, large-scale use of fossil fuels in production and transportation have added to greenhouse gas emissions. All these factors have contributed to climate change. The next section examines how these issues have been dealt with in recent times.

6.5 The Potential of the Existing Regime

India adopted the neoliberal regime with the announcement of the New Economic Policy in 1991. With this, the role of the private sector in the shaping of the economy has assumed a key role. Laws, rules, regulations, and policies were liberalized in a direction favourably disposed to the demand of the market. All these developments created the space for the entry of domestic and global private capital. This section attempts to assess the potential of the existing regime in addressing the issue of environmental governance in the scheduled areas.

The potential of the current regime to handle concerns and challenges is relatively weak. This is largely to do with the nature and type of development it is pursuing. A large proportion of people in India still live in poverty, with low level of literacy, poor health infrastructure, and health status. However, the thrust of the regime is not so much on development with a focus on equity but growth with the hope that higher growth will spill over and lead to the development of the people at large. Enhancing growth has been the key state agenda since 1991, irrespective of the government in power. Yet there has been a difference between the governments before and after 2014. The former had been cautious and slow in pursuing the agenda of reform and hence had come under severe attack from those championing greater reform. Alongside, they were concerned with the rights and participation of the people including tribes. This is evident from measures like the Mahatma Gandhi National Rural Employment Guarantee Act (MGNREGA), 2005, the Right to Information Act, 2005, the Forest Rights Act, 2006, the Right to Fair Compensation and Transparency in Land Acquisition, Rehabilitation and Resettlement Act, 2013 (LARR Act), and many such people/public-oriented acts. Some such measures of notable importance in the context of the Fifth Schedule areas are the FRA, the LARR Act as well as various kinds of rules and provisions, for example, for environmental impact assessment (EIA), social impact assessment (SIA), etc., which acted as safety nets over the acquisition of land for various kinds of projects. Such measures restrained unscrupulous moves to acquire land and divert forests for mines and infrastructure projects with devasting consequences on tribes as well as the environment in the Fifth Schedule areas.

The current regime has been attempting to do away with many of the provisions in the acts referred to above to facilitate ease of doing business. An attempt was made to amend the LARR Act through ordinance and later through a bill introduced in Parliament in 2015. Out of the total fifteen amendments in the bill, nine were substantial in nature to enable the government to exempt five categories of projects (defence, rural infrastructure, affordable housing, industrial corridors, infrastructure) from the requirements of SIA, restrictions on the acquisition of multi-cropped land, and consent for private projects and public-private partnerships. The government had to drop most of its contentious amendments to the LARR Act, bringing back crucial clauses related to the consent of affected families and SIA following sustained opposition pressure.[34] Following such an attempt at amendment at the Centre, the Fifth Schedule states with BJP as the political party in power such as the State of Jharkhand brought an ordinance and later a bill to amend the pro-tribal land tenancy acts such the Chhotanagpur and Santhal Pargana Tenancy Act, 1908. The Bill was passed but did not receive assent from the governor following massive resistance from tribal communities in Jharkhand.

Since the enactment of the LARR Act, all development projects need to go through the EIA process for environmental clearance. The projects are assessed based on their potential environmental impact and based on these assessments, they are granted or denied clearance. However, the present regime introduced a new draft EIA Notification in 2020 replacing the EIA Notification, 1994 and its 2006 amendments to reduce public participation in all the steps of the environment clearance process 'by lessening the notice period for public hearings and doing away with them for a large category of projects'. The two most significant changes in the new draft EIA Notification are provisions for post-facto clearance of projects and abandoning the public trust doctrine, which adversely impact tribal communities. The new draft significantly diminishes the scope of the EIA and fundamentally diminishes the process, by reclassifying industries that do not require an environmental clearance, limiting public engagement, and normalizing environmental violations. Environmental activists see it as a regressive approach and

34 Pradeep Kaushal and Ruhi Tewari, 'Land Bill: Modi Govt Gives in, Agrees to Bring Back UPA's Key Provisions' *The Indian Express* (4 August 2015) <https://indianexpress.com/article/india/india-others/bjp-takes-u-turn-on-land-bill-agrees-to-bring-back-upas-key-provisions/>.

departure from the existing 2006 version of the EIA Notification, that fosters non-transparency and encourages environmental violations.[35]

Further, the government enacted the Coal Mines (Special Provisions) Act, 2015 removing end-use restrictions meaning the use of the product only for select purposes such as cement, iron, and steel production, etc., and not for trade. In March 2020, the government passed the Mineral Laws (Amendment) Act with the aim to promote ease of doing business by removing restrictions and other measures. The 2019 CAG report on the mining activities of Coal India Limited reveals that many environmental norms were being flouted.[36] In 2009–10, the MoEF classified coal blocks into 'go' and 'no-go' areas in five states, based on forest cover. 'No-go' areas are those with biodiversity and should not be considered for mining. Out of 602 blocks in total, 153 were classified as 'no-go' areas. However, several blocks in the 'no-go' areas were opened for auction by the Mineral Laws (Amendment) Act, 2020.[37]

6.6 Perspectives for Addressing Existing and Emerging Concerns

Environmental concerns in the scheduled areas are varied. Until the advent of colonial rule and administration, environmental governance was with the people. The colonial government took it away from them and vested it in itself on the ground of protecting the environment through scientific management. It viewed people-centric governance as destructive of the environment. Yet environmental destruction did not stop under colonial rule. India after Independence has continued with the same perspective and environmental destruction has not come to a halt. The result has been massive environmental and ecological disturbance with a bearing on people's lives. At the same time, the key factor underlying this destruction has been the exploitation of resources for the development of the people. The perspective of conservation as envisaged so far has not worked. This entails rethinking an alternate perspective of environmental governance.

The discussion of environmental governance in the Fifth and Sixth Schedule areas points to the far better socio-economic status of people as well as the environment in the Sixth Schedule areas in comparison to the Fifth Schedule areas. This points to some merit in the institutional arrangement and regulatory mechanism at work in Sixth

[35] Bismee Taskin, 'What Modi Govt's EIA Draft Says and Why Environment Experts Think It'll Encourage Violations' *The Print* (New Delhi, 29 July 2020) <https://theprint.in/theprint-essential/what-modi-govts-eia-draft-says-why-environment-experts-think-itll-encourage-violations/470248/>.

[36] Ministry of Coal, Report of the Comptroller and Auditor General of India on Assessment of Environmental Impact due to Mining Activities and its Mitigation in Coal India Limited and its Subsidiaries for the year ended March 2018, No 12 of 2019 (2019).

[37] Pavithra KM, 'Government Auctions 41 Coal Blocks—What It Means?' *Factly.in* (26 June 2020) <https://factly.in/government-auctions-41-coal-blocks-what-it-means/>.

Schedule areas. This is not to deny the ecological and environmental damage caused in the Sixth Schedule areas especially due to opencast coal mining and timber business by the political and business elite of the society as well as violation of labour standards in the concerned enterprises.[38] Yet in comparison to environmental degradation and forest depletion plus the poor development status of the people in the Fifth Schedule areas, the Sixth Schedule areas experience miniscule environmental problems.

The positive features of the Sixth Schedule areas include the creation of an Autonomous District Council (ADC) which provides space not only for self-governance but also governance in terms of customary law and the traditional system of management. An important aspect of the Sixth Schedule provisions is that the ADC is protected from the encroachment of law enacted by Parliament and state legislatures on specific subjects. However, the ADC is not protected from the power of the state to acquire land for public purposes and hence the ADC is required to frame laws over issues arising from land acquisition as there is an absence of laws related to rehabilitation and compensation. The judicial powers of the ADC relate to the constitution of district and village courts for the trial of cases between parties belonging to scheduled tribes. At the same time, the provision of appeal and access to the higher judicial institutions of the state has been made. The executive power authorizes the ADC to establish and manage primary schools, dispensaries, markets, fisheries roads, road transport, and waterways; assess and collect land revenue and impose taxes; issue licenses or leases for purpose of prospecting or extraction of minerals; and make regulations for control of money-lending and trading by non-tribals.[39] At the same time, its ability to raise revenue to run the administration and execute development works is weak and remains dependent on the state for financial support which has remained an obstacle to the effective functioning of the ADC. An institutional correction is needed on this issue.

The Sixth Schedule provisions have merit but there are also problems and hence the Fifth Schedule needs to evolve governance that takes the best of the provisions inherent in the Sixth Schedule but addresses the issues that plague it, especially financial constraints. Unlike the Sixth Schedule areas where the district or territory or region is the unit, the unit of governance in the Fifth Schedule areas is the village assembly, the traditional institution of governance under PESA. However, the *Gram Sabha* remains unprotected from the onslaught of laws and policies enacted by Parliament and state legislatures as is the case in the Sixth Schedule areas. In the existing arrangement, this power is vested in the office of the governor, but governors throughout India have failed to discharge this constitutional responsibility. In fact, even today, one of the reasons why the *Gram Sabha* is ineffective is that laws and policies related to subjects under PESA have not been harmonized with the provisions of PESA. This makes space for an institutional arrangement that shifts power from the government department to the *Gram Sabha*. The Sixth Schedule areas pattern referred to in PESA without interfering or

[38] Human Rights Now, 'Report on Child Labour in the Mines of Meghalaya' (Human Rights Now 2011).

[39] The Constitution of India 1950 Art 244(2).

compromising the power of the *Gram Sabha* may be one of the ways out. Unless such arrangements are made, the *Gram Sabha* would not be able to function as an effective unit of governance. Conversely, in the Sixth Schedule areas, there is a need for the village to be formally recognized as the unit of governance and vested with the power conferred on villages under the Fifth Schedule of the Constitution. In other words, governance must move in the direction of legal pluralism and recognize customary law and tradition with some tinkering to address the problem of equity inherent in the traditional social structure.

Conclusion

Until the onset of colonial rule, tribal communities living in distant and inaccessible territory enjoyed autonomy and self-governance. Colonial rule led to colonialists' sovereignty over the territory. Yet the colonial rulers were constrained to extend some autonomy to tribal communities for administrative convenience and strategic reasons. Yet the actual functioning varied from region to region depending on the imperatives of control over natural resources for economic and commercial interests. The latter led to the extension of roads, railways, and other means of communication, opening the territory thereby for settlement of people from outside the territory. Such a development eventually led to the idea of excluded and partially excluded areas and later paved the way for the Fifth Schedule areas and the Sixth Schedule areas under the Constitution.

The nature and type of environmental governance, which was similar in the two areas, moved along different trajectories under colonial rule but became entrenched in independent India. The Fifth and Sixth Schedules of the Constitution represent two distinct paradigms of development for tribal people in India with diametrically opposite consequences both in respect of development and environmental governance. The Sixth Schedule represents self-determined governance and development, and the Fifth Schedule is marked by its absence. There was no superimposition of laws relating to natural resources such as land and forest enacted by Parliament or state legislatures in the Sixth Schedule areas. This was not the case in the Fifth Schedule areas. Rather, the executives of states in the Fifth Schedule areas were vested with the power not to extend those laws or to extend them with modifications, which they never exercised. Many of such laws were antithetical to protective provisions in the Constitution. The people in the Sixth Schedule areas framed their own laws and regulations as well as they themselves carried out the executive functions. In the Fifth Schedule areas, even the executive functions were carried out by officials who hardly belonged to tribal communities.

The outcomes of the two schedules have been striking. Dispossession and displacement have been negligible in the Sixth Schedule areas and development indicators such as people living below the poverty line and with poor educational and health status are much lower as compared to the Fifth Schedule areas. Development indicators in the Fifth Schedule areas in contrast have been poor. Loss of control over land and forest due to the extension of laws adverse to tribal interests and absence of self-governance are the key underlying factors of such poor development status.

Suggestions for Further Reading

Varsha Bhagat-Ganguly and Sujit Kumar (eds), *India's Scheduled Areas: Untangling Governance, Law and Politics* (Routledge 2019).

CR Bijoy, 'Forest Rights Struggle: The Making of the Law and the Decade After' (2017) 13(2) *Law, Environment and Development Journal* 73.

Apoorv Kurup, 'Tribal Law in India: How Decentralized Administration is Extinguishing Tribal Rights and Why Autonomous Tribal Governments are Better' (2008) 7(1) *Indigenous Law Journal* 87.

Ministry of Tribal Affairs and UNDP, 'Land and Governance under the 5th Schedule: An Overview of the Law' (2015).

David Stuligross, 'Autonomous Councils in Northeast India: Theory and Practice' (1999) 24(4) *Alternatives* 497.

CHAPTER 7

BILATERAL INVESTMENT TREATIES AND THE ENVIRONMENT

PRABHASH RANJAN

Abstract

Several investor-state dispute settlement (ISDS) cases demonstrate that the goal of investment protection and the state's right to adopt environment-related regulatory measures might come face to face. Given this global backdrop, this chapter studies India's bilateral investment treaties (BITs) and investment chapters in free trade agreements to find out whether they contain provisions that allow the host state to adopt measures for the protection of the environment. Most BITs signed by India during the period 1994 to 2010 contained very few provisions for the protection of the environment. India's new treaty practice heralded by the adoption of the Model BIT in 2016 has changed this pattern.

Introduction

Bilateral investment treaties (BITs) are treaties concluded for the reciprocal protection and promotion of foreign investment in the territories of the signatory countries. From 1994 to 2010, India signed more than eighty BITs to attract greater levels of foreign investment. However, from 2011 onward, India's approach towards BITs changed due to foreign investors bringing numerous claims against India before investor-state dispute settlement (ISDS) tribunals.[1] Consequently, India unilaterally terminated most of its BITs, though due to survival clauses these BITs will remain applicable for fifteen years for the foreign investment that came in before the unilateral termination. India adopted a guarded approach towards BITs with the ostensible objective of attempting to reconcile the objective of investment protection, on the one hand, and pursuit of other objectives such as protection of the environment, on the other.

India's guarded approach towards BITs is an outcome of not just the ISDS claims brought against India but also of foreign investors, globally, employing the ISDS mechanism in BITs, to challenge a wide array of sovereign regulatory measures including environment-related regulatory measures.[2] According to a recent study, from 1990 to 2015, there have been a mammoth 146 ISDS cases where foreign investors have challenged environment-related regulatory measures.[3] These cases have involved prohibitions on chemicals or products for environmental reasons;[4] imposition of environmental pollution charges and penalties on foreign investors;[5] denial of permits to run waste landfills;[6] and recently, numerous claims brought against Spain's renewable energy programme.[7] The central concern in all these disputes has been whether the environmental measures adopted domestically by countries conflict with that country's BIT obligations or not. The answer to this question often depends on whether BITs provide adequate policy space to host states to enact domestic environmental measures. In this regard, apprehensions have been expressed about whether the existing BITs and investment chapters in India's free trade agreements (FTAs) adequately safeguard India's right to regulate in the public interest, including the environment. Since a recent study points out that there is a positive relationship between foreign direct investment (FDI) inflows to India and carbon or CO_2 emissions,[8] India should be alert to the fact that it may have to enact domestic regulatory measures to counter the adverse impact of

[1] Prabhash Ranjan, *India and Bilateral Investment Treaties: Refusal, Acceptance, Backlash* (OUP 2019).

[2] For a discussion on BITs and environment, see Kathryn Gordon and Joachim Pohl, Environmental Concerns in International Investment Agreements: A Survey (OECD Working Papers on International Investment 2011/01) <http://dx.doi.org/10.1787/5kg9mq7scrjh-en>. See also Kyla Tienhaara, 'Regulatory Chill in a Warming World: The Threat to Climate Policy Posed by Investor-State Dispute Settlement' (2018) 7(2) *Transnational Environmental Law* 229.

[3] Tarald Laudal Berge and Axel Berger, 'Do Investor-State Dispute Settlement Cases Influence Domestic Environmental Regulation? The Role of Respondent State Bureaucratic Capacity' (2021) 12(1) *Journal of International Dispute Settlement* 1.

[4] *Ethyl Corporation v The Government of Canada* (1998) UNCITRAL, Award on Jurisdiction (1999) 38 ILM 708; *Methanex Corporation v United States of America* (2005) UNCITRAL, Final Award of the Tribunal on Jurisdiction and Merits (2005) 44 ILM 1345.

[5] *Campos de Pesé, SA v Republic of Panama* (2020) ICSID Case No ARB/20/19.

[6] *Tecnicas Medioambientales Tecmed SA v United Mexican States* (2003)] ICSID Case No ARB(AF)/00/2.

[7] Isabella Reynoso, 'Spain's Renewable Energy Saga: Lessons for International Investment Law and Sustainable Development (IISD 2019) <https://www.iisd.org/itn/en/2019/06/27/spains-renewable-energy-saga-lessons-for-international-investment-law-and-sustainable-development-isabella-reynoso/>.

[8] Tripura Sundari CU and Anindita Mitra, 'Development and Degradation: The Nexus between GDP, FDI, and Pollution in India' (2020) 6(1) *Emerging Economy Studies* 39.

foreign investment on the environment. Therefore, it is important to prudently study India's BITs along with the new ones that have been signed from the point of view of understanding to what extent they preserve India's policy space to adopt environmental measures domestically.

In order to achieve the objective, this chapter surveys India's BITs and investment chapters in FTAs by dividing them into two time periods. Section 7.1 discusses those BITs and FTA investment chapters that India signed from 1994 (the year of signing the first BIT with the United Kingdom) until 2015. Section 7.2 studies the 2016 Model BIT and the subsequent BITs that India has signed. Finally, the conclusion observes that it is one thing for BITs to provide ample regulatory space and another for India to make use of this regulatory space in enacting domestic environmental measures.

7.1 Indian BITs and FTA Investment Chapters: 1994 to 2015

Most BITs signed by India during this period do not contain environmental provisions (EP). Only a handful of BITs recognize the state's right to regulate in the interest of environment. Following the methodology of Manjiao Chi who has empirically studied the presence of EPs in Chinese BITs,[9] this chapter divides the EPs in Indian BITs and FTA investment chapter into three categories: EPs as part of the general exceptions clause; and EPs as part of substantive obligations; and a residual category of EPs being part of other treaty provisions.[10]

7.1.1 Environmental Provisions as Part of the General Exceptions Clause

Some BITs contain a general exceptions clause, also known as the non-precluded measures (NPM) provision. The general exception clause allows host states to adopt measures for the protection of certain public policy concerns that may otherwise constitute a violation of the treaty. The general exception provision bestows regulatory latitude to countries to deviate from the substantive obligations in circumstances that warrant giving preference to compelling non-investment policy goals over investment

[9] Manjiao Chi, 'The "Greenization" of Chinese Bits: An Empirical Study of the Environmental Provisions in Chinese Bits and its Implications for China's Future Bit-Making' (2015) 18(3) *Journal of International Economic Law* 511.

[10] See also Pushkar Anand who follows more or less the same approach for South Asian BITs. See Pushkar Anand, 'Environmental Regulation and International Investment Law in South Asia' in Marc Bungenberg and others (eds), *Asian Yearbook of International Economic Law 2023* (Springer forthcoming 2024).

protection. The general exception clauses should not be confused with those clauses in BITs that constitute an exception to a particular substantive obligation (for instance, environment-related exceptions to expropriation provisions discussed later in the chapter).

The chapter divides the general exception clauses into two types—general exception clauses that are modelled on the basis of Article XX of General Agreement on Tariffs and Trade (GATT) and general exception clauses that are not based on GATT Article XX.

General exception clauses based on Article XX of GATT: Article XX of GATT exempts certain classes of regulatory measures from the strictures of GATT.[11] The important attributes of a general exception clause like Article XX are that it contains a list of permissible objectives, provides a nexus requirement and contains a *chapeau*. Permissible objectives are those objectives for which the World Trade Organization (WTO) member countries can digress from its GATT obligations. They include public policy areas that form the core of governmental functions of the state such as safeguarding the environment. The nexus requirement is the causal link between the adopted measures and the permissible objective to be achieved through that measure. Stricter the nexus requirement, greater will be the scrutiny of the measure adopted to achieve the avowed objective. A very good example of a stringent nexus requirement is 'necessary'. The *chapeau* (preambular paragraph) is an important component of Article XX. Once a regulatory measure falls under one of the exceptions listed in Article XX, it then has to satisfy the requirement given in the *chapeau*.[12] In other words, the regulatory measure should be such that it is 'not applied in a manner which would constitute a means of arbitrary or unjustifiable discrimination between countries where the same conditions prevail, or a disguised restriction on international trade'.[13] The *chapeau* ensures that states do not adopt regulatory measures to pursue compelling non-trade objectives in an abusive or discriminatory manner.[14]

A typical example of such a general exceptions clause in Indian BITs, modelled on Article XX of GATT, is Article 13.5 of the India-Colombia BIT:[15]

> Subject to the requirement that such measures are not applied in a manner which would constitute a means of arbitrary or unjustifiable discrimination against the investors of the other Contracting Party or a disguised restriction on investment of investors of a Contracting Party in the territory of the other Contracting Party, nothing in this Agreement shall be construed to prevent the adoption or enforcement by a Contracting Party of measures:

[11] Michael Trebilcock, Robert Howse, and Antonia Eliason, *The Regulation of International Trade* (Routledge 2013) 664.

[12] ibid.

[13] ibid.

[14] United States—Standards for Reformulated and Conventional Gasoline, Report of the Appellate Body, 29 April 1996, Doc WT/DS2/AB/R.

[15] Agreement for the Promotion and Protection of Investments Between the Republic of Colombia and the Republic of India, New Delhi, 10 November 2009 ('India-Colombia BIT').

a. necessary to maintain public order;
b. necessary to protect human, animal, plant life or health;
c. relating to the protection of the environment or the conservation of exhaustible natural resources, if such measures are made effective in conjunction with restrictions on domestic production or consumption;
d. in pursuance of its obligations under the United Nations Charter for the maintenance of international peace and security.

Article 13.5 of the India-Colombia BIT, like Article XX of GATT, contains a list of permissible objectives, encompasses nexus requirements such as 'necessary' and 'relating to', and a *chapeau* to ensure that regulatory measures are not misused.[16] Article 13.5 recognizes the right of the host state, subject to the conditions given in the *chapeau*, to deviate from investment treaty obligations to adopt measures that are necessary or relating to certain compelling public policy objectives. In this regard, Article 13.5(c) specifically allows the host state to adopt measures 'relating to the protection of the environment or the conservation of exhaustible natural resources'. A similar general exception clause, modelled on Article XX of GATT, is also present in Article 10.18 of the India-Korea FTA's investment chapter. Article 10.18(1)(b) of the India-Korea FTA's investment chapter provides that subject to the chapeau requirement, the host state can adopt measures, in derogation from the investment treaty provisions, that are 'necessary to protect' the 'environment'. Additionally, Article 10.18(1)(e) of the same treaty allows the host state to adopt measures necessary for the conservation of exhaustible natural resources.

General exception clauses modelled on the basis of Article XX of GATT are also present in Article 6.11 of the India-Singapore FTA's investment chapter and Article 21 of the India-ASEAN Investment agreement. However, these two general exception clauses, unlike the India-Colombia BIT and the India-Korea FTA investment chapter, do not mention 'environment' as one of the permissible objectives. The general exception clause in these two treaties only talks of the conservation of exhaustible natural resources. For instance, Article 21(1)(e) of the India-ASEAN investment agreement provides that the state can deviate from its treaty obligations, subject to the requirements given in the *chapeau* (same as Article 13.5 of the India-Colombia BIT), and adopt regulatory measures 'relating to the conservation of exhaustible natural resources'. Only those environmental regulatory measures that are aimed at safeguarding exhaustible natural resources would fall within the ambit of the general exception clause. Consequently, the scope of the general exception clause from the point of view of addressing environmental concerns is much narrower.

The investment chapter (Article 11(2)) in the India-Japan FTA incorporates the general exceptions clause given in Article XIV of the General Agreement on Trade in

[16] See also Amelia Keene, 'The Incorporation and Interpretation of WTO-Style Environmental Exceptions in International Investment Agreements' (2017) 18(1) *The Journal of World Investment & Trade* 62.

Services (GATS) *mutatis mutandis*. Interestingly, the general exception clause in GATS, unlike the one in GATT, does not mention the conservation of 'exhaustible natural resource' as a permissible objective. Accordingly, the investment chapter of the India-Japan FTA also does not contain any permissible objective about the environment.

General exception clauses that are not based on Article XX of GATT: some Indian BITs contain a general exception clause narrower in scope in terms of the regulatory objectives for which derogation from the treaty is permissible. For example, Article 12 of the India-France BIT provides:

> The provision of this Agreement shall not in any way limit the right of either Contracting Party in cases of extreme emergency to take action in accordance with its laws applied in good faith, on a non-discriminatory basis, and only to the extent and duration necessary for the protection of its essential security interests, or for the prevention of diseases and pests in animals or plants.

A similarly worded general exception clause is also present in some other Indian BITs.[17] Although it allows the host state to adopt measures for certain permissible objectives even if they derogate from the treaty, its design and architecture are not the same as Article XX of GATT. It encompasses very few permissible objectives and, most importantly, does not contain a *chapeau*. For this chapter, this general exception clause does not mention the environment as a permissible objective. It refers to the environment obliquely by talking about 'prevention of diseases and pests in plants'. Thus, the scope of this general exception clause is heavily circumscribed. There is no mention of 'environment' or even 'exhaustible natural resource' as a permissible objective. India can resort to this general exception only in a situation of extreme emergency and that too only to prevent the spread of diseases in plants. This general exception clause would be of no avail for addressing other environmental concerns such as rising pollution levels or ensuring that all investors carry out an environmental impact assessment, etc.

In sum, EPs do not figure prominently in the general exception clauses of Indian BITs. Only India-Colombia BIT and the investment chapter in India-Korea FTA specifically recognize the goal of environmental protection. If India adopts domestic environmental measures such as cancelling permits or licenses given to foreign investors to counter any adverse impact their activities might have on the environment, India can rely on the general exception clauses to defend its actions. India should learn from the mistakes of countries such as Venezuela[18] and Costa

[17] E.g., Agreement between the Republic of India and the Czech Republic for the Promotion and Protection of Investments (signed 11 October 1996, entered into force 6 February 1998), Art 12; Agreement between the Republic of India and the Republic of France on the Reciprocal Promotion and Protection of Investments (signed 2 September 1997, entered into force 15 May 2000), Art 12 and Agreement between the Government of the Republic of India and the Government of the Republic of Mauritius for the Promotion and Protection of Investments (signed 4 September 1998, entered into force 20 June 2000), Art 11.3.

[18] *Crystallex International Corporation v Bolivarian Republic of Venezuela*, Award, ICSID Case No ARB(AF)/11/2, 4 April 2016; *Rusoro Mining Ltd v Bolivarian Republic of Venezuela* (2016) ICSID Case No

Rica[19] that failed to invoke the general exception clauses to guard their domestic environmental measures when foreign investors brought ISDS claims against these countries.[20]

But what happens in those BITs that do not contain any EP? This is a relevant question because the number of Indian BITs without EPs in any form is quite high. In such BIT, India will be able to defend its domestic environment-related regulatory measures by relying on the police powers doctrine, which was articulated in a case involving domestic environmental measures, *Methanex Corporation v USA*,[21] as follows:

> As a matter of general international law, a non-discriminatory regulation for a public purpose, which is enacted in accordance with due process and, which affects, inter alios, a foreign investor or investment is not deemed expropriatory and compensable unless specific commitments had been given by the regulating government to the then putative foreign investor contemplating investment that the government would refrain from such regulation.[22]

Recently, an ISDS tribunal in a case known as *Eco Oro Minerals Corp. v Republic of Colombia* allowed Colombia to safeguard its environment-related regulatory measures directed at preserving what are known as 'páramo ecosystems', (these are defined as 'high-mountain ecosystems that play a central role in maintaining biodiversity, premised on a unique capacity to absorb and restore water') under the police powers doctrine.[23]

7.1.2 Environmental Provisions as Part of Specific Exceptions

As against the general exceptions clauses, BITs also contain exceptions to specific provisions. These provisions provide latitude to countries to enact regulatory measures that may deviate from a specific substantive provision. A survey of Indian BITs shows that exceptions about the environment exist for the following specific substantive obligations: expropriation, national treatment, and performance requirement (PR).

ARB(AF)/12/5 IIC 850 (2016); *Gold Reserve Inc v Bolivarian Republic of Venezuela* (2014) ICSID Case No ARB(AF)/09/1 (2016) EWHC 153 (Comm).

[19] *Infinito Gold Ltd. v Republic of Costa Rica* (2021)] ICSID Case No ARB/14/5, 3 June 2021.

[20] E.g., Wolfgang Alschner and Kun Hui, 'Missing in Action: General Public Policy Exceptions in Investment Treaties' in Lisa Sachs, Jesse Coleman, and Lise Johnson (eds), *Yearbook on International Investment Law and Policy* (OUP 2019) 363.

[21] *Methanex Corporation v United States* UNICTRAL, Final Award of the Tribunal on Jurisdiction and Merits, 3 August 2005.

[22] ibid, para 7, Part IV, ch D, p 4.

[23] *Eco Oro Minerals Corp v Republic of Colombia* ICSID Case No ARB/16/41.

Expropriation: instances of direct expropriations—'taking' coming through the state actions thereby depriving investors of the legal title[24]—have become rare.[25] Given the complexities of modern states that involve adopting several regulations to regulate various spheres of life, instances of indirect interference with investors' property rights or indirect expropriation have assumed significance. Indirect expropriation implies denial of the substantial benefits flowing from the investment without a formal 'taking' of the property.[26] In other words, when a regulatory measure leads to substantial deprivation of foreign investment, it amounts to indirect expropriation. However, it is not easy to draw a line between legitimate state regulation and indirect expropriation.

It is in this context that we need to study the exception provision for indirect expropriation found in some Indian BITs. For example, clause 3 of the side letter on the interpretation of expropriation in Article 5 of the India-Iceland BIT provides as follows:

> Except in rare circumstances, non-discriminatory regulatory actions by a Contracting Party that are designed and applied to protect legitimate public welfare objectives including health, safety and the environmental concerns do not constitute indirect expropriation or nationalisation.[27]

A similar provision is also present in a few other Indian BITs.[28] Thus, this provision carves out certain regulatory measures from the ambit of expropriation, including domestic environmental measures 'except in rare circumstances' notwithstanding substantial deprivation of foreign investment. Such a provision may be effective to safeguard environmental concerns. For instance, let us assume that a foreign investor challenges before an ISDS tribunal India's regulatory measure directing the closure of certain foreign-owned polluting firms in the interest of environmental protection acting under the Air (Prevention and Control of Pollution) Act, 1981. To fight such a challenge, India can rely on this exception as a tangible defence to protect its environmental regulation from indictment by the ISDS tribunal.

[24] JW Salacuse, *The Law of Investment Treaties* (2nd edn, OUP 2015) 322

[25] Rudolf Dolzer, Ursula Kriebaum, and Christoph Schreuer, *Principles of International Investment Law* (3rd edn, OUP 2022) 101.

[26] ibid, 92.

[27] Agreement Between the Government of the Republic of India and the Government of the Republic of Iceland for the Promotion and Protection of Investments (signed 29 June 2007, entered into force 16 December 2008), Art 5.

[28] E.g., Agreement between the Government of the Republic of India and the Government of His Majesty the Sultan and Yang Di-Pertuan of Brunei Darussalam on the Reciprocal Promotion and Protection of Investments (signed 22 May 2008, entered into force 15 February 2009), cl (d) of Protocol to Art 5 (India-Brunei BIT); Comprehensive Economic Partnership Agreement between Japan and the Republic of India (16 February 2011, entered into force 1 August 2011) [India-Japan FTA], annex 10; Comprehensive Economic Cooperation Agreement between the Government of Malaysia and the Government of the Republic of India (18 February 2011, entered into force 1 July 2011) (India-Malaysia FTA), annex 10–1.

An important element in the interpretation of these clauses is the meaning of the words 'except in rare circumstances'. Very few Indian BITs that contain this environmental exception provide the meaning of the words, 'except in rare circumstances'. For instance, the India-Brunei BIT states that 'except in rare circumstances' implies that 'measures are so severe in light of their purpose that they cannot be reasonably viewed as having been adopted and applied in good faith'.[29] Another example is of the investment chapter of the India-Korea FTA where Annex 10A.3(b) states that 'except in rare circumstances' implies 'when measures are extremely severe or disproportionate in light of its purpose and effect'.

The language in both these treaty provisions signifies that to decide whether the measure falls in the category of 'except in rare circumstances', one will have to compare the regulatory measure adopted by India to achieve an environmental objective with the benefit that is expected to flow from it. In other words, if the measure's impact were too severe or disproportionate keeping in mind the purpose behind the measure, the measure will not qualify having been taken in 'rare circumstances'. Consequently, to judge whether the regulatory measure falls under the category of 'rare circumstances', an ISDS tribunal might have to undertake some sort of proportionality review. Arguably, the same meaning can be given to the words, 'except in rare circumstances' in those BITs that do not define these words.

In one of the BITs, the India-ASEAN investment agreement, the exception to indirect expropriation is not prefaced with the words, 'except in rare circumstances'. Article 8.9 of the India-ASEAN investment agreement provides:

> Non-discriminatory regulatory measures by a Party or measures and awards by judicial bodies of a Party that are designed and applied in pursuit of public policy to achieve legitimate public interest or public welfare objectives, such as the protection of public health, safety, and the environment, do not constitute expropriation of the type referred to in subparagraph 2(b) [indirect expropriation] of this Article.[30]

Thus, a host state adopting domestic measures for the protection of the environment shall not constitute indirect expropriation provided the measures are non-discriminatory.

One interesting variation in the formulation exists in the investment chapter of the India-Japan FTA,[31] which does not carve out domestic environmental measures from the scope of the expropriation provision. It, however, provides that 'objectives of the government action, including whether such action is taken for legitimate public objectives such as . . . protecting and preserving the environment' shall be taken into consideration

[29] India-Brunei BIT (n 28) Art 5.

[30] Agreement on Investment under the Framework Agreement on Comprehensive Economic Cooperation between the Association of Southeast Asian Nations and the Republic of India, (12 November 2014, yet to come into force) (India-ASEAN investment agreement), Art 8.9

[31] India-Japan FTA (n 28) ch 8.

while deciding in a fact-based inquiry that whether a given action or series of actions amounts of indirect expropriation.[32] Thus the regulatory measure adopted for environmental protection is a factor to mitigate the determination of indirect expropriation, not an exception to indirect expropriation. In other words, if India's domestic environmental measure is challenged as expropriation, the ISDS tribunal, in the India-Japan FTA, will take into account the concerned environmental measure while determining indirect expropriation. In those BITs, that do not carve out domestic environmental measures from the ambit of expropriation, India will have the regulatory space to enact domestic environmental measures that may adversely affect foreign investment provided they do not lead to their substantial deprivation.

Performance requirement: in addition to the expropriation provision, two Indian BITs—India-Kuwait and India-UAE—contain an environmental exception for imposing PR.[33] PR is a condition imposed on foreign investment by the host state to influence their behaviour and derive certain benefits such as mandating the foreign investor to export a fixed part of her production. Article 4.4 of the India-Kuwait BIT provides:

> Once established investment shall not be subjected in the host Contracting State to additional performance requirements which may hinder or restrict their expansion or maintenance or adversely affect or be considered as detrimental to their viability unless such requirements are deemed vital for reasons of public order, public health or environmental concerns and are enforced by law of general application.[34]

This provision prohibits the imposition of PRs on foreign investment barring those requirements that are deemed significant for certain reasons such as environmental concerns. For instance, if India wishes to impose a PR of conducting an environmental impact assessment (EIA) for environmental reasons on a Kuwaiti investment, it will be able to do so relying upon Article 4.4.

Likewise, Article 4.3 of the India-UAE BIT provides:

> Once established, Investments shall not be subjected in the host Contracting Party to additional performance requirements which may hinder or restrict the management, maintenance, use, enjoyment or disposal of Investments unless such requirements are deemed vital for reasons of public order, public health or environmental concerns and are enforced by law for general application.[35]

[32] ibid, Annex 10.

[33] Anand, South Asian Bilateral Investment Treaties (n 10).

[34] Agreement between the State of Kuwait and the Republic of India for the Encouragement and Reciprocal Protection of Investment (signed 27 November 2001, entered into force 28 June 2003), Art 4.4.

[35] Agreement between the Republic of India and the Republic of UAE on the Reciprocal Promotion and Protection of Investments (signed 12 December 2013, entered into force 21 August 2014), Art 4.3.

This provision is almost similarly worded as Article 4.4 of the India-Kuwait BIT. Although Article 4.3 of the India-UAE BIT bars the imposition of PRs on foreign investment, those PRs that are considered indispensable for certain policy goals such as addressing environmental imperatives can be adopted. In those BITs that do not outlaw imposition of PRs, India has the policy space to impose any domestic environmental measures such as the EIA provided these measures do not breach the substantive protection standards given in the treaty.

National Treatment: the national treatment provision in a BIT imposes an obligation on the host state to treat foreign and domestic investment that is in like circumstances at par. All Indian BITs contain this provision. However, none of these BITs contain an exception for environment-related regulatory measures. One exception to this rule is Article 3.5 of the India-ASEAN investment agreement, which provides:

> Extension of financial assistance or measures taken by a Party in favour of its investors and their investments in pursuit of legitimate public purpose including the protection of health, safety, the environment shall not be considered as a violation of this Article.[36]

Thus, Article 3.5 allows the host state to derogate from the national treatment obligation in terms of extending financial assistance or adopting other measures favouring domestic investors to pursue legitimate public purposes such as related to the environment. Let us assume that India offers financial incentives to local companies who possess a technology that is environmentally sustainable, and does not extend the same incentives to foreign companies working in the same sector, who lack the said technology. Article 3.5 will provide a safe haven for such domestic environmental measures. In the absence of a provision like Article 3.5, such a regulatory measure might constitute a violation of the national treatment obligation.

7.1.3 Residual Category: Environmental Provisions as Part of Other Provisions

A survey of other provisions in Indian BITs that talk of the environment shows that they can be divided into the following categories: health, safety, and environmental measures; treaty preamble; non-lowering of EP. Let us discuss each of them.

Health, safety, and environmental provisions: the investment chapters of India's FTA contain provisions for safeguarding the environment under the rubric of 'health, safety, and environmental provisions'. For instance, Article 10.16(1) of the India-Korea FTA's investment chapter provides:

36 India-ASEAN Investment Agreement (n 30) Art 3.5.

> Nothing in this Agreement shall be construed to prevent a Party from adopting, maintaining or enforcing any measure consistent with this Agreement that is in the public interest, such as measures to meet health, safety or environmental concerns.[37]

An almost similarly worded provision is given in the investment chapters of India-Malaysia FTA:

> Nothing in this Chapter shall be construed to prevent: (a) a Party or its regulatory bodies from adopting, maintaining or enforcing any measure, on a non-discriminatory basis; or (b) the judicial bodies of a Party from taking any measures, consistent with this Chapter that is in the public interest, including measures to meet health, safety or environmental concerns.[38]

Prima facie, a provision like this appears to provide greater regulatory latitude to the host state when compared with a general exception clause based on Article XX of GATT. However, a closer reading reveals a different story. This provision empowers the host state to adopt domestic measures addressing public interest imperatives such as the environment provided they are 'consistent with' the treaty. In other words, unlike the general exception clauses where the countries (subject to the requirements aimed at prohibiting regulatory abuse) have the leeway to adopt domestic environmental measures that may breach the treaty, Article 10.16(1) mandates states to adopt measures for the protection of the environment without breaching the treaty. Arguably, provisions like Article 10.16(1) in the investment chapter of the India-Korea FTA merely reiterate the sovereign right of states to enact treaty consistent regulatory measures for the protection of the environment.

Preamble: according to Article 31(2) of the Vienna Convention on Law of Treaties, the preamble plays an important part in helping us understand the context of the treaty. Several ISDS tribunals have taken the preamble into account in interpreting substantive treaty provisions.

Very few Indian BITs mention the environment in the preamble of the treaty. For example, the India-Trinidad Tobago BIT states in the preamble that the objectives of fostering foreign investment and creating an enviable environment for the same 'can be achieved without relaxing health, safety and environmental measures of general application'. Thus, there is a recognition of the fact that fortifying foreign investment should not be done by degrading environmental norms. Likewise, the preambles of the India-Japan FTA (which also contains an investment chapter) and the India-Korea FTA recognize the objective of sustainable development and talks of preserving the environment while boosting foreign investment.

[37] Comprehensive Economic Partnership Agreement between the Republic of Korea and the Republic of India (7 August 2009, entered into force 1 January 2010) (India-Korea FTA), Art 10.16(1).

[38] India-Malaysia FTA (n 28) Art 10.20.

Thus, the preamble of these treaties not only talk of environmental protection but also sustainable development. It is imperative to bear in mind that the preamble of the WTO agreement also contains the term, 'sustainable development'. The WTO Appellate Body in the *Shrimp Turtle* case,[39] while giving a broad and evolutionary interpretation to the term 'exhaustible natural resources' in Article XX (g), invoked the notion of sustainable development. It held that WTO member countries were conscious of the significance and legitimacy of environmental protection as an objective of national and international policy.[40] This case elucidates the significance of how environmental values given in the preamble of the treaty can come in handy in interpreting treaty provisions.

Non-lowering of environmental standards: it is often argued that having relaxed and lenient environmental standards can play a pivotal role in attracting foreign investment. One study finds that while the laxity of environmental norms in a host country is a significant determinant for attracting foreign investment from the United States (US) for heavily polluting industries, it plays an insignificant role in the case of non-polluting industries.[41] In the context of India, a recent study shows that weaker environmental governance does not necessarily lead to greater foreign investment.[42]

Notwithstanding the empirical data, countries might be tempted into considering that they would be able to attract higher foreign investment flows by diluting their environmental norms. Some Indian BITs specifically dissuade states from doing so. For example, Article 10.16(2) of the India-Korea FTA's investment chapter provides:

> The Parties recognise that it is inappropriate to encourage investment by relaxing domestic health, safety or environmental measures. Accordingly, a Party should not waive or otherwise derogate from, or offer to waive or otherwise derogate from, such measures as an encouragement for the establishment, acquisition, expansion or retention in its territory of an investment of an investor. If a Party considers that the other Party has offered such an encouragement, it may request consultations with the other Party and the Parties shall consult with a view to avoiding any such encouragement.[43]

Article 99 of the investment chapter in India-Japan FTA follows the same. Thus, there is a clear recognition of the fact that foreign investment should not be encouraged by relaxing environmental norms. Furthermore, if a country does so, the other country can request consultations to persuade against any such policy.

[39] United States—Import Prohibition of Certain Shrimp and Shrimp Products, Report of the Appellate Body, 12 October 1998, Doc WT/DS58/AB/R.

[40] ibid.

[41] Yuquing Xing and Charles D Kolstad, 'Do Lax Environmental Regulations Attract Foreign Investment?' (2002) 21 *Environmental and Resource Economics* 1.

[42] Vinish Kathuria, 'Does Environmental Governance Matter for Foreign Direct Investment? Testing the Pollution Haven Hypothesis for Indian States' (2018) 35(1) *Asian Development Review* 81.

[43] India-Korea FTA (n 37) Art 10.16(2).

Barring these few investment chapters in India's FTAs, other Indian BITs do not contain any such provision. In other words, whether to relax environmental standards to attract foreign investment is an issue that is left for individual countries to decide nationally. For instance, India's recent draft EIA has diluted many requirements in the name of making it easier to invest such as reducing the time for public consultations from thirty days to twenty days, and creating a mechanism for *post facto* approval of projects that violate environmental laws, etc.[44] This is an example of India unilaterally downgrading the environmental norms. Such unilateral action implies that instead of using the policy space in the relevant investment treaty, India is going in the opposite direction where on its own volition it is downgrading environmental norms instead of ratcheting them up. Such domestic actions will weaken India's stand internationally to ask for greater regulatory space while negotiating investment treaties.

Another flip side of unilaterally lowering domestic environmental standards is that BITs rarely impose binding environmental obligations on foreign investors. Thus, the only way foreign investors can be made accountable for complying with environmental norms is through reasonable domestic environmental measures.[45] However, when domestic environmental norms are diluted as is the case with draft EIA, then it also weakens the means through which foreign investors can be held accountable under domestic law for environmental degradation.

7.2 Indian BITs: 2016 and Afterwards

As already pointed out, India adopted a new Model BIT in 2016. Since then, India has signed BITs with a few countries such as Belarus, Kyrgyzstan, Taiwan, and Brazil. This part of the chapter discusses to what extent EPs find a place in India's new investment treaty practice. We divide this discussion into the following parts: EPs in general exception clauses, EPs as specific exceptions, EPs as part of investor obligations, and EPs in ISDS mechanism.

7.2.1 Environmental Provisions in General Exception Clauses

The 2016 Model BIT contains a general exception clause. Article 32.1 provides:

[44] Ministry of Environment, Forest and Climate Change, Draft Notification, March 2020 <http://environmentclearance.nic.in/writereaddata/Draft_EIA_2020.pdf>.

[45] See Madhav Mallya, 'India's Race to the Bottom: Bilateral Investment Treaties and the New Draft Environmental Impact Assessment Notification' (*Opinio Juris*, 9 October 2020) <http://opiniojuris.org/2020/10/09/indias-race-to-the-bottom-bilateral-investment-treaties-and-the-new-draft-environmental-impact-assessment-notification>.

> Nothing in this Treaty shall be construed to prevent the adoption or enforcement by a Party of measures of general applicability applied on a non-discriminatory basis that are necessary to: ...
> (ii) protect human, animal or plant life or health; ...
> (iv) protect and conserve the environment, including all living and non-living natural resources;[46]

A similarly worded general exception clause is also present in India-Belarus BIT,[47] India-Kyrgyzstan BIT,[48] India-Taiwan BIT,[49] and India-Brazil BIT.[50] *Prima facie*, Article 32.1 of the 2016 Model BIT looks like it is based on Article XX of GATT. It is partly true since Article 32.1, like Article XX of GATT, contains several permissible objectives and has a nexus requirement. However, the critical difference is that Article 32.1 does not contain a *chapeau* of the kind in Article XX of GATT. The *chapeau* of Article XX ensures that the manner in which a country applies a regulatory measure does not 'constitute a means of arbitrary or unjustifiable discrimination between countries where the same conditions prevail, or a disguised restriction on international trade'.

Article 32.1(iv) allows the host state to adopt measures, even if they are in breach of the BIT, that are necessary to protect and conserve the environment. The only requirement is that such measures should be non-discriminatory. The absence of a *chapeau* of the kind given in Article XX of GATT implies greater regulatory leeway to the host state to enact domestic environment measures. However, this greater regulatory freedom could also lead to regulatory abuse. For instance, the absence of the *chapeau* of the kind found in GATT Article XX means that there would be very limited scrutiny of the manner in which the host country imposes the environment-related regulatory measure. The measure could constitute a disguised restriction to international investment.

Additionally, Article 22.1 of the India-Brazil BIT contains a separate clause on 'investment and environment, labour affairs and health'. Article 22.1 provides:

> Nothing in this Treaty shall be construed to prevent a Party from adopting, maintaining or enforcing any measure it deems appropriate to ensure that investment activity in its territory is undertaken in a manner according to labour, environmental and health law of that Party, provided that this measure is not applied in a

46 Model Text for the Indian Bilateral Investment Treaty (Indian Model BIT) <https://dea.gov.in/sites/default/files/ModelBIT_Annex_0.pdf>, Art 32.1.

47 Treaty Between the Republic of Belarus and Republic of India on Investments (Signed 24 September 2018, Enforced 5 March 2020) (India-Belarus BIT), Art 32.1.

48 Bilateral Investment Treaty Between the Government of the Kyrgyz Republic and the Government of the Republic of India (Signed 14 June 2019, Yet to be enforced) (India-Kyrgyzstan BIT), Art 32.1.

49 Bilateral Investment Agreement Between the Indian Taipei Association in Taipei and the Taipei Economic and Cultural Centre in India (Signed 18 December 2018, Enforced 14 February 2019) (India-Taiwan BIT), Art 31.1.

50 Investment Cooperation and Facilitation Treaty Between the Federative Republic of Brazil and the Republic of India (Singed 25 January 2020, Yet to be enforced) (India-Brazil BIT), Art 23.

> manner which would constitute a means of arbitrary or unjustifiable discrimination or a disguised restriction.[51]

Thus, this provision empowers the host state, without worrying about the treaty provisions, to adopt measures that it deems appropriate to ensure that foreign investors comply with the domestic environmental norms.

7.2.2 Environmental Provisions in Specific Exceptions

The 2016 Model BIT, apart from containing a general exception clause for environmental protection, also comprises environmental exceptions for specific substantive provisions. For example, Article 5.5 provides:

> Non-discriminatory regulatory measures by a Party or measures or awards by judicial bodies of a Party that are designed and applied to protect legitimate public interest or public purpose objectives such as public health, safety and the environment shall not constitute expropriation under this Article.[52]

A similar provision is present in India-Belarus BIT,[53] India-Kyrgyzstan BIT,[54] India-Taiwan BIT.[55] This provision is like the environment-related specific exceptions from the expropriation provision given in some old Indian BITs discussed before. An important difference is that like Article 8.9 of the India-ASEAN investment, Article 5.5 is not prefaced with the words 'except in rare circumstances'.

Apart from the expropriation provision, the 2016 Model BIT also contains EP in the context of the national treatment obligation. Article 4 of the 2016 Model BIT imposes the national treatment obligation on the host state not to discriminate between domestic and foreign investment in 'like circumstances'. To determine whether domestic and foreign investments are in 'like circumstances', one of the factors that have to be taken into account is 'the actual and potential impact of the investment on third persons, the local community, or the environment'. In other words, the impact of investment on the environment can be an important factor in determining likeness. Thus, assuming a foreign investor and domestic investor are operating in the same sector, but the adverse impact of the foreign investor's activity on the environment is higher in comparison to the domestic investor, then it can be argued that the foreign and domestic investors are not in like circumstances. This would allow for differential treatment between the two without leading to a violation of national treatment obligation.

[51] ibid Art 22.1.
[52] Indian Model BIT (n 46) Art 5.5.
[53] India-Belarus BIT (n 47) Art 5.5.
[54] India-Kyrgyzstan BIT (n 48) Art 5.5.
[55] India-Taiwan BIT (n 49) Art 5.5.

7.2.3 Environmental Provisions as Part of Investor Obligations

An important critique of investment treaties is that they are one-sided international law instruments, which impose obligations on host states, thus constraining their right to regulate, but do not impose obligations on foreign investors.[56] To overcome this design flaw, several new generation BITs impose obligations on foreign investors also known as investor obligations. For example, Article 12 of the 2016 Model BIT provides:

> Investors and their enterprises operating within its territory of each Party shall endeavour to voluntarily incorporate internationally recognised standards of corporate social responsibility in their practices and internal policies, such as statements of principle that have been endorsed or are supported by the Parties. These principles may address issues such as labour, the environment, human rights, community relations and anti-corruption.[57]

A similar provision is present in Article 12 of the India-Belarus BIT and India-Taiwan BIT.[58] Thus, investors are under an obligation to endeavour to address several issues, including environmental requirements. However, this obligation on the investor is couched in the best endeavour language. In the same vein, Article 12.2(a) of the India-Brazil BIT provides that investors and their investments shall 'endeavour' to comply with voluntary principles and standards such as contributing to the economic, social, and environmental progress, aimed at achieving sustainable development.

7.2.4 Environmental Provisions as Part of ISDS

An important element of India's new treaty practice is to include mitigating factors in calculating monetary damages to foreign investors, in case the ISDS tribunal ruled in favour of the investor. Article 26.3 of the 2016 Model BIT provides:

> for the calculation of monetary damages, the tribunal shall also reduce the damages to take into account any restitution of property or repeal or modification of the measure, or other mitigating factors.[59]

Then, footnote 4 states:

[56] See Jean Ho, 'The Creation of Elusive Investor Responsibility' (2019) 113 *American Journal of International Law, Unbound* 10.

[57] Indian Model BIT (n 46) Art 12.

[58] India-Taiwan BIT (n 49) Art 12.

[59] Indian Model BIT (n 46) Art 26.3.

> mitigating factors can include, current and past use of the investment, the history of its acquisition and purpose, compensation received by the investor from other sources, any unremedied harm or damage that the investor has caused to the environment or local community or other relevant considerations regarding the need to balance public interest and the interests of the investor.

Similar provision is present in India's BITs with Belarus,[60] Taiwan,[61] and the Kyrgyz Republic.[62]

Some argue that the mitigating factors mentioned in the footnote would allow for the reintroduction of counterclaims through the back door.[63] As per footnote 4, the tribunal will have to take into account mitigating factors while calculating monetary damages to be paid to foreign investors. One such mitigating factor is damage caused to the environment. In other words, it would give opportunities to the host state to make submissions about any environmental harm that the investor may have caused. Here, the host state can advance arguments like the foreign investor has breached domestic environmental norms. The host state can bring counterclaims against the foreign investor indirectly for environmental breaches.

Conclusion

The following conclusions can be drawn from a survey of Indian BITs and investment chapters in FTAs from the point of view of environmental protection. First, the bulk of the Indian BITs signed before the adoption of the Model BIT did not contain EPs in any form. Thus, the concern is that most of these BITs do not specifically recognize the state's right to regulate to address environmental concerns. In such BITs, India may have to rely on doctrines like the police powers to protect its environment-related regulatory measures if challenged by foreign investors under BITs.

Second, out of the few investment treaties that contain EP, investment chapters in FTAs encompass the most detailed provisions recognizing the state's right to regulate for environmental purposes. Third, the provisions in these treaties recognizing state's right to regulate for environmental purposes range from general exception clauses to specific exceptions for certain substantive provisions such as expropriation. Fourth, India's new investment treaty practice starting from the 2016 Model BIT reflects a better greening of India's investment treaties. The right to regulate for environmental protection is not just restricted to general and specific exceptions but has also expanded

60 India-Belarus BIT 2018 (n 47) Art 26.3.

61 India-Taiwan BIT (n 49) Art 25.3.

62 India-Kyrgyzstan BIT (n 48) Art 26.3.

63 Jarrod Hepburn and Ridhi Kabra, 'India's New Model Investment Treaty: Fit for Purpose?' (2017) 1(2) *Indian Law Review* 95.

to other provisions like investor obligations and ISDS. The challenge for India will be to ensure that it continues with this practice in its future BITs and FTA investment chapters. Fifth, ensuring that there is adequate regulatory space within the BIT to adopt domestic environmental measures is one thing. However, India needs to make optimum use of this regulatory space at the domestic level. There are examples, such as the draft EIA, which shows that India has unilaterally diluted environmental protection standards. This creates a divergence between what India is arguing for internationally in terms of greater regulatory space in investment treaties for environmental measures and what India seems to be doing domestically. This contradiction needs to be ended expeditiously or else India's treaty negotiating partners will not take India's quest for environment-related regulatory space in BITs seriously.

Suggestions for Further Reading

Manjiao Chi, 'The "Greenization" of Chinese Bits: An Empirical Study of the Environmental Provisions in Chinese Bits and its Implications for China's Future Bit-Making' (2015) 18(3) *Journal of International Economic Law* 511.

Alison Giest, 'Interpreting Public Interest Provisions in International Investment Treaties' Treaties' (2017) 18(1) *Chicago Journal of International Law* 321.

G Van Harten and D N Scott, 'Investment Treaties and the Internal Vetting of Regulatory Proposals: A Case Study from Canada' (2016) 7(1) *Journal of International Dispute Settlement* 1.

Stephan W Schill, 'Do Investment Treaties Chill Unilateral State Regulation to Mitigate Climate Change?' (2007) 24(5) *Journal of International Arbitration* 469.

Kyla Tienhaara, 'Regulatory Chill in a Warming World: The Threat to Climate Policy Posed by Investor-State Dispute Settlement' (2018) 7(2) *Transnational Environmental Law* 229.

CHAPTER 8

ECONOMIC INSTRUMENTS AND ECONOMIC REGULATORS

M.N. MURTY AND SUSHAMA MURTY

Abstract

Laws and policies governing environmental management in India make it mandatory for the regulators: government, market, and communities to use various economic instruments for efficient management of the environment. The government uses taxes, prices, and quantities as economic instruments. The market provides incentives to consumers, producers, and stockholders to control pollution through market prices. Local and international communities assume importance in the context of efficient management of local and global commons. Government, market, and communities complement each other with their environmental management policies. In case of market failure, government intervention in the market, and in case of both market and government failure collective action assume importance. Government uses budgetary policy instruments and direct environmental policy instruments. Collective action takes place either as group action to deal with general environmental problems or as community action for the management of local or global common property resources.

Introduction

The government, market, and communities are economic regulators, who use a variety of regulatory instruments for enhancing social welfare. Given the laws protecting people's right to clean environment, the free market and its regulatory instruments of prices and quantities fail to secure, on their own, larger societal objectives, such as sustainable management of the environment. The government with its normal budgetary policies and specific laws uses policy instruments that are either substitutes for or complements to market prices for realizing societal objectives. Further, given the failure of the market and the government in the management of local and global common property resources, local and international communities often act as regulators for the efficient management of these resources.

Government is by far the major regulator using prices, quantities, taxes, subsidies, and public expenditure as instruments for achieving its objectives of welfare maximization and environmental sustainability. Price instruments are used for regulating the supply and demand of commodities. Quantity instruments are used to ensure the supply of essential goods such as food and fuel to the poor and essential inputs to agriculture and industry. Quantity restrictions are imposed on imports and exports of certain commodities for achieving trade policy and environmental objectives. Quantity instruments are also used to directly achieve the environmental objectives of reducing air and water pollution in the country.

There could be government failure in environmental management for various reasons. The market could supplement the government for better environmental management in the presence of environmental laws. The market instruments of prices and quantities could efficiently manage natural resource-based goods like water and power in the presence of laws governing their supply and demand. Also, there are specific regulations allowing the government and the market to supplement each other for supplying essential goods like water and power for household and industrial uses.

There could be a failure of the market and the government in the efficient management of local and global common property resources. Legal rights, regulations, and agreements governing common property resources could facilitate local and international collective action for the efficient management of these resources. The typical examples of local commons and global commons are groundwater and greenhouse gas emissions respectively.

The rest of the chapter is structured as follows. Section 8.1 discusses economic instruments and laws governing the government as a regulator for efficient environmental management in India. Section 8.2 explains how the market works as a regulator in the presence or absence of laws. Section 8.3 deals with local and international community action for efficient management of local and global common property resources respectively. The conclusion provides a way forward.

8.1 The Government

The government uses budgetary policies (revenue and expenditure policies) to achieve environmental and other social objectives in the economy. Tax policies are used to provide incentives to producers and consumers for taking decisions to protect the environment. Public expenditure policies are used to facilitate environmental expenditures. The government of India has enacted laws to integrate environmental objectives with budgetary policies. The government also uses direct environmental policy instruments such as pollution taxes and quantity controls taking recourse to special laws enacted by it to protect the environment.

8.1.1 The Environment and the Tax Policies of the Government

Environmental taxes and subsidies are the main budgetary policy instruments of government.[1] In a world with no externalities, including environmental externalities such as pollution,[2] welfare maximizing resource allocation with consideration of income distribution or equity could be obtained in a free-market economy provided the government can implement redistributive instruments of personalized lump-sum taxes/transfers. This may involve lump-sum taxation of the rich and using the proceeds to make redistributive lump-sum transfers to the poor. In addition to their role as instruments of redistribution, lump-sum taxes can also be used for financing government expenditures, for example, for providing public goods including environmental services. These are often called the first-best instruments (regulatory instruments ensuring welfare maximization in the economy) of tax policies as the use of these instruments does not involve distortions causing welfare losses in the economy.

In a world with environmental externalities, an environmental tax accompanied by personalized lump-sum taxes/transfers become the first-best policy instruments of redistribution and externality correction. Analogous to the case where there are no externalities, personalized lump-sum taxes/transfers continue to be instruments that help attain the redistributive/equity, revenue-raising, and environmental objectives of the government while the environmental tax is fixed at a level that reflects the social marginal damage caused by the environmental externality. In such a situation, the government's budget will be balanced: the revenue from environmental taxation and personalized lump-sum taxation will be equal to the government's revenue requirements for meeting its expenditure.

In practice, the first-best instruments of taxation such as personalized lump-sum transfers/taxes cannot be implemented by the government due to incomplete information about individual actions in the market. These instruments are not incentive compatible since there are incentives for people to under-report their wealth/true abilities to pay tax to escape personalized lump-sum taxation and to benefit from positive

[1] See Sushama Murty, 'Some Results from the Theory of Optimal Taxation and Their Relevance for Increasing the Progressiveness of Indian Tax Structure' (2019) 54(1) *Indian Economic Review* 19.

[2] The problem of externality arises when individual consumption and production decisions of consumers and producers affect everybody else in the society with the affected parties having no control over it.

personalized lump-sum transfers/subsidies. In such situations, the government has to take recourse to second best or more incentive-compatible tax instruments such as commodity taxes and income tax, which are based on observed incomes, to realize its revenue, equity, and environmental objectives. However, such tax systems are distortionary since they involve some efficiency or welfare losses in the economy.

The literature on optimal taxation[3] shows that such tax systems will balance the trade-offs between the objectives of equity, efficiency, and environmental protection. For instance, redistributive objectives of the government may require heavy taxation of luxuries that are consumed by the rich, while the objective of raising revenue most efficiently with least distortions may require taxing necessities, which are consumed disproportionately by the poor. Environmental objectives require the government to tax appropriately emission-causing goods such as fossil fuels. Thus, the regulatory instruments of commodity taxes serve the purpose of not only redistribution and revenue generation for the government but also of environmental externality correction. In the context of consumption externalities, the literature shows that under a second-best optimal commodity tax structure, the optimal commodity tax rate for each commodity can be decomposed into (i) a tax for achieving equity and efficiency objectives; and (ii) a tax for correction of an environmental externality.[4]

In a second-best world with production externalities—externalities generated by producers of goods—optimal commodity taxation will require that firms generating production externalities should pay an environmental tax on externality causing intermediate inputs purchased from other firms. An example is an environmental tax on purchase of coal as an input by a firm from a firm supplying coal. In the context of goods and service tax (GST) in India, the tax rebate given to a firm on the purchase of an externality causing input from other firms should be reduced by the amount attributed to the social cost of externality generation.[5]

8.1.2 The Environment and Public Expenditure Policies

The Government of India makes direct environmental expenditures/investments as part of its budgetary policy to achieve environmental objectives. These expenditures are made by both central and state governments and local self-governments in India to deal with water and air pollution abatement, groundwater conservation, forest conservation, conservation of coastal and inland ecosystems, non-conventional energy sources, disaster management, and climate change related issues. These expenditures are financed

[3] Anthony B Atkinson and Joseph E Stiglitz, *Lectures on Public Economics* (McGraw Hill 1980).

[4] Agnar Sandmo, 'Optimal Taxation in the Presence of Externalities' (1975) 77(1) *Swedish Journal of Economics* 86.

[5] See Sushama Murty, 'Some Principles for Corrective Taxation of Externalities in a Second-best World with Commodity Taxes' (Discussion Paper No DP1801, Centre for International Trade and Development, School of International Studies, Jawaharlal Nehru University, Delhi 2018).

partly out of the revenue directly generated by the relevant governments (centre, state or local) and partly out of revenue earned through inter-governmental resource transfers in the form of revenue sharing by centre and states and states and local governments. These transfers are facilitated by the centre and state Finance Commissions constituted as per the Constitution of India, 1950.

As some examples of environmental public expenditures in India, consider forest conservation, water resources, and renewable energy. In the case of forest conservation, the long-term national target is to increase forest cover to 33 per cent of the country's geographical area. This target was first set by the National Forest Policy, 1952 and reiterated in subsequent policies of the government, including the National Forest Policy, 1988.[6] The new draft National Forest Policy, 2018 also aims to maintain at least one-third of India's total land area under forest and tree cover. Furthermore, India has committed to creating an additional carbon sink of 2.5 to 3 billion tons of CO_2 equivalent through additional forest and tree cover by 2030 in its Nationally Determined Contribution (NDC) to the Paris Climate Change Agreement.

There are now two sources for funding forest conservation by states in India: statutory transfers through Finance Commissions and the Compensatory Afforestation Fund (CAF) created by the Union government. The transfers to states through Finance Commissions generally take two forms: (i) an earmarked grant specifically for forests; and (ii) inclusion of forest cover in the formula determining share of states in the total tax revenues of the Union government. CAF was created by the Union government through the Forest (Conservation) Act, 1980, restricting use of forest land for non-forest purposes by states. It is now mandatory for states to get approval from the Union government for using forest land for other purposes. In view of the Supreme Court's judgment in 2002,[7] there is a need for making payments when forests are cut down for industrial and other purposes based on the estimated value (net present value) of forest land lost. These payments form part of CAF, which will be eventually distributed among states depending upon their needs for forest conservation.

In the case of water resources, public expenditures both by Union and state governments are incurred on river cleaning projects, supply of water to households, industrial and agricultural uses, and conservation of coastal and inland ecosystems. All the three governments in the Indian federation: centre, states and local self-governments participate in river cleaning programmes. For example, in the case of the project for cleaning the river Ganges, the stakeholders are the central, state, and local governments, households and industries in the Gangetic basin. The centre and the concerned state governments are sharing the investments on sewage treatment and riverfront development along the river. As per environmental regulations in India, it is mandatory for the industries to invest in reducing industrial water pollution and for local self-governments (municipalities) to invest in reducing household borne pollution in the Gangetic basin.

[6] Ministry of Environment and Forest, Government of India, National Forest Policy (1988).

[7] *TN Godavarman Thirumulpad v Union of India and Others WP* (C) No 202 of 1995 (Supreme Court of India).

In the case of supply of fresh water, the centre and states share investment expenditure on major dams constructed on the rivers with state governments investing in watershed management and minor irrigation schemes on their own. The local self-governments or municipalities and *panchayats* incur expenditures for supplying water to households and industries. The central and state governments in India share expenditure on investments made for the conservation of coastal and inland wetlands.

There have been direct public sector investments in different sources of renewable energy as part of the budgetary policy of the government apart from significant investments by the private sector and public-private partnerships in India. For example, the central government budget of 2021–22 allotted INR 5,753 crores to the Ministry of New and Renewable Energy and INR 300 crores for the New Green Energy Corridor scheme. In addition, the budget of 2020–21 provided for a capital infusion of INR 1,000 crores to Solar Energy Corporation of India and INR 1,500 crores to Indian Renewable Energy Development Agency.

8.1.3 Integrating Environmental Policy with Budgetary Policies in India

The revenue policies of the government of India have undergone major reforms during the last two decades. These reforms take cognisance of their implications for central and state relations and environmental management. During the pre-tax reform period, highly differentiated tax rates were levied in the form of specific and *ad valorem* duties on goods and services by both the centre and states. The first major reform of commodity taxes took place during 2005 in the form of introduction of value added tax (VAT) in India. This has made the tax base relatively more comprehensive and replaced specific taxes by *ad valorem* duties, reducing the multiplicity of tax rates, and credits being given for taxes on inter-regional trade. Before the current GST was introduced in 2017 as a major tax reform in India, there were central VAT (MOD VAT or modified value-added tax) and state VAT on goods and services in India. Many states replaced several types of commodity taxes by VAT.

It is important to know how the environmental policy objectives of government could be realized using a VAT regime. Using the commodity tax regime to achieve environmental objectives requires significantly differentiated rates of taxes. Environmental pollution taxes must be commodity specific because commodities differ with respect to pollution intensities in production and consumption. Take for example, a tax on electricity. In the case of a uniform VAT, a 10 per cent tax levied on electricity does not distinguish between a hydro and coal-fired thermal power. However, from the point of view of environmental protection, different rates of taxes must be levied on thermal power and hydropower with probably a subsidy for hydropower. VAT on goods and services is levied to achieve the objectives of budgetary policies: revenue efficiency, equity, environmental objectives, etc. Since VAT is levied mostly as an *ad valorem* tax, any increase in the rate of tax to realize environmental objectives could result in welfare losses that have to be weighed against gains in environmental benefits.

Income taxes could be used to raise revenues for environmental expenditures of the government. A plethora of environmental valuation studies show that people would like to make direct payments for environmental improvements such as urban air quality, water quality, river cleaning, forest conservation, soil conservation, etc. These studies use voluntary direct contributions from people, pure environmental taxes or budgetary policy instruments like income taxes or commodity taxes as vehicles for these payments. Take for example, river cleaning in India. A study done to find out household valuation of cleaning the river Ganges shows that, on an average, an urban household in India as a non-user[8] is willing to pay INR 1,506 per year at 2018 prices to maintain the river quality at bathing levels.[9] These payments could be appropriated by the government to finance river cleaning in India as part of income tax paid by urban households (e.g., surcharge on income for river cleaning) or through a mechanism whereby the government receives direct payments from people. The income tax alternative introduces market imperfections, distorting work-leisure choices of people while a direct payment is a pure environmental instrument and hence is not expected to cause market inefficiencies.

It is important to discuss the efficacy of using GST,[10] for achieving the environmental objectives of the government vis-a-vis employing the pre-reform commodity taxes in India. Given that the central and state GST rates are less differentiated, they are not flexible enough to address environmental problems. Pure environmental policy instruments discussed in section 4 help achieve the environmental objectives by providing incentives to firms and households to reduce pollution at various stages of the production cycle. In the production cycle, environmental problems arise while making input choices, choices regarding the production processes to use, choices regarding product quality, etc. GST is levied as VAT on the value of the product at the final stage of the production cycle. Therefore, in its current form, the burden of any increase in this tax to achieve environmental objectives will not be immediately passed on to the intermediate stages of the production cycle, hindering the incentives of producers and consumers to adopt the required abatement methods. To correct this, the public economics literature suggests that the tax credits/rebates given to producers on purchases of intermediate inputs such as coal under the GST should be reduced by an amount that reflects the social damages due to the externalities generated by the use of these inputs by producers. It is possible under this correction that producers using such inputs actually end up paying positive pollution taxes on the use of such inputs, that is, the input tax rebates/credits are negative.

[8] People express non-user benefits of an environmental resource based on their bequest, altruistic, and spiritual motives. In the case of the river Ganges, people may also be religiously motivated.

[9] A Markandya and M.N. Murty, *Cleaning Up the Ganges: The Cost Benefit Analysis of the Ganga Action Plan* (OUP 2000).

[10] GST is a destination-based tax avoiding the cascading effects and other problems associated with VAT.

A uniform pollution tax on emissions could help reduce pollution by all industries to the desired level as discussed in section 4. However, in its current form with only four GST tax slabs, namely, 5 per cent, 12 per cent, 18 per cent, and 28 per cent, a proportionate increase in the GST rate to reduce pollution will affect both polluting and non-polluting industries equally without resulting in the desired reduction of emissions. A highly differentiated GST system for taxing polluting goods based on their pollution intensities may be more suitable for correcting environmental externalities but implementing it may pose significant administrative challenges. Hence, to achieve environmental objectives, a practical approach could be to group commodities into high, medium, low, and no pollution-intensity groups, and levy four different excises, which increase according to the pollution intensities of the groups, in addition to existing GST rates on the goods making up these groups. The tax changes attempted could be revenue neutral in that excise taxes on polluting commodities could be accompanied by excise subsidies (which reduce the effective tax rate) on non-polluting commodities.

Constitutional provisions and legislations for environmental management in India empower the centre and states to use central and state GSTs as environmental regulatory instruments. This could result in interstate tax competition, where each state, given the taxes of other states, has an incentive to lower environmental taxes for attracting investments and business. There is a need, therefore, for tax coordination among states to avoid inefficiencies in environmental management from tax competition. Inter-jurisdictional competition is encountered in a federal structure of taxation. Apart from domestic taxes, countries could be tempted to use trade taxes to achieve environmental objectives. Export taxes on pollution intensive commodities and import taxes on imports that cause domestic pollution could result in reduction of environmental pollution. But trade instruments while improving domestic environmental quality could cause trade distortion resulting in welfare loses to the country. Therefore, in general, trade-offs between efficiency and environmental objectives will have to be balanced while designing trade taxes.

8.1.4 The Government and Direct Environmental Policy Instruments

There are economic instruments suggesting direct taxation of pollution/emissions to control environmental externalities as opposed to taxing goods that directly or indirectly cause emissions.[11] The government uses both market-based economic instruments, which can involve both prices and quantities, and non-market-based instruments such as command-and-control instruments for dealing with pollution. The government can

[11] M.N. Murty, 'Designing Economic Instruments and Participatory Institutions for Environmental Management in India' (2010) South Asian Network for Development and Environmental Economics (SANDEE) Working Paper No 48–10.

use either of these two types of instruments or a combination of both. Command-and-control instruments take the form of fines and penalties on polluters for not attempting to reduce pollution. These instruments do not ensure full efficiency in pollution reduction, given that the polluters are not completely incentivized to use cost minimizing abatement technologies. Economic instruments are of three types: price-based instruments, quantity-based instruments, and hybrid instruments.[12] These instruments help in achieving market/allocative efficiency while reducing pollution. The price-based instruments include pollution taxes and subsidies, and the quantity-based instruments include tradable pollution permits.

Using economic instruments requires a lot of information on firm-level emissions, technology, etc., and individuals' valuation of pollution which are not easy to obtain. Similarly, the problems in estimation of damages to the affected people involve practical problems for the design of the socially optimal pollution tax, and the unavailability of information about the socially optimal level of pollution poses problems for fixing the emission cap for tradable permits. A hybrid method that uses both command-and-control and economic instruments includes the Pollution Control Boards fixing standards and using either pollution tax or marketable permits to induce the polluter industry to meet those standards. The major problem of estimating damages to all the affected people from pollution can be avoided once the environmental standards are set *a priori*. The marginal abatement cost schedules can be estimated given the firm-level data on pollution loads, costs of abatement, and production levels. Given the knowledge of these schedules, a rate of tax can be fixed, which will incentivize the firms to automatically reduce pollution to meet the standards.

In India, direct market-based economic instruments have not been used so far and only command-and-control instruments have been used by the government to deal with industrial pollution.[13] However, there are a couple of instances of cap-and-trade schemes in India: the renewable energy certificates scheme and the Bureau of Energy Efficiency's (BEE) Perform, Achieve, Trade (PAT) scheme. Also, the Gujarat Pollution Control Board recently launched a conventional cap-and-trade regulation for particulate pollution in Surat.[14]

In a market economy without informational uncertainties, either pollution taxes or pollution permits as explained above can be used to ensure efficiency in emission reduction. However, in a situation of incomplete information, a choice needs to be made between these two instruments. It has been shown in the literature that if there is uncertainty about the measurement of benefits and costs of pollution abatement, there will be efficiency losses associated with both tax and permit instruments.[15] Therefore, the

[12] William J Baumol and Wallace E Oates, *The Theory of Environmental Policy* (2nd edn, CUP 1988).

[13] M.N. Murty, 'Environmental Regulation in the Developing World: The Case of India' (1995) 4(4) *Review of European Community and International Environmental Law* 330.

[14] See Sukanya Das, M.N. Murty, and Kavita Sardana, 'Using Economic Instruments to Fix the Liability of Polluters in India: Assessment of the Information Required and Identification of Gaps' (2021) 4(2) *Ecology, Economy and Society—the INSEE Journal* 45.

[15] Martin L Weitzman, 'Prices vs. Quantities' (1974) 41(4) *The Review of Economic Studies* 477.

choice between these two instruments assumes importance in the context of climate change mitigation given uncertainty about future or long run benefits and costs.[16] A combination of carbon tax and carbon permit policy instruments is needed to minimize efficiency losses for achieving the objective of stabilizing carbon emissions in the future.

8.2 The Market and the Environment

The market provides incentives to consumers, producers, and investors to protect the environment given the laws protecting private property rights. For example, it regulates the use of natural resource-based commodities like water and power in the economy given the related acts and regulations. The market and the government complement each other to ensure safe supply of some essential (utility) services.

8.2.1 Market and Laws

If the government is benevolent and there are supporting legal and other institutions for enforcement in place, then empowering the government with environmental regulation will help in achieving environmental goals. But the government may not be benevolent, and the required environmental laws may be absent. Market mechanisms also complement government regulation in controlling environmental externalities. A competitive market ensures the efficient supply of goods and services in the economy. The efficient functioning of the market requires the presence of laws enacted by the government to protect the rights of producers and consumers. The market provides incentives to consumers, producers, and stockholders to control pollution. The consumers regulate the market for pollution intensive commodities by expressing a preference for green products. The investors have incentives to invest in industries using cleaner technologies. The polluting industries may suffer losses because of a reduced demand for their products and increased cost due to higher penalties imposed by the government for non-compliance with pollution standards and settlement of compensation for victims of pollution. This will contribute to the downward valuation of the industry's stocks in the market as stock markets react to the environmental performance of companies.

Laws protecting private ownership of property can be considered as protectors of the environment since they may allow the safe transfer of ownership and make people liable for damages caused to others' property. An effective liability system forces the polluting industries to insure their property with private insurance companies and avoid facing the courts. Presence of insurance markets for cleaner production will provide incentives

[16] Nicholas Stern, *The Economics of Climate Change: The Stern Review* (CUP 2006).

to the producers to protect themselves from liability for environmental damages. Private management of environmental quality is ensured to some extent through corporate social responsibility of companies whereby such companies incorporate environmental concerns in their planning and action. This is traditionally seen as a philanthropic activity of companies. In India, the introduction of section 135 in the Companies Act, 2013, statutorily mandates specified companies to practice corporate social responsibility. This Act requires companies with a net worth of INR 500 crore or more to spend two per cent of their net profits in a financial year on activities pertaining to corporate social responsibility, including sustainable environmental management.

8.2.2 Market and Laws for Availing Goods and Services Derived from Natural Resources in India

Water, fuel, and power are the prominent goods that are produced directly from natural resources. There are several laws in India to ensure sustainable supply of these goods in the market. In the case of groundwater, for example, these regulations are governed by issues about whether water is an economic good or a fundamental right. Various laws governing the power sector in India consider power as an economic good.

The Model Bill for the Conservation, Protection, Regulation and Management of Groundwater, 2016 includes various provisions for the just use of groundwater. They address the right to water for life, the legal status and groundwater use in India, groundwater security plans, duties of groundwater users, groundwater for livelihood and irrigation, social and environment impact assessment, and dealing with dispute resolution in using groundwater. Many states in India are yet to execute groundwater legislation along the lines of the Model Bill. Prior to the Model Bill, some states enacted legislations like the Bombay Irrigation Act, 1879. Karnataka and Maharashtra have passed a modified version of the Model Bill which is yet to be implemented. Also, different states in India are considering different versions of the Model Bill which are not enacted yet.

The debate over the proposed Model Bill by scholars and stakeholders in India is mostly centred around whether water is an economic good or a fundamental human right.[17] Farmers' groups resist the Bill pointing out that it gives the state the authority to restrict fundamental rights to expand groundwater use. It is criticized on the ground that the Bill does not provide for the possibility of participation by all stakeholders in groundwater management. There are calls for the right to groundwater to be vested at multiple levels.[18] However, there is a broad agreement among all people concerned about the efficacy of the economic good approach for pricing the use of groundwater.

[17] See Ashu Jain and Gary Lilienthal, 'Water Rights in India: Economic Good, Fundamental Rights or Human Rights' (2021) 47(3) *Commonwealth Law Bulletin* 501.

[18] E.g., Philippe Cullet, 'Groundwater Law in India: Towards a Framework Ensuring Equitable Access and Aquifer Protection' (2014) 26(1) *Journal of Environmental Law* 55.

The power sector relying mainly on inputs from natural resources has been governed historically by relevant laws in India. The Electricity Act, 2003 is the principal legislation governing the power sector in India. It has replaced all the old laws and been subjected to various amendments through bills introduced by the government in the years 2014, 2018, and 2020. The State Electricity Boards are autonomous bodies solely authorized to govern the generation, transmission, and distribution activities. The Act has facilitated private sector participation in the power sector in the distribution system or transmission lines. It has established the Appellate Tribunal for Electricity, a supreme tribunal that hears appeals against the adjudications of the state and the Central Electricity Regulatory Commission. It also provides for environmentally friendly power generation by promoting renewable energy projects. It has shifted the responsibility of managing renewable power obligations from state commissions to the central commission for meeting the national climate change goals. Also, failure in implementing renewable power obligations would amount to penalties as per proposed amendment. The Electricity Regulation Act, 2006 provides for the establishment of a national regulatory framework for the electricity supply industry. The National Energy Regulator is the custodian and enforcer of this framework. The regulator by providing licenses and registration regulates generation, transmission, distribution, trading, and the import and export of electricity.

8.2.3 The Market and the Government and the Provision of Utility Services

The government and the market complement each other in supplying essential goods and services. Water and electricity are essential economic goods supplied in the free market at a price. In the absence of laws for regulating their supply in the market, there may be a tendency to form natural monopolies to supply them. In a free market, they are produced without any concern for the effects on the environment and supplied at arbitrarily higher prices. The public utilities, as autonomous bodies to operate in the market for supplying these services, are created under special legislation by Parliament or state legislatures.[19] Public utilities have the freedom to follow their own price policies. In India, electricity boards and water supply undertakings are created by special acts of state legislatures. As in the case of the general budgetary policies of the government, the criteria employed for fixing the prices of these public utilities are based on promotion of the government's efficiency, redistributive and environmental objectives.

One of the characteristics of public utilities is that they supply jointly several services with increasing returns to scale. The cost structure of a utility is such that there are joint costs for all the services it supplies and a cost attributable to each service. In view of this,

[19] See N Satish Gowda and ML Shilpa, 'Legal Regulations on Public Utility Services in India: Issues and Contemporary Challenges' (2017) 2(4) *International Journal of Legal Research and Studies* 162.

a public utility must consider different regulatory approaches for fixing prices for the services it supplies.[20] One such approach involves two-tier pricing requiring the utility to charge full-cost prices with the general government giving subsidies to services that promote environmental objectives or that are availed by the poor. In another approach, the government finances or compensates the budgetary deficits of utilities arising out of subsidies given to certain services to achieve equity and environmental objectives. All these approaches require linking utility pricing with the general/aggregate expenditure policy of the government.

State electricity boards (SEBs), which are the public utilities supplying electricity in India, levy tariffs following the budgetary policy of cross-subsidization. State governments provide budgetary support to SEBs to finance the resulting budgetary deficits. SEBs charge different prices for different users: charging industries at cost plus prices and households and farmers at subsidized prices. Electricity subsidies given to the farmers for groundwater irrigation result in the substitution of electricity by diesel oil, a highly air pollution intensive fuel. Some SEBs supply electricity at very negligible prices or even free of cost for groundwater irrigation.

Municipal water supply undertakings (water boards) also follow the policy of discriminatory prices. They charge higher prices for industry and subsidized prices for households with non-linear pricing with respect to units of consumption. The state governments subsidize the use of water for irrigation by farmers from two sources: canal and groundwater. The cost of canal irrigation consists of costs of infrastructure and maintenance and the distribution cost. The irrigation fees charged by the government covers only a small part of the maintenance cost and ignores very high infrastructure cost. The use of water for household and industrial purposes causes the serious problem of water pollution affecting the quality of ground and surface water. Therefore, the price charged by water boards has two components: production cost and pollution treatment cost. The pollution treatment cost is towards the cost of municipal sewage treatment plants incurred by water boards to treat polluted water for maintaining water quality standards. Thus, the market demand for water, the most important natural resource, is met using various pricing schemes ensuring its environmentally safe supply.

8.3 Community and Environment

Community or collective action has emerged as an alternative to the government and the market for environmental management. In dealing with environmental externalities such as air and water pollution, it takes the form of collective action by groups of stakeholders. In the context of management of common property resources (local or

[20] See Raghbendra Jha, M.N. Murty, and Satya Paul, *Pricing of Postal Services in India* (National Institute of Public Finance and Policy 1990).

global), it takes the form of collective action by all parties having property rights to the resource. In the case of global commons problems (e.g., climate change), it takes the form of international collective action of all countries.

8.3.1 Community Action and Environment

Collective action for environmental management must be understood in two different contexts of natural resource management: (i) dealing with the problem of environmental externalities discussed above; and (ii) efficient management of local and global common property resources. In the case of failure of the government and the market to control environmental pollution, literature shows that creation of specific property rights related to pollution among concerned agents could solve the problem.[21] Property rights mean either rights to clean water and air to people or rights to pollute to the producers and consumers. Giving the initial property rights to any natural resource either to the generator of the externality (polluters) or to the affected party (public), and if the cost of bargaining is zero, bargaining between the parties results in the optimal control of externality. In a realistic situation, there could be many polluters and many affected people (e.g., river pollution). Giving the legal rights to both the parties, bargaining takes place between a coalition of affected people and a coalition of polluters. This means that collective action of affected people and collective action of polluters for the formation of relevant groups is required to facilitate bargaining for controlling pollution.

There are several practical problems for the Coase bargaining to work in practice.[22] First, in reality, the transaction costs or costs of bargaining are positive. Second, one of the key assumptions in the bargaining solution is that all the externalities are captured in the value of property rights. There could be a problem in the context of defining the property rights of the future generations for an environmental resource and capitalization of future benefits from this resource. One approach for respecting the rights of the future generation is to consider the government as its representative. The government can compete in the market for environmental property rights of the future generation and pay for it by issuing a debt which must be serviced by the future generation. Another approach assumes that the present generation has a bequest motive for the future and wants to bequeath to the future the preserved resources. In the bargaining solution described above, the government has a minimal role to play as far as the welfare of the current generation is concerned. Its role is only to create property rights and protect them and then the free-market bargaining between the current generation agents will optimally control the externality.

In the context of group action to control pollution, Becker shows that political influence exerted by pressure groups in the free market can have an impact like that exerted

[21] RH Coase, 'The Problem of Social Cost' (1960) 3 *Journal of Law and Economics* 1.

[22] See Barry Nalebuff, 'On a Clear Day You Can See the Coase Theorem' in Partha Dasgupta and KG Maler (eds), *The Environment and Emerging Development Issues*, vol 1 (Clarendon Press 1997).

by a benevolent government to deal with market failure.[23] There are several agents involved in the political economy of industrial pollution abatement: the affected people, elected representatives, bureaucracy, and industry. Incentives exist for forming sub-coalitions of affected people and elected representatives and coalitions of industry and bureaucracy. Existence of such incentives is a fertile ground for the emergence of politically active pressure groups. Following Becker's argument, competition among these pressure groups may result in the optimal control of externalities.

In the case of market and government failure to manage common property resources, collective action of people or entities having property rights to the resource could be a solution. A common property regime is defined as a situation in which individuals have mutual duties and rights. Individuals' right to limit the group size and the right to prescribe how the resource will be used by each member in the group will together constitute the common property.[24] In a free market, there could be a free rider problem resulting in the over-exploitation of the resource threatening its survival for present and future uses. In other words, the resource faces the problem of the tragedy of the commons which may happen when the rate of exploitation of a resource exceeds the physical or biological rate to renew itself. The conventional solution to the free rider problem is government intervention (public action) with penalties and incentives to regulate the behaviour of individuals. The other option is voluntary collective action of people having property rights to the resource. In the case of management of the commons, collective action might be setting and observing a rule of restrained access to a common property resource to sustain it for present and future use.

8.3.2 Community Action in Practice

Wade and Ostrom have reported several successful cases of collective action across the world.[25] In India, there are several cases in which organized groups of local people affected by pollution in areas surrounding various industrial estates resorted to legal action against polluting industries by filing public litigation cases in the courts. In one such public interest, litigation on water pollution abatement by an industrial estate in Hyderabad, India, the Supreme Court of India, on the advice of an expert group constituted by it, ordered that the affected people be appropriately compensated by the industrial estate and that the industry and government should take remedial measures

[23] Gary S Becker, 'A Theory of Competition among Pressure Groups for Political Influence' (1983) 98(3) *The Quarterly Journal of Economics* 371.

[24] M.N. Murty, 'Management of Common Property Resources: Limits to Voluntary Collective Action' (1994) 4(6) *Environmental and Resource Economics* 581.

[25] Robert Wade, 'The Management of Common Property Resources: Collective Action as an Alternative to Privatisation or State Regulation' (1987) 11(2) *Cambridge Journal of Economics* 95; Elinor Ostrom, *Governing the Commons: The Evolution of Institutions for Collective Action* (CUP 1990).

to prevent further pollution.[26] The political organization of affected people in this case had also enlisted the support of local elected political representatives (members of local State Assembly and Union Parliament). The Court's order requiring the industries in the industrial estate to comply with water pollution standards created a problem for the small-scale industries given the scale economies in pollution abatement. To deal with this problem, the industries formed a group to set up a common effluent treatment plant, and the local government provided an incentive to the industries by sharing a part of the capital cost.

Local communities can influence the pollution abatement decisions of industries even in the absence of regulation by the government or in a free market situation. In case of large factories located in different regions of India, it is found that the extent of compliance of factories with environmental standards is related to the characteristics of local communities like education, political activity, etc., apart from factory specific characteristics.[27] Even with government regulation, we see a trend of involvement of local communities and environmental groups in all activities of environmental management, including design, monitoring, and implementation of environmental laws. This is viewed as the privatization of environmental management with laws permitting local environmental groups and industries to compete with government regulation.

A good example of the community as a regulator is the management of common property in the village economies. Successful management of neighbourhood forests (common lands) in village economies has now been achieved in India under a regime known as Joint Forest Management. There is an agreement between the village community and the government for mutually beneficial sharing of management of local forests. The agreement can either involve the government conceding property rights over the local forest land to the village community or the government keeping property rights and sharing the benefits with the local community. In the case where the village community possesses property rights over village commons or forest lands, collective action for management of the commons is successful only if there is a complementarity between individual benefits and the community benefits derived from the commons.[28] For example, since conserved forest land increases the supply of water for irrigation and fodder for cattle, the households owning private assets like cattle have incentives to voluntarily contribute towards preservation of common lands.

[26] *Indian Council for Enviro-Legal Action v Union of India and Others* WP (C) No 1056 of 1990 (Supreme Court of India).

[27] See M.N. Murty, AJ James, and Smita Misra, *Economics of Water Pollution: Indian Experience* (OUP 1999); World Bank, *Greening Industry: New Roles for Communities, Markets and Governments* (OUP 1999).

[28] See Kanchan Chopra, Gopal K Kadekodi, and M.N. Murty, *Participatory Development: People and Common Property Resources* (Sage 1990); M.N. Murty, 'Management of Common Property Resources: Limits to Voluntary Collective Action' (1994) 4 *Environmental and Resource Economics* 581.

Conclusion

The government, the market (consumers and producers), and communities are three pillars of the economy using various economic instruments for the efficient management of environmental resources. The right to clean environment protected by the Constitution of India and defended by the judiciary and various laws enacted by the government empowers the three pillars to ensure the sustainable use of natural resources.

The government can use budgetary policy instruments of taxes and public expenditures for efficient management of the environment. Even though the government is currently using these instruments, their potential is yet to be fully exploited. There remains considerable scope for using these instruments to integrate further environmental objectives with other budgetary policy objectives. As an example, recent commodity tax reforms leading to GST have involved limited differentiation of tax rates among commodities. This has made commodity taxes less flexible as instruments for dealing with environmental problems in India. The current GST needs to be supplemented by additional excise taxes on commodities that create environmental problems.

Economic instruments that are targeted to directly tackle environmental problems include pollution taxes, subsidies, and marketable pollution permits. These instruments, which complement the traditional budgetary policy instruments of the government, provide incentives to producers and consumers to take decisions for environmental improvements. However, currently, the Indian government is mainly using command-and-control or arbitrary instruments for dealing with environmental problems. These are more arbitrary and less efficient in comparison to the economic instruments of pollution taxes and pollution permits. A legal provision that will allow the government to freely use and reap maximum benefits from these two powerful economic instruments of environmental policy is still to be made in the Indian context.

The specific laws governing the supply and demand for goods and services with consequences for environment management must be strengthened. Market instruments such as commodity prices and quantities could be used to efficiently manage natural resource related goods like water and power. The presence of laws protecting property rights to land and insurance markets incentivize industries to work toward the objective of corporate social responsibility for avoiding damage to others' property.

Ensuring legal rights, regulations, and agreements governing the local common property resources could facilitate collective action by groups of people for the efficient management of these resources. Budgetary policy reforms enable the government to use the instruments of taxes, prices and quantities, and public expenditure for the sustainable use of environmental resources. Property rights and liability rules provide incentives to market players to take environmentally friendly consumption and production decisions. In the case of government and market failure to ensure environmental safety, the presence of laws protecting the legal rights provide incentives to initiate group action to deal with the general environmental problems like air and water pollution, and community action for the efficient management of local and global common property resources.

Suggestions for Further Reading

Kanchan Chopra, Gopal K Kadekodi, and M.N. Murty, *Participatory Development: People and Common Property Resources* (Sage 1990).

M.N. Murty, *Environment, Sustainable Development and Well-being: Valuation, Taxes, and Incentives* (OUP 2009).

M.N. Murty, AJ James, and Smita Misra, *Economics of Water Pollution: The Indian Experience* (OUP 1999).

M.N. Murty, 'Environmental Regulation in the Developing World: The Case of India' (1995) 4(4) *Review of European Community and International Environmental Law* 330.

Robert Wade, *Village Republics: Economic Conditions for Collective Action in South India* (CUP 1988).

CHAPTER 9

LIABILITY

CHARU SHARMA AND VISHAVJEET CHAUDHARY*

Abstract

This chapter analyses the underpinning theoretical ideas that guide liability in Indian environmental law. It contextualises liability and its contours in the Indian landscape. The text focuses on liability from a criminal law perspective, as well as a civil law perspective. It lists and critically assesses the various pieces of legislation and their scope, including specific sections of relevance and landmark cases that have shaped the jurisprudence of liability. It also enumerates fundamental and common law principles and their corresponding provisions in criminal and civil liability, including in the law of torts. The authors also try to capture the recent shifts in jurisprudence and its impact on the future of liability under environmental law in the future.

Introduction

This chapter provides an insight into situations that give rise to liability under the main environmental and natural resource statutes, and under the common law of tort and criminal law in India. It is divided into six parts. Sections 9.1 and 9.2 discuss the nature of liability generally, liability recognized under the common law of tort,[1] its development in terms of absolute liability,[2] and liability that exists within criminal law. Section 9.3 addresses civil liability arising out of breach of environmental regulations

* The authors would like to thank Mr Shantanu Saha, PhD Scholar, Jindal Global Law School for his contributions.

[1] The Constitution of India 1950, Art 372(2).

[2] See *MC Mehta v Union of India* AIR 1987 SC 1086 (Oleum gas leak case).

under three statutes concerning insurance, corporate regulation, and nuclear suppliers' liability. Sections 9.4 and 9.5 address liability under significant environmental and natural resources statutes that provide a liability regime framework for India. This framework exhibits a complicated matrix of rights, duties and liabilities.[3] Section F provides insights into the role of the Supreme Court of India and also the National Green Tribunal (NGT) where the judiciary has provided directions for future regulation in cases where the statutes are silent or ambiguous. Courts have found not only individuals but also the executive liable for environmental law violations, thus expanding the scope of environmental liability. The last section concludes with observations and the way forward.

9.1 Nature of Liability

The violation of an environmental regulation, rule, standard, duty, or a recognized legal right entails liability which can be either civil or criminal (or sometimes both). The liability arises from environmental harm or damage to a person or to property whether public or private. Environmental harm is not defined under the law. What constitutes an environmental harm or damage can be derived from the definition of 'environment' in the Environment (Protection) Act, 1986.[4] Accordingly, environmental harm can be interpreted as an adverse interference with the 'environment' and its interrelationship with human beings. Liability for harm may be in the form of civil, criminal, common law, statutory or the violation of a constitutional right or duty.[5]

The imposition of liability can be for various reasons and may exhibit one or more primary functions. First, the environment can be protected by proscribing harmful conduct with the threat of penal sanctions to deter such conduct. Second, the environment can be protected through the prevention of damage by imposing a variety of enforceable legal obligations on various actors, including the state and citizens whereby expenses are incurred, insurance liabilities are imposed, costs upon commercial or domestic use occur, and regulatory outcomes follow. Third, there is environmental protection in the form of compensation for the damage that has already accrued as a *post facto* remedy to compensate or rehabilitate the victims, as well as to restore the environment.[6] Compensation for environmental harm will be in accordance with the polluter pays principle and forms part of the environmental jurisprudence in India.[7]

[3] Charu Sharma, Tort Liability for Environmental Claims in India: A Comparative View (Universal Law Publishers 2017) 18, 163.

[4] EP Act, 1986 s 2(a).

[5] See generally Jason Hochstatter, 'Legal Liability' in Ali Farazmand (ed), *Global Encyclopedia of Public Administration, Public Policy, and Governance* (Springer 2018) 3754.

[6] National Green Tribunal Act, 2010 s 15.

[7] *Vellore Citizens' Welfare Forum v Union of India* (1996) 5 SCC 647.

The relationship between the liability regime and the regulatory framework is that while liability laws determine how the compensation and remedial measures are to be addressed after harm has occurred, the regulatory framework also uses an *ex ante* approach where a party is held accountable for a breach even before harm has occurred. These frameworks are laid out by the state which also must ensure their enforcement.[8] Thus a discussion of the liability regime remains incomplete without discussing the relevant regulatory framework. Liability under various statutes usually operates through procedural standards but has the normative backing of the polluter pays principle.

9.2 Liability Under Common Law of Tort, Crime, and Civil Liability

Before specific environment protection laws were enacted, the common law torts of nuisance, strict liability, negligence, and trespass were used to claim compensation for harm to property and person. They provided an indirect mechanism for the protection of the environment. Alongside tort, criminal law, and the criminal procedure statutes were also used to impose liability for harm to the environment and to people's health. However, there was no general duty of care for environmental harm.[9] Statutory liability may both be a civil wrong or a crime based upon the burden of proof of damage. In civil liability, the burden of proof is based on the balance of probabilities/preponderance. In criminal liability, the burden rests with the state and the burden of proof is beyond reasonable doubt. The liability imposed under various statutes includes fines, imprisonment, and compensatory damages—a mix of civil and criminal liability. In recent cases, the judiciary has utilized both civil and criminal law provisions to impose liability to address the violation of environmental standards.[10]

9.2.1 Common Law Liability

Despite critiques of the role of tort in India,[11] liability in tort law for environmental damage has been increasingly recognized, especially after the Bhopal Gas tragedy and

[8] PM Prasad, 'Environmental Protection: The Role of Liability System in India' (2004) 39(3) *Economic & Political Weekly* 257. See also *Nathan Chaudhary v State of GNCTD* 2021 SCC OnLine NGT 98.

[9] Neil Gunningham, 'Should A General "Duty of Care" for the Environment Become A Centrepiece of A "Next Generation" Environment Protection Statute?' (2017) 34 *Environmental and Planning Law Journal* 198.

[10] E.g. *Himmat Singh Shekhawat v State of Rajasthan* 2019 SCC OnLine NGT 1357.

[11] See Marc Galanter, 'India's Tort Deficit: Sketch for a Historical Portrait' in David M Engel and Michael McCann (eds), *Fault Lines: Tort Law as Cultural Practice* (Stanford University Press 2009) 47.

has been used by the courts to form the basis for compensation.[12] Liability has been followed by the imposition of compensatory, reparative, rehabilitative damages, *ex ante* expenses and *post facto* rehabilitation for environmental torts of injury to the person or her property.[13] Environmental damage has also been recognized by courts in private nuisance[14] and negligence[15] cases where compensation has been rewarded to the plaintiffs. In *MC Mehta v Union of India* (Oleum gas leak case), the tort of strict liability metamorphosed into absolute liability or liability of an 'enterprise which is engaged in a hazardous or inherently dangerous industry which poses a potential threat to the health and safety of the persons working in the factory and residing in the surrounding areas'.[16] The Court further held that 'it should be no answer to the enterprise to say that it had taken all reasonable care and that the harm occurred without any negligence on its part'.[17]

Accordingly, no form of defence employed is sufficient to exempt the defendants from the liability arising out of any illegal action or non-performance of reasonable care towards society or the environment. The compensation under this principle also depends on the financial and operational size of the corporation. Higher damages have been imposed on bigger corporations.[18]

9.2.2 Criminal Liability

In addition to tort liability, liability for environmental damage is found under criminal laws. The Indian Penal Code, 1860 (IPC) *inter alia* deals with public nuisance actions, including poisoning of wells, or ponds, health safety, and convenience that makes a person or legal entity such as a company criminally liable for their action. Section 268 defines 'Public Nuisance' as any act or an illegal omission which causes any common injury, danger or annoyance to the public, and abatement of public nuisance is covered under sections 269 to 278. Sections 425 to 440 provide for liability in respect of mischief in maiming, killing, of an animal, cattle, or property of an individual or stray animal or cattle. Sections 133 to 144 of the Code of Criminal Procedure, 1973 (CrPC) contain procedural provisions for public order and public nuisance where a person who is guilty of violation of any of these provisions is liable to prosecution and punishment.

12 *Union Carbide Corporation v Union of India AIR* 1992 SC 248; *Charan Lal Sahu v Union of India AIR* 1990 SC 1480.

13 National Green Tribunal Act 2010 (NGT Act), s 15. See also *Municipal Corporation of Greater Mumbai v Ankita Sinha* 2021 SCC OnLine SC 897, paras 15(6) and 24.

14 *Ram Baj Singh v Babu Lal AIR* 1982 All 285; *V Lakshmipathy v State of Karnataka AIR* 1992 Kar 57; *C Galstaun v Dunia Lal Seal* (1905) 9 CWN 612.

15 *Naresh Dutt Tyagi v State of UP* 1995 Supp (3) SCC 144.

16 *MC Mehta v Union of India AIR* 1987 SC 965; *Oleum Gas* case (n 2).

17 See Sharma (n 3) 37.

18 *Vedanta Limited v State of TN* 2020 SCC OnLine Mad 14684.

The provisions under the IPC in respect of 'public nuisance' and harming of public property were not originally intended to provide any protection to the environment per se. Rather the law imposed criminal liability for harm to the public and provided deterrence against damaging a river, well or any other water body, including a well, stream or pond. By proscribing actions against the detrimental use of common property natural resources, the state directly asserted ownership or control over resources by imposing liability for violation or harm to any of these natural resources. The interest or the right that was protected related to harm to public property and public health. With increasing development of infrastructure and growth in population, environmental damage and pollution increased exponentially within towns and cities. Small fines and imprisonment of a few months to a year under criminal law was cost inefficient and did not act as a deterrent against an individual or the state.[19] However, the judiciary made good use of certain opportunities to make state actors liable for omissions resulting in environmental harm. For instance, in *Municipal Council, Ratlam v Shri Vardhichand*, the provisions under the CrPC, especially section 133, were ingeniously applied to hold municipal corporations liable for failing to perform their statutory duty and causing public nuisance.[20]

More recently, special environmental courts have been set up under section 11(1) read with section 14 of the CrPC at the district level with the power to impose criminal liability for violations of environmental laws and regulatory notifications issued by the Central Pollution Control Board (CPCB) and State Pollution Control Boards (SPCBs) under the Environment (Protection) Act.[21] These courts delineate power for imposing environmental liability with local magistracies.

9.2.3 Civil Liability

This section discusses civil liability under three statutes that are pertinent in finding liability for environmental or natural resources damage, whether to a person or to the environment. First, the Public Liability Insurance Act, 1991 (PLIA) sets out civil liability, creates an Environmental Relief Fund (ERF), and recognizes a unique exception to nuisance and strict liability under tort for accidental environmental damage. Before the enactment of this law, there was very little insurance liability in India for damage to the environment and natural resources. Following the findings of the Court vis-a-vis absolute liability in the Oleum gas leak case,[22] the Government of India recognized the need for comprehensive insurance liability for all manufacturing enterprises involved in

[19] E.g., *Westend Green Farms Society v Union of India* 2019 SCC OnLine NGT 1326.

[20] *Municipal Council, Ratlam v Shri Vardhichand AIR* 1980 SC 1622.

[21] For details regarding composition and jurisdiction of this special court, see the webpage of Department of Environment, Government of Haryana <http://harenvironment.gov.in/en/environment-courts>.

[22] See *MC Mehta v Union of India* AIR 1987 SC 1086 (Oleum gas leak case).

inherently dangerous activities. As a response, the PLIA was enacted which mandated a corpus for the same. It imposes a duty upon industries handling certain types of hazardous chemicals and other classes of flammable substances to take out a special insurance policy to cover the liabilities likely to arise due to any chemical (industrial) accident. ERF was also established under the PLIA, to provide immediate relief to victims of accidents involving hazardous substances. The PLIA thus requires industries dealing with hazardous substances to subscribe compulsorily to public liability insurance and contribute to the ERF under section 7A that was to be used, *inter alia*, for compensation for the victims. Furthermore, section 24 of the National Green Tribunal Act, 2010 that deals with damage to the environment and various forms of compensation awarded by the NGT forms part of the ERF.[23] However, the quantum of relief provided under the PLIA has never been revised. A report highlights that the ERF has been underutilized and there exist ambiguities in its legal (including tax) status.[24]

Second, civil liability is recognized under the Companies Act, 2013, where public listed companies and financial institutions with a certain paid up capital are required to have in place corporate social and environmental responsibility strategies, including steps to have an environmental audit annually, and bear liability for Environment Impact Assessments (EIAs) and environmental clearance under the Environment (Protection) Act and related legislation.[25] Since 2022, under the Securities and Exchange Board of India Act, 1992, the top 1,000 listed companies (by market capitalization) are duty bound to file a Business Responsibility and Sustainability Report that may include environmental costs, expenses, and any anticipatory monitoring or mitigation expenses.[26] Remediation liability has been imposed upon industries and companies that pose an environmental and health risk for the local communities.[27] Accordingly, companies and industries are liable to incur costs for evaluation of risks, inviting experts, social workers, and non-governmental organizations for monitoring, building infrastructure facilities for residents, relocating communities, or integrating them with the business, schools, day care centres, and health clinics.[28] Liability upon companies therefore includes environmental liability for violation of procedural regulations resulting in fines, penalties, compensatory damages, or even punitive damages.[29] Beyond this statutory environmental liability, there may be further scope for imposition of negligence liability upon

[23] Debadityo Sinha, 'The Management of Environment Relief Fund' (Vidhi Centre for Legal Policy 2020), <https://vidhilegalpolicy.in/wp-content/uploads/2020/06/Management_of_ERF_Debadityo_Sinha_VCLP_2020.pdf>.

[24] ibid.

[25] Companies Act 2013, Sch VII.

[26] Securities and Exchange Board of India, Business responsibility and sustainability reporting by listed entities, Circular SEBI/HO/CFD/CMD-2/P/CIR/2021/562 dated 10 May 2021.

[27] E.g., *TN Pollution Control Board v Sterlite Industries (I) Ltd* (2019) 19 SCC 479.

[28] ibid.

[29] ibid.

companies or the state based upon expansion of a larger environmental 'duty of care' under tort of negligence.[30]

Third, the liability of suppliers of nuclear materials for damage arising out of nuclear accidents in India caused due to any latent defects or substandard services has been laid out under section 17(b) of the Civil Liability for Nuclear Damage Act, 2010 and rule 24 of the Civil Liability for Damage Rules, 2011. The nature of liability leans closer towards the standards of absolute liability as it does not take into consideration any intention or *mens rea* while determining the liability. In addition, the limitation period as provided under rule 24 for claiming an amount by way of recourse is arbitrary and in violation of Article 14 of the Constitution.[31]

9.3 Liability under Environmental Statutes

There are numerous rules notified by the Ministry of Environment, Forests and Climate Change (MoEFCC) and the CPCB under environmental statutes, such as the Water (Prevention and Control of Pollution) Act 1974 (Water Pollution Act), the Air (Prevention and Control of Pollution) Act 1981 (Air Pollution Act), and the Environment (Protection) Act. The Environment (Protection) Rules, 1986 provide for standards that each sector of industry should follow. Failure to follow these rules attracts statutory liability in the form of fines, penalties, compensation, disconnection of power and water supply or injunctions to stop industrial activity completely and/or punishment. Sections 3, 5, and 6 of the Environment (Protection) Act are in respect of the prevention and control of pollution and environmental protection. They, for example, apply to waste (chemical, industrial residential biomedical), to sanitation and sewage, microplastics, hazardous waste, and E-batteries, among other things. For infraction of standards under the above rules, provision of citizen suits under section 19 allows individuals to seek remedial measures.[32] The Environment (Protection) Rules not only provide standards for reducing and managing pollution and effluents or discharges in each specific sector but also liability for violation of statutory provisions.

[30] For a discussion on expansion of 'environmental duty of care' and its scope, see Gunningham (n 9) 206–208.

[31] Arghya Sengupta and Sanhita Ambast, 'A Dangerous Recourse? A Critical Relook at Section 17 of the Civil Liability for Nuclear Damage Act, 2010' (2012) 3(4) *International Journal of Nuclear Law* 292.

[32] For similar citizen suit provisions, see Water (Prevention and Control of Pollution) Act 1974, s 49, and Air (Prevention and Control of Pollution) Act 1981, s 43.

9.3.1 Liability under the Water (Prevention and Control of Pollution) Act, 1974

The Water Pollution Act recognizes liability for non-compliance with its provisions. Chapter VII lists the liability for breach of statutory standards and directions. Section 41 imposes liability for breach of section 20(2) in respect of collection of effluent samples from the water source or stream, sewage, or trade effluents upon an occupier's premises. A person is liable for imprisonment or a fine or both, if she does not furnish the required information or provides false information to the SPCB under sections 25 and 26. Section 43 entails liability upon a person who contravenes section 24 and the punishment is imprisonment and a fine. Liability under this section aims to control pollution and deter poisonous noxious or polluting matter to be discharged into any stream, well or sewer or on land.[33] Sections 25 and 26 provide for restrictions and standards to establish and operate an industry for which permission must be obtained from the CPCB or the SPCB (licence and permit). These form the most important provisions of the water pollution regulatory regime.

Section 45 allows for enhanced conviction of imprisonment and a fine in cases where there has been a previous conviction in the preceding two years under sections 24, 25 or 26. Section 46 provides for deterrence by allowing courts to publish in newspapers or in such other manner the names, addresses, and information about a repeat offender at his own cost. Section 47 provides for the liability of companies and management personnel while section 48 provides for liability for government departments.

Apart from penalties for not having a valid environmental permit/consent, the Act includes provisions that impose sanctions. Section 33 empowers the SPCB or the CPCB to apply to the court, to restrain any person causing pollution if the pollution is likely to prejudicially affect water in a stream or a well. Section 33A empowers the Board to order the closure of any industry and to stop the electricity, water, and any other service to such industry. A legal duty was so created by virtue of the Act to protect water bodies. Despite these relatively harsher sanctions, rivers, ponds, and lakes in the country stay extremely polluted and statutory authorities remain 'negligent' in implementation.[34]

9.3.2 Liability under the Air (Prevention and Control of Pollution) Act, 1981

Provisions under the Air Pollution Act are like those of the Water Pollution Act. An occupier of land engaged in any kind of industrial venture, or commercial operation is required to follow standards and procure similar licence/permits, that is, consent to

[33] See also Water Pollution Act, s 24(1)(b) and s 24(2)(a–d).

[34] *Akhil Bhartiya Mengela Samaj Parishad v Maharashtra Pollution Control Board* OA No. 64 of 2016 (NGT—Western Zone Bench, Judgment dated 24 January 2022).

establish and operate any enterprise from the SPCB. Section 37 provides for criminal liability upon failure to comply with sections 21 or 22 that require the occupier to procure a license to establish and operate. Violation of directions issued by SPCBs or the CPCB attract criminal liability of imprisonment and fine.[35] Liability has been imposed on errant polluters by courts in the form of not only compensatory damages but also retributive and reparative damages for rehabilitation.[36] With recent reports of very poor air and water quality, extreme pollution deterrent and exemplary damages have been imposed.[37] In air pollution cases decided by the Supreme Court, especially in crop residue burning practice by the farmers in Northern India, the Court has imposed liability not only on errant individuals but also state and local authorities for failing to perform their constitutional and statutory duties to provide air free of pollution and accordingly take steps to control pollution as interpreted under Article 21 of the Constitution. Failure to administer air quality control and to stop the practice of burning crop residue, *inter alia*, has contributed to severe air pollution in North India and the state has been held liable for non-performance of its duty as the air pollution has caused serious health and environmental problems.[38] In *MC Mehta v Union of India*,[39] the NGT issued notice to the state authorities as to why they should not be asked to pay compensation as they had acquiesced and failed to prevent stubble burning which was in utter violation of the public trust doctrine,[40] and their duties under the Air Pollution Act.[41]

9.3.3 Liability under the Environment (Protection) Act, 1986

The Environment (Protection) Act is an umbrella legislation that empowers the central government to make rules in respect of protection of the environment. Central and state government authorities, that is, the CPCB and SPCBs are empowered to make rules and establish parameters for liability in accordance with the centre's direction. Section 6 confers rule-making power upon the central government in respect of matters in section 3. Section 7 imposes a duty not to discharge pollutants in excess of set standards. Violation or non-compliance with such standards attracts liability upon any legal person 'carrying on any industry, operation or process'. Section 15 recognizes liability in the form of penalties for contravention of the provisions of the Act as well as

35 Air Pollution Act, s 37(2).

36 *Aryavart Foundation v Vapi Green Enviro Ltd* 2021 SCC OnLine NGT 4.

37 For a detailed description of the CPCB's initiative under the National Air Quality Monitoring Program (NAMP), see <https://cpcb.nic.in/about-namp/>.

38 *Vardhaman Kaushik v Union of India* OA No 21 of 2014 (NGT—Principal Bench, Judgment dated 4 December 2014).

39 *MC Mehta v Union of India* (2020) 7 SCC 573.

40 *MC Mehta v Kamal Nath* (1997) 1 SCC 388.

41 *Central Pollution Control Board v News Item Published in, Asian Age* OA No 1038 of 2018 (NGT Principal Bench, Order dated 15 July 2022).

the Environment (Protection) Rules, and orders and directions issued under sections 3, 5, and 6. The punishment for such infraction can be imprisonment or fine or both. Section 16 lays down liability for companies and section 17 lays down liability for government departments. Under section 24(2), where any act or omission constitutes an offence punishable under this Act and under any other Act then the offender found guilty of such offence shall be liable to be punished under the other Act and not under this Act.

9.3.4 Liability under the National Green Tribunal Act, 2010

The NGT was established under section 3 of the NGT Act to provide effective and expeditious disposal of cases relating to environmental protection and conservation of forests and other natural resources as well as liability for infractions. The NGT exercises jurisdiction over all civil cases involving substantial questions relating to the environment including enforcement of any legal right relating to the environment (section 14(1)). The NGT deals with civil cases under the seven laws related to the environment listed under Schedule 1.[42] The NGT can order compensation for restitution in instances where the person or their property has been damaged due to pollution; for restitution of the property so damaged; and for restitution of the environment. The NGT can add to or award damages from the ERF under section 24 as mentioned above. The nature of liability as recognized under the NGT Act is civil and tort based—not only based on polluter pays principle but also under the PLIA and compliance obligations under the listed Acts. It is in form of compensatory damages for injury or loss to a person, their property, to the environment or ecology—for repair, remediation, rehabilitation. Even punitive and exemplary damages have been imposed upon errant individual industries and government authorities.[43] Under section 15(1), the NGT can divide the compensation or relief payable under separate heads as specified in Schedule II of the Act, which includes claims due to harm, damage or destruction to flora, including aquatic flora, crops, vegetables, trees, and orchards; including cost for restoration on account of harm, or damage to the environment including pollution of soil, air, water, land, and ecosystems and marine waters.[44]

A person may be found criminally liable upon failure to comply with an order or award or decision of the NGT. Non-compliance of the direction or award is punishable with imprisonment, or a fine or both (section 26(1)). A company is liable where it fails to comply with any order or award or decision of the NGT and punishable with a fine (section 26(2)). Where the failure or contravention continues, an additional fine applies.

[42] See NGT Act ss 1, 2, 14–34.

[43] *Samir Mehta v Union of India* 2016 SCC OnLine NGT 479.

[44] Wildlife (Protection) Act, 1972 and FRA 2006 are not covered under the NGT Act.

Where restitution damages are awarded, these are based on NGT rules and require a restitution plan with specific details of the damages caused and the repair required.[45]

9.4 Liability under Natural Resources Statutes

There are several laws for the protection, conservation, preservation, management, and governance of natural resources. They prescribe duties upon the state, compliance obligations upon the state, industry, and individuals, apart from civil and criminal liability in the form of fines and penalties.

9.4.1 Liability under Wildlife Laws

The Wildlife Protection Act, 1972 (WLPA) provides for the protection of wild animals, birds, and plants. It aims to protect the remaining population of endangered species by banning hunting, giving legal protection to their habitats, and restricting wildlife trade among other things. The WLPA was amended in 1990, 1992, and 2006 to include strict criminal liabilities to deter against violations and in accordance with India's international obligations under the Convention on International Trade in Endangered Species of Wild Fauna and Flora, 1975. The WLPA empowers the central and state governments to declare any area a wildlife sanctuary, national park, or closed area and provides varying degrees of liability based on the degree of protection accorded to the protected area.

Section 9 provides for liability in terms of prohibition of hunting and its regulation through a permit for any wild animal specified in Schedules I, II, III, and IV subject to certain exceptions. The Act provides for protection of the listed species of flora and fauna and establishes a network of ecologically important protected areas. A person is criminally liable if being in possession, *inter alia*, of the listed species or having entered a protected area without a valid permit. Further, there is prohibition on any industrial activity inside protected areas. Where it becomes necessary to carry on any activity that is non-forest related, a proponent needs to get an environmental clearance under the FCA and the Centrally Empowered Environment Committee constituted under the FCA. A person or a company may be liable if it operates without an environmental clearance or a forest clearance under these specific laws. Sections 18–35 declare protected areas (sanctuaries, national parks, bio reserves, and closed areas) and establish a procedure to notify or de-notify land and settlement of the rights of villagers. A person may be held liable for violation of any of the provisions that are declared to be illegal under

[45] NGT (Practices and Procedure) Rules 2011, rr 35–37.

the various rules once an area is declared to be a protected area. Each state may have different rules for entry, activities that are allowed or permits for entry, and activities that are prohibited. Furthermore, within National Parks and Biodiversity hotspots or Tiger reserves, all entry and activities are strictly prohibited and attract penal liability for violation. For example, criminal proceedings have been taken against wildlife traffickers and persons who have been caught hunting or smuggling scheduled animals and plants.[46]

The WLPA prohibits, *inter alia*, taking or hunting of wildlife, without a licence or permit, and its scheduled species and creates penalty in the form of fines and punishment for violations.[47] Thus a person may be liable, for example, for hunting without a licence, or hunting or taking without any permit or breaching any of the conditions of a licence or permit granted for different activities that are allowed under the Act,[48] such as taking away or collection of berries or leaves for livelihood, letting in cattle for grazing into a protected area, hunting, collecting feathers, hooves, nails, skin of dead animals, cutting trees for firewood or branches or bark of a tree, etc.[49] In *State of Rajasthan v Salman Khan*,[50] the accused person was prosecuted for killing a protected species of Indian black buck under the WLPA, among others.

A trial court empowered to conduct a criminal trial may convict a person who may then be punishable with imprisonment or a fine or both.[51] Under section 57, there is a presumption in certain cases against the accused, that is, where it is established that they are in possession, custody or control of any captive animal, animal, article, meat, etc. until the contrary is proved. The burden of proving lawful possession, custody or control of such article lies on the accused. Section 58 provides offences by companies and section 51(1) pins liability on the concerned officials of the company. The liability in respect of direct infringement of the provisions in respect of hunting, taking, smuggling, using, entering among others, translates into imprisonment and fines.[52] For instance in 2017, the Madhya Pradesh Tiger Strike Force caught a ring of Indian and international smugglers smuggling pangolin scales and protected species of turtles. The Task Force accused thirty-seven people, of which thirteen were arrested and criminally charged under the WLPA.[53]

[46] E.g., *Sansar Chand v State of Rajasthan* (2010) 10 SCC 604; *Salman Khan v State of Rajasthan* 2016 SCC OnLine Raj 4853.

[47] See WLPA, s 51.

[48] See WLPA, ss 11–17 (A–H), 51–58 (A–Y).

[49] See WLPA, ss 2(18), 2(23), 9, 51, 52 and 53.

[50] *State v Salman Khan* Criminal Case No 66 of 2011 (Chief Judicial Magistrate, Jodhpur District, Jodhpur, order of 5 April 2018 (WLPA, ss 9 and 51, etc.).

[51] WLPA, s 51.

[52] WLPA, s 51.

[53] P Naveen, 'Madhya Pradesh Court Acquits 11 in High Profile Wildlife Smuggling Case' *Times of India* (29 November 2021) <https://timesofindia.indiatimes.com/city/bhopal/madhya-pradesh-court-acquits-11-in-high-profile-wildlife-smuggling-case/articleshow/87971776.cms>.

9.4.2 Liability under Forest Laws

The Indian Forest Act and the FCA deal with acquisition, use, and conservation of natural resources. The Forest Act recognizes three kinds of forest, that is, village, reserve forests, and protected forests.[54] On a decreasing scale, reserve forests have a higher degree of protection, then protected forests, and lastly village forests. Unlike National Parks or wildlife sanctuaries under the WLPA, reserved forests and protected forests are declared by the respective state governments. Activities such as hunting and grazing in reserved forests are banned and entail criminal liability unless specific orders are issued otherwise. In protected forests, there is limited liability as such activities are sometimes allowed for communities living on the fringes of the forest, who sustain their livelihood partially or wholly from forest resources or products. A state government may declare any reserved, protected or village forest into a sanctuary or a national park with procedures prescribed under the WLPA and settlement of rights under the WLPA or the FRA. The procedure consists of multi stakeholder participation, inputs, and determination of rights of the villagers.[55] The Forest Act further deals with settlement of land rights and user rights, as well as criminal liability for infringement of various other provisions. Criminal liability for offences under the Forest Act is provided, under sections 42 and 63 read with the IPC. It provides for imprisonment or a fine or both for infraction of state forest rules.

The FCA was enacted to address the rampant deforestation and diversion of forest land for non-forestry purposes. An amendment was introduced in 1988, under which state governments were prohibited from assigning, by way of lease or otherwise, any forest land or any portion thereof to any private person or authority (that was not owned, managed, or controlled by government) without prior sanction of the central government. This imposed a duty upon state governments in the management of forest land, derogation of which entails liability. A state government that allows de-reservation of forests for any construction project or mining activity can be held liable if the project proponent and the state government have not been given a forest clearance under the FCA. It is important to reiterate that any environmental clearance required under the Environmental (Protection) Rules such as an EIA process also takes account of processes to be followed for forest clearance under the FCA. The infraction of the regulatory procedure for both an environmental clearance and forest clearance under the Environmental (Protection) Rules, including non-performance of an EIA and under the FCA Rules, attract liability. Further, an environmental clearance and a forest clearance may also entail settlement of rights of traditional forest dwellers under the FRA.

In the context of natural resources, one can observe not only conflicts between the centre and states in respect of coordination between government authorities but also between fair settlement of rights of traditional dwellers within forests and industries,

54 Indian Forest Act ss 3, 4–27 and 28–30.

55 WLPA s 35A.

and non-observance of regulatory procedures by project proponents whether private or state. One also observes a solution based judicial approach that has provided direction for resolution of such conflicts and an ingenious interpretation of law and policy while recognizing the polluter or wrongdoer's liability or duty under the public trust doctrine of state liability in allowing mining[56] by the Supreme Court.[57] Furthermore, the NGT has not only applied and followed environmental principles and found individuals and corporations or the state liable but has provided detailed direction to administrative environmental agencies.[58]

9.5 Emerging Trends and the Role of the Judiciary

This section provides an insight into emerging trends within environmental protection cases, creation of new instances of liability by the judiciary, and the challenges in the implementation and enforcement of statutes. It reflects on a few cases that illustrate how the Supreme Court and the NGT have been instrumental in shaping the environmental regulatory and liability regime. It also examines cases where the judiciary has resolved conflicts using various environmental principles in a nuanced manner to impose liability upon various actors to meet the objectives of specific statutes for the protection, preservation, and conservation of the environment. Certain cases reflect areas where conflict has arisen between the centre and states or where there have been lapses on the part of the administrative state authorities that have ignored environmental objectives. Some cases also reflect a hiatus or gap within federal or state statutes that the courts have addressed by relying upon policy and the constitutional mandate of environmental protection. In doing so, the courts have imposed liability in the form of mandatory duty or personal liability of state functionaries for non-compliance with the rules.

One instance of hiatus in the execution of forest related laws and rules in recent years is with respect to the application of the FCA, and the use of funds with the Compensatory Afforestation Fund Management and Planning Authority (CAMPA) for the benefit of tribal communities.[59] The FCA provides that each time forest land is diverted, the project proponent bears liability to pay the state to undertake plantation and liability to pay compensation for the ecosystem services lost due to diversion of forest land called

[56] E.g., *Goa Foundation v Union of India* (2014) 6 SCC 590.

[57] See e.g., the role of the Supreme Court in *TN Godavarman Thirumulpad v Union of India* 2022 SCC OnLine SC 1318 (in particular paras 12, 15, 16 of the order dated 9 May 2022 and paras 27–29 of the order dated 3 June 2022).

[58] E.g., *Sushil Bhatt v Moon Beverages Ltd* 2022 SCC OnLine NGT 76.

[59] *TN Godavarman Thirumulpad v Union of India* WP (C) No 202 OF 1995 (Supreme Court of India, Judgment dated 12 March 2014). See also *TN Godavarman Thirumulpad v Union of India* (1997) 3 SCC 312.

Net Present Value. A project proponent is also liable to pay the state for diverting forest land for non-forest purposes, such as industrial projects like mining or dams. All such approvals were to be done by the centrally empowered statutory committee constituted under the FCA, directly under the central government, namely the MoEFCC. After the decision in the *TN Godavarman Thirumulpad v Union of India* case, all states needed prior approval from the Supreme Court for any business activity in respect of forests. The Court also set up the monitoring committee for CAMPA and the Compensation Afforestation Fund (CAF). According to the MoEFCC, this fund has accumulated approximately INR 660 billion.[60] Monies from this fund ought to be deployed for carrying out compensatory afforestation across the country. However, it is not being allocated by the central government to the states for political or budgetary reasons. The hiatus can be clearly seen when the money is not allocated or used for the purpose that it was created. Accordingly, the liability for violating the FCA or any related rule becomes infructuous. Detailed guidelines were provided by the Supreme Court through various orders over the last thirty years in respect of all sectors related to activities within the forests. Supreme Court orders have also contributed significantly to the evolution and development of environmental law and recognition of liability for violation of such laws. However, there are no statutory rules or regulatory guidelines on how the central government is to allocate such a fund or how to use it based on a variable or suitable scientific formula within each state. There are no statutory state committees comprising forest experts nor locals or forest dwellers who could best advise upon the use of funds for tree/forest plantation or species introduction in every state. Accordingly, even if liability exists upon the state government under the statute or under an order of the court, if funds are underutilized, it makes the objective of environmental protection illusionary and the court's directions unachievable.

Additionally, in accordance with the FRA that recognizes the primacy of a *Gram Sabha* (village council) while deciding the fate of the forests, such funds need to be used with their consent and participation in different states. However, a new set of CAF Rules was introduced in 2018 in which participation of the *Gram Sabha* was ousted and replaced with state bureaucrats with state interests at heart rather than those of the community, clearly in violation of the FRA.[61] However, there have been only a couple of cases so far where the NGT has recognized and imposed liability on state governments—each state having failed not only in upholding respective constitutional duty under Articles 48 or 51A(g), but also having ignored or allowed infractions of various forest laws, such as the FCA, the FRA, and provisions for forest clearance along with environmental clearance under the Environment (Protection) Act in allowing project proponents to develop or proceed with projects for increasing state revenues.[62] This situation provides a classic example of conflict between the centre and states and administrative indifference

[60] Mayank Agarwal, 'India's New Compensatory Afforestation Rules Dilute Rights of Forest Dwellers' *Mongabay India* (23 August 2018) <https://india.mongabay.com/2018/08/indias-new>.

[61] ibid.

[62] *State of Meghalaya v All Dimasa Students Union* (2019) 8 SCC 177.

that exists for environmental fund management under state rules. Liability for misapplication or mismanagement of funds should then rest squarely on the state as well as the central government.

In such circumstances, the judiciary plays a vital role as a guardian of the environment, and in prioritizing development for state or citizen interests. An illustration of the same can be observed in *State of Meghalaya v All Dimasa Students Union*.[63] The NGT imposed liability to the tune of INR 100 crores upon the State of Meghalaya for allowing illegal mining in violation of the Forest Act and the FCA among others.[64] Upon appeal by the state government, the Supreme Court held that 'the direction of Tribunal will not come into force if the mining is done by Tribal community in accordance with the regulations contained in the relevant statutory provisions'. Furthermore, the state was liable to pay INR 100 crores and as this was 'neither a penalty nor a fine imposed upon State' but '[t]he amount has been directed to be deposited for carrying out steps regarding restoration of environment'.[65] The amount was in the form of civil statutory liability and the state was held liable for violating environmental norms and principles in respect of the protection of natural resources by allowing indiscriminate mining. The state was permitted to transfer the said amount from the Meghalaya Environment Protection and Relief Fund to the CPCB which was directed to utilize the same for restoration of the environment.

Similarly, in *Mantri Techzone Private Limited v Forward Foundation*,[66] the Supreme Court has interpreted the nature of liability impositions and remedies available to the Tribunal. It was held that liability in the form of compensation, and directions that could be restitutionary as well as remedial. Liability can also be imposed to repair the environmental damages caused to the administrative and other statutory authorities in respect of questions that raise substantial environmental issues.

Along with the Supreme Court, the NGT has played a pivotal role in recognizing liability situations based on tortious wrongs or regulatory violations and has provided a direction to the effective working of administrative and statutory authorities under various pollution laws. For instance, in *Paryavaran Suraksha Samiti and Another v Union of India*,[67] a much-needed impetus was infused into the prolonged attempts at capacity building and strengthening the administrative and statutory bodies, such as CPCB/SPCBs/pollution control committees (PCCs) under the Environment (Protection) Act, the Water Pollution Act and the Air Pollution Act. In another case, the NGT directed the state authorities to take measures and provided detailed directions for strengthening of SPCBs and PCCs in Union Territories and of the CPCB itself. The NGT also cautioned that upon inaction or non-compliance with the detailed directions, the relevant heads

[63] ibid.

[64] *All Dimasa Students Union Dima Hasao District Committee v State of Meghalaya OA* No 73 of 2014 (NGT Principal Bench, Order dated 4 January 2019).

[65] *State of Meghalaya* (n 62) para 179.

[66] *Mantri Techzone Private Limited v Forward Foundation* (2019) 18 SCC 494.

[67] *Paryavaran Suraksha Samiti v Union of India* 2021 SCC OnLine NGT 538.

and officers of state and central statutory administrative authorities would be personally liable to pay compensation from their salaries.[68] In *Samir Mehta v Union of India*,[69] the NGT imposed liability of INR 100 crores for environmental damage due to an oil spill and dumping of coal in the seabed and causing marine pollution based on the polluter pays principle as well as civil liability recognized under international conventions that India had signed but not ratified.[70]

The NGT has from time to time also issued regulatory guidelines along with imposing liabilities. In *Nathan Chaudhary v State of GNCTD*, the NGT disposed the case with a direction to the SPCB and the CPCB to ensure compliance with the Hazardous Waste Management Rules, 2016 and the recommendations of the Committee which, *inter-alia*, recommended the Indian Oil Corporation Limited to prepare uniform Standard Operating Procedure for E-auctioning of hazardous and other waste, including spent catalyst.[71] The above case illustrates the NGT's unique stance on filling gaps in regulatory frameworks by bringing together judicial function along with scientific expertise. Similarly, in *Bonani Kakkar v Oil India Limited*,[72] a case concerning a fire that broke out in one of the pipelines of Oil India Limited (OIL), the NGT laid out the process that needs to be followed to determine the biodiversity impact assessment. This assessment was deemed to be fundamental in determining the final liability of OIL and the compensation to the affected families in the area and the environmental restitution costs.[73] The role of the expert members of the NGT is highlighted in such orders as they are instrumental in laying out the technical details of such impact assessment and determination of liabilities. The above cases are examples of how the judiciary and particularly the NGT have been instrumental in shaping the environmental regulatory and liability regime.

Conclusion

It is not trite to state that the mixed spectrum of liabilities that exists in the environmental and natural resources law regime is being widely facilitated by the principles of common law and civil liability provisions. Criminal liability such as provided under the IPC, aiding the environment specific liabilities prove to be effective as the fear of censure and sanctions provide for a good jurisprudential reason to comply. While the polluter pays principle is a strong tool to ensure that offenders do not get away lightly in terms

[68] *Akhil Bhartiya Mengela* (n 34). See also *Shailesh Singh v State of Haryana* 2021 SCC OnLine NGT 1231.

[69] *Samir Mehta v Union of India* 2014 SCC OnLine NGT 927.

[70] ibid.

[71] *Nathan Chaudhary* (n 8).

[72] *Bonani Kakkar v Oil India Ltd* 2021 SCC OnLine NGT 519.

[73] ibid, para 12.

of monetary compensation, the penal provisions provide for incarceration in several cases thus attributing responsibility. Both civil and criminal liability for environmental damage reflect diverse functions. Liability rules arising from common law within the domestic environmental law regime in India can provide compensatory, rehabilitative, and corrective justice relief. For meaningful imposition of liability, there needs to be coordinated functioning of administrative institutions, which so far has been missing. Environmental law and its interpretation also need to ensure that the fear of censure and development can go hand in hand.

In this context, the role of the judiciary as an environmentally conscious body resonates from the judgments by the Supreme Court and orders of the NGT, which while providing relief, have also expanded the scope of environmental liability for compensatory damage in an unprecedented manner. Challenges are aplenty and full compliance is a long way from being realized. Among other environmental and natural resources governance and management issues as discussed above, the discussion, debate, and dissonance within the centre and state laws and policy have also provided an impetus to focus upon environmental rights of and injustice meted upon the most affected stakeholders, such as indigenous population and vulnerable communities, and determine the liability of the wrongdoers. Judicial innovation has also come a long way, for example, the power to publish details of the offenders is an unusual provision that affords public sanction and censure.

Environmental liability thus has a dual function to perform. On the one hand, it needs to reflect the societal and political needs. On the other, it provides an economic incentive in adhering to the standards or the rules of specific statutes, to carry out a corrective justice function, impose penal punishment and recompense the harm done.

Suggestions for Further Reading

Sunil Gulia and others, 'Evolution of Air Pollution Management Policies and Related Research in India' (2022) 6 *Environmental Challenges* 100431.

Neil Gunningham, 'Should a General "Duty of Care" for the Environment Become a Centrepiece of a "Next Generation" Environment Protection Statute?' (2017) 34 *Environmental and Planning Law Journal* 198.

Jason Hochstatter, 'Legal Liability' in Ali Farazmand (ed), *Global Encyclopaedia of Public Administration, Public Policy, and Governance* (Springer 2018) 3754.

Sridhar Rengarajan and others, 'National Green Tribunal of India—An Observation from Environmental Judgements' (2018) 25 *Environmental Science and Pollution Research* 11313.

Charu Sharma, *Tort Liability for Environmental Claims in India—A Comparative View* (Universal Publication 2017).

PART III

PRINCIPLES AND CONCEPTS

CHAPTER 10

SUSTAINABLE DEVELOPMENT

Exploring Jurisprudential and Policy Trajectories

NUPUR CHOWDHURY AND HAARIS MOOSA

Abstract

The chapter explores the inflection points and undercurrents in the evolution of the principle of sustainable development starting from the Brundtland Commission report. The jurisprudential evolution of the principle of sustainable development from the Supreme Court and carried on by the High Courts and the National Green Tribunal is surveyed through the matrices of environment protection, the imperatives of economic and social development and indeterminacy. Also analysed is the impact that natural disasters have on environmental decision making. The interplay of the principle of sustainable development with the reality of social development and the resultant policy formulations are also analysed in the backdrop of the balancing act of environmental protection and economic development.

Introduction

The Brundtland Commission Report of 1987 is the widely accepted benchmark in most academic and policy writings on sustainable development. The report provides the following definition for the term:

> humanity has the possibility of making development sustainable, which is of ensuring that it meets the needs of the present without compromising the ability

of future generations to meet their needs. The concept of sustainable development involves limits, but not absolute ones.[1]

The Brundtland Report passed the baton of sustainable development to the Rio Declaration of 1992. In the former, sustainable development was defined by combining the ideas of human needs and environmental limits, while the latter went on to give it a wider scope of intergenerational equity and intra-generational equity.[2] Inter-generational equity was based on the idea of regulating current consumption patterns[3] to ensure natural replenishment which would not undermine or threaten the security of future generations. Intra-generational equity is based on three pillars—social development, economic development, and environmental protection. These three pillars are not stacked in order of priority, and it is emphasized that these pillars are mutually supportive and therefore need to be pursued simultaneously.[4] Although this sounds eminently logical, how countries pursue sustainable development was left largely to them, and this is manifested quite starkly in how they have sought to address each of these three pillars.

In India, it was the higher judiciary and then later the National Green Tribunal (NGT) rather than the executive or the legislature, which played a leadership role in developing the domestic discourse on sustainable development.

The Supreme Court evolved a rich environmental jurisprudence which adopted sustainable development as its fulcrum. It extensively referenced the principle in evolving response to private and public acts of environmental pollution and enlarging public participation by allowing the ordinary public to bring to its attention such acts and in evolving new mechanisms for oversight like continuing mandamus. One aspect which suffered from relative under attention of the Court has been the disproportionate impact of environmental degradation on the poor. A review of the Court's jurisprudence on sustainable development beginning in the nineties provides insights into how the Court adopted the discourse of sustainable development in the Indian context and comments specifically on its attempt to balance the three pillars—social development, economic development, and environmental protection. Another critical outcome of the Court's early adoption and emphasis on sustainable development was the push to establish a specialized environmental court. Eventually, the NGT was established in 2010 and given an explicit statutory mandate to apply the principle of sustainable development, and this has led to an expansion of the discourse on sustainable development.

This chapter provides an overview of the most important benchmarks in the application of sustainable development in the Indian context. It is divided into three parts. The

[1] World Commission on Environment and Development, *Our Common Future* (OUP 1987) para 27.

[2] Rio Declaration on Environment and Development, 14 June 1992, UN Doc A/CONF.151/26/Rev. 1 (Vol. I), Annex II (1992), Principle 3.

[3] ibid, Principle 8.

[4] C Lemke, *Accounting and Statistical Analyses for Sustainable Development* (Springer Gabler Wiesbaden 2021).

first section focuses on how the Supreme Court and the NGT sought to emphasize the balance between the two pillars of economic development and environmental protection. Additionally, we also highlight how the frequent experience of natural disasters has provoked High Courts to explore new discourses on sustainable development. In the second section, we focus on the neglected question of social development in the context of environmental justice through the lens of court decisions. In the third section, we explore how the policy and legislative frameworks engage with the three pillars of sustainable development. The policy framework should be seen as an important adjunct to the Supreme Court's discourse on sustainable development because many of the policies were developed in response to the Court's nudge to the executive.

10.1 Environment Protection Versus Economic Development

As underlined earlier, the judiciary took an early lead domestically in developing a discourse on sustainable development, drawing inspiration from both the Brundtland Report and the Rio Declaration.[5] This section discusses some of the epochal judicial decisions on sustainable development in India, a discussion on certain outlier judgments of the Supreme Court, especially on the aspect of indeterminacy, and a survey of some progressive judgments of certain High Courts, together providing evidence of two interrelated aspects. First, there has been an overemphasis on economic development among the three pillars. The Supreme Court sought to justify economic development, even in the face of environmental degradation, by mandating environmental compensation to be provided for by project proponents. A natural corollary to this overemphasis has been the extensive application of the polluter pays principle. In contrast, the precautionary principle has been less applied, although it has been referenced extensively in judicial decisions.

10.2 Indeterminacy and Indian Environmental Law

The year 1996 was a watershed year in the development of environmental law in India. For the first time, the Supreme Court engaged with the idea of sustainable development in *Vellore Citizens' Welfare Forum v Union of India*.[6] Its essential features were identified

[5] Saptarishi Bandopadhyay, 'Sustainable Development and Indian Environmental Jurisprudence' in Shibani Ghosh (ed), *Indian Environmental Law: Key Concepts and Principles* (Orient Black Swan 2019)

[6] *Vellore Citizens' Welfare Forum v Union of India* (1996) 5 SCC 647.

as including the precautionary principle and the polluter pays principle.[7] Even though other principles were mentioned,[8] they were not made a part of the discourse on sustainable development.

The principle of sustainable development was interpreted inconsistently in the mid-1990s. In *FB Taraporawala v Bayer India Ltd*, while referring to *Vellore*, Justice BL Hansaria went on to say that 'maintenance of balance between development and its sustenance in future' has to be ensured.[9] This lays bare the divergence in the ideation of sustainable development even as early as in 1996. It was later that the idea of 'carrying capacity' of ecosystems was merged with the idea of sustainable development.[10]

The Supreme Court, in *AP Pollution Control Board v MV Nayadu*, officially sanctioned the use of writ remedies for enforcing environmental rights by linking the right to a clean environment with the right to life under Article 21 of the Constitution of India.[11] Here, sustainable development proved to be the perfect protean fit for the exercise of residuary powers under Articles 226, 136, and 32 of the Constitution.[12] The indeterminacy that was to mark Indian environmental law for the coming decades is the alchemy of this protean nature of sustainable development and the extraordinary residuary nature of writ remedies under the Constitution.[13]

This indeterminacy in environmental proceedings has meant that the real worth of the principle of sustainable development came to be tested later on and the Supreme Court held that a change in *status quo* need not be looked at with suspicion.[14] When faced with the future of a large-scale infrastructure project, the Supreme Court courted the possibility of 'mitigating' environmental harms even while pushing ahead with developmental projects.[15] Sustainable development as a principle was further nuanced by linking it to the vitality of the environment and natural resources of a certain 'quality' for 'continued economic and social development'[16] and it was also said that sustainable development can only be understood in relation to the 'right to development'.[17] Further the principle was linked with the preservation of human life and property and 'disaster management' was made a part of it.[18] The most jarring exposition of the genesis of the principle by the Supreme Court was in *Research Foundation for Science Technology National Resource Policy v Union of India* where the Court observed that:

[7] ibid 11.

[8] ibid (Inter-Generational Equity, Use and Conservation of Natural Resources, Environmental Protection, the Precautionary Principle, Polluter Pays principle, Obligation to assist and cooperate, Eradication of Poverty and Financial Assistance to the developing countries).

[9] *FB Taraporawala v Bayer India Ltd* (1996) 6 SCC 58 [4].

[10] *MC Mehta (Taj Trapezium Matter) v Union of India* (1997) 2 SCC 353[27].

[11] *AP Pollution Control Board v MV Nayadu* (1999) 2 SCC 718 [56].

[12] *Mathai v George* (2016) 7 SCC 700.

[13] See generally *Kunhayammed v State of Kerala* (2000) 6 SCC 359.

[14] *Narmada Bachao Andolan v Union of India (UOI) and Others* (2000) 10 SCC664.

[15] ibid [150].

[16] *KM Chinnappa v Union of India (UOI)* (2002) 10 SCC 606 [41].

[17] *ND Jayal v Union of India* (2004) 9 SCC362.

[18] ibid [56].

> Hazardous wastes are highly toxic in nature. The industrialisation has had the effect of generation of huge quantities of hazardous wastes. *These and other side effects of development gave birth to principles of sustainable development so as to sustain industrial growth.*[19]

Here, the Supreme Court unabashedly goes on to say that the object of sustainable development is to sustain industrial growth. Even though this statement was made in 2003, it illustrates the limitations of environmental adjudication in India, which emphasized that the principle of sustainable development was merely a sidekick of industrial development.[20] However, the Court has also had moments of sagacity wherein it engaged with the idea of economic growth and its ends.[21] For instance, in *Nandini Sundar v State of Chhattisgarh*, the Supreme Court established a link between lopsided developmental policies and resource conflicts.[22]

It is also relevant to note that remediation for environmental harm,[23] the precautionary principle,[24] the public trust doctrine,[25] and public participation in environmental decision-making[26] were read into the principle of sustainable development in later years, both as part of the polluter pays principle and otherwise.[27] The Court also tried to source the genesis of the principle of sustainable development to intergenerational equity and bring it under Article 21 of the Constitution.[28]

Although most of the jurisprudence on sustainable development has been rather pedantic, the decision in *Lafarge Umiam Mining (P) Ltd v Union of India* remains important insofar as it owns up to the over-deployment of the principle of sustainable development and its consequent meaninglessness and goes on to say that each case will have to be decided 'on the facts' and that the doctrine of margin of appreciation in favour of the decision maker will apply.[29] The Court goes on to say that once a proposed activity—

[19] *Research Foundation for Science Technology National Resource Policy v Union of India* (2005) 10 SCC 510, para 1.

[20] *Karnataka Industrial Areas Development Board v C Kenchappa* (2006) 6 SCC 371 [1].

[21] *Intellectuals Forum* v *State of AP* (2006) 3 SCC 549. See also *Lafarge Umiam Mining (P) Ltd v Union of India* (2011) 7 SCC 338 [31].

[22] *Nandini Sundar v State of Chhattisgarh* (2011) 7 SCC 547.

[23] *Deepak Nitrite Ltd v State of Gujarat* (2004) 12 SCC 402.

[24] *Karnataka Industrial Areas Development Board* (n 20).

[25] *Intellectuals Forum* v *State of AP* (2006) 3 SCC 549.

[26] *Karnataka Industrial Areas Development Board* (n 20) [30]. See also *Tirupur Dyeing Factory Owners Assn v Noyyal River Ayacutdars Protection Assn* (2009) 9 SCC 737; *Orissa Mining Corpn Ltd v Ministry of Environment and Forests* (2013) 6 SCC 476.

[27] *Deepak Nitrite Ltd.* (n 23).

[28] *TN Godavarman Thirumulpad v Union of India* (2006) 5 SCC 47 [1]. See also *Amarnath Shrine, In re (Court on its own Motion) v Union of India* (2012) 12 SCC 497.

[29] *Lafarge Umiam Mining Pvt Ltd* (n 21) [19] and [30].

> is fair and fully informed, based on the correct principles, and free from any bias or restraint. Once this is ensured, then the doctrine of 'margin of appreciation' in favour of the decision-maker would come into play.[30]

There has been no serious appraisal of this 'margin of appreciation', while in many cases, especially involving large infrastructure projects, the presumption in favour of the decision maker is eminently manifest.

From time to time, the Supreme Court has had spells of self-reflection. And it has contributed valuable *obiter dicta*, like in *TN Godavarman Thirumulpad v Union of India* and *Centre for Environment Law, WWF-I v Union of India* where the Court expounded on the anthropocentric undergirding of the principle of sustainable development.[31]

Recently, in *Citizens for Green Doon v Union of India*, the Supreme Court incorporated the idea of environmental justice under the umbrella of sustainable development.[32] It insisted on maintaining equity not only between the living and the unborn but also between various sections of present society. The Court also correctly identifies the arbitrariness in environmental adjudication created by the *nebulousness* of sustainable development.[33] The Court in *Bengaluru Development Authority v Sudhakar Hegde* refers to Article 14 of the Constitution (dealing with equality) for remedying the differential impacts of environmental adjudication because of the indeterminacies involved in the principle.[34] This judgment serves as a pointer for the future growth of environmental justice in India.[35] Also, linking sustainable development to 'environmental rule of law', as was done in *Hanuman Laxman Aroskar v Union of India*, acquires a certain importance when read with the need for environmental justice.[36]

More recently, the Supreme Court has emphasized the link between the precautionary principle and sustainable development.[37] It underlined the constitutional status of the principle of sustainable development in revoking the approval granted by the Standing Committee of the National Board of Wildlife for doubling of the existing railway line between Castlerock (Karnataka) and Kulem (Goa). It stated:

> A situation may arise where there may be irreparable damage to the environment after an activity is allowed to go ahead and if it is stopped, there may be irreparable damage to economic interest. This Court held[38] that in case of doubt, protection of environment would take precedence over the economic interest. It was further held

30 ibid.

31 *TN Godavarman Thirumulpad v Union of India* (2012) 3 SCC 277 [14]; *Centre for Environment Law, World Wide Fund-India v Union of India* (2013) 8 SCC 234.

32 *Citizens for Green Doon v Union of India* 2021 SCC OnLine SC 1243 [31]. See also *Municipal Corporation of Greater Mumbai v Ankita Sinha* 2021 SCC OnLine SC 897 [27.1].

33 ibid.

34 *Bengaluru Development Authority v Sudhakar Hegde* (2020) 15 SCC 63.

35 ibid [94].

36 *Hanuman Laxman Aroskar v Union of India* (2019) 15 SCC 401 [128].

37 *TN Godavarman Thirumulpad v Union of India* 2022 SCC OnLine SC 583 [18].

38 *MC Mehta v Union of India* (2004) 12 SCC 118.

> that precautionary principle requires anticipatory action to be taken to prevent harm and that harm can be prevented even on a reasonable suspicion. Further, this Court emphasises in the said judgment that it is not always necessary that there should be direct evidence of harm to the environment.[39]

Despite revoking the approval, based on both the enormous risk to biodiversity and the lack of economic utility of the project, the Court still allowed the project proponent to undertake a detailed environmental impact assessment of the project and reapply for approval.[40] This is emblematic of the Court's diffidence to focus on environmental protection as it firmly believes that the relationship between the three pillars is that of a zero-sum game and therefore cannot be mutually supportive.

10.3 The Jurisprudential Outliers

There are two cases which can be termed as outstanding outliers to the Court's diffidence in drawing consumption limits in the face of extensive evidence of environmental degradation and damage triggered by human action.

In *Goa Foundation v Union of India*, the Court took cognizance of the overwhelming evidence recorded by independent expert committees that illegal mining was rampant in the state, and this had led to extensive ecological damage and was detrimental to the health of the people of Goa.[41] The Court established that iron ore was primarily meant for export and that the state was not getting adequate royalty and was aiding the aggrandisement of private mine holders without any social benefit. Although accepting that mining was an important economic activity, the Court underlined the need for sustainable mining and held:

> We cannot, therefore, prohibit mining altogether, but if mining has to continue, the lessees who benefit the most from mining, must contribute from their sale proceeds to the Goan Iron Ore Permanent Fund … for the purpose of sustainable development and inter-generational equity.[42]

The Supreme Court's intervention was triggered by the extraordinary scale of illegalities resulting in extensive environmental damage, which was first established by the state and thereafter by independent judicial commissions. Subsequently, the Court only intervened to restore the sanctity of the legal process governing mining with the caveat that part of the proceeds accrued should be appropriated for sustainable development.[43]

39 *TN Godavarman Thirumulpad* (n 37)[19].
40 ibid [25].
41 *Goa Foundation v Union of India* (2014) 6 SCC 590.
42 ibid [78].
43 *Goa Foundation v Union of India* (WP(C) 435 of 2012) Supreme Court of India, Order dated 20 September 2017.

The state was given the liberty to decide how monies accrued could be spent for sustainable development. However, the judgment was soon *de facto* overturned by the state by allowing for a second renewal of lapsed mining leases.[44] While considering the challenge, Justice Lokur was scathing in his indictment of the state. He stated:

> Unfortunately, the State is unable to firmly stop violations of the law and other illegalities, perhaps with a view to maximize revenue, but without appreciating the long-term impact of this indifference. Another excuse generally put forth by the State is that of development, conveniently forgetting that development must be sustainable and equitable development and not otherwise.[45]

Consequently, the Court directed the state to grant fresh mining leases and nullified the decision for a second renewal of lapsed mining leases.[46] This case illustrates that often, the state blindly pursues economic development at the cost of environmental protection, thereby embracing the belief that economic development and environmental protection are inherently incommensurable, thus completely negating the principle of sustainable development.

The second case also involved a finding by independent expert committees established by the state. In *Orissa Mining Corporation Ltd v Ministry of Environment and Forests* (the Niyamgiri case), the judiciary found that large-scale illegalities were committed by Vedanta in operating its alumina refinery project and bauxite mining project in Odisha, resulting in environmental degradation.[47] The Court underlined the autonomy of the *Gram Sabha* under the Scheduled Tribes and Other Traditional Forest Dwellers (Recognition of Forest Rights) Act, 2006 (FRA), to consider not only individual and community claims over forests but also religious rights of the communities in assessing the application for grant of access to forests in the Niyamgiri Hills. It held that the Ministry of Environment and Forests would have to consider the decision of the *Gram Sabha* while reviewing the application for Stage II clearance for the bauxite mining project.

By upholding the fidelity to procedural requirements in statutes like the FRA and the Environmental Impact Assessment (EIA) Notification, 2006, the Supreme Court sought to remedy the wilful intransigence of the state in undermining the extant legal framework by turning a blind eye to violations by private industry. One can read this as diffidence on the part of the Supreme Court to limit its intervention only to cases where the violation has been documented by independent expert committees established by the state. Seldom has the Court reviewed and questioned the state's belief in the incommensurability between the goals of economic development and environmental protection to

44 Lisa Monteiro, 'Goa Mining Case: What Have you Done' *Times of India* (22 January 2022) <https://timesofindia.indiatimes.com/city/goa/mining-case-what-have-you-done-in-last-7-years-hc-asks-state/articleshow/88863428.cms>.

45 *Goa Foundation v Sesa Sterlite Ltd* (2018) 4 SCC 218[1].

46 ibid [154].

47 *Orissa Mining Corporation Ltd v Ministry of Environment and Forests* (2013) 6 SCC 476.

the exclusion of sustainable development. Additionally, the Court exhibits a firm belief in the restitution of the environment, apparent from the emphasis on the collection of monies for undertaking environmentally harmful activities. Nevertheless, the Court's interpretation of the FRA strengthens governance spaces, allowing for the expression of new bottom-up imaginations of sustainable development that are driven by *Gram Sabhas*.

Historically, the High Courts have closely followed the jurisprudence of the Supreme Court on the application and interpretation of the principle of sustainable development. However, the experience of environmental disasters like the floods in Kerala in 2018, repeated urban floods in Chennai, and the flash flood in Uttarakhand in 2013 have all had a discernible impact in igniting deeper reflections by those High Courts on sustainability in general and specifically in accepting that not all environmental harm is restitutive through *post facto* actions. High courts seem to be unwilling to accept fait accompli arguments, which show a casual disregard for environmental regulations.

While considering a case of illegal mining, the Kerala High Court exhorted the state in the following manner:

> It is time the law makers, the government and the administrators sat up and pondered upon (i) How to re-build by sustainable alternative methods?, (ii) What can be done to prevent recurrence of a like calamity? after introspecting on (iii) Why such a disaster occurred? We cannot shut our eyes or ears to the refrain that in reality the disaster inflicted by nature, is man made.[48]

Similar imperatives have driven the High Court of Kerala to extend a novel interpretation to Clause 8 (vi) of the EIA Notification to rule that residents had a right to be heard by the assessing authority when they raised objections against a grant of environmental clearance under the EIA process.[49] The High Court held that the public has a right to make representations to help the regulatory authorities to better verify the claims of the project proponent.

Sustainable development is comparable to the basic structure doctrine in limiting states' power to use natural resources.[50] Relying on this reasoning, the Madras High Court held:

> while the administration can tap the hills and hillocks for mineral resources, the exploitation cannot lead to their complete extinction … In all such cases, it must be demonstrated that all the other avenues have been exhausted and that in the interest of the general public, it is necessary to carry out limited mining in the hillock in question.[51]

[48] *EICL Ltd v Circle Inspector of Police* 2018 SCC OnLine Ker 3537 [35].

[49] *G Madhavan Kutty v District Environmental Impact Assessment Authority* 2017 SCC OnLine Ker 1197 reiterated in *Jayachandran Nair B v UOI* 2018 SCC OnLine Ker 3535.

[50] *K Santhaman v District Collector* 2021 SCC OnLine Mad 2092.

[51] ibid [15], [17].

The Madras High Court has repeatedly found fault with the state's actions in going ahead with land acquisition for projects in the absence of environmental clearance.[52]

In 2017, the Uttarakhand High Court halted the grant of new mining leases, arguing that the Himalayan ecosystem is fragile and excessive mining has led to environmental degradation and floods.[53] Although it found 'sufficient material on record of irreversible damage',[54] it established a high-powered committee with members having security of tenure to prepare a state level fifty-year plan that would address the issue of environmental limits to mining. This approach of the court represents a possible way forward in ensuring commensurability between the three pillars of sustainable development.

In comparing the records of the various courts, we find that the Supreme Court has perhaps been the most diffident in reviewing the policy choices of the state that continue to reflect the incommensurability between the three pillars. Only in certain exceptional circumstances of well-documented and widespread illegalities resulting in environmental degradation, the Court chose to intervene to emphasize the sanctity of environmental statutory processes, which have been blatantly ignored by the state regulators. Certain High Courts have shown remarkable ingenuity in adopting a proactive approach by aggressively reviewing state action and suggesting alternate models for developmental intervention that are both socially and environmentally sustainable.

Recently, there has been much celebration of the environmental rule of law and the idea of just sustainability, as discussed in recent judgments.[55] We are perturbed by this for several reasons. Despite Justice Chandrachud's frank acceptance of the problem of indeterminacy and his valiant attempt to posit an environmental rule of law to address this, the problem remains unresolved.[56] This is evident from his own lack of continuity in being unable to follow through with the logic of precedence in applying the same principle in similar circumstances. This is exemplified by the contrast in judicial reasoning between *Himachal Pradesh Bus Stand Management and Development Authority v The Central Empowered Committee* and *Hanuman Laxman Aroskar*.[57] These cases were similar in facts and circumstances in terms of involving a developmental project, which was approved without any due diligence, as was mandated under the current environmental legal regime. However, the outcomes of both cases were different.

The idea that the Court has developed a new and possibly path-breaking interpretation of sustainable development through the idea of just sustainability is intriguing. The idea that natural resources belong to the nation and are held by the state in public

[52] See *Pandarinathan Govindarajulu* v *Union of India* 2020 SCC OnLine Mad 809 reiterating the ratio of *PV Krishnamoorthy v The Government of India* 2019 SCC OnLine Mad 36205.

[53] *Naveen Chandra Pant v State of Uttarakhand* 2017 SCC OnLine Utt 389.

[54] ibid [126].

[55] Upendra Baxi, 'A Milestone for Environmental Justice' *India Legal* (20 July 2019); Stellina Jolly and Siddharth Singh, 'Critiquing Sustainable Development and Analyzing Avenues for Just Sustainability in India' (2021) 51(2) *Texas Environmental Law Journal* 187.

[56] ibid.

[57] *Himachal Pradesh Bus Stand Management and Development Authority v The Central Empowered Committee* (2021) 4 SCC 309; *Hanuman Laxman Aroskar* (n 36).

trust is well established,[58] as is the idea of intragenerational and intergenerational equity.[59] So, we disagree that *State of Meghalaya v All Dimasa Students Union* marked a new milestone and has unveiled a new discourse on sustainable development.[60]

10.4 Social Development

Social development requires that all individuals and communities have equal opportunity to access goods and services to pursue their mental and physical development. Equity is therefore the bedrock principle underlying social development.[61] Historically, some communities in India have suffered from a lack of social development. Social justice in the context of India requires the state to provide opportunities to communities which have been historically deprived in terms of access to opportunities.[62] Environmental justice at a *de minimum* requires that environmental harms are equitably distributed among individuals and communities in the society.[63] In India, this aspect is further complicated by the fact that historically disadvantaged communities like scheduled tribes and forest dwelling communities who depend on their immediate environment (including forest tracts) for subsistence needs often bear the brunt of environmental destruction and degradation which may either be caused by disasters or rampant industrialisation requiring diversion of their habitats.[64] Environmental justice demands that this reality of dependence of such communities, which is critical to their social development, is taken into consideration both by the executive in policymaking and the judiciary when confronted with legal challenges.

[58] Shalini Randeria, 'Glocalization of Law: Environmental Justice, World Bank, NGOs and the Cunning State in India' (2003) 51(3–4) *Current Sociology* 305; J Razzaque, 'Application of Public Trust Doctrine in Indian Environmental Cases' (2001) 13(2) *Journal of Environmental Law* 221; Lavanya Rajamani, 'Doctrine of Public Trust: A Tool to Ensure Effective State Management of Natural Resources' (1996) 38(1) *Journal of Indian Law Institute* 72.

[59] *Goa Foundation* (n 43); *MC Mehta v Union of India* (2009) 6 SCC 142; *Techi Tagi Tara v Rajendra Singh Bhandari* (2018) 11 SCC 734.

[60] *State of Meghalaya v All Dimasa Students Union* (2019) 8 SCC 177.

[61] Dan Cristian and others, 'The Components of Sustainable Development—A Possible Approach in Procedia Economics and Finance' (2015) *PEF* 806, 811.

[62] Council for Social Development, *India Social Development Report* (OUP 2006).

[63] Jennifer R Wolch, Jason Byrne, and Joshua P Newell, 'Urban Green Space, Public Health, and Environmental Justice: The Challenge of Making Cities 'Just Green Enough' (2014) 125 *Landscape and Urban Planning* 234, 244; Pankaj Kumar, 'Securing Environmental Justice: A Comparative Study of the National Green Tribunal in India with the Land and Environment Court in Australia' (PhD Thesis, Centre for the Study of Law and Governance, Jawaharlal Nehru University 2022).

[64] National Human Rights Commission, 'From the Margins to the Centre: A Study of the Health Inequities Among the Tribal Communities in selected districts of Chhattisgarh, Jharkhand and Odisha' (2018); Varsha Ganguly, 'Impact of Displacement on Quality of Life of Maldhari (Pastoral) Women of Gir Forest' (PhD Thesis, South Gujarat University Surat 2000).

Tribal communities in India have been given special protection for their ways of life in terms of allowing them substantial powers of local self-governance through the recognition of Fifth and Sixth Schedule areas in the Constitution. Additionally, legislations like the FRA recognize that tribal communities have rights to access forest resources alongside the responsibility of protection of such resources.

Interestingly, on the question of the state's power to alienate natural resources, the Supreme Court has clarified that although auction or competitive bidding is a preferable mode, there is no constitutional obligation to choose that.[65] However, it added the caveat that the state is justified in choosing to forfeit revenue to pursue other social goods or public goods. This would include, for instance, alienation with the aim of providing affordable housing to scheduled castes and scheduled tribes or other economically deprived communities.[66] Critically, therefore, the Supreme Court accepted that the state could address social justice claims also through its powers of allocation of natural resources. *Ipso facto,* the state cannot alienate natural resources to private individuals without due consideration in accordance with Articles 14 and 39(b) of the Constitution.

Courts have been frequently confronted with litigation wherein tribal and other local communities have challenged developmental projects sought to be pushed through by the state. As discussed in the earlier section, in the Niyamgiri case, the Court upheld the powers of the *Gram Sabha* to govern their immediate environment in determining whether forest tracks should be diverted for non-forest purposes.[67] The decision of the *Gram Sabha* is to be considered by the Forest Advisory Committee (FAC) while considering applications for diversion of forests. Clearly, there remains a possibility of the FAC disagreeing with the *Gram Sabha*, and in such cases, the Court should be able to intervene. However, for the Court to intervene, it would necessarily require the development of a jurisprudence that would squarely address the question of social justice in the context of environmental litigation. Consequently, the question here is whether such jurisprudence has been developed by the Court.

We address this question with reference to two cases: *Lafarge Umiam Mining* and *State of Meghalaya.*[68] Although some years apart, both these cases serve as important referential points in discussing the question of social development as an aspect of sustainable development.

The *Lafarge Umiam* case involved limestone mining in the tribal areas of Meghalaya. It was a unique case because the approval for mining by a private company was granted by the local body (the Khasi Hills Autonomous District Council). While the Court upheld the principle of sustainable development, it emphasized that in such cases of forest diversion for 'non-forest purposes', an over-broad approach should be abandoned in favour of a case-by-case approach, taking into consideration the local specificities. Consequently,

65 *Natural Resources Allocation, In re, Special Reference No 1 of 2012* (2012) 10 SCC 1 [148], [150].

66 *Goa Foundation* (2018) (n 45) [80].

67 *Orissa Mining Corpn Ltd v Ministry of Environment and Forests* (2013) 6 SCC 476.

68 *Lafarge* (n 21); *State of Meghalaya* (n 60).

it applied the margin of appreciation doctrine and rejected a merits review for such administrative decisions. Merits review generally involves a reappreciation of evidence in addition to an appraisal of procedural infractions.[69] In this context, the Court stressed that 'public participation provides a valuable input in the process of identification of forests', and tribals and other locally affected persons were ecologically aware and were cognizant of the relationship between poverty and environmental pollution and were able to balance economic development and environmental protection.[70]

The fact that tribals had expressly supported mining due to several social interventions undertaken by the private company was an important consideration for the Court in recognizing the role and sanctity of local decision-making on such issues. Admittedly, one can raise the counterfactual point of whether the Court would uphold such decision-making in non-tribal areas outside the North-East (for instance, where the FRA is in operation) and where the *Gram Sabha* may reject the project despite both its long-term economic benefits as well as local social welfare development interventions which may accompany them, based solely on environmental considerations or different ideas of social development. Indeed, the Niyamgiri case seems to suggest that the Court would support such an interpretation.

Alternatively, one can raise the question to what extent locally affected persons may be allowed to pursue economic activities towards their social development, even at the cost of environmental harm. In *State of Meghalaya*, the issue was large-scale illegal rat hole mining in Meghalaya, which resulted in environmental damage and was also inhumane and unsafe. The NGT imposed a state-wide ban on mining, which was challenged in the Supreme Court. The Supreme Court modified the NGT's order to limit it to illegal mining but allowed mining to continue under the lease mechanism of the Mines and Minerals (Development and Regulation) Act, 1957. While addressing the contentions of petitioners that the mining ban would lead to economic deprivation and hardship, the Court responded to it by emphasizing the principle of inter-generational equity.[71]

Scholars have argued that this inaugurates the concept of 'just sustainability' and marks a significant milestone in the Court's interpretation of sustainable development.[72] The judgment seems to suggest that the Court would not support large-scale illegal activities leading to environmental degradation even if supported by locally affected persons. Natural resources are held in public trust for present and future generations, and thus, the social development of local people (located close to the natural resources) cannot be presumed to be of primary interest in their governance.

Arguably, *Lafarge* and *State of Meghalaya* stand at two ends of the continuum and provide deep insights into the Court's thinking. The Court is willing, in some instances, to recognize that locals at the site of the project are equipped to make decisions about the

[69] *State of Meghalaya* (n 60) [75]. See also Ian Turner, 'Judicial Review, Irrationality, and the Legitimacy of Merits-Review' (2008) 29 *Liverpool L Rev* 309

[70] *State of Meghalaya* (n 60)[97].

[71] ibid [1].

[72] See for instance, Baxi (n 55); Jolly and Singh (n 55).

nature and scale of the project, taking into consideration their social and environmental impacts, and such decisions should be given due consideration within the regulatory process for forest diversion or environmental clearance. However, since environmental resources are not the sole preserve of local people, due consideration of local decision-making cannot extend to allowing for rampant environmental destruction in pursuit of illegal activities.

In comparison to the Supreme Court, the NGT has developed a more forthright jurisprudence on the link between economic development resulting in environmental destruction, which impacts the poor disproportionately and undermines their social development.

In *MP Patil v Union of India,* there was a legal challenge against the environmental clearance granted to a thermal power project.[73] The NGT established an explicit link between displacement and deprivation because communities stood distanced and removed from their natural environment wherein a large part of their subsistence could be sourced from the hinterland. It stated:

> Poverty and degraded environment are closely inter-related, especially where people depend primarily on natural resources based on their immediate environment for their livelihood. Restoring natural systems and improving natural resource management practices at the grass root level are central to a strategy to eliminate poverty.[74]

Thus, developmental imaginations cannot be singular in terms of focusing only on large scale infrastructure projects. The imagination should be expanded to include other forms of development which enrich natural habitats that continue to be a rich source of subsistence living for many rural communities and tribal populations in India. Similar reasoning was also advanced by the NGT in *Antarsingh Patel v Union of India.*[75] The Maheshwar Hydro Power Project was challenged by project-affected persons. The NGT, in this case, emphasized the need to put citizens at the centre of development and to avoid hardships for the affected persons.[76]

The Supreme Court's support is critical in deepening the NGT's jurisprudence on this aspect. Indeed, in 2021, the Supreme Court greatly expanded the NGT's jurisdiction by recognizing its *suo moto* powers.[77] However, this trend remains uncertain and tenuous, as is evident from a decision of the Supreme Court wherein it stated that the NGT cannot sit in appeal over the opinion rendered by an expert body.[78]

Questioning the NGT's statutory mandate to undertake a merits review is surprising given that, unlike other administrative courts, the NGT is a specialized tribunal which

[73] *MP Patil v Union of India* Appeal No 12/2012 (Decided on 13 March 2014), National Green Tribunal Principal Bench.

[74] ibid [69].

[75] *Antarsingh Patel v Union of India* 2012 SCC OnLine NGT 47.

[76] ibid [15].

[77] *Municipal Corporation of Greater Mumbai* (n 32).

[78] *State of UP v Uday Education and Welfare Trust* 2022 SCC OnLine SC 1469 [79].

includes expert members and therefore is uniquely capable and statutorily bound to undertake such reviews. This directly contradicts the earlier three-judge bench decision in the *Municipal Corporation of Greater Mumbai v Ankita Sinha* case.[79] Further, this again illustrates this bench's fallacy that sustainable development is incommensurable with the aim of environmental protection. More disturbingly, it seems to indicate that the economic impact of its decision should be an important consideration for the NGT.

The discussion above highlights that the social development aspect of sustainable development has emerged as a concern of the Court and the Tribunal. Although the Supreme Court has recognized that in certain cases, the economic activity is neither environmentally sustainable nor helping social development, it has been reluctant to undertake a forthright merits review of regulatory approvals (forest diversion or environmental clearance) by expert bodies working under the Ministry of Environment, Forest and Climate Change (MoEFCC). Instead, it has, in some instances, prodded regulatory authorities to give more careful consideration to the views of affected persons. It has also emphasized that large-scale projects should set aside a part of the profits generated and invest them in local-level social development projects, which would be immediately beneficial for those living in the vicinity of such projects. Ultimately, though, it has yet to fully accept the premise that social development as an aspect of sustainable development cannot be a top-down policy of the state. It includes a critical procedural aspect of allowing individuals and communities (especially those who face discrimination and economic deprivation) to have a voice in determining the nature and dimensions of their social development.

10.5 Sustainable Development in Policy and Legislation

In this section, we explore how specific environmental policies and laws have addressed the three pillars of sustainable development. The National Forest Policy, 1988 (NFP) provided a break from the past in directing the focus of government policy towards sustainable development. It represented a radical departure from the natural resource utilization model, which had dominated the earlier era of policymaking. There was the explicit acceptance that forests had been seriously depleted as they were only looked at as a resource for revenue generation. Although conservation was defined as including sustainable utilization of forests, the NFP clearly stated that 'the principal aim of Forest Policy must be to ensure environmental stability and maintenance of ecological balance … the derivation of direct economic benefit must be subordinated to this principal aim.'[80]

[79] *Municipal Corporation of Greater Mumbai* (n 32).

[80] The National Forest Policy (No 3-1/86-FP, 1988)cl 2.2.

Sufficient provisioning of fuel wood, fodder, and pasture in the forest hinterland was emphasized as critical to preventing the depletion of forests 'beyond the sustainable limit'.[81] Evidently, the idea of sustainability underpinned the approach to forests and following from that the need to restrict economic activities to a level which would not threaten the very existence of forests themselves. Environmental conservation was therefore the primary aim of the NFP.

The NFP also marked a procedural break from the past in terms of social development. It accepted that tribal people had a symbiotic relationship with forests, and their involvement was critical in the governance and management of forests. Indeed, it was accepted that the forest conservation programme could not be successfully implemented without the people's support and participation. Thus, sustainable development of forests required the active participation of the people. Admittedly, the role of the people was still largely envisaged as 'affected parties' or 'beneficiaries' of government policy. People had a limited role in providing substantive input into the policy itself. However, the policy was also an expression of the fact that the state understood that the ownership of the policy by people was critical to its success. Thus, there was more forward acceptance of the need for partnership between state agencies and people in implementing the policy.

The Draft National Forest Policy, 2018 (Draft NFP) seems to suggest that there is a shift underway to focus more on timber production through public-private initiatives. Although the Draft NFP uses the term sustainable forest management, the lack of a definition in the policy itself or its referencing with well-established definitions as provided in the Biological Diversity Act, 2002 has further strengthened the suspicion that the aim here is to prioritize economic development even at the cost of environmental protection.[82]

The National Environment Policy, 2006 (NEP) identified sustainable development as the most important environmental issue. Critics of the policy point out that it should have been renamed as a policy on sustainable development since the focus was not on environmental conservation or procedurally speaking on environmental rights or even rights of nature but on the right to development with reference to the relationship between poverty and environmental degradation.[83] It is relevant to note that NEP emphatically stated that legal recognition of traditional entitlement has to be granted to the forest-dependent communities to remedy the historical injustice that was embedded in the exclusionary philosophy of carving out non-human habitats exclusively for the use of wildlife and ensure that local cooperation could be incentivized in the protection of local environments and in effect contribute to social development.[84]

[81] ibid cl 3.4.

[82] Biological Diversity Act 2002, s 2(o). For a discussion on the Draft NFP, 2018, see Study Group, Jawaharlal Nehru University, 'Study Group's (SG) Comments on the Draft National Forest Policy 2018', <https://www.jnu.ac.in/sites/default/files/cslg/Draft-NFP2018-StudyGroupResponse.pdf>.

[83] Videh Upadhyay, 'National Environment Policy 2004: A Critique of the Draft' (2004) 39(39) *Economic and Political Weekly* 4306.

[84] Ministry of Environment and Forests, National Environmental Policy (2006), para 5.2.3

This statement in the NEP was realized through the enactment of the FRA. The FRA vests tenurial and other usufructuary rights in communities who have been living in forests and their hinterlands. These rights are balanced with responsibility for conservation and sustainable use. Procedurally, the FRA opened a deliberative space for such communities through their *Gram Sabha* to allow for the diversion of forest land for certain developmental purposes. The *Gram Sabha*, which includes all adult members of the community, now has the decision-making authority to decide what constitutes sustainable development at the micro, administrative level.

The Compensatory Afforestation Fund Act, 2016 (CAFA) was enacted in pursuance of the Supreme Court's orders in the Godavarman case. Before that, the Compensatory Afforestation Fund Management and Planning Authority (CAMPA) was established by the Supreme Court in 2006 to administer the funds which the Court had ordered to be collected whenever forests were diverted for 'non-forest purpose'. The enactment of the CAFA is testimony to the scale of monies collected in lieu of the diversion of forests for developmental activities. The funds were meant to be used for compensatory afforestation. Independent reports suggest that the funds did not lead to expansion in forest cover due to several reasons.[85] Finding non-forest or degraded land to undertake compensatory afforestation is difficult. Sometimes, non-native species are being planted indiscriminately, and finally, funds have been diverted away from afforestation towards other purposes, like in Punjab, where a part of the funds was used for litigation.[86]

Procedurally, CAFA operates largely through the project proponent and the forest bureaucracy, and it excludes the local communities living in these forests.[87] The form and function of CAFA are thus fundamentally opposed to the FRA, and in effect, this has led to the centralization of forest governance. Consequently, the governance space created by the FRA in allowing local communities to determine the contours of sustainable development within their own neighbourhood that was recognized in the Niyamgiri case or even to an extent in *Lafarge Umiam* by the Supreme Court has been narrowed down by CAFA.

A spate of recent amendments suggested to the EIA Notification and the Coastal Regulation Zone (CRZ) Notification has sought to exempt several projects from seeking clearance from the MoEFCC.[88] Exploration activities related to drilling of oil and natural gas are exempted from obtaining prior CRZ clearance as well as environmental clearance under the Draft EIA Notification, 2020. A reduced notice period for public hearing and the revision in post-clearance reporting requirements from biannual to

[85] Supriya Vohra, 'Compensatory Afforestation Unlikely to Make up for the Loss of Carbon Stocks' *Mongabay* 23 August, 2021); Manasi Karthik and Arpitha Kodiveri, 'The Great Indian Land Grab being Carried out in the Name of Compensatory Afforestation' *The Wire* (30 January 2018) <https://thewire.in/environment/great-indian-land-grab-carried-name-compensatory-afforestation>.

[86] Dipak Anand, 'CAMPA Funds Should be Used to Conserve Nature' *Down to Earth* (18 July 2019).

[87] KB Saxena, 'Compensatory Afforestation Fund Act and Rules: Deforestation, Tribal Displacement and an Alibi for Legalised Land Grabbing' (2019) 49(1) *Social Change* 23, 40.

[88] Stellina Jolly and Siddharth Singh, 'Environmental Impact Assessment Draft Notification 2020, India: A Critique' (2021) 5 *Chinese Journal of Environmental Law* 11, 36.

annual have been introduced. All these amendments suggest that first, the executive views environmental regulations primarily as impediments and has therefore reduced such regulations in pursuit of 'economic development'—and second, the space for people or community engagement in environmental policymaking is fast shrinking. The idea of balancing the three pillars of sustainable development is increasingly being abandoned in favour of a zero-sum race, where economic development will be pursued at the cost of environmental protection.

As is evident from the above discussion, the law and policy discourse on sustainable development has undergone significant changes. First, sustainable development is adopted in most legislative and policy documents explicitly. Second, allowing the decentralization of powers to communities for them to determine on a case-by-case basis as to what constitutes sustainable development is what was expanded in certain legislations. However, increasingly, we see a reversal from that position. Greater centralization of decision-making in the central executive, accompanied by reduced space for public scrutiny of development decisions, means that sustainable development may be essentially reduced to a phrase that is widely mentioned in policy documents but undermined in practice by the state.

Conclusion

The judicial approach to sustainable development is characterized by indeterminacy. This indeterminacy suggests that courts have had wide and unbridled discretion in their choice of precedents in developing a case-specific understanding of sustainable development. This has also meant that progressive judgments which have recognized important aspects of sustainable development, like intra-generational equity, remain outliers. Indeterminacy has also meant that there is no general standard of review. This means that litigants have no clear roadmap, allowing them no legal certainty as to what it means to argue for sustainable development as a ground for challenging any development project or policy decision of the state.

There are certain aspects of the judicial and policy discourse which represent progressive aspects of the principle of sustainable development that need to be more widely celebrated. First, the idea of absolute limits on consumption is necessary, and that all of nature cannot be restored needs to be appreciated. Second, intragenerational equity is critical in allowing for a fairer distribution of environmental burdens and benefits. Third, procedural rights are crucial in ensuring that indigenous communities have the space and facility to represent their own visions of sustainable development within policy and developmental plans. This must be recognized and strengthened not only within law and policy but also within judicial discourse.

Suggestions for Further Reading

Nupur Chowdhury, 'Sustainable Development as Environmental Justice: Exploring Judicial Discourse in India' (2016) 51(26/27) *Economic and Political Weekly* 84.

Stellina Jolly and Siddharth Singh, 'Critiquing Sustainable Development and Analyzing Avenues for Just Sustainability in India' (2021) 51 *Texas Environmental Law Journal* 187.

Sharachchandra M Lélé, 'Sustainable Development: A Critical Review' (1991) 19(6) *World Development* 607.

Bimal N Patel and Ranita Nagar, *Sustainable Development and India: Convergence of Law, Economics, Science, and Politics* (OUP 2018).

Geetanjoy Sahu and Ritwick Dutta, 'The Green Tribunal in India After 10 Years: From Ascendancy to Crisis' (2021) 56(52) *Economic and Political Weekly* 60.

CHAPTER 11

PREVENTION, PRECAUTION, AND POLLUTER PAYS PRINCIPLES

PREETA DHAR AND PARUL GUPTA

Abstract

This chapter explores the evolution and application of the prevention, precaution, and polluter pays principles in India. Early environmental regulations aimed at planning human activities within the assimilative capacity of the environment—reflecting an initial framing of the prevention principle. However, with the recognition of the limits of 'scientific certainty' in determining and addressing environmental harm, more proactive and precautionary measures were adopted. The precautionary and prevention principles are read together in setting environmental standards and regulating activities and substances. The polluter pays principle is a market-based mechanism to build in incentives to minimize and remedy environmental harm. The three principles play out in the allocation of responsibility and liability, but there are inherent limitations and tensions in their application. This chapter discusses some of these tensions through the regulatory framework and case law, and proposes a coherent reading of the three principles aligned with other emerging principles.

Introduction

Principles of environmental law are invoked at multiple levels to rationalize decisions, guide state actions, and bridge gaps in existing frameworks in response to emergent issues. They have been instrumental in explaining and making coherent the patchwork of laws, regulations, and judicial interpretations in terms of how environmental issues are framed, responsibilities are assigned, and remedies are implemented.[1] In international law, they are used for guiding actions of member states. Within domestic contexts, principles are explicitly or implicitly applied in developing the framework of environmental regulation and in adjudicating environmental disputes. However, there are tensions in how these principles are interpreted and applied. In both international and domestic contexts, environmental law is in a 'constant state of flux and contestation'.[2] Therefore, the scope and meanings of principles are relatively fluid, evolving with changing framings of environmental issues as well as other emerging principles of environmental law. This chapter explores these aspects in the context of three core principles of environmental law in India—the prevention, precautionary, and polluter pays principles.

In India, the precautionary principle (which has been interpreted to include the prevention principle) and polluter pays principle are read closely with the principle of sustainable development and recognized to be integral to the right to a clean and healthy environment within the fundamental right to life.[3] They have been read alongside other environmental principles to develop the framework of environmental protection and regulation. However, there is a fair degree of ambiguity, complementarity, and contradiction in how these principles are interpreted and applied.

The chapter is structured in four sections. Section 11.1 outlines the core ideas underlying the principles and how they have been conceived in Indian jurisprudence. Section 11.2 discusses the regulatory framework, while Section 11.3 discusses the allocation of responsibility and liability in relation to environmental harm. Section 11.4 flags the constraints and tensions that arise in applying the principles coherently. The chapter then concludes with the pathways and possibilities these principles provide in addressing present and future environmental challenges.

11.1 Prevention, Precaution, and Polluter Pays Principles—an Overview

The principles discussed in this chapter have mirrored evolving understandings of governance approaches and environmental issues.

[1] Eloise Scotford, *Environmental Principles and the Evolution of Environmental Law* (Bloomsbury 2017).

[2] Elizabeth Fisher, 'Environmental Law as "Hot" Law' (2013) 25(3) *Journal of Environmental Law* 347.

[3] *Research Foundation for Science Technology and Natural Resources Policy v Union of India* (2005) 13 SCC 186; *Bittu Sehgal v Union of India* (2001) 9 SCC 181.

Early approaches to environmental regulation reflected a strong reliance on the command-and-control approach. This is visible in the 1972 Stockholm Declaration, which emphasizes rational planning and management of natural resources.[4] It reflects the 'assimilative capacity' approach—which assumes that the capacity of the environment to assimilate the impacts of human activities can be accurately determined, and timely preventive actions can be taken to prevent irreversible harm.[5] Early conceptualizations of the prevention principle relates to this framing.

The principle of prevention entails a duty to prevent harm beyond a certain threshold. In the Indian context, this can be inferred from the definition of environmental pollution—which is defined as the presence of substances (solid, liquid, or gaseous) in concentrations which 'may be or tend to be' injurious to the environment.[6] This conception is echoed in the rules relating to hazardous material and chemical accidents, which set out thresholds of quantities and limits of concentration.[7]

The limitations of a narrow understanding of the prevention principle reflecting the assimilative capacity approach were soon realized.[8] It would involve determining thresholds—and the entailing course of action—based on conclusive scientific evidence. However, devising effective and timely environmental measures may not be feasible if they are postponed until 'scientific certainty' is achieved. Acknowledging the limitations of scientific certainty in both understanding environmental harm and devising remedies, the precautionary principle emerged to provide a useful consensus on a more prudent approach. The precautionary principle institutionalizes caution in setting standards[9] and entails states to undertake proactive measures to improve environmental quality. The reference to scientific uncertainty in the precautionary principle functions as a clarification, rather than a condition for taking proactive measures.[10]

[4] This can be made out from the logic of principles 6, 7, 13, and 14 of the Declaration of the United Nations Conference on the Human Environment, Stockholm, 16 June 1972, UN Doc A/CONF.48/14/Rev.1.

[5] Ellen Hey, 'The Precautionary Concept in Environmental Policy and Law: Institutionalizing Caution' (1991) 4 *Georgetown International Environmental Law Review* 303.

[6] ss 2(b) and 2(c), Environment (Protection) Act, 1986. This is reinforced in later provisions in which the role of the Central Government includes prescribing the 'maximum allowable limits of concentration' of environmental pollutants in different areas (ss 5(1)(ii), 6(2)(b), Environment (Protection) Act). The definition also indicates the application of the precautionary principle since the language makes room for uncertainty.

[7] The Hazardous and Other Wastes (Management and Transboundary Movement) Rules, 2016; the Manufacture, Storage and Import of Hazardous Chemicals Rules, 1989; the Chemical Accidents (Emergency Planning, Preparedness and Response) Rules, 1996.

[8] In the Wingspread Consensus Statement on the Precautionary Principle (1998), the need for a new approach is explicitly recognized.

[9] Ellen Hey, 'The Precautionary Concept in Environmental Policy and Law: Institutionalizing Caution' (1991) 4 *Georgetown International Environmental Law Review* 303.

[10] Arie Trouwborst, 'Prevention, Precaution, Logic and Law-The Relationship between the Precautionary Principle and the Preventative Principle in International Law and Associated Questions' (2009) 2(2) *Erasmus Law Review* 105.

Early references to a precautionary approach are seen in the context of avoiding activities which can cause possible serious or irreversible damage.[11] Later, international legal instruments like the United Nations Framework Convention on Climate Change, the Convention on Biological Diversity, and the Rio Declaration highlight the need to take measures to prevent serious or irreversible environmental degradation even if there is a lack of scientific certainty.[12] In this sense, the precautionary principle reflects a departure from the 'assimilative capacity' approach of the Stockholm Declaration.[13]

In the Indian context, the precautionary principle is explicitly invoked by the Supreme Court in *Vellore Citizens' Welfare Forum v Union of India*, drawing on the Rio Declaration.[14] In the judgment, the Supreme Court spells out three essential features of the precautionary principle in the Indian context—first, it places an onus on state authorities to 'anticipate, prevent and attack the causes of environmental degradation'. Second, it clarifies that the lack of scientific certainty should not warrant postponing measures to address threats of 'serious and irreversible damage'. And third, it reverses the burden of proof on the developer/industrialist—to demonstrate that the proposed activities are environmentally benign. Therefore, a 'strong version' of the precautionary principle is applied in India which subsumes the prevention principle.[15] This entails authorities to be proactive—both in terms of minimizing environmental harm and shifting to more sustainable pathways.[16]

The polluter pays principle was recognized as 'an economic principle for allocating the costs of pollution control' by the Organization for Economic Cooperation and Development (OECD) in 1972.[17] As the Rio Declaration articulates, it is premised on the understanding that the enterprise causing environmental pollution should internalize the costs of such pollution.[18] The application of the principle involves aligning economic responsibilities and incentives in order to prevent or abate environmental degradation.

[11] World Charter for Nature, UN General Assembly Resolution 37/7, 28 October 1982, UN Doc A/RES/37/7, Principle 11.

[12] UN Framework Convention on Climate Change, New York, 9 May 1992, 1771 UNTS 107, art 3; Convention on Biological Diversity, Rio de Janeiro, 5 June 1992, 1760 UNTS 79, Preamble; Rio Declaration on Environment and Development, 14 June 1992, UN Doc A/CONF.151/26/Rev 1 (vol I), Annex II (1992), Principle 15.

[13] *Andhra Pradesh Pollution Control Board v MV Nayudu* 1999(2) SCC 718.

[14] *Vellore Citizens' Welfare Forum v Union of India* (1996) 5 SCC 647; Rio Declaration (n 12).

[15] Lavanya Rajamani, 'The Precautionary Principle' in Shibani Ghosh (ed), *Indian Environmental Law—Key Concepts and Principles* (Orient BlackSwan 2019) 192.

[16] This is expressed in the *MC Mehta v Union of India* AIR 2004 SC 4016—'Precautionary principle requires anticipatory action to be taken to prevent harm. The harm can be prevented even on a reasonable suspicion. It is not always necessary that there should be direct evidence of harm to the environment.'

[17] OECD Environment Directorate, 'Polluter Pays Principle: OECD Analyses and Recommendations' (OECD 1992). On the evolution of the polluter pays principle, European Court of Auditors, 'The Polluter Pays Principle: Inconsistent Application Across EU Environmental Policies and Actions' (2021), <www.eca.europa.eu/Lists/ECADocuments/SR21_12/SR_polluter_pays_principle_EN.pdf>.

[18] Rio Declaration on Environment and Development, 14 June 1992, UN Doc A/CONF.151/26/Rev 1 (Vol I), Annex II (1992), Principle 16.

In the Indian context, the internalization of the responsibility for causing pollution was addressed directly in *MC Mehta v Union of India* (Kanpur Tanneries) case—units were held responsible for bearing the cost of effluent treatment, and those failing to do so were ordered to be closed.[19] The polluter pays principle is explicitly invoked for the first time in *Indian Council for Enviro-Legal Action v Union of India*.[20] The Supreme Court drew on international developments as well as the principle of absolute liability in the Oleum gas leak case to hold the industry liable to compensate the harm caused by them and defray the costs of remedial measures.[21] The polluter pays principle has thus been applied in holding industries responsible for bearing the costs of meeting environmental standards, as well as holding them accountable for environmental damage.

Some points of clarification have emerged in the course of the application of the polluter pays principle. Viewed isolated from other environmental norms and principles, it would imply that industries or activities may use natural resources, continue to cause pollution or fail to undertake remedial measures so long as they paid for it. This interpretation of 'pollute and pay' has been specifically rejected.[22] Further, in a limited sense, the principle might be understood to apply only to incidents of pollution as understood in the literal sense (of introducing harmful substances into an environment), after the pollution has taken place. However, in the Indian context, the principle has been applied for environmental restoration in a wider sense—for instance, ascribing liability of units extracting groundwater without necessary approvals.[23] Nevertheless, a deeper engagement is needed to identify the limits of applying the polluter pays principle in relation to natural resource use and 'non-polluting' environmental impacts. It is also important to locate the prevention, precaution, and polluter pays principles in relation to other evolving environmental law principles, which are briefly highlight in the concluding section of this chapter.

The principles are applied through the framework of environmental laws—including statutory provisions and regulatory practices.[24] Judicial interventions have also shaped the application of the principles discussed in this chapter. Notably, the NGT has a statutory mandate to apply the precautionary principle and the polluter pays principle.[25] Broadly, the prevention and precautionary principles can be made out in provisions relating to standard setting and regulation—discussed in section 2 of the chapter. Section 3 discusses how the polluter pays principle, along with the prevention and precautionary principles, finds application in the distribution of responsibilities and liability in relation to environmental impacts.

[19] *MC Mehta v Union of India* 1987 (4) SCC 463.

[20] *Indian Council for Enviro-Legal Action v Union of India* (1996) 3 SCC 212.

[21] *MC Mehta v Union of India* 1987 (1) SCC 395.

[22] *Research Foundation for Science* (n 3).

[23] *Sushil Bhatt v Moon Beverages Ltd.* 2022 SCC OnLine NGT 76.

[24] This includes departmental clarifications, procedures, and practices in the exercise of administrative power.

[25] National Green Tribunal Act, 2010 s 20.

11.2 Tracing The Principles in the Regulatory Framework

The prevention and precautionary principles are found in the logic of defining acceptable environmental standards and regulating activities and substances that can affect the quality of the environment.

11.2.1 Standards of Environmental Quality

Thresholds of acceptable environmental quality are set out through environmental standards. Standards for air quality[26] and water quality, as well as emissions and effluents of industrial activities, are prescribed by the Pollution Control Boards (PCBs) under the Air Act and Water Act.[27] The Environment (Protection) Act, 1986—an enabling legislation that empowers the central government with wide-ranging powers and functions—also includes provisions for setting standards relating to the quality of the environment.[28] In case of deterioration of environmental standards, authorities are responsible for conceiving and executing plans for the 'prevention, control and abatement' of pollution as well as improving the quality of the environment.[29] This forms the baseline for the application of the prevention principle—by setting standards of environmental quality and aligning responsibilities to restore acceptable environmental quality where standards are breached.

Thresholds and standards are not uniform. More stringent standards may be prescribed for areas based on their ecological sensitivity, reflecting another dimension of the prevention and precautionary principles. For ecologically sensitive areas—either specifically identified regions notified under the Environment (Protection) Act[30] or types of

[26] Under the Air Act, the Central Pollution Control Board (CPCB) has notified from time to time, the National Ambient Air Quality Standards—the current standards having been set in 2009.

[27] Taking into consideration the standards set by the CPCB, the State Pollution Control Board (SPCB) is responsible for setting out standards for emissions from industrial plants and automobiles (s 17(1)(g), Air Act), and sewage and trade effluents—including their treatment (s 17(1)(g),17(1)(k), Water Act).

[28] The Environment (Protection) Rules, 1986, sets standards for different industries. Sch I includes the parameters and levels of emissions or discharge, as well as the processes to be adopted by industries. These standards are updated from time to time through government notifications.

[29] The CPCB at the national level and the SPCB at the state level (under s 16(2)(b) and s 17(1)(a) respectively of the Air Act and the Water Act). The Air Act, in fact, includes the mandate to 'improve' air quality—in addition to the prevention or abatement of pollution—indicating a more proactive statutory responsibility. Likewise, s 16(2)(h) and s 17(1)(b), respectively, of the Water Act and s 3(2)(ii) of the Environment (Protection) Act contain similar provisions.

[30] Notifications have been made for special administration of areas including the Murud Janjira, Dahanu Taluk, Doon Valley, Mahabasehwar-Panchgani, Mount Abu. A compilation of the Notifications

ecosystems[31]—standards may be set with a view to preserving the ecological character of the area. For instance, the National Ambient Air Quality Standards (NAAQS) prescribe stricter air quality standards for ecologically sensitive areas.[32] Eco-sensitive zones and areas designated for salt pans, shellfish, and mariculture have the most stringent marine outfall water quality standards.[33]

11.2.2 Regulation and Restriction of Activities

Commercial and industrial activities are regulated through a system of appraisals and oversight. This includes granting environment clearance under the Environment Impact Notification, 2006, 'consent to establish' and 'consent to operate' from the relevant Pollution Control Board,[34] in addition to any sector-specific approvals. The precautionary and prevention principles find application in the appraisal of projects.[35] Where activities are approved, they include conditions intended to ensure that environmental standards are adequately maintained.

Precautionary and prevention principles are also built into the powers of the PCBs to refuse renewal of consents, withdraw consents of non-compliant units,[36] or restrain units causing (or apprehended to cause) pollution.[37] This is paralleled with mechanisms to hold units accountable for any prospective default. For instance, the practice of requiring industries to furnish bank guarantees has been held to be within the purview of the powers of the PCBs of regulating industries and 'remedying the apprehended wrong to the environment'.[38]

Additional safeguards are prescribed for activities which pose a greater degree of risk to health, environment, and public safety—like ship recycling, handling of genetically modified organisms, or activities involving chemicals and hazardous substances.[39]

under the EP Rules is available in *Pollution Control Act, Rules and Notifications Thereunder* (7th edn, CPCB, 2021) <https://cpcb.nic.in/7thEditionPollutionControlLawSeries2021.pdf>.

[31] For instance, the conservation and management of wetlands, coastal areas, eco-sensitive zones around protected areas, and ecologically fragile areas have been notified under the Environment (Protection) Act and Rules. In such areas, industries causing pollution and the production and use of hazardous substances are prohibited depending on the sensitivity of the landscape.

[32] Notification of the CPCB dated 18 November 2009 under the Air Act.

[33] Categorized as 'SW-I' under the EP Rules.

[34] s 25 of the Water Act and s 21 of the Air Act.

[35] *Alembic Pharmaceuticals v Rohit Prajapati* 2020 SCC OnLine SC 347.

[36] Tanneries operating in violation of norms and refused to relocate were directed to be closed down. *MC Mehta (Calcutta Tanneries' Matter) v Union of India* (1997) 2 SCC 411.

[37] Under s 22A, Air Act and s 33, Water Act, the SPCB can exercise this power by approaching a judicial magistrate.

[38] *State Pollution Control Board v Swastik Ispat Pvt. Ltd.* 2014 SCC OnLine NGT 13.

[39] For instance, on-site emergency plans and detailed disaster control measures are required to be drawn up by the occupier of industries under s 41B(4) of the Factories Act, 1948. Ship recycling facilities are required to maintain emergency preparedness and response plans (s 14, Recycling of Ships Act, 2019). Off-site emergency plans are required under r 17(1) of the Rules for the Manufacture, Use, Import, Export and Storage of Hazardous Micro-Organisms Genetically Engineered Organisms or Cells, 1989. The Chemical Accidents (Emergency Planning, Preparedness and Response) Rules, 1996, require the

The statutory requirements of preventive and anticipatory mitigation measures reflect the prevention and precautionary principles. Notably, the role of the polluter is not only restricted to paying for the pollution caused by it but also cooperating with the authorities for responding to/containing the pollution.[40] Likewise, the central government has the power to restrain persons from mishandling hazardous substances.[41] In such instances, it is adequate for the authority to act on a 'reason to believe', rather than a conclusive proof—reflecting the precautionary principle in a prevention measure.

Restrictions may also be imposed to improve or preserve the environmental quality of certain areas. For instance, in 'critically polluted areas'—identified by the CPCB based on a Comprehensive Environmental Pollution Index (CEPI)—additional requirements may be imposed with a view to lower levels of pollution.[42] The NGT ordered a moratorium on polluting industries (corresponding with the 'red' and 'orange' category industries of the CPCB) in such areas till their viability is assessed in relation to the 'carrying capacity' of the area. The NGT observed that in addition to recovering compensation for the damage to the environment, the SPCBs should apply the precautionary principle in developing 'Action Plans' for improving the environmental quality of these areas.[43]

The precautionary principle has also been invoked to restrict activities to preserve the integrity of sensitive areas like animal corridors[44] and wildlife habitats.[45] In some instances, orders have invoked the precautionary principle to impose a temporary ban on disruptive activities near wildlife sanctuaries till a full assessment of their impacts and mitigation measures is carried out.[46] Likewise, restrictions on commercial activities in the vicinity of significant heritage areas—built and natural—have been upheld.[47]

operating unit to have an on-site emergency plan, as well as an off-site emergency plan (rr 13 and 14). In addition, for chemical accidents or other disasters, guidelines are available under the National Disaster Management Act, 2005.

[40] This is reflected, for instance, in the National Oil Spill Disaster Contingency Plan, 2015.

[41] Public Liability Insurance Act, 1991 s 13.

[42] The evaluation was conducted first in 2009–10 and later in 2017–18 based on the criteria revised by the CPCB in 2016. The revised criteria considered the scale of industrial activity, the scale of exceeding environmental standards (air, surface water and groundwater), health-related statistics, and the compliance status of industries. Revised Criteria for CEPI <https://cpcb.nic.in/openpdffile.php?id=TGF0ZXN0RmlsZS9MYXRlc3RfMTIwX0RpcmVjdGlvbnNfb25fUmV2aXNlZF9DRVBJLnBkZg==>.

[43] *In Re: Central Pollution Control Board v News Item published in 'The Asian Age' authored by Sanjay Kaw titled CPCB to rank industrial units on pollution* (NGT—Principal Bench, Order dated 10 July 2019 and 13 December 2018 in OA 1038/2018).

[44] *Hospitality Association of Mudumalai v In Defence of Environment and Animals* (2020) 10 SCC 589; *Rohit Choudhury v Union of India* 2012 SCC OnLine NGT 66.

[45] *TN Godavarman Thirumulpad v Union of India and Others* WP(C) No 202/1995, Order dated 9 May 2022 (Supreme Court).

[46] *Pratap Bhanu Singh Shekhawat v Department of Mines and Geology* 2021 SCC OnLine NGT 264.

[47] *K Guruprasad Rao v State of Karnataka* (2013) 8 SCC 418; *M.C. Mehta (Taj Trapezium Matter) v Union of India* (1997) 2 SCC 353.

In instances of ambiguity or lapses in environmental governance, the precautionary principle (which includes the principle of prevention) has been invoked to strengthen environmental safeguards. To illustrate, the Supreme Court laid down minimum safeguards for declaring 'Ecologically Sensitive Zones' when the existing regulations were found inadequate.[48] Courts have also directed authorities to formulate rules or standards for aspects not included within the legal framework—holding that failing to regulate activities where the pollution potential is established goes against the precautionary principle.[49]

11.2.3 Prohibition of Harmful Substances

The prevention and precautionary principles also find application in the prohibition of certain products on account of their impacts on health and environment. In the Indian context, these have included ozone-depleting substances,[50] paints with high lead content,[51] and persistent organic pollutants.[52] The presence of some other harmful substances has been sought to be minimized—including the import of asbestos and identified hazardous waste.[53] In addition to prohibition of substances which have a clear, irreversible health risk, recent developments—like the ban of single-use plastic[54]—indicate that products or uses may be phased out even if there is no consensus on the health and environmental impacts. In the absence of prohibitions in the regulatory framework, the judiciary has been instrumental in applying the precautionary principle to ban harmful substances like endosulfan.[55]

[48] *TN Godavarman Thirumulpad v Union of India and Others*, WP(C) No 202/1995, Judgment dated 3 June 2022 in IA No 1000 of 2003 (Supreme Court).

[49] *Gauri Maulekhi v Union of India* 2021 SCC OnLine NGT 328.

[50] Ozone Depleting Substances (Regulation and Control) Rules, 2000.

[51] Manufacture, trade, import or export of household and decorative paints containing more than ninety parts per million is prohibited under the Regulation on Lead Contents in Household and Decorative Paints Rules, 2016.

[52] Following the Stockholm Convention on Persistent Organic Pollutants, 2004, India notified the Regulation of Persistent Organic Pollutants Rules, 2018, which prohibits the manufacture, trade, use, import, and export of seven identified chemicals.

[53] MoEFCC Notification on the Prohibition of the Import of Hazardous Waste, dated 13 October 1998. Import of additional substances was prohibited under the Hazardous and Other Wastes (Management and Transboundary Movement) Rules, 2016.

[54] Plastic Waste Management (Amendment) Rules, 2022 dated 11 March 2021.

[55] AD Kumar and C Jayakumar, 'From Precautionary Principle to Nationwide Ban on Endosulfan in India' (2019) *Business and Human Rights Journal* 1.

11.3 Principles in the Allocation of Responsibility and Liability

The legal framework contains a complex distribution of responsibilities and liability. In this chapter, the terms are used conceptually. Responsibility corresponds to the duty of an actor (state or non-state) to act in a certain manner or respond in a particular situation. Environmental responsibilities entail, *inter alia*, acting with due care, following prescribed requirements and ensuring that the activity does not degrade the quality of the environment. Liability arises when a particular actor is held financially accountable for fulfilling environmental responsibilities or making good any lapse in responsibility. The question of liability—closely associated with the issue of responsibility—most strongly reflects the polluter pays principle but also involves the application of the prevention and precautionary principles. This is discussed in this section under three heads: industrial units, state authorities, and dispersed actors.

11.3.1 Industrial Units

Entities undertaking industrial or developmental activities are responsible for following prescribed standards. In addition, they are liable for the environmental degradation caused by their activities. This entails the following issues:

First, it is not necessary to precisely establish the relationship between a breach of standards and environmental harm. This issue was considered by the Supreme Court in *Deepak Nitrite v State of Gujarat*, in which it was observed that 'mere violation of the law in not observing the norms' would not necessarily imply environmental degradation for applying the polluter pays principle.[56] This position was subsequently revisited in *Research Foundation for Science Technology and Natural Resources Policy v Union of India*, where the polluter pays principle was read with the precautionary principle. Rejecting the view that the polluter pays principle can be applied only in situations where the actual degradation of the environment is established, the Supreme Court held the polluter liable to bear the costs of environmental protection measures for 'avoiding or reducing environmental risks before specific harms are experienced'.[57] Subsequent judgments have also held that 'defaulting parties' can be held liable, even if the nexus between the activity in question and the consequential environmental damage is not established 'with exactitude'.[58]

[56] *Deepak Nitrite v State of Gujarat* (2004) 6 SCC 402.

[57] *Research Foundation for Science Technology and Natural Resources Policy v Union of India* (2005) 13 SCC 186.

[58] *Gurpreet Singh Bagga v Ministry of Environment and Forest and Others*, NGT Order dated 18 February 2016 in OA 184/2013.

Second, a unit may be held liable even without establishing 'fault'. The standard of no-fault liability has been accepted in Indian jurisprudence. In *Indian Council for Enviro-Legal Action*, the principle of absolute liability was invoked on account of the activity being 'hazardous or inherently dangerous'.[59] Later judgments have also included 'absolute liability for harm to the environment' caused by activities which are not hazardous *per se* within the ambit of the polluter pays principle.[60] Failure to take safeguarding measures—which reflect the precautionary principle—has been held to attract the polluter pays principle.[61]

Third, a range of considerations are weighed in determining liability. The application of the polluter pays principle has established that it covers compensating victims of pollution, as well as the restoration of the environment.[62] In some cases, the liability has included compensating affected people for the loss of livelihood.[63] Judgments have also highlighted that the liability amount should be calculated to have a deterrent effect, especially in cases of intentional violations.[64] This has been calculated in terms of the capacity of the enterprise or correcting for the profitability of the violation.[65] Following the direction of NGT to lay down guidelines to assess and recover compensation for environmental damage,[66] CPCB has developed a methodology for environmental compensation for different sectors.[67] These guidelines have underscored the need to account for the 'risk' posed by the violation—especially to human health, or sensitive ecosystems. In such cases, the deterrence of the liability imposed is also informed by the precautionary and prevention principles.

[59] (1996) 3 SCC 212.

[60] The principle of absolute liability has been held to apply in cases of pollution contributed by tourists (*Society for Preservation of Kasauli and its Environs v Bird's View Resort and Others* OA 69/2017, Judgment of 30 May 2017 (NGT—Principal Bench), conducting a public event which damaged the flood plains of the Yamuna (*Manoj Misra v Delhi Development Authority* OA 65/2016, Judgment of 7 December 2017 (NGT—Principal Bench).

[61] *Vimal Bhai v Tehri Hydro Development Corporation and Others*, NGT judgment dated 13 April 2016 in OA 196/2016.

[62] *Vellore Citizens' Welfare Forum v Union of India* (1996) 5 SCC 647.

[63] *Hazira Macchimar Samiti v Union of India and Others*, judgment dated 8 January 2016 in Appeal No 79/2013.

[64] *MC Mehta v Union of India* AIR 1987 SC 1086; *Saloni Ailawadi v Union of India* 2019 SCC OnLine NGT 1151.

[65] *MC Mehta v Union of India* (1987) 1 SCC 395; *Sterlite Industries (India) Ltd v Union of India and Others* (2013) 4 SCC 575; *Praveen Kakar v Ministry of Environment, Forest and Climate Change* 2022 SCC OnLine NGT 154.

[66] *Court on its own Motion v State of Karnataka* 2018 SCC OnLine NGT 694; *Paryavaran Suraksha Samiti v Union of India* 2018 SCC OnLine NGT 1316.

[67] 'Report of the CPCB In-house Committee on Methodology for Assessing Environmental Compensation and Action Plan to Utilize the Fund', 2019 <https://cpcb.nic.in/uploads/report-15.07.2019.pdf>.

11.3.2 State Authorities

Aside from the actions (or inactions) of polluting units, state authorities have clearly defined responsibilities. If a polluter fails to comply with any mitigation or remedial measures, the PCB can undertake the work and recover the cost from the polluter,[68] expressing an application of the polluter pays principle. In emergency situations of pollution or apprehended pollution, the PCB can directly undertake remedial measures.[69] This reinforces that the prevention or remedy of environmental harm is the first order of priority—for which the relevant authorities are directly responsible. The Supreme Court has therefore observed that for continuing pollution or environmental degradation, 'the entire machinery involved in the administration has to be held responsible'.[70]

State governments and local bodies have been held responsible in cases where they have not responded effectively to environmental degradation.[71] It has been clarified, however, that amounts payable by state authorities for restoration of the environment are 'neither a penalty not a fine imposed on the State'.[72] The responsibility of local bodies in relation to 'public health, sanitation conservancy and solid waste management' has been read into the constitutional scheme.[73] Following this reasoning, municipal councils have been held responsible for failing to implement door-to-door garbage collection,[74] providing drainage systems,[75] or allowing untreated discharge to flow into water bodies.[76]

A review of judgments indicates that this translates into holding the 'polluter' responsible in broadly two ways—while some cases have indicated that authorities may 'evolve norms to recover funds for the purpose of generating finances' for performing their responsibilities,[77] others have called for holding erring officers, contractors or subcontractors responsible.[78] The intent of personal liability is to ensure effective and timely response to correct abdication of duties.

[68] Water Pollution Act, ss 30, 33; Air Pollution Act, s 22A.

[69] Water Pollution Act, s 32; Air Pollution Act, s 23.

[70] *MC Mehta v Union of India* WP(C) No 13029/1985, Order of 13 January 2020 (Supreme Court).

[71] Polluting state governments would have to make monthly payments to the CPCB (*MC Mehta v Union of India* 2019 SCC OnLine NGT 274). Delhi, Haryana, and Uttar Pradesh state governments have been directed to furnish performance guarantees for failure to prevent discharge of pollutants in river Yamuna (*Manoj Mishra v Union of India* 2019 SCC OnLine NGT 644).

[72] *State of Meghalaya v All Dimasa Students Union, Dima Hasao District Committee and Others* (2019) 8 SCC 177.

[73] *Paryavaran Suraksha Samiti v Union of India* (2017) 5 SCC 326, referring to Arts 243-W to 243-Y of the Constitution.

[74] *Confederation of Trans Hindan RWA's Ghaziabad v UP State Pollution Control Board* 2019 SCC OnLine NGT 1977.

[75] *Municipal Council, Ratlam v Shri Vardhichand and Others* 1980 AIR SC 1622.

[76] *MC Mehta v Union of India AIR* 1988 SC 1115.

[77] *Paryavaran Suraksha Samiti* (n 73).

[78] *MC Mehta v Union of India* OA 200/2014, Order of 22 August 2019 (NGT—Principal Bench). In *Karnataka State Pollution Control Board v B Heera Naik* 2019 SCC OnLine SC 1528, the Supreme Court

11.3.3 Dispersed Actors

Dispersed activities and consumption can also result in environmental harm. Waste laws, especially, have been framed to integrate end-of-life collection and disposal responsibilities to minimize such harm. Generators of certain kinds of waste are required to make payments to the local authorities for the proper disposal of the waste.[79] The local authorities may also impose 'user fees' or 'waste management charge' on waste generators to cover costs of waste management.[80] In other cases, different actors in the lifecycle of products—manufacturers, importers, sellers, and users—are made responsible for the waste generated by their activities under Extended Producer Responsibility (EPR).[81] This is expressed in the obligation to set up mechanisms for collecting back items[82] and ensuring its proper disposal.[83] The costs for setting up these mechanisms—and penalties for failing to do so—can be viewed as an application of the polluter pays principle. Interestingly, operating without an EPR authorisation is 'deemed' to cause damage to the environment[84]—making explicit the connection with the polluter pays principle. Finally, there may be market-based mechanisms like deposit refund schemes, or discounts for returning used items, which puts an initial cost of 'pollution' on individual consumers,[85] which is reversed upon proper disposal.[86] In this sense, EPR extends the application of the polluter pays principle to the post-consumption phase.[87]

held that the head of the local authority, namely the Municipal Commissioner, can be prosecuted under the Water Pollution Act.

79 Construction and Demolition Waste Management Rules, 2016. The Solid Waste Management Rules, 2016 (SWM Rules) indicate that manufacturers or brand owners of disposable products and packaging material should pay local authorities to establish a waste management system. r 17, SWM Rules.

80 r 15, 20 SWM Rules.

81 The Guidelines on Extended Producer Responsibility for Plastic Packaging defines EPR as 'the responsibility of a producer for the environmentally sound management of the product until the end of its life'.

82 Mechanisms for collecting back items which may cause pollution include disposable items and packaging waste (r 17, SWM Rules), batteries (rr 4 and 7, Batteries (Management and Handling) Rules, 2001), electronic waste (E-Waste (Management) Rules, 2016).

83 The concept of extended producer liability features prominently in the waste rules introduced in 2016—it is explicitly spelt out in the PWM Rules and the Uniform Framework for Extended Producers Responsibility under PWM Rules notified in MoEFCC June 2020. The E-Waste Rules outline a particularly elaborate system of submitting EPR Plans with the CPCB and ensuring responsible recycling and dismantling under Extended Producer Responsibility—Authorisation or through the 'Producer Responsibility Organization'.

84 r 5(7) E-Waste Rules.

85 The Uniform Framework for Extended Producers Responsibility under PWM Rules, for instance, clarify that the definition of 'producer' includes individuals using plastic products or products with plastic packaging.

86 E-Waste Rules (3)k), PWM Rules; 4(v), Batteries Rules.

87 Antonio Massarutto, 'The Long and Winding Road to Resource Efficiency—An Interdisciplinary Perspective on Extended Producer Responsibility' (2014) 85 *Resources, Conversation and Recycling* 11.

11.4 Tensions and Concerns in the Contemporary Context

The application of the principles, however, is uneven. Principles are not enforceable by themselves. Within the legal framework, their application is contingent on how they are expressed in statutory provisions and regulatory practices. In environmental disputes, their application depends on how the issue is framed by the judiciary and the interpretation of the principles in specific disputes. The balance of considerations and consistency of application of the principles reflect underlying tensions in the framing of environmental responsibility.

First, a cohesive reading and application of these environmental law principles remain elusive. Gill highlights, for instance, the lack of conceptual coherence of the precautionary principle among key actors.[88] Bhullar argues that subjective perceptions of the decision-makers determine how the polluter pays principle is applied.[89] In judgments, the principles are held to be inapplicable in contexts which were not considered harmful in the opinion of the judiciary.[90] The standards are applied unevenly in governance as well. The response to the air quality of the National Capital Region illustrates this. While the period for compliance with emission standards and pollution mitigation measures has been repeatedly and significantly relaxed for thermal power plants,[91] a stricter view is taken regarding the pollution caused by farmers burning crop stubble in areas around the National Capital Region.[92]

Second, a conceptualization anchored in terms of 'pollution' as understood in a conventional sense has fundamental limitations. This viewpoint excludes aspects of environmental degradation that are not reflected in a limited understanding of pollution—for instance, habitat or biodiversity loss, impact on local communities, the resilience of ecosystems, or the cumulative impact of developmental or ancillary

[88] Gitanjali Gill, 'Precautionary Principle, Its Interpretation and Application by the Indian Judiciary: "When I Use A Word it Means Just What I Choose it to Mean-Neither More Nor Less" Humpty Dumpty' (2019) 21(4) *Environmental Law Review* 292.

[89] Lovleen Bhullar, 'The Polluter Pays Principle: Scope and Limits of Judicial Decisions' in Shibani Ghosh (ed), *Indian Environmental Law—Key Concepts and Principles* (Orient BlackSwan 2019) 152.

[90] These principles have been held to not apply in some cases. *Narmada Bachao Andolan v Union of India* (2000) 10 SCC 664; *Rajiv Suri v Delhi Development Authority* 2021 SCC OnLine SC 7.

[91] Standards notified in 2015 (through Notification No SO 3305(E) dated 7 December 2015) were relaxed first in 2017 (through directions in Notification No B-33014/07/2017-18/IPC-II/TPP dated 11 December 2017), and subsequently again in 2020 (through modified directions in Notification No. B-33014/07/2020/IPC-II/TPP).

[92] Notably, the Commission for Air Quality Management in the National Capital Region and Adjoining Areas Act, 2021, contains a provision for environmental compensation, in which only the pollution caused by stubble burning is mentioned. Section 15 states: 'The Commission may impose and collect environmental compensation from farmers causing air pollution by stubble burning, at such rate and in such manner, as may be prescribed'.

activities in a region. In several instances, relaxations have been made to the appraisal of industries based on their 'pollution' impacts. Following a categorization of industries based on their estimated pollution loads, requirements for obtaining consent were relaxed for some categories of industries.[93] Industries have been allowed to increase their capacity or change their operation without undergoing the Environmental Impact Assessment (EIA) process as long as there is 'no increase in pollution load'.[94] However, such relaxations arguably negate the safeguards intended to give effect to the precautionary and prevention principles.

Third, there is a distinct possibility that one principle may be invoked to effectively undermine or exclude the application of the other principles. This is observed particularly in the issue of *ex post facto* clearance, where the polluter pays principle (of imposing penalties or directing mitigation measures) is used to regularize illegalities.[95] The concept of an *ex post facto* clearance was held to be unsustainable in law—with a particular observation regarding the fact that it ran counter to the precautionary principle and sustainable development.[96] Nevertheless, subsequent Supreme Court judgments have diluted this position. The application of the EIA process with 'pedantic rigidity' has been relaxed to allow non-compliant units to regularize their operations.[97] Further, proposals to amend the EIA process have indicated provisions to mainstream *post facto* clearances with some financial penalties[98]—effectively allowing units to 'pollute and pay'.

Ultimately, an underlying tension between economic development and environmental protection shapes the application of these principles. The process of appraisal of projects explicitly or implicitly involves a 'cost-benefit analysis' of the viability of a developmental project.[99] However, framed in limited terms of economic viability, many environmental costs are not considered in such assessments. The cost-benefit analysis approach, if not consciously aligned with the precautionary principle,[100] can fundamentally weaken the appraisal process.

[93] Harmonisation of Classification of Industrial Sectors under Red/Orange/Green/White Categories, Directions of the CPCB dated 7 March 2016.

[94] Notifications number SO 3518(E) dated 23 November 2016, SO 236 (E) dated 16 January 2020, and SO 980 (E) dated 2 March 2021, MoEFCC.

[95] Notifications number SO 804(E) dated 14 March 2017, which proposed *ex post facto* clearance as a one-time condonation of irregular units.

[96] *Alembic Pharmaceuticals Ltd v Rohit Prajapati* 2020 SCC OnLine SC 347. Although the provision was struck down by the Supreme Court, it has reappeared in subsequent proposals to amend the EIA process. In fact, while the 2017 provision provided a one-time condonation, the draft EIA Notification, 2020, includes *post facto* appraisals as a regular avenue for industries, with some entailing financial penalties—in line with the position of 'pollute and pay'.

[97] *Electrosteel Steels Limited v Union of India* 2021 SCC online SC 1247.

[98] Draft EIA Notification, 2020.

[99] The CBA was originally part of the forest diversion proposals but has also been applied in some cases to include projects requiring EC/EIA. For instance, a CBA was recommended in the terms of reference for the environmental clearance of the Vishnugad Pipalkoti hydroelectric project. TOR dated 2 March 2021 granted by the MoEFCC to M/S THDC India Limited.

[100] David M Driesen, 'Cost-Benefit Analysis and the Precautionary Principle: Can they be Reconciled?' [2013] *Michigan State Law Review* 771.

This tension is mirrored in disputes involving non-compliant units. Although the courts have stated on multiple occasions that environmental protection takes precedence over economic interest,[101] a strong reading of the principles has been followed in very few decisions where industries or infrastructure projects are challenged.[102] Even in findings of clear violations, the 'principle of proportionality'[103] has been invoked to condone irregularities—especially when works have already commenced, or large-scale investments[104] and employment considerations[105] are weighed in. Very rarely are operations directed to be closed. It is often assumed that mitigation plans are adequate to offset the environmental impact of projects.[106] However, as some judgments have tellingly observed, it is difficult to apply the principles at the stage of adjudication without 'clear pathways to determine the harm caused'.[107] Such context-specific reliefs in *fait accompli* situations significantly compromise the rationale of the principles.

Conclusion

The wide acceptance of the principles—between different actors and in policies and judgments—provides valuable imaginaries in developing the framework of environmental protection and regulation in India. However, the translation of these principles to practice warrants more critical engagement. There are two dimensions to this—the reflection of the principles within the statutory and regulatory framework and their interpretation in judicial disputes. While elements of the principles are explicitly or implicitly found in statutory provisions and regulatory processes, they are not expressed consistently. Regulatory exemptions, relaxations, and condonations may undermine a coherent application of the principles. In judicial interpretations as well, there is a fair degree of variation in their interpretation and application in specific factual contexts. Principles by themselves are guiding but not determinative. They need to be integrated within the logic of the entire framework of governance and environmental decision-making.

[101] *MC Mehta v Union of India* (2004) 12 SCC 118; *TN Godavarman Thirumulpad v Union of India* WP(C) No. 202/1995, Order of 9 May 2022 (Supreme Court).

[102] E.g., *Debadityo Sinha v Union of India* Appeal No 79/2014, Judgment of 21 December 2016 (NGT—Principal Bench).

[103] *Alembic Pharmaceuticals* (n 96); *Lafarge Umiam Mining (P) Ltd v Union of India* (2011) 7 SCC 338.

[104] E.g., *Om Dutt Singh v State of Uttar Pradesh* 2015 SCC OnLine NGT 163.

[105] *Pahwa Plastics v Dastak NGO* 2022 SCC OnLine SC 362.

[106] In allowing the construction of a nuclear power project, the Supreme Court expressed confidence that previous disasters would not recur, given the protections in place under disaster management laws. *G Sundarrajan v Union of India* (2013) 6 SCC 620. Some judgments have called into question unviable mitigation measures instead of taking them for granted—*TN Godavarman Thirumulpad* (n 101).

[107] *Citizens for Green Doon v Union of India* 2021 SCC OnLine SC 1243.

It is also important to locate the prevention, precaution, and polluter pays principles in relation to other evolving environmental law principles. The principles discussed in this chapter were developed in an anthropocentric context. Since then, there has been growing recognition of the intrinsic value of biodiversity and ecological processes globally[108] as well as in India.[109] The emerging nature of environmental problems indicates the need for a paradigm shift—the regulatory framework needs to reflect a conceptualization of environmental harm which is more complex and diffuse than the context in which these principles were originally conceived. With climate change and frequent extreme climate situations, it is all the more important to preserve the resilience of ecosystems. The reading of the precautionary and prevention principles should evolve to respond to a broader understanding of environmental degradation.[110] Industries and developmental activities should account for long-term and cumulative impacts on landscape, biodiversity and ecological resilience[111] rather than limiting their responsibility to a narrow understanding of pollution as emissions and discharge of harmful pollutants.

The need for a more coherent governance approach to achieve environmental justice is also recognized through the concept of 'environmental rule of law',[112] which has been read into Indian jurisprudence through judgments of the Supreme Court.[113] Environmental rule of law emphasizes the need for consistent and progressive policymaking (principles of non-regression and progression), and aligning decisions to favour protection of environment in situations of uncertainty.[114] This highlights that the principles discussed in this chapter remain relevant—but in an evolving context, layered with meaning over time.

Read cohesively, these principles have significant potential in re-casting environmental governance. A consistent and meaningful—not merely pragmatic—application of the principles is necessary. The three principles discussed in this chapter should be read in a manner that strengthens rather than weakens environmental safeguards.

[108] E.g., UN General Assembly Resolution 66/288, The Future we Want, UN Doc A/RES/66/288 (2012) para 197.

[109] The shift from an anthropocentric to an ecocentric approach is found in judicial interpretations, including *TN Godavarman Thirumulpad v Union of India* (2012) 3 SCC 277; *Centre for Environment Law, WWF-I v Union of India* (2013) 8 SCC 234; *Animal Welfare Board of India v A Nagaraja* (2014) 7 SCC 547.

[110] The Supreme Court has observed in some instances that the 'Precautionary Principle makes it mandatory for the State Government to anticipate, prevent and attack the causes of environmental degradation'—indicating that it is not restricted to a limited understanding of pollution. *Hospitality Association of Mudumalai v In Defence of Environment and Animals* (2020) 10 SCC 589.

[111] To illustrate, the industrial unit was held responsible for obstructing the tidal drainage and destroying mangroves and the coastal ecosystem. *Krishnadevi Malchand Kamathia v Bombay Environmental Action Group* (2011) 3 SCC 363.

[112] The term first finds mention in Decision 27/9: Advancing justice, governance and law for environmental sustainability of the UNEP, 2013.

[113] *Hanuman Laxman Aroskar v Union of India* 2019 SCC OnLine SC 441; *Himachal Pradesh Bus Stand Management and Development Authority v Central Empowered Committee* (2021) 4 SCC 309.

[114] IUCN World Declaration on the Environmental Rule of Law, 2016, principle 5 states '*in dubio pro natura*'.

Suggestions for Further Reading

Chandra Bhushan, Srestha Banerjee, and Ikshaku Bezbaroa, 'Green Tribunal, Green Approach: The Need for Better Implementation of the Polluter Pays Principle' (Centre for Science and Environment 2018).

Shibani Ghosh (ed), *Indian Environmental Law—Key Concepts and Principles* (Orient BlackSwan 2019).

Gitanjali Nain Gill, 'Precautionary Principle, Its Interpretation and Application by the Indian Judiciary: "When I Use a Word it Means Just What I Choose it to Mean-Neither More Nor Less" Humpty Dumpty' (2019) 21(4) *Environmental Law Review* 292.

Nicolas de Sadeleer, *Environmental Principles: From Political Slogans to Legal Rules* (OUP 2020).

Arie Trouwborst, 'Prevention, Precaution, Logic and Law: The Relationship between the Precautionary Principle and the Preventative Principle in International Law and Associated Questions' (2009) 2 *Erasmus Law Review* 105.

CHAPTER 12

PUBLIC TRUST DOCTRINE

ROOPA MADHAV

Abstract

The principle of stewardship of natural resources by the state and the people is at the core of the public trust doctrine. Natural resources are imagined differently by the doctrine as being beyond exclusive private ownership or state control to contain a permanent easement enjoyed by the general public. This conception imposes obligations and duties on both the state and citizens to ensure effective management of resources, in the interest of both present and future generations. In the Indian context, the doctrine is extensively applied by the judiciary to a range of resources to protect public interest but as this chapter demonstrates, it is lacking in a rigorous outlining of the normative content of the doctrine and a reimagination to make it indigenous to environmental challenges within India.

Introduction

Historically, the public trust doctrine ensures that certain resources that have a public interest attached to them be protected from appropriation or exploitation by the government or private parties. The doctrine provides a public ownership status for resources critical for the common good of society and prohibits both state and private actions that would harm the public interest in these resources. In the absence of a clear universally accepted definition, it is important to begin by understanding the public trust doctrine.[1]

[1] See generally, Doug Quirke, 'The Public Trust Doctrine: A Primer' (University of Oregon School of Law Environmental and Natural Resources Law Center 2016) <https://law.uoregon.edu/sites/law1.uoregon.edu/files/mary-wood_0/mary-wood/PTD_primer_7-27-15_EK_revision.pdf>.

The public trust doctrine, simply put, classifies certain natural resources as trust resources that must remain within the stewardship of the public and cannot be handed over to private uses. First, the public trust doctrine carves out a separate category of public rights over select natural resources necessary for the greater common good and human development. Second, it is a judicial review of administrative decisions taken with regard to resource management and resource alienation. Third, it imposes obligations and duties not only on the state to protect the resource as a trustee but also imposes responsibilities on the public to act proactively to ensure the trust resources are well managed. In other words, it introduces the idea of stewardship over natural resources, the stewardship role is a joint responsibility of the state, citizens and private actors.[2] Fourth, the management of the trust resources must ensure that it benefits both present and future generations. In sum, the doctrine, in its traditional sense, creates public rights over resources that are necessary for the greater common good, imposes obligations and duties on the state and citizens, and provides judicial review of administrative action to prevent harm to the resource, while modern readings of the doctrine introduce the idea of stewardship and the principle of intergenerational equity to guide resource planning and management.[3]

The doctrine has also been interpreted as a fiduciary obligation borrowing from private trust law. It is understood as one party (trustee) managing the property (trust resources) on behalf of and for the benefit of another (beneficiary). The trustee is subject to fiduciary duties and is under an obligation to manage the trust resources and act in the best interest of the beneficiaries so as to ensure benefits accrue to them.[4]

This chapter, in the first section, provides an overview of the history, evolution, and current developments of the doctrine in multiple jurisdictions around the world. The exploration in the first section provides the scaffolding for an analysis of developments in Indian jurisprudence over three decades, as it borrows heavily from American jurisprudence. Courts in India significantly expanded the application of the doctrine to a wide range of natural resources but have been slow in building a robust normative framework that is specific to the Indian context. In the analysis, I consider only the key rulings of the Supreme Court to outline the developments and understand the normative content of the doctrine in India. Additionally, I argue in the final section that for a long time, the doctrine focused on state obligation, but robust citizen engagement is critical for the doctrine to be infused with meaning. The final section examines the potential, challenges, and limitations of the doctrine, with a specific focus on the need for the judiciary to provide a clear normative outline to better enable the scope and expansion of the doctrine in a more consistent manner.

[2] Haochen Sun, 'Toward a New Social-Political Theory of the Public Trust Doctrine' (2010) 35 *Vermont Law Review* 563.

[3] Quirke (n 1).

[4] See generally Mary Christina Wood, *Nature's Trust: Environmental Law for a New Ecological Age* (CUP 2014).

12.1 History and Evolution of the Doctrine

What is the source of the public trust doctrine? This is a question that the courts in India attempt to answer as being a settled legal certainty when, in fact, there is much debate on the civil law origins of the doctrine. The common law interpretations of the doctrine are largely developments within the American jurisprudence, while some jurisdictions like South Africa ground the doctrine additionally in statutory frameworks.[5] In India, it has been read into the Constitution of India 1950 as being a part of the right to life under Article 21.[6]

It is popularly understood that the historical origins of the doctrine are in Roman civil law. This is based on the Justinian Code. The Justinian Code states: 'By the law of nature these things are common to mankind—the air, running water, the sea, and consequently the shores of the sea'.[7] A closer examination, however, shows academic debate on the civil law origins of the doctrine.

12.1.1 Civil Law Origins

The traditional rights of the public over resources that are held in common, such as air, rivers, lakes, the sea, and its shore, have been protected since antiquity. Although the concept of public trust is traced back to civil law, the idea of both a 'trust' and the 'public' are an ambiguous notion in early Roman law. Based on historical evidence, it may be argued that both the idea of 'trusteeship' and the amorphous concept of 'public rights' is essentially a common law understanding evolved through judicial interpretation. The lack of a similar development of the doctrine in the civil law tradition further supports this assertion.[8] The sheer malleability of the doctrine is attributed more to its common law moorings than its origins in Roman law.

James Huffman, relying on Patrick Deveney's work, debunks the historical reading.[9] First, he notes that Roman law did not guarantee an inalienable public right to use and

[5] See generally, Andrew Craig Blackmore, 'Rediscovering the Origins and Inclusion of the Public Trust Doctrine in South African Environmental Law: A Speculative Analysis' (2018) 27(2) *Review of European, Comparative and International Environmental Law* 187.

[6] *MC Mehta v Kamal Nath* (1997) 1 SCC 388.

[7] Justinian, The Institutes of Justinian (Thomas Cooper ed, 3rd edn, 1852). Also see, James L Huffman, 'The Public Trust Doctrine: A Brief (and True) History' (2019) 10(1) *George Washington Journal of Energy and Environmental Law* 15, 16.

[8] Patrick Deveney, 'Title, Jus Publicum, and the Public Trust: An Historical Analysis' (1976) 1 *Sea Grant Law Journal* 13.

[9] James L Huffman, 'Speaking of Inconvenient Truths: A History of the Public Trust Doctrine' (2007) 18(1) *Duke Environmental Law & Policy Forum* 1.

access the sea and seashore. Second, certain resources were designated 'common to all' because they were in abundant supply. Thirdly, Roman law made no distinction between the public and the personal status of the ruler. Huffman concludes that 'Roman law seems to offer little to those seeking the comfort or reassurance of well pedigreed legal precedence'.[10] Similarly, Ruhl and McGinn carry out a more contemporary examination of Roman law narrative against the backdrop of the Atmospheric Trust litigation which relies on the doctrine. They note that the Roman doctrine can be traced much further back in time than Justinian's Institutes and that it involved a more complex property law doctrinal foundation than the Roman roots narrative that is presented in legal discourse.[11]

12.1.2 Common Law Developments

The earliest common law reference to the idea of the public trust doctrine is captured in the concept of common property or the doctrine of res communes. Paragraph 5 of the Magna Carta, 1215 made explicit reference to the guardianship of land and other related resources such as parks, fishponds, and other things pertaining to land. English law borrowed from Roman civil law in drafting the Magna Carta but also added its own perspectives to indigenize the doctrine.[12] English law was predominant in the United States of America until independence, but on gaining independence, the king's role as trustee of communal property was removed. From England, the public trust principle became part of American common law.

As early as 1821, the New Jersey Supreme Court, in *Arnold v Mundy*,[13] used the term 'public trust' in the course of stating a rule limiting a private party's capacity to own water-related resources. However, it is the American public trust doctrine that is more popularly associated with the Supreme Court's 1892 decision in *Illinois Central Railroad Co. v Illinois*.[14] This case pertains to a grant by the Illinois legislature to a railroad company a large parcel of land on the Chicago waterfront. The Court ruled in favour of the state, concluding that the original grant was void because the state did not have the power to alienate property in which the public had a trust interest for purposes such as navigation and fishing. The doctrinal basis for this conclusion is unclear, as the Court's opinion cited no authority for its conclusion.[15] The developments of the doctrine emerge from this judgment, but the common law basis and understanding of the doctrine are

[10] ibid.

[11] J B Ruhl and Thomas McGinn, 'The Roman Public Trust Doctrine: What Was It, and Does It Support an Atmospheric Trust?' (2020) 47(1) *Ecology Law Quarterly* 117.

[12] For more on the history, *see generally* Michael C Blumm and Courtney Engel, 'Proprietary and Sovereign Public Trust Obligations: From Justinian and Hale to Lamprey and Oswego Lake' (2018) 43(1) *Vermont Law Review* 1.

[13] *Arnold v Mundy* 6 NJL 1, 8 (1821).

[14] *Illinois Central RailRoad Co. v Illinois* 146 US 387, 452 (1892).

[15] ibid.

not clearly explicated.[16] The turning point in the public trust doctrine developments is arguably the academic article written by Prof Sax in 1970. Sax wrote a powerful piece that continues to reverberate even today, arguing for the extension of the doctrine beyond water resources and navigation to being applicable to natural resources more generally.[17] The evolution of the public trust doctrine as a modern-day doctrine coincides with the emergence and growth of the environmental jurisprudence. However, as Cohen notes, the old historical understanding may have little resemblance to what is emerging in modern-day case law and academic literature.[18] It is against this backdrop that the Indian judiciary must be careful in evaluating the precedents brought before them from other jurisdictions to understand the changing context and the nature of the academic discourse in each jurisdiction which has also contributed significantly (particularly in the context of American environmental jurisprudence) to the evolution of the public trust doctrine. The present-day discourse attempts to look at the public trust doctrine within the climate change debates and the international application of the doctrine to atmospheric pollution.[19]

The next major decision in the American context is the California Supreme Court ruling in *National Audubon Society v Superior Court*, more famously known as the Mono Lake case, which introduces the idea of 'public trust values' when the court stated: 'approval of such diversion without considering public trust values ... may result in needless destruction of those values'.[20] To quote the judges, who state: 'the core of the public trust doctrine is the state's authority as sovereign to exercise a continuous supervision and control over the navigable waters of the state and the lands underlying those water'.[21] Thus, apart from placing a public trust value, the judges imposed an obligation of continuous supervisory duty on the states to take such uses into account in allocating water resources.

As Blumm and Guthrie note,[22] the biggest developments in public trust doctrine after the Mono Lake case are outside the United States as they survey the developments in ten jurisdictions across the world, notable among these are India, South Africa,[23] and

[16] For more on the history, see generally Blumm and Engel (n 12).

[17] Joseph L Sax, 'The Public Trust Doctrine in Natural Resource Law: Effective Judicial Intervention' (1970) 68 *Michigan Law Review* 471, 476.

[18] Lloyd R Cohen, 'The Public Trust Doctrine: An Economic Perspective' (1992) 29(1) *California Western Law Review* 239.

[19] See generally, Joseph Orangias, 'Towards Global Public Trust Doctrines: An Analysis of the Transnationalisation of State Stewardship Duties' (2021) 12(4) *Transnational Legal Theory* 550. Also see, Mary Turnipseed and others, 'Reinvigorating the Public Trust Doctrine: Expert Opinion on the Potential of a Public Trust Mandate in US and International Environmental Law' (2010) 52(5) *Environment: Science and Policy for Sustainable Development* 6.

[20] *National Audubon Society v Superior Court* 658 P 2d 709 (Cal 1983)712.

[21] ibid 712.

[22] See Michael C Blumm and Rachel D Guthrie, 'Internationalizing the Public Trust Doctrine: Natural Law and Constitutional and Statutory Approaches to Fulfilling the Saxion Vision' (2011) 45 *University of California Davies Law Review* 741.

[23] South African law is an interesting mix of customary law, Roman Dutch law and the British Common Law. The South African Constitution, 1996 in s 24 (a) guarantees a right to an environment

the Philippines.[24] While South Africa has seen statutory incorporation of the doctrine, India and Philippines has seen more judicial incorporation. More recently, the mineral policy of India adopted the term for the very first time, thus bringing it into policy language.[25]

12.1.3 Historical Origins of Public Trust Doctrine in India

The normative content of the doctrine must take into account the historical moorings of the concept as the origins shape the contours of the idea and its future evolution. The application of the doctrine in the Indian context is justified as rooted in English jurisprudence and the common law. It has also been traced to the Indian Constitution. One of the first cases relying on the public trust doctrine is the *MC Mehta v Kamal Nath* case. The adoption of the public trust doctrine in Indian jurisprudence is with regard to a case pertaining to flood management measures adopted by a private motel without requisite permission. In tracing the origins of the doctrine and adapting the same to the Indian context, the judges state thus:

> The ancient Roman Empire developed a legal theory known as the 'Doctrine of the Public Trust' … Under the Roman law these resources were either owned by no one (res nullius) or by every one in common (res communis). Under the English common law, however, the Sovereign could own these resources but the ownership was limited in nature, the Crown could not grant these properties to private owners if the effect was to interfere with the public interests in navigation or fishing. Resources that were suitable for these uses were deemed to be held in trust by the Crown for the benefit of the public.[26]

The ruling then goes on to rely on the historical background provided by the seminal article by Sax and provides extracts in support of its arguments. The two key arguments worthy of note here are that there is a distinct class of property (now known as trust property) that is recognized in the public interest and that in these properties, a distinct perpetual use is protected in favour of the public. However, as Sax notes, it is not clear if the public has an enforceable right to prevent the infringement of the interests. Further,

that is not harmful to human health or well-being and to environmental protection for the benefit of present and future generations.

[24] In two significant rulings in the Philippines in recent years—the Metro Manila case and *Oposa v Factora*, the Filipino Supreme Court relied on the public trust doctrine and opined that its origins lay in natural law.

[25] Mineral Policy 2019. It affirms the public trust principle that minerals and their value are held by the state for the common good and supports intergenerational equity, stating that the state must receive the full value of extracted minerals.

[26] *MC Mehta v Kamal Nath* (1997) 1 SCC 388 [24].

noting the common law history of the doctrine, the ruling then concluded that English history also applies to the Indian context because of a shared legal history.

In *TN Godavarman Thirumulpad v Union of India*, the Court reiterated the ratio of *MC Mehta*. It was emphasized that the doctrine of Public Trust is founded on the idea that certain common properties such as rivers, seashores, forests, and the air were held by the government trusteeship for the free and unimpeded use of the general public. It was reiterated that the Indian legal system is based on the English common law. This includes the Doctrine of Public Trust, under which the state is seen as the trustee of all natural resources which are by nature meant for public use and enjoyment.[27]

Thus, the courts in India, while tracing the history of the doctrine to English law and the common law traditions, also rely on the American interpretations of the doctrine of the Roman law roots and modern interpretations of its continuing relevance. There is also the linking of the doctrine to the right to life in Article 21 and the right to environment, although this link is not backed by a robust legal argument.

12.2 Application of the Public Trust Doctrine in India—Expanding Scope and Normative Content

The emergence of the public trust doctrine within Indian jurisprudence coincides with the shift in the early 1990s from a nationalized command economy model to a deregulated liberalized economy. This shift introduced a range of private actors into the realm of economic activity, including the use and management of natural resources for commercial gain. The public trust doctrine thus emerged in the latter half of the 1990s for the very first time in response to a challenge of diversion of the course of a river by private actors.[28] The adoption of the doctrine is of significance as it attempts to place a check on private ownership of natural resources that are a gift of nature.

Although the doctrine has been prevalent for two decades in India, the judiciary has not clearly outlined the core elements of the doctrine and its application in the Indian context. In this chapter, an attempt is made to provide a broad outline of the normative content based on an analysis of the case law over the last three decades.

27 *TN Godavarman Thirumulpad v Union of India* AIR 2005 SC 4256.
28 *MC Mehta v Kamal Nath* (1997) 1 SCC 388.

12.2.1 Constitutional Aspects of the Public Trust Doctrine

The roots of the public trust doctrine have also been attributed to Article 21 of the Indian Constitution, which protects the right to life. It is a major leap in judicial interpretation worth discussing in some detail. The ruling in *MI Builders Pvt Ltd v Radhey Shayam Sahu* pertained to the construction of an underground air-conditioned shopping complex in Jhandewala Park—an important historical site in the city of Lucknow.[29] The project was challenged in the High Court, which held that the Corporation's decision was illegal, arbitrary, and unconstitutional. Aggrieved by this order, MI Builders approached the Supreme Court. What was not disputed was the historical importance of the park and its maintenance from the point of view of the environment. It was the only green space in a crowded commercial and residential area of the city.

The Court ruled on the primary contention in the appeal, that is, whether the Corporation is estopped from going back on the agreement and the building has been constructed in public good to relieve the congestion in the area. In deciding the case, the Court held that the agreement was wholly arbitrary and favoured the builder, thus enabling him to make huge profits. In its final order, the Court allowed for a partial dismantling of the buildings, restoration of the park in the area, and the remaining building to be handed over to the municipality to run as a parking lot.

The Court dwells very briefly on the public trust doctrine in two short paragraphs. The important aspect to note is the bald statement made by the judge without assigning any reasoning for his conclusion. After citing from textbooks and the *Illinois Central* ruling, he concludes the paragraph with a very important observation that the public trust doctrine in India, it would appear, has grown from Article 21 of the Constitution. This conclusion has no supportive reasoning either preceding it or succeeding it, making this a leap of faith in judicial law making without according sufficient reasons.

The carving out of certain resources as trust resources that need to be allocated with care, keeping in mind both citizens' rights and the need to protect the assets of the nation, seems to inform several justifications to lean towards the public trust doctrine. Locating an additional hook within the constitutional framing has further strengthened the reading of the doctrine as being supported within the constitutional framework.

12.2.2 Public Trust Doctrine as Public Easementary Right

The public trust doctrine flows from the idea of an easementary right of the public over resources. The doctrine emerged at the historical juncture when claims of the sovereign (the monarchy) over the commons were required to be balanced with the rights of the public over the resources. Such a claim of the public was couched within the idea of a public easementary right over resources.

[29] *MI Builders Private Limited v Radhey Shayam Sahu* (1999) 6 SCC 464.

Within the Indian jurisprudence, in applying the public trust doctrine, an important distinction is sought to be made with an easementary right of necessity (in this instance, one of access) that overrides and survives even a land acquisition process which in the normal course extinguishes all claims of easementary rights. In the *Fomento Resorts and Hotels Ltd v Minguel Martins* case,[30] the judge attempts to articulate this distinction but with limited success. However, the seed of the idea of an important distinction in the easementary claim is identified for a critical ruling in favour of the public in the second decade of court application and interpretation of the public trust doctrine.

The *Fomento* case deals with the right of access to the beach in the state of Goa. A private hotel sought to construct a building that blocked the traditional access of the public to the beach, which was a popular tourist spot. The private hotel, however, sought to provide an alternate route for the public and built a road, parking facility and a footpath. The Court notes in para 53 that the 'doctrine puts an implicit embargo on the right of the State to transfer public properties to private party if such transfer affects public interest, mandates affirmative State action for effective management of natural resources and empowers the citizens to question ineffective management thereof'.[31]

Importantly, this case raised a question about the easementary right being extinguished on the acquisition of land. The Court drew a distinction between easementary rights of necessity and those that are ordinary easements to conclude that the former survive even an acquisition by the state. The Court ordered the demolition of the portion of the hotel building so that public access to the beach is restored. This ruling thus provides the seed of an argument that may be lost entirely if it is not rescued and robustly discussed. In making this fine distinction between ordinary easements and those that survive in the public interest, the judgment provides a foothold in property law/easementary law discourse for the public trust doctrine to survive and thrive in.

12.2.3 Allocation of Trust Resources, Restrictions on Use of the Resources, and Duties of State

The doctrine imposes restrictions on governmental authority on the use and allocation of trust resources, and the judiciary, in the exercise of the powers of judicial review, has both outlined the restrictions on the use of resources, the duties, and obligations of resource administrators to be compliant with the doctrine. In *MC Mehta*, the judges held that the public trust doctrine primarily rests on the principle that certain resources like air, sea, waters, and forests have such great importance to the people as a whole that it would be wholly unjustified to make them a subject of private ownership.

Relying on Sax's interpretation, the Court acknowledged that the doctrine imposes restrictions on governmental authority. 'Three types of restrictions on governmental

[30] *Fomento Resorts and Hotels Ltd v Minguel Martins* (2009) 3 SCC 571.

[31] ibid.

authority are often thought to be imposed by the public trust: first, the property subject to the trust must not only be used for a public purpose, but it must be held available for use by the general public; second, the property may not be sold, even for a fair cash equivalent; and third the property must be maintained for particular types of uses'.

The public trust doctrine was explained by the Supreme Court in *Karnataka Industrial Areas Development Board v C Kenchappa*.[32] Primarily, it imposes restrictions on the use of the resources to the detriment of the general public, acknowledges that natural resources are a gift to humanity and should be accessible to all, irrespective of their status in society. Based on the ratio in the *MC Mehta* case, the Court observed that certain resources 'being a gift of nature should be made freely available to everyone irrespective of their status in life. The doctrine enjoins upon the Government and its instrumentalities to protect the resources for the enjoyment of the general public'.[33]

In *Centre for Public Interest Litigation v Union of India*, the Court concluded that people are the owners of natural resources.[34] Relying on the precedents on the public trust doctrine, it concluded that telecom spectrum is a resource that needs to be allocated keeping the public interest in mind. In applying the doctrine, it also derived that state action, especially in awarding contracts, must look to enhancing competition and fairness (doctrine of equality) in the allocation of resources. Thus, the Court extends the public trust doctrine beyond environmental jurisprudence to the allocation of resources in the national interest. This case subsequently led to a presidential reference being made with regard to mandatory auctions as the acceptable mode of transparent and fair allocation of natural resource. *In Re Natural Resources Allocation*, the Supreme Court explored the meaning of the doctrine in the Indian context at some length.[35] It clearly imposes limits on the private ownership of certain resources of public importance. It also held that while auctions may be the best way of maximizing revenue, the objective of revenue maximization may not always subserve the public good.

Against the backdrop of excessive sand mining, in *State of NCT of Delhi v Sanjay*, the Supreme Court held thus: 'There cannot be any two opinions that natural resources are the assets of the nation and its citizens. It is the obligation of all concerned, including the Central and the State Governments, to conserve and not waste such valuable resources'.[36] Relying on Article 48-A and Article 51-A of the Constitution, it took the view that the public trust doctrine rests on the principle that 'certain resources like air, sea, waters and forests are of such great importance to the people as a whole that it would be highly unjustifiable to make them a subject of private ownership'.[37]

In the *Fomento* case, the Court went on to note that the doctrine places limits on the state and its administrators with regard to trust resources. It noted that the public

[32] Karnataka Industrial Areas Development Board v C Kenchappa (2006) 6 SCC 371.

[33] ibid, para 83.

[34] *Centre for Public Interest Litigation v Union of India* (2012) 3 SCC 1.

[35] *In re Natural Resource Allocation, Special Reference No 1 of 2012* (2012) 10 SCC 735.

[36] *State of NCT of Delhi v Sanjay* (2014) 9 SCC 772.

[37] ibid, para 55.

trust doctrine imposes limits and obligations upon government agencies and their administrators on behalf of all people, especially future generations.

For example, renewable and non-renewable resources, associated uses, ecological values or objects in which the public has a special interest (i.e., public lands, waters, etc.) are held subject to the duty of the state not to impair such resources, uses or values, even if private interests are involved. The same obligations apply to managers of forests, monuments, parks, the public domain, and other public assets.[38]

In effect, this judgment lays down clearly the scope of the doctrine—(a) it places limits on the state and its administrators, (b) it protects the long-term public interest, thus enabling intergenerational equity, and (c) it is a public right protection against short-term private gains. It therefore imposes an obligation on the private parties to protect long-term public interest in the resource so as to not impair or diminish these long-term interests. And finally, the Court notes that the interests of the future generations also need to be accounted for by administrators in decision-making.

In *Intellectuals Forum, Tirupathi v State of AP*, the Supreme Court again invoked the public trust doctrine in a matter involving the challenge to the systematic destruction of percolation, irrigation, and drinking water tanks in Tirupati town.[39] Relying on rulings in *MC Mehta*, *MI Builders Pvt Ltd* and the US court ruling in *National Audubon Society (Mono Lake case)*, the judges observed that the doctrine imposes affirmative duties on the administrators of the trust resources. To quote:

> This is an articulation of the doctrine from the angle of the affirmative duties of the State with regard to public trust. Formulated from a negatory angle, the doctrine does not exactly *prohibit* the alienation of the property held as a public trust. However, when the State holds a resource that is freely available for the use of the public, it provides for a high degree of judicial scrutiny on any action of the Government, no matter how consistent with the existing legislations, that attempts to restrict such free use. To properly scrutinise such actions of the Government, the courts must make a distinction between the Government's general obligation to act for the public benefit, and the special, more demanding obligation which it may have as a trustee of certain public resources.[40]

The Court, in this case, went on to hold that the government orders were violative of the public trust doctrine, directed that no further construction be made in Peruru and Avilala tanks and corrective measures be taken for recharging them.

[38] *Fomento* (n 30) para 54.

[39] *Intellectuals Forum, Tirupathi v State of A.P.* (2006) 3 SCC 549.

[40] ibid [76].

12.2.4 Protection of Ecology and Public Trust Doctrine

In a range of cases, the courts have had to examine projects that impact public trust resources to weigh in favour of the ecology. In *Association for Environment Protection v State of Kerala*, the Supreme Court was called on to examine the grant of permission to build a hotel without carrying out the requisite Environmental Impact Assessment (EIA).[41] The Court held that the Government Order of 13 January 1978 is illustrative of the state government's commitment to protect and improve the environment as envisaged under Article 48-A. According to the Government Order, no project costing more than ten lakh rupees should be executed without a comprehensive EIA by the Environmental Planning and Coordination Committee. Such a review and assessment of environmental implications would have assessed whether it is desirable or feasible to construct a restaurant which could adversely impact the riverbed and the people in the region. It noted that the omission by the Department of Tourism to send the proposal for scrutiny by the commission resulted in a violation of the fundamental right to life guaranteed to the people of the area under Article 21 of the Constitution.

In *Association for Environment Protection*, the question before the court was the construction of a hotel/restaurant on the banks of the River Periyar in the absence of an EIA. The ruling carries out a detailed analysis of the doctrine and the evolving jurisprudence in India. It relies on earlier public trust doctrine precedents to hold that the construction of the hotel/restaurant violated the government order and directed the demolition of the structure.

12.2.5 Natural Resources Protected Under the Public Trust Doctrine in India

There is a narrow application of the doctrine to land below the water in seas or rivers, parklands, and wildlife in the case of American jurisprudence. A similar restriction is not evident in India, and it has truly been liberated beyond its historical shackles. However, a robust legal argumentation to justify this expansion is missing from the jurisprudence.

In *State of West Bengal v Kesoram Industries Ltd*, the Court applied the doctrine to groundwater taking the view that it is a part of national wealth, that it belongs to the entire society, and the state has a duty to protect groundwater against excessive exploitation.[42] Similarly, as outlined above, in *Intellectual Forum*, the Court held that natural resources, which include lakes are held by the state as a trustee of the public, and can be disposed of only in a manner that is consistent with the nature of such a trust.[43]

[41] *Association for Environment Protection v State of Kerala* (2013) 7 SCC 226.

[42] *State of West Bengal v Kesoram Industries Ltd.* (2004) 10 SCC 201.

[43] *Intellectual Forum v State of AP* (2006) 3 SCC 549.

Perhaps, the most detailed discussion with the public trust doctrine was in the single judge ruling of the Kerala High in the *Perumatty Grama Panchayat v State of Kerala* (Plachimada) case related to over extraction of groundwater by Coca Cola Pvt Ltd, in the *panchayat* limits of a Perumatty, a small village in the state of Kerala.[44] The court, in this case, relied on the public trust doctrine to rule that the state is trustee of natural resources and hence it is the duty of the state to protect groundwater resources against over exploitation.[45] However, the judgment is not a binding precedent as it was overruled by the higher bench of the Kerala High Court and subsequently by the Supreme Court, without engaging with the substantive issues, including the one on public trust doctrine, before disposing of the case.

Apart from an application to water resources, the doctrine has been expanded to include forests and mineral resources. In *KM Chinnappa v Union of India*, the renewal of the mining lease granted to Kudremukh Iron Ore Company in the Kudremukh National Park was challenged.[46] The Supreme Court held that western ghats and pristine forest resources cannot be allowed to be eroded or encroached unless the courts find it necessary in good faith and in the public interest. In *Goa Foundation v Union of India*, the Supreme Court invoked the public trust doctrine to ban illegal mining in the state of Goa and also create the Goan Iron Ore Permanent Fund, which provides for 10 per cent of the sale proceeds of iron ore excavated in the state of Goa and sold by the lessees to be appropriated for the purpose of sustainable development and inter-generational equity.[47] In *Fomento Resorts*, the Court observed that the natural resources, including forests, water bodies, and rivers are held by the state as a trustee on behalf of public and especially for future generations.[48]

The expansion of the scope of the doctrine was perhaps in *Centre for Public Interest Litigation*, where the Supreme Court held that telecom spectrum is a scarce commodity and a national resource held by the state as a trustee of the public at large.[49]

[44] See *Perumatty Grama Panchayat v State of Kerala* 2004(1) KLT 731.

[45] For a detailed discussion of the case, see Sujith Koonan, 'Groundwater: Legal Aspects of the Plachimada Dispute' in Philippe Cullet and others (eds), *Water Governance in Motion: Towards Socially and Environmentally Sustainable Water Laws* (CUP 2010) 159.

[46] *KM Chinnappa v Union of India* AIR 2003 SC 724.

[47] *Goa Foundation v Union of India* (2014) 6 SCC 590.

[48] See *Fomento* (n 30).

[49] *Centre for Public Interest Litigation v Union of India* (2012) 3 SCC 1.

12.3 The Normative Content and the Potential and Limitations for Application of the Doctrine

In the preceding paragraphs, the normative content of the doctrine, which is unclear, is sought to be extracted from the Indian jurisprudence, where the doctrine is applied to all natural resources. The doctrine seeks to fill a gap that the environmental law does not entirely address. While environmental law concerns are clearly addressed by the body of statutory law and legal principles such as precautionary principle and polluter pays, the doctrine still remains relevant in outlining the boundaries of administrative action with regard to natural resources. It is useful to summarize the core normative content of the doctrine below—

First, it seeks to provide guidance in decision-making to administrative authorities in charge of decision-making in the absence of a clear law or, in other words, the doctrine fills gaps in the law.

Second, it seeks to provide citizens with a say in natural resource governance by acknowledging that certain resources are the gift of nature, the corpus of which needs to be protected, and it cannot be subject to destruction through alienation from private actors, and even when an alienation occurs, the public rights over such resources do not diminish.

Third, it allows us to view the resource as a natural capital—the resource is a corpus that needs to be protected, it yields revenues for present and future generations and hence must be sustainably managed, with long-term planning being the essence of the doctrine.

Fourth, the idea of trusteeship reshapes the role of the state from that of an owner of resources to that of a trustee holding the resources on behalf of the citizen. Such a shift in the legal function of the state creates both rights and obligations. It creates rights on behalf of the citizens (as beneficiaries of the trust) but also imposes obligations and duties on the state.

In expanding the scope and application of the doctrine, it is important to also focus on the citizens as key beneficiaries and provide a critique of the doctrine. The doctrine offers a lot of promise, but it also comes with a range of challenges that need to be addressed in the long term.

The public trust doctrine is an evolving concept, being constantly adapted and interpreted to address modern-day challenges. Hence, the ambiguity built into the conceptual framing must be viewed as a strength. It provides the judiciary the legal space to interpret the doctrine as applicable to rapidly changing environmental challenges and also to ensure resource-specific tweaking that is inevitably necessary. For instance, the potential of the doctrine is currently being explored in climate change litigation challenges being brought before the courts in the United States.[50]

[50] See generally, Mary C Wood and Charles W Woodward IV, 'Atmospheric Trust Litigation and the Constitutional Right to a Healthy Climate System: Judicial Recognition at Last' (2016) 6(2) *Washington*

The potential for the future developments of this doctrine is immense. First, it reimagines the role of the state as a steward and trustee of natural resources, thus upending the long-held state ownership model that informed the colonial interface with natural resources. Second, more rigorous thinking through the doctrine can ensure that it provides clear guidance to resource administrators to act more effectively in their role as trustees. Third, it provides the potential for citizen engagement in decision-making as beneficiaries invested in the future of the resource, thus widening the doctrine beyond just state obligations and duties.

Perhaps a major challenge is the limited view of the public trust doctrine from a state lens, which restricts the discourse to that of the duties of the state. It is rarely viewed from the citizen beneficiary lens as the focus under the doctrine is the role of the state in resource management, along with restrictions on the state power to alienate certain public resources. For instance, the Constitution of Bhutan states that:

> Every Bhutanese is a trustee of the Kingdom's natural resources and environment for the benefit of the present and future generations and it is the fundamental duty of every citizen to contribute to the protection of the natural environment, conservation of the rich biodiversity of Bhutan and prevention of all forms of ecological degradation including noise, visual and physical pollution through the adoption and support of environment friendly practices and policies.[51]

It locates the citizen beneficiary as the primary trustee and imposes both rights and obligations on the citizen to protect and conserve the environment from degradation.

The private trust approach to the public trust doctrine conceives of the doctrine as consisting of three elements. The three elements are—(a) a trustee, who holds the trust property and is subject to fiduciary duties to deal with it for the benefit of another; (b) a beneficiary, to whom the trustee owes fiduciary duties to deal with the trust property for their benefit; and (3) trust property, which is held by the trustee for the beneficiary. This conception of the citizen as a beneficiary is an underdeveloped arena, with the focus largely being on the state as the duty bearer.

The other challenge is the lack of rigour in thinking through the normative content so as to provide a clear set of guidance to both the state and the citizen beneficiary. There is a need to expand our understanding of the doctrine beyond its conventional bounds within the judiciary and judicial review process to its broader potential as a legal tool to protect citizens' rights to public space and natural resources. The doctrine confers both rights as well as imposes responsibilities with regard to trust resources. It envisages an engaged citizenry that proactively works with the state to protect the trust resources. However, while this abstract notion is well outlined in the judicial discourse, it is weakly articulated in the administrative circles where resource administrators view citizens as subjects and not as primary beneficiaries who demand to know how the trust resources

Journal of Environmental Law and Policy 633.

[51] Constitution of the Kingdom of Bhutan, 2008, Art 5(1).

are used and allocated. The reconception of the role of the state and the citizen requires greater judicial engagement to outline the rights and duties of citizens as beneficiaries of the trust resources.

However, there are limitations to the evolution of the doctrine. The constitutional and statutory adoption of the doctrine may solidify the doctrine as a statutory or constitutional claim, but it may also create multiple contradictory interpretations. While the constitutional framing provides for a more rooted understanding of the role of the state in resource management and provides guidance to both the state and the citizens, the statutory evolution may be more rapid and responsive to changes and demands of everyday actions related to resource management. In the absence of a clearly articulated statement in the Constitution, the extension of Article 21 may lead to multiple formulations within the statutory framing that need to be harmonized in the long run. To avoid this, the judiciary may need to be proactive in articulating the core content of the doctrine into the Constitution.

Additionally, the doctrine also interfaces with other environmental principles, and this interface needs to be harmonized through effective judicial interpretation. A mapping of the interface is a much-needed academic exercise that needs to be carried out to help with the process of better articulating how the environmental principles impinge on each other. The doctrine may also evoke conflicting mandates for the trustees, which need to be negotiated by the administrators with some guidance on hand. This guidance can be provided both by the judiciary and resource administrators, contributing to thinking about their role as trustees of natural resources.

Conclusion

The public trust doctrine requires the state to manage certain natural resources (also called trust resources) in a sustainable manner keeping intergenerational equity in mind. The state, under the doctrine, has the obligation to actively take care of the resource, ensure the trust property does not deteriorate and is protected from environmental harm, and when the trust property is to be alienated, it must be done in the highest public purpose. Even when the trust property is alienated for private purposes, the state must oversee the process to protect the resource use. Judicial oversight or review of administrative action pertaining to trust resources is a critical aspect of the public trust doctrine.

The public trust doctrine steers the state and its citizens into the role of stewardship over trust resources. This reimagination of the role of the state is an evolving concept and can be further strengthened through rigorous engagement by the judiciary and the legislature in outlining the contours of the core ideas specific to the Indian context. It is further supported by the engagement with the doctrine in practice by the executive and the beneficiary citizens in a manner that makes the doctrine truly robust in its application.

The concept of the public trust doctrine is closely interlinked with two other key environmental principles. The notion of intergenerational equity emerges from the understanding that the current generation must protect and preserve natural resources for the use and enjoyment of future generations. This is also reflected in the concept of sustainable development, which notes that development undertaken must meet the needs of the present without compromising the ability of future generations to meet their needs. Resource administrators must take into account both intergenerational equity and sustainable development in their long-term planning.

However, at present, the conception of trusteeship remains limited to a rather Anthropocene understanding, with the citizens and state at the centre of the relationship. It does not quite account for the rights of the environment within this dyad of state and the citizen. It is a useful but limited conception that needs more careful examination by the judiciary to craft it to contemporary developments and jurisprudence on the rights of nature.

Suggestions for Further Reading

Shibani Ghosh, 'Public Trust Doctrine in Indian Environmental Law' in Shibani Ghosh (ed), *Indian Environmental Law: Key Concepts and Principles* (Orient BlackSwan 2019) 230.

Paromita Goswami, 'Public Trust Doctrine: Implications for Democratisation of Water Governance' (2016) 9(1–2) *NUJS Law Review* 67.

Jona Razzaque, 'Application of Public Trust Doctrine in Indian Environmental Cases' (2001) 13(2) *Journal of Environmental Law* 221.

Joseph L Sax, 'The Public Trust Doctrine in Natural Resource Law—Effective Judicial Intervention' (1970) 68 *Michigan Law Review* 471.

David Takacs, 'The Public Trust Doctrine, Environmental Human Rights, and the Future of Private Property' (2008) 16 *NYU Environmental Law Journal* 711.

CHAPTER 13

ENVIRONMENTAL DUTIES

SHALINI IYENGAR

Abstract

Environmental duties play a key role in environmental law in India. Mentioned in the Constitution of India, 1950 and in statutes, duties have often been relied upon by courts in imposing obligations on the state and on private actors. Taken as a whole, certain broad clusters of environmental duties are visible. These include the duty to protect and prevent environmental harm, the duty to provide the necessary elements for a clean and healthy environment, procedural duties, corporate duties, and the duties towards non-humans. Overall, while the polyvalence of duties makes them critical in imposing affirmative responsibilities and limits to state and corporate power, they also raise urgent questions on the desirability of individuating environmental responsibility.

Introduction

The enviro-legal landscape in India has long been distinguished by its diversity of legal and conceptual approaches. Home to multiple judicial forums and a rich array of legislative and constitutional tools, the legal system in India is also marked by fundamentally creative moves by litigants, courts, and legislators. Such moves have led to India's early articulation of both duty- and rights-based approaches towards the environment and the recognition that the right to life enshrined in Article 21 of the Constitution of India, 1950, includes the right to a clean and healthy environment guaranteed by the state within its ambit.

Although rights and duties are both firmly entrenched in the constitutional and broader enviro-legal landscape, the environmental conversation in India is still dominated by an emphasis on rights.[1] This subtle hierarchy has produced significant blind spots. Leaving duties undiscussed in the environmental context is particularly problematic since duties squarely impose obligations on both state and non-state actors, including individuals and corporations. That is, environmental duties have both vertical and horizontal dimensions insofar as they impact both citizen-state and citizen-citizen relationships. Significantly, the implications of this multi-dimensionality have been underexplored. There is thus little clarity into the scope and extent of such duties, even as they are constantly invoked by the courts. What is the relationship between environmental duties and rights? What is the scope of these obligations, and who owes these duties to whom? How, moreover, are these duties to be implemented?

This chapter attempts to address some of these issues. I first discuss the sources and duty-bearers of environmental duties in the legal landscape in India. I then examine how environmental duties have been interpreted and applied by courts in India. Within this section, I specifically focus on three broad trends in these cases—(i) duties to protect the environment and provide basic amenities, (ii) duties to non-humans, and (iii) corporate duties. I then conclude the chapter with some observations on the status of environmental duties in India.

13.1 Duties in the Indian Enviro-Legal Landscape

Environmental duties are a key element within the sprawling terrain of environmental law in India today. While the question of duties and obligations was extensively discussed in the Constituent Assembly debates, the present status of environmental duties owes much to events in India over the 1970s and 1980s. The first of such events was the Forty-second Constitutional Amendment in 1976, which included the addition of Article 48-A in the Directive Principles of State Policy (DPSP) and the creation of a dedicated Part IV-A outlining the Fundamental Duties of citizens in the Constitution. These specific inclusions took place against a backdrop where duties and obligations were sought to be elevated above a constitutional rights discourse. Although several of these changes were undone by later amendments and judicial pronouncements, it is

[1] See generally, Shibani Ghosh (ed), *Indian Environmental Law: Key Concepts and Principles* (Orient Blackswan 2019); Gitanjali N Gill, 'Human Rights and the Environment in India: Access through Public Interest Litigation' (2012) 14(3) *Environmental Law Review* 200; Lavanya Rajamani, 'The Right to Environmental Protection in India: Many a Slip between the Cup and the Lip?' (2007) 16(3) *Review of European Community and International Environmental Law* 274. But see, Lovleen Bhullar, 'Environmental Constitutionalism and Duties of Individuals in India' (2022) *Journal of Environmental Law* 1–20; Armin Rosencranz and Shiraz Rustomjee, 'Citizens' Right to a Healthful Environment' (1995) 25(6) *Environmental Policy and Law* 324.

notable that both Article 48-A and Part IV-A of the Constitution were left untouched. The landscape of duties would thus be forever changed by the events of 1976.

The second key event was the articulation of environmental rights by an increasingly assertive Supreme Court of India from the 1980s onwards. Judicial decisions dramatically expanded the scope and ambit of environmental rights in the Constitution by reading them into the fundamental right to life as set out in Article 21 of the Constitution. This articulation of an environmental rights discourse sparked the rise of a concomitant set of duty-based discourses. After all, if citizens had environmental rights, then by inference, these rights imposed correlative duties on the state to guarantee their fulfilment. Thus, the inclusion of the right to a clean and healthy environment in a so-called 'negative' right like Article 21 of the Constitution would be the harbinger of a host of 'positive' obligations on state authorities in relation to the environment.

Through the chapter, I seek to demonstrate three primary dimensions of environmental duties. First, that duties are polyvalent and multi-directional. This means they have been used in multiple contexts and directed towards multiple actors. Duties have thus been interpreted to include multiple obligations, including protection, prevention, remediation, procedure, and provisioning—indeed, in the finest deontological sense, duties have often subserved the environmental ends sought to be achieved. Duties also function across the traditional depiction of the 'three generations' of rights. They can represent the obligation to refrain from, the obligation to do, and the collective obligation imposed on members of a community. Moreover, rather than a classical exposition of duties being seen through a strictly vertical lens—that is, citizen's rights and state's duties, duties have been found to impose obligations on the state, individuals, and even the courts themselves. Second, duties have multiple sources. They do not merely arise from the Constitution, but also from statutes and common law, and perhaps most provocatively, there exists a reciprocal relationship between the power to do something and the duty to do it. That is, courts in India have suggested that the power and capacity to do something imply a duty to do it and, conversely, that the legal duty to do something implies that one has the power to do so. This, then, is a framing of environmental duties that sidesteps their popular conjoining with the idea of environmental rights. Third, in cases where courts have linked rights and duties, they have done so not just through the traditional framing of one's right being another's duty but also by holding that to have a duty *is* to have a right. Therefore, as we see in the case discussions, a citizen's fundamental duty in relation to the environment has been interpreted to create a *right* inhering in the same citizen in relation to the environment.

It is important to emphasize that there is no one 'environmental duty' that exists within the legal system in India. Instead, it would be more appropriate to identify a constellation of explicit and implicit environmental duties imposing different obligations on state and non-state actors. In the sections that follow, I map these sources of duties before turning to broad categories of the obligations that environmental duties impose.

13.1.1 Constitutional Sources

Directive Principles of State Policy: in contrast to environmental rights, environmental duties are clearly mentioned within the Constitution. While technically non-justiciable, Article 37 of the Constitution makes it clear that the DPSP are 'fundamental to the governance of the country and it shall be the duty of the state to apply these principles in making laws'. Article 48-A, which was added by the Forty-second Amendment to the Constitution in 1976, states that 'the State shall endeavour to protect and improve the environment and to safeguard the forests and wildlife of the country'.[2] Duties in relation to the environment are more indirectly implied in Articles 39(e), 47, and 48 of the Constitution which cast a general obligation on the state to pay heed to public health and animal husbandry.[3] In the hands of the judiciary, these articles have been interpreted to impose wide-ranging duties on the state in relation to the environment. This approach has hinged on first, adopting a broad interpretation of the word environment, secondly, on linking the physical environment with the state obligations in relation to public health and standard of living, and thirdly, on linking these DPSPs with the fundamental right to live with human dignity under Article 21 of the Constitution.

The Court's approach in *Virender Gaur v State of Haryana* is emblematic of this approach. In this case, the Court read Articles 47 and 48-A of the Constitution together and held that the word environment was 'of [a] broad spectrum which encompassed hygienic atmosphere and ecological balance'.[4] This extended the already broad definition given to the environment under the Environment (Protection) Act, 1986, and implied that the environment refers both to a certain state of affairs in the world as well as more subjective criteria like 'hygiene' and 'balance'.[5] Such a decision takes on even more importance when read against the backdrop of previous cases, such as *Bandhua Mukti Morcha v Union of India*, where the Court had already interpreted Articles 39(e) and (f), 41, and 42 of the Constitution as obliging the state to protect the 'minimum requirements' to 'enable a person to live with human dignity' guaranteed in Article 21 of the Constitution.[6] In later cases, the Court would interpret these provisions to oblige the state to ensure that citizens had access to clean air, water, and sanitation facilities.[7] Taken together, these cases wove together the different articles in the DPSP to impose a comprehensive set of environmental duties on the state. Given the open-ended and

[2] See Granville Austin, Working a Democratic Constitution: A History of the Indian Experience (OUP 2003).

[3] The Constitution of India, 1950, Arts 39(e), 47, and 48.

[4] *Virender Gaur v State of Haryana* (1995) 2 SCC 577.

[5] s 2(a), The Environment (Protection) Act, 1986, s 2(s): 'environment includes water, air and land and the inter relationship which exists among and between water, air and land, and human beings, other living creatures, plants, micro-organism and property'.

[6] *Bandhua Mukti Morcha v Union of India* (1984) 3 SCC 161.

[7] *MC Mehta v Union of India and Others* (2002) 4 SCC 356; *AP Pollution Control Board II v Prof MV Nayudu* (2001) 2 SCC 62; *Vishala Kochi Kudivella Samrakshana Samithi v State of Kerala* 2006 (1) KLT 919.

processual character of the DPSP, courts have used these articles to impose continuing obligations on the state.

Fundamental Duties: while debates in the Constitutional Assembly did not result in the inclusion of a proposed section on the duties of citizens,[8] by 1969, there was a clear assertion by the Supreme Court that citizens had both rights and duties under law.[9] However, the formal articulation would have to wait until the Forty-second Constitutional Amendment, which added the Fundamental Duties chapter to the Constitution. These duties impose obligations on 'every citizen of India' and although not subject to writ jurisdiction, they have been deemed to 'provide valuable guidance and aid to interpretation and resolution of constitutional and legal issues'.[10]

Within the broader chapter, Article 51A(g) of the Constitution refers to the environment and states that citizens are obliged to 'protect and improve the natural environment … and to have compassion for living creatures'. What the chapter leaves unmentioned is who these duties are owed to, their extent, and who possesses the correlative rights. For instance, if a citizen litters, can a case be filed against them by another citizen or by the government? Are these obligations best seen through the consciousness-raising paradigm rather than an enforcement paradigm?[11] At least some of these questions would be answered by the courts' continued reliance on this article in their environmental jurisprudence.

The courts have interpreted the fundamental duties chapter of the Constitution as being a source of both substantive and procedural obligations and as an important interpretive aid with respect to fundamental rights.[12] Citizens have been held to be 'fundamentally obligated' to abide by the duties, which have even been compared to the fundamental rights in the Constitution.[13] Article 51A(g) of the Constitution has been relied upon by the Supreme Court to require mandatory environmental education,[14] and the Court has held that it was a 'social obligation' for every Indian citizen to 'preserve the environment and keep the ecological balance unaffected'.[15] The judiciary's invocation of fundamental duties as being more than exhortatory statements is also visible in a 2022 case where the Supreme Court agreed to consider a Public Interest Litigation

[8] Kalyani Ramnath, '"We the People": Seamless Webs and Social Revolution in India's Constituent Assembly Debates' (2012) 32(1) *South Asia Research* 57.

[9] Bhullar (n 1); *Chandra Bhavan Boarding and Lodging Bangalore v The State of Mysore and Another* (1969) 3 SCC 84 [13].

[10] *AIIMS Students' Union v AIIMS* (2002) 1 SCC 428; *Mohan Kumar Singhania v Union of India* 1992 Supp (1) SCC 594; *TN Godavarman Thirumulpad v Union of India* (2002) 10 SCC 606; *State of WB v Sujit Kumar Rana* (2004) 4 SCC 129.

[11] Bhullar (n 1); Justice Kurian Joseph, 'Fundamental Duties in the Indian Constitution' in *Supreme Court of India, The Constitution at 67* <https://main.sci.gov.in/pdf/AnnualReports/The%20Constitution%20at%2067.pdf>; *MC Mehta v Union of India* (1988) 1 SCC 471.

[12] *Intellectuals Forum, Tirupathi v State of AP* (2006) 3 SCC 549 [82]; *Sachidanand Pandey v State of WB* (1987) 2 SCC 295 [4].

[13] *AIIMS Students Union* (n 10).

[14] *MC Mehta v Union of India* (1992) 1 SCC 358.

[15] *Rural Litigation and Entitlement Kendra v State of UP* (1986) Supp SCC 517.

that was seeking to enforce the Fundamental Duties through the enactment of specific legislation transforming them from moral to legal obligations.[16] Importantly, the fundamental duty to protect the environment has been used by courts even to the extent of curbing fundamental rights (a tension more fully explored in the later discussion on citizens' duties to non-humans).

A more innovative use of this provision, however, has been to use it as a source of standing in several environmental cases. In *LK Koolwal v State of Rajasthan*, the High Court of Rajasthan noted that 'right and duty co-exist' and that Article 51A(g) of the Constitution should be seen both as a source of both duties and rights since it inhered a right in citizens to move the court to ensure that the state's 'obligatory and primary duties are performed in accordance with the law of land'.[17] This position has been extended by the National Green Tribunal (NGT) in a case where the petitioners' *locus standi* was attacked on the basis that they were neither 'interested parties' nor 'aggrieved' nor 'injured' as required under the National Green Tribunal Act, 2010 (the NGT Act).[18] The NGT set aside this objection on the basis that since Article 51A(g) of the Constitution clearly stated that 'protecting and improving the environment' was the fundamental duty of every citizen of India, *ipso facto*, any citizen had the right to approach the Tribunal in relation to protecting the environment. 'Statutory provisions' under the NGT Act were 'subservient to the constitutional mandates', and the definition of an aggrieved person under the Act could not supersede the definition of every citizen as set out in the Constitution.[19] In essence, by reading the provisions of the NGT Act through the lens of Article 51A(g) of the Constitution, the Tribunal held that since the Fundamental Duties created an obligation for citizens to protect the environment, this obligation could be a source of their standing in cases before the NGT.

Fundamental Rights: the other key constitutional source for environmental duties arises out of Article 21 of the Constitution and its right-to-life jurisprudence. The courts' efforts have taken a Constitutional provision framed as an admonition to the state to avoid infringing on a citizen's right to life[20] and transformed and extended it into the source for a wide-ranging set of negative and positive duties on the state.[21] While this interpretation has often been linked to the DPSP, in some cases, the Court has derived the state's duty to protect the environment from Article 21 of the Constitution more directly. This was the High Court of Rajasthan's position in *LK Koolwal* cited above. It ruled that

[16] Krishnadas Rajagopal, 'In Supreme Court, AG Says No Need to Enact Specific Laws to 'Enforce' Fundamental Duties on Citizens' *The Hindu* (4 April 2022) <https://www.thehindu.com/news/national/in-sc-ag-says-no-need-to-enact-specific-laws-to-enforce-fundamental-duties-on-citizens/article65289221.ece>.

[17] *LK Koolwal v State of Rajasthan* 1986 SCC OnLine Raj 43.

[18] *Vimal Bhai v Ministry of Environment and Forests* 2011 SCC OnLine NGT 16.

[19] ibid.

[20] The Constitution of India, Art 21 reads: 'No person shall be deprived of life and liberty except according to the procedure established by law'.

[21] Lovleen Bhullar, 'The Judiciary and the Right to Environment in India' in Shibani Ghosh (ed), *Indian Environmental Law: Key Concepts and Principles* (Orient BlackSwan 2019) 21.

the 'maintenance of health, preservation of sanitation, and environment' fell within the purview of Article 21 of the Constitution and created obligations for the government,[22] and a number of cases have echoed this reasoning.[23] A similar reasoning was followed in the *AP Pollution Control Board II* v *Prof MV Nayudu* case where the petitioners challenged government plans to allow industrial development in the areas around the key water reservoirs of Hyderabad.[24] The Supreme Court did not refer to the DPSP in its decision but found that Article 21 of the Constitution protected the right to water by stating that 'the right to access to drinking water is fundamental to life and there is a duty on the State under Article 21 to provide clean drinking water to its citizens'.[25]

13.1.2 Statutory Sources

Procedural Duties: the evolution of procedural duties is a key development within the broader space of environmental duties. Much like procedural rights,[26] procedural duties have played an important role in ensuring the 'democratization of environmental decision-making' and include private and public obligations to provide information, ensure participation in environmental decision-making, and provide redress mechanisms.[27]

Broadly speaking, the duty to ensure citizens' access to environmental information flows from citizens' rights to information under Articles 19(1)(a)[28] and 21[29] of the Constitution and statutory legal duties under the Water (Prevention and Control of Pollution) Act, 1974 (Water Pollution Act), the Air (Prevention and Control of Pollution) Act, 1981 (Air Pollution Act), the Environmental Impact Assessment Notification, 2006 (issued under the Environment (Protection) Act, 1986) (EIA Notification), the Right to Information Act, 2005, and the Companies Act, 2013. These duties are owed by both state and private actors to the public, impacted peoples, and regulatory authorities. They have been interpreted as the obligation to proactively disclose information relating to environmental impacts, decision-making processes, environmental hazards, and corporate sustainability measures.[30] The peremptory character of such duties has been emphasized by courts,[31] and public authorities have been ordered to mandatorily

[22] *LK Koolwal* (n 17).

[23] E.g., *Intellectuals Forum Tirupathi* (n 12).

[24] *AP Pollution Control Board II* (n 7).

[25] ibid.

[26] Shibani Ghosh, 'Procedural Environmental Rights in Indian Law' in Shibani Ghosh (ed), *Indian Environmental Law: Key Concepts and Principles* (Orient BlackSwan 2019) 55.

[27] Philippe Cullet, 'Definition of an Environmental Right in a Human Rights Context' (1995) 13(1) *Netherlands Quarterly of Human Rights* 25.

[28] *State of UP v Raj Narain AIR* 1975 SC 865; *People's Union for Civil Liberties and Another v Union of India and Another* AIR 2003 SC 2363.

[29] *Rajiv Suri v Delhi Development Authority and Others* (2022) 11 SCC 1; *Reliance Petrochemicals Ltd v Proprietors of Indian Express Newspapers, Bombay Pvt. Ltd.* AIR 1989 SC 190.

[30] Ghosh (n 26).

[31] E.g., *Utkarsh Mandal v Union of India* (2009) SCC OnLine Del 3836.

disclose information[32] in the manner and timeframe contemplated by statutory obligations.[33] Moreover, both public and private actors have had their environmental clearances reviewed or suspended in cases where information was either not appropriately communicated or was incorrect.[34]

The duty to ensure public participation in decision-making is a critical obligation in India[35] and has been set out in the Environment (Protection) Act, the EIA Notification, and the Scheduled Tribes and Other Traditional Forest Dwellers (Recognition of Forest Rights) Act, 2006. Courts have relied on these statutes to hold that governments have an obligation to ensure public participation in environmental decision-making and have ruled that this obligation includes, at a minimum, conducting public hearings and consultations, and taking the inputs from the consultation into account in their decision-making.[36] In the specific context of hearings, a detailed exposition of the nature of such obligations can be found in *Samarth Trust v Union of India Ministry of Environment and Forests,* where the petitioners filed a writ before the High Court of Delhi to clarify the 'nature, scope, and methodology' of public hearings as required under the EIA Notification.[37]

Finally, the third limb of procedural environmental duties is the duty to ensure access to justice. This duty has been the basis for the Court's multiple orders in relation to setting up specialized environmental courts.[38] This wide-ranging and sprawling obligation derives from multiple sources, including Articles 32 and 226 of the Constitution, the NGT Act, the Air Pollution Act, the Water Pollution Act, and the Biological Diversity Act, 1992.

Corporate Duties: statutes have often been interpreted as creating specific obligations for private actors. In *Manoj Misra v Union of India,* the NGT stated that the Air and Water Pollution Acts require companies to operate only with the consent of the Pollution Boards.[39] Thus, the Acts' intention to prevent and control air and water pollution created statutory rights for citizens and obligations for corporations.

[32] *GK Krishnan v Ministry of Environment and Forests* CIC/SG/A/2012/000374/18316, 9 April 2012 (Central Information Commission).

[33] *Medha Patkar and Another v Ministry of Environment NGT Principal Bench,* 11 July 2013; *Save Mon Region Federation and Another v Union of India NGT Principal Bench,* 14 March 2013.

[34] *University of Delhi v Ministry of Environment Forest and Climate Change* Appeal No 17/2021, Judgment of 31 May 2022 (NGT—Principal Bench); *Hanuman Laxman Aroskar v Union of India* (2019) 15 SCC 401; *Rajiv Suri* (n 29); *Utkarsh Mandal* (n 31).

[35] Lavanya Rajamani and Shibani Ghosh, 'Public Participation in Indian Environmental Law' in Lila Barrera-Hernandez and others (eds), *Sharing the Costs and Benefits of Energy and Resource Activity: Legal Change and Impact on Communities* (OUP 2016) 393; *Orissa Mining Corpn Ltd v Ministry of Environment and Forests* (2013) 6 SCC 476; *Debadityo Sinha v Union of India* Appeal No 79/2014, Judgment of 21 December 2016 (NGT—Principal Bench); *Utkarsh Mandal* (n 31).

[36] *Cellular Operators Association of India v TRAI* (2016) 7 SCC 703.

[37] *Samarth Trust v Union of India Ministry of Environment and Forests* 2010 SCC OnLine Del 2127.

[38] AP Pollution Control Board (n 7); *Indian Council for Enviro-Legal Action v Union of India* (1996) 3 SCC 212; *MC Mehta v Union of India* (1986) 2 SCC 176.

[39] *Manoj Misra v Union of India* 2015 SCC OnLine NGT 840.

Another important set of corporate duties is articulated in the Companies Act, 2013, the SEBI (Listing Obligations and Disclosure Requirements) Regulations, 2015, and the SEBI Circular for Business Responsibility Reporting, 2015. Under the Companies Act, companies above a particular size have mandatory corporate social responsibility (CSR) obligations and directors owe duties to act for the benefit of the company, its employees, the shareholders, the community and 'for the protection of the environment'.[40] SEBI Regulations also make it mandatory for the 1,000 largest listed entities in India to publish this Business Responsibility Report. Failure to discharge these obligations could lead to penal sanctions or action being taken by the SEBI. Although non-binding, the voluntary Corporate Social Responsibility Guidelines, 2009 and the National Voluntary Guidelines on Social, Environmental and Economic Responsibilities of Businesses 2011 are also significant since they indicate the scope and extent of companies' statutory (CSR) obligations. The 2009 Guidelines require companies to draft policies on CSR, and the 2011 Guidelines set out a framework for drafting Business Responsibility Reports.

13.2 Environmental Duties: Limitation and Potential

If one examines judicial interpretations of environmental duties, a few clusters or themes emerge. While acknowledging the obvious overlaps within these categories, they can be broadly divided into (i) the duty to prevent, protect, and provide; (ii) duties to non-humans; and (iii) corporate environmental duties. In the sections below, I elaborate on each of these categories.

13.2.1 Duty to Prevent, Protect, and Provide

As discussed in the previous sections, the Constitution sets out broad environmental duties. Courts have relied on these constitutional provisions, in addition to common law principles and international environmental law, to hold that both government and private parties have an obligation to protect and safeguard the environment, prevent harm, compensate affected parties, remediate environmental damage, and provide access to a clean and healthy environment.[41]

[40] Companies Act, 2013 s 166(2).

[41] See generally *AP Pollution Control Board v Prof MV Nayudu* (1999) 2 SCC 718; *Vellore Citizens' Welfare Forum v Union of India* (1996) 5 SCC 647; *M/s Abhilash Textile v The Rajkot Municipal Corporation* (1987) SCC OnLine Guj 47 [7]; *Hinch Lal Tiwari v Kamala Devi* (2001) 6 SCC 496; *Vijay Singh Puniya v State of Rajasthan* (2003) SCC OnLine Raj 87 [31]; Rural Litigation and Entitlement Kendra (n 15); *The Principal, St Anthony's College v State of Meghalaya* WP No 294 of 2012, Judgment dated 17 April 2014 (High Court of Meghalaya).

The precautionary principle is a good example of an international environmental law principle that has been read into domestic law to impose environmental obligations and limitations on the state. While the classic exposition of the principle in international environmental law is found in Principle 15 of the Rio Declaration,[42] the clearest articulation of the principle in Indian jurisprudence is expressed in the *Vellore Citizens' Welfare Forum v Union of India (Vellore Tanneries)* case,[43] which held that the precautionary principle encompassed three aspects: (i) the state had an obligation to 'anticipate, prevent, and attack' the bases of environmental damage; (ii) a 'lack of scientific certainty' should not be used to defer measures to prevent environmental damage where 'threats of serious and irreversible damage' exist; and (iii) the proponent of the potentially harmful measure should be required to prove its non-damaging nature. In *AP Pollution Control Board*, the Court ruled, moreover, that the precautionary principle obliged the government to prevent irreversible environmental harms.[44] While this principle has been used in several cases, as Rajamani notes, a large proportion of these cases 'are, in reality, engaging the principle of prevention'.[45] However, at least in a few cases, this principle has been relied upon to order additional enquiries to gather more evidence.[46]

The public trust doctrine is another principle that has been relied upon by courts to find that the government has a duty to prevent public resources from coming under private ownership. Broadly construed, the public trust doctrine entails a state obligation to 'protect the people's common heritage of streams, lakes, marshlands and tidelands'.[47] In a series of cases beginning from the landmark *MC Mehta v Kamal Nath* decision, courts have ruled that under the public trust doctrine, it was the state's duty to protect environmental resources.[48] This meant that the state was the 'trustee of all natural resources', which placed it 'under a legal duty to protect the natural resources'.[49] Additionally, in *Fomento Resorts and Hotels Ltd and Another v Minguel Martins and Another*,[50] the Court stated that the 'heart of the public trust doctrine is that it imposes limits and obligations upon government agencies and their administrators on behalf of all the people and especially future generations'.[51] Moreover, not only was such an obligation imposed on the state, 'every person exercising his or her right to use the air, water, or land and associated natural ecosystems has the obligation to secure for the rest of us the

42 Rio Declaration on Environment and Development, 14 June 1992, UN Doc A/CONF.151/26/Rev. 1 (vol I), annex II (1992), Principle 15.

43 *Vellore Citizens' Welfare Forum* (n 41).

44 *AP Pollution Control Board* (n 7).

45 Lavanya Rajamani, 'The Precautionary Principle' in Shibani Ghosh (ed), *Indian Environmental Law: Key Concepts and Principles* (Orient BlackSwan 2019) 192.

46 *Democratic Youth Federation of India v Union of India* (2011) 15 SCC 530; *Shobha Phadnavis v State of Maharashtra* 2016 SCC OnLine NGT 3797.

47 *National Audubon Society v Superior Court of Alpine County* 33 Cal 3d 419.

48 *MC Mehta v Kamal Nath* (1997) 1 SCC 388; *TN Godavarman Thirumulpad v Union of India* AIR 2005 SC 4256; *Intellectuals Forum, Tirupathi* (n 12).

49 ibid.

50 *Fomento Resorts and Hotels Ltd v Minguel Martins* (2009) 3 SCC 571.

51 ibid.

right to live or otherwise use that same resource or property for the long term and enjoyment by future generations'.[52] Thus, private rights holders had 'an obligation to use such resources in a manner as not to impair or diminish the people's rights and the people's long-term interest in that property or resource, including down-slope lands, waters and resources'.[53]

The duty to provide refers to state obligations to provide safe and clean drinking water, sanitation facilities, and clean air and requires the state to guarantee access, address pollution, and remediate previous harms. These duties are rooted in the Constitution and statutes. An area where this is particularly evident is in a series of cases relating to clean air and water. In the *AP Pollution Control Board* case discussed earlier, the Supreme Court emphasized the state's responsibility to ensure clean air and reiterated that 'in such a matter of air and water pollution, it is the Constitutional duty enjoined upon all the stakeholders to do the needful for providing better air and potable water'.[54] The duty to access has also been relied upon in a prohibitory sense insofar as the state is restricted from taking any steps that might interfere with existing rights to public resources such as beaches.[55] Although provisioning duties inevitably involve costs to the public exchequer, the courts have rejected government efforts to plead straitened finances as a reason for inaction. This stance was most forcefully articulated in *Municipal Council, Ratlam v Vardichand*, a matter concerning the provision of sanitation facilities in a town in Madhya Pradesh.[56] Rejecting the respondent municipality's arguments on insufficient funds, the Court stated that finances could not be used as a pretext to avoid responsibility for constitutional and statutory obligations regarding sanitation and public health.

13.2.2 Environmental Duties to Non-Humans

The rights of non-humans and the duties owed to them have become a particular issue of judicial concern over the past two decades. This has aligned with the Supreme Court's concern over an overly anthropocentric focus in environmental cases[57] and has seen the courts move towards granting rights to non-humans, including, most notably, animals, rivers, glaciers, and associated landscapes.[58]

In several decisions addressing environmental duties to non-humans, the courts have invoked the doctrine of *parens patriae*.[59] While this doctrine is used to indicate state

52 ibid.
53 ibid.
54 *MC Mehta (Stubble Burning and Air Quality) v Union of India* (2020) 7 SCC 530.
55 *Fomento Resorts and Hotels Ltd* (n 50).
56 *Municipal Council, Ratlam v Vardichand* (1980) 4 SCC 162.
57 E.g., Centre for Environmental Law, *World Wildlife Fund v Union of India* (2013) 8 SCC 234.
58 E.g., *Lalit Miglani v State of Uttarakhand* 2017 SCC OnLine Utt 392; *Court on its own Motion v Chandigarh Administration* 2020 SCC OnLine P&H 4454.
59 E.g., *A Periyakaruppan v Principal Secretary to Government* 2022 SCC OnLine Mad 2077; *Animal Welfare Board of India v A Nagaraja* (2014) 7 SCC 547.

power and capacity in jurisdictions like the United States, courts in India have framed it in terms of duties cast upon the state, specific government functionaries, and even upon the courts themselves. For instance, in *Charan Lal Sahu v Union of India*, the Supreme Court noted that the essence of the doctrine was 'the obligation of the State to protect and take into custody the rights and privileges of its citizens for discharging its obligations'.[60]

Some aspects of the substance of these *parens patriae* obligations can be gleaned from court decisions such as *Nagaraja*,[61] where the practice of Jallikattu or bull-racing was challenged. The petitioners argued, *inter alia,* that Jallikattu caused unnecessary pain and suffering to animals and violated the Prevention of Cruelty to Animals Act, 1960 (PCA), read with Articles 21 and 51A(g) of the Constitution. The Court's decision noted that the PCA had been enacted prior to the addition of the the Fundamental Duties chapter in the Constitution. Moreover, the Court held that it had a 'duty under the doctrine of *parens patriae* to take care of the rights of animals, since they are unable to take care of themselves as against human beings'.[62] Ultimately, the Court rejected arguments rooted in tradition and custom to rule that the duties imposed on citizens under sections 3 and 11 of the PCA and Article 51(A)(g) of the Constitution, created corresponding rights granted to animals in addition to their rights to life guaranteed under Article 21 of the Constitution. By extending the environmental protections under Article 21 to animals, the Court underlined the illegality of Jallikattu and banned its continuance.

A related yet subtly different line of argument has been followed in the 'rights of nature' cases which have held that entities as disparate as the Sukhna Lake, the 'entire animal kingdom', the rivers 'Ganga and Yamuna and all their tributaries [and] streams', and the 'Himalayas, glaciers, streams, water bodies', have been granted the status of legal persons with 'all corresponding rights, duties, and liabilities' of a living person.[63] While this aligns to some extent with the *Nagaraja* ratio, the imposition of duties and liabilities in these cases is troubling. After all, although rights should not be seen through an anthropomorphic lens alone, duties presuppose a certain capacity tied to humanness. Imposing duties on non-humans is, thus, likely to lead to legal incoherence and unworkability. Would a river, for instance, have a duty to compensate flood victims? Could the government official declared to be *in loco parentis* in relation to a river's rights be sued for the river's flooding? How would a decision of this nature be implemented? This is arguably one of the reasons that the decision granting legal personhood to the Ganga and Yamuna rivers was swiftly stayed by the Supreme Court. Stay notwithstanding, it does appear, however, that the debate on the rights and duties of nature is very much here to stay. A May 2022 decision by the Madras High Court in a case concerning disciplinary proceedings against an official for improperly issuing *pattas* to forest land supports this

60 *Charan Lal Sahu v Union of India* (1990) 1 SCC 613.

61 *Animal Welfare Board of India* (n 59).

62 ibid.

63 *Lalit Miglani* (n 58); *Court on its own Motion* (n 58). See also ch 14 in this Handbook.

assessment.[64] In their decision, the judge noted that the appropriate punishment in this matter had to account for the official's violation of his 'duty to protect the forest land'.[65] After extensively discussed human obligations towards nature protection, the judge approvingly cited the *Lalit Miglani v State of Uttarakhand* case granting 'constitutional legal rights to the Mother Earth' before invoking its *parens patriae* jurisdiction and declaring that 'Mother Nature' was a 'living being' with rights, duties, and liabilities.[66]

Another vein of reasoning is visible in the controversial cow slaughter cases. In 2005, a seven-judge bench of the Supreme Court ruled on the constitutionality of state legislation banning cow slaughter.[67] This case built on previous judgments, including *Mohd. Hanif Quareshi v State of Bihar*, which had ruled a total ban on cow slaughter violated fundamental rights to religion and occupation and that Article 48 of the Constitution could not be used to validate provisions which were seen as violating fundamental rights.[68] However, in its 2005 decision, the Court took a somewhat different stance. Noting that Articles 48A and 51A(g) had not yet been introduced within the Constitution at the time of the 1958 *Quareshi* case, the Court stated that 'the State is, in a sense, "all the citizens placed together" and, therefore, though Article 51A does not expressly cast any fundamental duty on the State, the fact remains that the duty of every citizen of India is, collectively speaking, the duty of the State'.[69] The Court then went on to assert that the broad wording of Article 51A(g) specifically embraced the category of cattle referred to in Article 48 and that its call to have compassion for living creatures lent itself to the bans envisaged by the impugned legislations. As this decision shows, duties to animals can be used to undermine the fundamental rights of citizens.

The category of environmental duties to non-humans is, therefore, a still-emergent area of jurisprudence. Rooted in the Constitution, state obligations to protect entities as diverse as rivers and wild and domestic animals have been used as a basis for holding government officials to account as well as to infringe on the fundamental rights of citizens.

13.2.3 Corporate Environmental Duties

A notable example of the obligations of corporations regarding environmental harms is visible in the *MC Mehta v Union of India (Shriram—Oleum Gas)* and the *Indian Council for Enviro-Legal Action v Union of India* cases where the mismanagement of toxic chemicals from factories impacted the local environment and public health.[70] While the

64 *A Periyakaruppan* (n 59).
65 ibid.
66 ibid.
67 *State of Gujarat v Mirzapur Moti Kureshi Kassab* (2005) 8 SCC 534.
68 *Mohd. Hanif Quareshi v State of Bihar* AIR 1958 SC 731.
69 *State of Gujarat* (n 67).
70 *MC Mehta v Union of India (Shriram—Oleum Gas)* (1987) 1 SCC 395; Indian Council for Enviro-Legal Action (n 38).

Supreme Court notably declined to offer a definitive answer on whether a private corporation could be sued for their failures in relation to citizens' fundamental environmental rights, they held that the doctrine of absolute liability could be used to impose punitive and compensatory damages on corporations for their failure to prevent environmental harm and considering the environmental damage caused by their activities. In Shriram Mills, the Court thus held that:

> where an enterprise is engaged in a hazardous or inherently dangerous activity and harm results to anyone on account of an accident in the operation of such hazardous or inherently dangerous activity resulting, for example, in escape of toxic gas, the enterprise is strictly and absolutely liable to compensate all those who are affected by the accident.[71]

The Great Indian Bustard and the Lesser Florican cases have indicated how the courts are likely to interpret companies' CSR obligations.[72] These cases were filed to address the impact of overhead power lines on these highly endangered species. In its interim order, the Supreme Court relied on the provisions in sections 135 and 166(2) of the Companies Act to hold that the funds required to protect the birds might be partly realized through these statutory obligations placed on generating companies. Moreover, the Court ordered that future high voltage powerlines in priority areas must be laid underground by the companies concerned.

Finally, the obligation of due diligence has increasingly come to the forefront. Although imposed on public and private actors,[73] it is a particularly key obligation for corporate actors under domestic law. This is because the due diligence principle has been invoked to hold errant actors accountable as well as to provide a defence for them. For instance, section 40 of the Air Pollution Act, section 47 of the Water Pollution Act, and section 16 of the Environment (Protection) Act all note that when a company is found to have committed an offence under the Act, its personnel can avoid liability if they prove that they had taken due diligence to prevent the commission of such an offence. Due diligence is also an increasingly important word in the context of international and transnational law. It is present in international soft law principles such as the Equator Principles,[74] the United Nations Guiding Principles on Business and Human Rights,[75] the OECD Guidelines for Multinational Enterprises,[76] as well as in jurisdictions such

[71] ibid.

[72] *MK Ranjitsinh v Union of India* (2021) SCC OnLine SC 326.

[73] E.g., *Common Cause v Union of India* (2017) 9 SCC 499.

[74] The Equator Principles <https://equator-principles.com/about-the-equator-principles/>.

[75] United Nations Human Rights Office of the High Commissioner, Guiding Principles on Business and Human Rights, Implementing the United Nations 'Protect, Respect and Remedy' Framework (United Nations 2011) <https://www.ohchr.org/sites/default/files/documents/publications/guidingprinciplesbusinesshr_en.pdf>.

[76] OECD, *OECD Guidelines for Multinational Enterprises* (OECD Publishing 2011) <https://www.oecd.org/daf/inv/mne/48004323.pdf>.

as the European Union.[77] Given the international reach and presence of multinational companies, it is expected that these regulatory regimes would have a significant impact on companies operating in India.

Corporate environmental duties are an increasingly important area of environmental law. This importance is visible in the corporate statutes discussed above as well as in the steps to evolve corporate obligations at the international and supra-national levels.[78]

Conclusion

Explicitly mentioned in the Constitution, in statutes, and in judicial decisions, environmental duties are embedded within the enviro-legal framework in India. The line between duties and rights has always been blurred, but as this chapter makes clear, duties in the Indian environmental context do not exist merely as mirror images of rights but are also free-standing sources of environmental obligations. Perhaps most strikingly, in contradistinction to rights, duties are imposed on every actor. Individuals, the state, companies, and even non-humans have been invested with environmental obligations.

However, environmental duties raise a host of uncomfortable questions as well. To begin with, given the relationship between obligations and agentive capacity, it is still unclear what it might mean for non-humans to have environmental duties. Moreover, the scope and extent of citizens' environmental duties are also far from clear. While duty-based accounts of citizenship emphasize that reciprocal obligations between the state and citizens are critical to a healthy social contract and integral to fostering a sense of community,[79] the discussion in this chapter has shown that there is often a darker side to such approaches. After all, it is arguable that a duty-based ethic wrongly individuates environmental harms rather than affixing primary responsibility on the states and corporations that bear the chief responsibility for environmental degradation in the country. Finally, in the Indian context, the invocation of citizens' environmental duties has often been used to sidestep thorny questions arising from a clash of rights. The nadir of this approach is visible within the cow slaughter cases where decisions have been grounded in the argument that individuals had a duty to 'show compassion' rather than framing the issue as the state's obligation to balance competing fundamental rights, .[80]

With duties being used to both advance and curtail rights, the sprawling and fragmented edifice of environmental duties requires a close and careful examination to

[77] European Commission, 'Just and Sustainable Economy: Commission Lays Down Rules for Companies to Respect Human Rights and Environment in Global Value Chains' (2022) <https://ec.europa.eu/commission/presscorner/detail/en/ip_22_1145>.

[78] E.g., Julia Bialek, 'Evaluating the Zero Draft on a UN Treaty on Business and Human Rights' (2019) 9(3) *Goettingen Journal of International Law* 501; Olivier de Schutter, 'Towards a New Treaty on Business and Human Rights' (2015) 1(1) *Business and Human Rights Journal* 41.

[79] Andrew Dobson, Citizenship and the Environment (OUP 2003).

[80] *State of Gujarat* (n 67).

ensure proper apportionment of responsibilities on actors with the most power and capacity. At the very least, they provide a glimpse into the opportunities and limitations of environmental law in addressing some of the most urgent crises of our times.

Suggestions for Further Reading

Fernando Berdion Del Valle and Kathryn Sikkink, '(Re)discovering Duties: Individual Responsibilities in the Age of Rights' (2017) 26(1) *Minnesota Journal of International Law* 189.

Lovleen Bhullar, 'Environmental Constitutionalism and Duties of Individuals in India' (2022) 34(3) *Journal of Environmental Law* 399.

Radhika Govindarajan, *Animal Intimacies* (University of Chicago Press 2018).

Tarunabh Khaitan, 'Constitutional Directives: Morally-Committed Political Constitutionalism' (2019) 82(4) *Modern Law Review* 603.

K Sivaramakrishnan, 'Environment, Law, and Democracy in India' (2011) 70(4) *The Journal of Asian Studies* 905.

CHAPTER 14

RIGHTS OF NATURE

STELLINA JOLLY*

Abstract

In 2017, through two judgments (*Mohammed Salim v State of Uttarakhand* and *Lalit Miglani v State of Uttarakhand*), the High Court of Uttarakhand declared the Rivers Ganga and Yamuna and glaciers, respectively, as legal persons enjoying all the rights and duties of a living entity. The decisions proved impactful in articulating the legal personality of animals and other natural entities in subsequent cases. These decisions can be seen in the background of similar legal initiatives in other jurisdictions granting rights of nature, which constitutes a significant development in environmental law. However, there is a knowledge gap concerning the normative foundation and implementation mechanisms, and implications of recognizing the rights of nature. This chapter considers the main characteristics of the rights of nature with a focus on the rights of rivers and analyses its potential to shape the contemporary narrative and change the way in which environmental protection is envisaged.

Introduction

The idea of living in harmony with nature dominated the early Indian environmental ethos.[1] Living in harmony with nature was entrenched in traditions[2] and religious faith echoed in the daily lives of people, enshrined in myths, folklore, religion, arts, and

* The author acknowledges the research assistance provided by Samriddhi Chatterjee, student, GNLU, Gujarat.

[1] See generally Peter Marshall, *Nature's Web: Rethinking Our Place on Earth* (Routledge 1992).

[2] The concept of *Vasudhaiva Kutumkam* found in Hindu texts considers the world as one family.

culture.[3] The worship of plants, animals, forests, rivers, the sun, and considering the Earth itself as Mother Goddess, symbolizes living in environmental harmony and conservation of nature.[4] Sacred groves dedicated to local deities have been preserved since time immemorial.[5] Religious scriptures prescribed tree planting and condemned the destruction of plants and forests, stipulating that trees are like children.[6] The Mughal era in Indian history was characterized by the establishment of magnificent gardens and parks.[7]

The ancient Indian environmental ethic of living in harmony with nature was gradually relegated to the background during the British era that brought the plunder of natural resources in the name of development.[8] The post-Independence period witnessed the expansion of environmental law, characterized by a proliferation of legal measures and institutions influenced by developments in international environmental law, beginning with the Stockholm Declaration. In all the major international legal developments that followed the Stockholm Declaration, environmental protection was conceived in the context of its linkage with development, articulating a human-centric perspective.[9] In the environment–development matrix, the judicial acknowledgement of a right to environment was meaningful.[10] Despite the pronouncement of a right to environment, there is an understanding that environmental law has been unsuccessful in abating environmental destruction from crossing critical planetary boundaries.[11] The deepening crisis in nature has led scholars, communities, and activists to question the human-centric legal paradigm and initiate an interest towards recognizing the rights of nature as a possible tool to address and reverse environmental degradation.

Through two judgments (*Mohammed Salim v State of Uttarakhand* (Ganga and Yamuna)[12] and *Lalit Miglani v State of Uttarakhand (Glaciers)*,[13] the Indian judiciary followed developments in certain other jurisdictions,[14] declaring the Rivers Ganga and

[3] Julia Shaw, 'Religion, "Nature" and Environmental Ethics in Ancient India: Archaeologies of Human: Non-Human Suffering and Well-being in Early Buddhist and Hindu Contexts' (2016) 48(4) *World Archaeology* 517.

[4] ibid.

[5] P Leelakrishnan, *Environmental Law in India* (5th edn, Lexis Nexis 2019) 9.

[6] ibid.

[7] Michael H Fisher, *An Environmental History of India: From Earliest Times to the Twenty-First Century* (CUP 2018) 96.

[8] ibid 135–136.

[9] Louis J Kotzé and Duncan French, 'The Anthropocentric Ontology of International Environmental Law and the Sustainable Development Goals: Towards an Eco-Centric Rule of Law in the Anthropocene' (2018) 7(1) *Global Journal of Comparative Law* 5.

[10] Erin Daly, 'Constitutional Protection for Environmental Rights: The Benefits of Environmental Process' (2012) 17(2) *International Journal of Peace Studies* 71.

[11] Jan G Laitos and Lauren Joseph Wolongevicz, 'Why Environmental Laws Fail' (2014) 39(1) *William and Mary Environmental Law and Policy Review* 1; Susana Borras, 'New Transitions from Human Rights to the Environment to the Rights of Nature' (2016) 5(1) *Transnational Environmental Law* 113.

[12] *Mohammed Salim v State of Uttarakhand* SCC OnLine Utt 367.

[13] *Lalit Miglani v State of Uttarakhand* 2017 SCC OnLine Utt 392.

[14] Constitution of the Republic of Ecuador, 2008 Chapter 7, 71–74; Law on the Rights of Mother Earth, 2010 (Bolivia); Te Awa Tupua (Whanganui River Claims Settlement) Act 2017 (Public Act 2017 No 7)

Yamuna and glaciers, respectively, as legal persons enjoying all the rights and duties of a living entity. Granting rights to nature is considered a possible tool to address and reverse environmental degradation.

This chapter considers the main characteristics of the rights of nature, with a particular focus on India, and analyses its potential to shape the contemporary narrative and bring a substantial change in the way environmental protection is envisaged. Section 14.1 explores the reasons for articulating the rights of nature in the broader context of environmental protection. Section 14.1.1 and 2 explores the concept of rights of nature and examines how recognizing the rights of nature differs from conventional environmental protection. Section 14.2 provides a snapshot of the rights of nature elaborated in judicial developments in the Indian context, focusing on the rights of rivers. Section 14.3 focuses on whether the rights of nature can improve the existing environmental law framework and improve environmental protection in India. The chapter concludes by drawing out some suggestions for creating a legal framework.

14.1 Articulation of the Rights of Nature

The intensification of human pressure on the environment and the consequent environmental degradation[15] have prompted scholars to emphasize deep respect for ecology and the inherent value of all things in nature independent of their use by human beings.[16] The idea of recognizing animal rights was one of the focuses of this new strand. The idea was given a push by the laws essentially conceived in terms of rights and obligations,[17] and it became the basis for animal protection in many jurisdictions.[18] The second strand was dominated by environmental ethics scholars who focused on wide-ranging constellations of ideas ranging from wilderness conservation[19] to the irrevocable and intrinsic value of nature.[20]

(New Zealand); *Center for Social Justice Studies et al v Presidency of the Republic et al* Judgment T-622/16 Constitutional Court of Colombia (10 November 2016) (the Atrato River Case).

15 Laitos and Wolongevicz (n 11) 8; Johan Rockstrom and others, 'A Safe Operating Space for Humanity' (2009) 461 *Nature* 472.

16 Katherine V Kortenkamp and Colleen F Moore, 'Ecocentrism and Anthropocentrism: Moral Reasoning about Ecological Commons Dilemmas' (2001) 21(3) *Journal of Environmental Psychology* 261, 265.

17 Mihnea Tănăsescu, *Understanding the Rights of Nature: A Critical Introduction* (Transcript Verlag 2022) 10.

18 Bhumika Sharma and Priyanka Sharma, 'Legislative Framework vis-a-vis Animals: A Comparative Study' (2017) 18(3&4) *Nyaya Deep—The Official Journal of NALSA* 131.

19 John Muir, *Wilderness Essays* (Madison & Adams Press 2019).

20 J Baird Callicott, 'The Metaphysical Implications of Ecology' (1986) 8(4) *Environmental Ethics* 301.

Among the many streams of thought influencing the articulation of ecocentric approaches, the indigenous vision of harmony between living and non-living is significant.[21] A conspicuous plank of this ecocentric approach is fashioned around rights of nature or rights of Mother Earth.[22] It should be noted that though the two terms—rights of Mother Earth and rights of nature—are used interchangeably, they differ in their scope. The focus of rights of nature is on extending the rights to non-human species and inanimate objects for their existence unthreatened by human activities,[23] whereas the rights of Mother Earth encompass both humans and nature, and not nature alone.[24] The constitutional recognition of the Rights of Mother Earth in Bolivia is an example, which encompasses humans and nature as a unity[25] whereas the legal recognition of Whanganui River describes Te Awa Tupua as an indivisible and living whole, comprising the Whanganui River from the mountains to the sea, incorporating all its physical and metaphysical elements.[26]

With regard to the developments on the rights of nature, the earliest intellectual genealogy of rights of nature belongs to Stone, who identified the following as constituting the core rights of nature:

- nature can institute legal actions only through a guardian;
- the court should consider the injury to nature itself; and
- grant the relief in favour of nature itself.[27]

The idea of granting rights to nature was further built on a platform of ideas that differed from each other. From a philosophical perspective, Arne Naess talked about rights for plants and animals.[28] Thomas Berry, whose ideas were influenced by natural law, coined the term 'Earth jurisprudence'[29] and proposed that every Earth community essentially possesses three rights: (i) the right to be, (ii) the right to habitat, and (iii) the right to fulfil its role in the ever-renewing processes of the Earth community.[30] Berry

[21] Thomas J Demos, *Decolonizing Nature: Contemporary Art and the Politics of Ecology* (Sternberg Press 2016) 8; Boaventura de Sousa Santos, *The End of the Cognitive Empire: The Coming of Age of Epistemologies of the South* (Duke University Press 2018).

[22] Pablo Sólon, 'The Rights of Mother Earth' in Vishwas Satgar (ed), *The Climate Crisis: South African and Global Democratic Eco-Socialist Alternatives* (Wits University Press 2018) 107, 126.

[23] David R Boyd, *The Rights of Nature: A Legal Revolution that Could Save the World* (ECW press 2017) 137.

[24] Sólon (n 22) 108.

[25] Law of the Rights of Mother Earth 2010 (Law N^0 071 of the Plurinational State of Bolivia), art 3, 5.

[26] Te Awa Tupua Act (n 14).

[27] Christopher D Stone, 'Should Trees Have Standing? Toward Legal Rights for Natural Objects' (1972) 45 *Southern California Law Review* 450.

[28] Arne Naess, *Ecology, Community and Lifestyle* (CUP 1976).

[29] Thomas Berry, *The Great Work: Our Way Into the Future* (Bell Tower 1999). Also quoted in Cormac Cullinan, *Wild Law: A Manifesto for Earth Justice* (Chelsea Green Publishing 2011) 11.

[30] Michelle Maloney and Sister Patricia Siemen, 'Responding to the Great Work: The Role of Earth Jurisprudence and Wild Law in the 21st Century' (2015) 5(1) *Environmental Law Journal* 6, 9.

cogitated on the rights of nature as the creation of the universe and believed that human laws merely recognize the already existing rights of nature.[31] Providing a biocentric perspective, Laitos argues for (i) a right to exist, (ii) a right of personal protection, (iii) a right to liberty, and (iv) a right to have these rights legally recognized by the government, for natural resources.[32]

Cormac Cullinan underscored the persistence of environmental issues and questioned how to ensure that the wrongdoer is deterred or punished for their conduct if there is no tangible consequence in the form of rights available to the injured (nature)?[33] Some proponents of the rights of nature attempted to embed these rights within democracy through public participation.[34] Earth democracy promotes earth stewardship of the local communities and considers human rights interdependent with Earth rights.[35] These perspectives illustrate that the ecocentric approach does not operate with a single template and narrative, but differs in its concept, foundation, and genealogy.

On a conceptual level, it can be argued that nature lacks awareness and self-consciousness, which are essential elements of personality. How can a river or an animal want to exist and flourish? However, proponents of the rights of nature underplay the importance of awareness and consciousness, and argue that these cannot be the only criteria for the grant of personality.[36] In addition, there is no consensus as to what constitutes nature and its scope. For instance, while arguing for the rights of nature, Stone specifically limits himself to non-animals and natural objects.[37] Callicott considers animals' rights and environmental ethics as incompatible with each other.[38] Regan argues for the inherent value only for higher animals,[39] whereas Barry argues for the rights of all the components of the Earth community.[40] The lack of consensus as to what constitutes nature is also seen in the approach of jurisdictions. The Constitution of Ecuador defines nature broadly as the Andean Indigenous deity (Mother Earth) in all its encompassing nature.[41] By contrast, New Zealand's legislation only recognizes and specifies rights for particular ecosystems: the Whanganui River and the Te Urewera forest.[42] With all these challenges, the idea of granting rights to nature appears to be

[31] Berry (n 29) 56, 61.

[32] Jan Laitos, *The Right of Non-Use* (OUP 2012).

[33] Cormac Cullinan, 'Do Humans Have Standing to Deny Trees Rights' (2008) 11 *Barry Law Review* 11.

[34] Peter Burdon, 'Wild Law and the Project of Earth Democracy' in Michelle Maloney and Peter Burdon (eds), *Wild Law: In Practice* (Routledge 2014).

[35] F Stuart Chapin, *Grassroots Stewardship: Sustainability within Our Reach* (OUP 2020).

[36] PS Elder, 'Legal Rights for Nature: The Wrong Answer to the Right(s) Question' (1984) 22(2) *Osgoode Hall Law Journal* 285.

[37] Stone (n 27).

[38] Callicott (n 20) 311.

[39] Tom Regan, *The Case for Animal Rights* (University of California Press 1983).

[40] Berry (n 29) 163.

[41] Ecuador Constitution (n 14).

[42] Te Urewera Act 2014 (Public Act No 51 New Zealand).

taking hold in many jurisdictions,[43] and differs from the conventional mode of environmental protection.

14.1.1 Nature as a Holder of Rights

Conventional environmental protection is rooted in the revolutionization of rights, including the right to the environment.[44] However, all these rights are framed through the perspective of humans, illuminating the domination of humans over nature. Recognition of the rights of nature exalts nature as a subject of substantive rights, highlights the intrinsic worth of nature, and emphasizes the interconnectedness and shared existence of all elements of nature, including humans.[45] Going by the practice adopted in other jurisdictions, conferring rights on nature brings the community into focus and upholds the indigenous way of life.[46] For instance, under conventional environmental laws, the construction of an industrial unit and its potential health and environmental impact are addressed initially through public comments during an environmental impact assessment (EIA). Possible environmental effects can also be addressed by invoking the right to life under the constitution if the matter is taken before the courts through litigation. However, this approach evaluates environmental law from a human-centric perspective. Under the rights of nature, nature is protected independently of its human utility.[47] Conferring rights to nature also challenges the traditional understanding of looking at environmental protection through the prism of private property, which is discussed below.

14.1.2 Challenging the Idea of Property and Representing Nature

The prominent manifestation of anthropocentrism in law is built around the notion of 'nature' as private property.[48] At the international level, developing states' demand to claim state sovereignty over natural resources has culminated in the declaration by the United Nations of Permanent Sovereignty of Natural Resources.[49] At the

[43] See also Craig M Kauffman and Pamela L Martin, 'Constructing Rights of Nature Norms in the US, Ecuador, and New Zealand' (2018) 18(4) *Global Environmental Politics* 43; Abigail Hutchison, 'The Whanganui River as a Legal Person' (2014) 39(3) *Alternative Law Journal* 179.

[44] Daly (n 10) 73.

[45] Daniel P Corrigan and Markku Oksanen, *Rights of Nature: A Re-examination* (Routledge 2021).

[46] Mihnea Tanasescu, 'Rights of Nature, Legal Personality and Indigenous Philosophies' (2020) 9(3) *Transnational Environmental Law* 429.

[47] ibid.

[48] Sólon (n 22) 126.

[49] UN General Assembly Resolution 1803 (XVII), Permanent Sovereignty over Natural Resources, 14 December 1962, UN Doc A/RES/1803 (XVII).

domestic level, laws are established to guarantee property rights over land resources, reflecting that the overriding legal relationship between humans and nature has so far been through property.[50] The 'inherent value' of nature and the community perspective intrinsic to the rights of nature challenge the notions of property. For instance, recognizing legal personality of water bodies will modify the status of groundwater sources, which are considered part of land ownership in India and many jurisdictions.[51] With all the traction towards recognizing the rights of nature, India has also joined these jurisdictions in adopting an ecocentric approach to environmental protection, as outlined below.

14.2 Anatomy of the Right of Nature and its Manifestation in Indian Jurisprudence

The first initiative in the evolution of Indian jurisprudence towards an ecocentric approach was seen in the case of animals by relying on the expanded notion of the right to life under Article 21 of the Constitution of India, 1950. The rights jurisprudence acknowledged the inherent dignity of all persons, irrespective of the humanness of such persons. The idea that rights can be extended to non-humans is seen in *Animal Welfare Board v A Nagaraja*,[52] a case involving *Jallikattu* (a bull-taming sport), where the Supreme Court observed that every species has an inherent right to life and to be protected by law. A similar approach is also seen in *TN Godavarman Thirumulpad v Union of India* (Asiatic Wild Buffaloes case)[53] and *Centre for Environment Law, WWF-I v Union of India* (Asiatic Lions case),[54] where the Court recognized the extensive rights of animals, including fundamental rights and the necessity to drift away from the prevalent anthropocentric perspective to an ecocentric one. Subsequently, in 2018, in *Karnail Singh v State of Haryana*, 'the entire animal kingdom including avian and aquatic are declared as legal entities having a distinct persona with corresponding rights, duties and liabilities of a living person' and the Supreme Court made all the citizens living in the state persons *in loco parentis*.[55] Similarly, in *Narayan Dutt Bhatt v Union of India*, the petitioner sought restriction on the movement of horse carts/tongas from Nepal to

[50] Richard A Epstein, 'Property Rights, State of Nature Theory, and Environmental Protection' (2009) 4(1) *New York University Journal of Law and Liberty* 1.

[51] Philippe Cullet and Sujith Koonan (eds), *Water Law in India: An Introduction to Legal Instruments* (OUP 2018).

[52] (2014) 7 SCC 547.

[53] *TN Godavarman Thirumulpad v Union of India* MANU/SC/0122/2012 (Supreme Court of India).

[54] *Centre for Environment Law, WWF-I v Union of India* (2013) 8 SCC 234.

[55] *Karnail Singh v State of Haryana* 2019 SCC OnLine P&H 704.

India and vice versa.[56] Taking note of the conditions of animals as amounting to cruelty, the High Court of Uttarakhand declared the entire animal kingdom as a legal person having corresponding rights, duties, and liabilities of a living person.[57] In comparison to the rights of animals, the Indian jurisprudence has not explicitly considered flora as subjects of rights.[58]

In *Orissa Mining Corporation v Ministry of Environment and Forests* (Vedanta mining), while determining the legal question of mining and environmental sanctions, the Court went beyond conventional environmental law and placed tribal rights at the forefront.[59] The judgment provided a participatory mode of environmental governance and ruled that mining can take place only with the consent of the communities. As a result, all the *Gram Sabhas* voted against mining. Though the judgment did not pronounce on the legal personality of mountain ecosystems, it upheld the spiritual connection of the Dongria Kondh community with the Niyamgiri hills.[60] In that way, it can be considered as an ecocentric approach reflecting the tribal populations worldview of nature. In this context, an assessment of the Scheduled Tribes and Other Traditional Forest Dwellers (Recognition of Forest Rights) Act, 2006 (Forest Rights Act) is important. The Act recognizes the contribution of tribal populations to environmental preservation and attempts to restore their customary rights. Such an approach subscribes to the ecocentric perspective, as it recognizes the intrinsic relationship tribal population have with the forest and evidences the importance of human participation in conservation practices to achieve sustainability. The Act also places a responsibility on the *Gram Sabha* to conserve and protect biodiversity, wildlife, forests, water sources, and other ecologically sensitive areas, as well as to stop any destructive practices that harm these resources or the tribal populations' cultural and natural heritage.[61]

The strand of ecocentrism was taken forward in judgments in *Mohammed Salim* (Ganga and Yamuna) and *Lalit Miglani* (*Glaciers*).[62] In the Ganga and Yamuna case, the High Court of Uttarakhand relied on legal personality granted to non-human entities like corporations and idols of the legal person to define a juristic person, and held the Rivers Ganga and Yamuna to be legal/living entities with all corresponding rights, duties, and liabilities of a living person.[63] The court directed the Director of *Namami Ganga*, the Chief Secretary of the state of Uttarakhand, and the Advocate General of

[56] *Narayan Dutt Bhatt v Union of India* 2018 SCC OnLine Utt 645.

[57] ibid.

[58] Rita Brara, 'Courting Nature: Advances in Indian Jurisprudence' in Anna Leah Tabios Hillebrecht and Maria Valeria Berros (eds), *Can Nature Have Rights?—Legal and Political Insights* (2017) 6 *RCC Perspectives: Transformations in Environment and Society* 31, 33.

[59] *Orissa Mining Corporation v Ministry of Environment and Forests & Others* (2013) 6 SCC 476.

[60] Stellina Jolly, 'The Vedanta (Niyamgiri) Case: Promoting Environmental Justice and Sustainable Development' in Carmen G Gonzalez, Sumudu A Atapattu, and Sara L Seck (eds), *The Cambridge Handbook of Environmental Justice and Sustainable Development* (CUP 2021) 289.

[61] Scheduled Tribes and Other Traditional Forest Dwellers (Recognition of Forest Rights) Act, 2006 (India), s 5.

[62] *Mohammed Salim* (n 12); *Lalit Miglani* (n 13).

[63] *Mohammed Salim* (n 12).

Uttarakhand to be persons *in loco parentis* as the human face to protect, conserve and preserve the River Ganga and its tributaries.[64]

In the *Glaciers* case, the High Court of Uttarakhand held that 'Rivers, Forests, Lakes, Water Bodies, Air, and Glaciers have a right to exist, persist, maintain, sustain and regenerate their own vital ecology system'.[65] Injuries suffered by these natural bodies would be seen as akin to injuries suffered by human beings. The court appointed several officials as persons *in loco parentis* who were given the responsibility of protecting and conserving the glaciers feeding the river.[66] However, the Supreme Court stayed the operation of these decisions because of implementation problems. One of the administrative problems, as pointed out by the state, emanated from the River Ganga's interstate nature, making it difficult to be administered by a single state.[67]

Despite the stay order passed by the Supreme Court, the Ganga and Yamuna judgment continues to have judicial impacts. The High Court of Punjab and Haryana declared the Sukhna Lake to be a 'legal person', having the 'corresponding rights, duties and liabilities of a living person'.[68] The legal personality of the lake was sought for its *survival, preservation, and conservation* based on the *public trust doctrine*.[69] The court declared all the citizens of Chandigarh as '*loco parentis*' or 'the human face to save the lake from becoming extinct'.[70] The Madurai division of the Madras High Court declared 'Mother Nature' as a living being and accorded it rights similar to 'fundamental rights/constitutional rights for their survival, safety, and resurgence in order to maintain its status and also to promote their health and wellbeing'.[71]

The Ganga and Yamuna judgment has influenced the legal pronouncement of rights of nature in Bangladesh. In a public interest litigation filed by Human Rights and Peace for Bangladesh, the Supreme Court of Bangladesh recognized the River Turag as a legal person, to protect and preserve the river under Articles 18A, 21, 21(2), 31, 32, and 102 of the Constitution of Bangladesh, 1972, relying on the public trust doctrine and the human right to a healthy environment.[72] The Court appointed the National River Commission

[64] ibid 19.

[65] *Lalit Miglani* (n 13) 62.

[66] ibid 63; See also Stellina Jolly and KS Roshan Menon, 'Of Ebbs and Flows: Understanding the Legal Consequences of Granting Personhood to Natural Entities in India' (2021) 10(3) *Transnational Environmental Law* 467.

[67] *State of Uttarakhand and Others v Mohammed Salim and Others* Special Leave to Appeal (C) No 016879 of 2017 (Order of 7 July 2017, Supreme Court of India) (staying the ruling in the *Mohammed Salim* case); *Union of India and Others v Lalit Miglani and Others* Special Leave Petition (Civil) Diary No 34250 of 2017 (Order of 27 November 2017, Supreme Court of India).

[68] *Court on its own Motion v Chandigarh Administration* 2020 SCC OnLine P&H 4454.

[69] ibid [178].

[70] ibid.

[71] *A Periyakaruppan v The Principal Secretary to Government* 2022 SCC OnLine Mad 2077.

[72] *Human Rights and Peace for Bangladesh v Secretary of the Ministry of Shipping* Writ Petition No 13989 of 2016 (Supreme Court of Bangladesh); See also Mohammad Sohidul Islam and Erin O'Donnell, 'Legal Rights for the Turag: Rivers as Living Entities in Bangladesh' (2020) 23(2) *Asia Pacific Journal of Environmental Law* 160.

as the legal guardian responsible for the river's protection.[73] In comparison to the judicial statements in India and Bangladesh, which recognize the legal personality of rivers, the Bhutanese legal system reflects a deep reverence for nature. The Constitution of Bhutan, 2008 declares that 'every Bhutanese is a trustee of the Kingdom's natural resources and environment for the benefit of the present and future generations and it is the fundamental duty of every citizen to contribute to the protection of the natural environment, conservation of the rich biodiversity of Bhutan and prevention of all forms of ecological degradation'.[74] Whereas the constitutional provision in Bhutan entrusts citizens with trusteeship rights over natural resources, the High Court of Punjab and Haryana's decision on Sukhna Lake and the Madras High Court on the rights of Mother Nature proclaim all the citizens of the state to be guardians for the protection of nature. Trusteeship over natural resources is couched more in terms of the duty placed on citizens to protect the natural resources for the benefit of present and future generations. However, in guardianship, the guardian is responsible for discerning the interests and representing nature, which is treated as a perpetual minor.

The details and features of the judicial decisions in India are enumerated in Table 14.1.

The granting of legal personality to nature in India is part of the growing legal initiatives in jurisdictions that have recognized the rights of nature. These judicial statements set the stage for debating the implications of recognizing the rights of nature. The next section evaluates the implications of recognizing the rights of nature by examining the salient features and rationality employed by the judicial decisions in elevating and operationalizing the legal personality of the River Ganga and the glaciers.

14.3 Protection of Nature by Conferring Legal Rights: Implications and Impediments

Rights of nature are a normative improvement over conventional environmental law premised on anthropocentrism, and they can reinvigorate environmental principles and give a fillip to them. Sustainable development is the overarching environmental principle underlying the current environmental law framework in India.[75] As a dynamic principle, sustainable development was invoked by the courts in India through the doctrine of carrying capacity and proportionality, wherein they attempted to weigh

[73] ibid.

[74] Constitution of the Kingdom of Bhutan, 2008, art 5.

[75] Saptarishi Bandopadhyay, 'Sustainable Development and Indian Environmental Jurisprudence' in Shibani Ghosh (ed), *Indian Environmental Law: Key Concepts and Principles* (Orient BlackSwan 2019) 107.

Table 14.1 Details of Court Decisions on the Rights of Nature

Case	Scope/Entire nature/ Specific species/ Ecosystem	Catalogue of rights	Representation/ Implementation (appointment of persons *in loco parentis*)
Md. Salim v State of Uttarakhand	River	Broad rights concerning the right to life	State officials
Lalit Miglani v State of Uttarakhand	Rivers and glaciers	Broad rights concerning the right to life	Several state officials
Karnail Singh v State of Haryana	Entire animal kingdom	Right to honour Right to dignity Right to be protected from unlawful attacks.	All citizens of the state
Court on its own Motion v Chandigarh Administration	Sukhna Lake	Broad rights concerning the right to life	All citizens of the state
A Periyakaruppan v The Principal Secretary	Mother Nature	Broad rights concerning the right to life	All citizens of the State

Source: Author

economic and environmental parameters.[76] Recognition of the rights of nature focusing on the existence of nature and recognizing the limits of an ecosystem and planetary limits can provide an impetus for the courts to interpret sustainable development with a focus on the interests of the environment, rather than evaluating the balance of economic and environmental parameters. However, whether the rights of nature can effectively address environmental issues depends on how effectively they are conceived and implemented; otherwise, many of the problems of conventional environmental law would re-emerge.[77]

It is important to discuss here the rationality employed by courts in India. The *Glaciers* judgment refers to the intrinsic rights of nature when the High Court of Uttarakhand declared that 'Rivers and Lakes have intrinsic right not to be polluted. Polluting and damaging the rivers, forests, lakes, water bodies, air, and glaciers will be legally

[76] Stellina Jolly and Zen Makuch, 'Procedural and Substantive Innovations Propounded by the Indian judiciary in Balancing Protection of Environment and Development: A Legal Analysis' in Christina Voigt and Zen Makuch (eds), *Courts and the Environment* (Edward Elgar Publishing 2018) 142.

[77] Julien Bétaille, 'Rights of Nature: Why it Might Not Save the Entire World' (2019) 16(1) *Journal for European Environmental and Planning Law* 35; Erin L O'Donnell, 'At the Intersection of the Sacred and the Legal: Rights for Nature in Uttarakhand, India' (2018) 30(1) *Journal of Environmental Law*135.

equivalent to harming, hurting, and causing injury to a person'.[78] However, the reference to the inherent value of nature operates as wishful thinking and gets side-lined in lieu of the overt attention to religious precincts. The judgments in the Ganga and Yamuna case and the *Glaciers* case locate the rationale for conferring the rights of nature in the negligence of the government in protecting the rivers,[79] constitutional directive principles and fundamental duties,[80] and with reference to religion and faith. The justification for linking religion and faith to decide the legal personality of nature sits disturbingly within the democratic and secular legal system of India.

In addition, neither case included a specific reference to community rights. The sole reference to the community was made in the *Glaciers* case when the High Court stated that the Chief Secretary of the State of Uttarakhand is also permitted to co-opt as many as seven public representatives from all the cities, towns, and villages of the State of Uttarakhand to give representation to the communities living on the banks of rivers near lakes and glaciers.[81] However, that is a far cry from the elaborate system of community management envisaged under the legal developments in New Zealand and other jurisdictions.[82]

The problem of conventional environmental law cannot be addressed by implementing the rights of nature if effective representation of nature cannot be ensured.[83] In the Ganga and Yamuna case and the *Glaciers* case, the High Court of Uttarakhand, using the doctrine of *parens patriae*, identified government officials and specific individuals as legal representatives. This equates to and places water bodies as 'perpetual minors', which is a political device to subdue independence and cement state authority.[84] In comparison, the legal framework regulating the Whanganui River in New Zealand does not operate on the basis of *parens patriae*. All the stakeholders have created the institutional framework accommodating the worldviews of the indigenous community as a result of concerted efforts.[85] Such groundwork has not been undertaken in the Indian context. The analysis of the Uttarakhand cases reveals brazen violation of the fiduciary relations typifying the *parens patriae* doctrine and defies the whole purpose of personhood as the State is one of the leading polluting entities.[86] The Madras

[78] *Lalit Miglani* (n 13) [51]; Kelly D Alley, 'River Goddesses, Personhood and Rights of Nature: Implications for Spiritual Ecology' (2019) 10 *Religions* 502.

[79] *Mohammed Salim* (n 12) 9.

[80] ibid 18.

[81] *Lalit Miglani* (n 13); Armin Rosencranz and Dushyant Kishan Kaul, 'Are Rivers Really Living Entities'? (2017) 47(2) *Environmental Policy and Law* 54.

[82] Andrew Geddis and Jacinta Ruru, 'Places as Persons: Creating a New Framework for Māori-Crown Relations' in Jason Varuhas and Shona Wilson Stark (eds), *The Frontiers of Public Law* (Hart 2019) 255.

[83] Erin L O'Donnell and Julia Talbot-Jones, 'Creating Legal Rights for Rivers: Lessons from Australia, New Zealand and India' (2018) 23 (1) Ecology and Society 7.

[84] See generally Marlene Sway, 'Gypsies as a Perpetual Minority: A Case Study (1975) 3(1) *Humboldt Journal of Social Relations* 48.

[85] Elaine C Hsiao, 'Whanganui River Agreement—Indigenous Rights and Rights of Nature' (2012) 42(6) *Environmental Policy and Law* 371.

[86] Kelly D Alley and Tarini Mehta, 'The Experiment with Rights of Nature in India' in Cameron La Follette and Chris Maser (eds), *Sustainability and the Rights of Nature in Practice* (CRC Press 2019)

High Court, while referring to the judgment in the *Glaciers* case, noted the need for the establishment of a nature's rights Commission, but did not elaborate on this.[87]

In terms of implementation, it is contended that the language and framework of rights are essentially a human construct and do not operate in the natural world.[88] For instance, if a human being kills another being, it is actionable; however, even if a landslide or the flooding of a river kills a human being, it does not violate human rights. Any discourse on the rights of nature needs to engage with this dichotomy, especially because the articulation of legal personality also ascribes questions of liability. The High Court of Uttarakhand declared the Rivers Ganga and Yamuna and glaciers as legal persons with all the rights of human beings, and declared that any injury/harm caused to these bodies should be treated as harm/injury caused to human beings would be.[89] However, the judgments do not lend clarity to the content of the rights. Can they be read as the right to flow without restrictions, and in that case, what about the construction of dams; do the river and its catchment also get rights?[90] For the rights to be implemented, it is important to come to a common understanding of what those rights entail, and provide adequate guidance for the guardians to discern the interests of nature.[91]

The effectiveness of *parens patriae* also needs to be assessed in the context of the public trust doctrine that dictates that the state holds in trust natural resources to ensure access to and protection of resources for the benefit of the general public.[92] The courts in India have given an expansive definition to the contours of the public trust doctrine and have mandated governments to maintain and protect the environment.[93] The question arises that when the legal system has already provided for the responsibility of the state as a trustee of resources, instead of trying to implement the public trust doctrine effectively, what is the additional utility of granting legal personality to nature and appointing government officials as persons *in loco parentis*? Interestingly in the Sukhna Lake case, the High Court of Punjab & Haryana observed that *the preservation, conservation, and*

365; Palash Srivastava, 'Legal Personality of Ganga and Ecocentrism: A Critical Review' (2019) 4(1) *Cambridge Law Review* 151; Akshita Jha and Adrija Ghosh, 'Is Being a "Person" Essential for the Environment to Hold Rights? Assessing the Legitimacy of Environmental Personhood and Alternative Approaches' (2018) 11(3) *National University Juridical Law Review* 469.

[87] *A Periyakaruppan* (n 71) 21.

[88] Rolston Holmes, 'Rights and Responsibilities on the Home Planet' (1993) 18 *Yale Journal of International Law* 251.

[89] *Lalit Miglani* (n 13).

[90] Ashish Kothari and Shrishtee Bajpai, 'Rivers and Human Rights: We are the River, the River is Us?' *Vikalp Sangam* (3 November 2017) <https://vikalpsangam.org/article/rivers-and-human-rights-we-are-the-river-the-river-is-us/>.

[91] Gabriel Eckstein and others, 'Conferring Legal Personality on the World's Rivers: A Brief Intellectual Assessment' (2019) 44(6–7) *Water International* 1, 8, 9. See also Julia Talbott Jones, 'Flowing from Fiction to Fact: The Challenges of Implementing Legal Rights for Rivers' *Global Water Forum* (14 May 2018) <https://globalwaterforum.org/2018/05/14/flowing-from-fiction-to-fact-the-challenges-of-implementing-legal-rights-for-rivers/>.

[92] Shibani Ghosh, 'Public Trust Doctrine in Indian Environmental Law' in Shibani Ghosh (ed), *Indian Environmental Law Key Concepts and Principles* (Orient BlackSwan 2019) 230.

[93] *MC Mehta v Kamal Nath* (1997) 1 SCC 388; *Intellectuals Forum v State of AP* (2006) 3 SCC 549.

saving of the environment are based on the public trust doctrine.[94] Under this doctrine, the state is the trustee of natural resources, whereas the judgment designates citizens of Chandigarh as the guardian for the protection of Sukhna Lake. Guardianship and trusteeship are different, and how the linkage between both has been made has not been clarified in the judgment. The problem with the appointment of citizens as guardians lies also in the context of understanding and discerning the interests of nature.[95] How can humans discern the interest of nature? What they conceive as protective of the interests of nature depends on the value judgment from their side.[96] The Indian legal system already provides for public-spirited citizens to bring legal action through public interest litigation. In such a scenario, how will the newfound guardianship be different from the rights granted under public interest litigation?

Arguments can also be brought in the context of other environmental law principles, like the polluter pays principle and intergenerational equity. The polluter pays principle is interpreted to allow compensation to victims and compensation for damage to the environment.[97] Similarly, intergenerational equity, with its emphasis on the use and conservation of the environment and its natural resources for future generations, forces human activities within planetary boundaries.[98] In such a scenario, it would be better to strengthen the implementation of existing legal principles rather than relying on a new paradigm that a human agency must implement.

Scholars like Livingstone question the utility of recognition of the rights of nature, as their enforcement would still depend upon human entities due to the inability of nature to express itself.[99] They argue that when nature is represented through guardians, it has the effect of going back to anthropocentrism because such representation assumes that guardians can gauge the interest of nature. How can this be any different from the traditional model of environmental protection? It is only in the context of indigenous communities that the worldview of nature is built upon the foundation of co-existence with nature. For instance, the indigenous people and their relationship with nature are reflected in the Te Awa Tupua (Whanganui) Settlement Act, 2017, which articulates a co-governance scheme. It requires the Whanganui Iwi and the government to work together for the management of the river. While reflecting the indigenous worldview of nature, these developments can also be considered in the context of the increased

[94] *Court on its own Motion* (n 68) 161 [120].

[95] ibid.

[96] Peter D Burdon, 'The Rights of Nature: Reconsidered' (2010) 49 *Australian Humanities Review* 69, 79.

[97] *Indian Council for Enviro-Legal Action v Union of India* (1996) 3 SCC 212; Lovleen Bhullar, 'The Polluter Pays Principle: Scope and Limits of Judicial Decisions' in Shibani Ghosh (ed), *Indian Environmental Law Key Concepts and Principles* (Orient BlackSwan 2019) 152; Harshita Singhal and Sujith Koonan, 'Polluter Pays Principle in India: Assessing Conceptual Boundaries and Implementation Issues' (2021) 7(2) *RGNUL Student Research Review* 33.

[98] Tiina Häyhä and others, 'From Planetary Boundaries to National Fair Shares of the Global Safe Operating Space—How can the Scales be Bridged?' (2016) 40 *Global Environmental Change* 60.

[99] John A Livingston, *Rogue Primate: An Exploration of Human Domestication* (Roberts Rinehart 1994).

protections for indigenous peoples entrenched in international human rights law in relation to natural resources, land, and culture.[100]

This is not to argue that rights of nature can address the concerns of indigenous people and their struggle. Many argue that rights of nature provide only for a cultural right-to-be, and fail to address colonial atrocities.[101] Despite some linkage between the rights of nature and indigenous philosophies, overstating the linkage might constrain and dilute the political and legal foundations of indigenous ideas. Nonetheless, these rights are important in fostering actions to reclaim and implement these rights.[102] It is to be noted that the Indian judicial decisions on the rights of nature do not operate in the context of indigenous peoples' rights. In such a background, the development of deep respect for ecology through existing legal rules is essential for reversing the environmental crisis rather than simply elevating the legal personality of nature.

Conclusion: Creating a Framework for Rights of Nature

India has joined other jurisdictions in recognizing the rights of nature, as an innovative mode of environmental protection. Judicial decisions (highlighted in earlier sections) have elevated animals, rivers, and Mother Earth from being objects of environmental protection to subjects of legal person with rights, duties, and liabilities. It is too early to evaluate the experiences and success of these legal initiatives to see whether the legal personhood of rivers and nature can protect the environment effectively. As noted earlier, the Indian courts' reliance on *parens patriae* and *in loco parentis* to entrust guardianship to state entities and citizens over nature/rivers is problematic. In addition, lack of clarity as to the scope and content of the rights of nature will lead to discerning the rights as per the interests of guardians. Nevertheless, what is clear is that the idea of rights of nature will impact litigation and policy decisions. For instance, the People's Charioteer Organization (PCO) has filed public interest litigation with the Supreme Court of India to formally declare the country's entire animal kingdom to be legal persons and to require all citizens to stand as their legal guardians to protect them from cruelty and promote their welfare.[103] Similarly, the Supreme Court of India is due to hear

[100] Leena Heinämäki, 'The Protection of the Environmental Integrity of Indigenous Peoples in Human Rights Law' (2006) 17 *Finnish Yearbook of International Law* 187.

[101] Glen Sean Coulthard, *Red Skin, White Masks: Rejecting the Colonial Politics of Recognition* (University of Minnesota Press 2014).

[102] Rickard Lalander, 'Rights of Nature and the Indigenous Peoples in Bolivia and Ecuador: A Straitjacket for Progressive Development Politics?' (2014) 3(2) *Iberoamerican Journal of Development Studies* 148.

[103] Rajesh K Reddy, 'Groundbreaking Litigation Seeks to Extend Formal Personhood Status to India's Animal Kingdom' *Center for Animal Law Studies* (8 September 2020) <https://law.lclark.edu/live/news/44234-groundbreaking-litigation-seeks-to-extend-formal>.

the two Uttarakhand cases whose judgments may offer clarity concerning the normative issues plaguing the rights of nature, including what aspects of nature should be granted personality, what it entails, and how it will be implemented.

It is to be noted that Indian judicial decisions while recognizing the legal personality of nature, did not engage with the various discourses and literature on the rights of nature. Neither did the judgments engage with the historical evolution and imperatives for the recognition of the legal personality of nature in jurisdictions like New Zealand, Ecuador, and Colombia. The granting of legal personality to rivers in New Zealand and Colombia was influenced by the need to recognize the indigenous communities' relationship with nature. In contrast, the judicial statements in India operate in a non-indigenous context. It is primarily in the context of the indigenous communities whose way of life and beliefs represent a symbiotic relationship with nature. Thus, unless and until the way indigenous philosophies personify nature can be aptly translated into the concept of the legal person, environmental protection envisaged through the legal personality of nature will not be effective. Hence, the focus should be on developing respect for ecology rather than on simply claiming rights in their traditional sense.[104] As noted earlier, the judgment in *Vedanta*, without specifying the rights of nature, in practical terms, acknowledged the harmony of human life with nature. Hence, instead of trying to focus exclusively on the rights of nature as a panacea for environmental degradation, the need of the hour is to encourage a culture of profound respect for nature by engaging with the numerous streams of deep ecology and indigenous rights and Earth democracy and participation. Empowering the tribal and local communities through strengthening local institutions' participation in environmental policies and elevating their philosophical and cultural views can go a long way in promoting respect for nature. The Forest Rights Act, 2006, with its emphasis on the acknowledgement of the close relationship between forest dwellers and their customary rights on forests, offers tremendous potential to evolve respect for nature. Similarly, fundamental duties under the Indian Constitution that dictate the protection and improvement of the natural environment can also be leveraged to create an ecosystem of respect for nature. However, this is not to argue that recognizing the rights of nature as a subject of law with the right to representation is meaningless. It can be a powerful mode of promoting environmental protection through reorienting human behaviour, which calls for further research and discourse.

Suggestions for Further Reading

Julien Bétaille, 'Rights of Nature: Why it Might Not Save the Whole World' (2019) 16(1) *Journal for European Environmental Planning Law* 35.

Cormac Cullinan, *Wild Law: A Manifesto for Earth Justice* (Chelsea Green 2011).

[104] Michelle Maloney, 'Changing the Legal Status of Nature: Recent Developments and Future Possibilities' (2018) 49 *NSW Law Society Journal* 78.

Stellina Jolly and KS Roshan Menon, 'Of Ebbs and Flows: Understanding the Legal Consequences of Granting Personhood to Natural Entities in India' (2021) 10(3) *Transnational Environmental Law* 467.

Erin L O'Donnell, *Legal Rights for Rivers Competition, Collaboration and Water Governance* (Taylor and Francis 2018).

Erin L O'Donnell, 'At the Intersection of the Sacred and the Legal: Rights for Nature in Uttarakhand, India' (2018) 30(1) *Journal of Environmental Law* 135.

CHAPTER 15

PROCEDURAL ENVIRONMENTAL RIGHTS

SHIJU MAZHUVANCHERY

Abstract

Procedural environmental rights (PERs) provide a means for enforcing the substantive right to a clean and healthy environment. Though these rights do not guarantee any particular outcome, they are effective in preventing erosion of the substantive right. Principle 10 of the Rio Declaration is the most coherent articulation of PERs at the international level. The three components of PERs are: access to environmental information, public participation in environmental decision-making, and access to environmental justice. PERs in India have evolved and the perception as to their purpose has changed. This change is closely related to the shift in the character of environmental laws in India. From being considered as reasonable restrictions on the fundamental right to carry on trade or business, environmental laws have transformed into tools for the realisation of the fundamental right to a clean environment. An analysis of these laws reveals that PERs are entrenched to various degrees.

Introduction

The fundamental right to a clean and healthy environment finds recognition in many national constitutions.[1] In India, it was through judicial interpretation that this right was read into the Constitution of India, 1950.[2] Addressing environmental issues from

[1] James R May and Erin Daly, *Global Environmental Constitutionalism* (CUP 2014).
[2] E.g., *Subhash Kumar v State of Bihar* (1991) 1 SCC 598.

a rights perspective has its advantages. Such an approach enables citizens to challenge executive and legislative measures that can cause harm to the environment. In legal parlance, a distinction is made between 'substantive rights' and 'procedural rights'. Whereas the right to a clean environment is a substantive right, the right to approach a court to enforce this substantive right is a procedural right. Thus, procedural rights are means to achieve substantive rights. They are often characterized as weak versions of substantive rights as they do not secure a 'thing of value' like a clean environment.[3] Though they do not guarantee any particular outcome, they are very effective in preventing the erosion of rights. In that sense, procedural environmental rights (PERs) provide a means for enforcing the substantive right to a healthy environment.

At the global level, the UN Conference on Human Environment (Stockholm Conference 1972) was the first attempt to recognize PERs. While the Stockholm Declaration referred to the importance of education on environmental matters,[4] the Action Plan contained specific recommendations for access to information and public participation.[5] The 1992 Rio Declaration on Environment and Development was a major milestone in that direction. Principle 10 highlighted the importance of public participation and recognized the right of access to environmental information, participation in environmental decision-making, and access to justice.[6] These rights are the three components of PERs. This chapter examines PERs guaranteed under various laws in India. Section 15.1 describes the evolution of PERs in India, including the rationale behind the introduction of these rights. Sections 15.2, 15.3, and 15.4 discuss in detail the law in India relating to access to environmental information, public participation in environmental decision-making, and access to environmental justice. The last section concludes.

15.1 Evolution of Procedural Environmental Rights in India

PERs in India have evolved over time. The perception as to the purpose of these rights has also changed over the years. This change is closely related to the shift in the character

[3] Erin Daly, 'Constitutional Protection for Environmental Rights: The Benefits of Environmental Process' (2012) 17(2) *International Journal of Peace Studies* 71.

[4] Declaration of the United Nations Conference on the Human Environment, Stockholm, 16 June 1972, UN Doc A/CONF.48/14/Rev 1, Principle 19.

[5] Action Plan for the Human Environment, Recommendations 7 (a), 39 (a), and 97, Report of the United Nations Conference on the Human Environment, Stockholm, 5–16 June 1972, UN Doc A/CONF.48/14/Rev 1.

[6] Rio Declaration on Environment and Development, 14 June 1992, UN Doc A/CONF.151/26/Rev 1 (vol I), annex II (1992).

of environmental laws in India. From being considered reasonable restrictions on the fundamental right to carry on trade or business,[7] environmental laws in India have transformed into tools for the realization of the fundamental right to a clean environment.[8] The discussions in the House of People on the Water (Prevention and Control of Pollution) Bill, 1974 illustrate this. The members understood the legislative proposal as a reasonable restriction on the right to carry on business to protect public health in the interest of the general public.[9] A number of provisions in the legislation (the Water (Prevention and Control of Pollution) Act, 1974) reflect this. The detailed procedure laid down regarding the collection of samples that includes serving of notice, presence of the occupier and witness, sending the sample to a laboratory of the occupier's choice, etc., is one such example.[10] The decision in *Delhi Bottling Co. Pvt. Ltd v Central Board for the Prevention and Control of Water Pollution* is an apt illustration of the importance of these procedural safeguards.[11] In this case, the Delhi High Court quashed criminal proceedings against a polluting industrial unit on the ground that the samples were not divided into two parts as mandated by the law.

Similarly, rule 5 of the Environment (Protection) Rules, 1986, often cited as an example of public participation in environmental decision-making,[12] is intended to make the restriction a reasonable one. Such an understanding of procedural rights was not illogical given that the right to a clean/healthy environment was not recognized as a fundamental right both within the country and globally during the initial phase of the evolution of environmental laws in India. With the recognition of the right to a clean/healthy environment as a fundamental right under Article 21 of the Constitution,[13] legislations were perceived as tools for the enforcement of these rights. Thus, the preamble to the National Green Tribunal Act, 2010, mentions the judicial recognition of the right to a healthy environment as a fundamental right.[14] The implication of this is that lawmakers consider the legislation as a device to realize that right. Thus, access to justice, the primary aim of the National Green Tribunal Act, is couched as a procedural right intended to achieve the substantial right to a clean environment.

[7] The Constitution of India, 1950, Art 19(1)(g).

[8] This right is guaranteed under the right to life and liberty. Ibid, Art 21.

[9] Lok Sabha Debates 21 February 1974, Fifth Series vol XXXV, No 3, cols 240–302.

[10] Water (Prevention and Control of Pollution) Act, 1974, s 21.

[11] *Delhi Bottling Co. Pvt. Ltd v Central Board for the Prevention and Control of Water Pollution* 1985 SCC OnLine Del 263.

[12] Shibani Ghosh, 'Procedural Environmental Rights in Indian Law' in Shibani Ghosh (ed), *Indian Environmental Law: Key Concepts and Principles* (Orient Blackswan 2019) 55.

[13] *Subhash Kumar* (n 2).

[14] The preamble, *inter alia*, reads: 'AND WHEREAS in the judicial pronouncement in India, the right to healthy environment has been construed as a part of the right to life under Article 21 of the Constitution'.

15.2 Access to Environmental Information

Access to environmental information is the first component of PERs. An examination of the nature and origin of the right to information is necessary to better understand the content of this right.[15] There have been many explanations ranging from a derivative right under the fundamental right to freedom of speech and expression to viewing it as an essential attribute of democracy. In the Indian context, the initial view was that it derived from the right to freedom of speech and expression.[16] But in *SP Gupta v Union of India*, the Supreme Court linked the right to know to the democratic structure.[17] It was observed that for a society that accepted democracy as its credal faith it was elementary that the citizens ought to know what their government was doing.[18] The Court added that no democratic government could survive without accountability and the basic postulate of accountability was that the people should have information about the functioning of the government.[19] Thus, if this right is moored to the notion of democracy, the content of the right gets expanded. In that sense, the duty of the government relates not only to providing access to environmental information that is in its possession but also to gathering information and converting it into a language understood by the common person. For a meaningful realization of the right in the context of environmental democracy, the government must fulfil three major obligations: collection, access, and dissemination of information.

15.2.1 Collection of Information

There are several laws that authorize the collection of information relating to the environment. These take many forms, including the collection of information for the performance of statutory duties, collection of relevant information from an applicant for permitting certain activities, submission of periodic compliance reports by regulated entities, and the requirement of a person to provide information in the event of an accident or an unseen event. Reports submitted either to the legislature or to the government ensuring accountability are another source of information. As can be seen in the analysis below, environmental information is collected from different sources under various laws.

15 Shannon M Roesler, 'The Nature of the Environmental Right to Know' (2012) 39(4) *Ecology Law Quarterly* 989.

16 The Constitution (n 7) Art 19(1)(a). See also *State of UP v Raj Narain* (1975) 4 SCC 428.

17 *SP Gupta v Union of India* 1981 (Supp) SCC 87.

18 ibid [273].

19 ibid.

Two major pollution control laws, the Water (Prevention and Control of Pollution) Act, 1974 (the Water Pollution Act) and the Air (Prevention and Control of Pollution) Act, 1981 (the Air Pollution Act), contain provisions that either mandate or empower the Central Pollution Control Board (CPCB) and State Pollution Control Boards (the Board or SPCB) to collect information. These provisions primarily intend to help the Boards to carry out their statutory functions. Thus, under the Water Pollution Act, the SPCB can conduct surveys to gauge the flow, volume, and other characteristics of a stream or well; measure rainfall, etc.[20] In addition, the Board can seek information from persons abstracting water in substantial quantity or discharging sewage or trade effluents about such abstraction and discharge.[21] One could see similar powers given to the Boards under the Air Pollution Act.[22] The Boards also have a duty to collect, compile, and publish information, including technical and statistical data relating to water and air pollution.[23] These Acts also mandate the State Boards to collect information as part of its regulatory functions. Under these Acts, industrial units must obtain consent to establish and operate.[24] The application for consent under the Water Pollution Act requires furnishing of information relating to monthly consumption of water, other raw materials and chemicals used, the quantity of effluents discharged, the mode of discharge, solid waste generated, etc.[25] Similar requirements can be seen under the Air Pollution Act.[26] The maintenance of a Register containing particulars of the industrial units to which consent has been granted,[27] and the submission of Annual Reports[28] by the Boards are other provisions that are relevant to the collection of information. Another requirement under these Acts is the duty of the person in charge of an industrial undertaking to provide information about an accident to the State Board and other agencies prescribed by the government.[29]

The Environment (Protection) Rules, 1986, through an amendment in 1992, introduced the concept of an annual environmental statement.[30] The statement must be submitted by certain industrial establishments to the SPCB where the establishment is located. The details to be furnished include water and raw materials consumption, pollution discharged to environment, hazardous and solid waste generated and its disposal mechanisms, impact of pollution abatement measures taken on conservation of natural resources, and the cost of production, and proposed measures and investment plans

20 Water Pollution Act (n 10) s 20(1).
21 ibid s 20(2).
22 Air (Prevention and Control of Pollution) Act, 1981 s 25.
23 Water Pollution Act (n 10) ss 16(2)(f) and17(1)(c); Air Pollution Act (n 22) ss 16(2)(g) and (i) and 17(1)(c).
24 Air Pollution Act (n 22) s 21; Water Pollution Act (n 10) s 25.
25 Water (Prevention and Control of Pollution) Rules, 1975 r 32 and Form XIII.
26 Air (Prevention and Control of Pollution) (Union Territories) Rules, 1983 r 9 and Form I.
27 Air Pollution Act (n 22)s 51; Water Pollution Act (n 10) s 25(6).
28 ibid s 35; Water Pollution Act (n 10) s 39.
29 ibid s 23; Water Pollution Act (n 10) s 31.
30 Environment (Protection) Rules, 1986 r 14.

for the abatement and control of pollution.[31] There are several other rules promulgated by the Ministry of Environment, Forest and Climate Change (MoEFCC) under the Environment (Protection) Act, 1986 covering various activities, processes and products. Many of these rules contain provisions relating to collection of information.[32]

The Environmental Impact Assessment Notification, 2006 (EIA Notification) is another example of information collection at different stages. Once the Terms of Reference (TOR) are determined by the Appraisal Committee, an Environmental Impact Assessment (EIA) study must be carried out by an independent consultant. The EIA Report should contain details that include the description of the environment, anticipated environmental impacts, and mitigation measures, analysis of alternative technology and site, environmental monitoring programme, benefits of the proposed project, and environmental cost-benefit analysis.[33] The EIA Report is an important document for the effective realization of the other two procedural rights: public participation and access to justice. Faulty EIA reports have led to the cancellation of environmental clearance granted to projects. In *T Muruganandam v Ministry of Environment and Forests (MoEF)*, the National Green Tribunal (NGT) ordered a review of the environmental clearance granted to a thermal power plant as the report was flawed.[34] Once the clearance is granted, as part of the post-clearance monitoring mechanism, the project proponent is required to submit half-yearly compliance reports.[35]

15.2.2 Access to Information

Access to information in the possession of public authorities is the second component of this PER. The twofold obligation under this component, making available relevant information in the public domain and providing access to persons upon request without proving legal or other interest, is embedded in domestic law. The Air Pollution Act and the Water Pollution Act allow a court to take cognizance of offences on a complaint made by any person who has given sixty days' notice to the Board.[36] In such cases, the Board has an obligation to make available relevant reports in its possession to such a person upon demand.[37] Such a request can be refused only in public interest.[38] Though the Environment (Protection) Act provides for private complaints, there is no obligation on the part of the central government to provide information.[39]

[31] ibid, Form V.

[32] E.g., Hazardous and Other Wastes (Management and Transboundary Movement) Rules, 2016 r 6(1) and r 6(5)–(7).

[33] EIA Notification, 2006 Appendix VI.

[34] *T Muruganandam v Ministry of Environment and Forests* 2014 SCC OnLine NGT 7161.

[35] EIA Notification (n 33) para 10(ii).

[36] Water Pollution Act (n 10)s 49(1)(a) and Air Pollution Act (n 22)s 43(1)(b).

[37] ibid s 49(2) and ibid s 43(2).

[38] ibid.

[39] Environment (Protection) Act, 1986 s 19.

The EIA Notification imposes an obligation to make information available in the public domain at different stages. Once the TOR for the EIA study is finalized, the regulatory authority must display it on its website.[40] In order for the public consultation in the environmental clearance process to be meaningful, the SPCB must publish the summary of the Draft EIA Report on its website. In addition, the entire Draft Report should be made available for inspection for any concerned person at a notified place during normal office hours.[41] The public hearing proceedings must be videographed and displayed on the website of the SPCB.[42] Once the environmental clearance is granted, the project proponent should make it public along with the conditions attached. This must be done by displaying the information permanently on their website and by publishing it in two local newspapers of the district in which the project is located.[43] The regulatory authorities should also place it in the public domain.[44] Similarly, the half-yearly compliance report is considered as a public document and should be displayed on the website of the regulatory authority.[45]

However, a major fillip for the realization of this right came not through environmental legislation but through the Right to Information Act, 2005 (RTI Act). The RTI Act creates a mechanism for citizens to access information under the control of public authorities. From an environmental perspective, a major contribution of the Act is to provide an institutional mechanism to ensure that the rights to access granted under the various environmental laws discussed above are realized. In *Shibani Ghosh v MoEF*, the Central Information Commission (CIC) ordered mandatory disclosure of documents relating to the environmental clearance process.[46] Though the decision was made in pursuance of the provisions of the RTI Act,[47] many of these documents had to be published even under the EIA Notification. It does not mean that the scope of the RTI Act is limited to the provisions mandating disclosure contained in various environmental laws. As the Act makes it clear, the right to access extends to all the information held by public authorities unless specifically exempted. In *Shalini Bhutani v MoEF*, the CIC ordered the respondent 'to provide copies of the agreements of the approved projects and minutes of the meetings in which these approvals were granted' by the National Biodiversity Authority under the Biological Diversity Act, 2002.[48] It is worthwhile to note that there is no provision under the Biological Diversity Act for the disclosure of such information.

[40] EIA Notification (n 33)para 7(II)(ii). Depending on the category of the Project MoEFCC and State EIA Authority are the regulatory authorities under the Notification.

[41] ibid para 7(III)(vi).

[42] ibid Appendix IV, 5.0 and 6.6.

[43] ibid para 10(i)(a).

[44] ibid para 10(i)(c).

[45] ibid para 10(iii).

[46] *Shibani Ghosh v MoEF* 2012 SCC OnLine CIC 1047.

[47] Right to Information Act, 2005 s 4.

[48] *Shalini Bhutani v MoEF* 2008 SCC OnLine CIC 5180.

Two major issues that have come up in the context of the operation of the RTI Act vis-à-vis environmental laws are: (1) the scope of exceptions under the RTI Act, and (2) the disclosure of draft proposals and recommendations where a final decision is yet to be taken. In *GK Krishnan v MoEF*, the CIC dealt with both these issues.[49] This was an appeal against the refusal to provide a copy of the summary of the Western Ghats Ecology Expert Panel's Report. The MoEF refused disclosure, citing that the report was not finalized and a decision had not been taken by the Ministry. The first appeal was rejected on the ground that non-disclosure was protected under section 8(1)(a) of the RTI Act.[50] On the second appeal, the CIC rejected both these contentions. It was noted that nothing in the Act exempts draft reports, proposals, and recommendations from the purview of the Act. The exemption was narrowly construed, and it was held that information must be provided if the disclosure served a larger public interest.

15.2.3 Dissemination of Information

For the right of access to information to be meaningful, there should be proactive efforts on the part of the government to disseminate information. In *MC Mehta v Union of India*, the Supreme Court, while ordering school boards and universities to make the environment a compulsory subject, emphasized the importance of dissemination in a democratic society.[51] The Court held that in a democratic polity dissemination of information was the foundation of the system, and keeping the citizens informed was an obligation of the government[52].

There are provisions in environmental statutes that mandate public authorities to disseminate environmental information. The Air Pollution Act and the Water Pollution Act require the CPCB 'to organise through mass media a comprehensive programme regarding the prevention and control of water pollution'.[53] There are several other rules issued under the Environment (Protection) Act mandating the creation of public awareness.[54]

Labelling of products is often considered as furthering the consumers' right to know. Labels disseminate information about the potential impact of the product on human health and the environment.[55] Certain rules under the Environment (Protection) Act mandate compulsory labelling like the Hazardous Waste Rules, 2016.[56] An ambitious

49 *GK Krishnan v MoEF* CIC/SG/A/2012/000374/18316 decided on 9 April 2012. This decision was upheld by the Delhi High Court in *Union of India v G Krishnan* 2012 SCC OnLine Del 2869.

50 The RTI Act s 8(1)(a) exempts information 'disclosure of which would prejudicially affect the sovereignty and integrity of India, the security, strategic, scientific or economic interests of the State, relation with foreign State or lead to incitement of an offence' from the purview of the Act.

51 *MC Mehta v Union of India* (1992) 1 SCC 358, 359.

52 ibid.

53 Air Pollution Act (n 22) s 16(2)(f); Water Pollution Act (n 10) s 16(2)(e).

54 E.g., Solid Waste Management Rules, 2016 r 15(zg).

55 Roesler (n 15) 1031.

56 Hazardous Waste Rules (n 32) para 17, Form 8.

eco-labelling project was launched in India in the year 1991.[57] The objectives of the scheme were to incentivise manufacturers and importers to reduce adverse environmental impacts of the products, and to assist consumers by providing information to be environmentally responsible. Under this voluntary scheme, manufacturers could apply for certification of their products and could use the ECOMARK label. This scheme was not successful, with very few manufacturers applying for certification. Ten years later, the Energy Conservation Act, 2001, empowered the central government to introduce mandatory labelling for appliances that consume, generate, or transmit energy.[58]

The above analysis demonstrates that the right to access environmental information is well entrenched in domestic law. There are various provisions that empower the collection of information by different government agencies, guarantee access to information, and mandate disclosure of information. However, it does not mean the right is realized to its fullest extent in India. Many a time, the information is couched in complex scientific language beyond the grasp of the common person. The delay in providing information is another issue. In a multilingual country like India, the lack of availability of information in regional languages is also an issue. At the national level, most of the time, dissemination of information takes place only in English and Hindi, denying most people relevant information.

15.3 Public Participation in Environmental Decision-Making

Public participation in environmental decision-making is the second component of PERs. There are many arguments that support public participation, ranging from theoretical to pragmatic justifications. From a human rights perspective, it is argued that every citizen has a right to take part in the conduct of public affairs, and several treaties prescribe that.[59] Another argument is that the right to a clean environment includes the right to take part in legal and administrative procedures concerning environmental protection.[60] Promoting legitimacy and acceptance,[61] and 'cognitive improvement of decisions due to plurality of perspectives'[62] are other justifications advanced.

[57] MoEF, Resolution, GSR 85 (E) Dt. 20 February 1991.

[58] Energy Conservation Act, 2001 s 14(d).

[59] E.g., International Covenant on Civil and Political Rights, New York, 16 December 1966, 999 UNTS 171, art 25.

[60] *Research Foundation for Science Technology and Natural Resource Policy v Union of India* (2005) 10 SCC 510.

[61] Jonas Ebbeson, 'The Notion of Public Participation in International Environmental Law' (1998) 8(1) *Yearbook of International Environmental Law* 51.

[62] Naveen Thayyil, 'Public Participation in Environmental Clearances in India: Prospects for Democratic Decision-Making' (2014) 56 *Journal of the Indian Law Institute* 463.

Public participation can take place at different stages and levels. It can be in the form of pre-legislative consultation, public hearing before decision-making, participation in the review process, etc. For effective realisation of this right, the state must provide adequate information about opportunities for public participation,[63] make efforts to conduct public participation in a transparent and consultative manner, and provide adequate opportunities for the public to express their views,[64] make available all relevant information in 'an objective, understandable, timely and effective manner',[65] ensure that due account is taken of the comments in decision-making,[66] etc. The early pollution-related laws, the Air Pollution Act and the Water Pollution Act do not contain provisions relating to this. However, there are a few environmental and other laws in India that provide for public participation. These provisions are examined under the following two heads: obligation to provide information about public participation, and stages and manner of participation.

15.3.1 Obligation to Provide Information

The obligation under this head is two-fold: providing information about public participation and making available information relevant for decision-making. The EIA Notification is often cited as an example of public participation in environmental decision-making in India. Public consultation is one of the four steps in the environmental clearance process and comes at the third stage after screening and scoping. The Notification defines public consultation as 'the process by which the concerns of local affected persons and others who have plausible stake in the environmental impacts of the project or activity are ascertained with a view to taking into account all the material concerns in the project or activity design as appropriate'.[67] As per the Notification, there are two components of public consultation: 1) Public hearing at the site or in its close proximity 'for ascertaining the concerns of the local affected persons', and 2) obtaining 'responses in writing from other concerned persons having a plausible stake in the environmental aspects of the project or activity'.[68] The Notification lays down a detailed procedure for the conduct of the public hearing.[69] When it comes to the obligation to provide information, as discussed in the previous section, the Notification satisfies both the conditions.

[63] Guidelines for the Development of National Legislation on Access to Information, Public Participation and Access to Justice in Environmental Matters 2010 (Bali Guidelines) 8. UNEP/GCSS.XI/11, Decision SS.XI/5, pt A, 26 February 2010.

[64] ibid 9.

[65] ibid 10.

[66] ibid 11.

[67] EIA Notification (n 33)para 7(III)(i).

[68] ibid para 7(III)(ii)a, b.

[69] ibid app IV.

The Environment (Protection) Rules prescribe public consultation in certain instances. Under the Environment (Protection) Act, the central government can restrict the location of industries, operations or processes in areas or impose conditions for the same.[70] But under the Rules, before exercising such a power, the central government must issue a draft notification expressing its intention to bring in restrictions.[71] However, in public interest, the central government can dispense with this requirement.[72]

15.3.2 Stage and Mode of Participation

The effectiveness of public participation would depend upon many factors, including who can participate, at what stage one can participate, and what is the manner of participation envisaged. A wide definition of the term 'public' could include those affected by or having an interest in environmental decision-making and non-governmental organizations promoting environmental protection. Again, participation must be at an early stage when all the options including 'no action' are open.[73] For the participation to be effective, the process must be conducted in a transparent and consultative manner.[74]

Under the EIA Notification, public consultation is an important step. As mentioned in the previous section, public consultation comprises public hearings and written responses. Several projects are listed in the Notification that are exempt from public consultation.[75] Detailed procedure for the conduct of public hearing is part of the Notification. It prescribes that the public hearing should take place at the project site or in its proximity and be presided over by a high-ranking official. The Delhi High Court has held that persons not living in close proximity to the project site can also participate in the public hearing and express their views.[76] Videography of the entire proceeding and providing opportunity to the people present in the meeting to seek clarifications from the project proponent are some of the other requirements. A question that the courts have to frequently confront is what would be the impact of procedural lapse in the conduct of public hearings on the environmental clearance granted. In *Adivasi Majdoor Ekta Sangathan v MoEF*, the NGT set aside the environmental clearance granted to a coal mining project and a pithead washery on the ground that public hearing was not conducted properly.[77]

70 Environment (Protection) Act (n 39) s 3(2)(v).
71 EPR (n 30)r 5(3)(a).
72 ibid, r 5(4).
73 UNEP, Putting Rio Principle 10 into Action: An Implementation Guide (UNEP 2015) 84.
74 Bali Guidelines (n 63) 9.
75 EIA Notification (n 33) para 7(III)(i)(a)–(f).
76 *Samarth Trust v Union of India* 2010 SCC OnLine Del 2127.
77 *Adivasi Majdoor Ekta Sangathan v MoEF* 2012 SCC OnLine NGT 51.

The position of law after a perusal of cases decided by various High Courts and the NGT appears to be that if the lapse violated a mandatory provision of the Notification or the principles of natural justice, the process is liable to be struck down as invalid.[78]

Though the EIA procedure embodies principles of public participation, critics have highlighted its shortcomings. One such criticism is that public consultation is envisaged at the last stage, where many issues like the shortcomings in the TOR, etc. cannot be addressed.[79] The fact that concerns raised in the public consultation are not adequately addressed during appraisal is also a drawback of the process.[80] The long list of projects exempt from public hearing is also a concern.[81]

The Scheduled Tribes and Other Traditional Forest Dwellers (Recognition of Forest Rights) Act, 2006 (Forest Rights Act) contains two notable provisions that embody the principle of public participation. Under the Act, the *Gram Sabha* is given the primary responsibility for initiating the claims of forest rights and determining them.[82] The *Gram Sabha* is a village assembly consisting of all the adult members of the village with 'full and unrestricted participation of women'.[83] Another important provision that gives importance to the *Gram Sabha* is regarding the declaration of 'critical wildlife habitat'. These are areas of National Parks and Sanctuaries that are required to be kept inviolate for the purposes of wildlife conservation.[84] Such areas can be declared only after an open consultation by an expert committee with the affected people.[85] Another precondition for such a declaration is the preparation of a 'resettlement or alternatives package'. The same must be communicated,[86] and free informed consent of the *Gram Sabha* must be obtained in writing.[87]

The Wild Life (Protection) Act, 1972, was one of the first national-level legislation in the field of conservation. The legislation, as originally enacted, did not have any provision for public participation. However, later amendments have introduced participation in different forms. NGO participation is prescribed in various authorities constituted under the Act. The National Board for Wild Life,[88] the State Board for Wild Life,[89] the Advisory Committee for Sanctuaries,[90] and the Conservation Reserve Management Committee[91] must have NGO representation. These committees have an important

[78] MP Ram Mohan and Himanshu Pabreja, 'Public Hearings in Environmental Clearance Process: Review of Judicial Intervention' (2016) 51(50) *Economic and Political Weekly* 68.

[79] Thayyil (n 62) 484.

[80] ibid 486.

[81] Ghosh (n 12) 55.

[82] Scheduled Tribes and Other Traditional Forest Dwellers (Recognition of Forest Rights) Act, 2006s 6(1).

[83] ibid s 2(g).

[84] Forest Rights Act (n 82)s 2(b).

[85] ibid s 2(b).

[86] ibid s 4(2)(d).

[87] ibid s 4(2)(e).

[88] Wild Life (Protection) Act, 1972s 5A.

[89] ibid s 6.

[90] ibid s 33B.

[91] ibid s 36B.

role to play in the management of protected areas and the conservation of wildlife. 'Conservation Reserve' as a protected area was added by the 2003 amendment, and consultation with the local communities is a condition precedent for its declaration.[92]

The most significant provision relating to public participation in the Act is tiger reserves. Though these reserves came into existence in 1972–73 with the launch of Project Tiger, it was only through an amendment of the Act in 2006 that these were given statutory recognition.[93] It may be recalled that the Forest Rights Act, discussed above, also came into existence in 2006 and became operational on 1 January 2008 with the notification of the rules. The 2006 amendment considers the Forest Rights Act and recognizes the same. As per the amendment, a tiger reserve includes 'core or critical tiger habitat areas (CTH)' and 'buffer or peripheral area'.[94] Before declaring such an area, the concerned state government must reach a conclusion with the consent of the Scheduled Tribes and other forest-dwelling tribes in the area that their activities, or 'the impact of their presence upon wild animals is sufficient to cause irreversible damage and shall threaten the existence of tigers and their habitat'[95] and options of co-existence is not possible.[96] Once these conclusions are reached, a resettlement package must be finalized with the consent of the *Gram Sabha* and of the persons affected.[97] However, these significant provisions that are one of the best examples of participatory decision-making were not followed in letter and spirit when the CTH was declared. To complete the process before the implementation of the Forest Rights Act, the CTH was 'created overnight with little basis in science'.[98]

As the above analysis reflects, early laws like the Water Pollution Act and the Air Pollution Act do not contain provisions relating to public participation. However, today, several environmental laws prescribe public consultation before rule making and before taking decisions affecting the environment. Participation is envisaged at different stages and in different modes. Except in the case of declaration of the CTH under the Wild Life (Protection) Act, consent of the affected people is not a condition precedent for decision-making. Though the environmental clearance procedure under the EIA Notification contains detailed rules relating to public participation, the list of exempted projects from its ambit is increasing. Again, the consultation comes at a later stage after the TOR is finalized and the EIA study is completed. Non-adherence to these provisions by public authorities is another drawback. As seen in the declaration of CTH, these are seen as procedural bottlenecks that need to be managed somehow.

92 ibid.
93 ibid s 38V.
94 ibid s 38V(4) Explanation.
95 ibid s 38V(5)(ii).
96 ibid s 38V(5)(iii).
97 ibid s 38V(5)(v).
98 Valmik Thapar, 'Tourism Did not Kill the Tiger' *The Indian Express* (29 August 2012) <http://archive.indianexpress.com/news/tourism-did-not-kill-the-tiger/994472/1>.

15.4 Access to Justice

Access to justice is the third and final component of PERs. *Ubi jus, ibi remedium* is a well-known legal maxim and has particular significance in the Indian context. Though access to justice is not specifically mentioned as a fundamental right under the Constitution, there is a long line of Supreme Court judgments that held it to be a facet of the right to life under Article 21 and the right to equality under Article 14. The Constitution Bench, in *Anita Khushwaha v Pushap Sudan*, identified four main dimensions of the right of access to justice: an effective adjudicatory mechanism, accessibility in terms of distance, speedy adjudication, and affordability.[99]

Access to environmental justice would mean that natural and legal persons have access to a court of law or an independent tribunal to challenge: denial of access to environmental information, denial of public participation in environmental decision-making, and violation of any procedural or legal norms relating to environment. A broad interpretation of standing, not prohibitively expensive proceedings, 'prompt, effective and adequate' remedies, and timely and effective implementation of the decisions are other dimensions of this right.[100]

Early pollution control laws—the Water Pollution Act and the Air Pollution Act, stipulate the constitution of an authority to which appeals may be preferred against orders of the SPCBs.[101] Under the Water Pollution Act, appeals can be filed only against the order granting consent to establish and consent to operate, the conditions imposed in the consent order, and the order rejecting or withdrawing the consent. However, under the Air Pollution Act, an appeal can be filed against all orders issued by SPCBs. As far as *locus standi* is concerned, both the Acts use the term 'person aggrieved', leaving room for narrower and liberal interpretations. If one perceives these laws as reasonable restrictions on the fundamental right to carry on business, only industrial establishments can appeal against the denial of consent or conditions imposed in the consent order. A liberal interpretation would allow even a person affected by the grant of consent to approach appellate authorities. One could see wide variance among appellate authorities on the question of standing.[102] Though the qualification of the presiding officers is not prescribed under the Acts, the Supreme Court, in *AP Pollution Control Board v Prof. MV Nayudu*, observed that these appellate bodies should be headed by sitting or retired judges of the Supreme Court or High Court.[103] However, a recent study

[99] *Anita Khushwaha v Pushap Sudan* (2016) 8 SCC 509.

[100] Bali Guidelines (n 63) Part III.

[101] Water Pollution Act (n 10) s 28; Air Pollution Act (n 22) s 31.

[102] Shibani Ghosh, Sharachandra Lélé, and Nakul Heble, 'Appellate Authorities under Pollution Control Laws in India: Powers, Problems and Potential' (2018) 14 *Law, Environment and Development Journal* 45.

[103] *AP Pollution Control Board v Prof. MV Nayudu* (1999) 2 SCC 718 (737–738).

has found that bureaucrats hold ex-officio charge as presiding officers in most of the states.[104]

The NGT was established in 2010 as a specialized tribunal for the effective and expeditious disposal of cases involving environmental issues. The jurisdiction of the NGT extends to all civil cases where a substantial question relating to environment is involved,[105] appeals against various orders under the Water Pollution Act, the Air Pollution Act, the Environment (Protection) Act, the Biological Diversity Act, and the Forest (Conservation) Act, 1980,[106] and determination of liability and compensation under various statutes.[107] In terms of *locus standi*, the legislation uses a wide term 'person aggrieved'.[108] The NGT has adopted a liberal approach to the question of standing and has held that every Indian citizen can approach the Tribunal.[109] As far as physical accessibility is concerned, the NGT has its principal bench in Delhi and four regional benches in Chennai, Bhopal, Pune, and Kolkata. In a recent case, the Supreme Court rejected a plea for setting up of benches in all state capitals, citing the low caseload and observed that if the plea were to be allowed, 'the judges and other members in these forums might be left twiddling their thumbs'.[110] A separate chapter in this volume contains a detailed discussion on NGT (chapter 41).

Environmental laws in India, starting from the Water Pollution Act, have treated violations of these laws as criminal offences and provided for punishments and mechanisms for prosecution. Generally, it is the state that is the prosecuting agency in criminal proceedings. However, the Environment (Protection) Act enacted in the wake of the Bhopal gas tragedy introduced the concept of private/citizen prosecution. As per the provisions of the Act, a court can take cognizance of an offence either on a complaint made by the central government, any authority or officer authorized on this behalf or on a complaint made by any person.[111] However, such a person before filing a complaint must give notice of not less than sixty days to the central government or any authorized officer.[112] There were apprehensions at the drafting stages whether such a provision would open up the floodgates of litigation and harassment and blackmailing of industrial establishments.[113] However, the debates in the House of People and the Council of States show that there was genuine appreciation for this provision. It was hailed as a 'very significant landmark in the progress of environmental protection'.[114] There were suggestions that the cost of legal proceedings should be borne by the government.[115]

[104] Ghosh and others (n 102) 55.

[105] The National Green Tribunal Act, 2010s 14.

[106] ibid s 16.

[107] ibid s 17.

[108] ibid s 16.

[109] *Vimal Bhai v MoEF* 2011 SCC OnLine NGT 16.

[110] *Madhya Pradesh High Court Advocates Bar Association v Union of India* 2022 SCC OnLine SC 639.

[111] Environment (Protection) Act (n 39)s 19.

[112] ibid s 19(b).

[113] MK Ranjitsinh, *A Life with Wildlife* (Harper Collins 2017) 235.

[114] Rajya Sabha Debates, 14 May 1986 Session 138.

[115] Lok Sabha Debates, 8 May 1986.

Similar provisions were added to the Water Pollution Act,[116] the Air Pollution Act,[117] and the Wild Life (Protection) Act[118] by later amendments. Citizen prosecution provisions in one form or another is a common feature of environmental laws in India.[119]

15.4.1 Public Interest Litigation

The judiciary in India has been at the forefront in protecting the environment. Using writ jurisdiction, the Supreme Court and High Courts have intervened to enforce existing laws and hold the executive accountable for its failure to protect the environment. Many environmental issues have been brought to the Court by way of public interest litigation (PIL). In simple terms, PIL is the relaxation of the traditional rule of *locus standi*. Cunningham classifies PILs into two categories, 'representative standing' and 'citizen standing'.[120] In the former, the rule that only a person who has sufficient cause could approach the court is relaxed. Thus, petitions on behalf of the poor and marginalized filed by well-intentioned individuals and NGOs are entertained. In the latter case, public-spirited individuals and NGOs are allowed to approach the court for redressal of public injury rather than private injury. In *SP Gupta*, a lawyer with 'sufficient interest' could assert 'diffused', 'collective', and 'meta-individual rights'.[121] Most of the PILs in the field of environment can be classified under 'citizen standing'.

PILs in the Indian context are unique in certain other aspects. Instead of an adversarial process, in PIL, the approach is collaborative where the relief is often the result of negotiation between the parties. The judge is not a passive observer as in the case of a normal litigation but takes an active role in finding a solution. *MC Mehta v Union of India (Taj Trapezium)* is an example of such an approach.[122] During the many hearings, the Court negotiated, *inter alia*, the relocation of industries and a compensation scheme for the workers of the affected industries.[123] In many cases, the Court has appointed commissions, experts, and *amicus curiae* to assist the proceedings. Continuing mandamus to ensure the implementation of orders is another innovation seen in some environmental PILs.

The role of PILs in the development of Indian environmental jurisprudence is significant. Concepts like 'polluter pays',[124] 'precautionary principle',[125] 'sustainable

[116] Water Pollution Act (n 10) s 49 introduced by an amendment in 1988 (Act 53 of 1988).

[117] Air Pollution Act (n 22) s 43 introduced by an amendment in 1987 (Act 47 of 1987).

[118] Wild Life Protection Act (n 88) s 55(c) introduced by an amendment in 2003 (Act 16 of 2003).

[119] E.g., Public Liability Insurance Act, 1991 s 18(b); National Green Tribunal Act, 2010 s 30(1)(b).

[120] Clark D Cunningham, 'Public Interest Litigation in the Supreme Court of India: A Study in Light of the American Experience' (1987) 29 *Journal of the Indian Law Institute* 494.

[121] *SP Gupta* (n 17) 213–215.

[122] *MC Mehta v Union of India* (Taj Trapezium) (1997) 2 SCC 353.

[123] Shyam Divan and Armin Rosencranz, *Environmental Law and Policy in India* (2nd edn, OUP 2001) 268.

[124] *Indian Council for Enviro-Legal Action v Union of India* AIR 1996 SC 1446.

[125] *Vellore Citizens' Welfare Forum v Union of India* (1996) 5 SCC 647.

development',[126] and 'public trust'[127] were introduced into domestic law by the judiciary while adjudicating PILs. The judiciary has adorned many roles in its engagement with PILs. In one of the *MC Mehta* cases, the Supreme Court took up the role of a public educator in mandating the school and university curriculum to include environmental studies as a compulsory subject.[128] It overstepped its boundaries in making policy prescriptions in several cases including the Delhi Vehicular Pollution case.[129] It acted as a super administrator in micromanaging issues and making sure that its orders were implemented. The Forest Conservation case is a classic example of such an approach, where it kept the petition in its docket for more than two decades and, through the mechanism of continuing mandamus and appointment of *amicus curiae* and the Central Empowered Committee managed every aspect of forest governance in India.[130]

India's PIL jurisprudence and judicial activism have come under severe criticism. While giving voice to the voiceless (representative standing) has been one of the avowed objectives of PILs, at least on many environmental issues, it has alienated the marginalized them. While ordering the closure of polluting industries and eviction of encroachers from forests, the interests of the workers and the livelihood needs of the forest-dwelling communities were not given proper consideration.[131] The inconsistency in approach is another criticism.[132] Many a time the outcome of the litigation depends on the convictions of the individual judges. Especially in cases involving large infrastructure projects, courts have overlooked environmental concerns and have come down heavily on petitioners for delaying projects of national interest.[133]

Conclusion

An analysis of various laws indicates that PERs find recognition in various statutes in India. From being perceived as reasonable restrictions on the right to carry on trade or business, today, these rights are seen as facets of the right to a clean and healthy environment. These are also perceived as part and parcel of the principles of natural justice and an essential attribute of democracy. Coming specifically to the three components of PERs, the right of access to environmental information finds mention in almost all

[126] *ND Jayal v Union of India* (2004) 9 SCC 362.

[127] *MC Mehta v Kamal Nath* (1997) 1 SCC 388.

[128] *MC Mehta v Union of India* (1992) 1 SCC 358.

[129] *MC Mehta v Union of India WP* (C) 13029 of 1985.

[130] *TN Godavarman Thirumulpad v Union of India WP* (C) 202 of 1995.

[131] Ashok H Desai and S Muralidhar, 'Public Interest Litigation: Potential and Problems' in BN Kirpal and others (eds), *Supreme But Not Infallible: Essays in Honour of the Supreme Court of India* (OUP 2000) 159.

[132] S Muralidhar, 'Access to Justice' (2005) 545 Seminar <https://india-seminar.com/2005/545/545%20s.%20muralidhar1.htm>.

[133] *Goa Foundation v The Konkan Railway Corporation* 1992 SCC OnLine Bom 205.

the relevant environmental laws. There are provisions that mandate the collection, prescribing access, and directing dissemination of information. The RTI Act bolsters this right mainly by providing an institutional mechanism for enforcement. Publication of various regulations and notifications in regional languages will go a long way in ensuring access to environmental information.

Access to justice is entrenched in domestic law due to an active judiciary. One can cite many examples of judicial intervention in environmental matters due to a liberal interpretation of the principle of *locus standi*. Environmental jurisprudence in India has been enriched by the intervention of the higher judiciary in PILs. However, the relaxation of procedures has left the marginalized sections of society, like workers and forest-dwelling communities, voiceless and defenceless in many instances. Public participation in decision making in environmental matters appears to be the weak link in PERs in India. Very few laws contain this mandate and the procedure for ensuring it. Even in laws that mandate participation, like the EIA Notification, one can see a substantial dilution over a period of time. Strengthening these rights is a must for the enjoyment of the substantive right to a clean and healthy environment.

Suggestions for Further Reading

Ashok H Desai and S Muralidhar, 'Public Interest Litigation: Potential and Problems' in BN Kirpal and others (eds), *Supreme but Not Infallible: Essays in Honour of the Supreme Court of India* (OUP 2000) 157.

Shibani Ghosh, 'Procedural Environmental Rights in Indian Law' in Shibani Ghosh (ed), *Indian Environmental Law: Key Concepts and Principles* (Orient BlackSwan 2019) 55.

Manju Menon and Kanchi Kohli, 'Environmental Regulation in India: Moving Forward in the Old Direction' (2015) 50(50) *Economic and Political Weekly* 20.

MP Ram Mohan and Himanshu Pabreja, 'Public Hearings in Environmental Clearance Process: Review of Judicial Intervention' (2016) 51(50) *Economic and Political Weekly* 68.

Naveen Thayyil, 'Public Participation in Environmental Clearances in India: Prospects for Democratic Decision-Making' (2014) 56 *Journal of the Indian Law Institute* 463.

CHAPTER 16

DUE PROCESS AND ENVIRONMENTAL LAW

ARPITHA KODIVERI

Abstract

This chapter provides an overview of how due process requirements interact with environmental law. It looks at both procedural and substantive due process as an integral part of how to navigate the development and implementation of environmental law in India. Using due process as the lens the chapter unpacks how community-based consent and consultation requirements form a part of the procedural due process requirements. On substantive due process the chapter elucidates how public participation in environmental law making and the power of judicial review of legislative decision-making become avenues for the fulfilment of this requirement. The chapter argues that there exists a due process deficit by examining the consent provision under the Forest Conservation Act, 1980 (FCA) and the recent amendments being brought to the FCA. The chapter concludes by offering a few pathways to address the due process deficit identified in the examples above.

Introduction

Due process is a framing principle that guides the making and implementation of environmental law.[1] Though not explicit, it forms the core of ensuring that fundamental

[1] Robin Kundis Craig, 'Due Process Challenges in Environmental and Natural Resources Law', *FSU College of Law*, Public Law Research Paper No 453 (30 June 2010).

rights concerning the environment within the Constitution of India, 1950, namely the right to a healthy environment, are preserved. A due process reading of environmental law is where its making and implementation must adhere to the tenets of substantive and procedural due process. Substantive due process is where a statute can be challenged if it is considered arbitrary by the judiciary. Procedural due process is where rights deprivation, like the right to a healthy environment, requires a just, fair, and equitable process. Substantive due process includes two important aspects, namely, public participation in the process of law-making and the power of the judiciary to examine legislative changes as being fair and constitutionally valid.

In India, procedural considerations such as consultation with the communities impacted by a development project are an integral part of how decisions on deforestation or regulating pollution get made. Further, how can environmental considerations like the conservation of pristine areas be prioritized in making these decisions? Due process is closely related to environmental constitutionalism and is aimed at limiting government decisions, both administrative and legislative, that impede on fundamental rights like the right to a healthy environment.[2]

Environmental law has occupied the space within the larger legal framework charged with regulating excessive extraction, disciplining the rapid expansion of capital, and infusing the law with limitations of the finite nature of the environment. Legal principles like due process are used in efforts to regulate extractive activities and form an integral part of implementing environmental law. However, one can argue that environmental law has not been effective enough in protecting forests, rivers and other ecosystems.[3] In this chapter, I try to highlight the presence of due process in the larger enviro-legal framework and how far it has succeeded in regulating extraction and prioritizing the environment in state decision-making in India.

This chapter focuses on the way due process intersects with environmental law. The main points of such intersection in India are the role of the judiciary in examining environmental decision-making and law-making and the due process deficit in the procedural aspects of environmental law, especially in citizen participation.[4] The intersection with environmental law-making is the lack of substantive due process considerations resulting in rapid deregulation without sufficient judicial oversight. The method used in this chapter consists of a doctrinal analysis of the state of play of due process in Indian environmental law by mapping it across different natural resource laws such as forest laws, environment protection laws, biodiversity laws and jurisprudence. The chapter begins with an assessment of the existing regime at the intersection of due process and environmental law in India. I will then proceed to elaborate on the role of substantive

[2] Emmanuel Opoku Awuku, 'The Right to Clean Environment: Lessons from India and Tanzania' (1994) 27(4) *Verfassung und Recht in Übersee/Law and Politics in Africa, Asia and Latin America* 516.

[3] Michael M'Gonigle and Louise Takeda 'The Liberal Limits of Environmental Law: A Green Legal Critique' (2013) 30 *Pace Environmental Law Review* 1005.

[4] K Sivaramakrishnan, 'Environment, Law, and Democracy in India' (2011) 70(4) *The Journal of Asian Studies* 905.

and procedural due process in relation to environmental law. I will then unpack the due process deficit in environmental law-making and implementation. I will conclude with a set of recommendations to address the due process deficit.

16.1 Assessing the Existing Regime

The evolution of environmental law in India, when read through the lens of due process considerations, provides an understanding of the limitations of the existing legal framework. Due process in the Indian legal experience is largely procedural and selectively substantive. The critical gaze on Indian environmental law with due process considerations sheds light on the intersections of public participation in administrative as well as legislative decision-making, adherence of the executive and the legislature to procedural safeguards established by law and the role of the judiciary in scrutinizing environmental law-making. The literature, like the work of Caleb Hall and Ronald Klipsch, at the intersection of due process and environmental protection is growing as the increasing relevance of public participation and judicial review of vague environmental laws is seen as an effective strategy to check state power in decision-making.[5] This chapter adds to this growing body of work by offering insights from the Indian experience where due process is present in environmental law and jurisprudence implicitly as it is read into Article 21 of the Constitution and not mentioned explicitly in the Constitution, unlike in other jurisdictions like the United States where it is explicit. What, then, does a subtle presence of due process and a deficit of a stronger form mean for environmental decision-making? This chapter shows how unregulated economic growth at the cost of the environment thrives within this implicit and softer framing of due process in environmental law.[6]

Due process in India was a product of expansive judicial interpretation of the constitutional safeguard under Article 21, where the right to life and personal liberty could not be deprived except under the procedure established by law. The term 'procedure established by law' referred to procedural aspects that had to be complied with to legitimize the deprivation of the right to life and personal liberty.[7] The transition from procedure established by law to due process was made in *Maneka Gandhi v Union of India* where the Supreme Court held that the '«[p]rocedure established by law» must be fair, just and reasonable'.[8]

[5] Caleb Hall, 'A Right Most Dear: The Case for a Constitutional Environmental Right' (2016) 30(1) *Tulane Environmental Law Journal* 85; Ronald E Klipsch, 'Aspects of a Constitutional Right to a Habitable Environment: Towards an Environmental Due Process' (1974) 49(2) *Indiana Law Journal Article* 1.

[6] Hall (n 5).

[7] KK Nigam, 'Due Process of Law: A Comparative Study of Procedural Guarantees against Deprivation of Personal Liberty in the United States and India' (1962) 4(1) *Journal of the Indian Law Institute* 99.

[8] *Maneka Gandhi v Union of India* (1978) 1 SCC 248.

Due process includes procedural and substantive due process. Procedural due process refers to depriving rights under Article 21 of the Constitution following procedures that are fair, just, and reasonable and the requirement of a right to a hearing before such deprivation occurs.[9] Substantive due process is where the passing of the law can be challenged before the judiciary if the law is considered arbitrary or unfair.[10] The jurisprudence on substantive due process is unsettled as a 2016 judgment by the Supreme Court in *Rajbala v State of Haryana* stated that a statute cannot be invalidated merely because it is 'arbitrary'. It also went on to reject the US doctrine of substantive due process by holding that Indian courts 'do not examine the wisdom of legislative choices unless the legislation is otherwise violative of some specific provision of the Constitution'.[11] The unsettled jurisprudence on substantive due process by the judiciary creates a due process deficit by limiting the role of the courts in scrutinizing legislative choices to constitutional grounds.

Due process in the context of environmental law in India is visible in both its procedural and substantive forms. The Supreme Court, over the years, has expanded the right to life to include the right to a healthy environment, right to clean water,[12] right to livelihood,[13] and right to a pollution-free environment.[14] With the expansion of the right to life, the procedural safeguards and limitations then apply to these environmental rights too. Thus, any deprivation or violation of environmental rights must be based on the procedure established by law, including the environmental law framework.[15] The challenge, however, is the procedure established by law, and the implementation of these environmental rights remains vague within the jurisprudence. The procedure for deprivation of environmental rights is then derived from the regulatory processes embedded within the environmental law framework and, at times, other principles of environmental law like public participation and the public trust doctrine. The due process requirements are supplemented by these other principles. The public trust doctrine, which imposes a duty on the state to hold the resources as a trustee, can trigger a judicial review process of decisions made by the state in violation of the doctrine. Environmental law in India is rich in its procedural intricacies as the state decides on development projects informed by public participation. The key procedural legal tools used by the state include the environmental clearance (EC) process under the Environment (Protection) Act, 1986, the forest clearance process under the Forest Conservation Act, 1980 (FCA), and the process requiring industries to obtain consent to operate under the Water (Prevention and Control of Pollution) Act, 1974. Interestingly, the judiciary can be approached both for

[9] ibid [5].

[10] Herbert Hovenkamp, 'The Political Economy of Substantive Due Process' (1988) 40(2) *Stanford Law Review* 379.

[11] *Rajbala v State of Haryana* (2016) 1 SCC 463 [68].

[12] *MC Mehta v Kamal Nath* (1997) 1 SCC 388.

[13] *Olga Tellis and Others v Bombay Muncipal Corporation* 1986 AIR 180, 1985 SCR Supp (2) 51.

[14] *Subhash Kumar v State of Bihar* (1991) 1 SCC 598.

[15] Awuku (n 2).

the deprivation of environmental rights as well as the procedure harnessed in arriving at this decision, examining whether it is just, fair, and reasonable.[16]

In *MC Mehta v Union of India*, the Court stated that 'where the regulatory authorities, either connive or act negligently by not taking prompt action to prevent, avoid or control the damage to the environment, natural resources and peoples' life, health and property, the principles of accountability for restoration and compensation have to be applied'.[17] The remedies available for due process violations range from a reconsideration of state decision-making to restoration and compensation. Despite the presence of these jurisprudential developments, due process as the framing for environmental arguments made before the Court is subtle and not explicit. An example of this is environmental cases filed based on a violation of procedural requirements in granting environmental clearances where the environmental impact assessment process is challenged on the ground of lack of sufficient information on possible environmental damage, lack of an appropriate public hearing process, or violation of fulfilment of the procedural requirement of an EC by the project proponent or the conditions laid down in the clearance previously granted.[18]

Due process, both in its substantive and procedural form, if strengthened, can prevent the violation of environmental rights and correct the excesses of the state when it makes environmentally unsound decisions. The legal framework does provide opportunities to make up for the due process deficit, which I will address later in this chapter.

16.1.1 Due Process, Environmental Law-Making, and Implementation

To simplify how due process interacts with environmental law, I have chosen to divide the arenas of interaction into environmental law-making or judicial review of legislative action on the environment as the substantive element. For the procedural aspects of due process, I examine the implementation of procedures present in environmental legislation, that is, the judicial review of executive action or inaction in adhering to these procedures within environmental laws. This is by no means an all-encompassing categorization but assists in providing a clearer lens on how substantive and procedural due process are present in environmental law in a subtle form.

Due process in environmental law-making refers to where laws can be struck down if they are unjust, unfair, and unreasonable. Due process in the implementation of

[16] Deepa Badrinarayana, 'The "Right" Right to Environmental Protection: What We can Discern from the American and Indian Constitutional Experience' (2017) 43(1) *Brooklyn Journal of International Law* 75.

[17] *MC Mehta v Union of India* [2004] INSC 185 (18 March 2004).

[18] P Leelakrishnan, 'Environmental Impact Assessment: Legal Dimensions' (1992) 34(4) *Journal of the Indian Law Institute* 541.

environmental law refers to where deprivation of environmental rights can take place by adhering to the procedures established within environmental laws.

Due process, as an overarching legal principle, is primarily concerned with limiting state power when decisions violate the right to life, liberty, and property without following the standards of procedural safeguards and the legislative decision being just, fair, and reasonable. In a legal framework where the state enjoys wide discretionary power, attention to due process becomes pertinent to be able to hold the state accountable for environmental decision-making.

16.1.2 Substantive Due Process and Environmental Law-Making

As stated earlier in the chapter, the jurisprudence on substantive due process is unsettled. Judicial review of legislative action is restricted to examining the constitutionality of the Act. Thus, laws can be examined, amended, and struck down if they oppose the Constitution and its basic structure. This does allow for the operationalization of substantive due process and the examination of environmental legislation on whether they violate or undo fundamental rights.

In the 2015 case of *Sheikh Zahid Mukhtar v State of Maharashtra*, the Bombay High Court examined the constitutionality of the Maharashtra Animal Preservation Act, 1957 where a section of the Act criminalized the possession of the flesh of a cow, bull, or bullock that has been slaughtered.[19] This was challenged as violating the right to privacy under Article 21 of the Constitution. The court held that it was in violation of the right to privacy and struck down the said provision. In doing so, the court added two specific aspects to the jurisprudence on the substantive due process, which is of relevance to environmental law.[20] Firstly, it allowed for the test of constitutionality to include unenumerated rights like the right to privacy, and secondly, it challenged the legislative choices made by reading into the right to privacy the right to choose one's food. This expansive reading of substantive due process allows for environmental legislation to be scrutinized based on the unenumerated right to a clean environment and the right to livelihood.

Substantive due process in the Indian context is limited to the test of constitutionality. It does not extend to being able to examine if the law and legislative choices made are just, reasonable, and not arbitrary. This limit to the power of judicial review can curtail the ability of the courts to provide oversight on environmental laws being made, which may not pass the test of just, reasonable, and non-arbitrary.[21] This broader category of

[19] *Sheikh Zahid Mukhtar v State of Maharashtra* 2016 SCC OnLine Bom 2600.

[20] ibid.

[21] Manoj Mate, 'The Origins of Due Process in India: The Role of Borrowing in Personal Liberty and Preventive Detention Cases' (2010) 28(1) *Berkeley Journal of International Law* 216.

judicial review can enable the courts to strike down or re-visit legislative choices being made more recently with the deregulation efforts underway where environmental laws are being changed in ways that reduce the ability of regulatory authorities and citizens to challenge development projects that have an adverse impact on the environment. An example of such an effort is the amendments made to the FCA in 2021, where projects in and around areas of strategic importance are exempt from the need to obtain a forest clearance.[22] There are however examples of the dangers attached to the excessive reliance on courts as well. *Wildlife First v Ministry of Environment and Forests* was a case challenging the constitutionality of the Scheduled Tribes and Other Traditional Forest Dwellers (Recognition of Forest Rights) Act, 2006 (FRA), a law that, after many years, recognized the rights of forest-dwelling communities to use and conserve forest areas. This is an example where a progressive law was challenged through judicial review and has led, for instance, to an order calling for the eviction of one million forest-dwelling communities who remain dependent on these ecosystems.[23]

Another constraint to substantive due process in India is the inability of courts to examine the legislative procedure used to arrive at the legislation.[24] Article 122(1) of the Constitution does not allow for judicial review of the legislative process. In *Justice KS Puttuswamy (Retd) v Union of India*, the question of judicial review of irregularity of procedure came to the fore where the bill was designated a money bill.[25] A close reading of the judgment reveals that this irregularity of procedure contributed to substantive illegality. This is a deficit in substantive due process where the legislative procedure cannot be the basis of striking down laws. As the current government is amending many environmental laws and the legislative procedures being followed are not ideal, like the proposed amendments to the FCA in 2021, which had a limited window for providing comments, these laws cannot be subject to judicial review on these grounds. This deficit has been filled by a more general principle of environmental law, the principle of non-regression. The National Green Tribunal (NGT), while looking into the dilution of the Environmental Impact Assessment process, ruled that this was contrary to the principle of non-regression, which prevented environmental laws from being drafted in a way that would cause regression as opposed to progression in legislative developments.[26] In conclusion, as substantive due process is understood narrowly in the Indian context, it limits the ability to harness the role of courts in checking how environmental law is made and amended.

[22] Jacob Koshy, 'What are the proposed amendments to the Forest Conservation Act about?' *The Hindu* (5 October 2021) <https://www.thehindu.com/sci-tech/energy-and-environment/explainer-what-are-the-proposed-amendments-to-the-forest-conservation-act-about/article36840926.ece>.

[23] *Wildlife First v Ministry of Environment and Forests* 2018 SCC OnLine SC 3177.

[24] Dhananjay Dhonchak, 'The Case of Judicial Review of Legislative Process' *Indian Constitutional Law and Philosophy* (31 August 2021) <https://indconlawphil.wordpress.com/2021/08/31/guest-post-the-case-for-judicial-review-of-legislative-process>.

[25] *Justice KS Puttuswamy (Retd) v Union of India* (2017) 10 SCC 1.

[26] *Society for Protection of Biodiversity v Union of India* 2017 SCC OnLine NGT 981.

16.1.3 Procedural Due Process: Mapping Procedures in Environmental Laws

In this section, I provide a sampling of procedural provisions across some environmental legislation to give an essence of what the procedural due process requirements look like. These procedures are seen as preventing the deprivation of environmental rights identified as part of Article 21 of the Constitution. There are overlaps between procedural due process requirements and public participation, which are two-fold, namely (i) the need to be provided notice before the government takes any action, and (ii) the need to be heard before the decision is arrived at. These two elements of procedural due process are essential before the state takes a decision that may result in the deprivation of environmental rights. The possibility of judicial review has not been adequately harnessed in examining whether procedures established within environmental law in and of itself, as present in the statute, are just, reasonable, or fair. Where judicial review has stepped in is to see if it is reasonable, legal, and non-arbitrary in the implementation of these procedures present in environmental law. Table 16.1 below maps some of the procedures present in environmental law in India.

These procedures put in place a pathway for decision-making by the state when it takes key decisions of acquiring land for deforestation. A quick survey of the variety of procedures briefly identified above shows that there is a requirement for notice to be given, for those aggrieved to be heard, and for the decision arrived at to be a product of these processes. The due process requirements within the environmental law framework in India are visible in the public hearing process within the EIA requirement and the consent process under the forest clearance requirement. Each of these procedures requires adequate notice of the environmental harm and the need for permission and perspectives of the impacted community to be incorporated into the decision-making process. The challenge, however, has been the weak enforcement of these public participation provisions.[27]

An example of judicial review of procedural requirements within environmental law is in *Sterlite Industries (India) Ltd v Union of India*, where the Court held that there are specific grounds on which the grant of environmental clearance can be challenged, namely illegality, irrationality, and procedural impropriety.[28] The courts have interfered in examining administrative decisions on environmental issues in many instances. In *Adivasi Majdoor Kisan Ekta Sangathan v Ministry of Environment and Forests*, the NGT declared the environmental clearance invalid as the opposition by the citizens in the public hearing was not recorded, and no summary of the public hearing was provided in

[27] Manju Menon and Kanchi Kohli, 'From Impact Assessment to Clearance Manufacture' (2009) 44(28) *Economic and Political Weekly* 20.

[28] *Sterlite Industries (India) Ltd v Union of India* (2013) 4 SCC 575.

Table 16.1 Procedures in environmental law

Environmental law	Procedure
Environment Impact Assessment Notification, 2006	The EIA establishes a four-part process which includes screening, scoping, public hearing, and appraisal.
Forest Conservation Rules, 2016	The forest clearance process concerns two stages before providing permission to deforest. It also requires consent from the village assembly before granting clearance.
Right to Fair. Compensation and Transparency in Land Acquisition, Rehabilitation and Resettlement Act, 2013	The Act requires a social impact assessment process to be undertaken along with the consent of landowners to be obtained before the acquisition of land.
State laws on Water User Associations	Different state laws require water user associations to be consulted on irrigation use and distribution of water and their participation in planning and designing of micro-irrigation systems.
Biodiversity Act, 2002	The Act puts in place procedures for accessing and sharing benefits from the use of biodiversity. There is a requirement to apply for permission for accessing biodiversity with the national biodiversity authority which consults with the local communities through the state biodiversity boards and the biodiversity management committees.

Source: Author

the local language.[29] However, procedural due process while strong does not often result in a challenge to state decisions as the next section on the due process deficit will show.

16.2 Due Process Deficit

Despite due process being a framing principle in environmental law and environmental constitutionalism, it has not permeated the enforcement of existing environmental regulations or the procedure for re-engineering environmental laws. A due process deficit exists as the procedural provisions of environmental law are not adequately enforced, and amendments and passing of environmental laws are done without adequate public consultation and judicial oversight. The deficit in substantive due process

[29] *Adivasi Majdoor Kisan Ekta Sangthan v Ministry of Environment and Forests* 2012 SCC OnLine NGT 51.

is the limitation of the power of judicial review to questions of constitutionality, and the deficit in procedural due process is the weak enforcement of environmental procedures by the regulatory authorities and inconsistency in judicial review.[30] The due process deficit is where the procedural and substantive safeguards are often compromised and even changed to be able to facilitate the expansion of capital and development.[31]

Environmental law in India operates within a political economy of development where ecological concerns are seen as coming in the way of the ambitious development trajectory. As Pistor suggests, law and legal interpretation when operating within such a political economy seek to favour the interests of capital.[32] The courts, too, where the remedy can be sought for due process violations, have been inconsistent in regulating development projects.[33] The inconsistency here is where the courts at times prioritize the interest of safeguarding the environment and at times recognize the need for development. A recent example of this is the decision taken by the Supreme Court in the matter concerning the Kudankulam nuclear power project, especially in the context of Article 21 of the Constitution, which triggers the due process requirements as part of the right to a clean and healthy environment. The Court stated:

> While balancing the benefit in establishing ... [the nuclear power plant], with the right to life and property and the protection of the environment including marine life, we have to strike a balance, since the production of nuclear energy, is of extreme importance for the economic growth of our country, alleviate poverty, generate employment, etc. While setting up a project of this nature, we have to].have an overall view of the larger public interest rather than a smaller violation of the right to life guaranteed under Article 21 of the Constitution.[34]

The political economy of development and extraction can shape judicial decisions in ways that violate the right to life and liberty. The contestations over the enforcement of environmental law and the expansion of development projects become the site where decisions made—both legislative and administrative—are seen as just, fair, and reasonable.[35] A utilitarian approach to decision-making where the greatest good or larger public good is seen as a way to compromise on the rights of a few has been challenged repeatedly before courts where occasionally courts have secured the rights of a few, especially in the context of *Adivasi* rights to land and forests.[36]

[30] Jonathan H Adler, 'Wetlands, Property Rights, and the Due Process Deficit in Environmental Law' (2012) 9 *Cato Supreme Court Review* 139.

[31] ibid 17.

[32] Katharina Pistor, *The Code of Capital: How the Law Creates Wealth and Inequality* (Princeton University Press 2016).

[33] Geetanjoy Sahu, 'Public Interest Environmental Litigations in India: Contributions and Complications' (2008) 69(4) *Indian Journal of Political Science* 745.

[34] *G Sundarrajan v Union of India & Others* (2013) 6 SCC 620 [175].

[35] Kanchi Kohli and Manju Menon, *Developments in Environmental Law in India* (CUP 2021) 319–334.

[36] Sahu (n 33).

The inconsistency in the jurisprudence and adherence to due process requirements are framed by the economic considerations at play. I will unpack the due process deficit in both procedural and substantive aspects by closely examining the consent process in the forest clearance requirement and the recent amendments to the FCA. Through the examination of these provisions and legal amendments, I argue that due process can assist in finding more just and reasonable decisions.

16.2.1 The Consent Requirement and the Deficit in Procedural Due Process

The consent requirement within the FCA became part of the Indian environmental legal framework in 2009 through an administrative notification and as an amendment to the Forest Conservation Rules in 2016. The consent requirement refers to the requirement where the *Gram Sabha* or village assembly has the right to permit or prevent the diversion of forest land for different purposes.[37] The consent requirement has been a site of contestation where mining leases have been revoked and development projects curtailed because of the *Gram Sabha* asserting its power to say no. However, this is rare, and, in most instances, the consent requirement is either bypassed or not appropriately enforced to enable the diversion of forest land for development purposes.[38]

Procedural due process is violated here where, at times, adequate notice is not provided and on the aspect of being heard, procedural due process is limited in its ability to influence the eventual decision taken by the Ministry of Environment, Forest and Climate Change (MoEFCC) on the diversion of forest land. The due process deficit is deepened, where the applicability of the consent requirement is being diluted for particular projects like linear projects such as the construction of roads and bridges.[39] Choudhury and Aga, in their article on the Keonjhar takeover, alert the readers to how *Gram Sabha* resolutions have been manufactured and manipulated to be able to fulfil the consent requirement so forest land can be made available quickly for mining.[40]

The consent requirement in the coastal villages of Jagatsinghpur was violated to establish an integrated steel plant, highlighting the many aspects of the due process deficit. In 2005, the state of Odisha signed a Memorandum of Understanding (MoU) with the Pohang Steel Company for establishing an integrated steel plant in the agrarian villages of Jagatsinghpur.[41] The local community was not consulted as the MoU was being negotiated and decided upon. Protests ensued as part of the community opposed

[37] Forest Conservation Rules, 2016 r 6(3)(E)–(G).

[38] Chitrangada Choudhury and Aniket Aga, 'Manufacturing Consent: Mining, Bureaucratic Sabotage and the Forest Rights Act in India' (2020) 31(2) *Capitalism Nature Socialism* 70.

[39] ibid.

[40] ibid.

[41] Banikant Mishra and Birendra Kumar Nayak, 'Paan or POSCO' (2011) 46(26/27) *Economic and Political Weekly* 12.

the entrance of the steel major. In its articulation of dissent, the local community filed *Gram Sabha* resolutions under the FCA in 2011. Despite the submission of these *Gram Sabha* resolutions in 2011, the MoEFCC retained discretionary power on whether it would comply with the decision taken by the *Gram Sabha*.[42] In the exercise of this discretionary power, the MoEFCC granted the forest clearance by deferring to the state of Odisha and considering cooperative federalism where the centre and state arrive at decisions together. The due process deficit here was where the dissent of the local community was documented but failed to influence the eventual decision made.[43]

Protests on the ground continued against the acquisition of land and deprivation of the right to secure tenure. The Pohang Steel Company withdrew its proposal to construct the integrated steel plant in 2017 on account of the ongoing conflict, as well as changes to the Mines and Mineral Regulations in 2015, which required companies to go through an auction for mining leases. The retreat of POSCO did not put the idea of the development project on hold. In 2018, Jindal Steel Works (JSW) came into the picture and decided to pursue this project. As the new company began to acquire land, a few procedural innovations took place, enabling it to bypass the consent requirement. These procedural innovations were in the form of the creation of land banks and the ability to transfer an existing forest clearance to a new company.[44] Land banks are an administrative mechanism devised by the industrial development corporations in Odisha to identify small and large parcels of land and acquire them for future industrial use which in turn gets stored in what is termed as a land bank. The procedural requirements for the identification and acquisition of land for land banks remain unclear. The procedure laid down in the Land Acquisition Act, 2013, such as the requirement of a social impact assessment that must be conducted or the consent of the landowners needs to be obtained, have not been made applicable. In the villages of Jagatsinghpur, the local community was unaware that their land had been banked until a boundary wall was constructed by the Industrial Development Corporation of Odisha.[45]

A case was filed by Bhramarbar Das, a resident of Govindpur, before the NGT, claiming that the boundary wall was constructed in violation of the FRA and the FCA. The claim made in the petition was that the construction of the boundary wall was an illegal diversion of forest land which requires forest clearance.[46] Such forest clearance was not obtained, thus there is a need to stop the construction of the boundary wall. This petition resulted in a favourable judgment, where the construction of the boundary wall was ordered to be stopped.

The forest clearance granted to the Pohang Steel Company was transferred to JSW. The FCA allows for such transfer if the land is being provided for the same use and the

[42] ibid.

[43] ibid.

[44] Arpitha Kodiveri, 'Our Land is Banked: Forest Rights, Consent and the Invention of a Legal Exception as Land Banks' (2021) 25(7) *International Journal of Human Rights* 1148.

[45] ibid.

[46] ibid.

new user agency agrees to comply with the conditions of the earlier forest clearance. With the transfer, the consent requirement did not need to be fulfilled by JSW. In some ways, these procedural innovations and strategic use of discretionary power resulted in the local community not being able to articulate their dissent against the acquisition of their lands by JSW. This is an example of how due process is violated and the deficit is deepened to facilitate the current political economy of development and extraction.[47]

16.2.2 Amendments to the Forest Conservation Act, 1980: Deficit in Substantive Due Process

Forest law has been a subject of deregulation ever since India's economy was liberalized in 1991. A significant attempt to re-engineer environmental law was made in 2002 with the Govindarajan committee report, which sought to simplify environmental and forest clearances. The report identified the problem as being that:

> [e]nvironmental clearance perhaps takes the longest time and causes maximum delays to projects. Cumbersome procedures for environmental clearance and public hearing, submission of incomplete information, poor quality of EIA/EMP, disproportionate details required with applications, delays in the meetings of the Expert Committees and site visits, etc., are the major reasons behind delays.[48]

The suggested reforms and changes did not take on board the views of concerned stakeholders and citizens. India has a pre-legislative consultation policy that requires that a draft Act be placed in the public domain for thirty days before it is passed.[49] Here, too, the issue remains that there is no mandatory requirement that the comments received from citizens will shape what the law looks like.

Successive governments have adopted an authoritarian form of law-making with reduced parliamentary deliberation as well as citizen participation.[50] The changes in environmental law in such a context have meant rapid deregulation and the shaving away of hard-won legal gains, especially of procedural democracy like the recent amendment to the Forest Conservation Rules, 2022 where consent of the *Gram Sabha* is not required prior to state decisions on deforestation.[51] From this vantage point, environmental law

[47] ibid.

[48] Govindarajan Committee, Report on Reforming Investment Approval and Implementation Procedures (2002) iii.

[49] Ministry of Law and Justice, Decisions taken in the meeting of the Committee of Secretaries (CoS) held on 10 January 2014 under the Chairmanship of Cabinet Secretary on the Pre-legislative Consultation Policy.

[50] Tarunabh Khaitan, 'Killing a Constitution with a Thousand Cuts: Executive Aggrandizement and Party-State Fusion in India' (2020) 14(1) *Law and Ethics of Human Rights* 49.

[51] Mukta Joshi and Nitin Sethi, 'Government to Approve Cutting Down of Forests Without Consent from Tribals and Forest Dwellers' *Newslaundry* (7 July 2022) <https://www.newslaundry.com/2022/

has become a site of assertive state control to facilitate capital and not regulate it. The vibrant environmental movement, which has been active in opposing these autocratic amendments, has coordinated a campaign that opposed the passing of the draft EIA Notification 2020 that reduced the requirement of public hearings to specific projects.[52]

The MoEFCC received up to 1.7 million letters opposing the amendments to the EIA.[53] This is an instance where public participation was harnessed to oppose the dilution of environmental laws. However, public consultation in environmental law-making has not been consistently implemented. When environmental law is being deregulated, citizen participation has been avoided or conducted in an ad-hoc manner.[54]

The legal principles of quick decision-making to cultivate a regulatory environment that facilitates capital create three modalities of deregulation that I have come to identify. They are:

a) The use of delegated legislation: The amendments made and proposed are passed through delegated legislation so that they do not have to go through parliamentary scrutiny. The MoEFCC, under the Environment (Protection) Act, retains powers to pass such delegated legislation and use it as a mechanism to change the law.
b) The creation of legal exceptions or reducing the scope and applicability of the Act: Using delegated legislation and amendments to key laws, the state seeks to reduce the applicability of protective legislation like the Environment (Protection) Act and the FCA.
c) Emphasis on a compensatory approach to environmental law: The development of compensatory mechanisms like the Compensatory Afforestation Fund Act, 2016 provides a legal approach where ecological damage can be compensated for and restored. This draws from the civil law theory of compensating for harm done and has informed environmental law deregulation where it is permissive of capital with the conditionality of compensation as opposed to preventing the harm.

The use of delegated legislation allows for quick law-making in favour of capital, which is not subject to sufficient scrutiny. Similarly, the creation of exceptions ensures that industries like the mining sector are protected from the regulatory burden that comes with environmental and forest clearances. The desire for fast-tracking these clearances places undue pressure on the bureaucracy and local communities in arriving at a decision.[55]

07/07/government-to-approve-cutting-down-of-forests-without-consent-from-tribals-and-forest-dwellers>.

52 Abhijit Mohanty, 'Why Draft EIA 2020 Needs a Reevaluation' *Down to Earth* (6 July 2020) <www.downtoearth.org.in/blog/environment/why-draft-eia-2020-needs-a-revaluation-72148>.

53 Interview with Disha Ravi and Yash Marwah, 27 December 2021.

54 ibid.

55 Arpitha Kodiveri, 'The Visible Faultline of Development in India—The Right of Consent of Adivasi Communities and the Political Economy of Mining' in Alan P Diduck, Kirit Patel, and Aruna Malik (eds), *Advancing Environmental Justice for Marginalized Communities in India* (Routledge 2021).

In October 2021, the MoEFCC issued a consultation paper detailing fourteen proposed areas for amending the FCA. It included creating a large swathe of exceptions to the applicability of the Act, including land required for strategic projects, land alongside railway lines, and de-reserving forests without the approval of the central government.[56] These changes were made to liberalize forest law to facilitate development. The element of public participation was partially fulfilled when the consultation paper was released for public comment but with a short window of fifteen days. It was made available in a single language while these changes will impact a diverse community that lives in and depends on these forest areas.

The due process deficit here is experienced in the unsettled jurisprudence on the substantive due process on whether the courts can step in to examine if the law being passed is fair when it interferes with rights under Article 21 of the Constitution. In India, the courts can step in only to examine if the law has been passed by the competent authority and if a particular provision of the Constitution is being violated.[57] This limited scope of judicial oversight in legislative decision-making reduces the space available to mount a due process challenge against proposed amendments like to the FCA. There are, however, some exceptions, as seen in *Shaikh Zahid Mukhtar*.[58]

16.3 Potential of the Existing Regime in Strengthening Due Process Requirements

An analysis of due process in environmental law in India highlights the deficit that exists in the regime. The primary reasons for such a due process deficit are the large discretionary power enjoyed by the state in environmental decision-making and the unchecked legislative decision-making on environmental law, especially in deregulating it. The existing regime offers a few avenues that can strengthen the due process requirements and in turn secure the citizen's rights under Article 21 of the Constitution. The avenues available are:

a) Enforcement of environmental and forest clearances: The EIA and the forest clearance process ensure that citizen participation is incorporated as an essential element of the process. To strengthen procedural due process, it will be important for the MoEFCC to enforce these provisions and find ways for the local

[56] Kohli and Menon (n 35) 322.

[57] Vikram A Narayan and Jahnavi Sindhu, 'A Case for Judicial Review of Legislative Process in India?' (2020) 53(4) *Verfassung und Recht in Übersee / World Comparative Law* 358.

[58] *Sheikh Zahid Mukhtar* (n 19). This is an instance where judicial review of legislative decision-making occurred as the law was in violation of the right to life and personal liberty.

community and village assembly to impact the eventual outcome and for the local community to be adequately heard.[59]

b) Monitoring and compliance in environmental decision-making: India's environmental governance struggles with regulatory failure in monitoring and ensuring compliance with environmental and forest clearances which have been granted. The regulatory authority, by strengthening monitoring and compliance, will provide an additional opportunity for communities adversely impacted by development projects to be able to articulate their issues as well as ensure better adherence to the terms and conditions of the statutory environmental procedures.[60]
c) Judicial oversight over administrative decision-making and legislative procedures: There has been an excessive reliance on the courts to challenge environmental decisions taken by the administrative bodies on the grounds of non-compliance with existing procedures or the decision being against securing ecological balance or other rights like the right to life. The courts, as stated earlier, have been active in regulating development with environmental considerations. However, they have also deferred to the decision taken by the executive on aspects of development. The presence of an independent judiciary and the NGT act as important sites to check the discretionary power enjoyed by the state.[61] There is a need to extend the power of judicial review to include legislative procedures as environmental laws are being rapidly undone and changed in India.
d) Challenging delegated legislation: A large amount of environmental law and decision-making is found in delegated legislation derived from the power provided to the MoEFCC under the Environment (Protection) Act to pass notifications in the interest of protecting the environment. Delegated legislation can be challenged before the courts on the grounds of it being *ultra-vires* the parent statute. Thus, delegated legislation that reinterprets and bypasses existing environmental procedures like the creation of land banks can be challenged.[62]
e) Implementation of the pre-legislative consultation policy: The pre-legislative consultation policy passed in 2014 should form the basis of all environmental law-making and there must be a larger window of time to provide public comments as well as the proposed amendments being made available in many languages for citizens to be able to provide their inputs in legislative decision-making.[63] This policy does have its limitations, one being that the consultation policy does not clarify

59 ibid.

60 Manju Menon and Kanchi Kohli 'Environmental Decision-making: Whose Agenda?' (2007) 42(26) *Economic and Political Weekly* 2490.

61 Ayesha Dias, 'Judicial Activism in the Development and Enforcement of Environmental Law: Some Comparative Insights from the Indian Experience' (1994) 6(2) *Journal of Environmental Law* 243.

62 Manju Menon and Kanchi Kohli, 'Re-Engineering the Legal and Policy Regimes on Environment' (2008) 43(23) *Economic and Political Weekly* 14.

63 Tarunabh Khaitan, 'Reforming the Pre-Legislative Process' (2011) 46(25) *Economic and Political Weekly* 27.

how the comments received from citizens will be incorporated in the law-making process.

f) Using decentralized decision-making to check arbitrary environmental decision-making: Laws like the FRA and the Panchayats (Extension of Scheduled Areas) Act, 1991, require that environmental decision-making both on conservation and diversion are devolved to the *Gram Sabhas*. These laws should be effectively implemented so that unchecked discretionary power of the MoEFCC can be checked by these local bodies which will improve due process considerations.[64]

16.4 Addressing the Due Process Deficit

> It is difficult to negotiate with the bureaucracy. We are left with no other option but to approach the courts about these environmental issues.[65]

The regulatory failure to enforce environmental laws places an excessive burden on the courts to check administrative decision-making and burdens vulnerable litigants with the difficult task of approaching the courts. Provisions governing administrative procedures are derived from the rules of specific legislation and the Constitution. The checks and balances on the exercise of administrative discretion are through judicial review. Overcoming the need to go before the courts can be through the creation of an ombudsman within the MoEFCC which can receive complaints by citizens to expand public participation and secure procedural due process.[66] There will be challenges with such an arrangement in terms of ensuring the independence of the ombudsman and the nature of remedies that will be proposed as opposed to what can be achieved before the courts.

While the dependence on the judiciary is excessive for the review of administrative action and regulatory failure, when it comes to environmental law-making, it is largely absent. There is a need to strengthen the substantive due process requirements by using the courts to challenge the making and proposed amendments to environmental laws such that the courts can check the fairness of a given legislative decision. While bringing courts into the picture of legislative decision-making can be seen as being problematic as judicial interference in legislative functioning, it provides another window for citizens to challenge arbitrary deregulation of environmental laws.[67]

[64] Arun Agrawal, 'The Regulatory Community: Decentralization and the Environment in the Van Panchayats (Forest Councils) of Kumaon, India' (2001) 21(3) *Mountain Research and Development* 208.

[65] Interview with Manorama Kathua in Jagatsinghpur (July 2018).

[66] Menon and Kohli (2008) (n 62).

[67] Kohli and Menon (n 35) 319–334.

Both procedural and substantive due process can be effectively realized by scrutinizing the procedural innovations made within the executive, such as land banks. Environmental law in India consists of different pieces of delegated legislation both by the MoEFCC as well as other ministries like the Ministry of Mines or Coal. The creation of land banks that are part of delegated legislation of the Industries Department that violates forest law, as seen earlier in the chapter, requires inter-ministerial consultations to be able to resolve these conflicting legal approaches.[68]

In addressing the due process deficit, it becomes important to examine the ability of environmental law to discipline capital within the current political economy of development. Procedural and substantive due process offers protection against the violation of fundamental rights concerning the environment.[69] These rights are under threat from the present extractive development model, where environmental law is facilitating extraction instead of regulating and conserving these resources. A recent report speaks of the increase in the number of environmental and forest clearances that have been granted. It also documents how these decisions on granting clearances are made speedily and very often with limited information.[70] This prevents the MoEFCC from adequately considering the environmental impact of the clearances granted.

Conclusion

The chapter chronicles how due process as a legal principle interacts with environmental law in India. Both procedural and substantive due process are present in particular forms in the Indian context. The chapter focuses on how substantive due process can be used to strengthen judicial review of environmental law-making and procedural due process steps to examine how just, equitable, and reasonable decision-making processes around the environment are.

In conclusion, due process is a salient framing principle and provides an interesting point of entry to understanding environmental law in India. The primary argument presented in this chapter is the need to unpack and find creative ways to fill the due process deficit that has been identified. In this chapter, a due process deficit is seen due to existing legal frameworks, unsettled jurisprudence, and the political economy of development. The courts form an important site for the realization of both procedural and substantive due process, but there is a need for the inclusion of courts in the examination of legislative decision-making. As the climate crisis looms large, due process provides an

68 Sharachchandra Lélé, Navroz K. Dubash, and Shantanu Dixit 'A Structure for Environment Governance: A Perspective' (2010) 45(6) *Economic and Political Weekly* 13.

69 Kohli and Menon (n 35).

70 Nihar Gokhale, 'To Kickstart the Economy, India's Environment Ministry is Clearing Projects in 10 Minutes' *Quartz* (5 May 2020) <https://finance.yahoo.com/news/kickstart-economy-india-environment-ministry-045737759.html>.

effective tool in holding the state accountable for its environmental decisions, which are made in ways that can adversely impact the rights concerning the environment under Article 21 of the Constitution.

Suggestions for Further Reading

Anuj Bhuwania, *Courting the People: Public Interest Litigation in Post-Emergency India* (CUP 2017).

Shibani Ghosh, *Indian Environmental Law: Key Concepts and Principles* (Orient BlackSwan 2019).

Teresa Joseph and Siby K Joseph (eds), *Deliberative Democracy: Understanding the Indian Experience* (Routledge 2018).

Ranjana Padhi and Nigamananda Sarangi, *Resisting Dispossession: The Odisha Story* (Palgrave Macmillan 2020).

Geetanjoy Sahu, 'Public Interest Environmental Litigations in India: Contributions and Complications' (2008) 69(4) *Indian Journal of Political Science* 745.

PART IV

LAND, AGRICULTURE, AND BIODIVERSITY

CHAPTER 17

INDIVIDUAL AND COMMUNITY PROPERTY RIGHTS AND DUTIES IN LAND AND THE ENVIRONMENT

M.S. VANI

Abstract

The appropriation of land and its components for self-use has been one of the primary actions of humankind with respect to nature. Human society has evolved a range of value systems—economic, political, social, cultural, ethical and spiritual—to describe its relationship with land and other natural elements and the methods to establish such a relationship. These value systems coalesce broadly into two distinct philosophical approaches—anthropocentrism and biocentrism—engendering distinct legal, institutional and governance modes, representing western and non-western cultures generally. The chapter examines the property rights and duties of individuals and communities in India in land and environment. The chapter reflects on the need for a duty-based local governance system with dominant community property tenures, and a legal system infused with ethical and spiritual values to re-establish a balance between property rights and environment, securing both.

Introduction

Land is a primary element of critical importance for the survival of the human species. A basic unit of organization of land for human use is 'property tenure' or the human right to hold property. Property comes in at least three different forms: private, collective, and common.[1] One or the other form may be predominant in any society, but generally, more than one form is prevalent.[2] In the Western context, while economic, social, and political value systems have long been associated with property rights in land, a more recent perspective is the 'environmental' value of natural resources. Modern law-makers do not think of the environment as a whole but more as a generic word for natural 'resources',[3] an economic term in Western economic and legal frameworks. The term 'environment', however, goes beyond the sum of land-based 'resources' to include the dynamic interrelationship among them. Natural 'resources' exist not independently of each other but as components of ecosystems that impact one another in a continuous process of evolution.[4] Laws which address such dynamic interrelationships may be termed 'environmental laws', failing which they remain natural resources law.

Embedded in this distinction is the crucial question regarding the human–nature interrelationship—whether humans are separate from or intrinsic to the dynamic natural environment and whether nature has intrinsic value apart from humankind. The response to this question has been a matter of philosophical conceptual choice between two streams of thought and approach—anthropocentric and biocentric. In the former, humans are viewed as separate from nature, a basic belief embedded in many Western religions and philosophies.[5] In the latter, humans are regarded as an intrinsic part of nature—a position reflected in many non-Western cultures and traditions.[6] Each of these belief systems are manifested in political economy frameworks, including the concepts of property rights and modes of governance. The distinction crystallizes in the nature and extent of 'obligations' or 'duties'. Western concepts of property reflect the substantially anthropocentric view of envisaging rights only of humans and requiring duties only to other humans, often ignoring the ecological context.[7] In contrast, duties towards nature are a foundational principle of biocentrism,[8] in which rights to natural processes are balanced through duties.

The formal legal framework on land and the environment in India is derived from two sources—colonial natural resources law and Western environmental law. Both are

[1] Hugh Breakey, 'Property' in James Fieser and Bradley Dowden (eds), *Internet Encyclopedia of Philosophy* (undated) 3 https://iep.utm.edu/prop-con/.

[2] ibid.

[3] Klaus Bosselmann, 'Losing the Forest for the Trees: Environmental Reductionism in the Law' (2010) 2(8) *Sustainability* 2424.

[4] Bruce Pardy, *Ecolawgic: The Logic of Ecosystems and the Rule of Law* (Fifth Forum Press 2015) 17.

[5] W Warren Wagar, Book Review: William Leiss, '*The Domination of Nature* (Braziller 1972)' 14(3) *Technology and Culture* (1973) 480.

[6] Rex Weyler, 'A Brief History of Environmentalism' (*Greenpeace*, 5 January 2018) <www.greenpeace.org/international/story/11658>.

[7] Steven McMullen and Daniel Molling, 'Environmental Ethics, Economics and Property Law' in Mark D White (ed), *Law and Social Economics* (Palgrave Macmillan 2015) 21.

[8] Joseph R DesJardins, 'Biocentrism' Saving Earth: Encyclopaedia Britannica (undated) <https://www.britannica.com/explore/savingearth/biocentrism>.

founded on similar anthropocentric principles aimed at global resource extraction and regulation to serve colonial and neo-colonial economics.[9]

In addition to formal law, a substantial and significant body of non-formal or 'customary' legal frameworks on natural resources derived from pre-colonial legal traditions is also extant, founded on philosophical principles distinct from Western traditions.

The objective of this chapter is to examine the property rights of individuals and communities in land and the environment in India, considering the underlying philosophical, legal, and social value systems historically, identifying the dominant value systems of rights and duties reflected in governance systems currently, and their impact on rights and resources. Section 17.1 discusses conceptual approaches to property rights and governance in India from a historical perspective and the impact of colonial natural resources law on property rights to land. Section 17.2 examines constitutional and legal provisions on state, private and community property in land and the framework of associated duties of individuals and communities. Section 17.3 describes individual and community property rights and obligations under environmental laws. Section 17.4 outlines issues of concern and challenges in achieving human and environmental security through the prevailing governance structures on property rights in land and the environment.

17.1 Conceptual Approach to Property Rights in India

Private property dominates around the world today, but community property was the first mode of human cooperation for survival and development.[10] In the Western world, individual property rights emerged as a predominant form, leading to the commoditization of land. 'Ownership' rights - constituted by the right to exclusion, use and transfer[11] became central to the economic approach to land, to control part of the material world by a human, with corresponding duties of non-interference on the part of other humans.[12] This typically Western anthropocentric concept of ownership, was exported over most of the world through colonialism. Colonial land law in India perceived land

[9] Louis J Kotzé, Louise Du Toit, and Duncan French, 'Friend or Foe? International Environmental Law and its Structural Complicity in the Anthropocene's Climate Injustices' (2021) 11(1) *Oñati Socio-legal Series* 180.

[10] Liz Alden Wily, 'Collective Land Ownership in the 21st Century: Overview of Global Trends' (2018) 7(2) *Land* 68.

[11] Breakey (n 1).

[12] Mcmullen and Molling (n 7).

not as a 'biotic community'[13] but as a commodity, shorn of environmental, ethical, moral, and spiritual values.

Colonial anthropocentric ideology could not completely obliterate biocentric traditions in India, which accord the same moral or intrinsic value to all living and non-living elements. This approach, derived from Vedic philosophical traditions, established the unity of humans and the environment unequivocally through three interconnected principles: the *Pancha Bhutas* or Five Elements—Earth, Water, Fire, Air, and Ether formed the basic building blocks of the entire universe, including humans; *Brahman*, the ultimate creative principle underlying all phenomena, present in every person, molecule, and atom, endowing 'sacredness' to everything, living and non-living; and *Dharma*, the balancing, constant principle that 'supports' and 'sustains' life and order in all their forms.[14] The sustaining and balancing principles of *Dharma*, which being empirical were constantly observed and interpreted according to changing conditions of society and environment, were distilled into the concept of 'duties' in social and political life, forming the bedrock of customary law, a living and enduring legal tradition.[15]

The prevalence of both individual and community property and the use of the former closely tied to community decision-making, which included environmental decision-making on rights and duties,[16] was enabled by the absence of state ownership of territory in pre-British India. The king received taxes only for his function of protection as a sovereign and not for ownership of all land.[17] This was acknowledged by early colonial British administrators, judges, and historians.[18] Thus, right up to the nineteenth century, customs and traditions—evolved by the 'co-sharing village community—the primary tenure of Indian agrarian society'[19]—played a significant role in constraining individual property rights in village land and maintaining local arrangements to accommodate conflicting individual and collective rights.[20]

Impact of colonial rule on property rights: Colonial rule imposed fundamental changes in indigenous human-land interrelationships through several interconnected actions.[21] Private saleable property rights in land were introduced, severed from community tenure.[22] The government assumed 'sovereign rights over all the land', becoming

[13] Aldo Leopold, *A Sand County Almanac and Sketches Here and There* (OUP 1987) 204.

[14] Chaturvedi Badrinath, *Dharma, India and the World Order* (Saint Andrew Press 1993).

[15] M.S. Vani, 'Customary Law and Modern Governance of Natural Resources in India—Conflicts, Prospects for Accord and Strategies' in Rajendra Pradhan (ed), *Legal Pluralism and Unofficial Law in Social, Economic and Political Development* (ICNEC Kathmandu 2002) 409.

[16] Lallanji Gopal, 'Ownership of Agricultural Land in Ancient India' (1961) 4(3) *Journal of the Economic and Social History of the Orient* 240.

[17] ibid 240.

[18] Mark Wilks, *Historical Sketches of the South of India in an Attempt to Trace the History of Mysore* (Asiatic Society 1810) 65–138.

[19] Eric Stokes, *The English Utilitarians and India* (OUP 1959) 111.

[20] David Ludden, *Peasant History in South India* (OUP 1989) 184.

[21] Stokes (n 19) 82.

[22] ibid.

the universal landlord. The pre-British tradition of tax collection from the village as a whole as a percentage of gross produce was changed to rent collection from intermediary landholders and cultivators, which left no surplus for the community.

In 1856, the East India Company delegitimized community land tenure and assumed control over what was termed 'cultivable and uncultivable wastes' and offered them for sale to the public at large. Rules for selling waste lands were published in 1864 and the policy put into effect through survey and settlement operations,[23] severing the rights-duties dynamic in community shareholding property customs with respect to land. The substitution of customary law by state law and takeover of community property by the colonial regime struck at the heart of the biocentric approach.

Post-Independence, these changes were retained in land laws. The distribution of legislative powers and the pattern of 'listing' and wording of legislative subjects such as land, forest, wildlife, fisheries, etc. in the new Constitution of India, 1950, was a replica of the Government of India Act, 1935, continuing the 'natural resources' model, rather than the 'environmental' model. The term 'environment' did not feature in the Constitution till 1976, when the forty-second constitutional amendment introduced the concept of environmental 'duties'.

17.2 Individual and Community Rights and Obligations in Land

While individual property rights and state powers of eminent domain have constitutional recognition, there is no explicit mention of 'community property', even with respect to tribal populations, for whom special constitutional provisions exist. Article 244 of the Constitution, read with Schedules V and VI, was intended to protect tribal customary law, social and religious practices, and traditional community natural resource management practices. However, even though common ownership of land is a characteristic feature of tribal life, Schedule V does not refer to community 'tenure' in lands but to lands of 'members' of Scheduled Tribes, namely private rights.[24] In Schedule VI as well, the term 'community property rights' is absent. Powers of management of lands in these areas are vested in Regional and District Councils of Tribals, excluding Reserved Forests under the control of State Forest Departments. Eminent domain powers of state are explicitly protected in the Schedule, overriding community ownership traditions over land.[25] Even private rights are not entirely private. Schedule V empowers Governors of States to enact regulations to control the transfer of land by

[23] Ludden (n 20) 175–176.
[24] The Constitution of India, Schedule V, 5(2)(a)–(b).
[25] ibid, Sixth Schedule, 3(a).

and allotment to members of the Scheduled Tribes 'to protect tribes against usurpation of lands by outsiders'. Despite several state laws in Schedule V areas to this effect, tribal populations are the most dispossessed citizens.

Both the Constitution as well as land reform laws in the years after Independence failed to restore community tenure over common lands or Common Property Resources (CPRs) in non-tribal areas usurped by the colonial state and retained by the Indian state. CPRs include community pastures, community forests, wastelands, common dumping and threshing grounds, watershed drainages, village ponds, rivers, rivulets, as well as their banks and beds, on which villagers exercise *de facto* ownership, if not *de jure*.[26] Forests are under state control and not considered CPRs even though local communities have exercised collective rights and obligations over such lands traditionally. The importance of CPRs is manifold in terms of supplying food, fodder, and timber to farmers and livestock. The poorest households, particularly landless families, access CPR resources, particularly in arid and semi-arid zones, where 84–100 per cent of the rural poor depend on them.[27] CPRs sustain ecosystem functions, particularly the harvesting of monsoon rainwater, 80 per cent of which is received in about one hundred hours annually.[28]

The seventy-third and seventy-fourth constitutional amendments, which provide constitutional status and functions to urban and rural local governance institutions, missed the opportunity to transfer real powers of governance over land and other natural resources to them. Articles 243G and 243W of the Constitution merely suggest, using the word 'may', a transfer of administrative functions only, that too, entirely subject to existing laws enacted by states. The status quo—state sovereign rights over land and eminent domain powers—remains unchanged. As the seventy-third and seventy-fourth constitutional amendments excluded Scheduled Tribal Areas, the Panchayats Extension to Scheduled Areas Act (PESA) was enacted by Parliament in 1996. However, PESA failed to create any new tenurial rights to land and other natural sources—the one exception was 'ownership' in relation to 'minor forest produce'.[29]

The primary land legislation at the state level land revenue acts—declare state property rights over land and acknowledges private property, but not community property rights.[30] By virtue of these provisions, all lands 'which were not privately owned' belonged to the state.[31] State property rights over land include standing and flowing water, mines, minerals, and forests. Property rights of individuals acknowledged in

[26] NS Jodha, 'Rural Common Property Resources: Contributions and Crisis' (Society for Promotion of Wastelands Development 1990).

[27] Planning Commission of India, Report of Sub-Group on Institutions and Commons for 12th Five Year Plan (2012) 10.

[28] PR Pisharoty (1990), as cited in Anil Agarwal and Sunita Narain (eds), *Dying Wisdom—Rise, Fall and Potential of India's Traditional Water Harvesting Systems* (Centre for Science and Environment 1997) 315.

[29] PESA Act, 1996 s 4(m)(ii).

[30] E.g., Madhya Pradesh Land Revenue Code, 1959 s 57; Tamil Nadu Land Encroachments Act, 1905 s 2.

[31] ibid.

revenue codes refer to rights settled during survey and settlement operations and recorded in village registers and maps with specific survey numbers assigned to owners. These form the proof of ownership in rural areas. In urban areas as well, such records are officially maintained.

Similar to the transformation of ownership rights of local communities in forest and forest produce into 'concessions' or 'use rights' under colonial forest legislation[32] (as well as post-Independence forest law), customary ownership rights in common lands were transformed into 'use' rights under state land revenue laws, and are 'regulated' by the state. In Madhya Pradesh, for instance, the government regulates not only 'common use rights' in unoccupied government lands, termed *nistar*, but also common customary rights of irrigation, fishing, right of way, and other easements on private land. With respect to *nistar*, the state determines the nature of use—only for 'bonafide domestic consumption', prohibiting 'sale, gift, barter, export, or wasteful use'. Records of rights are prepared by government officers for rights on government lands (*Nistar Patrak*) and customary community rights on private land (*Wazib-ul-Urz*).

Duties of individuals and communities associated with property rights in land: Legal obligations associated with individual property rights are restricted to payment of land revenue or property tax and any other charges that may be imposed legally. An important obligation of all landholders is with respect to easements. The Easements Act, 1882 defines an easement as a right which the owner or occupier of certain land possesses over another person's land for the beneficial enjoyment of his own land.[33] Some illustrations are right of way, right to take water over another person's land, etc. The legal obligations of private property right holders include allowing easementary rights of adjoining property holders. Legal duties towards the 'environment' are not envisaged under laws conferring private rights to land.

Though community use rights are legalized, communities have no legal obligations for the conservation of non-forest commons, as land laws are command and control statutes conferring monopoly powers on the government. The anthropocentric, reductionist approach in land laws empowers revenue authorities to 'allocate' common land for various local purposes or change such allocation unilaterally, to remove encroachments on such lands, as well as to 'regularize' them on payment of land value by encroachers.[34] These powers not only transform the contours of commons property and thereby their access but also invalidate the collectively held decision-making powers of the village community, to allocate rights and duties among themselves based on changing local ecological conditions and human needs; monopolistic state legal power leads to frequent conflicts, often brought to courts.[35]

32 Vani (n 15) 27–30.

33 Indian Easements Act, 1882 s 4.

34 E.g., Tamil Nadu Land Encroachment Act, 1905; Karnataka Land Revenue Act, 1964.

35 *Gram Panchayat Dhooma v State of MP* 2021 SCC OnLine MP 5916.

In some states, local government laws provide for commons management by local committees of village *panchayats*. However, they may act only on the direction of the revenue departments, as in the case of Uttar Pradesh. In some states, such as Madhya Pradesh, the *Gram Sabha*'s resolution is required to divert to other uses land set apart for *nistar* use. In practice, the procedure is a mere formality. PESA provisions recognize the 'competence' of the *Gram Sabha* to 'safeguard and preserve community resources', including land,[36] but do not recognize customary tenure, which underwrites customary management.

In the customary legal domain, community control over land is important because rights are exercised in tandem with collective duties, as in many cases, private land rights are dependent on collective risk-sharing arrangements.[37] The concept of 'duty' translates into the practice of collectively imposing 'restraint' in resource use.[38] Some examples are quantitative restriction on the amount of harvest from a given locality, for example, the amount of wood or grass harvested by a family or their livestock from community lands; harvesting in certain seasons; certain species of trees may be wholly protected; and certain habitat patches may never be harvested. In the state of Mizoram, the community wood lots from which regulated harvests are permitted (supply forests) are complemented by sacred groves, aptly called 'safety forests', from which no harvests are permitted. Certain methods of harvest may be completely prohibited. In the Aravalli Hills of Rajasthan, there are patches of forests called *oraons* where harvesting by using metal tools is prohibited, though wood may be removed by breaking twigs by hand. Specific age-sex classes or social groups may be banned from employing certain harvesting methods or utilizing certain species or habitat patches.

Such duties restricting rights are also found in the context of water commons or surface water bodies in many states. In the state of Tamil Nadu, *Eris* or constructed surface water bodies – designed and constructed by ancient Tamil societies for the harvesting of monsoon rain water - are multipurpose water bodies serving human and ecological needs. Water is used simultaneously for irrigation, fish culture, drinking for humans and animals, bathing and washing, recharging groundwater and tree cultivation, and silt collected from tank beds is used for brickmaking and for improving soil fertility in agricultural lands.[39] Tanks are not only economic entities but also the fulcrum for the social and cultural life of the villages. In pre-colonial times, local institutions exercised a range of legal powers over water and land resources for the construction, use and maintenance of these systems.[40] This tradition continues today in the customary legal domain—local

36 PESA s 4(d).

37 Jodha (n 26).

38 Madhav Gadgil and Ramachandra Guha, *This Fissured Land—An Ecological History of India* (OUP 1993) 37.

39 Olivia Aubriot and P Ignatius Prabhakar, 'Water Institutions and the 'Revival' of Tanks in South India: What is at Stake Locally?' (2011) 4(3) *Water Alternatives* 325.

40 M.S. Vani, *Role of Panchayat Institutions in Irrigation Management: Law and Policy in Tamilnadu and Karnataka* (Indian Law Institute 1992) 15.

rules, multidimensional in nature, acknowledging the interconnectedness of natural sources—simultaneously address land, crops, water, fisheries, silt, trees, other vegetation, pastures, and use of modern technologies which impact on natural sources.[41]

Duties of restraint and cooperation in the use of tanks include restricting other uses to give priority to drinking water and groundwater recharge; extending or restricting cultivated area, or changing crops or cropping patterns collectively as per water availability in an equitable manner; and restricting tree cutting.[42] Comprehensive sets of rules are formulated collectively by the tank-related informal institutions for ensuring equity in access to water as well as a range of other resources from common lands and for mobilizing cash and labour contributions for maintenance of common properties.[43] Central to local tank management is the spiritual value ascribed to tanks which are considered sacred. Tanks are the focal point of many collective religious, spiritual, and cultural activities, with a symbiotic relationship with temples. Tanks are an integral part of the local human and natural ecosystem, representing, in practice, a combination of environmental, economic, spiritual, and ethical values, a far cry from the government's perception of them as 'minor irrigation sources'.

17.3 Individual and Community Property Rights and Obligations Under Environmental Laws

It is officially stated by the government that 'environmental laws' in India have been 'influenced and shaped' by international law, particularly after the Stockholm Conference, 1972. As such, the extension of the Western anthropocentric approach to the environment in India was inevitable.

The question of whether the environment can be owned as property arises in the Environment (Protection) Act, 1986, whose definition of the environment includes property. This term is undefined in the Act, and it remains unclear whether it refers to 'natural' goods or man-made 'things'. However, the inclusion of the term property in the definition of the environment reserves the potential for its subjection to human use. In the anthropocentric approach, nature-humankind has regularly been conceptualized

[41] M.S. Vani and Rohit Asthana, 'Customary Rights and their Relation to Modern Tank Management in Tamilnadu' (Development Centre for Alternative Policies 2004) part II.

[42] A Gurunathan and CR Shanmugham, 'Customary Rights and their Relevance in Modern Tank Management: Select Cases in Tamil Nadu' in Philippe Cullet and others (eds), *Water Governance in Motion—Towards Socially and Environmentally Sustainable Water Laws* (CUP 2010) 129.

[43] ibid.

'as a relation between the owner and the owned',[44] a perception that differs vastly from the Indic conception of the human-nature relationship.

Though the term 'environment' as defined by the Environment (Protection) Act includes various natural resources, humans, and the inter-relationship between them, environmental laws address only the first two components. Addressing the 'inter-relationship' would require an integrated legal approach to the environment, which is currently absent, evidenced by separate legislations for water, air, land, environment, biodiversity, forest, wildlife, and minerals. Since natural ecosystems are inherently integrated, the use of any one component requires the definition and fulfilment of duties in every ecological context, to exercise property rights in such a manner that they do not adversely impact the range of natural elements and processes and other property holders involved. However, the legal framework not only treats the resources as separable but also rights and duties in a true anthropocentric fashion.

A constitutional amendment of 1976 introduced Articles 48-A and 51A(g) to declare the duties of state and citizen respectively 'to protect and improve the environment'. However, such a provision by itself does not constitute a radical or fundamental change in the prevailing philosophical approach to nature-human relationships. The words 'protect and improve the environment' are more reflective of the anthropocentric method of 'externalizing' the environment for human beings to act upon. The environmental duty of the state is included in the Directive Principles of State Policy, which are non-justiciable. Thus, the duty is non-mandatory, hence a matter of human choice, again, an anthropocentric perspective. Provisions for the duties of citizens are included in Part IVA of the Constitution, conferring on them the value of 'principles', requiring legislative action for actualization, which the state has the liberty to undertake, or not, by reason of the 'non-justiciability' of Part IV. Constitutional provisions till 1976 reflected the instrumental value of natural resources, as evidenced by the pattern and wording of legislative lists of Parliament and states, and these remain unchanged.

The insertion of environmental duties in the Constitution was more in response to the obligations under (anthropocentric) international environmental laws than an intention to adopt a different biocentric approach. The Supreme Court of India, in *TN Godavarman Thirumulpad v Union of India*, succinctly described the conflict inherent in the two approaches by opining: 'Environmental justice could be achieved only if we drift away from the principle of anthropocentric to ecocentric. Many of our polluter pays principle, intergenerational equity have their roots in anthropocentric principles. Anthropocentrism is always human interest focused and that nonhuman has only instrumental value to humans'.[45]

All environmental resources, namely land, water, air, biodiversity, wildlife, and forests, are state property either by declaration or assumption. Most of the environmental laws

[44] Markku Oksanen, 'Nature as Property—Environmental Ethics and the Institution of Ownership' (University of Turku 1998).

[45] *TN Godavarman Thirumulpad v Union of India* (2012) 3 SCC 277 and reiterated in *MK Ranjitsinh v Union of India* 2021 SCC OnLine SC 326.

do not provide for 'rights'. The objective of the Water Pollution Act, the Air Pollution Act and the Environment (Protection) Act is pollution control through regulatory measures rather than environmental governance. In the interest of forest conservation, the Forest Conservation Act, 1980 (FCA) increased the central government's powers over forest resources, by restricting state governments' power to de-reserve a forest and use forest land for non-forestry purposes without the prior approval of the centre. The provisions of the FCA extend to all areas recorded as forest in government records and the areas which may be defined as forest as per its 'dictionary meaning', irrespective of ownership. The latter provision has provided a means for the government to take over non-forest commons and private lands of forest-dwelling communities, who thereafter are treated as 'encroachers'.[46]

India's first environmental law, the Wild Life Protection Act, 1972 (WLPA), introduced an exclusionary model of wildlife management, similar to the Indian Forest Act, 1927 (IFA), in the form of protected areas and wildlife sanctuaries[47] for the purpose of protection of wildlife for ensuring the 'ecological and environmental security of the country'. Hunting rights of all individuals and communities are banned except for the Scheduled Tribes of the Nicobar Islands.[48] With respect to other Scheduled Tribes in forest or notified areas, only personal 'use rights' of specified plants are provided for.[49]

The WLPA provides for the determination and acquisition of rights of any person in any area to be notified as a sanctuary, national park, conservation reserve or tiger reserve, as per the procedures laid down for land acquisition generally. Such designated areas could be established only after the settlement of all claimed or officially determined rights.

Rights in such areas are treated only as individual rights, without reference to any attached community cultures and traditions, which are also lost, for which there is no compensation. However, in the case of 'community reserves',[50] traditional and cultural conservation values and practices are recognized. These are to be protected in addition to fauna and flora—a concession allowed only because these reserves are to be set up based on volunteering by local communities on their own and not government land.

In the case of forests, the property right of the government derives its legitimacy from the colonial politico-legal principle that 'all land not actually under cultivation belonged to the State', which enabled the takeover of all forest areas, commodification of forest products, extinction of community ownership of forests, and industrial and commercial interests overriding environmental concerns.[51] The free access enjoyed by local

[46] Down to Earth, 'Forest Conservation is too Complex an Issue to be Resolved by Executive Fiat' *Down To Earth* (undated) <https://www.downtoearth.org.in/indepth/forest-conservation-is-too-complex-an-issue-to-be-resolved-by-executive-fiat-13145>.

[47] Ministry of Environment, Forest and Climate Change, 'India's National Wildlife Action Plan, 2017–2031' (2017) <https://wii.gov.in/nwap_2017_31>.

[48] Wild Life Protection Act, 1972 s 65.

[49] ibid s17A.

[50] ibid s 36C.

[51] Vani (n 15) 28–30.

communities was suspended. Thereafter, the use of forest was to be based on 'privilege' and not a 'right'. The government reserved the powers to grant, regulate, limit, suspend, transfer, or extinguish such privileges or concessions. Different classes of forests were defined—reserved, protected, and village forests. The third type was not constituted over most of the subcontinent.[52]

Full settlement of rights and community participation in management under the IFA remained unachieved goals for decades, in recognition of which the Forest Policy of 1988 addressed matters such as the sustainable management of forests, rights to forest resources and participatory management under Joint Forest Management. Less than moderate success of this policy led to the Forest Rights Act (FRA) in 2006. The limited rights of 'concessions' or 'privilege' allowed under the colonial era IFA underwent a major change in the FRA.

The FRA is unique as it seeks to establish the historicity of rights that pre-existed the colonial legal mode of settlement of forest rights. The rights recognized under this Act are significant in many ways. Individual and community ownership and use rights are provided for in tandem. Ownership rights are with respect to land, namely the right of residence within forests, with title deeds; to minor forest produce, habitat, and habitation; and community right to intellectual property and traditional knowledge related to biodiversity and cultural diversity. Use rights provided for include the right of cultivation to a composite of natural sources occurring within forests such as *nistar*, fish, other products of water bodies, and grazing of varied patterns involving customary geographical areas rather than official boundaries.

Rights of different occupational and social groups, such as grazing rights of nomadic or pastoralist communities, community tenures of primitive tribal groups and pre-agricultural communities, women's right to joint titling of land rights, and customary rights of tribals in Scheduled areas, are also recognized. Most importantly, community protection, regeneration, and management of community forest resources, namely local governance and environmental decision-making, are recognized as rights. Obligations are imposed on the village community to conserve and protect biodiversity, wildlife, forests, adjoining catchment areas, water sources, and other ecologically sensitive areas, as well as to stop any destructive practices that harm these resources or the tribals' cultural and natural heritage. For the first time since the onset of colonial natural resources law, legislation has created the opportunity for the restoration of the rights-duties dynamic of the community, linking individuals and the collective in customary practices of integrating their lives with natural phenomena as they experience it.

The Biological Diversity Act, 2002, on the other hand, is a single-focused, instrumentalist, anthropocentric tool to regulate trade in bio-resources internationally. The Act deals only with the issue of access to biological resources and knowledge for commercial purposes or research, the potential benefits that may arise, and the sharing thereof among stakeholders. The law is enacted on the presumption of state

52 ibid.

property over such resources, drawing legitimacy from the UN Convention on Biological Diversity, which reaffirms the sovereign rights of the states over their biological resources. Government agencies are vested with monopoly powers of regulation of access and use. The rights of individuals and communities under the Act are only of access to resources without interference. Individuals include 'growers and cultivators' of biodiversity (an anthropocentric view) and traditional healers who have been practising indigenous medicine. Intellectual property rights of individuals and communities derived from traditional practices are not recognized. Biodiversity Management Committees (BMCs) provided for by the Act have been vested with powers only to levy a 'collection' cess whenever the resources are accessed by outside agencies or individuals. There are no other management duties. The right to be 'consulted' when resources or knowledge are accessed does not empower BMCs in any real sense. There are no clearly defined rights of local communities, even in terms of 'benefit sharing'. The proceeds of transactions between accessors and government agencies are deposited in government-managed funds, and their expenditure is left to the discretion of central and state agencies. Local individuals and communities who have been traditional users and conservers of biodiversity resources are seen as 'beneficiaries'. In a landmark judgment in 2018, the Uttarakhand High Court held that 'biological resources are definitely the property of a nation where they are geographically located, but these are also the property, in a manner of speaking, of the indigenous and local communities who have conserved it through centuries'.[53]

17.4 Issues of Concern and Challenges

Land and environmental law in India suffer from the limitations inherent in anthropocentric, reductionist methods. These limitations manifest in sectoral, non-inclusive approaches creating islands of exclusivity; attempts to 'control' the environment through 'command and control' laws; avoiding systemic operation; compartmentalization giving rise to silos, which ignore the interdependencies within living systems, and relying on an incremental approach.[54] The outcome of such a framework is discussed below in terms of the status of the environment, individual property rights in land, CPRs and community rights, and individual and community rights under environmental laws.

[53] *Divya Pharmacy v Union of India* 2018 SCC OnLine Utt 1035.

[54] Pardy (n 4); Caer Smyth, '"Tick the Box and Move on": Compartmentalization and the Treatment of the Environment in Decision-Making Processes' (2021) 48(3) Journal of Law and Society 410.

17.4.1 Private Property Rights in Land—Inequity, Insecurity, and Loss

The reductionist approach in the implementation of land reform laws, which vested property rights in citizens soon after Independence, is starkly apparent. The choice of some land reform laws and property rights over others, their incomplete and uneven implementation, and abrupt changes in policy focus resulted in significant disparities in individual property rights. Laws for the abolition of intermediaries were implemented, but not land ceiling laws and redistribution of land to the landless.[55] All the other land reform laws were not fully implemented,[56] or they varied across states, districts, and various statutes.[57] As a result, according to the Census 2011, 279.3 million citizens (20 per cent) were landless. For Scheduled Castes and Scheduled Tribes, half and one-third of their population are respectively landless. Inequity prevails among the landed as well. Marginal (less than one hectare) and small (one–two hectares) holdings constitute 86.07 per cent of operational holdings but hold only 46.94 per cent of the operated area while large holdings account for only 0.57 per cent of operational holdings but hold 9 per cent of the operated area.[58]

Failure to implement land consolidation laws[59] resulted in uneconomic holdings, recourse to debts from banks and money lenders, and loss of crops due to adverse climate conditions have led to suicides by farmers across the country every year. A total of 296,438 farmers have committed suicide in India since 1995,[60] most of them small and marginal farmers with less than two hectares of land.[61] The current trend in states is the amendment of decades-old land reform laws to allow industries and non-farmers to buy large parcels of agricultural land and put them to non-agricultural uses—primarily industries and real estate.[62] This is an example of a sectoral emphasis which does not consider the impact on other components of the whole.

Land ownership in India is presumptive, determined by sale deeds (namely a record of transfer of property) and not government-guaranteed title deeds, and therefore

[55] RS Deshpande, 'Current Land Policy Issues in India' (2003) 3 Land Reform 155.

[56] ibid.

[57] Planning Commission of India, Implementation of Land Reforms—A Review by the Land Reforms Implementation Committee of the National Development Council (1966).

[58] Ministry of Agriculture and Farmers Welfare, 'Pocketbook of Agricultural Statistics' (2020).

[59] Deshpande (n 55).

[60] P Sainath, 'How States Fudge the Data on Declining Farmer Suicides' (*Rediff*, 1 August 2014) <www.rediff.com/news/column/p-sainath-how-states-fudge-the-data-on-farmer-suicides/20140801.htm>.

[61] Rina Chandran and Suchitra Mohanty, 'Bigger Land Holdings Key to Preventing Farmer Suicides in India, Activists Say' *Reuters* (31 January 2017) <https://www.reuters.com/article/us-india-landrights-farming-idUSKBN15F0T5>.

[62] Flavia Lopes and Mridula Chari, 'In 12 years 11 States Changed Land Ceiling Laws in Favour of Industry Over Farmers' *IndiaSpend* (10 February 2021) <https://www.indiaspend.com/land-rights/in-12-years-11-states-changed-land-ceiling-laws-in-favour-of-industry-over-farmers-724650>.

subject to challenge.[63] Land records at the state level are outdated and unreliable, as they are maintained by three different departments—Registration, Survey, and Revenue—which work in silos.[64] The average age of village/cadastral maps in most states, prepared during the British regime, is more than fifty years.[65] Contradictory, incorrect, or incomplete data impacts the value of land in transactions. Small landowners face the risk of reduced land security or creditworthiness with a decrease in the land value.

The status of property rights of women on land is an indicator of gender equity. At the national level, reliable data on Women's Land Rights are not available as multiple agencies collect data using differing parameters and methods. Some estimates include only agricultural land, others include homestead land, while still others include land leased for cultivation.[66] Despite laws codifying women's right to property, such as the Hindu Succession Act, 1956/2005, the Indian Succession Act, 1925, and the Muslim Personal Law (Shariat) Application Act, 1937, Women's Land Rights are reported to be twelve point nine per cent.[67]

A total loss of property rights in land and environment has occurred because of eminent domain powers of the state. Around five million people have been displaced due to development projects in over fifty years in India, including 1.64 million displaced by dams and 2.55 millions by mines.[68] Of these displaced, eighty per cent are tribals and other rural poor.[69]

17.4.2 Degradation and Disappearance of Community Property Resources

CPRs continue to be termed as 'wastelands'—a legacy of the erstwhile colonial government's anthropocentric and reductionist policy towards land resources. An outcome is that there is no official definition of CPRs or a systematic database on their status and ownership. A primary reason is the absence of a land use policy, which no state in India has enacted, despite the National Land-Use Policy Outline in 1986 and the Draft National Land Utilisation Policy, 2013, circulated by the centre to states. A land use policy could lay down norms and strategies for the integrated use and management of

[63] Prachee Mishra and Roopal Suhag, 'Land Records and Titles in India' (PRS India 2017) <https://prsindia.org/files/policy/policy_analytical_reports/Land%20Records%20and%20Titles%20in%20India.pdf>.

[64] ibid.

[65] Committee on State Agrarian Relations and the Unfinished Task of Land Reforms (Ministry of Rural Development 2009) 164.

[66] Centre for Land Governance, 'India: State of Land Report' (2018) <https://centerforland.org/wp-content/uploads/2019/04/SLR.pdf>.

[67] ibid.

[68] Lok Sabha Secretariat, Displacement and Rehabilitation of People due to Developmental Projects (No 30/RN/Ref./December/2013).

[69] ibid.

land, which would militate against the sectoral use of land currently in practice, which allows the diversion of CPRs for other purposes.

Significant shrinking of commons due to conversion to forests under the regulatory regime of forest law[70] has been at the cost of the rights of local populations in CPRs as well as the ecological cost of losing CPRs to commercial forestry. Between 1987 and 2021, the forest area has increased by 7.2 million hectares at the cost of CPRs.[71] Commons have been diverted for industry or infrastructure projects as well, for which no consolidated figures are available at the national or state level. Loss of rights occurs not only due to the diversion of commons for industry or infrastructure projects but also due to the degradation of commons surrounding polluting industries set up by the government on so-called 'wastelands', resulting in livelihood losses in diverted and surrounding impact areas.[72] There is large scale encroachment into common lands to acquire private rights taking advantage of rent-seeking in revenue departments, or illegally, by villagers and outsiders. The Supreme Court recognized the issue as a systemic problem relating to common lands across the country.[73] Lack of a participatory approach to CPR management in law, combined with the intense competitive control and diversion by the state, has eroded customary community shareholding practices integrated with conservation duties, pushing the commons to 'open access' status.

17.4.3 Denial and Destruction of Property Rights of Individuals and Communities

Sectoral, incremental, incomplete, and selective methods of implementing environmental and natural resources laws have debilitating impacts on the rights to resources. A range of environmental resources lost due to land acquisition for development projects were never replaced. Environmental impact assessments associated with land acquisition are in themselves 'inefficient' and the regulatory framework 'routinely manipulated'.[74] The actual compensatory mechanism for environmental loss under the National Green Tribunal (NGT) Act, 2010 and through the discretionary powers of the NGT are woefully inadequate, except in exceptional cases.[75]

[70] Shankar Gopalakrishnan, 'Undemocratic and Arbitrary: Control, Regulation and Expropriation of India's Forest and Common Lands' (Society for Promotion of Wastelands Development 2012).

[71] Forest Survey of India, 'State of Forest Report 2003' (2003) 16 <https://fsi.nic.in/documents/sfr_2003_hindi.pdf>; Forest Survey of India, 'Indian State of Forest Report 2021' (2021) <https://fsi.nic.in/forest-report-2021-details>.

[72] Gopalakrishnan (n 70).

[73] *Jagpal Singh v State of Punjab* (2011) 11 SCC 396.

[74] Centre for Science and Environment, 'Environment Impact Assessment' (undated) <www.cseindia.org/environment-impact-assessment-308>.

[75] Raghuveer Nath and Armin Rosencranz, 'Determination of Environmental Compensation: The Art of Living Case' (2019) 12 *NUJS Law Review* 1.

Under the WLPA, the area covered under Community Reserves is only 0.044 per cent of total geographical area, compared to 5.08 per cent for National Parks and Sanctuaries, and 0.144 per cent for Conservation Reserves.[76] Since the Act does not make any provisions regarding the relative focus to be given to the different designated areas, policy decisions determine the implementation of the Act according to the government's own priorities. Flouting the provisions of the Act to settle rights claims of people in wildlife reserves within two years, the government has 'dawdled indecisively for decades', and the process has been completed only in a handful of reserves.[77] Notifications of reserves have proceeded faster than the settlement of rights, with the government evicting 'encroachers' at will and clamping down on 'biotic pressures'.[78]

A major impediment in the settlement of rights is that forest-dependent communities' traditional rights to land and resources are mostly unrecorded.[79]

Under the FRA, 2.14 million individual rights covering an area of 4.6 million acres, and 100,000 community rights covering an area of 12 million acres have been registered,[80] with a potential of 150 million forest dwellers and 40 million hectares to be covered.[81] At this rate, considering individual rights, it would require seventy-eight years to cover the entire eligible population in this incremental approach. The recognition of individual rights by the state focuses on land rights for agriculture and habitation—which is only one of thirteen rights in the Act. While government data shows that community rights have been registered over a far larger area, a 2010 government report shows that recognition of individual rights has taken precedence over community or group rights, which number seven in the Act but which have been ignored by the implementing authority.[82]

Interdepartmental conflicts result in the denial of rights. Stiff resistance is reported from the Forest Department and wildlife authorities in implementing the FRA in their jurisdictions, resulting in a series of violations of the FRA on the ground.[83] The benefits of the FRA are limited to only specific areas. The rights and procedures defined in the IFA will continue to apply in wastelands taken over by the Forest Department for conversion into forests, where the FRA does not apply. Provisions in the PESA relating to the consent of the *Gram Sabha* to mining leases or diversion of lands are observed more

[76] Wildlife Institute of India, National Wildlife Database (2020).

[77] MD Madhusudan, 'Of Rights and Wrongs: Wildlife Conservation and the Tribal Bill' (2005) 40(47) *Economic and Political Weekly* 4893.

[78] ibid.

[79] Sarbani Sarkar, 'Settling Rights' (2000) 492 Seminar <https://www.india-seminar.com/2000/492/492%20s.%20sarkar.htm>.

[80] Forest Rights Act—Performance Dashboard <https://dashboard.tribal.gov.in/>.

[81] Rights and Resources Initiative, Vasundhara, and Natural Resources Management Consultants, 'Potential for Recognising Community Forest Resource Rights under India's Forest Rights Act' (Rights and Resources Initiative, Vasundhara, and Natural Resources Management Consultants 2015).

[82] Manthan—Report of the National Committee on Forest Rights Act (Government of India 2010)208.

[83] ibid 210.

in breach, due to which there is extensive illegal mining in these areas, with no state action against them.[84]

In contrast to such legislative and executive lacunae and lethargy, the judiciary has—upheld the rights of primitive tribal groups and dalit populations in the Niyamgiri Hills of Orissa to make decisions over their land, forests, resources, cultures and customs, including religion and spirituality, under the provisions of the Constitution, PESA and the FRA.[85] The Supreme Court of India decreed that the *Gram Sabha* has the authority to determine whether the proposed mining project would affect individual or community rights, including cultural and religious rights, under the FRA and that this is a precondition before the mining process in Niyamgiri Hills can proceed. By recognizing the tribal people's constitutional right to enjoy 'a distinctive spiritual relationship with the lands and resources in their use and occupation' under Articles 25 and 26 of the Constitution, the Supreme Court, for the first time, infused forest law with an ecocentric perspective by integrating religion, spirituality, and economy.

A policy initiative of the Government of India, which could have paved the way for integrated natural resource or 'environmental' policy and law eventually, is the National Watershed Development Program, started in 1980–81. However, it also suffers from the limitations of a sectoral, incremental, and divisive approach, being implemented in selected districts/locations in the country, in 'project mode', under varied funding programmes, with a focus on water conservation for agriculture in rainfed areas. After four decades, it remains a policy with no legal backing.

Conclusion

A review of property rights of individuals and communities in land and the environment in India yields the understanding that property rights are not merely economic concepts; they are multidimensional, reflecting political, social, ethical, moral, and spiritual values. In India, the philosophical constructs, institutional structures and practices in land and the environment underwent a foundational change under colonial rule. This change may be summarized as the shift from the philosophical approach of biocentrism to anthropocentrism. The institutional structure of community property rights as the fulcrum against which individual rights were balanced, non-interference by the state in local environmental decision-making, and the spiritual-philosophical anchor to human-nature interrelationships that upheld the integrity of all natural systems were the hallmarks of the earlier biocentric way of life, legacies of which are found in the customary legal domain on natural resources in India. The predominance and singularity of the 'economic' or utilitarian value of natural elements, consolidation of state power

[84] Ravi Rebbapragada, 'The Importance of the Samata Judgment: A Weapon of the Weak and the Marginalised' (2017) 36(3) *Common Cause* 15.

[85] *Orissa Mining Corpn Ltd v Ministry of Environment & Forests* (2013) 6 SCC 476.

over all resources, obliteration of community property rights, individual property rights dependent on state largesse, and a reductionist, divisive approach in natural resources governance—in short, the anthropocentric approach and method established through colonial rule, and retained after Independence, characterizes the legal framework in India on land and the environment.

Empirical evidence points to an alarming deterioration in environmental conditions and deplorable status of property rights on land of individuals and communities in India, particularly of socially and economically depressed groups, which threatens citizens 'right to life' guaranteed by the Constitution, despite decades and centuries of legal regulation and management. The evidence demonstrates the need for a radical transformation to a duty-based system of governance, with property tenure that would uphold the integrity of natural ecosystems through local environmental decision-making while fulfilling the economic needs of citizens equitably. There is a pressing need for an integrated natural resource or environmental perspective in legal research and education. Far greater attention is also required to the non-formal or customary legal, scientific, and cultural knowledge repository with respect to the natural world. Legal research on this subject in India is scanty, while it is significant in its absence in legal education.

Suggestions for Further Reading

Maarten Bavinck and Amalendu Jyotishi (eds), *Conflict, Negotiations and Natural Resource Management: A Legal Pluralism Perspective from India* (Routledge 2016).

Madhav Gadgil and Ramachandra Guha, *This Fissured Land—An Ecological History of India* (OUP 1993).

Robert Lingat, *The Classical Law of India* (University of California Press 1973).

Eric Stokes, *The English Utilitarians and India* (OUP 1959).

M.S. Vani, 'Customary Law and Modern Governance of Natural Resources in India—Conflicts, Prospects for Accord and Strategies' in Rajendra Pradhan (ed), *Legal Pluralism and Unofficial Law in Social, Economic and Political Development* (ICNEC Kathmandu 2002) 409.

CHAPTER 18

AGRICULTURE, FOOD SYSTEMS, AND THE ENVIRONMENT

ZAINAB LOKHANDWALA

Abstract

Despite extensive environmental impacts such as soil degradation, land use changes, biodiversity loss, water resource depletion, chemical and toxic release, and pollution, environmental law has remained virtually silent about agriculture and food systems. As a result, environmental law's prescriptive, administrative, and adjudicatory capacities to tackle environmental impacts of agriculture remain underdeveloped. India's agriculture and food systems continue to tread towards greater environmental damage owing to the combination of passive silences and active protections of the law. This chapter shows that since the 1960 Green Revolution, agricultural development in India idealises 'success' based on growth and productivism, technological and input intensity, and the ability to cater to a globalized commodity market. This chapter further explores a blend of interventions within environmental law, agricultural law, and other legal domains, along with a reimagination of agriculture and food systems that may prevent future environmental impacts.

Introduction

Agriculture has dramatically shaped the planet's environment for several millennia. Not only does farming impact the environment and ecological systems, but a 'farm' is itself a specialized ecosystem.[1] Yet, the role of agriculture has largely been framed in terms of providing food security, and this is arguably so for allied spheres such as land, water, soil, seeds, etc. Agriculture causes some environmental harm through its mere practice such as land degradation, habitat and biodiversity loss, depletion of water resources, soil erosion, and the release of toxins and pollution.[2] With the advent of industrialized agriculture in India in the 1960s, and its evolution towards catering to a global commodities market, the style of practising agriculture and its very purpose has undergone several major shifts. Watershed moments such as the 1960 Green Revolution and the 1991 economic liberalization have substantially shaped the trajectory of agriculture in India, which tolerated and/or neglected many types of environmental harm in the name of agricultural productivity.

In India, agriculture is a deep-rooted socio-cultural institution, and consequently, it is highly diverse across the country. Diversities based on region, ecosystems, local environment, and conditions exist. Economic diversities also exist with respect to links between producer-farmers, 'middlemen', and other market actors, consumer demands, economic volatility due to fluctuating farm profits, and differentiated capacities to deal with distresses.[3] Social diversities in the nature of the caste, gender, and religion of the farmers exist. Political diversities also play an important role. Agriculture remains one of the most politically significant sectors in India, despite its overall low-profitability and ever-decreasing contributions to India's economic growth.[4] A majority of the members of Parliament and State Assemblies have farming or agribusiness backgrounds.[5] Elected leaders and political party workers at the local level have a substantial farmer-voter base.[6] Collective political power that different farmer groups exercise determines the manner of distribution of sector allocations, concessions, and subsidies, and are crucial in determining the concentrations of agrochemical and food processing industries, and access to higher selling prices due to greater corporate presence.[7] Yet, one should not let these diversities and complexities conceal some generalized 'hard truths' about agriculture such as its adverse impact on the environment.

An environmental law critique of agriculture is, hence, long overdue, even if it is done at the risk of generalization. Environmental law has developed over the past decades, covering several key areas such as pollution, forests, and biodiversity

[1] Ian Wilkinson, 'The Farm as an Ecosystem' (2017) 18(2–3) *Biodiversity* 92.

[2] A Suresh and others, 'Agricultural Sustainability and Its Trends in India: A Macro-Level Index-Based Empirical Evaluation' (2022) 14 *Sustainability* 2540.

[3] JB Ruhl, 'Farms, Their Environmental Harms, and Environmental Laws' (2000) 27 *Ecology Law Quarterly* 263.

[4] The World Bank, 'Data—Agriculture, Forestry, and Fishing Value Added (% of GDP)', World Bank National Accounts Data (1 March 2021) <https://data.worldbank.org/indicator/NV.AGR.TOTL.ZS>.

[5] Simin Fadaee, 'Politics of Alliance in the Farmers' March to Parliament in India' (2021) 37(1) *International Sociology* 31.

[6] Diego Maiorano and Vani Swarupa Murali. 'The Indian Elections and the Rural Sector' Institute of South Asian Studies Insights, No 533, National University of Singapore (19 January 2019).

[7] Shoumitro Chatterjee and others, 'A Study of the Agricultural Markets of Bihar, Odisha and Punjab. Final Report' (Center for the Advanced Study of India (University of Pennsylvania 2020) 51–53, 110–120.

conservation. Yet, 'agriculture' and 'environment' have evolved as somewhat separate and compartmentalized law-policy fields. A combination of active protections under agricultural law and passive silences under environmental law has left environmental harm to continue unabated, as well as perpetuated the chasm between these fields of study.

The first section of this chapter describes Indian agriculture's productivist orientation, which has created severe environmental impacts. These are caused not only by farms but also by allied sectors such as large-scale irrigation infrastructure, chemical inputs to enhance yields and the hybrid seed industry. The second section explores the active (agricultural) and passive (environmental) laws and regulations that allow and exacerbate environmental harm. These include agricultural input subsidies, lack of adequate regulation of harmful chemicals and hybrid seeds, and an increasingly privatized market architecture that is driven by profitability and not ecological sustainability. The third and final section explores certain recent attempts at 'crossing the chasm'. These are environment-oriented agricultural laws, regulations, and programmes, expanding the focus area of environmental law into the fields of agriculture, and other approaches such as food sovereignty and peasants' rights that have the potential to address the environmental impacts of agriculture through other routes of law and policy.

18.1 Dominant Agricultural Models and Food Systems Shaped by the Green Revolution 'Success' Story

The 1960 Green Revolution is a watershed moment in Indian agricultural history, which pulled India out of an era of dire food shortages and an imminent threat of famine. 'Miracle wheat' was tested and introduced in 1962, followed by high-yielding rice in 1964. Within a few years, India became food secure and an exporter of wheat and rice internationally.[8] Despite the uptake of new seeds and agricultural technology being limited to north-western and western parts of India, the Green Revolution managed to create an enduring skeleton for policymaking in the decades to come.

Post 1960, India's agricultural institutional apparatus aggressively promoted and endorsed rapid agricultural transformation, at first with the aim of achieving national food security and later, following the 1991 economic liberalization, with the aim of increasing economic growth, agricultural infrastructure development and farmers' incomes through increases in yields.[9] The productivist shift in agricultural law and

[8] Govindan Parayil, 'The Green Revolution in India: A Case Study of Technological Change' (1992) 33(4) *Technology and Culture* 737.

[9] Mark Rosegrant and Peter Hazell, Transforming the Rural Asian Economy: The Unfinished Revolution (Asian Development Bank 2000) 10.

policy was coupled with other developments, such as the rise of globalized trade and the consequent commodification of food, a neoliberal wave of development ideals, and the valuation of agricultural success or failure in terms of its contribution to national gross domestic product (GDP). The central government, aided by its newly fashioned agricultural bureaucracy, initiated several demonstrations and awareness-building campaigns via press, radio, and cinema to convince farmers to adopt high-yielding varieties (HYV) seeds and agricultural technology. Within the first ten years, the land area covered by HYVs increased by 10.4 per cent.[10] An increased emphasis on productivism ignored several other parameters of crop diversity, environmental impact in terms of water and soil erosion, and retention of control over traditional knowledge in seeds, plants, and plant genetic resources, etc. A centralized supply of agricultural productivist knowledge via India's agricultural institutional apparatus has had profound effects on the rural, social, and organizational structures, labour relations and the socio-economic situation of small- and medium-scale farmers.[11] In terms of food production, per acre per season food production almost tripled between 1960–90.[12] Farmers could sow two crops within one year instead of one, and the profitability of cereals resulted in more land being deployed for cereals vis-à-vis other crops. This also increased the holdings of buffer stocks, thereby removing the need for food imports and food aid. Self-sufficiency with respect to food staples was achieved, a goal pursued aggressively in the 1960–75 period.[13]

National food security, which remained a core objective prior to 1980, gave way to new core objectives such as increasing agricultural growth and development. For instance, the 2020 Niti Aayog's (Policy Commission of India) Agricultural Vision continues to echo the productivist tone, where it points to low efficiency, sub-optimal fertilizer and chemical use, and problems in technology-diffusion and small landholding as the chief problems that affect agriculture and farmers.[14] It further elaborates the reasons for agriculture's overall under-development as low levels of technology, low quality of inputs, low investments, low availability of credit, and missing links within supply chains. Farmers' and rural poverty alleviation programmes have worked hand in hand with the idea that low productivity *is* unsuccessful agriculture.

Since the turn of the twenty-first century, agricultural profitability has been on a decline, creating an acute 'agrarian distress'. This silent crisis has been attributed to the practices of the Green Revolution, which idealizes high and intensive production 'at all

[10] Government of India, Directorate of Economics and Statistics, 'Area under High Yielding Varieties Programme (HVP) All India 1966-67 and 1968-69' (Ministry of Food and Agriculture 1969) Statements I and II.

[11] Raj Patel, 'The Long Green Revolution' (2013) 40(1) *Journal of Peasant Studies* 1.

[12] Michael Lipton and Richard Longhurst, *New Seeds and Poor People* (Unwin Hyman 1989) 1.

[13] Dana G Dalrymple, 'The Adoption of High-Yielding Grain Varieties in Developing Nations' (1979) 53(4) *Agricultural History* 704.

[14] Niti Aayog, Raising Agricultural Productivity and Making Farming Remunerative for Farmers (2015) <https://www.niti.gov.in/sites/default/files/2019-08/Raising%20Agricultural%20Productivity%20and%20Making%20Farming%20Remunerative%20for%20Farmers.pdf>.

costs'.[15] Agrarian distress has led to a wave of impoverishment and depeasantization. Eighty per cent of all poor in India comprise smallholder farmers, women, pastoralists, landless agricultural labourers, and shepherds; that is, a substantial majority of the poor are involved in agriculture.[16] Further, thousands of young people are opting out of agriculture as a profession. The average age of a farmer in India is fifty-one years.[17] Surveys analysing rural youth's aspirations for what they wanted to become in the future show that merely 1.2 per cent wished to join agriculture.[18] Agricultural labourers who are usually landless themselves filled this youth vacuum and they are employed under precarious conditions. Long-term decisions regarding environmental protection and sustainable use of resources cannot be taken by this kind of labour or absentee landlords who only care about farm profits in production terms. A study showed that between 2000 and 2010 the number of cultivators declined by 10 per cent (14 per cent for women farmers), while the number of agricultural labourers rose by 31 per cent in the same period.[19] Further, 76 per cent of farmers surveyed did not wish to remain in agriculture.[20] Since the advent of the Green Revolution in 1960, the number of farmers has reduced by a staggering 52 per cent, while landless female agricultural labourers increased by 47 per cent.[21] It is thus unfortunate that high production and profitability continue to remain the unit of measurement of success, which has not only caused severe environmental impacts but also disenfranchised several rural workers.[22]

18.2 Active Protections and Passive Silences that Allow Environmental Impacts

The body of agricultural law, regulations, and policies covering different sub-sectors in different states makes up a complex subject area. As stated above, most of these are

[15] Dan Banik, 'Human Rights for Human Development: The Rhetoric and the Reality' (2012) 30(1) *Nordic Journal of Human Rights* 4, 17.

[16] MS Swaminathan, '50 Years of Green Revolution: An Anthology of Research Papers' (World Scientific 2017) 33–36.

[17] Centre for the Study of Developing Societies, 'State of Indian Farmers: A Report' (CSDS 2014).

[18] Richard Mahapatra, 'Farmers Ageing, New Generation Disinterested: Who Will Grow our Food?' *Down to Earth* (24 July 2019) <www.downtoearth.org.in/blog/agriculture/farmers-ageing-new-generation-disinterested-who-will-grow-our-food—65800>.

[19] Nitin Gupta, 'Decline of Cultivators and Growth of Agricultural Labourers in India from 2001 to 2011' (2016) 12(2) *International Journal of Rural Management* 179.

[20] ibid.

[21] Sudha Pai, 'Class, Gender and Agrarian Change: An Analysis of the Status of Female Agricultural Labour in India' (1987) 15(6) *Social Scientist* 16.

[22] Arthur Goldsmith, 'Policy Dialogue, Conditionality and Agricultural Development: Implications of India's Green Revolution' (1988) 22(2) *The Journal of Developing Areas* 189.

focused on perpetuating a productivist drive, either ignoring environmental concerns or, in some cases, directly promoting negative environmental effects. Agriculture is a state subject under the Constitution of India, 1950,[23] yet agriculture is of national significance. The central government through its Ministry of Agriculture and Farmers' Welfare develops and provides finance for agricultural policies, schemes, and programmes. While the states implement these programmes and adopt state-specific legislations, the centre controls significant spheres, such as pricing, procurement and storage of grain, farmer cooperatives, and producer companies, foreign direct investment in chemical industries, transport trucks, agricultural technologies, etc., and seed-related research and diffusion of 'improved' seeds. It is impossible to analyze all these law-policy fields at the central and state levels, and therefore, only some prominent fields, such as water, chemical inputs, soil, land, and seeds, are analyzed here.

The most dominant varieties of crops, in terms of cultivation area, government procurement and profitability, are water-intensive. Many were introduced by the Green Revolution, such as HYV rice and wheat, and agricultural research since then has incentivized farmers to grow these crops rather than traditional cereals such as millet and sorghum. Rice and wheat require an extensive irrigation infrastructure, and this has resulted in severe water stress in many parts of India.[24] Approximately 91 per cent of all freshwater in the country is used in the agricultural sector.[25] India has the largest land area under irrigation (48 per cent) in the world, and the highest quantum of subsidies related to water. This includes subsidised pricing of water, of equipment used to extract groundwater and divert rivers or canal water, and of electricity used for irrigation.[26]

Water subsidies (including electricity) usually benefit landed farmers that are connected to the irrigation network or can afford the extraction technology.[27] India's Socio-Economic Caste Census data indicates that 56 per cent of rural homes have no land,[28] and the median Indian farmer is a labourer and not a landowner.[29] Further, most small and marginal landowning farmers are dependent on rainfall, while the landless are not the usual beneficiaries of these subsidies.[30] Furthermore, large-scale irrigation infrastructures such as dams, water distribution canals, and technologies that shift

[23] The Constitution of India, 1950, Entry 14, List II.

[24] S Subramanian and AV Manjunatha, 'Demystifying the Energy-Water-Soil-Food Nexus in Indian Agriculture' (2014) 20 *Ecology, Environment and Conservation* S303.

[25] Yoshihide Wada, LPH van Beek, and Marc Bierkens, 'Nonsustainable Groundwater Sustaining Irrigation: A Global Assessment' (2012) 48(6) *Water Resources Research* doi:10.1029/2011WR010562.

[26] Reena Badiani and Katrina Jessoe, 'The Impact of Electricity Subsidies on Groundwater Extraction and Agricultural Production' (2013) University of California at Davis Working Paper.

[27] Ramesh Chand, 'Doubling the Farmers' Income by 2022' (2017) Niti Ayog Working Paper No 1/2017.

[28] Ministry of Rural Affairs, 'SECC 2011– Highlights' <https://secc.govin/>.

[29] Rahul Tongia, 'India's Biggest Challenge: The Future of Farming' *The India Forum* (30 September 2019) <https://www.theindiaforum.in/article/india-s-biggest-challenge-future-farming>.

[30] G Ravindra Chary and others, 'Climate Resilient Rainfed Agriculture: Experiences from India' in Xavier Poshiwa and Ravindra Chary (eds), *Climate Change Adaptations in Dryland Agriculture in Semi-Arid Areas* (Springer 2022) 3.

the flow of rivers have massive environmental impacts.[31] For example, the gargantuan Sardar Sarovar Dam in the State of Gujarat was justified on the basis of food security and providing drinking water; yet, its chief beneficiaries are large-scale commercial farmers in North Gujarat that grow water-intensive cash crops.[32]

Pesticides, insecticides, weedicides, and chemical fertilizers are used in large quantities to maximize production. Since the 1960s, the use of fertilizers in Indian agriculture has increased at an average 8.1 per cent compound growth rate every year.[33] With the lessening of available manual labour and the consequent rising costs of labour, chemicals have been increasingly deployed to remove weeds and herbs, an activity previously carried out manually. Further, the high use of chemicals directly corresponds to the high production of cash crops; that is, such inputs are most used in the states of Punjab, Haryana, and Maharashtra.

The Insecticides Act, 1968 and the Insecticides Rules, 1971 regulate the use of insecticides and pesticides. They set up the Central Insecticides Board, which is empowered to regulate the use, manufacture, distribution, sale, and transport of insecticides. The rampant use of Endosulfan is an exemplary case study of the failures of this Act in preventing harmful health and environmental impacts.[34] Astonishing levels of toxic residues in the soil, water and within humans have been reported in many parts of India.[35] The marketing of Endosulfan, as is the case with many other chemicals, is allowed by the Central Insecticides Board after sufficient testing is done and its data is submitted by the manufacturing entity (usually domestic companies such as AMICO or Indian subsidiaries of larger multinational corporations such as Syngenta AG or Bayer Corp). These companies have the option of testing and collecting data in either government laboratories or in government-approved private commercial laboratories.[36] Most applicant companies prefer private labs, as the desired results can be generated more easily.[37] Safe use levels as advertised by the companies themselves are too high to begin with, coupled with the problem of high levels of use by farmers themselves owing to subsidized prices and little training and awareness.[38] In 2011, following the tragedy of Endosulfan poisoning in Kasargod, Kerala, the Supreme Court of India issued an

31 Philippe Cullet, The Sardar Sarovar Dam Project: Selected Documents (Routledge 2007)2–3.

32 ibid 14–19.

33 Research and Markets, 'Indian Pesticides Market: Industry Trends, Share, Size, Growth, Opportunity and Forecast, 2021–2026' IMARC Report (April 2021) i–v.

34 Centre for Science and Environment, 'Pesticide Regulations' (21 July 2012) <https://www.cseindia.org/pesticide-regulations-1031>.

35 Government of Kerala, 'Health Hazards of Aerial Spraying of Endosulphan in Kasaragod District, Kerala' –Report of the Expert Committee on Endosulphan Health Hazards (August 2003) <http://www.indiaenvironmentportal.org.in/files/KeralaGovt_FinalReport.pdf>.

36 Indira Devi, 'Pesticides in Agriculture—A Boon or a Curse? A Case Study of Kerala' (2010) 45(26–27) *Economic and Political Weekly* 199, 203.

37 Special Correspondent, 'Endosulfan Conspiracy' *Down to Earth* (15 July 2003) < www.downtoearth.org.in/coverage/endosulfan-conspiracy-38732>.

38 Chandra Bhushan, Avimuktesh Bhardwaj, and Savvy Soumya Misra, *State of Pesticide Regulations in India* (Centre for Science and Environment 2013) 3.

order banning its use.[39] Since then the government has been phasing out its use in the country.[40]

With respect to pesticides, the Pesticide Management Bill, 2017, released by the Ministry of Agriculture and Farmers' Welfare was heavily contested and later withdrawn. A later version was released in 2020, which sought to replace the Insecticides Act if passed. The Bill sets up a stricter and wider regulatory framework with the Central Pesticides Board under the Insecticides Act exercising the power to formulate standards and best practices for manufacturers, laboratories, and pest control. Typical of any delegated legislation, the success or failure of this Bill will depend on how vigorously its institutional authority carries out its functions, and because it does not change much of its preceding legislation, it is unlikely to change the status quo drastically.[41] The Bill resembles the current Act in most respects, and as such does not combat the 'network of toxicity' within the political economy of agrochemicals—where private actors are allowed a free hand in propagating their technologies.[42] Along with this Bill, a proposed ban on twenty-seven toxic pesticides is under review by a parliamentary expert committee. This is a positive development; however, it has been aggressively resisted by agrochemical companies across India. If implemented, this proposal will be the second ban imposed in a long-term phase-out programme of sixty-six identified chemicals, of which the first eighteen were banned in 2018.[43]

Fertilizers are the other major chemical inputs that farmers use, and similar problems with respect to overuse, active promotion by chemical companies and passive acquiescence by a weak regulatory framework can be seen here, too. Laws regulating fertilizers comprise mainly two sets of rules notified under the Environment (Protection) Act, 1986—the Environmental Protection Standards for Nitrogen Fertiliser Plants, 1989 and the Environmental Protection Standards for Phosphate Fertiliser Plants, 1989. These are technical standards meant for quality control and do not address the core issues of overuse to increase yield or misuse by mixing different fertilizers in the wrong proportions. Furthermore, the lack of adequate regulatory legislation promotes spurious manufacture, processing, and marketing of fertilizers.[44] The regulatory framework around chemical inputs can be described as one promoting their use and conducive to private companies operating in these sectors. This is because the framework, on

[39] *Democratic Youth Federation of India v Union of India and Others* (2011) 15 SCC 530.

[40] Dileep Kumar and C Jayakumar, 'From Precautionary Principle to Nationwide Ban on Endosulfan in India' (2019) 4(2) *Business and Human Rights Journal* 343, 349.

[41] Kavitha Kuruganti, 'Does the Government Really Need a New "Pesticides Management Bill"?' *The Wire* (7 March 2018) <https://thewire.in/agriculture/does-the-government-really-need-a-new-pesticides-management-bill>. Kuruganti's critique is applicable for the 2020 Bill as well.

[42] Aniket Aga, 'Draft Pesticide Management Bill is Out of Sync with the Agrarian Political Economy' (2018) 53 (18) *Economic and Political Weekly-Engage*.

[43] Prabhudatta Mishra, 'Decision on Banning 27 Pesticides by Agriculture Ministry Likely this Week' *The Hindu Businessline* (4 April 2022) <www.thehindubusinessline.com/economy/agri-business/decision-on-banning-27-pesticides-by-agriculture-ministry-likely-this-week/article65289983.ece>.

[44] Federation of Indian Chambers of Commerce and Industry, 'Study on Sub-Standard, Spurious/Counterfeit Pesticides in India' Report (2015) 6–7.

the one hand, comprises price subsidies[45] and, on the other, some form of quality control and marketing permits. India's agrarian distress and its underlying ecological distress have continued unabated while chemical inputs have been on the rise. Agricultural regulations, thus, have failed to account for losses due to environmental factors, which are, in turn, caused partly by the overuse of chemicals.

Chemical inputs are one component of a larger technological package available to farmers. The most salient element is seeds, which are improved varieties that are highly responsive to chemical inputs, ensuring a quick maturation period, and less sensitivity to local climatic factors, which ergo produce higher yields. One of the most profound impacts of the increasing uptake of improved seeds is the loss of traditional farm-saved seeds. Agricultural law and policymakers have routinely dubbed traditional self-replicating seed varieties as inferior vis-à-vis the improved or hybrid varieties owing to their low productive value.[46] Some studies with respect to particular plants or in particular regions have shown that in areas that grow 70–90 per cent hybrid varieties, an estimated 95 per cent of traditional varieties have been lost.[47] In northeast India, several varieties of sugarcane have given way to a single hybrid variety.[48] Thousands of varieties of rice, cotton, minor millets, pulses, and other crops are no longer in use.[49] The overall share of private hybrid seeds vis-à-vis open-pollinated traditional seeds is 70–88 per cent in India.[50] Across major crops, hybrids comprise shares between 7–8 per cent in paddy, 60–70 per cent in maize, 90 per cent in jowar, bajra, and some oilseeds, 95 per cent in cotton, and over 80 per cent in vegetables.[51]

The rise of private commercial interests in seeds has gone hand in hand with the rise of intellectual property rights (IPR) protection over seeds. India joined the World Trade Organization in 1995 and acceded to the Agreement on Trade-Related Aspects of Intellectual Property Rights (TRIPS), which required India to provide IPR protection for plant varieties.[52] In 2001, India enacted its *sui generis* legislation, the Protection of

[45] The government previously lowered the market price of inputs, but since 2018, these subsidies have been linked with the direct benefit transfer (DBT) system, wherein subsidy payment to the companies take effect after actual sales to farmers by retailers at a recorded point-of-sale (PoS) machine. Companies have to register themselves on the e-Urvarak platform to claim this subsidy.

[46] C Subramaniam, 'A New Strategy in Agriculture: A Collection of the Speeches by C Subramaniam' (ICAR 1972) 31; Swaminathan (n 16) 33–36.

[47] Sivaraj Natarajan and others, 'Agrobiodiversity in India: Status and Concerns' in Souliha Cambay and Charan Singh (eds), *Sustainable Agriculture for Food Security: Concepts and Approaches* (Springer 2018) 121, 123.

[48] Ashish Kothari, 'Reviving Diversity in India's Agriculture' *Grain* (25 October 1994) <https://grain.org/es/article/entries/514-reviving-diversity-in-india-s-agriculture?print=true>.

[49] Somnath Roy and others, 'Chakhao (Delicious) Rice Landraces of North-east India: Collection, Conservation and Characterization of Genetic Diversity' (2014) 12 *Plant Genetic Resources* 264.

[50] Pramod K Agrawal, 'Seed Industry Regulations in Relation to Seed Industry Development in India' in David Gisselquist and Jitendra Srivastava (eds), *Easing Barriers to Movement of Plant Varieties for Agricultural Development*, World Bank Discussion Paper 367 (World Bank Publications 1997) 105.

[51] IMARC Group, Report: Seed Industry in India: Market Trends, Structure, Growth, Key Players and Forecast, 2022–2027 (2021) <https://www.imarcgroup.com/seed-industry-in-india>.

[52] Agreement on Trade-Related Aspects of Intellectual Property Rights, 15 Apr 1994, Marrakesh Agreement Establishing the World Trade Organization, Annex 1C, 1869 UNTS 299 (1994), art 27(3b)

Plant Varieties and Farmers' Rights Act (PPVFRA) that recognizes plant breeders' rights and farmers' rights. This Act makes no distinction between commercial plant breeders and farmers and accords them equal status to register seed innovations and gain benefit therefrom. It also recognizes farmers' rights to save, use, exchange and sell farm-saved seeds.[53] This is important for a country like India where over 75 per cent of all food is grown using varieties saved by farmers.[54]

The real question, however, is whether the PPVFRA has been effective in promoting the use and conservation of farmers' traditional varieties. First, plant breeder rights can only be granted if the plant variety satisfies the criteria of distinctness, uniformity, and stability.[55] In most cases, farmers' traditional seeds, especially landraces, do not meet these criteria. Landraces are genetically diverse and locally adapted varieties which are unfit for uniform crop production on a large scale.[56] IPR protection over seeds promotes homogeneity and uniformity, as these characteristics are conducive to mass agricultural production.[57] Second, the implementation data of the PPVFRA shows that even though farmers comprise the largest group of applicants (between 45–50 percent across the years and different categories), the proportion of acceptance of their applications (only 7–8 per cent of all applications) is much lower than the proportionate acceptance of other parties such as public/private research organizations or biotech companies.[58] Until 2020, farmers have submitted the highest number of applications but have been issued the lowest number of certificates.[59]

The Seeds Bill, 2004, was drafted as an attempt to regulate private seed developers, which currently fall outside the regulatory parameters of the Seeds Act, 1966. This Bill was not passed, *inter alia*, due to conflicting provisions with farmers' rights under the PPVFRA by mandating all seeds sold, including farmers' varieties, to be registered. The Biotechnology Regulation Bill, 2013 was drafted but not passed due to strong opposition in the same vein, that is, the Bill would jeopardize farmers' interests by ushering in

states: 'Members shall provide for the protection of plant varieties either by patents or by an effective sui generis system or by any combination thereof.'

[53] International Treaty on Plant Genetic Resources for Food and Agriculture, Rome, 3 November 2001, 2400 UNTS 303, art 9.1.

[54] FAO, 'India at A Glance' (n.d.) <https://www.fao.org/india/fao-in-india/india-at-a-glance/en/>.

[55] Stephen A Marglin, 'Farmers, Seedsmen, and Scientists: Systems of Agriculture and Systems of Knowledge' in Frederique Apffel-Marglin and Stephen A Marglin (eds), *Decolonizing Knowledge: From Development to Dialogue* (OUP 1996) 205–206.

[56] Suman Sahai, 'Farmers' Rights in India: The Way it Always Was' *Development and Cooperation* (29 March 2010) <https://www.dandc.eu/en/article/indias-law-plant-variety-protection-and-farmers-rights>.

[57] Deborah Fitzgerald, *Every Farm a Factory: The Industrial Ideal in American Agriculture* (Yale University Press 2003); Pushpa Singh, 'Politics of Knowledge in Development: Explorations in Seed Sovereignty' (2021) 9(1) *Studies in Indian Politics* 105.

[58] PPVFR Authority, 'List of Registered Certificates Issued' in *Annual Report (2020–21)*, updated 28 February 2020 <http://www.plantauthority.gov.in>. See also sections titled 'Annual Reports' and 'Application Details'.

[59] ibid. For analysis of data until 2014, see Rajshree Chandra, 'Farmers' Rights in India: Globally Sui Generis' (2016) 6 *South Asia Chronicle* 119, 129–131.

biotechnological advances in agriculture. Most recently, the Seeds Bill, 2019 has received similar opposition as its predecessors on the issue of restricting farmers' rights.[60]

Today the development and diffusion of seeds in India is chiefly controlled by public bodies such as the Indian Council of Agricultural Research (ICAR), thirty-eight agricultural research universities across different states, 415 Farm Science Centres (KVKs) to demonstrate and distribute free 'improved' seeds, and central and state seed corporations (*Beej Nigams*) that develop, check, mark, certify, and distribute seeds, and a highly competitive and profitable private seed industry comprising over 850 companies in the formal sector as of 2017.[61] In the informal space, a plethora of farmers' associations, local companies, and seed systems of farm-saved, selected, and exchanged seeds are involved in seed production and supply, and some of these entities and systems function with governmental financial support. The growth of the private sector has changed the landscape in which seeds are opted for and the direction of research and development in seeds.

Environmental law has remained disengaged with the abovementioned environmental impacts of agriculture. The silofication of agricultural and environmental law is manifest, for instance, in the environmental impact assessment (EIA) law, namely the EIA Notification, 2006, which is highly limited in terms of the activities and impacts it covers. Strategic impact assessments of agriculture at a sectoral level[62] that could include EIA for particular crops, particular regions (perhaps starting with water-scarce or severely degraded lands), or particularly large agribusinesses remains absent. This assessment could provide a clearer picture of the impacts and allow the EIA departmental bureaucracy to scrutinize agriculture. This may be wishful thinking, considering that the Draft EIA Notification 2020[63] has a much-limited mandate compared to the 2006 Notification, and it consequently reduces the powers of the EIA Authority. The Pollution Control Boards (PCB) at the state and central levels routinely deal with air and water pollution issues caused by agriculture. Yet, aside from the censure of stubble burning in agricultural lands,[64] little has been done to curb environmental impacts caused by farming itself. The National Green Tribunal (NGT) is an important judicial institution that applies and interprets environmental law. Case analysis shows that albeit a wide range of matters has been argued before the Tribunal, they primarily

[60] Vandana Shiva, 'The Seed Bill 2019 is a Threat to India's Seed Sovereignty and Farmer's Rights' *Jivad* (4 November 2019) <https://seedfreedom.info/the-seed-bill-2019-is-a-threat-to-indias-seed-sovereignty-and-farmers-rights/>.

[61] Pepijn Schreinemachers and others, 'The Contribution of International Vegetable Breeding to Private Seed Companies in India' (2017) 64 *Genetic Resources and Crop Evolution* 1037, 1038–1039.

[62] Urmila Jha-Thakur and Asha Rajvanshi, 'Strategic Environmental Assessment in India: Trends and Prospects' in Thomas Fischer and Ainhoa González (eds), *Handbook on Strategic Environmental Assessment* (Edward Elgar 2021) 388.

[63] Stellina Jolly and Siddharth Singh, 'Environmental Impact Assessment Draft Notification 2020, India: A Critique' (2021) 5 *Chinese Journal of Environmental Law* 11.

[64] S Bhuvaneshwari, Hiroshan Hettiarachchi, and Jay Meegoda, 'Crop Residue Burning in India: Policy Challenges and Potential Solutions' (2019) 16(5) *International Journal of Environmental Research and Public Health* 832, 836.

focus on the activities of some industries, scrutiny of clearances by the Ministry of Environment, Forest and Climate Change, illegal land conversions, and construction of illegal structures on protected areas.[65] The NGT's jurisdiction does not prevent agricultural matters to be raised; yet a conceptual separation between agriculture and environment has apparently prevented agro-environmental impacts from being considered by the NGT.

Environmental law's most significant engagement with agriculture has been in the domains of wildlife and habitat protection and forest conservation. Enclosures created under the Indian Forests Act, 1927, the Forest (Conservation) Act, 1980, and the Wild Life (Protection) Act, 1972, have been used to disallow and displace tribal, forest-dwelling and other rural communities that engage in small-to-marginal farming in protected or peripheral areas. A well-rehearsed narrative against shifting or *jhum* cultivation, clearing of forest patches for agriculture, and using 'polluting' methods of farming such as burning of timber and wastes and overusing forest streams has been heard from India's forest administrators.[66] Yet, this needs to be put in perspective given environmental law's silence on the impacts of industrialized large-scale agriculture, which are incomparable to tribal and other small-scale farming practices.

This section has illustrated some examples of 'active protections' such as water and electricity subsidies that not only condone but, to a certain extent, encourage overuse of natural resources, or IPR protection of seeds that are improved or hybrid varieties, rather than traditional landraces; and 'passive silences' such as the complete absence of environmental impacts in agriculture within the environmental legal framework. On the one hand, the development and evolution of agricultural law and policy have been non-linear and ambivalent. It has rolled out laws and programmes for farmers' welfare and enhanced farming; yet these are entrenched within its own productivist outlook and in a political economy of several private players that stand to benefit from a perpetuation of productivism. A complex web of regulatory laws, commodity and income support programmes, government purchases, subsidies, and research and development focus have heavily influenced agriculture's environmental record. On the other hand, environmental law has remained disconnected from the agricultural sector and, arguably, its sub-sectors, too. The section below discusses the attempts made to reduce the environmental impacts of agriculture.

[65] Geetanjali Nain Gill, 'Environmental Justice in India: The National Green Tribunal and Expert Members' (2015) 5(1) *Transnational Environmental Law* 1.

[66] Lara Domínguez and Colin Luoma, 'Decolonising Conservation Policy: How Colonial Land and Conservation Ideologies Persist and Perpetuate Indigenous Injustices at the Expense of the Environment' (2020) 9(3) *Land* 65.

18.3 Efforts in Promoting Ecologically Sustainable Agriculture—Towards Non-Productivist Focused Food Systems

Attempts towards reducing the environmental impacts of agriculture reflect a rising environmental consciousness; however, the author reads them as the few exceptions in an overarching legal framework that has licensed environmental harms to continue unabated. Furthermore, these measures have largely been spearheaded by the agricultural administrative machinery in India rather than the environmental legal framework and machinery. As a result, environmental law's prescriptive, administrative, and adjudicatory outreach into the environmental impacts of agriculture remains stunted. Environmental law must, therefore, make meaningful inroads into the agricultural field to address environmental impacts. Years of productivity-focused agricultural policy-making have characterized what successful agriculture should look like.[67] Some government programmes and initiatives have tried to infuse environmental considerations within the existing model, which may lead to more ambitious measures in the future.

The central government's National Mission for Sustainable Agriculture (NMSA) is one such instance. It is one of the eight missions under India's National Action Plan for Climate Change (NAPCC) launched in 2008 to combat the adverse impacts of climate change.[68] The NMSA aims for the conservation of natural resources and development of rainfed agriculture while coping with the growing demands of food for the future. The NMSA promotes many objectives, including 'improved crop seeds', 'water use efficiency', 'pest management', 'credit support', 'markets', and 'livelihood diversification'. The NMSA has four main sub-missions: Soil Health Management, Rainfed Area Development, Sub-Mission on Agro-Forestry, and Climate Change and Sustainable Agriculture: Monitoring, Modelling and Networking.

Climate change has provided a much-needed link between environmental considerations and agriculture. Over the last five years, the NMSA architecture consolidated other schemes and programmes, including farmer welfare schemes to better streamline funding and implementation. Programmes under the NMSA have received a stagnant budgetary allocation during this time; however, only a little over half has been spent while the rest is diverted back towards the government in its 'revised budget'.[69] One reason for under-utilization is that only a quarter of these allocations were

[67] Raju J Das, 'Geographical Unevenness of India's Green Revolution' (1999) 29(2) *Journal of Contemporary Asia* 167.

[68] Along with other Missions such as National Solar Mission, National Water Mission, Mission on Sustainable Habitat etc.

[69] Niti Aayog, Evaluation of Centrally Sponsored Schemes in Agriculture, Animal Husbandry and Fisheries Sector—Volume 2: Agriculture, Report 2020/UCSS01/2 (2020) 6–10.

released to states during the 2021–22 fiscal year, while many states did not receive any funds.[70] Some programmes lack clarity and therefore are difficult to implement, such as the Rainfed Area Development Programme which lacks focus in terms of geographical areas and provides a generalized template for increasing productivity in rainfed areas as a one-size-fits-all solution for exploiting these areas.

Alongside the NMSA institutional framework, programmes such as 'Zero Budget Natural Farming' (ZBNF) have been propagated as a solution for rising costs of chemical inputs, increasing farmer indebtedness and agrarian distress. Zero budget or natural farming was first proposed by agriculturalist and activist, Subhash Palekar, who in the 1990s developed, tested, and propagated this concept to oppose the techno-chemical methods of farming introduced by the Green Revolution.[71] Palekar was closely associated with several peasant mobilizations in South India, and was a member of the Karnataka Rajya Raitha Sangha (KRRS), which, in turn, functions as the Indian chapter of the global farmers' movement—La Via Campesina.

ICAR has been testing the concept and techniques of ZBNF in basmati rice and wheat in some parts of India since 2017.[72] These studies and others have shown some positive impacts on soil health, including organic carbon and fertility; however, many productivity and economic impacts remain unproven. The National Academy of Agricultural Sciences, a research institute of leading agriculture scientists in India, have labelled this an 'unproven technology' that requires more data.[73] Scientific scepticism over ZBNF has largely centred around its (in)effectiveness in producing high yields.[74] Amidst such productivist entrenchment, even the government's own commitment towards ZBNF is questionable.[75] Aside from public campaigns, awareness programmes, training workshops, and lectures, hard funding and resource-allocation for switching to ZBNF has been minimal. The central government allocated a lump sum of only INR 325 crores to another umbrella scheme—*Paramparagat Krishi Vikas Yojana* (PKVY), of which ZBNF is one component among other programmes on soil health management under the NMSA. Out of this, INR 120 crores have been allocated to the Department of Agricultural Research and Education to carry out research on ZBNF.

Organic farming is another term that has caught the imagination of policymakers, farmers, and urban consumers connected to natural farming but is much broader.

[70] States such as Jharkhand, Telangana, Andhra Pradesh, Karnataka, Gujarat received no funds.

[71] Saikat Biswas, 'Zero Budget Natural Farming in India: Aiming Back to the Basics' (2020) 10(9) *International Journal of Environment and Climate Change* 38.

[72] Tests were conducted in Modipuram (Uttar Pradesh), Ludhiana (Punjab), Pantnagar (Uttarakhand), and Kurukshetra (Haryana), while other state-level agencies and NGOs have conducted their own field tests on ZBNF in the past five years.

[73] Harish Damodaran and Parthasarathi Biswas, 'Top Agricultural Scientists Body Rejects Zero Budget Natural Farming' *The Indian Express* (10 September 2019) <https://indianexpress.com/article/india/zero-budget-natural-farming-government-scientists-question-5981236/>.

[74] Sarah Duddigan and others, 'Impact of Zero Budget Natural Farming on Crop Yields in Andhra Pradesh, SE India' (2022) 14(3) *Sustainability* 1689.

[75] Jo Smith and others, 'Potential Yield Challenges to Scale-Up of Zero Budget Natural Farming' (2020) 3 *Nature Sustainability* 247.

Organic farming focuses more on using organic inputs rather than chemical inputs, but these may or may not reduce a farmer's input costs, as ZBNF intends to primarily do. The National Centre for Organic and Natural Farming has operated since 2004 as a nodal agency for the promotion of organic farming. Many regional centres have also been set up to conduct field research on organic farming. The central government has rolled out certain programmes, such as PKVY, that promote cluster-based organic farming, with governmental assistance in training, procurement of inputs, certification, and marketing. The Mission Organic Value Chain Development for the North-Eastern Region promotes organic farming of high-value 'niche' crops with a focus on exporting them and increasing farmer incomes. The Capital Investment Subsidy Scheme under the Soil Health Management Scheme aims to reinvigorate soil health by setting up fruit and vegetable market waste and agro-waste compost production units. Several similar programmes that provide financial assistance, organizational support, or procurement of organic produce for the Targeted Public Distribution System (TPDS) have been initiated on the demand and supply sides of organic farming. State-level initiatives, such as Sikkim becoming a fully organic state in 2016 and Andhra Pradesh pledging to be fully organic by 2024 are also significant.[76]

The measures described above represent the first step in ushering in agroecological approaches to farming. 'Agroecology' is the use of ecological concepts and methods for the long-term enhancement and management of soil fertility and agriculture productivity.[77] Aside from adopting 'natural' inputs and methods, this concept stresses the increasing diversity of plants and animals that, in turn, help in nutrient recycling, biomass creation and using natural resource systems in the production process. Agrobiodiversity is essential for securing adequate nutritious food, maintaining an ecological balance, and safeguarding socio-cultural norms surrounding food and agriculture.[78] In this context, any meaningful transition towards agroecology will necessarily require stronger conservation measures of farmers' saved seeds and landraces. The National Bureau of Plant Genetic Resources stores thousands of farmers' varieties and landraces to conserve them for future research and cultivation; the Traditional Knowledge Digital Library in New Delhi contains, *inter alia*, food and agricultural-related knowledge originating from many communities across India; and the ongoing work of Sristi, an organization that identifies and assists farmers to register their seeds under the PPVFRA is one way of making the PPVFRA more accessible to farmers, the same way it is for commercial breeders.[79] Organizations such as the MS Swaminanthan Foundation and many others that have worked both with the government and

[76] Government of Andhra Pradesh and Rythu Sadhikara Samstha, 'Andhra Pradesh 'Zero-Budget' Natural Farming Vision 2024: A Systemwide Transformation' (2013) <http://www.mcrhrdi.gov.in/94fc/week4/shilpa/ZBNF%20-%20COP14%20-%2013Sept2019-1.pdf>.

[77] Nimisha Tripathi and others, 'Agroecology and Sustainability of Agriculture in India: An Overview' (2015) 2 EC *Agriculture* 241.

[78] Lori A Thrupp, 'Linking Agricultural Biodiversity and Food Security: The Valuable Role of Agrobiodiversity for Sustainable Agriculture' (2002) 76(2) *International Affairs* 283.

[79] SRISTI, 'Advocacy and Policy Analysis' <https://www.sristi.org/advocacy-and-policy-analysis/>.

independently have set up many seed-gene-grain banks in several villages.[80] Yet these are islands of success in an ocean of ongoing seed loss.

For a more holistic engagement between the environment and agriculture, agricultural 'success' itself needs to be reframed outside the productivist paradigm. Some Western countries have started moving towards this framing.[81] There is no evidence of the same in India. A framing in terms of agriculture's primal role in satisfying local/regional food systems through ecologically sustainable practices rather than its orientation towards satisfying global commodity markets through long supply chains needs to be acknowledged. If agriculture is viewed through the parameters of crop diversity, environmental impact in terms of water and soil erosion, retention of control over traditional knowledge in seeds, plants and plant genetic resources and incomes of farmers, then the idea of a successful farmer would have to qualify more than the mere production bar.[82]

In this context, the food sovereignty approach may provide some guidance in moving towards such food systems. Food sovereignty is a concept developed by La Via Campesina (LVC) as an alternative to neoliberal agricultural policies. It is the right of peoples to define their own agricultural and food policy and includes prioritizing local agricultural production to feed the people, access of peasants and the landless people to land, water, seeds, and credit, the right of farmers and peasants to produce their own food, the right of people to take part in agricultural policy choices, and the right of countries to reject certain policies and guard against low-priced agricultural imports. In India, several movements and organizations like the KRRS, Alliance for Sustainable and Holistic Agriculture (ASHA) and Navdanya have advocated for food sovereignty at a local subsistence level. Food sovereignty rights have more recently been articulated within the United Nations Declaration on Rights of Peasants, 2018 (UNDROP).[83] UNDROP provides a good entry point to re-conceptualize the role of agriculture and food systems in India, as India has voted in favour of UNDROP, and has its own rich history of peasant and small farmer resistance movements, and a post-colonial legal tradition of using rights as an emancipatory tool for 'new' claims.

[80] MS Swaminathan Research Foundation, 'Promoting Community Seed Grain Banks' <https://mssrf.org/content/promoting-community-seed-grain-gene-banks>.

[81] Geoff Wilson, 'From Productivism to Post-Productivism ... and Back Again? Exploring the (Un) Changed Natural and Mental Landscapes of European Agriculture' (2001) 26(1) *Transactions of the Institute of British Geographers* 77.

[82] Ramesh Chand and Shinoj Parappurathu, 'Temporal and Spatial Variations in Agricultural Growth and its Determinants' (2012) 47(26–27) *Review of Rural Affairs, Economic and Political Weekly Supplement* 55.

[83] UN Declaration on the Rights of Peasants and Other People Working in Rural Areas, 17 December 2018, UN Doc A/RES/73/165.

Conclusion

This chapter has shown how agricultural and environmental law have evolved into separate conceptual categories. The complexities and diversities of agriculture in India make it a difficult subject for environmental impact scrutiny. As a result, several impacts go unnoticed and remain unaddressed. A combination of sanctions within agricultural law and silences within environmental law has abandoned the agricultural sector to market forces. In recent years, there has been a push towards promoting sustainable agriculture; yet several specific programmes remain underfunded, unclear in terms of mandate and limited in coverage. Adaptation to climate change has triggered many such measures. Yet, the role of environmental law has remained minimal. Environmental legislations, rules such as those on environmental impact assessment, and administrative and judicial institutions have not engaged with the question of environmental impacts of agriculture at the sectoral level. These gaps can be addressed by a more vigorous attempt to create linkages between agriculture and ecology, and by adopting new approaches such as food sovereignty and rights of peasants that redefine the role and purpose of agriculture and food systems.

Suggestions for Further Reading

Sejuti Das Gupta, *Class, Politics, and Agrarian Policies in Post-liberalisation India* (CUP 2019).

Alf Gunvald Nilsen and Kenneth Bo Nielsen, 'Social Movements, State Formation and Democracy in India: An Introduction' in Alf Gunvald Nilsen and Kenneth Bo Nielsen (eds), *Social Movements and the State in India: Deepening Democracy?* (Palgrave Macmillan 2016) 1–23.

Raj Patel, 'The Long Green Revolution' (2013) 40(1) *Journal of Peasant Studies* 1.

JB Ruhl, 'Farms, Their Environmental Harms, and Environmental Laws' (2000) 27 *Ecology Law Quarterly* 263.

S Subramanian and AV Manjunatha, 'Demystifying the Energy-Water-Soil-Food Nexus in Indian Agriculture' (2014) 20 *Ecology, Environment and Conservation* S303.

CHAPTER 19

AGRICULTURE AND TECHNOLOGY

JAGJIT KAUR PLAHE AND
WENDELL S.C.L. CORNWALL

Abstract

This chapter critically analyses the techno-capitalist neoliberal policies which India has adopted for the country's agri-food system. The chapter argues that farmers have been caught between two technological approaches to agriculture: the Green Revolution and the Gene Revolution. The authors contend that over time these policies have roped farmers into unsustainable agricultural practices of monoculture, increased their reliance on costly external inputs and heavy irrigation, and plunged them deeper into debt. They have also negatively affected the quality of soils and biodiversity in farms all over the country. The chapter analyses India's WTO-compliant domestic laws and policies which support the Gene Revolution. It uses the case of genetically modified (GM) cotton to investigate the laws and policies which support the Gene Revolution in India since cotton was the first GM crop to be commercialized in the country in 2002.

Introduction

This chapter critically analyses the techno-capitalist policies which India has adopted for the country's agri-food system. It argues that farmers have been caught between two technological approaches to agriculture: the Green Revolution (which the country adopted after independence) and the Gene Revolution, partly to comply with agreements of the World Trade Organization (WTO). The authors contend that over time, India's techno-capitalist policies have roped farmers into unsustainable agricultural practices of monoculture, increased their reliance on chemical inputs and heavy irrigation, and plunged them deeper into debt. They have also negatively affected the quality of soils and biodiversity in farms throughout the country. The chapter critically analyses India's WTO-compliant domestic laws and policies which support the Gene Revolution. Cotton was the first genetically modified (GM) crop to be commercialized in the country in 2002. It, therefore, uses the example of Bt cotton to investigate laws and policies, which support the Gene Revolution in India.

In the 1960s, the Indian government commenced a programme known as the Green Revolution to increase cash crop cultivation in the country. Through this new programme, which ran from 1967 to 1968, the Indian government endeavoured to make a strong and systematic effort to extend the application of science and technology in agriculture in the hope of increasing yields.[1] The Green Revolution was marked by three main features: the introduction of high-yielding varieties (HYVs), intensive use of fertilizers and pesticides, and expansion of irrigation facilities. Cultivation of HYVs led to monocropping and was highly dependent on an array of external inputs, including pesticides, synthetic fertilizers, and irrigation. While food output increased during the first few decades, over time, yields of HYVs began to decline. Genetic engineering of plant species and the application of biotechnology to agriculture, known as the Gene Revolution, was marketed as a technological solution to the problems of environmental degradation and livelihood insecurity that the Green Revolution had created. Contrary to expectations, Bt cotton has further exacerbated the problems of the Green Revolution.[2] Most studies on Bt cotton and the Gene Revolution have focused on the local context affecting farmers.[3] These studies list farmer indebtedness, crop failure, the lack of irrigation, and the rising costs of inputs as the leading causes of the crisis in the region. The existing research, however, does not consider how these problems are linked to the national law and policy context under neoliberalism.

Even though India commenced liberal economic reforms in 1991, national agricultural liberalization policies have, to a large extent, been influenced by India's commitments under the WTO. The establishment of the WTO in 1995 and its Agreement on Agriculture (AoA) institutionalized the process of agricultural liberalization on a global scale by restricting the rights of sovereign states to regulate food

[1] Uday B Mehta, *Agrarian Strategy in India* (Vora and Co 1975).

[2] Asmita Bhardwaj, 'Genetically Modified Cotton: Agrarian Distress and India's Emerging Economy' (DPhil thesis, Cornell University 2010).

[3] Tata Institute of Social Sciences, 'Causes of Farmer Suicides in Maharashtra: An Enquiry' (Final Report Submitted to the Mumbai High Court, 15 March 2005); Planning Commission, 'Report of Fact Finding Team on Vidarbha: Regional Disparities and Rural Distress in Maharashtra with Particular Reference to Vidarbha' (Maharashtra Reports, Government of India 30 May 2006); Amol R Dongre and Pradeep R Deshmukh, 'Farmers' Suicides in the Vidarbha Region of Maharashtra, India: A Qualitative Exploration of their Causes' (2012) 4(1) *Journal of Injury and Violence Research* 2; Guillaume Gruère, Purvi Mehta-Bhatt, and Debdatta Sengupta, 'Bt Cotton and Farmer Suicides in India: Reviewing the Evidence' (IFPRI Discussion Paper, International Food Policy Research Institute 2008).

and agriculture, instead leaving it in the hands of private corporations and international institutions, such as the WTO, that support them.[4] Gonzalez argues that the WTO's AoA systematically favours industrialized countries' agricultural producers at the expense of farmers in developing countries by exacerbating rural poverty and inequality and restricting developing country policy options to promote food security.[5] The AoA imposes 'a one–sided free–trade model on poor countries', while rich countries are legally permitted to continue to heavily subsidize their agricultural producers.[6] It is in this context that India was also obliged under the Agreement on Trade Related Aspects of Intellectual Property Rights (TRIPS) of the WTO to extend intellectual property rights to plants and plant genetic materials. Under TRIPS, India was required to amend its patent regime to allow for the patentability of life forms. India was also obliged to introduce an intellectual property rights regime to protect plant varieties. India amended its patent regime and introduced a *sui generis* (system-tailored) legislation to protect plant varieties, the Protection of Plant Varieties and Farmers Rights Act, 2001. However, even though this was a progressive regime, the government introduced a very conservative Seed Bill in 2004 (revised in 2019), compromising the rights of farmers. The Indian government has also instituted biosafety and biodiversity regulation in line with the international Cartagena Protocol on Biosafety, 2000, and the Convention on Biological Diversity, 1992.

Using a political economy approach, this chapter critically analyses India's laws and regulations under the Gene Revolution. The chapter begins by explaining the shift from the Green Revolution to the Gene Revolution. It then focuses on the political economy of the following domestic policies which support the Gene Revolution: India's biosafety regime, India's biodiversity governance, India's TRIPS-compliant patent regime, the Protection of Plant Varieties and Farmers' Rights Act, 2001, and the Seed Bill, 2019.

19.1 From the Green Revolution to the Gene Revolution

While India invested heavily in the development of hybrid varieties of various crops during the Green Revolution, it received mixed productivity gains. Intensifying the use of chemical inputs decreased soil fertility and affected surrounding vegetation. Before the Green Revolution, Indian farmers adopted mixed cropping, cultivating different varieties of rice, millets, sorghum, barley, wheat, and maize. In fact, the 'production of

[4] Eric Holt Giménez and Annie Shattuck, 'Food Crises, Food Regimes and Food Movements: Rumblings of Reform or Tides of Transformation?' (2011) 38(1) *The Journal of Peasant Studies* 109.

[5] Carmen Gonzalez, 'The Global Food System, Environmental Protection, and Human Rights' (2011) 26 *Natural Resources & Environment* 7.

[6] Shona Hawkes and Jagjit Kaur Plahe, 'Worlds Apart: The WTO's Agreement on Agriculture and the Right to Food in Developing Countries' (2013) 34(1) *International Political Science Review* 21.

rice and millets were higher than the production of wheat, barley, and maize combined all together'.[7] However, with the introduction of hybrid varieties, it is estimated that India has lost more than 100,000 indigenous rice varieties that took many thousands of years to evolve.[8] In the case of cotton, hybrid cotton was initially credited with increasing yields and reducing the land area required for cotton cultivation. However, over time, increased inputs, including fertilizer and pesticide, were needed to produce yields, which raised production costs for cultivators and led to environmental degradation. In the 1990s, cotton consumed almost half of all pesticides used in Indian agriculture, although it only accounted for five per cent of the total cultivated area in India.[9]

Hybrid varieties also became highly susceptible to pest attacks, and pests developed resistance to chemical inputs, disrupting natural ecosystem balances. The susceptibility of hybrid cotton to the American bollworm (*Helicoverpa Armigera*), a moth larva that devours cotton bolls, raised the first questions about the appropriateness of Green Revolution hybrid technologies for India. The Green Revolution was designed for monocropping and not for mixed cropping patterns. In contrast to traditional methods of farming, industrial agriculture under the Green Revolution required specific kinds of seeds and inputs. The requirement was to 'breed crop varieties that exhibit persistent genetic uniformity'; for market-led agriculture, uniformity is always paramount.[10]

The practice of monocropping stripped soils of essential nutrients required for healthy crop yields. Monocropping also made plants more susceptible to diseases and led to reduced yields due to decreased soil fertility. This roped farmers into a dependency on chemical inputs to increase soil nutrients as well as decrease the incidence of pests. With many local varieties disappearing, farmers had no choice but to buy HYV seeds each season. Another major drawback of the Green Revolution was the requirement of large inputs of irrigated water for HYVs, including crops such as wheat, rice, and cotton. In some states, such as Punjab, canal irrigation was introduced or extended to grow extremely water-intensive crops such as rice. Farmers throughout the state also pumped groundwater for cultivation, which rendered Punjab one of the most 'water depleted' regions in the country.[11]

The high production costs of HYVs also led to the widespread indebtedness of farmers, who could not afford the increased and often hidden associated costs of production. Moreover, farmers who were unable to receive loans from formal institutions to pay increasing production costs turned to private moneylenders, who represented less than optimal loan terms and greater safety risks if loans were not repaid. The risk of

[7] Ann Raeboline Lincy Eliazer Nelson, Kavitha Ravichandran, and Usha Antony, 'The Impact of the Green Revolution on Indigenous Crops of India' (2019) 6(8) *Journal of Ethnic Foods* 1.

[8] Special Correspondent, 'From 1,10,000 Varieties of Rice to Only 6,000 Now' *The Hindu* (6 April 2012) <https://bit.ly/3aSJXTa>.

[9] Cotton Corporation of India, 'Indian Cotton: A Profile' (Cotton Corporation of India 2000).

[10] Mohsen Al Attar Ahmed, 'Monocultures of the Law: Legal Sameness in the Restructuring of Global Agriculture' (2006) 11 *The Drake Journal of Agricultural Law* 139, 143–144.

[11] Daisy A John and Giridhara R Babu, 'Lessons from the Aftermaths of Green Revolution on Food System and Health' (2021) 5 *Frontiers in Sustainable Food Systems* 1.

debt was also compounded by the variable yield rates of HYVs. If farmers experienced a bad yield in one season, they had limited options for repaying private moneylenders, as few farmers possessed any extra capital to account for a bad harvest.[12]

Ironically, the problem of increased chemical inputs created by the development of HYVs informed the basis of the Gene Revolution, with promises of reduced pesticide use becoming a major rationalisation for the introduction of GM crops to India, the first being Bt cotton. The Bt cotton plant releases a toxin killing bollworm pests that might otherwise damage the plant, and therefore (according to claims by the technology's creators) produces higher crop yields and reduces pesticide use, decreasing production costs and increasing farmer's profits.[13] The agri-chemical giant Monsanto claimed 'agricultural productivity and the entailing profits would be maximised through controlling crop pests and eliminating pesticide sprays', thus benefitting farmers and the environment.[14] Beginning in 2002, farmers across the country turned to Bt technology in the great hope of solving their agrarian problems.

The rationality behind the introduction of Bt technology in India was 'constructed by a network of technocrats and their corporate partners' in order to create a market in the country.[15] The Indian state, multinational seed corporations, the privatized national seed industry, and certain powerful individuals led a strong and successful pro-biotechnology campaign advocating for the production of genetically modified (GM) crops in India.[16] Biotechnology was framed not only as 'politically neutral' and beneficial but as the 'technological answer' to the problem of declining rural productivity, increasing hunger, and environmental degradation in the country.[17] In line with this frame, the central and state governments have set up various institutions and policies to support biotechnology. These policies and institutions are based on the importance of modern agriculture and technical advancement through the application of scientific knowledge.[18] They do not focus on issues of inequity which arose due to the Green Revolution, nor are they concerned with food justice or environmental sustainability. The problem in India, like elsewhere, has been 'framed as purely a matter of supply; the solution to which is the technological improvement offered by biotechnology'.[19]

In providing a technological solution to feed people, the Gene Revolution was seen as a continuation of the Green Revolution. It is important to note that the Green Revolution for all its problems was sponsored by the public sector, and in India, it was supported by government services and policies such as subsidized seed, fertilizer subsidies, free

[12] Planning Commission (n 3) 52, 54–56.

[13] Monsanto, 'Bolgard II Cotton: Technical Manual' (Monsanto Australia 2011).

[14] Sunita Raina, 'Rationalising Bt Technology: Creating a Biopolitical Space Around Bt Cotton' (2012) 6(2) *History and Sociology of South Asia* 123, 126.

[15] ibid 124.

[16] Bhardwaj (n 2) 114–115.

[17] Sally Brooks, 'Biotechnology and the Politics of Truth: From the Green Revolution to an Evergreen Revolution' (2005) 45(4) *Sociologia Ruralis* 360.

[18] Raina (n 14) 132.

[19] Brooks (n 17)363.

or subsidized electricity and the minimum support price designed to protect agricultural producers from disruptive market forces. The Gene Revolution, however, is led by the private sector and clearly reflects the growing power of corporations in relation to states in the world food system.[20] The state sector in India is fully supporting the Gene Revolution through pro-biotechnology policies and institutions. Given this strong institutional network to support biotechnology, 'experts defined agbiotechnology and economic growth as intrinsically related to each other, thus reinforcing the desirability of Bt technology' in the agricultural sector.[21]

The following section will analyse the intellectual property rights (IPR) regime that supports the Gene Revolution in India, highlighting how India's agricultural technology policies are linked to international agreements.

19.2 Gene Revolution: Domestic Laws and Policies

Even though India commenced liberal economic reforms in 1991, national agricultural liberalization policies have largely been influenced by India's commitments under the WTO. This section focuses on the following domestic laws and policies: the biosafety regime, the WTO-compliant patent regime, Plant Variety Protection in India, and the Seeds Bill.

19.2.1 India's Biosafety Regime

Biosafety refers to 'the prevention of potential risks [to human, animal, and plants] from products derived from genetic engineering ... [including] the safe transfer, handling and use of GMOs'.[22] The rapid uptake of Bt cotton throughout India has raised some crucial questions about that country's biosafety regulations. Genetically Modified Organisms (GMOs) are regulated under the Environment (Protection) Act, 1986, which falls under the purview of the Ministry of Environment, Forests and Climate Change. In 1986, the National Biotechnology Board of India was upgraded to the Department of Biotechnology (DBT). In time, the DBT began to play a vital coordinating role in providing legitimacy to transgenic agriculture by creating a space for biotechnological research and development.[23] In 1989, the Indian government developed rules on the

[20] ibid 362.

[21] Raina (n 14) 132.

[22] Lianchawii, 'Biosafety in India: Rethinking GMO Regulation' (2005) 40(39) *Economic & Political Weekly* 4284.

[23] Raina (n 14) 132–134.

manufacture, use, import, export, and storage of Hazardous Micro-organisms and Genetically Engineered Organisms or Cells. These rules became legally binding in 1993 and constitute the regulatory framework for GMOs and 'other novel foods' in India. In 1990, the DBT introduced the 'Recombinant DNA Safety Guidelines', and in 1994, instituted 'Revised Guidelines for Safety in Biotechnology'. These were revised again in 1998, known as the 'Revised Guidelines for research in transgenic plants and guidelines for toxicity and allergenicity evaluation of transgenic seeds, plants and plant parts'.

Before GMOs can be marketed in India, they require the approval of six different bodies. The Institutional Biosafety Committee monitors research and development at the project level. The Review Committee on Genetic Manipulation oversees and monitors research activities as well as small-scale field trials. The Genetic Engineering Approval/Appraisal Committee (GEAC) is in charge of authorizing large-scale trials and releasing GMOs into the environment. The rDNA Advisory Committee operates under the DBT and regulates safety recommendations. It also monitors biosafety at the national and international levels. The State Biotechnology Coordination Committee (SBCC) oversees and coordinates all GMO activities at the state level with the central government. The District Level Committee (DLC) oversees GMOs at the district level.[24]

Despite having such a complex system for biosafety, the regulatory system is riddled with problems. Of these six bodies, only the first three are actively involved in approving GMOs in the country.[25] Lianchawii documents in detail the 'pitfalls' of biosafety regulation in India, when in 2002, GEAC approved the cultivation of Bt cotton in the state of Andhra Pradesh even though reports from the SBCC and the DLC were missing. The failures of the biosafety system led to the widespread use of Bt cotton across the country. Further, the GEAC is mainly composed of scientists with few personnel trained in risk assessment, specifically in ecological risk assessment.[26]

19.2.2 India's Biodiversity Governance

Biodiversity is regulated by the Biological Diversity Act, 2002, formulated after a consultative process with different stakeholders. The National Biodiversity Authority (NBA) was established in 2003 to implement the Act (in accordance with section 8 of the Act). Amongst its various functions, the NBA sets the guidelines and procedures that govern access to plant genetic matter and the sharing of benefits from IPRs with communities.[27]

[24] Lianchawii (n 22) 4285; Asheesh Navneet, 'A Co-Dynamic Model to Frame Controversies over Genetically Modified Crops in India' (2014) 16(3) *Asian Biotechnology and Development Review* 61.

[25] Navneet (n 24) 53–56.

[26] Lianchawii (n 22) 4827.

[27] Krishnamoorthy Venkataraman, 'India's Biodiversity Act 2002 and its Role in Conservation' (2009) 50(1) *Tropical Ecology* 23.

The problems of India's biodiversity regime came to the fore when Bt brinjal was introduced in India. In 2005, Bt brinjal (also known as eggplant or aubergine) was developed through a public-private partnership between the Indian government's institutions (including the Department of Biotechnology and the National Bureau of Plant Genetic Resources), public agricultural universities (University of Agricultural Sciences in Dharwad and Tamil Nadu Agricultural University in Coimbatore), and a private consulting firm.[28] In blatant violation of the country's biodiversity regime, the Maharashtra Hybrid Seed Corporation (Mahyco) and the public universities accessed various varieties of brinjal for research, without the permission of the states' biodiversity boards.

In 2012, the NGO Environment Support Group (ESG) filed a public interest litigation in the High Court of Karnataka.[29] According to ESG, this was a case of biopiracy because those who developed Bt brinjal failed to apply to the NBA for permission to use local varieties which is a requirement under the Biological Diversity Act.[30] Given the lawsuit and the publicity it created, the NBA filed a criminal prosecution case against those who had developed the Bt brinjal varieties.[31] According to Peschard and Randeria, 'this created a bizarre situation: the government was initiating criminal proceedings against a project in which some of its own leading bodies had taken an active part'.[32] In 2022, this case was still before the courts.

19.2.3 India's WTO-compliant Patent Regime

Exclusive monopoly rights of the biotech seed corporations are ensured by the WTO's TRIPs Agreement, which mandates the patentability of lifeforms. Article 27.3(b) of the TRIPS Agreement allows WTO members to exclude plants, animals, and essentially biological processes of producing them from patentability. However, micro-organisms and non-biological processes of producing plants and animals, as well as microbiological processes, should be patentable for a minimum of twenty years. In 2005, India's Patent Act, 1970, was amended to allow the patenting of micro-organisms and, significantly, to allow both process and product patents in the agri-food sector for up to twenty years. While seeds and plants are not patentable under the amended Patent Act, it allows for the patentability of micro-organisms and of non-biological processes for producing plants and animals.[33] Furthermore, the definitions of terms such as 'invention' and

[28] Jyotika Sood, 'Whose Germplasm is it?' *Down to Earth* (New Delhi, 15 October 2012) <https://bit.ly/3JVzoNR>.

[29] *ESG v NBA* Writ Petition N° 41532/2012 (2012) (High Court of Karnataka).

[30] Karine Peschard and Shalini Randeria, 'Taking Monsanto to Court: Legal Activism around Intellectual Property in Brazil and India' (2020) 47(4) *The Journal of Peasant Studies* 792.

[31] *NBA v UAS Dharwad* CC N° 579/2012 (PCR N° 267/2012) (2012).

[32] Peschard and Randeria (n 30) 803.

[33] Patents Act, 1970 s 3(j).

'inventive step' were kept unclear, broadening the scope of patentability for processes and products.[34]

IPRs that enable corporate control over seeds and plant varieties through exclusive rights have critical implications for farmers' rights. This is exemplified by the case of Bt cotton. Founded in 1964, Mahyco, in collaboration with Monsanto (now part of the Bayer Group), is the agricultural sciences company responsible for developing and releasing Bt technology in India. This partnership began in 1998 when Monsanto acquired a 26 per cent stake in Mahyco; today, Mahyco, known as Mahyco Monsanto Biotech (MMB), has a fifty-fifty joint venture with Bayer.[35] The introduction of GM Bt cotton to India began with limited field trials of the product in 1998, which subsequently expanded to forty locations in cotton growing areas throughout India.[36] By 2014, 7.7 million farmers had adopted Bt cotton on 11.6 million acres, around 95 per cent of the total cotton area of India.[37] In 2018, this figure was estimated to be 90 per cent.[38] Under the Gene Revolution, farmers cannot save seed for the next season. They have increasingly become dependent on the market for GM seeds.[39] Bollgard-I, with a single Bt gene (*cry1Ac*), was first released commercially in 2002, followed by Bollgard-II in 2006, which has two Bt genes (*cry1Ac* and *cry2Ab*). Both these genes are 'owned' by Monsanto through patent rights in the United States. Bt cotton hybrids expressing six events (different combinations of three Bt genes) have now been commercialized in India, and these have been introduced into 780 cotton hybrids.[40]

Monsanto had a patent in the United States on the event MON531, which expresses the *cry1Ac* gene, which expired in 2012. In September 2015, Monsanto stated that while it did not have a patent on MON531 in India, the company enjoyed 'proprietary rights over the MON531 event pertaining to regulatory data, biological materials, trade secrets, know-how and the like'.[41] Monsanto attested that it had 'proprietary rights over the MON 531 event by virtue of the various buckets of rights available' to the company.[42]

[34] Jagjit Kaur Plahe, 'The Implications of India's Amended Patent Regime: Stripping Away Food Security and Farmers' Rights?' (2009) 30(6) *Third World Quarterly* 1197; Patents Act, 1970 ss 2(j) and 2(ja).

[35] Monsanto, 'Mahyco Monsanto Biotech' (2022) <https://bit.ly/3emtGY7>; Rajesh Bhayani, 'Bayer, Monsanto Global Merger to Create $2.83 bn Firm in India' *Business Standard* (15 September 2016) <https://bit.ly/3QxOOJ2>.

[36] Navdanya International, 'The GMO Emperor has No Clothes: A Global Citizens Report on the State of GMOs–False Promises, Failed Technologies' (Navdanya International 2012).

[37] Bhagirath Choudhary and Kadambini Gaur, 'Biotech Cotton in India, 2002 to 2014: Adoption, Impact, Progress & Future' (International Service for the Acquisition of Agri-Biotech Applications 2015).

[38] KR Kranthi and Glenn Davis Stone, 'Long-term Impacts of Bt Cotton in India' (2020) 6 *Nature Plants* 195.

[39] Asheesh Navneet, 'Regulatory Approach Towards GM Technology in India, USA and EU: A Comparative Analysis' (2019) 65(4) *Indian Journal of Public Administration* 869.

[40] Choudhary and Gaur (n 37) 9.

[41] Makarand Gadgil, 'BT Cotton Sales by CICR may Bring Down Seed Cost of Farmers' *Mint* (21 September 2015) <https://bit.ly/3uV21mw>.

[42] ibid 1.

Since Bt cotton cultivation began in India, the debate on GM technology has deeply divided the country. Those who support the technology point to data that shows the immense growth in cotton production since Bt cotton was introduced. They argue that farmers have saved money on pesticides and their livelihoods have improved.[43] They also argue that Bt cotton was ushered in by farmers and not by the government since farmers started to exchange GM seeds 'illegally' because of its superior performance. Farmers thus 'chose' Bt cotton over local varieties.[44] On the other hand, other recent studies question the superior performance of Bt cotton. For example, an empirical study concludes that over the twenty years Bt cotton has been cultivated in India, it has only managed to control one pest, which is the American bollworm.[45] However, cotton farmers across the country have reported an increase in a large number of other pests which the Bt technology cannot control. The authors conclude that it 'now appears that Bt cotton's primary impact on Indian agriculture will be its role in this rising capital-intensiveness rather than any enduring agronomic benefits'.[46] Those who are critical of GM technology argue that the Gene Revolution has deepened the agrarian crisis in India, plunging farmers into a never-ending cycle of debt in many cases leading to farmer suicides. They point to the crisis in the cotton belt of Vidarbha in Maharashtra, where Bt cotton was introduced in 2002. Vidarbha comprises 50 per cent of cotton acreage in the state of Maharashtra; currently 1.4 million hectares in Vidarbha are under cotton cultivation, most of which is Bt cotton.[47] Farmers in this region are primarily small and marginal, cultivating less than five acres of non-irrigated land.[48]

Before Bt cotton was introduced in Vidarbha, farmers were already in a dire situation. Livelihoods were under such threat that in an act of complete desperation, in 2005, forty families put their village up for sale. A member of this village of 600 acres explained that the land was worth more than their debts.[49] 'We unanimously decided to sell our village, pay the dues and move out. It's better than committing suicide'.[50] Just as with the Green Revolution, while yields initially increased in Maharashtra, this was followed by a decline in productivity: a 17 per cent decline from 2010 to 2011 and a further 13 per cent decline from 2017 to 2018.[51] Bt cotton promised higher yields, less pesticide use, and

[43] Gruère and others (n 3); Ronald J Herring, 'On Risk and Regulation: Bt Crops in India' (2014) 5(3) *GM Crops & Food* 204.

[44] Navneet (n 39) 870.

[45] Kranthi and Stone (n 38)188.

[46] ibid 195.

[47] Parineeta Dandekar, 'Vidarbha: The Worst Place in the Nation to be a Farmer?' (*South Asia Network on Dams, Rivers and People*, 31 December 2014) <https://bit.ly/3w8uLc1>.

[48] Meena Menon, *Organic Cotton: Reinventing the Wheel* (Deccan Development Society and Kalpavriksh 2003).

[49] Pramit Bhattacharya, 'Vidarbha's Tryst with Bt Cotton' *Mint* (3 October 2012) <https://bit.ly/3cmaXux>.

[50] Jaideep Hardikar, 'Believe It or Not, This Village in Wardha is up for Sale' *GMWatch* (16 December 2005) 1 <https://bit.ly/3aSR4Lm>.

[51] Poorvi Kulkarni, 'As a Genetic Revolution Collapses, Vidarbha's Cotton Farmers Dread Coming Season' *BQPrime* (21 July 2018) <https://bit.ly/3v2EiAF>.

ultimately higher income. However, for many millions of farmers in Vidarbha, this has turned out to be an empty promise.

Bt cotton seeds alone account for approximately 40 per cent of the national seed market.[52] MMB has granted licences to forty-eight companies for the sale of hybrid cotton seeds. Together, these companies provide over 95 per cent of cotton seeds to farmers in India.[53] These licence arrangements bar companies from entering into agreements with any other technology provider, and the granting of the licence is at the sole discretion of MMB, securing the corporation's monopoly control in India. Under an international agreement, MMB can charge a royalty of 20 per cent for three years, and up to five percent for three more years.[54] When Bollgard-I was first introduced in the Indian market, between 2002 and 2006, royalties comprised 75 per cent of the cost of one packet of Bt cottonseed. It was also stipulated in the sublicensing agreements that seed companies were only allowed to introduce the Bt trait into proprietary hybrid varieties of cotton.[55]

Bt cotton cultivation is extremely expensive for small farmers. In 2018, they required two packets of Bollgard-II (US$12 per packet) for each acre of cultivation. They also required a further US$174–188 for inputs such as fertilizers and pesticides.[56] Monsanto licenses Bt technology to forty-nine companies in India for which it charges royalty fees. The high royalty fees have led to several legal disputes in various states in India. For example, under pressure from various farmers' groups, in 2006, the Andhra Pradesh government approached the Monopolies and Restrictive Trade Practices Commission (MRTPC) and issued a complaint against Monsanto for charging high fees (up to 75 per cent) for a packet of Bt cottonseed. The MRTPC ruled against Monsanto, and the government was allowed to fix the price of a packet of Bt cottonseed to INR 750 (down from a staggering INR 1700). Emboldened by the outcome, five other states took legal action against Monsanto in state high courts.[57]

In December 2015, the Union government issued the Cotton Seeds Price (Control) Order (CSP), which fixed the maximum price of Bt cottonseed as well as the royalties that can be charged. Under the CSP, the government took the decision in March 2016 not only to cap the price of Bollgard-II seeds (INR 800 or US$12 per packet of 450 gms) but also to cap the royalty paid to MMB to INR 49 per packet as opposed to INR 184 that was paid earlier. Monsanto reacted by taking legal action against the Indian government in the Delhi High Court and threatening to leave the Indian market.[58] Furthermore,

[52] G Seetharaman, 'These Two Issues Could put the Brakes on the Bt Cotton Story' *The Economic Times* (21 January 2018) <https://bit.ly/3PBciMk>.

[53] S Murali, 'Farmers up in Arms against Monsanto' *The Hindu* (6 September 2016) <https://bit.ly/3PYFgGv>.

[54] Navdanya International (n 36) 164.

[55] Madhvi Sally and Karunjit Singh, 'Monsanto Abused Dominant Position in India: CCI Probe' *The Economic Times* (22 May 2019) <https://bit.ly/3w8LoGa>.

[56] Seetharaman (n 52).

[57] Peschard and Randeria (n 30) 801.

[58] Seetharaman (n 52).

Monsanto had applied for proprietary rights over the Bollgard-II Roundup Ready Cotton from India's GEAC. The corporation withdrew its application for these rights in 2016, citing uncertainty in the Indian business and regulatory environment. While state and central governments have taken some action to protect Bt cotton farmers, the model of industrial agriculture that began with the Green Revolution and has continued through the Gene Revolution remains unchanged.

Monsanto also had problems with its Indian licensees, the most prominent being the conflict with Nuziveedu Seeds Ltd (NSL). The refusal of Monsanto to renegotiate its licensing arrangement with NSL in light of the CSP was the spark that ignited this conflict. In response, NSL stopped paying royalties to Monsanto in 2015, claiming that the Patents Act did not allow Monsanto to patent seeds. In 2016, Monsanto sued NSL in the Delhi High Court for infringement of its patent for Nucleotide Acid Sequence (NAS), which contains the Bt gene. Monsanto argued that NAS by itself was a patentable micro-organism that met the criteria for inventiveness under the Patents Act. NSL, on the other hand, filed a counterclaim, arguing that NAS could not be extracted from the seed after it was inserted and that the gene continued to be transmitted naturally through biological processes. As NAS now formed an integral part of the seed, Monsanto's patent was not valid since biological processes were not patentable under the Act. Furthermore, NSL disputed the argument that NAS was a micro-organism since it could not reproduce on its own. Rather, 'it was merely a chemical composition'.[59] The key question before the court was whether NAS became a part of the plant or seed following its insertion into the seed. The court upheld the validity of the patent.

Both parties then appealed to the division bench of the Delhi High Court, which revoked the patent, arguing that the Act does not allow for the patentability of NAS. The case then went to the Supreme Court in 2018, which stated that patents could only be revoked in accordance with the procedures laid out in section 64 of the Patents Act and the Code of Civil Procedure, 1908. Monsanto therefore maintains its patent on its GM cotton seeds in India.

19.2.4 Plant Variety Protection in India

As a signatory to the TRIPS Agreement of the WTO, not only was India obliged to extend patents to lifeforms, but it was also obliged to introduce an IPR regime to protect plant varieties. The government first developed a Bill to protect plant varieties in 1993; revised Bills were introduced in 1997, 1999, and 2000. In 2000, a Joint Parliamentary Committee was set up to conduct public hearings on the Bill due to public concerns.[60]

[59] Nidhisha Garg, 'Monsanto v Nuziveedu: A Missed Opportunity by the Supreme Court' *Kluwer Patent Blog* (27 January 2020) <https://bit.ly/3K6uw7d>.

[60] Jagjit Kaur Plahe, 'TRIPS Downhill: India's Plant Variety Protection System and Implications for Small Farmers' (2011) 41 *Journal of Contemporary Asia* 75.

In 2001, the Protection of Plant Varieties and Farmers' Rights Act (the Act or PPVFRA) was passed, and it came into force in 2005.

The Indian government also established the PPVFR Authority of India (the Authority), which began accepting registrations for plant varieties in 2007.[61] It was largely due to the strong advocacy of civil society groups in India that the final Act included the right of farmers to sell protected varieties of plants.[62] The PPVFRA stipulates that farmers are 'entitled to save, use, sow, resow, exchange, share or sell' produce from their farms, including varieties protected under the Act.[63] Farmers, however, cannot sell branded seed of a protected variety.[64] The implications of the Act for farmers have been extensively discussed in the literature.[65]

The PPVFRA allows for the protection of new varieties, extant varieties, farmers' varieties and essentially derived varieties. In India, the PPVFRA applies not just to commercial varieties but to all varieties, including those in the public domain. Under the Act, in order to register a variety with the Authority, the variety has to be new, distinctive, uniform and genetically stable (DUS). Farmers can register a 'new farmers' variety under the Act.[66] Farmers' groups or a community of farmers can register existing 'extant' varieties.[67] In order to register new varieties, they are required to conform to the DUS criteria.[68]

The Authority began to issue plant variety protection (PVP) registrations in 2009. From 2009 to 2018, the Authority has issued a total of 3,441 applications as follows: 1,143 (33.21 per cent) were issued to public research organizations/agricultural universities, 774 (22.49 per cent) to private seed companies, and 1,587 (46.1 per cent) to farming communities as well as individual farmers. Initially, the rate of success in registering farmers' varieties was very low. However, since 2015, this rate has increased quite dramatically, primarily for the registration of extant varieties. This indicates a higher rate of awareness of the PPVFRA among farmers. Whether farmers have gained from higher registrations, however, remains unclear.

Farmers' plant varieties, both extant and new, are developed through traditional and innovative breeding methods which involve 'skill, effort, patience of careful observation, selection, saving, sowing and re-sowing of seeds, sharing the seeds for cultivation'.[69] Farmers' varieties are therefore considered to be community varieties as opposed

[61] Prabhash Ranjan, 'Recent Developments in India's Plant Variety Protection, Seed Regulation and Linkages with UPOV's Proposed Membership' (2009) 12(3) *The Journal of World Intellectual Property* 219.

[62] Suman Sahai, 'Plant Variety Protection and Farmers' Rights Law' (2001) 36(35) *Economic & Political Weekly* 3338.

[63] The Protection of Plant Varieties and Farmers' Rights Act 2001 (PPVFRA 2001) s 39(1)(iv).

[64] Plahe (n 60)84–85.

[65] ibid 85–89; Karine Peschard, 'Farmers' Rights and Food Sovereignty: Critical Insights from India' (2014) 41(6) *The Journal of Peasant Studies* 1085.

[66] PPVFRA 2001s 39(1)(i).

[67] ibid s 39(1)(ii).

[68] Plahe (n 60) 83.

[69] Pankhuri Agarwal, 'Problems with the Indian Plant Varieties Regime (V): Farmers' Rights—A Myth or Reality (I)?' *Spicy IP* (26 October 2018) <https://bit.ly/3RHJZhj>.

to individual ones. However, through the PPVFRA, Indian farmers have been roped into a system of private protection for plant varieties, thus creating exclusive rights for some farmers at the expense of other farmers.[70] It seems though that these rights are not giving them much benefit. As Aggarwal argues, to register a new variety, farmers must comply with all the registration requirements that formal breeders have to comply with. The author argues that 'the outcome of informal breeding based on genetic variability (phenotype) has to be scientifically validated by modern scientists based on DUS standards set by the Authority on the basis of genetic makeup'.[71] Farmers also need to pay very high fees for registering new varieties which can amount to a minimum of US$3,000, including registration fees, lawyer fees, fees for establishing DUS, a yearly fee and a one per cent royalty fee if the farmer makes any profit. The DUS fees differ for each crop. While according to the Act, farmers would register new varieties so that they get exclusive marketing rights, this is unlikely to be the case because farmers use traditional breeding methods as opposed to commercial breeders who use modern technology.[72] A protected new farmers' variety could be used by other farmers since unlike hybrid crops, farmers' varieties can be saved and reused. Farmers therefore have very little incentive to protect new varieties. This is why very few farmers have applied for registration for 'new farmers' varieties' under the PPVFRA. The high number of farmers' variety registrations recorded by the Authority is mainly for extant varieties. Even though these varieties have been registered, there is nothing to stop other farmers from using them. Farmers have registered their extant varieties because there is no fee for doing so and because of the government's strong campaign to encourage farmers to register their seeds under the Act.

At the end of 2017, corporations from the private sector were issued PVP certificates for 73 per cent of all new varieties, while the public sector received only 27 per cent. Farmers did not receive any certificates. From 2009 to 2017, an average of thirty-seven varieties were registered yearly from the private sector as opposed to thirteen from the public sector.[73] Clearly, the private sector is way ahead in gaining exclusive ownership of hybrid and 'new' varieties of crops in India. Corporations, such as Monsanto, have been granted PVP certificates for several 'new' varieties of tetraploid cotton as well as some extant varieties which provide the corporation exclusive rights over these varieties for a period of fifteen years.[74]

The PepsiCo Case points to the problems with the PVP system in India. In 2019, twenty-five potato varieties were registered by the Authority with ten registered to private corporations and fifteen to public institutions. However, no farmers' varieties had

[70] Plahe (n 60) 81–82.

[71] Agarwal (n 69) 1.

[72] ibid.

[73] PA Lakshmi Prasanna and others, 'Intellectual Property Rights Protection for Plant Varieties in India: Status, Emerging Issues, and Challenges' (2019) 32(2) *Agricultural Economics Research Review* 259.

[74] Protection of Plant Varieties and Farmers' Rights Authority, 'Compendium of Registered Varieties under PPV&FR Act, 2001' (Department of Agriculture and Co-operation, Ministry of Agriculture 2018).

been registered. The giant multinational corporation PepsiCo sued four farmers from the state of Gujarat in 2019 for infringement of their PVP for a variety of potato FL 2027 potato variety (also known as the FL2027 variety), which the corporation uses to produce its well-known brand of Lays chips. The corporation sought close to US$1,30,743.00 from each farmer for allegedly breaching PepsiCo's exclusive right over the FL 2027 potato variety. PepsiCo argued that under Indian law, PVP registration gave the corporation exclusive rights to 'produce, sell, market, distribute, import or export the said variety', subject to other provisions of the law.[75] Legal experts, on the other hand, argued that according to section 39(1) of the PPVFR Act, farmers are allowed to 'save, use, sow, resow, exchange, share or sell' their farm produce, including seed of a variety which is protected under the Act.[76] This led to a nationwide backlash against the corporation following which PepsiCo withdrew its lawsuit.[77]

In June 2019, farm activist Kavitha Kuruganti filed an application for the revocation of PepsiCo's PVP certification before the Authority on various grounds, including that PepsiCo had provided incorrect information in its application and that the exclusive rights that the corporation was given were not in the public interest. In December 2021, the Authority revoked the registration granted in 2016 to PepsiCo for the FL 2027 potato variety.[78]

The PepsiCo cases attest to the fact that farmers' rights are not automatically guaranteed by the Authority. Farmers, with the help of activists, may have to fight each case as it arises. Furthermore, while this was a very important win for farmers and farming communities across India, the provisions of the 2019 Seed Bill (first introduced in 2004) seek to undermine farmers' rights enshrined in the PPVFRA.

19.2.5 The Seeds Bill, 2019

The Indian National Seed Corporation, founded in 1963, and the Seeds Act, 1966, were introduced to regulate seed quality in the country. The Seed Corporation and the Act played a very important role during the Green Revolution in terms of providing HYV seeds to farmers. The government introduced a New Policy on Seed Development in 1988, which enabled the general import of seeds and encouraged MNCs to enter the seed market in India, privatizing the industry.[79] The push toward a fully privatized seed system was hampered to some extent with the enactment of the progressive PPVFRA.

75 Latha Jishnu, 'Farmers' Rights are a Hot Potato' *Down to Earth* (14 May 2019) <https://bit.ly/3eluz3d>.

76 PPVFRA 2001 s 39(1)(iv).

77 Latha Jishnu, 'Plant Protection Authority Sets Right its Potato Blunder' *Down to Earth* (15 December 2021) <https://bit.ly/3Qyrj2G>.

78 ibid 1.

79 VR Gadwal, 'The Indian Seed Industry: Its History, Current Status and Future' (2003) 84(3) *Current Science* 399.

Indeed, some argue that to strengthen the rights of private plant breeders, the government introduced a conservative Seeds Bill in 2004.[80]

The Seeds Bill, 2004 was introduced to replace the 1966 Act 'to regulate the quality of seeds for sale, import and export and to facilitate the production and supply of seeds of quality and for matters connected therewith or incidental thereto'.[81] The 2004 Bill proposed 'to bring all the players, from the seed producer to the seed retailer, under the law to facilitate the effective regulation of the production, supply and distribution of seeds'.[82] The provisions of the 2004 Bill conflict with the PPVFRA for several reasons. The Bill states that 'a register of all kinds and varieties of seed to be called the National Register of Seeds shall be kept by the Registration Sub-Committee wherein all specifications, as may be prescribed, shall be maintained'.[83] The Bill further states that 'no seed of any kind or variety shall, for the purpose of sowing or planting by any person, be sold unless such seed is registered … by the Registration Sub-Committee in such manner as may be prescribed'.[84] Farmers in India therefore will not be permitted to sell seeds if they do not meet the criteria of genetic purity, a minimum period of germination and physical purity.[85] Farmers across the country organized against the 2004 Bill fearing that they would not be able to save, re-use, and exchange seeds. The Bill therefore was not passed. Fifteen years later, a revised Seeds Bill was introduced. A stark difference between the 2004 Bill and the 2019 Bill is that the former excluded any 'individual, company, trader or dealer who engages in the procurement and sale on a commercial basis'.[86] The latter, however, expands the definition of farmer to include 'any person who owns cultivable land or any other category of farmers who are doing agricultural work as may be notified by the Central/State Governments'.[87]

Farmers also have little protection if 'legally registered' seeds fail. According to the 2019 Bill: 'If, such registered seed fails to provide the expected performance under such given conditions, the farmer may claim compensation from the producer, dealer, distributor or vendor under the Consumer Protection Act, 1986'.[88] Kuruganti contends it will be very difficult for farmers to seek redress and compensation under the Consumer Protection Act. She further argues that this 'requires Bills and other paperwork to be in order. It is also expecting a farmer to actually compete with money power that a corporate seed entity has'.[89] Another concern is that unlike the PPVFRA, where all

[80] Ranjan (n 61) 234–238.
[81] ibid 221.
[82] ibid.
[83] The Draft Seeds Bill 2004 s 12(1).
[84] ibid s 13(1).
[85] Plahe (n 60) 92.
[86] The Draft Seeds Bill 2004 s 2(9).
[87] The Draft Seeds Bill 2019 s 2(11).
[88] ibid s 21.
[89] Akansha Kumar, Interview with Kavitha Kuruganti, Coordinator, Alliance for Sustainable and Holistic Agriculture, 'Why Modi Govt's New Seed Bill Might Be Unfair to Farmers' *The Quint* (6 December 2019) <https://bit.ly/3QuzE7v>.

applicants need to provide 'a complete passport data of the parental lines from which the variety has been derived' (including contributions made by farmers), there is no such requirement under the Seeds Bill.[90] The contribution of farmers in developing new plant varieties is not recognized and varieties originally developed by farmers can be claimed by the private sector.[91]

The liberalization of the Indian seed industry has greatly benefited multinational seed corporations. The mergers of top seed multinational corporations have led to a highly concentrated global seed market. It is estimated that the world's top three seed companies, Bayer-Monsanto, DowDuPont/Corteva and ChemChina-Syngenta, account for 60 per cent of the global proprietary seed market.[92] In this global environment, India has emerged as one of the biggest seed markets in the world. It is estimated that over half of India's seed production is now undertaken by the private sector,[93] and the Indian hybrid seed industry is worth INR 15,000 crore (US$2 billion).[94]

Conclusion

This chapter has shown that the Gene Revolution is based on the same highly input-intensive monocropping model of the Green Revolution, reproducing its problems on a much larger scale. It used the Bt cotton case to analyse the shift from the Green Revolution to the Gene Revolution in India. The Bt cotton story has been sold as a success story, one that is environmentally sustainable, providing an 'ecofriendly environment without compromising on profitable yield'.[95] A report by the International Service for the Acquisition of Agri–biotech Applications (ISAAA) celebrates India's emergence as the world's largest producer of cotton and importantly the 'resurgence of cotton, the white gold of rural India [which] can help resurrect the spirit of the Gandhian 'spinning wheel' and the glory of the cotton and textile sectors in the country'.[96] It points to a 50 per cent reduction in the use of insecticides in cotton production since 2001, a reduction in food insecurity in Bt cotton producing households by 15–20 per cent, and a 'substantial increase' in the net income of Bt farmers.[97] The aim of ISAAA—which is sponsored

90 PPVFRA 2001, s 18(e).

91 R Ramakumar, 'A Potential Seedbed for Private Profits' *The Hindu* (6 December 2019) <https://bit.ly/3PrXYFt>.

92 Koen Deconinck, 'From Big Six to Big Four' *Seed World* (6 May 2019) <https://seedworld.com/from-big-six-to-big-four/>.

93 Ramakumar (n 91).

94 Harish Damodaran, 'Explained: Sowing a New Seeds Regime' *The Indian Express* (New Delhi, 10 December 2019) <https://bit.ly/3JXIPeb>.

95 Deepak K Shah, 'Bt cotton in India: A Review of Adoption, Government Interventions and Investment Initiatives' (2012) 67(3) *Indian Journal of Agricultural Economics* 365.

96 Choudhary and Gaur (n 37) 4–5.

97 ibid.

by big corporations such as Bayer-Monsanto and United Phosphorous Limited as well as a range of government donor agencies—is to justify the use of Bt cotton and to further strengthen the institutional framework for biotechnology in India. The report blatantly ignores the distress of small cotton farmers, which is widely and routinely reported in the news. The words 'suicide', 'farmer distress' or 'debt' do not appear in this report. Such reports do not discuss the problems of monocropping, the privatization of agriculture, farmer dependence on a range of external inputs, and the lack of support for alternatives. The links between the neoliberal food regime and the livelihood crisis are not made. They cannot be made since they would negate the neoliberal frame of the profitable, 'eco-friendly' and 'simple' technological fix to the agrarian crisis in India.

Under the corporate food regime, control by large companies is highly concentrated both upstream and downstream. Upstream, agri-seed, and chemical corporations are now part of a multi-billion dollar global industry of which India is now a big part. The seed industry in India is strongly supported by the WTO-compliant national policies and institutions. The expansion of international IPR regimes has 'accelerated the solidification of asymmetrical power relations in the agricultural industry' negatively impacting smallholders.[98] For the first time in India's post-Independence history, life forms are patentable. Furthermore, plant genetic material and plant varieties can be privately 'owned' by commercial plant breeders. Plant breeders' rights make a distinction between growers and breeders, which assumes that commercial breeders are the legitimate suppliers of propagating material when the distinction between growers and breeders is often unclear in many developing countries where farmers develop new plant varieties and are the major suppliers of seed.[99] Farmers' rights provisions in the PPVFRA are undermined and eroded in the 2019 Seeds Bill.

The extension of private property rights to plant varieties has led to higher transgenic seed prices, further threatening the livelihoods of farmers. Not only do large agri-seed corporations hold plant breeders' rights and patents over plant varieties, seeds, and plant genetic matter in India, the same corporations also control the chemical inputs that are required to cultivate them.[100] India's biosafety and biodiversity regimes are struggling to regulate the biotechnology sector, especially developments which involve public-private partnerships. The cases discussed in this chapter attest to how farmers' rights are being undermined by the neoliberal policies that support the Gene Revolution.

India urgently needs to support farmers through sustainable climate-resilient agricultural policies that encourage seed saving and exchange, the use of bio-fertilizers and pesticides, and alternative markets development. In 2016, the state of Sikkim in India became one of the first organic states in India. This was achieved through strong state

98 Ahmed (n 10) 150.

99 Shaila Seshia, 'Plant Variety Protection and Farmers' Rights: Law-Making and Cultivation of Varietal Control' (2002) 37(27) *Economic & Political Weekly* 2741.

100 Ahmed (n 10) 150.

government support.[101] Sikkim has now become a model for other Indian states to promote organic agriculture across the country.

Suggestions for Further Reading

Mohsen Al Attar Ahmed, 'Monocultures of the Law: Legal Sameness in the Restructuring of Global Agriculture' (2006) 11 *The Drake Journal of Agricultural Law* 139.

KR Kranthi and Glenn Davis Stone, 'Long-term Impacts of Bt Cotton in India' (2020) 6 *Nature Plants* 188.

Karine Peschard, 'Farmers' Rights and Food Sovereignty: Critical Insights from India' (2014) 41 *Journal of Peasant Studies* 1085.

Jagjit Kaur Plahe, 'The Implications of India's Amended Patent Regime: Stripping Away Food Security and Farmers' Rights?' (2009) 30(6) *Third World Quarterly* 1197.

Jagjit Kaur Plahe, 'TRIPS Downhill: India's Plant Variety Protection System and Implications for Small Farmers' (2011) 41 *Journal of Contemporary Asia* 75.

[101] Lachlan Gregory, Jagjit Plahe, and Sandra Cockfield, 'The Marginalisation and Resurgence of Traditional Knowledge Systems in India: Agro-Ecological "Islands of Success" or a Wave of Change?' (2017) 40(3) *South Asia: Journal of South Asian Studies* 582.

CHAPTER 20

CONSERVATION AND USE OF BIOLOGICAL RESOURCES

ALPHONSA JOJAN

Abstract

This chapter provides an overview of laws and policies relating to biodiversity conservation and fair, equitable and sustainable use of biological resources and related knowledge in India. The first part of the chapter discusses existing central laws on biodiversity conservation focusing on area-based *in situ* conservation, agro-biodiversity, and community conservation. The second part of the chapter discusses the legal regime on access and benefit sharing focusing on the concept, access regulations, and benefit sharing aspects along with the existing issues and challenges. The chapter concludes by stating that the legal framework on biodiversity needs to be inclusive, participatory, democratic, equitable, clear, and based on human rights. The chapter also emphasises the need for further research in this area.

Introduction

The term 'biological diversity' (often referred to as 'biodiversity') means the variability among living organisms such as plants, animals, micro-organisms along with the ecological complexes they are part of.[1] The term became popular with the adoption of the Convention on Biological Diversity (CBD) in 1992. It was used with the intention of leveraging international political attention to the issues of habitat loss and mass

[1] Convention on Biological Diversity 1992 (CBD) art 2.

extinction of species which were already at crisis levels globally.[2] Loss of genetic diversity within crop species and their near extinction also became important issues for the international community to act upon. Consequently, the CBD recognized the conservation of biodiversity as a common concern of humankind which required international action, cooperation, and commitment.[3]

Global recognition of the importance of protecting biodiversity came about through the efforts of bodies such as the International Union for Conservation of Nature and the United Nations Environment Programme to move away from a fragmented and sectoral approach towards a comprehensive model of global biodiversity conservation.[4] In addition to the agenda of conservation, the use of biodiversity and bioresources for poverty alleviation and development were being raised by countries in the global South as part of the negotiating process for the CBD. Aligned with this, critical issues emanating from the deliberations of the Food and Agriculture Organization's (FAO) International Commission on Plant Genetic Resources were discussed during the CBD negotiations. These issues included sovereign rights over biological resources, rights of indigenous and local communities over their knowledge, innovations, and practices, access to genetic resources, and sharing of benefits and technology transfer in return for facilitated access to genetic resources. Consequently, the parties to the CBD adopted three main objectives, namely, conservation of biological diversity, sustainable use of its components, and fair and equitable benefit sharing arising from the use of genetic resources.[5] Along with the CBD, another prominent international treaty that is relevant for biodiversity is the International Treaty on Plant Genetic Resources for Food and Agriculture (ITPGRFA) which focuses on the conservation, exchange, and utilization of plant genetic resources.

With sovereignty over 8.1 per cent of the widely known plant and animal species, India is one of the seventeen mega-diverse countries in the world, considering its species' richness and endemism.[6] It also claims four of thirty-four globally identified biodiversity hotspots, namely the Western Ghats, the Nicobar Islands, parts of Assam and Meghalaya in the north-eastern region, and the Eastern Himalayas.[7] India has many farmers' crop varieties, landraces, wild relatives of cultivated crops and breeds of domesticated animals and fish, and is recognized as one of the Vavilovian centres of origin of cultivated plants of the world.[8] It is also home to diverse human communities who depend upon varied ecosystems, such as forest and coasts, which encourage

[2] RP Neumann, 'Biodiversity' [2009] *International Encyclopaedia of Human Geography* 308.

[3] Michael Pimbert, 'Issues Emerging in Implementing the Convention on Biological Diversity' (1997) 9(3) *Journal of International Development* 415.

[4] UNEP Training Manual on International Environmental Law <https://wedocs.unep.org/20.500.11822/20599> 184, para 10.

[5] CBD art 1.

[6] Ministry of Environment, Forest and Climate Change (MoEFCC), Government of India, 'Implementation of India's Biodiversity Action Plan: An Overview' (2019) 7.

[7] MoEFCC (n 6) 17.

[8] MoEFCC (n 6) 23.

the development of rich biocultural practices, extensive knowledge systems, and innovations based on local biodiversity and related knowledge. People in India have traditionally used biological resources for various purposes, including the production and trade of food, fibre, fodder, and medicine. They embrace various traditional lifestyles, such as hunter-gatherers, pastoralists, farmers, and fisherfolk in addition to urban lifestyles. Therefore, biodiversity in India is not just about the variety of natural resources; it is also about life and livelihoods.[9] Biodiversity, biological resources, and their genetic or biochemical information are also crucial to agricultural, pharmaceutical, and herbal medicinal companies seeking to produce new products commercially. Given the diverse and competing uses of biodiversity, the stated aim of biodiversity governance in India's domestic biodiversity law—the Biological Diversity Act, 2002 (BDA)—is, therefore, not only the conservation of biological diversity but also the sustainable use of its components along with fair and equitable sharing of the benefits of such use.

This chapter examines the national legal and regulatory framework relating to biodiversity in India through the lens of international biodiversity law. In addition, the three-fold objectives of the CBD are used to frame issues and map and analyse domestic laws. Biodiversity and associated cultural diversity have been used in the CBD and the BDA as an all-encompassing concept.[10] Due to the extensive and multi-disciplinary nature of this area, critical analysis of all aspects of laws relating to biodiversity in India is beyond the scope of this chapter. A few themes are selected based on existing law and jurisprudence in India.

Section 20.1 provides a descriptive analysis of the Indian legal and institutional framework for biodiversity protection focusing on area-based *in-situ* conservation with specific reference to agricultural biodiversity. It also discusses the legal recognition of community conservation practices that support conservation and sustainable use. Section 20.2 critically analyses the existing jurisprudence on access to bioresources and related knowledge, as well as fair and equitable benefit sharing from the utilization ofe the resources. The chapter concludes by highlighting the need for further research in this area.

20.1 Protection and Conservation of Biodiversity

Biodiversity conservation is carried out through two main strategies, namely, *in situ* conservation and *ex situ* conservation.[11] The CBD, in its preamble, requires the contracting

[9] Shalini Bhutani and Ashish Kothari, 'The Biodiversity Rights of Developing Nations: A Perspective from India' (2002) 32(4) *Golden Gate University Law Review* 587.

[10] CBD art 2.

[11] CBD, arts 8 and 9.

parties to conserve biodiversity through the conservation of ecosystems and natural habitats, and to maintain and recover species in their natural environment (*in situ* conservation). This section starts by providing a descriptive analysis of the legal and institutional framework relating to the *in-situ* conservation strategiesin India focusing on area-based conservation. It then moves on to examine a sub-category of biodiversity—agricultural biodiversity, followed by a discussion on community conservation.

20.1.1 Conservation of Biodiversity

Indian Parliament has enacted many legislations and policies that contribute towards biodiversity conservation. Biodiversity at the level of ecosystems such as forest, coast, and marine, and at the level of species, especially threatened and wild species, has been the focal point of these laws and policies. For example, forestry has received a high level of legislative and executive intervention with the Indian Forest Act, 1927, the Forest (Conservation) Act, 1980, and the National Forest Policy of 1988. Similarly, wildlife has received great attention following the enactment of the Wild Life (Protection) Act, 1972 (WLPA). Promulgation of the Environment (Protection) Act, 1986, was pertinent to the protection of ecological complexes supporting biodiversity such as water. Protection of coastal ecosystems and critical habitat of coastal species has benefitted from the issuance of the 'Coastal Regulation Zone Notification', which was initially notified in 1991 under the Environment (Protection) Act.

These laws and policies create an elaborate framework, including institutions for action towards conservation. One of the strategies is area-based conservation, primarily through the establishment of 'Protected Areas' (PAs), which are areas requiring special measures for biodiversity conservation.[12] Initially, in India, the definition of PAs under the WLPA was limited to areas identified for protection of wildlife and its environment. But later, it was extended to include protecting larger areas at the landscape and seascape level, and protecting traditional or cultural conservation values and practices. To illustrate, the initial two categories of PAs are national parks and sanctuaries, which are areas constituted for the purpose of protection, propagation, and development of wildlife and its environment.[13] Two further categories of PAs—conservation reserves and community reserves were added by an amendment to the WLPA in 2002.[14] According to the WLPA, conservation reserves are areas adjacent to national parks or sanctuaries and those areas that link one protected area to another, and are constituted for the protection of landscapes, seascapes, flora and fauna, and their habitat, whereas community reserves are areas under community or individual ownership set aside to protect traditional or cultural conservation values and practices with respect to flora and fauna.[15]

[12] CBD art 8(i).
[13] Wild Life (Protection) Act, 1972 (WLPA),ss 35, 18 and 26A.
[14] ibid ss 36A and 36C.
[15] ibid ss 36A(1) and 36C(1).

PAs are not just areas set aside for conservation. This legal classification has an extra layer of protection; that is, when activities such as mining, national highway construction or other developmental activities that affect PAs are proposed within the PA or 10 km of its radius, a Wildlife Clearance under the WLPA is required.[16]

The governance objectives of areas outside the PA classification have changed over time. Forests are an example. During the colonial period, forests were categorised into reserve, protected, and community forests primarily for commercial exploitation of forest resources. Independent India continued the colonial institutional and legal framework with slight modifications. For example, the 1952 Forest Policy recognized the economic role of forests.[17] A substantial change occurred through the passing of the Forest (Conservation) Act, 1980 which required forest clearance for the conversion of forest areas for non-forest purposes such as mining, construction of dams, reservoirs, or expansion of agriculture.[18] The National Forest Policy of 1988 also prioritized maintenance of environmental stability and ecological balance over direct economic benefits from the forest.[19]

There has been criticism that despite a rich tradition of community conservation, the Indian legal and policy framework on forests and wildlife has been modelled on exclusionary conservation methods, such as the creation of inviolate spaces with no human intervention, which has led to environmental justice issues such as the displacement of local communities from PAs and forests.[20] The governance and management structure and system will throw light on this exclusionary model of conservation. The management of National Parks and Sanctuaries is mainly undertaken by the Forest and Wildlife Departments of state governments under the WLPA after extinguishing people's rights over these areas. Other newer categories of PAs are represented through a mixture of government departments, local democratic institutions, and/or non-government organizations. As an example, the Conservation Reserve Management Committee, constituted under the WLPA for the governance of conservation reserves, comprises one representative of local self-government, three members of NGOs, and a representative each from the departments of Agriculture, Animal Husbandry, and Forest and Wildlife.[21] Five representatives of the local self-government and one representative from the Forest or Wildlife Department constitute the Community Reserve Management Committee constituted under the WLPA for the governance of community reserves. Exclusion is still manifested in how the community reserves and conservation reserves

[16] WLPA ss 29, 33(a) with respect to Sanctuaries, and ss 35(6), 35(8), and 33(8) with respect to National Parks.

[17] MoEFCC (n 6) 8.

[18] Forest (Conservation) Act, 1980 s 2.

[19] National Forest Policy, 1988 para 2.2.

[20] Ashish Kothari and others (eds), 'Recognising and Supporting Territories and Areas Conserved by Indigenous Peoples and Local Communities: Global Overview and National Case Studies' (Secretariat of the Convention on Biological Diversity, ICCA Consortium, Kalpavriksh and Natural Justice 2012) 130.

[21] WLPA s 36(b).

under the WLPA have only nominal/namesake local community participation, with the claims that the government retains much of the overarching control in practice.[22]

This exclusionary conservation model was challenged, and in 2006, historic legislation, namely, the Scheduled Tribes and Other Forest Dwellers (Recognition of Rights) Act, 2006 (FRA) recognizing various rights of forest-dwelling and forest-dependent communities was passed by Parliament.[23] The FRA has the potential of recognising another category of area based conservation. FRA grants, inter alia, the right to protect, conserve, or manage areas which have been traditionally protected or conserved for sustainable use.[24] In addition, FRA empowers the holders of forest rights, Gram Sabhas and committees constituted by Gram Sabhas to protect wildlife, forests, and biodiversity.[25]

A further 'area-based' conservation measure is Biodiversity Heritage Sites (BHS) under the BDA. BHS are areas of important biodiversity as declared by state governments.[26] The Voluntary Guidelines for Selection and Management of BHS prescribe the criteria for identification of BHS as not only diversity in forest or wildlife ecosystems but also diversity in domesticated biodiversity, representative agroecosystems, sacred groves, community conserved areas, and medicinal plant conservation areas.[27]

Other avenues of biodiversity conservation and protection are being undertaken in addition to the aforementioned area-based conservation. For example, the WLPA prevents poaching and illegal trade of wildlife and protects specified flora and fauna from activities such as hunting.[28] The BDA empowers the central government, in consultation with the state government, to declare species on the verge of extinction, or likely to become extinct, and prohibit their collection without approval from the relevant authority.[29]

Additionally, an important tool in ensuring that any encroachment upon biodiversity is justified or sustainable is environmental impact assessments (EIAs). Despite industrial and construction activities already being scrutinized for sensitivity towards biodiversity as specified in the Environment Impact Assessment Notification under the Environment (Protection) Act,[30] and the BDA also mandating the central government to undertake biodiversity-inclusive EIAs wherever necessary,[31] there are yet to be any comprehensive guidelines on how to conduct such an inclusive EIA.

[22] Kothari and others (n 20)130.

[23] Scheduled Tribes and Other Traditional Forest Dwellers (Recognition of Forest Rights) Act, 2006 (FRA) s 3. See further ch 27 in this volume.

[24] ibid s 3(1)(i) read with s 2(a).

[25] ibid s 5.

[26] Biological Diversity Act, 2002 (BDA) s 37(1).

[27] National Biodiversity Authority, Guidelines for Selection and Management of the Biodiversity Heritage Sites, para 4.

[28] BDA ss 5C and 9.

[29] BDA s 38.

[30] Environmental Impact Assessment Notification, 2006, Part III of App I/Form I and Parts 3 and 4 of App III.

[31] BDA s 36(4)(i).

20.1.2 Conservation of Agrobiodiversity

Laws on the conservation of forest and wildlife ecosystems have been in place in India even before the CBD. But through the CBD's emphasis on the importance of genetic diversity, a specific sub-set of biodiversity, namely 'agrobiodiversity', received a special space in law and policy. As a historically agrarian society, laws promoting agrobiodiversity are particularly important for India. Indians and the wider Indian subcontinent have traditionally cultivated landscapes, pastures and domesticated plant species and animal breeds. Communities in India have practised different agricultural practices like terrace farming, shifting cultivation like *jhum* cultivation, and mixed farming for centuries.[32] This diversity is evident since fifteen different agro-climate zones are identified in India based on the varieties of crops and animal breeds suited to the different climatic and geological features of the land.[33] India is considered to be at the centre of origin for rice, brinjal, citrus fruits, banana, and cucumber species,[34] due to the immense concentration of sub-species, races, and varieties of these plants.

These numerous varieties and subspecies have been cultivated through traditional farming practices, agricultural knowledge, and traditional plant varieties, which are now being eroded due to the emphasis on using modern varieties to achieve higher productivity. These changes have come about through government policies, such as the Green Revolution that focused on achieving higher productivity using inputs such as irrigation, chemical pesticides, and insecticides.[35] Another factor for the erosion of genetic diversity is the conversion of agricultural and forest land for non-agricultural purposes, such as construction projects and dams.[36]

To stem the decline of agrobiodiversity and genetic erosion, its conservation is being promoted through *ex situ* or *in situ* means. In the case of *in situ* conservation, cultivated and domesticated species are conserved in their natural surroundings or where they have developed their distinctive properties,[37] such as farmers' fields, on-farm areas, home gardens, etc. *Ex situ* conservation occurs outside the natural environment through gene banks, botanical gardens, zoological parks, seed banks, and culture collection.

In recognizing the importance of agrobiodiversity, certain laws support the protection of agro-ecosystems, traditional plant varieties, animal breeds, and associated knowledge.[38] For example, the BDA contains several provisions relating to agrobiodiversity.

[32] TPCG and Kalpavriksh, 'Securing India's Future: Final Technical Report of National Biodiversity Strategy and Action Plan' (2005).

[33] MoEFCC (n 6) 23.

[34] C Thomson Jacob, Ajay Parida, and NK Krishnakumar, 'Conservation of India's Agrobiodiversity Towards Increasing Food, Nutritional and Livelihood Security' (2020) 119(4) *Current Science* 607.

[35] Mrinalini Kochupillai, Promoting Sustainable Innovations in Plant Varieties (Springer 2016) 80; Ashish Kothari, Conserving India's Biodiversity: Prospects and Policy Implications (1997) 5–6.

[36] Prashant Reddy, 'Access to Plant Genetic Resources and Benefit Sharing: Has India Lost the Plot' [2018] *Intellectual Property Quarterly* 181.

[37] BDA s 36.

[38] TPCG and Kalpavriksh (n 30) 21.

Even though section 41 of the BDA empowers the Biodiversity Management Committee (BMC) constituted at the local level to, *inter alia*, conserve land races, folk varieties, cultivars, domesticated stocks and breeds of animals, and micro-organisms, rule 22(6) of the Biological Diversity Rules, 2004 (Biodiversity Rules) narrows down the main function of the BMC as the documentation of local biodiversity in a register called the 'People's Biodiversity Register' (PBR). PBRs may include various information relating to agrobiodiversity and domesticated biodiversity.[39]

Another prominent piece of legislation is the Protection of Plant Variety and Farmers Rights Act, 2001 (PPVFRA), which focuses on the protection of plant genetic resources. The PPVFRA enables the registration of, *inter alia*, new plant varieties, extant and farmers' varieties.[40] It gives recognition and reward to farmers who engage in the conservation of landraces and wild relatives of economic plants through the genome saviour award.[41] Section 45 of the PPVFRA creates a gene fund that can be used to support the conservation and sustainable use of genetic resources, and to build the capacity of *panchayats* to carry out conservation and sustainable use.[42] The Act also creates the PPVFRA Authority whose mandate is to protect farmers' and breeders' rights. A task force formed by this Authority has designated twenty-two agrobiodiversity hotspots,[43] which have since been identified by the Authority for protection as Biodiversity Heritage Sites.[44]

In addition to laws, there is an institutional framework relating to agrobiodiversity. The National Bureau of Plant Genetic Resources (NBPGR) undertakes the conservation of plant genetic resources such as landraces, wild relatives, farmers' varieties, modern cultivars, and biotechnological cell lines.[45] The formal agrobiodiversity sector has been focusing on *ex situ* conservation after collecting the genetic resources from farmers and pastoralists.[46]

As mentioned, the laws relating to agrobiodiversity are scattered and fragmented.[47] Despite the recognition of the importance of agrobiodiversity, there remains a lack of a comprehensive legal vision for conserving agrobiodiversity. Most current legal provisions emphasize documenting agrobiodiversity and favour registering the traditional varieties or associated knowledge. There is an argument that registration of a 'new variety' or 'traditional variety' has not incentivised *in situ* conservation of farmers'

39 National Biodiversity Authority, Revised PBR Guidelines 2013.

40 Protection of Plant Variety and Farmers Rights Act, 2001 (PPVFRA) s 39(1)(ii) read with s 2(l).

41 ibid s 39(1)(iii).

42 ibid s 45.

43 AK Singh, MP Nayar, and Narayanan K Nair, 'Agro-Biodiversity Hotspots in India: Conservation and Benefit Sharing' (PPV and FRA 2009) Vol 2, Annexure 1.

44 Jacob, Parida and Krishnakumar (n 32) 607.

45 MoEFCC (n 6) 89.

46 TPCC and Kalpavriksh (n 30) 24.

47 See also Zainab Lokhandwala, 'Peasants Rights as New Human Rights: Promises and Concern for Agrobiodiversity Conservation' (2022) 12(1) *Asian Journal of International Law* 106.

varieties.[48] Documentation of agrobiodiversity in PBR has not translated into ground-level conservation of these ecosystems or varieties. The recognition and award scheme under the PPVFRA is also criticized as it is only awarded if the genetic resources contribute to the development of modern varieties.[49] There is, therefore, a requirement for strategic laws for the conservation of agrobiodiversity. Additionally, more research is needed to understand, evaluate, and assess the existing laws.

20.1.3 Biodiversity and Indigenous Peoples and Local Communities

Indigenous culture and ways of living are increasingly recognized as contributing to the conservation of biodiversity. Article 8(j) of the CBD states that, subject to national legislation, contracting parties respect, preserve, and maintain not only knowledge and innovations but also practices by indigenous peoples and local communities (IPLCs) that embody traditional lifestyles relevant to conservation and sustainable use. Importantly, this provision deals with *in situ* conservation, thereby recognizing a critical link in IPLCs' contribution towards *in situ* conservation, which is otherwise ignored in law and policy.[50]

An example of this legal recognition enacted under national law is the farmers' rights as guaranteed in section 39 of the PPVFRA. The right of farmers with respect to traditional practices of seed saving, exchanging, using, and selling is an explicit provision protecting the traditional rights of farmers.[51] Innovations by farmers are also recognized by the right to register a plant variety, including farmers' own varieties. Traditional knowledge of farmers is included in the definition of farmer's variety under section 2(l) of the PPVFRA as the same as a variety that is traditionally cultivated and evolved by farmers in their field or is a wild relative or landrace of a variety about which farmers have knowledge. Other rights include the right to receive compensation for the contribution of the germplasm to develop another plant variety (premised on the benefit-sharing principle) and the right to recognition and reward.[52]

The FRA is another significant piece of legislation which recognizes certain parts of Article 8(j) of the CBD. These include the right to conserve a community forest resource for the purpose of sustainable use, the right of ownership over non-timber forest produce, and the right of access to biodiversity and traditional knowledge.[53]

[48] See generally NS Gopalakrishnan, 'Problems with Indian Plant Variety Regime: Old Vine in Newly "Enclosed" Bottle?' *Spicyip* (6 July 2018) <https://spicyip.com/2018/07/problems-with-the-indian-plant-variety-regime-old-vine-in-newly-enclosed-bottle.html>.

[49] PPVFRA s 39(1)(iii). See also Gopalakrishnan (n 46).

[50] Kabir Bavikatte and Morten Walloe Tvedt, 'Beyond the Thumbrule Approach: Regulatory Innovations for Bioprospecting in India' (2015) 11(1) *Law Environment and Development Journal* 1.

[51] See generally, Sujith Koonan, 'Farmers Rights in India: Assessing the Conceptual and Implementation Issues' (2012) 4(1) *Dehradun Law Review* 29.

[52] PPVFRA ss 41(3) and 39(1)(iii).

[53] FRA s 3(1)(i), (c), and (k).

Besides enactment of legislation, the judiciary also recognizes the cultural, social, spiritual, and religious significance of biodiversity and biological resources to IPLCs. The case of Dongria Kondhs of Orissa's Niyamgiri hill ranges is an example. The Niyamgiri hills are a biodiversity-rich forest with several endemic and threatened plants and animals.[54] Dongria Kondhs have a close spiritual relationship with the Niyamgiri hills and consider *Niyamraja* their most significant deity. Their way of life also prohibits unsustainable exploitation of forests and land. There has been judicial recognition of this relationship. In relation to environmental clearance for bauxite mining in the Niyamgiri hills, the Supreme Court focused on the various rights of Scheduled Tribes and Forest dwellers. It ruled that the right to practice rituals and observations, which are integral to their religion, is guaranteed under Articles 25 and 26 of the Constitution, and the right to worship their deity has to be protected and preserved.[55] Pursuant to the ruling, twelve *Gram Sabhas* rejected the mining proposal, and the MoEFCC subsequently rejected the environmental clearance for mining in the Niyamgiri hills.[56]

Despite these legal provisions, realizing all these rights suffers from various issues and challenges. Farmers' rights are conceived narrowly, and registration of farmers varieties has arguably led to the obliteration of farmers' varieties and innovation.[57] There are studies which show poor implementation of the FRA.[58] The BDA is another legislation which recognizes under section 2(a) conservers of biological resources and holders of knowledge as 'benefit claimers' for claiming benefits of use of their resources and knowledge. But, the BDA is different from the PPVFRA and the FRA since it does not directly give any right to IPLCs. The next section discusses the lack of explicit recognition of the rights of IPLCs in the BDA.

20.2 Access and Benefit Sharing

Access and benefit sharing (ABS) in the context of laws relating to biodiversity refers to the regulation of access to biological resources and related knowledge and benefits to be shared from the utilization of the accessed biological resource and/or knowledge. It was developed to address the issues of unauthorized and uncompensated use of genetic resources and traditional knowledge. It was also envisaged as a tool that can balance the interest of nations and communities possessing rich traditional knowledge against the interest of nations and corporates with advanced technology that use such traditional

[54] Meenal Tatpati, Ashish Kothari, and Rashi Mishra, 'The Niyamgiri Story: Challenging the Idea of Growth Without Limits?' (Kalpavriksh 2016) 5.

[55] *Orissa Mining Corpn Ltd v Ministry of Environment and Forests* (2013) 6 SCC 476 [55].

[56] Tatpati, Kothari, and Mishra (n 52) 11.

[57] TPCG and Kalpavriksh (n 30) 33; Gopalakrishnan (n 46).

[58] CR Bijoy, 'Democracy in the Forests: The Governance That Is to Be' (2021) 17(1) *Law Environment & Development Journal* 20.

knowledge to obtain private intellectual property rights. This section will, first, discuss the concept of ABS, second, deal with the regulations with respect to access to biological resources and knowledge, and third, examine the benefit sharing envisaged in the Indian legal framework. This section concludes by discussing issues and challenges identified with the Indian law relating to ABS.

20.2.1 Concept of ABS

The concept of ABS rests on the principle of sovereign rights of nation states over natural resources as recognized in the Preamble and Article 3 of the CBD. Accordingly, nation states have the authority to determine access to the genetic resources occurring in their jurisdiction as stated in Article 15(1) of the CBD, and Article 15(4) and (5) state that such access shall be based on mutually agreed terms and subject to the prior informed consent of the provider. Along with the access regulations, the user is also obligated to share the results of research and development fairly and equitably and the benefits arising from the commercial and other utilization of genetic resources with the providers of such resources, based on mutually agreed terms.[59] In addition to regulations of access to genetic resources, regulations relating to access to traditional knowledge held by IPLCs are dealt under Article 8(j) of the CBD. This Article encourages nation states to make laws that subject access to traditional knowledge to (a) the prior informed consent of those communities holding the knowledge and (b) a benefit-sharing obligation. These obligations are further expanded and elaborated in the Nagoya Protocol on Access to Genetic Resources and the Fair and Equitable Sharing of Benefits Arising from their Utilization (Nagoya Protocol) adopted in 2010.[60] Article 6(2) of the Nagoya Protocol states that prior informed consent of IPLCs is obtained where IPLCs have established legal rights over the genetic resources. Further, Article 7 requires contracting parties to take measures to ensure that traditional knowledge associated with genetic resources held by IPLCs are assessed with their PIC and on mutually agreed terms. The ITPGRFA is also important in the context of access to plant genetic resources and the sharing of benefits from their use. The CBD envisages a bilateral ABS contractual agreement between the provider and the user in relation to access conditions and benefit-sharing obligations. In contrast, Article 10 of the ITPGRFA offers a multilateral benefit-sharing mechanism for plant genetic resources that are important for food and agricultural purposes.

A contextual background focusing on the practice of global collection of plant genetic resources will provide a better understanding of the concept of ABS.[61] Plant

[59] CBD art 15(7).

[60] Protocol on Access to Genetic Resources and the Fair and Equitable Sharing of Benefits Arising from their Utilization, Nagoya, 29 October 2010, UN Doc UNEP/CBD/COP/DEC/X/1.

[61] See generally, Jack R Kloppenburg and Daniel Lee Kleinman 'Plant Germplasm Controversy' (1987) 37(3) *Bioscience* 190; James O Odek, 'Bio-piracy: Creating Proprietary Rights in Plant Genetic Resources' (1994) 2(1) *Journal of Intellectual Property Law* 141; Philippe Cullet, 'Environmental Justice in

genetic resources have been globally exchanged from time immemorial, arguably as an open access resource without many restrictions.[62] The emergence of agricultural and breeding technologies in the global North led to the development of new plant varieties often termed as 'improved' or 'modern' or breeders' varieties. The raw materials for the technological application were obtained from biodiversity-rich areas, and many of those areas then were under colonial rule, and these raw materials were stored and conserved *ex situ* in gene banks of technologically rich countries. This collection practice continued through the establishment of the Consultative Group on International Agricultural Research.

Parallel to the development of plant technology was the expansion of the legal regime on intellectual property rights to life forms, particularly plant variety protection, under the 1978 International Convention for the Protection of New Varieties of Plants (UPOV), which resulted in a restriction on the use of improved varieties. In response, in 1983, the FAO adopted the voluntary International Undertaking on Plant Genetic Resources, which considers all plant genetic resources as the common heritage of mankind free of all restrictions.[63] This included not only landraces and wild relatives of cultivars but also breeders' varieties and elite varieties.[64] This was not agreed upon by countries in the global North who wanted breeders rights over their modern varieties.[65] Countries in the global South could not agree to the system of open access to biological resources such as landraces, farmers varieties, and other biological resources occurring in their country.[66] This led to reaffirmation of sovereign rights over their biological resources including germplasm. The negotiations for the mandatory intellectual property rights protection for plant germplasm, either through plant patents, plant variety protection or other *sui generis* rights under the World Trade Organization's (WTO) Agreement on Trade Related Aspects of Intellectual Property Rights (TRIPS) escalated these tensions.[67] In addition to plant genetic resources, traditional knowledge on medicinal and other properties were also used by entities in the global North to produce modern medicines and other products that were protected under intellectual property rights. The legally binding CBD was used to counterbalance the development of TRIPS. The contracting parties to the CBD agreed to facilitated access in exchange for the sharing of benefits based on prior informed consent and mutually agreed terms in accordance with Article

the Use, Knowledge and Exploitation of Genetic Resources' in Jonas Ebbesson and Phoebe Okowa (eds), *Environmental Law and Justice in Context* (CUP 2009) 371.

[62] Elisa Morgera and Elsa Tsioumani, 'The Evolution of Benefit Sharing: Linking Biodiversity and Community Livelihoods' (2010) 15(2) *Review of European Community and International Environmental Law* 150.

[63] International Undertaking on Plant Genetic Resources, Resolution 8/83, Report of the Conference of FAO, 22nd Session, Rome 5–23 November 1983, Doc. C 1983/REP.

[64] ibid art 2(1)(a).

[65] Kloppenburg and Kleinman (n 59) 190.

[66] MoEFCC, 'Access and Benefit Sharing in India: A Handbook for Researchers (National Biodiversity Authority 2021) 7 <http://nbaindia.org/uploaded/pdf/IDB_ABS.pdf>.

[67] ibid.

15 of the CBD. Traditional knowledge-related norms were discussed in Article 8(j) of the CBD. As Schroeder argues, open access to biodiversity and traditional knowledge would be ideal, but the same is not suitable in a world marked by colonization and an unjust international economic order that led to significant human suffering.[68]

20.2.2 Regulation of Access to Bioresources and Knowledge

India signed the CBD on 5 June 1992, ratified it in 1994, and enacted the BDA in 2002 to give effect to the CBD. The regulation of access to biological resources and associated knowledge is primarily dealt with under the BDA, the Biodiversity Rules, and the 2014 Guidelines on Access to Biological Resources and Associated Knowledge and Benefit Sharing Regulations, 2014 (the ABS Regulations). The BDA regulates only certain uses of biological resources.

One of the regulated activities is research since it is considered as the starting point for commercial utilization of biological resources and therefore, such activities are considered paramount in implementing the ABS system.[69] One of the major criticisms of biodiversity regulation is that the CBD, the BDA and related biodiversity guidelines stifle taxonomical and other kinds of fundamental research due to the re-affirmation of national sovereignty over biological resources.[70] The concern is that national sovereignty would hinder the practice of collegiality and reciprocity that used to exist among biologists by virtue of considering biological resources as 'common heritage of humankind'.[71] Other commentators highlight the fact that the Green Revolution that benefitted millions was plausible due to the free international exchange of plant genetic resources among scientists who developed high yielding plant varieties such as IR8, dwarf wheat, etc.[72] There are also arguments to distinguish between commercial research and non-commercial research for the purpose of regulation of access.[73] While the BDA does not distinguish between commercial and non-commercial research,[74] paragraph 13 of the ABS Regulations requires the National Biodiversity Authority (NBA) to accord its approval within forty-five days for basic research and research for emergency purposes such as a pandemic. Article 8 of the Nagoya Protocol also makes special provisions for non-commercial research.

68 Doris Schroeder, 'Traditional Knowledge, Indigenous Communities, and Ethical Values' in Suneetha Subramanian and Balakrishna Pisupati (eds), *Traditional Knowledge in Policy and Practice: Approaches to Development and Human Well-Being* (United Nations University Press 2010) 97, 105.

69 MoEFCC (n 64) 14.

70 KD Prathapan and others, 'Biological Diversity Act, 2002: Shadow of Permit Raj Over Research' (2006) 91(8) Current Science 1006.

71 ibid.

72 Reddy (n 34) 181.

73 Prathapan and others (n 68) 1007.

74 MoEFCC (n 64) 47.

An example of the difficulty in distinguishing commercial and non-commercial research, especially research and development in sectors such as agriculture, medicine, etc., is where research leads to the development of a new product such as transgenic Bt Brinjal which may pose threats to the environment and biodiversity. Bt Brinjal was developed by inserting the proprietary Bt gene into indigenous/local brinjal varieties.[75] In relation to research activities for the development of transgenic brinjal, a criminal complaint was filed by the authorized officers of the NBA and others before the Court of Judicial Magistrate, Dharwad, for conducting unauthorized 'research' on local varieties of brinjal for development of Bt Brinjal.[76] The complaint was filed against Maharashtra Hybrid Seed Company (MAHYCO) which has a 26 per cent shareholding by Monsanto, an American seed company, bringing it under the unamended section 3(2) person of the BDA.[77] The case also accused the University of Agricultural Sciences of illegally transferring research results to MAHYCO. The accused had allegedly accessed local varieties of brinjal for the development of Bt Brinjal without the prior approval of the NBA. The case is still pending before the court.

In addition to access, applying for intellectual property rights, in or outside of India, for inventions based on research or knowledge of biological resources obtained from India is regulated under section 6 of the BDA.[78] Those applying for plant variety protection in India are exempted from section 6 of the BDA but are nevertheless governed by the PPVFRA.[79] The PPVFRA was enacted as a response to India's obligation under TRIPS, which requires intellectual property protection for plant varieties but permits its *sui generis* protection. The unique feature of the PPVFRA is farmers' rights under section 39. This provision entitles farmers, *inter alia*, to 'save, use, saw, resaw, exchange, share or sell his farm produce including the varieties protected under the Act'. It is important to note that farmers' rights are considered as rights that counterbalance intellectual property rights as they allow farmers to continue the use of protected varieties.[80]

Access to traditional knowledge is combined with access to biological resources in the BDA. There are suggestions for having separate provisions for accessing traditional knowledge considering the Nagoya Protocol, which recognizes clear rights of IPLCs over their traditional knowledge.[81]

[75] Kanchi Kohli and Shalini Bhutani, 'Chasing Benefits: Issues on Access to Genetic Resource and Traditional Knowledge with reference to India's Biodiversity Regime' (Kalpavriksh 2011) <http://awsassets.wwfindia.org/downloads/chasing_benefits.pdf>.

[76] Criminal Complaint No 579 of 2012 before the Magistrate, Dharwad as seen in para 1, *SA Patil v State of Karnataka*, Judgment of 11 October 2013 (High Court of Karnataka).

[77] ibid para 2.

[78] The section explicitly exempts applications for any right under the PPVFRA.

[79] BDA s 6(4).

[80] Koonan (n 49) 32.

[81] Pushpa Kumar Lakshmanan, 'Implementing the Nagoya Protocol on Access and Benefit Sharing in India' in Usha Tandon, Mohan Parasaran, and Sidharth Luthra (eds), *Biodiversity: Law, Policy and Governance* (Routledge 2018) 118–119.

20.2.3 Benefit Sharing

In India, there are two pieces of legislation that are important with respect to benefit sharing in the context of access to bioresources and knowledge. While benefit sharing for activities regulated under sections 3, 4, 6, and 7 is dealt with under the BDA, benefit sharing in relation to contribution to a new plant variety is dealt with under the PPVFRA. The scheme of benefit sharing under the BDA and the PPVFRA is different.

Benefit sharing is specifically mentioned in section 2(g) of the BDA, which defines 'fair and equitable benefit sharing' as the sharing of benefits as determined by the NBA under section 21. It is pertinent to note here that the CBD in Articles 15(4) and 15(5) envisaged facilitated access to be based on mutually agreed terms with the prior informed consent of the provider. In addition, obligations relating to fair and equitable sharing of benefits fall under Article 15(7) of the CBD, which also requires mutually agreed terms between the user and the provider. The unique feature of the BDA and the Biodiversity Rules is that the approval for access is in the form of a written agreement or contract between the NBA and the user, which mentions benefit-sharing obligations. Critics point out that the BDA intends to club 'access' obligations with the requirement of 'benefit sharing'.[82] Benefit sharing that is determined by the NBA under sections 21(1) and 21(2) of the BDA mandates that while regulating access, the NBA should ensure that the benefits of the use of the biological resource and related knowledge are based upon mutually agreed terms.[83] Even though a reading of the unamended section 21(1) of the BDA requires the NBA to facilitate negotiations between the user, local bodies and benefit claimers, the agreement for ABS is entered between the user and the NBA. According to the amended section 21(1), terms and conditions are mutually agreed between the user and the BMC represented by the NBA. This agreement is a standard fully fledged agreement which includes benefit sharing as a condition for utilizing biological resources and associated knowledge.[84] Critics have highlighted the challenge that neither the applicant nor the members of the Expert Committee which processes the ABS application are able to clearly specify the quantum of benefits likely to accrue at this early stage of research including the exploratory stage.[85] The Expert Committee on ABS and the NBA use certain estimations for the fast processing of ABS applications without truly ascertaining the potential and possibilities of each application for access.

In 2014, the NBA framed the Guidelines on Access to Biological Resources and Associated Knowledge and Benefit Sharing Regulations (ABS Regulations). These ABS Regulations enabled the State Biodiversity Boards (SBBs) to enter into benefit-sharing agreements. The Regulations explicitly require benefit-sharing obligations to be met by Indians and Indian entities who are using biological resources for commercial utilization or bio-survey or bio-utilization for commercial utilization except those who are

[82] Bavikatte and Tvedt (n 48) 11.

[83] BDA s 21.

[84] Bavikatte and Tvedt (n 48) 13.

[85] ibid.

exempted.[86] In a challenge to the ABS Regulations, the High Court of Uttarakhand held that the Regulations were *intra vires* to the BDA. The court put special emphasis on the term 'fair and equitable benefit sharing' as per section 2(g) of the BDA, which is defined as the sharing of benefits as determined by the NBA under section 21. The judgment explicitly mentioned the power of the NBA to determine benefit sharing under section 21(2).[87] It is important to note that these Regulations were notified under section 64, read with sections 18(1) and 21(4) of the BDA, which empowers the NBA to make guidelines on ABS. Although the court referred to Articles 8(j) and 15 of the CBD and Articles 5, 7, 12, and 15 of the Nagoya Protocol, which deal with prior informed consent and mutually agreed terms, the court did not specifically deal with the issue of whether predetermined benefit sharing as provided in the Regulations conflict with the CBD and the Nagoya Protocol. The issue of unilateral imposition of benefit sharing is being challenged before the National Green Tribunal (NGT).[88]

Benefit sharing under the PPVFRA is determined by the Plant Variety Protection Authority under section 26. This provision sets out a procedure for claiming the benefits. The determination of benefit sharing is not envisaged as a negotiated text but is determined by the Authority upon inviting claims and hearing the applicant of the registered variety and the benefit claimer. In addition, benefit sharing is limited to monetary compensation, whereas benefits sharing under the BDA is both monetary and non-monetary.

20.2.4 Other Issues

Several other issues need to be considered here. These include the ambiguous nature of regulation, its centralized nature, and the lack of effective recognition of the rights of IPLCs.

Ambiguous and excessive regulation: The BDA has been criticized for its ambiguous nature. Definitions of 'value-added products' and 'biological resources' are heavily contested by the users. Many petitions were filed before different fora, including various High Courts and different regional benches of the NGT, seeking clarification on these definitions, but those petitions were dismissed without any interpretation.[89]However, in *Biodiversity Management Committee v Western Coal Fields Ltd*, the NGT went into substantial definitional interpretation of the term 'biological resources'. In this case, the BMC of the village Eklahara in Madhya Pradesh contended that coal is a biological

[86] Guidelines on Access to Biological Resources and Related Knowledge and Benefit Sharing Regulations, 2014 regs 2, 3, and 14.

[87] *Divya Pharmacy v Union of India* 2018 SCC OnLine Uttarakhand 1035, para 104.

[88] *Dabur India v National Biodiversity Authority* Appeal No 54 of 2022 (NGT—Southern Zone Bench, Chennai).

[89] Alphonsa Jojan, 'The Curious Case of the Indian Biological Diversity Act' *Spicyip* (16 November 2017) <https://spicyip.com/2017/11/the-curious-case-of-the-indian-biological-diversity-act.html>.

resource, and therefore, the respondent must share benefits with the BMC. The NGT agreed with coal users and the NBA by stating that coal is not a biological resource and hence does not come under the regulatory purview of the BDA.[90]

Another criticism of the Act is excessive regulation by authorities. As mentioned above, the BDA intends to cover only certain activities, and therefore, it is argued that direct consumption and trading as commodities do not come under the purview of the BDA.[91] In fact, Indian biodiversity regulation should focus on 'end uses' instead of regulating all uses throughout the length and breadth of the country.[92] Nevertheless, the ABS Regulations stipulate that traders should share benefits with the NBA or the SBB for accessing biological resources. This requirement is evident from para 3 of the Regulations, which states that the benefit-sharing obligation of a trader who has not entered a prior benefit-sharing agreement shall be 1–3 per cent of the purchase price of the biological resources. Further, if this trader sells the biological resources to another trader, the benefit-sharing obligation of the buyer shall be 1–3 per cent of the new purchase price. An additional proviso is that 'where a buyer submits proof of benefit sharing by the immediate seller in the supply chain, the benefit-sharing obligation on the buyer shall be applicable only on that portion of the purchase price for which the benefit has not been shared in the supply chain'. This indicates that trading, the entire supply chain and the end use are regulated by the Regulations or at least benefits are claimed. It is clear from the definition of commercial utilization that only end uses are targeted, and trading of biological resources cannot be considered as 'end use' to fall under the definition of commercial utilization. This imposition of benefit is in addition to the collection fee that the BMCs are entitled to levy under section 41(c) of the BDA read with regulation 5 of the 2014 ABS Regulations. These aspects make the regulatory power of the authorities under the BDA excessive.

Centralized and bureaucratic regulation: The unamended BDA envisages regulation of access to biological resources as a negotiated process mediated by the institutions created by the Act. The role of the NBA, according to section 21(1) of the Act, is to grant approvals for access while ensuring that the terms and conditions secure equitable sharing of benefits arising out of the use of accessed biological resources and related knowledge.[93] Thereby, the original Act envisages a participatory, inclusive, and democratic regulation. But the Act was criticized as early as in 2000, while it was still in the legislative process, as giving the government and bureaucracy control over biological resources and knowledge.[94] Over the years, this prediction has proved correct as the regulation of ABS tends to involve more of bureaucratic control. The terms and

[90] *Biodiversity Management Committee v Western Coal Fields Ltd* Original Application No. 28 of 2013, Judgment of 6 October 2015 (NGT—Central Zone).

[91] Bavikatte and Tvedt (n 48) 10.

[92] Madhav Gadgil, 'Defining Biological Resources' (2000) 79(3) *Current Science* 280.

[93] BDA s 21.

[94] K Ravi Srinivas, 'Biodiversity Bill: Nice Words, No Vision' (2000) 35(45) *Economic and Political Weekly* 3916.

conditions are already fixed to ease the processing of applications whose statutory time limit is six months.[95] They are predetermined by the NBA through the ABS Regulations. There is minimal chance for actual negotiation. So far, except in one or two cases, there are no reported cases where benefit claimers are identified, nor are there cases in which local bodies have been active participants in the ABS negotiations.[96] In addition, more recognition is given to the role of Expert Committees for approval of the access application. Certain commentators have argued that the NBA acts as *parens patriae* on behalf of Indian citizens through which the NBA collects or negotiates user fees, royalties, and shares with benefit claimers.[97] While the international and national laws rely upon the concepts of prior informed consent and mutually agreed terms, especially involving IPLCs in ABS, the Regulations do not pay enough heed to it as the NBA acts as a mere fee collector,[98] as opposed to a body that promotes participatory decision-making in the ABS process.

Lack of real recognition of rights of indigenous peoples and local communities: The unamended section 21(1) of the BDA vests power with the NBA to ensure that the terms and conditions of access secure equitable benefits between the person applying for such approval, the local bodies concerned, and the benefit claimers on mutually agreed terms.[99] Despite this provision, currently there is no mechanism to identify benefit claimers under the Act. Even though the BDA recognizes conservers of biological resources, creators and holders of knowledge and information relating to the use of biological resources as 'benefit claimers',[100] benefit claimers rarely benefit from these provisions.[101] There are no effective pathways for realizing their rights, and therefore, they largely remain on paper and are unsecured. Under the existing regime, those seeking the NBA's approval must provide information, *inter alia*, on whether any identified individual/community is holding the traditional knowledge. The onus of identification of benefit claimers is neither shared by the NBA nor the SBB, even though the NBA has the responsibility to ensure equitable sharing of benefits in accordance with mutually agreed terms.[102] If the applicant does not identify the benefit claimer, benefit claimers are excluded from the entire process of determination of ABS. The Act does not provide any incentive or obligation for the applicant to identify the benefit claimer. Furthermore, the applications under the BDA are not published publicly, unlike the

[95] Biological Diversity Rules, 2004 r 14(3).
[96] Bavikatte and Tvedt (n 48) 15.
[97] Reddy (n 34) 192.
[98] Srinivas (n 92) 3918.
[99] BDA s 21.
[100] ibid s 2(a).
[101] Kanchi Kohli and Shalini Bhutani, 'Ten Years of Biological Diversity Act' (2012) 47(39) *Economic and Political Weekly* 15.
[102] Alphonsa Jojan, 'Developing Biocultural Jurisprudence for Securing Rights of Indigenous Peoples and Local Communities: Divya Pharmacy v UoI' *Spicyip* (6 March 2019) <https://spicyip.com/2019/03/developing-bio-cultural-jurisprudence-for-securing-rights-of-indigenous-peoples-and-local-communities-divya-pharmacy-v-uoi.html>.

applications for EIA under the Environment (Protection) Act. Unlike the mechanism under the PPVFRA, there are no legal measures under the BDA for a potential benefit claimer to engage with the approval process if they are not identified. They are at the mercy of the user applicant or the statutory body. In other words, benefit claimers do not have any mechanism to claim their benefits. The only provision is their right to file a complaint before the court under section 61 of the BDA in case of offences under the Act. The 2023 Amendment Act to the BDA has removed benefit claimers from the process of determination of benefit sharing envisaged in section 21(1).

Further, there is no mechanism to elaborate benefit sharing with benefit claimers even though the NBA has notified the 2014 ABS Regulations. This notification mentions the percentage of fees to be collected from the user applicants but does not provide a mechanism for involving benefit claimers in the process. This approach of the state and the authorities marginalizes IPLCs, who are the real beneficiaries of the Act. The funds that are deposited with the National Biodiversity Fund, the State Biodiversity Fund and the Local Biodiversity Fund are also to be used for channelling benefits to benefit claimers, conservation, and promotion of biological resources and development of areas from where such biological resources or associated knowledge have been accessed, and the socio-economic development of such areas in consultation with the local bodies.[103] Hence, the larger scheme of the BDA has a critical role for the benefit claimers who are yet to see any substantial benefits.

This importance given to benefit claimers is reflected in *Divya Pharmacy v Union of India*.[104] In this case, the primary issue was whether the SBB or the NBA has the power to impose fair and equitable benefit sharing as defined in section 2(g) of the BDA with respect to Indian entities since Indians are only required to give prior intimation to the relevant SBB as per section 7.[105] The court ruled that SBBs have the power to impose benefit sharing, and the NBA has the power to frame guidelines based on a purposive interpretation of the BDA, considering the long history of the movement for conservation and India's commitments under international law.[106] The court held that the BDA is a beneficial piece of legislation, and IPLCs who either grow biological resources or have traditional knowledge over the resources are the real beneficiaries of the Act.[107] Reliance was also placed on the Nagoya Protocol, particularly Articles 7, 12, and 15, which make no distinction between an Indian (domestic) user and a foreign user with respect to the obligations towards IPLCs.[108] The 2023 Amendment Act has amended section 7 of the BDA so as exclude activities using codified traditional knowledge from the regulatory scope of SBBs, thereby disentitling benefit claimers of the potential benefits from users such as Divya Pharmacy and other AYUSH industries.

103 BDA s 27(2),
104 *Divya Pharmacy* (n 85).
105 ibid para 16.
106 ibid paras 105–106.
107 ibid para 43.
108 ibid para 72.

Conclusion

The national legal framework on biodiversity aims to achieve biodiversity conservation, sustainable use of its components and fair and equitable benefit sharing. Section 20.1 mapped the legal framework for biodiversity conservation in India through themes such as approaches to conservation, particularly *in situ* conservation, agrobiodiversity conservation, and community conservation. It suggests that biodiversity conservation laws have the potential to govern not only wildlife, forests, and coasts, but also cultural landscapes and waterscapes, domesticated biodiversity, agroecosystems, and so on to be governed by diverse actors such as the concerned government departments, local bodies, and communities. This section also finds that agrobiodiversity conservation laws are weak, and relevant institutions on agrobiodiversity should go beyond their existing approaches, such as *ex situ* conservation, documentation, and registration of indigenous agricultural biodiversity. They should also focus on *in situ* conservation, including promotion, recognition, and support for the efforts of farmers and other communities in it. Further, this section highlighted that the role of communities in conservation should no longer be overlooked, but their efforts should receive adequate official recognition and support. Therefore, the current legal and institutional framework on biodiversity conservation and use should be made more inclusive, participatory, democratic, and human rights-based, focusing on all levels of biodiversity and all actors conserving biodiversity.

Section 20.2 discussed the ABS concept, the national framework of ABS and related issues and challenges. This discussion indicates that the ABS aspects of the BDA require a thorough review focusing on providing clarity and certainty on regulated activities under the BDA. Additionally, the ABS Regulations should construct mechanisms that secure the rights of IPLCs over their resources and traditional knowledge. Moreover, the impact of the BDA on international collaboration on basic and conservation research requires further investigation and special consideration. It is suggested that the regulation should promote such research by giving swift approvals and adequate sharing of benefits, especially non-monetary benefits such as education, training, capacity building, and information sharing. Therefore, the law on ABS should be amended to be clear, effective, equitable, and supportive of conservation and environmentally sound biodiversity-related activities.

This chapter explored biodiversity-related laws in India, highlighting the need for more research in this area. The chapter reveals that in addition to conservation and sustainability, laws relating to biodiversity are intrinsically linked to laws on human rights, especially those of indigenous people and local communities who depend on biodiversity. These laws also have implications on international and domestic trade, intellectual property protection of life forms such as plants, animals, and micro-organisms, agriculture, and technology such as biotechnology. Further research in this area of law should be informed by these linkages and their complexities to undertake a nuanced and comprehensive study of this area.

Suggestions for Further Reading

Kabir Bavikatte and Morten Walloe Tvedt, 'Beyond the Thumbrule Approach: Regulatory Innovations for Bioprospecting in India' (2015) 11(1) *Law Environment and Development Journal* 1.

Shalini Bhutani and Ashish Kothari, 'The Biodiversity Rights of Developing Nations: A Perspective from India' (2002) 32(4) *Golden Gate University Law Review* 5.

Sujith Koonan, 'Farmers Rights in India: Assessing the Conceptual and Implementation Issues' (2012) 4(1) *Dehradun Law Review* 29.

Doris Schroeder, 'Traditional Knowledge, Indigenous Communities, and Ethical Values' in Suneetha Subramanian and Balakrishna Pisupati (eds), *Traditional Knowledge in Policy and Practice: Approaches to Development and Human Well-Being* (United Nations University Press 2010) 97.

Meenal Tatpati, Ashish Kothari, and Rashi Mishra, *The Niyamgiri Story: Challenging the Idea of Growth Without Limits?* (Kalpavriksh 2016).

CHAPTER 21

BIOSAFETY IN SYNTHETIC BIOLOGY

SOPHY K.J.

Abstract

The 1992 Convention on Biological Diversity defines 'synthetic biology' as 'further development and a new dimension of biotechnology that combines science, technology and engineering to design, redesign, manufacture/construct and or modify genetic materials, living organism and biological systems'. Policy questions around the use of synthetic biology in plant genetic resources include discussions of equity, fairness and bio-safety/security. This chapter addresses these policy questions, focusing specifically on biosafety concerns of synthetic biology. It maps discussions on biosafety at international forums regulating biotech trade and its further expansion to synthetic biology and contrasts the domestic regulatory approach towards the new technology over the last two decades. It reviews recent policies governing bio-risk issues and emphasises the precautionary principle and the command-and-control approach to address the biological risks of synthetic biology.

Introduction

While the potential of the new technology, Synthetic Biology (SynBio), is widely recognized,[1] biodiversity, biosafety, and biosecurity concerns relating to it are a matter

[1] Laurie J Heyer and Jeffrey L Poet, 'Synthetic Biology: A New Frontier' (2014) 121 (9) *The American Mathematical Monthly* 866.

of debate in various international forums, such as the United Nations Environmental Programme (UNEP), World Trade Organization (WTO), Food and Agriculture Organization (FAO), and World Intellectual Property Organization (WIPO). SynBio is used in a wide range of fields such as food production, waste processing, water purification, and ecological restoration. However, concerns about its intervention with the environment and its implications for biodiversity are uncertain, and there is serious concern about its potential threats to cultures, rights, livelihoods, and nature itself.[2] This chapter discusses the need for regulatory initiatives to address these concerns, considering SynBio's pervasive interventionist character into the plant kingdom, environment, food security, and public health.

Biosafety concerns in SynBio mainly revolve around two challenges. The first is the accidental or deliberate release of modified organisms into the environment and its implications for the natural environment, biodiversity, food security, and public health.[3] Second, the fast pace of technology development today raises the question of unpredictable behaviours of the organisms themselves.[4] These challenges highlight the need for regulations to contain the modified organisms. Biosecurity regulations have focused on the containment of misuse or accidental misuse of processes and products. Biosecurity for SynBio raises regulatory concerns as policymakers and practitioners believe that it outpaces the established biosafety and biosecurity measures to prevent misuse.[5] Certain countries in Europe, America, and Asia have enacted laws and regulations to deal with the concerns of biosafety, biosecurity, and cyberbiosecurity arising from SynBio, to regulate its adverse effects on public health and the environment.[6] India is still at the nascent stage of framing policy and regulatory provisions.

This chapter starts by discussing the characteristics of SynBio to explain the importance of a new regulatory framework for this innovation. The discussion revolves around ethical, legal, and social concerns relating to SynBio raised by scientists and policymakers. Regulatory challenges to prevent violations that result in misuse/failure to comply with obligations of containment, interventions into biodiversity and other environmental hazards are also discussed in this chapter. Lastly, the current position of law relating to biosecurity and biosafety in India is covered to analyze the potential of these regulations to tackle issues arising from SynBio. The chapter then summarizes the discussion in the conclusion.

[2] Kent H Redford and others, 'Synthetic Biology and the Conservation of Biodiversity' (2014) 48 *Oryx* 330.

[3] Jing Li and others, 'Advances in Synthetic Biology and Biosafety Governance' (2021) 9 *Frontiers in Bioengineering and Biotechnology* <https://doi.org/10.3389/fbioe.2021.598087>.

[4] Timothy K Lu, Ahmad S Khalil, and James J Collins, 'Next-generation Synthetic Gene Networks' (2009) 27(12) *Nature Biotechnology* 1139.

[5] Benjamin D Trump and others, 'Building Biosecurity for Synthetic Biology' (2020) 16(7) *Molecular Systems Biology* e9723.

[6] National Academy of Engineering and National Research Council, *Positioning Synthetic Biology to Meet the Challenges of the 21st Century: Summary Report of a Six Academies Symposium Series* (The National Academies Press 2013).

21.1 SynBio and Policy Considerations

SynBio as a technology is a second-generation development in genetic engineering. This section introduces the technology in SynBio to explain its difference in application and outcome from the first-generation biotechnology processes. That will help us analyse the ethical, legal, and social concerns around SynBio to understand the policy challenges.

SynBio is the application of engineering principles and mathematical modelling to the design and construction of biological parts, devices, and systems with applications in medicine, environmental science, technology, and energy.[7] This indicates the use of multi-calculative and technological tools in genome editing. It creates a fully operational biological system from the stitching of the smallest constituent parts together, such as DNA, proteins, and other organic molecules.[8]

SynBio is like genome editing in Genetically Modified Organisms (GMOs), but it differs in how it creates change in genome sequencing. In genome editing in GMOs, there is an intervention with typical tools to make smaller changes to an organism's DNA, mostly through the addition or subtraction of DNA or transfer of existing genes between species. In SynBio, a genetic code is created by sewing different DNAs together and inserting them into another organism's genome. This results in the creation of new genetic codes which could not be found in an environment with new or existing traits.[9] Production of SynBio can be more challenging and there is uncertainty over its longer use as it increases potential toxicity due to multiple external factors, including change in climate and genomic behaviour.[10]

The use of engineering techniques with mathematical modelling and scientific precision in cells to create genes that perform desired functions has become common in medicine, agriculture, and manufacturing sectors.[11] Though basic scientific biological understanding helps to identify gaps in the creation of synthetic genomic sequences, there are instances where unexpected gaps get uncovered in the experimentation stage.[12] These challenges are related to resistance in living cells against the performance of the assigned tasks.[13]

[7] Heyer and Poet (n 1).

[8] Zheng-jun Guan and others, 'Biosafety Considerations of Synthetic Biology in the International Genetically Engineered Machine (iGEM) Competition' (2013) 63(1) *BioScience* 25.

[9] Paras Chopra and Akhil Kamma, 'Engineering Life through Synthetic Biology' (2006) 6(5) *In Silico Biology* 401.

[10] European Union, Final Opinion on Synthetic Biology III: Risks to the environment and biodiversity related to synthetic biology and research priorities in the field of synthetic biology (2015).

[11] Steven A Benner and A Michael Sismour, 'Synthetic Biology' (2005) 6(7) *Nature Reviews Genetics* 533.

[12] Jonathan B Tucker and Raymond A Zillinskas, 'The Promise and Perils of Synthetic Biology' (2006) 12 *The New Atlantis* 25.

[13] Gigi Kwik Gronvall, 'Mitigating the Risks of Synthetic Biology' (Council on Foreign Relations 2015).

As discussed above, there are potential risks of uncertainty, unpredictability, and unpreparedness to tackle the impacts of SynBio technology. These risks raise environmental challenges that include 'the potential for SynBio organisms to persist in the environment, become invasive, disrupt food webs, transfer genetic material via vertical gene flow or horizontal gene transfer, and impact biodiversity and ecosystems'.[14] The pervasiveness of this technology is unpredictable because of its 'much larger depth of intervention into the biological nature of the organism,—both by quality and quantity'.[15] Therefore, the regulation of SynBio to prevent biosecurity and biosafety concerns should contain a stronger precautionary regime to control its use and dissemination into the environment.

SynBio has been criticized for its unidentifiable and potential harm to the environment.[16] The omnibus question is whether human beings are leaping beyond moral boundaries to redesign lives and natural ecosystems with modern genome technologies. Other important questions involve the protection of the environment from potential bio-hazards, the possibility of risk assessments, accessibility to new SynBio curatives, the evolution of global and domestic biosafety regulations and protocols, etc. Bioethicists have raised three important concerns: (1) the argument of 'life' forms is used as a commodity for monopolization; (2) moral concerns about human intervention into the creation of life; and (3) deliberate misuse of SynBio innovations for ulterior motives.[17]

The argument regarding the monopolization of 'life forms' is a long-drawn ethical debate that started with the patenting of life forms. The clarity that the WTO's Agreement on Trade-Related Aspects of Intellectual Property Rights (TRIPs) provided under Article 27(3)(b) is that plants, animals, and essentially biological processes are excluded from patenting, but microorganisms and non-biological and microbiological processes are eligible for patents.[18] However, plant varieties are eligible for protection either through patent protection, a 'sui generis' system, or a combination of the two. Using the exemptions under this provision, patents are granted for biological molecules or microorganisms and methods for their production or uses of such molecules or microorganisms. A SynBio product consisting of different parts, such as molecules, microorganisms, etc., is protected through different patents. Patenting of seeds, plant varieties, and bacteria raises questions relating to private property rights or exclusive rights of the right holders to the prevention of access of others. The concern is over

[14] Michelle M Epstein and Theo Vermeire, 'Scientific Opinion on Risk Assessment of Synthetic Biology' (2016) 34(8) *Trends in Biotechnology* 601.

[15] M Engelhard, M Bolker, and Nediljko Budisa, 'Old and New Risks in Synthetic Biology: Topics and Tools for Discussion' in M Engelhard (ed), *Synthetic Biology Analysed: Tools for Discussion and Evaluation* (Springer 2016) 51.

[16] J Anderson and others, 'Engineering and Ethical Perspectives in Synthetic Biology' (2012) 13(7) 5 *EMBO Reports* 584.

[17] Thomas Douglas and Julian Savulescu, 'Synthetic Biology and the Ethics of Knowledge' (2010) 36(11) *Journal of Medical Ethics* 687.

[18] Agreement on Trade-Related Aspects of Intellectual Property Rights (TRIPS), Marrakesh, 15 April 1994, 1869 UNTS 299.

public access, exchange, and deterrence to utility for all. The second concern revolves around the moral debates on humans owning lives. The commercial control of any life form as a tradable commodity for private benefit raises an ethical debate to the extent that it is artificial, unnatural or inorganic and intervenes with the organic evolution of living organisms.

Considering the merit of the concerns as discussed above, more attention is given to the third concern—deliberate misuse of SynBio innovations for ulterior motives—for analysis. The serious concern about the misuse of knowledge for use in biological weapons has been raised by bioethicists. According to them, not only intended use but also the dual-use dilemma[19] plays an important role in risk enhancement of potential misuse. Selgelid has argued that 'the threat posed by the misuse of knowledge from synthetic biology will ultimately be greater than that posed by nuclear technology'.[20] Ethicists are of the view that any potential use of such technology requires the development of principles and strict protocol regarding due diligence studies, stages of production with challenges and gaps, safeguards against leakage, and dissemination and condensation processes and its future use.[21]

Endy records that 'SynBio will not achieve its potential until scientists can predict accurately how a new genetic circuit will behave inside a living cell'.[22] He challenges the reliability of the molecular processes of cells and the expertise of scientists to manipulate them accurately.[23] Inherent risks in SynBio are associated with its self-replicating character and capability of evolution, which may occur in the future.[24] The first risk which is preventable to an extent is by following a containment protocol to block the leakage of any synthetic microorganism from the research laboratory. Any deliberate attempt to release the same should be condemned through strict laws.

The assessment of potential risks associated with synthetic genomes depends upon familiarity with their genetic pedigree and emergent properties arising from the complex interactions of their constituent genes. Over time, the artificial or redesigned BioBricks raises concerns over its predictability and harmful characteristics.[25] The lack of natural genetic pedigree in SynBio demands a robust regulatory framework with biosafety

[19] This dilemma arises when scientific knowledge could be used in good and harmful ways, and the risk of harmful use is sufficiently high that it is no longer clear whether that knowledge should be pursued or disseminated. See Seumas Miller and Michael J Selgelid, 'Ethical and Philosophical Consideration of the Dual-use Dilemma in the Biological Sciences' (2007) 13(4) *Science and Engineering Ethics* 523.

[20] Michael J Selgelid, 'A Tale of Two Studies: Ethics, Bioterrorism and the Censorship of Science' (2007) 37(3) *Hastings Center Report* 35.

[21] ibid.

[22] Drew Endy, 'Foundations for Engineering Biology' (2005) 438(7067) *Nature* 449.

[23] ibid.

[24] Xiaomei Zeng and others, 'Regulation and Management of the Biosecurity for Synthetic Biology' (2022) 7 (2) *Synthetic and Systems Biotechnology* 784.

[25] *BioBrick* is a standard for interchangeable parts developed to build biological systems in living cells. BioBricks can be thought of as building blocks or legos that can be put together in different ways to assemble larger synthetic biological circuits that together have a unique function.

guidelines to prevent their accidental release into the environment. Following the precautionary principle would be important until these synthetic genomes are found harmless. This requires a biocontainment policy with a high level of safety standards demonstrated accurately. Church cautions against any release of synthetic genomes without clarity of their behaviour or potential consequences—both ecological and medical.[26] Rabinow and Bennett argue for rethinking the role that human sciences play in genetic engineering and adopting a 'human practices' approach to formulate a new approach to the ethical, legal, and social concerns of bio-engineering models.[27]

21.2 Biosafety for SynBio: Relevance of the Precautionary Principle

Biosafety in SynBio became a wider policy concern as it risks biodiversity, food security, and public health. The World Health Organization defines 'biosafety' as 'the containment principles, technologies, and practices that are implemented to prevent unintentional exposure to pathogens and toxins or their accidental release to the environment'.[28] Already existing debates on biosafety concerning GMOs, biodiversity, and traditional knowledge are relevant discussions before various international forums such as UNEP, FAO, WIPO, and WTO. This is primarily because SynBio is the next-generation biotech innovation, and issues of containment, contamination, and risks associated with use and misuse to the environment and health are also relevant for SynBio.

The precautionary principle in environmental law implies that if there is an apprehension about possible damage to the environment, it is better to avoid such adverse effects on the environment by waiting for incontrovertible scientific evidence.[29] Principle 15 of the 1992 Rio Declaration on Environment and Development, states that:

> In order to protect the environment, the precautionary approach shall be widely applied by States according to their capabilities. Where there are threats of serious or irreversible damage, lack of full scientific certainty shall not be used as a reason for postponing cost-effective measures to prevent environmental degradation.[30]

[26] George Church, 'Let Us Go Forth and Safely Multiply' (2005) 438 *Nature* 423.

[27] Paul Rabinow and Gaymon Bennett, *Designing Human Practices: An Experiment with Synthetic Biology* (University of Chicago Press 2012).

[28] WHO, Laboratory Biosafety Manual (3rd edn, 2004) 47 <https://www.who.int/publications/i/item/9241546506>.

[29] James Cameron and Juli Abouchar, 'The Precautionary Principle: A Fundamental Principle of Law and Policy for the Protection of the Global Environment' (1991) 14 *Boston College International and Comparative Law Review* 1.

[30] Rio Declaration on Environment and Development, 14 June 1992, UN Doc A/CONF.151/26/Rev 1 (vol I), annex II (1992) Principle 15.

This principle received particular interest in environmental litigation as it has weighed scientific risk evaluation and potential damage to the environment. This principle is extensively used to avoid public health crises due to unscientific environmental contamination.[31]

The biosafety debates became more prominent in the context of discussions on transgenic plants and GMOs. These debates are relevant for SynBio because of the commonalities of critical policy issues involved in biotech products. The debates on 'trade v. sustainable environment' in world forums emphasized fundamental questions relating to food security, feed supply, health care, and environmental governance.[32] The Preamble to the 1992 Convention on Biological Diversity (Biodiversity Convention) read with Article 8(g) and Article 19(3)[33] adopted the precautionary principle to impose restraints on biotech trade.[34] A joint reading of these provisions indicates that the principle is also applicable to SynBio but it remains advisory.[35] It should have been made a mandatory principle to strengthen protection measures.

The weak positioning of the precautionary principle under the Biodiversity Convention led to negotiations to formulate the Cartagena Protocol on Biosafety, 2000. The Protocol emphasizes the central role of the principle in stating that:

> lack of scientific certainty due to insufficient relevant scientific information and knowledge regarding the extent of the potential adverse effects of a living modified organism on the conservation and sustainable use of biological diversity in the Party of import, taking also into account risks to human health, shall not prevent that Party from taking a decision, as appropriate, about the import of the living modified organism in question ... to avoid or minimize such potential adverse effects.[36]

This provision empowers parties to take precautions before introducing living-modified organisms (LMOs) or such products into the environment.

[31] Kenneth R Foster, Paolo Vecchia, and Michael H Repacholi, 'Science and the Precautionary Principle' (2000) 288 Science 979.

[32] Robert Falkner, 'Regulating Biotech Trade: The Cartagena Protocol on Biosafety' (2000) 76(2) *International Affairs* 299.

[33] ibid, art 19(3).

[34] Convention on Biological Diversity, Rio de Janeiro, 5 June 1992, 1760 UNTS 79.

[35] Thomas P Redick, 'Biotechnology, Biosafety and Sustainable Development' (1997) 12(2) *Natural Resources & Environment* 114.

[36] Cartagena Protocol on Biosafety to the Convention on Biological Diversity, Cartagena, 29 January 2000, 2226 UNTS 208, art 10 (6).

21.3 The Cartagena Protocol: Biosafety and SynBio

The main objective of the Cartagena Protocol is to ensure protection in the safe transfer, handling, use, disposal, and transboundary movement of LMOs. LMOs are defined under Article 3(g) of the Protocol to mean 'any living organism that possesses a novel combination of genetic material obtained through the use of modern biotechnology'. The terminology 'modern biotechnology' according to the Protocol drafted in 2000 does not include techniques like genome editing.[37] Further, the definition of LMOs does not contain other constituents like DNA. Hence, the question remains unanswered as to whether the Protocol covers products of SynBio, which are non-living or cannot attain life in isolation. The definitions of 'transfer' and 'transboundary movement' do not include the possibility of local synthesis of DNA using publicly available sequence data.[38] The ambiguity in its definitions to cover products of SynBio leaves certain genetic constituents developed through SynBio out of this Protocol. Therefore, a conscious approach to enlarge the scope of the definition of LMOs to include any genetic constituent is required to cover SynBio products.

Article 18 of the Protocol requires each party to take appropriate measures while handling, packaging, or transporting LMOs under conditions of safety to avoid adverse effects on the conservation and sustainable use of biodiversity and to consider risks to human health. The detailed identification and documentation that this provision requires was contested by the Miami Group on the grounds of unfeasibility and administrative hazards.[39] This debate resulted in leaving out the provisions relating to detailed documentation to be decided within two years of the Protocol's entry into force. The Advance Informed Agreement (AIA) procedure includes the right of the importing nation to either approve or prohibit the transboundary movement of regulated goods.[40] A denial shall be based on a risk assessment that proves a threat to biodiversity or human health. AIA procedure gives power to the importing country to ask for details and reject LMOs if it risks the biosafety of the country.

There are two kinds of procedures to regulate the movement of LMOs. One is intended for direct introduction into the environment through AIA and the other is for LMOs used directly as food, feed, or processing (LMO-FFP). As mentioned above, under the AIA procedure, the exporter country is required to obtain prior consent from

[37] Ana Atanassova and Felicity Keiper, 'Plant Breeding Innovation: A Global Regulatory Perspective' (2018) 95 *Cereal Chemistry* 8.

[38] Felicity Keiper and Ana Atanassova, 'Regulation of Synthetic Biology: Developments Under the Convention on Biological Diversity and its Protocols' (2020) *Front Bioeng Biotechnol* <https://www.ncbi.nlm.nih.gov/pmc/articles/PMC7160928/#B1>.

[39] Argentina, Australia, Canada, Chile, Uruguay, and the USA.

[40] Cartagena Protocol on Biosafety to the Convention on Biological Diversity, Cartagena, 29 January 2000, 2226 UNTS 208, art 10 (3).

the potential importing countries. Risk assessment and decision-making regarding import or rejection of import are made by the importing country.

Under the procedure for LMO-FFP, countries that decide to put LMOs on the market make their decision public by entering it into a central information system known as the Biosafety Clearing House (BCH). Based on this information, a country can decide whether or not to import the products based on the precautionary approach. A country can consider its socio-economic factors before decision-making. Countries are required to do public consultations regarding the import of LMOs. If the decision is taken to import LMOs to be released into the environment, it is required to communicate its decision along with a summary of the risk assessment to the BCH.

The Protocol is an important step to balance trade and environmental concerns arising from LMOs. Though it was welcomed by environmentalists, it was criticized for deterring trade in agrarian innovations and new genetic resources.[41] There is also an argument that this raises public health concerns as stricter regulations impede R&D in pharmaceuticals.[42] The Protocol prioritises biosafety in the biotech trade, and it empowers states to make a scientific decision based on risk assessment. The procedures of international information sharing within the institutional framework of the BCH would assist developing countries to set biosafety standards and risk assessments.

The unresolved debates on liability and redress for damage resulting from transboundary movement of biotech products under the Cartagena Protocol resulted in the formation of an Open-ended Ad Hoc Working Group of Legal and Technical Experts on Liability and Redress.[43] After relentless efforts, the Nagoya–Kuala Lumpur Supplementary Protocol on Liability and Redress to the Cartagena Protocol on Biosafety was adopted on 15 October 2010.[44] The Protocol recommends 'parties to continue to apply existing legislation on civil liability or to develop specific legislation concerning liability and redress for material or personal damage associated with damage to the conservation and sustainable use of biological diversity'.[45] India ratified this Protocol in December 2014.[46] This is considered to be one of the important turning points in India's rethinking of the biosafety regulatory framework.

[41] Jonathan H Adler, 'More Sorry Than Safe: Assessing the Precautionary Principle and the Proposed International Biosafety Protocol' (2000) 35 *Texas International Law Journal* 173.

[42] ibid.

[43] Cartagena Protocol on Biosafety to the Convention on Biological Diversity, Cartagena, 29 January 2000, 2226 UNTS 208, art 3.

[44] Nagoya–Kuala Lumpur Supplementary Protocol on Liability and Redress to the Cartagena Protocol on Biosafety, 15 October 2010.

[45] ibid.

[46] Voluntary Peer-Review under the Convention on Biological Diversity (2016).

21.4 The Biodiversity Convention's Thirteenth Conference of Parties and Policy Decisions on SynBio

The thirteenth Conference of Parties (COP) to the Biodiversity Convention reiterated the use of SynBio and gene drives and reaffirmed the precautionary approach in the transboundary movement of LMOs. The policy recommendations on SynBio were carried out based on conclusions and recommendations of the report of the Ad Hoc Technical Expert Group on Synthetic Biology established by the Biodiversity Convention. The definition of SynBio by the COP posited it as a further development and new dimension of modern biotechnology that combines science, technology, and engineering to design new genetic material, living organisms, and biological systems.[47] This understanding of newness in technology brought in regulatory discussions specifically on SynBio.

The COP records that it is unclear whether LMOs through SynBio would fall under the definition of LMOs in the Cartagena Protocol and whether the result of a SynBio application is 'living' or not.[48] With this ambiguity, it went ahead to apply general principles and methodologies for risk assessment and existing biosafety frameworks for such LMOs with the understanding that as future developments and applications in SynBio demand, new methodologies need to be updated and adapted for parties to follow.[49] It also asks the parties to follow the three objectives of the Biodiversity Convention: (1) conservation of biological diversity; (2) sustainable use of the components of biological diversity; and (3) fair and equitable sharing of benefits; and to take appropriate domestic socio-economic, cultural, and ethical considerations into account while identifying adverse or advantageous effects of SynBio.[50] While it agrees to the ambiguity of coverage of SynBio under the definition of LMOs, the COP recommends the application of the same risk assessment procedure and management of the Protocol to products of SynBio. This shows the contradiction and callous decision-making of the COP without adopting a precautionary approach to restrain any trade or movement of LMOs out of SynBio, without clarity on its coverage, and adequate research into its behaviour in different ecosystems. Developing countries in Asia, Africa, and Latin America sought a moratorium on SynBio and gene drives until the concept is clearly understood and argued that the application of GMOs is still a subject of controversy.[51] However, the COP went

[47] Decision XIII/17, 'Synthetic Biology', Report of the Conference of the Parties to the Convention on Biological Diversity on Its Thirteenth Meeting, UN Doc CBD/COP/13/25 (2016) 126.

[48] ibid para 7.

[49] ibid para 6.

[50] ibid para 10.

[51] Abebiyi Adedapo, 'Developing Countries Oppose UN Ratification of Synthetic Biology, Gene Drives' *Earth Journalism Network* (18 December 2016) <https://earthjournalism.net/stories/developing-countries-oppose-un-ratification-of-synthetic-biology-gene-drives>.

ahead and recognized the use of SynBio and gene drives. This demonstrates the lack of commitment of international forums towards issues of biosafety and environmental governance. The importance of the precautionary principle in biosafety is diluted as advisory on the ground of trade prospects of industrialized nations, even in international forums.

From the discussion on international standards relating to biosafety in the trade of LMOs, the risks of modern biotechnology to the environment and health were the focus of discussion in international documents such as the Biodiversity Convention, the Protocol and the COP. There was a gradual understanding that SynBio, as a new biotechnological innovation, raises more contentious challenges to the environment. The lack of consensus to adopt the 'precautionary principle' and the command-and-control approach resulted in a weaker biosafety framework at the international level. This is particularly important for the protection of biodiversity and biosafety in the Global South as the ramifications of the technology on the communities are manifold, including its intrusion into their livelihoods and survival.

21.5 Regulatory Framework in India

Globally, SynBio advanced rapidly, though, in India, it is still at the nascent stage both in its application and policy framing. India ratified the Cartagena Protocol on 23 January 2003, and the Ministry of Environment and Forests (MoEF) (now Ministry of Environment, Forest and Climate Change) is the nodal ministry for its implementation. At the policy level, the initiatives to examine the regulatory issues relating to SynBio in India started with the establishment of a Task Force on Synthetic and Systems Biology Resource Network. The Report of this Task Force recommended more investment to augment research and development in SynBio and warned that significant regulatory and ethical issues would need to be dealt with before implementation.[52]

The Guidance Report by the Department of Biotechnology (DBT) recommended that '[i]t is time for India to consolidate its stand on the science of synthetic biology and communicate its interests and aspirations in relevant international fora with clarity and should avoid conflicting stands on science on one hand and policy on the other'.[53] Based on this, a National Policy on Synthetic Biology for India has been drafted.[54] There are Biosafety regulations under domestic environmental law and earmarked institutions

[52] Report of the Planning Commission Constituted Task Force on Synthetic and Systems Biology Resource Network—12th Five Year Plan (2011) <https://dst.gov.in/sites/default/files/3-tsk_ssbrn-report.pdf>.

[53] Anonna Dutt, 'National Policy Required for Synthetic Biology, Says DBT Paper' *Indian Express* (17 February 2022) <https://indianexpress.com/article/cities/delhi/national-policy-needed-for-synthetic-biology-says-dbt-paper-7777678/>.

[54] Jacob Koshy, 'Centre Moots Policy on Synthetic Biology' *The Hindu* (20 February 2022) <https://www.thehindu.com/news/national/centre-moots-policy-on-synthetic-biology/article65068405.ece>.

to deal with regulatory approvals of biotech-engineered LMOs, which would include SynBio. This section examines various regulatory laws and policies for biosafety to analyse their efficiency in arresting the risks associated with SynBio.[55]

India is one of the countries which came up with a regulatory regime for GMOs. The central government approved the Rules for the Manufacture/Use/Import/Export and Storage of Hazardous Microorganisms, Genetically Engineered Organisms or Cells (Rules) under the Environment (Protection) Act, 1986 on 5 December 1989. According to the Rules, there are six authorities for regulatory purposes: the Recombinant DNA Advisory Committee (RDAC),[56] the Review Committee on Genetic Manipulation (RCGM),[57] the Genetic Engineering Approval Committee (GEAC),[58] Institutional Biosafety Committees (IBSC),[59] State Biosafety Coordination Committees (SBCC),[60] and District Level Committees (DLC)[61] to look into approval for GMOs. As the name suggests, the Rules deal with activities such as use, manufacture, import, export, storage, and research. The GEAC is the competent authority to approve or disapprove the release of GM crops considering the environmental risks.[62]

The Rules primarily focus on the approval process for GMOs/Genetically Engineered Organisms (GEOs) and hazardous microorganisms (which may not be genetically modified). The definition of genetic engineering under the Rules was further revised in the Regulations and Guidelines for Recombinant DNA Research and Biocontainment, 2017 (2017 Regulations) to include any 'modification, deletion or removal of parts of heritable material'. By this revision, the Rules can cover SynBio and the new genome engineering technologies—gene editing and gene drives.[63] The approval for any activity

55 Regulations and Guidelines for Recombinant DNA Research and Biocontainment, 2017.

56 Its mandate is (1) to review developments in biotechnology at national and international levels; (2) to recommend suitable and appropriate safety regulations for Indian in recombinant research, use, and applications from time to time; (3) to evolve long-term policy for research and development in Recombinant DNA research.

57 This Committee monitors the safety-related aspects of ongoing research projects or activities involving hazardous microorganisms, GE organisms and cells, and products thereof.

58 GEAC is (1) to appraise activities involving large-scale use of hazardous microorganisms GE organisms or cells in research and industrial production from the environmental angle; (2) to appraise proposals relating to the release of GE organisms and products into the environment, including experimental field trials; (3) The committee or any persons authorised by it has powers to take punitive action under the Environment (Protection) Act, 1986.

59 The Committee will be the nodal point for the implementation of the biosafety guidelines and the interactions within the institution.

60 This committee has the powers (1) to inspect, investigate and take punitive action in case of violations of statutory provisions through the State Pollution Control Board (SPCB) or the Directorate of Health etc.; (2) to review periodically the safety and control measures established at various institutions handling GE organisms; (3) to act as a nodal agency at the state level to assess the damage, if any, due to the release of GE organisms and to take on-site control measures.

61 DLC is to monitor the safety regulations in installations engaged in the use of genetically modified organisms/hazardous microorganisms and their applications in the environment.

62 Food Safety and Standards Authority of India, *Operationalising the Regulation of Genetically Modified Foods in India* (Food Safety and Standards Authority of India 2010).

63 ibid 5.

mentioned under the Rules needs to be processed through the GEAC, and the Rules designate the MoEF and the DBT as authorizing agents for approval. Various stages of regulatory approval include the manufacture, use, sale, import, export, and storage of GMOs.[64] The regulatory system also comprises other legal instruments such as the Drugs and Cosmetics Rules, 1988 (8th Amendment), the Protection of Plant Varieties and Farmers' Rights Act, 2001 (PPVFRA), the Biological Diversity Act, 2002, and the Food Safety and Standards Act, 2006. Even the plant varieties registered under the PPVFRA must get the approval of the GEAC if they are GM varieties. The failure of Bt Cotton, the first GM variety approved by the GEAC, and its adverse consequences on the ecosystem called into question the safety regulatory assessment process followed by the Committee.

The Rules prohibit pathogenic microorganisms in the laboratory without proper measures set out in the Environment (Protection) Act, 1986. Any experiment in the field of gene technology, either inside or outside the laboratory, cannot be carried out without the approval of the IBSC. Further, different guidelines and protocols came from the DBT to deal with new biotech innovations, including SynBio. The 2017 Regulations contained elaborate principles, factors, and operational guidelines relating to containment. It is important to note that the 2017 Regulations stressed identifying levels of risks associated with GEOs and selecting appropriate containment facilities. The 2017 Regulations prescribe certification of containment facilities for risk levels 3 and 4 and this includes inspection from the RCGM and evaluation of the facilities that would conclude with the filing of the inspection report.

There were various guidelines after the 2017 Regulations, such as the Handbook for Institutional Biosafety Committees, 2020 (Handbook),[65] the Guidelines for Establishment of Containment Facilities, 2020, and the Guidelines for the Safety Assessment of Genome-edited Plants, 2022 (Guidelines, 2020 and 2022). These are guidelines and recommendations to be followed by the responsible Committees for approvals.[66] Only approval processes cannot ensure the biosafety of SynBio products. There must be continuous assessment and renewal process of these products to check their potential change in characteristics. This considers unpredictability and uncertainty over its longer use and behavioural changes due to climatic conditions. Moreover, scientists have termed SynBio as a dual-use technology,[67] and the scientific culture of

[64] Rules for the Manufacture, Use, Import, Export and Storage of Hazardous micro-organisms/Genetically Engineered Organisms or Cells, 1989 r 2(3).

[65] This Handbook is to explain the decentralized regulatory powers of IBSCs and the regulatory mechanism of online registration and renewal of IBSCs at the Indian Biosafety Knowledge Portal.

[66] Institutional Biosafety Committee (IBSC) under the Handbook for Institutional Biosafety Committees, 2020, IBSC/RCGM/DBT under the Guidelines for Establishment of Containment Facilities, 2020, and Genetic Engineering Approval Committee under the Guidelines for the Safety Assessment of Genome-edited Plants, 2022.

[67] The dual-use dilemma in which the same technologies can be used for the good of humans and misused for biodegradation and bioterrorism.

Do It Yourself[68] around SynBio disseminates this technology without any checks and balances.[69] From a policy perspective, any regulatory framework that aims only to regulate approval of SynBio at the beginning without its continuous assessment at later stages, becomes a 'window dressing' without a robust regulatory vision.

Further, the proposed Biotechnology Regulatory Authority of India Bill (BRAI) is a failed attempt pending approval in Parliament since 2013. The BRAI makes a provision for a six-tier review system, which includes a provision for the public and other stakeholders to express their views before final approval by the authority.[70] It was halted because of strong civil society resistance about the manner of framing the BRAI and processes incorporated in it. BRAI was criticized for not considering domestic agrarian conditions and consulting important stakeholders, farmers, in the decision-making process of the approval.[71] The state governments have only been given recommendatory powers relating to decision-making. The power to approve or reject vests with the centrally located authority. It is reported that states like Madhya Pradesh, Kerala, and Karnataka have formally written to the central government opposing the current BRAI proposal for this reason.[72] Civil Society Organisations have contended that the decisions relating to the commercial use of biotech products have to be left to the state government to 'allow commercial use of an approved GM plant within the state if it has concerns about its adverse effects on biodiversity/ecosystems within the state'.[73]

21.6 Critical Insights

Considering developments in SynBio, especially in the context of dual-use research, there is a need to coordinate the functioning of authorities and revise and update the regulations and guidelines. Of the authorities, the RDAC and the RCGM function under the DBT. The RDAC functions as a policy-level committee, and it reviews international

[68] Do It Yourself is biohacking and wetware hacking, namely using genetic material for varied purposes. This is generally shared through virtual world-biotech sharing platforms or open science platforms to bring the technology closer to the public. The disadvantage is the use/misuse of such precise technology by individuals, and any critical challenges, such as callous handling of sensitive technology, may cause to human lives and the environment.

[69] Bart Kolodziejczyk, 'Do-it-yourself Biology Shows Safety Risks of an Open Innovation Movement' (*Brookings*, 9 October 2017) <https://www.brookings.edu/blog/techtank/2017/10/09/do-it-yourself-biology-shows-safety-risks-of-an-open-innovation-movement/>.

[70] SR Rao, 'Development of Genetically Engineered Crops—Public Policy, Regulatory Framework and Scientific Risk Assessment: Imperatives for Commercial Use' (International Conference on Plant Biotechnology for Food Security: New Frontiers, New Delhi, 2012).

[71] Sophy K. Joseph, *Customary Rights of Farmers in Neoliberal India: Legal and Policy Analysis* (OUP 2020).

[72] Ananya Mehta, 'Food Sovereignty, GMOs and BRAI Bill' *Greenpeace.org* (2013) <https://www.greenpeace.org/india/en/story/405/food-sovereignty-gmos-and-the-brai-bill/>.

[73] ibid.

and national developments in the field of biotechnology in an advisory capacity to the government. IBSCs follow the Recombinant DNA Safety Guidelines, 1990 and the Revised Guidelines for Research in Transgenic Plants and Guidelines for Toxicity and Allergenicity Evaluation of Transgenic Seeds, Plants and Plant Parts, 1998. ISBCs recommend biosecurity clearance to the RCGM. State Biosafety Coordination Committees (SBCCs) and DLCs check compliance with statutory biosafety requirements. This current regulatory framework is also applicable to SynBio research and applications. Apart from updating the 1989 Rules through the 2017 Regulations and notifying certain guidelines and protocols, the enforceability of such guidelines or protocols is not clear from the wording of these policies. These policies would effectively act as advisories and recommendations. They do not impose any liability on misleading, malicious or manipulative applications that have the potential of callous or risky or dual use on approval. There is no clarity on any legal procedures to be followed regarding ambiguous or false information relating to risks or outcomes. Further, the provision of collateral liability on the evaluators in the approval process in case of any deliberate collusion with the applicants is left unaddressed in these policy documents.

In the biosafety regulatory regime, especially in respect of SynBio, containment regulations play an important role.[74] The Second Asilomar Conference (1975), bringing together scientists, legal experts, physicians, and journalists, adopted two basic principles: (1) containment should be an essential consideration in the experimental design, and (2) the effectiveness of the containment should match the estimated risk as closely as possible.[75] One of the limitations of the 1989 Rules is the lack of a robust containment policy at par with technological development. Risk assessment and management require regulation of containment measures and waste management apart from handling, storage, transport, packaging, and labelling of biological organisms. Lack of containment measures seriously affects all processes and risks human health and the environment. The Regulation and Guidelines on Biosafety of Recombinant DNA and Biocontainment, 2017, was brought in to update the policy considering the rapid advancement in biology and biotechnology research globally and in India, both in public and private sector institutions. The Guidelines aim to cover the regulations on biosafety of rDNA research and handling of hazardous microorganisms and GE organisms or cells in India. However, the records of its compliance and implementation by the respective authorities are not available.

India's biosafety regulations indeed deal with both microorganisms and genomic technology. However, SynBio requires a more expertise-oriented evaluation for gene drives and the creation of a database on BioBricks for risk assessment. Another important criticism of the Indian decision-making system in biosafety governance is its non-consultative framework, wherein it lacks public participation in decision-making. Though the regulatory space is governmental, industry and civic knowledge

[74] World Health Organization, *Laboratory Biosafety Manual* (3rd edn, WHO 2004).
[75] Asilomar Conference on Recombinant DNA Molecules, Pacific Grove, CA, 1975.

help to overcome their ignorance of the impacts of hi-tech products on the ecosystem. Therefore, it is argued that the 'top-down approach needs to be re-adjusted to alter the boundaries itself and seek to alter the boundaries of regulatory exclusiveness'[76] by making it more consultative and participatory in decision-making.

The Task Force of the Twelfth Planning Commission Report on Synthetic Biology dealt with the risk discourse, bringing interlinkages between the risks involved and its potential challenges to the environment and health.[77] However, it has failed to focus on mitigating the risks to the environment, but reduced it to approving the technology for work by the experts.[78] This missing link with the public interest is a contentious issue that still persists in the policy documents. The DBT also released a Foresight Paper in 2022 on Synthetic Biology, emphasizing the need for a national policy to consolidate India's stand on the issue. This document also does not contain any policy directions on mitigating the risks of SynBio, apart from general directions drawn from international policies and the need for coordination between science and policy.

India's reports about fulfilling obligations under the Cartagena Protocol also record that capacity building is ongoing to strengthen the biosafety management system in India, with special emphasis on risk assessment and management, handling, transport, packaging, and identification of LMOs, socio-economic considerations, and public awareness to ensure adequate protection of human health and biodiversity from potential harm arising from all LMO-related activities. However, the 2022 Foresight Paper does not mention any efforts to specifically deal with biosafety issues in SynBio. There is no clarity on whether there is any further policy development to deal with biosafety issues arising from SynBio products. To deal with biosafety issues relating to SynBio products, there needs to be expertise development and training, risk assessment, risk management as well as other scientific and technical expertise, public awareness, participation, and education in biosafety relating to SynBio.[79] A proactive approach to enforce the precautionary principle and the command-and-control approach should be included in the policy documents, be it guidelines or protocols to deal with SynBio.

Conclusion

Biotechnology has witnessed a major technological revolution with the evolution of SynBio-based innovations. SynBio, as a new technology, raises challenges for the

[76] A Damodaran, 'Re-Engineering Biosafety Regulations in India: Towards a Critique of Policy, Law and Prescriptions' (2005) 1(1) *Law, Environment and Development Journal* 1.

[77] Report of the Planning Commission (n 52).

[78] Krishna Ravi Srinivas, 'Synthetic Biology in India: Issues in Risk, Power and Governance' (2014) *Research and Information System for Developing Countries*, Discussion Paper # 194.

[79] Sheetal Menon and Shishir Kumar Jha, 'National Biosafety System for Regulating Agricultural Biotechnology in India' (2016) 14(2) *International Journal of Biotechnology* 151.

existing biosafety regulations. Most regulations for arresting biosafety from new biotechnological innovations in India are covered under the 1989 Rules. The ability of the 1989 Rules to assess the risks of new SynBio organisms, currently based on the known relatives of those organisms, is insufficient. This is particularly so because the presumption that a microbe does not change through technological intervention is not true in the case of the products from SynBio. The Handbook of 2020 and Guidelines of 2020 and 2022, known to be 'soft' regulations, have limitations when it comes to the enforcement of biosafety measures. There are international principles, such as the precautionary principle, and the command-and-control approach, for bringing strict rules for biosafety for SynBio.

The relationship between technology, society, and nature is interlocked in SynBio and raises ethical, legal, and social concerns about the impact of this technology on the environment and human lives. SynBio has a pervasive effect on living beings and creates a fundamental intervention in the relationship between humans and nature. The power of technology cannot justify all changes in the human experience of nature. It is this balance between technology, society, and nature that must be achieved through policy framing by practitioners and policy analysts.

To make a stronger regulatory base for biosafety in India, our legal discourse should contain the precautionary principle and the command-and-control approach. This will bring a more liability-based approach and indemnification of damages for misuse or potential misuse. A precautionary principle would deter approval of products of dubious use. The inclusion of the command-and-control approach would bring in the legality/illegality discourse to the policy, creating a possibility for offences and penalties to be included in the legal framework. Legality and illegality clauses can contain 'public interest' restraints to affirm the biosafety of the environment.

Another important recommendation is to constitute a participatory mechanism in the approval process of SynBio involving multiple stakeholders such as scientists from different disciplines, representatives of tribal and marginalized communities, Panchayati Raj Institutions, and legal professionals. This will ensure that the traditional farmers, breeders, forest dwellers and other traditional communities engaged with the conservation of biodiversity are informed, and their objections/comments are considered while deciding on the release of SynBio to the environment. The existing biosafety regime highlights the importance of having separate bodies for environmental assessment, risk management, risk communication, and knowledge dissemination to guide the scientists and researchers functioning in the discipline. Transparency and accountability relating to decision-making need to be ensured through the publication of documents relating to field trials, due diligence, post-release materials, and review materials.

Suggestions for Further Reading

Zheng-jun Guan and others, 'Biosafety Considerations of Synthetic Biology in the International Genetically Engineered Machine (iGEM) Competition' (2013) 63(1) *BioScience* 25.

Nicholas BW Macfarlane and others, 'Direct and Indirect Impacts of Synthetic Biology on Biodiversity Conservation' (2022) 25(11) *iScience Review* 105423.

Thomas P Redick, 'Biotechnology, Biosafety and Sustainable Development' (1997) 12(2) *Natural Resources & Environment* 114.

Sachin Sathyarajan and others, 'Regulating Risks in Synthetic Biology' (2021) 23(3) *Asian Biotechnology and Development Review* 101.

Andrew W Torrance, 'Synthesizing Law for Synthetic Biology' (2010) 11 *Minnesota Journal of Law, Science & Technology* 629.

PART V

FISHERIES AND MARINE ENVIRONMENT

CHAPTER 22

MARINE FISHERIES

DIVYA KARNAD

Abstract

India's marine fisheries laws are challenged by complex and dynamic fishers, fishing practices and the marine environment. The country has done well to simultaneously oversee different spaces at the state and national levels, but research on the ground demonstrates that further legal stratification is needed. Laws in India which concern the oceans are oriented towards capitalists furthering the economic growth of the country, while small-scale fishers who are the majority users of the oceans, function as communities interested in their livelihoods and ecological sustainability. These deep disconnects have given rise to communities taking to forming informal legal institutions at the village level, which address their concerns and make sense to them. India's legal machinery requires a considerable shift to promote the concerns of its fishing citizens, and meet global concerns about climate change, ecological sustainability and providing livelihoods to those living in poverty.

Introduction

Marine fishing in India provides livelihoods to about 4.9 million active fishers[1] and involves a huge diversity of fishing nets, lines, and techniques, from manually operated shore-seines to the mechanically operated hydraulic cranes of purse-seines. Marine fisheries are also one of the most difficult sectors to regulate, with enforcement

[1] Government of India, Ministry of Fisheries, Animal Husbandry and Dairying, Department of Fisheries, Fisheries Statistics Division, *Handbook on Fisheries Statistics: 2020* (November 2020) <https://dof.gov.in/sites/default/files/2021-02/Final_Book.pdf>.

requiring enormous manpower and resources for surveillance and patrolling. As a result, Illegal, Unregulated, and Unreported (IUU) fishing activities occur. Such activities not only pose a threat to food security by unsustainably depleting the marine environment of resources but also a threat to economic and political security.[2] Fishermen have reported lower per capita catches, the disappearance of particular species, adverse climate change impacts, and increased physical clashes between users of different fishing gear.[3] Attempts to regulate the marine space have worsened conflicts,[4] often because lawmakers in the country's national and state capital remain significantly disconnected from the current and ever-evolving issues that plague the marine fisheries sector. As the ocean becomes the new frontier for economic growth in India, the government is planning several interventions in a space historically used almost solely by marine fishers. Conflicts are likely to escalate, necessitating a different approach to law-making and regulations to ensure conflict resolution.

One of the main issues lawmakers must contend with is that the highly technical nature of marine fishing has meant that fishers continuously experiment with and adapt fishing technologies to suit local conditions. Rapid technological change also accompanies the environmental changes that fishermen are observing in the sea. Therefore, using a legal blueprint created elsewhere to regulate India's fisheries is not possible. Instead, lawmakers must regulate very diverse fisheries, operated not only from designated fishing harbours but also from beaches and bays across India's coastline. One fishing vessel may carry several different types of fishing gear, and the fishers may decide which type of net or gear to use based on ecological and weather conditions on the spur of the moment. This diversity has meant that laws about marine fisheries in India remain at a relatively broad level, preventing certain types of fishing gear and vessels but stopping short of regulating catch levels, amount of fishing effort, introducing new fishing technology, and so on. Fishing law in India is a Concurrent List subject in the Constitution of India, 1950: at the national level, the Indian Fisheries Act, 1897 devolves authority to the states within territorial waters,[5] while retaining the ability to regulate the Exclusive Economic Zone.

The practice of marine fishing is also connected to a seafood industry that supports more than fourteen million people,[6] and laws must ensure that this economy is not stifled even as they are concerned with regulating fisheries conflicts. Consequently, laws

[2] Pooja Bhatt, 'IUU Fishing as a National Security Threat: Revisiting India's Domestic Framework and Compliance with International Regimes' (2020) 96 *International Law Studies* 442.

[3] Divya Karnad, Mayuresh Gangal, and Krithi K Karanth, 'Perceptions Matter: How Fishermen's Perceptions Affect Trends of Sustainability in Indian Fisheries' (2014) 48(2) *Oryx* 218.

[4] Special Correspondent, 'Fishermen Protest Against Draft Marine Bill' *The Hindu* (Chennai, 20 July 2021) <www.thehindu.com/news/national/tamil-nadu/fishermen-protest-against-draft-marine-bill/article35416777.ece>.

[5] The Territorial Waters Continental Shelf–Exclusive Economic Zone and Other Maritime Zones Act (1976) identifies the area within twelve nautical miles of the high tide line as the territorial waters of India.

[6] Government of India (2020) (n 1).

are relatively lax at the interface of fishing and the seafood economy.[7] As the government promotes the modernization of fisheries, new technologies are being introduced whose social and ecological impacts are yet to be fully realized, and new markets are being reached. The consequences of such largely unregulated growth over the last fifty years have allowed unsustainable practices from the Global North to become widespread in India. Economically, marine fisheries now contribute 1 per cent of India's gross domestic product, but ecologically 86 per cent of the marine fish stocks are either fully exploited or depleted. The need for more appropriate fisheries laws that can keep up with modern needs and conflicts is felt by many fishers.[8] In this context, a critical question becomes how fisheries laws can evolve to ensure not only economic and social wellbeing but also ecological wellbeing.

This chapter will examine the diverse sets of laws that apply to India's fisheries at different scales: national, state, and local. It will also describe the rationale behind such law-making and thus provide some context to understand how fishermen perceive these laws. It will then lay out how these laws are implemented or enforced, with a view to identifying the gaps between the intent of the law and the ways in which the laws are applied. It will also provide a case study, demonstrating how fishermen overcome the inadequacies of state laws by implementing their own laws at the local level. Finally, it will identify the shortcomings of the ways in which fisheries laws in India are currently being amended and offer recommendations on how to improve law-making in such a way as to make it more relevant to Indian marine fisheries.

22.1 Understanding the Effectiveness of Fishing Law in India

Fishing law must be set against the context of fishing communities and practices in India. Fishing communities have traditionally remained at the edge of modern society, some officially classified as 'fishing castes' and typically at the lower end of the Hindu caste hierarchy. They have historically used fishing practices such as the shore-seine (known locally as *rampan*, *periya valai*, etc.). The shore-seine is significant because it was a community-building fishing practice, reflecting how fishers associated with each other and their environment. The manpower required to pull a shore-seine in from the sea may bring an entire village of fishermen together to work on the beach. The community would also work together to buy the equipment needed, such as the rowboat and the net. The catch from such an operation is diverse, especially of smaller fish that live

[7] Divya Karnad, Dhruv Gangadharan, and Yarlagadda Chaitanya Krishna, 'Rethinking Sustainability: From Seafood Consumption to Seafood Commons' (2021) 126 *Geoforum* 26.

[8] Divya Karnad, 'Navigating Customary Law and State Fishing Legislation to Create Effective Fisheries Governance in India' (2017) 86 *Marine Policy* 241.

in the shallow nursery areas of the coastal seas where these nets are deployed. This catch would support the local economy, consisting primarily of fisherwomen, who would be able to sell the fresh catch to a consumer base that was educated about how to utilize it. Such a community-based economy is significant in this modern era of individualization and disconnects.

Laws that support individual, capitalist fishers who sell seafood across the country to a relatively uneducated public (with respect to how to utilize diverse seafood), especially with their link to online sellers, are therefore sources of conflict. Further, by not placing effective restrictions on newer fishing technologies, such as the proliferating bottom trawls in areas traditionally used by shore-seines, the legal system effectively aided the demise of community economies while promoting a new class of 'capitalist fisherman' who often did not go fishing themselves. Instead, capitalist fishermen created another new class of fishers through employment: the fish-workers.[9] The demise of traditional fishing community relations was evident in the fact that this new economic structure of employer-employee was very different from the association of equals that characterized shore-seine operations. The ways in which laws for the mainstream undermined fishing communities were further cemented by the effort it took to get a legal reaction to how bottom trawls destroyed nearshore fisheries by dredging through the seabed and eliminating all sea life in its path. After decades of not regulating bottom trawls, many states in India have now designated exclusive shallow water zones for the operation of low capital input technologies, many of which have low ecological footprints and are operated entirely by fishing communities. However, for most fishing communities, this is too little, too late. The narrow nearshore strips restrict more 'eco-friendly' fishers to areas already severely overfished. As a result, these laws are regularly and blatantly flouted.[10]

22.2 History of Fishing Laws

Understanding India's marine fishing laws and fishermen's attitude towards these laws must consider the politics of their historical context. There is a development and colonial discourse that positions fishing communities as socially, politically, and economically backward. This is exemplified by the statement: 'The sea faring population of India is born and not made'.[11] The most direct interpretation of this statement is that fishing was considered an occupation restricted to certain castes, a sentiment that continues to be reflected in the idea of 'fishing castes' in the National Census.[12] That 'fishing castes'

[9] Ajit Menon, Subramanian Karuppiah, and Johny Stephen, 'Reconfiguring the Coast' (2008) 43(16) *Economic and Political Weekly* 35.

[10] Karnad, Gangal, and Karanth (n 3) 218.

[11] Government of Madras, 1906, Order No 222, Department of Revenue, 10 March 1906, p 38.

[12] Government of India, Ministry of Social Justice and Empowerment Resolution, Res F. No 12015/15/2008-BCC dated 16 June 2011 <www.ncbc.nic.in/Writereaddata/note29635288563679886826.pdf>.

are listed as backward castes suggests a social rigidity that would prevent economic efficiency, proving an obstacle to growth and development. Consequently the government's approach with respect to regulating and implementing regulations in this sector is quite different from other sectors that involve diverse mixtures of people.[13] Kaufmann points out that the rigid relationships and groupings of caste are merely a fiction of European making.[14] While there is some evidence from literature and inscriptions in the Sangam period (600BC–300AD) of the present-day state of Tamil Nadu that fisher people of the coast were considered subordinate to the agrarian castes,[15] the discourse of backwardness and its use as a rationale for developing fisheries was a colonial creation.[16]

From a legal perspective, this discourse has resulted in fishers not being allowed to participate in law-making despite knowing the most about how fishing and the marine system work. At present, fishing castes are characterized by stereotypes, such as independence, pride, aggression, and masculinity, as well as regarded with prejudice, as being alcoholics, violent, and culturally backward.[17] The lack of knowledge, both about the communities involved as well as about the marine environment has meant that instead of basing law on ground realities, fishing laws have been created based on how fisheries operate elsewhere in the world, to comply with global standards that often have no relevance to India. One clear example of this was the introduction of bottom trawl fishing for shrimp.[18] Sundar writes that the erstwhile colonial government recognized that the employed labour concept that is vital to bottom trawling was alien to the family-owned fishing operation structure of most Indian fisheries.[19] However the independent Indian government imposed bottom trawl fishing using the rationale of economic efficiency. NK Panikkar, a fisheries development advisor to the government of India, recommended further mechanization of fisheries as a means of progress, a way to increase yields while maintaining safety standards for fishermen.[20] Bottom trawling, made accessible through a technology transfer agreement with Norway, represented this mechanization.[21] The impacts on the fisheries were swift, both in terms of increased

[13] Divya Karnad, 'Locating Effective Commons and Community in Maharashtra State's Fisheries, India' (PhD Thesis, The State University of New Jersey-New Brunswick 2017).

[14] SB Kaufmann, 'A Christian Caste in Hindu Society: Religious Leadership and Social Conflict among the Paravas of Southern Tamilnadu' (1981) 15(2) *Modern Asian Studies* 203.

[15] Manu V Devadevan, 'Lying on the Edge of the Burning Ground: Rethinking Tinais' (2006) 49(2) *Journal of the Economic and Social History of the Orient* 199.

[16] Madras Fisheries Bureau, 1915. Paper from 1899 Relating Chiefly to the Development of the Madras Fisheries Bureau, vol 1, bulletin 1.

[17] Elisabeth Schoembucher, 'Equality and Hierarchy in Maritime Adaptation: The Importance of Flexibility in the Social Organization of a South Indian Fishing Caste' (1988) 27(3) *Ethnology* 213.

[18] John Kurien, 'Ruining the Commons and Responses of the Commoners: Coastal Overfishing and Fishermen's Actions in Kerala State, India' (1991) *United Nations Research Institute for Social Development*, Discussion Paper No 23 <https://www.files.ethz.ch/isn/28896/dp23.pdf>.

[19] Aparna Sundar, 'Capitalist Transformation and the Evolution of Civil Society in a South Indian Fishery' (PhD thesis, University of Toronto 2010).

[20] NK Panikkar, 'Impact of Technology on Indian Fisheries' (1964) 1(1) *Fishery Technology* 1.

[21] John Kurien, 'Entry of Big Business into Fishing: Its Impact on Fish Economy' (1978) 13(36) *Economic and Political Weekly* 1557.

conflicts and reduced catches.[22] Sundar identified the government of India's techno-cratic approach to developing fisheries as mirroring their promotion of the Green Revolution in agriculture. While they aimed to increase production for food supply and export while improving the living conditions of fishermen, this worked only in the short term. Such efforts at the national level have led to localized conflicts over dwindling resources, with state or even district-level lawmakers needing to step in and resolve problems.

Civil law, which is oriented to the individual or the family unit, has been insufficient to deal with the kinds of common property claims and conflicts that arise within India's fisheries. As a result, fishing communities often take matters into their own hands, with the result that when conflicts escalate, civil issues turn into criminal offences. In such criminal cases, state authorities come down hard on fishing communities for meting out what the latter perceive to be justice, creating greater mistrust between fishing communities and the state.[23]

22.2.1 Brief Introduction to State Fishing Laws

In the context of perceptions that laws are either biased against fishing community's relationships or do not suit the context of India's marine fisheries at present, the Indian Fisheries Act, 1987 is democratic in that it devolves authority to the coastal (and riparian) states to enact state fishing laws apropos to the types of fishing that occur in those states. As a result, state Marine Fishing Acts contain details about the types of fishing gear permitted, the use of bycatch reduction devices, the fishing ban period, the types of vessels banned, and so on. Despite this level of detail, more detail is needed to truly reflect the realities of conflicts in the water. For instance, one type of fishing gear that is regulated in the state Marine Fishing Acts is the purse-seine. This is typically a highly mechanized operation from a large vessel (>26 m), which has the capacity not only to fish within the Indian Exclusive Economic Zone but also in international waters. In states such as Maharashtra, large purse-seine vessels are not permitted to operate within territorial waters. However, such vessels are not legally required to have a Vessel Monitoring System (VMS), now a global standard to track the operations of large fishing vessels. As a result, such vessels can fish illegally in state and international waters without fear of detection, causing conflicts with Indian fishers or international fishing fleets. Another issue that has been repeatedly exploited is the difference between state Marine Fishing Acts. Fishing fleets in Kerala and Tamil Nadu, for instance, are known to travel between states to ensure that they can continue to fish along whichever coast

[22] Aaron Savio Lobo and others, 'Commercializing Bycatch Can Push a Fishery Beyond Economic Extinction' (2010) 3(4) *Conservation Letters* 277.

[23] Divya Karnad, 'Conservation Amidst Shifting Sands in India's Marine Fisheries' in Umesh Srinivasan and Nandini Velho (eds), *Conservation from the Margins* (Orient Blackswan 2018) 276.

permits fishing during the weeks when there is no overlap in the two states' fishing ban period.

While state laws for marine fishing differ in the details, they have some commonalities. All states have legislated an area adjoining the coast set aside only for 'traditional fishing'. The width of this zone varies in different states. Most states also prescribe minimum mesh sizes for different types of fishing gear. Tamil Nadu allows an Authorized Officer to set a maximum number for licensed vessels. Andhra Pradesh and West Bengal have made it mandatory to use turtle excluder devices. All states also prescribe an annual fishing ban period for mechanized vessels (and, in some states, for all fishing). However, this ban period also varies between states.[24] India's eastern coastal states impose their seasonal annual fishing ban from 15 April to 14 June, and the western coastal states from 1 June to 31 July. Even this coordination on the east coast (and the west coast) is relatively recent, before which each state had ban periods for different durations and starting on different dates.[25] For instance, West Bengal, Andhra Pradesh, Tamil Nadu, and Kerala imposed an annual fishing ban of forty-seven days (applied since 1988–89). Odisha, whose coastline is between West Bengal and Andhra Pradesh, had a sixty-day ban (applied since 2000). Gujarat, Maharashtra, and Goa imposed bans of sixty-seven days (effective from 1989–90), whereas neighbouring Daman and Diu banned fishing for seventy-five days, and Karnataka imposed a ban of fifty-seven days. This changed with a government order in 2021, which standardized the dates for each coast. In common parlance, the annual fishing ban is referred to as the monsoon fishing ban, a title which fits the circumstances on the west coast of India. However, on the east coast, the northeast monsoon is active from October to December; consequently, fishers have been pushing the state government to shift the ban period.[26]

Central and state governments offer compensatory basic income to registered fishermen during the ban period as part of a saving-cum-relief scheme, amounting to INR 4,500 (altogether) annually. However, the bureaucratic hurdles in state governments accessing money from the central government have led some states, like Tamil Nadu and Andhra Pradesh, to implement their own fishermen's compensation schemes. Tamil Nadu now provides registered fishermen with INR 5,000 per annum, and Andhra Pradesh now provides fishermen with INR 10,000 per annum. Other states, like West Bengal, have stopped offering fishermen's compensation altogether.[27]

[24] Rajesh KM, 'Fisheries Legislation in India' (Central Marine Fisheries Research Institute 2013) <http://eprints.cmfri.org.in/9871/1/Rajesh_8.pdf>.

[25] Government of India, Ministry of Fisheries, Animal Husbandry and Dairying, Department of Fisheries, Order No 30035/l 5t97-Fy (-f-l) vol V. dated 30 March 2021 <https://dof.gov.in/sites/default/files/2021-03/Fishing_Ban_Order_2021.pdf>.

[26] S Godson Wisely Dass, 'Demand for Shifting Fishing Ban to Year End' *The New Indian Express* (15 April 2021) <www.newindianexpress.com/states/tamil-nadu/2021/apr/15/demand-for-shifting-fishing-ban-to-year-end-2290259.html>.

[27] Supriya Vohra, 'During Monsoon Fishing Ban, India's Small-scale Fishers Flounder at the Deep End' *The Wire* (Panaji, 12 November 2021) <https://science.thewire.in/environment/india-monsoon-fishing-ban-small-scale-fishers-insufficient-relief-coverage/>.

Table 22.1 Difference in the scale and types of legal matters associated with different legal systems

	National Law	State Law	Customary Law
Example	Indian Fisheries Act	Maharashtra Marine Fisheries Act	Informal, society or *Panchayat*-based
Scale	Exclusive Economic Zone	Territorial waters	Villages
Types of law	Temporal and species restrictions	Gear, vessel and temporal restrictions	Space, gear, temporal, vessel and social restrictions

Source: Author

The central government now seeks to standardize and create uniform laws for India's entire Exclusive Economic Zone (EEZ) with the new Indian Marine Fisheries Bill, which could reduce some of these loopholes and centralize regulations in future.[28] The relationship between types of laws operating at different scales is presented in Table 22.1.

The gap between fisheries law and the actual conflicts that affect fishing communities is recognized by state fisheries officers, who often find themselves at the frontlines of these conflicts. The fisheries officers find themselves handicapped with respect to restoring the fisheries resources in the marine ecosystem beyond enforcing the annual fisheries ban. Although they could also involve themselves in issues pertaining to enforcing the traditional fishing zone, thereby protecting nearshore marine ecosystems, they cite several reasons why they do not do so. Firstly, there is confusion about jurisdiction. Technically, the region within which the artisanal fishing zone exists is the jurisdiction of the marine police, but the marine police believe that their role is to enforce issues related to the Indian Penal Code, 1860, particularly with respect to smuggling and terrorism. However, fisheries officers believe the marine police are also responsible for enforcing the traditional fishing zone. As a result, this aspect of domestic law is overlooked by both departments and creates conflicts among fishermen. Secondly, officers of the Department of Fisheries have adopted a position of non-interference in the fishing community's conflicts since they believe that they lack the legal basis to intervene. Instead, their policy appears to be to wait and hope that the community can resolve the issue, and if the situation escalates, to allow the police to deal with criminal offences. The implication of such a stance is that the fisheries department, and consequently fisheries law, is commonly understood (by both state fisheries officers and fishing communities) to have little bearing on regulating fisheries and, thereby, having no connection to ecological sustainability. Instead, fisheries officers perceive their

[28] Government of India, Ministry of Fisheries, Animal Husbandry and Dairying, Department of Fisheries, The Draft Indian Marine Fisheries Bill <https://dof.gov.in/sites/default/files/2021-10/Draft_Indian_Marine_Fisheries_Bill_2021.pdf>.

role as providing schemes to 'develop' fisheries, a vision that is typically at odds with maintaining or restoring marine ecosystems.

One way in which the state implements such development is by building fishing harbours. For instance, the Maharashtra Maritime Board (MMB) Act, 1996, authorizes the MMB to develop all minor ports in Maharashtra to boost economic activity. Since fishing harbours do not have a separate legal designation, they come under the purview of the MMB, a body that is not legally (or in practice) required to represent fishing interests. This automatically results in the MMB building fishing harbours for the state (based on their view of developed fisheries) rather than for the diverse types of actual fishing communities that may use the harbour. The consequence is that many such harbours are unusable by locals (who cannot afford the capital investment required to buy new fishing technologies), or they force the conversion of local fisheries into capital-intensive ones. The result adds to inter-sectoral conflict, as well as issues of overfishing and ecosystem decline due to unchecked fishing capacity being added. State authorities, including the marine wing of the police, are seldom acquainted with the fishing community's practices or concerns. In fact, members of the Maharashtra State Fisheries Department and Marine Police have reported that they receive only one week's marine training on board marine vessels (and often this is their only experience at sea) during their entire service period. Opportunities for the state to recognize the extent to which fisheries laws remain distant from the current and emerging concerns of fishing communities are therefore limited.

While government authorities forego regulation and focus on development, fishing communities create or identify other institutions primarily for the purpose of conflict resolution, which often has the fallout effect of preserving marine ecosystems. Customary fishing institutions step in where state institutions fail. By creating laws that pertain to the local context, customary fishing institutions become very relevant bodies whose workings match the timelines, language, and social norms of fishing communities. This creates a kind of legal pluralism, where the state's legal system operates at a larger scale, while the customary institution operates informally at a smaller scale for the same people. Customary law, in some cases, addresses the shortcomings of the state legal system but, in doing so, may contradict the state legal system. The implications of legal pluralism will be discussed further in the case study, but suffice to say that the official legal position is that such customary law is illegal.

The ecological integrity of India's marine environment rests on the effective functioning of customary legal systems, which depend on local ecological knowledge and generational investment by fishermen. Customary legal systems, in turn, are made powerful by the informal practice of state authorities ignoring fishing conflicts or not enforcing fisheries regulations. While such practices lend authority and legitimacy to customary legal institutions, the lack of formal recognition makes customary law vulnerable. The state can change its position and forcefully impose rules at any time, which could override customary law. Lawmakers and legal theorists could bridge the disconnect between state law and the lived reality of India's marine fisheries by paying more attention to the practices of customary fishing law.

22.2.2 Legal Pluralism in India's Fisheries

Customary law in Indian fisheries is generally associated with small-scale, artisanal, or traditional fishing.[29] However, recent research has begun to re-envision this association by studying mechanized fisheries, particularly bottom trawl fisheries, and finding evidence of emergent customary law.[30] With a focus on wellbeing, these customary legal institutions, whether small- or large-scale fisheries, appear to benefit fishing communities and the marine ecosystems that they depend on. Community rules, where present, are better enforced within a community than state regulations. After all, self-governance can only take place where at least a semi-autonomous social space exists.

The customary legal system had many components of structure and organization that were like state legal systems. For instance, the village or groups of villages that converged under these rules had a designated meeting space, often a temple, and followed rituals to ensure the truthfulness of participants at the meeting. Monitoring and enforcement involved all members, and rule-breaking was met with various degrees of punishment. Where customary legal systems varied from state legal systems was in the details of how rule-making, enforcement, and justice were achieved. For instance, within close-knit fishing communities, it was important that the meeting space was relatively inexpensive to reach and that the proceedings were in the local dialect to be completely understood by all participants. Compliance with local rules was achieved as much through social pressure since all participants could potentially monitor each other all the time, as legitimacy for local regulation was achieved through cultural rituals, caste and kinship ties, close spatial location, occupational homogeneity, and similar values of social justice and ecological sustainability.[31] Locally relevant, well-enforced customary law was effective at protecting common property rights, ethical concerns, and socio-ecological wellbeing in contrast to ineffective state legislation.

However, customary law could break down outside these small, closely knit communities. Multiple studies have found such systems in association with particular temples or predominantly Hindu communities but absent among fishing communities

[29] Maarten Bavinck and others, 'From Indifference to Mutual Support—A Comparative Analysis of Legal Pluralism in the Governing of South Asian Fisheries' (2013) 25(4) *The European Journal of Development Research* 621.

[30] Maarten Bavinck and V Vivekanandan, 'Qualities of Self-governance and Wellbeing in the Fishing Communities of Northern Tamil Nadu, India-the Role of Pattinavar ur panchayats' (2017) 16(1) *Maritime Studies* 1.

[31] Maarten Bavinck, '"A Matter of Maintaining Peace" State Accommodation to Subordinate Legal Systems: The Case of Fisheries along the Coromandel Coast of Tamil Nadu, India' (1998) 30(40) *The Journal of Legal Pluralism and Unofficial Law* 151; DS Johnson, 'The Values of Small-scale Fisheries' in Derek S Johnson and others (eds), *Social Wellbeing and the Values of Small-scale Fisheries* (Springer, Cham 2018) 1; P Thamizoli and Pushparaj I Prabhakar, 'Traditional Governance System of Fishing Communities in Tamil Nadu, India: Internal Mandate, Interfacing and Integrating Development' in Rajib Shaw and RR Krishnamurthy (eds), *Communities and Coastal Zone Management* (Research Publishing Services 2010).

that predominantly belonged to other religions.[32] Further the involvement of the state, in terms of promoting certain fishing technologies at the cost of others or by directly invalidating customary law could also lead to fishermen turning to the state for better governance.[33] This suggests opportunities for state and customary law to work together because customary law has a limited reach. Karnad found that customary law operates at the scale of groups of villages and remains contextually relevant to that group, while state law must act at the scale of the state in relation to the nation, sacrificing local concerns in the process.

The overlap between customary and state law creates unique opportunities for complementarity because state law can work effectively at politically relevant scales for the nation, while customary law allows for adaptive fisheries management at the local scale. The reluctance of fisheries department officials to apply state law at the village level reveals their recognition of the shortcomings of state legislation to deal with local concerns. Since they are bound by the inflexible and slow bureaucratic procedure, officials often find it easier to turn a blind eye to practices of customary law. Thus, these legal systems enable each other and cannot be studied in isolation. Emergent and modern customary law finds innovative ways of working with or within state legal practices. Both caste-based and non-caste-based trawl boat owners' associations in Tamil Nadu have worked with state authorities to create effective fishing rules aimed at restricting new entrants and further expansion of fisheries.[34] Bavinck describes customary law of small-scale fishermen being recognized by state officials in the Ramnad District of Tamil Nadu, possibly due to the latter's eagerness to remain uninvolved in micro-managing local affairs.[35] Such initiatives hint at grassroots movements towards creating co-management regimes.

Marine fisheries are a realm where there is abundant evidence of multiple legal practices.[36] Previous research on legal pluralism in fisheries governance suggests that after a period of struggle, customary law declines in the face of modern state interventions.[37] However, it is possible for the state to include, rather than overwhelm customary law.[38] There appears to be a close linkage between livelihoods filled with

[32] Antonyto Paul, 'Rise, Fall and Persistence in Kadakkodi: An Enquiry into the Evolution of A Community Institution for Fishery Management in Kerala, India' (2005) 10(1) *Environment and Development Economics* 33.

[33] Julia M Novak and Mark Axelrod, 'Patterns of Multi-Level Fisheries Governance and Their Impact on Fishermen's Adaptation Strategies in Tamil Nadu, India' (2016) 26(1) *Environmental Policy and Governance* 45.

[34] Johny Stephen, 'A Place to Live and Fish: Relational Place Making among the Trawl Fishers of Palk Bay, India' (2014) 102(Part A) *Ocean and Coastal Management* 224.

[35] Personal communication from Maarten Bavinck to the author (2014).

[36] Maarten Bavinck, *Marine Resource Management: Conflict and Regulation in the Fisheries of the Coromandel Coast* (Sage Publications 2001).

[37] John Kurien and AJ Vijayan, 'Income Spreading Mechanisms in Common Property Resource: Karanila System in Kerala's Fishery' (1995) 30(28) *Economic and Political Weekly* 1780.

[38] John Griffiths, 'What is Legal Pluralism?' (1986) 18(24) *The Journal of Legal Pluralism and Unofficial Law* 1.

ecological, social or political uncertainties, such as marine fishing, and legal pluralism because multiple legal systems allow people the flexibility to adapt to changing conditions.[39]

22.3 Current Issues

The marginalization of 'primitive and backward' fishermen who do not conform to the state's vision of a developed fishery continues in the draft Indian Marine Fisheries Bill. This Bill is the most updated version since the first draft in 2019 was hastily formulated in tandem with the politically charged discussions which were taking place in the World Trade Organization (WTO) on fisheries subsidies.[40] Rather than addressing the shortcomings of existing legislation by recognizing the diversity, needs, and conflicts within India's marine fisheries, this Bill pushes further in the direction of standardization and uniformity, by treating marine fishing 'as a whole'. The Bill proposes the centralization of power to govern fisheries in the Exclusive Economic Zone by weakening the role of state Marine Fisheries Regulation Acts. For instance, section 4 states, 'Indian fishing vessels shall engage in fishing and fishing related activities within the exclusive economic zone and in the high seas under a license issued by the licensing authority'. For small-scale fishers not licensed for high-seas operations, this appears to be an effort to restrict them to the territorial sea, where most fish resources have already been plundered by mechanized fishing. The Bill also proposes increased surveillance of the fisheries sector using the latest satellite equipment and technology. Yet it is unclear who will bear the financial burden of installing these technologies, and many small-scale vessels cannot install these technologies due to their small size or lack of protection from the elements. Further, there is an effort to promote mariculture in the sea, which until now was prevented by the open access and public nature of the sea. Mariculture will involve the recognition of private use rights in the ocean, automatically curtailing access for those who are not recognized users. The fear is that by adding hurdles to the fishing community's access to the ocean, the Bill will criminalize many small-scale fishing operations and eventually wipe out the small-scale sector. The declining marine ecological health that accompanies each new technological change has brought increased inter-sectoral conflict within the fisheries.

The definition of 'small-scale fisher' in the Bill (section 2(r)) as a person whose fishing vessel is less than twenty-four metres long is also problematic. The twenty-four-metre

[39] Ruth S Meizen-Dick and Rajendra Pradhan, 'Legal Pluralism and Dynamic Property Rights' (2002) *CAPRi* Working Paper No 22 <https://ebrary.ifpri.org/utils/getfile/collection/p15738coll2/id/127262/filename/127473.pdf.

[40] John Kurien, 'The Blue Lining—Indian Marine Fisheries Bill 2021' *Manorama Online* (21 July 2021) <https://www.onmanorama.com/news/straight-talk/2021/07/21/the-blue-lining-indian-marine-fisheries-bill.html>.

cut-off will also include most of the individually owned large-scale fishing vessels. Experts suggest other criteria, such as low horsepower engines and types of fishing gear, could be used to better effect. Further, the Bill continues to ignore participatory processes or the history of fishing community-led regulation of fisheries. The vast knowledge garnered by the resource users themselves could be put to great use in drafting effective legislation that is future-proof. Most importantly, the Bill completely ignores issues of sustainability, ecology, and biodiversity, which are crucial in this era of climate change impacts. Further, the Bill also ignores climate change impacts on the ocean.

In 2012, the Bharatiya Janata Party (BJP, currently the party that has formed the national government) brought out a national policy on fishing and fishermen, identifying fishing castes as isolated, ignored, and deprived of the benefits of economic development.[41] Their recommended solution included 'special efforts to transfer modern innovations and technological developments in harvesting, processing and marketing to fishing community'.[42] Hence, fishermen are making demands of government for help with accessing new and 'modern' fishing technology, better infrastructure, and access to markets. There is no mention of ecological sustainability or restoration.

The BJP has more recently laid out its plans to stimulate the Blue Economy through proposed legal provisions that allow parts of the ocean to be leased out to various activities, such as mariculture. However, these forms of development are visible by partitioning space in the ocean and reducing access to fishing communities, which could result in increased conflict. To ameliorate these conflicts, state laws have designated exclusively artisanal, near-shore zones within which modern, mechanized technologies such as trawl fishing or the more recent purse-seine fishing cannot operate. However, this is not sufficient given that conflicts are only increasing.[43] There is a need for greater legal intervention to ensure equitable access to resources, but such legislation does not appear to be forthcoming.

There are several international policy documents that could serve as good guides for better law-making in India, including the UN FAO Code of Conduct for Responsible Fisheries and their Small-Scale Fisheries Guidelines. In these and other documents, fisheries are viewed holistically as part of larger trade and economic networks rather than in isolation. The main significance is to promote the legal recognition of the role of women in fisheries trade and consequently to offer them some regulatory benefits.[44] While efforts have been made to translate the FAO guidelines so that both fishing

[41] Bharatiya Janata Party of India, National Policy on Fishing and Fishermen (2021) 19. https://www.bjp.org/files/books-monographs/national-policy-on-fishing-eng.pdf.

[42] ibid.

[43] Maarten Bavinck, Svein Jentoft, and Joeri Scholtens, 'Fisheries as Social Struggle: A Reinvigorated Social Science Research Agenda' (2018) 94 *Marine Policy* 46.

[44] Hillary Smith and Xavier Basurto, 'Defining Small-scale Fisheries and Examining the Role of Science in Shaping Perceptions of Who and What Counts: A Systematic Review' (2019) 6 *Frontiers in Marine Science* 236.

communities and policymakers can access and understand them,[45] the Bill suggests that this has had little impact on actual law-making.

The lack of fishing community participation in law-making is clearly a missed opportunity. Fishing communities have centuries of hands-on experience with what has worked and failed with respect to fisheries management. They can also be offered assistance to convert some of their knowledge into forms useful to lawmakers.[46] Further, they are organized into nationwide societies such as the National Fishworkers Forum and the National Platform for Small Scale Fish Workers who might be easily recognized by the government and be able to participate in some of these processes.

Much like fishing laws elsewhere, Indian fisheries are highly regulated on paper. While some of these laws are oriented towards reducing conflict and increasing ecological and economic sustainability, most of the laws are oriented towards smoothening the path for the development of the fisheries. Laws have very little to do with the reality of fisheries and often do not achieve the intended objectives for this reason. From an ecological and economic sustainability standpoint, regulating fishing alone cannot produce results. Instead, it is important to legally regulate the entire supply chain linked to those fisheries through complementary trade and transport legislation that ensures that the entire system shifts towards sustainability. India needs forward-thinking legislation that accounts for the realities of conflict within the fisheries sector. Therefore, India's fisheries laws need to take into consideration climate change, especially because fishing communities face the brunt of extreme weather, with fewer fishing days, more unpredictable catches, and faster storms. The emphasis of the legal system needs to be on supporting resilience within the fisheries. A combination of overfishing, pollution, and climate change have caused marine ecosystem declines at alarming rates. Therefore, the emphasis of the legal system needs to be on sustainability. While technological changes could bring in greater efficiency and less effort on the part of fishing communities, too much change, especially with an unproven ecological or climate-friendly track record, is affecting too many fishing communities too soon. Regulation is needed to ensure that new technologies are first tested in Indian conditions before being promoted or adopted in Indian fisheries. While the government has neglected the fisheries sector for over a century, fishing communities have had rich experience in facing issues on the water and regulating to ameliorate their impact. Therefore, it is critical that law-making for the future takes their experience and inputs into account.

[45] National Fisheries Policy, 2020 <http://www.indiaenvironmentportal.org.in/files/file/National%20Fisheries%20Policy%202020.pdf>.

[46] Divya Karnad, 'Incorporating Local Ecological Knowledge Aids Participatory Mapping for Marine Conservation and Customary Fishing Management' (2022) 135 *Marine Policy* 104841.

Conclusion

The question of whether marine ecological sustainability is of primary concern for India, given the current legal regime, seems to have been answered by the new Indian Marine Fisheries Bill. Clearly, the economy rather than ecology or sustainability is motivating the government's interventions in the marine sector, and laws are being framed to facilitate further exploitation rather than to ensure that livelihoods and life remain viable along the coast. Privatization of the oceans for purposes such as oil exploration, mariculture and so on is the new wave of land grabs. New legal terms, such as 'marine spatial planning' are emerging in policy documents without clear definitions,[47] albeit accompanied by the use of new technology, such as Geographic Information Systems. As policy shifts towards remote surveillance, and there is no legal requirement for local participation, fishers and marine species are left out of the picture. With the Marine Fisheries Bill suggesting the demise of 'small-scale fisheries', which are defined to cover most of India's fisheries, the type of fishing vessels and people who will come in to replace historic fishing communities will have a very different relationship with the coasts and the sea. India has an opportunity to operate differently. Reframing laws to support existing customary rules and building on customary rules to develop state- and nation-wide policies that make sense not only to fishing communities but also for ocean health would be the best way forward to promote resilience. Especially in an era of climate change, India's marine laws need to be highly adaptable and pave the way for resilience and adaptation to climate change and the environment, responding to local concerns rather than the country's economic desires.

Suggestions for Further Reading

Maarten Bavinck, '"A matter of Maintaining Peace"—State Accommodation to Subordinate Legal Systems: The Case of Fisheries along the Coromandel Coast of Tamil Nadu, India' (1998) 30(40) *The Journal of Legal Pluralism and Unofficial Law* 151.

Maarten Bavinck, *Marine Resource Management: Conflict and Regulation in the Fisheries of the Coromandel Coast* (Sage 2001).

Divya Karnad, 'Navigating Customary Law and State Fishing Legislation to Create Effective Fisheries Governance in India' (2017) 86 *Marine Policy* 241.

Rahul Muralidharan, 'What the 45-Day Annual Fishing Ban in Tamil Nadu Means for Fisheries Conservation' *The Wire* (15 April 2017) <https://science.thewire.in/environment/45-day-fishing-ban-trawler-tamil-nadu>.

Shinoj Parappurathu and C. Ramachandran, Taming the Fishing Blues Reforming the Marine Fishery Regulatory Regime in India' (2017) 45 *Economic and Political Weekly* 52, 73.

[47] Divya Karnad and Kevin St Martin, 'Assembling Marine Spatial Planning in the Global South: International Agencies and the Fate of Fishing Communities in India' (2020) 19(3) *Maritime Studies* 375.

CHAPTER 23

PROTECTING THE COASTAL AND MARINE ENVIRONMENT

TONY GEORGE PUTHUCHERRIL

Abstract

The coastal and marine environment performs several key functions—regulating the climate, sequestering carbon dioxide, and sustaining essential biological processes. With close to a quarter of the world's population living in coastal and adjacent areas and millions depending on coastal and marine ecosystems and resources for their livelihood and sustenance, the health of the marine and coastal environment is critical. Despite this, the coastal and marine environment is fast deteriorating, the degradation set to accelerate rapidly with climate change and sea level rise. This chapter provides an understanding of these developments and the current state of the law on the protection of the marine and coastal environment in India evaluating its capacity to respond to these challenges. In this regard, the focus will be on India's coastal law and the attempts to operationalize integrated coastal zone management which has global recognition as the primary pathway to secure sustainable coastal development.

Introduction

The Indian coastline is more than 7,500 kilometres long, with 5,500 kilometres of mainland coastline, and the rest falling to the Andaman, Nicobar and Lakshadweep Islands.[1]

[1] Ministry of Environment, Forest and Climate Change, 'Report of the Committee to Review the Issues Relating to the Coastal Regulation Zone Notification, 2011' (MoEFCC 2015) 13, 35–36.

Mainland coastal India is divided into nine states and two Union Territories. Those states are: (1) Gujarat, (2) Maharashtra, (3) Goa, (4) Karnataka, (5) Kerala, (6) Tamil Nadu, (7) Andhra Pradesh, (8) Orissa, and (9) West Bengal. Puducherry (Pondicherry) and Daman and Diu are the two Union Territories.[2] India's coastal seas and terrain are unique in terms of the marine environment and its resources. More than 1,382 islands, 1,093 beaches, corals (1,420 km^2), seagrass beds (360 km^2), salt marshes and mangroves (4,628 km^2), turtle nesting grounds (five species of sea turtles), several species of fish (2,546 species of fish), reptiles, crustaceans, and horseshoe crabs and their habitats are among the country's coastal ecosystems.[3] More importantly, the shoreline is home to massive swaths of people, industry, and construction projects. The coastal regions are vital to the national economy of India as well as the subsistence economies of local populations. One-fourth of India's population lives within fifty kilometres of the coast,[4] and the seventy-three coastal districts (out of a total of 593 districts) house about 17 per cent of the country's population.[5] The Indian coastline is dotted with seventy-seven cities, including Mumbai, Kolkata, Chennai, Kochi, and Visakhapatnam, which are among the largest and most densely populated in South Asia. The population density of coastal areas varies, ranging from less than twenty-five persons per square kilometre in some locations to seven hundred or more in others.[6] The coastal city of Mumbai, India's commercial capital, has about twenty million people.

Coastal and marine resources are critical for economic development, food production, and carbon sequestration from a socio-economic development standpoint. The country's Blue Economy assets are currently valued at trillions of dollars.[7] At the same time, coastal regions and resources are under severe strain. Unsustainable coastal development that affects coastal resources, land-based sources of marine pollution, and invasive species are all critical risks to coastal waterways and resources. These issues will be worsened by sea-level rise and climate change. India will be one of the twenty-seven countries most affected by sea-level rise.[8]

This chapter provides an overview of how India protects its coastal and marine environment and resources through law. It fulfils this goal in three sections. The first section provides an overview of the current legal regime for protecting the coastal and marine environment. Even though there is a broad overview of the applicable major legal instruments, the focus is on India's Coastal Regulation Zone Notification, 2019

[2] PondyCAN, 'The Challenged Coast of India' (2012) 7.

[3] MoEFCC (n 1) 14.

[4] PondyCAN (n 2) 7.

[5] ibid.

[6] R Krishnamoorthy and others, 'Environmental and Human Impacts on Coastal and Marine Protected Areas in India' in Guido Visconti and others (eds), *Global Change and Protected Areas* (Kluwer Academic Publishers 2001) 373.

[7] The World Bank, Enhancing Coastal and Ocean Resource Efficiency Project (2020) 1.

[8] Tony George Puthucherril, 'Operationalising Integrated Coastal Zone Management and Adapting to Sea Level Rise through Coastal Law: Where Does India Stand?' (2011) 26 *The International Journal of Marine and Coastal Law* 569, 573.

(CRZ Notification 2019). This is because the CRZ Notification 2019 is at the heart of India's complex regulatory framework in terms of its breadth and scope, which it has put in place over the years to protect the coastal and marine environment. The following section will assess this legal framework's in/ability to address ongoing and emerging concerns, such as unsustainable coastal development and sea-level rise. Thereafter, an overview of the Integrated Coastal Zone Management (ICZM) concept will be provided. The ICZM now has universal acceptance as a viable management paradigm that can help operationalize sustainable coastal development and this section will also explain how India is implementing the same. The final section will outline possible ways forward.

23.1 Law and Practice on the Protection of the Coastal and the Marine Environment

India is a signatory to all the major international legal instruments that prescribe legal obligations on states to protect the coastal and marine environment.[9] In pursuance of these international, binding, hard law instruments, and even otherwise, India has enacted legislation relevant to the protection of the coastal and marine environment. Mirroring the federal nature of India's polity, the legal regime stands diffused, emanating, and operating at the federal and state levels. Nevertheless, some of the more prominent pieces that form the essential pillars of this legal framework are the following federal laws, namely, the Wild Life (Protection) Act, 1972, with its mandate on the constitution of protected areas, including marine protected areas and protection to several marine species from poaching and illegal trade, the Territorial Waters, Continental Shelf, Exclusive Economic Zone, and other Maritime Zones Act, 1976, which establishes the different maritime zones and extends India's jurisdiction thereto, the Water (Prevention and Control of Pollution) Act, 1974, with emphasis on protecting the wholesomeness of water including the sea and tidal waters, and the Environment (Protection) Act, 1986.

The Environment (Protection) Act is India's most comprehensive environmental law that empowers the central government to formulate delegated legislation to regulate and

[9] Some of the major international environmental instruments which India has acceded to or ratified include the Convention on Wetlands of International Importance Especially as Waterfowl Habitat 1971, the United Nations Convention on the Law of the Sea 1982, the Convention on Biological Diversity 1992, the United Nations Framework Convention on Climate Change 1992, and the Basel Convention on the Control of Transboundary Movements of Hazardous Wastes 1989. See Tony George Puthucherril, 'A Case Study of India's Policy and Legal Regimes on Ocean Governance' in Biliana Cicin-Sain, David Vanderzwaag, and Miriam C Balgos (eds), *Routledge Handbook of National and Regional Ocean Policies* (Routledge 2015) 462.

provide protection to any aspect of the environment, including the coastal and marine environment. So potent is its framework that it is under this law that India has issued most of its environmental laws, including its coastal law and the Environment Impact Assessment Notification, 2006 (EIA Notification). The EIA Notification is particularly relevant in operationalizing sustainable coastal development. It subjects new projects or activities or their expansion and modernization to prior environmental clearance.

Apart from these laws, the Forest (Conservation) Act, 1980, which restricts the transfer of forest land for non-forest purposes, the Biological Diversity Act, 2002, which seeks to conserve biological diversity, ensure its sustainable use, and secure equitable benefit-sharing, the pre-independence Indian Fisheries Act, 1897, which proscribes fish destruction by poison and explosives, the Maritime Zones of India (Regulation of Fishing by Foreign Vessels) Act, 1981, which regulates fishing along a state's coastline, and the Coastal Aquaculture Authority Act, 2005, which provides rules for sustainable coastal aquaculture are all relevant to coastal and marine environment protection. Additionally, the Indian Ports Act, 1908, the Coast Guard Act, 1978, the Merchant Shipping Act, 1958, and the Customs Act, 1962 also have applicability.

As India's coastal law, the CRZ Notification emerges as the centrepiece of this complex legal maze. At the heart of this complex legal framework is the CRZ Notification 2019. It provides a blueprint to operationalize sustainable coastal development and lays down normative prescriptions to protect the coastal and marine environment[10] and to respond to the rising sea level. In the succeeding paragraphs, an overview of the essential features of the CRZ Notification is provided, explaining how this coastal law secures the protection of the coastal and marine environment.

The regulation of coastal zones has a chequered history. In 1991, India's federal government passed the CRZ Notification as a subordinate or delegated legislation under the Environment (Protection) Act to offer protection to coastal areas. This coastal law placed a strong emphasis on regulation. The CRZ Notification of 2011 attempted to replace the CRZ Notification of 1991 with a new legal framework stressing both regulation and management. This new Union coastal law effectively imposed enforcement responsibilities on the coastal states. However, the states experienced significant implementation issues due to a lack of resources and institutional capacity for coastal zone control and management. The Ministry of Environment, Forest and Climate Change (MoEFCC) formed a committee under the chairmanship of Dr Shailesh Nayak to address these concerns.[11] Based on the committee's findings, the MoEFCC published a draft CRZ Notification in 2018, which was subsequently notified as the CRZ Notification 2019, the present coastal law of the country.

Like its earlier iterations, the CRZ Notification 2019 is also a delegated legislation under the Environment (Protection) Act. It intends to conserve and protect the unique environment of coastal stretches and marine areas, ensure livelihood security to the

[10] *Rajakkamangalam Thurai Fishing Harbour Pvt Ltd v Union of India* MANU/GT/0169/2016 (using the CRZ Notification to protect olive ridley turtles and sand dunes).

[11] MoEFCC (n 1).

fishers and other local communities, and promote sustainable development based on scientific principles considering sea-level rise and other natural hazards.[12]

23.1.1 Definition of Coastal Regulation Zone

The CRZ Notification 2019 lays down a general but detailed definition of the CRZ. This is important as it helps to demarcate the area of applicability of the law. Accordingly, the CRZ is the country's coastal stretches and the water area that extends up to its territorial water limits.[13] The Andaman and Nicobar Islands, the Lakshadweep Islands, and their marine areas are excluded from the CRZ Notification's operational ambit.[14] Specifically, the CRZ includes the land area between the high tide line (HTL) and up to 500 metres on the landward side along the seafront.[15] Regarding tidally influenced water bodies connected to the sea, the CRZ includes the land area between the HTL and up to fifty metres or the creek's width, whichever is less on the landward side. The 'intertidal zone' (the land area between the HTL and the low tide line (LTL)),[16] the water and bed area between the LTL up to the territorial water limit (twelve nautical miles) in the case of the sea, and the water and bed area between the LTL at the bank to the LTL on the opposite side of the bank for tidally influenced water bodies all form part of the CRZ.[17]

Based on this comprehensive definition of the CRZ, the CRZ Notification 2019 classifies this entire area into five separate categories to conserve and protect the coastal areas and marine waters. These are the CRZ-I, CRZ-II, CRZ-III, CRZ-IV, and Areas that Require Special Consideration in the CRZ.

23.1.2 The Regulatory Scheme

The primary mode through which the CRZ Notification 2019 functions is that it imposes a general prohibitory scheme on eleven activities within the entire CRZ, and thereafter based on the CRZ category, it subjects the general prohibitions to various degrees of exceptions.[18] The eleven prohibited activities in the entire CRZ include the setting up of new industries, including new fish processing units and expansion of existing ones, situating port and harbour projects in high eroding stretches of the coast, the manufacture or handling of oil, the storage or disposal of hazardous substances, land reclamation, bunding or disturbing the natural course of seawater, and the discharge of untreated

[12] Coastal Regulation Zone Notification, 2019, preamble.
[13] ibid.
[14] ibid.
[15] ibid preamble cl (i).
[16] ibid cl (iii).
[17] ibid cl (iv).
[18] ibid para 4.

waste and effluents and the dumping of wastes, including industrial solid wastes, construction debris, and fly ash for landfilling.[19] In addition, the dressing or altering of active dunes, disposal of plastic into the coastal waters, and the withdrawal of groundwater, mining of sand, rocks, and other sub-strata materials also stand prohibited.[20]

The first zone identified by the CRZ Notification 2019 is the CRZ-I. These areas are environmentally the most critical.[21] The CRZ-I is further sub-classified into CRZ-IA and CRZ-IB. The CRZ-IA consists of ecologically sensitive areas (ESAs) whose geomorphological features play a critical role in maintaining the coast's integrity.[22] They also serve as natural defences against coastal hazards and help maintain the biological integrity of the coast by providing direct and indirect ecosystem services that sustain coastal livelihoods. Hence, their conservation and protection are highly essential. The CRZ Notification 2019 identifies the following sensitive coastal and marine ecosystems as falling under ESAs: mangroves, coral reefs, sand dunes, biologically active mudflats, protected areas, including biosphere reserves, salt marshes, turtle nesting grounds, horseshoe crabs' habitats, seagrass beds, nesting grounds of birds, areas or structures of archaeological importance, and heritage sites.[23] In the CRZ-IA areas, activities are generally not permitted. However, this is subject to exceptions like eco-tourism under an eco-tourism plan and road construction.[24] The CRZ Notification 2019 also prescribes general and specific conservation, protection, and management measures. The general measures require that the ESAs be identified and their boundaries delineated in the Coastal Zone Management Plan (CZMP). Special measures are proposed for the different ESAs considering their unique conservation requirements.[25]

The CRZ-IB is the inter-tidal zone, that is, the area between the LTL and HTL.[26] In this intertidal zone, certain activities like land reclamation and bunding for foreshore facilities and defence projects, coastal erosion control and salinity ingress prevention measures, activities that require foreshore facilities, non-conventional energy sources, facilities for receiving and storing petroleum products and liquefied natural gas, modernization of fish processing units, facilities for the intake of cooling water and outfall for discharge of treated wastewater or cooling water from thermal power plants are permitted.[27]

The CRZ-II consists primarily of urban coastal areas. It includes developed land areas up to or close to the shoreline, within the existing municipal limits or in other legally designated urban areas that are substantially built-up.[28] Generally, activities permitted

19 ibid.
20 ibid.
21 ibid para 2.1.
22 ibid para 2.1.1.
23 ibid.
24 ibid para 5.1.1.
25 ibid annex—I.
26 ibid para 2.1.2.
27 ibid para 5.1.2.
28 ibid para 2.2.

in the CRZ-IB are permissible in the CRZ-II. Furthermore, construction of buildings for residential purposes, schools, hospitals, institutions, etc., is permitted in this zone, provided the same is on the landward side of an existing road or authorized fixed structure. Vacant plots in designated areas can be used to develop tourism development-related projects subject to the Guidelines for Development of Beach Resorts, Hotels, and Tourism Development Projects in the Designated CRZ Areas.[29] Notable among the prescriptions contained in the Guidelines are those that require necessary arrangements to be made for treating effluents and solid wastes. While untreated effluents and solid wastes are not to be discharged into the water or onto the beach, the quality of treated effluents, solid wastes, emissions, and noise levels, etc., that emanate from the project should conform to the standards laid down by the competent authorities, including the Central or State Pollution Control Board.[30] Another essential requirement is that while private property owners can fence their properties, such fencing should not hamper public access to the beach.[31]

Predominantly rural areas (relatively undisturbed) fall under the CRZ-III classification. Based on population density, the CRZ-III is further sub-classified into CRZ-IIIA (if population density is more than 2,161 per sq km) and CRZ-IIIB (if population density is less than 2,161 per sq km). There is a no-development zone in CRZ-IIIA (area up to fifty metres from the HTL on the landward side) and CRZ-IIIB (area up to 200 metres from the HTL on the landward side). Generally, activities permitted in the CRZ-IB are also permissible in the CRZ-III. The CRZ Notification 2019 also sets out two legal regimes applicable to the CRZ-III. First, a common one applies to the no-development zone (NDZ) irrespective of whether the NDZ falls in the CRZ-IIIA or the CRZ-IIIB. The second regulates activities beyond the NDZ in the CRZ-IIIA or the CRZ-IIIB.

Regarding the permissible activities in the NDZ, the most important relates to tourism development. Accordingly, if a national or state highway passes through the NDZ of CRZ-III areas, temporary tourism facilities can be put up on the seaward side of an existing road. At the same time, resorts, hotels, and the like are permitted on such roads' landward side.[32] In areas beyond the NDZ, vacant plots can be developed for tourism development projects, wastelands and non-arable lands can be used for airport development. Fisherfolk and other local communities can set up a 'home stay'. While limestone and atomic mineral mining are permitted, groundwater withdrawal is prohibited except if used by local communities.[33]

The water area of the CRZ falls under the CRZ-IV and is sub-classified into CRZ-IVA and CRZ-IVB. The CRZ-IVA is the water and sea bed area from LTL up to twelve nautical miles into the sea.[34] The CRZ-IVB is the water and the underlying bed area between

[29] ibid annex—III.

[30] ibid annex—III, para 1.

[31] ibid.

[32] ibid para 5.3.

[33] ibid para 5.3 CRZ-III (iii).

[34] ibid para 2.4.1.

the LTL of the bank of tidally influenced water bodies to the LTL on the opposite side of that bank. It extends from the mouth of the water body at sea level up to where the tide exerts its influence.[35] This is measured based on a salinity concentration of five parts per thousand (ppt) during the driest period of the year.[36] Even though the CRZ-IV has a sub-classification, both are subject to a common regulatory scheme, which permits activities like traditional fishing, power generation through non-conventional energy sources, erosion control measures, the establishment of weather radar and ocean observation platforms, facilities for discharging treated effluents into the water, exploration and extraction of oil and natural gas, construction of memorials, and projects of the Department of Atomic Energy.[37]

As far as areas that require special consideration in the CRZ are concerned, the CRZ Notification 2019 identifies specific ecosystems within the existing CRZ and subjects them to a special regime for enhanced protection. In this regard, there are three important sub-classifications, namely, Critically Vulnerable Coastal Areas (CVCAs), the backwater and mainland islands, and the CRZ areas within the municipal limits of Greater Mumbai.[38] For the twelve ecosystems identified as CVCAs, Integrated Management Plans have to be prepared for their conservation and their management has to take place with the involvement of the coastal community.[39] Considering the space limitations in the coastal stretches of backwater islands, including islands on the mainland coast, a uniform CRZ of twenty metres from the HTL on the landward side applies.[40] The management of the backwater and mainland islands has to be by following Integrated Island Management Plans to be developed for this purpose.[41] For the CRZ-II areas that fall within the municipal limits of Greater Mumbai, all open spaces are declared as 'No Development Zones' to protect and preserve the green lung.[42] Even though such open spaces cannot be used for residential or commercial purposes, a floor space index of up to 15 per cent to construct civic amenities or sports or recreational activities is allowed.[43] If sewage treatment plants are to be constructed in the CRZ-I areas within the municipal limits of Greater Mumbai, there has to be the approval of the central government.[44]

35 ibid para 2.4.2.
36 ibid.
37 ibid para 5.4.
38 ibid para 3.1–3.
39 ibid para 10.1.
40 ibid para 10.2(ii).
41 ibid para 10.2.
42 ibid para 10.3.
43 ibid para 10.3.
44 ibid para 10.3(ii).

23.1.3 Obtaining the CRZ Clearance

Prior to commencing all permitted or regulated project activities, there must be CRZ clearance. For development activities or projects in the CRZ-I and the CRZ-IV, the MoEFCC, based on the recommendation of the concerned Coastal Zone Management Authority (CZMA), grants the CRZ clearance.[45] For the CRZ-II and the CRZ-III areas, CRZ clearance is the responsibility of the concerned CZMA.[46] Projects or activities that attract the CRZ Notification 2019 and the EIA Notification require a composite Environmental and CRZ clearance.[47] There are rules in the CRZ Notification 2019 that spell out the detailed procedure for CRZ clearance. Striking is the fact that there is a provision for post-clearance monitoring under which the project proponent must submit half-yearly reports (on 1 June and 31 December of each calendar year) in respect of compliance with the stipulated terms and conditions relating to environmental clearance in hard and soft copies to the regulatory authority concerned. These compliance reports must be published, and copies given to any applicant.[48] Such post-clearance monitoring and the requirement to place it in the public domain enhances transparency and accountability.

23.1.4 The Coastal Zone Management Plan

The CZMP is a critical document as the state government, the Union Territory administration, the local authority or the concerned Coastal Zone Management Authorities all have to work within the framework provided by an approved CZMP. Accordingly, there are detailed rules regarding its development and approval. In preparing or updating the CZMP, the state government or the Union Territory must engage reputed and experienced scientific institutions, including the National Centre for Sustainable Coastal Management (NCSCM).[49]

The draft CZMP must be prepared in a 1:25,000 scale map to identify and classify the CRZ areas within the respective territories.[50] The HTL and the LTL should be demarcated based on the demarcation undertaken by the NCSCM.[51] The CZMP should also reflect the Hazard Line, an essential tool used to develop disaster management plans and adaptation and mitigation measures.[52] The Guidelines also provide for the creation of CZM maps.[53] The various regulatory lines viz., those at a distance of twenty

[45] ibid para 7(ii).
[46] ibid para 7(iii).
[47] ibid para 7(iv).
[48] ibid para 8(vi)(a).
[49] ibid para 6(ii).
[50] ibid para 6(iii).
[51] ibid annex-IV, para 1.
[52] ibid annex-IV, para 2.
[53] ibid annex-IV, para 3.

metres, fifty metres, 200 metres and 500 metres from HTL, respectively, as applicable in the various CRZ categories, and the Hazard Line is to be demarcated and transferred to the CZM maps.[54] The ESAs or the CRZ-IA areas should also be clearly demarcated on the CZM maps.[55]

The draft CZMP should be submitted by the state government or the Union Territory to the concerned CZMA for appraisal, with appropriate consultations and recommendations. Once prepared, the draft CZMP is to be publicized, and suggestions and objections should be received by following the Environment (Protection) Act.[56] Public hearing on the draft CZMP is to be held at the district level by the concerned CZMA.[57] Based on the suggestions and objections received, the CZMPs are to be revised, and the MoEFCC's approval should be obtained.[58] The approved CZMP shall be placed on the MoEFCC website, the state or Union Territory CZMA, and hard copies made available in the *Panchayat* and the District Collector's Office.[59] Usually, the CZMP is revised once every five years.[60]

23.1.5 Enforcement

As far as the enforcement of the CRZ Notification 2019 is concerned, the MoEFCC, the concerned state government, the concerned Union Territory administration, the National CZMA and the concerned state or Union Territory CZMA have powers under the Environment (Protection) Act.[61] However, the concerned state government or the Union Territory CZMA is primarily responsible for enforcing and monitoring the CRZ Notification 2019.[62] And, it is this fixing of the primary responsibility on the state or the Union Territory, which often lacks the necessary resources, including the scientific and technical know-how, that has proved to be a major bane in securing effective enforcement. To assist them in this task, the state government and the Union Territory can constitute district-level committees under the chairmanship of the concerned district magistrate comprising at least three representatives from local traditional coastal communities, including fisherfolk.[63]

[54] ibid annex-IV, para 3(iii).
[55] ibid annex-IV, para 5.
[56] ibid annex-IV, para 6.
[57] ibid.
[58] ibid annex-IV, para 6(ii).
[59] ibid annex-IV, para 6(iii).
[60] ibid annex-IV, para 7.
[61] ibid para 9(i).
[62] ibid para 9(iii).
[63] ibid.

23.1.6 Discussion

Clearly, India has a highly complex legal framework for protecting the coastal and marine environment. As mentioned earlier, the coastal law is the centrepiece of this regulatory labyrinth. The coastal law's underlying approach to protecting the coastal and marine environment and even adapting to sea-level rise is regulation through zoning. It secures this by identifying the CRZ, classifying it into different categories, prescribing prohibitions and crafting exemptions depending on the category of the CRZ. Given that the idea of zoning has otherwise not taken off well in India's town planning, zoning through coastal law has its upside. However, this approach also has a downside, particularly when the law prescribes a uniform regulatory template applicable to the entire mainland coastal India. Due to the diverse and dynamic nature of India's coastal and marine ecosystems, zoning may lead to an over-indulgence in micro-management. This is one of the reasons why the CRZ Notification, even though placed in the statute book in 1991, has had to be amended now and then and even overhauled completely in 2011 and 2019 to assuage the states' concerns and to cater to local development requirements. This is perhaps the most critical weakness in the coastal law that has proved counterproductive to achieving its larger conservation objectives.

Rather than enacting a dedicated coastal law statute, India prefers the delegated and bureaucratic route to manage sensitive and dynamic coastal and marine ecosystems, which has led to several amendments, each amendment further diluting the stringency of the law. Even before its textual ink could dry, the CRZ Notification 2019, like its predecessors, has also met a similar fate. This major bane has reduced the potency of the coastal law, rendering it highly confusing and difficult to decipher and navigate, leading to situations like the *Maradu* case (discussed subsequently), where officialdom manipulated the law to favour unscrupulous builders.

23.2 Emerging Regulatory Challenges: Balancing Development with Environment and the Problems Posed by Climate Change and Sea-Level Rise

As pointed out earlier, the country's unique coastal environments and resources are under increasing stress due to rapid urbanization and development. Consequently, coastal zones are often the laboratories where sustainable development ideas are expounded, amplified, and applied. Even though it is the executive's responsibility to enforce and implement coastal law, given the judiciary's unique place in India's federal governance framework and the constitutional basis of environmental rights, the judiciary often emerges as the ultimate arbiter that adjudicates disputes when coastal development is pitted against coastal environmental protection.[64]

In accordance with the international understanding of sustainable development, the Supreme Court of India (Supreme Court or Court) has consistently emphasized that the idea of sustainable development is part and parcel of India's environmental law.[65] In securing sustainability in the coastal zones, the Supreme Court and the High Courts have implemented sustainable development ideas in a catena of cases.[66] One of the landmarks in this regard is *S Jagannath v Union of India*.[67] Drawing upon expert reports, the Court explained the adverse impacts of non-traditional and unregulated prawn farming. Despite arguments that intensive forms of aquaculture, though environmentally detrimental, have immense economic potential to bring the dollar into the country, the Supreme Court decided that prawn farming industries were prohibited in the coastal regulation zones under the CRZ Notification 1991 and other laws. It held:

> [t]he purpose of the CRZ Notification is to protect the ecologically fragile coastal areas and safeguard the aesthetic qualities and uses of the sea coast. The setting up of modern shrimp aquaculture farms right on the sea coast ... is per se hazardous and is bound to degrade the marine ecology, coastal environment and the aesthetic uses of the sea coast.

Accordingly, the Supreme Court held that only traditional aquaculture systems could be permitted.

Within a decade of its establishment, the National Green Tribunal (NGT or Tribunal), a specialized body with multi-disciplinary expertise in deciding environmental disputes[68] has begun to play a critical role in protecting the coastal and marine environment, implementing the CRZ Notification, and ensuring sustainability.[69] An important decision in this regard is *S Venkatesh v Union of India*.[70] The primary issue related to the East Coast Road (ECR) expansion in flagrant violation of the CRZ Notification 2011 and the EIA Notification. The ECR runs parallel to the coast within fifty to one hundred metres distance, and in many stretches, it passes through ESAs, like mangrove forests, coastal evergreen forests, dunes, agricultural fields, tidal flats, salt pans, bird and wildlife sanctuaries. It was claimed that the construction would lead to a severe adverse impact on the coastal environment. The primary purpose behind the widening was the many

[64] *Joseph Antonio D'Souza v State of Goa* MANU/GT/0234/2020 (linking mangrove protection to the constitutional mandate under art 47).

[65] *Goa Foundation v Sesa Sterlite Limited* (2018) 4 SCC 218.

[66] Centre for Environmental Education Research and Advocacy, *Cases and Materials Concerning the Coastal Environment* (National Law School of India University 1999).

[67] (1997) 2 SCC 87.

[68] National Green Tribunal Act, 2010, preamble and s 14.

[69] *Kheti Vikas Seva Trust v State of Gujarat* MANU/GJ/0182/2015; *Dileep B Nevatia v Union of India* MANU/GT/0275/2020.

[70] MANU/GT/0166/2016.

curves in the existing road, which led to several accidents and loss of life. In securing the balance, the Tribunal, while permitting the project, laid down several directions, like planting indigenous tree species where possible, constructing water harvesting structures, and providing for noise barriers to avoid adverse impacts, thereby securing sustainability.

Nevertheless, sustainable coastal development ideas and the balance are challenging to secure and implement. A primary reason is the critical role the coast, the marine environment, its resources, and the larger 'Blue Economy' play in sustaining the more significant economic interests of a developing country like India and that of a large percentage of its population who draw their sustenance primarily from these resources. Since India opened its economy in 1991, coinciding with its first CRZ Notification, there has been an increasing proliferation of various industries and economic activities on the coast. Power plants, Special Economic Zones, ports, urbanization, tourism projects, and desalination plants dot the coastline, often at the expense of fragile coastal and marine ecosystems. The CRZ Notification was amended several times to facilitate these projects, and even legally mandated action was put off.[71] India's coastal law has the dubious distinction of having been amended nearly thirty-four times and re-cast twice during its three decades of existence,[72] making it the most amended law in this country's history. These actions paved the way for regularizing violations and setting up new development projects, utterly disregarding environmental factors leading to increased coastal erosion and mangrove destruction, resulting in the levelling of dunes and the loss of intertidal zones.[73] It has also degraded fish habitats and nursery grounds, contaminated coastal aquifers, and increased the pollution of coastal and marine waters.

The decision of the Supreme Court, in *Indian Council for Enviro-Legal Action v Union of India*,[74] highlights the regulatory dilemma in several respects. The dispute arose over the non-finalization of the CZMPs mandated by the CRZ Notification by the state governments despite the passage of the statutory period. While directing the central and state governments to finalize the CZMPs, the Court lamented:

> [e]nactment of a law, but tolerating its infringement, is worse than not enacting a law at all ... Continued tolerance of such violations of law not only renders legal provisions nugatory but such tolerance by the enforcement authorities encourages lawlessness and adoption of means which cannot, or ought not to, be tolerated in any civilised society.[75]

[71] *Udaya Suvarna v The Deputy Commissioner/Chairman District Sand Monitoring Committee* MANU/GT/0016/2017 (sand mining in the CRZ rivers in total disregard of the law).

[72] Ishan Kukreti, 'Coastal Regulation Zone Notification: What Development are we Clearing our Coasts for?' *Down To Earth* (4 February 2019) <www.downtoearth.org.in/coverage/governance/coastal-regulation-zone-notification-what-development-are-we-clearing-our-coasts-for-63061>.

[73] Mayank Aggarwal, 'Industries Violating Coastal Zone Law Can Now Get Away with Paying Compensation' *Mongabay* (2 March 2021) <https://india.mongabay.com/2021/03/industries-violating-coastal-zone-law-can-now-get-away-with-paying-compensation/>.

[74] (1996) 5 SCC 281.

[75] ibid [26].

Accordingly, the Supreme Court directed the central government to constitute the state and National CZMAs to implement the CRZ Notification 1991 effectively. The Court also found two amendments that reduced the NDZ to be illegal.

More recently, the inconsistencies in coastal law administration led to the razing of four complexes that housed nearly 350 apartments in Maradu in Kerala for violating the CRZ norms. The *Kerala State Coastal Zone Management Authority v State of Kerala, Maradu Municipality* (Maradu Apartments Demolition) case[76] is a landmark for it underscored the importance of maintaining fidelity to the rule of law, even though, as will be seen, it came at a heavy price. Instances of non-compliance with judicial orders by the executive, particularly in coastal and marine environmental law matters, are aplenty. In this case, for the first time, the Supreme Court took the bull by the horns to ensure that the executive implemented its order in letter and spirit. However, whether this case was apt for this type of activism is doubtful.

Maradu is a small town located seven kilometres from Kochi in the State of Kerala and initially was a *grama panchayat*. In 2006, the Maradu *grama panchayat* granted building permits to four businesses to construct five waterfront apartment complexes facing the scenic backwaters of Kochi. The permit did not have the approval of the Kerala State Coastal Zone Management Authority (KSCZMA). The KSCZMA found that the construction was in critically sensitive regions classified as CRZ-III, where construction was prohibited within 200 metres of the coast. Consequently, the builders were issued a showcase notice alleging they had breached the CRZ Notification.

The builders petitioned the Kerala High Court and obtained an interim stay, allowing them to continue work on the project. The High Court's Single Judge Bench allowed their petition as Maradu was a well-developed area and could fall under the CRZ-II. Subsequently, the Division Bench affirmed this. The KSCZMA filed an appeal with the Supreme Court alleging violation of the CRZ Notification. The Supreme Court constituted a three-member technical committee to determine whether Maradu fell within the CRZ-III or not. The technical committee found that Maradu did indeed fall under the CRZ-III. Accordingly, the Supreme Court determined that the permit issued by the *panchayat* was illegal and void and that no development activity could take place. The Supreme Court ordered the demolition of the apartments as the construction violated the CRZ Notification 1991 and the 1996 KCZMA Plan, which classified the region as CRZ-III.[77]

However, the Government of Kerala began to drag its feet. Taking *suo motu* notice of non-compliance with its demolition orders, the Supreme Court set a deadline. Considering the hardship faced by the apartment owners, it directed the state government to compensate the flat owners to the tune of INR 2,500,000 each, to be recouped from the builders and others responsible. However, there was disagreement over the reasonableness of this amount. It did not consider the appreciation in the value of the

[76] *Kerala State Coastal Zone Management Authority v State of Kerala, Maradu Municipality* (2019) 7 SCC 248.

[77] ibid [108].

flats. Therefore, the Supreme Court ordered the builders to deposit about INR 615 million for disbursal. The apartment owners were permitted to take recourse to proper legal processes (civil or criminal) to resolve their issues.

Finally, in January 2020, the four illegal multi-storey apartment complexes were demolished through controlled implosion.[78] In the meantime, in 2010, the *grama panchayat* of Maradu was upgraded into a municipality. Accordingly, the area was re-classified as CRZ-II, where the NDZ was only fifty metres. The irony of the reclassification was not lost on those concerned since the buildings could now be rebuilt on the same plot where they once stood in flagrant violation of the law. That's so much for upholding the rule of law and protecting the coastal and marine environment!

The abovementioned cases are symptomatic of the malaise that plagues the legal regime relating to India's coastal and marine environment, which is hopelessly fragmented. There is utter disregard for the statutory processes, and even those entrusted with the enforcement of the legal norms are guilty of diluting them. This, unfortunately, leads to negative externalities and sub-optimal development. However, these issues will be magnified many times over when one considers the most significant threat that India's coastal and marine environment will face, that is, climate change and sea-level rise. India is one of the nations at high risk of sea-level rise. Several of India's port cities like Chennai, Kochi, Kolkata, Mumbai, Surat, and Visakhapatnam will be exposed to severe coastal flooding, displacing millions and exposing assets worth trillions of dollars to the rising waters.[79] An online visualization tool created by NASA that utilizes the projections developed by the Intergovernmental Panel on Climate Change (AR6) reveals that under a scenario where current levels of global emission in line with the collective nationally determined contributions persist, then by 2040, the sea levels would have risen by 0.15 metres in Kochi, 0.12 metres in Mumbai, and 0.10 metres in Chennai, Visakhapatnam, and Mangaluru.[80] At the global level, this rise would be about 0.14 metres. Thus, India's coastlines will be very severely affected by sea-level rise.

As of now, zoning under the CRZ Notification is one of the primary strategies envisaged to respond to sea-level rise. Given the various amendments and re-casts to the coastal law, which have resulted in more development in harm's way at the expense of sensitive coastal and marine ecosystems, implementing any retreat strategy in the future would be practically impossible. Several ecosystems would drown because of a coastal squeeze. In such a scenario, the policymakers would have very few options and would have to resort to the heavy fortification of the coastlines to protect the infrastructure, which may not always be the ideal adaptive response.

[78] Express Web Desk, 'Maradu Flats Demolition Highlights: Last of the 4 Illegal Apartment Complexes Demolished' *The Indian Express* (Kochi, 12 January 2020) <https://indianexpress.com/article/india/kerala-maradu-flats-demolition-today-kochi-live-updates-6210949/>.

[79] India Today Web Desk, 'These Indian Cities Likely to Go Three Feet Underwater by Century-End, IPCC Report Rings Warning Bell' *India Today* (New Delhi, 10 August 2021) <www.indiatoday.in/science/story/ipcc-climate-report-coastal-cities-in-india-sea-level-rise-environment-global-warming-indian-ocean-1839061-2021-08-10>.

[80] Sea Level Projection Tool <https://sealevel.nasa.gov/ipcc-ar6-sea-level-projection-tool>.

23.3 The Way Forward: Implementing Integrated Coastal Zone Management

In the context of these emerging challenges and the disconnect between the law and the factual realities, the ICZM has become highly relevant to India. As a continuous, iterative, and participatory process generally implemented over longer scales to achieve sustainable coastal development, the ICZM can help overcome several current challenges and provide a more effective system to protect the marine environment and even provide for coastal climate change adaptation.[81] The ICZM seeks to overcome fragmented decision-making, ensuring that the interventions and decisions regarding the coastal and marine environment are holistic and participatory. The concept has universal recognition, and almost every coastal country has an ICZM programme.

23.3.1 ICZM Implementation in India (Phase I)

As far as ICZM implementation in India is concerned, in 2010, the government of India embarked upon the ICZM project, implemented as a pilot with the World Bank's assistance in identified coastal stretches in the states of Gujarat, Odisha, and West Bengal.[82] The project's objectives were to develop institutional capacity to implement the CRZ Notification, address climate change, especially sea-level rise, conserve and protect fragile coastal ecosystems, address coastal pollution, and improve livelihood opportunities. The project had four components—one at the national level and three state components.

In the national ICZM component, the focus was on capacity building. This was important because the concerned authorities often found themselves hamstrung by a lack of capacity to implement the CRZ Notification. In this regard, the MoEFCC set up the Society of Integrated Coastal Management (SICOM) to implement the ICZM project. SICOM was designated as the National Project Management Unit.[83] SICOM coordinated efforts with various ministries, coastal states, and Union Territory governments, and project execution agencies.

An essential outcome of the project was the setting up of the NCSCM as an autonomous body under the MoEFCC. It advises the Union, the states and Union Territory governments and other associated stakeholders on policy and scientific matters relating

[81] Tony George Puthucherril, *Towards Sustainable Coastal Development: Institutionalizing Integrated Coastal Zone Management and Coastal Climate Change Adaptation in South Asia* (Brill Nijhoff 2015)Part II.

[82] Global Ocean Forum, 'Towards the Development of the Next Phase of Integrated Coastal Zone Management in India: Application of Lessons Learned from an International Review of Implementation of ICZM' (2019) 34.

[83] Society of Integrated Coastal Management, 'Origin of ICZM' (MoEFCC) <https://sicom.nic.in/projects/iczm-project-phase-1/origin-iczm>.

to the ICZM. The NCSCM is housed at Anna University in Chennai and has established six multi-disciplinary divisions to undertake research and development in ICZM practice and research.[84] The Centre is developing a repository of information and knowledge on ICZM practices in India and elsewhere. However, the most important function of the NCSCM is its role in the effective implementation of the CRZ Notification. In this regard, the NCSCM has successfully demarcated the hazard lines and the boundaries of ESAs along the entire coast of India.[85]

As mentioned, ICZM Phase I was implemented in Gujarat, Odisha, and West Bengal. The first step was to designate a State Project Management Unit to carry it out. In Gujarat, it was the Gujarat Ecology Commission,[86] in Odisha, the 'Integrated Coastal Zone Management Society, Odisha' was created,[87] and in West Bengal, the mandate was given to the Institute of Environmental Studies and Wetland Management.[88] The project had three main components: pollution abatement, resources conservation, and livelihood enhancement. Several successful projects, including the creation of ICZM plans, were implemented.

23.3.2 Achievements and Concerns

The pilot project approach and capacity building at the national and state levels established a strong foundation for the germination of the ICZM in India. The project's implementation enabled India to move away from a regulation-based approach to science-based coastal management. It also facilitated community participation. The project gave India the institutional frame to move towards a more ambitious ICZM agenda. Establishing the NCSCM as a world-class research institution on the ICZM was an important step. Despite India's complex governance structure, the project has proved that the ICZM can be implemented via Project Management Units. This is a valuable lesson. The concerned state government departments carried out most specific projects like mangrove plantation, eco-tourism, etc., without inter-departmental frictions or

84 National Centre for Sustainable Coastal Management, 'About NCSCM (MoEFCC)' <https://ncscm.res.in/about-us/>.

85 Ministry of Environment, Forest and Climate Change, 'National Centre for Sustainable Coastal Management' (Press Information Bureau, Government of India 2019) <https://pib.gov.in/Pressreleaseshare.aspx?PRID=1596334>.

86 Gujarat Ecology Commission, 'GEC as State Project Management Unit for ICZMP Gujarat' (Forests and Environment Department, Government of Gujarat) <https://gec.gujarat.gov.in/showpage.aspx?contentid=195&lang=English>.

87 Integrated Coastal Zone Management Project, 'Aims and Objectives' (Department of Forest, Environment and Climate Change, Government of Odisha) <http://www.iczmpodisha.org/aims-objectives.php>.

88 Institute of Environmental Studies and Wetland Management, 'About Us' <http://www.ieswm.org/about/aboutus.htm#>.

conflicts. The enhancing livelihood opportunities segment of the project, by tapping on existing resources and efficiently using them, demonstrated how effective linkages could be established between conservation goals and income opportunities. The focus on disaster management, enhancement of carbon sinks, and information awareness also boosted the project's utility for coastal communities.

As part of Phase I, certain ICZM plans were developed for specific coastal stretches. However, this raised several questions regarding the methodology adopted to develop these plans. Other areas that needed scrutiny related to the enhancement of local capacity, the involvement of the constitutionally stipulated local self-government institutions, and ensuring adequate finances would be available for implementing the project on longer-term scales. Perhaps at least in these three states, it was necessary to ensure that the officials of Phase I would be utilized for further ICZM efforts so that their accumulated wisdom would not be lost.

23.3.3 ICZM Implementation in India (Phase II)

Given the success of Phase I, the government of India has now moved to Phase II. In this Phase, the ICZM project has been extended to all the coastal states and union territories. The World Bank continues to support ICZM implementation through ENCORE set around three pillars, namely, 1) Institutional and Management Capacity for ICZM, 2) Climate Smart Growth, and 3) Information and science for evidence-based decision-making.[89] It seeks to pursue linkages between coastal conservation, climate resilience, and poverty reduction. Like in Phase I, the project activities for Phase II include preparing state-level ICZM plans, long-term support to implement marine spatial planning, and developing and protecting 'blue' resources to mitigate poverty and climate change.[90]

23.3.4 Discussion

As seen in ICZM Phase I and ICZM Phase II, the ICZM provides a methodology to harmonize marine environment protection and conservation (protection of olive ridley turtles, mangrove reforestation) with development (eco-tourism) and coastal climate change adaptation (coastal erosion). In this regard, the foundational lessons of Phase

[89] Society of Integrated Coastal Management, 'Environmental and Social Management Framework Volume II' (2019) 26 <http://iczmpodisha.org/images/documents/Environmental-Social-Management-Framework-Vol-II.pdf>.

[90] The World Bank, 'New World Bank Program to Strengthen Integrated Coastal Zone Management in India' (Press Release, 28 April 2020) <www.worldbank.org/en/news/press-release/2020/04/28/india-integrated-coastal-zone-management>.

I - World Bank support, capacity development, the science-based approach, focus on sustainable livelihoods, and poverty reduction have ensured that India is in the right direction in implementing the ICZM. This realisation prompted the government of India to initiate Phase II on a grander scale. This is highly significant since the ICZM efforts rarely surpass pilot efforts, particularly in developing countries. Most projects depend on donor support, and once that dries up, the effort comes to a standstill. All gains get squandered. In India's context, if the ICZM has to take deeper roots, appropriate linkages will have to be created between the CRZ Notification 2019 and other legislations on protecting the marine environment with ongoing ICZM programmes. The effort must be expended to ensure that the law and the project are mutually complementary and supportive.

Conclusion

Millions of impoverished local, traditional, and subsistence-based communities live on India's coastlines, which also house unique marine and coastal biodiversity. Surviving in deplorable social and economic conditions, those communities have to face the brunt of climate change and sea-level rise. If there is continued degradation of the coastal and marine environment, the socio-economic conditions of these already impoverished communities will correspondingly decline. This will render them even more vulnerable to climate change and sea-level rise. Therefore, protecting, conserving, and sustainably managing the coastal and marine environment and its resources is vital. While India has a comprehensive legal framework on this subject, it is highly fragmented, leading to ineffective management. In this context, the ICZM approach has been proposed to conserve and protect the coastal and marine environment, create more sustainable opportunities, and provide for climate change mitigation and adaptation. The ICZM can help create synergies between eco-restoration, sound management of coastal and marine resources and the communities that depend on them. It can also promote adaptation based on precaution and help increase coastal communities' adaptive capacities, rendering them more resilient to climatic perturbations.

Suggestions for Further Reading

Biliana Cicin-Sain and Robert W Knecht, Integrated Coastal and Ocean Management: Concepts and Practices (Island Press 1998).

RR Krishnamurthy and others (eds), *Coastal Management: Global Challenges and Innovations* (Academic Press 2019).

Shailesh Nayak, 'Coastal Zone Management in India: Present Status and Future Needs' (2017) 20(2) *Geo-spatial Information Science* 174.

Tony George Puthucherril, *Towards Sustainable Coastal Development: Institutionalizing Integrated Coastal Zone Management and Coastal Climate Change Adaptation in South Asia* (Martinus Nijhoff/Brill 2015).

Tony George Puthucherril, 'Operationalising Integrated Coastal Zone Management and Adapting to Sea Level Rise through Coastal Law: Where Does India Stand?' (2011) 26 *The International Journal of Marine and Coastal Law* 569.

PART VI

FORESTS, ECOSYSTEMS, AND PEOPLE

CHAPTER 24

FOREST MANAGEMENT AND CONSERVATION REGIME

SHARACHCHANDRA LELE

Abstract

Forest conservation involves ensuring sustainability in use-priority areas, preservation in biodiversity-priority areas, and regulation of the conversion of forests to non-forests. But forests provide multiple benefits to multiple stakeholders at multiple scales, and hence trade-offs between these benefits result in tradeoffs between stakeholders. Forest governance therefore requires addressing questions relating to the use, preservation and conversion of forests while incorporating the interests of multiple stakeholders. This chapter describes how these questions were resolved under the statist forest governance regime that prevailed during the colonial and post-colonial epoch, till the passage of the Forest Rights Act, 2006. An overview of the basic legal framework is followed by a description of key variations, nuances, and shifts over time in each. An assessment of this governance regime is then presented in terms of the fairness of priorities chosen for forest management, including attention to customary rights and social justice, effectiveness, sustainability and transparency and accountability in functioning.

Introduction: Forest Conservation and Management

'Forest conservation' is a broad concept, covering at least three dimensions: sustainable use of forests,[1] preservation of wildlife or biodiversity (often implying lower levels

[1] Sharachchandra Lele, 'Sustainable Use of Biomass Resources: A Note on Definitions, Criteria, and Practical Applications' (1994) 1(4) *Energy for Sustainable Development* 42.

of use), and the prevention or regulation of the conversion (both legally and illegally) of forests to non-forest land uses. Decisions about these three dimensions—whether to use, preserve or convert—are related to the different values or stakes that society may ascribe to having forests in the landscape—their direct tangible use benefits (such as timber, firewood or grazing), their indirect tangible benefits (such as soil conservation or carbon sequestration), and their intangible benefits (cultural value, recreational value, biodiversity value). Moreover, these benefits accrue to (or may be appropriated by) different stakeholders. This is especially the case in a country such as India, with a long history of millions of *Adivasis* and non-*Adivasis* residing in, dependent upon and culturally linked to forests and an enormously rich biota that has co-evolved with human presence over millennia,[2] and a more recent one of state interest in high-value products, or modern 'environmental' concern about the indirect and the intangible benefits. Forest 'management', which refers to specific actions relating to the protection and manipulation of the forest biota and landscape, may take many forms depending upon the benefits to be maximized. Forests may be managed to maximize timber production or a combination of firewood, grazing, and non-timber forest products, or prioritize the needs of wildlife, or (in the modern era) simply for carbon sequestration. In other words, forest management is shaped by the goals, processes, and institutions of forest conservation, which constitute forest governance. Forest conservation, however, must also engage with the process of conversion of forest land to other uses.

Any forest governance regime must, therefore, provide explicit or implicit answers to multiple questions relating to the three dimensions of conservation, that is, use, preservation, and conversion/non-conversion. These questions include: what constitutes sustainable use, conservation or conversion, whether and where to prioritize sustainable use versus conservation and where to permit conversion, who will manage the forest on a day-to-day basis given its spatial spread and complexity, through what process should decisions about assigning and changing priorities or about forest conversion be taken, and so on.[3] Furthermore, given the long history and ubiquitous presence of forest-dwelling or forest-dependent communities, one would naturally expect that they would have a formal role in the legal regime for forest conservation and management.

In India, however, the approach to the making of laws relating to all three dimensions of forest conservation falls into two epochs—a statist approach that began in 1865 under colonial rule and continued till 2006, and a new rights-based approach that has been pioneered by the Scheduled Tribes and Other Traditional Forest Dwellers (Recognition of Forest Rights) Act, 2006 (FRA). For the sake of compactness, the FRA is discussed separately in chapter 25, and the legal arrangements around wildlife conservation are discussed in chapter 26. This chapter will focus on the laws preceding the FRA that are premised on forest management and conservation by the state and primarily focused

[2] See Ramachandra Guha and Madhav Gadgil, 'State Forestry and Social Conflict in British India' (1989) 123 *Past and Present* 141.

[3] See Sharachchandra Lele, 'Understanding Current Forest Policy Debates through Multiple Lenses: The Case of India' (2019) 2(2) *Ecology, Economy and Society* 21.

on management for production and regulating conversion. The chapter begins with an overview of the basic legal framework for state management of forests that was set up by the colonial government starting in1865, then highlights important nuances, regional variations, and recent modifications in this framework before outlining the framework that emerged starting in 1980 for regulating forest conversion. Finally, an assessment of the socio-ecological outcomes produced by these management and regulatory frameworks is presented, which leads to insights into the kinds of changes that may be desirable.

24.1 Basic Legal Framework

The legal framework in India that enables state-led forest management is grounded in the colonial-era Indian Forest Act (IFA) of 1927 (built on its predecessor, the Forest Act, 1878[4] that laid the groundwork for colonial forestry in the country). The IFA continues to be in force in most states or has been copied with slight changes into eight state Forest Acts, namely, Andhra Pradesh, Assam, Jammu and Kashmir, Kerala, Karnataka, Orissa, Rajasthan, and Tamil Nadu. In brief, the IFA (and the state laws) (a) gives the state the legal authority to constitute three legal categories of forests (Reserved, Village and Protected), (b) declares certain valuable forest produce as state property, and (c) empowers the representatives of the state (forest officers) to regulate the use of and protect these forests (including their wildlife), and to manage, extract, and sell state-owned forest produce.

Reserved Forests (RFs) are fully controlled by the state, with trespass prohibited, while Protected Forests (PFs) are state-owned but with less strict regulation, so that entry into PFs does not require prior permission. Village Forests (VFs; carved out of RFs) would be RFs where managerial authority would be delegated to village councils (although VFs have almost never been notified). The IFA also empowers the state to notify privately held forested lands as Private Forests and thereby regulate their management. Supplementary laws passed after Independence primarily provided for (a) stricter regulation of Private Forests (various state Private Forest Acts) and (b) state ownership and regulation over certain valuable minor forest produce or non-timber forest produce.[5]

The IFA lists forest offences (actions prohibited in RFs—extendable to PFs) and vests very substantial powers with the forest officers, even more than those with policemen: power to arrest without warrant, power to release on a bond a person arrested, power to prevent commission of offence, power to try offences summarily, power to compound

[4] The first colonial legislation on forests was the Indian Forest Act of 1865, but it was seen as inadequate and quickly replaced with the 1878 Act.

[5] Sharachchandra Lele, Manoj Pattanaik, and Nitin D Rai, 'NTFPs in India: Rhetoric and Reality' in Sarah A Laird, Rebecca J McLain, and Rachel P Wynberg (eds), *Wild Product Governance: Finding Policies that Work for Non-Timber Forest Products* (Earthscan 2010) 85.

offences, and at the same time power to issue a search warrant and power of a civil court to compel the attendance of witnesses, and so on.[6] Indeed, being a parallel police force, much of the training of foresters is focused on understanding the principles and practice of criminal law because they use it constantly in their policing of the forest.[7]

Regarding prevention/regulation of forest conversion, one may assume that illegal deforestation (clandestine conversion of state forests to non-forest uses) can theoretically be prevented by the state forest officers exercising the powers given to them in the IFA. But the question of legal deforestation (conversion of state forest by the exercise of the state's power to 'de-notify' forest land, which is concomitant with the power to notify it in the first place) is more complicated. During colonial rule, the process (often called 'dis-forestment') was negotiated between the Forest and the Revenue Administration. Post-Independence, this power to de-notify RFs/PFs vested with the state governments because forests were in the State List of the Constitution of India, 1950, and the states were rather liberal in granting such conversion, both for development projects like dams and for agriculture.[8]

The Forty-second Constitutional Amendment of 1976 moved forests to the Concurrent List of the Constitution, and this enabled the central government to pass the Forest (Conservation) Act of 1980 (FCA), which requires[9] that 'de-reservation' or 'diversion' of forest land to non-forest purposes or 'clearing of forest land natural tree growth' be done only after concurrence from the central government.[10] A Forest Advisory Committee is constituted by the Ministry of Environment, Forest and Climate Change (MoEFCC) for considering and making recommendations regarding all such proposals.[11] The FCA also introduced the concept of 'compensatory afforestation', stipulating that the permission to divert for non-forest uses would be contingent on equivalent areas being afforested to compensate the forest lost.[12]

A major modification to the scope of the FCA was made by the Supreme Court of India in its 1996 orders in the famous *TN Godavarman Thirumulpad v Union of India* case.[13] Noting that many physically forested lands had been left out of the FCA's

[6] Indian Forest Act, 1927 ss 64–68, 72. What constitutes 'non-forest use' was defined in the 1988 amendment to the Forest (Conservation) Act, 1980.

[7] E.g., B Jagannath Shetty, *A Manual of Law for Forest Officers* (2nd edn, BJ Shetty 1981).

[8] E.g., MV Nadkarni, Syed Ajmal Pasha, and LS Prabhakar, *The Political Economy of Forest Use and Management* (Sage 1989).

[9] FCA s 2.

[10] Such concurrence is called 'forest clearance' in bureaucratic parlance. 'De-reservation' would cause the land to lose its legal status as forest land, whereas 'diversion' does not change the legal status of the land.

[11] FCA s 3.

[12] Forest Conservation Rules 2003 s 7(2)(d).

[13] *TN Godavarman Thirumulpad v Union of India* WP (Civil) No. 202 of 1995, Order dated 12 December 1996 (Supreme Court of India).

regulatory ambit because they had not been legally notified as either RF/PF/VF, etc., the Court extended the scope of the FCA to all lands, whether legally notified as forest or matching the 'dictionary definition' of forests. This has led to the creation of another category of forests ('deemed forests') where the land has not been legally notified as 'forest' under the categories defined in the IFA or state forest acts but fits the dictionary definition; hence, if it has to be diverted for non-forest uses, the FCA requirements would apply.

A second major modification introduced by the Supreme Court in 2002[14] in the FCA process was based on the argument that compensatory afforestation, which created plantations on equivalent land, could never adequately compensate for the loss of natural forests. Therefore, the project proponent (who was seeking the diversion of forest land) must not only pay the cost of compensatory afforestation but also pay the 'Net Present Value' (NPV) of the forest diverted, which would be far higher, ranging between INR 580,000 and INR 920,000 per hectare. Furthermore, the Court ordered all these funds to be deposited into a central Compensatory Afforestation Fund (CAF) rather than being paid directly to the states.

In short, the broad legal framework for management is one of state ownership of the forest and all its produce and the granting of police powers to the Forest Departments to protect the forest and obtain revenue from forest products. For regulation of conversion, the police powers were to prevent illegal conversion of rich forests, while initially, legal conversion of poorer quality forests was permitted by the states and even encouraged. Since the 1980s, the procedure for conversion has involved the central government and required meeting several conditions including compensatory afforestation. With the Supreme Court's interventions, the applicability of the FCA has expanded, the cost of conversion has increased, and the process has become even more centralized.

24.2 Reading Between the Lines: Key Nuances, Shifts, and Assumptions in the Forest Management Framework

The above broad brush picture hides many of the complexities and regional variations that remain ingrained but are often hidden from a superficial perusal of the legal framework.

[14] ibid, IA No 566, Order 30 October 2002.

a) Most of the landscape in the north-eastern states, dominated by Scheduled Tribe communities, is left out of the purview of the IFA,[15] as the states have special status under the Constitution,[16] and are also covered under the Sixth Schedule of the Constitution, giving their community institutions complete control over their lands, including the right to practice shifting cultivation which is banned in the rest of the country. These lands are administratively classified as 'unclassed forests' by the Forest Departments.
b) The IFA does not specify the physical condition of land that can be designated as RF or PF by the state: any land over which the government has proprietary rights can be declared RF/PF. In other words, RF/PF are legal classifications of land that vest the substantial powers over them provided in the IFA to Forest Officers (that is, to the Forest Department). So we see Himalayan glaciers or rocky outcrops in the Western Ghats, alpine or desert grasslands or even water bodies like urban lakes being designated as RFs/PFs.
c) Conversely, the IFA only empowers the state to notify lands as RFs and PFs, but the state may choose not to, and even in provinces directly administered by the British, many forested lands were left un-notified as a buffer for future expansion of agriculture.[17] Moreover, much of India was then under princely states, not directly administered by the colonial government, and each princely state had its own framework of forest law that only approximately matched the IFA and consciously left many forested areas for local use or agricultural expansion.[18] The Supreme Court's order in the *Godavarman* case mentioned above was explicitly aimed at bringing all such non-notified forested lands under the stricter regulation regime of the FCA. This required the identification of so-called 'deemed forests',[19] including the unclassed forests of north-eastern India and various categories of land under 'revenue classifications' such as *chhote jhaad ka jangal* in Central Province, *zudpi jangal* in Maharashtra, or the Assessed Waste Lands of South Canara. The *chhote jhaad ka jangal* had in fact become a terrain of dispute between

[15] Dhrupad Choudhury, 'The Forest Rights Act, Northeast India, and Shifting Cultivators: A Commentary' in Sharachchandra Lele and Ajit Menon (eds), *Democratizing Forest Governance in India* (OUP 2014) 339.

[16] Nagaland: art 371A; Manipur: art 371C; Mizoram: art 371G; Arunachal: art 371H; Meghalaya: art 371B.

[17] E.g., Assessed Waste Lands in South Canara District of Madras Presidency. See AS Shrinidhi and Sharachchandra Lélé, 'Forest Tenure Regimes in the Karnataka Western Ghats: A Compendium' (2001) *Institute for Social and Economic Change* Working Paper 90.

[18] Madhu Sarin, 'Laws, Lore and Logjams: Critical Issues in Indian Forest Conservation' (IIED Gatekeeper Series 116, 2005).

[19] A term created to represent lands not notified as RF/PF but meeting the 'dictionary definition' of a forest. The Karnataka High Court recently questioned this in *Dhananjay v State of Karnataka* WP No 54476/2016 (GM-MM-S) C/w WP 51135/2016.

the Revenue and Forest administration earlier, resulting in the Orange Areas of Madhya Pradesh and Chhattisgarh.[20]

d) On paper, the IFA provides for an elaborate process for ensuring that the declaration of land as RF/PF does not abridge any person's or community's prior rights. Sections 4–20 spell out steps for notifying a RF and section 29(3) for a PF. However, section 29(3) also provides an escape clause that allows land to be notified as PF 'pending' inquiry and record (or settlement) of such rights. Furthermore, the entire mindset of the colonial and post-colonial forest administration has been that the forest resources of the country always (historically) belonged to the government of the day. Being 'super-abundant', they were looked upon as 'waste' and used by villagers adjacent to the forests, but such use was only tolerated by the state and was never recognized as a 'right'.[21] Therefore, in practice, in the declaration of RFs and PFs, very few rights were ever admitted and recorded, especially in good quality forests that were notified as RFs; most other customary use was treated as a 'privilege'.[22] Even where extensive customary rights have been recognized in colonial law, such as the Chhota Nagpur Tenancy Act of 1908 where the *Mundari khuntikattidar* (effectively village headman) had the rights to manage the entire village lands as a trustee of the community, post-Independence notifications subsumed these lands under PFs.[23]

e) In particular pockets, however, the colonial rulers had to compromise with the resistance, protest, and even rebellion by local communities to the takeover of their forests.[24] This resulted in a complex tapestry of localized 'rights and privileges' recognized under various state-specific laws on the forested landscape and which continue today under the 'savings' clauses of the new state forest acts. For instance, the *soppinabetta privileges* of the erstwhile North Canara district recognized by the erstwhile Bombay Presidency and in other districts by the erstwhile Mysore Princely State or the *kumki privileges* in South Canara district of Madras Province were recognized as far back as the 1890s and have been 'saved' at the time of the passing of the Karnataka Forest Act of 1963.[25] These privileges provide exclusive usufructuary control over forest patches to certain individuals or groups of individuals on the basis of their ownership of particular agricultural lands and have virtually become rights. In Central Province, *nistari* (usufruct) rights of

[20] Anil Garg, *Orange Areas: Examining the Origin and Status* (National Centre for Advocacy Studies 2005).

[21] Shetty (n 7) 79. As Guha points out, the presumption that all land not under settled cultivation belonged to the state and that all customary rights were only 'privileges' was a colonial construct. See Ramachandra Guha, 'The Prehistory of Community Forestry in India' (2001) 6(2) *Environmental History* 213, 215.

[22] Shetty (n 7) 39.

[23] Sudha Vasan, 'Forest Law, Ideology, and Practice' in Nandini Sundar (ed), *Legal Grounds: Natural Resources, Identity and the Law in Jharkhand* (OUP 2005) 112.

[24] Guha (n 21) 227–229.

[25] S 117 (Repeals and Savings). See Shrinidhi and Lélé (n 17) for details.

firewood collection and grazing were extensively recognized, not only for villagers having forests inside their boundary (where they were codified in *nistar patraks* or registers) but even for distant villages. A major exception to state forestry was made in the Kumaon region of the erstwhile United Provinces, where, following multiple and sometimes violent protests,[26] the creation of *Van Panchayats* (village forest councils) was enabled,[27] and villagers were permitted to manage their forests themselves outside of the IFA.[28] None of these 'deviations' from the simple classification of RF/PF/VF/Private Forest is apparent when perusing any summary of forest law in India, but may become apparent when one scrutinizes the 'forest manuals' of individual states,[29] or other records on the ground.

f) The IFA does not spell out the objectives for which the RF/PF must be managed. The objective for the colonial state was clear: maximizing timber harvest and, indirectly, revenue generation, much of which was achieved by clear-felling multi-species natural forests and replacing them with single-species stands of teak or pine.[30] Sustaining timber yield was a secondary objective. Although again not mentioned in the statutes, the administrative requirement of managing harvest as per 'Working Plans', drawing upon principles of forestry developed in Europe, is assumed to ensure sustainability. The Supreme Court, concerned though it has been about forest conservation, only imposed the requirement that all felling of trees in forests must take place only under a Working Plan approved by the central government but did not explicitly impose any sustainability requirement.[31]

g) The National Forest Policy of 1988 (NFP88) sought to re-shuffle the priorities of state forest management, prioritizing 'maintaining environmental stability ... and ecological balance', and declaring that the 'derivation of economic benefit must be subordinated to this aim'.[32] It also acknowledged the need to meet 'the requirements of ... the rural and tribal populations'.[33] This had been preceded by a number of states (especially in the Himalayan and Western Ghats region) passing administrative orders prescribing a 'green felling ban', that is, no felling in natural forests. But felling continues there in forest plantations already created, and most central Indian states continue logging in natural forests. The NFP88, not having the status of a law, does not prevent such felling.

[26] Ramachandra Guha, *The Unquiet Woods: Ecological Change and Peasant Resistance in the Himalaya* (OUP 1989).

[27] Government of Uttar Pradesh, Kumaon Panchayat Forest Rules (1931) Forest Department, Government of United Provinces 441/XIV-366.

[28] Van Panchayats continue to exist today, although their rights have been significantly curtailed.

[29] E.g., NV Ramachandra Chetty, *The Karnataka Forest Manual* (Karnataka Forest Department, Government of Karnataka 1976).

[30] Guha and Gadgil (n 2) 147.

[31] Godavarman case, Order of 12 December 1996 (n 13).

[32] Ministry of Environment and Forests, National Forest Policy 1988 (No 3-1/86-FP dt. 7 December 1990) para 2.2.

[33] ibid para 2.1.

h) The NFP88, however, also mooted the 'creation of massive people's movement' for the regeneration of degraded forest lands, and this was followed by a central government circular in 1990 to all states[34] asking them to initiate participatory or 'joint' forest management programmes (JFM). Officially, JFM exists today across almost all states but has neither received statutory status nor has it significantly altered the objectives of forestry or empowered villagers to manage forests for their own benefits.[35]

i) With the emergence of climate change as a major environmental issue, the role of forests as ecosystems as repositories of carbon and, therefore, afforestation as a process that can sequester additional amounts to mitigate climate change has gained attention, especially in international discourses.[36] The government of India committed in the 2015 Paris Agreement to sequester a significant additional amount of carbon dioxide through afforestation and forest improvement. This international commitment is almost equivalent to a statutorily set objective for the forest sector. The central government attempted to incorporate this objective in a revised National Forest Policy draft in 2018[37] but had to shelve the draft amidst many objections, including by its own Ministry of Tribal Affairs.[38] Nevertheless, carbon sequestration has become a major additional goal of state forestry in India, apart from biodiversity conservation (limited to protected areas) and timber/softwood production, as, for example, it shows up in projects supported by international donors//lenders in this sector.[39]

j) Furthermore, although the IFA does not mention a 'forest department' at all, the creation of an Imperial Forest Service in 1869, renamed the Indian Forest Service in 1920, laid the foundation for a separate cadre of officers to run the provincial forest departments. Although discontinued in 1932, the Indian Forest Service (IFS) was reinstated in 1966 and is considered an 'All India Service' under Article 312(1) of the Constitution. All senior positions in state/union territory Forest

[34] Ministry of Environment and Forests, Government of India, Involvement of Village Communities and Voluntary Agencies for Regeneration of Degraded Forest Lands (Memorandum to Forest Secretaries of All States and Union Territories 6-21/89-FP, 1 June 1990).

[35] Sharachchandra Lele, 'What is Wrong with Joint Forest Management?' in Lele and Menon (eds) (n 15) 25; Oliver Springate-Baginski and Piers Blaikie (eds), *Forests, People and Power: The Political Ecology of Reform in South Asia* (Earthscan 2007).

[36] Sharachchandra Lele and Jagdish Krishnaswamy, 'Climate Change and India's Forests' in Navroz K. Dubash (ed), *India in a Warming World* (OUP 2019) 477.

[37] Ministry of Environment, Forests and Climate Change, Government of India, Draft National Forest Policy 2018 (F. No 1-1/2012-FP (Vol.4); Sharachchandra Lele, 'Smoke in the Woods' *The Hindu* (Chennai, 9 April 2018) <http://www.thehindu.com/opinion/op-ed/smoke-in-the-woods/article23475064.ece> for a critique.

[38] Kumar Sambhav Shrivastava, 'Tribal Affairs Ministry Opposes Centre's Draft National Forest Policy for its "Privatisation Thrust"' *Scroll* (17 July 2018) <https://scroll.in/article/886708/thrust-on-privatisation-tribal-affairs-ministry-opposes-centres-draft-national-forest-polic>.

[39] See, e.g., USAID's call for proposals at <https://www.grants.gov/web/grants/search-grants.html?keywords=Strengthening%20Landscape%20Management%20and%20Conservation%20Activity>.

Departments are staffed by IFS officers, as are all senior forest-related positions in the central Ministry, and their training and socialization are meant to create an elite group that swears by the 150-year-old (colonial) legacy of 'scientific' state-controlled forestry.[40]

k) Finally, through gradual changes in 'service rules', this elite group also staffs all senior positions in institutions of teaching and research related to forestry, thereby controlling the production of formal knowledge on forests, heads the forest monitoring agency (the Forest Survey of India) thereby controlling the evaluation of outcomes, and heads the Compensatory Afforestation Fund Management and Planning Authority (CAMPA) committees that disburse funds to their own departments. IFS officers are often also appointed to key positions in central and state tribal welfare departments as they are seen as the only officers with field experience in tribal areas.

In short, there is some regional variation in the implementation of the basic legal framework of state forestry, with the northeast largely left out of its ambit. In areas with full state control, the objective of management for more than a century was exclusively timber and other product extraction; post-NFP88, some dilution of this focus is visible without any statutory redirection. There is local nuance and concession to local needs through the recognition of usufructuary rights (in pockets) and privileges (on a wider scale), but almost nowhere is there a recognition of villagers' customary rights to *manage* the forest as per their needs (the exception being *Van Panchayats*). Management decisions and concomitant police powers rest solely in the hands of state Forest Departments, run by officers of the IFS, whose authority has gradually expanded beyond management into policymaking, funding, and even other sectors. The next chapter will show that the FRA seeks to radically shift these arrangements, although with limited success in the fifteen years of its implementation.

24.3 Reading Between the Lines: Gaps and Shifts in the Framework Regulating Forest Conversion

The legal framework for regulating forest conversion also has many nuances and has gone through several shifts over time that are not apparent from a superficial perusal.

[40] Kevin Hannam, 'Educating an Environmental Elite: The Training of the Indian Forest Service' (2000) 9(4) *International Research in Geographical and Environmental Education* 285.

a) The FCA contains no guidance on when a proposal to divert forests for non-forest use should be *rejected*. It only provides guidance on what procedures need to be completed for the proposal to be considered. The key step is the identification of land for compensatory afforestation and agreeing to pay the compensatory afforestation costs (and post-*Godavarman*, the NPV). The only substantive criterion is the suggestion that forests that fall within sanctuaries or national parks or are a habitat for threatened species of flora or fauna *might* not be diverted.[41] Attempts to define 'no-go' areas other than sanctuaries and national parks have not made headway. Since 2014, an administrative 'decision support system' has provided inputs for identifying 'inviolate' or high conservation' areas under an administrative order.[42]
b) As per the Forest (Conservation) Rules, 2022 (FC Rules), decisions regarding 'small' diversions (less than five hectares) and 'linear projects' (diversion of land for roads, railways, pipelines, and transmission lines) can be taken by a regional empowered committee. [Note: This chapter was written before the Forest (Conservation) Amendment Act 2023 was passed and so this Act and its implications are not discussed in this chapter.]
c) From an initial position requiring that compensatory afforestation be carried out close to the location where the forest is proposed to be cut down or at least in the same district to permitting it anywhere in that state, the FC Rules, 2022 permit 'Accredited Compensatory Afforestation' where land from anywhere in the country can be considered for compensatory afforestation for a particular project.
d) There has been a lengthy back and forth between the Supreme Court and the central and state governments on the question of the under-utilization and mis-utilization of compensatory afforestation funds, and the need for a proper mechanism to distribute these funds to the states and monitor their use.[43] The Court forced the setting up of a statutory authority to administer the CAF; the CAMPA bill was passed by the Lok Sabha (Lower House of Parliament) in 2008 but came into effect only in 2016 because of opposition in the Rajya Sabha (Upper House). The structures for deciding how to spend these funds are effectively in the hands of the forest bureaucracy, although the Supreme Court continues to want a say in how these funds are utilized.
e) In terms of who decides on forest diversion, the process laid down in the FCA is obviously centralized, technocratic, and state-dominated. The proposal is forwarded by the state government with comments from their Forest Department. The Forest Advisory Committee (FAC) consists overwhelmingly of technocrats (five bureaucrats[44] and three 'independent' experts from the fields of 'mining, civil

[41] Forest Conservation Rules, 2003 s 7(2)(a) or Forest Conservation Rules, 2022 s 9(5)(e)(ii)(E).

[42] Anonymous, Report of the Committee to formulate objective parameters for identification of inviolate forest areas (Ministry of Environment and Forests, Government of India 2012).

[43] Kanchi Kohli and others, 'Pocketful of Forests: Legal Debates on Valuating and Compensating Forest Loss in India' (Kalpavriksh and WWF-India 2011).

[44] Who may hesitate to go against the wishes of the government of the day.

engineering and development economics'),[45] so there is little chance of the socio-environmental impacts of forest conversion being taken into consideration, notwithstanding a prolonged tussle between the Supreme Court and the MoEFCC as to the composition of the FAC.[46]

f) The strongest challenge to this technocratic and centralized process came from the passing of the FRA in 2006, which, *inter alia,* recognizes access and management rights of forest-dwellers over forests. Consequently, the diversion of such forests to non-forestry uses would require either their consent or compensation of their rights. The first attempt to incorporate this requirement in the forest diversion process is a 2009 order.[47] Subsequently, in *Orissa Mining Corporation v MoEFCC,*[48] the Supreme Court confirmed the need for considering the opinions of affected forest-rights holders prior to deciding on any proposal for forest diversion. The FC Rules were therefore amended in 2014 and 2017 to incorporate the 2009 order, requiring that the process of recognition of forest rights be completed, and the informed consent (or otherwise) of the *Gram Sabhas* be sought. The MoEFCC tried to dilute this requirement in various ways, such as exempting 'linear projects' (railway lines, highways, transmission lines and pipelines) from this requirement of *Gram Sabha* consent, but this exemption was struck down by the High Court of Andhra Pradesh in 2019.[49] However, the FC Rules, 2022 have relegated the consent requirement itself to a footnote, with the process of FRA 'compliance' (not rights-holders' consent) to be carried out in parallel or even after forest clearance has been given.

In short, the process regulating forest conversion began as an attempt by the central government to regulate what seemed like an overly generous approach of state governments to forest conversion to non-forest uses. But over time, with economic growth taking the front seat, the central government itself has diluted these provisions to allow so-called 'development' projects to get forest clearance easily. We shall now assess the outcomes of this shifting framework for management and conservation.

[45] Modified to 'ecology, engineering and development economics' only in Forest Conservation Rules, 2022 s 3(2).

[46] Kanchi Kohli, 'Whose Expert is an Expert?' *IndiaTogether* (30 January 2007) <https://www.indiatogether.org/expert-environment#continue>.

[47] Ministry of Environment and Forests, Government of India, Diversion of forest land for non-forest purposes under the Forest (Conservation) Act 1980—ensuring compliance of the Scheduled Tribes and Other Traditional Forest Dwellers (Recognition of Forest Rights) Act 2006, 11-9/1998-FC(pt) dt. 3-Aug-2009.

[48] *Orissa Mining Corporation Ltd v Ministry of Environment & Forest* (2013) 6 SCC 476.

[49] *SAMATHA and EAS Sarma v Union of India* WP(PIL) 231 of 2013, Order dated 6 March 2019 (High Court of Andhra Pradesh).

24.4 Assessing Outcomes of the Legal Framework for Forest Management and Regulating Conversion

To assess the effectiveness of any legal framework for forest conservation, it is necessary to spell out first the normative dimensions along which one would carry out such an assessment. Forests provide multiple benefits to multiple stakeholders at different physical and social distances from the forest, starting from historical forest-dwellers who benefit in many material and cultural ways from the forest, downstream beneficiaries of hydrological services, national beneficiaries of forest products, and national and global beneficiaries of biodiversity and carbon sequestration. Moreover, and perhaps most importantly, these benefits cannot be simultaneously maximized; trade-offs are inevitable.[50] For instance, logging the forest for timber to supply to the urban economy will reduce the availability of many non-timber forest products harvested by the local community and will also affect wildlife adversely, not to mention reducing the amount of carbon sequestered in the forest vegetation and soils. Logging may also open up the forest for invasion by exotic species such as *Lantana camara*, thereby jeopardizing the natural regeneration of the forest as assumed in a logging plan. Clear-felling natural forest and replacing it with single-species plantations of teak or pine or more exotic species such as eucalyptus or *Acacia auriculiformis* may generate high volumes of timber or softwood but decimates biodiversity and provides almost nothing of use to local communities. Alternatively, managing the forest to maximize the production of small timber, firewood, fodder, grazing availability, and other non-timber forest products would result in a forest that is significantly different from an 'old-growth' forest, with intermediate levels of biodiversity and limited availability of large timber. If the priority is wildlife conservation, then logging must be banned (as it is in India's protected areas), and local use may have to be modified.

Therefore, to assess the 'effectiveness' of a forest conservation regime, one has first to know which of the competing objectives is forest conservation aimed at, that is, forest conservation 'for what?' and therefore 'for whom?'.[51] Note that the objectives may not be singular but a mix in which highest priority is given to different objectives in different locations. For instance, wildlife conservation may be prioritized in certain locations without implying complete displacement of local needs or communities. Moreover, land used for forests also has opportunity costs, and therefore, a forest conservation regime

[50] Sharachchandra Lele and Amit Kurien, 'Interdisciplinary Analysis of the Environment: Insights from Tropical Forest Research' (2011) 38(2) *Environmental Conservation* 211.

[51] Sharachchandra Lele, 'Rethinking Forest Governance: Towards A Perspective Beyond JFM, the Godavarman Case and FRA' in Anonymous (ed), *The Hindu Survey of the Environment 2011* (2011) 95.

must include mechanisms to determine when and where society may prefer to allow their conversion to non-forest uses.

The *effectiveness* of a legal regime will then refer to the extent to which particular priorities are achieved. The regime will also have to be assessed in terms of *sustainability*, that is, whether it promotes the continued availability of the prioritized benefits over time—whether timber, grazing or carbon. But, the setting of the priorities themselves involves considerations of *fairness* in the distribution of benefits across stakeholders. It would also include considerations of *customary rights*—whose rights? And who came first?—and also of *social justice*—which stakeholder is socio-economically the weakest and therefore more deserving of benefits? Clearly, in the Indian context, fairness from all perspectives (custom, social justice, and even aggregate social welfare) would mean that the interests and rights of the forest-dwellers, who have been historically living in and been materially dependent upon and culturally attached to the forests, ought to be given priority in most places. Finally, from the perspective of governance in a democratic country, the legal framework must be assessed in terms of the balance of discretionary power and *accountability* that it strikes, the *decentralization* it achieves in management, and the extent of *public voice* it provides in decisions regarding conversion.[52]

From this multidimensional point of view, the flaws in India's legal framework set up for state forest management and conservation are glaringly obvious.

a) **Premise of state ownership and control and consequent historical injustices**: The entire framework of 'state' ownership and management originated in the colonial interest in appropriating forest resources for colonial purposes, which after Independence was simply replaced by the goal of meeting 'national needs'.[53] This meant exclusion of local users from prime forests and at best 'tolerance' towards them in other forests. But given the ubiquity of forest-dwelling populations, their customary practices and their needs, this also meant the suppression of all shifting cultivation across mainland[54] India, extinguishment of customary rights to access forests and to collect of forest produce in most places and limiting them to paltry 'privileges', and criminalization of any attempts to satisfy needs beyond these privileges. The de-recognition of customary tenures led not only to the local community not being able to meet its needs, but also their alienation from the responsibility of protecting and sustainably managing forests. The founding concept of 'state ownership' of forested land, rooted in the idea of a vast unpopulated wasteland or pristine forest, thus guarantees enormous structural injustice—one of the major 'historical injustices' flagged in the FRA.

[52] Lele (n 3).

[53] National Forest Policy, 1952, para 3.

[54] This term refers to all of India, excluding the north-east.

b) **Extra layers of injustice**: A further dimension of historical injustice was added in the creation of 'Forest Villages',[55] where itinerant *Adivasis* were forcibly settled,[56] and they were forced to carry out free labour for the Forest Department in 'return for' the right to cultivate some land, which continues to be designated as 'forest land'. Even today, all rural development schemes and programmes in such Forest Villages are implemented only through the Forest Department.[57] Till the passing of the FRA in 2006, only one state (Maharashtra) had abolished Forest Villages and even post-2006, the process has barely begun in three states (Chhattisgarh, Odisha, West Bengal). Non-recognition of cultivated lands and habitation due to the peremptory declaration of land as RF/PF without adequate enquiry and rights settlement (even as prescribed by the IFA) has been another widespread form of historical injustice which the FRA attempts to redress (see the next chapter).

c) **Absence of legally mandated substantive goals**: The legal framework, even post-Independence, remains focused on establishing or perpetuating state control and provides almost no substantive goals or criteria for how forests should be managed. It does not statutorily require the conservation of *natural* forests. The colonial focus on timber extraction, therefore, remained till well into the 1980s and continues in many parts of the country even today. Even sustainable harvest is not a statutory requirement. The National Forest Policy of 1952 first articulated the need to ensure sustainable harvests and suggested using Working Plans to ensure this. The procedural requirement, now made virtually statutory by the Supreme Court, is that felling be done as per an approved Working Plan, which assumes that Working Plans ensure sustainability. In the absence of independent scrutiny (for reasons outlined above) of the science behind and the actual implementation of Working Plans, the assumption remains untested, but the evidence available suggests otherwise.[58] Moreover, the conversion of natural forests to single-species plantations—which has taken place on a large scale in the country—does not come under the sustainable harvest criterion: it is a question of priorities regarding what kind of benefits to maximize from a 'forest'. Thus, historical clear-felling and conversion of natural forests to plantations across the country, continued logging of natural forests in many parts, continued adherence to outdated methods of estimating sustainable yield without field verification,[59] and repetition of the same format and 'resource inventory' approach in the National Working Plan Code

[55] Not to be confused with Village Forests formed under the VF chapter of the IFA, where village communities are given some degree of autonomous control over the VF.

[56] Daniel John Read, 'Pugmarks and Footprints: Human-Wildlife Encounters and the Legitimacy of Conservation in Central India' (PhD Thesis, University of Georgia 2019).

[57] RR Prasad and MP Jahagirdar, *Tribal Situation in Forest Villages: Changing Subsistence Strategies and Adaptation* (Discovery Publishing House 1993).

[58] Madhav Gadgil, S Narendra Prasad and Rauf Ali, 'Forest Management and Forest Policy in India: A Critical Review' (1983) 33 *Social Action* 127.

[59] Madhav Gadgil, 'Empowering Gramsabhas to Manage Biodiversity: The Science Agenda' (2007) 42(22) *Economic and Political Weekly* 2067.

of 2014,[60] without explicitly debating and deriving different prescriptions for different objectives, have ensured that neither the productivity nor the biodiversity of the country's forests have been sustained.

d) **Decentralization**: Meeting the needs of local communities was never a priority in the legal framework; therefore, assessing effectiveness vis-à-vis this objective is pointless. The important thing to note is that in a country of this size with a very large forest-dwelling and forest-dependent population and a long history of customary tenure, the idea of decentralizing day-to-day management—in even part of the landscape—into the hands of the local community was never taken up seriously, despite the Village Forest chapter in the IFA. The Madras Presidency experimented at a small scale, first with VFs and then with similar '*Panchayat* Forests', but the VF experiment was short-lived and the *Panchayat* Forest experiment was also deemed unsuccessful and wrapped up (ironically) after Independence, with the Andhra Forest Act, 1957 dropping the VF chapter entirely.[61] Similarly, the princely state of Mysore and even Bombay Presidency had allowed the formation of some VFs in Shimoga and North Canara districts respectively, but these were dissolved after the passing of the Karnataka Forest Act, 1963, even though the Act had a VF chapter. Only two villages managed to obtain a stay on their dissolution and continued to protect and manage their forests.[62] JFM never went beyond the status of a superficially participatory programme run and controlled by the state Forest Departments.[63] Attempts to provide JFM with legal status were taken up only in the state of Karnataka by introducing an additional section for JFM committees in the VF chapter,[64] but even this amendment was never used.[65] It is only with the passing of the FRA and the recognition of Community Forest Resource rights under its section 3(1)(i) in a few states[66] that statutorily recognized and reasonably autonomous and democratic village-level forest management has come into existence in mainland India. Legal mechanisms for addressing intra-village inequities or inequities between settled villagers and nomadic communities that may have historically been using those forests are, however, yet to be put into place.

e) **Democratic accountability and transparency**: The (colonial-origin) legal regime also provides state forest officers with an enormous amount of discretionary

[60] Ministry of Environment and Forests, Government of India, National Working Plan Code 2014 <https://icfre.gov.in/UserFiles/File/Institute-FRI-2011/2014/NWPCode-2014_21May14.pdf>.

[61] VM Ravi Kumar, 'State, Forests and Communities: History of Community Forest Management in Colonial Andhra 1800-1947' (2012) 47(49) *Economic and Political Weekly* 53.

[62] H Rajagopal Shetty, *Study on Working of Forest Panchayats: Uttara Kannada District—Karnataka State*, SWED Forest Report submitted to Karnataka Forest Department (1988).

[63] Lele (n 35) and references therein.

[64] Amendment under Act 12 of 1998 s 31A.

[65] Committees have never actually been notified under this new section.

[66] Kundan Kumar, Neera M Singh, and Y Giri Rao, 'Promise and Performance of the Forest Rights Act: A Ten-year Review' (2017) 52(25–26) *Economic and Political Weekly* 40.

police power over largely illiterate and socio-economically marginalized forest-dwellers without proportionate accountability. Even in the post-Independence period, accountability to a democratically elected state government has translated into limited real accountability, as a powerful forest bureaucracy and elected governments in which forest-dwelling communities (especially *Adivasis*) were hardly represented, have continued to ignore the enormous oppression and injustice that have been perpetrated—the scale of which is only now being documented.[67] In addition to this gross misuse of power, the forest bureaucracy wields its powers in other unaccountable ways, such as not making all its documents including Working Plans and maps available in the public domain, not permitting independent reviews of the outcomes of their forest management activities, arbitrary delays and refusals in giving permission to carry out scientific research in forested areas,[68] and as mentioned above, being the policeman, the proprietor, the funder, the monitor, and the policy-maker all rolled into one.

f) **Conservation/diversion criteria**: The FCA curbed the power of the states to denotify forests and asked for some information (whether the area overlapped with a Protected Area; whether 'any rare/endangered/unique species of flora and fauna found in the area'[69] and even the 'cost-benefit analysis' of the project!). But it laid down no criteria for deciding in favour or against diversion using this information, and there is no record of the cost-benefit analysis ever being discussed. Implicitly, PAs were not to be diverted, but no-go areas beyond PAs were never identified. The attempt to use multiple criteria with the help of a computerized decision-support system since 2014 is a step forward, but there has been no public scientific debate on the criteria or how they would be operationalized. There is no official position on whether the purpose of diversion is to be given any consideration. Implicitly, however, 'developmental' projects (both public and private sector) have been prioritized while livelihood projects (such as diversion for agriculture) have been rejected.[70] Following the demand for NPV, the question of proposing diversion for agriculture by peasants simply did not arise. An analysis of six months of forest clearance decisions (January-December 2019) showed the rejection rate to be less than 2.5 per cent (most on procedural grounds), and more than half the approved diversions were in dense or very dense forest.[71]

[67] See Shomona Khanna and others, *Criminalisation of Adivasis and the Indian Legal System* (Indigenous Peoples Rights International 2021) ch 5 for details.

[68] MD Madhusudan and others, 'Science in the Wilderness: The Predicament of Scientific Research in India's Wildlife Reserves' (2006) 91 *Current Science* 1015.

[69] FC Rules, 2004, Form A item 7.

[70] Smriti Das, 'Pressure for Conversion of Forestland to Non-forest Uses in India' in Ramachandra Guha and others (eds), *Deeper Roots of Historical Injustice: Trends and Challenges in the Forests of India* (Rights and Resources Initiative 2012) 159.

[71] Mridhu Tandon and Rakesh Singh, 'Analysis of Forest Diversion in India, 2019' Clearance Trend Series, Legal Initiative for Forest and Environment (LIFE) (July 2020).

g) **Conservation/diversion process**: There have been multiple and repeated critiques of the process by which the permissions for diversion are given. First, given the size and diversity of the country, a set of experts sitting in the national capital can never on their own check the veracity of information submitted—such as whether information regarding forest quality and wildlife presence/absence is accurate. They need information from local concerned citizens, but the local public hearings are absent from the process; the process depends entirely on information provided by the forest bureaucracy. Second, the absence of a voice for those directly affected by the diversion, namely, the customary users of the forest, was a glaring gap for almost thirty years before the 2009 order required that the consent or otherwise of holders of forest rights under the FRA be recorded. Unfortunately, notwithstanding the judgement in the *Orissa mining* case, this order has been observed only in its breach.[72] Certifications that the FRA process is complete have been issued by Collectors without Community Forest Rights having been recognized or communities even being informed of these rights in the FRA, and where consent has been obtained, it is often found to be fraudulent.

h) **Compensation for diversion**: The idea of compensatory afforestation was a legislative innovation. But its implementation left a lot to be desired. The afforestation did not often take place in practice; it involved only monoculture plantations; it happens on village commons already under use without consulting the users; and the charging of NPV over and above the cost of compensatory afforestation is flawed for multiple reasons: the compensatory forest will over time surely produce some of the lost benefits, the NPV amount charged has a weak empirical and conceptual foundation (involving double counting and miscounting), and the NPV amount is not shared with the actual stakeholders who lose the forest benefits,[73] as the Supreme Court rejected the recommendations of its own Committee.[74]

i) **Federalism**: The IFA, a colonial creation, was no doubt a central act, but it coexisted with several state acts and regulations that were somewhat adapted to the local context.[75] Post-Independence, one would have expected much more regional specificity since forest was a state subject under the Constitution. But this did not transpire in practice—state acts are largely copies of the IFA and, in fact, they wiped out nuances already accepted by colonial-period regional laws. The creation of the IFS was another step towards indirect central control, but the shifting of forests to the Concurrent List of the Constitution in 1976 and the passing of

[72] Meenal Tatpati, The Scheduled Tribes and Other Traditional Forest Dwellers (Recognition of Forest Rights) Act, 2006 (FRA) and Diversion of Forests Under Forest Conservation Act 1980 (FCA): Briefing note examining on-ground realities in the implementation of the FRA in areas facing forest diversion (Kalpavriksh 2017).

[73] Kohli and others (n 43) 39.

[74] Kanchan Chopra, Gopal K Kadekodi, and VB Eswaran, Report of the Expert Committee on Net Present Value (2006).

[75] See Shrinidhi and Lélé (n 17).

the FCA in 1980 are sharper markers of increased central control. Central control may be justified on the grounds that forests provide certain benefits (biodiversity, hydrological regulation, and carbon sequestration) that accrue to stakeholders beyond state boundaries. Similarly, nudging by the central government also led to the launch of the attempt at participatory forestry (JFM), and the FRA is a central legislation that champions the rights of the local population on the ground of redressing historical injustice. So, the issue is not whether the central government should have a say in the forest sector, as much as whether state governments have developed (and the central government has fostered) independent capacities and regionally appropriate legal frameworks, whether central funds have given them the leeway to do so, and whether central scrutiny has been substantive or just bureaucratic in nature—whether in diversion proposals or for Working Plans. The answers here seem to be in the negative.

j) **Role of the Supreme Court**: Forests are an emotive issue that immediately triggers considerations of (the expanded interpretation of) Article 21 of the Constitution (right to life as the right to a clean environment) and provides a justification for intervention by an activist judiciary. The Court has played an important role in clarifying the scope of the FCA and, more generally, in drawing attention to the important issue of forest conservation that tends to get short shrift in the political process in a rapidly developing country. However, the *Godavarman* case is a globally unique case of an open-ended and unending intervention by a court in the domain of both law-making and day-to-day governance under the cloak of a 'continuing writ of mandamus'.[76] The number of interlocutory applications filed is in the thousands and the orders are also in the hundreds. Instead of dealing with one-off questions of the scope/applicability of the FCA, the Court has engaged in all kinds of questions and matters that fall beyond not only its constitutional purview but also its physical ability to delve into and monitor in any realistic manner. The consequence has been several conceptually flawed decisions as much as the creation of a parallel structure of micromanagement that is (and always will be) poorly informed of ground realities (especially with continuously changing judges—inevitable in a 26-year-old case). Court-managed forest governance reflects instead the judiciary's simplistic notion of 'conservation' as 'non-use' or 'preservation', ignoring the socio-ecological reality of India's forests and the continued belief in state control, ignoring the colonial roots of this approach and its devastating impacts on the lives of forest-dwellers.

[76] Armin Rosencranz, Edward Boenig, and Brinda Dutta, 'The Godavarman Case: The Indian Supreme Court's Breach of Constitutional Boundaries in Managing India's Forests' (2007) 37 *ELR News and Analysis* 10032; Armin Rosencranz and Sharachchandra Lélé, 'Supreme Court and India's Forests' (2008) 43(5) *Economic and Political Weekly* 11.

Concluding Remarks: Navigating Colonial Legacies with Statist and Conservationist Blinkers

As mentioned, forest law is perhaps the oldest environmental law in India. But this history, instead of making it the most mature legal framework, makes it the most contentious one. This is because the 'Indian' Forest Act is not an act created for the welfare of Indian citizens but very much a colonial construct, formulated with the singular purpose of establishing state control over forest resources for colonial gains while limiting their use by the local population. The replacement of the colonial purpose with a 'national' purpose did not change the foundational concept of forests as state property, to be managed by a technocracy for some (largely self-defined) public purpose, nor did it change the technocracy's colonial mindset of viewing local communities as 'abusers', 'encroachers' or 'degraders' who 'burden' their property. Consequently, the forest sector has been a site of enormous conflict since the 1878 Act to date. The conflict is as much over 'what are forests for' as 'whose forest is it'. But the answers are not binaries: to cast 'state' and 'community' in stark opposition to the second question is as simplistic as to cast 'local benefits' and 'global benefits' being mutually exclusive or 'forest' and 'non-forest' being neatly separable. Forests are complex socio-ecological entities that potentially provide multiple benefits at multiple scales but also impose costs (such as crop damage or human deaths due to wildlife or habitat for pathogens) and opportunity costs (land that could be used for other purposes). They are 'common-pool resources' but also provide positive environmental externalities. This creates a genuine tension between a purely 'communitarian' perspective and a broader 'environmental one',[77] where the positive externalities have become as important, especially in the context of a sharp decline in forest cover over the past 150 years.

Unfortunately, the 'broader' interest in India's forests has always come at the expense of local interests and the rights of forest-dwellers. The colonial interest was in products and revenues, though also sometimes cloaked in 'environmental concern' about the harm that deforestation causes.[78] After independence, when the Chipko movement was demanding rights to derive forest-based livelihoods, its message was misinterpreted

[77] Sharachchandra Lélé, 'Beyond State-Community Polarisations and Bogus "Joint"ness: Crafting Institutional Solutions for Resource Management' in Max Spoor (ed), *Globalisation, Poverty and Conflict: A Critical 'Development' Reader* (Kluwer Academic Publishers 2004) 283.

[78] Vasant K Saberwal, 'Science and the Dessicationist Discourse of the 20th Century' (1998) 4 *Environment and History* 309.

as being simply driven by a broad ecological concern.[79] This coincided with a rising modern urban conservationist discourse that simplifies forests to 'green cover', 'pristine ecosystems' or 'wildlife habitat' that provide benefits 'at a distance' and that must be saved at any cost for a (homogeneous) 'national public good'. This discourse rendered invisible the 250 million forest-dependent people in the country or the historical injustices they have faced and provided continued support for the idea of professionally managed state forestry, except with a modified objective of conservation or environmental balance. The IFA remained intact with the addition of the FCA. But the FCA itself became a forest diversion act, setting up hoops to jump and compensatory solutions rather than engaging with substantive issues and local stakeholders, allowing logging to continue as long as it was apparently 'scientific', denying diversion for agriculturalists while permitting it for mining and dams in the 'public interest'. This discourse informs the Supreme Court's judgements as well.

Thus, a re-establishment of community tenure has to be the foundation or the starting point of forest governance reform in India. These community-level institutions will have to meet norms of participatory democracy and embrace multi-objective forestry and multiple sources of knowledge. But community tenure alone cannot be the end-point: some form of multi-level governance is essential, given the legitimate broader environmental stakes. If, however, this governance is not to become the same old state control in a new garb, its structure would have to be radically democratic, with a separation of roles and powers—both vertical and horizontal—coupled with downward accountability. The upper levels will have to play different roles—protection support, technical support, financial support and regulation—but combining these roles into the same old forest bureaucracy or ministerial functioning would be a recipe for failure. The FRA—as the next chapter will show—does not provide answers to the question of how the upper levels are to be structured, but the question emerges—as did the conclusion that local rights-holders must have a say in forest diversion—as a logical corollary to the FRA's attempt to set the foundation right. Answering these questions wisely to produce a broad-based, environmentally sound, socially just, and democratic structure is the challenge before the next generation of forest lawmakers in India.[80]

Suggestions for Further Reading

Ritwick Dutta and Bhupender Yadav, *Supreme Court on Forest Conservation* (Universal Law Publishing 2005).

Ramachandra Guha and others, *Deeper Roots of Historical Injustice: Trends and Challenges in the Forests of India* (Rights and Resources Initiative 2012).

[79] Emma Mawdsley, 'After Chipko: From Environment to Region in Uttaranchal' (1998) 25(4) *The Journal of Peasant Studies* 36.

[80] Sharachchandra Lele, 'Forest Governance: From Co-option and Conflict to Multilayered Governance?' (2017) 52(25) *Economic and Political Weekly* 55.

Kanchi Kohli and others, *Pocketful of Forests: Legal Debates on Valuating and Compensating Forest Loss in India* (Kalpavriksh and WWF-India 2011).

Sharachchandra Lélé and Ajit Menon (eds), *Democratizing Forest Governance in India* (OUP 2014).

Chhatrapati Singh, *Common Property and Common Poverty: India's Forests, Forest Dwellers, and the Law* (OUP 1986).

CHAPTER 25

FOREST RIGHTS AND THE FOREST RIGHTS ACT

SHOMONA KHANNA

Abstract

The enactment of the Scheduled Tribes and Other Traditional Forest Dwellers (Recognition of Forest Rights) Act, 2006 (the FRA) advances international best practice in forest conservation, recognising that indigenous and local forest dwelling communities play a vital role in forest ecosystems, and their active involvement in forest governance is integral to climate change mitigation. It recognises the land rights of indigenous peoples and other local communities who depend on forest resources for their livelihoods and food security. The FRA necessarily sets about re-calibrating the forest law architecture and forest bureaucracy. While the FRA has been in force for more than sixteen years, it continues to be a site of fierce contestation. This chapter analyses these contestations from a legal perspective.

Introduction

International best practice has long recognized that indigenous and local forest-dwelling communities play a vital role in the conservation of forest ecosystems, and their active involvement in forest governance is integral to climate change mitigation. The February 2022 report of the Intergovernmental Panel on Climate Change (IPCC) estimates that Indigenous Peoples and local communities manage at least 17 per cent of total carbon stored in forests across sixty-four assessed countries.[1] The report is

[1] Intergovernmental Panel on Climate Change, 2022: Impacts, Adaptation and Vulnerability. Working Group II Contribution to the IPCC Sixth Assessment Report (2022) <https://www.ipcc.ch/report/

categorical that successful forest adaptation involves recognition of land rights and cooperation with Indigenous Peoples and other local communities who depend on forest resources for their livelihoods and food security. It also recognizes that restoring land access and rights via the transfer of formal land titles to indigenous and local communities improves biodiversity conservation and carbon sequestration.

Legislative advances in the direction of recognizing the rights of Indigenous Peoples and other local communities were made in India over a decade and a half ago. On 31 December 2007, a brief single-sentence notification appeared in the official Gazette of India, stating that on this date, the provisions of the Scheduled Tribes and Other Traditional Forest Dwellers (Recognition of Forest Rights) Act, 2006 shall come into force. Commonly known as the Forest Rights Act or simply the FRA, this legislation sent shockwaves through the existing forest law architecture and forest bureaucracy, and yet it was the culmination of a decades-long journey fraught with struggle. The FRA seeks to displace more than a century of received wisdom, where a centralized forest bureaucracy exerting authority over forests and wildlife conservation was considered the only bulwark against environmental degradation. A necessary corollary of this approach was the forcible exclusion of *Adivasis* and forest-dwelling communities from landscapes which needed 'protection', at complete odds with modern-day requirements of climate change mitigation.

It also marked the beginning of a different kind of struggle, a struggle to keep alive the aspirations the FRA represents. While the FRA has been in force in India for more than sixteen years, it continues to be a site of fierce contestation. At first glance, this may appear to be a simple confrontation between the forest bureaucracy on the one hand and the *Adivasi* and forest-rights movement on the other. However, there are deeper layers to the way in which the law has advanced, defying reductive categorization.

We begin this chapter by examining the core components of this law, its substantive components, and also the procedural mechanisms it endorses and creates. We also explore the interconnections between the FRA and other forest legislations, such as the Forest Conservation Act, 1980 (FCA), and how this dynamic has impacted the existing legal regime relating to forest governance. And finally, we explore how there has been sustained and persistent resistance, primarily from within the entrenched forest bureaucracy, to the FRA and everything it stands for.

25.1 Core Components of the Forest Rights Act

In many ways, the FRA is unique in that it combines substantive articulation of the law relating to forest rights while also providing the mechanisms through which such rights are to be recognized and advanced. It explicates the governance rights of *Adivasis* and

sixth-assessment-report-working-group-ii/>.

forest-dwelling communities to manage and preserve their traditional forests and the biodiversity therein and provides the architecture through which such governance is fructified. However, before we delve into these intricacies, we glance at the genesis of the law and the socio-economic-political realities from which it has emerged.

25.1.1 Forest Rights Act: The Back-Story

There is no dearth of writing on the colonial roots of the forest-law architecture and forest bureaucracy in India and on how the British government bent the forests to the needs of its industrial machine.[2] The forest laws put in place in the mid-nineteenth century by the colonial government, culminating in the Indian Forest Act, 1927, included mechanisms for 'settlement of rights' through a time-bound procedure before a forest bureaucrat. These mechanisms, however, were a complete failure, with vast swathes of forests taken over by the government by simply 'extinguishing' the pre-existing rights of *Adivasi* and forest-dwelling communities in these lands.[3]

Instead of addressing these failures, the newly Independent Indian state continued to reinforce the colonial forest law regime and buttress the authority of the forest bureaucracy through fresh legislation at both the central and state levels. The fortress conservation approach adopted under the Wildlife (Protection) Act, 1972 (WLPA), severely stunted the wildlife and environmental conservation movement in India for decades. Enacted a century after the first national park was notified over indigenous lands in Yellowstone, USA, this law provided a template that is utterly at odds with the realities in the Indian subcontinent. Not only did the law fail to acknowledge centuries of knowledge and experience of conservation within India's rich and diverse *Adivasi* populations, it also placed inordinate power in the hands of the forest bureaucracy to drive out local communities while policing their access to 'protected areas'.[4] Indeed, the heavy-handed use of the criminal law provisions of this law, while making a limited dent on the burgeoning trade in animal organs and artefacts, created an unhealthy animosity between those who sought to 'conserve' wildlife, and the indigenous populations who paid the price for such conservation. It certainly has not helped that such initiatives often displayed double standards when it came to providing access to luxury tourism and large capital.[5] Despite the antagonistic legal architecture and in the eye-teeth of

[2] Ramachandra Guha, *The Unquiet Woods: Ecological Change and Peasant Resistance in the Himalaya* (Orient BlackSwan 2013).

[3] Madhu Sarin, 'Undoing Historical Injustice: Reclaiming Citizenship Rights and Democratic Forest Governance through the Forest Rights Act' in Sharachchandra Lélé and Ajit Menon (eds), *Democratizing Forest Governance in India* (OUP 2014) 103.

[4] Shomona Khanna and others, *Criminalisation of Adivasis and the Indian Legal System* (Indigenous Peoples Rights International 2022).

[5] Shomona Khanna, 'Exclude and Protect: A Report on the WWF Case on Wildlife Conservation in the Supreme Court of India' (SRUTI 2008).

opposition from the forest bureaucracy, community-led forest governance and conservation efforts continued to proliferate in different parts of the country.[6]

The extent of oppression against *Adivasis* and forest dwellers was documented by the Commissioner for Scheduled Castes and Scheduled Tribes, Dr BD Sharma, in his seminal report to Parliament in 1989.[7] Although the Union executive made some efforts at course correction, these were marked by inertia and ennui.

The centralizing tendencies of the forest law regime only deepened in the early 1990s with the liberalization of the Indian economy, when commercial extractive industry began to make rapid inroads into forest areas. *Adivasi* communities who sought to protect their traditional homelands found themselves pitted against the combined strength of the legal regime, large capital, and hostile state machinery. While judicial remedies were available, access to the justice system was limited to communities which were well-resourced and resilient enough to absorb the crippling delays inherent to the legal process in India.

Things came to a head in 2001 when a routine order passed by the Supreme Court in *TN Godavarman Thirumulpad v Union of India* (*Godavarman* case),[8] relating to 'encroachments' in forests, was mischievously projected as an *en masse* order of eviction by the central Ministry of Environment and Forest (MoEF) (now renamed as the Ministry of Environment, Forest and Climate Change).[9] It is estimated that more than 300,000 *Adivasis* and forest dwellers were brutally evicted from their homes and lands inside the forests, purportedly in compliance with the court's order.[10]

Although the MoEF quickly remedied its 'error', this turn of events galvanized the many disconnected *Adivasi* communities and forest-rights organizations to come together under the umbrella of the Campaign for Survival and Dignity and demand structural changes in the legal regime.[11] Several years of political mobilisation, advocacy, and public pressure culminated in the enactment of the Forest Rights Act in 2006, under the charge of a separate central Ministry of Tribal Affairs.[12]

This fraught history finds resonance in the detailed Preamble to the FRA, which acknowledges that forest dwellers 'are integral to the very survival and sustainability of the forest ecosystem', and yet their 'forest rights on ancestral lands and their habitat were not adequately recognised in the consolidation of State forests during the colonial

[6] E.g., the Van Panchayat Rules, 1931, were applied in the hill areas of Uttar Pradesh (now Uttarakhand).

[7] Ministry of Labour and Welfare, Report of the Commissioner for Scheduled Castes and Scheduled Tribes, Twenty-ninth Report (1987–89).

[8] IA No 703 in WP (C) No 202 of 1995 (Order of 23 November 2001, Supreme Court of India, unreported).

[9] Ministry of Environment and Forests, Circular of 3 May 2002 to all state governments and Union territories.

[10] Campaign for Survival and Dignity, Endangered Symbiosis: Evictions and India's Forest Communities (Report of the Jan Sunwai, 19–20 July 2003).

[11] For a detailed description of the forest rights movement in India, see <www.forestrightsact.com>.

[12] Government of India (Allocation of Business) Rules, 1961 s 3(1) read with Second Schedule.

period as well as in independent India resulting in historical injustice'. The Preamble also asserts that the rights of forest dwellers 'include the responsibilities and authority for sustainable use, conservation of biodiversity, and maintenance of ecological balance and thereby strengthening the conservation regime of the forests while ensuring livelihood and food security'. It acknowledges that 'it has become necessary to address the long-standing insecurity of tenurial and access rights' of forest dwellers, which is what the statute now sets out to do.[13]

25.1.2 Substantive Shift in the Law

Prior to 2006, the access of forest-dwelling communities to forests and forest resources was, at best, at the peripheries of the mainframe forest laws which forbade such access and criminalized it.[14] While the overarching approach of the law was to treat forest dwellers as 'encroachers', scattered through the legal landscape were fragmentary access[15] and usufruct[16] privileges, and in a few rare cases, limited statutory rights.[17] Some communities were even allowed to 'participate' in forest management, most often subordinated to and at the pleasure of the forest bureaucracy.[18] These arrangements were made through a kaleidoscope of delegated legislations, executive instructions, and circulars, and sometimes simply through arrangements to look the other way. In the rare cases where the rights to cultivate land were recognized at all, these were under government initiatives to 'regularise encroachments',[19] couched very openly in the language and accoutrements of state patronage. Across all such arrangements, the common denominator, to a greater or lesser degree, was the insecurity of tenure.

Core principles and definitions: the FRA makes a significant departure from existing forest law as well as from forest governance mechanisms, as we will discuss. Therefore, it was necessary to clearly delineate certain core principles and definitions so that the scheme of the statute could work. While it is not possible to examine all these principles in the present chapter, we do need to point to the more important underlying fundamentals.

[13] Scheduled Tribes and Other Traditional Forest Dwellers (Recognition of Forest Rights) Act, 2006 (FRA), Preamble, paras 1–4.

[14] Khanna and others (n 4).

[15] E.g., the Orissa Government Land Settlement Act, 1962 specifically provides for earmarking of 'gochar' or grazing lands.

[16] Forest-dwelling communities in Himachal Pradesh have a legally recognized right to timber for house construction.

[17] Madhya Pradesh Land Revenue Code, 1959 recognizes the usufructuary right of forest-dwelling populations to access minor forest produce, known as 'nistari rights'.

[18] The most significant social forestry project in India is undertaken under the Joint Forest Management Scheme.

[19] Ministry of Environment and Forests, Circular of 18 September 1990, bearing F. No 13-1/90/-FP (I).

Section 4(1) of the FRA makes the core substantive statement of law vesting forest rights in the eligible forest dweller, both tribal and non-tribal. It states that '[n]otwithstanding anything contained in any other law for the time being in force ... the Central Government hereby recognises and vests forest rights in:

(a) the forest dwelling Scheduled Tribes ...;
(b) the other traditional forest dwellers.'

The *non-obstante* clause at the beginning of this provision is significant for the reason that by recognizing forest dwellers as 'right-holders', the FRA upends the extant forest law at the time. This included not only mainframe forest laws such as the Indian Forest Act, 1927 and the WLPA but also a plethora of state legislations and rules, along with a body of jurisprudence established through court orders and judicial precedents. This unambiguous and emphatic statement from the legislature that the legal terrain has altered continues to be vitally important today.

Another innovation is the wide definition of the term 'forest land', in order to ensure that the protective cover of the law has the broadest outreach possible. In this, the law mirrors the definition laid down by the Supreme Court in the *Godavarman* case,[20] becoming the first central legislation to provide a definition of forest land and thus filling an important void in the law.[21] The terms 'forest dwelling Scheduled Tribes' and 'other traditional forest dwellers', the two categories eligible to claim forest rights under the law, are also carefully defined, taking care to balance the constitutional distinction between tribals and non-tribals while acknowledging that the notification of Scheduled Tribes under Article 342 of the Constitution of India continues to be a work in progress.[22]

The most important core principle, however, is the definition of 'village', and, coterminously, the definition of the '*Gram Sabha*' of the village. As we will see further in this chapter, the *Gram Sabha* plays a pivotal role in the process of determination of rights and making decision-making regarding the protection and use of forest resources. Therefore, the specific description of the *Gram Sabha* is vital to the success or failure of the enterprise. Here, the FRA draws upon the Panchayats (Extension to Scheduled Areas) Act, 1996 (PESA) for inspiration. PESA defines the *Gram Sabha* as the smallest possible unit of a community for the purposes of governance, as follows:

> a village shall ordinarily consist of a habitation or a group of habitations or a hamlet or a group of hamlets comprising a community and managing its affairs in accordance with traditions and customs.[23]

[20] *TN Godavarman Thirumulpad v Union of India* (1997) 2 SCC 267.

[21] Numerous definitions of 'forests' and 'forest land' are found in various state legislation and even in state amendments to the central Indian Forest Act, 1927. There is limited coherence in these definitions.

[22] Even today, many petitions and applications remain pending before the Ministry of Tribal Affairs regarding the inclusion of some of the most marginalized tribes and communities in the Presidential Order, which lists Scheduled Tribes.

[23] Panchayats (Extension to Scheduled Areas) Act, 1996 s 4(b).

This is an important departure from most state-level *Panchayati Raj* legislations which define the limits of a *Gram Sabha* (and the co-terminus *Panchayat* jurisdiction) based on population numbers. As a result, a *Gram Sabha* under *Panchayati Raj* laws often comprises four or five, sometimes even more, villages which include different communities. It is impossible for such a body to perform any but the simplest decision-making functions. PESA, on the other hand, acknowledges that if the *Gram Sabha* is to be vested with decision-making authority and governance functions, it must be a smaller unit at the habitation or hamlet level to be a viable community. The FRA has adopted this definition of the village and the *Gram Sabha* from PESA.[24]

Definition of forest rights: an important advancement in the FRA is the consolidation of all the fragments of forest rights and usufructs and enumerating them under one statutory definition of 'forest rights'. Thus, while the statute does not create any new rights, it brings forest rights to aggregation at centre stage, when thus far, these had been at the peripheries of law as exemptions, exceptions, provisos, and privileges. At the same time, none of the forest rights listed under section 3 of the FRA (other than the right to minor forest produce or MFP) transition from usufructuary rights into the domain of private property rights. The statute also brings the concept of community property to centre stage in stating that all forest rights are 'individual or community tenure or both'. Some of the key forest rights enumerated are:

(i) *Forest right to land being occupied or cultivated*—the forest right to land under occupation for self-cultivation or residence,[25] also referred to as 'individual forest right', is one of the highlights of the law.[26] Separate forest rights relate to conversion of titles/leases/grants which had been given to forest dwellers under various state laws on a temporary lease, but were not renewed.[27]

(ii) *Forest right to MFP*—the FRA vests a specific forest right to ownership, access to collect, use and dispose of MFP traditionally collected within and outside village boundaries.[28] Also included are traditional *nistari* rights,[29] and 'other community rights of uses or entitlements such as fish and other produce of water bodies'.[30] The law acknowledges that access to MFP and other forest produce is not limited to personal subsistence use, but encompasses individual or collective

[24] FRA s 2(p) defines 'village' and FRA s 2(g) defines '*Gram Sabha*'.

[25] ibid s 3(1)(a).

[26] This forest right is restricted to land under occupation on the cut-off date (fixed as 13 December 2005) up to a maximum of four hectares.

[27] Here, the upper limit of four hectares is not applicable, although the right remains heritable but inalienable.

[28] FRA s 3(1)(c). FRA s 2(i) defines MFP as 'all non-timber forest produce of plant origin, including bamboo, brushwood, stumps, cane, tussar, cocoons, honey, wax, lac, tendu or kendu leaves, medicinal plants and herbs, roots, tubers, and the like'.

[29] ibid s 3(1)(b).

[30] ibid s 3(1)(d).

processing, storage, value addition, transportation, and sale of such produce for livelihood purposes.[31]

(iii) *Grazing*—the FRA mentions the nomadic and pastoralist communities several times, leaving no doubt that the rights of these forest-dwelling communities are an important part of the law. Therefore, there is a specific inclusion of the forest right to 'grazing (both settled or transhumant) and traditional seasonal resource access of nomadic or pastoralist communities'.[32]

(iv) *Forest villages*—perhaps the most marginalized forest dwellers are those who live in forest villages and other unsurveyed villages and hamlets inside forests. These villages usually comprise *Adivasi* forest dwellers who were taken into the forests as manual labour during the colonial period. Over the years, these communities formed into forest villages which remained unlisted in government records and severed from the mainstream. The FRA includes a specific forest right to conversion of old, unrecorded, unsurveyed, and other such forest villages into revenue villages.[33]

(v) *Customary habitat of particularly vulnerable tribal groups*—specific mention is made of the forest right to 'community tenures of habitat and habitation for (particularly vulnerable) tribal groups and pre-agricultural communities'.[34] The institutions responsible for rights recognition are under a duty to take proactive steps to ensure that the habitat and other forest rights of particularly vulnerable tribal groups are claimed and processed.[35]

(vi) *Community forest resource (CFR) rights*—in recognition of the well-established tradition of community conservation of forests in India, the CFR right is vested in the community of forest dwellers to 'protect, regenerate, conserve and manage' their traditional forests and forest resources.[36] We will be examining this forest right in some detail further below.

(vii) *Developmental rights*—the FRA also anticipates the provision of certain basic infrastructural facilities by the government, such as schools, dispensaries, *anganwadis*, and so on, which are exempt from the dreaded forest clearance under section 2 of the FCA. To qualify for this special dispensation, the proposed facility must obtain the recommendation of the *Gram Sabha*.[37]

[31] Scheduled Tribes and Other Traditional Forest Dwellers (Recognition of Forest Rights) Rules, 2008 (Forest Rights Rules) r 2(1)(d).

[32] FRA s 3(1)(d) read with s 2(a).

[33] ibid s 3(1)(h) read with Forest Rights Rules r 2A. See also Ministry of Tribal Affairs, Circular of 8 November 2013 bearing F. No 23011/33/2010-FRA.

[34] FRA s 3(1)(e) read with s 2(h). See also Ministry of Tribal Affairs, Circular of 23 April 2015, F. No 23011/16/2015-FRA.

[35] Forest Rights Rules rr 12(1)(d) and 12B(1).

[36] FRA ss 3(1)(i), 2(a), and 5.

[37] Each such initiative must be limited to one hectare of land and not require the felling of more than seventy-five trees. See FRA s 3(2).

(viii) *Other forest rights* include the forest right to *in-situ* rehabilitation in case of illegal eviction or forced displacement resulting from government development projects, community right of access to biodiversity and intellectual property in traditional knowledge, rights recognized under state or Autonomous District Council laws, and tribal rights accepted as traditional or customary law to the tribe in a particular state.

It is important to emphasize that while recognizing these forest rights, the nature of the land continues to remain 'forest land', and ownership continues to vest in the state.[38] This approach is in accord with the idea described in the Preamble of the FRA that 'ensuring livelihood and food security' for forest dwellers, who are part of the forest ecosystem, is not antagonistic to the long-term health of the forest itself.

Core commitment to conservation: the FRA marks an important and timely departure from the fortress conservation approach of wildlife conservation law in India. As seen in the previous section, the Preamble itself recognizes that vesting communities of forest dwellers with the responsibility and authority for sustainable use of forest resources actually 'strengthen(s) the conservation regime of the forests'.[39] Towards this end, the FRA includes the forest right to 'protect, regenerate or conserve or manage any community forest resource which they have been traditionally protecting and conserving for sustainable use'.[40] To remove all doubt regarding the nature and extent of this right, the statute also vests the *Gram Sabha* of forest dwellers with the power to 'protect the wildlife, forest and biodiversity (and) ensure that adjoining catchments area, water sources and other ecological sensitive areas are adequately protected' in section 5. Making a further departure from the pre-existing forest law regime, which had fragmented forests and forest produce into different components based upon their value to the state, these provisions recognize the interconnectedness of all the different parts of an ecosystem and a forest landscape and the need to address their conservation and management in a holistic manner.

Unlike numerous other beneficial legislations where noble statements of intent remain amorphous, the FRA provides a robust mechanism through which such rights are fructified. These CFR rights are, therefore, claimed and vested as community property in the *Gram Sabha* or the community as a whole. It is further provided that the *Gram Sabha* will appoint a CFR Management Committee and develop a CFR Management and Conservation Plan[41] for the proper execution of its responsibilities. Towards this end, the forest bureaucracy must provide the necessary assistance, including making necessary adjustments to its own management plan[42] for the forest. Further, we examine how these provisions have been harmonized with other forest 'conservation' laws.

[38] ibid s 4(4). Forest right conferred under s 3(1) 'shall be heritable but not alienable or transferable ... and in the absence of a direct heir, the heritable right shall pass on to the next-of-kin'.

[39] ibid, Preamble, para 2.

[40] ibid s 3(1)(i) read with s 2(a).

[41] Forest Rights Rules r 4(1)(e).

[42] The management plan of the forest department is known as the 'Working Plan'.

The FRA also makes provision for the creation of critical wildlife habitats, where forest rights are either 'modified or resettled' in the interest of protecting a particular species of flora or fauna. However, the creation of such critical wildlife habitat areas is markedly different from the protected areas under the WLPA. Here, it is necessary to first complete the forest rights recognition process in its entirety and then embark upon a rigorous consultative process involving the local communities, scientific experts, and state functionaries on a case-by-case basis. Through this process emerges an understanding of the contours of the conservation challenge at hand, including an exploration of whether co-existence is a viable option, and the extent to which forest rights need to be modified, curtailed, limited or stopped entirely. [43] This approach is prescient of the recommendations of the IPCC as recently as February 2022 regarding the need to collaborate with indigenous communities in advancing climate change mitigation and conservation, especially in forests.[44]

25.1.3 Procedural Innovation: Mechanism for Recognition of Forest Rights

The failure of the rights settlement mechanism under the colonial forest law regime and the post-colonial legislation which followed in their footsteps has been an important contributor to the 'historical injustice' perpetrated on forest dwellers since the mid-eighteenth century.[45] Efforts by some of the state governments, and even by the central government, to remedy the situation have been confounded by multiple hurdles.[46] Persistent and concerted efforts by the judiciary have also yielded limited results, as evidenced by the continuing mandamus in *Banwasi Sewa Ashram v Union of India*,[47] which has been pending for four decades.[48]

It is precisely this historical injustice the FRA sets out to address, described in its Preamble, by providing 'a framework for recording the forest rights so vested and the nature of evidence required for such recognition and vesting in respect of forest land'.[49]

[43] FRA s 4(2).

[44] IPCC (n 1).

[45] Khanna and others (n 4) ch 4.

[46] For instance, on 18 September 1990, the Ministry of Environment and Forests, government of India, issued a set of six Circulars (bearing Nos 13-1 to 6/90-FP) aimed at 'regularisation of encroachments' in forest areas in an attempt to correct the historical exclusion of forest-dwelling communities from the rights settlement process under colonial forest legislations such as the Indian Forest Act, 1927.

[47] AIR 1987 SC 374.

[48] The Supreme Court had established an alternative rights settlement mechanism manned by judicial officers for 433 project-affected villages in Uttar Pradesh. The matter remains unresolved to date. For a detailed account, see Shomona Khanna, 'Historical Wrongs and Forest Rights: Nascent Jurisprudence on FRA and Participatory Evidence Making' in Varsha Bhagat-Ganguly and Sujit Kumar (eds), *India's Scheduled Areas: Untangling Governance, Law and Politics* (Routledge 2020) 136.

[49] FRA, Preamble, para 1.

Drawing upon PESA, the FRA creates a three-tier rights recognition mechanism in which the *Gram Sabha* plays a pivotal role, and no single stakeholder dominates the decision-making process.

The *Gram Sabha* constitutes from among its members a Forest Rights Committee (FRC), which is tasked with receiving claims for forest rights and verifying them. The verification process includes, among other things, an on-site verification in the presence of the concerned officials from the forest and revenue departments. The recommendations of the FRC are scrutinized in a meeting of the *Gram Sabha*, which may approve or disapprove the claims through a resolution.

The claims are then forwarded to the Sub-Divisional Level Committee (SDLC), which comprises representatives of the revenue, forest, and tribal welfare departments and three representatives of the concerned *Panchayati Raj* institution. The SDLC prepares a draft proposed record of rights.

This draft is then forwarded to the District Level Committee (DLC)[50] with an analogous composition to 'consider and finally approve' the records of rights prepared by the SDLC. The decision of the DLC in this regard 'shall be final and binding'.

This three-tier mechanism is complementary rather than hierarchical so that each body performs a vital function, and yet its task is inchoate without the others. Neither is the verification of claims carried out by the *Gram Sabha* complete without the SDLC and the DLC performing their specific roles nor is the decision of the DLC complete without the *Gram Sabhas* having completed their statutory tasks.

Evidence: previous efforts by the state to 'regularise encroachments' by forest dwellers and *Adivasis* in forest lands relied heavily upon the rigid laws of evidence that govern the mainstream legal system. This is one of the key reasons these initiatives came up short, apart from their half-hearted implementation. Based upon this experience, the FRA provides a completely different template for evidence in support of forest rights claims. To begin with, the Scheduled Tribes and Other Traditional Forest Dwellers (Recognition of Forest Rights) Rules, 2008 provide a detailed list of the types of evidence an individual or a community can provide in support of a forest-rights claim.[51] This includes a wide variety of *documentary* evidence which would ordinarily not pass muster in a court of law, such as gazette reports, electoral lists, old records, and so on. Provision is also made for *oral* evidence of village elders and *physical* evidence such as old constructions, trees, and so on. Any two pieces of evidence from this list can be submitted in support of a claim.

In addition, every claim is subjected to two further layers of scrutiny, which also add to the evidence in its support. After receiving the claim, the FRC conducts an on-site physical verification of the claim jointly with officers of the state Revenue Department and the Forest Department. This is recorded in its recommendations on whether the claim should be approved or not. Thereafter, in a meeting of the village general body, or

[50] ibid s 6(5).

[51] Forest Rights Rules r 13.

Gram Sabha, the recommendation is scrutinized again, and a resolution passed either accepting or refusing the claim. The process is completely open and transparent, with little room for manipulation or falsification of records, while also being wholly accessible and comprehensible to the forest-dwelling claimant.

Despite its transformative potential, the actual implementation of the FRA has been sluggish and uneven. As of 31 December 2023, approximately 4.87 million claims for individual forest rights had been filed across India, of which a little over 2.5million titles extending over 18 million acres of forest land had been recognized and vested under these provisions of the FRA.[52] Where community rights are concerned, of a total of 189,553 claims filed, 114049 claims extending over 13.3 million acres of land had been recognized. While this may seem like a lot at first glance, according to reliable estimates, it barely scratches the surface of the FRA's true potential. A 2016 civil society report estimated that the extent of forest land where forest rights potentially ought to be recognized is forty million hectares, benefitting 150 million people, and this too is a conservative estimate.[53] Later in this chapter, we explore some of the structural barriers to the implementation of the FRA.

25.2 Operationalizing the Connection Between the Forest Rights Act and Other Laws

The last fifteen years have seen the FRA capture the imagination of *Adivasi* and forest-dwelling communities across India like no other legal venture. Thus, even though the number of claims filed, approved, and granted remains low, a wealth of ideation and conversation around the FRA has emerged over the years. These ideas and concepts have rapidly found their way into other laws, which either constitute the forest law architecture or are adjacent to it. While it is impossible to do justice in this brief chapter to the universe of laws impacted by the FRA, we briefly examine some of the more important developments.

[52] Ministry of Tribal Affairs, Monthly Update on the status of implementation of the Scheduled Tribes and Other Traditional Forest Dwellers (Recognition of Forest Rights) Act, 2006 (2023) <https://tribal.nic.in/downloads/FRA/MPR/2023/(A)%20MPR%20Dec%202023.pdf>.

[53] Rights and Resources Initiative, Vasundhara and Natural Resources Management Consultants, Potential for Recognition of Community Forest Resource Rights Under India's Forest Rights Act: A Preliminary Assessment (2015) 5–6.

25.2.1 The Forest Rights Act and the Forest Conservation Act

The FCA describes itself as '(a)n Act to provide for the conservation of forests', which it aims to do by restricting the de-reservation of forests or use of forest land for non-forest purposes without the express approval of the central government.[54] The objective of the statute was to decelerate the rate at which forests were being diverted for commercial purposes by state governments, and the resultant decline in forest cover. When the statute by itself did not have the desired results, the Supreme Court stepped into the breach in the *Godavarman* case, one of the longest-running, continuing mandamus public interest litigations in India. The Court brought in numerous innovations towards this end over the years, both in substantive law, such as an expansion of the definition of 'forest land',[55] as well as in the procedural domain, such as the establishment of the Central Empowered Committee.[56] The commercial diversion of forest lands, which are also *Adivasi* homelands, has nevertheless continued apace.[57]

With the FRA coming into force in 2008, it became quickly apparent that diversion of forest lands, despite all the procedural checks and balances in existence, can no longer take place without the active participation and consent of the forest dwellers since it is their specific forest rights which will be displaced by such diversion. In 2009, executive instructions were issued by the MoEF (as it then was) for ensuring compliance with the FRA when diverting forest land for non-forest purposes under the FCA.[58] Accordingly, before a forest approval can be granted, the process of identification and recognition of forest rights in the area must be completed. It is also mandatory that the *Gram Sabhas* 'have given their consent to the proposed diversion and the compensatory and ameliorative measures if any, having understood the purposes and details of proposed diversion'.

As often happens with advances in the law which run counter to the status quo, this instruction was largely ignored by state governments, project proponents, and even by the central government itself. In 2013, however, a three-judge bench of the Supreme Court in *Orissa Mining Corpn Ltd v Ministry of Environment and Forests* (*Niyamgiri* case) gave this process its imprimatur, requiring that it is the decision of the *Gram Sabhas* of forest dwellers which must eventually be binding on the state regarding whether approval for forest diversion be granted or not.[59] The Court observed:

54 Forest Conservation Act, 1980 s 2. For a detailed discussion on the FCA, see ch 28 in the present volume.

55 *TN Godavarman Thirumulpad* (n 20).

56 The Supreme Court established the CEC. See *TN Godavarman Thirumulpad v Union of India* 2002 (5) SCALE 6.

57 According to the Government's e-GreenWatch portal (Integrated e-Governance Portal for Automation, Streamlining and Effective Management of Processes related to Plantation and Other Forestry Works), 355,013 hectares of forest land was diverted under the FCA up to 10 October 2022. See <https://egreenwatch.nic.in/>.

58 Ministry of Environment and Forest, Circular of 3 August 2009 bearing F. No. 01-9/1998-FC(pt).

59 *Orissa Mining Corpn Ltd v Ministry of Environment and Forests* (2013) 6 SCC 476.

> Of late, we have realised that forests have the best chance to survive if communities participate in their conservation and regeneration measures. The Legislature also has addressed the long standing and genuine felt need of granting a secure and inalienable right to those communities whose right to life depends on right to forests and thereby strengthening the entire conservation regime by giving a permanent stake to the STs dwelling in the forests for generations in symbiotic relationship with the entire ecosystem.[60]

As it turned out, every *Gram Sabha* of the *Dongaria Kondh* tribe consulted with regard to this particular project unanimously expressed its disapproval, and eventually, the forest approval to the mining project was rejected and the project was shelved. It was the first time in India that one of the most marginalized *Adivasi* groups in the country had succeeded in a legal battle against the combined strength of a large multinational corporation and the state by asserting statutory rights vested in them under the FRA. The judgment and its outcome have been a shot in the arm for *Adivasi* and forest dwellers' rights movements across the country. The legal principle of *Gram Sabha* consent prior to forest diversion has found its way into numerous rules,[61] circulars,[62] and executive instructions issued by governments and has been reiterated and affirmed in several subsequent judgments and orders from courts.[63]

25.2.2 The Forest Rights Act and the SC/ST Prevention of Atrocities Act

While the FRA recognized a displacement of the old order, where the law perceived forest dwellers as encroachers on their own lands, this change simply was not sinking into the collective consciousness of the bureaucracy. Old habits die hard. Clearly, something more was needed.

60 ibid para 42.

61 Forest Conservation Rules, 2017, r 6(3)(e). On 29 November 2023, the MoEF notified the Van (Sanrakshan Evam Samvardhan) Rules, 2023, replacing the earlier Rules entirely, including the provisions requiring prior informed consent of *Gram Sabhas* before forest diversion. The 2023 Rules, however, are under a cloud. They have been challenged in a spate of public interest petitions before the Supreme Court. The National Commission for Scheduled Tribes, a constitutional authority under Article 338-A of the Constitution, has also questioned their validity.

62 See, for instance, Ministry of Tribal Affairs, Circular of 7 March 2014 bearing F. No 23011/02/2014-FRA.

63 For example, in *Chewang Pintso Bhutia v State of Sikkim* AIR 2014 (NOC) 596) 217, the Sikkim High Court passed a detailed judgment extending the principle laid down in the *Niyamgiri* case to environmental violations. Reiterating the articulation of Arts 25 and 26 (the fundamental right to freedom of religion and spiritual belief) of the Constitution in the *Niyamgiri* case, the court held that just because a site is not notified as sacred does not preclude its sacredness. There was a legal obligation upon the state to obtain the concurrence of the local population before diverting the site (in this case, a river) for a commercial purpose with significant environmental consequences.

This came with a 2016 amendment to the Scheduled Castes and Scheduled Tribes (Prevention of Atrocities) Act, 1989, which incorporated a new offence in the definition of 'atrocity'. The dispossession of a Scheduled Caste or Scheduled Tribe from their forest right, or prevention of their enjoyment of such forest right, is now a criminal offence inviting a minimum punishment of six months' imprisonment.[64]

Prior to this amendment, forest dwellers and *Adivasis* had rarely turned to this Act, and certainly not to protect their resource rights. In recent years, this seemingly innocuous provision has come as a categorical message from the criminal law regime that the balance of power between forest dwellers and the forest bureaucracy has shifted.[65] Its significance cannot be underestimated in the face of egregious and persistent violations of the FRA by government officials and private corporations. References to this legal provision and the shift it symbolizes have found their way into representations to district administrators and state governors, into complaints to the local police and petitions to constitutional courts, as also in statements to the media and *Gram Sabha* resolutions. It has entered the lyrics of traditional songs sung in remote villages and social media handles of young *Adivasi* influencers.

25.2.3 Forest Rights Act and Land Acquisition

The failure to recognize the pre-existing rights of forest dwellers while declaring forests not only created great uncertainty of tenure but also meant that when the state seconded any land or resources for commercial purposes, such as mining or industrial development, the forest dwellers received no compensation. According to one estimate, between 1950 and 1991, at least 2.6 million people were displaced by mining projects alone, of whom an incredible 52 per cent were tribals. Only 25 per cent received some sort of resettlement.[66]

The Right to Fair Compensation and Transparency in Land Acquisition, Rehabilitation and Resettlement Act, 2013 (LARR) promised a change to this situation. The LARR includes forest rights holders within the definition of 'affected persons' in acquisition proceedings and specifically mandates full and proper compensation for acquisition of forest rights. It also mandates consent of the *Gram Sabha* as a pre-condition for any land acquisition in Scheduled Areas. Unfortunately, the LARR undermines its own transformative potential by exempting numerous categories of land acquisition from its operation, such as acquisition in coal-bearing areas.

[64] Scheduled Castes and Scheduled Tribes (Prevention of Atrocities) Act, 1989 s 3(1). Where the offender is a government servant, the minimum imprisonment is one year.

[65] Gayatri Raghunandan, *Use of the Prevention of Atrocities Act to Advance Forest Rights: A Handbook* (Vasundhara, Odisha 2019).

[66] Centre for Science and Environment, 'Rich Lands, Poor People: Is "Sustainable" Mining Possible? State of the Environment Report' (Centre for Science and Environment 2008) 6.

Be that as it may, it is heartening that a land acquisition legislation articulates that the forest rights of *Adivasis* and forest dwellers must be duly accounted for and rehabilitation and compensation packages provided to them. This articulation has been important to communities who have earlier faced forcible displacement and erasure, sometimes multiple times, with all the attendant trauma and fragmentation of community.

25.3 Structural Resistance to the Forest Rights Act and its Implementation

Even before the Scheduled Tribes (Recognition of Forest Rights) Bill, 2005, an early version of the FRA, was placed before Parliament and from the robust and heated debates that were to follow, it was apparent that this law would be met with stiff resistance. Anticipating this, the Cabinet Secretariat of the government of India amended the rules governing the jurisdiction of the different ministries to bring '(a)ll matters including legislation relating to the rights of forest-dwelling Scheduled Tribes on forest lands' under the jurisdiction of the Ministry of Tribal Affairs and curtailing the jurisdiction of the MoEF (as it then was).[67]

Despite such clear reorientation of administrative authority, the forest bureaucracy has been loath to surrender power, whether to the forest-dwelling communities or to its own colleagues in the state tribal welfare departments. Intense resistance is also manifest from some in the Indian wildlife conservation movement, and challenges to the FRA have emerged in surprising avatars over the last fifteen years.

25.3.1 Legal Challenges

Shortly after the FRA came into force, a spate of quite similar writ petitions were filed in the Supreme Court and in several High Courts, challenging its constitutional validity on a variety of grounds, including the legislative competence of Parliament to enact such law.[68] They sought immediate injunction on the implementation of the FRA, and initially, some of the High Courts were swayed by the end-of-times scenario painted in these petitions. Rapid response from the government and forest rights organizations

[67] Government of India (Allocation of Business) Rules (n 12).

[68] The Bombay Natural History Society (BNHS) and three other conservation organisations filed WP (Civil) No 50 of 2008 in the Supreme Court. Several years later, the BNHS filed a formal application to withdraw as a petitioner in the case, which goes by the title '*Wildlife Trust of India and Ors v Union of India and Ors*' since then.

ensured there was no court-ordered impediment to the implementation of the FRA.[69] There have also been sporadic challenges in various courts to specific aspects of the statute.

25.3.2 A Recalcitrant Executive

The forest bureaucracy, at the centre and in the states, has found numerous ways to obstruct the implementation of the FRA. Two states in the North-East have refused to apply the FRA taking shelter under their special constitutional status.[70] Other states in the North-East, such as Meghalaya, have argued that the FRA does not apply to them because forests in their jurisdiction are overwhelmingly community owned. States with largely non-tribal forest-dwelling populations have either refused to implement the statute entirely or *en masse* rejected applications submitted by other traditional forest dwellers. Yet other states have failed to implement the FRA due to hyper-technical and often absurd objections raised by bureaucrats. The obstinate resistance of the forest bureaucracy to get with the programme, so to speak, requires a detailed study of its own.

25.3.3 Weaponizing Technology Against the Forest Rights Act

As early as 2009, an avalanche of rejections in Gujarat[71] revealed that the state government had issued a series of circulars directing that all FRA claims must be supported by satellite imagery maps. It is self-evident that forest dwellers did not have access to such expensive digital technology. It was only after a civil society organization approached the Gujarat High Court in a public interest litigation that a scathing judgment was delivered directing the state government to re-open and reconsider all the rejected claims, this time without the requirement of satellite maps.[72]

Yet efforts to use satellite mapping as a method to divest forest dwellers of their forest rights under the FRA continue unabated.[73]For instance, the Forest Survey of

[69] Since these matters are *sub judice* at the time of writing, further comment on the legal issues arising is not possible.

[70] Constitution of India art 371-A (pertaining to Nagaland) and art 371-G (pertaining to Mizoram).

[71] In the first week of May 2009, at a meeting of the State Level Monitoring Committee, the state government also declared that at the most, only about 10 per cent of the claims filed by the claimants were genuine claims.

[72] *Action Research in Community Health and Development (ARCH) v State of Gujarat* (2013) SCC Online Guj 2583.

[73] Forest Rights Rules, r 12A; Ministry of Tribal Affairs, Circular of 28 April 2015 bearing D.O. No 23011/18/2015-FRA.

India[74] has been making demands of state governments to provide GPS locations of 'encroachments' in forest areas. More recently, there have been efforts to insist upon additional GPS verification through satellite mapping of claims, despite their approval through the three-tier rights recognition process under the FRA before issuing the title document.

25.3.4 Systematic Subversion of the Right to Community Forest Resources

The Community Forest Resource (CFR) right is at the heart of the FRA and its aspirational shift towards democratic forest governance. Unfortunately, forest dwellers pursuing this right are actively discouraged, and their efforts are thwarted in every possible way.

Even where CFR titles have been issued, myriad devices are employed to stunt their true nature. The forest bureaucracy has, on occasion, simply refused to grant CFR titles inside protected areas governed by the WLPA, such as in Himachal Pradesh, rejected CFR claims over forest lands earmarked for proposed coal block allocations, such as in Jharkhand, or 'revoked' titles already granted when powerful mining corporations have laid claim to the same forest land, such as in Chhattisgarh. While the state governments have been taken to court for these blatantly illegal decisions, there does appear to be an overwhelming attitude of impunity, especially when mining interests are involved.

The forest bureaucracy has also attempted to subvert CFR rights under the FRA by insisting that these titles be vested in Joint Forest Management committees or notifying the CFR area as a 'village forest' under the Indian Forest Act, 1927 and imposing crippling conditions on the exercise of such rights. These are but a few instances of the relentless efforts by the forest bureaucracy at the centre and in the states to sabotage the CFR rights recognition process and stultify the democratic forest governance potential of the FRA.

25.3.5 Legislative Amendments Which Erode the Forest Rights Act

Legislative changes in statutes adjacent to the FRA have significant implications. The Compensatory Afforestation Fund Act, 2015 (CAF Act) sought to provide a statutory framework for the Compensatory Afforestation Fund established under the aegis of the Supreme Court in the *Godavarman* case as far back as 2006.[75] Aggregating payments

[74] In 2019, the Forest Survey of India ('FSI') was impleaded as a party respondent in the pending litigation regarding the constitutional validity of the FRA in the Supreme Court. See *Wildlife First v Union of India* WP(C) No 109 of 2008 (Supreme Court of India, pending).

[75] See *TN Godavarman Thirumulpad (87) v Union of India* (2006) 1 SCC 1. The constitutional validity of the CAMPA Rules, notified by the MoEF and CC pursuant to the Supreme Court's urging, was upheld.

collected over the years from project proponents seeking diversion of forest lands, paid towards compensatory afforestation, net present value, and penal payments for violations, this fund has grown exponentially since its inception.[76] The 2015 Act, however, makes no provision for involving *Gram Sabhas* of forest dwellers in decision-making regarding the lands on which activities under the CAF Act would be carried out. This has resulted in indiscriminate tree plantations across the country, often over CFR lands. Forest-dwelling communities have been confounded by the obdurate refusal of the forest bureaucracy to acknowledge the validity of their rights under the FRA in these confrontations.

The last few years have also seen a spate of amendments to forest and environmental laws, which seriously erode the authority of forest-dwelling communities under the FRA. This includes amendments to the Forest (Conservation) Act, 1980, the WLPA, the Biological Diversity Act, 2002, and changes to the Environment Impact Assessment Notification, 2006. Each of these amendments, to a greater or lesser degree, increase centralization of authority and control in the forest bureaucracy, relaxation of procedures for obtaining approvals for commercial activities, narrowing of spaces for public participation in decision-making, and invisibalization of the FRA and forest dwellers. Although some of these amendments were still under litigation at the time of writing, the architecture of environmental and conservation law and the environmental regulatory framework has already changed beyond recognition.

Conclusion

A text in travail, the law relating to forest rights and the FRA has advanced two steps forward, retreated one step back, stepped sideways, and done about-turns, often in unpredictable ways. From time to time, the central government and the state governments declare their intent to speed up the implementation of the law in a 'mission mode', but these declarations remain unrealized. Instead, the general message has percolated to the forest-dwelling communities across the country—that the promise of tenurial security and democratic forest governance under the FRA no longer has the backing of the state, which has turned its allegiance elsewhere. The promise of the FRA at the time of its enactment in 2006 has become somewhat tarnished.

Subsequently, in *TN Godavarman Thirumulpad (104) v Union of India* (2008) 7 SCC 126, the Supreme Court issued detailed directions regarding the collection and disbursal of Compensatory Afforestation and Net Present Value funds.

[76] By October 2019, the Compensatory Afforestation Fund amounted to nearly INR 748,250 million. Of this, about INR 653,780 million was released to the states, per government data. See CR Bijoy, 'How Land Diversion Laws Threaten Forests and Forest Dwellers' *IndiaSpend* (25 September 2020) <www.indiaspend.com/how-land-diversion-laws-threaten-forests-and-forest-dwellers/>.

Be that as it may, it is also true that the aspirations the FRA represents have irrevocably seeped into the discourse around *Adivasi* autonomy and their relationship with forest ecosystems. Promises of a truly democratic forest governance regime, of community-managed forests akin to the *Adivasi* homelands of old, of revitalized community and clan relationships advancing towards collective resource planning and distribution—these ideas have captured the *Adivasi* imagination, flourished, proliferated, and taken root. Where once *Adivasis* and forest dwellers were subjected to brutal evictions and abuse at the hands of forest departments if they dared object to the diversion of 'state-owned' forests for commercial exploitation, the settled law now is that they hold the final decision-making in their hands. The FRA has moved forward inexorably towards becoming an ineluctable part of the forest law architecture in India. That this dramatic paradigm shift has taken place in the short span of fifteen years is quite remarkable.

No amount of cunning, trickery, or guile on the part of the state can bring back the *status quo ante* which existed prior to 2006, nor push the forest dwellers back into the prison that was the colonial forest law regime. The project of decolonising India's forests commenced by the FRA is now an inexorable reality.

Suggestions for Further Reading

Varsha Bhagat-Ganguly and Sujit Kumar (eds), *India's Scheduled Areas: Untangling Governance, Law and Politics* (Routledge 2020)

Ramachandra Guha, *The Unquiet Woods: Ecological Change and Peasant Resistance in the Himalaya* (OUP 1989).

Shomona Khanna and others, *Criminalisation of Adivasis and the Indian Legal System* (Indigenous Peoples Rights International 2022).

Madhu Sarin, 'Undoing Historical Injustice: Reclaiming Citizenship Rights and Democratic Forest Governance through the Forest Rights Act' in Sharachchandra Lélé and Ajit Menon (eds), *Democratizing Forest Governance in India* (OUP 2014) 100.

BD Sharma, *Unbroken History of Broken Promises: Indian State and the Tribal People* (Sahyog Pustak Kuteer 2010).

CHAPTER 26

ECOSYSTEMS PROTECTION AND WILDLIFE

SANJAY UPADHYAY

Abstract

India has one of the most diverse and rich wildlife and ecosystems in the world. The approach towards conservation of species either involves protecting the species per se, regardless of their habitat or protecting the ecosystem inhabited by the species. In this background, this chapter discusses the evolution of different kinds of ecosystems in the country and examines if the existing legislations address the conflicting environmental, sociological, and economic needs that are specific to ecosystems. It also captures the institutional and administrative arrangements in law and the judicial interventions which continue to shape the discourse around ecosystem protection and wildlife in India.

Introduction

Wildlife has always occupied a prominent place in India's heritage and several legal instruments have been developed to further the conservation and protection of wildlife and its habitat. Until 1972, wildlife was largely managed at the state level with specific state legislation and sometimes targeting specific species.[1] In 1972, the first comprehensive central legislation for the protection of wildlife was enacted in furtherance of India's international commitment and the run-up to the Stockholm conference in 1972. The

[1] E.g., Madras Elephant Preservation Act, 1878; Rajasthan Wildlife Act, 1953; UP National Parks Act, 1955.

Wild Life (Protection) Act, 1972 (WLPA) aims to protect wild animals, birds, and plants for ensuring ecological and environmental security by establishing a uniform framework for the preservation of wildlife throughout the country, a network of Protected Areas such as National Parks and Wildlife Sanctuaries, and regulating hunting and illicit trade in wildlife and its products. The WLPA Amendment of 2022 has attempted to shift the preambular emphasis to conservation and management rather than only protection among others.

This chapter starts by analysing the historical evolution of ecosystems that exist to protect wildlife in India. Thereafter, the chapter discusses the institutions established for ecosystems and wildlife, the WLPA's approach to protecting and conserving species, and the bottlenecks in implementing the WLPA Amendment 2022. The chapter goes on to describe the legal and administrative classifications for Protected Areas apart from those prescribed under the WLPA and the participative strategies adopted by some of those classifications.

26.1 Ecosystem Protection and Management—Species-Specific or Habitat-Specific?

Since 1983, National Wildlife Action Plans have been developed to outline strategies and the course of action for wildlife conservation. Presently, the third National Wildlife Action Plan for the period 2017–31 is in effect, with the key focus areas being wildlife health, conservation of marine ecosystem, reduction of human-wildlife conflict, conservation of coastal ecosystem, and integration of climate change into wildlife planning, among others.[2] While the WLPA is the primary legislation advocating habitat conservation, programmes such as Project Tiger, Project Elephant, and Project Rhino adopt a species-based conservation approach.[3] This section of the chapter examines the different kinds of ecosystems in India and whether the existing legislations address their specific needs.

Wildlife and its preservation have been viewed differently at different times in the legal discourse in India.[4] However, the prominent place of conservation and protection of wildlife and its habitat has remained constant. Wildlife preservation laws have undergone a paradigm shift from being un-codified moral sanctions to codified legislation with provisions for penal punishment. The Ashokan edicts, which prohibited the

[2] Ministry of Environment, Forest and Climate Change, 'India's National Wildlife Action Plan, 2017–2031' (2017).

[3] Sanjay Upadhyay and Videh Upadhyay, *Handbook on Environmental Law—Forest Laws, Wildlife Laws and the Environment*, vol-I (Lexis Nexis 2002) 219.

[4] ibid.

killing of several species of wildlife, and Kautilya's *Arthshastra*, which prescribed death for killing elephants, are now folklore of legislative history. Also, areas called 'hunting reserves' were demarcated for royal recreation, and were mainly for game rather than conservation per se, but were clearly a habitat where wildlife would thrive. However, as per the current wildlife regime, hunting is a prohibited activity except in self-defence.[5] Having said that, it would be unfair not to credit the establishment of magnificent gardens, orchards, and parks to the Mughals and the policies of emperors such as Akbar who followed the principle of tolerance towards beasts and birds.

The colonial era witnessed the emergence of a plethora of laws for the consumption and use of natural resources such as water, forests, and minerals, which were vested in the state, but the principle of 'finders keepers' governed the fate of wildlife.[6] The late nineteenth century, however, witnessed sporadic efforts for wildlife preservation in the form of the Elephant Preservation Act, 1873, and the Wild Birds Protection Act, 1887, largely focusing on species conservation. The Wild Birds and Animals Protection Act, 1912, for the first time, prohibited the killing of wild animals and birds, and the disobedience of this mandate entailed penal consequences. However, there was no concept of protection for the area or the habitat for wildlife preservation. In other words, the ecosystem approach was still taking root.

Perhaps the biggest breakthrough in the efforts for wildlife conservation was the idea of 'protected areas', including wildlife preserves of all kinds, that is, Sanctuaries, National Parks, and other protected habitats.[7] The Wild Birds and Animals Protection Act, 1935, for the first time, empowered the provincial government to set aside an area to be a Sanctuary for the protection and growth of wild animals and birds.

26.2 The Wild Life (Protection) Act, 1972—Establishment and Protection of Protected Areas as Ecosystems

Following the Stockholm conference in 1972, India developed one of the most progressive and comprehensive legislations on the conservation and protection of wildlife. The Wild Life (Protection) Act, 1972 replaced all the existing state laws on wildlife and established a network of protected areas, national parks and sanctuaries. Post-2002, two new categories of Protected Areas, namely Conservation Reserves and Community Reserves, were added. The WLPA is based on the ecosystem approach and follows the command-and-control approach to regulation. It regulates and prohibits illicit wildlife trade. It also appoints authorities, prohibits hunting of any wild animal specified in

[5] ibid 220.
[6] ibid 228.
[7] ibid 229.

Schedules I, II, III, and IV, lays down permissions and prohibitions to protect specified plants, prohibits trade or commerce in wild animals, animal articles and trophies from certain animals, and provides for the prevention and detection of offences arising out of the Act. In 2006, the WLPA also gave a legal mandate to the tiger reserve concept and established the National Tiger Conservation Authority.

The most significant amendment of the WLPA was in December 2022, including a preambular shift from protection to conservation and management. An attempt has been made to streamline the Schedules to the WLPA from six to four. The central government is now empowered, apart from the state government, to declare Conservation Reserves, among other things.

26.2.1 Institutions on Ecosystem and Wildlife

The WLPA creates independent statutory institutions such as the National Board for Wildlife (NBWL) and the State Board for Wildlife as the highest recommending bodies on wildlife policies. Apart from the bureaucracy, headed by the Chief Wildlife Warden at the state level and the Director of Wildlife Preservation, who is often the Additional Director General of Forests (Wildlife), heading at the central government level, other autonomous institutions have been created as institutes of eminence for wildlife conservation. These include the Wildlife Institute of India, Dehradun, and the Indian Institute of Science, Bangalore.[8]

The apex body that opines on wildlife matters is the NBWL, which was set up via an amendment in 2003 and is headed by the prime minister of India. It includes representation from the central and state governments and eminent conservationists, ecologists, and environmentalists. The functions of the NBWL include the promotion, conservation, and development of wildlife and forests, and the impact assessment of various projects and activities on wildlife or its habitat.[9] The NBWL has also been empowered to constitute the Standing Committee of the NBWL to perform such duties as may be delegated to it by the NBWL.

The NBWL is mandated to meet at least annually to provide guidance on the laws and policies relating to wildlife conservation, including the prevention of illegal trade.[10] However, after its last reconstitution in 2014,[11] the NBWL has not even met once. The role of the NBWL becomes more significant as there is increasing evidence globally that illegal trade in wildlife is perhaps the cause of the current pandemic. In the absence of such a meeting of the Board, the policy-making powers have been taken over by the Standing Committee of the NBWL without any delegation.[12] This has huge legal

[8] Wild Life (Protection) Act, 1972 (WLPA) s 3.

[9] ibid s 5.

[10] National Board for Wildlife Rules, 2003 r 4.

[11] This reconstitution was the result of *Chandra Bhal Singh v Union of India and Another* CWP No 736 of 2014 (Order of 21 November 2014, Supreme Court of India).

[12] WLPA s 5B(1).

ramifications, and the same was taken up by the Supreme Court of India (Supreme Court or Court) in *Chandra Bhal Singh v Union of India*,[13] which is pending adjudication.

The State Board for Wildlife is responsible for recommending projects at the state level. Its primary duties include advising on the selection of national parks and sanctuaries, formulating policy on the protection of wildlife and plants, advising on any matter relating to the schedules, and taking suitable measures for harmonizing the needs of tribals and other forest dwellers with wildlife protection and conservation.[14] The WLPA Amendment of 2022 has also created a Standing Committee of the State Board, akin to the Standing Committee of the NBWL. The State Board may delegate its powers and functions to the Standing Committee. Given the state of the Standing Committee of the NBWL, the effectiveness of the Standing Committee at the state level remains questionable.

26.2.2 Protected Areas as the Primary Approach to Ecosystem Conservation in India Under the WLPA

The WLPA provides for five categories of ecosystems with varied legal protection, which is the *in situ* mode of conservation. The highest protection is accorded to National Parks, followed by Wildlife Sanctuaries. Notably, all rights are legally required to be extinguished in National Parks, whereas some rights can continue in sanctuaries with the permission of the Chief Wildlife Warden in accordance with the Management Plan.[15] Such a Management Plan would additionally require the approval of the *Gram Sabha* if the sanctuary falls under Scheduled Areas or an area where the Scheduled Tribes and Other Traditional Forest Dwellers (Recognition of Forest Rights) Act, 2006 (FRA) is applicable.[16]

In 2003, two more Protected Area categories were added, namely the Community Reserves and Conservation Reserves, which could be declared by the state government. This experiment was based on the status of land on which such ecosystems could be conserved. A Conservation Reserve is required to be constituted on government land, and a Community Reserve on community or private land. Although the institutional framework for these two categories is based on the concept of participative wildlife conservation, the conservation strategy has not taken off in the last two decades. One major reason is that Community Reserves would be treated as sanctuaries, thereby instilling no confidence in the private or community landholder to create such conservation zones.

Another significant amendment in 2006 created two important institutions: the National Tiger Conservation Authority and the Wildlife Crime Control Bureau. Tiger

[13] *Chandra Bhal Singh v Union of India* WP(C) No 1284 of 2020 (Supreme Court of India).

[14] WLPA s 8.

[15] Wildlife Protection (Amendment) Act, 2022 s 33.

[16] ibid.

reserves as a management concept were introduced as early as 1973 under the celebrated Project Tiger programme. From an ecosystem perspective, the tiger reserve is divided into the core area or the Critical Tiger Habitat (CTH) and the buffer area, which has a different framework for conservation. As the name suggests, CTHs are given higher protection than the buffer area. Interestingly, the term Protected Area is not defined in the WLPA. However, the Supreme Court clarified that this expression 'was intended to and does refer to all the areas which have had legal protection against non-forest activities that devastated the environment including poaching, mining, felling of trees etc'.[17] The WLPA also has provisions for *ex-situ* conservation through the concept of zoos, another significant amendment in 1991.

26.2.3 Key Issues and Concerns with the WLPA and its Latest Amendments

While the new amendments talk about introducing a new chapter to implement the Convention on International Trade in Endangered Species of Flora and Fauna, 1973, the regulation of invasive alien species, the enhanced role of the Wildlife Crime Control Bureau, converting the Management Plan into a legal document, regulation of invasive species, among others, there remain some key concerns which make the amendments insufficient and inadequate. For example, there is no word on specialized agencies, the role of institutions such as the Wildlife Institute of India and its linkage with the Central Forensic Science Laboratory, or the classification of offences and their conformity to the Code of Criminal Procedure, 1973. Similarly, maritime zones and their wildlife have been missed. The declaration of a Sanctuary, National Park or Tiger Reserve must have *Gram Sabha*'s concurrence, especially after the enactment of the FRA and the *Panchayat* (Extension to Scheduled Areas) Act, 1996. However, such provisions are still missing. There is no mention of the Elephant Reserve, Biosphere Reserve or Elephant Corridors. More importantly, the bar on the accrual of rights in proposed Sanctuaries/National Parks needs an explanation of those rights that are not settled within the statutory period. More clarity on deemed Sanctuaries is required.

Further, the regulation of angling is missed! Parameters on ecotourism/nature-based tourism need legal sanctity. Clarity in boundary demarcation by reconciling forest and revenue records is also extremely important. Importantly, the alteration of boundaries needs to exclude Critical Habitat and Critical Wildlife Habitat as envisaged in the FRA. The process of wildlife clearance, including court orders and the role of the Central Empowered Committee (CEC), among others, still leaves much to be desired in terms of clarity. The role of third parties (especially NGOs in wildlife cases) also needs to be expanded. There is a need for a comprehensive database/MIS on wildlife crimes, with a statutory requirement on reporting with reporting formats. The above

[17] *Tarun Bharat Sangh v Union of India* 1993 Supp (3) SCC 115.

concerns are merely illustrative, and clearly, a more comprehensive consultation needs to be carried out. In fact, the current amendments only capture a few suggestions of the Committee constituted to amend the WLPA in 2006, of which the author was a member.[18] The final report was submitted in 2008. Therefore, there is a need to discuss all the recommendations of the Committee and provide clear reasoning as to why only selective and perhaps low-hanging decisions were incorporated in the WLPA Amendment of 2022.

26.3 Other Laws for the Creation of Ecosystems for Wildlife Conservation

Apart from the WLPA, several other legislations mandate the establishment and protection of ecosystems for the purposes of wildlife conservation. The Environment (Protection) Act, 1986, attempts to cushion the Protected Areas created under the WLPA through the concept of Ecologically Sensitive Areas/Ecologically Sensitive Zones and Ecologically Fragile Areas, among others. Other laws such as the Biological Diversity Act, 2002 (concept of biodiversity heritage sites as well as conservation of ecosystems and species conservation while advocating sustainable use), the FRA (concept of Community Forest Resource areas and Critical Wildlife Habitats, perhaps the strongest conservation area under any law), and the Coastal Regulation Zone Notification, 2011 and 2019 (CRZ-I areas and Critically Vulnerable Coastal Areas), create special ecosystems for wildlife protection. It is important to explore these legislations to understand the nuances and overlaps with the WLPA for wildlife conservation.

26.3.1 Concept of Ecologically Sensitive Areas/ Ecologically Sensitive Zones and Ecologically Fragile Areas or Zones

The Environment (Protection) Act, 1986, is a landmark umbrella legislation that responded to a widely felt need for general legislation on environmental protection. The Act vests the central government with the power to take all such measures that are necessary for the purpose of protecting and improving the quality of the environment. The Act, read along with the Environment (Protection) Rules, 1986, empowers the central government to prohibit and restrict the location of industries if it is, *inter alia*, in proximity to a protected area under the WLPA.[19]

[18] Committee of MoEFCC to examine and suggest amendments in Wildlife Protection Act as per suggestions made in Tiger Task Force and Special Investigation Team of the CBI, 2006.

[19] Environment (Protection) Rules, 1986 r 5(1)(iii).

Initially, the Draft Environment (Siting for Industrial Projects) Rules, 1999, envisaged a distance of twenty-five km for the siting of industries. Subsequently, this provision was interpreted and utilized in the Wildlife Conservation Strategy, 2002, which for the first time specified that land falling within ten km of the boundaries of national parks and sanctuaries should be notified as eco-fragile zones under section 3(v) of the Environment (Protection) Act and rule 5(viii) and (x) of the Environment (Protection) Rules. Thereafter, the NBWL noted that delineation of Eco Sensitive Areas (ESAs) would be site-specific and relate to regulation rather than prohibition of specific activities in consultation and concurrence with the state governments.[20] A letter was issued by the then Ministry of Environment and Forest (MoEF) asking the Chief Wildlife Wardens of all the states to initiate steps for designating areas as ESAs.[21]

Two kinds of ESAs are notified under the Environment (Protection) Act. The first category is a specially created ESA or ecologically sensitive zone (ESZ) or ecologically fragile area (as variously called) which are unique habitats requiring protection through proper planning. Several such ESA/ESZ notifications have been issued for special areas across the country, for example, the Western Ghats ESA notification, the Mahabaleshwar—Panchgani ESA notification, the Matheran ESZ notification, the Dahanu Taluka ESA notification, and the Murud Jazira notification. The second category is notified as a buffer to existing 'Protected Areas' namely, national parks and sanctuaries.

Apart from the above, the Supreme Court has dealt with ESAs, especially in *TN Godavarman Thirumulpad v Union of India*, and more importantly, in *Goa Foundation v Union of India*. In a case pertaining to the safety zone for mining activities, the Court held that a one km safety zone has to be maintained for mining activity outside the Jamua Ramgarh Wildlife Sanctuary in Rajasthan.[22] This has been largely followed for the entire country as explained in later decisions of the Court. Significantly, the Court directed the government of India to convene a meeting of state governments and decide about ESA, and until such decision is taken and notified, the radius of ten km shall be treated as ESA.[23] However, this was partially distinguished when the Court stated that there was no finality to the concept of a buffer of ten km; however, the one km distance was given finality in the context of mining projects.[24]

The issue of declaration of ESA was again discussed by the Court wherein it was observed that the Ministry of Environment, Forest and Climate Change (MoEFCC) had notified ESZ in around 641 of 662 National Parks and Wildlife Sanctuaries in the

[20] Minutes of Meeting of the National Board for Wildlife dated 17 March 2005.

[21] Letter dated 27 May 2005 by the Ministry of Environment and Forest to Chief Wildlife Wardens of all states to initiate steps to declare Eco-Sensitive Areas.

[22] *TN Godavarman Thirumulpad v Union of India* WP (C) No 202 of 1995 (Order of 4 August 2006, Supreme Court of India).

[23] *Goa Foundation v Union of India* WP No 460 of 2004 (Order of 4 December 2006, Supreme Court of India).

[24] *TN Godavarman Thirumulpad v Union of India* (2014) 14 SCC 160.

country.[25] The Court therefore directed that an area of ten km around the remaining twenty-one National Parks and Wildlife Sanctuaries be declared as ESZ and once proposals for notification are received, the MoEFCC could move the Court again for a relaxation in the notified area of ESA.[26] Subsequently MoEFCC described the regulatory framework for such ESAs.[27]

The distance of the ESZ and the activities that may be undertaken in the ESZ were contested again before the Court in the context of mining activities in and around the Jamua Ramgarh Wildlife Sanctuary. After a detailed adjudication of the recommendations in the CEC's report and a supplementary note of the CEC, the Court directed a minimum ESZ of one km for each Protected Area, National Park, or Wildlife Sanctuary.[28] If the ESZ has already been prescribed, the side margin of the ESZ will prevail and where the Draft ESZ notification is pending, the ESZ covering an area beyond one km will be maintained. No new permanent structures were permitted in the ESZ and only those activities can be undertaken in the ESZ permissible per the MoEFCC's Guidelines for declaration of ESZ dated 9 February 2011.

The minimum width of the ESZ, however, may be relaxed in public interest by the Court based on the recommendations of the CEC and the MoEFCC.[29] Recently, different states have filed Interlocutory Applications before the Court for dilution of the minimum width of the ESZ, including a petition by the MoEFCC itself.[30]

The Court, while directing a default ten-km radius for Protected Areas, had also directed the MoEFCC to refer those cases to the Standing Committee of the NBWL, where Environment Clearance had been granted within the ten-km zone, adding another layer of permission for projects falling within the ESZ.[31] However, subsequently, the power of clearance was handed back to the NBWL and only in case of exception and any grievance, the CEC was given the power to move the Court by way of an Interlocutory Application.[32]

However, where the project proponents of activities within the ESZ have failed to obtain the requisite permission from the Standing Committee of the NBWL, the Court has not hesitated to restrict the establishment/operation of such projects. For example, the Supreme Court quashed the Environmental Clearance granted to a housing project for

[25] *TN Godavarman Thirumulpad v Union of India* IA No 1000 in WP (C) No 202 of 1995 (Order of 11 December 2018, Supreme Court of India).

[26] ibid.

[27] OM dated 16 July 2020 read with ON dated 8 August 2019.

[28] *TN Godavarman Thirumulpad v Union of India* WP No 202 of 1995 (Judgment of 3 June 2022, Supreme Court of India).

[29] ibid.

[30] IA No 131377/2022 by Ministry of Environment, Forest and Climate Change and IA No 205092/2022 by the State of Karnataka in *TN Godavarman Thirumulpad v Union of India* WP No 202 of 1995 (Supreme Court of India).

[31] *CEL-WWF-India v Union of India* CWP No 337 of 1995 (Order of 9 May 2002, Supreme Court of India).

[32] *TN Godavarman Thirumulpad v Union of India and Others* WP No 202 of 1995 and *CEL-WWF-India v Union of India* CWP No 337 of 1995 (Order of 5 October 2015, Supreme Court of India).

failing to acquire clearance since the project was located within the ESZ of the Sukhna Wildlife Sanctuary.[33]

It is interesting to note that even activities falling in the vicinity of the ESZ have been subjected to the requirement of prior clearance from the Standing Committee of the NBWL, among other conditions. Recently, the Court allowed the operation of certain stone quarries subject to the condition that the state of Odisha completes the process of declaration of the traditional elephant corridor as a Conservation Reserve under section 36A of the WLPA.[34]

Both the National Green Tribunal (NGT) and the Supreme Court have been stringent about the implementation of mitigation measures for any project which falls within an ESA.[35] In one case, the Supreme Court upheld the NGT's order directing that the Zonal Master Plan be brought in conformity with the ESZ Notification for Mount Abu.[36]

High Courts have also been particularly cautious of the activities undertaken in ESZ and ESA and have restricted construction activities,[37] the discharge of untreated sewage and effluents,[38] and the operation of brick kilns within the Dalma Wildlife Sanctuary[39] illegally and causing damage to the ESZ area. This does not mean a blanket restriction on development activities in the ESZ. The Madras High Court directed the state to allow the operation of stone quarry activities, which were suspended for the period before the final ESZ Notification was issued for the Kanyakumari Wildlife Sanctuary stating that the final ESZ has reduced the distance from three km to zero.[40]

26.3.2 Wetland Ecosystem Protection

The Wetlands (Conservation and Management) Rules, 2010 (Wetland Rules) (revised in 2017), framed under the Environment (Protection) Act, are a tool for protecting wetland ecosystems which are rich in biodiversity. Institutional arrangements such as the Central Wetlands Regulatory Authority have been envisaged.[41] Similarly, a Wetland Atlas is formulated for more effective conservation. While the country is in the process of identifying and notifying wetlands as per these rules, some decisions of the Supreme Court are milestones in protecting wetland commons[42] if sincerely implemented. Over the years, courts have been particularly active in restricting any encroachment

[33] *Tata Housing Development Co. Ltd v Aalok Jagga* (2020) 15 SCC 784.

[34] *Binay Kumar Dalei v State of Odisha* (2022) 5 SCC 33.

[35] *Hanuman Laxman Aroskar v Union of India* (2020) 12 SCC 1; *Citizens for Green Doon v Union of India* 2021 SCC Online SC 1243.

[36] *Pragnesh Shah v Arun Kumar Sharma* (2022) 11 SCC 493.

[37] *Alex J Fernandes v State of Goa* 2021 SCC OnLine Bom 2966.

[38] *Bombay Environment Action Group v State of Maharashtra* 2006 SCC OnLine Bom 1072.

[39] *M/s RDS Bricks v State of Jharkhand* 2016 SCC OnLine Jhar 2918.

[40] *N Mathias v K Rajeswaran* 2021 SCC OnLine Mad 1899.

[41] Environment (Protection) Act, 1986 s 3(3).

[42] *Hinch Lal Tiwari v Kamala Devi* (2001) 6 SCC 496; *Jagpal Singh v State of Punjab* (2011) 11 SCC 396.

on wetlands and ensuring that the principle of 'wise use of wetland' is implemented.[43] Given the ecological importance of wetlands, the Supreme Court has made it clear that rule 4 of the Wetland Rules restricting activities on wetlands will continue to apply to all the wetlands mapped by the Union of India in the National Wetland Inventory and Assessment.[44] Some international concepts such as Ramsar Sites under the Ramsar Convention on Wetlands of International Importance, 1971 also get legal validity under the above rules, which is a significant step to give national credence to India's international obligations.

26.3.3 Conservation of Ecosystems and Species While Advocating Sustainable Use and Biodiversity Heritage Sites

The Biological Diversity Act, 2002 (BDA) aims to conserve biological diversity, regulate access to biological resources, and ensure equitable benefit sharing arising from the utilisation of those resources. The Act also establishes various governing and regulatory bodies, including the National Biodiversity Authority (NBA) at the national level, the State Biodiversity Boards (SBBs) at the state level, and Biodiversity Management Committees (BMCs) at the local level.

The BDA advocates conservation at two levels, ecosystem and species conservation, while prescribing sustainable use and benefit sharing arising from such sustainable use. However, the unique concept of a special ecosystem approach under the BDA is Biodiversity Heritage Sites (BHS).[45] BHS are those areas of biodiversity importance that the state government notifies in consultation with local bodies and may also frame rules for its management and conservation in consultation with the central government. BHS are well-defined areas that are unique, ecologically fragile ecosystems—terrestrial, coastal and inland waters, and marine having a rich biodiversity.[46]

One of the basic objectives of creating BHS is to instil and nurture conservation ethics in society, put an end to the overexploitation of natural resources and avoid environmental degradation.[47] An essential criterion for creating BHS is identifying areas that have not been covered under the WLPA and extending protection to them.

The BMCs, in addition to their duties outlined in the BDA, may also take care of the management of BHS. When the BHS extends to more than one local body, it shall be the

[43] *Raja Muzaffar Bhat v State of Jammu and Kashmir* 2019 SCC OnLine NGT 1728 and 2019 SCC OnLine NGT 1508. See also *Col. Sarvadaman Singh Oberoi v Union of India* OA No 325 of 2015 (NGT—Principal Bench).

[44] *MK Balakrishnan (1) v Union of India* (2009) 5 SCC 507.

[45] Biological Diversity Act, 2002 s 37.

[46] For details, see Guidelines for Selection and Management of Biodiversity Heritage Sites, para 3.

[47] ibid.

responsibility of the BHS Management Committee, constituted by the BMC or other appropriate authority.

At present, there are forty-three BHSs in India. A glance at these BHSs further clarifies the diverse criteria adopted for their declaration. Thus, for instance, while the 'Nallur Tamarind Grove', believed to be a relic of the Chola dynasty, spread over an area of fifty-four acres in the Devanahalli Taluk of Bengaluru district, has been declared one owing to the dynamic pattern of plant diversity, 167 ha of the University of Agricultural Sciences, GKVK campus, Bengaluru has been declared a BHS owing to a critical repository of various forms of flora and fauna which need to be protected for posterity. The website of the NBA provides a detailed analysis and understanding of BHS.[48][49]

While there is a clear intent to protect BHS, what is substantially missing is the legal mandate under the BDA Act itself. No state has framed the rules under section 37(2) of the BDA for the management of BHS.

26.3.4 Concept of Critical Wildlife Habitats

Critical Wildlife Habitat (CWH) is a relatively new concept introduced in the FRA. It is a dedicated area for wildlife conservation, where for the first time, the rights of the people are being recognized and then modified, keeping in mind the nature of the habitat. It aims at keeping the interest of both people and wild animals in mind, as it not only creates inviolate zones for conserving threatened species of animals but also offers a resettlement and rehabilitation package to people whose rights may get affected owing to such declaration and consequent relocation based on their free and prior informed consent.

Thus, CWHs are areas within National Parks and Sanctuaries declared as critically important for wildlife conservation, which may be made inviolate under the FRA for the protection of wild plants and animals to create a sanctum sanctorum that cannot be diverted for any use other than forest and wildlife conservation. It is little wonder, then, that not a single CWH has been notified as of date.

While CWHs are established under the FRA, a CTH may be created under the WLPA. Legally, these two categories are distinct. A CWH under the FRA is necessarily a subset of a National Park or a Sanctuary. A CTH is a subset of the tiger reserve concept where such reserves are not necessarily only out of National Parks and Sanctuaries but may be in addition to them. A CTH ordinarily would be a core area and part of a National Park or a Sanctuary (sometimes the whole), but the concept of a tiger reserve is a core plus buffer, which may, in fact, mostly include areas beyond National Parks and Sanctuaries. Both categories are independent and mutually exclusive for two different purposes, with due process in law to constitute them. Incidentally, and in fact, by design, both

[48] National Biodiversity Authority <http://nbaindia.org/content/106/29/1/bhs.html>.

[49] ibid.

follow the same due process, albeit through two different legislations. However, the biggest difference is that while a CWH cannot be diverted for any other purpose once it is created, a CTH may be interfered with as a part of the broader tiger reserve concept under the WLPA.

Another critical concern in habitat management is the recognition, settlement, and vesting of rights in Protected Areas, which has often been adjudged with suspicion as one view believes that forest dwellers cannot co-exist with wildlife. This understanding initially led the Supreme Court in *Wildlife First v Union of India* to direct the states to carry out evictions of persons whose claims had been rejected.[50] Subsequently, the order was stayed temporarily when the Court was apprised of the fact that even though state governments had filed data on the status of claims, including the rejected claims, the reasons, and the procedure adopted for the rejections had not been stated adequately.[51] It is clear that effective implementation of the FRA would make it easier to identify and differentiate between genuine forest dwellers and encroachers and prevent future instances of blanket court orders disenfranchising genuine forest dwellers of their rights in the name of wildlife conservation.

26.4 Administrative Classifications that Recognize Ecosystems for Wildlife Conservation

Certain administrative classifications such as 'elephant reserves and corridors', 'GIB arc', 'important bird areas', and 'biosphere reserves', among others, are integral to wildlife conservation and are important ecosystems, while they are still administrative concepts and programmes in India. All these areas have not yet been accorded any legal protection and mandated under any law, although their parts may be a legally recognized category. These are landscapes for which a bigger conservation approach is adopted, sometimes as a matter of policy and programmes and sometimes for international optics, and it is hoped that the protection envisaged by them assumes the seriousness that it deserves for ecosystem conservation.

26.4.1 Elephant Corridors and Elephant Reserves

Even though the elephant is protected under Schedule 1 of the WLPA and has been given the highest level of protection, its habitat, comprising elephant reserves and corridors,

[50] *Wildlife First v Union of India* 2019 SCC OnLine SC 238.

[51] WP(C) No 50 of 2008 (Order of 28 February 2019, Supreme Court of India).

has neither been legally recognized nor protected. The attempts of tribunals and courts have been thwarted thus far, which will be described later. The only provision that comes closest to declaring a corridor, which connects two Protected Areas or two important wildlife zones, is the concept of a Conservation Reserve under sections 36A and 36B of the WLPA, which was introduced via an amendment in 2003. A Conservation Reserve is constituted out of government land after consultation with the community. The Supreme Court gave a shot in the arm to such an initiative by directing the State of Odisha to complete the process of declaring the traditional elephant corridor as a Conservation Reserve.[52] As important as elephant corridors are for wildlife conservation and especially for the protection and survival of the elephant, their declaration without any statutory back up does not impose any restrictions on what may be permitted and prohibited, which makes these classifications arbitrary and almost insignificant. However, Project Elephant, a scheme envisaged by the MoEFCC as early as 1992, has led to the identification and demarcation of approximately 101 elephant corridors in the country. The Supreme Court has also directed the MoEFCC to respond to the Gajah Report's recommendation to confer statutory status on the National Elephant Conservation Authority.[53]

Courts have adjudicated on the issue of elephant conservation, including its habitat. In one case, the Supreme Court held the power of the state government to take measures to be undeniable considering entries 17-A 'Forest' and 17-B 'Protection of wild animals and birds' in the Concurrent List of the Constitution of India, 1950. Therefore, it upheld the Tamil Nadu state government's order notifying an 'elephant corridor' and issuing directions to resort owners and other private landowners to vacate their land falling in the notified elephant corridor.[54] In another case, the Court ordered Numaligarh Refinery Ltd to demolish 2.2 km of wall with barbed wire and razor-edge fencing right in the middle of an elephant corridor for expansion of its township in the proposed Deopahar Reserve forest area, near the Kaziranga National Park. The Court orally ordered that 'elephants have first right over the forest'.[55] In certain cases, night safaris have also been questioned as they may affect the elephant corridor and disturb the movement of wild animals.[56]

Another important step is the NGT's direction to the central government to demarcate all elephant corridors and reserves as ESA, thereby bringing them under the ambit of the Environment (Protection) Act.[57] The Supreme Court has sought a status report

[52] *Binay Kumar Dalei* (n 34).

[53] *Prerna Singh Bindra v Union of India* WP No 1212 of 2021 (Order of 1 February 2023, Supreme Court of India).

[54] *Hospitality Association of Mudumalai v In Defence of Environment and Animals* (2020) 10 SCC 589; *In Defence of Environment and Animals v Principal Chief Conservator of Forest* WP No 10098 of 2008 (Order of 7 April 2011, Madras High Court).

[55] *Numaligarh Refinery v Rohit Chaudhary* Civil Appeal Diary No 41203 of 2018 (Judgment of 18 January 2019, Supreme Court of India).

[56] *BR Deepak v State of Karnataka* (2010) SCC OnLine Kar 4570.

[57] *Kashmira Kakati v Union of India* OA No 19 of 2014 (Judgment of 8 December 2017, NGT—Principal Bench). See also *Pradip Kumar Bhuyan v Union of India* OA No 246 of 2018.

from the Union of India regarding the steps taken in pursuance of the said direction.[58] It remains to be seen whether these directions are implemented, and if they prove to be beneficial for the overall welfare of the species.

26.4.2 The Great Indian Bustard Arc

The Great Indian Bustard (GIB) Arc landscape is another priority habitat area where the critically endangered Great Indian Bustard is regularly sighted. The GIB Arc extends from the northern part of Desert National Park towards Salkha and Mokla villages to the north and in the east to the extensive dry savannah controlled by the Indian Armed Forces and used for artillery testing near Pokhran.[59] It has been proposed as an 'eco-sensitive zone',[60] and the NGT, Bhopal has prohibited new wind turbines and powerlines in the area.[61]

In the Thar Desert in Rajasthan, 75 per cent of priority GIB conservation sites are outside Protected Areas, with most being 'threatened by hunting and unplanned land uses',[62] while the Mokla grassland (about 50 sq km) in the GIB Arc has been converted to scrub by misguided planting of exotic *Acacia tortilis*.[63]

A catena of judicial decisions has recommended GIB endemic states undertake adequate mitigation measures for ensuring the sustainable existence of wind power projects as well as the GIB.[64] The said GIB Arc was envisaged somewhere towards the end of 2018 and at the beginning of 2019 when the Jaisalmer Forest Department withheld clearances for projects that fell within the ambit of the said Arc.

The Arc mostly covers areas outside the Desert National Park. Though the GIB Arc is not a legal concept, the presence of windmills and high-tension power lines in the Arc has been seen as a red flag, and projects have been rejected on this ground alone. Similar experiments have been carried out for the Terai Arc as well. The Supreme Court is also taking cognizance of such initiatives and giving them credence through orders

58 *Coal India Limited v Dr Kashmira Kakati* Civil Appeal No 9710-9711 of 2018 (Order of 7 January 2022, Supreme Court of India).

59 Sutirtha Dutta and others, 'Status of Great Indian Bustard and Associated Wildlife in Thar' (Wildlife Institute of India and Rajasthan Forest Department 2014).

60 *CWEL v Union of India* OA No 385 of 2019 (NGT Principal Bench, Report dated 11 July 2019 submitted by the MoEFCC).

61 *Mahendra Singh Boravat v State of MP* OA No 63 of 2016 (Order of 26 July 2021, NGT—Central Zone Bench).

62 Dutta and others (n 59).

63 NJ Collar, PS Patil, and Gobind Sagar Bhardwaj, 'What Can Save the Great Indian Bustard'? (2015) 23 *Birding ASIA* 15.

64 *Centre for Wildlife and Environment Litigation v Union of India and Others* OA No 385 of 2019 (Judgment of 23 December 2020, NGT—Principal Bench). See also *Suo Motu v Principal Secretary and Others* DB CWP (PIL) No 825 of 2019 (High Court of Rajasthan); *Sunil Kumar Jain v SEIAA Rajasthan and Others* Appeal No 1 of 2019 (NGT—Central Zone Bench); *MK Ranjitsinh v Union of India* (2021) 15 SCC 1.

and directions for regulating habitats which may impact endangered species.[65] For example, there is an injunction on installing fresh overhead transmission lines. Further, the Court has directed the installation of bird divertors in priority areas of Gujarat and Rajasthan. It remains to be seen whether such measures would suffice to facilitate long-term protection of the critically endangered GIB.

26.4.3 Important Bird Areas

An administrative initiative for the avian ecosystem is the Important Bird Areas (IBA) programme of Birdlife International, which aims to identify, monitor, and protect a global network of IBAs for the conservation of the world's birds and associated biodiversity.[66] The IBAs serve as conservation areas for the protection of birds at the global, regional, or sub-regional level. The designation of IBAs is based on standardized criteria, namely (i) hold significant numbers of one or more globally threatened bird species, (ii) be one of a set of sites that together hold a suite of restricted-range species or biome-restricted species, and (iii) have exceptionally large numbers of migratory or congregatory birds.[67] The IBAs contain a range of habitats, such as wetlands, mudflats, microhabitats in biodiversity hotspots, grasslands, and scrublands, making them excellent indicators of biodiversity richness.[68] The Bombay Natural History Society and Birdlife International have identified 467 IBAs in India.[69] Forty per cent of these IBAs fall outside the Protected Areas network and thus form an important tool for landscape-level conservation planning for avian species.[70] BNHS has also prepared a list of ninety-six new/potential sites which can be designated as IBAs in the future.[71] Here again, the conservation community has taken up the importance of IBAs, and courts have favourably examined their relevance for conservation of bird population, especially in the case of infrastructure projects.

65 *MK Ranjitsinh v Union of India* 2022 SCC OnLine SC 1051.

66 Paul F Donald and others, 'Important Bird and Biodiversity Areas (IBAs): The Development and Characteristics of a Global Inventory of Key Sites for Biodiversity' (2019) 29(2) *Bird Conservation International* 177.

67 Envis Centre on Wildlife and Protected Areas, 'Important Bird Areas (IBAs) in India' <http://wiienvis.nic.in/Database/ImportantBirdAreas(IBAs)inIndia_8463.aspx?format=Print.

68 Ministry of Environment, Forest and Climate Change, 'India's 5th National Report to the Convention on Biological Diversity' (2014).

69 MZ Islam and AR Rahmani, 'Important Bird Areas in India: Priority Sites for Conservation' (Bombay Natural History Society and Bird Life International 2004).

70 Envis Centre on Wildlife and Protected Areas (n 67).

71 ibid.

26.4.4 Biosphere Reserves

One of the oldest programmes on landscape management is the concept of biosphere reserves under UNESCO's Man and the Biosphere (MAB) Programme, initiated in 1971.[72] Biosphere Reserves are sites established by countries to promote sustainable development based on local community efforts and sound science. The purpose of the Biosphere Reserve is to conserve, *in situ*, all forms of life, along with the support system, in its totality so that it could serve as a referral system for monitoring and evaluating changes in natural ecosystems. The network of biosphere reserves has increased to 631 in 119 countries across the world, and there are eighteen notified biosphere reserves in India.[73]

26.4.5 Participative Strategies for Ecosystem Management

Numerous approaches have been followed to give effect to effective conservation. The conventional command-and-control approach under statutes borrowed from the colonial past has evolved into new approaches to participative conservation. From the early 1990s, concepts such as Joint Forest Management, NGO initiatives such as Joint Protected Area Management, and Community Wildlife Management have been debated and experimented with mixed successes and failures. The latest trend is to recognize the formal, decentralized approach to conservation, reflected in the latest amendments to the WLPA, as well as the enactment of legislation such as the FRA.

The policy thrust through the recent Wildlife Conservation Strategy also advocates a similar decentralized approach. The *Gram Sabha* or the village assembly, even down to the hamlet level, are now significant stakeholders in ecosystem management. Other concepts, such as ecotourism, also advocate an incentive-based approach to conservation. The concept of Community Forest Rights under the FRA and the planning process, which is now statutorily mandated, again strengthens the decentralized approach to conservation. While the foundation for participative conservation has been established, it needs to percolate through all the planning processes for ecosystem management. Whether it is the Management Plan of Protected Areas, the People's Biodiversity Registers (PBRs) under the BDA, the Conservation and Management Plan under the FRA, or the Tiger Conservation Plan under the WLPA, the effective and authentic role of the community must be a *sine qua non* for ecosystem management.

Another quiet development that has a bearing on ecosystem management is the land reform legislation where the state machinery takes over the control of land in favour of larger private gains rather than the good of the community dependent on it, thereby

72 UNESCO, Man and the Biosphere (MAB) Programme <https://en.unesco.org/mab>.

73 Wildlife Institute of India, Biosphere Reserves <https://wii.gov.in/nwdc_biosphere_reserves>.

impacting conservation. Even where there are regulations to hand over control to the *panchayats*, state discretion looms large. An example is the inadequate legal framework of Madhya Pradesh and Chhattisgarh, where the record of transferred land has been contested by both the Revenue and Forest departments, leading to a long-drawn dispute of what is now termed as 'orange areas' and impacting the livelihood of tens of thousands of families and obviously the conservation regime itself.

In another instance, the MoEFCC and the Ministry of Tribal Affairs (MoTA) issued a joint communication stating that both ministries would resolve any clarifications pertaining to the implementation of the FRA.[74] The joint communication envisages greater support to the state Forest Department for verification of forest rights, mapping of forest lands, provision of necessary evidence, preparation of conservation plan for management of Community Forest Resource, and capacity building schemes for forest dwellers for sustainable use of forest resources. While the active involvement of the Forest Department with the Tribal Department is crucial for preventing future conflicts over implementation of the FRA, the tendency of the state to take over processes meant to be led by the community cannot be over-emphasized. For example, state authorities have outsourced the formation of PBRs to external agencies in contravention of the BDA, which mandates the BMCs to spearhead the formation of PBRs.

26.5 Challenging the Narrative: A Way Forward

The evolution of ecosystem management is strongly rooted in the legal framework and is further sprinkled with administrative concepts to fill gaps in ecosystem management as a landscape approach. But the crucial missing piece in the puzzle is institutional streamlining. The MoEFCC and its co-ordination with ministries dealing with extractive industries, on the one hand, and strengthened support from ministries, such as the MoTA and the Department of Science and Technology on the other, is inadequate, as is evident from several disputes.

Other statutory institutions such as the NBWL and the National Biodiversity Authority, State Biodiversity Boards, the State Board for Wildlife, and the Chief Wildlife Warden's Office at the state level and the BMCs, Joint Forest Management Committees, Eco-Development Committees, and the *Gram Sabha*, often overlap and contradict each other. These are serious gaps that need immediate attention for smooth and effective ecosystem management.

Another crucial component is the role of extractive industries and public infrastructure undertakings, linear or otherwise, and the way they impact ecosystems and attempt

74 Ministry of Environment, Forest and Climate Change and Ministry of Tribal Affairs, Joint Communication for more effective implementation of the Forest Rights Act (July 2021).

to mitigate such impacts. The monitoring framework for such coordinated approaches to impact assessment and its management is rather weak unless pointed out by conscious citizens. In fact, the citizens' role needs to be enhanced to strengthen effective monitoring when ecosystems are under threat.

It would not be out of place to emphasize the inadequacy of institutional capacities, either dealing with regulating such ecosystems or those in the position of oversight, judicial or otherwise, which needs immediate attention. Another myth that needs to be debunked is that conservation is always at the cost of development.

Conservation must be a strength to meaningful development as the longevity of natural ecosystems is an elixir to life itself!

Suggestions for Further Reading

ELDF and WWF India, *Conserving Protected Areas and Wildlife: A Judicial Journey* (WWF India 2009).

Arjya B Majumdar, Debosmita Nandy, and Swayambhu Mukherjee, *Environment and Wildlife Laws in India* (Lexis Nexis 2013).

Manoj Misra, 'Evolution, Impact, and Effectiveness of Domestic Wildlife Trade Bans in India' in Sara Oldfield (ed), *The Trade in Wildlife: Regulation for Conservation* (Earthscan 2014) 78.

Ghazala Shahabuddin and K Sivaramakrishnan (eds), *Nature Conservation in the New Economy: People, Wildlife and the Law in India* (Orient BlackSwan 2019).

Sanjay Upadhyay and Videh Upadhyay, *Handbook on Environmental Law: Forest Laws, Wildlife Laws and the Environment*, vol I (Lexis Nexis Butterworth 2002).

PART VII

AIR, CLIMATE CHANGE, AND DISASTERS

CHAPTER 27

AIR QUALITY REGULATION

SHIBANI GHOSH*

Abstract

This chapter unpacks the key components of air quality regulation in India. It provides an overview of the regulatory and institutional framework that governs some of the major sources of air pollution in the country, focusing primarily on national laws and policies. It identifies four main challenges in regulating air quality: weaknesses in regulatory design; capacity and capability constraints in regulatory institutions; flawed policy-making; and the inadequacy of hard regulation in delivering cleaner air. The chapter concludes by suggesting certain pathways for reform: through legal amendments, institutional strengthening, and development of technical capacity for sound policy-making.

Introduction

Air pollution has remained a pressing concern in India over the last several decades. Data on air pollution in India points unequivocally to a very grave situation. Thirty-five of the fifty most polluted cities in the world are in India,[1] and the annual average particulate matter (PM2.5) concentration in India was estimated to be more than twice the acceptable national standards.[2] Two hundred and forty-one out of 331 cities in India do

* I would like to gratefully acknowledge Sharon Mathew's valuable research assistance in the writing of this chapter.

[1] IQ Air, 'World Air Quality Report: Region & City PM2.5 Ranking' (2020) <https://www.iqair.com/world-most-polluted-cities/world-air-quality-report-2020-en.pdf>.

[2] Health Effects Institute (HEI), 'State of Global Air 2020 Country Profile- India' (2020) <https://www.stateofglobalair.org/sites/default/files/documents/2020-11/soga-country-profile-india.pdf>.

not comply with air quality standards for particulate matter.[3] Notably, poor air quality is a nation-wide problem, with no significant urban-rural gap. Eighty-three per cent of the Indian population is exposed to air quality that does not meet the national standards on particulate matter,[4] and according to a study, in 2019, the permissible annual ambient PM2.5 concentration standard was exceeded in most states in the country.[5]

Equally disturbing is the mounting evidence regarding the health impact of such severe levels of pollution and its effect on the Indian economy. The number of deaths attributable to air pollution in India has shown a steady upward trend in the last twenty-five years.[6] In 2019, air pollution—both ambient and household—was found to be the leading risk factor for premature deaths in the country, accounting for nearly 1.67 million deaths.[7] While air pollution is commonly associated with respiratory and cardiovascular diseases, it is also linked to diabetes, neo-natal disorders, and cataracts, and emerging evidence shows it may lead to other adverse health outcomes like dementia and loss of intelligence quotient.[8] Assessing the economic losses due to premature mortality and morbidity attributable to air pollution is not easy, but the available estimates are startling—one study calculated it to be 3 per cent of India's GDP in 2019,[9] while another estimated the total welfare losses to be 7.7 per cent of the GDP.[10]

Research and monitoring are increasing, public awareness is growing, and the nature and scale of the problem of poor air quality are becoming more evident. The myth that it is largely an urban and seasonal problem is being dispelled. From being primarily the concern of an 'activist' judiciary, air pollution now figures in parliamentary debates, emergency law-making (ordinances), political manifestos, and widespread civil society agitations.

[3] Sunil Dahiya, 'Airpocalypse III: Assessment of Air Pollution in Indian Cities and National Clean Air Programme (NCAP)' (Greenpeace 2019) <https://www.greenpeace.org/static/planet4-india-stateless/2019/08/8d46f0c0-airpocalypse-iii-report.pdf>.

[4] Joshua S Apte and Pallavi Pant, 'Toward Cleaner Air for a Billion Indians' (2019) 116 *Proceedings of the National Academy of Sciences* 10614.

[5] Sagnik Dey and others, 'A Satellite-Based High-Resolution (1-Km) Ambient PM2.5 Database for India over Two Decades (2000–2019): Applications for Air Quality Management' (2020) 12(23) *Remote Sensing* 3872 (the six states which did not exceed the permissible PM2.5 standards are sparsely populated and mountainous).

[6] GBD MAPS Working Group, 'Burden of Disease Attributable to Major Air Pollution Sources in India' (HEI 2018) Special Report 21 <https://www.healtheffects.org/system/files/GBD-MAPS-SpecRep21-India-revised_0.pdf>.

[7] HEI (n 2).

[8] Anamika Pandey and others, 'Health and Economic Impact of Air Pollution in the States of India: The Global Burden of Disease Study 2019' (2021) 5(1) *The Lancet Planetary Health* e25.

[9] Confederation of Indian Industry and others, 'Air Pollution and its Impact on Business: The Silent Pandemic' (2021) <https://s40026.pcdn.co/wp-content/uploads/01042021_Business-Cost-of-Air-Pollution_Long-Form-Report.pdf>.

[10] The World Bank and Institute for Health Metrics and Evaluation, 'The Cost of Air Pollution: Strengthening the Economic Case for Action' (2016) <https://openknowledge.worldbank.org/bitstream/handle/10986/25013/108141.pdf?sequence=4&isAllowed=y>.

This chapter gives a snapshot of how India is responding to the problem of air pollution through regulation and government action. I define air quality regulation as the body of laws legislated by Parliament and the rules and notifications issued under them, along with the policies and programmes of the government of India and central agencies, to preserve the quality of air,[11] prevent and mitigate air pollution, and prescribe institutional mechanisms for monitoring and enforcing air quality standards. Due to space constraints, I do not refer to laws and policies issued at the sub-national level, though they critically impact air quality. The emphasis on central laws and policies in this chapter is also appropriate given the enormity of the crisis—the centre needs to provide leadership through legislation, finance, policy, and technical know-how. The chapter is divided into three sections. Section 27.1 lays out the broad contours of the regulatory and institutional framework for air quality governance in India. Section 27.2 identifies the four main challenges in regulating air quality: weaknesses in regulatory design, capacity and capability constraints in regulatory institutions, flawed policy-making, and finally, the inadequacy of hard regulation in delivering cleaner air. Section 27.3 suggests certain pathways for reform: legal amendments, institutional strengthening, and development of technical capacity for sound policy-making.

27.1 Regulatory and Institutional Framework

Air quality regulation in India has its origin before Independence. The Indian Penal Code, 1860, considered the beginning of modern environmental regulation in India,[12] penalizes the voluntary vitiation of the atmosphere.[13] Other laws like the Bengal Smoke-Nuisances Act, 1905 and the Bombay Smoke-Nuisances Act, 1912 also regulated sources of smoke. Post-independence, two legislations have been passed by Parliament on this issue—the Air (Prevention and Control of Pollution) Act (Air Act) in 1981,[14] and the Commission for Air Quality for the National Capital Region and Adjoining Areas Act (CAQM Act) in 2021.

In this section, I begin with an overview of the key regulatory frameworks that govern the major sources of air pollution. This is followed by a brief discussion of the institutional and policy framework and systems for air quality monitoring and communication. I then identify the tools regulators use to ensure compliance with the law. Finally,

[11] E.g., Air (Prevention and Control of Pollution) Act, 1981, preamble [hereafter Air Act].

[12] CM Jariwala, 'Changing Dimensions of Indian Environmental Law' in P Leelakrishnan (ed), *Law and Environment* (Eastern Book Company 1992) 1.

[13] The Indian Penal Code, 1860 s 278. See also 'public nuisance' under IPC s 268.

[14] 'Air' is not an entry in Schedule VII to the Constitution. The Air Act was legislated by Parliament to implement decisions taken relating to air quality at the United Nations Conference on Human Environment held in Stockholm in 1972.

as the judiciary has played a crucial role in air quality governance in India, I discuss some of the significant judicial pronouncements on the issue.

27.1.1 Key Regulatory Frameworks Governing Major Pollution Sources

The major sources of air pollution in India are industries, power plants, transport, households (cooking and heating), biomass burning (including crop residue and waste), roads, construction sites, and diesel generators.[15] Source apportionment studies reveal that the significance of each source varies in different parts of the country.[16] Each source is regulated by a different set of regulations.

The Air Act focuses largely on point sources of pollution—industrial plants and power plants. To some extent, it also regulates vehicular emissions.[17] Under the Air Act, definitions of key terms—air pollutant, air pollution, and emissions—are broad[18] and potentially allow the government to regulate sources quite comprehensively.[19] The Act empowers state governments to declare air pollution control areas (APCAs), and within these APCAs, different standards for fuel, appliances, etc. can be notified to address specific causes of air pollution.[20]

The Environment (Protection) Rules, 1986 (EP Rules) issued under the Environment (Protection) Act, 1986 prescribe the emissions standards for various industry categories and processes. The Rules include emission norms for thermal power plants, diesel engines and generators, and dust mitigation measures for construction and demolition sites.[21] Notifications issued under the Environment (Protection) Act regulate specific sources of pollution—the Noise Pollution (Regulation and Control) Rules, 2000,[22] the Construction and Demolition Waste Management Rules, 2016, and the Solid Waste Management (SWM) Rules, 2016. Other notifications, such as the EIA Notification, 2006 and the Coastal Regulation Zone (CRZ) Notification, 2019, as well as the designation of areas as critically polluted based on the Comprehensive Environment Pollution

[15] E.g., Sarath K Guttikunda, Nishadh KA, and Puja Jawahar, 'Air Pollution Knowledge Assessments (APnA) for 20 Indian Cities' (2019) 27 *Urban Climate* 124, 138.

[16] ibid.

[17] Air Act (n 11) s 20.

[18] ibid s 2.

[19] The definition of air pollutant is sufficiently broad to cover GHG emissions. The Air Act therefore offers a potential legislative hook for climate action.

[20] Air Act (n 11) s 19(3)–(5).

[21] Environment (Protection) Rules, 1986 (EP Rules) sch I, sl nos 25, 95–96, 106–107; Central Pollution Control Board (CPCB), 'Guidelines on Dust Mitigation Measures in Handling Construction Material and C&D Wastes' (2017) <https://prana.cpcb.gov.in/assets/pdf/c_and_d_guidelines_1.pdf>.

[22] Noise is included in the definition of 'air pollutant'. See Air Act (n 11) s 2(a). This chapter does not discuss the regulatory framework governing noise pollution, as the focus is on air pollution caused by emissions.

Index,[23] lead to the prescription of compliance conditions for specific categories of projects and activities. To that extent, they regulate potentially polluting sources.

Vehicular emissions are regulated by the Motor Vehicles Rules, 1989. Apart from setting out emission standards (referred to as Bharat Stage or BS standards) for different types of vehicles, the Rules also set out requirements for Pollution Under Control (PUC) certification, and procedures and penalties in case of non-compliance.[24]

Burning crop residue before the next sowing season has become a significant source of pollution, albeit for two to three weeks, particularly in northern India. Fire counts in Punjab and Haryana have increased in recent years, and due to the wind direction and peculiar topography of the Indo-Gangetic Plains, the smoke from these fires envelopes large swathes of downwind area, including the National Capital Region (NCR). Several measures have been taken at the centre and state levels to discourage crop residue burning, including prohibition under the Air Act[25] and imposition of payment of environmental compensation.[26] Apart from this, financial incentives are being given to farmers to adopt *in-situ* and *ex-situ* management of crop residue.[27]

Household air pollution is the single largest source of air pollution exposure in India.[28] The primary source of household pollution is the burning of biomass like firewood as fuel. There is no law regulating the type of fuel that households must use. However, the government, through schemes like the Pradhan Mantri Ujjwala Yojana (PMUY), has been encouraging the use of cleaner fuels like LPG.[29]

27.1.2 Institutional and Policy Framework

There is an 'institutional thicket'[30] governing the air quality landscape, and policies vary according to the sector. This section provides an overview of the main institutional actors and the National Clean Air Programme 2019 (NCAP)—India's only air

[23] CPCB, 'Comprehensive Environmental Pollution Index (CEPI) Monitoring for Polluted Industrial Areas (PIAs)' <https://cpcb.nic.in/comprehensive-environmental-pollution-index-cepi/>.

[24] Central Motor Vehicles Rules, 1989 rr 115, 116.

[25] E.g., Government of Punjab Department of Science, Technology and Environment, Notification No. 3/162/2006-STE(4)/946 dated 22 October 2013 <http://www.cja.gov.in/Important%20Instructions/Air%20Pollution.pdf>.

[26] Commission for Air Quality Management in National Capital Region and Adjoining Areas Act, 2021 s 15 [hereafter CAQM Act].

[27] E.g., Government of India, 'Central Sector Scheme on Promotion of Agricultural Mechanisation for In-Situ Management of Crop Residue in the States of Punjab, Haryana, Uttar Pradesh and NCT of Delhi' (2018) <https://agrimachinery.nic.in/Files/Guidelines/CRM.pdf>.

[28] Zoe Chafe and others, 'How Much Do Households Contribute to Ambient Air Pollution in India?' (*Ideas for India*, 19 August 2019) <https://www.ideasforindia.in/topics/environment/how-much-do-households-contribute-to-ambient-air-pollution-in-india.html>.

[29] Ministry of Petroleum and Natural Gas, 'Pradhan Mantri Ujjwala Yojana 2.0' <https://www.pmuy.gov.in/index.aspx#>.

[30] Santosh Harish, 'Renewing India's Air Quality Management Strategy in the Shadow of COVID-19' (Centre for Policy Research (CPR) 2021) 11.

quality-focused national policy. The State Pollution Control Boards (SPCBs) in the states and the Pollution Control Committees (PCCs) in the Union Territories, set up under the Water (Prevention and Control of Pollution) Act, 1974 (Water Act) and the Air Act, are the main institutional actors implementing air quality regulations in India. The Central Pollution Control Board (CPCB) performs a largely supervisory and technical advisory role, occasionally issuing directions to SPCBs to take appropriate measures. The nodal agency implementing the powers of the central government under the Environment (Protection) Act (and rules and notifications issued under it) is the Ministry of Environment, Forest and Climate Change (MoEFCC). State governments exercise their statutory powers (for instance, under the Air Act) through their environmental departments.

Apart from the MoEFCC and the Boards, an institution that has played a key role in air quality governance—although only in the NCR—is the Environment Pollution (Prevention and Control) Authority (EPCA). It was set up in 1998 through a notification issued by the central government[31] at the direction of the Supreme Court.[32] It had a comprehensive mandate in the NCR for protecting the environment. It advised the Supreme Court and suggested policy measures for air pollution control. Although its functioning came under criticism,[33] some of its recommendations have been significant, particularly on the adoption and incentivization of cleaner fuel, transitioning to higher vehicular emission standards, the Graded Response Action Plan, and the Comprehensive Action Plan for the NCR.[34]

The EPCA was succeeded by the CAQM, constituted by an Ordinance promulgated in October 2020.[35] This Ordinance lapsed in March 2021. A second Ordinance was promulgated in April 2021.[36] A significant revision in the second Ordinance was the exclusion of stubble burning or mismanagement of agricultural residue from the definition of punishable offences. This was in response to demands raised by farmer unions during their protests against three controversial farm laws.[37] Instead, the Ordinance empowered the Commission to impose and collect environmental compensation from farmers causing air pollution by stubble burning.

[31] Ministry of Environment and Forests (MoEF), Notification S.O. 93(E) dated 29 January 1998.

[32] *MC Mehta v Union of India and Others* (1998) 2 SCC 435.

[33] E.g., Ritwick Dutta, 'Twenty Years of EPCA: Lessons for the New EPCA' (Legal Initiative for Forests and Environment, 2018) <https://indiaaq.files.wordpress.com/2018/10/20-years-of-epca.pdf>.

[34] CPCB and MoEFCC, 'Graded Response Action Plan for Delhi & NCR' (July 2017) <https://cpcb.nic.in/uploads/final_graded_table.pdf>; MoEFCC, Notification S.O. 118(E) dated 12 January 2017, <https://cpcb.nic.in/uploads/GRAP_Notification.pdf>.

[35] The Commission for Air Quality Management in National Capital Region and Adjoining Areas Ordinance, 2020.

[36] The Commission for Air Quality Management in National Capital Region and Adjoining Areas Ordinance, 2021.

[37] The Wire Staff, 'Farm Law Talks: Centre, Farmers Reach Consensus on Power Tariff, Stubble Burning', *The Wire* (30 December 2020) <https://thewire.in/government/farmers-protesting-delhi-borders-talks-centre-farm-unions-underway>.

The 2021 Ordinance was replaced by the CAQM Act in August 2021. Similar to the Ordinances, the Act puts in place a statutory mechanism to deal with issues relating to air quality in the NCR, as well as its adjoining areas.[38] Unlike the EPCA, the CAQM has full-time members, apart from the *ex officio* members; it has the necessary statutory powers to appoint full-time staff, and its territorial jurisdiction is wider than the NCR.[39] The Act gives the Commission exclusive jurisdiction over air quality issues in the region, and significant overriding powers over other central, state, and local agencies and statutory authorities working on the issue.[40]

The National Environment Policy 2006 included a section on air pollution that proposed actions like city-level action plans and certain sectoral initiatives.[41] In 2019, the first policy focusing on air quality—the NCAP—was launched by the government of India.[42] The NCAP is expected to guide the CPCB as it executes a nation-wide programme for prevention of air pollution.[43] The national-level target of the programme is to attain 20–30 per cent reduction of particulate matter by 2024 while keeping 2017 as the baseline year.[44] The programme identifies mitigation measures across various sources of pollution, suggests ways to augment monitoring capacity and knowledge databases, and lists actions for institutional strengthening. Although the NCAP acknowledges the need for regional-level and sectoral planning for air quality, it adopts a city-centric approach.[45] The CPCB has identified several 'non-attainment cities'—the number now stands at 131[46]—based on data which shows emissions of core pollutants exceeding prescribed limits for over five years. City-level action plans have been prepared, approved and are in the process of implementation for these non-attainment cities, and funds have been released by the central government as well as through a Finance Commission grant.[47]

[38] CAQM Act (n 26) s 2(1)(a).

[39] ibid s 1(2).

[40] ibid s 12(6); Santosh Harish, Shibani Ghosh and Sharon Mathew, 'The CAQM Act 2021: An Overview' (CPR 2021).

[41] National Environment Policy 2006, 36–37.

[42] MoEFCC, 'National Clean Air Programme' (2019) <https://moef.gov.in/wp-content/uploads/2019/05/NCAP_Report.pdf>.

[43] Air Act (n 11) s 16(2).

[44] This target has been reportedly revised upwards to 35–50 per cent by 2026 in the identified non-attainment cities. Vishwa Mohan, 'Govt to Revise Target to Cut PM Levels by 50% in 4 Yrs' *The Times of India* (18 December 2021) <https://timesofindia.indiatimes.com/india/govt-to-revise-target-to-cut-pm-levels-by-50-in-4-yrs/articleshow/88351133.cms>.

[45] 'First Meeting of National Apex Committee under National Clean Air Programme Held' *Press Information Bureau* (17 December 2021) <https://pib.gov.in/PressReleasePage.aspx?PRID=1782722>.

[46] MoEFCC, 'Portal for Regulation of Air Pollution in Non-Attainment Cities' <https://prana.cpcb.gov.in/#/home>.

[47] Lok Sabha Unstarred Question No 2046; Answered on: 14 March 2022 (Grants for Air Quality).

27.1.3 Air Quality Monitoring and Communication

To monitor air quality, the CPCB executes the National Ambient Air Quality Monitoring Programme (NAMP) through manual monitoring stations in 931 locations covering 398 cities/towns.[48] These stations monitor four pollutants: sulphur dioxide, oxides of nitrogen, respirable suspended particulate matter (RSPM/PM10), and fine particulate matter (PM2.5). Apart from these, there are 540 Continuous Ambient Air Quality Monitoring Stations (CAAQMS). They also measure other pollutants like carbon monoxide, ozone, ammonia, and lead. Data from CAAQMS can be used for short-term air quality forecasting.[49]

In recent years, the CPCB has been using data from the CAAQMS to calculate the Air Quality Index (AQI) of an area.[50] The AQI is a tool for communicating air quality to the public in a simplified form. Based on the AQI, air quality is described as 'good', 'poor', 'severe' levels, etc., and categories of activities are discouraged if the AQI reaches a particular level.[51]

27.1.4 Regulatory Tools to Ensure Compliance

Sources of emissions are primarily regulated in two ways—first, they are required to meet the prescribed emissions standards, and second, they must obtain consent or approvals under the appropriate regulations. Emission standards for specific industries, operations and processes have been issued by the central government as Schedules to the EP Rules. For instance, the National Ambient Air Quality Standards (NAAQS) 2009 are included as Schedule VII of the EP Rules.[52] The Boards also have the power under the Air Act to prescribe emission standards,[53] and they may adopt more stringent standards than those specified in the EP Rules.[54]

Point sources of emissions, such as industrial plants, are not permitted to establish or operate without the SPCB's consent under the Air Act.[55] A consent typically stipulates several conditions, including the approved fuel and equipment, permissible emissions, and compliance reporting requirements. Consent requirements, as well as industry siting guidelines, depend on the categorization of the industry by the CPCB as red, orange, green, or

[48] CPCB, 'Manual Ambient Air Quality Monitoring Stations in the Country (As on 30.06.2023) ' <https://cpcb.nic.in/uploads/Stations_NAMP.pdf>.

[49] CPCB, 'Central Control Room for Air Quality Management' <https://app.cpcbccr.com/ccr/#/login>.

[50] CPCB, 'How is AQI Calculated' <https://app.cpcbccr.com/ccr_docs/How_AQI_Calculated.pdf>.

[51] CPCB, 'National Air Quality Index' < https://app.cpcbccr.com/AQI_India/>.

[52] The NAAQS are much below the 2021 revised WHO standards for air quality.

[53] Air Act (n 11) s 16(2)(h) and 17(1)(g).

[54] EP Rules r 3(2).

[55] Air Act (n 11) s 21.

white.[56] Clearances and regulatory oversight mechanisms are also prescribed in other laws such as the EIA Notification, the CRZ Notification, the SWM Rules, and the Motor Vehicles Rules.

To ensure compliance with emission standards, consent conditions, and other statutory requirements, the regulators—the Boards or the relevant government department—usually select one or more of the following regulatory tools.

First, Boards have the power to issue directions to any person bound by law to comply with them.[57] This power is broadly worded, and the directions could be of any nature, including for closure of the regulated entity or stoppage of electricity or water supply.[58] The Environment (Protection) Act gives similar powers to the central government, and these powers have been delegated to the CPCB in case of violations of notified general emission standards under the EP Rules and other standards.[59] Apart from polluting entities, the CPCB can also issue directions to SPCBs under the Air Act directing them to initiate measures in their jurisdictions.[60]

Second, a polluting entity may be directed to forfeit a bank guarantee deposited by it. This mechanism is not mentioned in the Air Act or the Environment (Protection) Act, but as a non-punitive condition, the National Green Tribunal (NGT) has upheld its validity.[61] Boards include a condition in consents directing regulated entities to deposit bank guarantees which may then be forfeited in part or full in case of default.[62] Bank guarantee is also used to ensure time-bound implementation of pollution control measures. Boards calculate the guarantee amount after considering factors like the cost of pollution control equipment, annual turnover of entity or applicable consent fee.

Third, a polluting entity may be directed to pay environmental compensation. Although environmental compensation is not statutorily prescribed, the PCBs are increasingly adopting this route against polluting industries.[63] The CPCB, on directions of the NGT, has devised a formula for the calculation of environmental compensation.[64]

[56] CPCB, 'Final Document on Revised Classification of Industrial Sectors under Red, Orange, Green and White Categories' (29 February 2016) <https://mpcb.gov.in/sites/default/files/consent-management/CPCBCategorizationdirection.pdf>.

[57] Air Act (n 11) s 31A.

[58] Air Act (n 11) s 31A, explanation.

[59] MoEF, Notification S.O. 157(E) dated 12 February 1996.

[60] For instance, the letter dated 5 February 2014 from the Chairman, CPCB, to the Chairman of all SPCBs/PCCs <http://cpcb.nic.in/displaypdf.php?id=Q1BBLoJfRGlyLnBkZg==> (directions to install online emissions monitoring systems (CEMS) in seventeen categories of highly polluting industries).

[61] *State Pollution Control Board, Odisha v M/s Swastik Ispat Pvt Ltd* 2014 SCC OnLine NGT 13; *Tarun Patel v Chairman, Gujarat Pollution Control Board* 2014 SCC OnLine NGT 1383.

[62] Consent dated 27 April 2020 issued by Uttar Pradesh PCB <https://upocmms.nic.in/UPOCMMS/applicationProcessingDetails/openCerificate/2572643>.

[63] E.g., Letter dated 26 November 2020 from Chairman, CPCB to M/s Assam Petrochemicals Limited <https://cpcb.nic.in/openpdffile.php?id=UHVibGljYXRpb25GaWxlLzM5MzNfMTYwNjgyNTU3OF9tZWRpYXBob3RvMzE4MzUucGRm>.

[64] CPCB, 'Report of the CPCB In-House Committee on Methodology for Assessing Environmental Compensation and Action Plan to Utilize the Fund' (2019) <https://cpcb.nic.in/uploads/report-15.07.2019.pdf>.

The CAQM Act specifically gives the Commission the power to award environmental compensation in cases of crop residue burning.[65]

Fourth, criminal cases may be initiated in case of offences. Violations of certain provisions of the Air Act, the Environment (Protection) Act, and the CAQM Act are criminal offences, and a complaint must be filed in an appropriate criminal court. For instance, emissions exceeding permissible standards may constitute an offence.[66] The penalty could be in the form of imprisonment and/or fine.[67] However, this is not a preferred enforcement route.[68]

27.1.5 Judicial Discourse on Air Quality

Regulating through judicial directions has been an important feature of air quality governance in India for more than three decades. The Supreme Court, the High Courts, and the NGT have issued directions on various factors affecting air quality.[69] In 1991, the right to pollution-free air was expressly acknowledged by the Supreme Court as a fundamental right enshrined in Article 21 of the Constitution.[70]

The Supreme Court's most notable contribution to air quality governance is perhaps its direction that all public transport vehicles running on diesel in Delhi have to convert to CNG.[71] The decision led to chaos and protests across the city,[72] but by some estimates is considered to have brought down pollution levels in the city at least in the initial years.[73] The 1985 writ petition in which this direction was issued continues to be heard by the Court on different aspects of air quality. For instance, through judgments in this case in 2017[74] and then in 2018,[75] the Supreme Court upheld notifications that

[65] CAQM Act (n 26) s 15.

[66] Air Act (n 11) s 37.

[67] ibid ss 37–41. The Jan Vishwas (Amendment of Provisions) Act, 2023 amends several provisions of the Air Act, including those on offences and penalties. However, these amendments are yet to come into force.

[68] E.g., the Maharashtra State Pollution Control Board (SPCB) did not file any case under the Air Act in 2018–19. See Maharashtra Pollution Control Board, Annual Report 2018–19 at 95 <https://www.mpcb.gov.in/sites/default/files/about-us/annual-report/MPCB_AR_Eng16032020.pdf>; similarly, the Gujarat SPCB did not file any cases under the Air Act in 2020–21. See Gujarat Pollution Control Board, Annual Report 2020–21 at 231 <https://gpcb.gujarat.gov.in/uploads/AR_2020_21_ENGLISH.pdf>.

[69] E.g., *Bittu Sehgal v Union of India* (2001) 9 SCC 181; *Vivek Srivastava v Union of India* 2005 SCC OnLine All 1555; *Vardhaman Kaushik v Union of India* 2016 SCC OnLine NGT 4176.

[70] *Subhash Kumar v State of Bihar* (1991) 1 SCC 598; *MC Mehta v Union of India* (2004) 12 SCC 118.

[71] *MC Mehta v Union of India* (1998) 6 SCC 63.

[72] Anuj Bhuwania, 'The Case that Felled a City: Examining the Politics of Indian Public Interest Litigation Through One Case' (2018) 17 *South Asia Multidisciplinary Academic Journal* <https://doi.org/10.4000/samaj.4469>.

[73] Urvashi Narain and Alan Krupnick, 'The Impact of Delhi's CNG Program on Air Quality' (2007) Resources for the Future, Discussion Paper RFF DP 07-06 <https://media.rff.org/documents/RFF-DP-07-06.pdf>.

[74] *MC Mehta v Union of India* (2017) 7 SCC 243.

[75] *MC Mehta v Union of India* (2019) 17 SCC 490.

permitted only vehicles meeting higher emissions standards to be sold and registered in the country after a cut-off date.

Apart from vehicular pollution, two other sources of pollution in particular have come under the judiciary's scanner in recent years—bursting firecrackers and burning of crop residue. In a case filed in 2015 seeking mitigation of air pollution caused by various sources, the Supreme Court has passed significant orders, including prohibiting the manufacture of certain types of firecrackers,[76] permitting the use of only 'green crackers', and a ban on the bursting of firecrackers during Diwali in parts of the country.[77] Separately, the Court also recognized the rights of the residents of Delhi and neighbouring areas to breathe unpolluted air, and their right to the protection of health.[78]

The Supreme Court has issued several directions to government agencies to address the issue of air pollution in the NCR due to the burning of crop residue, primarily in the states of Punjab and Haryana. The Court at one point held every person—from the farmer burning the residue to the Chief Secretary of the state—individually liable to pay for the tortious act of burning, observing that farmers cannot jeopardize the life of a sizeable population.[79] Two days later, the Court softened its stance holding that punishing farmers cannot be the ultimate solution and that it was the duty of the central and state governments to provide support through basic facilities, modern equipment, and financial incentives to the farmers.[80]

The issue came up again before the Court through a fresh writ petition filed in 2020. The Court appointed a one-person committee of retired Justice Madan Lokur to monitor the situation of crop residue burning in Punjab, Haryana, Uttar Pradesh, and Delhi.[81] On the next date of hearing, the Court was informed that the government was considering legislation to tackle the problem of stubble burning. Considering this, the Court put its order setting up the Justice Lokur Committee in abeyance.[82] Subsequently, the first Ordinance setting up the CAQM was promulgated. With the CAQM issuing orders and directions on specific sources of pollution, including stubble burning, the Court appears to have taken a step back on this issue, for now, while directing 'both the State Governments to persuade the farmers and impress upon them not to set fire to stubble at least for a period of two weeks'.[83]

[76] *Arjun Gopal v Union of India* (2019) 13 SCC 523.

[77] *Arjun Gopal v Union of India* 2017 SCC OnLine SC 1203.

[78] *Arjun Gopal v Union of India* 2017 SCC OnLine SC 1071, para 70.

[79] *MC Mehta (Stubble Burning & Air Quality) v Union of India* (2020) 7 SCC 573.

[80] *MC Mehta (Stubble Burning & Air Quality) v Union of India* (2020) 7 SCC 581.

[81] *Aditya Dubey (Minor) v Union of India* WP (Civil) No 1135 of 2020, Order of 16 October 2020 (Supreme Court).

[82] ibid Order dated 26 October 2020.

[83] ibid Order dated 15 November 2021.

While the rights-based discourse has been an important part of environmental jurisprudence in India,[84] the formulation of the right to life has not been consistently applied in all air quality cases. For instance, in the *Oleum Gas* case,[85] the *Taj Trapezium* case,[86] and the relocation of heavily polluting industries outside Delhi case,[87] the Supreme Court has issued detailed directions in response to deteriorating air quality but does not refer to the right of the citizens to breathe clean air.

27.2 Challenges in Regulating Air Quality

As the preceding section reveals, every major source of air pollution in India is governed by a regulatory instrument. Regulatory agencies like the PCBs have been established for several decades, and they are empowered with a diverse set of regulatory instruments. The judiciary is (mostly) sympathetic to the cause of better air quality. Yet, the quality of air in most parts of India does not meet the prescribed NAAQS. There are several factors contributing to this dismal scenario. I discuss four of them here.

27.2.1 Weaknesses in the Regulatory Design

The Air Act and the Environment (Protection) Act, along with the rules and notifications issued under them, regulate a significant wedge of the emissions pie in India. Consent/approval granting processes are focal points in these legal instruments. There are at least two flaws in the design and implementation of these processes.

First, the consent-granting processes focus on the source of emissions, not the airshed receiving the emissions or the increased risk of exposure to pollutants. While hazardous air quality can create local hotspots, air is shared by a region defined by topographical and meteorological conditions. Air quality regulation in India does not address the problem at the airshed level. The institutional framework and the corresponding administrative and financial powers are based on geographical state boundaries or city limits. This makes regional planning complicated and unappealing to policymakers.

According to the EP Rules, the cumulative effect of emissions from all sources in an area should not exceed the relevant concentrations as stipulated in the NAAQS.[88]

[84] E.g., Lovleen Bhullar, 'The Judiciary and the Right to Environment in India: Past, Present and Future' in Shibani Ghosh (ed), *Indian Environmental Law: Key Concepts and Principles* (Orient BlackSwan 2019) 1.

[85] *MC Mehta (Shriram—Oleum Gas) v Union of India* (1987) 1 SCC 395.

[86] *MC Mehta (Taj Trapezium Pollution) v Union of India* (1997) 2 SCC 353.

[87] *MC Mehta v Union of India* (1996) 4 SCC 750.

[88] EP Rules r 3B.

Consents should therefore be granted to only those entities in an airshed whose combined effect does not exceed the NAAQS, as individual compliance of emission standards will not be sufficient. But while granting consents presently, SPCBs do not consider the ambient air quality, locally and in the region. Three years after the launch of the NCAP, carrying capacity studies planned under it were not completed in any of the non-attainment cities.[89]

Second, the emission standards are set through processes that are unclear and sub-optimal. Standard setting is a crucial part of the regulatory process, and it must reflect what is required to keep the air quality within acceptable standards. For this reason, emission standards need to be updated regularly, considering new sources, emerging evidence on pollutants, technology, and health impacts, and periodic data on local and regional air quality. The process must be procedurally robust to ensure high public acceptance, leading to potentially higher compliance. The processes presently in place leave much to be desired. In a 2017 order, the Supreme Court observed that the emissions standards for SOx and NOx had not even been set for thirty-five industries.[90] Of the seventeen most polluting industry categories, emission standards for eleven were not revised in more than a decade.[91] Apart from guidelines issued by the CPCB on location-specific stringent standards,[92] there is no document laying down how emission standards are designed,[93] and the process of emission standard setting is often non-transparent and non-consultative.[94]

Standard setting can be a hugely contested process. An excellent, though sobering, case study for this is the repeated pushing back of deadlines of the 2015 emissions norms for thermal power plants.[95] If implemented effectively, the norms could lead to drastic reductions in particulate matter, NOx and SOx emissions by 2026–27.[96] But the

[89] Centre for Research on Energy and Clean Air (CREA), 'Tracing the Hazy Air: Progress Report of the National Clean Air Programme (NCAP)' (2022) 23 <https://energyandcleanair.org/wp/wp-content/uploads/2022/01/NCAP-Report_Jan22_.pdf>.

[90] *MC Mehta v Union of India* (2017) 14 SCC 488, 494.

[91] CREA (n 89) 26.

[92] CPCB, Guidelines for Development of Location Specific Stringent Standards (2009).

[93] Ricardo India Pvt Ltd, 'A Review of the Process for Setting Industry-Specific Emission Standards in India' (2016) <https://shaktifoundation.in/report/review-process-setting-industry-specific-emission-standards-india/>.

[94] Shripad Dharmadhikary, 'Setting Environmental Standards Comparing Processes in Thermal Power Plants in India, US, and EU' (2017) 52(19) *Economic and Political Weekly* 93.

[95] Anubha Aggarwal, 'Environment Ministry Finalises Coal Thermal Power Plant Categories: What Does it Say About Emission Norms Compliance' *Down to Earth* (22 December 2021) <https://www.downtoearth.org.in/news/pollution/environment-ministry-finalises-coal-thermal-power-plant-categories-what-does-it-say-about-emission-norms-compliance-80795>.

[96] CSE, 'Status of Coal Power Stations in Delhi NCR Off Target' (CSE 2018) 3 < 0.97959800_1530874694_Off-Target—-Coal-Power-Plants-Status-Report-in-Delhi-NCR.pdf>; Sunil Dahiya and Lauri Myllyvirta, 'Health and Economic Impacts of Unabated Coal Power Generation in Delhi-NCR' (CREA 2021) 2 <https://energyandcleanair.org/wp/wp-content/uploads/2021/03/Health-and-economic-impacts-of-unabated-coal-power-generation-in-Delhi-NCR_Report-22nd-March-2021_Final-Report.pdf>.

government is willing to give a long rope to polluting power plants at huge environmental and health costs.

27.2.2 Capacity Constraints in Regulatory Institutions

Improving air quality in India depends significantly on the ability of the regulatory institutions to function effectively. Each source of pollution in India is governed by a different institutional framework—involving a multitude of national and sub-national actors. Each of these actors needs adequate capacity and appropriate capability to effectively discharge its mandate. In this section, I focus on the SPCBs.

Initially set up under the Water Act, the mandate of the Boards was enhanced through the Air Act and over the years, they have been given an expanding list of functions relating to other sources of environmental pollution like noise and waste. Several factors undermine the Boards' ability to discharge their statutory mandate.[97]

First, the composition of the Boards is problematic. Most Board members are government officials or represent government interests. State governments can nominate a maximum of three Board members to represent the interests of agriculture, fishery, industry, trade, labour, or any other interest.[98] Although 'any other interest' may be represented on the Board, representatives from academia, public health, civil society organizations, etc. are rarely nominated. The Air Act also requires the state government to ensure that at least two Board members have special knowledge and experience in air quality. Of the ten states in the Indo-Gangetic plains, only one SPCB (Uttarakhand) identified two such members with special expertise.[99] Apart from the lack of diverse views and expertise and the real possibility of conflict of interest in cases of polluting government agencies, there is also no evidence that the present structure of the Boards, with one or two full-time members, is a successful model for environmental regulators in India.[100]

Second, the quality of leadership—the chairperson and the member secretary—is a matter of serious concern. The leadership in several Boards does not have the basic educational qualifications and professional experience necessary to effectively lead a

97 Departmental Parliamentary Standing Committee on Science and Technology and Environment and Forests, '192nd Report on the Functioning of Central Pollution Control Board' (2008); Centre for Science and Environment, 'Turnaround: Reform Agenda for India's Environmental Regulators' (CSE 2009); Geetanjoy Sahu, 'Environmental Regulatory Authorities in India: An Assessment of State Pollution Control Boards' (TISS 2013).

98 Air Act (n 11) s 5(2).

99 Reply dated 23 September 2021 of the Uttarakhand SPCB to RTI application dated 30 August 2021 filed as part of a research project at CPR. Bihar and Chhattisgarh SPCBs identified government posts (not persons) on the board as air quality specialists.

100 Shibani Ghosh, 'The Environment' in Devesh Kapur and Madhav Khosla (eds), *Regulation in India: Design, Capacity, Performance* (Hart 2019) 203, 220; Sharachchandra Lélé, Priyanka Jamwal, and Mahesh Menon, 'Challenges in Regulating Water Pollution in India: Standards, Monitoring, Enforcement and Accountability' (2021) 56(52) *Economic and Political Weekly* 46, 49.

technical institution like the SPCBs.[101] In 2017, the Supreme Court expressed deep anguish at the attitude of state governments in making such appointments.[102] The ability of the top officials to perform is also affected by frequent transfers. For instance, the Haryana SPCB has had five chairpersons from January 2017 to September 2021, and the Punjab SPCB has had four member secretaries from September 2017 to November 2021.[103]

Third, a high number of vacancies in the SPCBs affects their performance.[104] This issue has been highlighted in several reports, including in a comprehensive assessment undertaken by the CPCB and submitted to the NGT in 2020.[105] The CPCB reported that of the 9,438 sanctioned posts across all SPCBs, 4,342 posts were vacant—that is 46 per cent vacancy. For the CPCB, the vacancy number stands at 15 per cent.[106] In 2021, the NGT directed Chief Secretaries of all states to ensure that vacancies in the SPCBs are filled forthwith and specifically held that its order may be construed as overriding any contrary administrative order.[107] The extent of compliance of this direction is not known.

27.2.3 Flawed Policy-Making

Flaws in regulatory design and institutional capacity constraints are aggravated by *ad hoc*, non-deliberative, and non-participative policy-making. Policy-making around air quality has been mostly reactionary—mainly in response to judicial orders. A major flaw has been the treatment of air pollution as an environmental problem that is to be dealt with by environmental departments. The current regulatory framework does not, for instance, consider the massive economic and health costs of air pollution. Total exposure reduction is not a stated objective.[108] At the same time, myopic policy-making is leading to *ad hoc* technical fixes (like those for crop residue burning) while

[101] Several examples were highlighted by NGT in *Rajendra Singh Bhandari v State of Uttarakhand & Others* 2016 SCC OnLine NGT 456.

[102] *Techi Tagi Tara v Rajendra Singh Bhandari* 2017 SCC OnLine SC 1165.

[103] Reply dated 15 September 2021 of the Haryana SPCB to RTI application dated 1 September 2021; reply dated 18 November 2021 of the Punjab SPCB to RTI application dated 1 September 2021 (as part of a research project at CPR). See Shibani Ghosh and others, 'The State of India's Pollution Control Boards: Who is at the Helm?' (CPR 2022).

[104] It is noteworthy that the number of posts currently sanctioned is unlikely to be adequate for the Boards to discharge their broad mandate, and there needs to be a reassessment of staff requirements.

[105] Report of the Performance Audit of State Pollution Control Boards/Pollution Control Committees in compliance with an NGT Order (*Aryavart Foundation v M/s Vapi Green Enviro Ltd* 2021 SCC OnLine NGT 4).

[106] Lok Sabha Unstarred Question No 2746—Vacancies in Central and State Control Boards; Answered On: 6 March 2020.

[107] *Aryavart Foundation* (n 105).

[108] Ministry of Health and Family Welfare, 'Report of the Steering Committee on Air Pollution and Health Related Issues' (2015) <https://main.mohfw.gov.in/sites/default/files/5412023661450432724_0.pdf>.

procrastinating about difficult policy choices on minimum support prices and crop diversification.[109]

The focus of air quality policies has been the NCR, in part because of the Supreme Court's regular monitoring through the *MC Mehta* case and the EPCA's special mandate. While undoubtedly the NCR suffers from severe air pollution for several weeks in the year, many other parts of the country experience similar, or worse, levels of pollution but do not receive as much political, public, or judicial attention.[110] Baseline data of air quality is not available for vast parts of the country. India needs 1,600–4,000 air quality monitors, but there were only 804 as of September 2021, and most of these are in the urban areas;[111] and even urban areas are grossly under-monitored.[112]

The NCAP is an explicit recognition of the air pollution crisis in the country, but its focus on the non-attainment cities is problematic. It overlooks the regional nature of the problem and excludes urban areas that may not be covered by the existing monitoring network and non-urban areas. State Action Plans envisaged under the NCAP that could potentially address these lacunae did not materialize in any state as per the timeline prescribed in the NCAP.[113] Further, there are no interim targets or markers to assess the progress of the national-level PM concentration reduction target, even assuming this number is adequate from a public health point of view. Three years after the launch of the NCAP, little progress had been made in terms of air quality improvements in the country.[114] Analyses of city action plans reveal that many do not contain basic information, are identical for different cities, and will need significant strengthening for ground-level impacts.[115]

[109] Bhargav Krishna and Shibani Ghosh, 'Bad Air: Ad hocism won't Work Anymore' *Hindustan Times* (24 December 2021) <https://www.hindustantimes.com/opinion/bad-air-ad-hocism-won-t-work-anymore-101640282173777.html>.

[110] Anumita Roychowdhury and Avikal Somvanshi, 'Winter Air Pollution in Cities of Madhya Pradesh and Chhattisgarh' (CSE 2021) <https://www.cseindia.org/Central-India-air-pollution-analysis-note-Jan3.pdf>.

[111] Tanvi Deshpande, 'India doesn't have Enough Air Quality Monitors to Show the True Extent of Pollution in the Country' *Scroll.in* (19 December 2021) <https://scroll.in/article/1012865/india-doesnt-have-enough-air-quality-monitors-to-show-the-true-extent-of-pollution-in-the-country>.

[112] Anumita Roychowdhury and Avikal Somvanshi, 'Breathing Space: How to Track and Report Air Pollution Under the National Clean Air Programme' (CSE 2020) 21.

[113] Ritwick Dutta and Kankana Das, 'Neither Action nor Plan' (LIFE 2021) <https://ncaptracker.in/wp-content/uploads/2021/09/State-Action-plan.pdf>.

[114] PTI, 'Minimal or No Improvement in Air Pollution Levels, Ghaziabad Most Polluted: NCAP Report' *ThePrint* (10 January 2022) <https://theprint.in/india/minimal-or-no-improvement-in-air-pollution-levels-ghaziabad-most-polluted-ncap-report/800056/>.

[115] Tanushree Ganguly, LS Kurinji, and Sarath K Guttikunda, 'National Clean Air Programme (NCAP) for Indian Cities: Review and Outlook of Clean Air Action Plans' (2020) 8 *Atmospheric Environment: X* 100096.

27.2.4 Hard Regulation is Not Enough

India has typically regulated emissions from sources through 'hard' regulation—consent management, compliance with emission standards, monitoring, and enforcement action. But when sources of pollution are deeply linked with people's life choices and economic aspirations, hard regulation is not enough to bring down the pollution levels. In such situations, policy measures need to nudge behavioural changes[116] in an environmentally positive direction and incentivize the adoption of alternatives. We see this clearly in the context of several pollution sources.

The government has been trying to de-incentivize crop burning by providing financial support and subsidies for technical solutions like happy seeders, creating market value for the stubble, and issuing prohibitory orders. Yet burning the residue remains the most economically viable option for farmers.[117] Increasingly, research suggests that solutions have to incorporate the farmers' points of view and develop strategies to convince them to adopt alternatives to crop burning—through upfront financial transfers, awareness campaigns on crop diversification, use of technology, and health impacts of crop burning, or using the peer group as an example.[118]

Burning biomass for cooking and heating is a major source of household and ambient air pollution. A straightforward solution is to provide households with access to cleaner fuel like LPG. Through the PMUY, LPG connection has reached eight million households. However, the subsidy on LPG was rolled back in May 2020, and there is a risk that the gains of the scheme may be lost as beneficiaries revert to using traditional fuels.[119] Therefore, the sustained usage of LPG depends on continued affordability and accessibility of LPG. But alongside this, people's willingness to overcome personal and cultural preferences and overlook easier access to (free) biomass are important factors to consider.[120]

[116] See generally Richard H Thaler and Cass R Sunstein, *Nudge: Improving Decisions about Health, Wealth, and Happiness* (Yale University Press 2008).

[117] Chetan Bhattacharji, 'Delhi Drowns In Smog while Rural Punjab Farmers Burn Rice Stubble As Subsidies Discourage Alternative Crops' *Health Policy Watch* (17 November 2023) < https://healthpolicy-watch.news/as-delhi-drows-in-smog-rural-punjab-farmers-burn-rice-stubble-as-subsidies-discourage-alternative-crops/>

[118] Kelsey Jack and others, 'How to Get Farmers to Not Burn Crop Residue' *The Indian Express* (13 October 2021) <https://indianexpress.com/article/opinion/columns/paying-farmers-stubble-burning-pollution-7566129/>; L S Kurinji and Srish Prakash, 'Why Paddy Stubble Continues to be Burnt in Punjab? Meeting Challenges with Solutions' (CEEW 2021) <https://www.ceew.in/sites/default/files/ceew-study-on-paddy-stubble-burning-in-punjab-and-how-to-solve-challenges-with-solutions.pdf>.

[119] Santosh Harish, 'Air Quality Management in India at the Crossroads' (2021) 56(52) *Economic and Political Weekly* 38, 43.

[120] Sunil Mani and others, 'State of Clean Cooking Energy Access in India: Insights from the India Residential Energy Survey (IRES) 2020' (CEEW 2021) <https://www.ceew.in/sites/default/files/ires-report-on-state-of-clean-cooking-energy-access-in-india.pdf>.

Individual behavioural choices can play a significant role in air quality improvement.[121] But these decisions are influenced by several considerations—awareness of health impacts, affordability and accessibility of alternatives, availability of reliable infrastructure like buses and waste management facilities, and guilt caused by public pressure. Reform measures in the regulatory space need to be supported by an informed citizenry willing to make difficult behavioural choices.

27.3 Pathways for Reform

India was an early mover on a national air quality law, but as in other areas of environmental regulation, poor implementation, competing policy imperatives, lack of political salience, and conflicting interests have meant the law has been a failure. The chapter identifies key features of the regulatory architecture and some of the important challenges in air quality governance. But where do we go from here?

Legal amendments can address certain types of regulatory failure. Assuming the political viability of amendments being passed by Parliament, air quality regulation—broadly defined—will benefit from amendments that, in effect, introduce three reforms. First, regional or airshed-level governance mechanisms. There are hooks in the existing framework for inter-agency coordination across jurisdictions. However, a clear acknowledgement in law and the creation of statutory mechanisms to undertake coordinated planning and implementation at the airshed level is likely to provide a stronger impetus for effective measures. The CAQM Act was an opportunity for the government to do so. Instead, it restricted the CAQM's jurisdiction to the region around Delhi. However, CAQM's experience could provide a useful reference point for future legal amendments.

Second, markers of progress in the law and subsequent notifications that are defined in terms of environmental and health outcomes—for example, improvement in ambient air quality across a region (not just fewer 'severe' AQI days), reduction in exposure, fewer hotspots, decrease in COPD cases, etc. Progress can also be measured in terms of increased transparency in the system. Decision-making processes of regulators and their outcomes, monitoring data, and information submitted for regulatory compliance—all this should be actively and regularly disclosed in the public domain.

Third, nimbleness in the law that allows regulators to respond appropriately while being cognizant of institutional constraints and adapting to emerging science and technology. As an illustration, SPCBs should have the flexibility to adopt a graded enforcement protocol, allowing them to come down heavily, but certainly, on the few most

[121] Navroz K. Dubash, Shibani Ghosh, and Radhika Khosla, 'Air, An Election Issue' *The Indian Express* (20 April 2015) <https://indianexpress.com/article/opinion/columns/air-an-election-issue/>; Anumita Roychowdhury, 'Diwali: Nudge Practice of Not Tolerating Personal Harm' *Down to Earth* (14 November 2020) <https://www.downtoearth.org.in/blog/air/diwali-nudge-practice-of-not-tolerating-personal-harm-74241>.

egregious offenders on the top of the pyramid of offenders and lightly on first-time offenders with minimal environmental impact. This could act as a deterrent for future polluters and reduce monitoring costs.

Perhaps the low-hanging fruit for regulatory reform is strengthening the institutional framework. Government agencies, in particular SPCBs, need to fill sanctioned posts rapidly with competent people. Several reports, including the 2020 CPCB assessment, have revealed most Boards do not face financial constraints. They need to undertake staff adequacy assessments and initiate the process of creating more posts where necessary.

The four major sources of air pollution in India have to be tackled in parallel for there to be significant improvement in air quality.[122] It will require government agencies, in collaboration with civil society groups and other private actors, to prioritize policy actions. This will have to keep in mind the costs involved, institutional capabilities, potential impact (particularly on vulnerable groups), and political and social acceptability. Agencies across the spectrum—from the Environment Ministry to the urban local bodies—need to develop internal technical capacity and access external expertise to deal with specific sources of pollution through a deliberative and technically sound process.

Air pollution is an all-year-round, nation-wide public health crisis in India. It is caused by a multitude of factors, each of which is influenced by a different set of regulatory actors and measures. There is no silver bullet that can solve this wicked problem, but a strengthened regulatory apparatus is certainly a step in the right direction.

Suggestions for Further Reading

Joshua S Apte and Pallavi Pant, 'Toward Cleaner Air for a Billion Indians' (2019) 116(22) *Proceedings of the National Academy of Sciences* 10614.

Tanushree Ganguly, LS Kurinji, and Sarath K Guttikunda, 'National Clean Air Programme (NCAP) for Indian Cities: Review and Outlook of Clean Air Action Plans' (2020) 8 *Atmospheric Environment: X* 100096 <https://doi.org/10.1016/j.aeaoa.2020.100096>.

Shibani Ghosh, 'The Environment' in Devesh Kapur and Madhav Khosla (eds), *Regulation in India: Design, Capacity, Performance* (Hart 2019) 203.

Santosh Harish, 'Air Quality Management in India at the Crossroads' (2021) 56(52) *Economic and Political Weekly* 38.

Anamika Pandey and others, 'Health and Economic Impact of Air Pollution in the States of India: The Global Burden of Disease Study 2019' (2021) 5(1) *The Lancet Planetary Health* e25.

[122] Navroz K. Dubash and Sarath Guttikunda, 'Delhi has a Complex Air Pollution Problem' *Hindustan Times* (22 December 2018) <https://www.hindustantimes.com/india-news/delhi-has-a-complex-air-pollution-problem/story-xtLhB9xzNYeRPpoKBf9WGO.html>.

CHAPTER 28

CLIMATE CHANGE

Policy, Institutional, and Legal Framework

NAVROZ KERSI DUBASH, ADITYA VALIATHAN PILLAI, AND ANIRUDH SRIDHAR

Abstract

Transforming towards a low-carbon, climate-resilient society will require reimagining existing governance arrangements. This chapter documents how India's policies, institutions, and legal structures have changed in response to climate change. These developments have been opportunistic in character, with policy changes preceding institutional development. Policies are many and widespread, therefore, but lack strategic coherence. A more deliberate approach would bring with it enhanced governance requirements, including new structures for coordination, deliberation, and strategy-setting. This chapter pays attention to the prospects for climate law in India in this context, discussing different approaches to constructing firmer legal foundations for climate action.

Introduction

Addressing climate change poses major governance challenges due to the all-encompassing scope of the problem. Because modern economic processes are highly dependent on fossil fuel use, reducing greenhouse gases (or mitigation) requires reversing this dependency in areas as diverse as electricity production, industry, urbanization, transport, agriculture, and household consumption. Moreover, climate impacts will diminish development prospects through more extreme weather events (like storms, droughts, wildfires, and heat waves) and disruptions to water and agriculture systems, among other effects, unless appropriate adaptation and mitigation measures are undertaken.

These mitigation and adaptation challenges will require envisioning new forms of state capacity to direct transitions towards a low-carbon and climate-resilient future while simultaneously protecting the most vulnerable. This will likely require far-reaching changes in laws, policies, and institutions across countries. At a minimum, countries will have to consider building capabilities for long-term thinking, cross-government coordination, and the political management of disruptive change.

Over the past decade, India has seen shifts in its approach to climate governance. Somewhat counter-intuitively, policies have expanded while changes in climate-relevant institutions have been minor and uneven. Climate policies arose from opportunistic development-oriented objectives with additional mitigation synergies—such as energy security, energy efficiency or air pollution abatement, and, more recently, policies focused on green industrialization.

The logic of opportunism follows directly from adherence to the long-held principle of Common but Differentiated Responsibilities and Respective Capabilities (CBDR-RC) in the United Nations Framework Convention on Climate Change (UNFCCC), which India advocated for and helped cement.[1] By this principle, developed countries bear greater responsibility for causing, and therefore solving, climate change. Policies are consequently geared towards development objectives that may bring mitigation gains rather than outright decarbonization.

This opportunistic approach has meant a generally marginal role for purpose-built climate institutions. After early efforts at creating a bespoke institutional framework proved short-lived, India's climate policies have largely operated within a patchwork of pre-existing environmental and energy laws.

This *ad hoc* pursuit of climate policies through the filter of development objectives, here referred to as climate opportunism, is being tested in three ways. First, the need for coordinated, strategic action is becoming apparent in some areas, particularly in industrial policy for green technologies. 'Green growth' is now seen as a national objective.[2] Second, the proliferation of climate policies nationally and subnationally over the last decade challenges overall policy coherence. Third, the costs of climate change are becoming hard to ignore: the Intergovernmental Panel on Climate Change (IPCC)'s Sixth Assessment Report projects worsening near and long-term climate impacts—which makes adaptation urgent and raises the question of whether a more stringent

[1] Chandrashekar Dasgupta, 'Present at the Creation: The Making of the Framework Convention on Climate Change' in Navroz K. Dubash (ed), *India in a Warming World: Integrating Climate Change and Development* (OUP 2019) 142.

[2] Government of India, 'Budget 2022–2023: Speech of Nirmala Sitharaman, Minister of Finance' (1 February 2022) <www.indiabudget.gov.in/doc/budget_speech.pdf>.

approach to low-carbon transformation is needed.[3] Given these shifts, is the current legal and institutional landscape adequate?

The structure of this chapter mirrors the arc of Indian climate governance, whose evolution has been led by policies rather than institutions. Section 28.1 identifies key moments and significant trends in an expanding policy landscape. Section 28.2 probes the corresponding institutional framework upon which these policies are built, showing that it has lacked durability and impact over three decades. In Section 28.3, we turn to the prospects for climate law, a nascent conversation that holds deeply contrasting futures for the Indian climate effort. To conclude, we reflect on whether India needs new laws and institutions in this changing context.

28.1 An Expanding Climate Policy Landscape

Climate policies—an umbrella term covering all actions with climate effects, even if conceived for non-climate reasons—have proliferated nationally and subnationally over the last decade. This happened against the backdrop of global climate negotiations under the UNFCCC. Though India has consistently emphasized the differentiated responsibilities of developed and developing countries in the climate sphere, its policy-making is nonetheless impacted by both international and domestic drivers.

The National Action Plan on Climate Change (2008), for example, was formulated in response to international pressures as a set of tightly scripted, sectorally delimited actions shaped foremost by India's development imperatives.[4] It was established ahead of the Copenhagen Conference of Parties (COP) in 2009, where India issued its first pledge to decrease its emissions intensity (emissions per unit of GDP) by 20–25 per cent from 2005 levels by 2020.[5] The NAPCC laid out eight policy 'missions': solar power, energy efficiency, and forests for mitigation; water, agriculture, and Himalayan conservation for adaptation; and cities and knowledge, relevant to both mitigation and adaptation. The missions were led by nodal ministries but with links to related ministries to facilitate coordination.

This policy expansion was a diplomatic shift: whereas India had previously been resistant to signalling openness to domestic mitigation actions—which it saw as the

[3] Aditya Valiathan Pillai, Mandakini Chandra, and Sharon Mathew, 'IPCC Report on Climate Impacts Sounds Alarm Bells for India, South Asia' (Centre for Policy Research 2022) <https://environmentality.cprindia.org/blog/ipcc-report-on-climate-impacts-sounds-alarm-bells-for-india-south-asia>.

[4] Navroz K. Dubash and Shibani Ghosh, 'National Climate Policies and Institutions' in Navroz K. Dubash (ed), *India in a Warming World: Integrating Climate Change and Development* (OUP 2019) 329.

[5] Anjali Jaiswal, 'India Records Its Climate Actions by Copenhagen Accord Deadline' *Natural Resources Defense Council Expert Blog* (1 February 2010) <www.nrdc.org/experts/anjali-jaiswal/india-records-its-climate-actions-copenhagen-accord-deadline>.

responsibility of the developed world—it now enshrined in the NAPCC the idea of 'co-benefits' driving climate policy. The Plan notes that the approach would 'promote ... development objectives while also yielding co-benefits for addressing climate change effectively'.[6]

This had two significant governance ramifications. First, it allowed the state to formally consider climate policies and assign bureaucratic personnel to their pursuit.[7] Second, it prompted the national government to turn to the states, resulting in many states preparing a State Action Plans on Climate Change (SAPCC) developed by state governments but remaining close to a template prescribed by the central government.[8] These plans reflected the central government's diplomatic priorities by underplaying mitigation and focusing on adaptation.[9] Significantly, neither the NAPCC nor the SAPCCs were bound by law; they arose from executive actions in the Prime Minister's Office (PMO) and the Ministry of Environment, Forest and Climate Change (MoEFCC or the environment ministry) respectively.

The framework laid out in these plans has now been overtaken by a growing, organically evolved stock of climate policies. In its 2021 biennial update to the UNFCCC, India reported thirty-nine national mitigation policies spanning energy, agriculture, forestry, and transport.[10] Only some of these are housed within the NAPCC; most are driven by the developmental priorities of various ministries, leading to a policy sprawl.[11] Significantly, this sprawl suggests a broad definition of 'climate policy', consistent with global practice, to include both policies intended to achieve climate outcomes as well as those motivated by developmental objectives but with complementary climate effects.[12]

These policies, among other objectives, focus on subsidizing and scaling up new technologies and efficiency practices with clear economic benefits, such as generating jobs, reducing the cost of electricity, and improving energy security. Significantly, their intended effect is to limit the increase in future emissions rather than reduce current emissions, consistent with India's global position and domestic priorities.

[6] Government of India, National Action Plan on Climate Change (2008) s 3.

[7] Dubash and Ghosh (n 4).

[8] Ministry of Environment, Forest and Climate Change, 'Towards a Common Framework for Preparation of State Level Strategy and Action Plans on Climate Change', *National Consultation Workshop*, New Delhi (19 August 2010) <http://moef.gov.in/wp-content/uploads/2018/01/Experts-SAPCC-Preeti.pdf>.

[9] Navroz K. Dubash and Anu Jogesh, 'From Margins to Mainstream?: State Climate Planning in India as a "Door Opener" to a Sustainable Future', Climate Initiative (Centre for Policy Research 2014) < www.cprindia.org/research/reports/margins-mainstream-state-climate-change-planning-india-door-opener-sustainable>.

[10] Government of India, 'India: Third Biennial Update Report to the United Nations Framework Convention on Climate Change' (Ministry of Environment, Forest, and Climate Change 2021) <http://folk.uio.no/roberan/ind/india_proj201709.shtml>.

[11] ibid. India counts all policies with emissions or resilience benefits, even if incidental, as climate policies in its Biennial Update Reports to the UN.

[12] Navroz K. Dubash and others, 'Chapter 13: National and Sub-National Policies and Institutions' in *Climate Change 2022: Mitigation of Climate Change* (Intergovernmental Panel on Climate Change 2022).

The maturation of low-carbon technologies has led to a politically attractive 'green growth' framing that focuses on creating jobs and wealth. The national government's policy-making approach has consequently taken a more strategic turn, with a raft of interlocking policies meant to stimulate industrial growth. This includes generous subsidies for the manufacture of renewables and electric vehicles, protectionist tariffs for solar manufacturers, and attempts at developing a more robust financial system for green technology.

Despite an early focus on adaptation, India's states are now an increasingly important force in mitigation policy. A large and growing stock of renewable energy and electric vehicle policies are the most noticeable trend in recent years;[13] actions also cover areas like demand management and efficiency, afforestation, and building codes.[14]

The states are central to adaptation because they are responsible for a host of related policy domains under the Constitution of India, 1950, like agriculture and water.[15] The first set of adaptation-oriented SAPCCs were prepared with varying levels of adherence to the underlying science,[16] and, in some cases, amounted to a wish list of policies and infrastructure of unknown climate salience. The states have been asked by the MoEFCC to update their plans (states like Gujarat, Himachal Pradesh, and Haryana have updated theirs, while others like Kerala and Madhya Pradesh are in the process of doing so at the time of writing); it is too early to tell if these new SAPCCs will have greater impact than the previous round.

This spread of climate policies is supported by a growing but unevenly distributed pool of climate finance. State support for climate plans has been minimal, with state and national action plans receiving little to no additional funding beyond routine budgetary allocations for implementing departments.[17] However, the scope and complexity of market-driven financial instruments for mitigation has increased (particularly for renewable energy), supported by state guarantees, foreign capital, and government-backed funds.[18] While mature technologies are successfully being scaled with private capital (like renewables and electric vehicles), there is a deficit in less financially attractive areas that require state support, such as research and development for future

[13] Energy Policy Tracker, 'India' <https://www.energypolicytracker.org/country/india/>; Arunesh Karkun, 'Can EVs Solve India's Air Pollution Crisis?' (*Environmentality*, 9 December 2021) <https://environmentality.cprindia.org/blog/can-evs-solve-the-air-pollution-crisis>.

[14] Nehmat Kaur and Jarnail Singh, 'Driving Climate Action: State Leadership in India' (The Climate Group 2019).

[15] Aditya Valiathan Pillai, Navroz K. Dubash, and Parth Bhatia, 'Unlocking Climate Action in Indian Federalism' (Centre for Policy Research 2021).

[16] Vineet Kumar, 'Coping with Climate Change: An Analysis of India's State Action Plans on Climate Change' (Centre for Science and Environment 2018).

[17] Elizabeth Gogoi, 'India's State Action Plans on Climate Change: Towards Meaningful Action' (Oxford Policy Management 2017); Aditya Valiathan Pillai and Navroz K. Dubash, 'The Limits of Opportunism: The Uneven Emergence of Climate Institutions in India' (2021) 30 *Environmental Politics* 93.

[18] Gopal K Sarangi, 'Green Energy Finance in India: Challenges and Solutions' (ADB Institute 2018) 863 <www.adb.org/sites/default/files/publication/446536/adbi-wp863.pdf>.

technologies, including those that tackle hard-to-abate industrial emissions, the scale-up of scientific capacity for adaptation, and climate-resilient infrastructure, among others. New institutions and policies will be required to shape incentives and balance financial flows.

This continually expanding base of domestic policies, technologies, and investments has afforded India the diplomatic room to put forward steadily more ambitious international pledges. In Paris in 2015, India enhanced its Copenhagen emissions intensity target of 20–25 per cent reduction from 2005 levels by 2020 to a pledge of 33–35 per cent reduction by 2030 and added a significant jump in non-fossil generation capacity and an expansion of forest cover for the Paris Agreement in 2015.[19] In 2022, India upgraded its Nationally Determined Contribution (NDC), committing to a 45 per cent reduction in emissions intensity and to half its installed power capacity being non-fossil fuel-based by 2030, and a net-zero target by 2070.[20]

This scan of Indian climate policies suggests that policymaking has steadily expanded from the contained, if porous, vessel of the NAPCC. Consistent with an expansive construct of what constitutes climate policymaking, these policies emerge opportunistically from sectoral ministries and states with a mix of objectives and approaches. We now turn to how India has fared in building complementary institutional foundations and whether and how these may be needed for a more focused approach.

28.2 India's Climate Governance Framework

India's 'climate institutions', defined as the bodies, processes, and laws that give rise to climate action and structure its ambitions, have waxed and waned at the national level and have failed to take root in the federal system. They played an important role in the early phase of climate policymaking from 2009 to 2013 but have been mainly bypassed since. Policymaking has responded instead to bureaucratic and political priorities in individual ministries, the PMO, and agencies such as the NITI Aayog, the government's influential policy think tank.

[19] Government of India, 'India's Intended Nationally Determined Contribution: Working Towards Climate Justice' <https://nmhs.org.in/pdf/INDIA%20INDC%20TO%20UNFCCC.pdf>.

[20] Press Information Bureau (Government of India), 'Cabinet Approves India's Updated Nationally Determined Contribution to be Communicated to the United Nations Framework Convention on Climate Change' (3 August 2022) <https://pib.gov.in/pib.gov.in/Pressreleaseshare.aspx?PRID=1847812>.

28.2.1 The Evolution of Indian Climate Institutions

The evolution of Indian climate institutions over three decades has been substantially shaped by India's emphasis on differentiated responsibility for mitigation action globally. This approach has led to a scattered, opportunistic pursuit of co-benefits at the expense of a climate-focused institutional structure. The result is a loosely structured institutional network, with climate nodes spread across various ministries, knit together by unstable coordination and strategy bodies (Figure 28.1).[21] These institutions have worked with the grain of long-standing bureaucratic priorities of sectoral growth, stable energy prices, and energy security, rather than by creating new incentives or imposing costs.

The evolution of Indian climate institutions can be divided into four phases, each marked by a shift in underlying political context.[22] The first period, between 1992 and 2007, involved only the environment and foreign ministries, which coordinated around international climate summits to defend India's developmental space. Some important institutional foundations were laid in this period in the form of the national Clean Development Mechanism Authority under the environment ministry and two energy-related acts (the Energy Conservation Act, 2001 and the Electricity Act, 2003, discussed further below), which helped unlock low-carbon policies and infrastructure in subsequent decades.

In the second period, in the build-up to the Copenhagen COP between 2007 and 2009, a new phase of institution-building began in response to shifts in global climate politics, as developed countries placed pressure on large developing countries to announce more ambitious mitigation policies. India, by then seen as an emerging power alongside China, constituted the Prime Minister's Council on Climate Change (PMCCC), led by the prime minister and composed of several ministers and leading civil society organizations and think tanks. The body was to establish a national strategy for climate action. This led to the creation of the NAPCC, discussed earlier. In addition, a Prime Minister's Special Envoy for Climate Change was appointed to coordinate India's international positioning and domestic policy, including drafting the NAPCC and navigating the progress of its solar and energy efficiency missions through the bureaucracy.

In the third period, from 2009–14, the centre of gravity shifted to the Ministry of Environment and Forest (MoEF, with 'climate change' added to the title in 2014), with the appointment of a proactive new environment minister. This led to a change in negotiation strategy, with suggestions of more ambitious international pledges publicly opposed by former negotiators, opposition parties, civil society, and the PM's Special Envoy. The institutional conflict between the office of the Special Envoy and the MoEF led to the closure of the Special Envoy position in 2010.

[21] Dubash and Ghosh (n 4).

[22] For further details and underlying sources for these four periods, see Pillai and Dubash (n 17) s 3: 'Evolution of Climate Governance'.

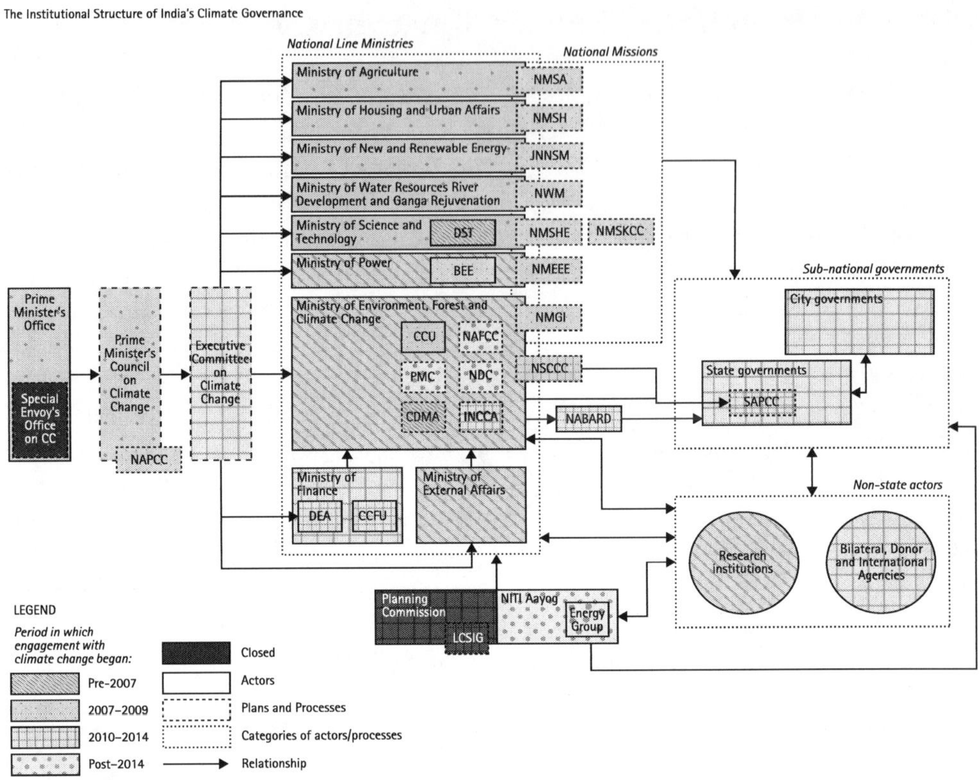

List of abbrevations

BEE	Bureau of Energy Efficiency	NAPCC	National Action Plan on Climate Change
CC	Climate Change	NDC	Nationally Determined Contribution
CCFU	Climate Change Finance Unit	NMEEE	National Mission on Enhanced Energy Efficiency
CCU	Climate Change Unit	NMGI	National Green India Mission
CDMA	Clean Development Mechanism Authority	NMSA	National Mission for Sustainable Agriculture
DEA	Department of Economic Affairs	NMSH	National Mission on Sustainable Habitat
DST	Department of Science and Technology	NMSHE	National Mission for Sustaining the Himalayan Ecosystem
INCCA	Indian Network on Climate Change Assessment	NMSKCC	National Mission on Strategic Knowledge for Climate Change
JNNSM	Jawaharlal Nehru Solar Mission	NSCCC	National Steering Committee on Climate Change
LCSIG	Expert Group on Low Carbon Strategies tor Inclusive Growth	NWM	National Water Mission
NABARD	National Bank For Agriculture And Rural Development	PMU	Project Management Unit
NAFCCC	National Adaptation Fund on Climate Change	SAPCC	State Action Plan on Climate Change

Source: Compiled by the authors

FIGURE 28.1 *The evolution of India's climate governance institutions in four periods* (Source: Compiled by the authors based on Navroz K. Dubash and Shibani Ghosh, 'National Climate Policies and Institutions' in Navroz K. Dubash (ed), *India in a Warming World: Integrating Climate Change and Development* (OUP 2019) 329).

The MoEF spearheaded a significant expansion of climate policies by introducing the SAPCCs, a long-term low-carbon plan under the erstwhile Planning Commission (NITI Aayog's predecessor) and a new climate science network. It also considered embedding performance targets for the NAPCC in a climate law.

Yet, while the MoEF is responsible for climate change under the Allocation of Business Rules that defines ministerial responsibilities, it lacks the bureaucratic clout to move larger ministries such as finance and power. Other organizations, such as the PMO for coordination, the foreign ministry for negotiations, and the Planning Commission (later NITI Aayog) for knowledge played key roles during the period. In part due to bureaucratic tensions, many of the MoEF's initiatives, except for the SAPCCs, were short-lived.

A governance vacuum emerged, with the MoEF losing its expansionary impulse after the leadership change and with the PM's Special Envoy, which had usefully wielded the imprimatur of the PMO in climate decision-making, no longer functional. To coordinate the implementation of the sprawling NAPCC in this context, a committee of senior bureaucrats headed by the Principal Secretary to the Prime Minister, called the Executive Committee on Climate Change (ECCC), was created in 2013.

The fourth period, from 2014 to the present, typifies the paradox of proliferating climate policies without the institutional bindings to tie them into a coherent whole. The core institutional elements of previous periods, the PMCCC and the ECCC, met infrequently in this period. Decision-making has defaulted to regular venues, such as the PMO, ministries, and the NITI Aayog (notably for electric vehicles and battery technology). In 2020, this structure was supplemented by the Apex Committee for the Implementation of the Paris Agreement (AIPA), led by the MoEFCC.[23] It is unclear whether this body wields adequate power to influence decisions in other ministries.

Across these four periods, it is worth noting that policies have been shaped by para- and non-state actors. For example, the PMCCC saw the active participation of leading think tanks and media representatives in its early agenda-setting years. Similarly, the private sector and consultants have played a role in shaping electricity and transport policy. Large state-owned companies play a pivotal role in India's rapid build-out of renewables. Yet, external inputs are sporadic, *ad hoc* and vary by sector in the absence of permanent deliberative institutions.

28.2.2 The States in Climate Policymaking

The division of powers in the Constitution places several important areas of climate action in the jurisdiction of the states (such as water, health, land, and local administration), making them indispensable in effective climate governance. States have experimented in areas such as electric vehicles, energy efficiency, renewable energy, and afforestation, as well as institutionally with new climate change departments (Orissa and Gujarat), councils (Maharashtra), and even public companies (Tamil Nadu) to implement climate programmes.

This activity is mostly the result of uncoordinated bottom-up impulses. The most visible federal coordination mechanism is the SAPCC, thirty-three of which were

[23] Press Information Bureau (Government of India), 'Government Constitutes High-Level Ministerial Committee for Implementation of Paris Agreement' (2 December 2020) <https://pib.gov.in/PressReleaseIframePage.aspx?PRID=1677630>.

mandated and approved by the national government.[24] Climate-specific federal co-ordination institutions do not exist; coordination is instead limited to existing sectoral forums in areas like water and electricity.[25] Underlying this framework are questions about tensions between cooperative and coercive approaches to climate federalism in India's highly centralized federal structure. For example, a proposed 2022 amendment to the Electricity Act, 2003 would have forced states to comply with minimum renewable energy purchase targets established by the central government under threat of penalty,[26] and a proposed national net-zero law for 2050 might carry implications for the division of responsibility of such targets to states.[27] Legal amendments are further discussed in the next section.

28.2.3 Functional Attributes of Indian Climate Institutions

This thinly institutionalized framework raises a fundamental question: if policies are proliferating, does climate change really require new governance structures? A partial response is that while *ad hoc* policies might somewhat limit Indian emissions and result in some adaptive gains, the transformational change needed for low-carbon development and climate resilience may require a more deliberate approach.

Specifically, climate change presents three pressing and complex governance challenges to the state: in areas of coordination, consensus building, and strategy development.[28] First, because climate change demands economy-wide emission outcomes, governments will need to coordinate across several policy areas; for example, the coal, renewable, and financial sectors will need to be coordinated while maintaining energy security. This also applies to resilience, where, for example, siloed sectors like transport, health, and energy will need to be brought into alignment in planning for extreme events. Box 28.1 lists India's coordination institutions.

Second, these transitions will inevitably create political losers, such as coal miners and internal combustion engine workers, who have the potential to disrupt or reinforce the transition. Institutions can usefully mediate these political shifts by designing deliberative bodies that allow losers to be heard and compensated. India has had no dedicated consensus-building institutions.

Third, long-term transition requires an analytically sound strategic approach, with adequate consideration of the synergies and trade-offs between climate change and

[24] Government of India, 'India: Third Biennial Update Report to the United Nations Framework Convention on Climate Change' (n 10).

[25] Pillai, Dubash, and Bhatia (n 15).

[26] Electricity (Amendment) Bill, 2022 [187 of 2022].

[27] Climate Change (Net Zero Carbon) Bill, 2021 [41 of 2021].

[28] Navroz K. Dubash and Others, 'National Climate Institutions Complement Targets and Policies' (2021) 374 *Science* 690.

Box 28.1 India's Coordination Institutions (*italicized entries represent institutions that are no longer functional*) (Source: Compiled by authors based on Aditya Valiathan Pillai and Navroz K. Dubash, 'The Limits of Opportunism: The Uneven Emergence of Climate Institutions in India' (2021) 30 *Environmental Politics* 93):

1. *Prime Minister's Office. Established the position of a Special Envoy for Climate Change (2007–10) to lead India's multilateral engagement on climate change and, by extension, spearhead development of India's NAPCC.*
2. Executive Committee for Climate Change (2013–present). A body of senior bureaucrats, led by the Principal Secretary to the Prime Minister, meant to coordinate the implementation of the NAPCC, particularly by coordinating across ministries jointly implementing 'missions'.
3. Apex Committee for Paris Agreement (2020–present). An inter-ministerial coordination body helmed by the Environment Ministry, focused on coordinating NDC implementation.
4. Ministry of Environment, Forests and Climate Change (formalized in 2014). Lead agency for climate policymaking under the Allocation of Business Rules, which allocates responsibilities to ministries.
5. Climate cells, small implementation and coordination units established in ministries. Responsible for implementing 'missions' in solar energy, energy efficiency, Himalayan protection, etc., under the NAPCC.
6. NITI Aayog: Plays a role in executing multi-ministerial actions in important long-term areas of policy intervention, such as electric vehicles and battery development.

development. The specialized nature of this task calls for dedicated and permanent institutions in government capable of thinking through long-term goals and international commitments, tracking development and climate outcomes, and updating strategies and targets. Box 28.2 lists India's strategy-setting institutions.

Boxes 28.1 and 28.2 reveal an absence of consensus-building institutions. Traditionally, policymaking within the co-benefits approach has occurred at the ministerial level, with consultations occurring within sectors but not at the level of national strategy.[29] But because policies have thus far been oriented towards conferring benefits rather than imposing costs, Indian institutions have not had to deal with political losers, the need for which will likely increase with more stringent decarbonization targets and more severe climate impacts. The column on coordination captures a variety of institutional experiments and an uneasy balancing act involving the PMO and the

[29] Pillai and Dubash (n 17).

Box 28.2 India's Strategy-setting Institutions (*italicized entries represent institutions that are no longer functional*) (Source: Compiled by authors based on Aditya Valiathan Pillai and Navroz K. Dubash, 'The Limits of Opportunism: The Uneven Emergence of Climate Institutions in India' (2021) 30 *Environmental Politics* 93):

1. *Prime Minister's Council on Climate Change (2007–15). A body chaired by the prime minister, ministers, and several civil society representatives; responsible for envisioning and ratifying the NAPCC and its missions. Stopped intervening after NAPCC establishment.*
2. *Planning Commission. Published documents that attempted to place climate change in India's overall developmental strategy, particularly the Low Carbon Strategy for Inclusive Growth (2014).*
3. *Prime Minister's Special Envoy for Climate Change, as part of Prime Minister's Office. Played a role in establishing the architecture of the NAPCC.*

environment ministry in negotiating bureaucratic tussles. Finally, there are no active institutions for strategy-setting.

This institutional history raises questions: how do we make institutions more resilient? How do we mainstream climate priorities in quotidian governance? What standards of accountability must be created? We turn to the idea of climate law next, an area of governance growing in prevalence globally in response to climate challenges.

28.3 Prospects for Climate Law

Globally, climate laws have proliferated since 2007. There has been a surge both in direct laws—whose primary objective is to contend with climate change—and indirect laws—that bear incidentally on mitigation and/or adaptation—from 342 in 2010 and 558 in 2015 to 694 laws as of 2020.[30] Depending on country context, these laws differ in their primary objective, which can be green growth, directly regulating emissions or adaptation. Their form can also vary and is often shaped by national context—laws designed for emission regulation may take a different form to those designed to facilitate green growth in developing contexts.

Law, as an instrument, has certain unique virtues in dealing with the climate governance challenges previously discussed. Through the legislative process, laws become the most formalized expressions of political will among a people, allowing laws to at once

[30] Dubash and others (n 12).

dictate, authorize, and make acceptable transformative government action, orchestrate cooperation, and enforce accountability while remaining resilient to political change. Notably, the most tenacious climate institutions are often those invested with the authority of law.[31]

In India, however, there are almost no direct climate laws or cases.[32] This, and the fact that climate policies have not had an organizing force or unifying vision, has led to many pressing climate governance challenges remaining unfulfilled. Nevertheless, certain laws and judgments that indirectly or partially affect climate governance are worth discussing as concrete starting points for the progression of climate law in India. And as the conversation and scope for a climate law widen—with private member's bills and reports calling for direct legal intervention in climate change—it is also important to identify the potential pathways that climate law could take in the country. In this context, we will also discuss the existing laws that can be amended to serve certain important climate governance roles and the all-encompassing and globally popular framework law, which has also received some traction in India in recent years.

28.3.1 Climate Change in Statutes and Case Law

While a climate law has not yet been passed in India, there are existing laws with other objectives that nonetheless perform certain roles salient to governance and policymaking in climate-relevant arenas.

Examples of statutory instruments that demonstrate capacity for climate governance are briefly discussed below:[33]

- The Electricity Act, 2003, established a framework for the development of the power sector in India, requiring the preparation of a regularly updated National Electricity Policy and National Tariff Policy based more on the optimization of existing resources—which includes coal, natural gas, nuclear, hydrogen, and renewables—than low-carbon opportunities. Yet, in part driven by the Act's 'promotion of efficient and environmentally benign policies',[34] it includes explicit

[31] Alina Averchenkova, Sam Fankhauser, and Jared J Finnegan, 'The Impact of Strategic Climate Legislation: Evidence from Expert Interviews on the UK Climate Change Act' (2020) *Climate Policy* 1; Eloise Scotford and Stephen Minas, 'Probing the Hidden Depths of Climate Law: Analysing National Climate Change Legislation' (2019) 28 *Review of European, Comparative & International Environmental Law* 67.

[32] A direct climate case, analogous to a direct law, is one whose judgment directs a measure specifically to contend with climate change.

[33] Most examples are drawn from Chandra Bhushan and Tarun Gopalakrishnan, 'Environmental Laws and Climate Action: A Case for Enacting a Framework Climate Legislation in India' (iForest 2021); and from the authors' analysis of the Climate Change Laws of the World Database <climate-laws.org/geographies/india>.

[34] See Electricity Act, 2003, preamble.

provision for low-carbon opportunities by, for instance, mandating distribution licensees to purchase a specified minimum of their requirements from renewable sources (known as Renewable Purchase Obligations).

- The Energy Conservation Act, 2001, established measures to promote energy efficiency, including energy audits for designated consumers, conservation codes for buildings, and energy labels for notified appliances. A subsequent amendment established an energy efficiency trading certificate mechanism to incentivize companies to invest in energy-use reduction.[35] An amendment in 2022 builds the legal foundations for the trading of carbon credits and further expands energy conservation levers in buildings, manufacturing, and transport.[36]
- The Clean Energy Cess Rules imposed in 2010 a cess on domestic and imported coal, out of which a National Clean Energy and Environment Fund was crafted for promoting research on renewable energy and technology—these were issued under the Finance Act, 2010.[37]
- The Disaster Management Act, 2005, bears most significantly on adaptation. Section 2(d) comprehensively defines a disaster as 'a catastrophe, mishap, calamity or grave occurrence in any area, arising from natural or man-made causes', including extreme weather events that could now be classified as climate events. The government had previously assumed a relief-based role in disasters, but with this Act came an additional focus on prevention. The Act aims through the institution of National and State Disaster Management Authorities and Funds to prevent, build capacity for, reduce risk and severity of, and reconstruct after disasters.
- The Compensatory Afforestation Fund Act, 2016, recognizes 'carbon sequestration' and 'flood moderation' as environmental services provided by forests and aims to establish a framework for the funding of compensatory afforestation.[38] There are also legal checks on deforestation, such as the Forest (Conservation) Act, 1980, which establishes a mandatory clearance process before forest land is diverted for other uses.[39]
- Given section 3(3) of the Environment (Protection) Act, 1986, permits the central government to establish new authorities to carry out its functions under the law, it was used to create an Apex Committee for Implementation of the Paris Agreement in 2020.[40] In addition, a judgment of the National Green Tribunal (NGT) reasoned that greenhouse gases (GHGs) would fall within the definition of a pollutant

[35] Energy Conservation (Amendment) Act, 2010 s 7.

[36] Energy Conservation (Amendment) Bill, 2022.

[37] In 2017, this cess (and fund) was renamed and repurposed for GST compensation. From the amount collected from the cess prior to 2017, a very small portion has been spent on green energy research and promotion.

[38] Compensatory Afforestation Fund Act, 2016 s 2(e)(ii).

[39] Forest (Conservation) Act, 1980 s 2.

[40] Press Information Bureau, 'Government Constitutes High-Level Ministerial Committee for Implementation of Paris Agreement' (2 December 2020) <https://pib.gov.in/pib.gov.in/Pressreleasesh are.aspx?PRID=1677630>.

in the Act.[41] Although the application itself was dismissed, that GHGs would be considered pollutants in common law is significant.

- The National Green Tribunal Act, 2010, which invested the NGT with jurisdiction over all civil cases turning on a substantial question of the environment, has used its authority on multiple occasions to pronounce on matters concerning GHGs.[42] The NGT can become an instrument of accountability and enforcement if India makes a significant foray into direct climate law.

In the parlance of climate law, however, many of these laws—with some exceptions such as the Energy Conservation (Amendment) Bill that explicitly refers to carbon credits—would be termed indirect climate laws: laws that have the capacity to affect mitigation or adaptation through the decision-making arenas they regulate though that is not their primary intent. But given the scale of the problem, they do not, perhaps, constitute a sufficient legal infrastructure to tackle climate change.

Besides statutes, courts can also produce a body of jurisprudence that impacts and becomes a part of climate law. Generally, the hooks for climate litigation internationally have been civil codes and constitutional and common law, read against the standard of international law and commitments under the UNFCCC and NDCs. Ghosh states that in India, '[w]hile there have been cases where courts have referred to climate concerns, there is yet to be a judicial decision on the justiciability of climate claims, or one that directs measures specifically for mitigation or adaptation'.[43] And given the separation of powers, courts are unlikely to pronounce on matters infringing on the government's plans for energy and the economy unless they can be shown to impinge on rights. But given India's abundant rights-based environmental jurisprudence and the judiciary's inclination to refer to international law and broadly worded statutory provisions, there are several potential hooks for climate litigation.

Judges have already interpreted the right to the environment into the Indian constitution—particularly from Articles 21, 48A, and 51A(g).[44] In *Indian Council for Enviro-legal Action v MoEFCC*, the judge proclaimed it a right, based on the Articles mentioned above, to demand steps be taken for protection from global warming.[45] The rights claim is apt to feature more in cases where climate adaptation is an explicit issue. Though there has not yet been a judgment based on India's internationally facing policies, *Hanuman Laxman Aroskar v Union of India* did mention India's NDCs while discussing strengthening the environmental rule of law in India.[46] There is also an NGT order—*Society for Protection of Environment and Biodiversity v Union of India*—that

[41] *Indian Council for Enviro-legal Action v MoEFCC*, Original Application No. 170/2014, Judgment of 10 December 2015 (NGT—Principal Bench).

[42] Shibani Ghosh, 'Climate Litigation in India' in Francesco Sindico and Makane Moïse Mbengue (eds), *Comparative Climate Change Litigation: Beyond the Usual Suspects* (Springer 2021) 357.

[43] ibid 357.

[44] ibid.

[45] Indian Council for Enviro-legal Action (n 41).

[46] *Hanuman Laxman Aroskar v Union of India* 2019 SCC OnLine SC 441.

found a regulatory exemption for a high-emitting industry in derogation of India's responsibilities under the Paris Agreement.[47] Seen together, though, climate case law in India bears on climate change as indirectly as its statutes. But judgments like the *Indian Council for Enviro-legal Action* and its discussion of GHGs indicate that the courts can, in the future, play a significant role in scaffolding the regulatory edifice of Indian climate governance.

28.3.2 Future Directions for Climate Law

A nascent conversation on new and direct climate law has emerged in India in recent years. In 2015, a private member's bill was introduced to Parliament, which had as its main purpose the setting of annual carbon budgets by the central government, the institution of a climate advisory body, and the integration of existing climate-relevant laws.[48] Subsequently, in 2021, another private member's bill on climate change, drawing on the design of the UK and New Zealand climate acts, proposed setting a net-zero target and dividing the labour of mitigation among sectors and subnational governments.[49] Also in 2021, a premier law school in India proposed a report and recommendation for a Climate (Protection) Bill, which focused exclusively on adaptation.[50] Arguably, no bill has yet been proposed that addresses both mitigation and adaptation and in a manner consistent with the Indian context and India's approach to climate change, as discussed further below. Besides bills, there have been reports assaying the climate competence of existing laws in India[51] and op-eds calling for an enabling framework law.[52]

But before writing climate change explicitly into Indian law, it is important to study how climate law can answer specifically to the Indian context. One general approach to taking the national context seriously is to focus on the climate governance functions that laws could help fulfil in any context, noting that the manner of fulfilment may vary based on the national legal context. These functions include high-level direction-setting; integration of disparate laws and policies to complement efforts; mainstreaming of climate considerations into key line ministries, subnational governments, and policy processes; the collection of information and production of knowledge necessary to

[47] *Society for Protection of Environment and Biodiversity v Union of India* Original Application No. 677/2016, Judgment of 8 December 2017 (NGT—Principal Bench).

[48] See Climate Change Bill, 23/2015.

[49] See Climate Change (Net Zero Carbon) Bill, 148/2021.

[50] ibid.

[51] Bhushan and Gopalakrishnan (n 33).

[52] Anirudh Sridhar, 'Designing a Climate Law for India' *Hindustan Times* (24 August 2021) <www.hindustantimes.com/opinion/designing-a-climate-law-for-india-101629800791590.html>; Anirudh Sridhar, 'In India's Climate Law, Focus More on Process, Less on Outcomes' *Hindustan Times* (25 August 2021) <www.hindustantimes.com/opinion/in-india-s-climate-law-focus-more-on-process-less-on-outcomes-101629893051858.html>.

make rational choices; the mobilization of finance for climate infrastructure and action; and oversight and accountability.[53]

Future climate law in India might usefully focus on these governance functions, given that most, if not all, remain unfulfilled. There are two main paths forward to closing these gaps: a dispersed upgrade of existing laws or a framework law on climate change.

A dispersed upgrade can be thought of as a patchwork quilt approach, wherein existing laws with climate governance potential are identified and upgraded for purpose across all relevant sectors until a comprehensive design of climate governance is achieved. The amendment to the Energy Conservation Act represents an example of such an upgrade. If this becomes India's approach to climate law, it will require amendments in other arenas of climate action, such as adaptation, finance, measurement, reporting, and verification (MRV), and other gaps in climate governance functions. Below are a few upgrades that might be effected in due course.

To enhance knowledge and accountability, the MOEFCC's mechanism for evaluating the environmental harm of large-scale projects, the Environmental Impact Assessment (EIA) Notification, could be deployed for climate governance. The NGT has considered including climate change within the scope of the EIA Notification process.[54] Though the case was dismissed, the Environment (Protection) Act or Notification could yet be amended, or a new Notification could be issued, to mandate the compilation of, say, a Climate Change Impact Assessment report. In a similar vein, the Right to Fair Compensation and Transparency in Land Acquisition, Rehabilitation and Resettlement Act, 2013, requires a Social Impact Assessment study to be conducted before land acquisition. Climate change arguably already enters this equation indirectly through consideration of food security, wherein multi-cropped agricultural land (that happens to be more climate resilient)[55] is deemed the last resort for acquisition.[56] This Act can be amended to make climate change a more central consideration in land management. Also, in the ambit of accountability, the Air (Prevention and Control of Pollution) Act, 1981, and the Water (Prevention and Control of Pollution) Act, 1974, could be amended in concert to respectively classify GHGs as air pollutants and task the Central and State Pollution Control Boards with monitoring greenhouse gases.

There are also hooks in Indian law for mainstreaming climate considerations across sectors. The Indian Companies Act, 2013, for instance, could be amended after the fashion of the UK's Companies Act, 2006, to make mandatory the inclusion of a

[53] Anirudh Sridhar and others, 'Climate Law and Governance as Indicators of "Ability" to Implement the Paris Agreement' <https://unfccc.int/sites/default/files/resource/202202281725_GST_19_CMA1_Proposal_Climate_Law_and_Governance_0.pdf>.

[54] (2017) SCC OnLine NGT 187.

[55] Forest Isbell and others, 'Biodiversity Increases the Resistance of Ecosystem Productivity to Climate Extremes' (2015) 526 *Nature* 574.

[56] Right to Fair Compensation and Transparency in Land Acquisition, Rehabilitation and Resettlement Act, 2013 s 10.

GHG report for all listed companies.[57] The prospect of surveillance could result in a mainstreaming of climate considerations across industries. Similarly, the Real Estate Regulatory Authority established under the Real Estate (Regulation and Development) Act, 2016, which currently makes recommendations to the government on the environmental sustainability of buildings[58] could be amended to mainstream climate considerations into its recommendations. This would have the benefit of promoting an understanding of mitigation and adaptation possibilities in this sector.

This is merely a small sample of potential upgrades. Given the ever-changing nature of climate impacts across sectors and populations, a dispersed upgrade approach will have to be agile in response to new knowledge and relentless to close the widening gaps in climate governance. Such an approach might end up requiring tremendous legislative effort—the last time substantial amendments were made to the Air Pollution Act, for instance, was in 1987, indicating the obstacles to amending long-standing laws.

'Framework laws', on the other hand, create an overarching legal basis for climate action.[59] They are motivated by the fact that climate change involves almost all essential sectors of the state from energy, water, land-use, urban planning, transportation, and more. Framework laws, in one stroke, carry the potential of integrating past climate-relevant legislation, setting clear directions for the future, and creating necessary processes and institutions.[60] They have also been adept at establishing climate-specific MRV systems.[61] As regards mitigation, they can either pursue a 'target and implementation' approach or seek to 'mainstream climate objectives through sectoral plans and integrative institutions'.[62]

As discussed, there have been initial discussions, if embryonic, of pursuing a framework climate change law for India. Yet, there has been inadequate consideration of the overarching direction such a law might take and how it may be tailored to the Indian context. One oft-cited model is that of the UK, which decrees a cap on carbon emissions supported by regulatory functions to implement the said cap.[63] Another is an enabling

[57] This argument is also made by Nilesh Beliraya K, 'The Need of Introducing Mandatory Climate Change Risk Disclosure by Companies in India' (2022) *NLUJ Law Review Blog* < www.nlujlawreview.in/the-need-of-introducing-mandatory-climate-change-risk-disclosure-by-companies-in-india/>.

[58] Real Estate (Regulation and Development) Act, 2016 s 32(e).

[59] Michal Nachmany and Joana Setzer, 'Global Trends in Climate Change Legislation and Litigation: 2018 Snapshot' (London School of Economics and Political Science, Grantham Research Institute on Climate Change and the Environment, Centre for Climate Change Economics and Policy April 2018) <www.lse.ac.uk/GranthamInstitute/wp-content/uploads/2018/04/Global-trends-in-climate-change-legislation-and-litigation-2018-snapshot.pdf>.

[60] Averchenkova, Fankhauser and Finnegan (n 31); Dubash and others (n 12); Scotford and Minas (n 31).

[61] Catherine Higham and others, 'Accountability Mechanisms in Climate Change Framework Laws', *Grantham Research Institute on Climate Change and Centre for Climate Change Economics and Policy* (2021) <www.lse.ac.uk/granthaminstitute/wp-content/uploads/2021/11/Accountability-mechanisms-in-climate-change-framework-laws.pdf>.

[62] Dubash and others (n 12) 13–14.

[63] Averchenkova, Fankhauser, and Finnegan (n 31).

rather than regulating instrument, such as the 2010 South Korean Framework Act on Low Carbon, Green Growth, which set up an institutional infrastructure for green growth and low-carbon development;[64] the Peruvian law which attempts to build an inclusive climate governance architecture; and the Kenyan law, which focuses mainly on adaptation and climate finance.[65] These laws have attempted to address the national context first and build capacity from the bottom up through procedural rather than outcome duties.[66] Given an Indian climate change narrative that prioritizes the pursuit of development and mitigation synergies, and its store of thin institutions, the latter, enabling approach would seem a better starting point from which to tailor a framework law, if pursued, to the Indian context.

In light of the opportunistic layering of climate policies in India and the transient institutions they have inspired, an approach more unifying than a dispersed upgrade one, such as a framework law, might, in the long run, be necessary to identify collaborative potentials across and mainstream climate change within a range of siloed sectors in India.

Conclusion

Indian climate governance is at an important juncture. Opportunistic climate policymaking has been accompanied by halting, scarcely durable institutional layering. A turn toward a 'dispersed upgrade' of climate law would constitute a further layering in the legal realm. However, the context for policymaking is shifting. A narrative of strategic economic opportunity may slowly supplant the more static co-benefits narrative. In adaptation, strategically mainstreaming resilience as a governance priority is the next step as vulnerabilities become harder to ignore. But, strategic approaches to mitigation and adaptation carry far greater governance requirements than approaches adopted thus far. As discussed above, they, at minimum, require institutions for coordination, strategy-setting, and consensus-building.

This raises the prospect that India's legal and institutional structure unless also transformed, could limit the ambition and effectiveness of climate policymaking. If it is to be transformed, concerted layering and a more fundamental reset—with new climate institutions and laws—both remain possible pathways. The choice depends not just on design considerations but crucially on the extent of political consensus for

[64] Myungjun Jang, Jin-Ah Kim, and Soon-Tak Sun, 'Development and Evaluation of Laws and Regulation for the Low-Carbon and Green Growth in Korea' (2010) 14 *International Journal of Urban Sciences* 191.

[65] Olivia Rumble, 'Facilitating African Climate Change Adaptation through Framework Laws' (2019) 13 *Carbon and Climate Law Review* 237.

[66] Colin T Reid, 'A New Sort of Duty? The Significance of "Outcome" Duties in the Climate Change and Child Poverty Acts' (2012) 4 *Public Law* 749.

transformative change. Powerful new institutions, while carrying greater possibility, also risk being undone, but more layering is administratively burdensome and potentially discordant. Ignoring the institutional challenge, however, carries the risk of undercutting the effectiveness of future climate action in India.

Suggestions for Further Reading

Chandra Bhushan and Tarun Gopalakrishnan, 'Environmental Laws and Climate Action: A Case for Enacting a Framework Climate Legislation in India' (iForest 2021) <https://shaktifoundation.in/report/environmental-laws-and-climate-action-a-case-for-enacting-a-framework-climate-legislation-in-india/>.

Navroz K. Dubash and others, 'National Climate Institutions Complement Targets and Policies' (2021) 374 *Science* 690.

Shibani Ghosh, 'Climate Litigation in India' in Francesco Sindico and Makane Moïse Mbengue (eds), *Comparative Climate Change Litigation: Beyond the Usual Suspects* (Springer 2021) 347.

Aditya Valiathan Pillai and Navroz K. Dubash, 'The Limits of Opportunism: The Uneven Emergence of Climate Institutions in India' (2021) 30 *Environmental Politics* 93.

Anirudh Sridhar and others, 'Climate Governance Functions: Towards Context-specific Climate Laws' (Centre for Policy Research and Grantham Research Institute, LSE 2022) <https://cprindia.org/briefsreports/climate-governance-functions-towards-context-specific-climate-laws/>

CHAPTER 29

ENVIRONMENTAL DISASTERS AND CLIMATE CHANGE

BIRSHA OHDEDAR

Abstract

This chapter analyses the legal framework for environmental disasters in India in the context of intensifying climate impacts. The Disaster Management Act, 2005 (DMA) is the primary legal framework governing disasters. In addition, other areas of law, regulation and policy are relevant to each disaster, such as flood plain zoning legislation for floods. The links between these laws and the disaster management framework are significant in providing a coherent response to disasters. This chapter analyses the law and policy framework for environmental disasters through a broad lens by examining disaster-specific laws and broader environmental law and policy. The chapter first analyses the DMA and outlines the institutional and policy framework it produces. It then examines laws relating to specific disasters, such as floods and droughts. Finally, a case study is provided of coastal disasters, which outlines the challenges in coordinating a coherent framework to respond effectively to disasters.

Introduction

Environmental disasters are a regular feature across India.[1] For instance, between 2015 and 2020, cyclones have increased by 32 per cent; during this period, many parts

[1] UNDRR, 'Disaster Risk Reduction in The Republic of India: Status Report 2020' (United Nations Office for Disaster Risk Reduction, Regional Office for Asia and the Pacific 2020).

of the country have also been experiencing drought conditions and seen a marked increase in forest fires.[2] During the monsoon, wet and dry spells have become increasingly intense.[3] Significant gas leaks, oil spills, and toxic pollution also manifest into environmental disasters that differentially affect human and non-human life.[4] Climate impacts are also intrinsically linked to environmental disasters. Climate change will increase the frequency and magnitude of droughts, floods, sea-level rise, wildfires, and other potential events that risk becoming disasters.[5] Often, such disasters are framed as 'natural' disasters. However, this does not mean that their causes, consequences, and impacts are entirely 'natural'. As disaster scholarship has argued, there is nothing 'natural' about natural disasters.[6] Social, political, and economic relations embedded in the law drive and co-produce the catastrophic consequences in uneven and differentiated ways.[7]

The legal framework for environmental disasters in India consists of laws and policies from several areas. Legislation is crucial for 'mainstreaming' disaster risk reduction into development planning.[8] The law can play an important role in placing responsibilities on government agencies and ministries to act. Policies also play a significant role in directing state actions, providing more specific and detailed guidance for decision-makers. A starting point is the Disaster Management Act, which is comprehensive

[2] Neha Madan, '32% Rise in Number of Cyclones in Past 5 Years: IMD' *The Times of India* (13 November 2019) <https://timesofindia.indiatimes.com/india/32-rise-in-number-of-cyclones-in-past-5-years-imd/articleshow/72031005.cms>; Shagun Kapil, 'Drought Watch: More than 44% of India Now Suffers' *Down to Earth* (17 June 2019) <https://www.downtoearth.org.in/news/climate-change/drought-watch-more-than-44-of-india-now-suffers-65127>; Dakshiani Palicha, 'Forest Fires in India: Alerts since April 1 Nearly Double That of 2020' *Down to Earth* (19 April 2021) <https://www.downtoearth.org.in/news/forests/forest-fires-in-india-alerts-since-april-1-nearly-double-that-of-2020-76559>.

[3] Deepti Singh and others, 'Observed Changes in Extreme Wet and Dry Spells During the South Asian Summer Monsoon Season' (2014) 4 *Nature Climate Change* 456.

[4] Recent examples in India include: 'India Gas Leak: At Least 11 Dead after Visakhapatnam Incident' *BBC News* (7 May 2020) <https://www.bbc.co.uk/news/world-asia-india-52569636>; Scroll, 'Tamil Nadu: At Least 2 Tonnes of Oil Spills into Sea Near Chennai After Tanker's Fuel Hose Snaps' *Scroll.in* (19 November 2018) <https://scroll.in/latest/902660/tamil-nadu-at-least-2-tonnes-of-oil-spills-into-sea-near-chennai-after-tankers-fuel-hose-snaps>.

[5] Valerie Masson-Delmotte and others, 'IPCC, 2018: Summary for Policymakers, Global Warming of 1.5°C. An IPCC Special Report on the impacts of global warming of 1.5°C above pre-industrial levels and related global greenhouse gas emission pathways, in the context of strengthening the global response to the threat of climate change, sustainable development, and efforts to eradicate poverty' (World Meteorological Organisation 2018) <https://www.ipcc.ch/site/assets/uploads/sites/2/2022/06/SR15_Full_Report_LR.pdf>.

[6] Jacob Remes, Kevin Gould, and Magdalena Garcia, 'Beyond "Natural-Disasters-Are-Not-Natural": The Work of State and Nature after the 2010 Earthquake in Chile' (2016) 23(1) *Journal of Political Ecology* 93; Paul J Govind and Robert RM Verchick, 'Natural Disaster and Climate Change' in Shawkat Alam and others (eds), *International Environmental Law and the Global South* (CUP 2015) 491–507.

[7] E.g., Remes, Gould, and Garcia (n 6); Daanish Mustafa, *Water Resource Management in a Vulnerable World: The Hydro-Hazardscapes of Climate Change* (IB Tauris 2013); Danny Marks, 'Assembling the 2011 Thailand Floods: Protecting Farmers and Inundating High-Value Industrial Estates in a Fragmented Hydro-Social Territory' (2019) 68 *Political Geography* 66.

[8] Anil Kumar Gupta, 'Disaster Governance and Legal Systems in India' in Indrajit Pal and Rajib Shaw (eds), *Disaster Risk Governance in India and Cross Cutting Issues* (Springer 2018) 39, 51.

legislation that institutionalized pre-disaster and post-disaster responses. Beyond the Disaster Management Act, there are laws and policies, at both the national and subnational levels, that are relevant to specific types of disasters. This chapter examines environmental disasters in India through a broad lens and goes beyond just disaster law and policy. It argues that analysis of disasters must focus on how different laws and policies interact in any disaster. The chapter also examines the gaps in the frameworks and challenges in implementing the law.

This chapter has four sections. Section 29.1 introduces the law and policy of environmental disasters. It examines the Disaster Management Act, relevant institutions, laws, and policies related to specific disasters, and the relevance of human rights and climate change policy. Section 29.2 then examines coastal disasters as a case study highlighting the issues and challenges in the legal frameworks for environmental disasters in India. The section specifically looks at the Sundarbans, one of the most climate-vulnerable coastal areas in the country. Section 29.3 provides a discussion and commentary on the themes from the preceding sections in the chapter. Finally, the chapter ends with a short conclusion.

29.1 Law and Policy of Environmental Disasters

Different areas of law and policy are relevant for any disaster that occurs. For instance, during a drought, the rules around water extraction are of particular concern. For an earthquake, building regulations and planning laws come into focus. This section surveys some of the areas of law that are relevant to environmental disasters. This is by no means comprehensive; rather, it gives a sense of the different types of laws and policies that can come into focus for different disasters.

29.1.1 Disaster Management Law

Historically, India's disaster management framework focused on post-disaster relief. Many states had 'relief codes' that were a hangover from the colonial relief-centric disaster regimes.[9] The Disaster Management Act, 2005 (DM Act) significantly departs from the old paradigm. The DM Act introduces a multi-level framework that links from the national to the district level. At the institutional level, several interlinked institutional bodies are established and tasked with specialized disaster management responsibility (see Table 29.1).

[9] Rajendra Kumar Pandey, 'Legal Framework of Disaster Management in India' [2016] *ILI Law Review* 172.

Table 29.1 Disaster Management Institutions

Institution	Level	Role
National Disaster Management Agency	National	Laying down policies on disaster management and guidelines which would be followed by different ministries, departments and state government
National Executive Council	National	Constituted to assist the National Disaster Management Agency in the performance of its functions. Wide-ranging role under s10 DM Act, including acting as the coordinating and monitoring body for disaster management, preparing a National Plan, monitoring the implementation of National Policy, etc.
National Institute of Disaster Management	National	Developing training, capacity building, education on disaster management. (Ss 42–43, DM Act)
National Disaster Response Force	National	Specialized force constituted for rescue, relief and response measures. (Ss 44–45, DM Act)
State Disaster Management Authority	State	Laying down policies and plans for disaster management in the State. (Ss 14–19, DM Act)
State Executive Council	State	Coordinating and monitoring the implementation of the National Policy, the National Plan and the State Plan. (Ss 20–24, DM Act)
District Disaster Management Authority	District	Planning, co-ordination and implementing body for disaster management at the District level and take all necessary measures for the purposes of DM in accordance with the guidelines laid down by the National Disaster Management Agency and State Disaster Management Authority (Ss 25–34, DM Act).

Source: Author

The DM Act also calls for the establishment of policies and plans at different governance levels (see Table 29.2).[10] Plans consist of the framework for mobilization and coordination of all spheres of disaster prevention, preparedness, response, and recovery. In other words, the plans provide granular details on disaster management actions that will be carried out.

The National Disaster Management Authority (NDMA) has also released several disaster-specific plans. These plans provide further information on the nature of specific types of disasters (e.g., cyclones, droughts, etc.) and the role and coordination required between different agencies in relation to those disasters. For instance, in relation to cyclones, the plans emphasize the need for early warning systems, communication and dissemination of cyclone warnings, coordination with the Indian Meteorological Department, best practices in relation to cyclone shelters, and other cyclone-specific actions.[11]

[10] DM Act ss 18, 23, 31

[11] National Disaster Management Authority, Government of India, 'National Disaster Management Guidelines: Management of Cyclones' (2008) <https://ndma.gov.in/sites/default/files/PDF/cyclone/cyclones.pdf>.

Table 29.2 Disaster Management Policies

Level	Policy
National	• National Policy on Disaster Management (2009) • National Disaster Management Plan (2016)
State	• State Disaster Management Policy
District	• District Disaster Managing Plan

Source: Author

Most importantly, the DM Act brings a holistic approach to disaster management, at least in comparison with what preceded it. The DM Act embeds an approach based on pre-disaster mitigation and post-disaster relief and recovery. It shifts the approach from the 'relief-centric' approach that preceded it. The National Disaster Management Plan includes measures for the prevention of disasters and the mitigation of their effects. It calls for the integration of these measures into development planning.[12] These reforms reflected a broader global shift in disaster management that focused on mitigation and also on the social causes of vulnerability. These are reflected in the Hyogo Framework for Action in 2005 and the Sendai Framework for Disaster Risk Reduction in 2015.[13] The National Disaster Management Plan also expressly links to the Paris Agreement and the Sustainable Development Goals. Overall, it reflects a significant step forward in how disasters are governed in India.

29.1.2 Laws Relating to Specific Disasters

As mentioned in the introduction, there are a variety of types of environmental disasters in India. While an exhaustive discussion of every disaster is out of the scope of this chapter, this section highlights some of the laws and policies relevant to two major environmental disasters: floods and droughts.

Floods: floods are a major environmental disaster in India, impacting millions of people every year. In 1976, the Ministry of Agriculture and Irrigation set up a national

[12] DM Act ss 11(3)

[13] The Sendai Framework for Disaster Risk Reduction 2015–30 is the leading international policy document. It lays out a voluntary pathway for the next fifteen years of disaster risk reduction. The Sendai Framework includes four priority areas, and seven global targets to assess global progress on disaster risk reduction. See: 'Sendai Framework for Disaster Risk Reduction 2015–2030' UN Doc A/CONF.224/CRP.1. Prior to the Sendai Framework, the Hyogo Framework for Action (2005–2015) was the leading international policy document on disaster reduction. See: World Conference on Disaster Reduction, Hyogo Declaration UN Doc A/CONF.206/6 (2005).

commission on floods, the *Rashtriya Bargh Ayog* (RBA), to examine India's flood control and response measures. The RBA made 207 recommendations and four broad observations.[14] Importantly, the RBA observed that it was not the increase in rainfall but the anthropogenic factors such as deforestation, drainage congestion, and development work that were the leading cause of flood-related devastation. Thus, it demonstrated a need for disaster management to focus on these key areas that exacerbated the scale and intensity of floods.

One key area is development activity in the floodplain zones of rivers. Floodplain regulation involved surveying areas adjacent to rivers and restricting development according to the vulnerability and frequency of flooding. This is a key strategy to minimize flood damage. Responsibility to regulate floodplains is under the purview of individual states.[15] However, the central government produced a model bill for floodplain zoning in 1975 for states to use as a starting point to create their own legislation.[16] Unfortunately, only Manipur, Rajasthan, Uttarakhand, and Jammu and Kashmir have enacted their own floodplain legislation to date.[17] Furthermore, implementation is a major issue even where legislation has been enacted, with the delineation and demarcation of the flood zone yet to be undertaken. In recent years, the issues of 'encroachment' and development on the flood plains have also come up in courts and tribunals. For instance, in 2015, the National Green Tribunal constituted a committee to produce norms relating to floodplain zoning and development in Odisha.[18]

Beyond restricting floodplain development, a common way of protecting communities from flooding has been structural interventions, such as building embankments. The basic idea of the embankment is to protect land from water. However, embankments have been widely criticized as a flood protection mechanism in India.[19] From a law and policy perspective, embankment laws are an area of law that has not undergone any fundamental changes in decades, despite vast technological, climatic, political, and social changes.[20] States are responsible for legislating on embankments,

[14] National Commission on Floods, 'Report of the Rashtriya Barh Ayog, Vol I' (Ministry of Energy and Irrigation, Government of India 1980).

[15] Both the regulation of land and 'drainage and embankments' are on the State List. Constitution of India 1950, List II, 17 and 18.

[16] Central Water Commission, 'Model Bill for Flood Plain Zoning, 1975' <https://www.ielrc.org/content/e7503.pdf>.

[17] Manipur Flood Plain Zoning Act, 1978; Uttarakhand Flood Plain Zoning Act, 2012; Rajasthan Flood Plain Zoning Act, 1990; and Jammu and Kashmir Flood Plain Zones (Regulation and Development) Act, 2005.

[18] *Dilip Kumar Samantaray v State of Odisha Board & Others* [2020] National Green Tribunal, Principal Bench, New Delhi 22/2020 (EZ).

[19] Rashmi Kiran Shrestha and others, 'Institutional Dysfunction and Challenges in Flood Control: A Case Study of the Kosi Flood 2008' (2010) 45(2) *Economic and Political Weekly* 45; Kuntala Lahiri-Dutt, 'Imagining Rivers' (2000) 35(27) *Economic and Political Weekly* 2395; Amitangshu Acharya, 'Engineering a Season of Floods' *Livemint* (18 November 2019) <https://www.livemint.com/mint-lounge/features/engineering-a-season-of-floods-11573832077930.html>.

[20] Philippe Cullet and Sujith Koonan, *Water Law in India: An Introduction to Legal Instruments* (2nd edn, OUP 2017) 288.

and they are often tied to irrigation laws. Some states, such as West Bengal, have embankment laws that are around 150 years old,[21] while others have legislated soon after independence.[22]A common theme is that the law gives significant powers to the state (namely the Irrigation Department) in building and maintaining embankments, with very little participation and accountability. This is discussed further in section 29.2 in relation to coastal flooding.

Water policy also has a role in managing floods. National Water Policy (NWP) in India puts an emphasis on flood forecasting, flood planning, and the need for flood plan zoning and floodproofing.[23] In recent years, there has also been a spotlight on the role of hydropower dams and related infrastructure in exacerbating the impacts of flooding.[24] Under the NWP, water storage projects should also provide for adequate flood cushioning, and in highly flood-prone areas, flood control should trump other considerations (such as electricity generation). However, the translation of these policies into state water policies has been patchy. For instance, in the aftermath of the Kerala floods in 2018, an official audit concluded that flood management provisions in the Kerala State Water Policy were inadequate and not in line with the NWP.[25] Finally, there are flood-specific guidelines that have been issued by the NDMA.[26] The guidelines, among other things, press state governments to implement flood plain zoning by legislation, as well as outline other measures to be taken by state governments.

Droughts: similar to floods, droughts have been a persistent feature in India in recent decades. Droughts will become more frequent and severe in the coming years as climate change intensifies across South Asia. As with floods, several different laws and policies can come into focus during a drought. The Disaster Management Act operates as an overarching governance framework. Individual states are primarily responsible for droughts since agriculture and water are both responsibilities of the state. However, the centre provides guidelines and norms that should be followed, although they are not binding as such. The Drought Management Manual ('Drought Manual') is the most important such document from a national perspective.[27]

21 E.g., Bengal Embankment Act, 1882; Bengal Irrigation Act, 1876.

22 E.g., Rajasthan Irrigation and Drainage Act, 1954.

23 Government of India Ministry of Water Resources, National Water Policy, 2012 s 10.

24 Prakash Kashwan and Neelima Vallangi, 'Hydropower Projects Are Wreaking Havoc in the Himalayas' *Al Jazeera* (19 March 2021) <https://www.aljazeera.com/opinions/2021/3/19/hydropower-projects-are-wrecking-havoc-in-the-himalayas>; SANDRP, 'Role of Dams in Kerala's 2018 Floods' (*SANDRP*, 4 October 2018) <https://sandrp.in/2018/10/04/role-of-dams-in-keralas-2018-floods/>.

25 Government of Kerala, 'Report of the Comptroller and Auditor General of India on Preparedness and Response to Floods in Kerala' (2021) 8 <https://cag.gov.in/uploads/download_audit_report/2021/Kerala_Au.I_Rep_6_2021-0618cb7f2db0035.98377057.pdf>.

26 National Disaster Management Authority, 'Guidelines on the Management of Floods' (2008) <https://ndma.gov.in/sites/default/files/PDF/Guidelines/flood.pdf>.

27 Department of Agriculture, Cooperation and Farmers Welfare, 'Manual for Drought Management' (Ministry of Agriculture and Farmers Welfare 2016) <https://agricoop.nic.in/en/divisiontype/drought-management>.

The Drought Manual provides guidance for state governments and agencies engaged in the prevention, mitigation, and management of droughts. A key area of concern has been the declaration of drought. The Drought Manual was first published in 2009. A revised version was published in 2016, to comply with a Supreme Court order, after several states failed to declare and respond adequately to drought.[28] The Drought Manual provides indices and parameters to guide decision-makers in declaring a drought. These include rainfall, agriculture, soil moisture, hydrology, and remote sensing. The rationale is to provide decision-makers with an objective criterion for declaring droughts. The revisions in 2016 are an attempt to move away from traditional crop-cutting methods as a parameter for drought declaration. The declaration of drought signifies the beginning of intervention and response. Thus, once a drought is declared, several plans and guidelines are provided by the centre to assist state and district authorities in their responses.[29] These plans assist with delineating responsibilities for different actors to respond to a drought situation so that droughts can be dealt with effectively.

The declaration of drought has often been a highly politicised decision. Both the state and central governments can delay or try to circumvent an official declaration to avoid providing compensation and relief.[30] Moreover, the level of severity (of drought) triggers whether there would be assistance from the centre or not. Despite the shift towards a standardized and objective set of parameters for drought declaration, the manual has proven controversial. For instance, several reports have stated it has become more difficult for a drought to be declared under the new parameters set by the 2016 revisions.[31] Meanwhile, the centre has also rejected drought declarations by states, meaning thousands of farmers were not able to gain adequate compensation and relief packages.[32] Accordingly, the relationship between the centre and the state is a key theme. Drought responses are primarily at the state level; however, the centre has an integral role in providing standards, guidelines, norms and for large-scale disasters, funding. The manual and guidelines are not binding on states and states remain the ultimate decision-makers. The Supreme Court, in *Swaraj Abhiyan v Union of India*, was

[28] *Swaraj Abhiyan v Union of India & Others* (2016) 7 SCC 498, para 109.

[29] These include the Crisis Management Plan and the Drought Management Plan. Both are available at: <https://agricoop.nic.in/en/divisiontype/drought-management>.

[30] Jitendra, 'Farmers Suffer as States yet to Declare Drought' (*Down to Earth*, 9 November 2018) <https://www.downtoearth.org.in/news/agriculture/farmers-suffer-as-states-yet-to-declare-drought-62079>.

[31] Nidhi Jamwal, 'India's Criteria for Classifying Drought-Hit Regions are Causing Many Cases to Go Unreported' (*Scroll.in*, 27 January 2018) <https://scroll.in/article/866262/indias-criteria-for-classifying-drought-hit-regions-are-causing-many-cases-to-go-unreported>; Jitendra (n 30); Jitendra, 'Why Is Karnataka Protesting Change in Definition of Drought?' (*Down to Earth*, 6 July 2017) <https://www.downtoearth.org.in/news/natural-disasters/why-is-karnataka-protesting-change-in-definition-of-drought—58229>.

[32] Sanjoy Dey, 'Centre Rejects Jharkhand's Drought Relief Proposal, No Compensation for 7 Lakh Farmers' *Hindustan Times* (19 July 2020) <https://www.hindustantimes.com/india-news/centre-rejects-jharkhand-s-drought-relief-proposal-no-compensation-for-7-lakh-farmers/story-ZqNr4invKWYPGJzRZiwWUJ.html>.

aware of the balancing act. The Court states that both the centre and the state must do more, and it orders the centre to revise the manual and various guidelines, but it is at pains to emphasize that it is not suggesting 'that the authority of the State Government to declare a drought of any other similar power is diluted'.[33]

Apart from drought-specific policies, several other areas of law and policy are significant during a drought. As livelihoods are severely impacted during a drought, the Mahatma Gandhi National Rural Employment Guarantee Act (MGNREGA) has been used in drought-prone regions to both provide jobs and carry out drought-prevention works.[34] The implementation of MGNREGA has been shown to increase rural wages, provide access to regular and predictable employment, reduce labour migration and decrease hunger.[35] Implementation is an issue however, and a lack of political will, administrative capabilities, and engagement with civil society in some states are seen as reasons for not succeeding.[36] Although results have been mixed, where it has been successfully deployed in drought-prone regions, it is a potentially transformational tool in both preventing and responding to drought.[37]

Similarly, the importance of water during a drought means rules around the extraction of groundwater are vital to prevent over-exploitation of water sources. However, groundwater laws in India have notoriously allowed for unbridled exploitation. The legal framework is still centred upon the common law right of landowners to access and control groundwater beneath their land, with very limited restrictions adopted in certain states.[38] Such a legal framework has thus contributed to worsening drought conditions. Even during a drought, a state government only has limited powers to restrict the rights of landowners to exploit.

Overall, each disaster has a number of laws and policies that are relevant. Both the centre and states have produced policies and guidelines that assist decision-makers in their responses. However, gaps remain in relation to implementation, enacting legislation in key areas (such as flood plain zoning or groundwater regulation), and the

[33] *Swaraj Abhiyan v Union of India & Others* (2016) 7 SCC 498, para 94.

[34] G Ram Mohan, 'Secure from Drought: How MGNREGA Changed Lives in Bandlapalli' *Down to Earth* (18 March 2021) <https://www.downtoearth.org.in/news/water/secure-from-drought-how-mgnrega-changed-lives-in-bandlapalli-75967>.

[35] Tanya Jakimow, '"Breaking the Backbone of Farmers": Contestations in a Rural Employment Guarantee Scheme' (2014) 41(2) *The Journal of Peasant Studies* 263, 278.

[36] Rachel Godfrey-Wood and Benjamin CR Flower, 'Does Guaranteed Employment Promote Resilience to Climate Change? The Case of India's Mahatma Gandhi National Rural Employment Guarantee Act (MGNREGA)' (2018) 36(S1) *Development Policy Review* O586; Puja Dutta and others, 'Right to Work? Assessing India's Employment Guarantee Scheme in Bihar' (World Bank Group 2014) <https://documents1.worldbank.org/curated/en/104331468266411269/pdf/Right-to-work-assessing-Indias-employment-guarantee-scheme-in-Bihar.pdf>.

[37] Jakimow (n 35) 279.

[38] Sujith Koonan, 'Revamping the Groundwater Legal Regime in India: Towards Ensuring Equity and Sustainability' (2016) 12(2) *Socio-Legal Review* 45.

relationship between the centre and state can be a challenge. Section 4 of this chapter, below, returns to some of these key themes.

29.1.3 Environmental Rights

Human rights are also central to disaster management frameworks. There is no legal departure from the state's obligations under human rights law when a disaster occurs.[39] The Sendai Framework states that disaster risk should be managed 'while promoting and protecting all human rights, including the right to development'.[40] In the Indian context, a wide range of social and environmental rights, such as water,[41] food,[42] and environment,[43] have been recognized by the Supreme Court under Article 21 of the Constitution.[44] The Court has reinforced the relevance of rights in disaster settings.[45] Environmental rights are relevant both before and after disasters. Rights are relevant to disaster risk reduction and preparation. After a disaster strikes, states have a duty to provide at least a bare minimum of food, water, shelter, clothing, and health services.

Environmental rights have both substantive and procedural content. For instance, in responding to disasters, substantive rights obligations relate to water, food, environment, and other rights. To this end, the NDMA has provided minimum relief standards.[46] However, states can make their own, more detailed norms and standards.[47] In the relief context, NGOs, charities, and humanitarian organizations play a vital role. Often, these actors have their own internal guidelines and norms relating to relevant rights.[48] However, it is important to remember that such actors are not the primary duty-bearers of human rights, and therefore, these do not substitute for the obligations on governments.

[39] Kristian Cedervall Lauta, 'Human Rights and Natural Disasters' in Susan Breau and Katja Samuel (eds), *Research Handbook on Disasters and International Law* (Edward Elgar 2016) 94.

[40] 'Sendai Framework for Disaster Risk Reduction 2015–2030' (n 13), para 19.

[41] *Subhash Kumar v State of Bihar & Others* [1991] AIR SC 420.

[42] *People's Union for Civil Liberties (Rajasthan) v Union of India & Others W.P.* (C) No 196 of 2001.

[43] *Virendra Gaur & Others v State of Haryana & Others* (1995) 2 SCC 577.

[44] On environmental rights in India, see: Lovleen Bhullar, 'The Judiciary and the Right to Environment in India: Past Present and Future' in Shibani Ghosh (ed), *Indian Environmental Law: Key Concepts and Principles* (Orient BlackSwan 2019) 21–54; Gitanjali Nain Gill, 'Human Rights and the Environment in India: Access through Public Interest Litigation' (2012) 14(3) *Environmental Law Review* 200.

[45] *Swaraj Abhiyan (II) v Union of India & Others* (2016) AIR SC 2953.

[46] National Disaster Management Authority, 'Guidelines on Minimum Standards of Relief' (2015) <https://nidm.gov.in/PDF/pubs/NDMA/19.pdf>.

[47] E.g., Kerala State Disaster Management Authority, 'Minimum Standards of Relief' (2020) <https://sdma.kerala.gov.in/wp-content/uploads/2020/10/Minimum-Standards-of-Relief-Kerala.pdf>.

[48] E.g., the Sphere Project, a coalition of NGOs involved in humanitarian and disaster response, operates in India. Sphere have specific requirements on how they respond to water provision during a disaster. See: The Sphere Project, *The Sphere Handbook: Humanitarian Charter and Minimum Standards in Humanitarian Response* (The Sphere Project 2011).

The role of procedural human rights is also vital to providing a voice to people in disaster-prone regions. In India, procedural environmental rights can be divided into rights to access justice, information, and public participation.[49] Disaster management policies in India have emphasized the need for community participation. For instance, the National Disaster Management Policy includes sections on 'community-based disaster preparedness' and 'stakeholder participation'.[50] However, research has shown significant gaps in facilitating and implementing this.[51] Thus, there is a need for more substantial legislative obligations on the state to facilitate and implement participation. Finally, the relationship between environmental rights and disaster management should be analysed broadly, considering the scope of different laws and policies that interact in any disaster. In other words, it is not just about disaster-specific statutes and policies but also laws related to water, food, and other subjects relevant to environmental rights in a disaster context.

29.1.4 Climate Change Policy

Climate change policy is also of importance in a disaster context.[52] However, climate change policy remains underdeveloped in India and insufficiently integrated into the policies and laws that deal with environmental disasters. The National Action Plan on Climate Change (NAPCC) is the only comprehensive national-level climate policy. The primary intervention of the NAPCC is the launch of eight 'national missions' that deal with different aspects of climate change. Otherwise, there is very little specific content to the NAPCC besides normative goals. Instead, each mission sets up an institutional structure that links with the work of ministries in the government.[53]

Individual states were asked to develop State Action Plans on Climate Change (SAPCC).[54] SAPCCs hold much potential to mainstream climate resilience and adaptation, which are essential for governing environmental disasters.[55] However, the promise has not been adequately realized. Dubash and Jogesh find that SAPCCs have

[49] Shibani Ghosh, 'Procedural Environmental Rights in Indian Law' in Shibani Ghosh (ed), *Indian Environmental Law: Key Concepts and Principles* (Orient BlackSwan 2019) 55–106.

[50] 'National Policy on Disaster Management' (2009) s 5.

[51] Natasha Goyal, 'Disaster Governance and Community Resilience: The Law and the Role of SDMAs' (2019) 1 *International Journal of Disaster Risk Management* 61; Subhajyoti Samaddar and others, 'What Constitutes Successful Participatory Disaster Risk Management? Insights from Post-Earthquake Reconstruction Work in Rural Gujarat, India' (2017) 85 *Natural Hazards* 111.

[52] For a more detailed introduction to climate policy in India, see ch 28.

[53] Navroz K. Dubash and Shibani Ghosh, 'National Climate Policies and Institutions' in Navroz K. Dubash (ed), *India in a Warming World: Integrating Climate Change and Development* (OUP 2019) 329–348, 331.

[54] Navroz K. Dubash and Anu Jogesh, 'From Margins to Mainstream? State Climate Change Planning in India' in Navroz K. Dubash (ed), *India in a Warming World: Integrating Climate Change and Development* (OUP 2019) 349–370, 350.

[55] ibid 365.

often been used merely to generate implementable actions rather than comprehensively redirecting development planning in line with adaptation and mitigation.[56] Thus, in a disaster context, SAPCCs could be vitally important in the future. However, for now, states are using it as an opportunity to gain funding for specific actions rather than more structural shifts to how disaster-related planning occurs.

29.2 Coastlines: A Case Study of Environmental Disasters

Building on the analysis above, the following section analyses the legal regime for disasters and climate change along coastlines. Coastlines are an important site of disasters today. India has nearly 7,000 km of coastlines. Almost one-third of India's coastline was lost to soil erosion between 1990 and 2016.[57] Much of this is linked to human activity along the coastline, but climate impacts have also become more relevant in recent years.[58]

Coastal regulation is vital to how disasters manifest. For instance, permitting more intensified coastal development can drive further vulnerability to disasters through ecosystem losses. In Chapter X, India's coastal law and regulations were introduced in detail. Briefly, the Coastal Regulation Zone (CRZ) Notification, subordinate legislation under the Environment Act 1986, is the primary regulation over India's coastlines. The regulation prohibits coastal development except in accordance with the permissions stipulated in the CRZ Notification. The CRZ Notification states, as an overall purpose, the need to regulate the coast to protect the environment, 'taking into account the dangers of natural disasters, sea-level rise due to global warming'.

As this chapter has emphasized, several areas of law and policy are also relevant to how disasters manifest. Accordingly, this section examines India's coastal zone regulations and embankment laws and their interactions with disasters, climate change, and human rights. The Sundarbans region in West Bengal is discussed here as an example of how the law operates along the coast in disaster-prone regions. Cyclones and sea-level rise in the Sundarbans

[56] ibid 365–367.

[57] RS Kankara, MV Ramana Murthy, and M Rajeevan, 'National Assessment of Shoreline Changes along Indian Coast: Status Report for 26 Years (1990-2016)' (Ministry of Earth Sciences & National Centre for Coastal Research 2018) <https://www.nccr.gov.in/sites/default/files/schangenew.pdf>.

[58] Manish Kumar, 'Eastern Indian Coast Erodes Faster with Rise in Human Activity' *Mongabay-India* (7 December 2020) <https://india.mongabay.com/2020/12/eastern-indian-coast-erodes-faster-with-rise-in-human-activity/>.

29.2.1 Cyclones and Sea-Level Rise in the Sundarbans

The Sundarbans in India is one India's most climate-vulnerable and disaster-prone areas.[59] Much of the population in the area lives in extreme poverty and are marginalized.[60] Coastal erosion, floods, and cyclones are common. Recent studies have shown it is the most cyclone-prone region in the country, with Cyclone Amphan (2020) and Cyclone Aila (2009) two of the most devastating cyclones in recent times.[61] Law and policy frameworks are vital in responding to these environmental disasters. This section highlights some of the key issues that arise.

Coastal planning and regulation: under the CRZ Notification, the entire Sundarbans region is categorized as a 'critically vulnerable coastal area'. As a critically vulnerable coastal area, the Sundarbans is recognized as needing greater levels of protection and needs an 'integrated coastal management plan'.[62] The area should be managed with the 'involvement of coastal communities including fisherfolk who depend on coastal resources for their sustainable livelihood'.[63] Such explicit recognition of the communities is an important development for coastal management in India. It is also an important way to realize procedural environmental rights. However, operationalizing such a plan has been an issue. There has been no official plan to date, apart from the 1996 West Bengal Coastal Zone Management Plan produced under the previous regulatory regime. In 2018, after numerous outcries and orders by the National Green Tribunals,[64] the state government finally published a draft version of the integrated coastal management plan.[65]

Rule implementation has also been poor in controlling development along the coastline. Similar to floodplain zoning, discussed in section 2 above, restricting development along the coast is important to reduce the scale of disasters. However, in the Sundarbans,

[59] Susmita Dasgupta and others, 'Coping with Climate Change in the Sundarbans: Lessons from Multidisciplinary Studies' (World Bank Group 2020); Sugata Hazra and others, 'Temporal Change Detection (2001–2008) Study of Sundarban' (Jadavpur University 2010) <http://www.iczmpwb.org/main/pdf/ebooks/WWF_FinalReportPDF.pdf>.

[60] World Bank, 'Building Resilience for Sustainable Development of the Sundarbans: Strategy Report' (World Bank Group 2014) 88061-IN 13.

[61] Jayanta Basu, 'Sundarbans is Cyclone Capital of India: IMD Report' *Down to Earth* (24 January 2022) <https://www.downtoearth.org.in/news/natural-disasters/sundarbans-is-cyclone-capital-of-india-imd-report-81244>.

[62] Integrated coastal zone management is viewed as an effort to manage coastal zones through proactive planning, integrating different policy areas, sectors and levels of administration, integrating terrestrial and marine components of the region, and reducing conflicts through facilitative and participatory management. For a detailed discussion, see: Tony George Puthucherril, *Towards Sustainable Coastal Development: Institutionalizing Integrated Coastal Zone Management and Coastal Climate Change Adaptation in South Asia* (Brill Nijhoff 2015) 182–210.

[63] 'The Coastal Regulation Zone Notification 2019' (Ministry of Environment Forests and Climate Change, Government of India 2019) EGD. No D. L.-33004/99 s 3.1.

[64] *Tribunal on its own motion v Union of India and others* [2017] National Green Tribunal (Eastern Bench, Kolkata) O.A. No 20/2014/EZ.

[65] Draft Coastal Zone Management Plan of West Bengal 2018.

there are problems with both legal and illegal development. Reports over the last decade show widespread reporting flouting of the rules and norms of the CRZ in the region.[66] The tourism demands in the region, supported by the government and the private sector, have been a primary driver. Since 2018, changes in the CRZ have allowed for 'eco-tourism' activities within the most protected and ecologically sensitive areas. There is no definition of 'eco-tourism' in the CRZ Notification, meaning a potential legal loophole could intensify further development along the coast. In the Sundarbans, tourism has already been a significant contributor to coastal degradation and disaster vulnerability.[67] The changes, which dilute protection and risk intensifying coastal development, have been heavily criticized by environmental groups and researchers.[68]

Outdated embankment law and governance: as coastal erosion and flooding are regular features of life in the Sundarbans, protecting communities who live in the region has primarily been through building embankments. These embankments, often made of mud and clay, are vital for protecting the coastline. There are 4,000 km of embankment that protect the coastline along the Sundarbans. They play a vital role in how disasters unfold in the region. Embankments are vested as state property under the Bengal Embankment Act, 1882.[69] Responsibility for these embankments largely falls under the purview of the state Irrigation Department.

The Irrigation Department's engineers have wide-ranging powers. This includes maintenance and the power to remove, dismantle, or demolish embankments.[70] The Irrigation Department primarily operates through a top-down governance structure. For instance, there is no obligation on the Irrigation Department to build or maintain an embankment due to coastal erosion in a particular area. While individuals can make an application to the District Collector,[71] the Collector is the ultimate arbiter as to any

[66] Upasona Ghosh, Shibaji Bose, and Rittika Bramhachari, 'Living on the Edge: Climate Change and Uncertainty in the Indian Sundarbans' (2018) Steps Working Paper 101, 40.

[67] The National Green Tribunal has intervened several times to order construction bans and bans on noise and solid waste pollution in the Sundarbans area, emanating from the tourism industry. E.g., Venkatesan R, 'NGT Orders Ban on Noise in Sundarbans' *Hindu Business Line* (15 January 2018) <https://www.thehindubusinessline.com/news/national/ngt-orders-ban-on-noise-in-sundarbans/article9386805.ece>; Jayanta Gupta, 'NGT Orders Ban on All Construction in the Sundarbans' *The Times of India* (6 August 2015) <https://timesofindia.indiatimes.com/city/kolkata/ngt-orders-ban-on-all-construction-in-the-sundarbans/articleshow/48377535.cms>.

[68] Ishan Kukreti, 'Coastal Regulation Zone Notification: What Development are We Clearing Our Coasts for' *Down to Earth* (4 February 2019) <https://www.downtoearth.org.in/coverage/governance/coastal-regulation-zone-notification-what-development-are-we-clearing-our-coasts-for-63061>.

[69] Embankments were vested in the state through the Bengal Embankment Act, 1873. Currently, the state has authority through Bengal Embankment Act, 1882 s 4.

[70] Bengal Embankment Act, 1882 ss 28–40.

[71] The District Collector or Magistrate is the most senior civil servant for each district. West Bengal is divided into twenty-three districts, and each district has a District Collector. The District Collector is appointed by the state government. District Collectors have a number of powers and roles (that vary from state to state) including maintaining law and order in the district and the collection of taxes.

benefits from the project.[72] There is no guidance on how such decisions shall be made, nor is the decision-making process integrated with the planning aspects of the Disaster Management Act, the CRZ Notification, or climate policy. In sum, a large amount of authoritative power is vested in the Irrigation Department and the District Collector (both civil servants of the state government) without much scope for input from the local population, for example, through the democratically elected village government (*panchayat*). Accordingly, decisions about embankments, which profoundly impact how people experience disasters, are largely about who has power. Thus, it is not surprising that literature from the field demonstrates widespread discretion and partisanship in the governance of embankments.[73]

Gaps in coordination and coherence of law: the coherence of different laws, policies and coordination between different institutions is vital to effectively preparing and responding to disasters. Overlaps of responsibility between key actors, are identified as an ongoing challenge in disaster management in India.[74] This is no different in responses to coastal disasters in the Sundarbans.[75] There are multiple departments with responsibilities that overlap regarding development and disaster management in the region. For instance, the Sundarbans Affairs Department (SAD), a specialized government department, has the responsibility to structure, plan, monitor, and evaluate activities conducted by other agencies in the region. The SAD has the potential to play an important coordinating role within the region. However, the relatively weaker political and financial power of the SAD over other departments has meant that it has not acted in such a capacity. For instance, despite the importance of embankments to managing disasters and development, the SAD has shied away from having any input into embankments and leaving it to the discretion of the Irrigation Department.[76] Today, the SAD mainly carries out smaller development projects such as constructing brick-paved roads or sinking tube-wells, which duplicates the work of other departments.[77] Other institutions, such as the state coastal authority (West Bengal Coastal Zone Management Authority) also

[72] Bengal Embankment Act 1882 s 7. Before the execution of works a notice must be given to affected villages. The form of notice is set out in Schedule III of the Act. Any person interested is competent to raise objections against the scheme under s 7. However, in case of imminent danger to life or property, the collector can execute works without going through formalities of notice, hearing the objections and inquiry first (s 25).

[73] See generally the ethnographic work of: Amites Mukhopadhyay, *Living with Disasters: Communities and Development in the Indian Sundarbans* (CUP 2016); Aditya Ghosh, Sustainability Conflicts in Coastal India: Hazards, Changing Climate and Development Discourses in the Sundarbans (Springer International 2018).

[74] Aditya Bahadur, Emma Lovell, and Florence Pichon, 'Strengthening Disaster Risk Management in India: A Review of Five State Disaster Management Plans' (ODI-CDKN 2016) <https://cdkn.org/sites/default/files/files/India-disaster-management-web.pdf>.

[75] See: Mukhopadhyay (n 73) 46–72; CSE, 'Living with Changing Climate: Indian Sundarbans' (2012) <http://cdn.cseindia.org/userfiles/adaptation_paradigm.pdf>.

[76] Mukhopadhyay (n 73) 53–54.

[77] Ghosh (n 73) 45.

do not have the ability to act as a coordinating agency nor resolve the contradictions and duplications regarding coastal disaster management and development.[78]

Relief-centric disaster management: disaster management in the Sundarbans continues to focus largely on rescue and relief rather than reflecting the broader shifts in disaster policy towards the preparation and mitigation of disasters.[79] The continuous cycle of disaster and relief has also led to institutional apathy in searching for different development pathways that would emphasize long-term planning for the region.[80] Relief work in the region has dependent on both state and non-state actors (e.g., NGOs). One area where progress has been made is early forecasting and communication of information about cyclones. This was vital during Cyclone Amphan in 2020 in mitigating the loss of life despite the scale of the cyclone.[81]

Climate change adaptation is vital in the region to mitigate disasters, and climate policy could play a more prominent role. The West Bengal SAPCC lays out 'actions and targets' concerning the Sundarbans, including (i) mangrove plantation to enhance the buffer zone from cyclones and floods; (ii) development of water and road networks; (iii) enhancing farming, including organic farming; and (iv) revamping school and market infrastructure.[82] However, these actions are worded vaguely, making it difficult to gauge progress. Moreover, there are contradictions. For instance, the development of concrete road networks, depending on the scale, could be seen to intensify development and increase vulnerability. The actions are also programmatic, thus limited to individual projects. Therefore, while holding the potential to integrate a broader shift in how disasters are governed in the region, today, the SAPCC is of limited relevance in the Sundarbans.

29.3 Environmental Disasters and Climate Change: Challenges Ahead in Coordinating a Coherent Framework

The sections above have introduced the legal framework for environmental disasters in India and demonstrated, through the case study of coastal disasters, how different laws, policies and institutions interact in a disaster context. This final section provides five general points that arise from the analysis above.

[78] Ministry of Environment and Forest, 'Order S.O. 1757(E)' (2008) <http://extwprlegs1.fao.org/docs/pdf/ind72739.pdf>.

[79] Aditya Ghosh, 'Invisible Disasters Left in the Wake of the Visible Storm' *The Wire* (29 May 2020) <https://thewire.in/rights/cyclone-amphan-sundarbans-disaster>.

[80] Mukhopadhyay (n 73) 46–73; Ghosh (n 79f).

[81] Sunny Chug and others, 'Recent Advances in Communication Infrastructure of IMD for Early Warning System' (2021) 72 *Mausam* 935.

[82] Government of West Bengal, 'West Bengal State Action Plan on Climate Change, 2017-2020' (2017) 65–70 <http://www.environmentwb.gov.in/pdf/WBSAPCC_2017_20.pdf>.

First, there is a major challenge in coordinating how different laws, policies and institutional actors respond to environmental disasters. Political relations between the centre and state and mistrust of government actors by communities and civil society have been highlighted in many disaster contexts in India.[83] The Sundarbans example above explains how overlaps of responsibility between departments are an ongoing issue. The centre has often responded to these challenges by producing new policies and plans. However, this does not necessarily provide a way forward. An example is the National Disaster Management Plan clubs, which, together several ministries and agencies tasked with different activities and tasks. However, there is no clarity about the roles of each of these actors. Nor is there any guidance or blueprint for inter-ministerial coordination.[84]

Second, the DM Act has made significant strides in instituting a framework incorporating pre-disaster preparedness, moving away from a post-disaster, relief-centric paradigm. However, there is still much work to institute this on the ground. As commentators have noted, while there is now a suite of disaster and climate-related laws, policies, and guidelines, going beyond producing documents and translating these to action is a significant task.[85] Furthermore, a political vision for mitigation and long-term paradigm changes requires social, cultural, and political shifts in how institutions and actors operate. Disaster management processes have been shown to be top-down, with local-level input restricted to the planning stage.[86] However, the emphasis continues to lie on technology-driven disaster strategies.[87] For example, the overwhelming focus on building embankments in the Sundarbans. Nevertheless, there are some examples of success. In Odisha, for example, political leadership and the establishment of decentralized and polycentric networks to respond to cyclones have significantly reduced the loss of life.[88] In this context, the environmental rights regime in India, discussed in section 29.1, should be further integrated into all aspects of disaster management.

[83] Jessica Field, 'Caught between Paper Plans and Kashmir Politics: Disaster Governance in Ladakh, India' (2020) 8(4) *Politics and Governance* 355; Mukhopadhyay (n 73); Pratik Dash and Milap Punia, 'Governance and Disaster: Analysis of Land Use Policy with Reference to Uttarakhand Flood 2013, India' (2019) 36 *International Journal of Disaster Risk Reduction* 101090.

[84] Anshu Ogra, 'The National Disaster Management Plan, 2019' (2022) 57(3) *Economic and Political Weekly* 16.

[85] Field (n 83) 360.

[86] RR Krishnamurthy and others, 'Managing the Indian Coast in the Face of Disasters & Climate Change: A Review and Analysis of India's Coastal Zone Management Policies' (2014) 18(6) *Journal of Coastal Conservation* 657.

[87] Virginie Le Masson, 'Considering Vulnerability in Disaster Risk Reduction Plans: From Policy to Practice in Ladakh, India' (2015) 35(2) *Mountain Research and Development* 104.

[88] Colin Walch, 'Adaptive Governance in the Developing World: Disaster Risk Reduction in the State of Odisha, India' (2019) 11(3) *Climate and Development* 238; Nibedita S Ray-Bennett, 'Learning from Deaths in Disasters: The Case of Odisha, India' (*Middle East Institute*, 9 June 2016) <https://www.mei.edu/publications/learning-deaths-disasters-case-odisha-india>.

Third, laws and policies can permit activities that exacerbate disasters and undermine disaster management efforts. A clear example of this is in relation to flooding. On the one hand, flood planning and disaster management policies promote flood resilience. On the other hand, the absence of legislation, or implementation of legislation, to prevent activities along flood plains or coastal areas can exacerbate flooding. For instance, it was found that floods in Uttarakhand in 2013 and 2019 were exacerbated by infrastructural development in the flood path, particularly hydropower projects.[89] The absence of effective flood plain zoning regulation that prevents the intensification of development in vulnerable areas was thus critical to driving the flood.[90]

Fourth and relatedly, disasters can be exacerbated by legislation that has not been revised to be informed by principles of environmental, disaster, and climate law. Earlier sections have discussed how groundwater laws can be an important tool to conserve water during droughts and coastal disasters, and embankments are vital for protecting coastal communities. However, many of the relevant laws have not been updated since the colonial era. Meanwhile, international and domestic legal systems have recognized principles such as precautionary principle, public trust, environmental democracy, and substantive and procedural aspects of environmental rights. However, these are not reflected in many such important laws.

Finally, international law and policy can play an important role in managing environmental disasters in India. India was one of the first countries to align its National Disaster Management Plan with the Sendai Framework. NAPCC was also instituted after developments at the international level. State-level climate and disaster policies have often been published as a result of development activities by international agencies and driven by international commitments.[91] This will continue to be an area that drives change, with new developments under the climate change regime, for instance. At the same time, if policies are enacted primarily due to external drivers, it is more difficult to translate into meaningful action.[92] For example, the lack of organic development of climate policies meant that many state institutions saw it as an opportunity for an additional source of funding from the central government to continue existing projects rather than a broader paradigm shift essentially.[93]

[89] Arun B Shrestha and others, 'Understanding the Chamoli Flood: Cause, Process, Impacts, and Context of Rapid Infrastructure Development' (ICIMOD 2021) <https://www.icimod.org/article/understanding-the-chamoli-flood-cause-process-impacts-and-context-of-rapid-infrastructure-development/>.

[90] Dash and Punia (n 83) 9.

[91] Climate policies at the state level, for instance, were supported by the German Development Agency (GIZ GmBH).

[92] Anshu Ogra and others, 'Exploring the Gap between Policy and Action in Disaster Risk Reduction: A Case Study from India' (2021) 63 *International Journal of Disaster Risk Reduction* 102428; Field (n 83) 359–360.

[93] Navroz K. Dubash and Anu Jogesh, 'State Climate Change Planning in India: From Margins to Mainstream' (2014) 49(48) *Economic & Political Weekly* 86; Matthew I England, 'India's Water Policy Response to Climate Change' (2018) 43(4) *Water International* 1.

Conclusion

Disasters in India will continue to be a regular feature, with increasing intensity due to climate change. This chapter has introduced and outlined the law and policy framework to deal with disasters. The DM Act, 2005 brought a significant shift to disaster management in previous decades. Under the framework brought in by the DM Act, various policies and plans have been enacted, and a nested institutional structure has been created to prepare, mitigate, and respond to disasters. However, research has shown significant core challenges to how the Act works in practice, particularly concerning disaster mitigation. As this chapter has emphasized, various laws, policies, and institutions are also relevant in dealing with environmental disasters in India. The chapter has focused on a few of these disasters—namely floods, droughts, and coastal disasters. Several laws, policies, and institutions operate with different objectives and aims, creating significant issues in how disasters are governed. This chapter has also shown a lack of meaningful participation in critical aspects of disaster governance in the legal framework. India's climate policy is still underdeveloped and not adequately integrated within relevant laws. These gaps mean that environmental disasters lead to significant losses of life and destruction, with disparities and injustices regarding who is most affected by disasters. Accordingly, while India's legal and policy framework in responding to disasters has developed over the last two decades, substantial effort across different levels of government, engagement with various actors, and legislative changes are still required to deal with the challenges that lie ahead.

Suggestions for Further Reading

Jessica Field, 'Caught between Paper Plans and Kashmir Politics: Disaster Governance in Ladakh, India' (2020) 8(4) *Politics and Governance* 355–365.

Paul J Govind and Robert RM Verchick, 'Natural Disaster and Climate Change' in Shawkat Alam and others (eds), *International Environmental Law and the Global South* (CUP 2015) 491–507.

Anil Kumar Gupta, 'Disaster Governance and Legal Systems in India' in Indrajit Pal and Rajib Shaw (eds), *Disaster Risk Governance in India and Cross Cutting Issues* (Springer 2018) 39–60.

RR Krishnamurthy and others, 'Managing the Indian Coast in the Face of Disasters & Climate Change: A Review and Analysis of India's Coastal Zone Management Policies' (2014) 18(6) *Journal of Coastal Conservation* 657–672.

Anshu Ogra and others, 'Exploring the Gap between Policy and Action in Disaster Risk Reduction: A Case Study from India' (2021) 63 *International Journal of Disaster Risk Reduction* 102428.

PART VIII

WATER

CHAPTER 30

GROUNDWATER LAW

Protection and Use

HIMANSHU KULKARNI AND KUMAR SATYAM

Abstract

Groundwater extraction has increased manifold over the last five decades and India's groundwater footprint is perhaps the world's largest. Uncontrolled extraction of groundwater and negligent waste and wastewater management have led to serious consequences. Law and policy making on groundwater has generally lagged behind the deepening crisis of groundwater. Groundwater legislation was mooted in the 1970s, although it took time for the States to legislate on groundwater use. Major gaps in the form of rights—equity, fairness and justice—and the lack of a coherent institutional framework continue to exist. The dual challenge of integrating aquifer diversity and complex groundwater contamination issues has impeded the effectiveness of some of these legislative measures. Hence, the Model Groundwater (Sustainable Management) Bill 2017, holds promise to address many of those issues, such as protection of aquifers and water security for the users with participation by communities and overarching law.

Introduction

Groundwater has enabled millions of users worldwide to reduce the hardships resulting from climate uncertainty and the shortcomings of centralized water supply (usually surface water supply). While the transition from traditional to modern means of sourcing, access, and distribution of groundwater has been quite varied across different regions of the world, the overall usage of groundwater worldwide has increased significantly. Some salient features of the groundwater story of the last century include certain interesting statistics:[1]

- There has been a six-fold increase in the extraction of groundwater throughout the world over the last fifty years.
- Nearly 1,000 km^3 of groundwater is pumped every year at the global scale.
- India, the USA, and China account for nearly half of the global groundwater use.
- India, with nearly a quarter of the total global extraction, is the country with the largest pumping by volume of groundwater today.
- India has remained the largest extractor of groundwater in the world since the 1980s.

Haphazard and rampant groundwater extraction has led to three obvious consequences, namely, groundwater depletion, groundwater contamination, and reduced base flows in streams and rivers, even as the dependencies on groundwater continue to grow and the vulnerabilities to depletion and contamination increase. The individualization and privatization of a common pool resource have also meant that the above three consequences often hide serious socio-economic impacts such as inequities, competition, and potential conflict.[2]

The legal regime on groundwater, even internationally, has begun to evolve only recently.[3] Even under international law, while treaties on surface water abound, the representation of groundwater is merely tokenistic despite the socio-economic, environmental, and political importance of groundwater. If groundwater is included in the scope of these legal instruments at all, it is 'related' to surface water or otherwise tends not to be addressed.[4]

The global emergence of the groundwater crisis has necessitated a discussion of international law on groundwater management and convergence. It is perhaps for this reason that the United Nations' International Law Commission's (ILC) portfolio of work now includes 'shared natural resources', including groundwater (the other two are oil and gas). There is a growing trend to include groundwater in international agreements, non-binding instruments, and interstate compacts, both from the resource management and environmental standpoints.[5] At the same time, given the complex nature of aquifers, legislation is often oversimplified to come to terms with the reality of a rather complex groundwater situation.

[1] Jean Margat and Jac van der Gun, *Groundwater Around the World: A Geographic Synopsis* (CRC Press 2013) 123; Tushaar Shah, *Taming the Anarchy? Groundwater Governance in South Asia* (Resource for the Future and IWMI 2009) 37.

[2] Himanshu Kulkarni and PS Vijay Shankar, 'Groundwater Resources in India: An Arena for Diverse Competition' (2014) 19(9) *Local Environment* 990.

[3] Stefano Burchi and Kerstin Mechlem, 'Groundwater in International law: Compilation of Treaties and Other Legal Instruments' (Food and Agriculture Organization of the United Nations 2005) 11.

[4] ibid 11.

[5] ibid 12.

Water is primarily a state subject under the Constitution of India, 1950. Progressively, through time, water has come to occupy the position as a point of national concern in the wake of issues and challenges such as a lack of safeguarding for the fundamental right to water, the emergence of a serious water crisis, and the invisibility of groundwater, resulting in a set of socio-ecological problems as invisible as the groundwater itself. These problems are compounded by the effects of a changing climate on the one hand and the growing demand for water on the other.

The policy regime on water evolved, particularly in response to the needs of a time when exploration and development of sources for access to water and systems of distribution often took precedence over the management of a finite resource. Therefore, regulation of water usage, particularly groundwater, was not considered highly relevant until about the 1990s. Today, 90 per cent of rural settlements in India depend entirely on groundwater, about 65 per cent of India`s irrigation, on average, is based on groundwater,[6] while nearly half of urban water usage is groundwater-based.[7] With about forty million wells (includes dug wells, bore wells and tube wells), India is facing a big challenge in balancing the overwhelming dependencies on its aquifers and the depletion and deterioration of groundwater resources. Groundwater exploitation and contamination in many districts in the country have reached alarming levels—about 60 per cent of districts either have a problem with depleting groundwater resources or face groundwater contamination challenges or even, in a few cases, both.[8] Moreover, springs—natural sources of groundwater—that form one of the most reliable sources of water supply in the mountains are drying up.[9]

The integrated nature of surface water and groundwater in addition to the interrelationship between various ecosystems and the environment are often ignored in discussions about resolving the crises of groundwater in India. Socially derived norms—for instance, users or the *Gram Panchayat* decide not to drill deep boreholes for irrigation—of regulating and moderating groundwater extraction have been piloted in different forms across India.[10] However, their limited spatial scales have often led to the 'free-riding' of the benefits of water conservation and protection by extractors who remain outside the ambit of the social initiative but can tap into the same resource. This is arguably the main reason why groundwater legislation has become necessary. Moreover, legislation is fundamental to maintaining water security for all the sectors that show large but variable dependencies on groundwater. Protecting groundwater

[6] BM Jha and SK Sinha, 'Towards Better Management of Ground Water Resources in India' (Central Ground Water Board 2009) 1.

[7] Sunita Narain, 'Sanitation for All' (2012) 486 *Nature* 185.

[8] Kulkarni and Vijayshankar (n 2) 992.

[9] Niti Aayog, 'Inventory and Revival of Springs in the Himalayas for Water Security, Report of Working Group I, Contributing to Sustainable Development in Indian Himalayan Region' (Niti Aayog, Government of India 2018) 1.

[10] Bishwadeep Ghose and others, 'Peoples' Participation for Sustainable Groundwater Management' in Dipankar Saha, Sanjay Marwaha, and Arunangshu Mukherjee (eds), *Clean and Sustainable Groundwater in India* (Springer 2018) 215.

resources, therefore, has become the core purpose of initiating groundwater legislation that integrates various dimensions of aquifers and their interconnectedness to both the environment and society.

Groundwater legislation is part of a wider groundwater governance framework that is as much about the management of aquifers as about the management of various stakeholders of groundwater from those aquifers. India's aquifer diversity is not only defined by its hydrological and hydrogeological settings but also by its social and economic diversity. This makes the development of water laws challenging but necessary.

This chapter situates groundwater within the National Water Policy of India and as part of the evolution of groundwater legislation more generally. It further highlights the main concerns and limitations and discusses the two interrelated topics of rights and institutions in groundwater management. This section will be followed by sections on the diverse aquifer typology and groundwater contamination, both vital to developing good governance and effective legislation. The emerging concept of groundwater governance is presented next along with the topics of the confluence of aquifers, society and laws. This chapter concludes by summarising how groundwater legislation can be made more effective and impactful.

30.1 The National Water Policy and Groundwater Legislation

It is necessary to distinguish between a policy and a legislation. A water policy provides the necessary oversight of the problems in the water sector and the relevant approaches to resolving those problems. Apart from a variety of technical solutions, a water policy often points to the regulatory instruments that restrict and control actions that are detrimental to developing a sustainable management and governance framework around water. Water legislation, in contrast, is more specific and has clear statements, provisions, and rules that enable it to be used as a legal instrument in regulating water usage, controlling contamination, and allocating available water for different uses among many other applications. This section discusses India's water policy framework and legal regime with specific reference to groundwater.

30.1.1 Groundwater and the National Water Policy

The National Water Policy is formulated by the Ministry of Water Resources (presently called the Ministry of Jal Shakti) of the government of India. The National Water Resources Council was constituted in 1983 and, in 1987, formulated the first National

Water Policy.[11] The main purpose of the policy is to govern the planning and development of water resources and their optimum utilization. The National Water Policy was reviewed and updated in 2002 and later in 2012. The policy of 1987 recognized that groundwater resource management should be tackled by common policies. However, the policy document was very general, and the planners failed to conduct an important as well as difficult job.[12] It included neither any institutional mechanisms nor any legal ones.[13] The document overemphasized surface water, irrigation, and water quality issues but groundwater concerns were missing from the document.[14]

The National Water Policy, 2002, broadly mentions the same arguments as the policy document of 1987 but again, with little on the implementation of legal obligations and regulations for groundwater over-extraction.[15] Coincidentally, this was also the period during which groundwater extraction in India grew in leaps and bounds. Consequently, the subsequent policies needed to become more dynamic, with revisions required on a regular basis.[16] Revisions to meet new challenges emerged over the next ten years due to complex problems and limitations in earlier versions of the legislation.[17]

The National Water Policy (NWP) of 2012 provided a detailed account of water-related challenges in India and the ways to address them. It highlighted the need for an overarching National Water Framework Law while also alluding to the modification of existing Acts based on the principle of managing groundwater as a common pool resource to be held in the trusteeship of the state under the public trust doctrine. Some of the provisions of the policy most likely to have a large impact on the water scenario in India refer to the need to arrest declining groundwater levels with improved technologies of water use, efficiency in usage and community involvement in managing aquifers.[18]

One of the main drawbacks of India's groundwater approaches until approximately 2010 was the absence of aquifer-based information on a large scale. But gaps continue to exist in the NWP 2012, such as the need for demystification in capacity, availability of content, information, and communication for an improved institutional framework on groundwater management and governance. Moreover, the need for the intersection

[11] Ramaswamy R Iyer, 'Federalism and Water Resources' (1994) 29(13) *Environment and Political Weekly* 733.

[12] Haris Umar, 'Legal Control on Groundwater Resources' (PhD Thesis, Aligarh Muslim University 2008) 72.

[13] IH Olcay Unver and Rajiv K Gupta, 'Water Resource Management; Cross Cutting Issues' (Middle East Technical University Development Foundation 2002) 124.

[14] P Rema Devi 'Groundwater Development and Legal Regulation' (1991) 33(4) *Journal of the Indian Law Institute* 614.

[15] Unver and Gupta (n 13) 101.

[16] Government of India, National Water Policy, 2002, para 9.

[17] Philippe Cullet, 'Groundwater Law in India—Towards a Framework Ensuring Equitable Access and Aquifer Protection' (2014) 26(1) *Journal of Environmental Law* 55.

[18] Krishna M Singh and others, 'A Review of Indian Water Policy' (ICAR-RCER 2013) 17.

of multiple disciplines becomes crucial in connecting aquifer behaviour under various stresses with human behaviour.

30.1.2 The Central Model Groundwater Bill and State Legislations

The legislative framework for the management of water resources differs from country to country or even region to region. Groundwater and surface water are seen as two different resources even though their unitary nature and their interrelationship have been discussed over time.[19] However, an acceleration in legislative activity has been seen because of the over-exploitation of groundwater,[20] particularly after the 1990s. At the same time, there was also a push for decentralized governance in India, particularly after the Seventy-third and Seventy-fourth Amendments of the Constitution of India, in 1950 and 1992, in addition to the inclusion of 'water' in all its functions and provisions in List II (State List) of the Constitution. All these factors prompted the states to devise their respective regulatory frameworks on groundwater.

'Model' bills were regularly introduced in 1992, 1996, and 2005 by the Ministry of Water Resources of that time. Driven by these model bills, several states began developing their groundwater regulation in the form of 'Acts' but there was also a growing need for groundwater regulation among states. For instance, the state of Maharashtra introduced the Maharashtra Groundwater (Regulation for Drinking Water Purposes) Act of 1993. This Act focused on regulating groundwater with the sole purpose of protecting drinking water sources, especially in rural areas where groundwater constituted the main source of drinking water supplies. Other states like Andhra Pradesh, Gujarat, Himachal Pradesh, Kerala, Maharashtra, West Bengal, and Madhya Pradesh have tried to legislate on groundwater based upon the model bills.[21] So far, nineteen states/Union Territories have enacted legislations in line with the Model Bill circulated by the Ministry of Water Resources, while eighteen other states/Union Territories are in the process of enacting similar legislation.[22] The problems, however, persist because these laws were only trying to manage the crisis at hand, and therefore remain far from ensuring long term sustainability.[23]

There have been efforts over the years to bring about a statutory framework governing groundwater before drafting the Model Groundwater (Sustainable Management) Bill,

[19] Cullet (n 17) 3.

[20] Philippe Cullet, 'Water Law Reforms; Analysis of Recent Developments' (2006) 48(2) *Journal of Indian Law Institute* 218.

[21] M.S. Vani, 'Groundwater Law in India: A New Approach' in Ramaswamy R Iyer (ed), *Water and the Laws in India* (Sage 2009) 178.

[22] Central Ground Water Board (CGWB), Frequently Asked Questions (FAQ's) <https://cgwb.gov.in/index.php/faq>.

[23] Umar (n 12) 84–85.

2017 (Model Groundwater Bill, 2017). For example, there was the 'Model Bill to Regulate and Control the Development and Management of Ground Water 1970'. This model legislation was then recast several times up to the last version of 2005, wherein there was some evolution from 1970 to 2005, but the basic regulatory structure proposed remained unchanged.[24]

One of the salient features of the Model Groundwater Bill, 2017, is that it includes 'protection principles' in international law, which were necessary yet missing in the environmental laws for decades.[25] The 'prevention principle' included in the Bill states that if the environmental damage is foreseeable, then it should be prevented rather than remedied through compensation after the damage is done. By including this prevention principle as well as the polluter pays principle, the Bill tries to give groundwater regulation a strong environmental perspective.[26]

The Bill identifies that the protection of aquifers is a crucial dimension of groundwater regulation and thus introduces groundwater protection zones and security plans. These protection zones include areas where livelihoods are dependent on groundwater, for example, in areas where arsenic or fluoride is present in groundwater and where the aquifers need to be protected from specific threats such as land use pattern changes.[27] It becomes necessary to change protection zones when a rural area dominated by agriculture merges into the neighbouring urban local body (municipality or municipal corporation) when urban infrastructure replaces cropped land use. These protection zones are necessary to foster groundwater security plans, including safe and sufficient water for livelihood use. It, therefore, ringfences water security even during droughts or floods and includes measures to improve groundwater quality.[28] The Bill emphasizes that groundwater resources are a public resource and recommends aquifer management measures for the development of water security plans at the *panchayat* and urban local body levels which also has the aim of prompting decentralized governance of groundwater resources.[29]

The government disclosed to Parliament in 2019 that nineteen states and Union Territories have adopted state groundwater legislation based on the Model Bill framed by the central government.[30] These are Andhra Pradesh, Assam, Bihar, Goa, Haryana, Himachal Pradesh, Karnataka, Kerala, Maharashtra, Odisha, Punjab, Telangana, Uttar Pradesh, West Bengal, Dadra and Nagar Haveli, Jammu and Kashmir, Lakshadweep, and Pondicherry. A few salient aspects from a few of these laws are provided below.

[24] Philippe Cullet, 'Model Groundwater (Sustainable Management) Bill, 2017: A New Paradigm for Groundwater Regulation' (2018) 2(3) *Indian Law Review* 7.

[25] ibid 10.

[26] ibid 10.

[27] ibid 11.

[28] ibid 12.

[29] ibid; Model Groundwater (Sustainable Management) Bill, 2017 s (10).

[30] PTI, 'Parliament Proceedings: Govt. Says 19 States, UTs have Adopted Model Groundwater Law so far' *The Hindu* (10 August 2021) <https://www.thehindu.com/news/national/parliament-proceedings-govt-says-19-states-uts-have-adopted-model-groundwater-law-so-far/article35836950.ece>.

The Maharashtra Groundwater (Development and Management) Act, 2009, includes regulation and control of pumping in areas experiencing groundwater over-exploitation. The Act emphasizes the maintenance of water quality, polluter pays principle, aquifer mapping, as well as facilitating participation by communities in the process of regulation and management.[31]

The Andhra Pradesh, Water, Land and Trees Act, 2002, the Kerala Groundwater (Control and Regulation) Act, 2002, and the Groundwater Resources (Management, Control, and Regulation) Act, 2005, specify the creation of an authority with the power to control groundwater extraction and regulation in the state if it is causing damage. The Karnataka Ground Water (Regulation and Control of Development and Management) Act, 2011, notifies the areas where groundwater development needs to be regulated; according to this Act it permits the extraction and registration of drilling agencies, and it mandates the recharge of groundwater.[32]

A few states considered it necessary to pass special laws[33] that deal with the problem of groundwater contamination by including penalties to ensure their effective enforcement. Examples are the Odisha River Pollution Prevention Act, 1953, the Maharashtra Prevention of Water Pollution Act, 1970, the Goa Groundwater Regulation Act, 2004, and the Kerala Groundwater (Control of Regulation) Act, 2002. All these edicts include penalties. Apart from such state legislations, the Parliament of India enacted pollution control laws, namely the Water (Prevention and Control of Pollution) Act, 1974, and the Environment (Protection) Act, 1986, as the overarching umbrella to address water pollution, among other things.

30.2 Emerging Concerns and Major Limitations of the Existing Legal Regime, with Particular Reference to Rights and Institutions

Groundwater is primarily a state subject under the Constitution of India. However, given the scale of the compounded problems of aquifer depletion and contamination, not to mention the social, economic, and environmental implications of the groundwater crises, groundwater is a subject that has come to occupy national significance,

[31] Umar (n 12) 92; Government of India, 'National Groundwater Management Improvement Program Environmental and Social Systems Assessment' 2016; Maharashtra Groundwater (Development and Management) Act, 2009, ch 3 (20, 21, 22, 26, 33).

[32] Umar (n 12) 85.

[33] ibid 132–133.

particularly in the context of the following issues, four of which are discussed in the following sections:

1. the rights question—the right to water as part of the fundamental right to life;
2. the emergence of a water crisis because of the mounting pressure on groundwater, a finite resource;
3. conflicts over sourcing and access to groundwater between users and uses that have led to adjudication in courts;
4. the threat to groundwater resources by waste generation and the severe pollution and contamination caused by poor groundwater management;
5. the implications of sourcing, access, and distribution of groundwater without due consideration to aquifers;
6. the usage and control of groundwater vis-à-vis the inequity between uses, users, and sectors, along with questions of fairness and justice;
7. the emerging concerns about the impact of climate change on groundwater and the need for appropriate responses at different scales, from local to national and even global scales.

30.2.1 Rights, Equity, Fairness, and Justice

The legal status of groundwater in India continues to be governed by British common law of the nineteenth century, the provisions of which give landowners the right to take all water below their own land. The legal status of groundwater, therefore, gets linked to the land above it. The Easements Act, 1882, describes the right pertaining to water as the landowners' right 'to collect and dispose within his own limits of all water under the land which does not pass in a defined channel'. This vague statement is then translated into the Transfer of Property Act, 1882,[34] whereby the right to water underneath the land gets transferred during the transfer of property from one owner to another.[35] Hence, the right to groundwater is handed out as a form of inheritance connected to land ownership.

Access to groundwater for agriculture is defined largely through the Easements Acts but drinking water provision even when the source is groundwater is provisioned through a service by the government. The courts recognized the right to clean and safe drinking water as a fundamental right to life guaranteed by the Indian Constitution through different judgments over the last forty years.[36] In order to ensure sustainable development and equitable development of groundwater, the nature of rights over it

[34] Vani (n 21) 444.

[35] ibid 445.

[36] *Subhash Kumar v State of Bihar* (1991) AIR SC 420; *Mullin v UT of Delhi* (1981) AIR SC 746; *Olga Tellis v Bombay Municipal Corporation* (1986) AIR SC 180; *Attakoya Thangal v Union of India* (1990) (1) KLT 550.

must, however, be defined. It is equally vital to know if the rights to groundwater are individual or group rights, positive or negative rights, private or public rights, usufructuary or riparian rights, etc.[37] For instance, a person can dig a borewell and extract groundwater and stop it from going to another person's well as per the provisions of land and groundwater under the Easements Act, 1882. This makes the right to groundwater an individual negative right.[38] In other words, a person is free to exercise their right to access water underneath their land even if it affects others in some way or the other, making this an individual negative right.

Further, the Constitution directs the state to maintain social welfare by ensuring social, economic, and political justice. It also directs the state to distribute resources to serve the common good. Understanding equity in land rights becomes important for the understanding of equity in groundwater rights,[39] in this regard. Linking a parcel of land to the aquifer below, its ownership and the means of access primarily create the first order of iniquities in access to groundwater. Rights to groundwater are derived from both statutory (written) as well as customary (unwritten) laws. Groundwater has been missing from many statutory laws on water, while customary laws have evolved because of socio-ecological transitions and sometimes from provisions for collective decisions and actions such as reservation of wells for community usage.[40] This is especially relevant to India's agricultural expansion through the green revolution during the last fifty years when groundwater sources grew exponentially leading to intensive irrigation in many parts.[41] the numbers of wells, depths of wells, and the rates at which wells get pumped have all risen, creating a competitive arena that has had implications on factors of sustainability and equity, especially with growing land division in agriculture.[42]

According to the World Bank,[43] India has more arable land than China, the USA, and the UK. However, the average size of operational holdings decreased from 2.28 hectares in 1970 to 1.08 hectares in 2015.[44] Hence, with land division came the increase in water sources for irrigation, leading to specific issues of access and distribution.[45] However, each region and even some states had their own specificities around the dual problem of shrinking landholding and increasing water sources.[46] Farmers owning wells and tapping the same aquifer end up with different well yields because of

[37] Devi (n 14) 4.
[38] ibid 4–5.
[39] ibid 4–5.
[40] Vani (n 21) 441.
[41] Shah (n 1) 36–50.
[42] Kulkarni and Vijay Shankar (n 2) 990–992.
[43] The World Bank, 'India: Issues and Priorities for Agriculture' (World Bank, Feature Story, 17 May 2012).
[44] Government of India—Ministry of Agriculture and Farmers Welfare, All India Report on Agriculture Census 2015–16 (2020) 26.
[45] Kulkarni and Vijayshankar (n 2) 994.
[46] Kumar Satyam, 'The Experience of Using Solar PV Water Pumping Systems for Irrigation in Bihar: Design, Implementation, Equity and Efficiency' (MSc Thesis, Shiv Nadar University 2021) 25.

aquifer heterogeneity, such inequities are further compounded by social and economic factors.[47] In simple words, two neighbouring farmers may own wells that show differing properties. For instance, one well can be a perennially high-yielding source, whereas the adjoining well may be a seasonally high-yielding source. This depends upon the lateral variation in the intensity of openings that hold (store) and carry (transmit) groundwater to these wells. Further, if the farmers who own the first well are rich, they can dig or drill another well to produce more water for intensifying agricultural production on their land. The neighbouring farmers may not have the wherewithal to make similar investments and may have to limit their agriculture to what can be sustained by their single, low-yielding well.

The other major policy instrument that has attempted to tackle questions of equity has been the approach to groundwater markets. Groundwater markets ensure water access to even small and marginal farmers[48] and are perceived as the instrument enabling improvements in access to groundwater. However, their superficial efficiency and equity benefits produce a euphoric projection missing the legal vacuum in which such water markets operate, leading to negative ecological, equity and efficiency effects.[49] For instance, water markets may give the impression that water availability to many becomes possible through transactions around groundwater, but they hide aspects like the ability or inability to enter into such transactions or even the acceptance into entering such transactions, both determined by the social and economic backgrounds of the sellers and buyers.

Water markets have sometimes found their way into legislation. The Maharashtra Water Resources Regulatory Authority Act, 2005 (MWRRA), for instance, tries to separate land and groundwater rights. It uses the terms 'entitlements' and 'quotas' and converts groundwater rights into a usufructuary right that is tradable.[50] However, it does not redefine property rights. In the absence of redefined property rights it is challenging to separate groundwater rights from land rights.[51] The MWRRA Act states that every landholder is entitled to water and in times of scarcity every landholder will get a quota of water enough to irrigate one acre of land. It also ensures that tailenders get an adequate and equitable share of water.

Legislation on aspects such as markets was sometimes preceded by experiments around cooperation and sharing of water. As far back as the 1970s, institutional

[47] Himanshu Kulkarni and R Gokhale, 'Managing Deccan Basalt Aquifers: Understanding Aquifer Heterogeneity, Iniquitous Access and Groundwater Competition' (2020) 1(2) *INC-IAH—e-Journal of Geo-hydrology* 9.

[48] Aditi Mukherji, 'Groundwater Markets in Ganga-Meghna-Brahmaputra Basin: Theory and Evidence' (2004) 39(31) *Economic and Political Weekly* 3514; Tushaar Shah and others, 'Solar Power as a Remunerative Crop' Water Policy Research Highlight—10 (International Water Management Institute 2016).

[49] R Maria Saleth, 'Towards a New Water Institution: Economics, Law and Policy' (1994) 29(39) *Economic and Political Weekly* A147.

[50] Vani (n 21) 457.

[51] ibid 444.

experiments like the *Pani Panchayat* in Maharashtra promoted community action and ensured equity and sustainability.[52] However, despite the *Pani Panchayats'* effort at delinking land and water rights and equitable distribution through equal allocation (even to the landless), their scale being quite small (although their numbers were large), led to 'free-riding' by individual users pumping groundwater, drilling deeper and shifting to water-intensive cropping of the conservation benefits created by a *Pani Panchayat*.[53]

30.2.2 Institutions/Organizations Dealing with Groundwater

Institutions are defined as complex composites of rules existing in a common language of a group of individuals rather than as the physical components of any external environment.[54] In simple words, groundwater institutions are described as the set of rules, norms, and values that consider groundwater as a common pool resource.[55] In more common parlance, institutions in groundwater are said to represent organizations responsible for the management and governance of groundwater. Established in 1971, the Central Ground Water Board (CGWB) grew out of a small organization with the purpose of drilling exploration wells to assess groundwater resources and then provide guidance/advice on where and how to harness the resource for various purposes. The CGWB is the arm of the Ministry of Jal Shakti, which deals with groundwater resources in India. The CGWB operates through various regional, divisional, and some state unit offices. Apart from these institutions, state governments also have their own institutions dealing with groundwater. The CGWB's relationship with the state agencies dealing with groundwater includes the periodic assessment of groundwater resources. Despite this relationship, the groundwater regulatory framework under the state groundwater Acts is directly governed by the state groundwater agencies. However, in most cases, the executive powers to invoke the legislation or some clause within a groundwater act are often vested with District Collectors. The Central Ground Water Authority (CGWA) has been constituted under section 3(3) of the Environment (Protection) Act, 1986, to regulate and control the development and management of groundwater resources in the country. The CGWA's mandate is to develop and promulgate technologies, implement policies, and

[52] Manish K Thakur and Binay K Pattnaik, 'How Effective are "Pani Panchayats"? A Fieldview from Maharashtra' (2002) 51(2) *Sociological Bulletin* 243.

[53] COMMAN, 'Managing Groundwater Resources in Rural India: The Community and Beyond' British Geological Survey Commissioned Report CR/05/35N (British Geological Survey 2005).

[54] Larry L Kiser and Elinor Ostrom, 'The Three Worlds of Action: A Metatheoretical Synthesis of Institutional Approaches' in Elinor Ostrom (ed), *Strategies of Political Inquiry* (Sage 1982) 179.

[55] Himanshu Kulkarni, Mihir Shah, and PS Vijay Shankar, 'Shaping the Contours of Groundwater Governance in India' (2015) 4(PA) *Journal of Hydrology: Regional Studies* 172.

keep track of them in the long run to work towards socio-scientific objectives and achieve sustainable development and management of groundwater. The CGWA is responsible for providing leadership and oversight to the exploration of groundwater to assess groundwater resources, including conservation augmentation, distribution and especially protection of groundwater resources.[56] In 2020, the CGWA released new guidelines to regulate and control groundwater extraction in India. These guidelines include detailed provisions for different kinds of groundwater usage, application to different sectors, reference to specific areas and contexts like saline water, wetlands, restoration, and the aspects of penalties.[57] More specifically, there is a reference to environmental compensation and deterrents towards compensation of losses and environmental damages.

Many organizations operating at the national, state, and local levels and are vested with certain executive and legislative powers and responsibilities that define the institutional structure for regulating and controlling groundwater extraction and contamination.[58] The CGWB and the CGWA are part of the Ministry of Jal Shakti (earlier called the Ministry of Water Resources). The ministry also periodically works towards framing policy guidelines for the regulation of groundwater and is responsible for implementing programmes on drinking water and sanitation. The Ministry of Agriculture and Farmers Welfare works towards framing policy and programmes related to agriculture and irrigation. These two ministries deal directly with larger water-related issues such as agriculture, the largest sector using water in India. Other important ministries and authorities which deal with water-related issues are the Ministry of Rural Development (MoRD), the Ministry of Housing and Urban Affairs (MoHUA), and the Ministry of Environment, Forest, and Climate Change (MoEFCC). Water being a state subject under the Constitution has meant that some state government agencies or departments were also set up to control water use.

The crises of groundwater extraction and contamination demand a robust groundwater governance framework. The typology is a function of both hydrogeological as well as socio-economic aspects and needs an understanding of the challenges around groundwater.[59] For instance, aquifers in the Himalayan Mountains are located at different elevations, and groundwater is accessed through natural springs around which communities have designed (traditionally) use practices and distribution. In the alluvial plains, in contrast, the expansive nature of aquifer has provided the notion of unlimited access and large swaths of the region have offered opportunities for large-scale groundwater irrigation, the consequences notwithstanding. The occurrence and movement of groundwater in these two contrasting settings and how societies

[56] Mandate provided to the CGWA <https://cgwb.gov.in/cgwb-organogram>.

[57] Central Ground Water Authority (CGWA), Ministry of Jal Shakti, Notification—Guidelines to Regulate and Control Ground Water Extraction in India, 2020, *The Gazette of India (Extraordinary)*, II (3(ii), S.O. 3289(E), (24 September 2020) paras 7, 8, and 16.

[58] Umar (n 12) 84.

[59] Kulkarni, Shah, and Shankar (n 55) 172.

in the regions source and access groundwater determine the sustainable availability and quality of groundwater resources. Hence it becomes particularly important to look at groundwater from an interdisciplinary perspective. This interdisciplinary science should be used as a medium of promoting both groundwater management and groundwater governance instead of using it for only infrastructure-based, supply-side resource management.[60]

30.2.3 Aquifer Diversity

The regulatory framework governing groundwater has not been updated since the nineteenth century and is based on a mistaken understanding of hydrogeology. The present legal regime gives precedence to the individual interests of landowners, precluding the basis for aquifer-wide protection measures.[61] The typology of aquifers cannot be painted with a single colour, and therefore, there cannot be application of a common groundwater legislation approach across to such a diverse set of aquifer and socio-economic settings. As the properties such as storativity and transmissivity of groundwater vary across India's aquifer typology, the methodologies for the assessment, governance and management of groundwater resources will also vary.

India's aquifer diversity is defined through a broad set of six hydrogeological settings, as reflected in Figure 30.1.[62]

30.2.4 Groundwater Contamination and its Implications for Human Health

The growing arsenic, fluoride, nitrate, and uranium contamination of groundwater is one of the significant water quality problems in India today.[63] Water quality is closely linked to changes in land use, waste disposal practices, especially urban sewage disposal, over-extraction of groundwater, agronomical practices by way of increased agrochemicals, poor sanitation practices, the disposal of industrial effluents, and poor water management at industrial sites.

[60] ibid 172.

[61] Cullet (n 17) 55.

[62] Himanshu Kulkarni, 'Groundwater Overdraft: A Physical Perspective' in Roger Calow and David Macdonald (eds), *Community Management of Groundwater Resources in Rural India* (British Geological Survey Commissioned Report CR/05/36N, British Geological Survey 2005) 1; Kulkarni and Vijayshankar (n 2) 996; Dhaval Joshi, Himanshu Kulkarni, and Uma Aslekar, 'Bringing Aquifers and Communities Together: Decentralised Groundwater Governance in Rural India' in Amarjit Singh, Dipankar Saha, and Avinash C Tyagi (eds), *Water Governance: Challenges and Prospects* (Springer 2019) 157.

[63] Madan Kumar Jha, Ankit Shekhar, and M Annie Jenifer, 'Assessing Groundwater Quality for Drinking Water Supply Using Hybrid Fuzzy-GIS-based Water Quality Index' (2020) 179 *Water Research* 1.

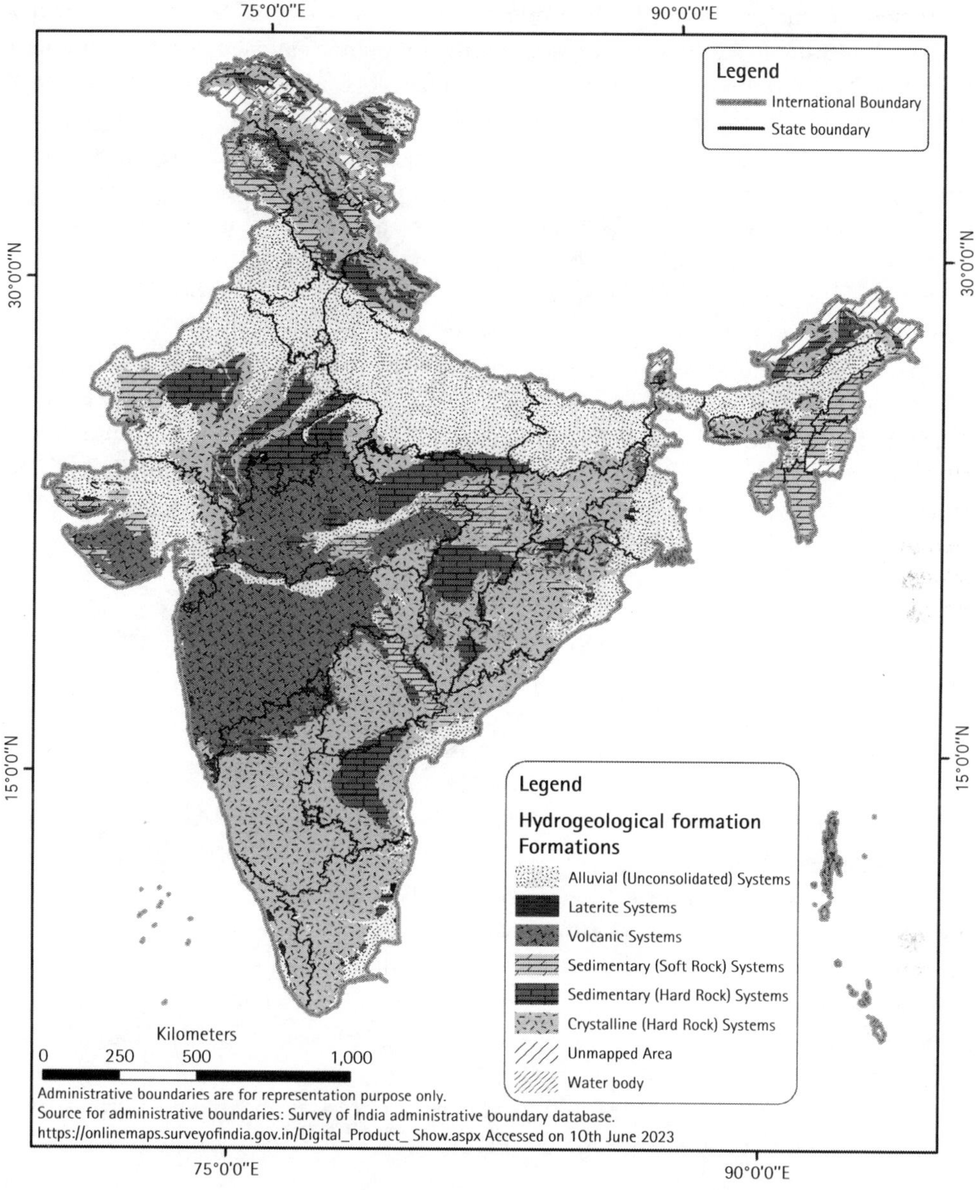

FIGURE 30.1 Hydrogeological settings that define India's aquifer typology

(Source: Prepared by the authors based on Himanshu Kulkarni, 'Groundwater Overdraft: A Physical Perspective' in Roger Calow and David Macdonald (eds), Community Management of Groundwater Resources in Rural India (British Geological Survey Commissioned Report CR/05/36N, British Geological Survey 2005) 1)

The biggest impact of deteriorating water quality is on drinking water sources and agriculture, the two demands that are dominantly met by groundwater. Deteriorating water quality is one of the major factors affecting infant mortality rates, especially among the poor and marginalized communities. Some 337 districts in the country show the presence of nitrates beyond the permissible limit in samples drawn from the shallow aquifers,[64] leading to a high level of vulnerability for people exposed to such contamination. Apart from drinking water, these contaminants enter the food chain and result in a range of health issues that remain unexplored.

Swachh Bharat Abhiyan, or Clean India Mission, the country-wide campaign to eliminate open defecation and improve solid waste management, was launched in 2014. This was followed by the launch of Jal Jeevan Mission, a national programme to provide tap water to every household in India, both rural and urban. The unitary nature of water and the role of aquifers as both sources and sinks for water provides the ideal setting for various loads ranging from sullage to sewage and from industrial waste to agricultural residues to make groundwater vulnerable to groundwater contamination.[65]

India's water pollution law missed the opportunity to create adequate legal protections against groundwater pollution. The limited scope of the Water Pollution Act, 1974, the failure to enforce the Model Groundwater Bills, and the omission in implementing simple solutions to contaminated water violate the fundamental rights of not only the present generation but also the future generation.[66]

30.3 Groundwater Governance at the Intersection of Aquifers, Society, and Laws

Singh and others define water governance as the set of rules, practices, and processes through which decisions for the management of water resources and services are taken and implemented.[67] South Asia's groundwater problem, for instance, requires groundwater governance that deals with a clear integration of conjunctive management of rain-surface water-groundwater, addressing the energy-irrigation nexus, participatory groundwater recharge, conveying water through pipes rather than channels, but most significantly dealing with externality.[68] With more than forty million wells, it is not surprising to find that the groundwater in an aquifer has come under a perpetuating scenario of competitive extraction; the nature of such competition and the aquifer

[64] CGWB: Central Groundwater Board, 'Overview of Groundwater Quality' 2018 <https://cgwb.gov.in/ground-water-quality>.

[65] Mihir Shah and Himanshu Kulkarni, 'Urban Water Systems in India: Typologies and Hypotheses' (2015) 50(30) *Economic and Political Weekly* 57.

[66] S Manjula and Namrata Kabra, 'Groundwater Pollution in India, and the Law' in Sarfaraz Ahmed Khan, Tony George Puthucherril, and Sanu Rani Paul (eds), *Groundwater Law and Management in India: From an Elitist to an Egalitarian Paradigm* (Springer 2021) 77.

[67] Shailesh Kumar Singh and others, 'Potential Groundwater Recharge Zones Within New Zealand' (2019) 10(3) *Geoscience Frontiers* 1065.

[68] Shah (n 1).

characteristics govern the outcomes from such competition.[69] The competitive arena is quite complex and a result of whether the same type of users (wells for irrigation) compete or whether it is a question of different uses or sectors extracting water from the same aquifer.[70] When competition turns into conflict, courts have intervened. Usually, competition turns into conflict when an aquifer used to supply water for a certain purpose suddenly begins to also serve another purpose. The well-known case involving Plachimada *Gram Panchayat* (village-level local government institution formed through a constitutional process) and the Coca-Cola Company is a case in point with a variety of judgments by the courts. The Division Bench of the High Court of Kerala affirmed the primacy of the control of landowners over groundwater in the absence of a law prohibiting groundwater extraction, while prior to this judgment, the single judge of the High Court of the state used the principle of public trust and its link to the right to life and stated that a system leaving groundwater extraction to the discretion of the landowners could result in negative environmental consequences.[71] A prolonged phase of groundwater competition usually occurs before groundwater conflicts come out in the open as in the case of *Velliyur village v the Chennai Metrowater Board in the State of Tamil Nadu*.[72] The competition over an aquifer between irrigators and the industry or between the drinking water demand of a village and a water-intensive industry is not uncommon in India. For instance, in Goa, competition between tourism, construction and industry with rural needs over groundwater is evident through tacit markets even as inadequate municipal supplies have led to a reckless rise in groundwater exploitation. In another example, tourism, construction, and industry in Goa are in competition with rural needs over groundwater through tacit markets, as inadequate municipal supply has led to a reckless rise in groundwater exploitation.[73]

Increasingly, the concept of groundwater governance is taking shape as part of larger institutional reform around groundwater management. There are multiple ways in which groundwater governance is defined and described. Groundwater governance is the governance of aquifers given their vulnerabilities and importance in providing essential reserve supplies of water.[74] Groundwater governance is also a system that attempts to address three problems—water quality and contamination, conflicts

[69] Kulkarni and Vijayshankar (n 2) 991.

[70] Himanshu Kulkarni and Siddharth Patil, 'Competition and Conflict Around Groundwater Resources in India' (Forum for Policy Dialogue on Water Conflicts in India 2017) 10.

[71] Environment Law Research Society (ELRS), 'Governing Water in India: Review of Law and Policy Developments' (ELRS 2012).

[72] S Janakarajan, 'Unequal Power, Unequal Contracts and Unexplained Resistance: The Case of the Peri-urban Areas of Chennai' in K.J. Joy and others (eds), *Water Conflicts in India: A Million Revolts in the Making* (Routledge 2008) 54.

[73] Sujeetkumar M Dongre and Govind S Potekar, 'Rural Needs or Tourism: The Use of Groundwater in Goa' in K.J. Joy and others (eds) (n 72) 33.

[74] Andrew Ross, 'Groundwater Governance: A Shared Global Vision for 2030' <http://www.oecd.org/cfe/regional-policy/8-Tour-de-table-Andrew-Ross.pdf>.

between users, and declining groundwater levels.[75] Globally too, groundwater governance is being synthesized through many lenses, including that of regulation and participation. However, from a practical standpoint, groundwater governance is the art of co-ordination between administrative action and decision-making at different jurisdictional levels.[76] Further, groundwater governance comprises the promotion of responsible collective action to ensure socially sustainable utilization and effective protection of groundwater resources for the benefit of humankind and dependent ecosystems.[77] While the socio-ecological context of governance becomes important, the hydrogeological diversity, such as in India, also requires a 'socio-hydrogeological' approach to groundwater governance.

Currently, the lack of robust groundwater governance mechanisms, mainly in the form of institutional frameworks including legislation, limits the impacts of processes such as bottom-up approaches of decentralized participatory groundwater management in India.[78]

The paradox of pushing for participatory forms of groundwater management in India while attempting to deal with governance through stringent legislation represents a clear dichotomy in the thinking around groundwater management and governance. Hence, the meaning and relevance of groundwater governance in India can be defined as the process that enables institutional support to help sustain aquifer-based, decentralized participatory groundwater management bearing in mind the objectives of efficiency, equity, and sustainability around groundwater resources.

The potential of the Model Groundwater Bill, 2017, in protecting aquifers and regulating overuse can be realized if states can incorporate some key elements of the aquifer settings that dominate in a state while developing or amending their Groundwater Acts. Salient points for specific legal appropriations (indicative only) for each of the hydrogeological settings mentioned in Figure 30.1 are provided below with specific reference to developing a national groundwater governance framework:

- Himalayan Mountain System: spring-water management and governance, protecting recharge areas, and protecting the spring source from impacts by artificially created sources such as waste disposal sites and effects of changing land and use.
- Alluvial System: avoiding undesired competition through lateral interference of wells, controlling heavy-duty individual irrigation wells by managing energy

[75] Sharon B Megdal and others, 'Groundwater Governance in the United States: Common Priorities and Challenges' (2015) 53(5) *Groundwater* 677.

[76] Robert G Varady and others, 'Groundwater Governance: A Global Framework for Country Action' Thematic Paper No 5: Groundwater Policy and Governance (GEF and others 2012) 7.

[77] Stephen Foster and others, 'Groundwater Governance—Conceptual Framework for Assessment of Provisions and Needs' Strategic Overview Series Number 1 (World Bank 2009) 3.

[78] Joshi, Kulkarni, and Aslekar (n 62) 157.

required for pumping, and encouraging water user groups or co-operatives with socio-hydrologically relevant institutions.

- Sedimentary Systems (Hard and Soft): integrating a variety of groundwater dependencies, keeping in mind the variety of demands on aquifers, a combination of well interference zones along with depths of drilling, water budgeting needs at multiple scales ranging from villages, aquifers to larger watersheds, groundwater user co-operatives at scales.
- Volcanic and Crystalline Systems (many common features, with local nuances): integrated watershed management, protection of catchment areas of watersheds and the natural recharge areas of aquifers, efficient management of the shallow aquifers, enabling equitable access by limiting the rate of pumping and depth of drilling, reducing vertical interference between multiple aquifers.

Conclusion

When groundwater is extracted, the complex legal regime of linked land-groundwater ownership has led to an often implicit behaviour that encourages the extraction of unlimited volumes of groundwater from a well. Slip-backs of villages into water scarcity even after drinking water schemes that are dependent on groundwater sources are implemented are often a result of complex interference between irrigation wells and drinking water wells. The long-term continuity of such a phenomenon has led to declining groundwater levels in different parts of India, but there is an emerging provision for legal protection against such consequences in certain state Groundwater Acts.

The protection of aquifers and water security must become the priority for groundwater governance in India, an example set forth in the Model Groundwater Bill of 2017. Aquifers occur in a variety of biophysical environments and are overlain by a diverse society. Hence, effective management of groundwater cannot be based on a licence-based one-stop solution. Participatory groundwater governance can form the backbone of India's groundwater programmes, a management and governance system that should be based on information such as aquifer boundaries, groundwater storage capacity, and flows in aquifers, as well as changing people's behaviour around groundwater usage. Communities must be encouraged to develop social norms for sustainable and equitable management of groundwater. Social norms so developed may be incomplete in sustainable groundwater management unless backed by strong and proactive legislation. Here again, a protection-based approach can ensure the provision of basic water needs from the aquifer such as drinking and domestic water.

Protection strategies, especially in legislation, must recognize the role of aquifers in different ecosystems and that an aquifer is an ecosystem in itself.

Further, it becomes important to develop a paradigm on equitable rights to groundwater and introduce legislative provisions dealing with such rights. Redefining the property rights in water to reflect commonality rather than private interests should be part of developing more effective legislation on groundwater. Managing and governing groundwater as a common pool resource through legislation complementary to incentivizing groundwater management as a community resource rather than a private one can become the backbone of any regulatory framework. Groundwater legislation must also become an instrument in fair and just conflict resolution. Conservation, recharge, and groundwater governance cannot be complete without a balanced approach to integrated supply and demand management of groundwater.

The availability of groundwater in an aquifer, at any given time, is a function of the natural state of the aquifer, its properties, and the impacts of use (pumping, contamination and a complex set of socio-economic conditions that determine how supply and demand match each other). Approaches that improve the efficiency of groundwater usage and include equitable distribution of groundwater resources must be included in every effort of groundwater governance with integrative legislation. Legislation will become more effective if an understanding of the aquifers that define 'groundwater availability and quality' and how aquifers are sourced, accessed, and pumped as a consequence of the 'supply of and demand from groundwater', both functions of human behaviour, can be integrated into a single system of groundwater management and governance.

Suggestions for Further Reading

Uma Aslekar, Dhaval Joshi, and Himanshu Kulkarni, 'What are We Allocating and Who Decides? Democratising Understanding of Groundwater and Decisions for Judicious Allocations in India' in Josselin Rouillard and others (eds), *Water Resources Allocation and Agriculture—Transitioning from Open to Regulated Access* (IWA Publishing 2022) 173.

Sarfaraz Ahmed Khan, Tony George Puthucherril, and Sanu Rani Paul (eds), *Groundwater Law and Management in India: From an Elitist to an Egalitarian Paradigm* (Springer Nature 2021).

Sujith Koonan, 'Revamping the Groundwater Legal Regime in India: Towards Ensuring Equity and Sustainability' (2022) 12(2) *Socio-Legal Review* 45.

François Molle and Alvar Closas, 'Groundwater Governance' in Patricia A. Maurice (ed) *Encyclopedia of Water: Science, Technology and Society* (John Wiley 2019).

Margreet Zwarteveen and others, 'Transformations to Groundwater Sustainability: From Individuals and Pumps to Communities and Aquifers' (2021) 49 *Current Opinion in Environmental Sustainability* 88.

CHAPTER 31

WATER QUALITY AND WATER POLLUTION

AVIRAM SHARMA

ABSTRACT

This chapter focuses on regulations, policies, and laws developed in India to deal with water quality and water pollution over the last seven decades. It traces the roots of the historical developments of regulatory and legal measures and chalks out the fundamental systemic challenges, such as weak institutions, ambiguous and conflicting goals, procedural inefficiencies, lack of coordination among institutions, and shifting goals, which create hurdles in the development of an effective regulatory and legal system to deal with water pollution and water quality concerns. In addition, the chapter discusses the emerging regulatory, judicial, and legal responses which are being devised to deal with the existing and emerging issues and challenges relating to water pollution and water quality regulation.

INTRODUCTION

THE purity and quality of water have always attracted the attention of humans.[1] However, the ways of perceiving and understanding water purity, cleanliness, and quality have

[1] Maggie Black, *The No-nonsense Guide to Water* (Verso 2004) 31, 108; Philippe Cullet and Joyeeta Gupta, 'India: Evolution of Water Law and Policy' in Joseph W Dellapenna and Joyeeta Gupta (eds), *The Evolution of the Law and Politics of Water* (Springer 2009) 158–165; Aviram Sharma, 'Drinking Water Quality in Indian Water Policies, Laws, and Courtrooms: Understanding the Intersections of Science and Law in Developing Countries' (2017) 37(1) *Bulletin of Science, Technology and Society* 45.

evolved.[2] The conventional understanding of purity relies on sensory perceptions of taste, odour, and sight. Modern scientific knowledge of water quality relies on scientific parameters, rather than sensory perceptions or religious dictums.[3] The legal discourse on water quality and pollution was formulated in response to the heightened concerns raised in public spheres on issues related to water pollution and its impact on public health.[4] Developed countries devised an elaborate scientific and explicit legal response to measure, monitor and regulate water pollution and water quality concerns. For example, the UK adopted the River Pollution Prevention Act in 1876. The USA enacted the Federal Water Pollution Control Act, 1948, which became the Clean Water Act in 1972. Similarly, Germany adopted the Federal Water Act in 1957 and the Effluent Charge Law in 1976.[5]

Most developing countries were relatively late formulating a comprehensive legal response to water pollution and water quality concerns. India, one of the emerging economies in South Asia, established explicit legal recourse to deal with water pollution and safeguard water quality from 1970 onwards.[6] However, even after more than five decades of regulatory and legal interventions, India has not been able to provide clean and safe drinking water to a large chunk of its population[7] and water pollution remains a perennial policy concern.[8]

Around 70 per cent of the surface water in India is contaminated with different kinds of pollutants.[9] In addition, groundwater in many districts of the country faces a threat

[2] Mark Harvey, *Drinking Water: A Socio-economic Analysis of Historical and Societal Variation* (Routledge 2015) 47, 149, 151; Black (n 1) 31, 102.

[3] Charles E Closmann, 'Chaos and Contamination: Water Pollution and Economic Upheaval in Hamburg, 1919–1923' (2007) 33(5) *Journal of Urban History* 828.

[4] Black (n 1) 31.

[5] For details, see Jan C Bongaerts and Andreas Kraemer, 'Permits and Effluent Charges in the Water Pollution Control Policies of France, West Germany, and the Netherlands' (1989) 12(2) *Environmental Monitoring and Assessment* 127.

[6] CM Abraham and Armin Rosencranz, 'An Evaluation of Pollution Control Legislation in India' (1986) 11 *Columbia Journal of Environmental Law* 101; Susan G Hadden, 'Statutes and Standards for Pollution Control in India' (1987) 22(16) *Economic and Political Weekly* 709; Cullet and Gupta (n 1) 178; Philippe Cullet and Sujith Koonan (eds), *Water Law in India: An Introduction to Legal Instruments* (OUP 2018).

[7] R Srikanth, 'Challenges of Sustainable Water Quality Management in Rural India' (2009) 97(3) *Current Science* 317; Aviram Sharma, 'Meeting SDG6: Ensuring Safe Drinking Water for All in Rural India' in Robert Brears (eds), *The Palgrave Encyclopedia of Urban and Regional Futures* (Palgrave Macmillan 2021) 3.

[8] Shyam Divan and Armin Rosencranz, *Environmental Law and Policy in India—Cases and Materials* (3rd edn, OUP 2022); Sulhi Ridzuan, 'Inequality and Water Pollution in India' (2021) 23(4) *Water Policy* 985.

[9] Debesh Chakraborty and Kakali Mukhopadhyay, 'Status of Water Pollution in India and Other Countries of Asia' in Debesh Chakraborty and Kakali Mukhopadhyay (eds), *Water Pollution and Abatement Policy in India: A Study from an Economic Perspective* (Springer 2014) 23; Yahua Wang and others, 'Combating River Pollution in China and India: Policy Measures and Governance Challenges' (2016) 18(S1) *Water Policy* 122.

due to excess arsenic, nitrate, fluoride, and many other contaminants.[10] Moreover, pesticides and fertilizer concentrations in water and soil have increased due to the intensification of agricultural activities.[11] The impact of point and non-point sources of water pollution has intensified over the years.[12] According to one estimate, the health costs of water pollution in India amount to around $6.7–8.7 billion per year.[13]

Besides the human and environmental health-related concerns, water unavailability and water scarcity are other emerging concerns, especially with increasing climate-change-induced factors.[14] The quantity (physical unavailability of freshwater) and quality are intertwined and cannot be separately understood. The issues of water quality and pollution are complex and need to be analysed, in a rapidly transforming India with more than 17 per cent of the world population and around 4 per cent of freshwater resources.[15]

Before moving further, it is important to delineate and dwell on water pollution and quality. According to the UN, water pollution implies 'chemicals or other substances in concentrations greater than would occur under natural conditions in the water. Major water pollutants include microbes, nutrients, heavy metals, organic chemicals, oil and sediments.'[16] Scientific studies have adequately established the composition of water in its natural state.[17] The presence of pollutants in higher concentrations than the natural state is termed water pollution.[18]

Water quality is a more standardized and specific term to denote the nature and characteristics of water and its suitability for different types of human use. Water quality is defined in relation to varying types of water uses, such as drinking water, river water, and wastewater quality. Water quality not only focuses on the excess of certain pollutants under natural conditions but also emphasizes the absence of certain substances which are essential for human health.[19] For instance, the lack of the scientifically permitted amount of fluoride in drinking water can compromise the drinking water quality and may create public health concerns.[20] Bartram and Balance explain that '"[w]ater quality"

[10] V Subramanian, 'Water Quality in South Asia' (2004) 1(1–2) Asian Journal of Water, Environment and Pollution 41, 49.

[11] Pradip Kumar Biswas and Kasturi Mandal, 'Drinking Water in Rural India: A Study of Deficiency, Quality and Some Social Implications' (2010) 12(6) *Water Policy* 885; PS Vijay Shankar, Himanshu Kulkarni, and Sunder Rajan Krishnan, 'India's Groundwater Challenge and the Way Forward' (2011) 46(2) *Economic and Political Weekly* 37.

[12] Subramanian (n 10) 52.

[13] Ridzuan (n 8) 985.

[14] NK Garg and Q Hassan, 'Alarming Scarcity of Water in India' (2007) 93(7) *Current Science* 932.

[15] Michael Greenstone and Rema Hanna, 'Environmental Regulations, Air and Water Pollution, and Infant Mortality in India' (2014) 104(10) *American Economic Review* 3038.

[16] UN Water <www.un.org/waterforlifedecade/quality.shtml>.

[17] Black (n 1) 9. Satinder Ahuja (ed), *Handbook of Water Purity and Quality* (Academic Press 2009) 6–7.

[18] UN Water (n 16).

[19] ibid.

[20] Antoine Aoun and others, 'The Fluoride Debate: The Pros and Cons of Fluoridation' (2018) 23(3) *Preventive Nutrition and Food Science* 171.

is a term used to express the suitability of water to sustain various uses or processes'.[21] It is expressed in terms of set standards and is more prominent and relevant from legal and regulatory perspectives. Different water quality indexes have been developed using multiple parameters over the years to express the overall water quality.[22]

In this background, this chapter traces the evolution of the policies, laws, and supporting institutions developed over the years to tackle the challenges related to water pollution and water quality in India. Section 31.1 offers an overview and background information on water pollution-related laws, policies, and water quality-related regulations. Section 31.2 discusses critical governance challenges while developing and implementing law and policy instruments on water quality and pollution-related issues. Section 31.3 considers the emerging pathways and the way forward, and finally, Section 31.4 offers concluding remarks.

31.1 Water Quality and Water Pollution Regulations, Policies, and Laws: an Overview

This section traces the roots of the historical developments of regulatory and legal frameworks developed over the years to deal with water quality and pollution in India. The legal response, especially during colonial times and early decades after Independence, was based on public nuisance laws and common law, namely unwritten rules based on legal precedents. For instance, Chapter XIV of the Indian Penal Code, 1860, describes offences affecting public health, safety, convenience, and morals. The Indian Easements Act, 1882 guaranteed the property rights of riparian owners against unreasonable pollution by upstream users, and the Shore Nuisance (Bombay-Kolaba) Act, 1853, discussed marine pollution.[23]

After Independence, commissions such as the Environmental Hygiene Committee of 1949 were set up to analyse the water pollution situation and address public health concerns. The government of India introduced the National Water Supply and Sanitation Program to improve access to safe water in 1954.[24] Subsequently, the Union government introduced programmes such as the National Rural Drinking Water Supply

[21] Jamie Bartram and Richard Balance, 'Water Quality Monitoring—A Practical Guide to the Design and Implementation of Freshwater' *Quality Studies and Monitoring Programmes* (UNEP and WHO 1996).

[22] Mobarok Hossain and Pulak Kumar Patra, 'Water Pollution Index—A New Integrated Approach to Rank Water Quality' (2020) 117 *Ecological Indicators* 106668.

[23] Prakash Nelliyat, 'Water Pollution: Extent, Impact and Abatement' in Vishal Narain and Annasamy Narayanamoorthy (eds), *Indian Water Policy at the Crossroads: Resources, Technology and Reforms* (Springer 2016) 131.

[24] Sharma (n 7) 2.

Programme in 1969 and the Accelerated Rural Water Supply Programme in 1972 to increase the coverage of drinking water supply through 'improved' sources.[25] Improving water supply and ensuring safe drinking water remained crucial in policy terms. Yet water quality was not explicitly defined in policies and water supply programmes, and 'improved' sources remained loosely defined. In the absence of an explicit legal framework, the state continued to use common law and nuisance laws to deal with pollution issues till the 1970s.[26]

The explicit legal response to deal with water pollution was formulated under the Water (Prevention and Control of Pollution) Act, 1974 (Water Pollution Act), the Water (Prevention and Control of Pollution) Rules, 1975 and the Water (Prevention and Control of Pollution) Cess Act, 1977 (to generate revenue for funding abatement-related interventions). State-level efforts such as the Orissa River Pollution Act, 1953, and the Maharashtra Prevention of Water Pollution Act, 1969, were the precursor for the Water Pollution Act.[27] Domestic and international environmental developments (such as the Orissa River Pollution Act, 1953, and the UN Conference on the Human Environment, 1972) eventually led to the enactment of the Water Pollution Act.[28]

Till 1971, there was no specific government department with the mandate to deal with environmental concerns under the government of India. After the 1972 Stockholm conference, the central government created the National Council for Environmental Policy and Planning to deal with environmental pollution and planning. Late, the Department of Environment was established in 1980 to plan, promote, regulate, and coordinate different environmental programmes of the central government.[29] Finally, in 1985, a full-fledged Ministry of Environment was created for planning, controlling, and governing environmental issues. This specific government institution directly dealt with water pollution-related concerns.

The central government formulated the Water Pollution Act at the request of multiple state governments. Interestingly, the legislation does not categorically define or specify 'water pollution' and does not dwell on the idea of water quality standards. Water comes under the State List in the Constitution of India, 1950. The state governments are responsible for formulating laws and regulations for developing, managing, and governing water resources (surface water and groundwater) and pollution abatement. The Union government has a constitutional mandate to legislate on navigation in national waterways, tidal and territorial waters, and interstate water disputes.[30]

Under the Water Pollution Act, the Union government created the Central Pollution Control Board (CPCB), whereas states were supposed to establish State Pollution

[25] Dipankar Chakraborti, Bhaskar Das, and Matthew T Murrill, 'Examining India's Groundwater Quality Management' (2011) 45(1) *Environmental Science and Technology* 27.

[26] Divan and Rosencranz (n 8) 91–100.

[27] CM Jariwala, 'Indian Water Pollution Law: The History and Prospects' (1989) *Banaras Law Journal* 21.

[28] Sharma (n 1) 52.

[29] Abraham and Rosencranz (n 6) 106.

[30] Cullet and Gupta (n 1) 165.

Control Boards (SPCB) to carry out the government's duties. The CPCB became one of the central units for planning and regulating environmental matters and pollution under the Environment Council/Department/Ministry over the years. The SPCBs remained a major institution at the state level to enforce environmental standards. As per the Water Pollution Act, the CPCB/SPCBs were supposed to be constituted with representatives from government institutions and other spheres with knowledge and experience in environmental protection and conservation at the central and state levels. The Act laid down the power and functions of boards, charts out the funds, accounts, and audit details for the functioning of the boards, rules and procedures for penalties, and the power to set up laboratories.[31]

Around twelve years after the enactment of the Water Pollution Act, the Union government formulated the Environment (Protection) Act, 1986. It is an umbrella legislation which attempted to fill the gaps in earlier regulations related to the environment.[32] In the Act, the environment 'includes water, air and land, and human beings, other living creatures, plants, micro-organisms and property', and environment pollution implies 'any solid, liquid or gaseous substance present in such concentration as may be, or tend to be, injurious to environment'.[33] Unlike the Water Pollution Act, pollution is defined explicitly in the Environment (Protection) Act.

Under the Environment (Protection) Act, the Union government is empowered to take necessary action to protect and improve the quality of the environment and prevent environmental pollution. The central government can make rules to carry out this Act's purposes, establish or recognize laboratories as environmental laboratories, and set ambient environmental standards. Using sections 6 and 25 of the Environment (Protection) Act, the central government formulated the Environment (Protection) Rules, 1986. These legal provisions predominantly focused on surface water; groundwater use remained largely unregulated.

Groundwater is a major source of drinking water in large parts of India (80 per cent of rural and 50 per cent of the urban population depend on it).[34] Development and regulation of groundwater emerged as a major policy concern over the last four decades. Under section 3(3) of the Environment (Protection) Act, the central government has created the Central Ground Water Authority to regulate, control development, and manage groundwater resources. Several state governments have formulated their own laws for groundwater governance.[35] The central government has drafted several model groundwater bills over the years to broaden state control over groundwater, mainly used as a common pool resource and public good in the country. Yet, rapid groundwater extraction and exploitation have led to severe water stress and aquifer pollution during

[31] ibid 165.

[32] Augustin Maria, 'The Costs of Water Pollution in India' (Conference on Market Development of Water and Waste Technologies through Environmental Economics, New Delhi, October 2003).

[33] Divan and Rosencranz (n 8) 673.

[34] Chakraborti, Das, and Murrill (n 25) 28.

[35] Cullet and Gupta (n 1) 166.

the last three decades. Pollution abatement of groundwater sources is crucial for public health and has emerged as a major concern in recent decades.[36]

From the 1970s onwards, several scientific standards for measuring water quality and pollution were formulated by different organizations, such as the Bureau of Indian Standards (BIS), the Indian Council of Medical Research (ICMR), and the CPCB. These standards and guidelines define water pollution and water quality of different kinds of water as per their use such as drinking water, outdoor bathing, propagation of wildlife and fisheries, irrigation, industrial cooling, and controlled waste disposal.[37] The ICMR published the drinking water quality standards in 1975.[38] The CPCB published the water quality monitoring and general guidelines for measuring pollution in 1976.[39] The BIS formulated drinking water standards (IS 10500) in 1983, standards for natural water minerals (IS 13428) in 1992, and for packed bottled water (IS 14543) in 1998; these standards were revised later on several occasions.[40] There are no uniform water quality standards for normal drinking water, barring the bottled water standards which were made mandatory in 2001.[41] For other uses, water standards set by CPCB are considered legitimate in legal discourse. Yet, no law explicitly adopts any of the water quality standards set by these different regulatory institutions in India.

After the late 1980s, several policies/programmes/interventions were formulated to deal with water pollution, water use, and water governance concerns. Different programmes were planned, such as the Global Environment Monitoring System (GEMS) since 1977, Monitoring of Indian Aquatic Resources (MINARS) in 1984, Ganga Action Plan (GAP) in 1985, and the National River Conservation Plan (NRCP) in 1995 for pollution abatement.[42] Special initiatives were designed to tackle water pollution challenges, such as the NRCP, the National Lake Conservation Plan, Waste Minimization initiatives in the 1990s, the plan for setting up Common Effluent Treatment Plants, relocation strategies for polluting industries and many more.[43]

The Environmental Action Programme was initiated to mainstream environmental concerns in developmental projects. The Coastal Regulation Zone Notification, 1991, was formulated to regulate activities around the coasts and in oceans. Similarly, several other laws and interventions, for example, the Environmental Impact Assessment Notification, the Solid Waste Management Rules, and the Wetlands (Conservation and

[36] Chakraborti, Das, and Murrill (n 25) 28.

[37] CPCB, Status of Water Quality in India, 2011 (Ministry of Environment and Forests 2011); Sharma (n 1) 47–49.

[38] Indian Council of Medical Research (ICMR), Manual of Standards of Quality for Drinking Water Supplies. Special Report Series No 44 (ICMR 1975).

[39] CPCB, Guidelines for Water Quality Monitoring (CPCB 2008).

[40] Aviram Sharma and Saradindu Bhaduri, 'Consumption Conundrum of Bottled Water in India: An STS Perspective' (2013) 33(5–6) *Bulletin of Science, Technology and Society* 172.

[41] Saradindu Bhaduri and Aviram Sharma, 'Public Understanding of Participation in Regulatory Decision-making: The Case of Bottled Water Quality Standards in India' (2014) 23(4) *Public Understanding of Science* 475.

[42] Maria (n 32) 2.

[43] ibid 7; Nelliyat (n 23) 140.

Management) Rules, included provisions that deal with water pollution abatement-related concerns in a piecemeal manner. Unfortunately, none of these interventions has been fully able to achieve their set objective, but they have contributed to the large array of initiatives designed to control pollution.

The first comprehensive national-level Water Policy was formulated in 1987, followed by a second in 2002, and the third in 2012. These water policies engaged with water pollution and quality concerns but failed to define or adopt any specific water quality standards. However, they prioritized different kinds of water use practices.[44] For general monitoring of water quality, the Ministry of Environment and Forest established the Water Quality Assessment Authority (WQAA) in 2001 to coordinate the activities of different water management agencies.[45] The National Environment Policy, 2006 discussed water quality, pollution-related concerns, and environmental standards; yet the policy has not adopted any specific standards. Even the most recent interventions, such as the *Jal Jeevan Mission* and *Har Ghar Jal* (2019), emphasize increasing access to 'safe' water but fail to promote any of the existing water quality standards.[46]

31.2 Challenges for Water Quality and Water Pollution Regulation

During the last five decades, India has developed a strong and wide-ranging legal response to deal with water pollution and quality concerns. The central and state governments have established organizational structures, regulatory procedures, and supporting legal frameworks.[47] However, despite all the reforms and legislation, there is no comprehensive law or policy framework to deal with water pollution and quality-related challenges.

Command-and-control mechanisms with many administrative approvals and penal provisions were established to deal with pollution-related issues in the 1970s.[48] The industrial zones in India developed as hotbeds of pollution during this period. By the 1980s and 1990s, industrialization and rapid and unregulated urbanization became the driving force of the Indian economy, but both remained patchy and uneven.[49] In the last three

44 Sharma (n 1) 49.

45 Chakraborti, Das, and Murrill (n 25) 31.

46 Sharma (n 7) 3.

47 Abraham and Rosencranz (n 6) 104–106; Chakraborty and Mukhopadhyay (n 9) 142–143; Philippe Cullet, 'Water Law Reforms—Analysis of Recent Developments' (2006) 48(2) *Journal of the Indian Law Institute* 206.

48 Abraham and Rosencranz (n 6) 105–107; Chakraborty and Mukhopadhyay (n 9) 144.

49 Kaushik Basu, 'A Short History of India's Economy: A Chapter in the Asian Drama' (The United Nations University World Institute for Development Economics Research (UNU-WIDER) Working Paper 2018/124; Mahalaya Chatterjee 'Regional Variation in Urbanisation in India and the Emergence of New Towns' (fifty-fourth Congress of the European Regional Science Association, St Petersburg, Russia, 2014).

decades, de-regulation and privatization led to the growth of private industries and the Indian economy. The nature of the economy started shifting from an overtly agrarian-based and state-dependent economy to a private capital-led economy diversifying into manufacturing and services accompanied by rapid urbanization in several pockets of India.[50] The national economy's size and scope grew significantly during this period. In this background, we will discuss a few major challenges witnessed while enforcing water pollution and water quality-related regulations, policy interventions, and legal remedies.

31.2.1 Weak Institutions

The departments, ministries, and regulatory institutions (CPCB, SPCB, CGWB) established during the last five decades to control and regulate water and environmental pollution remain weak and ineffective in handling the situation.[51] One of the primary reasons for the weak performance of regulatory institutions and lack of enforcement had been inadequately trained staff, staff shortage, lack of clear source of revenues, and lack of funding.[52] Abraham and Rosencranz argued that the Water Pollution Act was 'neither readily enforceable nor effective, and the elaborate administrative machinery they set up are poorly staffed and do little more than routine paperwork'.[53] The size of the pollution monitoring network has grown over the years (from eighteen monitoring stations on river Yamuna to up to 200 stations by 1987–88, around 1,000 by 2005–06 and above 2500 by 2010–11).[54] Yet, it is inadequate to effectively cover all the country's water bodies (surface water and groundwater). The ill-trained and insufficient workforce involved in monitoring and regulating regulatory institutions led to severe under-reporting of cases. The poorly manned command-and-control-based mechanism of pollution control has remained largely ineffective.[55]

From the formative years, the SPCBs lacked effective enforcement. Maria explains, 'By 1987–88, all the state boards had filed a total of only 1,602 cases for prosecution under the Water Act. Of these, 288 had been decided and 1,314 cases were still pending.'[56]

[50] Chatterjee (n 49) 3–9.

[51] Abraham and Rosencranz (n 6) 101–102; Sharachchandra Lélé, Priyanka Jamwal, and Mahesh Menon, 'Challenges in Regulating Water Pollution in India: Standards, Monitoring, Enforcement and Accountability' (2021) 56(52) *Economic and Political Weekly* 46.

[52] Chakraborti, Das, and Murrill (n 25) 31; Abraham and Rosencranz (n 6) 102, 106, 109; Keren Priyadarshini and Omprakash K Gupta, 'Compliance to Environmental Regulations: The Indian Context' (2003) 2(1) *International Journal of Business and Economics* 9.

[53] Abraham and Rosencranz (n 6) 106–107.

[54] CPCB (n 39) 6.

[55] Greenstone and Hanna (n 15) 26.

[56] Maria (n 32) 3.

Several studies have highlighted weak institutional capacity, inadequate monitoring, and lack of enforcement and compliance.[57] Lack of enforcement by the regulatory authorities led to an increase in non-compliance among industry actors as the cost of compliance is often more than non-compliance.[58] Self-regulation did not start till this period, and predominantly state-based regulations emerged as the norm. SPCBs emerged as the major environmental regulators at the state level. The performance of different SPCBs drastically varies from each other, with some working more effectively than others.[59] Unfortunately, state-level analyses of the performance of SPCBs are few and far between.[60]

31.2.2 Ambiguous and Conflicting Goals

The goals envisioned in environmental regulations, policies, and even water legislation are often too broad and contradictory.[61] There is a lack of clarity regarding rights and obligations at individual and institutional levels.[62] The lack of mandatory standards for measuring drinking water quality is one example. Without specific standards, achieving the desired goals becomes illusory and impractical.

The environmental goals of water pollution regulations and acts often conflict with the state's economic plans and developmental agendas. The regulators and bureaucrats working for environmental institutions often only offer lip service to formal rules and regulations for pollution control. Their concern remains more focused on employment generation and economic growth.[63] Such a situation has led to a bureaucratic-industrial complex in many contexts, further weakening regulatory institutions' authority.

Legal doctrines (based on Articles 21 and 47 of the Constitution) interpret water as a public good and fundamental right. In several crucial judgments, the judiciary articulated that it is the responsibility of the state to provide 'safe' water to every individual under the above-mentioned constitutional provisions.[64] The judiciary has significantly shaped the water policies and legislation in India.[65] The Constitution does not

[57] Abraham and Rosencranz (n 6) 102, 106,109; Lélé, Jamwal, and Menon (n 51) 48–51; Aviram Sharma, 'Science-based Mandatory Standards and the Implementation Gap: The Case of Bottled Water Regulations in India' (2018) 114(1) *Current Science* 29.

[58] Priyadarshini and Gupta (n 52) 10, 17.

[59] ibid 18.

[60] Sanchita Talukdar, 'A Review of Water Pollution Abatement Strategies in India: The Case of Gujarat' (3rd International Conference on Public Policy (ICPP3), Singapore, June 2017).

[61] Philippe Cullet, 'Right to Water in India—Plugging Conceptual and Practical Gaps' (2013) 17(1) *The International Journal of Human Rights* 56.

[62] ibid 63.

[63] Sheoli Pargal and Muthukumara Mani, 'Citizen Activism, Environmental Regulation, and the Location of Industrial Plants: Evidence from India' (2000) 48(4) *Economic Development and Cultural Change* 829.

[64] Cullet (n 61) 61; Sharma (n 1) 50–52.

[65] Cullet (n 61) 62.

recognize the human right to water; yet, the right to water has emerged mainly from case law.[66] Access to drinking water has been argued as a matter of a human right.[67] However, a right to water is not often realized for everyone. Contrary to the consensual judicial principles, the policy regimes increasingly promote water as a commodity and an economic good.[68] Even the legal framework is not binding for meeting the human right to adequate (amount of water required per person to meet all needs) and safe drinking water. Public institutions, in practice, are not providing adequate and safe water to every citizen. The conflicting positions of different institutions further complicate the situation and create hurdles in realizing the right to adequate and safe water.

Moreover, water quality standards need to be clearly and explicitly defined to be enforceable in any court or to meet human rights requirements. There are no explicit and uniform standards for drinking water quality in India. Without specific mandatory standards, even judicial interventions fail to ensure 'safe' drinking water availability.[69]

Yet, in rural areas, to accelerate the coverage of 'safe' drinking water, the government kept promoting access to 'safe' water as a public good (through programmes such as the National Drinking Water Mission, 1986, which was renamed the Rajiv Gandhi National Drinking Water Mission in 1991 or even through the *Jal Jeevan* (Water is Life) Mission 2019).[70] The current policy aims to provide functional household tap connections to every household by 2024.[71] All these interventions envisioned water as a public good; however, water is not always seen as a pure public good in law and policy terms or even social and economic spheres.

31.2.3 Procedural Inefficiency and Lack of Public Participation

Monitoring, regulatory activities and legal recourse face several kinds of procedural inefficiencies. For instance, under the Water Pollution Act, effluent discharge is permitted only after prior consent of SPCBs, and penal provisions exist for non-adherence. However, courts were not allowed to entertain a suit under this Act unless the suit was brought by the SPCB or had its sanction during the early years.[72] The consent and permit procedure has been argued to be an ineffective mode of regulation, especially against big industries, as prosecution under the Act is a lengthy and time-consuming exercise with under-staffed SPCBs.[73] In addition, the Water Pollution Act

66 ibid 61; Sharma (n 1) 45.

67 Cullet (n 61) 61–64.

68 ibid 57.

69 Sharma (n 1) 52.

70 Sharma (n 7) 3.

71 Government of India, *Jal Jeevan Mission* (Department of Drinking Water and Sanitation, Ministry of Jal Shakti, 2021).

72 Abraham and Rosencranz (n 6) 106.

73 ibid 107.

does not cover municipal waste, which is responsible for two-thirds of India's water pollution.[74]

Public participation in the regulation-making, monitoring, and implementation stages is crucial for effective legislation. However, most water pollution-related laws, policies, and interventions are developed in a top-down manner with little emphasis on broader participation. During the command-and-control regime, public involvement in the inquiry stage, permit-granting, and appeal stages was absent. The information related to the permission granting process and outcomes was made available only to 'interested' or 'affected' parties and was not readily available to the general public.[75] There was excessive government control over the boards, and these boards mostly acted as an advisory body, and they had limited enforcement powers and offered little space for public participation in the regulation process.[76] The situation has not changed much in later years. The democratization of decision-making and public participation in environmental regulations has not occurred as expected.[77]

The PCBs mostly failed to function as independent regulatory institutions. For instance, in terms of the expertise of the board members, environmental expertise is required only for the chairman and the secretary; no such criteria are prescribed for other members.[78] Government and public institutions' representatives in the CPCB and SPCBs are mostly officials heading different agencies, who are overburdened with administrative work and hardly have environmental expertise.[79] In the current SPCB of Bihar, only the chairman of the board has domain expertise in environmental pollution and environmental science. No other member from academia or other spheres with environmental expertise is on the Board. The board is dominated by bureaucrats representing different government organizations. In the case of Gujarat, apart from the secretary of the Board, no other member has environmental expertise, and the Board is dominated by bureaucrats.[80] The trend that started in the formative years of the CPCB and SPCBs is continuing. These institutions have failed to develop as independent regulatory institutions, having representatives and active engagement from different sections of society, and remain highly bureaucratized government institutions.

The lack of participation of the general public in regulatory decision-making has led to challenges in the effective implementation of the regulatory standards in the early years and continued.[81] However, citizen movements and individual efforts in different parts of India have forced government agencies to set up inquiry committees and

[74] ibid 105.

[75] ibid 110–111.

[76] ibid 110

[77] Poonam Pandey and Aviram Sharma, 'NGOs, Controversies, and "Opening Up" of Regulatory Governance of Science in India' (2017) 37 (4) *Bulletin of Science, Technology and Society* 199.

[78] Abraham and Rosencranz (n 6) 108.

[79] Lélé, Jamwal, and Menon (n 51) 48–49.

[80] See Gujarat Pollution Control Board <https://gpcb.gujarat.gov.in/webcontroller/viewpage/members-of-the-gujarat-pollution-control-board>.

[81] Abraham and Rosencranz (n 6) 110

effectively enforce laws and policies.[82] In many cases, citizen and community involvement led firms to alter their polluting activities and change their production processes.[83] Yet, no significant administrative reforms have occurred in the regulatory governance of environmental administration and institutions. India has not witnessed any broad-based environmental movement on issues related to water pollution at the regional or national level. However, pollution-related disputes and conflicts have grown at the local level. Water pollution has not yet become an electoral issue at the regional or national level, and political commitment to address water pollution remains low.[84]

31.2.4 Lack of Coordination and Conflicting Jurisdictions

Coordination among different government agencies/departments and ministries (such as the Ministry of Environment, Forest and Climate Change, the Ministry of Water Resources, the Ministry of Agriculture, the Ministry of Finance, etc.) to govern water and environment has remained missing.[85] Institutions often shift the blame on others and rarely develop active collaboration at the local or higher level. For example, the growth of bottled water and purification technologies are rampant in India,[86] and groundwater extraction for commercial purposes puts enormous stress on groundwater. However, BIS, which regulates the bottled water industry, does not regulate groundwater over-extraction.[87] Groundwater is regulated in principle by the Central Groundwater Board and state-level authorities, but they do not actively coordinate with BIS or other institutions (such as local municipalities or water supply boards).

Regulatory authorities (CPCB/SPCBs) faced jurisdictional opacity around implementation from their formative years.[88] In addition, conflicting objectives of different regulatory departments/institutions, from promoting economic growth to enforcing environmental regulations, have created coordination problems. Often, public policy discourses in developing and emerging economies are settled in favour of economic growth rather than environmental conservation or protection, and India is no exception.[89] In a nutshell, the sectoral and compartmentalized approach to water pollution and water quality management has failed to address the interwoven nature of water quality problems in India.[90]

[82] Divan and Rosencranz (n 8) 42.

[83] Priyadarshini and Gupta (n 52) 20; Pargal and Mani (n 63) 830.

[84] Sunita Narain, 'Changing Environmentalism' (*Seminar*, August 2002) <www.india-seminar.com/2002/516/516%20sunita%20narain.htm>.

[85] Aviram Sharma and Mark Harvey, 'Economies of Water in Delhi: A Neo-Polanyian Analysis' (2022) *Water International* 9; Sharma (n 57) 31.

[86] ibid; Sharma and Bhaduri (n 40) 172.

[87] Sharma (n 57) 30.

[88] Hadden (n 6) 715; Greenstone and Hanna (n 15) 26.

[89] Wang and others (n 9) 126; Lélé, Jamwal and Menon (n 51) 51.

[90] Chakraborti, Das, and Murrill (n 25) 32.

31.2.5 Shifting Goals and Inadequate Response

The science of water pollution existed much before the introduction of regulatory and legal procedures to deal with water pollution.[91] Yet, the scientific, regulatory, and socio-legal response to understanding the complex science of pollution remains inadequately developed in India. The existing scientific studies focus more on water pollution monitoring. Epidemiological and toxicological studies are not adequately carried out to analyse the impact of different kinds of pollutants.[92] In addition, social science studies analysing water pollution and its impact are rare, barring those coming from economics.[93] The science required to study the effect of water pollution is becoming interdisciplinary[94] and technology-intensive, as new and emerging pollutants (nanoparticles, microplastics, hormones, traces of pharmaceuticals) are becoming difficult to monitor and regulate.

Contrary to this rapidly evolving science of water pollution, the Indian judiciary is ill-equipped to deal with many water and environment-related cases due to a lack of capacity to engage with complex science in a timely manner. For instance, in *ICELA v Union of India* (the Bichhri Industrial Cluster case), the judiciary took twenty-two years to deliver the final judgment. In the Patancheru-Bollaram industry cluster case in Telangana, the court took twenty-seven years to deliver a final judgment. Till 2016, 21,000 industrial pollution cases were pending in Indian courts.[95] Various legal reforms were pushed over the years to address the question of qualification of the judges on the environmental matter and expedite the process.[96] The problem has become even more complex today, and the judiciary has not been able to address these concerns.

Moreover, several regulatory standards (water, sewage, and industrial effluent standards) have largely remained unchanged since their formulation and are ill-defined, even though scientific understanding of the pollutants and their human and environmental health impacts has drastically changed over the years.[97]

[91] William A Jury and Henry Vaux, 'The Role of Science in Solving the World's Emerging Water Problems' (2005) 102(44) *Proceedings of the National Academy of Sciences* 15715.

[92] Aviram Sharma 'Standards, Technology and Public Participation: Regulation Making for Bottled Water Quality in India' (PhD Thesis, Jawaharlal Nehru University, New Delhi, India 2014).

[93] E.g., Greenstone and Hanna (n 15); Chakraborty and Mukhopadhyay (n 9).

[94] Jury and Vaux (n 91) 15717.

[95] Rajit Sengupta and Kiran Pandey, 'Here are 3 of 21,000 Industrial Pollution Cases Pending in Indian Courts' *Down to Earth* (17 December 2018) <www.downtoearth.org.in/news/urbanisation/here-are-3-of-21-000-industrial-pollution-cases-pending-in-indian-courts-62508>.

[96] Gitanjali Nain Gill, 'Mapping the Power Struggles of the National Green Tribunal of India: The Rise and Fall?' (2020) 7(1) *Asian Journal of Law and Society* 93.

[97] Chakraborti, Das, and Murrill (n 25) 31; Lélé, Jamwal and Menon (n 51) 47–48.

31.3 Emerging Regulatory and Legal Landscape

Water pollution concerns have intensified over the years despite the growth of legal and policy interventions. '[F]rom 2009 to 2015, the number of polluted river stretches doubled from 150 to 302, while the urban sewage generated increased from 38,000 MLD in 2009 to 57,000 MLD in 2015'.[98] Around 70 per cent of the wastewater is dumped untreated in the rivers, even after hundreds of Sewage and Common Effluent Treatment Plants are established in urban India.[99] The agricultural sector (nitrate contamination from fertilizers and pesticide contamination) has emerged as another major polluter and non-point sources are still unregulated and difficult to monitor and regulate.[100] The non-point source-led pollution has led to excessive nutritional enrichment of water bodies, eutrophication, the proliferation of algal blooms, sedimentation, and elimination of native species.[101]

In recent years, water pollution and water access concerns have attracted the attention of academics, policy actors, and even the political class.[102] As a result, several new interventions (Clean Ganga Mission, *Swachh Bharat* Mission, *Jal Jeevan* Mission) were planned to address the pollution challenge and to ensure 'safe' access to drinking water for the masses. This section describes some of the emerging trends in terms of governing water quality and pollution concerns and the judicial and legal measures that are being developed.

31.3.1 Hybrid Regulatory Governance

In the last few decades, the command-and-control regime has given way to hybrid regulatory governance, especially when the state-controlled economy was giving way to a market-led economy in the current era of economic globalization.[103] In the new model, apart from the state-led regulatory actors and institutions, market-based mechanisms and community and individual participation of citizens have been envisioned in the overall governance of water.

The overt state-led control has started losing, and new ways of governance for monitoring, controlling, and regulating pollution have emerged. With broad changes in the Indian economy since the 1990s[104] and the rise of varieties of environmentalism

[98] Akash Vashishtha 'They're Raising a Stink: Polluted Rivers in the Country Have Doubled Over Past Five Years' Mail Online India (4 April 2015) cited in Wang and others (n 9) 126.

[99] For details, see <https://www.indiaspend.com/70-of-urban-indias-sewage-is-untreated-54844/>.

[100] Chakraborti, Das, and Murrill (n 25) 28.

[101] Wang and others (n 9) 126.

[102] Chakraborti, Das, and Murrill (n 25) 28, 32; Wang and others (n 9) 123.

[103] Kuldeep Mathur, Public Policy and Politics in India: How Institutions Matter (OUP 2013).

[104] Basu (n 49) 10.

(including middle-class environmentalism, greening of firms, and movements for the protection of livelihood and resources),[105] firms and industrial actors have too initiated the processes of ecological modernization.[106] In the early years, ecological modernization was mainly pursued in response to regulatory pressure and requirements.

In recent years, firms have started recognizing the market potential of 'green' production processes and products. Several players have started believing that the economy will benefit from the environmentalization of production processes, leading to ecological modernization.[107] Regulatory agencies have pushed disincentivization and incentivization to firms for adopting alternate production processes and mechanisms. The focus is not on penalizing non-compliant firms but has shifted to incentivizing them (for instance, the use of carbon credit as a tool) to adopt pro-environmental measures. Cases of self-regulation by firms and voluntary-based technological adoptions to modernize production processes are increasing.

During the last decade, the 'digitalization' of the Indian economy and society happened in a big way.[108] India has one of the world's highest numbers of mobile phones. Digital technologies can be used to improve public services and strengthen citizen-centric e-governance.[109] The regulatory actors, too, have started promoting digital technologies for communicating, monitoring, and governing water pollution and water supply systems.[110] The e-governance paradigm in India has its limitation, given the digital divide, which still exists even after the large-scale adoption of information and communication technologies and weak institutions of governance. At the same time, this would be an exciting area to watch in the coming years.

Several studies have argued for increasing public participation in monitoring, regulation, and enforcement of standards for pollution abatement and safeguarding water quality.[111] Public involvement and engagement can further enhance the voluntary adoption of standards and clean technologies.[112] Public engagement is carried out in different ways. For instance, the Green Rating Project (GRP) was launched for big industrial plants in India in 1997 to evaluate industries' environmental performance and

[105] Aviram Sharma, 'The Environment and Development Debate in India: The "Greening" of Developmental Discourse' in Rahma Bourqia and Marcelo Sili (eds), *New Paths of Development: Perspectives from the Global South* (Springer 2021) 109.

[106] Amit Kumar Gupta and Narain Gupta, 'Environment Practices Mediating the Environmental Compliance and Firm Performance: An Institutional Theory Perspective from Emerging Economies' (2021) 22 (3) *Global Journal of Flexible Systems Management* 160.

[107] ibid 160, 171.

[108] Pradip Ninan Thomas, *Digital India: Understanding Information, Communication and Social Change* (Sage 2012); Robin Jeffrey and Assa Doron, *Cell Phone Nation: How Mobile Phones Have Revolutionized Business, Politics and Ordinary Life in India* (Hachette 2013).

[109] Michael E Milakovich, *Digital Governance: Applying Advanced Technologies to Improve Public Service* (Routledge 2011) 88.

[110] Sharma (n 7) 4.

[111] Lélé, Jamwal, and Menon (n 51) 50; Bhaduri and Sharma (n 41) 472.

[112] Priyadarshini and Gupta (n 52) 20.

awarding ratings.[113] Some studies reported that the GRP employed by pulp and paper plants in India significantly reduced the pollution load of many dirty plants.[114] Duflo and others find that having a paid third-party auditor who is externally selected results in more accurate reporting of firms' water pollution emissions in India.[115] In addition, citizen science, whereby individuals voluntarily participate in the data collection and monitoring process, can also function as a form of third-party monitoring. Third-party-based certification and monitoring is relatively low in India.[116] Yet this is an exciting area that can help India monitor and regulate water pollution and quality in the coming decades. All such changes are pursued under the broader domain of hybrid regulatory governance.

31.3.2 Judicial and Legal Developments

The Indian judiciary has developed rich environmental jurisprudence during the last five decades. Many of the early environmental court cases dealt with issues of water pollution and water quality (*MC Mehta v Union of India*—Ganga Pollution Case 1988, *Vellore Citizens Welfare Forum v Union of India* 1996, *Subhash Kumar v State of Bihar* 1991).[117] Judges of the Supreme Court of India and High Courts interpreted constitutional rights to protect the citizens from water pollution or degradation of the environment having a detrimental impact on human health and life.[118] In addition, ideas on the line of the precautionary principle, polluter pays principle, and public interest litigation were developed due to judicial activism in cases related with water pollution and environmental degradation.[119] Yet, even with all these progressive developments, the judicial decisions failed to comprehensively shape the legal and administrative domain of water governance to ensure access to safe water. The judicial approach was predominantly piecemeal.

Legal activism and reform led to the establishment of the National Green Tribunal (NGT) in 2010 under the National Green Tribunal Act, 2010, to cater to environmental matters and speed up the justice delivery process.[120] The Tribunal has appellate jurisdiction to settle all environmental disputes. Unlike the Water Pollution Act, the NGT

[113] Sheila Olmstead and Jiameng Zheng, 'Water Pollution Control in Developing Countries: Policy Instruments and Empirical Evidence' (2021) 15(2) *Review of Environmental Economics and Policy* 261.

[114] Nicholas Powers and others, 'Does Disclosure Reduce Pollution? Evidence from India's Green Rating Project' (2011) 50(1) *Environmental and Resource Economics* 131.

[115] Esther Duflo and others, 'Truth-telling by Third-party Auditors and the Response of Polluting Firms: Experimental Evidence from India' (2013) 128(4) *The Quarterly Journal of Economics* 1499.

[116] Sharma (n 7) 5.

[117] Divan and Rosencranz (n 8) 50, 111, 148.

[118] Cullet (n 61) 71.

[119] Lavanya Rajamani, 'Public Interest Environmental Litigation in India: Exploring Issues of Access, Participation, Equity, Effectiveness and Sustainability' (2007) 19(3) *Journal of Environmental Law* 293.

[120] Gill (n 96) 86.

Act allows all aggrieved parties to approach the court, including representative bodies and organizations active in the environmental field.[121] However, the NGT is going through a turbulent and transitory phase, where different opposing forces are trying to curb its power and roll through legislative and other interventions.[122] NGT is also facing similar challenges as the environmental regulators.[123] In NGT, more than 3,573 cases were pending till 2018.[124] Overall, the Indian judiciary is in a transition phase, like the economy and society, where environmental and pollution-related lawsuits are getting filed at an increased rate; however, appropriate judicial remedies are not yet delivered on time. Whether the legal sector can develop a more comprehensive plan to deal with water pollution and quality concerns can only be answered in the future.

Conclusion

The earliest explicit legal frameworks to deal with water pollution and quality were based on command-and-control mechanisms and were predominantly state-led. During the last three decades, policy and legal regimes have started moving towards hybrid regulatory governance. However, state-based actors are still dominant in monitoring and regulating water pollution.

Water pollution remained a perennial policy concern, yet the intensity of water pollution increased over the years, and regulations remained largely ineffective. Economic growth without abiding by regulations or 'greening' production processes remained the primary mode of industrial and other developments. The overall policy and legal regime have only partially succeeded in tackling the complex water pollution concerns. Moreover, the impact of neo-liberalization and hybrid-governance models on regulation-making and implementation in the water pollution and water quality domain is understudied. Any effective and long-lasting change will be difficult to bring unless the societal and political response to pollution starts emanating from the grassroots level and policy and legal processes do not remain only driven by top-down environmental management principles.

The relationship between different forms of inequality and water pollution is an understudied topic in India.[125] Specifically, how water pollution impacts marginalized sections of Indian society along caste and gender lines, does not attract much attention among Indian academia, except for a few notable efforts.[126] Even though marginalized

[121] Ibid.

[122] ibid 120.

[123] Lélé, Jamwal, and Menon (n 51) 50.

[124] PIB, 'Cases Pending in Supreme Court and NGT' <https://pib.gov.in/Pressreleaseshare.aspx?PRID=1541784>.

[125] Ridzuan (n 8) 986.

[126] Philippe Cullet, *Water Law, Poverty, and Development: Water Sector Reforms in India* (OUP 2009).

sections have faced the maximum environmental and health-related harms in terms of facing water pollution, occupational hazards, and consuming contaminated water; yet, issues of environmental justice are rarely analysed in the context of water pollution in India.

Water pollution and access to 'safe' water cannot be comprehensively understood from the legal perspective until it is supported by a thorough social and political analysis. Broad economic, social, and political approaches to environmental pollution greatly affect the legal and administrative systems. Pollution concerns cannot be addressed when the dominant ideology of the government and industry and societal values prioritize economic interests and growth agenda at all costs. The impact of broader debates on legislative and policy interventions requires more thorough and critical reading.

Suggestions for Further Reading

Dipankar Chakraborti, Bhaskar Das, and Matthew T Murrill, 'Examining India's Groundwater Quality Management' (2011) 45(1) *Environmental Science and Technology* 27–33.

Philippe Cullet and Joyeeta Gupta, 'India: Evolution of Water Law and Policy' in Joseph W. Dellapenna and Joyeeta Gupta (eds), *The Evolution of the Law and Politics of Water* (Springer 2009) 157–173.

Sharachchandra Lélé, Priyanka Jamwal, and Mahesh Menon, 'Challenges in Regulating Water Pollution in India—Standards, Monitoring, Enforcement and Accountability' (2021) 56(52) *Economic and Political Weekly* 46–52.

Sheila Olmstead and Jiameng Zheng, 'Water Pollution Control in Developing Countries: Policy Instruments and Empirical Evidence' (2021) 15(2) *Review of Environmental Economics and Policy* 261–280.

Aviram Sharma, 'Drinking Water Quality in Indian Water Policies, Laws, and Courtrooms: Understanding the Intersections of Science and Law in Developing Countries (2017) 37(1) *Bulletin of Science, Technology and Society* 45–56.

CHAPTER 32

WATER SHARING AND PROTECTION

Inter-State Dimensions

K.J. JOY, NEHA BHADBHADE, SARITA BHAGAT, AND ABRAHAM SAMUEL

Abstract

In India, inter-state water sharing is more about allocating water amongst the co-basin states for various uses and less about protection of the river basin. The chapter argues that inter-state water sharing cannot be seen only as a legal and constitutional issue; there is a need to engage with geo-politics, history, ethno-linguistic identities, political economy and developmentalism, geographies and natural resources, including the emerging issues of climate change. Most of the established tribunals lack agreed upon principles and norms for water sharing, further fuelling the disputes. Further, most of the tribunal awards do not pay any serious attention to river protection. There is a need for an alternative approach based on agreed upon principles amongst the stakeholders along with nested institutions including multi-stakeholder platforms. The alternative approach is discussed through the case of the ongoing Mahanadi water dispute between Chhattisgarh and Odisha states.

Introduction

> None of the States in a river-basin owns the river but as public trustees of the water resources of the river, all of them have rights to use the water of the river: *Provided* that such use does not violate the right to water for life of any person in the river basin.[1]

[1] Ministry of Water Resources, Draft National Water Framework Bill, 2016 s 29(2)a.

THE hydrological boundaries of most of the major river basins in India cut across multiple states and Union Territories, characterizing them as inter-state rivers. The sharing of water among the basin states has been a problem leading to recurring contestations and disputes. Inter-state water sharing issues have cropped up or resurfaced in many basins—between Andhra Pradesh and Telangana over Krishna and Godavari, Karnataka and Tamil Nadu over Cauvery, Punjab, Haryana and Delhi over Sutlej, Karnataka and Goa over Mahadayi, and Odisha and Chhattisgarh over Mahanadi.

Three important factors that have made inter-state water sharing and disputes rather intractable are one, constitutional provisions for the management of inter-state rivers (water) that created jurisdictional ambiguity; two, policies promoting water-intensive crops like wheat and rice leading to water demands that exceed water availability; and three, lack of an integrated ecosystems approach in the management of inter-state rivers.[2] The latter two factors directly relate to conservation issues in the context of inter-state water sharing. Coupled with this, many still view that 'every drop of the water flowing into the sea is waste'. This has led to a dam(storage)-centric approach, leading to competition among various states to tap the available resources within their administrative boundaries. This is evident as most of the riverine conflicts have arisen because of the construction of a dam or diversion project on an inter-state river.[3] Over the years, such an approach has adversely impacted riverine ecosystems.

Inter-State River Water Disputes Act, 1956 (ISWD Act) is the main legal instrument in India to deal with inter-state water sharing and disputes. Experience shows that this has not really worked, and the case of the river Cauvery is a good example. The Cauvery Water Dispute Tribunal (CWDT) was constituted by the government of India on 2 June 1990 to adjudicate the dispute over sharing of Cauvery waters among its riparian states. All the riparian states approached the Supreme Court of India after CWDT gave the final award in 2007.[4] The ISWD Act was first amended in 2002 on the recommendations of the Sarkaria Commission and later in 2019. As per the 2019 amendment, the concerned state government needs to request the government of India to establish a Disputes Resolution Committee to resolve water disputes through negotiations before such disputes are referred to the Tribunal. It also introduced a single Standing Tribunal with multiple benches for different disputes.[5] However, it does not discuss principles and norms of water sharing among basin states.

[2] Nilanjan Ghosh, 'Three Stressors of Inter-State Water Conflicts in India' *Observer Research Foundation* (13 August 2020) <www.orfonline.org/expert-speak/three-stressors-of-inter-state-water-conflicts-in-india/>.

[3] K.J. Joy and Suhas Paranjape, 'Interstate Water Allocations, Dams and Conflicts' in Shantha N Mohan and Sailen Routray (eds), *Sharing Blue Gold: Locating Water Conflicts in India* (National Institute of Advanced Studies 2015) 41.

[4] Cauvery Water Disputed Tribunal, Final Order, 2007.

[5] K.J. Joy and others, 'Mahanadi Basin: An Alternative Approach to Inter-state Water Sharing and Management—An Approach Paper' (Forum for Policy Dialogue on Water Conflicts in India 2021).

The other legal window for inter-state water sharing and dispute redressal is the River Boards Act, 1956, which has not been used because of resistance from the states.[6] The Ministry of Water Resources circulated the draft River Basin Management Bill, 2018 (draft RBM Bill) to replace the River Boards Act. The draft RBM Bill proposes to set up River Basin Organizations (RBOs) to foster the 'development, management and regulation of waters of an inter-State river basin'.[7] Among the tasks of RBOs will be the development of a River Basin Master Plan.[8] The principles underlying the work of the RBOs include equitable and sustainable utilization of water, conjunctive and integrated management, and the common pool character of water.[9] The draft Bill contains provisions that can lead to sustainable and equitable use of water among basin states but it has not been adopted yet.

In Section 32.1, we discuss water sharing and conservation in the context of inter-state river disputes in India. The main proposition in this section is that the present legal instruments, especially tribunals, have engaged with water sharing among basin states from the perspective of dispute resolution and not conservation. We find that the absence of agreed-upon principles and norms of allocation has been one of the central gaps in the discourse around inter-state water sharing in India. In Section 32.2, we argue that inter-state conflicts need to go beyond the existing tecno-legal framework, contextualized in the geography, culture, identities, and pluralistic knowledge, which are more grounded. While taking such an approach, the ongoing developments in the water sector, especially in terms of large infrastructure and their effects on water sharing, cannot be ignored. In Section 32.3, we present the alternative approach through a case study of the Mahanadi basin and in the last section, we talk about the institutional processes and arrangements required to implement the alternative framework for water sharing among the co-basin states.

32.1 Inter-State Water Sharing: Protection of Rivers Missing from the Frame

Since the passage of the ISWD Act, nine major tribunals[10] have been established in India. The review of the final orders of these tribunals shows that river protection/conservation

[6] K.J. Joy and S Janakarajan, 'Inter-State Water Disputes Among the Riparian States: The Case of Cauvery River from Peninsular India' (Pakistan Institute of Legislative Development and Transparency 2011) <www.indiawaterportal.org/sites/default/files/iwp2/interstate_water_disputes_among_the_riperain_states_the_case_of_the_cauvery_river_kj_joy_and_s_janakarajan_pildat_2011.pdf>.

[7] Draft River Basin Management Bill, 2018 s 11.

[8] ibid s 17.

[9] ibid ss 5–8.

[10] The Godavari Water Dispute Tribunal (1969), the Krishna Water Dispute Tribunal- I (1969), the Narmada Water Dispute Tribunal (1969), the Ravi and Beas Water Dispute Tribunal (1986), the Cauvery

has been mostly out of their frame. The arguments and negotiations among the basin states are mostly based on the sharing of the quantum of water available in the river. A few examples presented below highlight the implications of the Tribunal processes, which also bring out the issues of river basin planning and management in the country.

Tribunals assess the total flow in the rivers using the dependability of the flow as an important parameter. Dependability indicates the degree of assuredness of the flow or water availability in the river. For example, 75 per cent dependable flow means that out of 100 years the assumed flow will be available for 75 per cent of the years. Thus, a 75 per cent dependable flow is much more assured as compared to a 65 per cent or 50 per cent dependable flow. The Krishna Water Dispute Tribunal I (KWDT-I) assessed the 75 per cent dependability flow to be 2060 TMC (Thousand Million Cubic Feet). The Tribunal allocated this entire flow among the three states of Maharashtra, Karnataka, and undivided Andhra Pradesh.[11] Such an apportionment leaves nothing for the river as environmental flow. The Krishna basin is one of the closed basins in peninsular India, which means the water is completely utilized by its riparian states, and there is no consideration for maintaining the health of the river.[12] The Tribunal provided for a review of its award after 31 May 2000 with a caveat that the unutilized water by the three states would be open for renegotiation.[13] The Tribunal did not provide any clarity as to what 'utilization' means and the states conveniently equated utilization with storage resulting in over-designed storages and setting up very high river lifts. The Krishna Water Dispute Tribunal II (KWDT- II) brought down the dependability to 65 per cent for the apportionment of water among the three states. The verdict stipulated that each state should make available a certain quantity of water for 'minimum flows in the stream', and the quantities prescribed for each state totals sixteen TMC, which works out to a meagre 0.7 per cent of the 65 per cent dependable flow estimated to be 2293 TMC.[14] Though the Introduction to the Tribunal award very clearly says that 'the aim is to maximize utilizable water and provide maximum benefits to maximum number of people while *preserving the river and its flow*' (p 3–4), the award itself does not provide much for the river.

The CWDT, in its order, reserved fourteen TMC of the 50 per cent dependable flow, estimated to be 740 TMC, for environmental protection (ten TMC for environmental protection and four TMC as inevitable outflows into the sea).[15] This reserved water

Water Dispute Tribunal (1990), the Krishna Water Dispute Tribunal-II (2004), the Vansadhara Water Dispute Tribunal (2010), the Mahadayi Water Dispute Tribunal (2010), and the Mahanadi Water Dispute Tribunal (2017).

[11] Krishna Water Disputes Tribunal, 'The Report of Krishna Water Disputes Tribunal with the Decision' vol I (2010) 800.

[12] Jean-Philippe Venot and others, 'Shifting Waterscapes: Explaining Basin Closure in the Lower Krishna Basin, South India' (2007) *International Water Management Institute Research Report* 121 <www.iwmi.cgiar.org/Publications/IWMI_Research_Reports/PDF/PUB121/RR121.pdf>.

[13] Joy and Paranjape (n 3) 41.

[14] Krishna Water Disputes Tribunal (n 11) 800; also, see Joy and Paranjape (n 3) 41.

[15] Cauvery Water Disputes Tribunal, 'The Report of the Cauvery Water Disputes Tribunal (with the Decision)' vol V (2007) 238.

amounts to less than 2 per cent of the total flows. The Godavari Water Dispute Tribunal (GWDT) and the Narmada Water Dispute Tribunal (NWDT) do not take into account the water requirement for environmental flows.[16] The Vansadhara Water Dispute Tribunal order too allocates the entire flow on a 50:50 basis to the conflicting states of Andhra Pradesh and Odisha leaving nothing for environmental flows.[17]

Probably for the first time in the context of inter-state water disputes in the country, the state of Goa used the environmental flow argument against Karnataka in the case of the Mahadayi water dispute. The dispute was around the construction of the Kalsa-Bhanduri project by Karnataka to divert the water from the Mahadayi river basin into the Malaprabha basin. Goa, during the hearing of the Mahadayi Water Dispute Tribunal, asserted that reduced flows in the Mahadayi river would cause large ecological degradation of the Mhadei Wildlife Sanctuary, lead to sea-water intrusion, and result in loss of livelihoods and social disharmony. The state of Goa also asserted that the project did not take the required clearance from the National Board of Wildlife (NBWL) under section 29 of the Wildlife (Protection) Act, 1972.[18] The Tribunal took the stand that environment, forest and wildlife need to be protected. With respect to environmental flows, the Tribunal ordered that the guidelines set by the Ministry of Environment, Forest and Climate Change (MoEFCC) should be followed. The guidelines say that during monsoon season, the flows in the river should be maintained at 30 per cent of the monsoon flows and during the lean season, the flow should be 20 per cent of the average lean season flow of 90 per cent dependability.[19] Probably this is the first and the only verdict of an inter-state water dispute tribunal where ecosystem needs were considered in the context of inter-state water sharing.

The allocation of water by the Tribunal is based on the dependable yield of the river, derived from the historical river flows. Seventy-five per cent dependable flow ensures that there is greater reliability in terms of water availability as compared to 65 per cent dependable yield, even though the quantum of water is higher in the latter. Allocation made on the basis of less dependable flows can lead to states over-designing the water resources infrastructure, leaving less unbound flows in the river that will degrade the riverine ecosystems. This is especially relevant in the case of peninsular rivers, as they are not perennial and are prone to frequent droughts. Moreover, the variability and uncertainty caused by climate change require a higher level of dependability (at least 75 per cent) in all water management, which will allow better flows in most years. This will also

[16] Godavari Water Disputes Tribunal, 'The Report of the Godavari Water Disputes Tribunal (with the Decision)', vol I (1) (1979) 38; Narmada Water Disputes Tribunal, 'The Report of the Narmada Water Disputes Tribunal' vol IV(1) (1978) 75.

[17] Vansadhara Water Disputes Tribunal, 'The Further Report on The Vansadhara Water Disputes Tribunal' (2021) 124.

[18] Mahadayi Water Disputes Tribunal, Report cum Decision—vol VI (2018) 1253.

[19] ibid 1248 http://cwc.gov.in/sites/default/files/7report-mahadayi-water-dispute-tribunal-part-ii-vol.vi-2018.pdf.

help downstream communities cope with ongoing and future demographic, economic and land use changes, and climate change.[20]

Another important aspect related to river flows that is not taken into account in water sharing among states is sediment transport. As an integral part of the fluvial processes, sediment transport is responsible for shaping different landforms and habitats, including the floodplains on which human civilizations are highly dependent. The Cauvery delta, which supports a large population of cultivators, has shrunk by 20 per cent because of the significant reduction in sediment flows.[21]

Groundwater does not enter the equation of inter-state water sharing. For example, Clause I of GWDT Final Order states that '[a]ll the states can make use of underground water within their respective State territories in the Godavari basin and such use shall not be reckoned as use of the water of the river Godavari'.[22] This goes against the unity of water and surface water—groundwater interactions. An integrated approach to river basin planning and management is the need of the hour, and tribunals should make informed decisions based on scientific studies that consider both groundwater and surface water availability. There should also be scientific studies carried out for the quantification of base flows in inter-state rivers and their impacts on river health, habitats, and livelihoods that depend on them.

Water quality is equally neglected. None of the awards of the tribunals have addressed the repercussions of increased urbanization and industrialization on riverine ecosystems, including the actions of the upstream riparian states on the downstream ones. In the case of the Mahanadi water dispute between the states of Chhattisgarh and Odisha, more than the reduced inflows into the Hirakud dam, the real issue is the immense water use and polluted return flows by the expanding thermal power plants in the basin. The Forum for Policy Dialogue on Water Conflicts in India's study of the basin over a decade reveals that the basin is heavily industrialized, causing heavy pollution not only severely degrading the riverine ecosystem but also rendering the waters of many of the tributaries unutilizable.[23] Since the Mahanadi Tribunal is still adjudicating the dispute, it can only be hoped that some of these aspects would be considered by the Tribunal in its proceedings.

[20] Based on Water Conflict Forum, 'Sharing the Waters of the Cauvery: An Alternative Vision and Approach' (October 2016) <https://waterconflictforum.org/lib_docs/Cauvery%20joint%20statement_final%20with%20signatories_26%20Oct%202016.pdf>.

[21] Vidya Venkat, 'Tamil Nadu's Granary Losing Substantial Ground: Delta Region Shrinks by 20%' *The Hindu* (15 July 2017) <www.thehindu.com/news/national/tamil-nadu/states-granary-losing-substantial-ground/article19286764.ece>.

[22] Godavari Water Disputes Tribunal (n 16) 38.

[23] Abraham Samuel, K.J. Joy, and Sarita Bhagat, 'Integrated Water management of the Mahanadi Basin: Water Resources, Water Allocation and Inter-Sectoral Use' (Forum for Policy Dialogue on Water Conflicts in India 2017) <https://waterconflictforum.org/lib_docs/Integrated-Management-of-the-Mahanadi-basin.pdf>; K.J. Joy and others, 'Mahanadi Basin: An Alternative Approach to Inter-state Water Sharing and Management'- An Approach Paper (Forum for Policy Dialogue on Water Conflicts in India 2021) <https://waterconflictforum.org/lib_docs/Report-Mahanadi-2021.pdf>.

With respect to environmental protection, none of the Tribunal orders have any provisions or mechanisms that could hold the states accountable if they do not maintain the prescribed minimum flows. Thus, the current legal and institutional architecture in India is largely ineffective when it comes to the protection of rivers and their ecosystem services, though in recent times, there is a ray of hope as the Mahadayi case shows.

Thus, it is important that river basin planning and management shift from a conventional technocratic approach focusing on volumetric or proportionate allocation and consumption to an integrated and alternative approach in which protection and conservation of the river are a priority along with livelihood needs. The fundamental principle of river basin planning and management should be to maintain naturally functioning ecosystems in the river by conserving and managing the available water in the form of groundwater, wetlands, and surface water, at the same time meeting the demands of the people. In doing so, environmental protection, equity, participation of all the stakeholders, and improvement of water efficiency must be considered.

32.2 Changing Contexts of Inter-State Water Sharing in India

Inter-state water sharing in India is often viewed from a legal and constitutional viewpoint, which blurs other possible explanations and solutions to a complex issue which has its links to politics, history, ethno-linguistics identities, political economy, and developmentalism, geographies and natural resources, scarcities and excesses in water cycle including the emerging issues of climate change. Techno-legal approaches have dominated the understanding of inter-state water disputes.[24] Given this scenario, it is important to explore various dimensions that revolve around inter-state water sharing that can help understand the issues from various explanatory angles and perspectives.

32.2.1 Beyond Techno-Legal Discourse of Inter-State Water Sharing: History, Geography, and Culture

Looking at inter-state water sharing solely through a legal, hydrological, or technical perspective leads us into a reductionist trap, failing to fully appreciate the multidimensionality of the issue at hand and possible solutions to address it. Geography, history, subnationalism, culture, and identity play a crucial link in understanding and deciphering some of the most contentious issues emerging in the current conflicts around water sharing among co-basin states. The immediate explanation is the

[24] Srinivas Chokkakula, 'Disputes, (de)Politicization and Democracy: Interstate Water Disputes in India' (Centre for Economic and Social Studies 2012).

mismatch between political boundary (which also, to some extent, binds the linguistic and cultural expressions of people) with the natural boundary of a basin spread over more than one political boundary and ethno-linguistic units.[25] While the natural boundary of the basin remains unaltered to a great extent, the political boundaries have undergone historical evolutions and shifts which also see conflicts around sharing of inter-state river waters in accordance to the shifting historical political boundaries. For example, the historical dispute between the princely state of Mysore and the Madras presidency on Cauvery water sharing is playing out now between the states of Karnataka and Tamil Nadu. Thus, the colonial historical legacy of water sharing is being carried forward in most of the present situations either as a continuity or as restructuring to accommodate the neoliberal agenda of developmentalism based on resource extraction.

Elements of nature such as rivers, land, and forests are also culturally and historically embedded with political formation and (sub)national identities. This identity formation is often criticized and to a large extent denigrated as undesirable and standing in the way of 'national interest'. A deeper understanding of cultural and ethno-linguistic identity and its relations with water and rivers is an important aspect if one has to look for sustainable solutions.[26]

32.2.2 Federalism vs Centralization: What is the Way Out?

The constitutional provisions for managing inter-state rivers are in the realm of both central and state subjects within the ambit of constitutional federalism. The ISWD Act (later amended in 2002 and 2019), and the River Boards Act, 1956, were introduced, along with the States Reorganisation Act, 1956, as the political, constitutional block for federal management of the Indian polity and geography. This is significant and points towards the need to address the issue of sharing the inter-state waters within the spirit of constitutional federalism. However, lingering disputes over many years, in the absence of long-term solutions between states, have seen voices demanding more intervention by the centre using its powers vested in various provisions such as entry 56 of the Union List, entry 20 in the Concurrent List, the River Boards Act, etc.[27] While entry 16 in the State List accords the responsibility of water resource development and management including water supplies, irrigation and canals, drainage and embankments, water storage and water power, etc. to states, it is subject to entry 56 of the Union List, which

[25] Radha D'Souza, 'At the Confluence of Law and Geography: Contextualising Inter-State Water Disputes in India' (2002) 33(2) *Geoforum* 255.

[26] Narendar Pani, 'Inter-State Water Conflicts and Linguistic Identity in India: The Case of the Cauvery' in K.J. Joy and S Janakarajan (eds), *India's Water Futures: Emergent Ideas and Pathways* (Routledge 2019) 253.

[27] Ramaswamy Iyer, 'Inter-State Water Disputes Act 1956: Difficulties and Solutions' (2002) 37(28) *Economic and Political Weekly* 2907.

states: 'Regulation and development of inter-state rivers and river valleys to the extent to which such regulation and development under the control of the Union is declared by Parliament by law to be expedient in the public interest'. While the states are accorded the right to manage their water resources (including water that belongs to inter-state rivers in their jurisdiction), the centre can intervene in case it deems fit. Entry 20 in the Concurrent List stipulates states get water resource development projects of a certain size cleared by the centre, which paves the way for the centre to play a higher role in water resource development by states.

The overall push towards centralization in recent times has threatened federalism in the country, and the water sector has not escaped this. One of the striking examples in this regard is the recent constitution of the Godavari River Management Board (GRMB), the Krishna River Management Board (KRMB), and the constitution of an Apex Council for the supervision of the functioning of these boards. The centre's intervention in inter-state water disputes is seen as a pretext for making water a central subject.[28] The central government, in the exercise of the powers conferred under section 85 of the Andhra Pradesh Reorganisation Act, 2014 (APRA), constituted two River Management Boards effective from 2 June 2014 for the administration, regulation, maintenance, and operation of projects on Godavari and Krishna rivers. The notification from the Jal Shakti Ministry on 16 July 2021 details the roles and responsibilities of the respective Boards, their constitution, etc. The notification enlists all head works (barrages, dams, reservoirs, regulating structures), part of the canal network, and transmission lines of the projects/components over which the respective Board will have jurisdiction in taking decisions over the regulation, maintenance, and operation of projects on the two rivers. It brings thirty-five projects in the Krishna basin and seventy-one in the Godavari basin under the Boards' purview.[29] The respective Board will take care of water sharing as per awards made by the GWDT and the KWDT, which is against the original intent of the River Board Act. For example, the Narmada Control Authority, set up to implement the Narmada Tribunal Award, is not a River Board.[30] In the case of the newly constituted KRMB and the GRMB, they will have the power to direct the respective state governments for the maintenance of the projects or components specified by the two Boards. No person from Andhra Pradesh and Telangana will be appointed as the Chairman, Member-Secretary, Members, and Chief Engineers of either the KRMB or the GRMB. The representation from the respective states is limited to only two members: a technical member and an administrative member. The two

[28] Amarnath K Menon, 'Andhra Pradesh and Telangana: The River Water Wars' *India Today* (2 August 2021) <www.indiatoday.in/magazine/up-front/story/20210802-andhra-pradesh-and-telangana-the-river-water-wars-1831858-2021-07-23>.

[29] Vishwa Mohan, 'Centre Notifies Krishna and Godavari River Management Boards, New Tribunals in Pipeline to Address States' Concerns' *Times of India* (New Delhi, 16 July 2021) <https://timesofindia.indiatimes.com/india/centre-notifies-krishna-and-godavari-river-management-boards-new-tribunals-in-pipeline-to-address-states-concerns/articleshow/84477201.cms>.

[30] Srinivas Chokkakula, 'Why Do Interstate Water Disputes Emerge and Recur? An Anatomy of Ambiguities, Antagonisms and Asymmetries' (Centre for Economic and Social Studies 2017).

state governments have to stop all the ongoing works on unapproved projects effective from the date of publication of the notification until the said projects are appraised and approved as per the provisions of the said Act.[31] This draws us to the issue of how to share inter-state river waters among co-basin states democratically and amicably, based on the principles and values of federalism, equity across states and sectors and the long-term sustainability of the river and its resources.

32.2.3 Inter-State Water Disputes and Emerging Infrastructure Interventions

Apart from large dams, two other major interventions need to be critically examined in the context of inter-state water sharing and disputes—the National Inland Waterways Project and the Inter-Linking Rivers Project. Most of the 111 officially notified Inland National Waterways in India identified for the purposes of inland water transport as per the National Waterways Act, 2016, are on inter-state rivers. The nomenclature 'national waterways' itself is problematic and can be seen as another attempt towards centralization as they will be operationalized under the Inland Waterways Authority of India. Studies show that national waterways involve large infrastructure development, massive dredging of riverbeds, alteration of the river morphology, bringing new conflicts around water use between sectors, say, fisheries, irrigation, transport, etc.,[32] with the potential of creating additional stressors in the already contentious inter-state water issues. The Interlinking of Rivers projects too envisages the construction of infrastructures, diversion of water, and hereby creating new contestations around water.

32.2.4 Climate Change: Emerging Trigger

Climate change and its impact on water resources and river systems could become a significant issue in water sharing between states, whether it is induced because of drought and scarcity or excess rainfall and floods. The impact would not only be on the available resources across states and regions but also on sharing the cost and losses resulting

[31] For discussions on the implications of this notification, especially from the point of centralization of powers in the context of inter-state rivers, see M Sridhar Acharyulu, 'The Great Indian River Question: Three Bills Threatening Federalism' *Down To Earth* (19 August 2020) < www.downtoearth.org.in/news/water/the-great-indian-river-question-three-bills-threatening-federalism-72913>; Biksham Gujja, 'Why Centre's "Unjustified" Role in Andhra-Telangana Water Dispute is Worrying' *The Wire* (6 August 2021) <https://thewire.in/government/why-centres-unjustified-role-in-andhra-telangana-water-dispute-is-worrying>.

[32] Shripad Dharmadhikary and Avli Verma, 'Grand Plans, Many Questions: A Status Review of Claims, Progress and Impacts of the National Inland Waterways Program' (Manthan Adhyayan Kendra 2021) <www.manthan-india.org/wp-content/uploads/2021/05/Grand-Plans-Many-Questions_CompressPdf.pdf>.

from the same. Most often, inter-state water sharing issues peak during times of scarcity and are further compounded by political compulsions within the states. This is also true for excess runoff and issues related to reservoir management and operations where a particular infrastructure project is in upstream states (flood as in the case of Maharashtra) or downstream regions (as in the case of Kerala). The uncertainty in rainfall and the rate of precipitation (cloud burst, intensive spells of short duration, etc.) means that the problem will be amplified in the future and add a new dimension to the already fragile inter-state water relations.

In the past few years, many inter-state conflicts have emerged in India and the section highlights the ongoing shift in the management and control of the rivers from the state to the centre. The inter-state water sharing has many complexities related to political dimensions and the influence of power, and the current techno-legal approaches are not working. Hence, there is a need to look at an alternative approach that is more participatory and takes into account the practical nuances on the ground. In the next section, we articulate the alternative approach for inter-state water sharing for the Mahanadi River.

32.3 Inter-State Water Sharing: the Case of the Mahanadi River Basin

Inter-state water sharing is mainly driven by a dispute resolution-centric approach and not by concern for the holistic conservation of the river basin. In this section, we suggest an alternative approach to address inter-state water sharing issues, which considers the needs of the people of both the states as well as the health of the basin, taking the Mahanadi basin as an illustrative case.

32.3.1 Mahanadi River Basin: Water Availability and Use

Mahanadi, an east-flowing peninsular river, covers a total area of 141,589 km^2. Chhattisgarh (73,214 km^2) and Odisha (65,847 km^2) are its major riparian states. The water availability and use are presented in Table 32.1.

32.3.2 Conflict in the Mahanadi Basin Around Water Sharing

In the past, there have been strong contestations in the basin as farmers resisted the increased allocation of water from the Hirakud reservoir for industrial use.[33] In 2016,

[33] Pranab Choudhury, Jinda Sandbhor, and Priyabrata Satapathy, 'Floods, Fields and Factories: Towards Resolving Conflicts Around Hirakud Dam' (Forum for Policy Dialogue on Water Conflicts in India 2012).

Table 32.1 Total water availability and use in the Mahanadi basin

Description	Water availability and use (BCM)		
	Mahanadi Basin	Chhattisgarh	Odisha
Annual surface water	66.8	36.9	29.9
Utilizable average surface water[a]	50.0	27.5	22.5
Total available groundwater[b]	13.6	6.8	6.8
Total utilizable water	63.6	34.3	29.3
Estimated surface and groundwater use for irrigation	18.8	8.0	10.8
Estimated industrial water use	2.1	1.1	1.0

(*Source*: Prepared by the authors drawing on data from: Central Water Commission and National Remote Sensing Centre, 'Mahanadi Basin' (Ministry of Water Resources and Indian Space Research Organisation 2014); Abraham Samuel, K.J. Joy and Sarita Bhagat, 'Integrated Water management of the Mahanadi Basin: Water Resources, Water Allocation and Inter-Sectoral Use' (Forum for Policy Dialogue on Water Conflicts in India 2017) <https://waterconflictforum.org/lib_docs/Integrated-Management-of-the-Mahanadi-basin.pdf>)

[a] The contribution of utilizable surface water from Chhattisgarh and Odisha is assumed to be on 55:45 basis based on the percentage of geographical area occupied by both the states in the basin.

[b] The contribution of replenishable groundwater from Chhattisgarh and Odisha is assumed to be on a 50:50 basis.

the conflict between Chhattisgarh and Odisha emerged allegedly because of the construction of barrages, diversion and pick-up weirs across the Mahanadi in Chhattisgarh including the Arpa-Bhaisajhar barrage and two under construction projects (the Pairy-Mahanadi Intra State Link Project and the Tandula Reservoir Augmentation Scheme). Odisha is apprehensive of these upstream developments because they may reduce the inflow into the Hirakud dam.

Irrigation water has increasingly been diverted for industrial use in recent times in both states. For example, an assessment of eight new barrages and one anicut in Chhattisgarh shows that the water from these structures is earmarked for industrial use, primarily to supply water to thermal power plants.[34] Civil Society Organizations in both states are of the opinion that the real conflict is between agriculture and industry though it is framed as one of inter-state water sharing. According to them, both the state governments are treating the Mahanadi water as a commodity to benefit the industries and are completely ignoring the needs of the farmers.[35]

[34] Craig D'Souza and others, 'Water Allocation and Use in the Mahanadi Basin: A Study of the Agricultural and Industrial Sectors' (Forum for Policy Dialogue on Water Conflicts in India 2017) <https://waterconflictforum.org/lib_docs/Water-Allocations-and-Use-in-Mahanadi-River-basin.pdf>.

[35] Keshab Chandra Ratha, 'Revisiting the Mahanadi Water Dispute Discourse: A Reflection of Diverse Perspectives' (2019) 18(1) *Maharshi Dayanand University Research Journal ARTS* 103.

32.3.3 Efforts by the Government to Resolve the Issue

In 2016, the Odisha government filed a petition against the Chhattisgarh government with the Ministry of Jal Shakti for constructing a series of 'illegal' barrages upstream of the Hirakud dam that can reduce the inflows to the Hirakud reservoir. The Odisha government sought to refer the dispute to a tribunal for adjudication under the ISWD Act. The central government initially constituted a Negotiation Committee to settle the ongoing disputes. However, the Odisha government did not participate in the proceedings. The Negotiation Committee submitted its report in May 2017, stating that efforts to bring about mutual agreement had failed. The central government, therefore, constituted the Mahanadi Water Disputes Tribunal on 12 March 2018, and as per the notification dated 3 June 2021, the period for submission of the report has been extended to March 2023.[36]

32.3.4 Alternative Approach for Water Sharing

One of the central gaps in sharing water among the basin states through the tribunals is that there are no commonly agreed-upon principles and norms for water allocation. Different tribunals have used different allocation norms. For example, in the case of the Narmada Water Dispute Tribunal Award, it is alleged that Gujarat got a much larger share of Narmada waters as compared to its contribution to the Narmada flows because large tracts of Gujarat are drought-prone. Also, different basin states use different principles of water sharing to get a better deal for themselves. In the case of the river Cauvery, Tamil Nadu argued its case based on the prior appropriation principle while Karnataka used the Helsinki principles.[37] It is hoped that the alternative approach presented below can be used as the starting point for a dialogue among all concerned stakeholders to evolve consensus on the principles and norms of water sharing and allocation.[38]

Based on the engagement—research and stakeholder meetings—in the Mahanadi basin for over a decade on water conflict-related issues, the Water Conflicts Forum developed an alternative approach to inter-state water sharing and management of the basin.

Alternative approach to inter-state water sharing: the techno-anthropocentric approach to rivers and waters, especially in terms of water use and allocation, has resulted in many river basins getting depleted with reduced flows. There are several

[36] Ministry of Jal Shakti, 'Mahanadi Water Disputes Tribunal' (2021) <http://jalshakti-dowr.gov.in/interstatedisputesactsandtr/mahanadi-water-disputes-tribunal>.

[37] S Saraswathi, 'Water Sharing: Principles to Replace Politics' *Sarkaritel.com* (undated) <https://www.sarkaritel.com/water-sharing-principles-to-replace-politics/>.

[38] This section is based on K.J. Joy and others (n 23) 11.

examples where all the utilizable water is allocated to the states as part of the tribunal awards resulting in over-exploitation and damning of the rivers by the respective states. In the alternative approach, we propose a set of guiding principles and norms for allocation based on these principles, which would result in sustainable water use and equitable allocation, as well as ensure the health of the river ecosystems. These are drawn from the learnings of managing transboundary waters as propounded by international conventions such as the Convention on the Law of the Non-Navigational Uses of International Watercourses (1997) and national water policies as well as the Water Conflicts Forum's engagement with water disputes and with various stakeholders trying to address these issues.[39]

Alternative principles for water sharing:[40] an alternative vision and approach are needed for managing the waters of the entire river basin, including, but not confined to, the visible flows in the river or allocations between states. Such a vision for integrated water management in the river basin should be embedded in equitable and sustainable resource use and democratic governance, grounded in a hierarchy of principles, and drawing upon a rigorous and nuanced understanding of the prevailing ecological and socio-economic situation.

The hierarchy of principles in the sharing of Mahanadi waters could be:

1) *Water for life*: providing adequate water of acceptable quality for drinking, cooking and sanitation needs of all the people in the basin, including water allocations for livestock as a separate category.
2) *Water for the ecosystem*: ensuring adequate water flows in the river system for aquatic life and other ecological functions.
3) *Water for sustaining livelihoods*: enabling productive activities (agriculture, artisan work, etc.) while ensuring equitable use and protecting public health.
4) *Water for adaptation to change*: keeping reserves and margins for ongoing and future demographic, economic and land use changes and climate change.

Based on the above hierarchy of principles for different uses and making assumptions of water required for each of these uses,[41] the alternative water allocations for both the states for the years 2030 and 2050 are summarized in Table 32.2.

[39] ibid.

[40] The alternative principles and their hierarchy were first articulated in a joint statement on the Cauvery dispute. See Water Conflicts Forum (n 20).

[41] We have used the following norms for different uses: (1) Water for life (domestic water): 100 lpcd (litres per capita per day) for all households in the basin, (2) Water for livestock: 30 litres per animal unit, (3) Water for the ecosystem (environment flows): 24 per cent of the total renewable water resource of 66.9 BCM, i.e., about 16 BCM, (4) Water for sustaining livelihoods: Every rural household (an average of five members) gets 4,000 m^3 of applied water (at source) for their livelihood needs including agriculture, (5) Water for adaptation to change: this is taken as 10 per cent of the utilizable water, i.e., 6.36 BCM, and (6) Water for industrial/commercial water use: the same as in BAU scenario (present use: 2.07 BCM, in 2030: 4.08 BCM and in 2050: 4.5 BCM). For details, see Joy and others (n 23) 20.

Table 32.2 Water use projection under alternative approach-based scenario (in BCM)

Uses	2030			2050		
	Chhattisgarh	Odisha	Total	Chhattisgarh	Odisha	Total
Water for life	1.13	0.94	2.07	1.92	1.28	3.02
Water for livestock	0.28	0.28	0.56	0.28	0.28	0.56
Water for the ecosystem	8.39	6.97	15.36	8.39	6.97	15.36
Water for agriculture livelihoods	16.5	15.6	32.10	18.3	14.7	33.00
Water for adaptation to change	3.50	2.86	6.36	3.50	2.86	6.36
Water for industrial water use	2.50	1.58	4.08	2.8	1.81	4.61
Total use/allocation	32.30	28.23	60.53	35.19	27.90	63.09
Utilizable water	34.30	29.30	63.60	34.30	29.30	63.60
Overall water balance	2.00	1.07	3.07	-0.89	1.40	0.41

(*Source*: Prepared by authors based on K.J. Joy and others, 'Mahanadi Basin: An Alternative Approach to Inter-state Water Sharing and Management' (Forum for Policy Dialogue on Water Conflicts in India 2021) <https://waterconflictforum.org/lib_docs/Report-Mahanadi-2021.pdf>).

The proposed alternative approach-based water allocation scenario shows that we are operating within the available water except in the case of the 2050 scenario for the Chhattisgarh, where there is a small gap between availability and requirement. This gap can be covered by improving water use efficiency, reusing and recycling of wastewater and effluents, and adopting water saving techniques both in agriculture and thermal power plants. Domestic water use, especially in urban areas, can be brought down by the reuse of treated grey water for flushing, gardening, washing vehicles, etc., which presently get clubbed together with domestic water.

We would like to emphasize that the numbers given here are not absolute; they would change if we got more reliable data and with changes in the agreed upon norms for different uses. The alternative approach shows that the first step is for the diverse stakeholders in the basin to agree on the hierarchy of principles for water allocation and use norms for different uses.

32.4 Institutional Arrangements and Processes for Basin Management

To ground the alternative approach discussed above would require a different institutional architecture and process, as the present process is top-down and limited to only state actors. Non-state actors (like civil society organizations, academic institutions and communities) have no role. Against this, we suggest a participatory and transparent process and boundary conditions for deciding on water sharing. We propose three preconditions. First, sharing the river waters cannot be left to a centralized political or bureaucratic process alone; water governance must be democratic, decentralized, and participatory. Second, all information and data pertaining to water at all scales and locations—rainfall, runoff, evaporation, surface and groundwater stocks and withdrawals, land use and cropping—that is gathered by any agency using public funds must be publicly available. Third, collaborative networks of citizens, civil society organizations, academic institutions, and state agencies dedicated to analysing and communicating this information for use by decision-makers at all levels—village, town, tehsil, district, state, and basin—should be enabled. [42]

Various international declarations/treaties[43] like the UNECE Convention on the Protection and Use of Transboundary Watercourses and International Lakes, 1992 and the Convention on Law of the Non-navigational uses of International Watercourses, 1997 around transboundary rivers bring forth two important conditions for transboundary

[42] This section draws on Samuel, Joy and Bhagat (n 23) 25.

[43] Atlas of International Freshwater Agreements <https://na.unep.net/siouxfalls/publications/treaties/2_WorldsAgreements_atlas.pdf>.

water sharing treaties to work: first, the treaty should not jeopardize the legitimate rights of others, and second, it should not cause any 'significant harm' to others. These two conditions can provide a good framework for building a relationship of cooperation among the co-basin states.

32.4.1 Institutions and Policy/Legal Regimes Should be Informed of the Biophysical Characteristics of Water

The legal and institutional mechanisms around water governance are fragmented and, in most cases, not informed by the biophysical characteristics—including the common pool character—of water as a resource. The biophysical characteristics of water include: (i) water is divisible and amenable to sharing, (ii) it has multiple uses and users and involves resultant trade-offs, (iii) a unit of water allocated to use or user becomes unavailable to another use or user, (iv) excludability is an inherent problem, especially with regard water in its natural form and exclusion costs involved, are very often high, (v) it requires consideration and understanding of expanding scales and boundaries from the local watersheds to basins as rivers and aquifers cut through state and national boundaries, and (vi) the way water is planned, used, and managed causes externalities—both positive and negative—and most of them are unidirectional (as water in its natural form flows in one direction, from upstream to downstream) and asymmetric (the actions of upstream users impact the downstream people and not vice versa).[44]

32.4.2 Bureaucratic River Basin Organizations Would not Work

The current institutional structures do not enable integrated and participatory governance of water resources. The proposed alternative scenario would require an inclusive and democratic/participatory institutional mechanism where all stakeholders (officials as well as various water users and interest groups) are involved in river basin planning, management, and governance, including conflict resolution. In recent times, there has been an emphasis on the formation of RBOs as part of the Integrated Water Resource Management (IWRM) strategy. Various water-related policy documents, including the National Water Policy, 2012 also refer to the need to create RBOs. But so far, our

[44] Sharachchandra Lélé, 'Beyond State-Community Polarisations and Bogus "Joint"ness: Crafting Institutional Solutions for Resource Management' in Max Spoor (ed), *Globalisation, Poverty and Conflict: A Critical 'Development' Reader* (Kluwer 2004) 283.

experience shows that such initiatives have been highly top-down, centralized, and bureaucratic.

32.4.3 Nested Institutions at Different Scales

We need effective institutions from the bottom up, starting from the micro-watershed and then moving to a milli-watershed, sub-basin, and then basin scale within a nested and delegated democratic framework. These institutions should have representation of various stakeholders, and they should be a platform for democratic decision-making. The institutions at various hydrological scales must function within the principle of subsidiarity. Also, these institutions must be legally mandated so that the decisions they make are legally enforceable.

32.4.4 Separate Institutions for Governance and Management

Institutions play two roles: governance, which is political in nature, and management. Governance functions involve deciding on the norms and principles of resource allocation, water rights and entitlements, pricing, operation and maintenance (O&M), and conflict resolution. Management functions involve activities like day-to-day functioning, implementation of governance decisions, actual O&M, data collection, and so on. Separate institutions are required to carry out these different functions. The decentralized RBOs (or multi-stakeholder platforms) could be the governance institutions at different scales, and these institutions can set up smaller teams for the management functions.

32.4.5 Periodic Review

The award of the tribunal should not be seen as a one-time effort or event. All the tribunal awards have a provision for review and possible reallocation of unutilized water. As discussed earlier in the context of KWDT-I, this leads to very desperate and often socially and ecologically unsustainable measures to utilize each state's share of water. This type of situation needs to be avoided by adopting transparent processes and implementing them within the alternative framework presented above. A shorter time span for reviews, which are undertaken more frequently, say, once in five years, ideally or at the most ten years is also important because of the rapid changes taking place (and the resultant uncertainties) in people's livelihood patterns and aspirations, land use, cropping and agronomical practices, and climate.

32.4.6 Adaptive Management

An important lesson in the context of water sharing among co-basin states is that one-time, prescriptive, top-down solutions—either by the tribunal or the Supreme Court—may not resolve the issues meaningfully. For a socially and environmentally just solution, we need to move to an adaptive management approach. In light of various *lacunae* in the functioning of tribunals (as discussed earlier), increasing uncertainties, and knowledge gaps, we need an adaptive management approach. Adaptive management allows us to make changes in the water sharing plan in the light of an improved understanding of the biophysical and social systems, new information resulting from changed or unforeseen circumstances, and new or updated models. It provides the space to review and make changes in the water sharing plan as per the changing context and stakeholder preferences. It encourages stakeholders to discuss water sharing issues in an orderly fashion while environmental uncertainties are being investigated and better understood. It uses uncertainty as an important factor in decision-making. The approach also needs to be embedded in an alternative set of principles of sharing (that we discussed in Section 32.4), sound science and participatory processes with active participation from non-state actors.

Conclusion

As discussed in Section 32.2 above, for socially and environmentally just water sharing among co-basin states along with water, it is important to engage with issues of subnationalism, identity, culture, history, and power asymmetries. Contestations related to sharing river waters among co-basin states are logical developments in the absence of proper democratic, legal and institutional mechanisms for negotiated settlements. The policy, legal and institutional mechanisms are fragmented and also are, in most cases, not informed of the biophysical characteristics—including the common pool character—of water as a resource. Neither non-state actors nor the local riparian communities have any role to play in the functioning of the tribunals, and their needs and aspirations are not often considered, though the inter-state water sharing agreements impact the lives and livelihoods of local riparian communities in different ways. It is important to recognize that communities are at the forefront of the consequences of inter-state water sharing agreements or tribunal awards.

One of the central gaps in inter-state water sharing through tribunals is the absence of clear principles and norms of allocation that guide the tribunal's processes. As a result, different riparian states use different doctrines as per their relative advantage. A clear understanding of sharing shortages among co-basin states is equally important as water sharing arrangements get stretched during times of scarcity and drought, resulting in contestations. The chapter tries to bridge this gap by proposing a set of principles and norms for water allocation. Also, the chapter proposes a democratic, nested and legally mandated institutional space at different scales for all the stakeholders to participate in and build consensus around water allocation and all other aspects of water governance and management.

We suggest three necessary conditions to prevent and/or resolve inter-state conflicts, namely, a) reliable and agreed-upon data on water at all scales and locations—rainfall, runoff, evaporation, surface and groundwater stocks and withdrawals, land use and cropping—that is gathered by any agency using public funds must be publicly available; b) an agreed-upon framework for determining entitlements and allocations, for each agro-ecological-social context; and c) legally mandated multi-stakeholder platforms at different scales for all the stakeholders to participate in and build consensus. Collaborative networks of citizens, civil society organizations, academics, and state agencies dedicated to analysing and communicating this information for use by decision-makers at all levels—village, town, taluk, district, state, and basin—should be enabled.

Referring to the quote in the introduction, which essentially says that the co-basin states must be responsible trustees of the river, and all the people in the basin have a right to use the water, but without violating the right to water for life for others in the river basin. To this, we would add the use of water should not compromise the ecological integrity and functions of the river basin.

Suggestions for Further Reading

Srinivas Chokkakula, 'Disputes, (De)politicization and Democracy: Interstate Water Disputes in India' (2012) *Centre for Economic and Social Studies*, Working Paper No 108) <https://cess.ac.in/wp-content/uploads/2019/12/CESS-Working-Paper-No.108.pdf>.

Srinivas Chokkakula, 'Why do Interstate Water Disputes Emerge and Recur? An Anatomy of Ambiguities, Antagonisms and Asymmetries' (Centre for Economic and Social Studies 2017).

Ramaswamy R Iyer (ed), *Water and the Laws in India* (Sage 2009).

K.J. Joy and S Janakarajan, 'Inter-State Water Disputes among the Riparian States: The Case of Cauvery River from Peninsular India' (Pakistan Institute of Legislative Development and Transparency 2011) <www.indiawaterportal.org/sites/default/files/iwp2/interstate_water_disputes_among_the_riperain_states_the_case_of_the_cauvery_river_kj_joy_and_s_janakarajan_pildat_2011.pdf>.

K.J. Joy and others, 'Mahanadi Basin: An Alternative Approach to Inter-state Water Sharing and Management—An Approach Paper' (Forum for Policy Dialogue on Water Conflicts in India 2021) <https://waterconflictforum.org/lib_docs/Report-Mahanadi-2021.pdf>.

CHAPTER 33

WATER DISPUTES AND THE ENVIRONMENT

Transboundary Dimensions

SRINIVAS CHOKKAKULA*

Abstract

The chapter presents a historical perspective of India's transboundary relationships to engage with water disputes and environmental risks. This offers a nuanced understanding of India's engagement with the narratives about its role as a hydrohegemon and its preference for bilateralism. Additionally, despite the uneven responses to the UN Watercourses Convention, 1997, the evolving water disputes case law shows an encouraging trend of accommodating for climate change and other environmental risks. Building on these strands and the emerging context of transboundary environmental risks surrounding India, the chapter posits that India's development interests and the collective concerns of transboundary environmental risks in South Asia align. This allows for building a case for an incremental evolution of regional institutional architecture, beginning with a pursuit of disaster resilience in South Asia. The new rationalities of transboundary environmental risks may be the basis for addressing the structural deficiencies and rebuilding the existing dormant regional institutions.

* Acknowledgements: I thank Debarshee Dasgupta for the research assistance; Ashwin Pandya and Shyam Babu for their comments on an earlier draft.

Introduction: India's Transboundary Relations

India's transboundary relationships with its South Asian neighbouring countries are embedded in the Indus, the Ganges, and the Brahmaputra (more comprehensively, GBM—Ganges-Brahmaputra-Meghna) river systems. The interdependencies constituted by these shared river ecosystems in the intersection of water resources development and the environment are diverse. They range from irrigation and hydropower development to coping with disasters and other environmental risks.

There is extensive literature characterizing the transboundary interactions in South Asia and, more so by India, as 'bilateralism' driven.[1] Indeed, bilateralism is the dominant descriptor of the transboundary relationships. It is often used to present a power relationship in support of the argument that India is a regional 'hydrohegemon'. This chapter, while exploring the intersection of transboundary water disputes and the environment, seeks to present two less-explored perspectives and offers a nuanced narrative of this imagination of India's dominant role in South Asia.

The first is a historical perspective of India's transboundary relationships, which is useful to critically engage with these narratives. Most transboundary relationships are initiated and invested in by India, usually to pursue the goals of development and coping with risk. These early initiatives, though conceived with progressive goals, were fragmented and were not always consistent with the later environmental sensibilities. These are perceived, often in retrospect, as poorly conceived. These perceptions also extend credence to the 'hydrohegemony' narratives. In contrast, the history of the contingent rationalities of the transboundary relationships offers a textured understanding to raise doubts about such overarching assessments. The purpose is to suggest that such assessments can be a hurdle for exploring effective multilateral options for future engagement.

The second is that the growing and emerging risks, such as climate change, floods, and deteriorating water quality, warrant a nuanced reading of the transboundary context and interdependencies for coping with the risks. The advantages of conventional power asymmetries in transboundary water sharing—whether produced geographically or historically—are disrupted and can potentially be normalized by the evolving collective risks and governance challenges. Political economy-driven power asymmetries are no exception to these normalization possibilities. The chapter provides a glimpse of the

[1] Anamika Barua, Sumit Vij, and Zulfiqur Rahman, 'Powering or Sharing Water in the Brahmaputra River Basin' (2018) 34(5) *International Journal of Water Resources Development* 829; Sumit Vij and others, 'Non-decisions are also Decisions: Power Interplay Between Bangladesh and India over the Brahmaputra River' (2020) 45(4) *Water International* 254; Punam Pandey, 'The Ganges River Negotiation: Idealism of Regional Cooperation or Pragmatic Bilateralism' (2018) 74(4) *India Quarterly* 438.

potential of using the lens of transboundary interdependencies for mobilizing collective action.

To pursue these perspectives, the chapter is organized in the following manner. In Section 33.1, I briefly revisit India's 'chosen' paradigm of bilateralism in its transboundary water relations to suggest that the rationalities are likely driven more by contingent and historical demands rather than a deliberate choice of bilateralism. This is further supported by a review of the existing—or rather lack of—legal and institutional architecture for a more holistic pursuit of transboundary river governance in South Asia. The section closes with a brief discussion of India's aligning interests in development and environmental risk coping. In Section 33.2, I pursue the theme of the absence of a comprehensive framework and the preference for a contingency approach (as in bilateralism) by engaging with empirical examples of transboundary water governance. These instances focus on environmental management dimensions of transboundary governance as an underlying or emerging concern for India. The examples will be discussed under two subheads: 33.2.1 international—focusing on India's transboundary engagements with its neighbours, and 33.2.2 inter-state (intra-national)—focusing on transboundary governance challenges between states within India. The objective is to show how India's domestic water security interests are deeply linked to its environmental management imperatives internally as well as externally, and increasingly so with effective transboundary governance. Section 33.3 returns to the existing regimes for governance for a critical examination of their relevance to addressing the challenge of transboundary environmental risks in the region.

33.1 Existing Transboundary Water Regime

33.1.1 Bilateralism: the Character of India's Transboundary Water Relations

None among India's neighbouring nations have shared territorial boundaries. This itself should offer a unique perspective on India's history of bilateralism. Besides, the evolution of transboundary river water relationships between India and its neighbours is marked by responses to contingencies and exigencies. This is primarily for coping with risks, followed by development interests and imperatives. The risk-coping interests are all about floods, though invariably accompanied by other benefits of irrigation and power generation. One of the first transboundary projects of Independent India, the Kosi Barrage—under the 1954 agreement between India and Nepal—was built essentially to address flood risk to the downstream Indian state of Bihar.[2] The more recent

[2] India-Nepal transboundary cooperation goes back to British India under colonial rule.Dharma Raj Bagale, 'Nepal–India Water Cooperation: Consequences of Mutuality or Hegemony?' (2020) 22(6)

transboundary arrangement for data sharing between India and China is also about coping with flood risk.

The rest of the transboundary arrangements of India, as Table 33.1 indicates, are for development objectives—water sharing, irrigation benefits, and power generation. Table 33.1 also shows that the transboundary arrangements along all its borders are largely initiated by India and executed bilaterally. The Indus Treaty negotiations were initiated by India and mediated by the World Bank. The agreements with Nepal over the rivers Mahakali, Gandak, and Kosi were essentially proposed and driven by India. The transboundary hydropower projects with Bhutan, as well as data sharing with China, were pursued by India. With Bangladesh, the most visible cooperation over the Farakka barrage is an outcome of Bangladesh's demand for a water sharing agreement. This was in response to India's proposals to divert water to address the problem of sedimentation in Kolkata Harbour. Most other India-Bangladesh cooperation initiatives were also established in a similar manner, propelled by India's developmental interests.

A perusal of this history of transboundary relationships presented in Table 33.1 does establish that bilateralism is undoubtedly the dominant strategy. At the same time, it is also India-driven. But the two do not necessarily translate to making India a hegemon; India happens to be the early initiator of transboundary relations. Yet bilateralism is used to argue that India has always pursued transboundary relationships as a 'hegemon'. The India-Nepal transboundary relationship is often used to support the popular theoretical framework, hydrohegemony.[3] The framing implies that a hydrohegemon tends to get favourable outcomes—serving its own interests at the cost of its neighbours. The evidence does not unequivocally support this view if we consider the varied outcomes between India and Nepal. Nepal forced India to renegotiate over river Kosi and did not agree to the proposals for a supplementary High Dam, upstream of the existing barrage. While India may have pursued its interests, Nepal has a long history of successfully renegotiating the agreements over the rivers Kosi, Gandak, and Mahakali.[4]

This happens to be so with Bangladesh, its downstream country as well—where India, as an upstream state, is supposedly at an advantage. As Table 33.1 shows, India and Bangladesh have had the most intense and consistent bilateral interactions over transboundary rivers. This is natural considering the scale, scope, and extent of the geographically determined transboundary interests extending over the Ganges, Brahmaputra, and Barak basins. As evident from Table 33.1, Bangladesh was reasonably successful in negotiating this asymmetry to pursue and protect its interests. The long-negotiated Ganges Treaty and the projects on the Feni River are illustrative, besides Bangladesh's rejection of India's proposed hydropower projects in more than one instance. When the proposals for the development of transboundary rivers posed environmental and disaster risks, Bangladesh resisted these initiatives, which led to

Water Policy 1098; Subash P Rai, Aaron T Wolf, and Nayan Sharma, 'Hydropolitics and Hydropolitical Dynamics between India and Nepal: An Event-based Study (2017) 19(5) *Water Policy* 791.

[3] Naho Mirumachi, Transboundary Water Politics in the Developing World (Routledge 2015).

[4] Rai and others (n 2).

Table 33.1 India's Transboundary Water Relationships

Country	River System	Transboundary waters relationship (conflictual and/or cooperative relationship)	Institutional Arrangements
Pakistan	Indus	• Indus Water Treaty, 1960, for sharing Indus waters. • Conflict over Tulbul Navigation Project—mouth of Wullar Lake (1980s) • Conflict over the Baglihar Hydroelectric Project on Chenab (1990s) • Conflict over Kishanganga Hydroelectric Project on Neelum (2000s)	• Permanent Indus Commission—bilateral • When the Commission fails to resolve, the World Bank coordinates resolution through a Neutral Expert or a Court of Arbitration.
Nepal	Ganges	• Kosi Agreement, 1954 (amended in 1966) to build Kosi barrage for flood protection, sharing irrigation, and power generation benefits o Agreement for renovation and extension of Chandra Canal (Western Kosi) 1978 for maintenance and additional works • Gandak Agreement, 1959 for Gandak Irrigation and Power Project • Mahakali Treaty, 1996 for Sarada Barrage, Tanakpur Barrage, and Pancheshwar Multipurpose Projects • Sapta-Kosi High Dam Project 2004 related joint investigations • Kamla and Bagmati Multipurpose Projects—joint studies under progress. • Karnali Multipurpose Project: DPR preparation under consideration	• Joint Nepal-India Ministerial Commission on Water Resources (post-2008 floods) • Joint Committee on Kosi and Gandak Projects • Mahakali River Commission (dispute resolution through arbitration by a jointly constituted tribunal) • Pancheshwar Development Authority for implementing Pancheshwar Project
Bhutan	Brahmaputra	• Jaldhaka Hydropower Project Agreement, 1961 • Chikha Hydropower Project Agreement, 1987 • Tala Hydropower Project Agreement, 1996 • Agreement to Cooperate in Hydropower Generation 2006 (signed in 2009) to generate a minimum of 10,000 MW power by 2020. Three projects initiated: Punatsangchhu-I & II and Mangdechhu. • Agreement to Cooperate in Hydropower Generation, 2014 to develop four projects of 2120 MW capacity: Kholongchhu, Bunakha, Wangchhu, and Chamkharchhu.	• Joint Hydro-meteorological and Flood Forecasting Network monitored by a Joint Experts Team. • A Joint Group of Expert (JGE) on Flood Management to discuss and assess the probable causes and effects of recurring floods.

(continued)

Table 33.1 Continued

Country	River System	Transboundary waters relationship (conflictual and/or cooperative relationship)	Institutional Arrangements
China	Brahmaputra Satluj (Indus)	• MoU 2002 (renewed again in 2013 and 2018) for sharing hydrological information on Yaluzangbu/Brahmaputra River (also of Sutlej in Indus) during flood season by China to India. o During the Doklam standoff in 2017, China did not share data. • India's resistance to China's hydropower projects in the upstream, November 2020	• Joint Expert Level Mechanism
Bangladesh	Ganges	• Establishment of the Joint River Commission 1972 to augment development potential from the 54 shared rivers. • Protocol on Inland Water Trade and Transit, 1972, for inland waterways connectivity and promote trade. o Addendum in 2020 with new routes • Farakka Barrage conflict (1975) and cooperation (1977, 1983, 1988); Ganges Water Treaty, 1996 for sharing Ganga river waters during the lean season (until 2026) • Framework Agreement on Cooperation for Development, 2011 for enhancing cooperation in trade, investment, economic cooperation, connectivity, water resources, management of natural disasters, generation, transmission and distribution of electricity, including renewable sources. o Formation of a Joint Technical Committee to conduct a feasibility study of the proposed Ganges-Padma Barrage Project in Bangladesh.	• Joint River Commission (JRC) • Joint Committee to give effect to the Treaty. Any dispute if not resolved by the Joint Committee, shall be referred to JRC.
	Brahmaputra (Teesta)	• Teesta (ad-hoc) waters sharing agreement 1983 o Interim arrangement for 15 years 2011: shelved due to resistance from West Bengal.	• JRC

	Barak	• Conflict over Tipaimukh Hydropower Project 1999: proposed by India with Bangladesh, raising environmental and other concerns about floods and other disaster-preparedness. o A Prime-Ministerial Dialogue in 2010 led to assurance from India of no steps that would lead to adverse impacts in Bangladesh. • Conflict and Cooperation over Feni Water Sharing 2019: the dispute over the sharing of Feni River waters goes back to pre-independence times of Bangladesh in 1958 with then Pakistan. o At a Prime Minister level meeting in 2019, it was agreed to firm up a draft framework for interim water sharing of Feni River along with multiple MoUs on connectivity and water resources development over six rivers, namely, Manu, Muhuri, Khowai, Gumti, Dharla, and Dudhkumar. o Following Secretary-level meeting led to an agreement allowing withdrawal of water from Feni River for drinking water of Sabroom town of Tripura. o Maitri Setu 2021: built over Feni River connecting the North-Eastern region in India and Chittagong Port	• Joint Committee of Experts in 1997, followed by a Joint Technical Group in 2004 to make recommendations. In 2013, a joint study was to be taken up under JRC.
Myanmar	Barak	• Agreement for building two hydropower projects 2008 over Tamanthi and Shwesayay rivers. o Myanmar scrapped the projects	

Source: Author

negotiated settlements across the shared Ganges, Brahmaputra, and Barak basins. Such rejection of India's proposed projects has happened in other instances, too. Myanmar scrapped a bilateral agreement for hydropower projects in the Barak basin.

Yet the dominant perceptions characterizing India as a regional hydrohegemon persist. The retracing of the history of transboundary relations is not to make this argument, though. The idea is to place for consideration a historical narrative not always determined by supposed power differentials. And thus, to suggest that other substantive and material aspects mattered in transboundary negotiations. The dominant lens of politics of power and political economy must be qualified by the nuanced dimension of contingent and contextual political ecology shaping the transboundary arrangements.

Unfortunately, scholarship is not very helpful in enabling such a qualified approach. The narratives often tend to be, at best, partial and lack comprehensive engagement. Consider the following. A recent narrative of India-Nepal's history of transboundary water sharing argues that India is a hydrohegemon.[5] Another version of the same history argues that the arrangements are fair and historically contingent.[6] This is illustrative of the nature and character of the literature in South Asia, often subjective to positionalities of knowledge production. Any discussion about India's transboundary water relationships must consider these limitations and ambiguities.

33.1.2 Regional Context

The history presented in Table 33.1, though India-centric, provides an idea of transboundary water governance for water disputes and environmental management in South Asia. Bilateralism drives and thrives. Neither surprising nor exclusive to South Asia, it is the preferred approach globally.[7] Multilateral responses are rare. This is also why the global history of the evolution of a framework for transboundary water governance is not very inspiring. It took more than five decades for the global community to arrive at a framework convention addressing the challenge. The UN General Assembly initiated the process of drafting a framework in the early 1970s, which eventually led to the 1997 UN Convention on the Law of the Non-navigational Uses of International Watercourses (UN Watercourses Convention).[8] It took close to another two decades for

[5] Bagale (n 2).

[6] Hari Bansh Jha, 'Nepal–India Cooperation in River Water Management' (2013) 37(2) *Strategic Analysis* 217.

[7] See, for instance, Meredith Giordano, Mark Giordano, and Aaron Wolf, 'The Geography of Water Conflict and Cooperation: Internal Pressures and International Manifestations' (2003) 168(4) *The Geographical Journal* 293.

[8] Asit Biswas, 'Cooperation or Conflict in Transboundary Water Management: Case Study of South Asia' (2011) 56(4) *Hydrological Sciences Journal* 662; Gabriel Eckstein, 'The Status of the UN Watercourses Convention: Does it Still Hold Water?' (2020) 36(2–3) *International Journal of Water Resources Development* 429.

it to eventually gain the minimum required ratifications to come into force in 2014. The pace of ratifications after coming into force has also been low.[9]

The UN Watercourses Convention may be seen as the sole legal framework guiding transboundary governance in South Asia—other than the bilateral agreements in place. The response of South Asian nations to the convention is like that of the rest of the world—slow and uneven. China voted against the convention. India and Pakistan abstained. Bangladesh and Nepal voted in favour. Afghanistan and Bhutan did not attend the voting.[10] But none of the South Asia nations have ratified the convention yet.

This uneven geography of responses to the convention reflects the fractured landscape surrounding India. For India, China's choice in the upstream to stay out of the convention can be a factor in its own positioning. India, being the central and key driver of the transboundary relationships in the South Asia region, has implications for developing transboundary waters and coping with associated risks. The tenuous geopolitical relations between India and China have direct implications for development opportunities and ecological interdependencies in the shared GBM river systems.[11] On the other hand, the UN Watercourses Convention's apparent weaknesses impacted its relevance and adaptation, especially with respect to its prescriptive nature. Both India and China had reservations about these.[12]

Despite the not-so-inspiring history of the UN Watercourses Convention, it is possible to glean some silver-lining elements from transboundary governance experiences in South Asia. First, despite the absence of ratification, the international customary law principles of transboundary cooperation embodied in the convention—such as its earlier version in the form of the Helsinki Rules[13]—have always informed the negotiations between India and its neighbouring nations and shaped their transboundary relationships.[14] Second, the history of international customary law

[9] Eckstein (n 8).

[10] 'United Nations General Assembly Press Release GA/9248' (21 May 1997) <www.internationalwaterlaw.org/documents/intldocs/convention_press.html>.

[11] Lei Xie, Yanbing Zhang, and Jagannath P Panda, 'Mismatched Diplomacy: China–India Water Relations Over the Ganges–Brahmaputra–Meghna River Basin' (2018) 27(109) *Journal of Contemporary China* 32.

[12] Eckstein (n 8). See also, Huiping Chen, Alistair Rieu-Clarke, and Patricia Wouters, 'Exploring China's Transboundary Water Treaty Practice Through the Prism of the UN Watercourses Convention' (2013) 38(2) *Water International* 217.

[13] See Salman MA Salman, 'The Helsinki Rules, the UN Watercourses Convention and the Berlin Rules: Perspectives on International Water Law' (2007) 23(4) *International Journal of Water Resources Development* 625.

[14] The Indus Water Treaty was mediated by the World Bank. Though the Treaty has some exceptional provisions, international principles have guided the negotiations. On other fronts, India has always defended its position as informed by international customary law principles, though there are counter perspectives of advantage to India—especially with Nepal. The Indo-Bangladesh transboundary water relations, though, had gone through contentious negotiations informed by the international customary law principles. See Ravindra Pratap, 'Building Peace over Water in South Asia: The Watercourses Convention and SAARC' (2018) 4(1) *Athens Journal of Law* 7; Salman MA Salman and Kishor Uprety, *Conflict and Cooperation on South Asia's International Rivers: A Legal Perspective* (The World Bank 2002).

principles has had a deep and sustained influence on India's internal water conflicts—between Indian states—that are known to be complex and intractable. India's track record of resolving its inter-state water disputes through adjudication by tribunals showcases an extensive and innovative application of the principles of international customary law.[15] India's experiences of international and inter-state water disputes contribute to the repository of case law and influence transboundary water relationships. The rich and rigorous use of international customary principles in India's inter-state dispute tribunals can inform international negotiations in South Asia.

Other than the UN Watercourses Convention, it is difficult to mention any other institutional and legal frameworks for managing water disputes and the environment in South Asia. The South Asian Association for Regional Cooperation (SAARC) stands out as the most visible regional institutional architecture, in addition to the South Asia Cooperative Environment Programme (SACEP)—a parallel intergovernmental institution focused on regional environmental management. Despite their ambitious beginnings, the two institutions have turned dormant in recent times. We will revisit these institutional spaces in the fourth section to critically examine their relevance and potential with the emerging risks as discussed in the following section.

33.1.3 Aligning Development and Environmental Interests

In South Asia and for India, the transboundary context is shifting in a manner that the development interests align with managing collective environmental risks. Besides being the largest untapped market in the world, the development potential of water resources in South Asia is still untapped. The potential for pursuing development goals is widely emphasized.[16] The lamentations about the failure to realize this potential in South Asia remain valid.[17] The India-Bhutan cooperation is a powerful example of this potential. Bhutan, having the lowest per capita GDP in the 1980s in the region, has become the country with the highest per capita GDP in the region in three decades.[18] This growth is attributed rightly to the India-Bhutan cooperation over hydropower generation.[19]

[15] See Srinivas Chokkakula, *Why Do Interstate Water Disputes Emerge and Recur? An Anatomy of Ambiguities Antagonisms and Asymmetries* (CESS 2017).

[16] BG Verghese and Ramaswamy R Iyer, *Harnessing the Eastern Himalayan Rivers: Regional Cooperation in South Asia* (South Asia Books 1994); BG Verghese, *Waters of Hope: From Vision to Reality in Himalaya-Ganga Development Cooperation* (Centre for Policy Research 2007).

[17] Biswas (n 8).

[18] The World Bank, 'GDP per Capita (Current US$)—South Asia' <https://data.worldbank.org/indicator/NY.GDP.PCAP.CD?locations=8S>. Bhutan's per capita GDP is US$3,266.4 in 2021 compared to India's US$2,256.6, Nepal's US$1,208.2, Bangladesh's US$2,457.9, and Pakistan's US$1,505.0.

[19] Biswas (n 8).

The unharnessed development potential, and the growing realization of environmental risks make an ineluctable argument for greater transboundary cooperation. While there is growing evidence about the impact of climate change over the hydrological cycle, ambiguities about implications over space and time at local and regional scales persist. There is a greater probability of extreme water-related events in Asia affecting the most vulnerable populations.[20] The IPCC's recent Assessment Report—6 offers a less ambiguous picture of these impacts, especially flood and water quality risks.[21] Some of these impacts are more immediate for consideration by policymakers.

These impacts resonate in India, manifesting in flash floods that the Indian Himalayan Region (IHR) has been experiencing lately. These received extensive attention in the public discourse as well as policy discussions. The Standing Committee on Water Resources of the Parliament of India has tabled a report on glaciers in IHR recently. It prominently discusses the flash floods in IHR due to glacial melting and associated risks such as glacial lake outburst floods (GLOF), landslide lake outburst floods, avalanches, and flash floods.[22] Taking note of the emerging risks, the Committee made several recommendations to deal with the challenge of glacial management. It focused on the need for data gathering and monitoring of glaciers in IHR to develop actionable plans. The Committee recognized transboundary coordination as the core challenge, though limited to that at an international scale. It pointed to an absence of a multilateral mechanism and the lack of provisions within existing treaties for dealing with glacier-linked risks.[23] It urged the Ministry of Jal Shakti to take up the matter with the Ministry of External Affairs about India entering into a treaty/agreement for the purpose. This growing recognition from policymakers in India is an opportunity to address the shared transboundary environmental risks in South Asia. Along with India, South Asian nations can align their development interests with efforts to cope with the collective environmental risks through robust transboundary cooperation.

33.2 Contemporary Context of Transboundary Environmental Risks

The growing and emerging environmental risks in South Asia bring the fractured and dormant regional institutional spaces into sharp focus. A greater appreciation of the transboundary (or extra-territorial) nature of these risks can aid and advance the

[20] UN Water, *UN World Water Development Report: Water and Climate Change* (UNESCO 2020).

[21] MA Caretta and others, 'Water' in HO Pörtner and others (eds), *Climate Change 2022: Impacts, Adaptation, and Vulnerability*, Contribution of Working Group II to the Sixth Assessment Report of the Intergovernmental Panel on Climate Change (CUP 2022) 562–563.

[22] Lok Sabha Secretariat, *Glacier Management in the Country- Monitoring of Glaciers/Lakes including Glacial Lake Outbursts leading to Flash-floods in the Himalayan Region* (Standing Committee on Water Resources, Twenty-third Report 2023).

[23] ibid 39.

conception and reimagination of a regional institutional architecture to cope with the risks. I discuss these through empirical examples of transboundary water disputes under two categories. One is international—between India and its neighbours. Under this category, I focus on the environmental dimensions of disputes between India and Pakistan. I also make references to India's other transboundary relations, highlighting the extra-territorial environmental externalities warranting collective responses. Two, inter-state—between states within India that are invariably linked to the international transboundary governance in the Indus and the GBM basins. This focuses on the recent incidents of cloud bursts and GLOFs posing risks to Indian states downstream, necessitating greater transboundary coordination between states to cope with the environmental risks.

33.2.1 International Transboundary Spaces

The Indus Water Treaty (IWT or the Treaty) is a celebrated transboundary cooperation arrangement globally.[24] There is extensive literature exploring the explanatory variables for its success. One of the prominent ones is about the unique geographic division of rivers instead of allocations between the parties.[25] A more compelling and interesting argument is about the institutional arrangements in place for giving effect to the Treaty in the form of a Permanent Indus Commission and the other institutional practices provided by the Treaty for resolving differences or disputes arising between the parties.[26] Over the six decades of its existence, the IWT was tested by several events—related to water as well as those unrelated. The institutional arrangements in place did well to provide resilience to the Treaty.

Disputes under the IWT, as noted earlier, have advanced international case law.[27] Remarkably, dispute resolution has also contributed to advancing the environmental management agenda.[28] The IWT case law often involved reinterpretation of the Treaty's provisions to address climate change and other environmental risks. The Baglihar and Kishenganga disputes illustrate this.

Both Baglihar and Kishenganga projects are run-of-the-river hydroelectric projects of India on the Western rivers of the Indus—over which non-consumptive use by India is allowed under the Treaty provisions. Pakistan objected to both of these projects. The

[24] It is also perhaps the only treaty that has a global institution such as the World Bank as a co-signatory besides the beneficiary sovereign nations.

[25] Ramaswamy R Iyer, *Towards Water Wisdom: Limits, Justice, Harmony* (Sage 2007).

[26] Neda A Zawahri, 'India, Pakistan and Cooperation Along the Indus River System' (2009) 11(1) *Water Policy* 1.

[27] Bharat H. Desai and Balraj K Sidhu, 'The Kishenganga Final Award: Is the Indus Waters Treaty at the Crossroads?' (2014) 49(7) *Economic and Political Weekly* 10; Salman MA Salman and Kishor Uprety, *Shared Watercourses and Water Security in South Asia: Challenges of Negotiating and Enforcing Treaties*, Brill Research Perspectives in International Water Law (Brill 2018) 1.

[28] Salman and Uprety (n 27).

dispute escalated to different levels, and involved a Neutral Expert (NE) in Baglihar and the Permanent Court of Arbitration (PCA) in Kishenganga.

In the Baglihar dispute, one of the issues is about the maximum design flood. India estimated the value at 16,500 m^3s^{-1}, while Pakistan valued it at 14,900 m^3s^{-1}. Though the NE felt both values could be accepted, he favoured the value of 16,500 m^3s^{-1} to accommodate climate change implications.[29] The IWT had no reference to climate change, yet Baglihar set a precedent in accommodating climate change impacts. Another contentious issue was about the location of the sluice gates below the Dead Storage Level (DSL). Though it was a legally valid objection, the NE chose to be prudent and progressive in approaching the issue.[30] The NE felt that the proposed level of sluice gates was acceptable, considering the advances in reservoir sedimentation management since the IWT ratification in 1960. These developments recommend sluicing and flushing below DSL to enhance the life of a reservoir.[31]

The Kishenganga dispute was dealt with by a Court of Arbitration (CoA) set up by the PCA. The project, as proposed by India, involved the diversion of water from the Kishenganga (in India)/Neelum (in Pakistan) river. Kishenganga/Neelum is a tributary of Jhelum, a Western river—allocated to Pakistan under the IWT. The Kishenganga Hydroelectric Project (KHEP) involves a dam on Kishenganga diverting water through a tunnel system to a powerhouse a few kilometres away to take advantage of an elevation difference of 666 metres and generate 1,350 gigawatt hours of electricity. It also involves a sluice gate below DSL. Pakistan raised two key objections, among others.

First, the diversion adversely affects the downstream flow in Neelum (Pakistan side of Kishenganga) and the Neelum-Jhelum Hydroelectric Project, Pakistan's own run-of-river hydroelectric plant on the Neelum. Second, the proposed drawdown below DSL violates the provisions of the Treaty.[32] In its Final Award, the CoA restricted the drawdown below DSL but allowed the diversion with an obligation on India to ensure a minimum flow of 9 m^3s^{-1} in the Kishenganga/Neelum. The minimum flow obligations may be reviewed after seven years of KHEP's operation.[33]

The two cases illustrate how the IWT's institutional arrangements enabled it to remain resilient despite the unforeseen technology changes and environmental risks. The dispute resolution accommodated for (a) climate change impacts, (b) more sustainable sedimentation management, and (c) minimum flows. Besides making the IWT more resilient, it also advanced the agenda of environmental management. These precedents

[29] Raymond Lafitte, Baglihar Hydroelectric Plant: Expert Determination on Points of Difference Referred to by the Government of Pakistan Under the Provision of the Indus Water Treaty (2007).

[30] Salman MA Salman, 'The Baglihar Difference and Its Resolution Process—A Triumph for the Indus Waters Treaty?' (2008) 10(2) *Water Policy* 105.

[31] ibid.

[32] This contradicts the earlier Baglihar decision about sluicing below DSL on account of advances in sedimentation engineering. For further discussion on this issue, see the Court of Arbitration, Award in the Arbitration Regarding the Indus Waters Kishenganga between Pakistan and India (PCJ 2013) and Salman and Uprety (n 27).

[33] ibid.

help exploring new avenues for pursuing environmental management goals. On an equally attractive note, the instances also show how collective environmental risks can be deployed as a compelling avenue for mitigating and resolving water disputes.

India's transboundary relations on other fronts are also driven by similar concerns. The Kosi Barrage project, between India and Nepal, was the first in the early 1950s, but had a contentious history. The acrimonious trajectory of bilateral cooperation can claim success over agreements for multipurpose projects like the Gandak Agreement, 1959, and the Mahakali Treaty, 1996. Yet the Kosi agreement dominates the narrative of India-Nepal transboundary relations, somewhat obscuring the successes. This dominance can be traced to three sets of factors. One, the early history of negotiations and renegotiations of the project colours the narrative. The Kosi agreement was first signed in 1954 and then renegotiated later. Nepal's discontent with the agreement led to these renegotiations and amendments. Two, unlike the rest of the projects, Kosi's purpose—flood protection—tested the project and the institutional arrangements frequently due to recurring floods in the basin. The project's effectiveness in addressing the problem often provides an opportunity to revisit the tenuous history of the agreement. Third, the partial nature of the Kosi project. The Kosi Barrage was meant to be only an interim solution to the problem of floods. It was to be followed by a 'High Dam' upstream of the barrage. The suboptimal performance of this partial solution and the dissatisfaction between the two parties about the respective benefits accrued resulted in much rancour between the two nations.

In a similar manner, India-Bangladesh transboundary relations—again primarily defined by the Farakka agreement over the river Ganges—also bring environmental risks into focus. The project was an early transboundary project with a contentious history and attracted criticism on environmental grounds with adverse impacts for Bangladesh.[34] In recent times, and with the Farakka Treaty's review due in 2026, the environmental risks acquired a different colour. The Indian state of Bihar linked the floods in 2016 to sedimentation in the river Ganges due to the Farakka barrage downstream.[35] The state's claims received extensive attention with an added angle of federal politics; the state and the centre (federal government) were under the rule of different political parties. The centre had the Central Water Commission (CWC) investigate this, which eventually submitted a report ruling out Farakka's role in Bihar floods, instead pointing to agriculture practices and other meteorological factors as possible causes.[36]

On other fronts too, flood risk draws attention and generates collective concerns. Though the India-Bhutan cooperation in hydropower is celebrated, there are growing

[34] Shafqat Kakakhel, 'Agreements and Institutions Related to Shared Rivers within South Asia and Beyond' in Imtiaz Ahmed (ed), *South Asian Rivers: A Framework for Cooperation* (Routledge 2018).

[35] Times News Network, 'Farakka not to Blame for Bihar Floods: CWC' *The Times of India* (24 February 2017) <https://timesofindia.indiatimes.com/city/patna/farakka-not-to-blame-for-bihar-floods-cwc/articleshow/57318767.cms>.

[36] Central Water Commission, 'Flood Storage Estimates of Ganga Basin' (CWC 2016).

concerns about the social and environmental impacts of this cooperation.[37] The India-China cooperation over the sharing of hydrological data is also concerned with similar risks.

33.2.2 Inter-state Transboundary Risks Interconnected to the International

Transboundary environmental risks challenge the 'hydrohegemon' narratives as well. The risks reveal an inherent flaw of these narratives that is associated with the well-known 'Territorial Trap'—where the domestic imperatives tend to get obscured.[38] The risks also extend to the transboundary governance spaces within nation-states. This is often less appreciated, and as a result, the power of these risks to generate cooperation and collective action is neglected.

The perceived flood risk due to the Farakka barrage in Bihar discussed above—though unsubstantiated—is a case in point. The flood risk perceptions in Assam and other states in North-East India due to hydropower projects in Bhutan—mentioned earlier—are other examples. In more recent times, the concerns included water quality related risks as well. The excessive turbidity levels during the 2017 floods in the Indian state of Arunachal Pradesh triggered debates about transboundary risks in the Brahmaputra basin. These concerns, though lacking evidence, have amplified the national narrative in India about the tenuous India-China transboundary relations.[39] Though these may have contributed to exacerbating antagonisms between the two countries, the perceptions of risks can be channelled to generate collective action if supported by appropriately designed institutional avenues.[40]

Water quality is an emerging parameter inducing conflict and cooperation globally.[41] In line with the IPCC Assessment Report—6 projections, Indian states in the IHR are vulnerable to extreme climate related events like floods and diseases.[42] The impacts accompany water quality issues as well. The GLOF and other outbursts induced floods in

[37] Udisha Saklani and Cecilia Tortajada, 'India's Development Cooperation in Bhutan's Hydropower Sector: Concerns and Public Perceptions' (2019) 12(2) *Water Alternatives* 734.

[38] John Agnew, 'The Territorial Trap: The Geographical Assumptions of International Relations Theory' (1994) 1(1) *Review of International Political Economy* 53.

[39] Arundhati Deka and others, 'Media Reporting on Conflicts and Cooperation: What does it Mean for the Brahmaputra Basin?' (2023) *International Journal of Water Resources Development* <https://doi.org/10.1080/07900627.2022.2163478>.

[40] See Srinivas Chokkakula, 'Interstate Water Disputes: Perils and Prospects of Democratization' (2014) 49(9) *Economic and Political Weekly* 75.

[41] Lucia De Stephano and others, 'Tracking Cooperation and Conflict in International Basins: Historic and Recent Trends' (2010) 12(6) *Water Policy* 871.

[42] Nishikant Gupta and others, 'Interstate Cooperation for Climate Change Adaptation in Indian Himalayan Region' (2018) 53(12) *Economic and Political Weekly* 35.

recent times—Parechu (2005), Kedarnath-Chorabari (2013) and Chamoli (2021)—are indicative of these increasing vulnerabilities.

Among these, the GLOF incident on 7 February 2021 induced floods in the Chamoli district of the Indian state of Uttarakhand is illustrative. It was one of the most severe of its kind and was caused by a massive avalanche of glaciers and rock from the steep heights of Ronti Peak in the Himalayas, leading to extensive damages and loss of nearly 200 lives. A combination of factors contributed to the severity: the extraordinary fall, the ratio of ice and rock debris, and the downstream impact on the hydropower projects and settlements.[43] The flood waters had high levels of turbidity due to the high proportion of rock and debris. These entered the Upper Ganga Canal, which brings water to the Indian state of Delhi for its water supply needs. With the turbidity levels exceeding 8,000 NTU as against the normal seasonal values of 100 NTU,[44] this disrupted the water supply in parts of Delhi, besides raising concerns about the health and safety of its citizens.[45]

The debates about addressing the floods, however, missed out on these extended transboundary environmental risks: the adverse impacts on water quality and supply in the downstream settlements. The committees constituted following the floods, from the Parliamentary Standing Committee[46] to the studies carried out by the National Disaster Management Authority (NDMA)[47] do not engage with this transboundary element of coping with drinking water security risks. They choose to keep their focus on coping with flood risk.

This discussion about interstate transboundary risks offers the following takeaways. First and foremost, there is a need to recognize that the conceptions of environmental risks at a solely international scale are flawed. Such conceptions elide the extended scope of transboundary risks such as water supply, quality, health impacts, and, in all likelihood, the impacts on fisheries and other aquatic ecosystems. Second, such conceptions fail to consider the potential for conflicts due to the distributional effects of risks. More importantly, they neglect the potential of these risks and their accompanying perceptions to mobilize cooperation and collective action at the international scale. Domestic imperatives and their perceptions invariably shape international transboundary outcomes. Third, the preceding two takeaways accentuate the dimension of federal governance.[48] To address transboundary (extra-territorial) risks

[43] DH Shugar and others, 'A Massive Rock and Ice Avalanche Caused the 2021 Disaster at Chamoli, Indian Himalaya' (2021) 373 *Science* 6552, DOI: 10.1126/science.abh4455.

[44] NTU is Nephelometric Turbidity Unit—used to measure turbidity.

[45] Shivam Patel, 'How did Uttarakhand Flash Floods Affect Water Supply in Parts of Delhi?' *The Indian Express* (16 February 2021) <https://indianexpress.com/article/explained/uttarakhand-flash-floods-delhi-water-supply-7191208/>.

[46] Lok Sabha Secretariat (n 22).

[47] National Disaster Management Authority, 'Study of Causes & Impacts of the Uttarakhand Disaster on 7th February 2021 in Raunthi Gadhera, Rishiganga & Dhauliganga Valley: Measures to Reduce Disaster Risks' (NDMA April 2022).

[48] This applies to all other countries in South Asia. Except for Bhutan, India and its neighbours are federal in nature.

and build climate resilience in the IHR, interstate cooperation is critical.[49] A more comprehensive and enduring response would require building an ecosystem of coherent federal governance to cope with the environmental risks.[50]

33.3 Potential of Existing Regimes

Despite its ambitious beginnings in 1985, SAARC has contributed little to advance overall regional cooperation either over water disputes or environmental management. The primary goals of SAARC were augmenting regional development and geopolitical potential.[51] It also aspired to address environmental governance issues. SAARC engaged with these collective concerns in its own limited ways. Its earliest engagement with environmental issues goes back to the 1987 Kathmandu Declaration on environmental risks and climate change. SAARC eventually set up a Technical Committee on the Environment and produced an Action Plan for the Environment.[52] It commissioned technical studies and made some key recommendations on the environment, including cooperation over water. SAARC also stressed the capacity building of member countries to monitor climate change impacts, focusing on disaster responses.[53] In 1997, it was resolved that the Environment Ministerial Meeting would be an annual event, with each event focusing on a theme. But these plans suffered due to political tensions in the region ever since. Despite some intermittent episodes of engagement, SAARC has generally withered into a dysfunctional space now. Bhargava's observation about how the SAARC has 'hardly progressed beyond signs and symbols' remains valid even now.[54]

SACEP predates SAARC and was founded in 1982 to pursue environmental cooperation at a regional scale by the South Asian governments. This was the South Asian governments' response to calls for pursuing an environmental agenda by global agencies like the UN Environment Programme in the late 1970s. Though its initial focus was air pollution, SACEP has increased its scope with an elaborate set of

[49] Gupta and others (n 42). For a more comprehensive discussion, see Srinivas Chokkakula, Debarshee Dasgupta, and Rakshita Goyal, 'Integrating India: Interstate River Water Cooperation' Ministry of Jal Shakti, Government of India (under review).

[50] Srinivas Chokkakula, Avani Kapur, and Arkaja Singh, 'Water Federalism: Working with States for Water Security' TREADS Working Paper (Centre for Policy Research 2021); Srinivas Chokkakula (ed), 'India's Water Federalism: New Perspectives for Public Policy' (Hanns Seidel Foundation and Asian Confluence 2022).

[51] Brookings India, *Reinvigorating SAARC: India's Opportunities and Challenges* (Brookings 2014); Wakana Takahashi, 'Environmental Cooperation in South Asia' in Kazu Kato and Wakana Takahashi (eds), *Regional/Subregional Environmental Cooperation in Asia* (IGES 2001).

[52] Takahashi (n 51). See also Ashok Swain, 'South Asia, Its Environment and Regional Institutions' in Lorraine Elliott and Shaun Breslin (eds), *Comparative Environmental Regionalism* (Routledge 2011).

[53] Takahashi (n 51).

[54] Kant K Bhargava, 'EU—SAARC: Comparisons and Prospects of Cooperation' (ZEI Discussion Paper C15 1998).

fifteen subject areas covering various environmental themes but does not include water disputes. SACEP pursued the environmental cooperation agenda focusing on activities related to environmental information gathering, producing action plans and capacity building of the member countries concerning national environmental law-making. In 1994, it established a SACEP Environmental and Natural Resources Information Centre (SENRIC) to gather information. Other key initiatives led to the production of the South Asian Seas Action Plan and the South Asian Environmental Education and Training Action Plan. However, SACEP's activities are dependent on external funding and member-country contributions. In the absence of sustained funding and proactive support from member countries, its activities suffered from inadequate financial and human resources.[55]

Though these institutional avenues and agendas sound promising, their efforts have not led to any significant consolidation of collective response to environmental or climate risks. This is so for a variety of reasons; geopolitics and political mistrust are identified as primary factors.[56] SAARC is also constrained due to a structural feature in its chapter, which restricts it from engaging with bilateral concerns in the forum.[57]

Related literature generally indicates an absence of resilient foundational structures—political, institutional, and financial—to cope with the demands of environmental risk management.[58] Both SACEP and SAARC suffered from these weaknesses. Between the two, SAARC is a more appealing avenue to anchor the regional responses to environmental risks, especially because of its endogenous origins as opposed to SACEP's apparent exogenous origins. SAARC also enjoys the advantage of integrating environmental action with its primary goals of augmenting the economic and geopolitical potential of the region. Though it pursued an environmental agenda, it could not lead to any treaties or other forms of cooperation for environmental management.

SAARC and SACEP, however, have the necessary synergy to address the regional environmental governance challenges. With its core focus on environmental cooperation and its embeddedness in international networks, SACEP has informed and shaped regional responses through SAARC—an avenue endogenously evolved and led by India. This potential synergy between the two institutional avenues has led to advancing the theme of disaster risk management better than the other themes. The Male Declaration of 2006 by the SAARC Environment Ministers was an important milestone. Though it was ostensibly a response to the UN's Hyogo Framework for Action for disaster resilience building, the Male Declaration resulted in tangible responses. It called for increased cooperation over environmental hazards and coping with disaster risks and led to the formulating of a Comprehensive Framework of Disaster Management in South Asia.

[55] Takahashi (n 51).

[56] Biswas (n 8); Swain (n 52); Brookings India (n 51); Takahashi (n 51); UC Jha, 'Environmental Issues and SAARC' (2004) 39(17) *Economic and Political Weekly* 1666; Imtiaz Ahmed, *South Asian Rivers: A Framework for Cooperation* (Routledge 2018).

[57] Swain (n 52); Takahashi (n 51).

[58] Takahashi (n 51).

SAARC eventually set up a South Asia Disaster Management Centre running a real-time portal of the South Asia Disaster Knowledge Network (SADKN).[59] These interventions, too, withered along with the SAARC, with the SADKN being in an abandoned state.

There are two clear lessons from this experience. One, themes such as coping with disaster risks can galvanize resilient collective action. The rising transboundary environmental risks expand the scope for this. Despite the intermittent and tenuous functioning of SAARC, it could advance the theme of coping with disaster risk in useful ways. Two, regional institutional architecture for cooperation is crucial for mobilizing collective action. It is imperative that regional institutions like SAARC or a more effective regional institution are active and functional.

Conclusion

This chapter began with a call for a historical perspective of India's transboundary relationships for a nuanced understanding of its role. The idea is to go beyond the dominant narratives of bilateralism and regional hydrohegemon. The purpose here is not just to point out that these narratives are not entirely unequivocal but also to argue that these assessments can be a hurdle for imagining and conceiving a regional institutional architecture for coping with emerging environmental risks and transboundary river water governance. Such assessments exacerbate existing and deep-rooted mistrust and hostilities.[60] India's transboundary context confronts an expanse of environmental risks that are increasingly transboundary in nature. This can be beneficially employed to serve South Asian nations' interests in harnessing the potential of transboundary water resources development and, at the same time, address the collective concerns of environmental risks in IHR, the Indus and GBM basins.

India's history of transboundary relations, the review of existing regional regimes, and the emerging transboundary context of water disputes and environmental risks allow us to arrive at a set of conclusions.

First, the historical perspective of transboundary relationships allows for an optimistic consideration of a possible negotiated and collective action in South Asia. Despite India's early and proactive pursuit of transboundary interests, there is enough empirical experience to argue that India has not always had its way. Notwithstanding the general preference for bilateralism, the lack of aligning interests among nations can be a reason for fragmented transboundary projects and the dominance of bilateralism in South Asia.

Second, the rich history of negotiations between India and its neighbours, and in some instances, the successful rejections of India's proposals, can be a useful basis for

[59] SAARC Disaster Management Centre, 'Genesis' (n.d.) <https://saarc-sdmc.org/genesis>.

[60] Biswas (n 8).

imagining a future with multilateral and deliberative transboundary interactions in the region. It is also true that negotiated settlements do not necessarily imply that the arrangements came into place in the best spirit of cooperation. Cooperation can be an outcome of coercion by the powerful.[61] But the history of bilateralism sans non-India initiatives buttresses this optimism. On the other hand, the emerging scope and expanse of transboundary environmental risks build a compelling case for transboundary cooperation and collective action. Pursuing disaster resilience can be the 'low-hanging fruit' because it forces all the parties to the negotiating table. This can help rebuild regional consensus for transboundary cooperation.

Third, in line with optimistic readings into transboundary interactions, water disputes in South Asia—both international and interstate—show an encouraging trend of accommodation for environmental risks, including those associated with climate change. Despite the uneven geopolitical responses to the UN Watercourses Convention, water disputes build on international customary principles for transboundary water governance to address complex and unforeseen challenges. This evolving repository of case law responding to environmental risks can be useful for informed thinking about regional transboundary institutional architecture.

Finally, India's transboundary context is shifting, with environmental risks weighing in along with its development interests. With India's proactive outlook on transboundary interactions, reflected by the recent Standing Committee recommendations,[62] coping with environmental risks such as floods can be a theme for reviving South Asia's regional institutional architecture within SAARC or otherwise. Despite the diminishing roles of SAARC and SACEP, the theme of disaster resilience, especially floods, highlights the relevance of these institutional spaces. India's emerging challenges in coping with the environmental risks, from climate change to water quality, can be a potent enabler for mobilizing collective action in South Asia.

Suggestions for Further Reading

Shlomi Dinar and others, 'Climate Change, Conflict, and Cooperation: Global Analysis of the Resilience of International River Treaties to Increased Water Variability' (2014) *The World Bank*, Policy Research Working Paper 6916.

Niranjan D Gulhati, *Indus Waters Treaty: An Exercise in International Mediation* (Allied Publishers 1973).

Ramaswamy R Iyer (ed), *Water and the Laws in India* (Sage 2009).

Claudia W Sadoff and David Grey, 'Cooperation on International Rivers: A Continuum of Securing and Sharing Benefits' (2005) 30(4) *Water International* 420.

Mark Zeitoun and Jeroen Warner, 'Hydrohegemony—A Framework for Analysis of Transboundary Water Conflicts' (2006) 8(5) *Water Policy* 435.

[61] Mark Zeitoun and Naho Mirumachi, 'Transboundary Water Interaction I: Reconsidering Conflict and Cooperation' (2008) 8(4) *International Environmental Agreements: Politics, Law and Economics* 297.

[62] Lok Sabha Secretariat (n 22).

PART IX

HEALTH AND SANITATION

CHAPTER 34

HEALTH AND ENVIRONMENT

AWADHENDRA SHARAN

Abstract

This chapter concerns the relationship between health and environment. Laws framed during the colonial period were of two kinds. Municipal management of the environment to ensure better health remained rather restrictive geographically and socially. The anti-smoke law, aimed at reducing respiratory harms, was somewhat more effective, but remained limited to large cities. Towards the middle of the twentieth century, the notion of public health expanded to include nutrition, poverty, housing and the state of physical environment. Health, however, only found a place in the Directive Principles of State Policy. Courts have occasionally taken recourse to this provision to rule on matters of public nuisance. Further, laws relating to water and air pollution and management of hazardous waste have been enacted. Poor implementation, however, has led to the Supreme Court to intervene, while including clean air, water and a healthy environment as essential components of the right to life.

Introduction

In the time of the pandemic, health outcomes loom large in our consciousness. Scientists have warned of emerging infectious diseases for some time, drawing our attention to environmental transformations that have enhanced the possibility of interspecies transfer of viruses and the spread of zoonotic diseases. However, this is environmental transformation at a distance happening over time and across widely dispersed ecosystems that do not always permit an immediate experiential grasp. On the other hand, the impact of the virus on the functioning of human bodies is immediate and graspable, measured in body temperatures, lowering of oxygen levels, loss of smell and taste, etc. And so, attention tends to be focused on the possibility of care—on the difficulties regarding the supply of medical oxygen, availability of trained medical staff, and the availability of vaccines, awaiting which hygienic practices of masking and social distancing are encouraged. In brief, we are reminded yet again of the environmental aspect of health, especially regarding preventive aspects of disease outbreak and transmission, but these dimensions are often eclipsed by the overwhelming medicalization of the pandemic discourse.

Epidemics and pandemics, however, are only the latest instances of attention being drawn to the health/environment interface in India. We have become increasingly familiar with other environmental transformations over the past two or three decades, most notably the fast-deteriorating air quality in cities of the global South. As the winter approaches, the skies of Delhi turn hazy, and the quality of air becomes intolerably toxic. Perhaps the air is toxic the year round, but it is most certainly visibly so in the winter. In this gloomy, toxic scenario, talk starts of loss of workdays, diseases of the heart and lungs and regarding high levels of fatality. *The State of Global Air 2020* reports that air pollution is now the world's leading environmental risk factor and that there is broad scientific consensus that long-term exposures to air pollution contributes to increased risk of illness and death from ischemic heart disease, lung cancer, chronic obstructive pulmonary disease (COPD), lower-respiratory infections (e.g., pneumonia), stroke, type 2 diabetes, and adverse birth outcomes.[1] The figures are indeed startling in this regard. In 2019, over 90 per cent of the world's population experienced annual average PM 2.5 concentrations that exceeded the WHO Air Quality Guideline of 10 μg/m^3(micrograms/cubic meter of air). India ranked at the very top, with PM 2.5 concentration measured at 83.2 ug/m^3, reflecting a serious ambient air quality issue.[2] Ozone pollution and household pollution are other aspects estimated to impact human health in large measures, though India may have fared somewhat better over the past decade.[3] Not surprisingly, then, air pollution features as one of the seven priority areas of preventive health under India's National Health Policy 2017.[4]

The pandemic and the pollution of air are thus both related and differ in how we posit the links between the harms caused by them to human bodies and what may be done to mitigate such harms. Among the critical differentiating elements is how the health/environment interface has been addressed in law. While the pandemic has been addressed in India through the colonial era Epidemic Diseases Act, 1897, and within the framework of disaster management, air pollution has seen a slew of recent laws and regulations, starting with the Air (Prevention and Control of Pollution) Act, 1981, to the

1 Health Effects Institute, 'State of Global Air 2020', Special Report (2020) 15.

2 ibid 6 Table 1.

3 ibid 11 Figure 7, 13 Figure 10.

4 Other areas include sanitation and nutrition, as also newer concerns around work-related stress and gender violence. Government of India, Ministry of Health and Family Welfare, 'National Health Policy' (2017) 6.

Commission for Air Quality Management in National Capital Region and Adjoining Areas Act, 2021. In what follows, I elaborate on these different linkages of environment, health, and law over time, beginning with the focus on environmental sanitation in colonial times and ending with the recent approaches linking a clean environment and better health outcomes to the right to life enshrined in the Constitution of India, 1950. To the extent that these laws and court rulings tend to be about urban environments, this chapter also has a city focus.

In Section 34.1, I elaborate on colonial municipal laws, laws of public nuisance and the Criminal Procedure Code, 1860, and the Bengal and Bombay Smoke Nuisances Act, enacted in 1905 and 1912, respectively, which remained important till new laws to prevent air and water pollution were enacted from the 1970s. I next look at the background context for the enactment of the Water (Prevention and Control of Pollution) Act, 1974 (Water Pollution Act) and the Air (Prevention and Control of Pollution) Act, 1981 (Air Pollution Act). The prospect of securing development while limiting the negative impacts of pollution, I suggest, were twin concerns in which these Acts were anchored. The administrative structures put into place following these Acts are detailed, along with an assessment of their relative success or failure in addressing pollution. This section ends with a discussion of the Environment (Protection) Act, 1986 and its provisions regarding health in the context of dealing with hazardous substances.

By the 1990s, the limits of the Water and Air Pollution Acts had become quite evident. The institutional location for addressing environmental harms also began to change, with the Supreme Court of India (and some High Courts) taking the lead in suggesting measures that the government and public authorities must adopt to protect human health. The most important development in this regard was elaborating the constitutional right to life to include a clean environment and health as fundamental rights. These developments are discussed in Section 34.2 of the chapter. Specific decisions of the Supreme Court to tackle environmental and health harms, especially in the context of air pollution in Delhi, are discussed through four case studies related to (i) industrial pollution, (ii) vehicular pollution, (iii) the bursting of firecrackers, and (iv) waste-to-energy plant. I conclude with reflections on this transformation, what has been gained in the process, and what more needs to be done.

34.1 Existing and Emerging Challenges in the Contemporary Context

Modern legal regimes relating to health and the environment first emerged in the colonial context. The 'tropics' were seen by the British as being especially pathogenic, a view that was consolidated with the emergence of the discipline of 'tropical medicine' in the late nineteenth and early twentieth centuries.[5] Municipal laws framed thus took environmental sanitation as an important local concern, but financial allocation remained limited and practical impacts negligible. The closing years of colonial rule and the early years after independence, however, witnessed an important shift with an emerging discourse of health as a fundamental right which the state was duty-bound to deliver. This was but a brief flicker, and post-independence, delivering on health, both preventive and curative, while mandated as a duty of the state in the Constitution, did not translate into a fundamental right. Recognition of public health dimensions of the environment instead found space within laws enacted to deal with air and water pollution that resulted from industrialization, which broadly set the stage for the contemporary framing of the issue.

34.1.1 Colonial Laws

The earliest historical interventions regarding health in modern times were anchored in a miasmatic conception of disease—a view that gases and vapours that arose from rotten matter corrupted the air and consequently caused disease. Public health measures, however, were designed to largely serve Europeans, with rather limited efforts made to improve environmental conditions more generally.[6] Two kinds of laws were framed, the first and the more widely used being municipal laws that addressed local risks, especially in parts of the town where the British resided, hoping to secure potable water, provide for adequate drainage and ensure better ventilation, all these being the standard features of municipal laws throughout British India.[7] Authorities variously interpreted issues of environmental harm as nuisances, sometimes to emphasize damage to property or offensiveness alone, and at other times to include health harms. Some considered nuisances merely irritants, as distinct from poisons; others defined the term more broadly to include any act that could cause injury, pose a danger, or cause harm to health and property. The Indian Penal Code promulgated in 1860 adopted this broader definition, much wider than what would have been acceptable in England at the time, to include the negligent spreading of disease, the fouling of any public spring, rendering the atmosphere noxious to health, etc. as public nuisances.[8] These provisions were also swiftly incorporated into local laws, expressly forbidding traditional activities such as washing in rivers, urinating by the side of the street or fishing practices that relied on

[5] David Arnold, 'The Place of the "tropics" in Western Medical Ideas Since 1750' (1997) 2(4) *Tropical Medicine and International Health* 303.

[6] Gyan Prakash, 'Body Politic in Colonial India' in Timothy Mitchell (ed), *Questions of Modernity* (University of Minnesota Press 2000) 189.

[7] Mark Harrison, *Public Health in British India: Anglo-Indian Preventive Medicine, 1859–1914* (CUP 1994); Ishita Pande, *Medicine, Race and Liberalism in British Bengal: Symptoms of Empire* (Routledge 2009).

[8] Michael Anderson, 'Public Nuisance and Private Purpose: Policed Environments in British India, 1860–1947' (1992) SOAS Law Department Working Paper No 1.

weirs or bamboo traps thereby impeding water flows. The reasoning for forbidding these practices could be varied—the practice in question could be a potential polluter or could be seen as obstructing free movement—but the consequence was largely an adverse impact on poor and marginalized communities that were reliant on common property and public resources for performing everyday tasks.[9] Waste was equally a concern and when disposal of rubbish by incineration began to be debated in major Indian cities around the 1860s, municipal authorities and local newspapers alike asked the question whether one form of pollution (on account of waste) was being exchanged for another (smoke and stench), with potentially adverse effects on the health of residents who lived in the vicinity of these incinerators. Similarly, laws were enacted to ensure that the places of slaughter of animals for meat did not become a source of disease.[10] And when modern factories were set up, it was expected that they would take care to consume their smoke to the maximum extent possible, subject to the availability of requisite technology.[11] Such technology being limited, and finances always difficult to secure for purposes other than policing, health interventions during the colonial period, however, remained rather circumscribed, notwithstanding the frequent mention of health issues in relation to the quality of air in municipal laws.

A second set of laws, specifically concerning smoke and air pollution, was enacted in the colonial period, but only for major cities such as Bombay and Calcutta, in 1892 and 1893, respectively. These Acts, however, were deemed to be of limited efficacy, and their operation was often amateurish, leading to a call for greater use of expertise in managing environmental pollution beyond what was available within municipal bodies. And so, the Bengal and Bombay Smoke Nuisances Acts were passed in 1905 and 1912, respectively, setting up Smoke Nuisances Commissions in both cities but operating outside municipal remits. These commissions were assisted by trained engineers working as smoke inspectors to advise industry on how to minimize smoke or, failing which, impose fines. In time, they also began to promote new technologies to ensure better combustion and the dispersal of smoke at a height, carrying it away from sites of emission within the major urban centres to other places. The spirit was one of co-operation with industry and the legislation was framed in a manner where industry and the use of local resources could continue to be encouraged while providing some protection to the public regarding damage to property and health, especially regarding respiratory diseases.[12] Ironically, while inspectors of the Smoke Nuisances Commissions were constantly at pains to point to the harmful impacts of smoke on human health, as also on plants and animals, municipal authorities remained rather reluctant to acknowledge modern industrial pollution as a factor in disease causation till well into the 1930s

[9] ibid 9.

[10] Awadhendra Sharan, *In the City, Out of Place: Nuisance, Pollution and Dwelling in Delhi, c.1850–2000* (OUP 2014) ch 2.

[11] Awadhendra Sharan, *Dust and Smoke: Air Pollution and Colonial Urbanism, India, c.1860–c.1940* (Orient BlackSwan 2020).

[12] ibid xvii.

when they began to conjoin absence of adequate nutrition, lack of suitable clothing, overcrowding, dampness, and want of fresh air with smoke caused by industry as responsible for high death rates among the poor. In doing so, they also signalled a significant shift in thinking about health in the last decades of colonial rule as it came to be related to ideas of national development.

The Indian National Congress also stepped up the development ladder, setting up a National Planning Committee in 1938 to chart the path for planned growth and India's future as an independent democratic nation. Several committees and sub-committees were set up, including one on health. The report of the sub-committee on health, published in 1947, made three crucial observations.[13] First, it noted the poor condition of the health of the people of India, putting a serious question mark on the claims of the colonial state regarding social and material improvements of Indians. Second, it linked the question of ill-health to poverty, the state of the physical environment, nutrition, etc., reflecting more expansive conceptions of public health that had begun to emerge in the 1930s. Third, and perhaps most crucially, it cast a duty on the state to deliver a public health service that could improve the environment and living conditions and thus prevent diseases. Health would no longer be a matter of charity but 'a matter of right to the individual through an organized public service'.[14] Interestingly, these views were echoed in the report and recommendations of the Health Survey and Development Committee (1946) which continued to influence thinking about health and health administration in India for several decades.[15] Health was again defined rather broadly, implying not just the absence of illness but instead as a state of harmonious functioning of the body and the mind in relation to the social and physical environment. Environmental sanitation, adequate nutrition, higher standards of living, and the availability of health protection were all argued to be crucial determinants of health. And while the criticism of the state was more muted, there was a clear and bold recommendation that a comprehensive health scheme financed by the government, providing both preventive and curative health care, should be available to all, irrespective of the ability to pay. Internationally, the WHO also proclaimed health as a fundamental right to which every human being, without distinction of race, sex, language or religion, was entitled.[16]

34.1.2 Environmental Law Post-Independence

The stage for delivering universal health, irrespective of means, through improvement in a broad set of conditions of life, ranging from adequate nutrition to better sanitation,

[13] National Planning Committee Series (Report of the Subcommittee), 'National Health' (Vora and Co 1947).

[14] ibid 12.

[15] Government of India, 'Report of the Health Survey and Development Committee' (Delhi 1946).

[16] Sunil S Amrith, *Decolonizing International Health: India and Southeast Asia, 1930–65* (Palgrave Macmillan 2006) 74.

and through better curative facilities, *as a matter of right*, had been articulated. The task would now be to translate it into actual state capacity and delivery. However, the Constituent Assembly which deliberated over the future Constitution in 1946–48 failed to realize this ambition. Health failed to find a place in the chapter on Fundamental Rights, being mentioned instead as a Directive Principle of State Policy that was not enforceable by law, even as it cast a duty on the state to improve public health. Article 47 of the Constitution of India 1950 specifically referred to the duty of the state regarding matters of health, tasking it with the responsibility of raising the level of nutrition and the standard of living of the people.[17] Read together with section 133 of the Criminal Procedure Code that authorized magistrates to take immediate action in the case of public nuisances that could cause obstruction or be injurious to health, a context thus emerged for the courts to remind functionaries of the state about their duties in matters of public health, even if this was not yet a fundamental right.

This latent possibility, however, had to await the emergence of a more activist court post the period of Emergency from 1975–77 for it to be realized. Among the most cited judgments in this regard was the case of *Municipal Council of Ratlam v Shri Vardhichand*, wherein the Supreme Court spoke of the social justice dimension of public health and, in doing so, also made an unambiguous statement regarding the duty of the state to ensure this by providing toilets and drainage facilities.[18] If public streets were being used for purposes that were causing the nuisance, the Court held, it signalled not wilful disobedience of law by the poor, but a failure on the part of the authorities to provide adequate facilities. And a responsible municipal body could not run away from its public duties merely on account of financial difficulties. To do so would be contrary to the mandate imposed on the state by Article 47 of the Constitution. The difference in interpretation regarding colonial laws of public nuisance that had often criminalized the behaviour of the poor in the past could not have been put in starker terms! And what is more, this interpretation continued to find resonance for about a decade more in most judgments related to slums and public nuisances until the courts once again began to take a less sympathetic view of the poor 'causing' public nuisances.[19]

Alongside the issue of environmental sanitation and public health as enunciated in municipal laws and the Directive Principles of State Policy in the Constitution, a new set of laws began to be enacted in the 1970s to deal with other kinds of pollution, prompted by concerns raised at the 1972 UN Conference on the Human Environment, the first international conference to focus entirely on environmental issues. India's position was two-fold—continuing to stake a claim for developmental goals while recognizing the immense importance of the issue of environmental harm. New laws that were enacted spoke to this emerging concern, especially regarding the protection of forests, rivers and

[17] The Constitution of India, Art 47.

[18] *Municipal Council, Ratlam v Vardhichand AIR* 1980 SC 1622.

[19] Asher Ghertner, 'Analysis of New Legal Discourse Behind Delhi's Slum Demolitions' (2008) 43(20) *Economic and Political Weekly* 57.

wildlife.[20] In other instances, these new laws spoke more directly to the relation of the environment to health, while tackling pollution that resulted from modern economic activities. These included the Water Pollution Act, followed by the Air Pollution Act. Both these Acts defined pollution rather broadly. In the case of water pollution, the term implied:

> such contamination of water or such alteration of the physical, chemical or biological properties of water or such discharge of any sewage or trade effluent or of any other liquid, gaseous or solid substance into water ... as may, or is likely to, create a nuisance or render such water harmful or injurious to public health or safety ... or to the life and health of animals or plants or of aquatic organisms.[21]

In the Air Pollution Act, the term was simply defined as 'the presence in the atmosphere of any air pollutant', though air pollutants themselves were described in some detail to mean any solid, liquid or gaseous substance 'present in the atmosphere in such concentration as may be or tend to be injurious to human beings or other living creatures or plants or property or environment'.[22]

The Water Pollution Act and the Air Pollution Act also set up similar structures to ensure the abatement of pollution, though they had different locations in the federal structure, with water being a state subject, and air being something that the central government could legislate on its own with greater authority.[23] Both provided for the setting up of Pollution Control Boards at the centre (Central Pollution Control Board or CPCB) and in the states (State Pollution Control Board or SPCB), with members drawn from the government, from companies owned by the government and experts whose advice could be required on a specific issue. Under the Water Pollution Act, the CPCB was expected to advise on matters concerning the prevention and control of water pollution, coordinate the activities of the SPCBs, provide technical assistance, sponsor research and training programmes and publish technical and statistical data on the subject. SPCBs were expected to perform some of the same tasks at the state level and lay down effluent standards for sewage and trade effluents and for the quality of receiving waters (not being water in an inter-state stream) resulting from the discharge of effluents. The task of inspecting effluents and evolving mechanisms for utilization or efficient disposal of sewage was also left to them. So was the task of advising state governments regarding the location of industries that may pollute a stream or well. The CPCB, under the Air Pollution Act, was similarly mandated to advise the government on matters of air pollution, coordinate with State Boards, provide technical assistance, sponsor training programmes, etc. They were also mandated to plan and help execute a nation-wide

[20] The Forty-second Constitutional Amendment in 1976 made protecting the environment part of the Directive Principles of State Policy in the Constitution.

[21] Water (Prevention and Control of Pollution) Act, 1974 s 5.

[22] Air (Prevention and Control of Pollution) Act, 1981 s 2.

[23] The Constitution, Sch VII.

programme for the prevention, control or abatement of air pollution and lay down standards for the quality of air. The State Boards were expected to render similar tasks at the level of states and, as in the case of water pollution, inspect manufacturing plants and air pollution control areas and take necessary steps to help prevent, control, or abate pollution. Later amendments granted further powers to the CPCB and SPCBs to ensure compliance, including closure or regulation of an industry or denial of supply of electricity, water, etc. However, the Boards could not impose these fines by themselves, and it was mandated that they could initiate criminal prosecution only through a court of law. Over time, thus, while the CPCB and SPCBs have endeavoured to set up networks for monitoring river water, air quality, and noise levels, the effectiveness of these Boards in mitigating pollution remains open to question.[24] Given the command-and-control style of regulation, the lack of adequate funds and technical staff, and the relative ineffectiveness of criminal prosecution as a measure of pollution control, serious limitations in their functioning have thus come to the fore.[25]

At the administrative level, a Department of Environment was set up in 1980, later elevated to the Ministry of Environment and Forests in 1985. An ambitious Environment (Protection) Act, 1986, was passed the following year, granting powers to the central government to take all such measures as it deemed necessary for protecting and improving the quality of the environment and for preventing, controlling, and abating environmental pollution. Among these, the question of health was specifically articulated in the sections related to hazardous substances, defined as substances which, on account of their chemical or physio-chemical properties, were liable to cause harm to human beings, other living creatures, microorganisms, property, or the environment. As we saw above, the relationship of waste to health had been spelled out in colonial times, too, especially regarding the disposal of waste through landfills or incineration. In contemporary times, this has been further elaborated on account of wastes that pose more complex risks and whose storage, transport and disposal require special rules. The case of hazardous solid waste was especially difficult given the impossibility of storage on site. So, following the Environment (Protection) Act, several other rules have also been passed, including the Bio-medical Waste (Management and Handling) Rules, 1998, to ensure that every occupier of a facility that generates bio-medical waste takes all necessary steps to ensure that it is handled in a manner that does not cause any adverse effect to human health and environment. The Municipal Solid Waste (Management and Handling) Rules, 2000, seek to facilitate the scientific handling of waste and prevent pollution at landfill sites. The Hazardous Wastes (Management, Handling and Transboundary Movement) Rules, 2008, concern those waste materials that, on account of their physical, chemical, reactive, toxic, or other properties, can cause harm to health

[24] Prakash Chand, 'Environmental Protection and Regulations in India: Role of the Central Pollution Control Board' (2018) 64(4) *Indian Journal of Public Administration* 645; Shibani Ghosh, 'Reforming the Liability Regime for Air Pollution in India' (2015) 4 *Environmental Law and Practice Review* 100.

[25] Chand (n 24) 660.

or the environment. More recently, the E-Waste (Management) Rules, 2016, made provision for extended producer responsibility in handling electronic waste.

In brief, starting from the 1970s, several laws have been passed and rules enacted to deal with the question of environmental pollution, guided by a twin perspective—a perceived need for development on the one hand and a simultaneous awareness of its negative environmental consequences on the other. In the process, they have also helped to create awareness of the negative health consequences of contaminated soil or polluted air and water. Important as these are. though, it is possible to suggest that practical outcomes have remained limited and executive authorities have been lax in discharging their duties, creating a context for a greater role of the courts in matters of health and environment.

34.2 Right to Life, Environment, and Health

The 1990s may be said to mark a watershed in Indian legal jurisprudence with the emergence of Public Interest Litigation and the widespread use of right-to-life arguments to seek a variety of social rights, including the rights to health and a clean environment.[26] As we saw above, the idea of health as a fundamental right of citizens had made a brief appearance in the 1940s, only for these hopes to be dashed. It now emerged in another guise, as part of the understanding of life itself, as guaranteed by the Constitution of India. The path to this transition lay through an expansive reading of Article 21 of the Constitution: 'No person shall be deprived of his life or personal liberty except according to procedure established by law'. Earlier concerned largely with issues of procedure, this provision gradually began to be read in a manner that could allow for the articulation of social rights. In *Subhash Kumar v State of Bihar*, the Supreme Court thus ruled that the right to life was a fundamental right under Article 21, and as such, it included the right to enjoyment of pollution-free water and air.[27] Similarly, in a judgment concerning stone crushing in Delhi region, the Supreme Court noted that while environmental changes were the inevitable consequence of industrial development, the quality of environment could not be permitted to be damaged by polluting the air, water and land to such an extent that it became a health hazard.[28] Together with Article 32 of the Constitution which authorizes the Supreme Court to take necessary action regarding the protection of fundamental rights, this expanded notion of life in Article 21 of the Constitution has opened still newer possibilities to address the environment and public

[26] Gitanjali Gill, 'Human Rights and the Environment in India: Access Through Public Interest Litigation' (2012) 14 *Environmental Law Review* 200.

[27] *Subhash Kumar v State of Bihar* (1991) 1 SCC 598.

[28] *MC Mehta v Union of India* (1991) 2 SCC 353.

health relationship. We can gauge just how swift this transition has been from two contemporary assessments. Writing in 1986, Abraham and Rosencranz, in their evaluation of pollution control legislation in India, noted that 'although various cases have been argued in the High Courts of several states, the Supreme Court of India has very rarely heard such cases. The environment enjoys no special protection from the Indian judiciary'.[29] Some two decades later, Dam and Tewary offer a diametrically opposite reading: 'The Indian Supreme Court has ... skilfully reinvented itself as a constitutional alchemist, transforming all problems of life into problems of law- in fact into problems of constitutional law', going on to suggest that notwithstanding some of the earlier gains, 'the Court's overenthusiasm in environmental matters has severely dented India's institutional balance and has contributed to a polity that is becoming consistently reliant on the judiciary for remedying all its problems, of both life and law'.[30]

I discuss this changing contemporary situation through the case of air pollution in Delhi, with a focus on industrial pollution, vehicular pollution, waste-to-energy plants and pollution from the bursting of crackers during Diwali. Each of these cases has occupied the attention of the courts over a length of time, though my presentation here of these cases is rather brief and only draws one key inference from each.

34.2.1 Industrial Pollution

Starting in the 1980s, the lawyer-activist MC Mehta filed several petitions before the Supreme Court of India highlighting various environmental risks Delhi faced, including smoke and highly toxic gases that were being allowed to pass into the air and effluents discharged into the river. The pollution that resulted from the numerous industries in Delhi, he argued, posed immense health dangers, from the increase in cases of tuberculosis to asthma, skin diseases, and cancer. Stone dust was a severe pollutant in south Delhi, and nose, throat, and eye ailments had become commonplace.[31] The Supreme Court, in its various judgments that have stretched over years, took cognisance of these health burdens and ruled that if pollution on account of industry was to be curbed, it was imperative that hazardous and polluting industries move out of the city limits as per the provisions of the Master Plan. Deadlines were fixed to give effect to this ruling, even as political parties made a strong plea that those residential areas where 70 per cent or more housed industrial units be recognized as industrial areas. Only thus could the livelihood of workers be protected, they reasoned. This plea that the livelihood of workers deserved equal constitutional protection was countered, however, by the argument

[29] CM Abraham and Armin Rosencranz, 'An Evaluation of Pollution Control Legislation in India' (1986) 11(1) *Columbia Journal of Environmental Law* 101, 104.

[30] Shubhankar Dam and Vivek Tewary, 'Polluting Environment, Polluting Constitution: Is a "Polluted" Constitution Worse than a Polluted Environment?' (2005) 17(3) *Journal of Environmental Law* 383,385.

[31] *MC Mehta v Union of India* (1996) 4 SCC 750.

that the health of the many deserved greater protection than the livelihood of the few. Industry, especially polluting industry, thus had little option but to shut operations or to move out.[32]

34.2.2 Vehicular Pollution

At any rate, conditions within Delhi did not improve even after some industrial units had relocated. In part, this may have had to do with the fact that industry alone was not responsible for the pollution of the city. Vehicular pollution was also of a significant magnitude. And unlike industry, relocation could not be an answer to pollution from motor vehicles. There was thus a sense of an unfolding crisis on hand, even greater in its potential to lead to degradation of public health than had been the case in the Bhopal gas tragedy.[33] The latter could be imagined as a one-time accident while the former had an ever-increasing polluting effect. The Delhi government, the Supreme Court observed, had failed to discharge its constitutional obligations in this regard and had done little regarding the emission of smoke, noise, etc., from vehicles operating in Delhi.[34] For this reason, and with a view to protecting the health of the present and future generations, the Court felt that it had no option but to step in. Having thus justified the ground for its own intervention, the Court then went on to pass several rulings, including the much-debated directive that no bus more than eight years old could operate on the roads of Delhi except on compressed natural gas (CNG) or any other clean fuel after 31 March 2001.[35] There was much hue and cry once again, and several groups made the plea that other fuels such as ultra-fine diesel also be considered as a clean fuel.[36] The evidence generated, however, was uncertain leading the Court to suggest that a precautionary approach be adopted, while going on to cite several studies that provided evidence for health harms on account of air pollution.[37]

34.2.3 Firecrackers

Matters of culture have provided a third context for considering the relationship of the environment to health, as elaborated in a case concerning the banning of firecrackers brought before the Supreme Court on behalf of three children in 2015.[38] The case of the petitioners was that while numerous sources could cause air pollution, the bursting

[32] Sharan (n 10) 199–210.

[33] *MC Mehta v Union of India* 2002 (2) SCR 963. On the Bhopal disaster, see further ch 38 in this volume.

[34] ibid.

[35] *MC Mehta v Union of India and Others* Writ Petition (Civil) 13029 (2002) AIR 2001 SC 201.

[36] *MC Mehta v Union of India and Others* Writ Petition (Civil) 13029 (2001) 2002 (2) SCR 963.

[37] *MC Mehta v Union of India and Others* Writ Petition (Civil) 13029 (2002) 2002 (2) SCR 963.

[38] *Arjun Gopal v Union of India* (2019) 13 SCC 523.

of firecrackers at the time of Diwali led to an additional massive spike in levels of PM 2.5 and PM 10. Second, while all residents were adversely affected by such pollution, children were especially vulnerable to exposure that may aggravate asthma, coughing, bronchitis, nervous system breakdown, and even cognitive impairment. The contrary argument presented was that the evidence about harms that could be attributed exclusively to firecrackers was not conclusive and that a ban on firecrackers would adversely affect the livelihood of workers engaged in the industry. Further, according to one respondent, any such ban would deny the freedom to practice one's religion. In response, the Court once again marshalled studies regarding health harms on account of pollution and took recourse to the precautionary principle, suggesting that even if not conclusive, the evidence was sufficient to recommend regulation. It did not impose a complete ban on the sale of firecrackers, however, but urged that there was a need to move in the direction of green celebrations, allowing for the production and use of firecrackers with reduced emissions.[39] For the same reason, the Court suggested that religious practices must be conducted in a manner that did not cause health harms.

34.2.4 Waste-to-Energy Plant

Finally, in the matter of incineration of waste, we encounter yet another dimension of the environment/health relation. Dealing with waste through incineration, which had been sparingly used during colonial times, came back to policy attention in the 1990s as a part of the Clean Development Mechanism to deal with climate change, the expectation being for a reduction in the emission of greenhouse gases such as methane that would otherwise be emitted from landfill sites. A proposal for a waste-to-energy plant was approved in Okhla in south Delhi in 2005. Ironically, opposition to the plant soon emerged based on a similar logic of health harm, viz., the potential pollution of the air and adverse health impacts of the dioxins emitted by the incinerators. Once again, the matter went to the courts, eventually reaching the National Green Tribunal (NGT).[40] The petitioners urged that once the plant became operational, it would create environmental and ecological disasters and the chemicals released into the environment would cause air and water pollution and constitute a health hazard. Further, the residue left after the burning of Refuse Derived Fuel (RDF) pellets would be in the form of highly toxic ash, which would pollute the entire carriageway wherever it was dumped. In brief, the plant was dangerous not only for the lives of residents in its vicinity but also for the people in the city in general. The Delhi High Court, however, did not grant a stay, and the plant became operational in 2011/12. The matter then went to the NGT, which, based on reports of expert committees, ruled that while the plant may have been polluting initially, this was no longer so, the petitioner having taken several measures to ensure

[39] ibid.

[40] Federico Demaria and Seth Schindler, 'Contesting Urban Metabolism: Struggles over Waste-to-Energy in Delhi, India' (2016) 48(2) *Antipode* 293.

that the emissions were within the prescribed limits. Thus, while a fine was mandatory for the earlier failure, the plant must be allowed to operate in the present. Given the huge amount of waste generated in the city and the paucity of landfill sites as well as the pollution at these sites, waste-to-energy plants, if not polluting, were a necessity, they ruled.[41]

Cumulatively, it is evident that air pollution has had a serious impact on the health of the residents of the city of Delhi.[42] An expansive reading of the right to life by the Supreme Court has also opened novel ways for considering environmental pollution and its impact on human health. This has happened at the same time as air pollution has been recognized as a critical area of concern in the domain of public health policy. Notwithstanding these developments, however, areas of concern remain. In the case of industrial pollution, there is little clarity whether industries that are relocated continue or cease to be polluting units at the new sites, leading some commentators to suggest that a possible (even if unintended) outcome of industrial relocation is the social and spatial redistribution of environmental and health risks, rather than its mitigation.[43] In the instance of vehicular pollution, the use of precautionary principle, together with the citation of available scientific evidence regarding health harms on account of pollution, has resulted in major policy changes. However, the scientific and technical consensus that courts have sought to achieve on matters of environmental harm remains elusive.[44] Regarding the use of firecrackers, the Supreme Court has tried to balance various aspects of the issue—religious freedom, economic costs, environmental pollution, and health harms. Such balance, however, is not easy to achieve, and matters of essential religious practice are not so easily settled. In this context, it is instructive to note that while in an earlier case concerning noise pollution in 2005, the Supreme Court had held that the festival of Diwali was mainly associated with *pooja* (prayer) and lights and not with firecrackers, by 2018, it proceeded on the assumption that burning of crackers during Diwali was part of religious practice.[45] On both occasions a 'balance' and a 'limit' was suggested, but based on different reasoning about what constituted an essential religious practice! And in the case of waste-to-energy plant, there remains the distinct possibility that the solution suggested to tackle one problem (waste) may lead to an entirely new environmental issue viz., the release of dioxins and consequent harm to the health of those exposed to these.

[41] *Sukhdev Vihar Residents Welfare Association v State of NCT of Delhi & Others* Original Application No 22 (T_{HC}) of 2013, Judgment of 2 February 2017 (NGT—Principal Bench).

[42] Sarath Guttikunda and Rahul Goel, 'Health Impacts of Particulate Pollution in a Megacity-Delhi, India' (2013) 6 *Environmental Development* 8.

[43] Usha Ramanathan, 'Communities at Risk: Industrial Risk in Indian Law' (2004) 39 (41) *Economic and Political Weekly* 4521.

[44] Rohit Negi and Prerna Srigyan, *Atmosphere of Collaboration: Air Pollution Science, Politics and Ecopreneurship in Delhi* (Routledge 2021).

[45] *In Re: Noise Pollution* AIR 2005 SC 3136; *Arjun Gopal v Union of India* (2019) 13 SCC 523.

Conclusion

In their pioneering writings on the environment in India, Madhav Gadgil and Ramachandra Guha have made a compelling case for understanding ecological concerns through their close link with issues of livelihood and equity.[46] My suggestion is that in urban contexts, environmental concerns are better addressed through their imbrication in issues of health. However, this relationship is complex in its own way. This chapter has suggested three trajectories that have emerged over time.

First, given the assumptions about the tropics being especially pathological spaces, environmental sanitation emerged as a key component of public health in the colonial period. Municipal and public nuisance laws spoke to this concern, seeking to regulate practices contributing to filth and pollution. However, they could also achieve rather little by way of improvement of the health of the general populace. In response, two developments took place. From the 1930s, the conception of public health was expanded to include nutrition, the standard of living, literacy, etc., and for a brief period health also began to be imagined as a potential fundamental right, though eventually, it could find constitutional space only as a duty of the state in the Directive Principles of State Policy. Post-1970s, occasionally, this provision in the Directive Principles was used, together with provisions of the Criminal Procedure Code, to radically reinterpret the public nuisance laws to advance a social justice conception of health and environment.

Second, the colonial period also saw laws passed that sought to move beyond the municipal remit, setting up special expert commissions to tackle the question of smoke. Smoke Nuisances Commissions that were set up in Calcutta and Bombay, from the very beginning, highlighted the health dimensions of air pollution, but it was only by the 1930s that they could persuade municipal authorities to take pollution on account of smoke seriously. These laws and commissions continued to be operational until well into the post-colonial period. Eventually, new laws regarding water and air pollution came to be passed in 1974 and 1981 respectively, providing scientific expertise and regulatory power through Pollution Control Boards to tackle the issue of pollution. However, financial limits, lack of technical staff, and difficulties in levying fines have meant that the outcomes of these laws have also been mixed, and the extent of pollution continued to remain high.

These two trajectories have since yielded to a third one in which the Supreme Court has interpreted the constitutional the right to life to include rights to clean air and water and, by implication, right to good health of the citizens. This also coincided with a greater appreciation of air pollution as a matter of public health concern within the policy domain. Older laws relating to the environment are still referenced, and administrative structures set up in previous decades are drawn upon, but the novelty of

[46] Madhav Gadgil and Ramachandra Guha, *Ecology and Equity: The Use and Abuse of Nature in Contemporary India* (Routledge 1995).

the interpretation of the right to life also marks a critical difference from earlier times. Important decisions have been taken regarding industrial (re)location, use of particular fuels, and adoption of new technologies to abate pollution through an expansive understanding of life.

The gains of the right-to-life rulings, however, do not imply that all are equally well served. As Baviskar has reminded us, often the voice and aspirations of the middle class substitute for what is described as a matter of public interest.[47] To this, we may add that conceptual and practical linkages between public health and clean environment have largely remained a matter of expert knowledge, and rarely draw upon the experience of vulnerable segments of the population, especially those suffering from the greatest exposure. Indeed, we may need to push the boundary of the environment-health relationship even further. Recognizing the intensification of outbreaks of pandemics in the twenty-first century, it is perhaps equally imperative that we move beyond conceptions of social justice that have remained enmeshed within an anthropocentric view of health towards a One Health paradigm, acknowledging the interdependence of human and non-human animal health and ecological change in ensuring well-being and survival.

Suggestions for Further Reading

Sunil Amrith, 'Political Culture of Health in India: A Historical Perspective' (2007) 42(2) *Economic and Political Weekly* 114–121.

Michael Anderson, Public Nuisance and Private Purpose: Policed Environments in British India, 1860–1947 (1992) *SOAS Law Department*, Working Paper No 1.

Amita Baviskar, 'The Politics of the City' (2002) 516 *Seminar* 40–42.

Shubhankar Dam and Vivek Tewary, 'Polluting Environment, Polluting Constitution: Is a 'Polluted' Constitution Worse than a Polluted Environment?' (2005) 17(3) *Journal of Environmental Law* 383–393.

Sarath Guttikunda and Rahul Goel, 'Health Impacts of Particulate Pollution in a Megacity-Delhi, India' (2013) 6 *Environmental Development* 8–20.

47 Amita Baviskar, 'The Politics of the City' (2002) 516 *Seminar* 40.

CHAPTER 35

SANITATION

Linkages with the Environment and Public Health

TANVI BHATKAL AND LYLA MEHTA

Abstract

Sanitation has been the object of much attention over the past couple of decades. The construction of toilets has been at the centre of policy interest, and given particular emphasis in the context of the Swachh Bharat Mission. There are multiple environmental and public health aspects that arise in the context of sanitation. These include the links between open defecation or the absence of wastewater treatment and contamination of surface and groundwater. Some of these challenges are addressed in part through the construction of toilets but these, in turn, create new challenges, such as concerning the disposal of septage. Sanitation also raises various rights-related issues in a context where there has been a strong link between caste and sanitation, most clearly articulated in the context of the practice of manual scavenging. This chapter highlights the various environment and health-related dimensions of sanitation policy and law.

Introduction

Sanitation is critical to realizing sustainable development through several different dimensions. Once viewed as the 'the last taboo' in international development,[1] sanitation is now considered a distinct human right and acknowledged to be pivotal for

[1] Maggie Black and Ben Fawcett, *The Last Taboo: Opening the Door on the Global Sanitation Crisis* (Routledge 2010).

human wellbeing and the realization of the UN Sustainable Development Goals. Access to safe, sustainable sanitation is closely linked to the realization of various rights such as food, life, health, housing, education, security, and political rights of participation. Despite acknowledgement of these linkages, the lack of adequate sanitation remains a major cause of disease in low- and middle-income countries like India, and there are considerable hurdles in realizing the right to sanitation.

Historically, those at greatest risk from environmental threats have been the poor—people without economic assets, social capital, and political power.[2] For sanitation, linkages with the environment emerge through two distinct environmental agendas: the green agenda, which prioritizes long-term global ecological sustainability and problems relating to the impacts of industrialization-based production, consumption and waste generation on ecosystems, resource depletion, and climate change,[3] and the 'brown agenda' which emphasizes social justice and the immediate local environmental needs of marginalized people.[4] Although the green and brown agendas are two sides of the same coin, there is a perceived tension between them. Many have argued that the 'green agenda' dominates discussions on the environment, neglecting social justice and governance.[5] Others have advocated for a holistic approach that focuses on the linkages and overlaps between the two agendas to achieve ecological sustainability and human wellbeing.[6] In countries like India, critical environmental challenges remain, especially in low-income settlements that demand prioritizing local environmental health issues such as sanitation. Thus, we recognize the connections between 'green' and 'brown' environmental concerns, but in the context of the persisting challenges associated with low levels of safe sanitation, we emphasize concerns relating to the brown agenda for environment in this chapter.

In India, the fundamental right to life includes the right to water and sanitation, yet the right to water has received greater attention than sanitation for a long time. Until recently, India had the world's highest prevalence of open defecation.[7] In recent years, sanitation has received increasing policy attention through high profile national government programmes such as the *Swachh Bharat* Mission (SBM). These interventions have tended to focus largely on hardware issues of toilet construction and stopping open

[2] Christopher J Murray and Alan D Lopez (eds), *The Global Burden of Disease: A Comprehensive Assessment of Mortality and Disability from Diseases, Injuries and Risk Factors in 1990 and Projected to 2020: Summary* (WHO and World Bank 1996).

[3] Adriana Allen and Nicholas You, *Sustainable Urbanisation: Bridging the Green and Brown Agendas* (UN-HABITAT 2002); Gordon McGranahan and David Satterthwaite, 'Environmental Health or Ecological Sustainability? Reconciling the Brown and Green Agendas in Urban Development' in Cedric Pugh (ed), *Sustainable Cities in Developing Countries* (Earthscan 2000) 73.

[4] Allen and You (n 3).

[5] Michael Redclift, 'Sustainable Development, (1987–2005): An Oxymoron Comes of Age' (2005) 13 *Sustainable Development* 212; Josef Leitmann, *Sustaining Cities: Environmental Planning and Management in Urban Design* (McGraw-Hill 1999).

[6] Susanna Myllylä and Kristiina Kuvaja, 'Societal Premises for Sustainable Development in Large Southern Cities' (2005) 15(3) *Global Environmental Change* 224; McGranahan and Satterwaite (n 3).

[7] World Bank, 'World Development Indicators' (2015).

defecation. While India now claims to be open defecation free, this claim remains highly disputed.[8] Equally, although recent sanitation efforts have led to an exponential rise in toilets, they have systematically neglected issues of sustainability and equity, failing to address gender and caste-based inequalities that reinforce the discrimination and marginalization of vulnerable groups in the sanitation sector.[9]

In this chapter, we outline the evolution of legal and policy regimes for sanitation in India and unpack their impacts and remaining challenges. Here, we view sanitation not only in terms of access to toilets and safely managed sanitation but also through the lens of the rights of the workers who maintain sanitation systems across the sanitation chain. While we emphasize the connections between sanitation and the environment, we focus on local needs and the environmental and health impacts of sanitation systems and interventions.

35.1 Evolving Sanitation Policy in India

Sanitation has gained increasing policy visibility in the last two decades. The human right to water and sanitation has been recognized in various international treaties and political commitments, including through the UN General Assembly Resolution, 2010,[10] and the explicit recognition of the right to sanitation in 2015.[11] In India, the history of the right to sanitation precedes these international declarations: In 1994, the Supreme Court of India declared the right to sanitation a constituent part of the fundamental right to life under Article 21 of the Constitution of India 1950.[12] The judiciary has also addressed other issues closely related to sanitation, such as manual scavenging.[13] However, in practice, constitutional provisions, laws and judicial verdicts have generally been superseded by government-led schemes and programmes.[14]

[8] Bilal Kuchay, 'Modi Declares India Open Defecation Free, Claim Questioned' *Al Jazeera* (2 October 2019) <https://www.aljazeera.com/news/2019/10/2/modi-declares-india-open-defecation-free-claim-questioned>.

[9] Philippe Cullet, Sujith Koonan, and Lovleen Bhullar (eds), *The Right to Sanitation in India: Critical Perspectives* (OUP 2019); Lyla Mehta and Synne Movik (eds), *Shit Matters: The Potential of Community-Led Total Sanitation* (Practical Action Publishing 2011).

[10] UN General Assembly Resolution, 'The Human Right to Water and Sanitation' UN Doc A/RES/64/292 (2010).

[11] UN General Assembly Resolution, 'The Human Rights to Safe Drinking Water and Sanitation' UN Doc A/RES/70/169 (2015).

[12] *Virendra Gaur v State of Haryana* (1995) 2 SCC 577.

[13] *Safai Karamchari Andolan and Others v Union of India and Others* (2014) 11 SCC 224.

[14] Philippe Cullet, 'Policy as Law: Lessons from Sanitation Interventions in Rural India' (2018) 54 *Stanford Journal of International Law* 241; Sujith Koonan, 'Right to Sanitation in India, Nature and Scope' in K.J. Joy and Sarita Bhagat (eds), *Right to Sanitation in India: Nature, Scope and Voices from the Margins* (Forum for Policy Dialogue on Water Conflicts in India 2016) 1.

Broadly, sanitation policy in India has taken a public health perspective. In a context where ending open defecation has been viewed as a first step to ensure safe sanitation, government interventions have mainly focused on the most visible and tangible infrastructure of toilet construction and access to such infrastructure. Although the modalities of sanitation programmes have varied over time—moving from a supply-driven approach towards more demand-centric efforts, at least in policy design, and from a primarily rural remit to increasingly focusing on urban areas—many recurring challenges and limitations persist. In this section, we outline the evolution of sanitation policy in India and identify some broad trends within the national approach to sanitation.

The first national sanitation programme was introduced in 1986: the Central Rural Sanitation Programme (CRSP), which was a supply-led toilet construction campaign for rural areas. After years of slow progress, it was restructured into the Total Sanitation Campaign (TSC) in 1999, marking a shift towards a demand-driven approach.[15] The TSC prioritized a 'community-led' approach: awareness-raising activities received 15 per cent of the budget, and the *Nirmal Gram Puraskar*, an award rewarding villages declared Open Defecation Free (ODF), was introduced to emphasize a collective approach.[16]

Over time, the programmes were revised a few times, with subsidies replaced by incentives for poor households that self-constructed household toilets in 2004,[17] and sanitation-related construction work merged with the Mahatma Gandhi National Rural Employment Guarantee Act (MGNREGA) through the *Nirmal Bharat Abhiyan* in 2012.[18] Alternate approaches were also attempted, such as Community Led Total Sanitation (CLTS), introduced by Kamal Kar in Bangladesh in 2000 and promoted by the World Bank's Water and Sanitation Programme. Here, rural communities were urged to analyse their own sanitary situation and inspire collective action and toilet construction as per their capacity, usually without subsidies or technical prescriptions.[19]

During the 2000s, sanitation policy also began to address the challenges of urban areas. The national government encouraged state and local funding and planning for sanitation at the city level through, for instance, the Jawaharlal Nehru National Urban Renewal Mission (JNNURM) and the National Urban Sanitation Policy (NUSP).

In terms of progress on sanitation coverage, officially, rural sanitation coverage reported impressive progress, increasing from 22 per cent in 2001 to 68 per cent in 2011.[20] Yet, as the TSC monitoring focused on subsidy disbursement, administrative

[15] Government of India, *Central Rural Sanitation Programme: Total Sanitation Campaign* (Department of Drinking Water Supply, Ministry of Rural Development 2001).

[16] Nisheeth Kumar and J P Shukla, 'CLTS in the Context of a Countrywide Programme in India: Public Good, Private Good?' in Mehta and Movik (n 9) 131.

[17] Government of India, 'Guidelines on Central Rural Sanitation Programme: Total Sanitation Campaign' (Ministry of Rural Development 2004).

[18] Government of India, 'Modification in Nirmal Bharat Abhiyan Guidelines' (2013).

[19] Robert Chambers and Kamal Kar, *Handbook on Community-Led Total Sanitation* (Plan and IDS 2008).

[20] Government of India, 'Towards Nirmal Bharat: Rural Sanitation and Hygiene Strategy, 2010–2022' (Ministry of Rural Development 2011).

monitoring systems were highly inaccurate. The 2011 Census revealed that about 80 per cent of these toilets were 'missing' in reality, millions of 'missing' latrines were either never constructed or partially constructed and abandoned. The target-driven approach meant progress and toilet construction was often reported without proper verification, and the programme experienced substantial leakages and corruption.[21]

As of 2014, India still had 597 million people defecating in the open, the highest in the world.[22] Toilets were highlighted in the campaigns of the two largest political parties during the 2014 parliamentary elections. Subsequently, the government of India launched the SBM, the largest programme on sanitation in India, which included an aggressive public campaign and brought sanitation into mainstream public and political discourse.[23] In 2019, the government of India declared the country open defecation free. This claim has been disputed as evidence suggests open defecation persists in many states.[24]

When considering the sanitation chain beyond open defecation, the need for Faecal Sludge and Septage Management (FSSM), particularly in urban areas, has received increasing recognition, but progress has lagged behind. In 2008, the NUSP recommended safe disposal of human waste, including septic tank sludge, but prioritized sewer-based planning and paid little attention to truck-based emptying. In 2013, the Ministry of Urban Development issued an advisory note on septage management, which promoted safe truck-based FSM. Investment in truck-based emptying increased after the Prohibition of Employment as Manual Scavengers and their Rehabilitation Act, 2013. In 2017, the National Policy on Faecal Sludge and Septage Management was published,[25] explicitly recommending that urban local bodies be provided with trucks whose operations be regularized as part of SBM (Urban). In 2020, the Department of Drinking Water and Sanitation launched Phase II of SBM-Gramin (rural) to focus on ODF Plus, which includes sustaining ODF and solid and liquid waste management. Subsequently, in 2021, the Urban *Swachh Bharat* Mission 2.0 was announced focusing on sludge management and wastewater treatment among other issues.

Thus, over the past decades, domestic policy and legal frameworks have addressed various issues relating to sanitation. Yet, the focus on increasing access to toilets and achieving "open defecation free" status driven a construction-driven infrastructure-centric approach. This narrow approach has often been at the expense of the wider environmental sustainability and equity issues. The next section analyses various challenges

[21] Andrés Hueso and Brian Bell, 'An Untold Story of Policy Failure: The Total Sanitation Campaign in India' (2013) 15(6) *Water Policy* 1001-17.

[22] WHO/UNICEF, 'Progress on Drinking Water and 2014 Sanitation' (2014).

[23] Ministry of Drinking Water and Sanitation, Swacch Bharat Mission (Gramin), 2014.

[24] Special Rapporteur on the Human Rights to Safe Drinking Water and Sanitation (2020); Report of the Comptroller and Auditor General of India for the year ended March 2017, Report No 1 of 2018, Government of Uttarakhand; Report of the Comptroller and Auditor General of India on local bodies for the year ended March 2017, Report No 5 of 2018, Government of Gujarat.

[25] Government of India, 'National Policy on Faecal Sludge and Septage Management (FSSM)' (Ministry of Urban Development 2017).

within the existing regime and draws out remaining issues across the sanitation chain, including FSSM.

35.2 Challenges Associated with Existing Sanitation Policies

Sanitation has become a key policy priority in recent years. Although legal and policy frameworks take a broad view of sanitation, in practice, policy has primarily focused on household toilet construction.[26] Several concerns persist, spanning issues relating to continuing open defecation, poor septage management, water pollution, and associated health impacts; gender, health, and safety concerns; and manual scavenging and inadequate protections for sanitation workers who suffer occupational illnesses and accidental deaths. In this section, we examine three main challenges: unequal access to sanitation, the need for FSSM to address environmental health challenges, and sanitation work, especially relating to manual scavenging and caste-based exploitation.

35.2.1 Politics and Inequalities Determining Access to Safe Sanitation

Increasing concerns over the consequences of inadequate sanitation and water for poverty, health, livelihoods, and education have spurred global declarations on the human right to sanitation. Although multiple sanitation policies have been introduced in India over the years to provide sanitation infrastructures to marginalized groups, large inequalities remain across and within regions, as well as between social groups.

The cultural politics of access to sanitation: Marginal people lacking access to sanitation are often deemed 'illegal' and 'invisible', and these framings are moulded by caste, gender, and other social power relations that maintain marginalization, such that these groups experience severe risks and vulnerabilities, trapping them into endemic cycles of poverty and ill being.[27] Yet, marginality, in this case, is not only about unequal access but also relates to a range of exclusions and discriminations linked to notions of pollution and purity which intersect and are compounded by exclusionary practices related to gender, caste, poverty, and religion.[28]

[26] Cullet (n 14).

[27] Deepa Joshi and Joy Morgan, 'Pavement Dwellers' Sanitation Activities—Visible but Ignored' (2007) 25(3) *Waterlines* 19; Art Cohen, 'Calling for an End to Second-class Shitizenship' (2010) 42(2) *Review of Radical Political Economics* 269.

[28] Arjun Appadurai, 'Deep Democracy: Urban Governmentality and the Horizon of Politics' (2001) 13(2) *Environment and Urbanization* 23; Assa Doron and Ira Raja, 'The Cultural Politics of Shit: Class, Gender and Public Space in India' (2015) 18(2) *Postcolonial Studies* 189.

Uneven power relations leave poor and marginalised people to depend on diverse informal arrangements and negotiations to meet their sanitation needs.[29] They are often forced to depend on vote bank politics to access resources. Yet, marginalized people also take recourse to the law and demand its fair application, as struggle and protest—to be recognized, measured, and mapped in government surveys—are often the only means by which they can claim their rights as citizens.[30] Although several policies and programmes have been introduced aiming to achieve universal access to sanitation, these efforts often remain depoliticized and fail to address power relations that shape and cement social and spatial inequalities in access.[31] Even when legal and policy frameworks identify the complexity of provision of and access to sanitation, and how they are shaped by power relations and governance systems, these issues remains secondary concerns within programmes.

Gendered challenges: Girls and women disproportionately suffer from poor sanitation access due to biological factors, socio-cultural norms, and safety-related risks relating to gender-based violence.[32] A gendered aspect of sanitation with specific environmental linkages relates to the safe management of menstruation. Without appropriate means for disposal, menstrual products are frequently disposed of through sanitation systems, clogging sewers, and blocking the chambers leading to septic tanks. Safe disposal of menstrual products is essential to safeguard both the health and hygiene of menstruating users, society, and the environment. The disposal of menstrual waste is shaped by various rules and policies, for example, the Solid Waste Management Rules 2016, the Bio-medical Waste Management Rules 2016, the Central Pollution Control Board guidelines for the management of sanitary waste, and the Menstrual Hygiene Management National Guidelines 2015 included in the SBM Guidelines, but their differing recommendations cause ambiguity in implementation.[33] Moreover, most interventions are guidelines rather than enforceable rules or laws, and challenges in coordination between various agencies, capacity differences, and misalignment of incentives further complicate their implementation.[34]

[29] Colin McFarlane and Renu Desai, 'Sites of Entitlement: Claim, Negotiation and Struggle in Mumbai' (2015) 27(2) *Environment and Urbanization* 441.

[30] Deepta Chopra, Philippa Williams, and Bhaskar Vira, 'Politics of Citizenship: Experiencing State–Society Relations from the Margins' (2011) 19(3) *Contemporary South Asia* 243; Nikhil Anand, *Hydraulic City: Water and the Infrastructures of Citizenship in Mumbai* (Duke University Press 2017).

[31] McFarlane and Desai (n 29); Renu Desai, Colin McFarlane, and Stephen Graham, 'The Politics of Open Defecation: Informality, Body and Infrastructure in Mumbai' (2015) 47(1) *Antipode* 98.

[32] Tina Khanna and Madhumita Das, 'Why Gender Matters in the Solution Towards Safe Sanitation? Reflections from Rural India' (2016) 11(10) *Global Public Health* 1185; Sujith Koonan, 'Sanitation Interventions in India: Gender Myopia and Implications for Gender Equality' (2019) 26(1–2) *Indian Journal of Gender Studies* 40.

[33] NFSSM Alliance, 'Menstrual Waste Disposal in India' A study by TQH Consulting for the NFSSM Alliance (2020).

[34] ibid.

35.2.2 Beyond Toilets: Are They Really Improved Sanitation Systems?

For a long time, India's sanitation policies and programmes focused on the front end of sanitation: toilet construction and use. There has been a significant increase in the number of toilets built over the past decade. Official records indicate that the share of rural households with toilet access increased from 43.8 per cent in 2014–15 to 100 per cent in 2019–20.[35] Improving access to toilets was certainly a necessity in the context of over 500 million people practising open defecation in India.[36] Yet, claims about India being ODF are widely contested. The Fifteenth Finance Commission noted that open defecation remained prevalent.[37] The Standing Committee on Rural Development also questioned the construction quality of toilets and inflation of government data, which counted non-functional toilets. Similarly, the Standing Committee on Urban Development noted in 2020 that SBM toilets were often very poorly built and maintained.

Moreover, the focus on toilets left the wider sanitation service chain unattended, with uncertain environmental impacts and continuing sustainability concerns.[38] A sanitation system needs to collect and isolate human waste, safely transport it, and then treat it before reusing or disposing it in the environment. Thus, proper treatment of faecal sludge and septage is critical to safe and sustainable sanitation, but in most places, the collected waste continues to be dumped without treatment.[39] Poor liquid and solid waste management and the resultant untreated or partly treated sewage/septage are key causes of water pollution, leading to environmental and public health challenges.

Only a small proportion of urban regions in India have sewerage networks, and not a single city or town has universal coverage. As of 2020, the installed capacity of sewage treatment plants (STPs) was only enough to treat 44 per cent of sewage generated in urban India, and only 64 per cent of this capacity was actually being utilized—meaning only 28 per cent of the total sewage generated was being treated, with the rest flowing untreated into rivers, lakes, ponds and groundwater, making the water sources extremely polluted.[40] Where sewerage networks exist, they are often badly maintained leading to frequent blockages, siltation, missing manhole covers, and gully pits.[41] In our research in urban Maharashtra and Kerala, we found that poor household connections to the sewage network mean that wastewater often spills out into the streets, cross-contaminating water sources. Similarly, stormwater may enter sewers, which are not

[35] Dashboard of SBM (Gramin), Ministry of Jal Shakti.

[36] WHO/UNICEF Joint Monitoring Programme 2017 report (2017).

[37] Fifteenth Finance Commission (2020).

[38] Kavita Wankhade, 'Urban Sanitation in India: Key Shifts in the National Policy Frame' (2015) 27(2) *Environment and Urbanization* 555.

[39] ibid.

[40] CPCB, National Inventory of Sewage Treatment Plants—March 2021 (2021).

[41] Wankhade (n 38).

designed to take such large loads, leading to overflow. Improper disposal of solid waste also tends to block sewer lines.

Smaller towns and rural areas predominantly have on-site sanitation, often without arrangements for treatment or disposal of faecal sludge.[42] Many on-site systems are poorly constructed, and faecal sludge may leach into and contaminate groundwater making them unsafe.[43] Given the multiple routes through which faecal exposure takes place, neglect of safe emptying, transportation, and treatment mean 'improved toilets' will need not improve health outcomes. For on-site systems to be considered safe, they must fulfil certain criteria: pit latrines should be at a certain minimum distance from drinking water sources to avoid water contamination, and septic tanks should have soakaways or drain fields. This is challenging for poor households, especially in dense urban settlements, and current modes of emptying pits and septic tanks and disposing of sludge often harm both public health and the environment. In some unsewered cities, faecal sludge management services are provided by state-managed cleaning trucks with suction pipes, but in most cases, these services are privately run and unregulated.[44] Septage from pit latrines is often dug out and covertly dumped untreated in nearby holes dug in the ground, open areas, into water bodies or in vacant sites—often manually without proper desludging equipment.[45] The physical and social mechanisms through which these practices are organized are generally ignored—or denied—by officials given the caste-related exploitations faced by sanitary workers and manual scavengers who provide these services.[46]

There is now a growing recognition of the fact that centralized sewerage systems are expensive to build, operate, and maintain, and the traditional importance accorded to sewered systems is starting to give way to a preference for non-sewered sanitation systems.[47] While City Sanitation Plans (CSP) required under the NUSP recommended FSSM planning since 2008, uptake was poor. In practice, CSPs were often considered a checkbox activity for municipal governments to secure national funding.[48] Human resource-constrained urban local governments often outsourced CSPs to external consultants who lacked the time, budget, and technical capacity for comprehensive sanitation planning, particularly community engagement and gender-sensitive

[42] ibid.

[43] WSP, *Technology Options for Urban Sanitation in India* (WSP 2008).

[44] CS Sharada Prasad and Isha Ray, 'When the Pits Fill up (in)visible Flows of Waste in Urban India (2019) 9(2) *Journal of Water, Sanitation and Hygiene for Development* 338.

[45] WSP-TARU, *Review of Sewerage and Sanitation Interventions in Urban India* (WSP-South Asia 2008).

[46] Prasad and Ray (n 44).

[47] Government of India, *National Urban Sanitation Policy* (Ministry of Housing and Urban Affairs 2008); Martin Gambrill, Rebecca J Gilsdorf, and Nandita Kotwal, 'Citywide Inclusive Sanitation—Business as Unusual: Shifting the Paradigm by Shifting Minds' (2020) *Frontiers in Environmental Science* 201.

[48] Abishek S Narayan, Max Maurer, and Cristoph Lüthi, 'The Clean Plan: Analysing Sanitation Planning in India Using the CWIS Planning Framework (2021) 11(6) *Journal of Water, Sanitation and Hygiene for Development* 1036.

planning, and often reproduced 'template solutions' rather than addressing contextual needs. Since 2014, SBM and Atal Mission for Rejuvenation and Urban Transformation (AMRUT) have diluted the requirement, and detailed project reports of sanitation infrastructure have replaced city-level planning.

Nevertheless, FSSM has received increasing attention in recent years. Many states and cities have begun introducing and scaling FSSM in urban areas. By 2021, more than 700 cities and towns across India were in various stages of FSSM implementation,[49] especially in Maharashtra, Tamil Nadu, Andhra Pradesh, Telangana, and Odisha. Progress notwithstanding, from a policy perspective, funds allocated for FSSM in the flagship programmes have been limited. In practice, the operationalization of non-sewered sanitation systems such as faecal sludge treatment plants has often proved challenging due to operational and governance struggles.[50] Moreover, AMRUT only covered 500 large cities, excluding over 4,000 small, rapidly growing towns.

Important labour dimensions of sanitation are relevant here. To date, faecal sludge management is largely a service-based industry characterized by informal septic tank desludging operators. However, the existing guidelines for FSSM fail to acknowledge the extent of current truck-based FSM practices as well as the ways in which caste hierarchies and prejudices are tightly intertwined with the tasks of cleaning pits and septic ranks, and transporting human waste.[51] Even at the stage of treatment, Faecal Sludge and Septage Treatment Plants handle lower volumes of sludge compared to STPs, and often relying on non-mechanised treatment processes. These processes expose workers to a range of hazards through contact with faecal matter. In this context, the occupational health and safety of sanitation workers involved in faecal sludge management remains a critical challenge. We turn to these next.

35.2.3 Manual Scavenging and Caste-Based Discrimination

Manual scavenging is a caste-based practice in which workers collect and dispose waste from unsewered latrines. Most people forced into scavenging are *Dalit*, and specific *Dalit* castes are designated 'scavenging castes' based on toxic notions of purity and

[49] NFSSM Alliance and Niti Aayog, 'Faecal Sludge and Septage Management in Urban Areas: Service and Business Models' (2021).

[50] Philippe Reymond, Rohit Chandragiri, and Lukas Ulrich, 'Governance Arrangements for the Scaling up of Small-scale Wastewater Treatment and Reuse Systems—Lessons from India' (2020) 8 *Frontiers in Environmental Science* 72; Reeba Devaraj and others, 'Planning Fecal Sludge Management Systems: Challenges Observed in a Small Town in Southern India' (2021) 281 *Journal of Environmental Management* 111811.

[51] Sarah Jewitt, 'Geographies of Shit: Spatial and Temporal Variations in Attitudes towards Human Waste' (2011) 35(5) *Progress in Human Geography* 608; Diane Coffey and Dean Spears, *Where India Goes: Abandoned Toilets, Stunted Development and the Costs of Caste* (HarperCollins 2017).

pollution.[52] As Ambedkar wrote, 'a man is not a scavenger because of his work. He is a scavenger because of his birth irrespective of the question whether he does scavenging or not'. Even formally, in many ways, scavenging is an inherited profession: if a sanitation worker dies before retirement, their spouse or son can often inherit their job.[53] Women constitute 90 per cent of workers, generally doing the lowest paid work, cleaning, and carrying faeces from toilets.[54] Men typically clean septic tanks and sewers—one of the most dangerous forms of labour, as they often must descend into septic tanks or drains.

The Constitution unequivocally abolished untouchability and its practice in any form, and manual scavenging has been banned through several statutes.[55] Post-Independence policies focused on the living and working conditions of manual scavengers but viewed the practice as 'inevitable' due to the pervasiveness of insanitary latrines.[56] Legal discourse changed in the late 1980s, partly due to collective mobilization by the manual scavenging community. Subsequently, the Employment of Manual Scavengers and Construction of Dry Latrines (Prohibition) Act, 1993 prohibited the construction and use of dry latrines and the employment of manual scavengers.[57] Yet, the Act was criticized for prioritizing sanitation over the human rights and dignity of manual scavengers.[58] Moreover, most state governments failed to implement the Act, and pit latrines remained manually emptied.

With continued deaths of sanitation workers engaged in hazardous work, the *Safai Karmachari Andolan* (SKA) and others conducted prolonged agitation and lobbying. This led to two important changes: a public interest litigation filed in the Supreme Court in 2003[59] and the enactment of the Prohibition of Employment as Manual Scavengers and their Rehabilitation Act, 2013. The 2013 Act explicitly emphasized the 'historical injustice and indignity' inflicted upon manual scavengers,[60] adding important caste dimensions. It imposed a legal obligation to demolish dry latrines or convert them into sanitary latrines and forbade employing workers for hazardous cleaning of septic tanks or sewers without proper safety measures. It also imposed sanitation-related obligations on local governments, including constructing and maintaining of community latrines

[52] Shiva Shankar and Kanthi Swaroop, 'Manual Scavenging in India: The Banality of An Everyday Crime' (2021) 2(1) *CASTE/A Global Journal on Social Exclusion* 67.

[53] Sripad Motiram and Ashish Singh, 'How Close does the Apple Fall to the Tree? Some Evidence from India on Intergenerational Occupational Mobility' (2012) 47(40) *Economic and Political Weekly* 56; Pradeep S Salve, Dhananjay W Bansod, and Hemangi Kadlak, 'Safai Karamcharis in a Vicious Cycle: A Study in the Perspective of Caste' (2017) 52(13) *Economic and Political Weekly* 38.

[54] Human Rights Watch, 'Cleaning Human Waste: "Manual Scavenging", Caste, and Discrimination in India' (Human Rights Watch 2014); Bhasha Singh, *Unseen: The Truth about India's Manual Scavengers* (Penguin Books 2014).

[55] Sujith Koonan, 'Manual Scavenging in India: State Apathy, Non-implementation of Laws and Resistance by the Community' (2021) 5(2) *Indian Law Review* 149.

[56] ibid.

[57] Employment of Manual Scavengers and Construction of Dry Latrines (Prohibition) Act, 1993.

[58] Koonan (n 55).

[59] *Safai Karmachari Andolan v Union of India* (2014) 11 SCC 224 directing the implementation of the Prohibition of Employment as Manual Scavengers and their Rehabilitation Act, 2013.

[60] Koonan (n 14).

to replace dry latrines. Although the 2013 Act marked progress, significant gaps remain, and it does not prescribe a cut-off date to eliminate manual scavenging.[61] Even the 2013 Act has had limited impacts, with poor implementation and little punitive action to serve as a deterrent.[62] Systemic indifference towards caste-based discrimination and marginalization has allowed exploitation and violence involved in manual scavenging to be invisibilized.[63]

Despite these two laws, manual scavenging continues across India. The rapid expansion of pit and septic tank-linked toilets under SBM has created new challenges without clear strategies to empty them. Toilets are seldom connected to sewage, drainage, and water facilities, and there has been relatively low investment in procuring mechanized sludge and pump machines for faecal sludge removal. As SKA founder Bezwada Wilson pointed out, 'Swachh Bharat represents toilet users, not toilet cleaners'.[64]

Moreover, it is not only private individuals and contractors but also public agencies that have perpetuated manual scavenging.[65] The Indian Railways have been one of the largest employers of manual scavengers; for a long time, trains contained open toilets that dumped faeces onto tracks, which was manually cleaned, without any protective or safety equipment.[66] It was claimed that this was not classified as manual scavenging as workers did not carry human excreta on their heads.[67] It was only in 2021 that Indian Railways shifted entirely to bio-toilets, eliminating the need for manual cleaning of faecal waste. Many urban local bodies also employ workers to clean sewers, toilets, and open defaecation areas manually—contractors managing this work often pressure workers to remain manual scavengers by withholding payments or threatening eviction from government housing.[68] The fact that public sector agencies have themselves utilized manual scavenging represents a paradox where the protectors of workers' rights also perpetrate their exploitation.[69]

A key challenge relates to defining manual scavenging. The government does not classify manual cleaning of sewers and septic tanks as manual scavenging. Yet, experts and activists argue that any direct contact with faecal waste is an extension of manual scavenging. Official figures appear to greatly underestimate the extent of manual scavenging, and the practice exists in places where it is declared to have been

[61] Koonan (n 55).

[62] Jayati Ghosh, 'Sanitation Project a Sham' *Frontline* (30 August 2017) <https://frontline.thehindu.com/columns/Jayati_Ghosh/sanitation-project-a-sham/article9831518.ece>.

[63] Koonan (n 55).

[64] Pankaj Srivastava, 'Swachh Bharat Represents Toilet Users, not Toilet Cleaners' *Governance Now* (24 August 2016) <https://www.governancenow.com/views/interview/swachh-bharat-represents-toilet-users-not-cleaners-bezwada-wilson>.

[65] Human Rights Watch (n 54).

[66] Singh (n 54); Ghosh (n 62).

[67] Singh (n 54).

[68] Human Rights Watch (n 54).

[69] Koonan (n 55).

eradicated.[70] Similarly, official figures often grossly underestimate the number of deaths of sanitation workers.[71] [72]

Sanitation is critical to human health, and the main objective of environmental sanitation is to reduce the risk and transmission of pathogens from hazardous human waste to water and food. However, it is critical that policies and programmes take a broad view of sanitation as not only access for citizens but also safeguarding the rights, health, and safety of sanitation workers often directly exposed to pathogens and dangerous gases. It is important that the burden of maintaining environmental safety through sanitation systems does not further entrench historical discriminations and exploitations experienced by marginalized workers and communities.

35.3 Looking Forward: Addressing Emerging Challenges

Despite increasing policy focus and budget allocation on sanitation, many critical challenges persist. Public policy and government programmes must take a holistic view of the right to sanitation that encompasses various dimensions of sanitation, including social equity, environmental sustainability, and public health. This section outlines some of the ways in which the existing regime can address existing and emerging challenges.

35.3.1 Addressing the Sanitation Chain Beyond Access to Toilets

Although the provision of sanitation services has increased significantly in recent years, the construction of toilets alone without a hygienic service chain poses considerable risks to the environment and public health. In terms of collection and treatment of wastewater, centralized systems have traditionally been considered the most desirable solution in urban areas. These rely on complex and capital-intensive infrastructure, consistent energy for pumps, and expert engineering management to collect wastewater and transport it to a treatment unit, usually far from the point of its origin,[73]

[70] Cullet and others (n 9).

[71] Shiv Sahay Singh, 'Manual Scavenging Left 282 Dead Since 2016' *The Hindu* (21 December 2019) https://www.thehindu.com/news/national/manual-scavenging-left-282-dead-since-2016/article30369014.ece.

[72] Ghosh (n 62).

[73] Neelam Rana and NC Narayanan, 'The Centralized Approach to Wastewater Management and Implications for Sanitation Governance: An Analysis of the Intent and Practice of the National Urban

with collection costs accounting for more than 60 per cent of the total budget.[74]

India is still establishing sanitation systems, which provides an opportunity to establish and mainstream sustainable approaches that address all dimensions of sustainability. Notwithstanding the adoption of policies for FSSM in 2017, systematic uptake of non-sewered sanitation systems has been challenging, with urban local governments often facing considerable operational and governance struggles.[75] Although technologies and policies for sanitation have advanced to accommodate contextual needs, planning practices have remained dominated by expert-driven approaches. The complexity of urban sanitation demands borrowing solutions from varied technical and non-technical sources. There is growing recognition by sanitation practitioners, policymakers, and researchers that solutions to the sanitation crisis must not repeat past mistakes of building socially inappropriate infrastructures or using engineering techniques and technologies that disproportionately benefit wealthier, more powerful groups.[76] In this context, urban sustainability challenges of inadequate sanitation and deteriorating water quality can be met by using integrated approaches including nature-based solutions that prioritize wastewater treatment close to where it is created, and emphasizing community-scale and community-managed systems that build on local skills, needs, and materials.[77]

Here, the concept of circular economy is an appealing one—providing an alternative to the largely linear, 'take-make-dispose' economy; it proposes capturing value in waste materials.[78] Millions of tonnes of faecal sludge generated every day in on-site sanitation systems is rich in nutrients and organic compounds.[79] A key challenge and opportunity relates to capturing value remaining in this waste. While SBM-II has begun to focus on faecal sludge and wastewater management and reuse, its operationalization and institutionalization need proper consideration. Importantly, issues of equity and marginality remain neglected in discussions on the circular economy in India and

Sanitation Policy in India' in K.J. Joy and S Janakarajan (eds), *India's Water Futures: Emergent Ideas and Pathways* (Routledge India 2018) 119.

74 Maya A Massoud, Akram Tarhini, and Joumana A Nasr, 'Decentralized Approaches to Wastewater Treatment and Management: Applicability in Developing Countries' (2009) 90 *Journal of Environmental Management* 652.

75 Narayan and others (n 48); Devaraj and others (n 50).

76 Mehta and Movik (n 9).

77 Shubhagato Dasgupta, Neha Agarwal, and Anindita Mukherjee, 'Moving up the On-Site Sanitation Ladder in Urban India through Better Systems and Standards' (2021) 280 *Journal of Environmental Management* 111656; Tatjana Schellenberg and others, 'Wastewater Discharge Standards in the Evolving Context of Urban Sustainability—The Case of India' (2020) 8 *Frontiers in Environmental Science* 30.

78 Patrizia Ghisellini, Catia Cialani, and Sergio Ulgiati, 'A Review on Circular Economy: The Expected Transition to a Balanced Interplay of Environmental and Economic Systems' (2016) 114 *Journal of Cleaner Production* 11.

79 Miriam Otoo and Pay Drechsel, *Resource Recovery from Waste: Business Models for Energy, Nutrient and Water Reuse in Low-and Middle-income Countries* (Routledge 2018); Miriam Otoo, Pay Drechsel, and Munir A Hanjra, 'Business Models and Economic Approaches for Nutrient Recovery from Wastewater and Fecal Sludge' in Pay Drechsel, Manzoor Qadir, and Dennis Wichelns (eds), *Wastewater: Economic Asset in an Urbanizing World* (Springer 2015) 247.

globally.[80] Analysis of the opportunities in the circular economy must address existing power relations, socio-political institutions, and the legacy of caste-based exploitation involved in sanitation work.

Thus, as national policies plan sanitation beyond toilets and focus on FSSM, it is critical that they create an enabling environment to facilitate the adoption of decentralized, low-cost, nature-based infrastructures to enable the safe treatment of faecal sludge and wastewater through modes that ensure the safety and dignity of sanitation workers.

35.3.2 Rights-Bearing Citizens Rather than Beneficiaries

Globally, the right to sanitation has progressively been integrated into human rights frameworks. In India, courts have repeatedly affirmed the right to sanitation as part of the fundamental right to life under Article 21 of the Constitution, highlighting the importance of equity and human rights in sanitation. Despite the presence of laws and constitutional norms, policy frameworks have not reflected the judicial recognition of the right to sanitation, and sanitation governance has functioned through programmes and schemes.[81]

Government policies and administrative measures rarely frame residents—indeed citizens—as rights holders, but instead as beneficiaries.[82] This framing has not changed even with the shift from the supply-driven CRSP to demand-led approaches of the TSC and SBM. Where right holders are considered beneficiaries, it is difficult to hold the state accountable for not performing its duties.[83] Recent policy measures requiring households to build their own toilets impose duties on citizens rather than recognizing their right to sanitation. The fact that the right to sanitation has been explicitly recognized, however, demands the creation of a framework and institutions to enable citizens to remedy violations of their right.[84]

Going forward, it is important that sanitation policies and programmes recognize the fundamental right to sanitation and be accompanied by mechanisms and institutional frameworks to ensure the accountability of implementing agencies.[85] As it stands, there are no accountability frameworks or avenues for recourse (beyond approaching the judiciary for the violation of fundamental rights) if the government fails to provide citizens with sanitation.[86] Thus, the existing policy framework needs to be further integrated around a rights-based approach.

[80] Roberto Merli, Michele Preziosi, and Alessia Acampora, 'How do Scholars Approach the Circular Economy? A Systematic Literature Review' (2018) 178 *Journal of Cleaner Production* 703; Patrick Schröder, Alexandre Lemille, and Peter Desmond, 'Making the Circular Economy Work for Human Development' (2020) 156 *Resources, Conservation and Recycling* 104686.

[81] Koonan (n 14).

[82] Cullet (n 14).

[83] ibid.

[84] Koonan (n 14).

[85] ibid.

[86] Cullet (n 14).

35.3.3 Need for Attention to Neglected Dimensions Across the Sanitation Chain

Sanitation programmes and policies in India have focused on access to sanitation, particularly toilets. As these have begun to address the sanitation chain, it is important to recognize the linkages between the flows of waste with labour and risk. The emptying and transportation of faecal waste shifts health and safety risks from households to sanitation workers and to the environment.[87] Although constitutional and legal provisions deem it a criminal act for someone to employ a manual scavenger, caste-related power asymmetries render implementation of the existing statutory framework poor. Even the limited implementation of the statutory framework has largely occurred due to the manual scavenging community organizing and asserting their rights politically and legally to seek the emancipation of historically marginalized *Dalit* communities.[88]

Despite laws aiming to eliminate manual scavenging based on a human rights perspective, FSSM policies and guidelines fail to explicitly engage with the caste-based discriminations and human rights violations involved in manual scavenging based on sanitized discourses of a Clean India, which is presented as caste-neutral.[89] Socio-political caste-based discriminations must be explicitly addressed within provisions for safe handling of faecal waste in policy frameworks, as well as in strategies and business models for reusing faecal waste. Going forward, the policy framework must take a holistic understanding of sanitation and address not only the environmental health issues implicated in access to sanitation but also the concerns and needs of sanitation workers. Without this, sanitation policies will fail to address a critical component of the sanitation challenge.

35.3.4 Governance and Financing Priorities

Lack of adequate sanitation planning has been a key cause of failure to provide sustainable sanitation in India.[90] It is critical to address the governance, regulatory, and institutional challenges and develop sustainable sanitation systems that can serve the needs of marginalized groups, enable environmental justice, and ensure dignity and safety for sanitation workers.

Although financing for urban sanitation has increased in the last two decades through the NUSP, JNNURM, SBM and AMRUT, various challenges persist. Across these

[87] Prasad and Ray (n 44).

[88] Koonan (n 55).

[89] Prasad and Ray (n 44); Subhash Gatade, 'Silencing Caste, Sanitising Oppression: Understanding Swachh Bharat Abhiyan' (2015) 50(44) *Economic and Political Weekly* 29.

[90] Ruth Kennedy-Walker and others, 'Challenges for the Future of Urban Sanitation Planning: Critical Analysis of John Kalbermatten's Influence' (2014) 4(1) *Journal of Water, Sanitation and Hygiene for Development* 1.

programmes, dedicated resources for sanitation planning were lacking; this meant city governments had to fund the planning process themselves, and sanitation often fared low among competing priorities.[91] There was often a lack of will for effective sanitation planning as the process is costly, time-consuming, and asynchronous with election cycles.[92] However, for investment in sanitation infrastructure to effectively address contextual needs, it is important to allocate financial and human resources for comprehensive and coordinated sanitation planning and implementation.

In addition, public funding has traditionally been directed to Class I cities, particularly those with a population over a million, partly because of their visibility. Megacities often have separate utilities for sanitation provision and at least ten times more skilled labour than secondary cities. Chaplin argues that urban local governments have been unwilling to upgrade sanitation infrastructure partly due to funding concerns: municipal governments have often been unable to raise tax collections and service revenues due to pressure from both politicians and the middle classes.[93] Yet, increasingly, there have been calls, and greater national investment into smaller cities, which suffer huge service deficits. There is a need for much more attention, political prioritization, and financing for urban infrastructure appropriate for small towns and cities. While this has begun to occur, with technical support from various agencies, this has so far taken the form of pilot projects. In the future, infrastructure planning must be institutionalized across small towns without resorting to 'one-size-fits-all' solutions.

A focus on quantifying construction has meant that other elements needed to strengthen sanitation systems remain neglected. In India, the top-down construction-led model has commonly failed as communities consistently require funding for operations and maintenance.[94] Although certain states have made marked progress towards safeguarding environmental and public health concerns through FSSM at the city level, continued investment is needed to ensure that urban local bodies can manage operations and maintenance to ensure the sustainability of progress towards safely managed sanitation. Similarly, retrofitting challenges need to be addressed: millions of toilets do not meet standards, and leach pits and septic tanks are frequently inappropriate, posing a considerable risk of groundwater contamination. In this context, it is important to have funds and plans to facilitate retrofitting current systems to meet proposed quality standards, especially in highly dense urban areas.

A further challenge is that municipal governments often struggle to manage infrastructure projects due to coordination challenges and administrative and jurisdictional ambiguities, especially in peri-urban areas.[95] Multiple agencies are often responsible for

[91] ibid.

[92] Susan E Chaplin, 'Cities, Sewers and Poverty: India's Politics of Sanitation' (1999) 11(1) *Environment and Urbanization* 145; Hueso and Bell (n 21).

[93] Susan E Chaplin, 'Indian Cities, Sanitation and the State: The Politics of the Failure to Provide' (2011) 23(1) *Environment and Urbanization* 57.

[94] Hueso and Bell (n 21).

[95] Fiona Marshall and others, 'On the Edge of Sustainability: Perspectives on Peri-urban Dynamics' (2009) STEPS Working Paper 35; Mehta and Movik (n 9).

different aspects of the sanitation chain, and state governments frequently supersede municipal authority, creating bureaucratic silos that prevent the implementation of sanitation solutions.[96] Thus, when considering sanitation planning and financing, it is also critical to look beyond simple quantifications of progress—such as number of toilets built—and to address the complex interrelated political, institutional, governance, and financing concerns that shape the implementation and sustainability of sanitation systems.

Conclusion

Policy interventions in India in recent years have given sanitation visibility at all levels. Yet, big gaps remain between rhetoric and reality, and there is a long way to go to achieve universal rights to safely manage sanitation. It is critical that these considerations be addressed across the entire sanitation chain to ensure equity and sustainability in sanitation infrastructures. Consequently, sanitation laws and policies must consider the flow of faecal sludge and wastewater beyond toilets through containment, transportation, treatment, and disposal or reuse. Going forward, these aspects of sanitation across the chain, which have often remained hidden, must be made visible in addressing the existing and emerging challenges relating to sanitation.

A crucial dimension of realizing the human right to sanitation relates to its justiciability and holding public entities accountable for non-compliance in terms of both the right to safe, sustainable sanitation and the constitutionally mandated human rights of sanitation workers. These two considerations must be brought together to address sanitation needs and plan for sanitation infrastructures. Victims of violations of the right to sanitation are often among the most marginalized in society, and persisting taboos prevent open discussion of the indignities linked to unhygienic and hazardous conditions. The right to sanitation needs to be understood not just about access to sanitation but also encompassing the rights and dignity of sanitation workers who have often been neglected. Violations of the right to sanitation and the rights of sanitation workers are both connected to unequal power relationships and systemic patterns of exclusion, and the structural causes of these violations must be addressed to empower marginalized groups to secure effective remedies.

Suggestions for Further Reading

Susan E Chaplin, 'Indian Cities, Sanitation and the State: The Politics of the Failure to Provide' (2011) 23(1) *Environment and Urbanization* 57.

Philippe Cullet, Sujith Koonan, and Lovleen Bhullar (eds), *Right to Sanitation in India: Critical Perspectives* (OUP 2019).

[96] Chaplin (n 93).

Sujith Koonan, 'Manual Scavenging in India: State Apathy, Non-Implementation of Laws and Resistance by the Community' (2021) 5(2) *Indian Law Review* 149.
Sujith Koonan, 'Sanitation Interventions in India: Gender Myopia and Implications for Gender Equality' (2019) 26(1–2) *Indian Journal of Gender Studies* 40.
Kavita Wankhade, 'Urban Sanitation in India: Key Shifts in the National Policy Frame' (2015) 27(2) *Environment and Urbanization* 555.

PART X

RESOURCE EXTRACTION, INDUSTRIAL DEVELOPMENT, AND ENERGY

CHAPTER 36

MINING AND THE ENVIRONMENT

SARVAJEET KUMAR SINHA AND ROOPA MADHAV

Abstract

Mining impacts the environment and the ecosystem. It poses critical challenges for regulators with a range of issues to be addressed: sustainable practices, pollution, mine closure and reclamation, and benefit sharing to balance negative externalities for the present and future generations. This chapter reviews the interface between mining and environmental regulation and examines six key areas in depth: (a) the challenge of making extractive industries align with sustainability goals; (b) protecting the corpus of mineral resources to ensure equitable distribution of resource wealth and also inter-generational equity; (c) efforts to curb illegal mining which contributes to unregulated extraction and significant damage to the environment; (d) preventive measures through the environmental impact assessment mechanism; and finally (e) the institutional effectiveness of regulatory bodies, the robustness of which can ensure long-term environmental protection.

Introduction

The adverse impacts of mining on the environment include significant damage to natural resources and human health—both the upstream and downstream extractive phases of mineral production cause significant pollution. The pollution depends on the type of minerals mined, the extraction method—open-cast or underground mining, and the beneficiation needed. The geophysical aspects of the mined area can also contribute to or aggravate pollution. Open-cast mining leads to large-scale loss of vegetation and deforestation. Drilling and blasting during the mining operations cause dust and noise pollution.[1] Mining processes such as dry crushing or grinding cause air pollution and heavy metal contamination with adverse health impacts for humans and the surrounding flora and fauna. Waste dumps and ore beneficiation lead to pollution of water sources, both surface water and groundwater. Acid mine drainage is another serious concern, the remediation of which takes many years. Land degradation due to surface mining and land subsidence in the case of underground mining require careful environmental planning and oversight.[2] Overall, mining leads to a large amount of waste that needs to be handled well beyond the operational life of the mine, requiring planning and oversight over a long period.[3] India has many abandoned mines, closed without a scientific process, compounding these environmental concerns.[4]

Environmental regulation of mining activities is a critical aspect of mineral development. It has progressively become an important element of the mine plans that the industry must adhere to.[5] In fact, sustainable and scientific mining are buzzwords regularly used in both government and industry reports.[6] Under the mining Sustainable Development Framework, after 2016, a star rating system was introduced to ensure greater compliance with environmental safeguards and to provide incentives for the adoption of best practices.[7] Despite awareness and knowledge, effective implementation remains a challenge.

Mineral regulation differs for major minerals (iron ore, bauxite, manganese, etc.), fuel minerals such as coal and lignite, petroleum, natural gas, atomic minerals, and minor minerals such as sand and granite. Although this complex mineral-specific regulatory framework impacts environmental regulation, this chapter highlights the issues pertaining to the two major classifications—major and minor mineral resources, the latter being entirely within the domain of state governments. Apart from the vertical division of powers between the centre and states, the horizontal division between several institutions, including the Ministry of Environment, Forest and Climate Change (MoEFCC) and the Revenue Department, require effective coordination to take care of institutional overlaps and ensure regulatory robustness.

[1] See generally, ELAW, 'Guidebook for Evaluating Mining Project EIAs' (Environmental Law Alliance Worldwide 2010) Ch 1 https://www.elaw.org/mining-eia-guidebook.

[2] ibid.

[3] See generally, Pradeep K Singh and Raj S Singh, 'Environmental and Social Impacts of Mining and their Mitigation' (National Seminar ESIMM, Kolkata, September 2016).

[4] See generally, the Ministry of Coal, Mine Closure Framework to be Implemented in Two Phases, PIB Oct 2021 <https://pib.gov.in/PressReleaseIframePage.aspx?PRID=1761414>.

[5] See generally, Government of India, 'National Mineral Policy—Report of the High Level Committee (Hoda Committee)' (Planning Commission, Government of India 2006).

[6] ibid. See also Government of India, Planning Commission and ISID, 'Sustainable Development: Emerging Issues in India's Mineral Sector' (Planning Commission 2012).

[7] The star rating scheme is designed to have a built-in compliance mechanism for environment and forest safeguards, recognize good performers, and adopt and share best practices within the sector. For more details, see <https://mines.gov.in/writereaddata/UploadFile/f.pdf>.

Against this backdrop, this chapter outlines the regulatory framework for mining and the environment in Section 36.1, explores key challenges impacting the sector in Section 36.2, and concludes with critical reflections on the broader issues that arise in ensuring that environmental concerns around mining are addressed effectively.

36.1 Mining and the Environment—Regulatory Framework

This section broadly outlines the regulatory framework that governs the interface between mining and the environment in India, highlights the key aspects of the policy and law framework, and briefly outlines the interface with the international framework on mining.

Being a federal state, environmental regulation is divided between all three levels—the centre, states, and local bodies in India—depending on the type of mineral resource. The mining regulatory framework has a bearing on environmental regulation and must be read with the broader environmental statutory framework. A significant part of national legal instruments on environmental regulation are crafted due to and influenced by international environmental law. It is, therefore, useful to make a brief detour to examine the international law relating to mining before diving into the specific regulatory aspects of mining in India.

It is important to note that no overarching international treaties regulate the environmental concerns arising from mining activities. The international instruments that have a bearing on mining are the International Labour Organization (ILO) Convention No. 169 (on the rights of Indigenous Peoples to their culture and way of life), the UN Declaration on the Rights of Indigenous Peoples, 2007 (which acknowledges the rights to natural resources, including land), and the Minamata Convention, 2013, which seeks to regulate the use of mercury in artisanal and small-scale gold mining. In the absence of a guiding international treaty framework, the development of the mining regulatory framework in India is episodic, responding to nudges for policy changes by the industry or the judiciary.

However, soft law measures to ensure greater accountability in sourcing minerals through the global supply chain are being introduced with some measure of success. The UN Guiding Principles on Business and Human Rights, 2011 and the OECD's Due Diligence Guidance for Responsible Supply Chains of Minerals from Conflict-Affected and High-Risk Areas, 2016, are efforts to ensure accountability in global supply chains. This broad law and policy shift from command-and-control mechanisms such as the polluter pays to ensure environmental protection to other measures such as supply chain regulation or performance-based standard setting is now evident in international and national regulatory instruments, including mining and the environment. While this chapter focuses on the national context, the lack of an international discourse on how best to regulate the sector to protect the environment has a bearing on the lack of standards and guidance for national governments to develop their regulatory trajectory.

36.1.1 National Policy Framework

Over the years, a discernible shift has been evident in national mining policy to address environmental impacts through scientific and sustainable mining. While defining the sustainability of a non-renewable resource remains tricky, efforts to increase the recycling of extracted materials to decrease the fresh extraction of resources are part of the larger sustainability framework.

The first National Mineral Policy was introduced in 1993, primarily encouraging investment and opening the sector to private participation. The policy recognized the need to protect the environment and acknowledged the need to prohibit mining in bio-diverse areas and ecologically fragile zones. The policy encouraged the adoption of an environmental management plan to ensure minimal environmental damage while facilitating reclamation and afforestation alongside mineral extraction. It also mentioned the Sustainable Development Framework for optimum utilization of the country's mineral resources. This National Mineral Policy was revised in 2008 (the 2008 Policy) following the recommendations of the Hoda Committee Report set up by the central government to review the mining policy and law framework.[8]

The Hoda Committee Report also examined the Sustainable Development Framework (SDF) developed by the International Council of Mining and Metals (ICMM) along with IUCN and recommended that a similar SDF framework be developed for the Indian mineral sector (a more detailed discussion is in the contemporary challenges in section 36.2). The 2008 Policy sought to promote the idea of scientific mining within the broader framework of sustainable development and environmental protection.[9] Apart from SDF, the 2008 Policy also introduced the concept of zero-waste policy to ensure optimum utilization of available mineral resources.

In 2017, the Supreme Court of India, in a case about illegal mining in the state of Orissa, observed that the 2008 Policy was outdated and unable to meet the challenges of the day.[10] It ordered the government of India to revise the policy to cater to present day needs. In pursuance of the Court's order, the government released the 2019 version of the National Mineral Policy. It has three key provisions about the environment. It proposes to identify critically fragile ecosystems and declare them as 'inviolate areas' where no mining will be permitted. It introduces the concept of inter-generational equity in mineral resource exploitation to ensure the interests of present and future generations are factored into long-term planning. It also proposes an overarching inter-ministerial body under the aegis of the Ministry of Mines to expedite clearances for mining projects

[8] Hoda Committee Report (n 5).

[9] Government of India, *Indian Minerals Yearbook, 2013* (September 2015).

[10] *Common Cause v Union of India* (2017) 9 SCC 499.

and facilitate horizontal institutional collaboration. The policy also identifies the need for adequate financial resources for mine closure.

While the policy documents see a progressive engagement with the environmental and social concerns around mining, they have also expanded manifold the deregulation of the mineral sector to enable greater ease in developing it. The contradictions inherent in the approach play out where the balancing act between development and environmental safeguards is difficult to maintain, with environmental safeguards steadily being whittled away.

Apart from the mining policy, some related policy documents that have a bearing on the mining sector, such as the National Environment Policy, 2006, the Industrial Policy, and the National Forest Policy, 1988, are critical for a better understanding of the policy environment. For instance, the National Forest Policy requires that the diversion of forest land for non-forest (including mining) purposes be examined carefully for environmental impact, with compensatory afforestation being built into the mining closure plans.

36.1.2 Constitutional Aspects of Mining and Environmental Regulation

Despite mining being in the Concurrent List of the Seventh Schedule of the Constitution of India, 1950, the central government exercised vast powers over mineral resources. Concerning major minerals, it determined control over important aspects such as royalty rates, terms of auctions, etc. State governments exercise powers under entry 23 of List II of the Seventh Schedule of the Constitution to regulate mines and the development of minerals, subject to the powers of the central government under List I of the Seventh Schedule of the Constitution. State governments have the power to impose taxes on mineral rights under entry 50 of List II of the Seventh Schedule.

Against the backdrop of regulating mining pollution, courts have a significant role to play. Article 21 (right to life) of the Constitution was expanded to include the right to a clean environment. The first major environmental litigation in India pertains to limestone quarrying in the Dehradun Valley. The Supreme Court was called upon to balance the competing needs of ecological protection and development, a difficult trade-off that continues to pose a challenge for both the judiciary and the administrators, and the Court looked towards constitutional provisions to resolve this issue. In 1982, the government of Uttar Pradesh refused to renew the mining leases for limestone as the blasting of rocks, destruction of forest cover, landslides, and impact on water bodies led to adverse effects on agricultural land in the nearby areas. The government move was challenged before the Allahabad High Court, and the court stayed the action taken by the state government.

In response to this order, in 1983, the Rural Litigation and Entitlement Kendra wrote a letter to the Supreme Court outlining the ecological destruction caused by limestone quarrying, and this was converted into a writ petition. The Court appointed the Bhargava committee to assess the issues arising from mining. Considering the hardships caused to mine owners and workers in the region and based on the expert committee report, the Court permitted the working of a select few mines in some areas of the valley. It is important to note here that during the pendency of this litigation, the Environment (Protection) Act was enacted in 1986. The Court concluded that mining violated the Forest (Conservation) Act, 1980 (FCA).[11] In this ruling, the Court read into Article 21 of the Constitution the right to a wholesome environment, making it a fundamental right.

Since then, there has been a steady reading into constitutional provisions of the need to ensure environmental protection and to incorporate legal principles into their interpretation. In *TN Godavarman Thirumulpad v Union of India*, the Supreme Court observed that the state and the citizens are obliged to protect and improve the environment, including forests, lakes, rivers, and wildlife. It further noted that a duty is cast upon the government under Article 21 of the Constitution to protect the environment, and the two principles which govern the law of environment are the principle of sustainable development and the precautionary principle.[12] These observations arose from public interest challenge to the actions of the state of Tamil Nadu in permitting the destruction of the tropical rain forest in the Gudalur and Nilgiri areas, resulting in serious ecological imbalances affecting lives and livelihood of the people in the region.

Against the backdrop of mining, more recently, a significant ruling on ownership of natural gas provides an interesting insight into the constitutional framing of non-renewable resources. In *Reliance Natural Resources Ltd v Reliance Industries Ltd*, Justice Reddy noted that although natural resources within the territory of India are vested with the Union government under the Constitution, the government does not enjoy complete discretion in the allocation of these resources.[13] The government must be guided by constitutional provisions in making critical decisions about the use of the resource and must attempt to balance the safeguards primarily contained in the fundamental rights (Part III of the Constitution) and guidance provided by the Directive Principles of State Policy (Part IV of the Constitution).

Another important aspect that has a bearing on mining and environmental protection is the rights of local communities under the Fifth Schedule and the Sixth Schedule of the Constitution. These provisions must also be read with Article 13 of the Constitution, which acknowledges customary law as an important source of law. The complex legal ordering of rights over mineral resources has implications for our understanding of the legal schema and its impact on environmental regulation. Mineral resources are available abundantly in the Fifth and Sixth Schedule areas. In the Fifth Schedule areas (predominantly tribal areas in peninsular India), large projects require additional clearances from the communities. In *Samatha v State of Andhra Pradesh*, the Supreme Court

[11] *Rural Litigation and Entitlement Kendra & Others v State of Uttar Pradesh* (1985) 2 SCC 431.

[12] *TN Godavarman Thirumulpad v Union of India* (2002) 10 SCC 606.

[13] *Reliance Natural Resources Ltd v Reliance Industries Ltd* (2010) 7 SCC 1.

noted that the grant of a mining lease amounted to transferring the land to a non-tribal, violating the provisions of the law and the spirit of the Fifth Schedule.[14] The grant of the mining lease was held to be illegal, and the Court ruled further that mining leases in Scheduled Areas in Andhra Pradesh could only be granted to the state government mining corporations or a cooperative set up by Scheduled Tribes.

In the areas falling within the Sixth Schedule, that is, largely the semi-autonomous tribal areas in the North-East, the central laws pertaining to mining are not automatically extended. The North-eastern states (and Jammu and Kashmir) have the right to decide whether a Union law about ownership and transfer of land and its resources would apply to them. This includes the central mining enactments. Given this, ensuring that the broader mining regulatory framework and environmental protections under mining laws apply to the Sixth Schedule areas is difficult. A share of the royalties will be paid to the Autonomous District Councils after an agreement between the state government and the district council. However, in a recent case on regulation of rat hole mining in the state of Meghalaya, the Supreme Court read down the role of the District Councils in mining regulation.[15]

The constitutional and statutory framework on land, mining, forests, and the environment overlap and must be considered together to better understand the interface between mining and the environment.

36.1.3 Mining Statutory Framework

The mining regulatory framework contains provisions for environmental compliance and oversight. It is useful, therefore, to examine the provisions of the primary legislation on mining to examine the impact on the environment. The regulation of mineral extraction is broadly divided into four categories—atomic minerals, fuel or energy minerals, major minerals, and minor minerals. For the sake of brevity, we exclude a discussion of atomic minerals and fuel minerals, except coal.

The overarching legislation—the Mines and Minerals (Development and Regulation) Act, 1957 (MMDRA) provides guidance on the abatement of pollution, mine closures, and environmental protection. There are two major rules under the enactment—the Mineral Concession Rules, 1960 (MCR), which pertain to the grant of licence to mining and the Mineral Conservation and Development Rules, 1988 (MCDR) regarding the conservation and adoption of scientific mining in the country. Scientific mining for the coal sector is governed by a separate enactment—the Coal Mines (Conservation and Development) Act, 1974. The Coal Controller under this legislation is responsible for the enforcement of provisions on conservation.[16]

[14] *Samatha v State of Andhra Pradesh* (1997) 8 SCC 191.

[15] For a discussion of the case, see Roopa Madhav, 'Rights over Mineral Resources: Mapping Recent Judicial Trends' (2022) 17(2) *Law Environment and Development Journal* 145.

[16] Hoda Committee Report (n 5); ISID Report (n 6).

Major Minerals: the MMDRA is the umbrella legislation regulating mining in India. The primary focus of this legislation is to facilitate reconnaissance, prospecting, and development of mines. Significant changes to the legislation about environmental safeguards were introduced through an amendment in 1986. This amendment introduced sanctions for violations such as termination of mining licence (section 4A) in the event of failure to comply with environmental protection measures and introduced proactive measures (sections 13–15) to restore and rehabilitate the degraded areas after mining.[17] This amendment also introduced the Mining Plan which takes into account the potential environmental damage at the stage of planning the fresh mine site with a clear plan for restoration and closure built into the larger mine plan. Over the years, more amendments introduced provisions needed to make the mining industry compliant with environmental standards.[18]

The central government framed the Mineral Conservation and Development Rules, 1988 (MCDR), which require the mining leaseholders to ensure safe and scientific mining to protect the environment. The MMDRA empowers the central government to issue directions to the state governments to ensure sustainable development and exploitation of minerals to reduce adverse air, groundwater, and ambient noise impacts. All mines, irrespective of their size and nature of mineral (major and minor), operating in the country must obtain an Environmental Clearance (EC) under the Environment Impact Assessment Notification, 2006 (EIA Notification). Mines operating without an EC are considered illegal.

The other mining laws related to environmental protection for mining activities in India include the Coal Mines (Conservation and Development) Act, 1974. The Coal Controller appointed by the Ministry of Coal (MOC) under this legislation is also empowered to monitor coal mine closure and operate the escrow account created by the mine owner in relation to such activities. As per the Guidelines for Preparation of Mining Plan (2011), information related to the environment management plan, progressive and final mine closure plans, and the results of any investigation carried out for environmental protection are also required to be included in the mining plan submitted by mine owners to MOC for approval. The approved mining plan must then be submitted to the MoEFCC by the mine owner as part of the forest and/or environmental clearance application.

Minor Minerals: minor minerals are regulated by state governments, and each state has enacted legislation to regulate the issues of licensing and collecting revenue from the sale of minerals. However, large-scale illegal mining and environmental impacts on forests and rivers led to guidelines being issued by the MoEFCC on sand mining, thus ensuring some uniformity in the regulation of sand mining across the country.[19] Court

[17] ibid.

[18] For instance, amendments to the Mineral Conservation and Development Rules, 1988, provide for generating environmental baseline data commencing prospecting operations; in 2003, the rules were amended to provide for a progressive mine closure plan.

[19] GoI, MoEF&CC, 'Sustainable Sand Mining Management Guidelines, 2016' <http://environmentclearance.nic.in/writereaddata/SandMiningManagementGuidelines2016.pdf>.

rulings, particularly directions from the National Green Tribunal (NGT), guided these proactive measures.

In *Deepak Kumar v State of Haryana*, the Supreme Court addressed the issue of environmental clearances for minor mineral leases.[20] The state of Haryana issued auction notices for extraction of minor minerals, particularly sand mining, in various state districts. This was challenged as the mining areas were in fragile ecological areas in the Himalayan foothills and riverbeds. The lack of an EIA requirement was highlighted as the areas sought to be auctioned were below five hectares. In deciding the case, the Court laid down guidelines for conducting mining in a manner that is not harmful to the environment and biodiversity in the region. It noted that unrestricted sand mining damages the ecosystem of rivers, altering the habitat characteristics of in-stream biota and the associated riparian habit.

Despite the case being about auction notices in the state of Haryana, the Court noted that it is relevant for other states in the country. It called for better regulation of minor minerals, including small-scale leases. In this context, the Court directed the state governments to two reports—the MoEFCC Report on Environmental Aspects of Quarrying of Minor Minerals (2010) and the Indian Bureau of Mines' (IBM) Report on the Model Mining Framework for Minor Minerals (2010), which provided guidelines on aspects such as size and period of mining lease, requirements of a mining plan, and mine closure. The MoEFCC recommendations also provided specific guidelines for riverbed mining. All state governments and Union territories were asked to give effect to the MoEFCC's recommendations.

Despite the numerous orders by the Supreme Court and the NGT,[21] illegal sand mining continues unabated. In several cases, the NGT was called on to adjudicate illegal mining in the guise of dredging and desiltation activity. It reiterated that the mandate of the law as laid down in *Deepak Kumar* and the Sustainable Sand Mining Guidelines issued by the MoEFCC under the Environment (Protection) Act be complied with.[22] Despite these developments, minor minerals lack a framework that can enable a more comprehensive and cooperative approach for wider uptake of environmental safeguards in a manner that is also economically viable.

36.1.4 Environment Statutory Framework

Before a mining project is operational, a slew of environmental clearances is required. The four key legislations to be noted here are the Environment (Protection) Act, 1986,

[20] *Deepak Kumar v State of Haryana* (2012) 4 SCC 629.

[21] ibid. See also *National Green Tribunal Bar Association v Virender Singh* (State of Gujarat) OA No 360 of 2015 (Orders of 4 September 2019 and 5 April 2019, NGT—Principal Bench); *Sudarsan Das v State of West Bengal & Others* 2018 SCC OnLine NGT 2380.

[22] ibid. See also *RELA v State of Andhra Pradesh* 2019 SCC OnLine NGT 1798 and 2020 SCC OnLine NGT 594.

the Water (Prevention and Control of Pollution) Act, 1974 (Water Pollution Act), the Air (Prevention and Control of Pollution) Act, 1981 (Air Pollution Act), and the Forest Conservation Act, 1980 (FCA). Additionally, the Coastal Zone Regulations, 1991, prohibits industrial activities, including mining, within a strip of 520 metres from the seashore. Forest clearance under the FCA also requires compliance with the Panchayats (Extension to Scheduled Areas) Act, 1996, and the Scheduled Tribes and Other Traditional Forest Dwellers (Recognition of Forest Rights) Act, 2006 (FRA).

Aside from these legislations, it is necessary to emphasize here that the FCA and the EIA Notification under the Environment (Protection) Act are two regulations the mining sector engages with more consistently. As noted above, an EIA is now required for minor mineral leases under five hectares. By an amendment, the EIA Notification also established the District Environment Impact Assessment Authority (DEIAA) and the District Expert Appraisal Committee (DEAC) to evaluate EC for medium- and small-scale leases for minor minerals. A cluster of small-size mining leases where the cluster size is greater than five hectares but less than twenty-five hectares can also be considered by the DEIAA.[23]

The environmental requirements can be summarized to include the following key steps. First, the mining lease holder must obtain an environmental clearance under the Environment (Protection) Act and the EIA. Second, the EIA Notification divides projects into categories 'A' and 'B' projects. The MoEFCC regulates the grant of EC to category A large-scale projects and the SEIAA regulates the smaller category B projects. Third, forest clearance is a two-stage process under the FCA for the diversion of forest land for mining purposes. A Stage I clearance for non-forest activities on forest land is provided by the concerned state government, followed by a Stage II approval by the central government, following which the application reverts to the state government for final clearance. Finally, the leaseholder is also required to comply with the requirements of the Water Pollution Act and the Air Pollution Act. The State Pollution Control Board (SPCB) is required to provide prior consent before the establishment and operation of any industry that may pollute water sources or cause air pollution. These broad steps are also applicable to mining projects.

Apart from the MoEFCC, the other major regulatory body is the IBM. It ensures that environmental protection and pollution regulations contained in the MMDRA and its regulations, particularly the MCDR, are implemented. The mining and closure plans mandated under the MMDRA and the Mineral Concession Rules also provide for environmental safeguards.

The grant of EC under the Environment (Protection) Act is the first step and the best safeguard to ensuring that pollution is minimized and steps to mitigate the costs of pollution are in place. In *Lafarge Umiam Mining Private Limited v Union of India*, the Supreme Court examined the grant of an EC to a limestone mining project in East

[23] Srestha Banerjee, 'EIA Notification Amended to Bring Small-scale Mining Under its Ambit' *Down to Earth* (28 January 2016) <https://www.downtoearth.org.in/news/mining/eia-notification-amended-to-bring-small-scale-mining-under-its-ambit-52628>.

Khasi Hills in the State of Meghalaya.[24] The Chief Conservator of Forests alleged that the project proponent had not disclosed the presence of trees and had not obtained the necessary forest clearance under the FCA. The Supreme Court upheld the grant of the EC based on the following factors: (i) mining of limestone was an integral historical part of the Khasi Hills region; (ii) the site was cleared after consultation with the custodian of the land, who decided to lease the land for the mining project; (iii) the headman of the Nongtrai village and the villagers who participated in the public hearing supported the project and certified that no damage would be caused to adjacent lands; (iv) the MoEFCC based its decision on the certificates issued by the Khasi Hills Autonomous District Council and the DFO, Khasi Hills Division, Shillong, certifying that there were no forests in the proposed project site; (v) the 2006 Notification was not applicable; and (vi) the MoEFCC had, at multiple stages, sought clarifications from the project proponent and requisite care and caution to protect the environment had been made. Upholding the grant of the EC and the forest clearance, Chief Justice SH Kapadia noted that the Court should review the decision-making process to ensure that the MoEFCC is fairly and fully informed, based on the correct principles, and free from any bias or restraint.

36.2 Contemporary Challenges

The challenges for environmental regulation of the mining sector are myriad, complex, and evolving. We focus on some key contemporary issues below.

36.2.1 Mineral Resources and Sustainability

With mineral resources, IBM's approach to sustainability takes the form of zero-waste where feasible and adopting efficient technological solutions to reduce or recycle waste. It also requires minimizing environmental damage and recourse to environmental restoration is adopted as soon as possible. In keeping with the Brundtland Commission's definition of sustainable development, it also incorporates the idea of ensuring the well-being of present and future generations.[25]

The principle of sustainability applies at all stages of the mine's life cycle—exploration, mine planning, construction, mineral extraction, mine closure and post-closure reclamation and rehabilitation.[26] In 2011, the SDF based on the approach of the ICMM established several key principles including—(a) incorporation of environmental and

[24] *Lafarge Umiam Mining Private Limited v Union of India* (2011) 7 SCC 338.

[25] See generally, Planning Commission and ISID Report (n 6). See also World Commission on Environment and Development, *Our Common Future* (OUP 1987).

[26] ibid.

social sensitivities in decisions on leases; (b) undertake strategic assessment of mining regions at periodic intervals; (c) manage impacts at the mine level through sound management systems; (d) address land, resettlement and rehabilitation and other social impacts upfront; (e) promote community engagement, benefit sharing, and contribution to socio-economic development; (f) ensure orderly mine closure planning and implementation and post-closure activities; and (g) install systems for assurance and credible reporting.[27]

SDF was introduced by an amendment to the MMDRA and the MCDR, and it incorporates standards for scientific, sustainable, and environmentally sound mining practices. It also provides for rating of mining companies based on their compliance with the SDF.[28] The oversight body under the MCDR is the IBM, and it monitors the implementation of SDF through inspections at regular intervals and ensures that the key principles of scientific mining are followed at every step in the mine operations.

The move to a standard-setting and self-regulatory model of regulation is evident in the adoption of the rating system in 2017 through an amendment to the MMDRA to ensure scientific mining. A four-star rating is necessary to ensure the continuation of the mining licence, and a defaulting company may be asked to stop operations if it fails to meet the required standards. The rating system presumes that there are self-regulating mining companies that are economically sound, committed to environmental goals and are deploying their resources towards achieving sustainability. However, many small and medium scale operations get left unregulated and a more streamlined command-and-control regulatory mechanism along with cooperative management of environmental concerns, where feasible, would accommodate the needs of a diverse mining industry.[29]

The two key principles of sustainable development and intergenerational equity are now a part of mining law and policy in India. As noted earlier, in *TN Godavarman Thirumulpad (104)*, the Supreme Court has read the principle of sustainable development into the Constitution and courts are required to balance development needs with the needs of ecology.[30] However, the contemporary policy encourages development, particularly power generation, along with an overall dilution of environment protection sending a powerful message to the executive that for now, the balance of executive action is in favour of development at the cost of environment.

[27] S Vijay Kumar, 'Mining and Sustainable Development Goals' a contribution to the compendium on 'Extraction Industry & Sustainable Development', released during the 'National Conference on Extractive Industry and Sustainable Development', 9 September 2017, New Delhi <https://www.google.com/url?sa=t&rct=j&q=&esrc=s&source=web&cd=&ved=2ahUKEwiglYzJu5z8AhVkXWwGHTTODx0QFnoECA4QAQ&url=https%3A%2F%2Fwww.teriin.org%2Fsites%2Fdefault%2Ffiles%2Ffiles%2FSDGs-files%2Fmining-and-SDGs.pdf&usg=AOvVaw2pbwHMC6Z_RhUNzpN96dEh>.

[28] See Ministry of Mines, Annual Report 2016–17 (Government of India 2016). See also CUTS International and Indian Chamber of Commerce, 'Sustainable Mining in India: Overview of Legal and Regulatory Framework, Technologies, and Best Process Practices' (2018).

[29] For a more detailed discussion, see Madhav (n 15).

[30] *TN Godavarman Thirumulpad (104) v Union of India* (2008) 2 SCC 222.

36.2.2 Intergenerational Equity

Intergenerational equity is a concept now widely acknowledged in environmental planning and the discourse on equity. It states that the environment is held in common between generations, and each generation should pass on the environment in no worse a condition than it received it from the previous generation.[31] It therefore mandates responsible use while encouraging preservation with future generations in mind. However, although the principle has been adopted quite extensively, its operationalization, keeping in mind the future needs of the next generation, is a difficult task.

Adoption of the principle by the Supreme Court in *Goa Foundation v Union of India* has led to innovation in how intergenerational equity is to be operationalized in the context of mineral resources.[32] In 2012, the Goa Foundation filed a public interest litigation challenging the rampant illegal mining leading to damage to the biologically diverse hotspots in the state of Goa. The Supreme Court upheld the principle of intergenerational equity and the public trust doctrine and read it into the right to life under the Constitution. It also held that the state is a trustee of all natural resources for the present and future generations.[33] The Court appointed an expert committee to develop a framework for implementing intergenerational equity.

Relying on the Shah Commission report, the Court also imposed a partial ban on mining in the state of Goa until the expert committee's final report was submitted. In this landmark judgment, the Court, for the first time, acknowledged the need for establishing a fund so that citizens benefit directly from the mining of resources. It directed the state government to develop a comprehensive scheme for a Goa Iron Ore Permanent Fund, to further sustainable development and intergenerational equity.[34] It is a first step in the right direction, but we need more rigorous engagement with the contours of implementation challenges of the principle of intergenerational equity.

36.2.3 Illegal Mining

Illegal mining is characterized by unscientific mining with severe consequences to the environment. Long-term planning of resource conservation and protection is upended by extensive illegal mining, depriving the states and communities of revenue and resource rights.

Illegal mining is a recurring challenge with wider economic and socio-political implications for society. Inadequate implementation of laws, opening up of the sector

[31] EB Weiss, 'In Fairness to Future Generations and Sustainable Development' (1992) 8(1) *American University of International Law Review* 19.

[32] *Goa Foundation v Union of India* (2014) 6 SCC 590.

[33] ibid.

[34] ibid.

to private actors without the backing of a regulatory framework that provides adequate oversight and the race to profit from the boom periods in the mining sector are some of the primary reasons for the persisting problems of illegal mining in the country. In November 2010, the central government set up a Commission of Inquiry headed by Justice Shah to examine the illegal mining of iron ore and manganese in the state of Goa. The Commission was tasked with examining a wide range of issues to relieve the governance crisis at that time. The Commission identified several irregularities, including mining without a licence; mining outside the lease area; undertaking mining in a lease area without taking approval; mining in contravention of a mining plan; mining and transportation of raised minerals in contravention of applicable laws; and conducting multiple trade transactions to obfuscate the origin and source of minerals to facilitate their disposal.

While illegal mining of iron ore and manganese in the three states of Goa, Karnataka, and Orissa is one clear recorded instance of large-scale illegal mining, several such instances are regularly brought to light through media reports. This points to a failure in the governance mechanisms and the lack of effective oversight. At times, legislative gaps contribute to illegal mining; at other times, the delays in granting approvals and renewal of licences aggravate existing problems. While not all illegal mining is egregious, deviations from the mining plan have a bearing on overall environmental management plans.

Several amendments to the MMRDA have been made to empower state governments to take action against illegal mining and transportation.[35] Efforts on the ground to increase patrolling, the inspection of mines, setting up of weighbridges to weigh vehicles that transport ore, and better monitoring of production data are underway.[36] This streamlining of institutional processes while also plugging regulatory gaps is a necessary iterative process and this is evident in the several amendments introduced. In 2011, rule 45 of the MCDR was amended to mandate the registration of miners, traders, consumers, and exporters of minerals with IBM. It also requires compulsory filing of monthly and annual returns on production, sale, and consumption of minerals, and in case of traders and exporters of minerals, the source, sale/export, or end-use. These measures enable governments to closely monitor mining activities and reduce illegalities while also enhancing revenue collection.[37]

Mining in forest areas remains challenging despite court orders to provide oversight to ensure compliance. In *TN Godavarman Thirumulpad (60)*, the Court prohibited and banned mining activity in Aravalli Hills, especially in that part which has been

[35] Mines and Minerals (Development and Regulation) Act, 1957 s 23C empowers the state governments to frame rules to prevent illegal mining, transportation, and storage of minerals.

[36] The Ministry of Mines, through the Indian Bureau of Mines, introduced the Mining Surveillance System (MSS) to use space technology to report any illegal mining activity to the state government to take necessary action. The MSS detects illegal mining activity beyond the lease area through satellite images.

[37] Sharad Matade, 'Govt Amends Rule 45 to Curb Illegal Mining' *Money Life* (25 February 2011) <https://www.moneylife.in/article/govt-amends-rule-45-to-curb-illegal-mining/14268.html>.

regarded as a forest area or protected under the Environment (Protection) Act.[38] The governments of Haryana and Rajasthan were directed to file compliance reports. The Court also stated that mining activity cannot be carried out at the cost of ecology or to the detriment of the environment. Once an area is declared a protected forest and a no-go area, state governments should ensure no mining operation is carried out.

Ending illegal mining requires political will, financial resources, and human power to monitor large tracts of mineral-rich areas. It is rarely acknowledged that small-scale and artisanal mining continues to thrive in the absence of employment in many regions of the country, contributing further to the problem of illegal extraction of resources. Drawing up environmental management plans for these small operations is an important challenge that must be addressed.

36.2.4 Environmental Clearance, Environmental Impact Assessment, and Implementation

Between 2013 and 2018, the Comptroller and Auditor General (CAG) of India conducted a study assessing the environmental impact of mining activities and their mitigation in Coal India Limited and its subsidiaries. The report submitted in 2019 noted the extent of non-compliance in the coal mines—(a) twelve out of the twenty eight mines studied did not comply with the SPCB's directives for the installation of continuous ambient air quality monitoring stations; (b) eight mines released pollutants into the water stream far over the limits prescribed by Bureau of Indian Standards; and (c) thirty-five mines closed between April 1946 and July 2009 did not have the required Mine Closure Status Report. The report also found that as of March 2018, sixteen units were operating without valid environmental documents—nine did not have an environment clearance, six units did not have the consent to operate, and one did not have the consent to establish. Although this snapshot of non-compliance is limited to the coal public sector undertakings, it provides insight into the widespread non-implementation of legal mandates regarding environmental protection.

Two critical elements in a proactive environmental governance framework are granting EC and EIA. The EIA Notification mandates that mining leaseholders obtain EC for new projects and those that are being expanded. Over the years, through court orders and subsequent guidelines issued by the MoEFCC, the EC is now mandated not just for major minerals but also for minor minerals.[39]

With mineral resources, to ensure greater ease in granting EC, powers have been sub-delegated to different levels of governance. The centre is responsible for the grant of EC for mining projects that are larger than fifty hectares, the state for projects between five and fifty hectares, and the DEIAA are responsible for five hectares and below.[40]

[38] *TN Godavarman Thirumulpad (60) v Union of India* (2009) 17 SCC 764.

[39] See *Deepak Kumar* (n 20).

[40] ibid.

However, the EC process is viewed by industry as time-consuming and in the absence of a robust monitoring mechanism at the ground level, it lacks meaning. To enable faster development of the mining sector, several aspects pertaining to EC have been relaxed, thus diluting the effectiveness of the safeguards built into the law.[41] Another concern is the requirement of a public hearing under the EIA Notification. Project-affected people and communities near the mining site can obtain a copy of the draft EIA report and evaluate and identify the loopholes in the draft EIA report. This is an important process for engagement with communities impacted by the mining projects, but compliance with this requirement is unsatisfactory, with no meaningful engagement initiated on the ground. Monitoring and post-EIA audits are largely missing, and this gap needs to be filled for the EIA process to close the loop. One suggestion is to evolve an Environmental Management System as recommended by ISO 14001.[42] Other than putting systems in place, respecting the value of the EIA process in safeguarding the environment is imperative for the mining sector.

36.2.5 Institutional Overlaps

The regulatory framework for environmental and mining governance needs streamlining. Currently, there are several authorities with overlapping jurisdictions, and nearly twelve approvals are required to be obtained by a mining leaseholder before starting operations. This overlapping jurisdiction leads to duplication of work, inconsistencies between statutory approvals granted by different authorities, and unnecessary regulatory burden.[43] For instance, the approval for the discharge of pollutants is not just granted through an EC but a separate application to the respective SPCB is also required to be made. The EC is granted by the MoEFCC after the final EIA/EMP is appraised by an Expert Advisory Committee. The final EIA/EMP incorporates decisions taken during the statutory public hearing conducted by the relevant SPCB. The EC, *inter alia*, specifies the environmental protection measures and other conditions to be implemented by the leaseholder to control the discharge of various pollutants. However, even after the EC is granted as per law, the leaseholder must obtain consent to operate from the relevant SPCB under the Water Pollution Act and the Air Pollution Act before the commencement of mining operations. Before the grant of consent, SPCBs can add fresh conditions in addition to those already included in the EC. This process can be streamlined to provide for a comprehensive EC, which ensures that monitoring is done by a single institution and the process of delays in commencing mining operations due to unnecessary delays due to multiple permissions is avoided.[44] Similarly, the

[41] For more on dilution of the EIA safeguards, see the chapter on EIA in this volume.

[42] Gurdeep Singh, 'Environmental Impact Assessment of Mining Projects' (Proceedings of International Conference on TREIA-2008, Nagpur, 23–25 November 2008).

[43] See Sarvajeet Kumar Sinha and others, 'Why India Needs a Coal Mines Environment Authority' (2021) 56(51) *Economic and Political Weekly* 32.

[44] ibid.

multiplicity of institutions does not lend itself to easy horizontal coordination, and the fragmentation of powers leads to ineffective governance.

Even when regulations are in place, implementation is hampered by institutional challenges such as a lack of resources and a lack of political will. For instance, it is well documented that the Central Pollution Control Board and the SPCBs have limited capacities as they are understaffed, lack the required technical capacity, and lack access to resources and staff training.[45] Institutional overlap adds additional layers of complexities, unnecessary delays adding to the difficulties of effective enforcement. The lack of personnel to police forest areas or mining areas contributes to the growing problem of illegal mining. Added to these are other institutional issues, such as a lack of continuity of institutional processes and building of institutional integrity through effective monitoring and enforcement.

36.3 Critical Reflections

Significant reforms in the mining sector are underway to attract private investment, spur growth and address the social and environmental concerns raised at regular intervals through courts and civil society interventions. Apart from a major overhaul of the MMDRA in 2015, a new National Mineral Policy was introduced in 2019. Successive amendments to the broader environmental regulation framework, including the EIA Notification, dilute existing protections while steadily moving the regulatory framework towards a self-regulatory model.

In recent years, the changes in law and policy focus on opening the sector to private participation with a reduced focus on environmental safeguards. The dilution of legal protections runs parallel to an increased uptake of self-regulatory models of governance. The move within the regulatory framework towards corporate self-regulation, incentives, and standard-setting norms yields mixed results. On one hand, it contributes to a more engaged corporate work culture; on the other hand, compliance may only be on paper, with the dangers of greenwashing evident without effective monitoring.

Pollution from mining activities, particularly unscientific mining practices in small- and medium-sized mining units, remains challenging as the units find it difficult to adopt sustainable mining practices. There is also the lacuna of mining-related pollution standards under the broad umbrella of environmental legislation. For instance, pollution standards have only been developed for coal and iron-ore mining in the country.[46]

[45] See generally, Armin Rosencranz and Videh Upadhyay, 'Some Suggestions and Recommendations Towards a Model State Pollution Control Board (SPCB) in India' (2011) 1 *Environmental Law and Practice Review* 106.

[46] See government of India, CPCB Report, Development of Clean Technology for Iron Ore Mines and Development of Environmental Standards (2007).

Given the range of challenges in the mining and environment interface, the regulatory framework must tread the careful path of fostering development while ensuring a sustainable and equitable path for mineral development. In recent times, permission for the location of extractive industries in forest areas has been granted with greater ease. The protections provided by the FCA and the FRA are also being steadily whittled away. Gaps in the legislative framework are another area of concern. For instance, legislation relating to water resources rarely examines the interface between mining, waterbodies, and groundwater aquifers. The legal and institutional failures are compounded in the light of environmental degradation, depletions of forests, water scarcity, and the looming challenge of climate change.

In this chapter, we have not dealt with the issue of legacy mines (abandoned or shut down) and the impact of climate policy on the mining sector, particularly coal mines. These critical issues remain an unrecognized issue within the environmental regulatory framework.

Conclusion

Responsible and sustainable mining across the globe has brought the necessary transformation to the mining sector in India. It has attempted to address the three pillars of sustainability—economic, environmental, and social. However, much more needs to be done as enforcement at the ground level remains a challenge. In the face of the contemporary challenge of climate change and the need to transition to a decarbonized economy, the mining sector is set to face major transitions related to the adoption of technology, closures, and workforce management and the more difficult issue of legacy mines that need to be managed for many more years. Going forward, the mining sector must focus on technologically superior modes of resource extraction and adoption of zero-waste models, enable greater recycling of extracted resources and find substitute materials that can ensure mineral extraction is reduced and gradually phased out.

Suggestions for Further Reading

Rahul Basu, 'Implementing Intergenerational Equity in Goa' (2014) 49(51) *Economic and Political Weekly* 33.

Chandra Bhushan and Monali Zeya Hazra, 'Rich Lands Poor People: Is "Sustainable" Mining Possible?' (Centre for Science and Environment 2008).

Institute for Studies in Industrial Development, 'Sustainable Development: Emerging Issues in India's Mineral Sector' (Planning Commission 2012).

Baniateilang Majaw, 'Ending Meghalaya's "Deadly Occupation": India's National Green Tribunal's Ban on Rat-Hole Mining' (2016) 49(1) *Verfassung und Recht in Übersee/Law and Politics in Africa, Asia and Latin America* 34.

Aijaj Ahmed Raj and Zubair Ahmed, 'Environmental Impact Assessment of Mining in India: A Review of Legal and Institutional Mechanism' in KM Baharul Islam and Zafar Mahfooz Nomani (eds), *Environment Impact Assessment: Precept and Practice* (CRC Press 2021) 339.

CHAPTER 37

HAZARDOUS WASTE

T.R. SUBRAMANYA AND ARUNA L.

ABSTRACT

The management, treatment, and disposal of hazardous waste is a growing concern. This chapter addresses issues related to hazardous waste and its management in India. While the 1989 Basel Convention on hazardous wastes is considered as a leap in this direction, its limitations in the Indian scenario are discussed, drawing specific examples from the various rules made by the Government of India, such as the Bio-Medical Waste (Management and Handling) Rules, 1998 and the Batteries (Management and Handling) Rules, 2001. The role of the judiciary has also been highlighted by shedding light on a few cases which have drawn a beneficial construction in addressing the gaps between the regulatory framework and the practical implication issues which lie with the authorities. The chapter also offers pragmatic workable solutions in order to avoid future problems. A holistic approach is the need of the hour and the chapter highlights all such areas.

INTRODUCTION

THE history of waste management in India dates back to the Indus Valley civilization.[1] The whole culture was based on organic usage; there was no hazardous waste as a by-product, and any waste generated would eventually turn into organic manure, which in turn, was used for agricultural purposes.[2]

[1] M Jansen, 'Water Supply and Sewage Disposal at Mohenjo-Daro' (1989) 21(2) *World Archaeology* 177.

[2] Gorbatov Research Centre for Food Systems and others, 'Internal Audit of the Food Safety Management System in Accordance with the New Requirements of GOST R ISO 19011–2021' (2021) *Vsyo o myase* 3.

Reduce, reuse, and recycle was a motto and a way of life. Hence, waste and hazardous waste were never a concern in India. Industrialization during the colonial period greatly boosted the economy and people's lives. At the same time, this led to the generation of waste in large quantities, including hazardous waste. India was not prepared for this as it was unexpected. In 1947, when India became independent, the primary concern of the independent country was to stabilize and address the political, social, and economic crisis. A major focus was on agrarian reforms since India still generated a huge part of its income from the agricultural sector. In catching up with globalization, India opened up to foreign investments; manufacturing units were set up, industries burgeoned, and with it, waste generation multiplied by enormous amounts. This was when hazardous waste became a huge issue which required immediate attention and action. The gap between waste generation and the shortage of energy resources to treat them has been widening over the years, causing major environmental and health concerns. Sustainable development goals include optimal usage of existing resources, generating sustainable resources, and reducing the environmental impact of the waste generated to ensure a cleaner environment for future generations. If it is not disposed of properly, its impact on the health of humans and animals, and the environmental catastrophe will be beyond repair, leaving behind a dump yard for the future generations. Since many developed countries failed to treat their own waste and started exporting it to developing countries which had inadequate methodologies to treat them, the Basel Convention emerged and agreements between the importing and exporting countries were required to ensure the safe movement of transboundary hazardous waste and its disposal as it was not only a threat to the parties involved but a global concern to avoid further depletion of the environment.

Hazardous waste, according to Article 1 of the Basel Convention, and rule 3(17) of the Hazardous and Other Wastes (Management and Transboundary Movement) Rules, 2016 in India, means and includes any waste which can cause danger to health or the environment. All the rules discussed in this chapter have relied on this definition. A brief introduction to the Basel Convention and the initiatives that India has taken, which not only comply with the provisions of the Convention but also have gone beyond it in a few cases, have been highlighted in the initial discussion of this chapter, which establishes the nexus between international and domestic laws. Since the Basel Convention addresses only issues concerned with the transboundary movement of hazardous waste and since India is a signatory to it, management and handling of the transboundary hazardous waste is dealt with under the Hazardous Waste Management (HWM) Rules. Other hazardous wastes are generated on a routine basis. These issues have been addressed through various rules by the Ministry of Environment, Forest and Climate Change (MoEFCC), drawing power from the Environment (Protection) Act, 1986. The legislative framework available in India regarding hazardous waste is undertaken by examining and analysing rules regarding hazardous waste, wastes generated due to batteries, biomedical waste, plastic waste, and e-waste. MoEFCC has framed several other rules. The discussion here is restricted to the limited scope of the chapter, and these rules have been prioritized over the rules on chemical accidents, fly ash, genetically engineered microorganisms, etc. since these hazardous wastes are generated in huge quantities and are serious environmental concerns. The effectiveness of any legislation depends on its enforcement and interpretation. In India, the formulation of rules and their implementation lies predominantly with the MoEFCC. The role of the judiciary is also very crucial. The Indian judiciary, in a plethora of cases, has identified the implementation issues and has been very progressive in addressing the problems, which have not been elaborated in the statute. In India, matters relating to hazardous wastes is heard by the National Green Tribunal (NGT),[3] the High Courts and the Supreme Court. The implementation issues of these rules and the role and approach of judiciary are critically evaluated here to emphasize the gravity of attention required to address the issues regarding hazardous wastes. The final section of this chapter, while providing an estimate of the law on hazardous waste, provides a few practical suggestions to overcome the same in a sustainable manner.

37.1 Indian Legal Framework to Combat Hazardous Waste

A brief historical evolution of the environmental protection laws is necessary to understand and appreciate the legislative initiatives to address hazardous waste. This jurisprudential development is noteworthy since all the rules on hazardous waste are made under the power drawn from the provisions of the Environment (Protection) Act, 1986. The Stockholm Conference of 1972 was vital in leading India to legislate on environmental protection. The Forty-second Amendment to the Constitution of India in 1976 incorporated Articles 48A and 51A(g) as part of the Directive Principles of State Policy and the Fundamental Duties respectively, introducing environment as part of the Constitution for the first time. The Environment (Protection) Act, 1986, was legislated not only to protect and improve the environment but also to regulate the production, disposal, treatment, and prevention of accidents which can influence the environment or cause any health hazards. However, neither the Act nor the rules[4] define or even mention hazardous waste.

The first few five-year plans, made after Indian Independence, emphasized the agrarian reforms. Environmental issues started receiving much attention at the national level only subsequently. In the Ninth Five-Year Plan (1997–2002),[5] the need to address the rapid urbanization and the resultant production of waste in huge quantities within a short period was observed. Due to the growth of chemical industries and the effect of rapid industrialization, which resulted in accelerated population growth, there was

[3] See further ch 41 in this volume.

[4] Environment (Protection) Rules, 1986.

[5] Government of India, 'Ninth Five Year Plan' 1 <https://niti.gov.in/planningcommission.gov.in/docs/plans/planrel/fiveyr/9th/vol1/v1c1-2.htm>.

an increase in hazardous waste generation, requiring immediate attention and action. During the Eleventh Five-Year Plan (2007–2012),[6] it was felt that though the Pollution Control Board (PCB) is responsible for enforcing the safe disposal of hazardous waste, the use of programmes like JNNURM[7] and UIDSSMT[8] to dispose of waste, including e-waste was required due to the sudden rise in its quantity.

Furthermore, funding of Treatment Storage and Disposal Facilities (TSDFs) for hazardous waste and Common Biomedical Waste Treatment and Facilities (CBMWTFs) for biomedical waste was undertaken by the MoEFCC and the Hazardous Waste (Management, Handling and Transboundary Movement) Rules, 2008 were notified. The Sub-group on Environment for the Twelfth Five-Year Plan[9] has elaborately dealt with the waste disposal mechanism on hazardous wastes and the subsequent developments that have taken place since the Eleventh Five-Year Plan. The tenure between the Ninth and Twelfth Five-Year Plans brought about substantial changes into the regulatory framework since most of the rules discussed in this chapter have their genesis during this period.

According to the powers conferred under sections 6, 8, and 25 of the Environment (Protection) Act, 1986, the central government has adopted several rules. A discussion of the following rules on HWM is undertaken here, since these rules are important and path-breaking due to their objectives and significance in the current scenario. The discussion starts with the 2016 Rules on HWM and proceeds to other rules that address additional hazardous wastes. It is significant to note here that all the rules discussed have been amended since their adoption and, in some instances, amended more than once. These amendments have echoed the readiness of the nation to embrace every possible opportunity to address hazardous waste in a progressive and environmentally sound manner. The discussion starts with the rules regarding hazardous waste and then proceeds chronologically to the other rules.

1. Hazardous and Other Waste (Management and Transboundary Movement) Rules, 2016.
2. Batteries (Management and Handling) Rules, 2001.
3. Bio-Medical Waste Management Rules, 2016.
4. E-Waste Management Rules, 2016.
5. Plastic Waste Management Rules, 2016.

[6] Government of India, 'Eleventh Five Year Plan' 1 <https://niti.gov.in/planningcommission.gov.in/docs/plans/planrel/fiveyr/11th/11_v1/11th_vol1.pdf>.

[7] Jawaharlal Nehru National Urban Renewal Mission launched on 3 December 2005.

[8] Urban Infrastructure Development Scheme for Small and Medium Towns, launched on 5 March 2012.

[9] 'Report of the Sub-Group on 'Environment' for Twelfth Five Year Plan' (Ministry of Environment and Forests 2011) <https://niti.gov.in/planningcommission.gov.in/docs/aboutus/committee/wrkgrp12/enf/wg_envr.pdf>.

37.2 Rules on Hazardous and Other Waste

The HWM Rules have been notified to ensure and address all aspects of hazardous waste[10] management, including safe handling, generation, processing, treatment, package, storage, transportation, use, reprocessing, collection, conversion, offering for sale, destruction, and disposal of hazardous waste. In 1997, a High-Powered Committee under the aegis of Prof MGK Menon[11] was constituted by the Supreme Court to assess, examine, and give a detailed, in-depth report covering all aspects of hazardous waste. Based on the report, the Supreme Court Monitoring Committee was constituted to oversee the implementation of the legislation, rules, regulations, directions of the court, and the objectives of the ministry with no laxity or delay.

The Hazardous and Other Waste (Management, Handling and Transboundary Movement) Rules, 2016, have superseded the Hazardous Waste (Management, Handling and Transboundary Movement) Rules, 2008, which had replaced the Hazardous Wastes (Management and. Handling) Rules, 1989. It was further amended in 2019 and 2021 mainly to accommodate the changes brought by the Basel Convention. The fundamental difference between the earlier rules and these rules is that there is a clear demarcation between hazardous and other wastes, which includes not only hazardous waste but also indigenous wastes.[12] The rules consist of six chapters and twenty-four rules which apply to designated categories of wastes as listed in its Schedule. Rules 4 and 5 outline the responsibility of the occupier and the State regarding the management of hazardous waste. Occupiers must ensure no accidents or adverse effects on human health. The occupiers should employ well-trained staff and the necessary equipment to avert such eventualities. They should approach the State Pollution Control Board (SPCB)[13] and obtain its prior authorization to store the hazardous waste for not more than ninety days with a few specific exceptions, as mentioned under rule 8. Rules 11–15 under Chapter III deal with the export and import of hazardous waste. This chapter provides clear guidelines regarding importing and exporting hazardous and other wastes to and from India and no prohibited waste imported. It further requires the prior consent of the importing country in case India wants to export hazardous or any other waste. This

[10] According to the Hazardous Wastes (Management and Handling) Rules, 1989, s 3(14), 'hazardous waste' means any waste which by reason of any of its physical, chemical, reactive, toxic, flammable, explosive or corrosive characteristics causes danger or is likely to cause danger to health or environment, whether alone or when in contact with other wastes or substances.

[11] Sukumar Devotta and CV Chalapati Rao, *Environmental Status of India* (Atlantic Publishers and Distributors 2008).

[12] Rule 3(23) 'other wastes' means wastes specified in Part B and Part D of Sch III for import or export and includes all such waste generated indigenously within the country.

[13] Constituted under s 4 of the Water (Prevention and Control of Pollution) Act, 1974 or a SPCB constituted under s 5 of the Air (Prevention and Control of Pollution) Act, 1981.

is exactly what the Basel Convention has put forth. While interpreting the requirements of rule 5 of the HWM Rules, 1989 (which is rule 6 under the 2016 Rules), the Court observed in *Sheo Kumar Agarwal Sunil Kumar, A Partnership Firm v Shagun Udyog, Pvt. Ltd* that authorization is a prerequisite to handle waste as prescribed under the Rules and that there is no specific requirement to be registered as a recycler or re-refiner.[14] While this shows that the rules have been broadly framed to encompass the accountability of every occupier, it also reflects the strictness in its implementation by the court of law. Rule 17 prescribes the packaging and labelling of hazardous waste according to the guidelines[15] of the Central Pollution Control Board (CPCB)[16] to impart precautionary measures and prevent any disaster. Though the Basel Convention does not impose such a requirement, it has been incorporated in the rules, as an additional measure and these guidelines are amended from time to time by incorporating best practices and eliminating administrative errors.

In *ITC Ltd v Norasia Container Lines Ltd*, the High Court of Madras decided upon what appeared to be rival contentions pertaining to the Customs Act, 1962; the Major Ports Trusts Act, 1963, and the HWM Rules, 1989, regarding the responsibility of disposal of cargo which had hazardous substances.[17] The court, while applying rule 15 regarding illegal traffic, observed that the obligation to dispose of cargo according to the Customs Act cannot be construed as imposing a liability on the authorities under the HMW Rules to dispose of the same. On the other hand, the liability is on the importer and exporter under the HWM Rules. Also, since the Customs Act and the HWM Rules apply to different realms, non-obligation to dispose under the Customs Act cannot automatically absolve them of their liability under rule 15(3) of the HWM Rules. Hence, it categorically decided that if it is hazardous waste, such cargo shall be disposed of under the provisions of the HWM Rules. Notably, when this decision was made, waste was not defined under the 1989 Rules, which was later included in the 2008 Rules.

In an interesting observation made by the Supreme Court in the *Karuna Society for Animals and Nature v Union of India case*,[18] the Court opined that merely constituting committees and holding meetings would not resolve the issues regarding implementing the rules. The case was a Writ Petition filed under Article 32 of the Constitution wherein, the CPCB and twelve states were named respondents.

The Court expressed its displeasure against the state of Rajasthan for claiming to have implemented the rules effectively, but photographs submitted proved the contrary. Hence, an order to form a committee was issued to report on adopted compliance measures. Furthermore, the Court observed that the situation in the state of Karnataka

[14] *Sheo Kumar Agarwal Sunil Kumar, A Partnership Firm v Shagun Udyog, Pvt. Ltd* 2007 SCC OnLine Jhar 4.

[15] Guidelines for Preparation of Inventories on Hazardous and Other Waste Generation and their Management, June 2019.

[16] Constituted under s 3 of the Water (Prevention and Control of Pollution) Act, 1974.

[17] *ITC Ltd v Norasia Container Lines Ltd* MANU/TN/2029/2008, 21 November 2011 (High Court of Madras).

[18] *Karuna Society for Animals and Nature v Union of India* (2016)14 SCC 303.

was equally bad. It observed that the committee did not comply with the rules and required the presence of the Principal Secretary, Ministry of Urban Development, government of Karnataka, to show what actions have been taken to effectively implement the rules. It further observed that the other eleven states had not filed their reply and granted them two weeks to do so, failing which action would be initiated against them and the prayers of the Petitioners would be granted. The inaction by appropriate authorities can be seen as a common bane across all these rules regarding HWM.

The ship dismantling industry in India is another controversy in the context of the management of hazardous waste. In *Research Foundation for Science, Technology and Natural Resource Policy v Union of India*, the Supreme Court, while hearing a matter regarding hazardous waste oil, upheld the polluter pays and precautionary principles and gave a landmark judgment which was holistic and a much needed one.[19] In this case, 133 containers were lying at Nhava Sheva Port. When tested, they were found to hold hazardous waste oil, and the Court issued directions to fifteen importers to show cause why the containers should not be re-exported or destroyed at their cost, since they were attempting to import waste oil under the guise of lubricating oil. One of the crucial observations made in this case was that according to Article 9(2)(a) of the Basel Convention on the Control of Transboundary Movements of Hazardous Wastes and their Disposal, 1989, also incorporated in the municipal laws of India, the exporter and the state of the exporter is required to ensure the re-return of the waste exported and mandated it to be identified as illegal traffic within thirty days. But, due to various protocols and other prevailing circumstances, there is always an inordinate delay, which was more than four years in this case.

Yet another highlighted issue was that since these hazardous oils had been lying on the coasts for a long period, some of them had exploded, causing great harm to the environment. As such, there was a fire hazard as well. The Court after considering the facts, circumstances and reports concluded that it was a more viable option to destroy the hazardous oil by incineration and required this to be done expeditiously rather than applying the return of such illegal waste to the exporter's country. An obiter worth mentioning here is the 'Basel Convention are only guidelines and the individual countries can provide different criterion in their national law'; enumerates that the Indian Courts intended to go beyond the basic benchmark to protect its citizens with a higher level of environment protection and safety which is a constitutional guarantee under Article 21 of the Indian Constitution. Hence, it established that in such cases, Indian laws apply, and under no circumstances can refuge be taken in any of the provisions of the Basel Convention.

Another question answered in the same case in an Interim Application decided on 11 September 2007[20] regarded the dismantling of a ship called *Blue Lady* in

[19] *Research Foundation for Science, Technology and Natural Resource Policy v Union of India* (2005) 13 SCC 661.

[20] *Research Foundation for Science Technology and Natural Resource Policy v Union of India* (2007)15 SCC 193.

Alang[21] (Gujarat, India), which is the largest ship-recycling yard in the world. According to the Basel Convention and the Indian regulations, ships identified for dismantling are regarded as hazardous waste, and the International Labour Organization (ILO) considers this job as one of the most dangerous jobs.[22] The Supreme Court has ignored the calamitous effect of the presence of asbestos in such dilapidated ships, which can cause serious health hazards and expose the workers to risks of cancer. The relief provided and the interpretation of specific clauses regarding ship-breaking have not been consistently followed by the courts, leading to a lot of confusion and criticism. However, an Act in 2019 seems to have addressed most of these issues.[23]

The HWM Rules were recently amended in July 2022 to broaden the Extended Producer Responsibility (EPR) for waste tyres. The amendment included Schedule IX, which exclusively elaborates the EPR for waste tyres. In its further amendment in 2023, which will come into effect from 1st April 2024, Extended Producer Responsibility for Used Oils has been incorporated as chapter VII.

37.3 Rules on Bio-Medical Waste

Any waste generated by the health care establishments can be referred to as biomedical waste. Improper disposal of biomedical waste leads to public health and environmental crises. Many viruses like HIV, hepatitis, and diseases like pneumonia and tuberculosis, spread due to bio-waste[24] which was not treated or disposed of properly. COVID-19 has educated people in every part of the world regarding the hazards of biomedical waste[25] and has made it all the more meaningful for legislation to ensure proper management of bio-waste. It not only brings with it contagious diseases which cause fatality to human lives but also affects the soil and groundwater if not disposed of properly. According to the World Health Organization, 15 per cent of the biomedical waste generated is hazardous, and if it is disposed of in an environmentally sound manner, this can prevent adverse effects on health and prevent chemical, biological, and environmental hazards.[26]

Biomedical waste has been defined under rule 3(f) of the Bio-Medical Waste (Management and Handling) Rules, 2016[27] and divided into categories specified

[21] Florent Pelsy, 'The Blue Lady Case and the International Issue of Ship Dismantling' (2008) 4(2) *Law, Environment and Development Journal* 135.

[22] Anonymous, 'Ship Breaking' (India Environment Portal) <www.indiaenvironmentportal.org.in/content/348097/ship-breaking/>.

[23] Recycling of Ships Act, 2019.

[24] Guidelines for Management of Healthcare Waste as per Biomedical Waste Management Rules, 2016 <https://cpcb.nic.in/uploads/Projects/Bio-Medical-Waste/Guidelines_healthcare_June_2018.pdf>.

[25] Parul Saxena, Indira P Pradhan, and Deepak Kumar, 'Redefining Bio Medical Waste Management During COVID- 19 in India: A Way Forward' (2022) *60 Materials Today: Proceedings* 849.

[26] WHO, 'Health-Care Waste' (2018) <www.who.int/news-room/fact-sheets/detail/health-care-waste>.

[27] These Rules superseded the Bio-Medical Waste (Management and Handling) Rules, 1998.

in Schedule I of the Rules, while Schedule II prescribes the standard for treatment technologies.[28] There are eighteen rules in total and apply to all persons from the waste generator to the disposer. Rules 4 and 5 impose a duty on the 'occupier'[29] and the 'operator',[30] respectively, to ensure safe disposal of the biomedical waste. The prescribed authority to issue authorization under the rules is the SPCB. Under rule 13, there is a requirement to furnish an annual report to the CPCB regarding the category and quantity of bio-waste disposed in the previous year. As far as the legislative lacuna is concerned, one major area has not been addressed regarding biomedical waste handling is the health care system,[31] which should be extended to each individual connected with generation to disposal.

Since this is an occupational hazard for health workers, educating them about the safety measures is very important and is not emphasized under these rules. In addition, strict action for non-disposal in an environmentally sound manner and not providing the safety measures for proper disposal of the biomedical waste needs enforcement with huge penalties to ensure compliance. Regarding implementation issues, one of the most cost-effective and simple methods of disposal of biomedical waste is incineration. However, it has been found that this is not an environmentally sound method, which has been banned in some countries, including the Philippines and Denmark.[32] India should adopt alternative measures like using newer technologies and biomedical waste management should be a top priority right from the planning stage of health care institutions and should cater to meeting the day to day demands of safe disposal.

37.4 Rules on Batteries Management

We use batteries extensively in wristwatches, TV remotes, wall clocks, toys, and mobile phones to electric vehicles. Depending on the type of battery, various chemicals are used, including toxic metals and corrosive materials. After its use, large amounts of chemicals like cobalt, electrolytes, lithium, manganese oxide, and nickel[33] remain as residues in the battery. Due to their chemical composition, worn-out batteries cannot

[28] This includes incineration, autoclave, microwaving, chemical disinfection, dry heat sterilization, and burial. Read more on Guidelines for Management of Healthcare Waste as per Biomedical Waste Management Rules, 2016 (n 24).

[29] Bio-Medical Waste (Management and Handling) Rules, 2016 r 3(m).

[30] ibid r 3.

[31] Mrinalini Goswami and others, 'Challenges and Actions to the Environmental Management of Bio-Medical Waste During COVID-19 Pandemic in India' (2021) 7(3) *Heliyon* e06313.

[32] Priya Datta, Gursimran Kaur Mohi, and Jagdish Chander, 'Biomedical Waste Management in India: Critical Appraisal' (2018) 10(1) *Journal of Laboratory Physicians* 6.

[33] Ka Ho Chan, Monu Malik, and Gisele Azimi, 'Separation of Lithium, Nickel, Manganese, and Cobalt from Waste Lithium-Ion Batteries Using Electrodialysis' (2022) 178 *Resources, Conservation and Recycling* 106076.

be treated as dry waste and cannot be disposed of in a similar manner. Since they are toxic, the pollutants can cause serious damage to the environment, including soil, air, and water.[34] They also cause cancer in several instances. One astonishing case was that of a child poisoned by the breast milk of his mother, who was an employee of a battery recycling unit which emits high levels of lead.[35] Several such instances of the hazards of the lethal threat of battery disposal and recycling have been recorded worldwide.[36]

The Batteries (Management and Handling) Rules, 2001, were notified by the central government and amended in 2010.[37] They exhaustively covered the activities of manufacture, purchase, sale, processing, and usage in relation to batteries.[38] Rules 4, 7, and 8 enumerated the responsibilities of the manufacturer, importer, assembler, and reconditioner of batteries, dealer, and recycler. Rule 10 emphasized the responsibilities of the consumers and bulk consumers and rule 11 imposed responsibilities on the auctioneer. These included collecting back used batteries, their transportation, buy-back, filing reports, and creating public awareness.

The limitations of these Rules in terms of effectiveness and implementation led the MoEFCC to adopt the Battery Waste Management Rules, 2022, which supersede the earlier rules.[39] The 2022 Rules have strengthened EPR and include a new definition of battery, which is comprehensive in terms of including new or refurbished battery/cells when compared to the definition mentioned under rule 3(e) of the 2001 Rules which dealt only with lead acid battery.[40] It applies to all batteries except those used specifically for military purposes. Electric vehicle batteries not included in the 2001 Rules have been included and defined under rule 3(j).[41] Further, rule 4 gives more emphasis to EPR by mandating the producers to file annual reports and also requires batteries to be labelled and packed, as elaborated under Schedule I to the rules.

[34] Piyush Kuchhal and Umesh Chandra Sharma, 'Battery Waste Management' (2017) 5 *Environmental Science and Engineering* 141.

[35] Fred Pearce, 'Getting the Lead Out: Why Battery Recycling is a Global Health Hazard' *Yale Environment360* (2 November 2020) <https://e360.yale.edu/features/getting-the-lead-out-why-battery-recycling-is-a-global-health-hazard>.

[36] Lead from a battery recycling plant in Senegal, Africa, led to the poisoning of people and the death of some children; children near such factories and dump sites have been reported to have developed brain issues, lives of aquatic plants and animals are harmed. See, e.g., Faridah Hussein Were, 'Africa's Growing Lead Battery Industry is Causing Extensive Contamination' (*IPEN*, 16 February 2020) <https://ipen.org/news/africa%E2%80%99s-growing-lead-battery-industry-causing-extensive-contamination>.

[37] Batteries (Management and Handling) Rules, 2001 (as amended).

[38] ibid r 3(e) defines a battery as a lead acid battery, a source of electrical energy and contains lead metal.

[39] Battery Waste Management Rules, 2022, Gazette of India, Part II—s 3—sub-section (ii), 24 August 2022.

[40] Batteries (Management and Handling) Rules, 2001 (as amended) r 3 (c): Battery means new or refurbished cell and/or Battery and/or their component, including accumulator, which is any source of electrical energy generated by direct conversion of chemical energy and includes disposable primary and/or secondary battery.

[41] Battery Waste Management Rules, 2022 (n 39) r 3(j): 'Electric vehicle battery means any Battery specifically designed to provide traction to hybrid and electric vehicles for road transport.

One uniqueness of these rules is that while producing new batteries, the quantity of minimum use of recycled materials is prescribed and must increase in a phased manner.[42] This is one contribution to fostering a circular economy. In order to make the stakeholders more accountable, rule 9 requires recyclers to recover battery materials in a phased manner by fixing a recovery target for every year and type of battery starting from 2024–25. Rules 11 and 12 empower the CPCB and SPCB to conduct audits and to suspend or cancel registration in case of non-compliance with the Rules. This is an additional power provided under the new Rules, which was in fact a limitation for the smooth functioning of the earlier Rules. Furthermore, environmental compensation can be levied under rule 13 of the 2022 Rules, which shall follow section 15 of the Environment (Protection) Act, 1986. The Rules emphasize the need to foster the environmentally sound management of batteries.

On the whole, the Rules seem to have comprehensively covered all the lacuna in the previous rules. They have become progressive by including electrical batteries and cells. In order to complement the work of the CPCB and SPCB, *panchayat* waste management authorities have been identified under the rules so that accountability and efficiency desired can be a reality. The one area which found its place in the 2010 and the 2020 draft Rules but is not addressed in the 2022 Rules is the position of bulk consumers.[43]

37.5 Rules on E-Waste Management

Due to the rapid rise in electronic gadgets, there is an increase in e-waste generation. According to the Ministry of Information and Technology, India is among the top contributors, and there has been an increasing trend recently due to COVID-19. Approximately three to five million tonnes of e-waste are generated annually.[44] A suggestion by the World Economic Forum in providing a solution to e-waste is to maintain standards not only while producing but also while reusing and refurbishing the electronic products.[45] This is all the more important since e-waste is not biodegradable and accumulates in the environment which causes health hazards.

Treating and disposing of e-waste is imperative since it may erode the soil due to landfilling and contaminate water, including rivers and wells and air due to the leakage of certain gases and burning of e-waste. Due to the multitude of chemicals involved in their manufacture and the prodigious use of electrical and electronic equipment[46] in

[42] Battery Waste Management Rules, 2022 (n 39) r 4(14).

[43] Rule 2(f) of the 2010 version of the Batteries (Management and Handling) Rules, 2001, had defined bulk consumers as any consumer who purchased a hundred or more batteries in a year.

[44] Sejal Mehta, 'The Why and How of Disposing Electronic Waste' (*Mongabay*, 25 August 2020) <https://india.mongabay.com/2020/08/explainer-the-why-and-how-of-disposing-electronic-waste/>.

[45] 'A New Circular Vision for Electronics: Time for a Global Reboot' (World Economic Forum 2019) <https://www3.weforum.org/docs/WEF_A_New_Circular_Vision_for_Electronics.pdf>.

[46] Toxic substances found in e-waste include lead (Pb) and cadmium (Cd) in printed circuit boards. Lead is primarily found in all electronic products/assemblies, cathode ray tubes (CRT), etc. Cadmium

our daily lives, care has to be taken at every step so that the waste created as an outcome of this usage does not turn hazardous. Waste disposal in India happens more through an informal methodology rather than a formal one.[47] It is estimated that more than 95 per cent of the e-waste disposal happens through the informal sector, wherein waste is collected from rag pickers and precious metals like gold, silver, aluminium, copper, etc., are extracted and the chemicals are not treated due to non-employment of technology.[48] The remaining waste is dumped in a landfill or river or burnt leaving the hazardous substances in this area to leech in soil, water or air respectively. The formal sector follows a more scientific and environmentally friendly manner of disposing of the e-waste sometimes leaving no residue at all. The E-Waste (Management) Rules, 2016, have replaced the erstwhile E-Waste (Management and Handling) Rules, 2011, and exclude radioactive waste,[49] used lead batteries[50] and micro enterprises.[51] The new rules emphasize the principle of EPR and include the informal sector since it is one of the major contributors to the e-waste production. Chapter II lays down elaborately the responsibilities of the various stakeholders like the producers, collection centres, dealers, refurbishers, consumers or bulk consumers, dismantlers, recyclers, and the state government.[52]

Rules 7 and 9 of the E-Waste (Management) Rules, 2016, impose responsibility on dealers and consumers regarding take-back service wherein the producers take the product back after its life. This is one methodology to ensure the safe disposal of these wastes. The CPCB and SPCBs are the administrative authorities identified to enforce these rules. Rule 15 under Chapter IV prescribes a maximum storage period of e-waste as 180 days, which is extendable to 365 days by the SPCB if it concurs that the storage is specifically required to develop a process for its recycling or reuse. While Chapter II imposes a responsibility to dispose of the e-waste, rule 16 under Chapter V requires a reduced use of hazardous substances in manufacturing electronic and electrical equipment. The 2016 Rules have included Compact Fluorescent Lamp (CFL) and other mercury lamps since this was not discussed under any other regulations. Another best practice adopted is that the ERP authorization, earlier sought from each state separately, was made pan India by making the CPCB responsible for issuing such authorization. This makes the process easier and faster since there was a delay in implementation, which was noticed due to this bottleneck alone. This is a commendable policy, and if

is found in monitors/CRTs, while mercury may be in switches and flat-screen monitors. Mercury is also found in CFL.

47 S Chatterjee, 'Electronic Waste and India' Ministry of Environment and Forest, Government of India <www.meity.gov.in/writereaddata/files/EWaste_Sep11_892011.pdf>.

48 Lakshmi Raghupathy and others, 'E-Waste Recycling in India—Bridging the Gap Between the Informal and Formal Sector' <http://greene.gov.in/wp-content/uploads/2018/01/Krueger.pdf>.

49 This is addressed under the Atomic Energy Act, 1962, and the rules made there under.

50 This is dealt with under the Batteries (Management and Handling) Rules, 2001.

51 The applicable law is the Micro, Small and Medium Enterprises Development Act, 2006.

52 E-Waste (Management) Rules, 2016 rr 5 to 12.

safety measures are adopted and mandated to be followed during the manufacturing stage, the waste disposal becomes much easier.

While hearing a petition[53] against unscientific disposal of e-waste, the NGT opined that environmental crimes are as serious as assaults but have failed to catch the attention of the authorities. It further observed that despite there being strong legislation on e-waste management, the action taken by the concerned authorities is highly inadequate.[54]

Since the disposal of e-waste happens predominantly at the consumer's end, consumer awareness and sound disposal mechanisms must be imparted through awareness programmes. This has to be the responsibility of the manufacturer, the dealer, and the government. 'Take back' should be popularized and consumers should be left with little or no choice but to dispose e-wastes in an environmentally friendly way.

37.6 Rules on Plastic Waste Management

Plastic waste management caught the attention of environmentalists mainly because it does not degenerate and destroys the ecosystem. Plastic is cherished as one of the best inventions and is used in nearly all aspects of our everyday life. It has become an intrinsic part of every action of human life. However, the hazards of using it and the inability to dispose of it without causing environmental damage is close to impossible and hence needs to be addressed.[55] In 1999, Recycled Plastics Manufacture and Usage Rules were notified by the government of India with the primary objective of regulating the manufacturing, sale, using, and recycling of plastic bags. Subsequently, it was amended in 2003 and replaced by the Plastic Waste (Management and Handling) Rules, 2011. This was superseded by the Plastic Waste Management Rules, 2016, and amended in 2021 by the Plastic Waste Management (Amendment) Rules, 2021.

Rule 5 of the 2021 rules enumerates plastic waste management, which requires the recycler and recycling process to fall in tune with the Indian Standard: IS 14534:1998 titled Guidelines for Recycling of Plastics, amended regularly. The responsibility of a waste generator is outlined in rule 8. The seventeen rules comprehensively address every waste generator, local body, *Gram Panchayat*, manufacturer, importer, and producer. Penalties for contravention of the rules lie with the procedure prescribed under the Environment (Protection Act), 1986.

[53] *Mahendra Pandey and Others v Union of India*, OA No 621 of 2018, Order of 16 January 2019 (NGT—Principal Bench).

[54] PTI, 'Ensure Scientific Management of E-Waste, Environmental Crimes as Serious as Assault: NGT to CPCB' *The Hindu* (18 January 2021) <www.thehindu.com/news/national/ensure-scientific-management-of-e-waste-Environmental-crimes-as-serious-as-assault-ngt-to-cpcb/article33601362.ece>.

[55] Abdul Rafey and Faisal Zia Siddiqui, 'A Review of Plastic Waste Management in India—Challenges and Opportunities' (2021) *International Journal of Environmental Analytical Chemistry* 1

While the rules have been amended to plug all hazards related to plastic waste, the High Court of Madras, in a fateful case[56] dismissed a case on technical grounds since the search and seizure of plastic bags[57] in contravention of the prescribed guidelines was conducted by an official who was not empowered to do so and thus vitiating the entire criminal proceedings initiated against the wrongdoer. There was clear violation of the prescription of the rules and the wrongdoer was fully aware of it but could not be punished not because of the lacuna in the law but because of the actions of the implementing authorities.

Several states in India banned the use of plastic in the wake of these rules.[58] However, strict enforcement has not materialized, and hence, the use of banned plastics has made a comeback.[59] In order to address the issue more stringently, a press note by the CPCB on implementation of Single Use Plastic Ban was issued in June 2022. While exploring alternatives like compostable plastics, directions were also issued to the E-commerce companies to phase out single-use plastic items.[60] Suitable alternatives to replace the use of plastics have not been provided. These alternatives should be effective and economically viable to encourage users to shun low-grade plastic and adopt the alternatives.

The 2022 amendment to the Plastic Waste Management Rules has introduced the definition of 'biodegradable plastics', which was not dealt with in the earlier rules. Concepts like 'End of Life Disposal' and 'Plastic Waste Processors' have been defined where plastic waste can be used to generate energy subject to guidelines. This makes the Rules highly progressive since they focus on environmentally sound disposal of plastic waste and have made provisions to use the waste to generate energy. Additionally, to ensure compliance with these Rules, rule 18 has been introduced to impose environmental compensation. This is a common inclusion that can also be seen in the Battery Waste Management Rules, 2022.

[56] *A Mahendran v M Dwarakanath*, Crl. OP No. 2532 of 2015, Judgment of 25 March 2021 (High Court of Madras).

[57] The accused was fully aware that the storage and sale of polythene/plastic bags are forbidden and banned and had wilfully violated sub-rule 5 of the Plastic Waste (Management and Handling) Rules, 2011 and the order of the government of Puducherry and also violated the provisions of law to make unlawful gain, thereby, committed offences punishable under s 15 of the Environment (Protection) Act, 1986.

[58] Around twenty-five states have banned plastic, Simrin Sirur, 'From Spoons to Flags, How Govt's Plastic Ban Aims to Phase out "Low-Utility" Single-Use Items' *The Print* (8 July 2022) <https://theprint.in/theprint-essential/from-spoons-to-flags-how-govts-plastic-ban-aims-to-phase-out-low-utility-single-use-items/1030371/>.

[59] 'Plastic Waste Management' (INSIGHTSIAS) <www.insightsonindia.com/environment/environment-pollution-and-control/waste-management/plastic-waste/>.

[60] CPCB's Actions to implement the Single-Use Plastic Ban (2022) <https://cpcb.nic.in/uploads/Press-release-SUP-ban-17062022.pdf>.

37.7 Challenges and Way Forward

The above discussion has focused mainly on outlining the rules made under the Environment (Protection) Act, 1986, to address issues related to hazardous waste. A noteworthy observation is the diversity of the legal and regulatory framework provided under these rules. This has led to a few grey areas. For instance, theoretically, the regulatory framework can be discussed and dissected under each set of rules, and solutions can be offered. However, in practice, one manufacturer may have to deal with all the above rules. Approvals under each rule need to be obtained and renewed periodically, in a few cases. Annual reports are required to be sent under some rules. Due to the multitude of applications of varied laws, compliance becomes a challenge. The entire object of addressing hazardous wastes then meets a dead-end since the requisite benchmark may not be attainable at all levels in all cases.

An administrative challenge in implementing the rules is that, the authority to overlook all these rules, over and above the implementation of Environment (Protection) Act is the CPCB with the assistance of the SPCB and other authorities like the *panchayat* under the Plastic Waste Management Rules. Given the magnitude of hazardous waste generation, the authorities are not fully equipped with infrastructure, personnel, financial assistance, and support from other departments of the state. The issues regarding waste already generated before the enactment of these rules are still unresolved, and fresh waste is dumped every day. According to its Annual Report for 2019–20, the CPCB has recycled 39 per cent of hazardous waste collected,[61] any other data regarding implementation, success, and areas of improvement are not available and difficult to find. It is pertinent to mention that the PCBs are overburdened, and sixteen activity heads are identified on its official website with multiple sub-activities under each main head.

In spite of these challenges, commendable work done by the concerned stakeholders and the authorities cannot be completely ignored. Considering the vast expanse, huge population, standard of living, and inadequate infrastructure in India, the advancement towards a sustainable environment is very much visible. In spite of the hurdles, there are several success stories and best practices.[62]

The very object of adopting these rules is to avert further degeneration of the environment. The liability on the erring officers has not been elaborated and they have not been made accountable. Lack of data on action taken and penalty imposed, if any, is not available, and hence, it does not induce confidence among the general public about accountability and liability. If these are stringent then there will be automatic deterrence to flouting the rules among the people. Not only penalties but tax concessions may be extended to ensure compliance with waste disposal. This will be a positive reinforcement

[61] CPCB, 'Annual Report 2019–20' (Ministry of Environment, Forest and Climate Change).

[62] CPCB, Best practices/Success Stories in Environmental Management (2021) <https://cpcb.nic.in/success-stories/>.

methodology; and hence, public participation will increase, and stakeholders will also put their best foot forward since it will be a lucrative incentive to comply with the rules and be rewarded for adhering to them. As an additional initiative, the concerned authority, while issuing the appropriate approvals, may require the applicant to deposit an amount as a 'security deposit'. The computation of this security deposit may be based on possible future damages incurred if an applicant fails to adhere to the rules. The security deposit may be adjusted towards the damage rather than initiating proceedings for recovery on default.

The need for a comprehensive code is indispensable at this point in time. By making one common law and facilitating a single platform for adhering to the statutory requirements, it becomes easy for the applicants to approach a hassle-free methodology, and implementation will also become easier for the authorities. Wherever applicable, a Public-Private Partnership model (PPP) can be adopted. This model has many success stories and if implemented well, it will not be long before India becomes a role model to the entire world regarding effectively addressing environmental issues along with sustainable development. Furthermore, every stakeholder and the general public need to initiate steps and take responsibility, as environmental degeneration is everybody's concern. Though awareness programmes are organized and reported in the annual reports, their effectiveness is not measured.

Conclusion

With globalization and the advancement of technology, human lives are more sophisticated and consequently, a huge amount of waste and, in particular, hazardous waste is generated. The best way to overcome the issue of hazardous waste is by ensuring that it is not generated or at least kept at an optimal minimum where it can be disposed of in an environmentally safe manner. The rules regarding hazardous waste and the amendments made to them affirm that India is not only adhering to the international conventions and resolutions on HWM but also includes principles like EPR and promoting a circular economy, thus emerging as a global player in not only protecting the environment but also promoting sustainable development. Though the legislative framework is strengthening, its effectiveness will be holistic only when all the stakeholders engage in it. Perhaps by applying the public trust doctrine, each of us should act as a trustee with only one object: securing the best use of the property for the beneficial utilization of its ultimate beneficiaries, who are the future generations. As observed rightly by a judge, 'Illiteracy and lack of information are only two among the reasons for failure in waste management'.[63]

[63] *All Kerala Plastic Dealers v Union of India* 2011 SCC OnLine Ker 4203.

Suggestions for Further Reading

Sairam Bhat (ed), *Handbook on Chemicals and Hazardous Waste Management and Handling in India* (CEERA, National Law School of India University, and MoEFCC 2019).

Shantanu K Dutta, VP Upadhyay, and U Sridharan, 'Environmental Management of Industrial Hazardous Wastes in India' (2006) 48(2) *Journal of Environmental Science and Engineering* 143.

Lakshmi Raghupathy and others, 'E-Waste Recycling in India—Bridging the Gap Between the Informal and Formal Sector' (2010) <http://greene.gov.in/wp-content/uploads/2018/01/Krueger.pdf>.

T.R. Subramanya, 'The Basel Convention on the Control of Transboundary Movements of Hazardous Wastes and Their Disposal of 1989 and Related Developments: An Overview' (2006) 46 *The Indian Journal of International Law* 406.

T.R. Subramanya, *Hazardous Substances in India and the World: Legislations, Frameworks and Management* (Routledge 2021).

CHAPTER 38

THE BHOPAL DISASTER AND THE ENVIRONMENT

ARPITHA KODIVERI AND SALIL TRIPATHI

Abstract

The industrial disaster in Bhopal, India, in 1984 was catastrophic: nearly 2,000 people died in the immediate hours, and thousands more over the next few years. The Indian subsidiary of an American corporation owned the plant. The Indian government negotiated a settlement with the US corporation, but the compensation process was bureaucratised and many victims are still seeking redress. The chapter highlights how environmental governance and law had to evolve to address concerns relating to industrial disasters. The changes in India's environmental laws are important, but not sufficient to prevent the recurrence of such incidents. Post-liberalization, India has amended erstwhile strong laws which raise the risk of future accidents.

Introduction

The catastrophic incident in Bhopal, India, when a poisonous gas, methyl isocyanate, leaked out of a fertilizer plant, has become emblematic of what can go wrong in a situation where a major industrial disaster takes place involving a foreign multinational company in a developing country.[1] The US multinational Union Carbide Corporation had nearly 51 per cent of equity in its Bhopal subsidiary. In December 1984, a major

[1] Ingrid Eckerman, *The Bhopal Saga: Causes and Consequences of the World's Largest Industrial Disaster* (Universities Press 2004).

industrial disaster occurred, which killed thousands of people immediately, and nearly 20,000 more died in the years that followed. A series of critical factors, including inadequate implementation of local laws and rules, insufficient supervision by the parent corporation, the unclear relationship between the parent corporation and the subsidiary, ambiguity about jurisdiction, and the absence of remedy contributed to the untenable situation where many victims are still seeking justice, and regulatory changes have not been put in place.[2] While India has introduced some laws since then, those are neither sufficient nor effective, in preventing a similar catastrophe.

For the purposes of this chapter, we define an industrial disaster as a catastrophic accident in which numerous deaths and/or serious injuries occur to workers and/or surrounding communities. In many instances, the impacts are long-lasting. In theory, this represents a liability for the entity that owns and operates the unit where the accident has occurred. The company has an obligation to ensure that workers and surrounding communities are safe and not harmed due to direct or indirect company activities.

Such disasters also have adverse environmental impacts, including the accidental discharge or release of hazardous materials or chemical substances during manufacturing processes or while being transported. Using synthetic chemicals and mishandling these products can lead to noxious effects on the environment.

Such incidents occur due to negligence, which could have been preventable. Besides negligence, such disasters occur due to insufficient training, inadequate supervision, inadequate supply of safety equipment, use of defective equipment, poor maintenance, unsafe storage of materials, insufficient ventilation, hazardous work conditions, and poor lighting. Workers asked to do overtime beyond reasonable limits can also lead to situations in which industrial disasters can occur due to human fatigue.

The unprecedented nature of the Bhopal disaster led to many calls, in India and abroad, for greater regulation of companies. The focus was rightly on multinational companies operating in countries with lax regulation, but the record of domestic companies was no less problematic. In India, new laws and regulations were passed to prevent recurrence. While there has not been a tragedy on such a scale in India since, it is not necessarily due to stronger laws, better supervision, or enhanced enforcement. Rather, it is a matter of chance. Indeed, since India liberalized its economy in 1991, and particularly in the last decade, its governments have removed some restrictions businesses considered onerous, including opening areas reserved to protect the environment or wildlife for mining or other industrial interests.

This chapter begins with an overview of the Bhopal disaster followed by locating the disaster within India's legal and judicial context as one of weak environmental governance. We then delve into the role of courts and jurisprudence in addressing the legal gaps for holding corporations accountable. Finally, we turn to the role of domestic environmental law and international law in regulating such industrial disasters. We conclude

[2] Sanjoy Hazarika, *Bhopal: The Lessons of a Tragedy* (Viking Penguin 1987).

with a set of policy recommendations on international and domestic environmental law to prevent such large-scale industrial disasters.

38.1 Context

The *Bhopal* case shows many failures. Union Carbide Corporation (UCC), incorporated in the US, was meant to transfer technology to its subsidiary Union Carbide India Ltd (UCIL), but either adequate safeguards were not included or implemented, or the supervision and inspection by Indian authorities were cursory. After the tragedy, the host government, India, did not permit US trial lawyers to represent Indian victims and chose to represent the victims themselves in the legal proceedings in the US, in effect denying the victims' agency. There were concerns about the most appropriate jurisdiction to address questions relating to compensation. The US court refused to hear the matter on the grounds of *forum non conveniens* and sent the case back to India with the specific condition that the company participate in the case in the Indian court. Later, the government settled the matter with UCC. While an amount of compensation was agreed upon, it was neither sufficient,[3] nor distributed properly, and did not anticipate future liabilities.

The Bhopal disaster was a tragedy on many counts. It reveals the inadequacy of existing laws and regulations and insufficient legal preparedness in coping with the aftermath of such disasters. It also showed a few fundamental problems about how multinational companies operate by using the corporate veil, where the parent company can transfer the profits of a business to another interlocked entity and make key managerial appointments, as it can evade penalties when liabilities arise. The lines of command and control between the parent corporation and its subsidiary are complex.

38.2 The Disaster and Beyond

Bhopal continues to remain one of the gravest industrial disasters of all time. Human error was often responsible for those disasters.[4] But the Bhopal disaster stands apart for the sheer scale of human lives lost.

UCC invested in India when the country was poor enough to qualify for concessional aid from development finance institutions. Its agricultural productivity was low, and the

[3] The government of Madhya Pradesh record of relief provided is available only through the web archive site, Wayback Machine <https://web.archive.org/web/20120518020821/http://www.mp.gov.in/bgtrrdmp/relief.htm>.

[4] Doru Costin Darabont, Daniel Onut Badea, and Alina Trifu, 'Comparison of Four Major Industrial Disaster from the Perspective of Human Error Factor' (2020) 305 *MATEC Web of Conferences* 00017.

country suffered from food shortages. In the 1960s, India decided to boost food production through a Green Revolution by introducing fertilizers, chemicals, and mechanization to Indian farms.

India needed the investment, but it had weak regulatory capacity. UCIL operated in an environment where the state—the Indian government at the centre and the Madhya Pradesh government at the state level—lacked the capacity to adequately scrutinize or supervise the project.

The UCC plant in Bhopal produced a fertilizer called Sevin to meet India's agricultural needs. The plant's design was like the company's other plants, including one in Virginia, US. The decision to locate the plant in Bhopal was controversial and invited criticism.[5]

On the night of 2 December 1984, a cloud of deadly methyl isocyanate gas escaped from the plant. Establishing a large industrial factory in India inevitably attracts poor people to live in its vicinity, hoping to get jobs or provide services. When the accident occurred, by the official count, 2,259 people died immediately,[6] and by one estimate, nearly half a million people were exposed to the gas.[7] Over the years, about 20,000 more died earlier than they would have expected, making it the world's worst industrial disaster[8] in terms of the number of fatalities and longevity of its impacts.

Soon after the incident, the company claimed in its public responses that the disaster was due to sabotage,[9] possibly by a disgruntled employee, although the company did not make such an allegation in any formal proceedings. UCC's then chief executive, Warren Anderson, promptly flew to India after the disaster. He was arrested soon after he arrived. In circumstances never clearly explained, he was allowed to leave the country within days. He never returned to India and was declared a 'proclaimed offender'.

In the days following the disaster, US industry officials defended US companies' safety record and expressed surprise that so many people could live in the vicinity of the plant.[10] That argument was, however, moot since people living miles away from the

[5] Sanjoy Hazarika, 'Indian Journalist Offered a Warning' *New York Times* (11 December 1984) <https://www.nytimes.com/1984/12/11/world/indian-journalist-offered-warning.html>.

[6] Prabhash K Dutta, 'Bhopal Gas Tragedy: What had Happened 33 Years Ago that Killed 1000s?' *India Today* (3 December 2012) <https://www.indiatoday.in/india/story/bhopal-gas-tragedy-what-had-happened-this-day-33-years-ago-that-killed-thousands-1099247-2017-12-03>.

[7] Edward Broughton, 'The Bhopal Disaster and its Aftermath: A Review' (2005) 4(6) *Environmental Health: A Global Access Science Source* <http://www.ehjournal.net/content/4/1/6>.

[8] Apoorva Mandavilli, 'The World's Worst Industrial Disaster is Still Unfolding' *The Atlantic* (19 July 2018) <https://www.theatlantic.com/science/archive/2018/07/the-worlds-worst-industrial-disaster-is-still-unfolding/560726/>.

[9] The Report of the ICFTU-ICEF Mission to study the Causes and Effects of the Methyl Isocyanate Gas Leak at the Union Carbide Pesticide Plant in Bhopal, India, on 2/3 December 1984, 2010 (ICFTU-ICEF Mission Report) <https://www.bhopal.net/the-report-of-the-icftu-icef-mission/>.

[10] Geraldine Cox, then an official of the US chemical industry, appeared frequently in the media, expressing sympathy for the victims and surprise over the proximity of settlements near the plant. One of the authors of this chapter saw the telecasts in the US in 1984.

plant too were affected, and many among them died. The UCC officials also pointed out India's poor inspection regime, with a view to mitigate UCIL's responsibility.

Initial accounts suggest that Indian doctors who were treating the victims were frustrated because UCIL officials did not reveal the precise composition of the chemicals used in the plant, making it harder for them to treat the affected patients.[11] Prominent trial lawyers from the US arrived in India immediately to represent Indian clients based on charging contingency fees, but the Indian government prevented Indian citizens from contracting with the lawyers. When the case was argued in a US court, India sent a high-powered legal team that claimed that the case should be tried in India. UCC, too, wanted the case to be tried in India, where tort law was not well-developed, and an Indian court, it assumed, would require UCC to pay lower compensation than an American court. Citing the doctrine of *forum non conveniens*, the US court agreed to transfer the case to India.

In 1989, the Indian government settled the case with UCC for $470 million, and an Indian Supreme Court ruling later essentially absolved UCC from future litigation.[12] In 1994, UCC sold UCIL to an Indian state-owned entity with interests in tea. In 1999, another large US multinational, Dow Chemicals, acquired UCC for $11.6 billion, making UCC its wholly owned subsidiary, but without the Indian subsidiary. The effect of these transactions (regardless of the intent) was that should there be any future liabilities related to the Indian operations, those would be the responsibility of UCIL or its new Indian parent and not Dow Chemicals. Whether the liability of a subsidiary should transfer to its new owners or whether the old owners continue to remain liable for the acts of its subsidiary during the time they controlled it is a contested matter.[13]

Over the years, activists in Bhopal and around the world have attempted to secure justice for the victims, continuing their campaign first against UCC and later, Dow. The new Indian parent of UCIL has rarely been mentioned. Indian courts have indicted UCIL and its officers in a criminal case in India, although UCC's American officers had left India and refused to appear in the criminal case, which is why the Indian legal system considers the chief executive an absconding offender.

Besides the accident *per se*, there has been another environmental crisis in Bhopal.[14] Activists and victims' lawyers say that poor storage by UCC of toxic materials in the Bhopal plant has contaminated the city's water supply, adversely affecting people's health.

In the Indian case, Dow had refused to accept legal liability for the Bhopal disaster, even though it owns UCC, the parent corporation of UCIL, by saying that the disaster occurred before Dow acquired UCC. UCIL, in any case, had already been sold before

[11] ICFTU-ICEF Mission Report (n 9).

[12] *Union Carbide Corporation (2) v Union of India* (1989) 2 SCC 540.

[13] E.g., Erin Brokovich, 'This Lawyer Should be World Famous for His Battle with Chevron—But He is in Jail' *The Guardian* (8 February 2022) <https://www.theguardian.com/commentisfree/2022/feb/08/chevron-amazon-ecuador-steven-donziger-erin-brockovich>.

[14] Broughton (n 7).

Dow acquired UCC. This creates a legal lacuna.[15] The extent to which a company is liable for the legacy of its corporate acquisitions remains an under-explored area and affects other major cases involving multinational companies in developing countries. To what extent can future owners of a corporation be held liable for acts that occurred before the acquisition and in which they had no role? Corporate lawyers argue that mergers and acquisition transactions would be impossible if future owners were to be held accountable for actions that had occurred much earlier and over which they had no control. Regardless of the merits of that argument, it does not offer any meaningful remedy to the victims.

38.3 Weak Environmental Governance

The history of environmental law and governance in India has been defined and shaped by the growth priorities of a developing economy. Implementing these laws has been challenging, pitting competing interests against one another: development, environment, and the rights of local communities. This requires a skilful balancing act which continues to define the struggles of environmental governance in India. In arriving at this balance, however, as former environment minister Jairam Ramesh argues in his book *Green Signals*, the interests of the environment and those dependent on it do get compromised.[16] To locate the past and present injustices in Bhopal, it becomes imperative to understand the political economy in which environmental law is made and used.

In their work on governance gaps, Penelope Simons and Audrey Macklin highlight how multinational companies choose to locate polluting industries (which are difficult to operate in developed countries because of their rigid pollution control norms) in what can be identified as zones of weak governance, where the regulatory and compliance burden is light, and cost-cutting is easier.[17] This is at the heart of the Bhopal gas tragedy, where the decision to locate the plant was made without sufficient consultation with the local community and ignored warnings, and regulatory oversight was weak.

When India approved the UCC project to be located in Madhya Pradesh, there were no comprehensive guidelines on the siting of hazardous industries. UCIL's plant was to be located at a site in a crowded part of the city, which was criticized as a failure on the part of the state to take into consideration the environmental impact on the local communities of living next to a fertilizer plant that was dealing with toxic substances.[18] It

[15] Dow has consistently maintained that it cannot responsible for what happened in 1984 because it bought UCC years after the disaster (the transaction was completed in 2001), and UCC had sold off UCIL to another Indian company in 1994.

[16] Jairam Ramesh, *Green Signals: Ecology, Growth and Democracy in India* (OUP 2015).

[17] Penelope Simons and Audrey Macklin, *The Governance Gap: Extractive Industries, Human Rights and the Homestate Advantage* (Routledge 2014).

[18] Usha Ramanathan, 'Bhopal: As the Law Develops' (2010) 45(34) *Economic and Political Weekly* 82; Armin Rosencranz, 'Bhopal, Transnational Corporations and Hazardous Technologies' (1988) 17(5)

should be noted that in 1975 a new master plan for the city of Bhopal was established, in which a zone was designated for hazardous industries. This would have meant moving the UCIL plant away from its location at Kali Parade. However, in 1976, the Madhya Pradesh Town and Country Planning Board categorized UCIL as a 'general' industry instead of a 'hazardous' industry, allowing it to remain in the same location. This showed that the local government lacked sufficient capacity to make complex decisions or may have been compromised or influenced due to pressures. Nevertheless, it showed how decisions were made without prioritizing the rights of the people living in and around the area.[19]

India had passed laws regulating industrial pollution in 1972, water pollution in 1974, and air pollution in 1981, and the UCIL plant was built in 1969. However, these laws were not retrospectively applied to the UCIL plant. UCIL had begun operations with minimal regulatory scrutiny on the adverse impacts on the water and air.[20] These gaps in the law continued to reinforce the weak framework of environmental governance. The compromises on safety have been extensively documented in the case papers gathered during the court proceedings and in the literature. For instance, the safety alarms to warn residents did not work on the night of the gas leak. The cooling system and vent gas scrubber meant to prevent leaks were not operational.[21] Critics have alleged that the company cut costs in a weak regulatory zone where safeguards to protect people were absent.[22] The plant could operate as it did because of the shaky foundation of the regulatory framework or laws.[23]

The absence of legal standards to regulate hazardous substances was another gap, which became part of the Indian legal framework only in 1989 through the Manufacture, Storage and Import of Hazardous Chemicals Rules, five years after the tragedy. The Rules aim to regulate industrial activity, use, and transport of hazardous chemicals by requiring industries to identify hazardous chemicals to prevent and control damage and provide information on their impact to ensure safe transportation.

The Factories Act, 1948, was amended in 1987, three years after the tragedy, when the occupational health and the safety of workers handling hazardous substances were included within the Act. The amendment also expanded the meaning of 'persons at risk' to include the population around the factory and not just the workforce.[24]

Ambio 336; Usha Ramanathan, 'Communities at Risk: Industrial Risk in Indian Law' (2004) 39(41) *Economic and Political Weekly* 4521.

[19] Delhi Science Forum, 'Delhi Science Forum Report: Bhopal Gas Tragedy' (1985) 13(1) *Social Scientist* 32.

[20] CM Abraham and Sushila Abraham, 'The Bhopal Case and the Development of Environmental Law in India' (1991) 40(2) *The International and Comparative Law Quarterly* 334.

[21] Amnesty International, 'Clouds of Injustice: Bhopal 20 Years On' (2004) <https://www.amnesty.org/en/wp-content/uploads/2021/09/asa201042004en.pdf>.

[22] Satinath Sarangi, 'Six Historical Mistakes of Bhopal' *The Statesman* (5 December 2014) <ielrc.org/content/n1403.pdf> and Delhi Science Forum (n 19).

[23] ibid.

[24] Ramanathan (n 18).

UCIL's decisions concerning safety were problematic.[25] In a 1981 gas leak, one worker died. Another leak in 1982 led to twenty-five deaths.[26] These initial incidents forewarned a larger disaster, yet neither the state nor the company proactively addressed safety concerns. In fact, in 1982, UCIL delinked the safety alarm so that only the employees of the company would be warned about a gas leak or any other disaster within the plant. While UCIL received a legal notice following allegations by Bhopal-based lawyer Shahnawaz Khan, the company denied the allegations and continued to operate the plant, allegedly without adequate safety considerations.[27] These lapses have been documented in several news articles and we rely on them to offer the trail of bad legal and administrative choices and existing legal gaps which undermined safety and environmental considerations in the state and company's decision-making.[28]

38.4 The Judicial Quagmire

The case posed significant challenges involving a multinational corporation operating in a developing country. To what extent is a subsidiary solely accountable for the harm caused? Does the liability extend to the parent corporation? Can the parent absolve itself of its responsibility because the disaster occurred at the subsidiary? Does the extent of a parent company's stake make any material difference?

The incident occurred in India, but the foreign parent company had majority control. But all affected litigants—victims and survivors—were in India, and many were not well-versed with legal systems in India or the US. Two jurisdictions were involved—the US, where UCC was headquartered, and India, where the operations were, where UCIL was headquartered.[29] Each jurisdiction brought with it its own set of legal strategies that could be pursued and judicial decisions that examined the quest for justice by the victims.

The first legal action was a case of 145 claims, consolidated into a single case before the Southern District Court in New York to be heard by Judge Keenan. Some critics

[25] Madhuresh Kumar, 'Bhopal and the Struggle for Social Justice in India' (2014) 41(1/2 135–136) *Social Justice* 186; Nityanand Jayaraman, 'Lessons we Refuse to Learn' *The Statesman* (2 December 2014) <ielrc.org/content/n1403.pdf>.

[26] NDTV Correspondent, 'Bhopal Disaster: The Ignored Warnings' *NDTV News* (14 June 2010) <https://www.ndtv.com/india-news/bhopal-disaster-the-ignored-warnings-420495>.

[27] ibid.

[28] Tomás Mac Sheoin and Frank Pearce, 'Introduction: Bhopal and After' (2014) 41(1/2) *Social Justice* 135; HR Sharma, 'Globalizing Disaster, Provincializing Law: Bhopal 25 Years Later' (2009) 9(3) *Global Social Policy* 321; Niaz Dorry and Nityanand Jayaraman, 'Chemical Industry vs Public Interest: Redefining the Public Debate on Chemical Security' (The No More Bhopals Alliance 2004) <https://www.greenpeace.org/usa/wp-content/uploads/legacy/Global/usa/report/2007/7/chemical-industry-vs-public-i.pdf>.

[29] Jayanth K Krishnan, 'Bhopal in the Federal Courts: How Indian Victims Failed to Get Justice' (2020) 72(3) *Rutgers University Law Review* 705.

saw the arrival of American lawyers in Bhopal as an instance of ambulance-chasing and had serious concerns over legal processes, whether the victims were being consulted adequately and whether their consent was informed.[30] To curb what it saw as possible exploitation of the victims, the Indian government passed the Bhopal Gas Leak Disaster Processing of Claims Act, 1985 (BGLDA), making the central government the sole representative of the interest of the victims of Bhopal. Legal scholar Shruti Rajagopalan has incisively argued that by retaining the right to represent the victims exclusively, the state undermined the agency of the victims. This, she argues, was paternalistic, and in doing so, it created hurdles for the victims to access justice through the adversarial system of courts.[31] After passing the Act, India pursued litigation in the US where the judicial panel for multi-district litigation transferred the class action suits to the Southern District of New York.

UCC argued that the court should declare that adjudicating the conflict in India was more appropriate. The primary reason for referring the case back to India was the assumption that Indian courts were well-placed to handle the dispute by pointing out how the use of public interest litigation signified a crucial innovation in Indian courts. An affidavit by Marc Galanter, Professor of Law at the University of Wisconsin-Madison, provided evidence that Indian courts were ill-equipped to deal with the dispute, especially since India lacked robust jurisprudence in tort law. The affidavit was ignored. Indian lawyers NA Palkhiwala and JB Dadachanji, who represented the Indian state, also argued for transferring the cases to India. The other reason to move the dispute to India was that the contracts were drafted in India under Indian laws, and if the dispute were to be dealt with in American courts, it would place an undue burden on US courts to discover the evidence needed for establishing the liability of UCC.[32] As noted earlier, Judge Keenan dismissed the case on the grounds of *forum non conveniens*. Drawing from Galanter's affidavit, one consequence of the transfer to India was that the legal outcome rested on a shaky foundation where tort law jurisprudence in the context of industrial disasters remained underdeveloped.

The struggle to hold UCC accountable continues in India with civil and criminal liability cases. In 1989, the Supreme Court settled the civil case with a compensation of $470 million from UCC. The settlement is seen as the final closure of the dispute and intended to terminate all civil and criminal proceedings, but it has been reopened after the judgment on criminal proceedings.[33] The settlement does not account for environmental damage. Bhopal-based human rights activist Satinath Sarangi examined the failure of the judiciary to redress the grievances of the victims. He highlighted the constraints of translating the injustice into quantifiable damages and compensation.

[30] Shruti Rajagopalan, 'The Bhopal Gas Tragedy: Paternalism and Filicide' (2012) 5 *Journal of Indian Law and Society* 201.

[31] ibid.

[32] ibid 9.

[33] Satinath Sarangi, 'Bhopal Disaster: Judiciary's Failure' (1995) 30(46) *Economic and Political Weekly* 2907; Abraham and Abraham (n 20).

Apart from the challenge posed by relying on remedies in the form of monetary compensation, the BGLDA created a bureaucratized process for access and distribution of compensation, which was cumbersome. To assess claims, the government appointed welfare commissioners mandated to investigate claims and decide their validity, creating another barrier.

There had been another litigation before the settlement. In 1987, India's Central Bureau of Investigation (CBI) filed a charge sheet before the Chief Judicial Magistrate (CJM) of Bhopal against Anderson and eleven other accused. The list included UCC (USA), UCIL, and Union Carbide (Eastern) Hong Kong. Those charges led to a judgment that has been contested because the charge was seen as too diluted and ended in dismissal. But Anderson and other foreign directors never appeared before the court. After the settlement was announced, there was no scope to continue with the criminal charges until a review petition reopened the case before the CJM in Bhopal.[34] The CBI approached the CJM to reduce the charge against Anderson from 'culpable homicide' to 'criminal negligence'. The court rejected that, and the CBI was asked to pursue Anderson's extradition. In 1996, the Indian Supreme Court diluted the charges for those who had appeared before the court, but that did not include the accused, who were foreigners, and since they had chosen to stay away from the proceedings.

In 2001, when Dow Chemical took over UCC, the civil society group Bhopal Group for Information and Action pursued criminal action against Dow. Meanwhile, Bhopal courts continued to issue summons against Dow, but to no avail. A few senior Indian officials accused in the case were arrested on less grievous charges in 2010.[35]

This brief and potted history shows failures at three levels—the difficulty in holding companies accountable for environmental and human rights abuses, the failure of regulatory mechanisms, and the inability of the judiciary to deliver justice. The state, through the BGLDA, took over the rights of its citizens by making itself the victims' sole representative. Gaps in law led to judicial failures, including the lack of jurisprudence on tort law and environmental laws as they apply to industries.

38.5 Bhopal and Absolute Liability

The Bhopal tragedy occurred when international environmental law was evolving after the 1972 Stockholm conference. There were precedents for the judiciary to draw from in creating new normative frameworks. In its judgment, the Indian Supreme Court also identified the legal gap in regulating hazardous substances and called for laws to be

[34] Tim Edwards, 'Criminal Failure and "The Chilling Effect": A Short History of the Bhopal Criminal Prosecutions' (2014) 41(1/2 135–136) *Social Justice* 53.

[35] ibid.

passed to fill it. As a result, a new normative framework was created in the form of the Environment (Protection) Act, 1986.[36]

Indian jurisprudence also evolved at the intersection of tort liability and hazardous substances. This included the principle of absolute liability in *MC Mehta v Union of India* (the *Shriram* case).[37] In this case, an Indian company, Shriram Foods and Fertilizers, which manufactured hazardous substances like caustic soda, oleum, and chlorine, was located in the densely populated Kirti Nagar area in Delhi. In December 1985, oleum gas leaked from the plant, causing significant harm to the residents living around it. The Court here devised the principle of absolute liability, as it was not part of Indian law till then.[38]

This principle entails that if an industry undertakes hazardous activities, it is liable for the harm that emerges from its activities, and the defence of 'reasonable care' is not sufficient to avoid liability. In the *Bhopal* case, the Court invoked this principle but did not apply it to its entirety, as it accepted the settlement to provide immediate relief for the victims. As the judgment notes:

> In the present case, the compulsions of the need for immediate relief to tens of thousands of suffering victims could not, in our opinion, wait till these questions, vital though they are, are resolved in the due course of judicial proceedings. The tremendous suffering of thousands of persons compelled us to move in the direction of immediate relief which, we thought, should not be subordinated to the uncertain promises of the law, and when the assessment of the fairness of the amount was based on certain factors and assumptions not disputed even by the plaintiff.[39]

In addressing absolute liability, the court relied on the corrective process of justice delivery to work in its favour. Social movements have criticized the Court's delay in taking on this important legal question as it moved to settle the case; they assert that it has paved the way for UCC to evade liability. It also prevents future claims from the victims and limits corporate liability. Despite such criticism, when the Court admitted the review petition, it refused to reopen the question of compensation. This judicial failure to address future claims, given the generational impact of the disaster and the claims of environmental damages, has pushed local groups to attempt to file cases in the US to seek redress.

The other legal question addressed insufficiently is the location of liability—is it with the parent company or the subsidiary? Evidence derived through litigation suggests that UCIL operated with strict oversight from UCC. As K Subramanian has noted: 'From the affidavits and other documents filed by UCC and the Indian Government, it was clear that the progress of the Sevin project was anything but smooth. UCIL needed assurances

36 Usha Ramanathan, 'Bhopal: As the Law Develops' (2010) 45/34 *Economic and Political Weekly* 82.

37 *MC Mehta v Union of India* (1986) 2 SCC 176.

38 ibid.

39 *Union Carbide Corporation (2) v Union of India* (1989) 2 SCC 540.

from UCC over the project design, safety, etc. It entered into separate agreements with the parent company.'[40] And yet UCC chose to attribute blame and liability to its subsidiary on faulty design and lack of safety measures. The Indian courts did not explicitly rule on this question, but a close reading of the judgment permits the inference that UCC was liable despite its attempts to shift the blame to UCIL because the Court held UCC liable for compensation.[41] This question continues to play out in the context of other environmental issues.[42]

Besides environmental law, the *Bhopal* case also poses significant questions about the model of the modern multinational corporation and where effective control rests. Many multinationals may want full control over their subsidiaries, but local laws often prevent them from owning the entire stake. The Foreign Exchange Regulations Act, 1976, sets clear rules about foreign ownership of companies in India. Some companies in the priority sector had the right to own up to 74 per cent, and progressively, the proportion was diluted to 51 per cent in some cases. In most 'non-priority' sector areas (including the manufacture of consumer durables), the foreign entity's stake could not exceed 40 per cent. In the late 1970s, two major US multinationals, IBM and Coca-Cola, chose to divest from India, rather than dilute their equity to 40 per cent.

The fact remains that UCC did own 50.9 per cent of UCIL. Being the majority shareholder, controlling the technology and appointing the subsidiary's key executives as the parent company, it held responsibility. UCC's critics have pointed out how the UCIL plant was designed as per the specifications of UCC and how its managerial and manufacturing processes mirrored similar plants in the US. UCC argued that even if it controlled more than half the shares, it did not effectively control the company since it had Indian management and responded to Indian regulators. Courts never got to rule on this issue.

Another issue was the notion of piercing the corporate veil. UCC's critics alleged that Union Carbide was a seamless organization, where the local affiliates followed strict rules and targets set by the parent corporation. To understand that better, it was necessary to 'pierce the corporate veil', that is, to remove the layers that separated the subsidiary from the parent to show the relationship. Citing competitive reasons, UCC would not make all the information accessible, strengthening critics' suspicions.

Multinational firms may have legitimate reasons for complicated ownership structures to comply with regulations, tomeet obligations of foreign exchange rules, or even to simplify their tax liabilities. The clear line linking the parent with the subsidiary may appear visible. As the cases never went to trial, these questions remained unanswered.

Then, there was the question of extraterritoriality. Which laws and penalties would apply? Should it be US standards since UCC was a US-based company complying with

[40] K Subramanian, 'Corporate Responsibility for Bhopal: How Union Carbide Exploited a Government Loophole' (2015) 50(3) *Economic and Political Weekly*.

[41] *Union Carbide Corporation* (2) (n 39).

[42] ibid.

US standards? Or should it be Indian standards? What were the Indian standards? Or did the liability exclusively rest with UCIL? In seemingly contradictory jurisdictions, what is the policy response on safety, compensation, and its quantum? As the 9/11 cases showed in the United States, it is difficult to arrive at compensation figures even for people working in the same building: should the compensation for a thirty-year-old immigrant working at the revolving restaurant on the top floor of the World Trade Center, who died during the attacks, be the same as what a thirty-year-old hedge fund trader working two floors below? There are ethical, actuarial, and legal questions—in the *Bhopal* case, such questions were not even addressed.

And there is the question of corporate liability. Is liability dictated by the size of the economy and the income potential of the victim, or should it be applied equally? Had the disaster occurred in Virginia, where UCC had a similar plant, what would have been the compensation per victim compared to what was ultimately offered to each Bhopal victim? This is not a moot question; the British oil company BP has paid $18.7 billion in full settlement of its liabilities over the 2010 Deepwater Horizon incident off the US, in which eleven people died. In comparison, in the Bhopal disaster, in which 2,259 died, the compensation figure was $470 million, which, in 2010, was worth about $1 billion (in 2022, it was worth $1.3 billion).

What is the value of a human life? Does it change according to profession, location, or nationality? Or does it depend on an individual's lifetime earnings? Compensation figures from different countries show a lack of consistency, uniformity, or equity.

Indian criminal investigators sought to prosecute UCC's officials under Indian criminal laws with a high evidentiary threshold to prove criminal conduct, where the jurisprudence for 'command and control' is relatively underdeveloped. While international criminal law and international humanitarian law provide theoretical grounds to prosecute in cases involving corporations where the intent (*mens rea*) is identifiable, in complicated corporate relationships, where 'piercing the corporate veil' is a cumbersome process, the absence of full discovery of the paper trail between the parent and the subsidiary, makes proving charges difficult.

The global movement to rein in corporate power was relatively limited when the Bhopal disaster occurred. In the years since, there has been some progress. In 1975, the UN established a Centre for Transnational Corporation, which developed a code of conduct for multinationals, but the end of the Cold War took energy away from that project and the centre was wound up in 1992. At the turn of the millennium, the UN Global Compact was launched, in which more than 10,000 companies and associations participate, committing to upholding ten principles of good behaviour, of which two deal with human rights—to respect rights and not to be complicit in abuses. However, it has no means or mechanism to evaluate companies' adherence to international standards, provide a remedy to victims or affected parties, or pass rulings that can affect corporate behaviour. And while the former UN Sub-Commission for the Protection and Promotion of Human Rights had developed a set of norms to guide corporate behaviour with regard to human rights, it was ultimately ineffective, partly because those norms transferred state obligations onto the private sector, which lacked legal obligation to abide by UN conventions or international law (which applies only to state parties), a point over which some international lawyers had conceptual and principled disagreement with the norms. In 2005, the UN appointed Harvard academic John Ruggie (and former senior UN official) to identify and clarify standards that apply to all companies—state-owned or private, large or small, multinational or local—and after six years of consultations, he developed the UN Guiding Principles for Business and Human Rights (UNGPs), which the UN Human Rights Council adopted unanimously in 2011. Those standards restate that governments have the responsibility to *protect* human rights, businesses have the responsibility to *respect* human rights, and where there are protection gaps, there is a need for effective *remedies* that are consistent with international standards. While the principles are a step in the right direction, the UNGPs lack the mechanism to measure or evaluate corporate performance and cannot enforce compliance. However, civil society groups have begun citing the UNGPs, and companies have begun to tailor their policies to align with the UNGPs. Whether that would prevent another incident like Bhopal is impossible to tell. The UNGPs call upon companies to undertake 'due diligence', but even if a company undertakes rigorous due diligence and puts in place measures to prevent accidents and complies with all standards, such moves can only be seen as 'necessary', but not 'sufficient'. For an incident like Bhopal, softer, normative measures are not the answer; serious investigations, evidence-based prosecution, and effective remedies for the victims are the only way forward.

38.6 Contaminated Water

In 1992, the international environmental group Greenpeace released a report examining groundwater pollution in and around the Bhopal plant. It revealed high levels of heavy metals and Sevin in the water. Critics have described it as the second disaster of the Bhopal Gas Tragedy.[43] As UCC had sold its Indian operations, and the plant was closed, it had not cleaned up the plant, nor were any remaining toxic substances removed. To hold UCC accountable for environmental remediation, victims pursued legal action in the US, as the Indian courts refused to revisit the question of compensation and environmental damages.

The US court, however, held that UCC was not liable for the ongoing pollution and that liability rested with UCIL and the state government. The Madhya Pradesh government has failed to clean up the UCIL site. Since Dow Chemical acquired UCC in 1999, civil society groups wanted Dow Chemical to clean up the site. However, the title belongs to the state government, which is considered responsible for the clean-up.[44] In

[43] Krishnan (n 29).

[44] ibid.

this legal process of shifting liability across actors, the toxic trail of the tragedy persists, and no environmental remediation has taken place.

The twists and turns of the case show a systematic failure that has impacted the victims. They continue to await justice while the law and courts have closed avenues of justice or redress, leaving crucial questions such as future claims, environmental damage, and remediation unattended.

38.7 Environmental Law and Industrial Disasters

Industrial disasters (*Bhopal* and the *Shriram* case, cited earlier) forced the Indian state to create a framework of environmental governance, developing new norms, laws, jurisprudence, and legal avenues. The disasters laid bare the inadequacies of India's environmental law, which is far from being equipped to address complex disasters. Nor is there much clarity about liability. But now, tools exist to address them.

The *Shriram* case (cited earlier) was key in the normative evolution of corporate liability. Here, the Court devised the principle of absolute liability, which is crucial in regulating hazardous substances. After the *Bhopal* case, the Factories Act, 1948, which assesses the risks in siting industries in specific locations, was extended in scope so that it did not consider only the risk of exposure to workers and factory premises but also to the population residing in the vicinity.[45] This was significant since it brought to light the complications involved in siting an industry. Other subsequent amendments to the Factories Act included the creation of disaster management plans.[46]

Another legal gap was the need for rules on handling hazardous substances, which led to the drafting of the Hazardous Wastes (Management and Handling) Rules, 1989. The Public Liability Insurance Act, 1991 (PLIA) was adopted to ensure quick compensation, which requires industries handling hazardous substances to be insured. The measure is now being reconsidered and draft amendments are up for comment. However, the amount has a cap of INR 500 million, which is insufficient. These laws now provide a semblance of a legal shield that victims of industrial disasters can use.[47] Bhopal has shaped environmental law to be more cognizant of the implications of industrial disasters and the need for corporations to be held accountable. At the same time, the PLIA is presently being diluted by decriminalizing non-compliance by hazardous industries.[48]

[45] Ramanathan (n 36).

[46] ibid.

[47] Abraham and Abraham (n 20).

[48] Ayaskant Das, 'Center Proposes Decrimininalizing Law Providing Safety of Workers' *NewsClick* (8 July 2022) <https://www.newsclick.in/centre-proposes-decriminalising-law-providing-safety-workers>.

The normative evolution shows legal preparedness as precautionary and includes elements of post-disaster relief mechanisms. The passing of the Environment (Protection) Act, 1986, strengthened the precautionary approach and authorized the central government to pass rules and set up authorities and procedures to protect the environment. The Act specifically refers to the handling of hazardous substances. The Environment (Protection) Act is the parent legislation that has led to legal mechanisms like the Environment Impact Assessment (EIA) and rules to handle hazardous and other kinds of waste. The recent wave of changes proposed to the Environmental Impact Assessment Notification, 2006, include exceptions to the need for environmental clearance (for instance, if projects are located a hundred kilometres away). The weakening of the precautionary approach and dismantling of environmental laws like the EIA perpetuate the aura of weak environmental governance.[49] Environmental law has generated ways to manage risk and redress harm. But these remain inadequate as remedies. Compensation for victims remains elusive as an effective remedy, and aspects of remediation and restoring ecosystems are yet to be adequately addressed.[50]

38.8 Looking Ahead

The UN Guiding Principles rest on three pillars—the state duty to protect human rights, the corporate responsibility to respect human rights, and the need for a remedy where gaps exist. The fundamental problem in the discourse of business and human rights lies in the gap. Businesses must comply with the law and adhere to standards that the state must regulate and implement, but the state is often unwilling or unable to play its role. Where the state is absent, the private sector acts with impunity. Campaigners have sought corporate accountability for human rights for a long time. The movement gathered momentum after the tragic executions of Ogoni activists, including Ken Saro-Wiwa, in the Niger Delta in 1995. Despite global revulsion over abuses, effective remedies have remained elusive. The UNGPs restate international law but do not offer a binding remedy. The UNGPs hold the state accountable and are also right in reminding companies that they have a responsibility to respect rights. However, the notion of responsibility to respect is often inadequately understood, and companies interpret it as it suits them. And governments are only now considering making due diligence mandatory. In such an environment, there is no guarantee that a disaster like Bhopal will not recur.

That no corporate entity has been held to account over Bhopal is a tragedy as well as a travesty. Remedies are essential. Whether such remedies should be through private

[49] Jayashree Nandi, 'Recent Environmental Rules Mirror Controversial Draft' *The Hindustan Times* (5 June 2022) <https://www.hindustantimes.com/india-news/recent-environment-rules-mirror-controversial-draft-101654367194857.html>.

[50] Sarangi (n 33).

litigation, public interest litigation, arbitration, criminal prosecution, the use of tort law to seek compensation, or a new binding international treaty that may enable prosecution for the most egregious human rights violations remain open questions.

Movement in international law tends to be glacial, and victims of abuses linked with companies should not have to wait decades for redress. Governments must use existing laws to prosecute cases quickly, enforce laws fairly and swiftly, and secure remedies domestically to send a powerful signal that in their legitimate pursuit of profits, human rights cannot be expendable. Future environmental legislation in India should take into account the following:

- Reconsider the recent spate of dilutions of the PLIA and the Draft EIA Notification, 2020, and strengthen the regulatory framework to enable industries to be held accountable.
- Establish a clear legal framework and mechanism for victims of industrial disasters to access compensation.
- Re-introduce rules for the siting of industries to prevent establishing hazardous industries in populous areas.

Bhopal was a wake-up call for India, but its relevance applies beyond India. Multinationals continue to operate in countries with weak governance or lax regulation.

The stories that novelist and activist Indra Sinha told in his Booker Prize-nominated novel *Animal's People*[51] and the images (e.g., 'Burial of an Unknown Child') that Indian photographers Raghu Rai and Pablo Bartholomew captured in the early hours of the tragedy should remind all of us of the urgency of the task ahead.

Suggestions for Further Reading

Dorothée Baumann-Pauly and Justine Nolan (eds), *Business and Human Rights: From Principles to Practice* (Routledge 2016).
Amita Baviskar, *Uncivil City: Ecology, Equity and the Commons in Delhi* (Sage 2020).
Anuj Bhuwania, *Courting the People* (CUP 2017).
John Braithwaite and Peter Drahos, *Global Business Regulation* (CUP 2000).
John Ruggie, *Just Business: Multinational Companies and Human Rights* (Norton Global Ethics Series 2013).

[51] Indra Sinha, *Animal's People: A Novel* (Simon and Shuster 2009).

CHAPTER 39

ENERGY AND SUSTAINABILITY

UDAY SHANKAR AND ARINDAM BASU

Abstract

Energy contributes immensely to the growth of a country and facilitates in improving the quality of life. Energy in the form of electricity has transformed the civilizational outlook of society. Electricity started being regulated since the nineteenth century on the matter of licensing, generation, distribution, consumer interests. While extracting the maximum benefits of electricity, a concern has been raised about the collateral damage cause to the environment on account of its generation from fossil fuels. Consequently, the scientific community introduced greener sources of energy through renewables and attempts are being made to regulate clean energy in every jurisdiction. Cleaner energy promises a better future for the coming generation. In view of this, this chapter examines the interface between energy and sustainability.

Introduction

We do not exist without energy, and our increasing addiction to energy reveals our cultural preference to harvest more as far as science and technology allow us to do so. But our progress towards an improved civilization has come at a serious cost as we keep exhausting our valuable non-renewable resources. Hence, we need to look for alternatives. In fact, we have already initiated our makeover by harnessing new renewable energy sources capable of large-scale production. Our aspiration is premised upon two standpoints: gradually replacing existing non-renewable energy sources with renewables and creating an independent demand for new sources by changing socio-cultural perceptions. This is what we call the cultural transformation towards green freedom.

The temptation for a colossal, if not total, energy transition is shaped by numerous policies and laws representing conflicting interests of various socio-economic segments. In India, energy policies now essentially revolve around simple binaries—upgrade the living standard of the enormous population by fostering economic development and adopt the path of sustainable development where green energy plays a prominent role. The policy prescriptions and legal instruments attempt to convert the competitive approach into a collaborative ecosystem.

The Indian judiciary is also slowly shaping India's energy jurisprudence. At least two recent decisions of the Supreme Court of India have pointed in opposite directions.[1] India's energy laws are to be understood in this complex set-up. What we understand as energy law is broader than exploration, exploitation, and distribution of electricity *simpliciter*. In its current state, the arms of energy law are spread in international politics, environmental law, economics, and obligations towards social justice.

In this chapter, we divide the relevant issues considering the far-reaching impact of energy law. Section 39.1 lays down the regulatory framework for energy in India identifying the separate regulatory discourses for non-renewable and renewable energy sources. Section 39.2 highlights a more sensitive yet inescapable dimension of energy laws, that is, access to energy premised upon a 'right to energy'. Subsequently we look towards market mechanisms in search of a suitable solution. Section 39.3 analyses the investment opportunities and probable pitfalls in India's energy sector. The line of argument meanders through the international arena before returning to India. Before the concluding remarks, Section 39.4 turns to judicial trends to assess the extent to which renewable energy is a real policy concern.

39.1 Regulatory Landscape Governing Energy and Sustainability in India

The regulation of the energy sector in India dates back more than a century and was almost exclusively connected to the laws related to electricity. For many years, dependence on non-renewable sources guided the regulatory aspects. This started to change after the new wave of environmentalism hit India during the 1980s. Soon the demand for clean energy sources and the rise of sustainable development as a guiding principle began to shape laws and regulations.

[1] *Power Exchange of India v SEBI* 2022 SCC OnLine SC 1051; *MK Ranjitsinh v Union of India* 2021 SCC OnLine SC 326.

In the context of this chapter, the broader international framework is relevant to our discussion on access to clean energy. Sustainable Development Goal (SDG) 7 that aims to '[e]nsure access to affordable, reliable, sustainable and modern energy for all' is particularly relevant.[2] This goal falls within the broader context of SDGs that call for 'leaving no one behind', a framing applicable equally to public, private, civil society organizations, and citizens. Further, SDGs are interdependent in nature indicating that the envisaged solutions would require collective participation.[3]

Electrifying India—History that Enlightens: In 1898, the government of Bengal enacted the Calcutta Electric Lighting Act. The Act made it possible to introduce electric lights on Indian streets, and then electricity was supplied to houses, too.[4] More comprehensive pan-India legislation came into force in 1900 in the form of the Indian Electricity Act. For the first time an electric meter was made mandatory and an electric inspector was made responsible for ensuring compliance with the Act. The 1900 Act paved the way for the smooth transition of Indian society into the age of electrification.[5] One remarkable feature of this legislation was that it also accommodated the private sector by introducing a licence regime, a method sincerely followed by India's post-Independence legislation, the Electricity (Supply) Act, 1948.

Within a decade, another comprehensive law, the Electricity Act, 1910, was enacted that laid down a basic regulatory framework for the electricity supply industry by introducing provisions for 'grant of license for bulk supply',[6] and for the purchase of electrical undertakings by the state.[7] The Act did not dwell upon non-conventional sources of energy and dealt only with electrical energy.[8] Just after Independence, a new legislation on electricity, the Electricity (Supply) Act, 1948, was enacted with the mandate to ensure availability of 'energy' in rural areas along with cities by creating state electricity boards. The Act also dealt with the statutory powers and functions of the Central Electricity Authority and provided for rationalizing the production and supply of electricity to boost the energy sector through a Grid System. It also dealt with 'water-power' whereby it allowed the Board to consider the installation of hydro-electric power without negotiating the interest of irrigation, navigation, and flood control.[9]

India professes a federal set-up by entrusting responsibilities between central and state governments, individually or jointly along with shared obligations on selected

[2] Sustainable Development Goals and Targets, in UN General Assembly Resolution 70/1, Transforming our World: The 2030 Agenda for Sustainable Development, UN Doc A/RES/70/1 (2015).

[3] Richard Gilbert and Jane Nelson, 'Advocating Together for the SDGs: How Civil Society and Business are Joining Voices to Change Policy, Attitudes and Practices' (2018) <https://www.hks.harvard.edu/sites/default/files/centers/mrcbg/files/Advocacy_Collaboration_SDGs.pdf>.

[4] E.g., Siddhartha Chandra Mukherjee, 'Steps of Power: Notes on the History of Electrification in India (1883–1930)' (2017) 78 *Proceedings of the Indian History Congress* 498.

[5] ibid.

[6] Electricity Act, 1910 s 3 dealt with the grant of licences.

[7] ibid s 6 dealt with the purchase of undertakings.

[8] ibid s 2(g).

[9] Electricity (Supply) Act, 1948, s 30.

subject matters. With electricity placed in the Concurrent List of the Constitution of India, 1950,[10] the legal instrument is enacted by the central government with an adequate decision-making space available for the state governments to regulate intra-state affairs on production, distribution, and tariff determination.

To align with the policy on liberalization in the infrastructure sector, the Electricity Regulatory Commission Act, 1998, was enacted to bring transparency, accountability and professionalism in the fixation of tariffs for meeting the energy crisis. This legislation has also created the Central Electricity Regulatory Commission to regulate the tariff of central generating companies and other generating companies in the case of a composite scheme for generation and sale of electricity to two or more states.[11] It also provided for establishment of the State Electricity Regulatory Commission, though optional, to regulate licences and others involved in the electricity sector in the state.[12] Notably, till this period, all the legislations were silent regarding 'clean energy'.

Against this backdrop, the Electricity Act, 2003, may be considered the most important legislation as it attempts to introduce renewable sources of energy in the league of conventional sources by inserting a few provisions dealing with issues of promotion and generation. The 2003 Act repealed all the existing laws dealing with electricity and ushered in a new beginning in the power sector by de-licensing generation, introducing open access in transmission and distribution, and fostering non-renewables for energy security. The Act lays down a comprehensive framework for power development, *inter alia*, recognizing the role of renewable energy in the National Electricity Policy and stand-alone systems.

39.2 Touch of Economics, Triggering Reasons, and Policies

India has two prime objectives—ensuring the economic health of the country, and backing up such development by promoting a sustainable energy policy. Both these objectives are demand-driven. Usually, almost a primeval way of thinking dominates; that is, poverty is the root cause of all environmental problems. Obviously, eradication of poverty buttresses the postmodern belief that for environmental wellbeing in a country like India the market will certainly find the solutions for all ecological problems.[13] This is where green energy steps come in. It is not very difficult to see that in India the demand

[10] The Constitution of India, 1950, Seventh Schedule, List III, Entry 38.

[11] Electricity (Supply) Act, 1948, ch II dealt with Central Electricity Regulatory Commission, and ch III with powers and functions of the Commission.

[12] ibid ch IV dealt with State Electricity Regulatory Commission, and ch V with powers and functions of the Commission.

[13] Ramachandra Guha and Joan Martínez Alier, *Varieties of Environmentalism: Essays North and South* (Earthscan 1997).

for renewable energy is more of an oxymoron. A vast population is to be lifted from poverty and it just does not make any sense to claim that underprivileged people en route to economic comfort will voluntarily adopt a sustainable lifestyle. That cultural shift may take years. In these fluid societal conditions, designing policies becomes tricky as it becomes too difficult to predict consumer choices.

Aside from pure paternalism, nudging may certainly help,[14] but many uncertainties remain.[15] It is a given that for India and elsewhere, the development process should be subject to optimal utilization of natural resources. One can understand what challenges lie ahead. India's burgeoning population (1.3 billion and growing) demands massive energy. Almost 10 per cent of the growth in the world's energy demand has originated from India since the dawn of this millennium. At the same time, India's per capita energy demand has increased by more than 60 per cent simply because its overall economic health and standard of living have improved. However, the shortcoming is that approximately 80 per cent of India's energy demand is satisfied by non-renewable sources such as coal, oil, natural gas, and solid biomass. In addition, it is astonishing that with such low per capita emission, India still occupies the third place in terms of greenhouse gas emissions in the world.[16] It is, however, easy to see what ails India as the co-relation between its population, unsustainable energy consumption pattern, and lack of alternatives is entirely visible.

It can be argued that nuclear power may also be a viable option. The government of India is committed to expanding its nuclear power programme to meet the demand for clean electricity. Though nuclear energy only contributed around 3–3.5 per cent since 2014 to total electricity generation, the scenario is likely to change in the future as India is engaged in developing a three-stage nuclear power programme.[17] In this regard, the Central Electricity Authority, while seeking to fulfil its obligation under section 4 of the Electricity Act,[18] released the draft National Electricity Plan for public consultation that indicated the increase in nuclear power generation capacity by 2032.[19]

[14] See Richard H Thaler and Cass R Sunstein, *Nudge: Improving Decisions about Health, Wealth and Happiness* (Penguin 2009) 185–198.

[15] For example, at the beginning of 1980, a long-forgotten economic concept called Jevon's paradox resurfaced, providing an alternative to energy efficiency formulation. See e.g., Vinola Vincent Munyon, William M Bowen, and John Holcombe, 'Vehicle Fuel Economy and Vehicle Miles Traveled: An Empirical Investigation of Jevon's Paradox' (2018) 38 *Energy Research and Social Science* 19.

[16] Sweety Pandey and others, 'State Energy and Climate Index: Round-I' (2022) (Niti Aayog 2022) 16 <https://www.niti.gov.in/sites/default/files/2022-04/StateEnergy-and-ClimateIndexRoundI-10-04-2022.pdf>.

[17] DTE Staff, 'As told to Parliament (10 February 2022): India Investing in Nuclear Power to Provide Clean Electricity' *Down To Earth* (10 February 2022) <https://www.downtoearth.org.in/news/governance/as-told-to-parliament-february-10-2022-india-investing-in-nuclear-power-to-provide-clean-electricity-81516>.

[18] Section 4 provides that '[t]he Central Government shall, after consultation with the State Governments, prepare and notify a national policy, permitting stand alone systems (including those based on renewable sources of energy and other non- conventional sources of energy) for rural areas'.

[19] Ministry of Power, National Electricity Plan (Draft) Generation Vol I (2022) <https://cea.nic.in/wp-content/uploads/irp/2022/09/DRAFT_NATIONAL_ELECTRICITY_PLAN_9_SEP_2022_2-1.pdf>.

This sounds encouraging but there are risks beneath. The first risk is the perilous nuclear fallout that may arise from any nuclear accident. Accidents on Three Mile Island in Chernobyl and Fukushima have already warned us against the devastation that nuclear accidents might bring. But it is also a fact that nuclear energy can potentially address the climate change problem. Hence, it has stayed on the policy agenda for many governments as an alternative clean energy solution. For India, nuclear programmes bring another challenge—acquiring land and dealing with the protests of local people who believe that the benefits do not correspond to their right to life. The Supreme Court of India was petitioned to prohibit the commissioning of the nuclear power plant in Kudankulam, Tamil Nadu, on the grounds of violating environmental norms. However, the Court dismissed the petition and highlighted the significance of access to energy for better living conditions.[20]

Nonetheless, if India expects to fulfil all its energy demands from renewables and improve innovation and technological capability, the government of India must meet two tough challenges. First, it has to tackle the problem of double externalities arising out of green innovation. If the gap between social and private return is not reduced,[21] there will certainly be fewer incentives to produce green goods and services, such as energy-efficient products and services. As a consequence, there will be a direct negative impact on the innovation market.[22]

Second, we must bring colossal technological changes on the scientific, engineering, and institutional front to achieve sustainability. To put this in context, electric vehicles constitute an interesting example. India is currently promoting a green hydrogen-based ecosystem and expects that car manufacturers will soon be able to launch cars suitable for Indian roads based on Fuel Cell Electric Vehicle (FCEV) technology powered by hydrogen. The idea is to be energy self-reliant by 2047 with the help of technologies that advance zero-emission solutions.[23] It is necessary to assess this ambition with caution because India cannot carry on this mission with a narrow mindset that the resulting benefits would be enjoyed by the transportation sector only.

A recent study reveals a different perspective, affirming that relying on green hydrogen may not be as safe as many countries think.[24] Initially, there may be exponential growth, but the major concern is the supply of green hydrogen in the long run. It is estimated that green hydrogen is likely to supply less than one per cent of the energy we

20 *Sundarrajan v Union of India* (2013) 6 SCC 620.

21 An understanding that takes us to the externality problem and, in a rudimentary sense, allows us to set the prices of the products based on (among other things) the environmental cost at an optimal level. Another way to look at this is to create a system that is transparent enough for producers and consumers to make informed decisions.

22 William D Nordhaus, *The Spirit of Green: The Economics of Collisions and Contagions in a Crowded World* (Princeton University Press 2021).

23 Ministry of Road Transport and Highways, 'Shri Nitin Gadkari Launches World's Most Advanced Technology' (16 March 2022) <https://www.pib.gov.in/PressReleasePage.aspx?PRID=1806563>.

24 Robert W Howarth and Mark Z Jacobson, 'How Green is Blue Hydrogen?' (2021) 9(10) *Energy Science and Engineering* 1676.

need by 2035. Even if there is a high possibility of making a substantial technical breakthrough by 2040 that may boost the market, the percentage is likely to be 3.2–11.2 per cent for the EU and 0.7–3.3 per cent globally. Such a prospect is far less encouraging.[25] This is a classic setting where uncertainties can dislodge future investment, which may endanger countries' ambitious climate targets. Certainly, the future is not dependent on green hydrogen alone and it is possible to implement ingenious policies to do away with additional complications. But at the moment we are looking too far ahead in the future with far too meagre solutions at our disposal.

In any case, we know that to internalize the social cost, putting a price on pollution (or polluting activities) is important. For example, to encourage investment in low-carbon technologies, carbon prices should be high enough so that investors can expect secure payoffs.[26] This is notwithstanding the environmental tax burden that an industry ordinarily bears. The question is about the correct policy choices to get there. Already, we have noticed the apparent uncertainties in the green hydrogen market.

The 2022 UN Sustainable Development Goals Report covers two important elements.[27] First, it isolates three reasons—COVID-19, climate change, and conflict—that have sufficiently slowed the progress toward achieving the 2030 Agenda for Sustainable Development. Second, the Report offers a visual progress chart of the SDGs, which shows that the Asian region and Latin American countries have done fairly well in achieving universal access to electricity. For developed nations, the same has been achieved. In contrast, the progress is depressing on the rate of energy efficiency improvement parameter. We can draw several lessons once again. The main problem is the consumption pattern and a clear disconnect between access to energy and access to clean energy. This should open further discussion about our 'rights'—the right to energy, the right to clean energy, and the right to affordable clean energy. This progression is a must for all countries; at least for India, we can say that the journey has begun.

39.3 Climate Change, Renewable Energy, and Decision-Making—A Game of Dice

The Electricity Act is perhaps the only relevant law for addressing the challenges in the Indian energy sector. The current Act can be seen from two different perspectives. First, we need to understand how far the Act can secure a clean and affordable energy supply,

[25] Adrian Odenweller and others, 'Probabilistic Feasibility Space of Scaling up Green Hydrogen Supply' (2022) 7 *Nature Energy* 854.

[26] Nordhaus (n 22) 223.

[27] United Nations, 'The Sustainable Development Goals Report 2022' 3 <https://unstats.un.org/sdgs/report/2022/The-Sustainable-Development-Goals-Report-2022.pdf>.

which consequently takes society toward low-carbon and sustainable energy consumption. Second, the Act's role in providing guidance towards fair, equitable and efficient energy distribution is yet to be explored adequately. Understanding these two aspects is necessary as it can tell us how India's solution for the access to energy problem can be synced with the international legal framework.

It is also important to remember that climate change remains a major influencing factor in the context of a sustainable energy solution. Though a bigger deterrent against developing international consensus to counter the impact of climate change appears to be inflexible political will, we can still trace some notable international legal initiatives. For example, the 2015 Paris Agreement includes Nationally Determined Contributions (NDCs) that require state parties to reduce their national emissions and adapt to the impacts of climate change.[28] Parties acknowledge and understand it as an obligation of conduct. But the question is the extent to which NDCs can be a game changer in the energy context. The Paris Agreement lays down a dynamic framework, and parties are required to design optimal choices. In that sense, the constitutive elements of the Paris Agreement are supposed to develop normativity that should guide parties' future behaviour. But this bare framework provided by the Paris Agreement is yet to be developed significantly as the countries continue to fail to stand on a uniform platform. Of course, it can be argued that uniformity is the antithesis to climate negotiations as the main debate is about who has been more responsible for causing climate change and thereby, responsible for maximum affirmative actions to mitigate. We see a fundamental flaw in this argument. After all, from the very beginning, the parties tried to develop something that would bring uniformity to the process. Unfortunately, the targets have always remained unfulfilled. But, a shortfall in results must not be interpreted as a lack of aspiration supporting uniformity. At best parties can be questioned on the quality of their consent. It is an entirely different matter that only a few states are somewhat proudly holding the Common but Differentiated Responsibilities principle as the commanding baton to orchestrate the climate talks, and gradually, the true essence of the negotiations is getting affected unnecessarily by their slender aspirations.[29] This was amply reflected at COP 26. This begs the question of how this is connected to the sustainable energy discourse. The answer is relatively straightforward: To reduce the impact of climate change offsetting carbon emission is a must. Reducing enormous amounts of carbon dioxide (or other harmful greenhouse gases), other than technological sophistication, requires viable alternatives to run the fossil fuel-based economy. Therefore, if we solve the energy crisis, we also mitigate the problem of climate change. To that extent the fate of climate politics is entwined with nations' ability to harness renewables to keep society going. We believe that successful conclusion of climate change negotiations provides a valid reason

[28] Paris Agreement, Paris, 12 December 2015, in Report of the Conference of the Parties on its Twenty-First Session, UN Doc FCCC/CP/2015/10/Add.1, art 4(2).

[29] E.g., Lavanya Rajamani, 'Ambition and Differentiation in the 2015 Paris Agreement: Interpretative Possibilities and Underlying Politics' (2016) 65(2) *International and Comparative Law Quarterly* 493.

for participating countries to make commitments cautiously in their domestic energy market.

The COP 26 President Alok Sharma sounded positive in his opening speech when he said that Glasgow should be seen as the 'last best hope' to answer the problems of climate change.[30] In reality, Glasgow left the biggest challenge unaddressed—the agreement of parties over legally binding commitments.[31] However, the parties have unleashed a host of aspirations such as limiting the usage of coal, minimizing deforestation, and cutting methane emissions. The most promising is progress over Article 6 of the Paris Agreement. Conceivably, international carbon trading can be the game changer for countries to meet their climate targets, provided the system is backed by transparent and strong accounting processes. This begs the question of the rules that should guide international carbon trading and how carbon prices should be set. Article 6 of the Paris Agreement provides the basic idea leaving much to be decided by the parties. Parties answered some tricky questions in COP 26 by reaching a new agreement on market mechanisms. The anticipation is to effectively engage the private sector and operationalize the transfer of emission reductions between countries.[32] A country like India can benefit significantly as international institutions and agencies are expected to work collaboratively with developing nations on the carbon offsetting process. Also, the opportunity is to go beyond NDCs with the help of additional mitigation reduction endeavours. This may particularly be a game changer for India.

India has announced its revised NDC as per the commitments given at COP26. Keeping in mind its long-term net-zero goal by 2070, India now is committed 'to reduce Emissions Intensity of its GDP by 45 per cent by 2030, from 2005 level and achieve about 50 per cent cumulative electric power installed capacity from non-fossil fuel-based energy resources by 2030'.[33] According to the communiqué, there has to be programmes and schemes in collaboration with different ministries and government departments.[34] There is no reference to India's long-term concern, that is, conversion of Certified Emission Reductions (CERs) and projects from Clean Development Mechanism (CDM) to Sustainable Development Mechanism (SDM), envisaged under Article 6.4 of the Paris Agreement as updated at COP 26.

At COP 27 in Sharm El-Sheikh, Egypt, member states took a significant step forward by adopting the loss and damage framework for countries either vulnerable or affected

[30] Alok Sharma, COP26 President, Opening Speech at COP26 (31 October 2021) <https://www.gov.uk/government/speeches/cop26-president-alok-sharmas-opening-speech-at-cop26>.

[31] Glasgow Climate Pact, Decision 1/CMA.3, 13 November 2021, UN Doc FCCC/PA/CMA/2021/10/Add.1.

[32] For more details of art 6, see UNFCCC, COP26 Outcomes: Market mechanisms and non-market approaches (art 6) <https://unfccc.int/process-and-meetings/the-paris-agreement/the-glasgow-climate-pact/cop26-outcomes-market-mechanisms-and-non-market-approaches-article-6>.

[33] Cabinet, 'Cabinet Approves India's Updated Nationally Determined Contribution to be communicated to the United Nations Framework Convention on Climate Change' (3 August 2022) <https://pib.gov.in/PressReleaseIframePage.aspx?PRID=1847812>.

[34] ibid.

by climate change-related events. However, no further progress was made on improving the emission-reduction commitments.[35] This development suits India just fine. The Sharm El-Sheikh Implementation Plan, the most important outcome of COP 27, which is to launch a work programme on just transition into renewable energy, may perfectly suit India's future energy planning. The reason is that problems like distribution and access to energy in India make any plan for a fast transition problematic and dependent on multiple factors. The government of India may use the same argument as a shield and a sword. For example, it can raise a valuable defence against any mandatory imposition of international law to protect its domestic conditions. At the same time, downplaying the risks associated with the energy market it can aggressively put policies in motion, such as the electrical vehicle policy. We have touched upon this aspect in section 39.2. Here, we want to focus on another element that may prove contentious for India in the long run.

One of the important outcomes of COP 27 was a decision on a mitigation work programme that parties are to initiate promptly and continue up to 2026. This may be further revised thereafter. This work programme is important for developing new technology in developing countries that may successfully address climate change problems. This will essentially be a transformative process.

India is already committed to reducing the emissions intensity of its GDP by 45 per cent by 2030. It is supposed to review its position in one year. After that, if required, it may accelerate its coal phase-down efforts alongside eliminating inefficient fossil fuel subsidies.[36] Now, what ideally is to be done is to reconsider the predominant thinking that only a reduction in coal consumption will be a sufficient way out from climate change. At this point, the paths leading to energy efficiency and the solution to the problem of climate change cross each other. If India can reduce the emission of other greenhouse gases, in addition to coal, then energy efficiency will be the result. Unfortunately, this possibility was not covered in the discussions during COP 27.

This was certainly a significant omission. Nonetheless, to stand by its climate commitments, India is currently proceeding with three policies—improving solar power capacity, encouraging the population to use electric transport, and utilizing its hydrogen reserves as a substitute for fossil fuels. It is yet to be seen if these strategies will help India to achieve its net-zero target. How India develops its energy infrastructure and provides enough economic incentives to its private sector remains crucial. We have briefly touched upon these issues in section 39.2. An extended analysis is beyond the scope of this chapter but we can state that without proper energy infrastructure and economic modelling, we may fall short of our net-zero target.

Before closing this discussion, we need to touch upon another historically important point in international climate politics: emission-reduction mechanisms under the

[35] For decisions taken at the Sharm El-Sheikh Climate Change Conference, see <https://unfccc.int/cop27/auv>.

[36] For matters relating to the work programme for urgently scaling up mitigation ambition and implementation referred to in para 27 of decision 1/CMA.3, see <https://unfccc.int/documents/624428>.

United Nations Framework Convention on Climate Change (UNFCCC). For India, among the available choices,[37] the CDM is the most relevant. CDM was crucial for developing nations. Under CDM, emission-reduction projects, run by any developed nation in a developing country, can generate CER credits, each equivalent to one tonne of CO_2. These credits are saleable and can be used by that developed nation to meet some of their emission-reduction targets under the Kyoto Protocol. The CDM has been the constant source of income for the UNFCCC Adaptation Fund, set up to finance adaptation projects in vulnerable developing countries.[38] The credits earned under CDM will be more valuable for developing countries if they are counted as part of their NDCs. COP 26 allows countries to use their credits towards NDCs if they originated under projects registered after 2013. For ongoing projects, the same can also be done, but the modalities are yet to be finalized.[39]

Therefore, the door is ajar for India. The agreed Article 6 (of the Paris Agreement) rules in COP 26 are not perfect, but at least they provide India with the perfect opportunity to advance its renewable energy projects. A couple of long-term benefits are in sight. First, India's playing field for carbon mitigation gets expanded, allowing it to design and approve projects with much more freedom according to its specific needs. Second, India will benefit because knowledge flow from developed countries will certainly boost domestic employment opportunities. Two important aspects stand out in India's revised NDCs. India now wants 'to achieve about 50 per cent cumulative electric power installed capacity from non-fossil fuel-based energy resources by 2030, with the help of transfer of technology and low-cost international finance including from Green Climate Fund (GCF)'.[40] At the same time for better adaptation India will boost investment in sectors vulnerable to climate change. Both these objectives are going to be market-driven for sure. It is to be seen how India can keep the rules of the game transparent enough so that its international climate pledges do not become a rhetoric.

39.4 Policy-Making and Some Ideas

By now, we have come to terms with climate change and started to believe that the solution is within our reach if we are ready to sacrifice some comforts in our lives. We may

[37] The link goes back to the Kyoto Protocol. Under the Protocol parties were required to reduce their GHG emissions. Parties assigned economic value to their efforts through three different mechanisms—Emission Trading (ET), Joint Implementation (JI) and Clean Development Mechanism (CDM). The first two were available only to Annex I parties.

[38] UNFCCC, 'What is the CDM' https://cdm.unfccc.int/about/index.html.

[39] ibid. The application of Article 6 of the Paris Agreement is the key provision guidance, included in a COP 26 decision. This will remain crucial for developing nations as they can decide further to characterize their voluntary carbon market.

[40] Ministry of Environment, Forest and Climate Change, Climate Change Performance Index (19 December 2022) <https://pib.gov.in/PressReleaseIframePage.aspx?PRID=1884764>.

feel positive that a better future with clean energy solutions is at the horizon. But it is important to remember that the magnitude of the problem is enormous and electrification with clean energy or launching energy-efficient cars will only take us to the halfway mark. The goal is to decarbonize our world and each of us can contribute by choosing a lifestyle with a smaller carbon footprint.[41]

The challenge is how people should be encouraged to optimize their lifestyles. For policymakers the guidance is found in SDG7. But, it will d be a mistake if the focus remains limited to SDG7 only. Instead, we need to go beyond the conventional approach towards wider participation. Industries will certainly play their part. However, the fruits taste sweeter if the distributive and procedural justice concerns are properly addressed.[42] The challenge is about balancing the different SDGs while acknowledging trade-offs. A study found that out of 169 SDG targets, 113 require actions to change our energy use pattern. It further confirmed the relationship between 143 targets (143 synergies, sixty-five trade-offs) that policymakers should consider to achieve SDG7. Three important areas were identified—realizing aspirations of greater welfare and wellbeing, building physical and social infrastructures for sustainable development, and achieving sustainable management of the natural environment.[43]

Noticeably, the paths to deliverance from the twin evils of climate change and resource scarcity twist and turn through the complex network of formal and informal dilemmas. However, an early identification and prioritization of actions mostly through utilizing the conventional governance structure can offer us more solutions to most problems. Here, the flow of things is typically hierarchical, and the role of the state is central to the success of any scheme.[44] The Indian experience suggests that such a role is well-understood by the government and differing with disagreement if any, we appreciate the efforts put by the Indian government, thus far.

For example, in addition to the bulk of the laws on electricity regulation, the current energy policies of India stand apart as the government is providing large financial support to the energy sector. Simultaneously, constant efforts are being made to reduce the subsidies provided to the fossil fuel-based economy. To that effect, any demeaning argument must give way to the fact that India's demographic challenges are significantly different compared to other nations. On the other hand, the moral dimension breaks down the analogy of short-sighted and one-dimensional patterns of control.[45]

Distinctive from this archetype, the utilities in the market bring forth the ubiquitous equity argument wrapped up in their profit maximization motives.[46] It is not difficult to follow the argument because, in a larger context, the same equity argument—who pays

[41] Saul Griffith, *Electrify: An Optimist's Playbook for Our Clean Energy Future* (MIT Press 2021) 184.

[42] Shelley Welton and Joel B Eisen, 'Clean Energy Justice: Charting an Emerging Agenda' (2019) 43 *Harvard Environmental Law Review* 307, 308.

[43] Francesco Fuso Nerini and others, 'Mapping Synergies and Trade-offs between Energy and the Sustainable Development Goals' (2018) 3(1) *Nature Energy* 10, 13–14.

[44] Welton and Eisen (n 42) 308.

[45] ibid.

[46] ibid.

for clean energy and who benefits from it—is advanced by the developing countries in a much larger context. Sure enough, the cost that consumers are required to pay cannot be too disproportionate across the different groups in society. In fact, the preambular dicta of the Electricity Act sets the goal of catering to the interests of consumers, thus making affordability an integral policy of electricity pricing. The task of ensuring affordability of electricity has been entrusted to an independent regulatory body, Central and State Electricity Regulatory Commissions, which decides based on commercial principles coupled with safeguarding the consumer's interest.[47] Though the fixation of tariff is based on the principle of cost recovery in a reasonable manner, the pricing of electricity through non-conventional energy is becoming competitive vis-a-vis conventional sources of energy.[48] Additionally, the Act also directs the government to incrementally reduce cross-subsidy to make the power sector competitive and sustainable.

How we walk the path of economic and social justice with a clean energy mandate depends on a combination of three aspects—long-term decision-making, distributive justice, and effective market control. The Union Budget 2023 focused on allocating funds to enhance energy capacity under different heads. This included INR 350 billion outlays for energy security, transition, and net-zero objectives. There has been a target to increase the annual production of green hydrogen too under the Green Hydrogen Mission.[49] India is also expanding its nuclear power production capabilities. INR 9.4 billion is allocated to the Nuclear Power Corporation of India Limited to augment nuclear power capacity. With twenty-two nuclear power reactors currently operational in the country, India would push hard to produce more nuclear power as a source of clean energy.[50]

Again, there is need for caution here. Allocation of funds can be seen as a part of the government's larger vision. We have already discussed the potential traps that India may find itself if not set its goal to what is realistically achievable. The dangers may come from freeing the market too much to impending environmental catastrophes that may further raise serious issues of social justice. For example, pushing the electrical vehicle market too far and too early needs quick development of infrastructure across the country which is, as of now, uncertain. Problems range from deploying untested technology (the explosion of electrical vehicle batteries is certainly a part of such technology) to making enough charging stations available and solving the grid load problem when too many owners try to charge their vehicles at once in any given area.

[47] Electricity Act, 2003 s 61.

[48] International Energy Agency, Renewables 2021: Analysis and Forecast to 2026 <https://iea.blob.core.windows.net/assets/5ae32253-7409-4f9a-a91d-1493ffb9777a/Renewables2021-Analysisandforecastto2026.pdf>.

[49] See Ministry of Finance, 'Highlights of the Union Budget, 2023–24' (1 February 2023) <https://pib.gov.in/PressReleasePage.aspx?PRID=1895315>.

[50] See Department of Atomic Energy, 'Union Minister Dr Jitendra Singh says, 22 Nuclear Power Reactors operational in the country' Press Release (9 February 2023) <https://pib.gov.in/PressReleasePage.aspx?PRID=1897803>.

Similarly, nuclear power brings the challenge of dealing with nuclear waste. Besides, in the case of any nuclear accident, addressing environmental harm has remained a difficult challenge.[51] As a matter of fact, all these issues form a part of the access to energy debate, which must not be viewed narrowly limited only to providing electricity to remote areas at affordable cost. Instead, one must look at it as an unbroken chain of progression. A break in any part will certainly have damaging repercussions for the other parts.

Finally, a quick look at judicial trends is necessary to gain insight into the approach of the judiciary in promoting the cause of greener energy. At least two cases provide us a canvas to argue that courts, thus far, have not provided adequate direction regarding how the government should balance its decisions in respect of the energy market vis-a-vis persuasive issues of species conservation.

The first case, *Power Exchange of India v SEBI*, was a long-standing issue between CERC and SEBI regarding whether electricity should be traded like other commodities through a forward contract.[52] A decade-long dispute had its origin when CERC passed an order against Multi Commodity Exchange of India Limited (MCX) and Forward Market Commission, Ministry of Finance, the Government of India (FMC). Both MCX and FMC filed a writ petition before the Bombay High Court. The court noted the incompatibility between the Forward Contract (Regulation) Act, 1952 (FCRA) and the Electricity Act, 2003. It observed that 'the development of power market nowhere contemplates speculative business/market in electricity'. Hence, CERC was not specifically empowered to do speculative trading or forward trading by overlooking the mandate of the FCRA.

While the appeal was pending before the Supreme Court, the Ministry of Power constituted a committee in 2018 to resolve the issues related to the efficient regulation of electricity derivatives. The committee submitted its report in 2019 and following its recommendations CERC and SEBI have entered into an agreement under which CERC will regulate all the physical delivery-based forward contracts and SEBI will regulate the financial derivatives. Subsequently, the Ministry of Power issued an order in September 2020.[53] Surprisingly, the Supreme Court, in a short judgment, upheld the aforesaid agreement and CERC order. No further explanation was provided as if that long-pending matter had lived its time. Nonetheless, a nagging doubt remains about the division of jurisdiction between CERC and SEBI. It is expected that it will lead to better allocation of risks as it can provide options to the parties to draft the terms of their contracts as per situations.

[51] For understanding risks that are associated with nuclear power plants, see Brice Smith, *Insurmountable Risks: The Dangers of Using Nuclear Power to Combat Global Climate Change* (IEER Press and RDR Books 2006); Saurabh Bhattacharjee, 'Nuclear Energy and Liability—An Environmental Perspective' in Philippe Cullet and Sujith Koonan (eds), *Research Handbook on Law, Environment and the Global South* (Edward Elgar 2019) 322.

[52] *Power Exchange of India v SEBI* 2022 SCC OnLine SC 1051.

[53] Ministry of Power, 'Gate Opened for the Power Market Reforms' (7 October 2021) <https://pib.gov.in/PressReleasePage.aspx?PRID=1761701>.

In contrast, *MK Ranjitsinh v Union of India* was less complicated considering the issues of sustainability presented before the court for adjudication.[54] The issue related to power lines in the states of Rajasthan and Gujarat running through the habitat of the Great Indian Bustard. This was the unfortunate outcome of several ongoing solar and wind power projects in these areas. In April 2021, the Supreme Court directed all concerned agencies to opt for underground power lines on a priority basis and install diverters on the power lines in the interim. The Court constituted a committee to address the technical aspect of putting underground power lines. However, progress was slow, and in April 2022, the Court strongly observed that governments in Gujarat and Rajasthan must install bird diverters in priority areas immediately.

The difference between the two approaches strikes us almost immediately. In Power Exchange, the issue was related to market regulation, and the Court took the side of the government. Neither did the Court deal with the impact of arms-length transactions in electricity market nor did it engage in an analytical discussion of the jurisdictional conundrum unlike the Bombay High Court. Providing much leeway to the government, it was almost the sacred acceptance of a governmental arrangement by the Court. But in *MK Ranjitsinh*, the Court entered into a detailed discussion over environmental harms. However, regarding managing the cost of the transformation of power lines, the Court's solution was unusually simple and clearly, more importance was placed on the conservation of species than on economic and infrastructural challenges that a state government may have to overcome.

The Supreme Court has also contributed to the growth of the non-fossil fuel-based power sector by upholding the regulation on renewable purchase obligations for captive generating units. The Court has highlighted the interrelationship between renewable energy sources and the mandate of the right to a clean environment, read into Article 21 of the Constitution of India.[55] Environmental law has developed through judicial activism in India. Judicial pronouncements such as *Hindustan Zinc Ltd v Rajasthan Electricity Regulatory Commission* and *MK Ranjitsinh* are a precursor to the role of the judiciary in mainstreaming the agenda of renewable energy in India's law and policy discourse by stressing the need to prioritize renewable energy and conservation of species.

Conclusion

Overall, India's renewable energy solutions should address two major challenges—access and affordability. Our discussion reveals that both are interdependent, but they cannot necessarily be solved through linear policy approaches. Climate change, the increasing demand for basic rights, and embedded technological uncertainties have

[54] *MK Ranjitsinh v Union of India* 2021 SCC OnLine SC 326.

[55] *Hindustan Zinc Ltd v Rajasthan Electricity Regulatory Commission* (2015) 12 SCC 611.

only complicated the matter. Several options are on the table for the government and prioritization must be done to share benefits among consumers and producers fairly. Simultaneously, decarbonizing the world does not only depend on intransigent market-based solutions. Rather, a universal change in the energy consumption pattern should be the goal. It is a daunting task to attract investment to make access to renewable energy competitive and an affordable replacement for consumers, bulk or retail. Possibly, a dedicated law to promote renewable energy with a defined role for all the stakeholders is the need of the hour.[56]

Suggestions for Further Reading

Penelope Crossley, *Renewable Energy Law—An International Assessment* (CUP 2019).

Anshuman Gupta and Narendra N Dalei (eds), *Energy, Environment and Globalisation* (Springer 2020).

Tina Soliman Hunter and others (eds), *Routledge Handbook of Energy Law* (Routledge 2020).

Mohammed Naseem and Saman Naseem, *Energy Law in India* (4th edn, Wolters Kluwer 2021).

Usha Tandon (ed), *Energy Law and Policy* (OUP 2018).

56 The Ministry of New and Renewable Energy drafted the National Renewable Energy Act and put it to public consultation in July 2015. See Uday Shankar and Sachin Kumar PP, 'National Renewable Energy Act 2015: A Critical Analysis' (2020) 45 *Cochin University Law Review* 69.

PART XI

ENFORCEMENT AND LITIGATION

CHAPTER 40

PENALTIES AND COMPENSATION

DHVANI MEHTA AND DEBADITYO SINHA*

Abstract

This chapter examines the different legislative and judicial routes for the imposition of penalties and the award of compensation for harm to the environment. An important aspect is the development of the standard of absolute liability by the Supreme Court of India, the incorporation of the polluter pays principle, and the creation of long-term mechanisms to remediate the long-term harms of activities like the diversion of forest land and mining. The chapter focuses on the manner in which the National Green Tribunal assesses damage to the environment and quantifies compensation. It argues that the Tribunal continues to be influenced by some of the mechanisms used by the Supreme Court to grant compensation, such as the use of expert committees, and calculating compensation as a percentage of the project cost. It further argues that Indian environmental regulation needs compliance and enforcement mechanisms other than the criminal penalties prescribed under its statutes.

Introduction

INDIAN environmental law can broadly be characterized as command-and-control regulation bolstered by the jurisprudence of the Supreme Court of India (Supreme Court),

* The authors are grateful to Tarika Jain and Himanshu Ahlawat for their research assistance with this chapter.

and more recently, the National Green Tribunal (NGT). Penalties and compensation are very important components, forming the bedrock of enforcement and redressal. While penalties have their foundation in Indian environmental statutes, compensation evolved with the Supreme Court's development of the standard of absolute liability[1] and its incorporation of the polluter pays principle.[2] The concept of compensation for environmental harm found statutory expression, with the enactment of the National Green Tribunal Act, 2010 (NGT Act), and the NGT has developed its own jurisprudence on environmental compensation.

This chapter provides an overview of the different ways in which penalties and compensation find expression in Indian environmental law and analyses, critically, their use and limitations . This chapter is based on laws as of 15 May 2023.

Section 40.1 discusses the rationale for using penalties and compensation as enforcement and redressal tools. It also maps the different mechanisms through which penalties and compensation are awarded under Indian law. Section 40.2 critically analyses the use of penalties and compensation. Since there is already a substantial body of literature on the Supreme Court's environmental jurisprudence,[3] we discuss the NGT's cases in greater detail. Section 40.3 identifies an emerging challenge to Indian environmental law in how the NGT imposes what it calls 'environmental compensation charges' followed by the conclusion.

40.1 Statutory and Judicial Expressions of Penalties and Compensation

This section provides an overarching view of the different penalties and mechanisms for compensation in Indian environmental law and describes how penalties and compensation are understood in the literature.

40.1.1 Theoretical Conception of Penalties and Compensation

Penalties: regulatory theory in environmental law recognizes that 'the core aim of a sanctioning system should not be to punish per se but to change behaviour'.[4] Keeping

[1] *MC Mehta v Union of India (Shriram–Oleum Gas)* (1987) 1 SCC 395.

[2] *Indian Council for Enviro-legal Action v Union of India and Others* (1996) 3 SCC 212 (Bicchri case); *Vellore Citizens' Welfare Forum v Union of India* (1996) 5 SCC 647.

[3] E.g., Geetanjoy Sahu, *Environmental Jurisprudence and the Supreme Court* (Orient BlackSwan 2014); Shibani Ghosh (ed), *Indian Environmental Law: Key Concepts and Principles* (Orient BlackSwan 2019).

[4] Richard Macrory, *Regulation, Enforcement and Governance in Environmental Law* (2nd edn, Hart 2014) 14.

this aim in mind, regulatory agencies may choose between 'deterrence' and 'advise and persuade' as two broad enforcement styles, with the former referring to 'the sanctioning of rule-breaking behaviour' and the latter emphasizing 'cooperation' and 'conciliation'.[5] In this chapter, penalties are part of the former strategy—as later sections demonstrate, the Supreme Court and the NGT see punishment and deterrence as key factors driving their imposition.

As far as the legislative expression of penalties is concerned, Indian primary laws generally define the offence and prescribe the punishment. While the punishment can sometimes be delegated to subordinate legislation, as a safeguard, the legislature must fix the maximum punishment in the primary statute.[6] Where the power to prescribe punishments is delegated to an authority other than the state or central government, it ought to be exercised with the prior sanction or subsequent approval of such government.[7] It is also clear that penalties cannot be imposed by an authority unless specific powers to this effect have been bestowed on it by a statute.[8]

Compensation: unlike penalties, which, if effectively deployed, are intended to achieve certain kinds of environment-protecting behaviour, liability regimes, of which compensation is a key component, have been described as far removed from being tools to achieve the optimal enforcement of environment protection law.[9] In contrast with penalties, 'liability mechanisms do not usually contain a preventive action dimension, but apply once environmental damage has occurred'.[10] Traditionally, compensation was awarded for individual harm, while penalties were seen as serving a wider, societal function.

Both these conceptions are now turning on their heads. As we move away from an anthropocentric understanding of environmental harm, compensation for environmental damage is treated as harm in its own right, in addition to its impact on humans and their property.[11] This is reflected in the provisions of the NGT Act, described in more detail in the next section. Similarly, there is also a recognition that penalties have a restorative component in addition to performing a sanctioning and deterring function.[12] It is in this expansive sense that compensation is used in this chapter.

[5] Robert Baldwin, Martin Cave, and Martin Lodge (eds), *The Oxford Handbook of Regulation* (OUP 2010) 121.

[6] BR Atre, *Legislative Drafting* (4th edn, Universal Law Publishing 2014) 229.

[7] ibid.

[8] *Khemka & Co (Agencies) Pvt Ltd v State of Maharashtra* (1975) 2 SCC 22.

[9] Martin Hedemann-Robinson, *Enforcement of European Environmental Law: Legal Issues and Challenges* (2nd edn, Routledge 2015) 593.

[10] ibid.

[11] ibid 594–600.

[12] Macrory (n 4) 43.

40.1.2 Penal Provisions Across Indian Environmental Statutes

Penalties in Indian environmental law are criminal penalties that follow the template first set by early environmental statutes—the Water (Prevention and Control of Pollution) Act, 1974 (Water Pollution Act), the Air (Prevention and Control of Pollution) Act, 1981 (Air Pollution Act), and the Environment (Protection) Act, 1986 (Environmental Protection Act).

Violations under these Acts are punished with imprisonment and/or a fine only after a criminal trial results in a conviction. There are some exceptions to this model. For instance, rule 21 of the E-Waste (Management) Rules, 2016, and rule 23 of the Hazardous and Other Wastes (Management and Transboundary Movement) Rules, 2016 empower the State Pollution Control Boards (SPCBs) to impose financial penalties directly for violations. However, criminal penalties are the dominant norm, including in conservation laws like the Wild Life (Protection) Act, 1972 (WLPA), the Forest (Conservation) Act, 1980 (FCA), and the Biological Diversity Act, 2002 (BDA). Most offences are also no-fault liability offences,[13] with an exception under the Water Pollution Act.[14]

The next sub-section describes the statutory scheme in greater detail across two broad categories of environmental laws: pollution control and conservation.

Pollution control laws: the Air Pollution Act and the Water Pollution Act prescribe specific penalties for specific acts or omissions—discharging air pollutants in excess of the standards prescribed by the SPCBs,[15] discharging sewage or trade effluents without the previous consent of the SPCBs,[16] obstructing any person acting under the orders or the directions of the Pollution Control Boards (PCBs) or failing to furnish information required by them.[17]

These laws also contain a general catch-all provision that prescribes a penalty for the contravention of any provisions for which a specific penalty has not been provided.[18] The Environmental Protection Act contains a single, blanket provision that prescribes a maximum penalty for a violation of any of the provisions of the Act or rules, orders or directions issued under it.[19] There are no specific offences or penalties prescribed in subordinate legislation. The E-Waste Rules and Hazardous Waste Management Rules link these penalties to those provided under the Environmental Protection Act.

[13] Environment (Protection) Act, 1986 s 15; Water (Prevention and Control of Pollution) Act, 1974 s 44; Air (Prevention and Control of Pollution) Act, 1981 s 22.

[14] Water Pollution Act s 24 prevents persons from 'knowingly' using a stream or well to dispose of polluting matter.

[15] Air Pollution Act s 37.

[16] Water Pollution Act s 44.

[17] Air Pollution Act s 38 and Water Pollution Act s 42 contain similar provisions as regards the latter two actions.

[18] Air Pollution Act s 39 and Water Pollution Act s 45A.

[19] Environment Protection Act s 15.

The power to initiate prosecutions under these pollution control laws forms one of the two principal enforcement tools at the disposal of PCB officials, the second being the power to issue orders closing down or prohibiting any industry, operation or process and stop or regulate the supply of water and electricity.[20]

Conservation laws: forest and wildlife conservation laws are similar but enforced by different officials. These laws also contain provisions on compounding. For instance, under the Indian Forest Act, 1927, the state government may empower a Forest Officer not below the rank of a Ranger to accept compensation to compound an offence.[21] The FCA has a single penalty of simple imprisonment for up to fifteen days for violating any restrictions that the Act places.[22] The WLPA also has a general overarching penalty for violating any of its provisions,[23] and permits compounding of offences.[24]

40.1.3 Judicial and Legislative Routes for Compensation

This sub-section provides an overview of the different judicial and statutory mechanisms through which compensation can be obtained, with particular emphasis on the Supreme Court's contribution to this jurisprudence.

Common law and writ jurisdiction: apart from statutory penalties, civil remedies for environmental harms have always existed under the common law.[25] Ordinary civil courts have rarely been used in the recent past to bring claims for compensation for environmental harms. Tortious actions have often involved private disputes regarding environmental nuisances.[26]

After the Supreme Court opened its doors to public interest litigation in the 1980s, large-scale environmental harms have been addressed through its writ jurisdiction. Although the Supreme Court does not traditionally award compensation in petitions under Article 32 of the Constitution, there have been several instances in which the Court has ordered such relief in environmental cases.

Perhaps the first seminal contribution of the Supreme Court to the award of environmental compensation was in its development of the standard of absolute liability.[27] The standard laid down by the Court has gone on to inform later statutory regimes, with both the Public Liability Insurance Act, 1991 (PLIA) and the NGT Act incorporating no-fault liability.[28]

[20] Air Pollution Act s 31A and Water Pollution Act s 33A.

[21] Indian Forest Act, 1927 s 68.

[22] Forest (Conservation) Act, 1980 s 3A.

[23] Wild Life (Protection) Act, 1972 s 51.

[24] ibid s 54.

[25] Shyam Divan and Armin Rosencranz, *Environmental Law and Policy in India: Cases and Materials* (3rd edn, OUP 2022) 152.

[26] *JC Galstaun v Dunia Lal Seal* (1905) 9 CWN 612, 617; *Venkatappa v B Lovis AIR* 1986 AP 239; *Ram Baj Singh v Babu Lal AIR* 1982 All 285.

[27] *MC Mehta (Shriram–Oleum Gas)* (n 1).

[28] Divan and Rosencranz (n 25) 836–837.

Apart from this, the Court's incorporation of the polluter pays principle into domestic environmental law has formed the principal basis for the award of compensation, with the NGT now applying this principle while passing its orders and decisions.[29] The polluter pays principle was used for the first time by the Court in *Indian Council for Enviro-legal Action v Union of India (Bichhri)* case.[30] In contrast to the *MC Mehta v Union of India (Oleum Gas Leak)* case, where the industry in question was not operating in violation of the law,[31] the *Bichhri* case involved many years of illegalities, with the offending chemical industries having operated without the appropriate statutory consent, and dumping toxic sludge, to the detriment of the health of villagers and their environment. Therefore, the Court located the liability of the polluting industries to take remedial measures in the absolute liability standard, as well as the polluter pays principle.[32] Since the *Bichhri* case, the Court has applied the polluter pays principle to impose liability for remedial measures in other cases as well.[33] The polluter pays principle brought about an evolution in domestic Indian environmental jurisprudence in the sense that it recognized the liability of the offender to take remedial measures in addition to compensating individual and community harms. However, in the cases through which this jurisprudence was developed, the offending activities in question violated environmental laws. It has been argued that the Court has also developed another form of the polluter pays principle for the indiscriminate use of natural resources, called the 'user pays principle'.[34] Thus, in *Goa Foundation v Union of India*,[35] the Court recognized the limits of regulatory authorities in restoring environmental damage due to mining operations, and therefore, ordered the creation of a Goa Iron Ore Permanent Fund. This Fund is to comprise 10 per cent of the sale proceeds of iron ore excavated in Goa and will be used for sustainable development and inter-generational equity. The Court has similarly applied its mind to the question of recouping ecological loss in *TN Godavarman Thirumulpad v Union of India* by requiring users of forest land to pay the 'net present value' of such land to compensate for the loss of benefits flowing from it.[36]

The Court's articulation of absolute liability and its incorporation of the polluter pays principle are its key contributions to the understanding of compensation in Indian environmental law. A more critical analysis of these follows in the next section.

[29] National Green Tribunal Act, 2010 s 20.

[30] *Indian Council for Enviro-legal Action v Union of India* (1996) 3 SCC 212. See also Lovleen Bhullar, 'The Polluter Pays Principle: Scope and Limits of Judicial Decisions' in Shibani Ghosh (ed), *Indian Environmental Law: Key Concepts and Principles* (Orient BlackSwan 2019) 152.

[31] *MC Mehta (Shriram–Oleum Gas)* (n 1).

[32] ibid paras 66 and 67.

[33] *Vellore Citizens' Welfare Forum* (n 2); *MC Mehta v Kamal Nath* (1997) 1 SCC 388.

[34] Bhullar (n 30) 173.

[35] *Goa Foundation v Union of India* (2014) 6 SCC 590.

[36] *TN Godavarman Thirumulpad v Union of India* (2006) 1 SCC 1. For a more detailed discussion of the Court's articulation of 'net present value', see Srilekha Sridhar, *Compensatory Afforestation and Net Present Value Payments for Diversion of Forest Land in India* (Kalpavriksh 2012).

Environmental compensation under the NGT Act: the NGT was created as a specialized agency to provide quick relief for environmental harms by applying judicial and technical expertise. It has the power to award 'relief and compensation to the victims of pollution and other environmental damage arising under the enactments specified in Schedule I'.[37] Additionally, the NGT may also order the restitution of the property damaged and of the environment[38] under any or all of the fourteen separate heads listed in Schedule II of the NGT Act. Relief can be claimed for death, disability, medical expenses, damages to crops, trees, orchards, milch and draught animals, and a loss of business or employment. Relief can also be awarded for]damage to the environment or to fauna and flora. The latter is more complicated to quantify, and it is here that the specialized expertise of the NGT is particularly needed. The second section of this chapter discusses whether and how the NGT uses this expertise.

Relief under the Public Liability Insurance Act, 1991: PLIA gave legislative expression to the principle of absolute liability developed by the Supreme Court. The Act makes industries that handle hazardous substances absolutely liable to provide relief for death or injury to persons (other than workmen) or damage to property due to an accident. The owner of any such industry must subscribe to an insurance policy, and remit an additional sum to the insurer. This additional sum is, in turn, to be deposited in the Environment Relief Fund (ERF). When an accident occurs, claims are to be made to the Collector, who can order the insurer to deposit money, make disbursals from the ERF, and require the owner of the industry to deposit an additional amount.[39] The ERF plays a dual role in environmental law. Under the NGT Act, where any amount is ordered to be paid by the Tribunal for compensation or relief, it is first to be credited to this ERF. However, disbursals from the ERF, whether for industrial accidents or for compensation awarded by the NGT, appear to be low and do not correspond either to the scale of accidents that have taken place or the orders of the NGT respectively.[40]

40.2 Critical Analysis of the Use of Penalties and Compensation

This section critically analyses the different legislative and judicial mechanisms for imposing penalties and compensation under Indian law. Given the limited tortious

[37] NGT Act s 15(1)(a).
[38] ibid ss 15(1)(b) and (c).
[39] Debadityo Sinha, *The Management of Environment Relief Fund* (Vidhi Centre for Legal Policy 2020).
[40] ibid.

actions for environmental wrongs in Indian law, we focus on the different ways in which the Supreme Court and the NGT assess and quantify damages and award compensation.

40.2.1 Weak Penalties and Lengthy Trials

The deterrent value of penalties under the existing law is weak—the highest named penalty under the Environmental Protection Act is only INR 100,000. This weak deterrent effect is further diluted by the delay inherent in the trial process in India. According to data from the National Crime Records Bureau (NCRB), overall court pendency in 2020 for offences against the environment stands at 75.1 per cent, with an even higher rate of 98.2 per cent for offences specifically under the Environmental Protection Act.[41]

Data from the NCRB provides some insights into the kinds of environmental offences prosecuted, their conviction rate and the pendency rate. For 2020, the Bureau reports a 78.1 per cent increase in cases registered under environment-related offences from the previous year. However, when these cases are disaggregated by type, it is cases under the Cigarette and Other Tobacco Products Act, 2003, register the highest number (49,710), forming 80.5 per cent of the total cases registered. This is followed by cases under noise pollution laws at the central and state level with a total of 7,318 cases.[42]

This crime data, although it ostensibly demonstrates an upward tick in the registration, prosecution, and conviction of environment-related cases,[43] largely confirms previous analyses of the state of Indian environmental law enforcement—that it is slow and ineffective, partially because of the limited resources of enforcement authorities and the lengthy trial process in lower courts necessitated in the absence of civil penalties.

The structure of Indian environmental regulation also makes it difficult to tailor penalties to the many kinds of violations that might be committed. Penalties are only prescribed in primary legislation, such as the Environmental Protection Act, which contains a catch-all penalty for any violation of any of its provisions, as well as the many rules, orders, and directions that might be issued under it.[44] There is a vast array of violations that fall within this net, all of which are technically liable to the same criminal penalty—from operating a coal washery without obtaining environmental clearance,[45] to recycling plastic bags without registration,[46] to failing to maintain records of the incineration of biomedical waste.[47]

[41] Only thirty-two cases under the Environment Protection Act were disposed in 2020, with 1,786 pending. See National Crime Records Bureau, Ministry of Home Affairs, *Crime in India 2020: Statistics*, Volume 1 (NCRB 2020).

[42] ibid.

[43] ibid 7, Table 1.3.

[44] Environment Protection Act s 15.

[45] Environment Impact Assessment Notification, 2006.

[46] Plastic Waste (Management and Handling) Rules, 2011 r 9(b).

[47] Bio-Medical Waste Management Rules, 2016 r 4(s).

While the liability to pay environmental compensation has now been codified through the NGT Act, the tribunal has also liberally interpreted provisions under the Air Pollution Act, the Water Pollution Act, and the Environmental Protection Act to empower itself and the PCBs to impose 'environmental compensation charges' that more closely resemble penalties than compensation. However, before discussing the legal authority (or lack of it) for exercising such powers, the following section provides an overview of how environmental damage has been assessed and compensation quantified.

40.2.2 Inconsistent Methodology in Awarding Compensation

This sub-section discusses and compares the way the Supreme Court and the NGT assess environmental damage and quantify compensation.

The Supreme Court: there are at least three distinct mechanisms that the Supreme Court has employed in its decisions involving compensation. The first is the correlation between the magnitude and capacity of the enterprise, and the amount of compensation payable by it. This was laid down by the Court in the *Oleum Gas Leak* case and continues to be used by it.[48]

Another similar method of arriving at a compensatory amount is to order a deposit of some percentage of the project cost towards the restoration of the environment. However, the basis for this calculation is not always clear. For instance, in *Goa Foundation*, the Court ordered the deposit of 10 per cent of the sale proceeds from iron ore in Goa in a Permanent Fund.[49] In a more recent case, the Court awarded damages to the tune of INR 1 billion or 10 per cent of the project cost by stating that it was the 'general law' that damages be awarded as a certain component of a particular project's costs.[50]

Since the Supreme Court does not have specialized expertise itself, it has used a range of fact-finding or expert bodies to assess environmental damage and report on the cost of remedial measures.[51] These expert bodies include the National Environmental Engineering Research Institute, specifically constituted committees, or, as in *Vellore Citizens' Welfare Forum v Union of India*, an authority that the central government was ordered to constitute under its powers under section 3 of the Environmental Protection Act.[52]

[48] *MC Mehta (Shriram–Oleum Gas)* (n 1); *Sterlite Industries Limited v Union of India* (2013) 4 SCC 575.

[49] *Goa Foundation* (n 35).

[50] *Goel Ganga India Developers Private Limited v Union of India*, through Secretary, Ministry of Environment, Forest (2018) 18 SCC 257.

[51] Dhvani Mehta, 'The Judicial Implementation of Environmental Law in India' in Shibani Ghosh (ed), *Indian Environmental Law: Key Concepts and Principles* (Orient BlackSwan 2019) 286.

[52] *Vellore Citizens' Welfare Forum* (n 2).

As the next sub-section demonstrates, all these mechanisms are also visible in the NGT's functioning. However, the NGT has unduly co-opted the Supreme Court's approach, resulting in a reduced quantum of compensation without any accompanying rationale.[53]

The NGT: while the Supreme Court's limitations in adjudicating environmental questions are understandable, this is not the case for the NGT. As we have already emphasized, the legislative intention underlying the creation of the NGT was to apply specialized expertise to the resolution of environmental issues, in particular, the assessment of environmental damage and the quantification of compensation. The inherent polycentric nature of environmental problems might make it difficult to calculate the exact amount of environmental compensation precisely. However, what has marked the NGT's functioning over the last ten years or so is the absence of a concerted effort to use its specialized expertise and develop a methodology to this effect.

In this sub-section, we argue that, broadly, the NGT has not used its specialized expertise to develop a sound, scientific, and principled basis for the assessment and quantification of environmental harm, and that there is no consistency in the way in which it awards compensation.[54] We draw these conclusions based on our analysis of orders passed by all benches of the NGT between 2014 and 2017, with the specific objective of studying how the NGT awarded compensation.[55]

Guesswork: two examples of cases where the NGT has resorted to guesswork relate to large-scale environmental violations by industries, one regarding the discharge of untreated effluents by various industries into the river Ganga,[56] the other relating to the illegal mining, crushing, and transportation of minor minerals from the river Yamuna in the states of Uttar Pradesh and Haryana.[57] In the first case, the NGT stated that it was not possible to assess the cost of environmental damage and restoration accurately, given the long duration over which the violations had been occurring. It cited the Supreme Court's decision in the *Oleum Gas Leak* case on absolute liability and ordered environmental compensation of INR five crores to be deposited, which was to be used to clean and prevent pollution in water canals. In the second case, the NGT goes so far as to say that the application of limited guesswork is an accepted principle, although the inability of the NGT to assess the extent of the damage was also partially because state governments did not place on record the amount of money that would be required to restore the ecological damage to the Yamuna.

[53] Raghuveer Nath and Armin Rosencranz, 'Determination of Environmental Compensation: The Art of Living Case' (2019) 12 *NUJS Law Review* 1.

[54] ibid.

[55] Research available on file with the authors.

[56] *Krishan Kant Singh v National Ganga River Basin Authority* MANU/GT/0130/2014 (NGT-Principal Bench) para 51.

[57] *Gurpreet Singh Bagga v Ministry of Environment and Forests* MANU/GT/0022/2016 (NGT-Principal Bench).

Capacity to pay: like the Supreme Court cases discussed earlier, the NGT has also linked environmental compensation to the capacity to pay, especially when it awards a percentage of the project cost as compensation. In *Forward Foundation v State of Karnataka,* the NGT, relying on the Supreme Court's judgment in *Goa Foundation,* required the defaulting companies to pay 5 per cent of the project cost to compensate for environmental damage.[58]

Anthropocentric approach to assessing environmental damage: where the NGT has applied some methodology to quantify compensation, such cases have involved losses to human life or property. This was the case in *Ramdas Janardan Koli v Ministry of Environment and Forests,* which related to the loss of fishing rights in Mumbai because of industrial activity.[59] The NGT dismissed the initial compensation amount determined by the government and developed its own methodology to calculate the appropriate amount that would be required to recompense the affected 1,630 families. The NGT made estimations about the average size of the family, factored in the daily income of a family of this size, the number of years for which their earnings were likely to be affected, and the time it would take them to switch to another trade.

Even in cases where the NGT recognizes the impact on the ecology or biodiversity, it has been unable to provide a detailed assessment of this impact or a comprehensive methodology to calculate compensation. In *Samir Mehta v Union of India*, the NGT was called on to assess the damage caused by the sinking of a ship carrying large quantities of petroleum oil and coal near the Mumbai coast.[60] Although the Tribunal relied on expert reports and case studies from other jurisdictions to conclude that the oil spill would have a significant negative impact on the marine ecology, it ultimately resorted to a form of guesswork while ordering the shipping company to pay environmental compensation amounting to INR 100,00,00,000.

Delegation: the NGT frequently delegates the task of assessing environmental damage and quantifying compensation. Specific measures required for environmental restoration are also delegated, often to regional authorities like the District Collectors, PCBs, Forest Departments, or expert committees specifically constituted for the purpose. The reliance on external experts must be understood in the context of vacancies and appointments to the NGT. The ability of the NGT to play the specialized role intended for it is directly dependent on the appointment of its members. Under the NGT Act, a minimum of ten full-time judicial members and ten full-time expert members are required for the Tribunal to function. According to an NGT report dated 1 January 2021, the NGT was functioning with just one chairperson, two judicial and two expert members.[61] Although more members, including expert members, have been appointed

58 *Forward Foundation v State of Karnataka* MANU/GT/0089/2015 (NGT-Principal Bench); Goa Foundation (n 35).

59 *Ramdas Janardan Koli v Ministry of Environment and Forests* OA No 87 of 2013, Order of 18 February 2014 (NGT-Western Zone Bench).

60 *Samir Mehta v Union of India* MANU/GT/0104/2016 (NGT-Principal Bench).

61 See Information relating to the National Green Tribunal under s 4(1)(b) of the Right to Information Act, 2005 < https://greentribunal.gov.in/sites/default/files/rti_gazette_notification/RTI%20MANUAL%20upto%2001.01.2021.pdf>.

recently, none of them appears to have specialized knowledge related to ecosystems and biodiversity.[62] This impacts the way the NGT is able to perform its primary function of assessing damage and calculating and awarding environmental compensation.

The objective of this section was to provide a critical analysis of one aspect of the role of the Supreme Court and the NGT in performing a function that is a particular challenge of environmental law—quantifying harm and assessing loss. It demonstrated that despite creating a specialized Tribunal, no especially unique methods, significantly different from those that the Supreme Court had adopted, have been developed by the NGT. Instead, as the next section will demonstrate, an emerging concern is that the NGT is not performing the function that it was intended for but straying into the domain of the legislature and the executive.

40.3 Blurred Boundaries Between Compensation and Penalties

This section discusses a specific aspect of the deployment of compensation and penalties under Indian environmental law and presents it as one of the emerging challenges to the credibility of the NGT and an indication of the failure of the existing regulatory regime. It argues that both the Supreme Court and the NGT do not always award environmental compensation in the way it is theoretically described in the first section of this chapter.

The Supreme Court has always been mindful of the need for environmental damages to perform both a compensatory and a deterrent function. For example, in *Vellore*, the Court used the polluter pays principle to impose a fine on the offending tanneries.[63] Similarly, in *MC Mehta v Kamal Nath*, the Court ordered the motel to show cause why an additional pollution fine ought not to be imposed on it.[64]

Both these are landmark cases in Indian environmental jurisprudence. Both cases also make a distinction between penalties and compensation—the penalty is the punishment for illegal action, and the compensation is the amount that is required to restore the damaged environment to its original state, although the penalty is also to be used for such restoration. Nevertheless, the deterrent function of compensatory damages has always been prominent in the Court's orders, beginning with the *Oleum Gas Leak* case. One of the reasons for linking the compensation payable to the magnitude and capacity of the enterprise was the need for it to have a deterrent effect.[65] While the compensatory amounts might have changed over the years, the principle that such amount should also have a deterrent effect continues to be reflected in the Court's judgments. In *Sterlite*

62 See <https://greentribunal.gov.in/judicial-present-members>.

63 *Vellore Citizens' Welfare Forum* (n 2).

64 *MC Mehta v Kamal Nath* (n 33).

65 *MC Mehta (Shriram–Oleum Gas)* (n 1) para 32.

Industries Limited v Union of India, the Court's order to deposit INR 1 billion is based on the argument that a smaller amount would not have the desired deterrent effect.[66]

The use of 'environmental compensation charges' as a regulatory tool to disincentivize certain kinds of behaviour or to recover the cost of some activities that necessarily have an adverse environmental impact is also seen in one of the Supreme Court's orders in its long-running air pollution case.[67] The Supreme Court declared that light and heavy-duty commercial vehicles entering Delhi after a particular date would have to pay an environmental compensation charge, which was later doubled. This use of environmental compensation charges, even beyond the imposition of a pseudo-penalty is now a mechanism regularly adopted by the NGT.

40.3.1 The NGT and Environmental Compensation Charges

The static nature of penalties under Indian environmental law has meant that the concept of environmental compensation has expanded to include things it was not traditionally intended to encompass. The NGT and PCBs, through the device of environmental compensation charges, have been filling the regulatory void created by the absence of civil penalties. While there is certainly a case to be made out for such penalties, their imposition by the NGT and the PCBs, without express statutory authorization, casts doubt over their legitimacy and leaves them open to legal challenge.

This sub-section describes the different ways the NGT awards environmental compensation, or as the NGT sometimes terms them, 'environmental compensation charges'. These charges more closely resemble penalties because they are either awarded as punishments for illegal action or intended to operate as standardized, prospective fines for certain violations. However, it should be noted that the NGT does not have the power to award penalties under the NGT Act for general violations of environmental law. Its power is restricted to the award of compensation or relief. It may only impose penalties for non-compliance with its own orders, awards, or decisions.[68]

Link Between Compensation and Illegal Action: as mentioned earlier, the NGT often relies on the 'magnitude, capacity and prosperity' of the polluting units to determine liability for compensation.[69] This imparts the character of a penalty to the final compensation award. The size of the polluting unit and the extent of environmental damage do not need to be linked. A small polluting unit emitting a hazardous substance could have far-reaching and damaging effects on the environment. As demonstrated

66 *Sterlite Industries Limited v Union of India* (2013) 4 SCC 575.

67 *MC Mehta v Union of India* Interlocutory Application No 365 of 2015 in WP (Civil) No 13029 of 1985, Order of 9 October 2015 (Supreme Court).

68 National Green Tribunal Act, 2010 s 26.

69 *Krishan Kant Singh* (n 56).

earlier, the intention of the Supreme Court in linking this capacity to pay to the compensation awarded was specifically to have a deterrent effect. However, a deterrent function is usually performed by penalties (see Section 40.1).

Apart from this, the NGT has also held companies 'liable to pay compensation under the polluter pays principle, for the illegal and unauthorized construction carried out in violation of the environmental laws and prior to grant of environmental clearance'.[70] The NGT links violations to compensation, not by assessing the extent of environmental damage, but by recognizing that violations are necessarily likely to affect the environment adversely, and therefore require compensation. In such cases, compensation awarded by the NGT has the character of a penalty, especially when it states that the 'liability *primarily* accrues on account of the illegal and unauthorised activities'.[71]

In other cases, the NGT makes it clear that the compensation being awarded is necessary both for the restoration and restitution of the environment as well as an expression of liability for illegal actions.[72] In fact, in *Krishan Lal Gera v State of Haryana*, the NGT awarded two separate sums: an initial deposit of 5 per cent of the project cost as environmental compensation, and a sum of INR five crores for commencing the project without the appropriate authorization.[73]

In this manner, the NGT routinely orders the payment of compensation, which is a penalty for a violation of the law. In some cases, a specific link is drawn between such violation and environmental damage; in others, it is clear that the NGT wishes to attribute liability separately for the contravention. This is why a standard amount is usually ordered to be deposited in the first instance, only to be adjusted later against a more exact determination of the extent of environmental damage.[74]

Prospective Environmental Compensation Charges: in other cases, the NGT appears to be performing functions of a legislative nature by prescribing fixed environmental compensation charges to be imposed for past and prospective activities that might damage the environment. Here, there is no significant assessment of the damage or calculation of environmental compensation; instead, a pre-determined minimum amount is ordered as a token to be adjusted should significant damage be established.

For example, in *Manoj Mishra v Union of India*, the NGT imposed a minimum fixed compensation of INR 50,000 for dumping construction debris onto the floodplain or the riverbed of the river Yamuna, and another INR 5,000 for throwing worship material into the river.[75] The rationale that the judges provided was that such activity was bound to pollute the river; at the same time, it was not practically possible to determine the exact amount of compensation, so a fixed charge was calculated based on an estimate of the resources that it would take to remove waste and debris from the river. This

[70] *Forward Foundation* (n 58).

[71] ibid.

[72] *SP Muthuraman v Union of India* MANU/GT/0116/2015 (NGT-Principal Bench).

[73] *Krishan Lal Gera v State of Haryana* MANU/GT/0140/2015 (NGT-Principal Bench).

[74] *SP Muthuraman* (n 72).

[75] *Manoj Mishra v Union of India* 2015 SCC OnLine NGT 840.

pattern repeats itself in several cases. The NGT has ordered environmental compensation of INR 50,000 to be imposed on builders dumping construction and demolition waste in the biodegradable waste collection system.[76] In the same case, lower amounts were directed to be paid for the failure to segregate biodegradable waste and for the open burning of solid waste. This kind of prospective compensation was also extended beyond polluting activities. In *Rohit Choudhary v Union of India*, the NGT ordered environmental compensation of INR 5,000 over and above the *challan* prescribed under the Motor Vehicles Act, 1988, in all accidents involving over-speeding of vehicles and causing animal deaths near Kaziranga National Park.[77]

In these cases, the NGT is not responding only to an actual violation before it and determining the environmental compensation or relief. Instead, it is defines a violation and prescribes the consequence for such violation whenever it should occur. This is a classic legislative function. Like the Supreme Court case mentioned earlier that imposed environmental compensation charges on certain kinds of vehicles, the NGT has authorized public authorities or municipal corporations to require the general public to contribute to the expenditure related to sewage treatment or disposal in the National Capital Territory of Delhi, citing the polluter pays principle.[78]

The NGT has certainly been very creative in its interpretation of 'environmental compensation'. There is no doubt that violating an environmental rule causes damage and harm and that harm requires compensation. Neither is there any doubt that most daily activities in modern life, whether driving vehicles or disposing of sewage have an environmental cost. It is also not in question that these environmental harms and costs must be recompensed. The NGT sees all of these as integral to the polluter pays principle and has been awarding environmental compensation on this basis.

However, the danger with the imposition of such penalties or taxes by the NGT in the guise of environmental compensation is that it does not necessarily reflect societal understanding of the harm of a particular activity. Since the NGT also does not attempt to quantify the impact that such activity comprehensively has on the environment, it makes the imposition of such charges even less legitimate.

40.3.2 Pollution Control Boards and Environmental Compensation Charges

The PCBs do not explicitly have the power to impose penalties or award compensation under the existing legal framework. However, they have been conferred some powers in this regard by the NGT. One of these is the power to lay down guidelines/methodology

[76] *Sangli Zilaha Sudhar Samiti v Commissioner, Sangli Miraj* OA No 115 of 2014 (NGT-Western Zone Bench).

[77] *Rohit Choudhary v Union of India* OA No 174 of 2013, Order of 17 May 2017 (NGT-Principal Bench).

[78] *Manoj Mishra v Union of India* OA No 6 of 2012, Order of 8 May 2015 (NGT–Principal Bench).

for calculating environmental compensation charges for different kinds of pollution, which challenges the traditional notions of penalties and compensation.

Methodology Developed by the CPCB to Impose Environmental Compensation: the NGT had not developed a sophisticated methodology for assessing and quantifying the damage. In fact, it is the CPCB that claims to have made the first attempt in India to develop a methodology for assessing environmental compensation.[79] This attempt was made in compliance with the orders of the NGT in a case dealing with the lack of functional effluent treatment plants.[80] Among other things, the NGT empowered the CPCB to take penal action for those failing to set up the appropriate effluent treatment plants. In addition, the CPCB was empowered to assess and recover compensation for environmental damage in the form of environmental compensation charges.

The guidelines developed by the CPCB in response to this direction take several important steps towards quantifying environmental compensation. The CPCB has developed a formula that factors in the number of days for which a violation continued, the scale of the operation, its location, and the pollution index, which denotes the degree of pollution hazard from a particular category of industry.[81] All of these are relevant factors in determining the environmental compensation to be levied.

However, aspects of the CPCB guidelines appear to conflate environmental compensation charges and penalties. For instance, in the introduction to its report, the CPCB states that the objective of imposing environmental compensation charges is 'to make defaulters realise their mistake'. The guidelines prescribe a *minimum* environmental compensation charge that must be imposed, irrespective of the formula developed, and exponentially increase such charges so as to have a *deterrent* effect on violators. The guidelines also list specific instances in which environmental compensation charges are to be imposed. In some instances, these charges are linked to the actual environmental damage caused by a particular action (accidental or intentional discharges of effluents), but in others, such as the intentional avoidance of data submission, there appears to be no such link. All of these suggest that the NGT, and therefore, the CPCB, view the latter's power to award environmental compensation as a way to penalize unlawful action.

In fact, in another part of the report, the CPCB also levies fixed environmental compensation charges for different kinds of violations of the Graded Response Action Plan to improve air quality in the Delhi National Capital Region.[82] These charges are graded depending upon the ambient air quality, with fixed amounts for different kinds of activities such as industrial emissions and violations at construction sites. These fixed charges presumably reflect the difficulty of quantifying the impact of emissions from a

[79] CPCB, 'Report of the CPCB In-house Committee on Methodology for Assessing Environmental Compensation and Action Plan to Utilize the Fund' (2019) (CPCB Methodology).

[80] *Paryavaran Suraksha Samiti v Union of India* OA No 593 of 2017, Order of 28 August 2019 (NGT-Principal Bench).

[81] CPCB Methodology (n 79) 4–5.

[82] ibid 9.

particular industry on air quality, but precisely because of their fixed nature, they closely resemble penalties.

There are other kinds of actions for which the CPCB has developed a methodology to calculate environmental compensation charges, all of which reflect some attempt to quantify environmental damage. For example, for untreated solid waste dumped in violation of existing rules, the CPCB has recommended that the compensation charges recover the costs saved by the offending unit by not installing the appropriate waste treatment system.[83] Similarly, the CPCB has developed detailed guidelines on environmental compensation charges for violations of rules on plastic waste management, e-waste management, biomedical waste management, and hazardous waste management.[84] These guidelines adopt different criteria to quantify environmental damage—cost per ton of plastic waste management, environmental concern factor, and health risk factor. However, the environmental compensation charges developed under these guidelines also have some elements of penalties. They refer to the 'levying' of charges, rather than awarding compensation, allowing for the imposition of spot fines, setting minimum and maximum amounts, including a scale for the imposition of charges intended to deter violators.

The guidelines for imposing liability for environmental damage due to hazardous wastes most closely align with the traditional understanding of environmental compensation. Where the handling of hazardous waste causes direct damage resulting in a loss of livelihood, health effects, or losses to property or crops, the District Magistrate or other agency of the state government or union territory is to determine the compensation payable. The guidelines also provide an indicative list of parameters that may be used to determine indirect compensation liability.[85] The guidelines also provide an indicative cost of site assessment and remediation.[86] They provide a spectrum of the costs that might be incurred and a set of factors that will help PCBs determine at which end of this spectrum liability should be fixed.

The fact that these guidelines are detailed and understand the nature of environmental compensation is at least partially a reflection of the clear legislative intent to impose liability under the Hazardous Waste Management Rules.

[83] ibid 10.

[84] E.g., CPCB, 'Guidelines on Implementing Liabilities for Environmental Damages due to Handling and Disposal of Hazardous Waste and Penalty' (Hazardous Waste Guidelines) (2016).

[85] ibid 21, Table-1.

[86] ibid 23, Table-2.

CONCLUSION

The Indian environmental regulatory toolbox is limited. Even introducing as basic an enforcement tool as civil penalties has not yet been introduced successfully,[87] although their need has long been recognized. The Ministry of Environment, Forest and Climate Change made another attempt—in July 2022, it proposed draft amendments to the Air Pollution Act, Water Pollution Act, and Environmental Protection Act that proposed to decriminalize most offences under these laws, raise the monetary limit on fines that may be imposed, and to appoint Adjudicating Officers to impose civil penalties.[88] In December 2022, a version of these amendments was incorporated in the Jan Vishwas (Amendment of Provisions) Bill, 2022. The Bill considerably reduces the quantum of penalties proposed in the July version of the draft while decriminalizing all existing offences under the Environmental Protection Act, the Air Pollution Act, the PLIA, and the Indian Forest Act, 1927.

The analysis in this chapter suggested that environmental compensation is not satisfactorily awarded and is used by the NGT to perform a deterrence function in addition to a remediation one. This is partly because of the lack of effective compliance and enforcement mechanisms in the Indian environmental regulatory arsenal. The Jan Vishwas Bill presented an opportunity to set this right and explore other mechanisms. However, the Bill's introduction of Adjudicating Officers and civil penalties falls short. The appointment of Joint Secretaries to the government of India as Adjudicating Officers is not sound, given their lack of judicial and technical expertise. The maximum amount for penalties remains capped, and while there is some attempt made to lay down guiding factors in determining the quantum of penalties, they do not go far enough in incorporating modern understandings of ecosystem and biodiversity loss.[89]

In more sophisticated regulatory environments, the discourse concerns regulatory mechanisms other than criminal law. However, in India, the discourse has moved the other way. The ineffectiveness of the existing penal regime has led the Supreme Court and the NGT to evolve compensatory mechanisms that can also function as deterrent penalties. These innovations raise concerns about the credibility and legitimacy of the NGT and question the enforcement actions of PCBs.

[87] The draft Environmental Laws (Amendment) Bill 2015 was criticized for the discretion it vested in the executive to classify non-compliance as 'substantial', 'non-substantial', and 'minor'. See Dhvani Mehta, 'The Environmental Rule of Law in India' (Thesis submitted for the Doctor of Philosophy in Law, University of Oxford, 2017).

[88] Ministry of Environment, Forest and Climate Change, Proposal for amendment in the Environment (Protection) Act, 1986-regarding (1 July 2022) <https://prsindia.org/files/parliamentry-announcement/2022-07-21/Press%20Release%20_EPA-Bill.pdf>.

[89] Debadityo Sinha, Himanshu Ahlawat and Shashank Pandey, 'Analysis of Proposed Amendments to the Environmental Laws in Jan Vishwas (Amendment of Provisions) Bill, 2022' <https://vidhilegalpolicy.in/research/analysis-of-proposed-amendments-to-the-environmental-laws-in-jan-vishwas-amendment-of-provisions-bill-2022>.

Suggestions for Further Reading

Shibani Ghosh, 'Reforming the Liability Regime for Air Pollution in India' (2015) 4 *Environmental Law and Practice Review* 100.

Raghuveer Nath and Armin Rosencranz, 'Determination of Environmental Compensation: The Art of Living Case' (2019) 12 *NUJS Law Review* 1.

PM Prasad, 'Environmental Protection: The Role of Liability System in India' (2004) 39(3) *Economic and Political Weekly* 257.

Charu Sharma, *Tort Liability for Environmental Claims in India* (Lexis Nexis 2017).

Usha Tandon, 'Green Justice and the Application of Polluter-Pays Principle: A Study of India's National Green Tribunal' (2020) 13(1) *OIDA International Journal of Sustainable Development* 35–46.

CHAPTER 41

NATIONAL GREEN TRIBUNAL AND THE ENVIRONMENT

GITANJALI NAIN GILL

Abstract

The establishment of specialised environmental courts or tribunals as specialist adjudicatory forums is shaping the normative interpretation of environmental law. India stands as an exemplar for developing nations through the establishment of the National Green Tribunal (NGT) in 2010. This was a bold and innovative initiative. Its working practices encompass judges working alongside scientific experts with environmental knowledge as joint decision-makers, participatory mechanisms that express equal opportunity for an aggrieved party, and expansive procedural powers. However, new challenges have arisen that question the effectiveness and efficiency of the Tribunal. These include availability and independence of a specialist range of scientific knowledge, the exercise of its jurisdictional power, and controversial self-expansionist powers. This chapter suggests the need for an evaluation of membership, timeframes, outreach, transparency and outcomes. The awareness and willingness to review, reform, and change are hallmarks of a successful tribunal thereby reinforcing its legitimacy and trust across India.

Introduction

Environmental problems are global, and associated disputes are polycentric, multidisciplinary, complex, and often political. International declarations and institutions call for judicial specialization, envisaging expert courts and judges trained in environmental matters to advance the environmental rule of law and promote sustainable development. A consequence of these international calls and developments is the global establishment of specialized environmental courts or tribunals (ECTs). As specialist, dynamic, adjudicatory forums, they are better suited than generalist courts to develop creative responses and comprehensive solutions to environmental problems by offering flexible mechanisms for dispute resolution.

The global proliferation of ECTs is shaping the normative interpretation of environmental law and related policies, recognizing the linkage between human rights and environmental protection, the threat of climate change, and the public dissatisfaction with existing general judicial forums. A comprehensive study of ECTs in 2009 identified over 350 ECTs in forty-one countries.[1] In 2021, there were 2,115 operational ECTs in sixty-seven countries.[2] This growth suggests ever wider recognition that a specialist court can more ably deliver consistency in decision-making, decrease delays (through its understanding of the characteristics of environmental disputes), and facilitate the development of environmental laws, policies, and principles.[3]

In India, tribunals, as quasi-judicial adjudicatory institutions for speedy disposal of cases and specialized expertise, operate in tandem with the traditional court system.[4] The foundations for an Indian ECT were laid by a progressive judiciary that identified the need for specialized environmental adjudication. India's commitment to a 'green court' assumes significant practical importance. The National Green Tribunal of India (NGT or Tribunal) was established by a statute in 2010. Subsequently, the NGT acquired a national and international reputation based on its progressive and innovative environmental decisions far beyond the courtroom door. The widespread recognition of this

[1] George Pring and Catherine Pring, *Greening Justice: Creating and Improving Environmental Courts and Tribunals* (The Access Initiative, World Resources Institute 2009); UNEP, *The ABCs of the ECTs: A Guide for Policy Makers for Designing and Operating a Specialised Environmental Court or Tribunal* (United Nations Environment Programme 2016).

[2] UNEP, *Environmental Courts and Tribunals 2021: A Guide for Policy Makers* (United Nations Environment Programme 2022) i.

[3] Ceri Warnock, *Environmental Courts and Tribunals: Powers, Integrity and the Search for Legitimacy* (Bloomsbury 2021); Brian J Preston, 'Benefits of Judicial Specialisation in Environmental Law: The Land and Environment Court of New South Wales as a Case Study' (2012) 29(2) *Pace Environmental Law Review* 395; George Pring and Catherine Pring, 'Twenty-first Century Environmental Dispute Resolution—Is There an 'ECT' in Your Future?' (2015) 33(1) *Journal of Energy and Natural Resources Law* 10.

[4] Arts 323A and 323B, introduced through the Forty-second Amendment to the Constitution of India, 1950, provide for the establishment of administrative and specified subject tribunals. As of June 2021, 159,783 cases were pending in the Supreme Court and High Courts in India. See PRS Legislative Research, 'The Tribunal System in India' (24 July 2021) <https://prsindia.org/files/bills_acts/bills_parliament/2021/Note%20-%20Tribunal%20system%20in%20India.pdf>. See also Nupur Chowdhury and Nidhi Srivastava, 'The National Green Tribunal in India: Examining the Questions of Jurisdiction' (2018) 21(2) *Asia-Pacific Journal of Environmental Law* 190; Law Commission of India, 'Assessment of Statutory Frameworks of Tribunals in India' (Law Commission No 272, 2017). For a critique on the Indian tribunal framework and its functioning, see Arun K Thiruvengadam, 'Tribunals' in Sujit Choudhry, Madhav Khosla, and Pratap Bhanu Mehta (eds), *The Oxford Handbook of the Indian Constitution* (OUP 2016) 413–414.

bold, innovative Tribunal is fulsome and positive. It stands as an exemplar for developing nations. However, with the passage of time, new challenges have arisen that question the effectiveness and efficiency of the Tribunal. This chapter sequentially presents the establishment of the NGT, its working practices, and the challenges of practice. Finally, it addresses current issues.

41.1 India's Specialized Environmental Tribunal: Genesis and Establishment

The development of a specialized Indian ECT on environmental matters was driven by external and internal demands reflecting subject specificity and complexity. The external demand was triggered by the Indian government's commitment to promote its international obligations under environmental conventions. India's constitutional provisions mandate constituent states to foster respect for international law and treaty obligations.[5]

Internal demand for judicial expertise was fuelled by scientific and interpretive limitations and the tardy progression of environmental cases. The Supreme Court of India (Supreme Court), in three cases, acknowledged that judges faced difficulties due to the lack of scientific knowledge coupled with inadequate exposure to and training in environmental matters.[6] In particular, the Court was concerned with the complexity and uncertainty that underpinned scientific evidence presented to the court. Such externally generated evidence created tensions and fear in claimants and the credibility of assurances given by defendants. There was judicial concern about the Court's ability to evaluate and incorporate this scientific input in complex environmental cases. Uncertainty becomes a problem when scientific knowledge, claims, and counterclaims are accepted as the basis for decision-making by the court. Scientists may refine, modify, or discard variables or models as more information becomes available. However, courts must make choices based on existing scientific knowledge. In addition, evidence generally presented in a scientific form may prove difficult to test or refute. Therefore, inadequacies in the record arising out of uncertainty or insufficient knowledge may not be properly acknowledged or considered.[7]

Initial legislative support for creating an NGT existed in two statutes—the National Environment Tribunal (NET) Act, 1995, and the National Environmental Appellate Authority (NEAA) Act, 1997. The NET Act was legislation dealing specifically with

[5] The Constitution of India, 1950, Arts 253 and 51.

[6] *MC Mehta v Union of India* (1986) 2 SCC 176; *Indian Council for Enviro-Legal Action v Union of India* (1996) 3 SCC 212; *AP Pollution Control Board v Prof MV Nayudu* (1999) 2 SCC 718.

[7] Gitanjali Nain Gill, *Environmental Justice in India: The National Green Tribunal* (Routledge 2017) 57; C Barton, 'The Status of the Precautionary Principle in Australia: Its Emergence in Legislation and as a Common Law Doctrine' (1998) 22 *Harvard Environmental Law Review* 509.

environmental issues and compensation. It provided strict liability for damages arising from any accident occurring while handling any hazardous substance and for establishing a tribunal for effective and expeditious disposal of cases arising from such accidents, with a view to giving relief and compensation for damage to persons, property, and the environment. The composition of the tribunal consisted of members who were required to have adequate knowledge and experience in or capacity to deal with administrative, scientific, or technical aspects of problems relating to the environment, including judicial experience. Unfortunately, the 1995 Act was not notified 'due to the sheer neglect and/or lack of political will to take the risk on the part of the executive to pave the way for the establishment of such a specialised environment tribunal'.[8]

The NEAA Act provided for the establishment of the NEAA to hear appeals with respect to the restriction of areas in which any industries, operations or processes shall be carried out or not, subject to safeguards under the Environment (Protection) Act, 1986. Expertise or experience in administrative, legal, management or technical aspects of problems relating to environmental management law or planning and development were essential qualifications for appointment to the NEAA. The NEAA was established on 9 April 1997 to address grievances regarding the process of environmental clearance (EC) and implement the precautionary and polluter pays principles. However, the NEAA did little work because its role was limited to examining complaints regarding ECs. After the first chairperson's term expired, no replacement appointment was made. In *Vimal Bhai v Union of India*, the High Court of Delhi expressed concern that the government was unable to find qualified members to fill positions in the NEAA.[9] The posts of the chairperson and the vice-chairperson remained vacant from July 2000 until the NEAA Act was repealed by the NGT Act, 2010. Thus, both environmental statutes were or became non-operational.

This background contextualizes the various interventions and dicta by the Supreme Court. Subsequently, the 186th Report of the Law Commission of India on the 'Proposal to Constitute Environment Courts' strongly advocated the establishment of 'environment courts'.[10] The Law Commission of India observed that an environmental tribunal would reflect India's commitments undertaken at international meetings including the UN Conference on the Human Environment, 1972, and the UN Conference on Environment and Development, 1992. The creation of a dedicated specialized court would benefit from the expert advice of environmental scientists and technically qualified persons as part of the judicial process. Such courts could have wider powers to make local inspections and hear oral evidence from resident panels of environmental scientists.[11]

[8] Bharat H. Desai and Balraj Sidhu, 'On the Quest for Green Courts in India' 2010 3(1) *Journal of Court Innovation* 79, 103.

[9] *Vimal Bhai v Union of India* 2009 SCC OnLine Del 289.

[10] Law Commission of India, 186th Report on Proposal to Constitute Environment Courts (Government of India 2003).

[11] ibid 8–9.

Accordingly, the government of India, through the Ministry of Environment and Forests (MoEF), introduced the NGT Bill, 2009, in the Lower House (*Lok Sabha*) of the Indian Parliament on 31 July 2009. The Bill was strongly criticized both within and outside Parliament. Criticisms included limitations or restrictions on matters relating to jurisdiction regarding substantial questions on environment, standing, administrative experience appointment provision, a sixty-day time-limitation clause from the date when the cause of action first arose, a narrow scope of remedial orders, and generally a promotional approach. Accordingly, the Bill was amended seven times to introduce necessary changes.[12] According to the then environment minister, Jairam Ramesh, the tribunal was 'one element of a reformist approach' to environmental governance.[13] The NGT was established on 18 October 2010. The NGT, as a specialized body, was created with the promise of a speedy, effective, and decentralized dispensation of environmental justice, including appropriate membership expertise and knowledge in environmental matters. It became operational on 5 May 2011, with New Delhi selected as the site for the principal bench. The regional benches are in Bhopal for the central zone, Chennai for the south, Pune for the west, and Kolkata for the east.[14] Additionally, to become more accessible, especially in remote areas, the NGT follows the circuit procedure of courts going to the people and not people coming to the courts.[15]

The establishment of the NGT encouraged the Supreme Court to review its own environmental case load and reconsider its stated limited environmental expertise. In *Bhopal Gas Peedith Mahila Udyog Sangathan v Union of India*, the Supreme Court transferred all environmental cases, both active and prospective, to the NGT to render expeditious and specialized judgments and to avoid the likelihood of conflicts of orders between High Courts and the NGT.[16] In 2015, the Supreme Court transferred more than 300 cases to the NGT. The Green Bench of the Supreme Court, headed by Chief Justice HL Dattu, decided to release several cases for swift decisions, thereby shedding its pendency.[17] Thus, these developments identified and reinforced the NGT's role as a specialized tribunal. It was hallmarked as a significant and effective contributor to environmental governance.

[12] Gitanjali Nain Gill, 'A Green Tribunal for India' (2010) 22(3) *Journal of Environmental Law* 461; Domenico Amirante, 'Environmental Courts in Comparative Perspective: Preliminary Reflections on the National Green Tribunal of India' (2012) 29(2) *Pace Environmental Law Review* 441; Kaleeswaram Raj, 'Decentralising Environmental Justice: Debating the National Green Tribunal' (2014) 49(48) *Economic and Political Weekly*.

[13] Statement made by Jairam Ramesh, former Minister of Environment and Forests, in the Indian Parliament (April 2010) <www.igovernment.in/news/31968/india-sets-up-national-green-tribunal>.

[14] MoEF, Government of India, Notification, 17 August 2011, SO 1908 E; NGT/PB/157/2013/331, 20 December 2013 (office order); NGT/PB/266/2013/281, 2 December 2013 (office order); NGT/PB/Pr/CB/97/2014/M78, 29 November 2014 (office order); NGT/PB/266/2016/299, 16 April 2016 (office order).

[15] Ramesh (n 13).

[16] *Bhopal Gas Peedith Mahila Udyog Sangathan v Union of India* (2012) 8 SCC 326.

[17] *TN Godavarman Thirumulpad v Union of India* (2016) 13 SCC 586.

41.2 The National Green Tribunal: Working Practices

The NGT is a creation of a statute; its jurisdiction, powers, and procedures are construed with reference to the language of the legislation.[18] The NGT is empowered to decide civil cases relating to environmental protection and the conservation of forests and other natural resources (including the enforcement of any legal right relating to the environment) and to give relief and compensation for damages to persons and property. The NGT has wide original (section 14),[19] appellate (section 16),[20] and special jurisdiction (section 15)[21] in relation to a substantial question relating to the environment (section 2(m))[22] and such questions that arise out of the implementation of the enactments specified in Schedule I to the Act. The enactments in Schedule I include the following: Water (Prevention and Control of Pollution) Act, 1974; Water (Prevention and Control of Pollution) Cess Act, 1977; Forest (Conservation) Act, 1980; Air (Prevention and Control of Pollution) Act, 1981; Environment (Protection) Act, 1986; Public Liability Insurance Act, 1981; and Biological Diversity Act, 2002. The jurisdictional power of the NGT is of a wide and overriding nature and may be exercised *ex debito justitiae* (that is, in the interests of justice).[23] The NGT Act mandates a low-cost fee to file an application or appeal and a fast-track process requiring the decision of cases within six months of application or appeal.

Since its inception in 2010, the NGT's adjudicative process involves judges working alongside scientific experts with environmental knowledge as joint decision-makers of equal standing. The benefit of this multi-faceted, multi-skilled body is that it produces a coherent and effective institutional mechanism to apply complex laws and principles in a uniform and consistent manner while simultaneously reshaping the approach to solve the environmental problem at its source rather than being limited to predetermined remedies. The scientific experts are 'central' and are not 'advisors' within the NGT's

[18] *Madhya Pradesh Pollution Control Board v Commissioner Municipal Corporation Bhopal* 2013 SCC OnLine NGT 56.

[19] The subject matter of an original application should therefore be a civil case and relate to a substantial question concerning the environment.

[20] The Tribunal is the appellate authority competent to decide questions of law and fact against orders and decisions passed by authorities under the enactments specified in Sch I.

[21] The Tribunal has special jurisdiction to order relief and compensation to victims of pollution and other environmental damage arising under the enactments specified in Sch I for restitution of damaged property and restitution of the environment in such areas as the Tribunal may think fit.

[22] The word substantial implies the real and tangible rather than the imaginary and does not demand a strictly quantitative or proportional assessment. See *Rohit Choudhary v Union of India* 2012 SCC OnLine NGT 66; *Forward Foundation v State of Karnataka* 2015 SCC OnLine NGT 5; *State of MP v Centre for Environment Protection Research and Development* (2020) 9 SCC 781.

[23] *Wilfred J v Ministry of Environment and Forests* MA No in 182 of 2014 and MA No 239 of 2014 in Appeal No 14 of 2014, etc. (Judgment of 17 July 2014, NGT–Principal Bench).

institutional structure. For the current purpose, the terms 'expert' and 'expertise' do not include judicial members but refer to the technical members exercising specialized scientific knowledge, including environmental sciences, environmental studies, environmental engineering, technology, ecology, forestry, plant sciences, soil sciences, zoology, and related categories. Experienced scientists, practising ecologists, and natural resource managers are considered experts.[24]

The involvement of experts and expert knowledge in policy and decision-making commands a place in academic discourse.[25] A scientific consensus that applies regulations and promotes scientific input focusing upon environmental sustainability and human welfare creates the 'epistemic community'. The engagement of the NGT's scientific experts as 'constructive science scholars' in the decision-making process is akin to Peter Haas's theoretical concept of 'epistemic communities'. Haas describes distinctive features of 'epistemic communities' as 'networks of knowledge-based experts with an authoritative claim to policy-relevant knowledge within their domain of expertise.[26] Consequently, scientific expertise may provide appropriate solutions to technical or complicated environmental problems.

This chapter acknowledges the NGT's efforts to reach decisions by recognizing scientific experts as full tribunal members within the decision-making process, thereby promoting a collective, symbiotic, interdisciplinary bench that seeks to harmonize legal norms with scientific knowledge.[27] The engagement of legal and scientific judges of homologous standing results in the NGT expanding and developing substantive and procedural dimensions that guide its decision-making in environmental matters. Substantively, the NGT has developed environmental jurisprudence and its practical application by preserving the link between life and a healthy environment and by successfully placing human rights within environmental discourse. In judicial pronouncements, the right to a healthy environment has been construed as a part of the right to life under Article 21 of the Constitution of India, 1950.[28] The substantive approach also includes the derivative application of principles of international law read in conjunction with the domestic constitutional right to a wholesome environment. Section 20 of the NGT Act mandates that the NGT apply the principles of sustainable

[24] Michael Drescher and others, 'Toward Rigorous Use of Expert Knowledge in Ecological Research' (2013) 4(7) *ECOSPHERE* 1.

[25] Tiina Paloniitty and Niina Kotamäki, 'Scientific and Legal Mechanisms for Addressing Model Uncertainties: Negotiating the Right Balance in Finnish Judicial Review?' (2021) 33(2) *Journal of Environmental Law* 283; Sheila Jasanoff, 'Quality Control and Peer Review in Advisory Science' in Justus Lentsch and Peter Weingart (eds), *The Politics of Scientific Advice* (CUP 2011) 19.

[26] Peter M Haas, *Epistemic Communities, Constructivism, and International Environmental Politics* (Routledge 2016) 5.

[27] Gitanjali Nain Gill, 'Environmental Justice in India: The National Green Tribunal and Expert Members' (2016) 5(1) *Transnational Environmental Law* 175.

[28] *National Centre for Human Settlements and Environment v State of MP* 2020 SCC OnLine NGT 2578; *Federation of Rainbow Warriors v Union of India* 2018 SCC OnLine NGT 831; *Manoj Mishra v Union of India* 2015 SCC OnLine NGT 840.

development,[29] the precautionary principle,[30] and the polluter pays principle[31] in its decision-making process.

The NGT has developed and expanded its procedures and powers in its commitment to resolving environmental disputes, and furthered participatory mechanisms that express equal respect for all participants and ensure equal opportunity. Environmental disputes in the NGT are not simply adversarial in nature. They are quasi-adversarial, quasi-investigative, and quasi-inquisitorial. For instance, under section 18(2) of the NGT Act, standing has been given a liberal construction and a flexible interpretation as expressed in the term 'aggrieved person'. The NGT has created receptive, accessible opportunities for the dispossessed and for representative non-governmental organizations by liberally interpreting the term aggrieved party, the genesis of which is derived from public interest litigation.[32] By championing parity of participation, the Tribunal aims to alleviate inequality and promote recognition, capabilities, and functioning of individuals and communities in India's environmental justice discourse. In environmental matters, the damage is not necessarily confined to the local area as the effects of environmental degradation might have far-reaching consequences beyond the immediate locality. Therefore, an aggrieved person need not be a resident of the local area; any person—whether a resident of that area or not and whether personally, directly, or otherwise aggrieved—may approach the NGT.[33] Additionally, the NGT employs technology to facilitate quick access to environmental justice. This includes e-petition throughout India, the use of geo-tagging, video-conferencing technologies, and a user-friendly website with detailed information about cases, reports, and guidance documents.

The NGT has employed sections 19(2) and 25 of the NGT Act to expand its procedural power to resolve environmental disputes and infuse accountability. These include adopting on-spot investigative procedures, stakeholder consultation, and appointment of committees. The on-spot investigative procedures, approved by the Supreme Court,

[29] *Sandeep Mittal v Ministry of Environment and Forests, and Climate Change* 2021 SCC OnLine NGT 554; *Sumit Kumar v State of Himachal Pradesh* 2020 SCC OnLine NGT 187; *Leo Saldanha v Union of India Application* No 6 of 2013 (Judgment of 27 August 2014, NGT–Southern Bench).

[30] *Dinesh Chahal v Union of India* 2019 SCC OnLine NGT 1559; *Saloni Ailawadi v Union of India* 2019 SCC OnLine NGT 1151.

[31] *Mantri Techzone (P) Ltd v Forward Foundation* (2019) 18 SCC 494; *LG Polymers v Union of India* 2020 SCC OnLine NGT 129; *Ramdas Janardan Koli v Secretary, Ministry of Environment and Forests* 2015 SCC OnLine NGT 4.

[32] Geetanjoy Sahu, 'Implications of Indian Supreme Court's Innovations for Environmental Jurisprudence' (2008) 4(1) *Law, Environment and Development Journal* 1; Lavanya Rajamani 'Public Interest Environmental Litigation in India: Exploring Issues of Access, Participation, Equity, Effectiveness and Sustainability' (2007) 19(3) *Journal of Environmental Law* 293; *State of Uttranchal v Balwant Singh Chaufal* (2010) 3 SCC 402.

[33] *Krishan Lal Gera v State of Haryana* 2015 SCC OnLine NGT 194; *Betty C Alvares v State of Goa* MA Nos 32 and 33 of 2014 in Application No 63 of 2012 (Judgment of 14 February 2014, NGT–Western Zone Bench); *Goa Foundation v Union of India* MA No 49 of 2013 in Application No 26 of 2012 (Judgment of 18 July 2013, NGT–Principal Bench).

involve inspecting affected sites by the expert members.[34] The procedure involves comparing contradictory claims filed by the parties or obtaining further details and assessing the ground realities. Stakeholder consultation is a problem-solving process that seeks solutions to environmental cases of national importance and wider ramifications, such as the ongoing Ganga river,[35] Yamuna river,[36] and air pollution[37] cases. The blame game attitude and buying of more time by regulatory authorities has been replaced by the submission of time-bound, clear-cut proposals and suggestions. Initially, there was indifference or reluctance on the part of regulatory authorities to take this process seriously. However, the determination of and enforcement by the NGT have made the authorities respond in an appropriate, timely manner.

Since 2018, the NGT has categorized and prioritized cases[38] and established more than 175 monitoring expert committees[39] where non-compliance with its orders reveals a stark account of the shortcomings and continuing challenges facing India's environmental governance. For example, in *Manoj Mishra v Union of India*, the Tribunal observed:

> we have already recorded a clear finding of the failure of the administration [regulatory agencies] in handling the situation and repeated failure in carrying out binding directions in various orders. Even information given from time to time has been found to be incorrect on several occasions.[40]

The purpose of these expert committees is to review, monitor, and implement the environmental rules, prepare suitable time-bound action plans, infuse accountability within different authorities, and submit a compliance report to the Tribunal.

The exercise of the powers of judicial review and *suo motu* (on its own motion) proceedings are other examples of NGT's procedural expansion. Interestingly, the Law Commission of India's 186th Report did not expressly recommend granting the powers of judicial review and *suo motu* to the Tribunal.[41] The NGT claimed widespread authority to enforce environmental rights, clarifying that it has the complete identity of

[34] *Forward Foundation v State of Karnataka* OA No 222 of 2014 (Judgment of 10 September 2015, NGT–Principal Bench); *MoEF v Nirma Ltd* (Order of 4 August 2014, Supreme Court of India); *Krishan Kant Singh v National Ganga River Basin Authority* MA No 403 of 2014 in OA No 299 of 2013 (Judgment of 16 October 2014, NGT–Principal Bench).

[35] *Indian Council for Enviro-Legal Action v National Ganga River Basin Authority* OA No 10 of 2015 (Judgment 10 December 2015, NGT–Principal Bench).

[36] *Manoj Misra* (n 28).

[37] *Vardhman Kaushik v Union of India* and *Sanjay Kulshrestha v Union of India* OA No 21 of 2014 and OA No 95 of 2014 (Order of 7 April 2015, NGT–Principal Bench).

[38] These cases include solid waste management, air and water pollution, plastic waste, and sand mining.

[39] Ritwick Dutta, 'Ministerial Panel Questioning NGT Mandate, but Forgets the Body is Always on Centre's Side' *The Print* (Delhi, 22 December 2020) <https://theprint.in/opinion/ministerial-panel-questioning-ngt-mandate-but-forgets-the-body-is-always-on-centres-side/571184/>.

[40] *Manoj Mishra v Union of India* 2018 SCC OnLine NGT 1430, para 5.

[41] Law Commission of India (n 10).

a civil court and that the power of judicial review is implicit and essential for expeditious and effective disposal of its cases. The NGT in *Wilfred J v Ministry of Environment and Forests* used 'textual ambiguity to expand its jurisdiction and claim the power of judicial review'.[42] The NGT Act does not expressly provide the Tribunal with the authority to initiate *suo motu* proceedings. As the NGT is a creation of statute, it cannot assume the inherent powers under Articles 32 and 226 of the Constitution. In *Baijnath Prajapati v Ministry of Environment and Forests*, the NGT commented that 'at the same time it is mentionable that we are not conferred with *suo motu* powers'.[43] However, in 2014, the NGT's position changed, and it claimed *suo motu* jurisdiction. The NGT took *suo motu* cognisance of letters, representations, and media reports based on the larger public interest and environmental protection.[44] For example, between January 2019 and October 2021, approximately seventy-six *suo motu* cases were entertained by NGT benches.[45] In 2021, the controversial *suo motu* power was validated by the Supreme Court for its exercise by the NGT.[46] The apex court, for the effective functioning of the NGT, stated:

> the duty to safeguard Article 21 rights cannot stand on a narrow compass of interpretation. Procedural provisions must be allowed to fall in step with the substantive rights that are invoked in the environmental domain, in larger public interest. The specialised forum is bestowed with the responsibility to ensure protection of the environment.[47]

The institutionalization and transformation sought by the NGT are a metamorphosis of societal and environmental interests that encapsulate the wellbeing of not only the individual but also the larger public interest. The NGT's willingness to resolve environmental issues reflects its expansive self-created procedure. Yet, the very success of the NGT has brought significant challenges concerning which judicial institution ultimately shapes and controls India's environmental regulation and decision-making, as discussed below.

[42] *Wilfred J* (n 23); Chowdhury and Srivastava (n 4) 215.

[43] *Baijnath Prajapati v Ministry of Environment and Forests* 2012 SCC OnLine NGT 21, para 9.

[44] *In Re: News item published in the local daily 'Indian Express Sunday Express' dated 28.06.2020 titled 'Gas Leak in Agro Company Claims Life of One'* OA No 107 of 2020 (Order of 8 January 2021, NGT–Principal Bench); *In Re: Gas Leak at LG Polymers Chemical Plant in RR Venkatapuram Village Visakhapatnam in Andhra Pradesh* OA No 73 of 2020 (Order of 8 May 2020, NGT–Principal Bench); *Tribunal on its own Motion v Govt. of NCT of Delhi* OA No 496 of 2016 (Order of 30 August 2018, NGT–Principal Bench).

[45] The author reviewed the NGT website to gather this data.

[46] *Municipal Corporation of Greater Mumbai v Ankita Sinha* 2021 SCC OnLine SC 897.

[47] ibid para 74.

41.3 The National Green Tribunal: Challenges

Initially, the NGT faced major institutional challenges due to the limited cooperation and hesitant operational commitment of both federal and state governments. The under-staffed bench and inadequate logistic and infrastructure facilities, coupled with inappropriate housing for bench appointees, was described by the Supreme Court as 'utterly disgusting'.[48] There is an explanation for this dismal treatment, which affected the establishment and early operational effectiveness of the NGT. An unresponsive and dysfunctional state administration existed that failed to appreciate the importance of green issues. The MoEF Minister Jairam Ramesh was known for raising the green profile and was hailed by many as an outstanding environment minister. Nevertheless, he was fighting battles within his ministry, the MoEF. Personally, 'he remained accessible and responsive, but he could not ensure that his ministry officials were also accessible and responsive'.[49] Ramesh described the ministry's environmental working position as 'it's a huge bureaucracy. There is a structural problem ... It's easier to reform laws and procedures and hope that would create a new mind-set in these people rather than try for a structural change.'[50]

Further, and more importantly, the NGT's decisions, especially during 2014–17, produced a political backlash as politicians, government policymakers, and bureaucrats were unexpectedly exposed to critical examination by the NGT and were often found wanting. The MoEF was severely criticized by the NGT for failing to observe its own procedural rules, such as the improper granting of licences without prior environmental impact assessments being completed or appropriately conducted or appointing members without appropriate qualifications to the expert appraisal committees. The NGT called senior regulatory authorities to the Tribunal only to hear inappropriate or implausible explanations for MoEF decisions. A similar obfuscatory response pattern occurred in other cases. For example, the NGT stated that members of senior regulatory authorities might face a term of 'state hospitality' (jail) for statements that bordered on contempt.[51] The bench further asserted that 'it is really unfortunate that the Ganges continues to be polluted. Why don't you [the state and federal governments] do something? You raise

[48] Legal India Admin, 'SC Slams Poor Facilities for Green Tribunal' *Legal India* (20 September 2012) <www.legalindia.com/news/sc-slams-poor-facilities-for-green-tribunal>; See Gill (n 7) 210–211.

[49] Himanshu Thakkar, 'What Jairam Did and Didn't Do as Green Minister' *Rediff.com* (20 July 2011) <www.rediff.com/news/column/what-jairam-ramesh-did-and-did-not-do-as-green-minister/20110720.htm>.

[50] Janaki Lenin, 'Green Fundamentalism will not Work, Says Jairam Ramesh' *First Post* (18 July 2011) <www.firstpost.com/blogs/green-fundamentalism-will-not-work-says-jairam-ramesh-42646.html>.

[51] Anonymous, 'Why Contempt should not be Initiated Against Delhi Govt, DJB: NGT' *The Economic Times* (New Delhi, 23 October 2017) <https://economictimes.indiatimes.com/news/politics-and-nation/why-contempt-should-not-be-initiated-agnst-delhi-govt-djb-ngt/articleshow/61185784.cms>.

slogans [about cleaning the river] but do exactly opposite of that.'[52] The NGT further stated that the MoEF is the 'most messy' ministry.[53] Such public statements embarrassed both regulatory authorities and politicians to such an extent that there was a reluctance to provide appropriate support in the expectation that it would restrict the activities of the NGT. Neither the ministry and state governments nor the various environmental statutory bodies were accustomed to being questioned in a probing, informed and systematic manner nor having their decisions subjected to regular public merit review.

The vulnerability felt by the MoEF as the result of the activity and willingness of the NGT to publicly criticize the ministry resulted in a practical attempt to curb and dilute the powers of the NGT through legislative intervention. For example, the Finance Act, 2017, was amended. The amended rules gave unbridled power to the central government to provide for the appointment, term of office, salaries, and allowances, registration, removal, and other terms and conditions of service of the chairpersons and members of tribunals, including the NGT. The amendment was designed to create systemic changes to undermine the system of institutional checks and balances and potentially create a conflict of interest.[54] However, the Supreme Court in February 2018 stayed the provisions of the Finance Act, 2017, that amended the rules of appointment to tribunals, including the NGT. The position since 2018 seems to have changed due to a new NGT chairperson. His appointment was questioned in the Indian Parliament as being a 'reward' for supporting the government's policy while sitting as a Supreme Court judge.[55]

Second, the NGT's self-declared expansion of powers to include judicial review and *suo motu*, as described, are controversial, questionable, and a case of judicial overreach. Tribunalization may result in serious encroachment on the judiciary's independence and power, thereby causing institutional confusion and complexity. The colonization of intellectual space by the NGT, partly by public awareness of its jurisdiction and through its effectiveness in protecting both the environment and the interests of affected parties, was not well received by some High Courts and the MoEF.[56] In an affidavit before the Supreme Court in 2013, the MoEF stated 'the government of India has not agreed to confer *suo motu* powers on the Tribunal. It is for the NGT, an adjudicatory body, to follow the provisions of the NGT Act 2010 . . . resulting in embarrassment to the

[52] Anonymous, 'India Environment Watchdog Anger over Ganges Pollution' *BBC News* (20 January 2016) <https://www.bbc.com/news/world-asia-india-35359089>.

[53] *Goa Foundation* (n 33).

[54] Gitanjali Nain Gill, 'Mapping the Power Struggles of the National Green Tribunal of India: The Rise and Fall?' (2020) 7(1) *Asian Journal of Law and Society* 85.

[55] Anonymous, 'Congress Raises Issue of Appointment of Justice Adarsh Kumar Goel as NGT Chairman in Lok Sabha' *The New Indian Express* (26 July 2018) <https://www.newindianexpress.com/nation/2018/jul/26/congress-raises-issue-of-appointment-of-justice-adarsh-kumar-goel-as-ngt-chairman-in-lok-sabha-1848938.html>.

[56] *P Sundararajan v Deputy Registrar*, NGT (2015) 4 Law Weekly 23, 27; *Central India Ayush Drugs Manufacturers Association v State of Maharashtra AIR* 2016 Bom 261.

government before Parliament'.[57] The exercise of judicial review over time has evoked mixed responses. Environmentalists felt a strong message was delivered that the NGT is concerned with the merits of the decision and the decision-making process.[58] As an independent body, the NGT aims to protect individuals against abuse or misuse of power by the authorities. Constitutional experts and governmental authorities, on the other hand, consider that the NGT seeks to acquire the powers of superior courts. They argue the NGT can only examine decisions but cannot challenge a statute.[59] However, the Supreme Court settled this vexed matter in *TN Pollution Control Board v Sterlite Industries (India) Ltd.*[60] It declared that it would be 'fallacious to state that the NGT has the power of judicial review akin to the High Court.... It is a statutory tribunal set up under NGT Act'.[61]

Although the Supreme Court validated the NGT's *suo motu* power for procedural flexibility and environmental exigencies, the progressive judgment opens the door to the dangers of jurisdictional overreach. Questions may include the veracity of the media source, the criteria for the selection of the news item may not be subject to rigorous scrutiny for examination, and *suo motu* might become a recognitional opportunity for activist judges.[62] For example, in the southern NGT bench, twenty-three of the sixty-six *suo motu* cases between January 2019 and October 2021 were drawn from one newspaper, Dinamalar Chennai edition. This power allows the NGT to initiate proceedings and permits the Tribunal to roam far and wide, searching for pressing environmental issues that 'it' considers to be in the public interest.

Third, the availability and independence of a specialist range of scientific knowledge reflecting the wide range of cases heard by the NGT remains an issue to be fully addressed. Since 2017, the NGT has experienced an acute shortfall of legal and scientific bench judges. Section 4 of the NGT Act mandates a full-time chairperson and at least ten, but not exceeding twenty, judicial and expert members. In 2021, the NGT had five judicial and four expert members. The current expert judges are specialists in forest-related matters, resulting in the diminution of a previously wide spectrum

57 Utkarsh Anand, 'SC Fumes as MoEF Says NGT Causing Govt Embarrassment' *Indian Express* (New Delhi, 13 September 2013) <https://indianexpress.com/article/news-archive/web/sc-fumes-as-moef-says-ngt-causing-govt-embarrassment/ >.

58 Statement by environmental activists (who are also lawyers) Ritwick Dutta and Rahul Choudhary in Pallavi Polanki, 'National Green Tribunal Asserts Independence, Is Environment Minister listening?' *Firstpost* (19 July 2014) <www.firstpost.com/india/national-green-tribunal-asserts-independence-environment-minister-listening-1625527.html>.

59 Statement of Rajeev Dhavan, senior advocate, in Yukti Choudhary, 'Tribunal on Trial' *Down to Earth* (30 November 2014) <https://www.downtoearth.org.in/coverage/tribunal-on-trial-47400>. See also Gopal Krishna, 'When Tribunals Undermine the Judiciary' *Rediff.com* (25 October 2013) <https://www.rediff.com/news/column/when-tribunals-undermine-the-judiciary/20131025.htm>.

60 *TN Pollution Control Board v Sterlite Industries (India) Ltd* (2019) 19 SCC 479.

61 ibid 524.

62 Marc Galanter and Vasujith Ram, 'Suo Motu Intervention and the Indian Judiciary' in Gerald N Rosenberg, Sudhir Krishnaswamy, and Shishir Bail (eds), *A Qualified Hope: The Indian Supreme Court and Progressive Social Change* (CUP 2019) 92.

of scientific expertise. Additionally, the appointment of two serving expert members has been questioned. They were senior officials in the Ministry of Environment, Forest and Climate Change involved in deciding forest clearance issues and now hear appeals against their own previous decisions.[63]

This limited expertise impacts the delivery of environmental justice. For instance, due to the shortfall of bench experts, the NGT has outsourced work to over 175 *ad hoc* committees.[64] Questions have been raised about the membership of these committees regarding independent advice and assistance to the Tribunal in implementing its orders. The Supreme Court was 'wholly disappointed' by the NGT order as the NGT accepted the managing director of Oil India Limited as a member of the enquiry committee. The same company was accused of polluting wetlands.[65] As noted by Dutta, most of these expert committees are composed of government nominees from regulatory authorities and government institutes, even in cases where the government is the defaulting party. There is no membership representation from independent environmental experts or civil society.[66] This has a knock-on effect on the quality of judgments. The limited range of scientific knowledge does not provide a balanced bench capable of comparing possible options that result in informed decision-making. For instance, in 2019, the Supreme Court critically commented on the failure of the NGT to carry out a merit review when it discharged in a perfunctory paragraph its adjudicatory function concerning a vital technical evaluation in the grant of environmental clearance.[67] Similarly, the NGT 'since July 2018, has disposed of over 700 cases, all at different stages of hearing, with largely generic orders directing the concerned authorities to look into the matter and take appropriate action in accordance with law'.[68]

Fourth, in recent times, the NGT has been criticized concerning the exercise of its jurisdictional power regarding both its limited and extended usage. For example, in *TN Pollution Control Board*, the Supreme Court found that the NGT passed an order

[63] Ritwick Dutta, 'Woes of the National Green Tribunal: Are the Recent Appointments Unconstitutional?' *Bar and Bench* (9 October 2019) <https://www.barandbench.com/columns/new-appointments-national-green-tribunal-unconstitutional-judicial-independence>.

[64] Remya Nair and Neelam Pandey, 'NGT Decisions Causing Losses to Industry, Need to Look at Its Mandate—Ministerial Panel' *The Print* (10 December 2020) <https://theprint.in/india/governance/ngt-decisions-causing-losses-to-industry-need-to-look-at-its-mandate-ministerial-panel/564194/>; Matham Ramesh, 'Turning a Decade-Old, NGT Faces Some Tough Questions' *The Hindu Business Line* (16 October 2020) <https://www.thehindubusinessline.com/news/national/turning-a-decade-old-ngt-faces-some-tough-questions/article62194300.ece>.

[65] *Bonani Kakkar v Oil India Limited* 2020 SCC OnLine NGT 954; Anonymous, 'Wholly Disappointed'—SC Stays NGT Order Forming Panel on Assam's Baghjan Oil Well Fire' *The Print* (1 July 2021) <https://theprint.in/judiciary/wholly-disappointed-sc-stays-ngt-order-forming-panel-on-assams-baghjan-oil-well-fire/688003/>.

[66] Dutta (n 39).

[67] *Hanuman Laxman Aroskar v Union of India* (2019) 15 SCC 401.

[68] Maya Ramesh, 'Nearly a Decade Old, Is the National Green Tribunal Losing Its Bite?' *The Wire* (11 May 2019) <https://thewire.in/environment/nearly-a-decade-old-is-the-national-green-tribunal-losing-its-bite>; *Hariram Singh v State of Bihar* 2019 SCC OnLine NGT 128; *Rajeshwar Prasad Raja v State of Jharkhand* 2019 SCC OnLine NGT 1854.

ultra vires its statutory power and without jurisdiction.[69] The NGT entertained a leap-frog appeal against an original order despite the matter being pending before the appellate authority under the Water (Prevention and Control of Pollution) Act, 1974, and the Air (Prevention and Control of Pollution) Act, 1981.[70] In *State of MP v Centre for Environment Protection Research and Development,* the Supreme Court stated that the NGT could not direct the state government to issue orders and directions to the petrol pumps or retail outlets or dealers not to supply fuel to vehicles not having a valid pollution control certificate.[71] In essence, the NGT's power is to examine and decide questions of violation of any specific statutory obligation which affects or is likely to affect a group of individuals or the community at large.

Fifth, speedy, reasoned, and transparent decisions reflect the mandate of the NGT and help 'build predictability of law and confidence in legal process and institutions'.[72] The official figures between July 2011 and September 2022 state that 39,125 cases were filed, out of which 37,150 were disposed and 1,975 remain pending.[73] However, the true picture is different. The 'new 4-D approach to dealing with cases—"dismiss, dispose, delegate and de-reserve" without providing due reasons' is disturbing.[74] For instance, in 2020, the NGT dismissed twenty-two appeals, mostly from local residents against green clearances issued on the grounds of delay without due consideration and process.[75] This contradicts the previous ruling of the NGT regarding a pragmatic justice-oriented approach towards condonation of delay.[76]

Finally, using technology can be a two-edged sword by working either for the benefit or to the detriment of parties. Technology offers speed and removes issues of 'distance'. However, hearings also indicate a limited benefit. Video conferences have been cancelled without notice, or the parties were offered insufficient time.[77] It is reported that lawyers have been put on 'mute settings' while presenting their arguments from regional benches.[78] These practices strike at the very heart of the NGT's mandate that offers environmental justice and increased public confidence.

[69] *TN Pollution Control Board* (n 60).

[70] ibid 513–514.

[71] *State of MP* (n 22).

[72] UNEP, *Environmental Rule of Law: First Global Report* (United Nations Environment Programme 2019) 212.

[73] National Green Tribunal <https://greentribunal.gov.in/>.

[74] Ramesh (n 68).

[75] Jay Mazoomdaar, 'Against Environmental Clearances: Green Tribunal Cited Delay in Filing as Reason to Dismiss Every Second Plea' *The Indian Express* (New Delhi, 1 March 2021) <https://indianexpress.com/article/india/green-tribunal-cited-delay-in-filing-as-reason-to-dismiss-every-second-plea-7208897/>.

[76] *Nikunj Developers v M/s Veena Developers* MA No 247 of 2012 (Judgment of 14 March 2013, NGT–Principal Bench); *Paryavaran Sanrakshan Sangarsh Samiti Lippa v Union of India* MA No 23 of 2011 (Judgment of 15 December 2011, NGT–Principal Bench).

[77] Geetanjoy Sahu, 'Whither the National Green Tribunal?' *Down to Earth* (23 September 2019) <https://www.downtoearth.org.in/blog/environment/whither-the-national-green-tribunal—66879>.

[78] Dutta (n 63).

41.4 The NGT: Addressing the Challenges and a Way Forward

It is more than a decade since the establishment of the NGT. It has gained an international reputation in global judicial circles through its progressive decisions, innovative structure, and practices. Becoming a showpiece from the global South, along with its national standing with the public, has been hard won. Nevertheless, the awareness and willingness to review, reform and change are hallmarks of a successful tribunal. A judicial institution founded on the environmental rule of law 'solidifies its legitimacy and trust across society'.[79] The constitutional courts welcome the establishment of the NGT as a 'multifunctional body, with a capacity to provide redressal for environmental exigencies ... working within the contours of its statutory mandate and with procedural safeguards'.[80]

There needs to be an evaluation of membership, timeframes, outreach, transparency, outcomes, and overall practical utility of the NGT. Currently, some weaknesses require remedial action. The following suggestions focus only on NGT's internal working practices and require no legislative amendment. First, bench membership and expertise must reflect the statutory minimum requirement. Further, the spectrum of expertise should match the wide range of subject matters covered by the NGT Act. A balanced bench is a *sine qua non* for an effective decision-making process. On one hand, having too many experts can lead to the slowing down or even paralysis of the decision-making process; at the same time, too few experts can affect the quality of the decisions.[81] The membership should be free from executive encroachment.[82] Judicial independence serves as a 'bulwark against political attack',[83] and ensures impartiality.

Second, the practical utility of establishing *ad hoc* committees since 2018 is yet to be established. The truism that committees take minutes but may waste years is illustrated by these committees. An abrogation of responsibility alongside a failure to meet statutorily fixed deadlines for the disposal of cases is a consequence of the increasing number of these committees, as is their tardiness in reporting promptly to the NGT.

Third, an independent assessment of the NGT would improve its functioning and promote a progressive move towards excellence. An internationally accepted evaluated

[79] UNEP (n 72) 19.

[80] Municipal Corporation of Greater Mumbai (n 46) paras 98 and 106.

[81] See generally, Lukasz Gruszczynski, 'The Role of Experts in Environmental and Health-Related Trade Disputes in the WTO: Deconstructing Decision-Making Processes' in Monika Ambrus and others (eds), *The Role of 'Experts' in International and European Decision-Making Processes: Advisors, Decision Makers or Irrelevant Actors?* (CUP 2014) 228.

[82] *Rojer Mathew v South Indian Bank Ltd* (2020) 6 SCC 1, 154.

[83] Paul L Stein, 'Specialist Environmental Courts: The Land and Environment Court of New South Wales, Australia' (2002) 4 *Environmental Law Review* 5, 7.

procedure is the International Framework for Court Excellence.[84] The framework provides a methodology for assessing a court's performance against seven areas of court excellence and guidance for courts intending to improve their performance. These involve court leadership and management, court planning and policies, court proceedings, public trust and confidence, user satisfaction, court resources, and affordable and accessible services.[85] These seven areas present a holistic approach to the tribunal's performance concerning the provision of quality services that result in the access to and delivery of justice. Fair, accessible, and efficient ECTs are essential to building public trust and confidence. Any absence of these core areas acts as a feedback loop in the NGT and raises questions about the quality and effectiveness of justice.

The NGT should be asked questions (often difficult) to improve its functioning. It is timely for the NGT to be made subject to independent review. This process will strengthen public trust and its institutional legitimacy, thereby promoting the delivery of environmental justice.

Suggestions for Further Reading

Domenico Amirante, 'Environmental Courts in Comparative Perspective: Preliminary Reflections on the National Green Tribunal of India' (2012) 29 *Pace Environmental Law Review* 441.

Nupur Chowdhury and Nidhi Srivastava, 'The National Green Tribunal in India: Examining the Question of Jurisdiction' (2018) 21(2) *Asia Pacific Journal of Environmental Law* 190.

Gitanjali N Gill, *Environmental Justice in India: The National Green Tribunal* (Routledge 2017).

Sridhar Rengarajan and others, 'National Green Tribunal of India—An Observation from Environmental Judgements' (2018) 25 *Environmental Science and Pollution Research* 11313.

Sudha Shrotria, 'Environmental Justice: Is the National Green Tribunal of India Effective?' (2015) 17(3) *Environmental Law Review* 169.

84 International Framework for Court Excellence (3rd edn, 2020) <www.courtexcellence.com/__data/assets/pdf_file/0023/66605/The-International-Framework-3rd-Edition-Amended.pdf>.

85 The NSW Land and Environment Court (NSWLEC), 'Annual Review 2020' 27–29.

CHAPTER 42

COURTS AND SOLID WASTE MANAGEMENT IN URBAN AREAS

KAVERI GILL*

Abstract

This chapter examines the invocation of the meta-narrative of the environment in urban governance and solid waste management. It outlines key interventions by the Supreme Court of India resulting in the framing of rules governing solid waste management. It then explores the implications of public interest litigation (PIL). It draws on a particular PIL concerning the informal plastic waste recycling market of Delhi. The chapter uses this to set out an empirical critique of law in action. It explores the PIL's workings as process, as providing a solution, and as resulting in specific policy and practice. The chapter concludes by pointing to the dangers of the judiciary using the trope of the environment to exercise fiat via the instrument of PIL cases related to solid waste management, not just to disproportionately disregard the well-being and livelihoods of the poor, but ironically, to the actual detriment of the environment.

* Acknowledgments: I would like to thank advocates Aditya Verma and Rigved Prasad for help accessing recent cases related to solid waste management, as well as the editors of this volume for their helpful comments.

Introduction

Development and changing consumption patterns in cities and towns of India have resulted in an increasing amount of waste generated annually. Estimates suggest between sixty-two and sixty-nine million tons of solid waste are produced each year in urban India.[1] By 2031, it is projected to increase to 165 million tons per year, with the urban share of the total population touching six hundred million, and the urban share of GDP rising to 75 per cent.[2] The management of such waste, a by-product of the growing affluence of certain classes and castes of urban dwellers, involves a choice between its formal collection by the urban local municipal body, or a company subcontracted by it, primarily for disposal in landfills, and increasingly, waste-to-energy plants; recycling by the informal sector, with attempts to divert combustible refuse to waste-to-energy plants as well; and waste that remains uncollected.

If development is the cause of ever greater volumes of solid waste to be managed, it is the meta-narrative of *the environment*, as proposed below, which has been extended as a justification for progressively more intervention of the courts in the sphere of solid waste management in India in the last three and a half decades.

> The sheer ubiquitous presence of the environment in contemporary social discourse, addressed in diverse forms, expressing distinct, disparate, even contradictory social concerns, suggests its emergence as a dominant discourse, a narrative structure that can be imbued with multiple and varying meanings, a floating signifier, and, potentially, a meta-narrative.[3]

In the particular case of urban waste policy and practice in India, especially since the mid-2000s, the meta-narrative of *the environment* is extended as a benign discourse, one that disguises the neoliberal policy agenda of the state, even as in practice it materially reproduces and legitimizes class and caste asymmetries in newer and structurally more damaging forms for informal labour, as well as results in and justifies a more degraded environment.[4] This is illustrated in a recent primary study in a medium Himalayan hill town that is representative, with some contextual variation, of the situation in other urban towns and cities of India.[5]

[1] Planning Commission, 'Report of the Task Force on Waste-to-Energy—In the Context of Integrated Municipal Solid Waste Management—Volume 1' (Government of India 2014).

[2] High Powered Expert Committee (HPEC), *Report on Indian Urban Infrastructure and Services* (Ministry of Urban Development, Government of India 2011).

[3] Sudha Vasan, 'The Environment as Meta-Narrative: Introduction to a Special Issue' (2021) 37(2) *Journal of Developing Societies* 143.

[4] Kaveri Gill, 'The Environment as Disingenuous Trope: Tracing Waste Policy and Practice in a Medium Hill Town of the Himalayas, India' (2021) 37(2) *Journal of Developing Societies* 184.

[5] ibid.

The present chapter restricts itself to looking at the invocation of *the environment* as the driving force propelling much proactive judicial intervention in recent decades by the Supreme Court of India in urban governance and solid waste management in India. Rather than exhaustively surveying these cases, this chapter will outline key interventions in the Supreme Court that resulted in framing the first-ever rules governing solid waste management in India. It will then lay out the salient features of the rules, as well as those of an updated set of rules, notified a decade and a half later, the most critical of which turns out to be the promotion of waste-to-energy plants as a standardized technocratic solution financially underwritten by the state.

The chapter will go on to explore the specific implications of public interest litigation (PIL) being the key instrument of these legal interventions, exploring its workings as a process, as providing a solution, and as resulting in specific policy and practice to judge outcomes and whether the environment improved as a consequence, as was the stated goal. Hailed by many as India's unique and laudable contribution to contemporary jurisprudence, it is a jurisdiction that emerged in the country post the political Emergency of 1975–77 as a means to democratize legal recourse in the truest sense.[6] One would, therefore, expect such an instrument to provide both a socially just and environmentally sound panacea to the solid waste management conundrum.

Drawing on an in-depth primary study of a particular PIL that severely disrupted the workings of the informal plastic waste recycling market of Delhi and negatively impacted those belonging to subordinate classes and castes working in it, as well as a follow-up on PIL directed against this market that did the same, the chapter will set out an empirical critique of law in action on various dimensions. It will conclude by pointing to the dangers of the judiciary using the trope of *the environment* to exercise fiat via the instrument of PIL cases related to solid waste management, not just to disproportionately disregard the well-being and livelihoods of the poor, but, ironically, to the actual detriment of the environment as well.

42.1 The Environment, Solid Waste Management, Judicial Activism, and Policy

This section discusses interventions in the Supreme Court that were critical to the drafting of the first-ever rules governing solid waste management in the country, highlighting the main features of the initial rules of the year 2000, as well as subsequent rules notified in 2016.

[6] Anuj Bhuwania, Courting the People: Public Interest Litigation in Post-Emergency India (CUP 2016).

Table 42.1 Key Supreme Court Cases Related to Solid Waste Management in India

Case
MC Mehta v Union of India (2004) 6 SCC 588
BL Wadhera v Union of India (1996) 2 SCC 594
Almitra H Patel and Another v Union of India (2000) 2 SCC 679

Source: Author

42.1.1 The Initial Framing of Solid Waste Management Rules in India: Key PILs

Solid waste management is categorized as a public health and sanitation concern, falling under the State List in the Constitution of India, 1950. As a public good with significant potential negative externalities in the case of deficient supply, the responsibility for its adequate provision lies with the government. At the central and state government levels, there is the involvement of various ministries (Urban Development, Environment, Forest and Climate Change; Non-conventional Energy Resources; and Health and Family Welfare), as well as several institutions falling under their purview.[7]

At the local level, responsibility falls to the decentralized tier of the municipal authority, alternatively called the urban local body. Although the Seventy-Forth Constitution Amendment Act of 1992 ought to have resulted in the empowerment of this local third tier of urban governance, in reality, the promise of both functional and financial devolution remains unfulfilled. Many municipalities are bankrupt, with inadequate formal provision of solid waste management widely prevalent.[8]

Beginning in the mid-1980s, numerous PIL petitions were filed in the Supreme Court, seeking to protect the environment, including from the indiscriminate dumping of municipal solid waste. If a violation of fundamental rights is asserted, as it was in these cases, Article 32 of the Constitution permits the Supreme Court to be directly approached.[9] Table 42.1 lists the historically most prominent cases related to solid waste management filed in the Supreme Court, selected due to their instrumentality in the subsequent framing of the first-ever rules in this sphere in the country.

[7] For instance, the CPCB reports to the Ministry of Environment, Forest and Climate Change, Government of India, falling under the Water (Prevention and Control of Pollution) Act, 1974 and the Air (Prevention and Control of Pollution) Act, 1981.

[8] KC Sivaramakrishnan, *Governance of Megacities: Fractured Thinking, Fragmented Set Up* (OUP 2015).

[9] Lavanya Rajamani, 'Public Interest Environmental Litigation in India: Exploring Issues of Access, Participation, Equity, Effectiveness and Sustainability' (2007) 19(3) *Journal of Environmental Law* 293.

The petitioners in these cases may be described as 'public-spirited citizens', for whom the Supreme Court opened its doors via the PIL's procedural originality and doctrinal license in relaxing the rule of *locus standi*.[10] But of the two—representative standing on behalf of the poor and downtrodden, as well as citizen standing seeking to enforce the performance of public duties, it is largely the latter category they fell into, which is ironic given the original purpose of the PIL. All were middle class, and many were 'career public interest litigators'.[11]

Such escalating environmental jurisprudence in India during this period was supported by liberal interpretations of the fundamental right to life, including the right to live with dignity, bestowed by Article 21 of the Constitution. In a novel interpretation, these have been perceived to include the rights to a clean and healthy environment, clear air and so forth.[12] As Bhuwania observed 'In narrating the story of PIL, these cases are usually read as signalling a new era, shifting the focus of PIL away from the dominant concerns of poverty and judicial reform to the subject of the environment'.[13]

Environmental PILs became pervasive. The right of enjoyment of pollution-free water and air was recognized as part of the right to life in 1991, and in seven years, the Court has faced so many public interest environmental cases that it was moved to note, '[a]t this point of time, the effect of the quality of the environment on the life of the inhabitants is much too obvious to require any emphasis or elaboration'.[14]

Few areas of environmental governance remained free of judicial intervention, with the judiciary seeing itself as responsible for holding to account state institutions perceived by them as recalcitrant and renegade.

In the specific domain of solid waste management, in *BL Wadhera v Union of India*, an order in favour of the petitioner begins by addressing various government bodies: 'The authorities, responsible for pollution control and environment protection, have not been able to provide clean and healthy environment to the residents of Delhi'.[15] It proceeds:

> It is no doubt correct that rapid industrial development urbanisation and regular flow of persons from rural to urban areas have made major contribution [*sic*] towards environmental degradation but at the same time the Authorities—entrusted with the work of pollution control—cannot be permitted to sit back with folded hands on the pretext that they have no financial or other means to control pollution and protect the environment.[16]

[10] ibid 293.
[11] ibid 296. See also Bhuwania (n 6) 15.
[12] Kaveri Gill, *Of Poverty and Plastic: Scavenging and Scrap Trading Entrepreneurs in India's Urban Informal Economy* (OUP 2009) 224.
[13] Bhuwania (n 6) 50.
[14] Rajamani (n 9) 294–295.
[15] *BL Wadhera v Union of India* (1996) 2 SCC 594.
[16] ibid.

Similarly, in *Almitra H Patel v Union of India*, the other prominent PIL case listed above, it was argued that anywhere from 20–80 per cent of waste remains uncollected by urban municipal bodies, with a significant proportion of that which is formally collected being illegally dumped on the peripheries of India's metropolitan cities and towns, and that therefore various government bodies, as respondents, had failed to fulfil their constitutional and statutory duties as regards the collection, storage, segregation, transportation, processing, and hygienic disposal of municipal solid waste.[17] The respondents were charged with remedying the above, by stopping the practice of dumping waste; identifying and setting up waste processing and disposal facilities (including upgrading existing, and locating new, landfill sites); and otherwise taking steps to ensure improved management of solid waste. The Court and the parties to the PIL also constituted a Committee with representation from various ministries and municipalities, with the Court directing statutory authorities to comply with their recommendations.[18]

This expansive judicial role in governance has been welcomed in some quarters as 'chemotherapy for the carcinogenic body politic'. The ability of public-spirited individuals to use the Supreme Court as a fulcrum to leverage public policy is perceived as a testament to Indian democracy. Judicial intervention has led to changes in policy as well as rules and arguably to discernible improvements in the environment.[19]

Whether, in the actual workings of environmental PILs, they have more closely approximated the authoritarianism of the Emergency years rather than deepened democracy will be explored in the next section, as will the supposed discernible betterment of the environment.[20]

42.1.2 Solid Waste Management Legislation in the Wake of the PILs

What is demonstrably true, in the case of solid waste management, is that such environmental action litigation resulted in the first-ever rules in the domain, that is, the Municipal Solid Wastes (Management and Handling) Rules, 2000 (the Rules), that closely complied with the recommendations made by a Committee constituted by the Supreme Court. The Rules begin by setting out the responsibilities of the municipal authority, for instance, to 'implement' the provisions of the Rules and for infrastructure development for the management of municipal waste, specifically, collection, storage, segregation, transportation, processing, and disposal of waste, set out in Schedule-II of the Rules, with Schedule-III entirely devoted to landfill specifications, and Schedule-IV

[17] *Almitra H Patel v Union of India* (1998) 2 SCC 416.

[18] Final Report of the Committee Constituted by the Hon. Supreme Court of India, Solid Waste Management in Class I Cities in India (March 1999) <https://swachcoop.com/pdf/BarmanCommitteeReport.pdf> [Barman Committee].

[19] Rajamani (n 9) 295.

[20] Gill (n 12); Bhuwania (n 6).

to standards for composting, treated leachates, and incineration; the responsibility of the state government and Union Territory administrations to 'enforce' the provisions of the Rules; and the responsibility of the Central Pollution Control Board (CPCB) and equivalent state or Union Territory board or committees to 'monitor' the compliance of the standards as regards groundwater, ambient air, leachate quality, compost quality, and incineration standards set out in the Rules.

Motivated by addressing environmental concerns stemming from the disorderly disposal of waste, the Rules focus almost exclusively on disposal in landfills and, to some extent, on composting for biodegradables and incineration for non-biodegradables.

Neglected altogether is the vast and sophisticated informal sector recovery and recycling sector,[21] that goes a long way towards propping up inadequate municipal waste management and ensuring a cleaner environment, in so far as recycling is a greener option over incineration or disposal.[22] The Court constituted Committee, while acknowledging the contribution of the informal sector and suggesting it be integrated into the formal system, demonstrated complete ignorance of the highly organized system and the prior existence of itinerant waste buyers in suggesting that a door-to-door collection system should be piloted in high income areas to collect dry, segregated waste.[23] Not only do the Rules suggest the municipal authority organize house-to-house collection, a task already engaged in by the informal sector, but also engage NGOs or resident welfare associations, both middle-class organizations, via regular meetings at quarterly intervals, to promote recycling or reuse of segregated materials, again something already done by the informal sector.

In terms of processing, defined as 'the process by which solid wastes are transformed into new or recycled products', a single line is devoted to recycling, that is 'mixed waste containing recoverable resources shall follow the route of recycling', with the municipal authority tasked with adopting a 'suitable technology or combination of such technologies to make use of wastes so as to minimise burden on landfill (*sic*)' via biological transformation (composting, vermicomposting, anaerobic digestion) and 'incineration with or without energy recovery, including pelletisation'.[24] The Rules also make it mandatory for existing informal sector recycling units to register themselves with the SPCB, even as they open the door to the private sector by defining the operator of a facility as a 'person who owns or operates a facility for collection, segregation, storage, transportation, processing and disposal of municipal solid wastes and *also includes any other agency appointed as such by the municipal authority for the management and handling of municipal solid wastes in respective areas*' (emphasis added).[25]

[21] Gill (n 12).

[22] In India, every ton per day of recyclables collected by the informal sector saves bankrupt municipalities INR 24,500 per year, as well as avoiding the emission of 721 kg of carbon dioxide per year—still, in a representative year like 2011, 6.7 million tons of recyclables ended up in insanitary landfills. See RK Annepu, 'Sustainable Solid Waste Management in India' (MSc Thesis, Columbia University 2012).

[23] Barman Committee (n 18) 77.

[24] Municipal Solid Waste (Management and Handling) Rules, 2000 r 9.

[25] ibid r 3.

The perspective of the Court, the Committee constituted by it and the resultant Rules mirror the government's framing both of the problem—viewed in terms of the environmental fallout of inadequate urban service delivery (in this case, of solid waste management), and ascribed simply to a lack of governance capacity, infrastructure, and finance of municipalities—as well as the perceived solution, that is, privatization and technological fixes as a one-size-fits-all solution.[26] Accordingly, the management of solid waste in the country has been privatized from the mid-2000s, a phase during which urban governance itself has taken a broader neoliberal turn.[27]

The central government's key programmes in this sphere, requiring cooperation from individual states, such as the Jawaharlal Nehru National Urban Renewal Mission (JNNURM) (2005–12), the *Swachh Bharat* Mission (SBM) (2014–19), affiliated to the Atal Mission for Rejuvenation and Urban Transformation (AMRUT) (2015–ongoing), and Smart Cities Mission (2015–ongoing), have all welcomed the entry of the private sector in urban service delivery. In the management of municipal waste, this has largely taken the form of the municipal authority signing a concessionaire agreement with a private company to oversee its formal collection, transportation, treatment, and disposal.

These programmes too remain oblivious to the actual reality of the vast informal sector engaged in waste work, and deeply segmented labour markets in all waste work in India, both formal and informal, on the basis of finely-policed caste differentiation especially between wet and dry waste work.[28] If there is a mention of the informal sector at all in the policy documents underpinning these programmes, it is to reductively cull the entire intricate chain with its division of labour to the level of waste pickers alone, with a token suggestion to upgrade their work conditions by absorbing them into the formal system of waste management.[29]

The most radical departure from the *de jure* decentralized urban governance envisaged by the Seventy-fourth Amendment of the Constitution, in favour of *de facto* centralized and corporate governance, lies in the Smart Cities Mission and its introduction of a Special Purpose Vehicle deemed a limited company, in which states/municipalities have the status of promoters with a 50:50 equity holding. It recommends 'smart' solutions for better urban infrastructure and services, which, in the sphere of waste management, takes the form of waste-to-energy plants.

The abject failure of the Rules of 2000, wherein many municipal authorities merely sub-contracted a private company to transport the urban solid waste to the peripheries of the cities to be dumped in unsanitary landfills, led to the notification of the Solid Waste Management Rules, 2016. These differed from the previous Rules in the following

[26] High Powered Expert Committee (n 2).

[27] Kaveri Gill, 'The Informal Waste Sector: "Surplus" Labour, Detritus and the Right to the Post-colonial City' in Philippe Cullet and Sujith Koonan (eds), *Research Handbook on Law, Environment and the Global South* (Edward Elgar 2019) 452.

[28] Kaveri Gill, 'Interlinked Contracts and Social Power: Patronage and Exploitation in India's Waste Recovery Market' (2007) 43(8) *The Journal of Development Studies* 1448.

[29] Ministry of Urban Development, *Guidelines for Swachh Bharat Mission (Urban)* (Government of India 2014).

salient ways: First, rather than commencing with the responsibility of the local municipal authority to implement them, followed by the responsibility of the state government/union territory to enforce them, and the CPCB and equivalent federal bodies to monitor them, as prescribed in the Rules of 2000, the Rules of 2016 begin by listing the duties of consumers and waste generators, which are largely to segregate waste and pay a user fee for the management of solid waste.

The onus on waste generators and consumers precedes the listing of the duties of the central government's Ministry of Environment, Forest and Climate Change. This is *inter alia*, to monitor the implementation of the Rules in the country, via a Central Monitoring Committee required to meet annually and renewed every three years. Its membership is drawn from the Ministry of Urban Development, Ministry of Rural Development, Ministry of Chemicals and Fertilizers, Ministry of Agriculture, CPCB, and their equivalent bodies at the state/Union Territory level, three urban local bodies, and two census towns by rotation, as well as industry representatives from the Federation of Indian Chambers of Commerce and Industry, and the Confederation of Indian Industry, in addition to two subject experts.

Further, and herein lies the most radical departure, the key duty of the Ministry of Urban Development listed is to formulate the national policy and strategy on solid waste management, with the policy focus on waste to energy, in consultation with stakeholders within six months of the date of notification of these rules; that of the Ministry of Power is to decide tariffs or charges for the power generated from waste-to-energy plants based on solid waste and organize the compulsory purchase of power generated from such waste-to-energy plants by distribution companies; and that of the Ministry of New and Renewable Energy Sources is to facilitate infrastructure creation for waste-to-energy plants and provide appropriate subsidy or incentives for such waste-to-energy plants.[30] Likewise, the duty of the Department of Fertilizers, Ministry of Chemicals and Fertilizers is to provide market development assistance on city compost.[31]

In short, in a significant departure from the Rules of 2000, the Rules of 2016 explicitly promote waste-to-energy plants, with the state directly or indirectly underwriting the risk and financing of such plants. There is far greater mention of the role of the informal sector, and a more expanded version of the various actors involved therein, for instance, suggesting that the Secretary for Urban Development in the states and union territories draft their solid waste management policy and strategies 'in consultation with stakeholders, including representative of waste pickers'[32] and that these should '*acknowledge the primary role* played by the informal sector of waste pickers, waste collectors and recycling industry in reducing waste and provide broad guidelines regarding integration of waste picker [*sic*] or informal waste collectors in the waste management system' (emphasis added).[33]

[30] Ministry of Environment, Forest and Climate Change, *Solid Waste Management Rules, 2016* (Government of India 2016) 56–57.

[31] ibid.

[32] ibid 57.

[33] ibid.

Fundamentally, however, decades after recognition by researchers and practitioners of the immense role and sophistication of the informal sector to the management of solid waste in the country, the Rules of 2016 persist in their narrow lens of who the actors are (focusing primarily on waste pickers); ignorance of the system (suggesting the organization of door-to-door collection where it is already undertaken by informal waste collectors); attention to 'formalising' the system, presumably to better their work conditions ('register' waste pickers, processors and dealers; 'integrate' waste pickers and informal waste collectors by establishing a system that includes those 'authorised' and provide ID cards to this end); and a focus on 'training' waste pickers and waste collectors, when it might be more reasonable to assume their decades-long activity in this area equips them to better train the trainers.[34] Sanctioned solid waste processing explicitly mention private sector participation, and favour 'suitable technology', such as waste to energy, with the well-intentioned provision that the operator of a facility 'ensure' personal protection equipment to all workers handling solid waste and that these are used by them. The above are all duties that are assigned to the municipal authority.

Lastly, another significant departure from the Rules of 2000 that points to an attempt at redressal of their lack of implementation, is that the Rules of 2016 set out a specific time-limit of a set number of years from the date of notification of rules, for the creation of the necessary infrastructure for the implementation of each of the salient rules by various local bodies or other authorities, by sub-contracting agencies if need be.[35]

42.2 Proactive Judicial Intervention in Solid Waste Management: Law in Action

The case selection in this section is made on the following grounds: The first case, *MC Mehta v Union of India*, was instrumental in the framing of the solid waste management rules in the country and cited in the previous section of this chapter.[36] Its devastating impact on the informal plastic recycling market located in the peripheries of Delhi from 1999 to 2001 was extensively researched by me,[37] and subsequently by a lawyer academician for what the case reveals about the nature of proliferating environmental litigation,

[34] ibid 58–60.

[35] ibid 62–63.

[36] *MC Mehta v Union of India* (2004) 6 SCC 588.

[37] Gill (n 12) ch 7, 'Bourgeois Environmentalism', the state, the judiciary, and the 'urban poor'. The Supreme Court's industrial relocation order of 1999–2000 aimed at 77,000 informal enterprises, judged 'polluting' and 'non-conforming' by the standards of the Master Plan of Delhi 2001. It ruled in the petitioner's favour, resulting in a sealing drive of 2000–01, which wreaked havoc on the informal recycling market.

via the instrument of the PIL, in the country at the time.[38] The second case, *Mahavir Singh v Union of India*, was lodged in the High Court of Delhi,[39] on which I again engaged first-hand as it impacted the aforementioned informal recycling market.[40] This section also relies on recent empirical research on the policy and practice of solid waste management in India, especially since the mid-2000s.[41] It examines law in action, in the wake of judicial interventions. Specifically, this section analyses whether the PIL process results in socially just decisions, whether the PIL provides a solution to perceived state inaction in protecting the environment, and whether the outcomes of such environmental litigation suggest an improvement in solid waste management policy and practice in the country.

42.2.1 PIL as a Process Providing a Socially Just Solution

In theory, the instrument of the PIL was introduced to further the democratic reach of the common person to petition the Supreme Court and high courts, and for the latter in turn to influence both the making and implementation of policy in a favourable direction for the people. But in reality, both the above cases illustrate how the PIL process subverts the existing democratic channels to unilaterally seek to impose the diktat of a middle-class career public interest litigator, in the first instance, and an allegedly disgruntled petitioner seeking to settle personal scores in the second, appealing to a court bench, whose interests cohered with and lay in passing orders that over-represented the interests of privileged sections of society, which during this phase was their interpretation of benefiting *the environment* over the very real concerns of poverty.

The experiences and testimonies of the urban poor affected by the orders in both case studies illustrate how their ability to politically mobilize to protect their interests—in this case for protecting their fundamental but thus far legally unenforceable claims, such as the right to work in the urban sphere—is nullified by judicial fiat. Key informants from the recycling market likened the process of the sealing drive ensuing from the Supreme Court order in *MC Mehta* to the Emergency of 1975 for two reasons. First, there was no avenue of appeal against misidentification of a unit and wrongful closure, and no legal records of proceedings. Second, the Supreme Court refused to hear from the lawyer representing the collective body of small-scale traders and manufacturers devastated by the relocation order. These findings are consistent and representative of the process of environmental PILs of this era.[42]

[38] Bhuwania (n 6) 50–79.

[39] *Mahavir Singh v Union of India* Writ Petition (Civil) No 7302 of 2009 (High Court of Delhi).

[40] Kaveri Gill, 'Poverty Invisibility Litigation?' *The Indian Express* (13 March 2010) <https://indianexpress.com/article/opinion/columns/poverty-invisibility-litigation>; Kaveri Gill, *Of Poverty and Plastic: Scavenging and Scrap Trading Entrepreneurs in India's Urban Informal Economy* (paperback edn, OUP 2012) 243 (Postscript on PILs).

[41] Gill (n 4).

[42] Bhuwania (n 6) 57.

Representatives of the informal recycling market also pointed to the fact of so-called environmentally beneficial decisions on the categories deemed 'polluting' and 'non-conforming' being arbitrary, changeable, and politicized, a charge levelled against the orders in *Mahavir Singh* as well,[43] and accused the state of following a divide-and-rule policy much like the colonial powers, to allay any organized collective pushback by the informal units. An activist and interventionist judiciary could and did take this bias much further, so that *MC Mehta* has been described as that 'which changed the face of Delhi more than any other case'.[44] Bhuwania notes: '[W]hat marks Delhi's dislocations as distinct is their source and their basis—they are based not, as in the past, on administrative or municipal policy or executive directions, but on judicial directions in a single PIL case concerning pollution in the city'.[45]

On hearing of *Mahavir Singh* in 2009 and the court's order, in an attempt to formally intervene using research undertaken for my book and to produce evidence as to why the environmental basis for it lay on shaky ground, I engaged with the petitioner's advocate. It was soon apparent that misconceptions abounded as regards the facts of the case and none of the lawyers, not even the junior most amongst them, had ever visited or planned to visit the site of the dispute themselves, rather relying on the petitioner's account or other second-hand sources' testimonies. Most tellingly, in my briefest window of time with the senior advocate, it was plainly articulated to me that the only ground that mattered in the PIL process and that might shift the position of the Court was environmental arguments—they were not concerned with the survival of scores of the urban poor employed in the informal sector.

In late 2010, the first advocate for the petitioner withdrew from the case altogether, and as happened in many of these PILs, the Delhi High Court appointed an amicus curiae in his place. Once admitted by the court, legal procedure dictates a PIL cannot be dismissed, as a regular case might be, and it becomes a 'proxy battle' between the court and the respondents. A lawyer explained, '[e]ven if the origination and starting point of a case is not worthy and not a PIL, it ends up as a PIL. Moreover, once an *amicus curiae* is appointed, the petitioner is a non-entity. This happens when the standing of a petitioner is not very sound'.[46] I met the amicus curiae, who appeared sympathetic to the plea that the book's research findings refuted the petitioner's arguments, but he could not spare the time for further engagement, either by visiting the area or calling me to depose before the next hearing. It became clear that there was nothing further I could do to represent the plastic recycling market's case in court.

The empirical details of law in action following judicial action, in this case the process of PILs, reveal two clear systemic critiques, one epistemic and the other ideological. First, the information-basis of PILs is thin on the ground, with over-stretched lawyers having no incentive or capacity to gain a sound understanding of the ground

43 *Mahavir Singh* (n 39).

44 Bhuwania (n 6) 58.

45 ibid 51.

46 Gill (n 12) 244.

reality required to make a comprehensive judgment for themselves. PILs are relatively far weaker than the no doubt imperfect information elicited and inconsistently acted upon before elections by the legislative and executive arms of the government and vote bank politics. While the latter is far from ideal, the system and process are incentive-compatible in terms of gathering and analysing necessary data for decisions, especially polycentric disputes impacting large numbers of people, including the poor.

Second, the PIL process tilts heavily towards elite bias. In the case studies, *the environment* is the benign metaphor to quickly push forwards coercive and wide-ranging urban transformation, to remake the city into the global metropolis of elitist imaginations impatient with the reality of cities of the global South. Those allowed to depose in court, as well as the benches, are likely to take ideological positions wherein the social reproduction and survival of the teaming masses in the informal economy are simply irrelevant. This is the only way to explain the marked inconsistency and simultaneous consistency in judgments with environmental consequences of this era, freely allowing for slum demolitions and sealing and closures affecting the poor, on the one hand, but passing no orders impacting the better off, on the other hand, where both are equally 'illegal'—or not.[47] Fears about the trespass of the judiciary over executive and legislature functions is therefore very real in a democracy.

42.2.2 PIL as a Solution for State Inaction

If an amicus curiae is disinclined to pursue a PIL case, an implicit stalling strategy is to slow it down procedurally and let it drag on for decades, wasting the judiciary's scarce time and resources. To avert such a possibility, among other things, the National Green Tribunal (NGT) Act, 2010 established the NGT as a body for the effective and expeditious disposal of cases relating to environment protection, including enforcement of any legal right relating to the environment and giving relief and compensation for damages to person and property. Section 29 of the NGT Act is a provision regarding the bar of jurisdiction of the civil court. All environmental matters covered under the Act had to be transferred, instituted, and litigated only before the NGT to render quick justice.[48]

So, it was with the case studies. The orders passed from time to time had noted how the limbs of the state machinery were falling short in curbing the menace of environmental pollution caused by industrial activities due to lack of coordination between them.[49] Enumerated respondents included multiple arms of the Union of India, Union

[47] Especially prior to the Commonwealth Games in Delhi in 2010, the judiciary was complicit in redefining the urban poor as encroachers, with scant attention to their rights to housing, shelter, or livelihood in the city.

[48] *Bhopal Gas Peedith Mahila Udyog Sangathan v Union of India* (2012) 8 SCC 326.

[49] *Satish Kumar v Union of India and Others* MA No 561 /2013 in Application No 56(THC) of 2013 and *Mahavir Singh v Union of India* and MA No 205/2013 in Application No 57(THC) of 2013 (Order of 12 December 2013, NGT–Principal Bench) 8.

Territory of Delhi, and state governments of Haryana—from ministries to municipal authorities, police and pollution control committees—all summoned at various points to take appropriate action.

By an order of 6 February 2013, the High Court of Delhi passed the petition to the NGT in the hope that this would yield quick and positive results. *Mahavir Singh*—along with a similar PIL, *Satish Kumar v Union of India*,[50] also alleging environmental pollution caused by 'illegal' industries in the same northwest area of Delhi—thereby became Application Nos 57(THC) of 2013 and 56(THC) of 2013 respectively.

The order of the NGT states that the sealing team, acting on the High Court's orders of 6 January 2010, faced resistance from offended industrial units because the Mundka area was reported as an industrial area by the Industries Department, which indeed it was as evidenced by a notification of the Industries Department dated 17 September 2007. However, the NGT still pointed out that 'the industrial activities carried out in the said area were highly polluting and the industry had to be closed down forthwith'.[51] It is worth illustrating the continuity in how the NGT sees the informal plastic recycling market, akin to how the courts did previously, in an *a priori* prejudiced way.

On 29 April 2013, the PVC Plastic Waste Dealers Association, including 600 dealers of plastic waste registered under the Societies Registration Act, 1860, was impleaded as a party Respondent in Application No. 57 of 2013 vide order passed in MA No 205/2013. Just as they had a decade and a half ago,[52] the newly impleaded party argued that their involvement was limited to segregating plastic waste in Village Mundka and the surrounding areas. They contended that about fifty thousand people were engaged in the segregation of plastic waste, either directly or indirectly, and made their living by sending the segregated plastic waste for recycling, which was beneficial for the environment. They repeated exactly what they had argued about fifteen years earlier in *MC Mehta*, namely, they moved on account of a fire which gutted the market in 1995 and settled at Tikri-kalan, five km away from Village Mundka. But despite acquiring land at Tikri-kalan, they were not allotted and given possession and were left in limbo without any site for the resettlement of their business, and it was these circumstantial compulsions that led them to carry on their activities from the place presently occupied by them.

The party's deposition was true, in so far as previous research recounted and mapped how the market had faced repeated eviction and displacement due to alleged environmental concerns over their activities and by a changing definition of what constituted the city's periphery as it grew beyond all recognition.[53] Their reiteration that on the contrary, they engaged with segregation and recycling of non-biodegradable material, that was environmentally beneficial and not harmful, was also a fact. Their pleas fell on deaf ears, however, with the NGT bench unmoved by these factual arguments.

[50] *Satish Kumar v Union of India* Writ Petition (Civil) No 3013 of 2010 (High Court of Delhi).

[51] *Satish Kumar* (n 49) 7.

[52] See Gill (n 12).

[53] ibid.

The NGT order was, in fact, baselessly dismissive of the second claim. After a lengthy diatribe on *the environment* and the waste management hierarchy that ironically lists recycling as the more environmentally beneficial option over energy recovery and disposal,[54] the Plastic Waste (Management and Handling) Rules, 2011, and an injunction for the informal actors to register themselves as per the rules, the order closes with a plea to the municipal and other authorities to enforce the aforesaid rules very diligently, and thereby summarily dismissed the petitions.[55]

Echoing Vasan, 'Entering the frame of the NGT involves the presentation of the self as green or environment friendly. While this is not required by law, as the NGT is formally empowered to assess compliance with the law, the discursive environment of the court demands and impels parties to perform their environmentality'.[56] Despite doing that, and despite being a polycentric 'dispute' in that it is a situation of interacting points of influence, with affected parties having various competing claims and interests in a fluid situation, and wherein a PIL in theory provides mechanisms for all to be heard, *Mahavir Singh* illustrates how in empirical terms, what is given weight—in this case, *the environment*—and how it is differentially perceived, despite all actors singing to that tune sheet (in this case, with *a priori* bias against the segregation and recycling activities of subordinate castes and classes working in the informal sector) is predetermined and a closed loop.

Moreover, if coordination, oversight, and other governance failures on the part of the legislature and the executive in contentious urban issues, whether by design or by inability, invite judicial intervention and activism in the first place,[57] the causes underlying them also predict and underwrite the courts' and the NGT's ineffectiveness to order and implement a superior outcome. Indeed, in *MC Mehta*, the chaotic closure of units following a Court order of 1992 led to legal experts commenting, 'one may wonder whether the Supreme Court of India can have the time and resources for the above sort of micro-management'.[58] The NGT was set up in part to deal with this inefficiency.

The NGT however, found itself unable to properly monitor the implementation of the Rules of 2016 across the country. The NGT noted that although it had earlier issued directions for implementing the Rules, they had simply not been complied with. The NGT proposed to direct the formation of Apex, Regional and State Level Committees for monitoring the implementation of the Rules, as well as the directions of the NGT and the submission of quarterly reports to them.[59] Therefore, that was done.

[54] From an environmental perspective, on a scale of successively less desirable options, a waste management hierarchy widely adhered to is prevention, followed by reuse, recycling, energy recovery, and finally, disposal as the last resort options.

[55] *Satish Kumar* (n 49).

[56] Sudha Vasan, 'We Are All Environmentalists! Framing Life in the National Green Tribunal, India' (2021) 37(2) *Journal of Developing Societies* 3.

[57] See Rajamani (n 9).

[58] Divan and Rosencranz quoted in Bhuwania (n 6) 58.

[59] *In re: Compliance of Municipal Solid Waste Management Rules, 2016 and other environmental issues* OA No 606 of 2018 (Order of 31 August 2018, NGT–Principal Bench).

42.2.3 Policy Outcomes and Practice in the Wake of Environmental PILs

Key juridical interventions did result in the much-needed framing of the first-ever rules, and the subsequent framing of policy, as well as the notification of an updated set of rules in the arena of solid waste management in the country, as outlined in Section 42.2 of this chapter. However, the policy outcomes they gave rise to and how they have worked in practice fail if judged by the metric of improving *the environment*, which was their original purpose. In the interests of brevity, two illustrations will suffice.

The first is the introduction and promotion of waste-to-energy plants between the passing of the Rules of 2000 and the revised Rules of 2016, despite so much well-known research that has existed for decades on their lack of efficacy for the composition of Indian waste. The government's position may have been gleaned from the stance of some official documents.[60] What is to be noted, however, is that despite the opposition to waste-to-energy plants of one of the key petitioners in PILs filed on municipal solid waste management, *Almitra Patel*,[61] they nonetheless become a key fulcrum of the revised Rules of 2016.[62] It is surprising that key functionaries in the making of policy resulting from public interest environmental litigation appear to have little say in the content and direction of final policy.

Second, recent empirical work undertaken in a Himalayan medium town illustrates how the scientific and technological policy solutions geared to achieve sustainable and zero waste outcomes in the management of municipal waste since 2005 especially, outlined in Section 42.2 of this chapter, have produced dismal results on the ground.[63] To replace large open-barrel containers with 'smart' dustbins, to achieve 100 per cent door-to-door collection and waste segregation, from the abysmally low starting point, to set up waste to biogas plants to generate electricity; to build compost pits as a green solution for biodegradable waste, and to construct a sanitary landfill to absorb the waste disposed of—none of these new measures has fructified to yield better environmental outcomes, five years after they were proposed and initiated. This is far from an anomaly in the larger landscape of practice in municipal social waste management in the country.

[60] For instance, Planning Commission (n 1).

[61] *Almitra H Patel v Union of India* (2000) 2 SCC 679.

[62] Isher Judge Ahluwalia and Almitra Patel, 'Waste-to-Energy Plants that Use Solid Waste as Feedstock Pose Threat to Environment' *Indian Express* (30 January 2019) <https://indianexpress.com/article/opinion/columns/toxic-plants-waste-to-energy-national-green-tribunal-waste-incineration-5560270/>.

[63] Gill (n 4); Kaveri Gill, 'Waste Management in a Himalayan Medium Town: Revisiting Informality, Centralization, and the Indian State', IRGS Policy Paper Series (2021) <https://irgs.snu.edu.in/sites/default/files/HimalayanStudies-Kaveri.pdf>.

Conclusion

This chapter has examined an era of pervasive judicial activism in the sphere of solid waste management in India, with the meta-narrative of *the environment*, as well as state negligence and inaction in this regard, invoked as the motivation for increasingly active judicial trespass into the territory of the legislature and the executive. The first-ever rules in this sphere, as well as subsequent rules, were the product of such intervention. Notably, the biggest departures from the Rules of 2000 in the Rules of 2016 were the introduction and financial underwriting of risk of waste-to-energy plants by the state, despite their well-proven lack of efficacy in the Indian context.

'The discursive environment of the court demands and impels parties to perform their environmentality'.[64] And so, given a chance to do so, the various parties involved in the polycentric disputes presented here, including especially the subordinate informal sector workers and units involved in waste management and its recycling, the various arms and levels of government and parastatal organizations entrusted with formal waste management, and the petitioners, their legal representatives, and the court and NGT benches—have all performed accordingly.

Following judicial action, this chapter offers a close-up look at the law in action. Contrary to the abstract possibilities for socially just as well as environmentally sound decisions presented by the innovative and novel instrument of the PIL, empirical reality has revealed a process that is systematically inaccessible and inequitable to the very subordinate class and caste groupings to whom they were meant to give voice; a solution to state inaction that is itself no better and as ineffective, so that courts pass on the monitoring and implementation of the rules to the NGT, who in turn passes it on to expert committees; and resultant policy outcomes and practices that are environmentally suspect as well as at times worse than what preceded them. It appears little has been gained from judicial action in the sphere of urban solid waste management in the country.

Suggestions for Further Reading

Anuj Bhuwania, *Courting the People: Public Interest Litigation in Post-Emergency India* (CUP 2016).

Kaveri Gill, *Of Poverty and Plastic: Scavenging and Scrap Trading Entrepreneurs in India's Urban Informal Economy* (OUP 2012).

Kaveri Gill, 'The Environment as Disingenuous Trope: Tracing Waste Policy and Practice in a Medium Hill Town of the Himalayas, India' (2021) 37(2) *Journal of Developing Societies* 184.

64 See Vasan (n 56) 3.

Lavanya Rajamani, 'Public Interest Environmental Litigation in India: Exploring Issues of Access, Participation, Equity, Effectiveness and Sustainability' (2007) 19(3) *Journal of Environmental Law* 293.

Sudha Vasan, 'We are All Environmentalists! Framing Life in the National Green Tribunal, India' (2021) 37(2) *Journal of Developing Societies* 1.

INDEX

For the benefit of digital users, indexed terms that span two pages (e.g., 52–53) may, on occasion, appear on only one of those pages.

Tables, figures, and boxes are indicated by *t*, *f*, and *b* following the page number